# CHESS OPENINGS

## THEORY AND PRACTICE

*I. A. Horowitz*

# CHESS OPENINGS

## THEORY AND PRACTICE

*A Fireside Book Published by*
*Simon and Schuster, New York*

*For Edna* 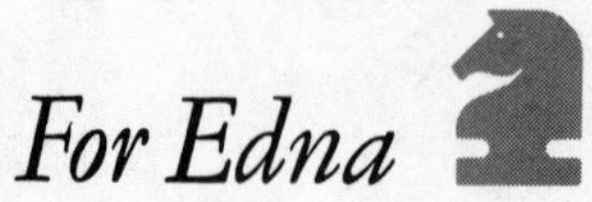


A Fireside Book
Published by Simon and Schuster
A Division of Gulf & Western Corporation
Simon & Schuster Building
Rockefeller Center, 1230 Avenue of the Americas, New York, N.Y. 10020
FIRESIDE and colophon are registered trademarks of Simon & Schuster

4 5 6 7 8 9 10 11 12 13
15 16 17 18 19 20 21 Pbk.

ISBN 0-671-13390-X
ISBN 0-671-20553-6 Pbk.

Library of Congress Catalog Card Number 64-24336
Manufactured in the United States of America

# CONTENTS

### SECTION TWO: QUEEN'S PAWN OPENINGS



### SECTION THREE: OTHER OPENINGS

# INTRODUCTION

ACCORDING to William Cook's *The Evolution of the Chess Openings,* the oldest work on the openings is a thirty-page manuscript by an unknown author, written in 1490 and discovered at the University of Göttingen in the latter part of the nineteenth century. While present-day nomenclature was naturally not then in use, this early text contains such openings as the Petroff Defense, the Philidor Defense, the Ruy Lopez, the Giuoco Piano, the English Opening and Bird's Opening. The manuscript, of course, is more interesting for its age than its utility.

It may be noted in passing that before the appearance of this ancient work, rules of play were quite different from those in the modern game. For example, there was no provision for castling; at one time the King could leap like a Knight once during a game; a Pawn could not initially traverse two squares; the Queen's move, far from being all-powerful, was severely limited.

Following the 1490 tract were others by Vincentz (1495), Lucena (1497), Damiano (1512), Ruy Lopez (1561), Polerio (1590), Captain Bertin (1735) and Philidor (1749). These prepared the ground for more comprehensive works. Bilguer's *Handbuch* was the dominant reference for some time until it was superseded by a number of international treatises, which, in the English-speaking countries, included *Modern Chess Openings* and *Practical Chess Openings.*

Chess openings are definitive patterns of play formed in the first dozen or so moves. Their names are derived variously from the locality or tournament where they made their debut, from the players who originated or popularized them, from common consent as it has crystallized over the years, and occasionally even from the caprice of some prominent eccentric.

Popularity, as well as soundness, plays an inevitable part in determining how much space may be usefully devoted to the discussion of any particular opening. Needless to say, if a variation is unquestionably refuted, nothing more can be said. Certainly no informed player will permit the Tarrasch Trap in the Ruy Lopez. But the Giuoco Piano, an old-time favorite, is also not seen much these days, even though no one could reasonably maintain that it is unplayable. The fianchettoes, on the other hand, are currently fashionable and therefore extensively analyzed, in startling contrast to the time not so long ago when they languished in the archives.

Designed to replace older works on openings, which have become obsolete, this book stresses completeness, ease of reading and reference, currency of material and exhaustive analyses culled from the most authoritative sources.

Prefaced by a diagram and a theoretical discussion, the analysis of each opening is categorized into Idea Variations, Practical Variations and Supplementary Variations. Idea Variations, as the term implies, present the inherent ideas and objectives of an opening before it has been subjected to the rough-and-tumble of tournament play. Practical Variations are just that—lines developed through practice, honed and shaped by innumerable tests in masters' tournaments and matches. Branching off from the main lines are by-products and mutations designated as Supplementary Variations. Entire games from major chess events are presented, illustrating salient opening features in depth; and such important openings as the Ruy Lopez, the Queen's Gambit Declined, the King's Indian, the Sicilian, the French, the Caro-Kann, the Nimzo-Indian and many others are worked out step by step, variation by variation.

Each variation is appraised by means of a symbol placed at the foot of the column:

$\pm$ *means* a better game for White
$\mp$ *means* a better game for Black
$=$ *means* approximate equality

Further signs indicating "hopelessly lost" or "markedly superior but without immediate forced win" have been dispensed with, for such symbols would not only clutter the text with unnecessary complexity, but would tend to stifle even a minimal initiative by the reader in forming a basic judgment. *Chess Openings: Theory and Practice* is a guide, not a gospel.

I am deeply indebted to former world champion Dr. Max Euwe and a large company of collaborators who have made this work possible. They are Jack Straley Battell, Hans Bouwmeester, Theodore A. Dunst, Arthur Feldman, Ernst Grünfeld, William Mühring, P. L. Rothenberg, Aben Rudy, Theodor D. Van Scheltinga, H. L. Tan, and Carel B. van den Berg.

This double-distilled essence of master play, which has been centuries in the making and reflects judicious thinking on contemporary practice, is offered both to present-day and future generations in the confidence that it will prove an "open sesame" to the creative and strategic planning of the openings.

—AL HOROWITZ

# Section One:
# KING'S PAWN OPENINGS

# chapter 1—Bishop's Opening

1 P–K4, P–K4
2 B–B4, N–KB3[A]
3 P–Q4[B], PxP
4 N–KB3[C]

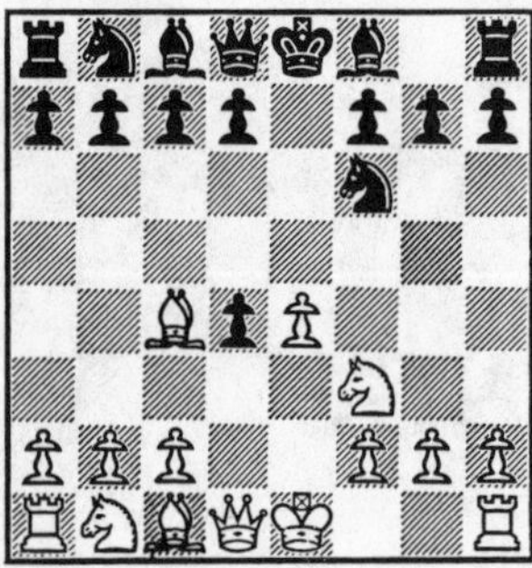

KEY POSITION

## OBSERVATIONS ON KEY POSITION

[A] The so-called Berlin Defense, which is the most active. Other good moves are 2 . . . N–QB3 and 2 . . . B–B4. There is a chance for transposition into other openings: the Giuoco Piano, the Vienna and the King's Gambit. But 2 . . . P–QB3? is inferior: 3 P–Q4, N–B3 4 PxP, NxP 5 Q–K2 and White has the edge.

[B] Other moves transpose into other openings. After 3 P–Q3, Black can play advantageously 3 . . . P–QB3.

[C] On 4 P–K5, Black plays 4 . . . P–Q4! Or 4 QxP, N–QB3 which leads to a variation of the Center Game favorable to Black.

Today this is considered the most important position of the rarely played Bishop's Opening. White sacrifices his King Pawn for the sake of an advance in development. A specialist in this gambit is the Russian master, F. Estrin, who has had a number of fine successes with White.

The defense is indeed rather difficult for Black. Emanuel Lasker's recommendation (Prac. Var. 3) is probably suitable for the safe maintenance of Black's extra Pawn.

If Black wishes to avoid the complications arising from 4 . . . NxP, he can satisfactorily decline the gambit in several ways: 4 . . . N–B3, 4 . . . B–B4, or 4 . . . P–Q4.

It is worth mentioning that the key position may also be arrived at via the Steinitz Variation of Petroff's Defense in this manner: 1 P–K4, P–K4 2 N–KB3, N–KB3 3 P–Q4, PxP and now not 4 P–K5 but 4 B–B4.

## IDEA VARIATIONS 1–5:

(1) 4 . . . NxP 5 QxP, N–Q3? 6 O–O! N–B3 (6 . . . NxB 7 R–K1† B–K2 8 QxNP and wins) 7 R–K1†, N–K2 8 B–N3. White has a winning position; Black is completely tied down.

(2) 4 . . . NxP 5 QxP, P–Q4? 6 BxP, N–KB3 (6 . . . N–Q3 7 O–O) 7 BxP†, KxB 8 QxQ, B–N5† 9 Q–Q2 and White is a Pawn to the good.

(3) 4 . . . NxP 5 QxP, N–B4 (only 5 . . . N–KB3 is correct; see Prac. Var. 1–3) 6 B–KN5!, P–KB3 7 B–K3, P–B3 8 N–B3, P–Q4 9 O–O–O, B–K2 10 Q–R4, QN–Q2 (10 . . . O–O 11 NxP! or 10 . . . B–K3 11 KR–K1!) 11 NxP!, PxN 12 Q–R5† with a winning attack for White (Estrin–Taimanov, Leningrad 1949).

(4) 4 . . . N–QB3, which is a sound way of declining the gambit, leads into the Two Knights Defense: 5 O–O, NxP 6 R–K1, P–Q4.

(5) Most comfortable for Black is probably 4 . . . P–Q4 5 PxP, B–N5† P–B3, Q–K2†.

PRACTICAL VARIATIONS 1–5:

1 P–K4, P–K4 2 B–B4, N–KB3 3 P–Q4, PxP 4 N–KB3

| | *1* | *2* | *3* | *4* | *5* |
|---|---|---|---|---|---|
| *4* | – – | – – | – – | – – | – – |
| | NxP | – – | – – | B–B4 | – – |
| *5* | QxP | – – | – – | O–O | P–K5 |
| | N–KB3 | – – | – – | P–Q3 | P–Q4 |
| *6* | B–KN5 | – – | – – | P–B3 | PxN |
| | B–K2 | – – | – – | P–Q6 | PxB |
| *7* | N–B3 | – – | – – | QxP | Q–K2† |
| | P–B3[1] | N–B3! | | N–B3[8] | B–K3 |
| *8* | O–O–O | Q–R4 | – – | ∓ | PxP |
| | P–Q4 | P–Q3 | P–Q4! | | R–N1 |
| *9* | KR–K1 | O–O–O | O–O–O | | B–N5 |
| | B–K3 | B–K3 | B–K3 | | Q–Q4[9] |
| *10* | B–Q3 | B–Q3 | KR–K1 | | = |
| | QN–Q2[2] | Q–Q2 | O–O![6] | | |
| *11* | Q–KR4 | B–N5 | B–Q3 | | |
| | N–B4[3] | O–O | P–KR3[7] | | |
| *12* | N–Q4![4] | N–Q4[5] | ∓ | | |
| | ± | = | | | |

*Notes to practical variations 1–5:*

[1] For 7 . . . O–O?, see Game 1.

[2] Steinitz recommended 10 . . . Q–R4 11 K–N1, QN–Q2 12 N–K5, NxN 13 RxN, O–O–O with a satisfactory game for Black. But Keres' recommendation, 11 B–B5!, is stronger for White.

[3] 11 . . . Q–R4 12 N–Q4, O–O–O 13 NxB, PxN 14 RxP, B–N5. White has recovered the Pawn with a likely edge (Estrin–Klaman, 1945).

[4] Black is in great danger according to Estrin: 12 . . . N–N1 13 P–B4, K–B1 14 P–QN4! Or 12 . . . KN–Q2 13 BxB, QxB 14 QxQ†, KxQ 15 P–B4, threatening 16 P–B5.

[5] White has good chances for the Pawn (Mieses–Rubinstein, Breslau 1912). See Game 2. A strong continuation for White is 12 N–K5, Q–Q1 13 NxN, PxN 14 B–Q3, P–KR3 15 P–B4.

[6] The text move is recommended by Emanuel Lasker. Inferior for Black is 10 . . . P–KR3 11 BxN, BxB 12 Q–R5, BxN 13 RxB† K–B1 14 RxQP with a winning attack (Terestchenko–Rotlevi, St. Petersburg 1909).

continued ▸

[7] Now the sacrifice 12 BxP is met by 12 . . . N–K5 13 Q–B4, B–Q3 14 Q–K3, B–QB4 15 Q–B4, NxP! Or 15 . . . B–Q3 which leads to a draw by repetition of position.

[8] Spielmann–Alekhine, Stockholm 1912.

[9] The position is similar to the Max Lange and hard to assess:

1) 10 N–B3, PxN 11 R–Q1, BxP† 12 K–B1! with obscure complications.
2) 10 N–B3, PxN 11 R–Q1, PxP 12 O–O, P–N8(Q) 13 RxQ/5, BxP†, again without clear results.
3) 10 N–B3, B–N5 11 O–O–O, BxN 12 PxB, N–B3 13 B–B6! with an edge for White.

### *Bishop's Opening Game 1*

*WHITE: Schlechter* *BLACK: Neustadt and Mieses*

*Carlsbad 1907*

| | WHITE | BLACK | | WHITE | BLACK |
|---|---|---|---|---|---|
| 1 | P–K4 | P–K4 | 26 | RxQR | RxR |
| 2 | B–B4 | N–KB3 | 27 | Q–B7! | R–K1 |
| 3 | P–Q4 | PxP | 28 | QxBP | N–Q3 |
| 4 | N–KB3 | NxP | 29 | NxN | B–N4† |
| 5 | QxP | N–KB3 | 30 | K–N1 | B–Q2 |
| 6 | B–KN5 | B–K2 | 31 | Q–QB3 | R–K6 |
| 7 | N–B3 | O–O? | 32 | Q–Q2 | R–K4 |
| 8 | O–O–O | P–B3 | 33 | Q–Q3† | B–B4 |
| 9 | KR–K1 | P–Q4 | 34 | Q–KN3! | R–Q4 |
| 10 | Q–R4 | P–KR3? | 35 | Q–KB3 | B–K3 |
| 11 | BxQP! | QN–Q2 | 36 | NxP! | R–K4 |
| 12 | B–QB4 | P–N4 | 37 | Q–KN3 | B–B5 |
| 13 | B–Q3 | PxB | 38 | Q–B2 | B–N4 |
| 14 | KNxP | R–K1 | 39 | N–Q4! | B–K6 |
| 15 | B–R7† | K–B1 | 40 | Q–R4† | K–N3 |
| 16 | B–B5! | K–N1! | 41 | NxB | RxN |
| 17 | NxP! | KxN | 42 | P–R4 | K–B4 |
| 18 | B–K6† | K–N3 | 43 | Q–R5† | P–N4 |
| 19 | P–B4 | N–R4! | 44 | P–R4 | R–K5 |
| 20 | Q–N4† | K–R3 | 45 | Q–B7† | K–K4 |
| 21 | B–B7? | NxP | 46 | P–KR5 | R–R5 |
| 22 | R–K6† | K–R2 | 47 | Q–N7† | K–B4 |
| 23 | N–K4! | N–K4 | 48 | P–R6 | B–Q5 |
| 24 | QxN | BxR | 49 | P–N4† | Resigns |
| 25 | RxQ | NxB | | | |

### *Bishop's Opening Game 2*

*WHITE: Mieses* *BLACK: Rubinstein*

*Breslau 1912*

| | WHITE | BLACK | | WHITE | BLACK |
|---|---|---|---|---|---|
| 1 | P–K4 | P–K4 | 15 | RxN | P–B4 |
| 2 | B–B4 | N–KB3 | 16 | R–N3! | K–R1 |
| 3 | P–Q4 | PxP | 17 | N–B3 | N–N1 |
| 4 | N–KB3 | NxP | 18 | BxB | QxB |
| 5 | QxP | N–KB3 | 19 | N–KN5 | N–R3 |
| 6 | B–KN5 | B–K2 | 20 | R–K1 | Q–Q2 |
| 7 | N–B3 | N–B3 | 21 | R/3–K3 | KR–K1 |
| 8 | Q–R4 | P–Q3 | 22 | N/3–K4 | B–B4 |
| 9 | O–O–O | B–K3 | 23 | N–B6! | PxN |
| 10 | B–Q3 | Q–Q2 | 24 | QxN | B–N3 |
| 11 | B–N5 | O–O | 25 | NxRP! | BxN |
| 12 | N–Q4 | P–QR3 | 26 | R–KN3 | RxR† |
| 13 | B–Q3 | N–K4 | 27 | K–Q2 | R–K7† |
| 14 | P–B4 | NxB† | | Draw | |

# chapter 2—Center Game

1 P–K4, P–K4
2 P–Q4, PxP
3 QxP, N–QB3
4 Q–K3, N–B3
5 N–QB3[A]

KEY POSITION

## OBSERVATIONS ON KEY POSITION

[A] 5 P–K5 is premature: 5 . . . N–KN5 6 Q–K4 (or 6 Q–K2, P–Q3!), P–Q4! 7 PxP e.p.†, B–K3 8 B–QR6 (if 8 PxP, Q–Q8†!), QxP 9 BxP, Q–N5† 10 QxQ, NxQ 11 N–QR3, R–QN1 12 B–K4, B–QB4 and Black has a promising game.

This opening is rarely adopted today. White immediately opens and exerts pressure on the Queen file, bringing, however, his Queen somewhat prematurely into play. Black has two ways to obtain a fully satisfactory game:

(1) Enterprisingly, with 5 . . . B–N5, intending to put the King Pawn under fire after . . . O–O and . . . R–K1. In this case, White can sacrifice his King Pawn for good attacking chances. Black, on the other hand, can reject the sacrifice, still obtaining a good game.

(2) Staidly, with 5 . . . B–K2, soon followed by . . . P–Q4, and establishing full balance in the center.

## IDEA VARIATIONS 1-3:

(1) 5 . . . B–N5 6 B–Q2, O–O 7 O–O–O, R–K1 8 B–B4, BxN!? 9 BxB, NxP 10 Q–B4, N–B3 11 N–B3, P–Q3 12 N–N5, and White has a dangerous attack (Winawer–Steinitz, Nuremberg 1896; See Game 1).

(2) 5 . . . B–N5 6 B–Q2, O–O 7 O–O–O, R–K1 8 B–B4, P–Q3! 9 N–B3 (nor is 9 P–B3 satisfactory [see Prac. Var. 1], but 9 Q–N3 deserves consideration), B–K3 10 BxB, RxB 11 N–KN5, R–K1 12 P–B4, P–KR3 with complications favoring Black (Tartakover–Reshevsky, Stockholm 1937; see Game 2).

(3) 5 . . . B–K2 6 B–B4, O–O (also good is 6 . . . N–QN5 so as to meet 7 B–N3 or 7 Q–K2 with . . . P–Q4) 7 KN–K2 (better is 7 B–Q2, followed by O–O–O or 7 N–KB3), N–KN5! 8 Q–Q2 (if 8 Q–N3, B–R5! 9 QxN, P–Q4),B–B4 9 N–Q1 (9 O–O fails: . . . Q–R5 10 Q–B4, B–Q3), Q–K2 with a promising game for Black (Troianescu–Spasski, Bucharest 1953; see Game 3).

*Center Game 1*

*WHITE: Winawer* *BLACK: Steinitz*

*Nuremberg 1896*

| WHITE | BLACK | WHITE | BLACK |
|---|---|---|---|
| 1 P–K4 | P–K4 | 3 QxP | N–QB3 |
| 2 P–Q4 | PxP | 4 Q–K3 | N–B3 |

| WHITE | BLACK | WHITE | BLACK |
|---|---|---|---|
| 5 N–QB3 | B–N5 | 13 B–Q3 | P–KR3 |
| 6 B–Q2 | O–O | 14 P–KR4 | N–Q4 |
| 7 O–O–O | R–K1 | 15 B–R7† | K–R1 |
| 8 B–B4 | BxN | 16 RxN | BxR |
| 9 BxB | NxP | 17 B–K4 | P–B3? |
| 10 Q–B4 | N–B3 | 18 BxB | BPxN |
| 11 N–B3 | P–Q3 | 19 PxP | N–K4 |
| 12 N–KN5 | B–K3 | 20 P–N6! | Resigns |

*Center Game 2*

*WHITE: Tartakover* *BLACK: Reshevsky*

*Stockholm 1937*

| WHITE | BLACK | WHITE | BLACK |
|---|---|---|---|
| 1 P–K4 | P–K4 | 32 RxR | R–B8† |
| 2 P–Q4 | PxP | 33 K–N2 | K–B2 |
| 3 QxP | N–QB3 | 34 P–B4 | P–KR4 |
| 4 Q–K3 | N–B3 | 35 K–B3 | P–KN4 |
| 5 N–QB3 | B–N5 | 36 P–B5 | PxP |
| 6 B–Q2 | O–O | 37 K–B4 | P–N5! |
| 7 O–O–O | R–K1 | 38 KxP | P–N6 |
| 8 B–B4 | P–Q3 | 39 K–Q4 | P–R5 |
| 9 N–B3 | B–K3 | 40 P–B4 | P–N3 |
| 10 BxB | RxB | 41 P–R4 | R–B7 |
| 11 N–KN5 | R–K1 | 42 R–K4 | RxP |
| 12 P–B4 | P–KR3 | 43 RxP | R–QR7 |
| 13 P–KR4 | Q–B1 | 44 R–N4 | P–N7 |
| 14 Q–B3 | K–B1! | 45 P–R5 | PxP |
| 15 N–Q5 | NxN! | 46 K–B3 | P–R5 |
| 16 PxN | N–Q5 | 47 P–B5 | K–B3 |
| 17 Q–Q3 | N–K7† | 48 R–N8 | K–B2 |
| 18 K–N1 | BxB | 49 R–N4 | P–R4 |
| 19 RxB | NxP | 50 P–B6 | K–K2 |
| 20 N–R7† | K–N1 | 51 R–N6 | K–B2 |
| 21 N–B6† | PxN | 52 R–N4 | R–B7! |
| 22 Q–N3† | N–N3 | 53 P–Q6 | P–R6 |
| 23 P–R5 | Q–B4 | 54 PxP | P–R7 |
| 24 PxN | PxP | 55 P–B8 (Q) | P–R8 (Q) † |
| 25 R–B2 | Q–N4 | 56 K–B4 | R–B7† |
| 26 Q–QB3 | Q–K4! | 57 K–N5 | Q–B8† |
| 27 RxBP | QxQ | 58 K–R4 | R–R7† |
| 28 PxQ | K–N2 | 59 K–N3 | Q–N8† |
| 29 R–B2 | R–KB1 | 60 K–B3 | R–B7† |
| 30 R–K2 | QR–K1 | 61 K–Q4 | P–N8/Q† |
| 31 R/1–K1 | RxR | Resigns | |

*Center Game 3*

*WHITE: Troianescu* — *BLACK: Spasski*

*Bucharest 1953*

| | WHITE | BLACK | | WHITE | BLACK |
|---|---|---|---|---|---|
| 1 | P–K4 | P–K4 | 22 | B–B4 | N–K3 |
| 2 | P–Q4 | PxP | 23 | NxN | PxN |
| 3 | QxP | N–QB3 | 24 | K–K3 | B–N7 |
| 4 | Q–K3 | B–K2 | 25 | R–KN1 | B–R6 |
| 5 | N–QB3 | N–B3 | 26 | B–K5 | P–KN3 |
| 6 | B–B4 | O–O | 27 | R–N3 | P–QN4 |
| 7 | KN–K2 | N–KN5 | 28 | B–N3 | P–B4 |
| 8 | Q–Q2 | B–B4 | 29 | P–B4 | B–B8 |
| 9 | N–Q1 | Q–K2 | 30 | PxP | P–B5 |
| 10 | P–KB3 | Q–R5† | 31 | B–B2 | QR–Q1 |
| 11 | P–N3 | N/5–K4! | 32 | P–R5 | B–Q6 |
| 12 | PxQ | NxP† | 33 | R–N2 | R–B8 |
| 13 | K–B1 | P–Q4! | 34 | BxB | RxB† |
| 14 | K–N2 | NxQ | 35 | K–K2 | R–B8 |
| 15 | BxP | B–KN5 | 36 | R–B2 | R–QR8 |
| 16 | BxN | BxN | 37 | P–QR3 | R–QB8 |
| 17 | N–B3 | B–R4 | 38 | PxP | R–B7† |
| 18 | B–KB4 | N–Q5 | 39 | K–B1 | RxR† |
| 19 | N–R4 | B–B6† | 40 | KxR | PxP |
| 20 | K–B2 | BxR | | Resigns | |
| 21 | NxB | P–B3 | | | |

PRACTICAL VARIATIONS 1–5:

1 P–K4, P–K4 2 P–Q4, PxP 3 QxP, N–QB3 4 Q–K3, N–B3 5 N–QB3

| | *1* | *2* | *3* | *4* | *5* |
|---|---|---|---|---|---|
| *5* | — — | — — | — — | — — | — — |
| | B–N5 | — — | — — | B–K2 | — — |
| *6* | B–Q2 | — — | — — | B–Q2 | — — |
| | O–O | — — | — — | P–Q4 | — — |
| *7* | O–O–O | — — | — — | PxP | — — |
| | R–K1 | — — | — — | NxP | — — |
| *8* | B–B4 | — — | Q–N3 | Q–N3 | NxN |
| | P–Q3 | N–QR4![2] | RxP![4] | NxN | QxN |
| *9* | P–B3 | B–Q3 | B–KN5 | BxN | N–K2 |
| | N–QR4 | P–Q4 | BxN | B–B3 | B–KN5 |
| *10* | B–Q3 | P–K5 | QxB | B–Q3 | N–B4 |
| | P–Q4 | P–Q5 | P–KR3 | BxB† | Q–Q2 |

| | 1 | 2 | 3 | 4 | 5 |
|---|---|---|---|---|---|
| 11 | Q–N5 | Q–N3 | P–B3 | PxB | P–KB3 |
| | P–KR3 | PxN | R–K1 | O–O | B–B4 |
| 12 | Q–R4 | B–KN5[3] | B–R4 | N–K2 | O–O–O |
| | P–Q5[1] | ∓ | P–Q3[5] | Q–K2[6] | O–O–O[7] |
| | ∓ | | ∓ | ∓ | = |

*Notes to practical variations 1–5:*

[1] 13 N–K2, BxB† 14 RxB, P–B4 and Black has a strong attack (Feilitsch–Keres, Correspondence Game 1933).

[2] A suggestion by Keres, which Sokolski has elaborated.

[3] Sokolski now proceeds 12 . . . N–K5 13 BxQ, NxQ 14 RPxN, B–KB4! 15 BxB, QRxB 16 BxP†, K–B1 17 RxR, RxR 18 B–Q3!±. However, Black has better by playing first 12 . . . PxP† 13 K–N1 and then 13 . . . N–K5!

[4] After 8 . . . NxP 9 NxN, RxN White obtains good chances with 10 P–QB3, followed by 11 B–Q3 and 12 N–B3. In the above line, weaker is 10 B–KB4? Q–B3! (Mieses–Capablanca, Berlin 1913). And if Black varies from the text with 8 . . . P–Q3?, the continuation favors White: 9 P–B3, B–K3 10 N–R3, Q–K2 11 N–B4 (Mieses–Spielmann, Munich 1914).

[5] White lacks sufficient compensation for the Pawn.

[6] White's Queenside Pawn structure is perforated.

[7] White's initiative is at a minimum.

# chapter 3—Danish Gambit

1 P–K4, P–K4
2 P–Q4, PxP
3 P–QB3

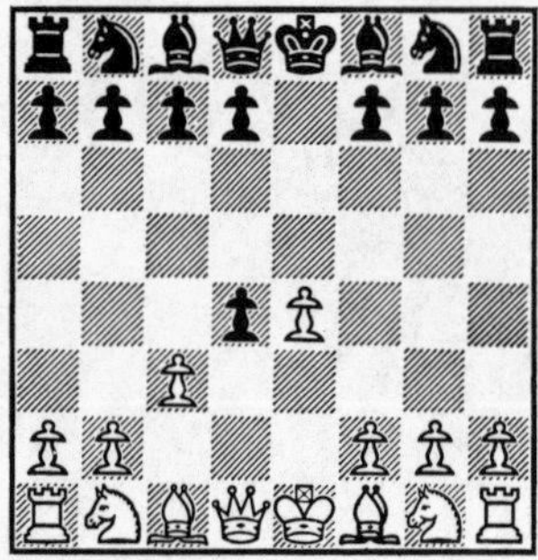

KEY POSITION

OBSERVATIONS ON KEY POSITION

White intends to accelerate his development by the sacrifice of two Pawns. If both are taken, he may obtain a very strong attack. Black faces a difficult task if he wants to keep his material advantage, but he has it in his power to get a satisfactory position by returning the Pawns in good time. Simpler, however, is to decline the gambit by 3 . . . P–Q4, whereupon Black easily obtains equality.

IDEA VARIATIONS 1–3:

(1) 3 . . . PxP 4 B–QB4, PxP 5 BxP, B–N5† 6 K–B1 (the most enterprising move, though Mieses' continuation of 6 N–B3 is also promising), N–KB3 (6 . . . K–B1 or 6 . . . B–B1 may be better) 7 P–K5, P–Q4 (recommended by theory but unsatisfactory; for 7 . . . N–N1 see Game 1) 8 B–N5†, KN–Q2 (if 8 . . . B–Q2? 9 Q–R4! and if 8 . . . P–B3 9 PxN, PxB 10 PxP, R–N1 11 Q–B2!) 9 Q–N4 (Bilguer's *Handbuch* now gives 9 P–K6, PxP 10 BxP, K–B2!, when 11 B–N2 offers White good chances), B–B1 10 P–K6, PxP 11 Q–R5†, K–K2 12 B–R3†, P–B4 13 BxP†, NxB 14 Q–N5† winning the Queen (Keres).

Note also 3 . . . PxP 4 B–QB4, PxP 5 BxP, P–QB3! This move has hardly been tested professionally, though it may well be the refutation of the Danish. Against a move like 6 Q–N3, Black plays . . . Q–K2 and threatens to exchange Queens by . . . Q–N5† and also . . . P–Q4, neither of which White can afford. But in addition, Black threatens to play a game of attrition with some such series of moves as . . . P–Q3, . . . N–Q2–B4, followed by . . . B–K3. In this way Black builds a barrier difficult to penetrate and in the long run, after beating back White's initiative, assumes the lead — and with two Pawns ahead. The difference between this and Prac. Var. 2 is the sequence of the moves.

(2) 3 . . . PxP 4 B–QB4, PxP 5 BxP, P–Q4! This is Schlechter's Defense. Black returns his material advantage for a steady position. 6 BxQP (not 6 PxP, N–KB3 7 N–QB3, B–Q3 which blocks White's attacking lines), N–KB3 7 BxP† (Keres suggests 7 N–QB3, B–K2 8 Q–N3, O–O 9 O–O–O or 9 R–Q1, and White has good attacking chances; in this line not 7 . . . NxB because of

8 NxN, threatening N–B6†), KxB 8 QxQ, B–N5† 9 Q–Q2, BxQ† 10 NxB, P–B4 =.

(3) 3 . . . P–Q4! 4 KPxP, N–KB3 (better than 4 . . . QxP; see Prac. Var. 4) 5 PxP (if 5 P–QB4, P–B4; if 5 B–N5, B–K2; and if 5 B–QB4, NxP 6 QxP, B–K3), B–N5† 6 B–Q2, BxB† 7 QxB, O–O 8 N–KB3, N–K5 9 Q–B4, QxP 10 B–Q3, Q–R4† 11 QN–Q2, NxN 12 QxN, R–K1† 13 N–K5, QxQ† 14 KxQ, B–K3 and the end game slightly favors Black (Reti–Schlechter).

For 5 N–B3, see Prac. Var. 5.

PRACTICAL VARIATIONS 1–5:
1 P–K4, P–K4 2 P–Q4, PxP 3 P–QB3

| | *1* | *2* | *3* | *4* | *5* |
|---|---|---|---|---|---|
| *3* | – – | – – | – – | – – | – – |
| | PxP | – – | – – | P–Q4![6] | – – |
| *4* | B–QB4[1] | – – | – – | KPxP | – – |
| | PxP | – – | – – | QxP | N–KB3! |
| *5* | BxP | – – | – – | PxP | N–B3 |
| | N–KB3 | Q–K2 | P–Q3 | N–QB3 | NxP |
| *6* | N–QB3 | N–QB3 | P–B4 | N–KB3 | QxP |
| | N–B3 | P–B3 | B–K3 | B–N5 | N–QB3 |
| *7* | N–B3 | Q–B2 | BxB | B–K2 | B–QN5 |
| | B–N5 | P–Q3 | PxB | N–B3[7] | B–K2! |
| *8* | Q–B2 | O–O–O | Q–N3 | N–B3 | O–O[11] |
| | P–Q3 | B–K3 | Q–B1 | Q–QR4![8] | O–O |
| *9* | O–O–O | N–Q5! | N–KB3 | O–O | BxN |
| | BxN[2] | PxN | N–QB3 | B–Q3[9] | PxB |
| *10* | QxB | PxP | N–N5 | B–K3 | R–K1 |
| | B–K3 | Q–N4† | N–Q1 | O–O[10] | B–N2 |
| *11* | KR–K1 | R–Q2 | O–O[5] | = | N–R3 |
| | BxB | B–B4 | ± | | KR–K1! |
| *12* | QxB | Q–N3[4] | | | N–B4 |
| | O–O[3] | ± | | | P–QB4[12] |
| | = | | | | = |

*Notes to practical variations 1–5:*

[1] Alekhine's recommendation is 4 NxP, which transposes into the Goring Gambit of the Scotch.

[2] Weaker is 9 . . .O–O? 10 P–K5, N–N5 11 P–KR4, P–KR3 12 K–N1, R–K1 13 N–Q5!, B–K3 14 N–N5! with a winning attack for White. In the above line Black may vary at his 11th turn: 11 . . . QNxP, then 12 N–KN5, P–KN3 13 QN–K4, B–KB4 14 Q–N3 with complications favoring White.

[3] 13 P–K5, N–K1 14 R–K3 and, according to Fine, White has sufficient compensation for the Pawns.

[4] In the opinion of Mieses, White has a strong attack for continued ▸

the piece: 12 . . . N–Q2 13 N–B3, Q–R3 14 QxP, R–N1 15 Q–B7.

[5] White has excellent compensation for the Pawns, according to the analyst Nielsen. If 11 . . . P–KR3, then 12 Q–KR3!

[6] Inferior is 3 . . . Q–K2 because of 4 PxP! QxP† 5 B–K2 (5 B–K3 is also playable), QxNP 6 B–B3, Q–N3 7 N–B3, B–N5 8 N–K2, and White obtains good attacking chances for the Pawns.

[7] Or 7 . . . O–O–O 8 B–K3, B–N5† 9 N–B3, KN–K2 10 O–O, Q–Q2 11 Q–R4 with even chances.

[8] Weaker is 8 . . . B–N5 9 O–O. Also weaker than the text move is 8 . . . Q–KR4 9 P–KR3, O–O–O 10 Q–R4.

[9] The text is safer here than 9 . . . O–O–O 10 B–K3, B–QB4 11 Q–N3.

[10] White's center and easy development compensate for his isolated Pawn.

[11] If 8 QxNP, B–B3 followed by . . . Q–K2† and the development of the Queen Bishop and . . . O–O–O favors Black (Alekhine).

[12] Black has a fair game (Alekhine–Moling, handicap game, Buenos Aires 1926). After 13 Q–Q1, however, he should have played 13 . . . R–QN1 (if 14 N–R5, then 14 . . . B–R1).

*Danish Gambit Game 1*

*WHITE: Denker* *BLACK: P. Gonzalez*

*Simultaneous Exhibition 1945*

| | WHITE | BLACK | | WHITE | BLACK |
|---|---|---|---|---|---|
| 1 | P–K4 | P–K4 | 10 | N–B3 | B–K2 |
| 2 | P–Q4 | PxP | 11 | N–Q5 | O–O |
| 3 | P–QB3 | PxP | 12 | N–B6†! | K–R1 |
| 4 | B–QB4 | PxP | 13 | N–R3 | BxN |
| 5 | BxP | B–N5† | 14 | PxB | P–KN3 |
| 6 | K–B1 | N–KB3 | 15 | Q–B4 | N–B4 |
| 7 | P–K5 | N–N1 | 16 | N–N5 | N–Q3 |
| 8 | Q–N4 | B–B1 | 17 | NxP†! | NxN |
| 9 | Q–B3 | N–KR3 | 18 | Q–R6! | Resigns |

# chapter 4—Four Knights' Game

This once popular opening arising after 1 P–K4, P–K4 2 N–KB3, N–QB3 3 N–B3, N–B3, is rarely played today. Especially well known is the Spanish Four Knights' Game resulting from 4 B–N5. The continuations 4 B–B4 and 4 P–Q4 are dealt with under the Giuoco Piano and the Scotch Opening.

The Three Knights' Game is briefly handled in Sup. Var. 3–5.

The Spanish Four Knights' Game disappeared from the immediate scene about 1910 after Rubinstein introduced 4 . . . N–Q5. Nowadays, this line is considered an effective means for White to play for a draw. There are, of course, some finesses to know and some problems not to be underestimated. Black is well advised not to maintain the symmetry too long which, by the way, is a rule to be observed in all openings with a symmetrical beginning.

Sound play on Black's part leads rather easily to equality, which is why this debut has little popularity today. Rubinstein contributed a great deal to the theory of this opening, particularly by introducing the defense which bears his name.

## part 1—METGER VARIATION

1 P–K4, P–K4
2 N–KB3, N–QB3
3 N–B3, N–B3
4 B–N5, B–N5[A]
5 O–O[B], O–O
6 P–Q3[C], P–Q3[D]
7 B–N5[E]

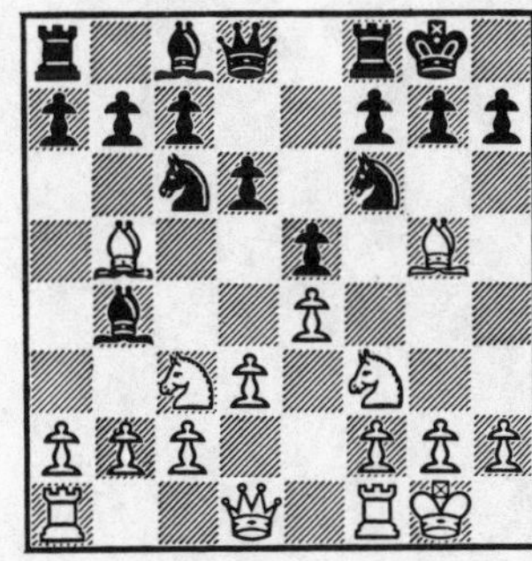

KEY POSITION 1

### OBSERVATIONS ON KEY POSITION 1

[A] This is the classical way to handle the Four Knights' Game. The move 4 . . . P–Q3 gets Black into an unfavorable variation of the Ruy Lopez. Playable, however, is 4 . . . P–QR3. See Sup. Var. 1.

[B] A little known mistake is 5 P–Q3?, N–Q5!

[C] 6 N–Q5, NxN 7 PxN, P–K5 leads to a good game for Black.

[D] Marshall's 6 . . . P–Q4 is risky because of 7 NxQP, NxN 8 PxN, QxP 9 B–QB4, Q–Q3 10 P–QR3, B–QB4 11 P–QN4! with pressure on both wings. Playable for Black, however, seems to be 6 . . . N–Q5, and after 7 B–QB4, P–B3 8 NxN (if 8 NxP, Q–R4!), PxN 9 N–K2, B–B4, the chances are even.

[E] The most energetic. For the quiet 7 N–K2 (Maroczy), see Part 3.

This set-up occurs with comparative frequency; the pin of the Knight offers White a slight initiative, requiring accurate counterplay. The best examples are the so-called symmetrical variations treated in Idea Var. 1. Idea Var. 2 deals with the Metger System proper, in which

Black anticipates White's N–Q5 and is able to strengthen his center. He obtains a steady but somewhat passive position.

IDEA VARIATIONS 1 and 2:

(1) 7 . . . B–N5? 8 N–Q5, N–Q5 9 NxB, NxB 10 N–Q5, N–Q5 11 Q–Q2!, NxN† (Black also loses with other moves: e.g., 11 . . . Q–Q2 12 BxN, BxN 13 N–K7†, K–R1 14 BxP†, KxB 15 Q–N5† and mate next move.) 12 PxN, BxP 13 P–KR3! (not 13 BxN?, PxB 14 Q–R6, K–R1 15 NxKBP, R–KN1† and wins), P–B3 14 NxN†, PxN 15 B–R4, K–R1 16 K–R2, R–KN1 17 R–KN1, R–N3 18 Q–K3, B–R4 19 P–KB4.

(2) 7 . . . BxN 8 PxB, Q–K2 (preparing the characteristic maneuver . . . N–Q1–K3, which counteracts White's impending P–KB4) 9 R–K1 (the following alternative is of no promise for White: 9 BxQN, PxB 10 P–KR3, P–KR3 11 B–K3, B–K3), N–Q1 10 P–Q4, N–K3 (best; for 10 . . . P–B3 and 10 . . . B–N5, see Prac. Var. 1 and 2 respectively) 11 B–QB1, P–QB4 (the too passive 11 . . . P–B3 leads again to Prac. Var. 1) 12 PxKP (introduced by Keres and most likely best; the alternative lines are comfortable for Black: 12 B–KB1, BPxP! 13 PxP, Q–B2 or 12 P–Q5, N–B2 13 B–Q3, P–QN4!), PxP 13 B–QB4 (if 13 NxP, N–B2 wins a piece). White has a slight edge but experience to the point is lacking.

PRACTICAL VARIATIONS 1 and 2:

1 P–K4, P–K4 2 N–KB3, N–QB3 3 N–B3, N–B3 4 B–N5, B–N5 5 O–O, O–O 6 P–Q3, P–Q3 7 B–N5

| | 1 | 2 |
|---|---|---|
| 7 | – | – – |
| | BxN[1] | – – |
| 8 | PxB | – – |
| | Q–K2 | – – |
| 9 | R–K1 | – – |
| | N–Q1 | – – |
| 10 | P–Q4 | – – |
| | P–B3 | B–N5[5] |
| 11 | B–KB1 | P–KR3 |
| | N–K3 | B–R4 |
| 12 | B–B1 | P–N4 |
| | R–Q1[2] | B–N3 |
| 13 | P–N3 | N–R4[6] |
| | Q–B2 | P–KR3! |
| 14 | B–N2[3] | B–QB4![7] |
| | P–B4 | N–K3[8] |
| 15 | P–Q5 | NxB |
| | N–B1 | PxN |
| 16 | N–R4 | P–B4 |
| | N–N3 | PxB |
| 17 | N–B5 | P–B5 |
| | N–K2 | PxP |
| 18 | P–N4 | NPxP |
| | N–K1 | P–KN3! |
| 19 | R–K3![4] | BxN† |
| | ± | K–N2[9] |
| | | = |

*Notes to practical variations 1 and 2:*

[1] For 7 . . . N–K2, see Part 2.

[2] Nor is 12 . . . Q–B2 any better. See Game 1.

[3] Somewhat risky is 14 N–R4, P–Q4 15 P–KB4!?, NxKP! 16 BPxP, NxBP 17 Q–B3, N–K5 and the chances are hard to assess.

[4] Black is cramped.

[5] Preferred by Capablanca.

[6] 13 P–Q5 is probably a little better. After 13 . . . P–B3, the chances are even.

[7] For 14 NxB, see Game 2.

[8] Also so good is 14 . . . B–R2.

[9] Dangerous for both sides.

### *Four Knights' Game 1*

*WHITE: Duras* — *BLACK: Rubinstein*

*Carlsbad 1917*

| | WHITE | BLACK | | WHITE | BLACK |
|---|---|---|---|---|---|
| 1 | P–K4 | P–K4 | 20 | B–Q2 | N/1–R2 |
| 2 | N–KB3 | N–QB3 | 21 | N–B3 | R–K2 |
| 3 | N–B3 | N–B3 | 22 | P–KR4 | P–B4! |
| 4 | B–N5 | B–N5 | 23 | N–R2 | R/1–K1 |
| 5 | O–O | O–O | 24 | R–K3 | P–QN3 |
| 6 | P–Q3 | BxN | 25 | B–B3 | B–N2 |
| 7 | PxB | P–Q3 | 26 | R/1–K1? | P–B5 |
| 8 | B–N5 | Q–K2 | 27 | Q–K2 | BxP |
| 9 | R–K1 | N–Q1 | 28 | Q–N2 | P–Q4 |
| 10 | P–Q4 | N–K3 | 29 | B–B1 | BxB |
| 11 | B–QB1 | P–B3 | 30 | NxB | RxR |
| 12 | B–B1 | Q–B2 | 31 | BxR | R–K5! |
| 13 | N–R4 | R–K1 | 32 | Q–R3 | R–N5† |
| 14 | Q–Q3 | B–Q2 | 33 | K–R1 | R–N6 |
| 15 | P–N3 | QR–Q1 | 34 | Q–R2 | N–N5 |
| 16 | B–N2 | B–B1 | 35 | B–N1 | NxQ |
| 17 | P–KB4 | PxBP | 36 | BxN | Q–B5 |
| 18 | PxP | N–B1 | 37 | N–N1 | QxRP |
| 19 | P–B5 | P–KR3 | | Resigns | |

*Four Knights' Game 2*

*WHITE: Wolf* *BLACK: Rubinstein*

*Teplitz–Schonau 1922*

| | WHITE | BLACK | | WHITE | BLACK | | WHITE | BLACK |
|---|---|---|---|---|---|---|---|---|
| 1 | P–K4 | P–K4 | 22 | P–R5 | N–N3 | 43 | R–N1 | Q–N1 |
| 2 | N–KB3 | N–QB3 | 23 | P–B3 | N–B5 | 44 | R–R1 | P–R4!! |
| 3 | N–B3 | N–B3 | 24 | B–B1 | K–R1 | 45 | B–N2 | P–R5 |
| 4 | B–N5 | B–N5 | 25 | BxN | NPxB | 46 | Q–K1 | Q–KR1 |
| 5 | O–O | O–O | 26 | Q–B2 | P–KN4 | 47 | Q–QB1 | R–R3 |
| 6 | P–Q3 | P–Q3 | 27 | P–Q5 | P–R4 | 48 | B–B1 | R–R1 |
| 7 | B–N5 | BxN | 28 | B–N2 | K–N2 | 49 | B–B4 | P–QR6 |
| 8 | PxB | Q–K2 | 29 | Q–K2 | R–KR1 | 50 | B–R2 | Q–R2 |
| 9 | R–K1 | N–Q1 | 30 | K–B2 | R–QR1 | 51 | R–R3 | N–Q2 |
| 10 | P–Q4 | B–N5 | 31 | KR–QN1 | N–Q2 | 52 | Q–B1 | Q–R1 |
| 11 | P–KR3 | B–R4 | 32 | Q–N5 | RPxP | 53 | R–R1 | N–B4 |
| 12 | P–N4 | B–N3 | 33 | KRPxP | N–B4 | 54 | Q–QB1 | R–QN1!! |
| 13 | N–R4 | P–KR3 | 34 | R–R1 | R–R5! | 55 | QxP | R–R1 |
| 14 | NxB? | PxN | 35 | RxR | PxR | 56 | Q–N2 | P–R6! |
| 15 | B–B4† | K–R2 | 36 | B–R3 | PxP! | 57 | B–B4 | Q–R5 |
| 16 | B–R4 | P–KN4 | 37 | QxP | Q–Q1 | 58 | B–K2 | Q–B7!! |
| 17 | B–KN3 | N–B2 | 38 | R–QN1 | R–N1 | 59 | RxP | Q–K6† |
| 18 | Q–B3 | QR–K1 | 39 | R–N4 | P–R3 | 60 | K–K1 | N–R5 |
| 19 | Q–K3 | P–QN3 | 40 | K–K2 | R–N3 | | Resigns | |
| 20 | B–N5? | R–Q1 | 41 | Q–R1 | K–N3 | | | |
| 21 | P–QR4 | N–R1! | 42 | K–Q2 | K–N4 | | | |

---

## part 2—PILLSBURY VARIATION

1 P–K4, P–K4
2 N–KB3, N–QB3
3 N–B3, N–B3
4 B–N5, B–N5
5 O–O, O–O
6 P–Q3, P–Q3
7 B–N5, N–K2[A]

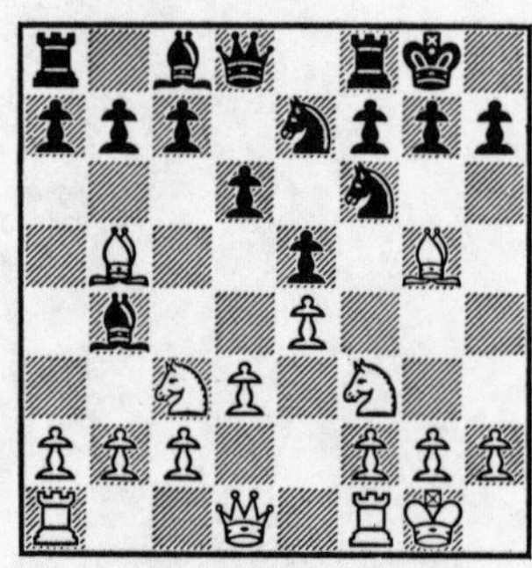

KEY POSITION 2

### OBSERVATIONS ON KEY POSITION 2

[A] If Black wants to play this variation, he should omit the capture of the Queen Knight. Here is a single example of the disadvantage following 7 . . . BxN: 8 PxB, N–K2 9 N–R4, P–B3 10 B–QB4, P–Q4 11 B–N3, Q–Q3 12 P–KB4 (12 . . . Q–B4† 13 P–Q4!), PxKP 13 QPxP, Q–B4† 14 K–R1, N–N5 15 P–B5!, N–K6 16 Q–B3!, NxR 17 RxN with an overwhelming attack.

Black allows the doubling of his King Bishop Pawn, but experience shows that accepting the challenge is not to be recommended for White. It remains to be seen, though, whether White can achieve something tangible with a quieter method. Usually Black can simplify the situation by a timely . . . P–Q4, possibly preceded by . . . P–QB3, in which case White has no more than an even game.

### IDEA VARIATIONS 3 and 4:

(3) 8 BxN (tempting but not effective; White lacks the means to profit from the weakening of the Pawn struc-

ture), PxB 9 N–KR4, P–B3 (the immediate 9 . . . N–N3 also serves well) 10 B–B4, N–N3 11 NxN (White actually admits that his plan has failed; but 11 Q–R5 leads to nothing because of 11 . . . NxN 12 QxN, P–KB4!), RPxN 12 P–B4, K–N2 13 Q–B3, B–B4† 14 K–R1, B–K3 and Black has the better of it.

(4) 8 N–KR4 (theoretically White's best chance), P–B3 9 B–QB4, P–Q4 (for other possibilities see Prac. Var. 3 and 4 as well as Game 3) 10 B–N3 (or 10 PxP, N/2xP! 11 KBxN, PxB=), Q–Q3 (also good is 10 . . . PxP 11 PxP, B–N5) 11 P–KR3 (Tarrasch–Yates, Hastings 1922; sharper is 11 P–B4, although it allows . . . B–B4† 12 K–R1, N–N5), P–KR3 12 BxN, QxB 13 Q–R5, BxN 14 PxB, PxP (in the aforementioned game, Yates played 14 . . . K–R2, getting into trouble, however, after 15 N–B3, N–N3 16 PxP) 15 PxP, B–K3. The game is even, according to Filip.

PRACTICAL VARIATIONS 3 and 4:

1 P–K4, P–K4 2 N–KB3, N–QB3 3 N–B3, N–B3, 4 B–N5, B–N5 5 O–O, O–O 6 P–Q3, P–Q3 7 B–N5, N–K2

| | 3 | 4 |
|---|---|---|
| 8 | N–KR4 | – – |
| | P–B3 | – – |
| 9 | B–QB4 | – – |
| | N–N3 | N–K1 |
| 10 | NxN | Q–R5[2] |
| | RPxN | N–B2 |
| 11 | P–B4 | N–B5 |
| | B–K3[1] | QBxN |
| 12 | = | PxB |
| | | P–Q4 |
| 13 | | P–B6 |
| | | P–KN3![3] |
| 14 | | PxN[4] |
| | | BxP |
| 15 | | BxB |
| | | QxB[5] |
| | | ∓ |

*Notes to practical variations 3 and 4:*

[1] For the enticing 11 . . . Q–N3†, see Game 3. The text move offers Black sufficient counter chances.

[2] 10 P–B4 constitutes a dubious sacrifice: 10 . . . BxN 11 PxB, P–Q4 12 B–N3, P–B3 13 PxKP, PxB 14 RxR†, KxR 15 Q–B3†, K–N1 16 R–KB1, N–B2 17 Q–B7†, K–R1 18 Q–B8†, QxQ 19 RxQ†, N–N1!

[3] Too dangerous is 13 . . . PxP 14 BxBP, Q–Q2 15 P–B4!. Also risky is 13 . . . PxB 14 PxNP, R–K1 15 N–K4 with a winning attack.

[4] Not 14 Q–R6?, N–B4!

[5] Black recovers the piece.

*Four Knights' Game 3*

*WHITE: Opocensky* *BLACK: Hrdina*

*Prague 1913*

| | WHITE | BLACK | | WHITE | BLACK |
|---|---|---|---|---|---|
| 1 | P–K4 | P–K4 | 10 | NxN | RPxN |
| 2 | N–KB3 | N–QB3 | 11 | P–B4 | Q–N3†? |
| 3 | N–B3 | N–B3 | 12 | K–R1 | N–N5 |
| 4 | B–N5 | B–N5 | 13 | Q–K1! | N–K6 |
| 5 | O–O | O–O | 14 | P–B5! | NxB |
| 6 | P–Q3 | P–Q3 | 15 | P–B6 | B–N5 |
| 7 | B–N5 | N–K2 | 16 | Q–R4 | B–R4 |
| 8 | N–KR4 | P–B3 | 17 | P–N4 | N–K6 |
| 9 | B–QB4 | N–N3 | 18 | PxB | NxR |
| | | | 19 | P–R6!! | Resigns |

## part 3—SVENONIUS AND MAROCZY SYSTEMS

1 P–K4, P–K4
2 N–KB3, N–QB3
3 N–B3, N–B3
4 B–N5, B–N5
5 O–O, O–O
6 P–Q3

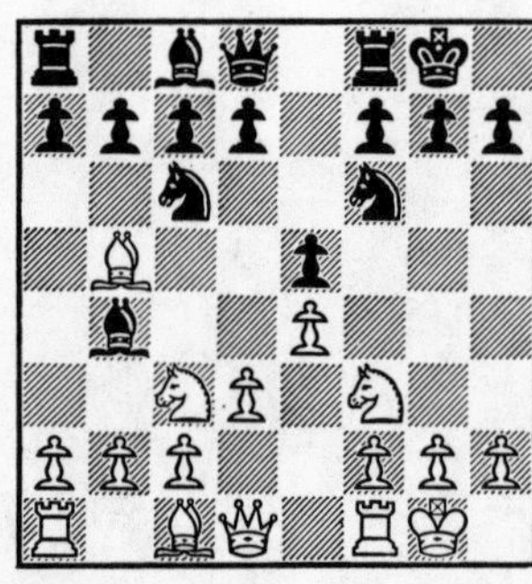

KEY POSITION 3

OBSERVATIONS ON KEY POSITION 3

The above position leads to two different lines. (1) The Svenonius — Idea Var. 5 — is sharp and risky and involves the sacrifice of a Pawn on Black's part. It is best for White to decline the offer and exercise pressure instead on the enemy King Pawn. In doing so, White gets the edge. (2) the Maroczy is safe and steady, but of little promise for the first player.

IDEA VARIATIONS 5 and 6:

(5) 6 . . . BxN 7 PxB, P–Q4 8 PxP (also important is 8 BxN; see Prac. Var. 5), QxP (or 8 . . . NxP 9 BxN, PxB 10 NxP, NxP 11 Q–Q2, N–Q4, 12 P–QB4, with an edge for White, according to Keres; but not 12 NxQBP?, Q–B3!) 9 B–QB4 (also good is 9 P–B4, Q–Q3 10 BxN, PxB 11 B–N2, R–K1 12 Q–K1!), Q–R4 10 R–N1, P–QR3 11 R–K1, P–QN3 12 Q–K2, B–N5 13 B–KN5 and White has the better of it (Lasker–Reti, Moscow 1925).

7 . . . P–Q4 initiates the system of the Swedish analyst Svenonius. Instead 7 . . . P–Q3 8 B–N5 transposes into a variation of Part 2.

(6) 6 . . . P–Q3 7 N–K2, N–K2 (best; for 7 . . . Q–K2 or 7 . . . B–N5, see Prac. Var. 6 and Game 4) 8 P–B3 B–R4 9 N–N3, P–B3 10 B–R4, N–N3 11 P–Q4,

R–K1 (safer than 11 . . . P–Q4 12 B–KN5!) 12 B–N3, PxP (another satisfactory move is 12 . . . P–KR3) 13 PxP, B–K3 14 N–N5, BxB 15 QxB, Q–Q2 = (Alekhine–Euwe, Amsterdam 1936).

7 N–K2 is characteristic of the Maroczy. White avoids the exchange of his Queen Knight.

PRACTICAL VARIATIONS 5 and 6:

1 P–K4, P–K4 2 N–KB3, N–QB3 3 N–B3, N–B3 4 B–N5, B–N5 5 O–O, O–O 6 P–Q3

| | 5 | 6 |
|---|---|---|
| *6* | – – | – – |
| | BxN | P–Q3 |
| *7* | PxB | N–K2 |
| | P–Q4 | Q–K2 |
| *8* | BxN | P–B3 |
| | PxB | B–QB4 |
| *9* | NxP | N–N3[3] |
| | Q–Q3 | ± |
| *10* | B–B4 | |
| | R–K1 | |
| *11* | PxP[1] | |
| | RxN | |
| *12* | P–Q4 | |
| | R–K8! | |
| *13* | BxQ | |
| | RxQ | |
| *14* | KRxR | |
| | PxB | |
| *15* | PxP | |
| | B–K3[2] | |
| | ± | |

*Notes to practical variations 5 and 6:*

[1] 11 Q–B3 is of no promise: 11 . . . PxP 12 PxP, RxN 13 QR–Q1, B–N5 14 RxQ, BxQ 15 RxN, PxR 16 BxR, PxB 17 PxB, R–N1=.

[2] The position is obscure, though 16 KR–N1 offers some winning chances.

[3] Black has difficulty bringing out his pieces (Maroczy–Swiderski, Vienna 1908).

*Four Knights' Game 4*

*WHITE: Rubinstein* *BLACK: Marshall*

*Lodz 1908*

| | WHITE | BLACK | | WHITE | BLACK |
|---|---|---|---|---|---|
| 1 | P–K4 | P–K4 | 20 | Q–K2 | KR–QN1 |
| 2 | N–KB3 | N–QB3 | 21 | P–B4 | PxP |
| 3 | N–B3 | N–B3 | 22 | BxP | P–B5 |
| 4 | B–N5 | B–N5 | 23 | NPxP | R–N8† |
| 5 | O–O | O–O | 24 | RxR | RxR† |
| 6 | P–Q3 | P–Q3 | 25 | R–B1 | R–N7 |
| 7 | N–K2 | B–N5 | 26 | P–K5 | N–K1 |
| 8 | B–K3 | N–KR4? | 27 | B–N3 | Q–R5 |
| 9 | BxN | PxB | 28 | P–B6! | B–B1 |
| 10 | N–K1 | P–Q4 | 29 | Q–N4 | P–N3 |
| 11 | P–KB3 | B–K3 | 30 | P–K6! | RxBP |
| 12 | P–N4! | N–B3 | 31 | N–K1! | RxQRP |
| 13 | N–N3! | P–Q5? | 32 | PxP† | KxP |
| 14 | B–Q2 | B–K2 | 33 | N–B3! | NxP |
| 15 | N–N2 | R–N1 | 34 | N–N5† | K–N2 |
| 16 | P–N3 | P–B4 | 35 | RxN! | KxR |
| 17 | N–B5 | BxN | 36 | Q–B4† | K–K2 |
| 18 | NPxB | R–N3 | 37 | Q–B7† | K–Q1 |
| 19 | R–B2 | Q–Q2 | 38 | N–K6† | Resigns |

---

## part 4—RUBINSTEIN VARIATION

1 P–K4, P–K4
2 N–KB3, N–QB3
3 N–B3, N–B3
4 B–N5, N–Q5

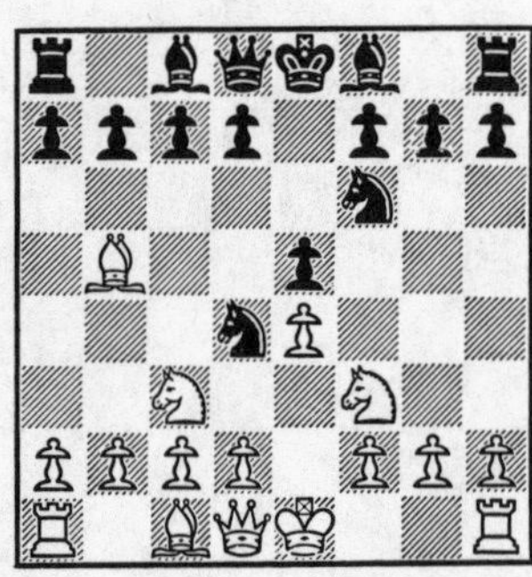

KEY POSITION 4

OBSERVATIONS ON KEY POSITION 4

It is Rubinstein's move, 4 . . . N–Q5, which actually drove the Four Knights into disrepute. The counter on his Bishop presents White with a difficult problem. True, he can simply play for a draw (see Idea Var. 7); but any attempt to achieve more leads to great complications involving some risk. The point is that Black gets excellent chances by parting with one or more Pawns, as has been demonstrated by Rubinstein in a number of brilliant games.

As to the best way of meeting the defense, there is still difference of opinion.

IDEA VARIATIONS 7 and 8:

(7) 5 NxN (an entirely harmless continuation), PxN 6 P–K5 (better than 6 N–Q5, NxN 7 PxN, Q–B3! 8 O–O, B–K2), PxN 7 PxN, QxP (not 7 . . . PxP†? 8 BxP, QxP 9 O–O and White has good chances) 8 QPxP, Q–K5† 9 Q–K2, QxQ† 10 BxQ=.

(8) 5 B–R4 (the most important continuation, according to present opinion; for other continuations see Prac.

Var. 7, 8 and 9), B–B4 (this gambit is characteristic of the system) 6 NxP, O–O 7 N–Q3 (for 7 P–Q3 see Game 5), B–N3 8 N–B4 (Canal's move; interesting is 8 P–K5, N–K1 9 O–O, P–Q3 10 PxP, N–KB3! 11 P–Q7 (11 PxP?, Q–Q3!), BxP 12 BxB, QxB 13 N–K1, QR–K1 and Black has sufficient compensation for the Pawn), P–Q4 9 P–Q3, B–N5 10 P–B3, N–R4 11 NxN (or 11 PxB, Q–R5† 12 P–N3, NxP 13 N–N2, Q–B3 14 PxN, N–B6† 15 K–K2, N–Q5† 16 K–K1, N–B6†, with perpetual check), BxN 12 NxP, P–QB3! (an important improvement by Keres) 13 NxB (if 13 N–B4?, NxKBP†!), PxN 14 B–N3, Q–R5† 15 K–B1 (not good is 15 P–N3, Q–R6 and Black holds all the threats), NxB 16 BPxN, P–KB4 and Black has powerful compensation for the Pawns.

PRACTICAL VARIATIONS 7–9:

1 P–K4, P–K4 2 N–KB3, N–QB3 3 N–B3, N–B3 4 B–N5, N–Q5

| | 7 | 8 | 9 |
|---|---|---|---|
| 5 | NxP | O–O | B–B4 |
| | Q–K2![1] | NxB | B–B4![7] |
| 6 | P–B4[2] | NxN | NxP |
| | NxB | P–B3 | Q–K2 |
| 7 | NxN | N–B3 | N–B3[8] |
| | P–Q3 | P–Q3 | P–Q4 |
| 8 | N–KB3 | P–Q4 | NxP[9] |
| | QxP† | Q–B2 | QxP† |
| 9 | K–B2[3] | P–KR3 | N–K3 |
| | N–N5† | P–QN4![6] | B–KN5 |
| 10 | K–N1[4] | = | B–K2 |
| | Q–B3 | | NxB |
| 11 | Q–K2† | | QxN |
| | B–K2 | | O–O–O |
| 12 | P–KR3 | | P–Q3 |
| | Q–N3† | | Q–K3 |
| 13 | P–Q4 | | O–O |
| | N–B3 | | N–Q4[10] |
| 14 | K–R2 | | = |
| | B–Q2 | | |
| 15 | R–K1 | | |
| | O–O[5] | | |
| | ∓ | | |

*Notes to practical variations 7–9:*

[1] The correct reply. 5 . . . B–B4 is effectively met with 6 B–K2!

[2] Safer is 6 N–B3. However, 6 . . . NxB 7 NxN, QxP† 8 Q–K2, QxQ† 9 KxQ, N–Q4! gives Black a good game.

[3] 9 Q–K2 leads to nothing.

[4] For 10 K–N3, Q–N3! see Game 6.

[5] Black has the edge, according to Keres.

[6] Black's Bishop pair compensates for White's center control.

[7] Here, too, a promising gambit.

[8] Not 7 BxP†?, K–B1! Nor 7 NxBP?, P–Q4! And if 7 N–Q3 then the effect of 7 . . . P–Q4 is even stronger.

[9] For 8 NxN see Game 7.

[10] White can free himself by returning the Pawn or permitting the doubling of his King Bishop Pawn.

*Four Knights' Game 5*

*WHITE: Tarrasch* *BLACK: Rubinstein*

*San Sebastian 1912*

| | WHITE | BLACK | | WHITE | BLACK |
|---|---|---|---|---|---|
| 1 | P–K4 | P–K4 | 30 | PxP | B–Q5 |
| 2 | N–KB3 | N–QB3 | 31 | QR–B1 | R–N2 |
| 3 | N–B3 | N–B3 | 32 | R–B2 | K–B2 |
| 4 | B–N5 | B–B4 | 33 | N–B2 | R–N7! |
| 5 | NxP | N–Q5 | 34 | RxR | BxR |
| 6 | B–R4? | O–O | 35 | R–Q2 | B–Q5 |
| 7 | P–Q3 | P–Q4 | 36 | N–R3 | K–K3 |
| 8 | B–KN5 | P–B3 | 37 | R–QB2 | K–Q3 |
| 9 | Q–Q2 | R–K1 | 38 | P–B5 | R–QB1! |
| 10 | P–B4 | P–N4! | 39 | B–Q1 | RxR† |
| 11 | B–N3 | P–KR3 | 40 | BxR | K–K4 |
| 12 | B–KR4 | NxP! | 41 | P–N4 | B–K6 |
| 13 | BxQ | NxQ | 42 | K–B3 | K–Q5 |
| 14 | KxN | RxB | 43 | B–N3 | B–N2 |
| 15 | N–K2 | NxN | 44 | K–K2 | B–QR3 |
| 16 | KxN | R–K1 | 45 | B–B2 | B–QN4! |
| 17 | K–B1 | B–N2 | 46 | P–R4 | B–Q2! |
| 18 | P–B3 | P–B3 | 47 | K–B3 | K–B6 |
| 19 | N–N4 | P–KR4 | 48 | KxB | P–Q5†! |
| 20 | N–B2 | B–K6 | 49 | K–K2 | KxB |
| 21 | B–Q1 | P–R5 | 50 | N–B4 | BxRP |
| 22 | P–KN3 | P–R4 | 51 | N–K6 | B–N6! |
| 23 | B–B3 | P–N5 | 52 | NxP† | K–N7 |
| 24 | K–N2 | NPxP | 53 | N–N5 | P–R5 |
| 25 | PxBP | B–R3 | 54 | K–K3 | P–R6 |
| 26 | P–B4! | QR–Q1 | 55 | NxP | KxN |
| 27 | BPxP | BPxP | 56 | K–Q4 | K–N5! |
| 28 | KR–Q1 | R–K2 | | Resigns | |
| 29 | N–N4 | PxP | | | |

*Four Knights' Game 6*

*WHITE: Spielmann* *BLACK: Rubinstein*

*Baden–Baden 1925*

| | WHITE | BLACK | | WHITE | BLACK |
|---|---|---|---|---|---|
| 1 | P–K4 | P–K4 | 8 | N–KB3 | QxP† |
| 2 | N–KB3 | N–QB3 | 9 | K–B2 | N–N5† |
| 3 | N–B3 | N–B3 | 10 | K–N3 | Q–N3! |
| 4 | B–N5 | N–Q5 | 11 | Q–K2† | K–Q1 |
| 5 | NxP | Q–K2 | 12 | R–K1 | B–Q2 |
| 6 | P–B4 | NxB | 13 | N/5–Q4 | N–K6† |
| 7 | NxN | P–Q3 | 14 | K–B2 | NxBP |

| | WHITE | BLACK | | WHITE | BLACK |
|---|---|---|---|---|---|
| 15 | NxN | QxN | 31 | Q–Q3 | Q–KR4 |
| 16 | P–QN4 | P–QR4! | 32 | N–K5 | KRxP!! |
| 17 | B–R3 | PxP | 33 | KxR | PxN |
| 18 | BxP | Q–KB4 | 34 | RxP | Q–N5† |
| 19 | Q–K3 | P–R3! | 35 | Q–N3 | QxQ† |
| 20 | QR–QB1 | R–KN1! | 36 | KxQ | B–Q3 |
| 21 | K–N1 | P–KN4 | 37 | KxP | RxP |
| 22 | Q–B3 | R–B1 | 38 | K–N1 | RxP! |
| 23 | PxP | PxP | 39 | R–KR5 | P–N3 |
| 24 | K–R1 | P–N5 | 40 | B–K5 | B–B4† |
| 25 | N–Q4 | Q–Q4! | 41 | K–B1 | K–N2 |
| 26 | Q–K3 | P–N6! | 42 | B–N3 | B–N4† |
| 27 | B–B3 | R–QR1 | 43 | K–K1 | R–K7† |
| 28 | N–B3 | PxP | 44 | K–Q1 | R–KN7 |
| 29 | B–B6† | K–B1 | 45 | R–B3 | B–K7† |
| 30 | Q–B3 | Q–QB4 | | Resigns | |

*Four Knights' Game 7*

*WHITE: Spielmann* *BLACK: Rubinstein*

*San Sebastian 1912*

| | WHITE | BLACK | | WHITE | BLACK |
|---|---|---|---|---|---|
| 1 | P–K4 | P–K4 | 24 | P–R5? | K–B1 |
| 2 | N–KB3 | N–QB3 | 25 | R–Q7? | B–B4! |
| 3 | N–B3 | N–B3 | 26 | RxQP | B–K3! |
| 4 | B–N5 | N–Q5 | 27 | R–N1 | R–B2! |
| 5 | B–B4 | B–B4 | 28 | R–R6 | R–R1 |
| 6 | NxP | Q–K2 | 29 | RxB | PxR |
| 7 | N–B3 | P–Q4 | 30 | N–N5 | K–K2 |
| 8 | NxN | PxB | 31 | R–K1 | K–B3! |
| 9 | N–B3 | NxP | 32 | P–B4 | R–B3 |
| 10 | O–O | O–O | 33 | NxP† | K–K2 |
| 11 | P–Q4 | PxP e.p. | 34 | N–N5 | K–Q2 |
| 12 | PxP | NxN | 35 | R–K5 | R–KB1 |
| 13 | PxN | B–KN5 | 36 | P–Q5 | PxP |
| 14 | P–Q4 | B–Q3 | 37 | RxP† | R–Q3 |
| 15 | Q–Q3 | QR–K1 | 38 | R–N5 | K–B3 |
| 16 | P–KR3 | B–R4 | 39 | R–N4 | R–B4 |
| 17 | P–QR4 | B–N3 | 40 | R–B4† | K–Q2! |
| 18 | Q–B4 | Q–K7! | 41 | N–K4 | R–QB3 |
| 19 | QxQ | RxQ | 42 | R–R4 | R–QR3 |
| 20 | B–R3! | R–B7 | 43 | P–N4 | R/4xRP |
| 21 | BxB | PxB | 44 | R–Q4† | K–B2 |
| 22 | KR–K1 | RxQBP | 45 | N–B3 | R–Q3 |
| 23 | R–K7 | R–N1 | | Resigns | |

## SUPPLEMENTARY VARIATIONS 1–5:
### 1 P–K4, P–K4 2 N–KB3, N–QB3 3 N–B3

(The Russian Three Knights' Game — 1 P–K4, P–K4 2 N–KB3, N–KB3 3 N–B3, B–N5 — is treated under "Petroff's Defense.")

| | *1* | *2* | *3* | *4* | *5* |
|---|---|---|---|---|---|
| *3* | – – | – – | – – | – – | – – |
| | N–B3 | – – | B–B4 | P–KN3 | B–N5 |
| *4* | B–N5 | – – | NxP! | P–Q4 | N–Q5! |
| | P–QR3 | B–B4 | NxN | PxP | N–B3 |
| *5* | BxN[1] | O–O | P–Q4 | N–Q5! | B–B4[11] |
| | QPxB | P–Q3[6] | B–Q3[8] | B–N2 | O–O |
| *6* | NxP | P–Q4 | PxN | B–KN5 | O–O[12] |
| | NxP[2] | PxP | BxP | P–B3 | ± |
| *7* | NxN | NxP | P–B4 | B–KB4 | |
| | Q–Q5 | B–Q2 | BxN† | P–Q3 | |
| *8* | O–O | N–B5! | PxB | NxP[10] | |
| | QxN/4 | O–O | P–Q3 | ± | |
| *9* | R–K1 | B–N5 | Q–Q4 | | |
| | B–K3 | BxN | Q–R5† | | |
| *10* | P–Q4 | PxB | P–N3 | | |
| | Q–KB4![13] | N–Q5 | Q–K2 | | |
| *11* | B–N5 | B–Q3[7] | B–KN2 | | |
| | P–R3![4] | ± | N–B3 | | |
| *12* | Q–Q3 | | O–O | | |
| | K–Q2 | | O–O | | |
| *13* | B–R4 | | B–QR3[9] | | |
| | Q–QN4[5] | | ± | | |
| | = | | | | |

*Notes to supplementary variations 1–5:*

[1] 5 B–R4 establishes the Ruy Lopez.

[2] 6 . . . Q–K2 is insufficient because of 7 P–KB4.

[3] Faulty is 10 . . . Q–Q4 because of 11 N–N5!, O–O–O 12 NxB, PxN 13 Q–N4!, QxQP 14 QxP† with a substantial positional advantage.

[4] 11 . . . B–Q3 12 P–KN4!

[5] There is no good way to penetrate Black's King position, awkward though it may appear.

[6] Or 5 . . . O–O 6 NxP, R–K1 7 N–B3!±.

[7] With a clear advantage for White, according to Pachman.

[8] An offhand game won by Reti (White) went as follows: 5 . . . BxP 6 QxB, Q–B3 7 N–N5!, K–Q1 8 Q–B5!

[9] White's center, two Bishops, and threat of P–K5 are in his favor.

[10] White's development is far superior.

[11] Instead 5 NxB, NxN 6 NxP, P–Q3 leads to no advantage.

[12] White has a minimal initiative.

# chapter 5—Giuoco Piano

The Giuoco Piano is one of the oldest openings; and the first ever subjected to close analysis. The Portuguese, Damiano, used to play it at the beginning of the sixteenth century and the Calabrian, Greco, at the beginning of the seventeenth. Variations were worked out then which are valid even today. Greco can be considered as the father of opening theory.

The Giuoco Piano arises after 1 P–K4, P–K4 2 N–KB3, N–QB3 3 B–B4, B–B4. One can imagine what great appeal this enterprising deployment must have had for the players of the nineteenth century, when the immediate attack on the King was the ruling passion of the chess fraternity. Both King Bishops are actively placed, and White's Bishop particularly is more or less at the point of crashing into B7 in kamikaze fashion.

Together with some related openings, the Giuoco Piano was extremely popular for many years; but the gradual change of insight, as far as handling of the opening is concerned, tended more and more to a lasting initiative rather than a splurge of brief fireworks and has slowly replaced the Giuoco Piano and the King's Gambit with the Ruy Lopez and the Queen's Gambit. The frequency of the Giuoco Piano has dropped from about 30 per cent to probably not more than 1 per cent.

Even so, the Giuoco Piano must still be considered as a good opening. Black has to know a great deal to emerge from this enterprising debut without damage. The ensuing discussions of the opening will explain why.

---

## part 1—MÖLLER VARIATION

1 P–K4, P–K4
2 N–KB3, N–QB3
3 B–B4, B–B4
4 P–B3[A], N–B3[B]
5 P–Q4, PxP[C]
6 PxP[D], B–N5†[E]
7 N–B3[F], NxKP[G]
8 O–O

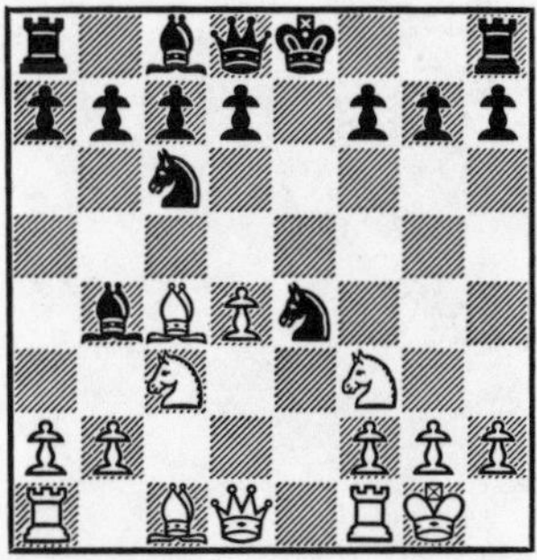

KEY POSITION 1

### OBSERVATIONS ON KEY POSITION 1

[A] The consistent continuation: White aims at building a strong center. The quieter continuations, 4 P–Q3, 4 N–B3 and 4 O–O are treated in the supplementary variations.

[B] In attacking the King Pawn, Black actually meets his opponent's plans. 4 . . . Q–K2 is treated in Part 3 and 4 . . . P–Q3 in the supplementary variations. The continuation 4 . . . B–N3 leads, after 5 P–Q4, Q–K2 to Part 3. Other moves are less commendable:

1) 4 . . . P–B4? 5 P–Q4 (also good is 5 P–Q3), BPxP (5 . . . KPxP 6 N–N5!) 6 NxP, NxN 7 Q–R5† with great advantage for White.

2) 4 . . . Q–B3 5 P–Q4!, PxP 6 P–K5, Q–N3 (6 . . . NxP? 7 Q–K2 and White wins a piece) 7 PxP, B–N5† 8 N–B3, QxP 9 R–KN1, Q–R6 10 BxP†! Or, in this line, 5 . . . B–N3 6 O–O, P–KR3 (6 . . . P–Q3 7 B–KN5, Q–N3 8 PxP, PxP 9 NxP!) 7 P–QR4, P–QR3 8 PxP, NxP 9 NxN, QxN 10 Q–B3 with advantage for White.

C 5 . . . B–N3 costs Black a Pawn, e.g., 6 NxP, NxN 7 PxN, NxP? 8 BxP† or 8 Q–Q5.

D 6 P–K5 is treated in Sup. Var. 1.

E 6 . . . B–N3? concedes White the center. After 7 P–Q5, N–K2 (if 7 . . . N–QR4, then 8 B–Q3, threatening 9 P–QN4) 8 P–K5, Black is in difficulties because of 8 . . . N–N5 9 P–Q6, PxP 10 PxP, BxP† (10 . . . NxBP 11 Q–N3!) 11 K–K2, N–B4 12 Q–Q5 winning a piece.

F For 7 B–Q2, see Part 2. On 7 K–B1, the so-called Cracow Variation, Black's best reply is 7 . . . P–Q4, e.g., 8 PxP, NxP/4 9 N–B3, B–K3 10 Q–K2, O–O 11 N–KN5? NxP!

G The consistent continuation. Black must take the Pawn or face difficulties:

1) 7 . . . P–Q3 8 P–Q5, BxN† (forced) 9 PxB, N–K2 10 O–O and White stands better.

2) 7 . . . O–O 8 B–KN5, P–KR3 9 BxN, QxB 10 O–O and White for choice. We may add that 8 P–K5 is of less promise because of 8 . . . P–Q4!

3) 7 . . . P–Q4 8 PxP, NxP 9 O–O, B–K3 10 B–KN5, B–K2 11 BxN, QBxB 12 NxB, QxN 13 BxB, NxB 14 R–K1, P–KB3 15 Q–K2, Q–Q2 16 QR–B1, K–B2! yet White has a tiny edge. If 11 BxB, N/3xB 12 Q–N3, NxN 13 BxB, Black's best is now 13 . . . N/6–Q4. For 16 . . . P–B3, see Game 1.

A wild position. Black is a Pawn to the good, but White has an advantage in development while the position is open. White therefore must depend on energetic play, regardless of the loss of additional Pawns or even greater material. Black's aim is consolidation; especially, safety for his King. His task is anything but simple, often requiring radical methods. Black must not forsake this aim on behalf of merely retaining a material advantage.

*Giuoco Piano Game 1*

*WHITE: Steinitz* *BLACK: Von Bardeleben*

| | WHITE | BLACK | | WHITE | BLACK |
|---|---|---|---|---|---|
| 1 | P–K4 | P–K4 | 6 | PxP | B–N5† |
| 2 | N–KB3 | N–QB3 | 7 | N–B3 | P–Q4 |
| 3 | B–B4 | B–B4 | 8 | PxP | KNxP |
| 4 | P–B3 | N–B3 | 9 | O–O | B–K3 |
| 5 | P–Q4 | PxP | 10 | B–KN5 | B–K2 |

| WHITE | BLACK | WHITE | BLACK |
|---|---|---|---|
| 11 BxN | QBxB | 24 R–N7†!! | K–R1 |
| 12 NxB | QxN | 25 RxP† | K–N1 |
| 13 BxB | NxB | 26 R–N7† | K–R1 |
| 14 R–K1 | P–KB3 | 27 Q–R4† | KxR |
| 15 Q–K2 | Q–Q2 | 28 Q–R7† | K–B1 |
| 16 QR–B1 | P–B3? | 29 Q–R8† | K–K2 |
| 17 P–Q5! | PxP | 30 Q–N7† | K–K1 |
| 18 N–Q4 | K–B2 | 31 Q–N8† | K–K2 |
| 19 N–K6 | KR–QB1 | 32 Q–B7† | K–Q1 |
| 20 Q–N4 | P–KN3 | 33 Q–B8† | Q–K1 |
| 21 N–N5† | K–K1 | 34 N–B7† | K–Q2 |
| 22 RxN† | K–B1 | 35 Q–Q6 mate | |
| 23 R–B7†! | K–N1 | | |

IDEA VARIATIONS 1-5:

(1) 8 . . . NxN 9 PxN, BxP 10 Q–N3, BxR? (10 . . . P–Q4!) 11 BxP†, K–B1 12 B–N5, N–K2 13 N–K5!, BxP 14 B–N6!, P–Q4 15 Q–B3†, B–B4 16 BxB, BxN 17 B–K6†, B–B3 18 BxB, and White wins.

(2) 8 . . . NxN 9 PxN, P–Q4 10 PxB, PxB 11 R–K1†, N–K2 12 Q–K2, B–K3 13 N–N5, Q–Q2 14 NxB, QxN 15 B–N5, QxQ 16 RxQ, P–KB3 17 QR–K1, O–O–O!, and Black has a satisfactory game.

(3) 8 . . . BxN 9 P–Q5! (the Möller Variation proper), N–K4 10 PxB, NxB 11 Q–Q4, N/B–Q3 (11 . . . P–KB4!) 12 QxNP, Q–B3 13 QxQ, NxQ 14 R–K1†, K–B1? (14 . . . N/B–K5 15 N–Q2, P–B4 16 P–B3, and White for choice) 15 B–R6†, K–N1 16 R–K5, N/Q–K5 (16 . . . N/B–K5 17 QR–K1, P–KB4 18 R–K7, and White wins) 17 N–Q2! P–Q3 18 NxN, PxR 19 NxN mate.

(4) 8 . . . BxN 9 P–Q5, B–B3 10 R–K1, N–K2 11 RxN, P–Q3 12 B–KN5, BxB 13 NxB, O–O 14 NxRP, KxN 15 Q–R5†, K–N1 16 R–R4, P–KB4 17 R–R3 (preventing 17 . . . N–N3), P–B5 18 P–KN4! PxP e.p. 19 Q–R7†, K–B2 20 Q–R5†, K–N1 (not 20 . . . N–N3? 21 RxP, Q–B3 22 B–Q3) 21 Q–R7 with perpetual check.

(5) 8 . . . BxN 9 P–Q5, B–B3 10 R–K1, N–K2 11 RxN, O-O 12 P–Q6, PxP 13 QxP, N–B4 14 Q–Q5, P–Q3 (safer is 14 . . . N–K2 with a repetition of position) 15 N–N5, BxN 16 BxB, QxB? 17 QxBP† and mate follows.

## PRACTICAL VARIATIONS 1–8:

1 P–K4, P–K4 2 N–KB3, N–QB3 3 B–B4, B–B4 4 P–B3, N–B3 5 P–Q4, PxP 6 PxP, B–N5† 7 N–B3, NxKP 8 O–O

| | *1* | *2* | *3* | *4* | *5* | *6* | *7* | *8* |
|---|---|---|---|---|---|---|---|---|
| 8 | – – | – – | – – | – – | – – | – – | – – | – – |
| | NxN[1] | – – | – – | BxN | – – | – – | – – | – – |
| 9 | PxN | – – | – – | P–Q5[12] | – – | – – | – – | – – |
| | BxP | – – | P–Q4! | B–R4 | N–K4 | B–B3 | – – | – – |
| 10 | Q–N3 | B–R3[5] | PxB | PxN | PxB | R–K1 | – – | – – |
| | P–Q4[2] | P–Q4[6] | PxB | O–O[13] | NxB | N–K2 | – – | – – |
| 11 | BxP | B–N5 | R–K1† | Q–Q5 | Q–Q4 | RxN | – – | – – |
| | O–O | BxR | N–K2 | N–Q3 | P–KB4[15] | O–O | P–Q3 | – – |
| 12 | BxP† | R–K1† | B–N5[8] | B–Q3 | QxN/B | P–KN4[16] | B–KN5 | – – |
| | K–R1[3] | B–K3 | P–KB3 | B–N3 | P–Q3 | N–N3 | BxB[18] | – – |
| 13 | QxB | Q–R4[7] | Q–K2 | BxP† | N–Q4 | P–Q6 | NxB | – – |
| | RxB | ± | B–N5[9] | KxB | O–O | PxP | P–KR3[19] | O–O |
| 14 | Q–N3 | | B–B4 | Q–R5† | P–B3 | P–N5 | B–N5†! | NxRP |
| | R–B4 | | K–B2 | K–N1 | N–B3 | B–K2 | P–B3[20] | KxN |
| 15 | R–K1 | | QxP† | N–N5[14] | B–N5 | B–Q5[17] | NxP! | Q–R5† |
| | B–Q2 | | N–Q4 | ± | P–KR3 | = | KxN | K–N1 |
| 16 | P–Q5[4] | | N–Q2[10] | | = | | Q–B3† | R–R4 |
| | ± | | B–K3 | | | | B–B4[21] | P–KB4[23] |
| 17 | | | B–N3 | | | | PxP | R–K1[24] |
| | | | P–B3 | | | | PxP | N–N3! |
| 18 | | | N–K4[11] | | | | BxP | R–R3 |
| | | | ± | | | | R–QB1[22] | R–B3![25] |
| | | | | | | | ± | ∓ |

*Notes to practical variations 1–8:*

[1] The Greco Variation, which is not quite satisfactory for Black.

[2] Suggested By O. Bernstein. For 10 . . . BxR see Idea Var. 1. Another inferior variation for Black is 10 . . . BxP? 11 BxP†, K–B1 12 B–N5, B–B3 13 QR–K1, N–K2 14 B–R5, P–Q4 15 RxN!, QxR 16 R–K1 with an irresistible attack for White.

[3] Not 12 . . . RxB because of 13 N–N5, B–K3 14 QxKB.

[4] 16 . . . N–K2 fails against 17 B–N5.

[5] This may be even stronger than 10 Q–N3.

[6] Or 10 . . . N–K2 11 Q–N3!, or 10 . . . Q–B3 11 R–B1, B–N5 12 BxB, NxB 13 R–K1† with a great advantage for White.

[7] White has a winning attack. See Game 2.

[8] For 12 Q–K2, see Idea Var. 2.

[9] 13 . . . PxB 14 QxP offers White excellent attacking chances.

[10] 16 BxP fails against 16 . . . QR–B1.

[11] White has a slight edge, despite his isolated Pawn.

[12] After 9 PxB, P–Q4 Black has a satisfactory game. The text was suggested by the Danish analyst, Möller.

[13] White also gets the advantage after 10 . . . QPxP 11 Q–R4, B–N3 12 BxP† and 10 . . . NPxP 11 N–K5, N–Q3 12 Q–N4.

[14] White has a winning attack.

[15] For 11 . . . N/B–Q3, see Idea Var. 3.

[16] For 12 P–Q6, see Idea Var. 5.

[17] White exercises strong pressure — at the heavy expense, however, of two Pawns.

[18] Or 12 . . . O–O, which is met by 13 BxB, PxB 14 Q–Q2, N–N3 15 QR–K1, and now 15 . . . P–KB4 has the serious drawback of allowing 16 Q–R6! (Spielmann–Duras, Karlsbad 1907).

[19] After 13 . . . B–B4 14 Q–B3! White has a superior game, e.g., 14 . . . Q–Q2 15 B–N5, QxB 16 QxB, P–KB3 17 RxN†, and White wins.

[20] Or 14 . . . B–Q2 15 Q–K2, K–B1 16 QR–K1, with a promising game for White.

[21] 16 . . . K–K1 loses to 17 PxP, as does 16 . . . K–N1 to 17 QR–K1. Also bad for Black is 16 . . . K–N3 because of 17 RxN! Finally, 16 . . . N–B4 leads to a great advantage for White after 17 PxP, PxP 18 BxP, R–QN1 19 P–KN4, P–N3 20 QR–K1.

[22] With 19 QR–K1, White maintains a strong attack.

[23] White seems to have a promising attack, yet he can hardly achieve more than a draw.

[24] The text is White's best, though it offers no winning chances. No more promising is 17 B–K2, R–K1 18 R–K1, K–B1. And after 17 Q–R7†, K–B2 18 R–R6, R–N1 19 R–K1, K–B1, it is Black who can play for a win. For 17 R–R3, see Idea Var. 4.

[25] Black is out of danger, e.g., 19 Q–R7†, K–B2 20 R–K6, N–B1! 21 Q–R5†, P–N3 22 Q–R8, BxR 23 PxB, RxP and White's attack has spent itself.

*Giuoco Piano Game 2*

*WHITE: Corte* — *BLACK: Bolbochan*

| | WHITE | BLACK | | WHITE | BLACK |
|---|---|---|---|---|---|
| 1 | P–K4 | P–K4 | 10 | B–R3! | P–Q4 |
| 2 | N–KB3 | N–QB3 | 11 | B–N5 | BxR |
| 3 | B–B4 | B–B4 | 12 | R–K1† | B–K3 |
| 4 | P–B3 | N–B3 | 13 | Q–R4 | R–QN1 |
| 5 | P–Q4 | PxP | 14 | N–K5 | Q–B1 |
| 6 | PxP | B–N5† | 15 | BxN† | PxB |
| 7 | N–B3 | NxKP | 16 | QxP† | K–Q1 |
| 8 | O–O | NxN | 17 | NxP† | BxN |
| 9 | PxN | BxP | 18 | B–K7 mate | |

# part 2—7 B-Q2 VARIATION

1 P–K4, P–K4
2 N–KB3, N–QB3
3 B–B4, B–B4
4 P–B3, N–B3
5 P–Q4, PxP
6 PxP, B–N5†
7 B–Q2[A], BxB†[B]
8 QNxB, P–Q4
9 PxP, KNxP
10 Q–N3, QN–K2[C]
11 O–O, O–O
12 KR–K1, P–QB3

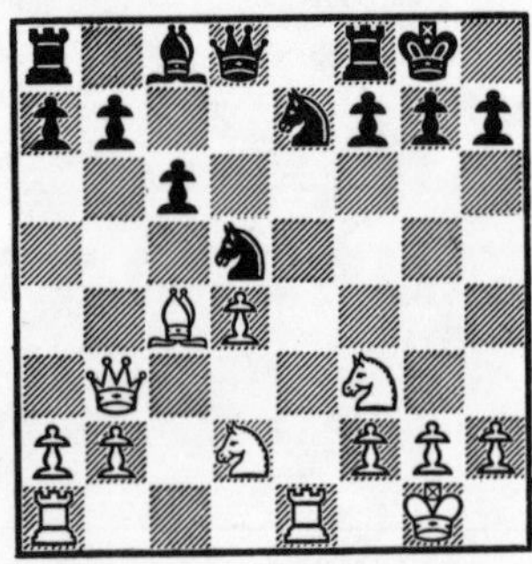

KEY POSITION 2

## OBSERVATIONS ON KEY POSITION 2

A This quiet continuation enables White to avoid a material sacrifice, but his advantage in the center is substantially diminished.

B 7 . . . NxKP may take the bold course of 8 BxB, NxB 9 BxP†, KxB 10 Q–N3†, P–Q4 11 N–K5†, K–K3 (11 . . . K–B3 12 P–KB3) 12 QxN, P–B4 13 Q–R3, PxP 14 N–KB3 or 14 N–Q3 with an adventurous game. The risk, however, is all Black's.

C 10 . . . B–K3 is answered by 11 QxP, N–R4 12 B–N5†, K–B1 13 Q–R6, P–QB3 14 B–R4. 10 . . . N–R4 is unfavorable for Black, as in 11 Q–R4†, P–B3 12 BxN, QxB 13 O–O, in which Black's Knight is ill-placed. But 10 . . . O–O!? 11 BxN, N–R4 deserves consideration.

White has an isolated Queen Pawn, but he enjoys far greater freedom of movement. A situation like this may become dangerous for either side. Failure to act energetically may hurt White in that his isolated Queen Pawn becomes a liability. On the other hand, even a slight inaccuracy may cause serious damage to Black.

## IDEA VARIATIONS 6 and 7:

(6) 13 P–QR4, Q–N3 14 P–R5, QxQ 15 NxQ, B–B4 (15 . . . R–Q1!) 16 N–K5, N–N5 17 QR–B1, KN–Q4 18 P–R6 with an edge for White.

(7) 13 N–K4, N–QN3 14 N–B5, NxB 15 QxN, P–QN3 16 N–Q3, B–K3? (16 . . . Q–Q3 or 16 . . . B–N2 gives an even game) 17 RxB!, PxR 18 QxP†, K–R1 19 QN–K5, Q–K1 20 N–N5 and White wins.

## PRACTICAL VARIATIONS 9–11:

1 P–K4, P–K4 2 N–KB3, N–QB3 3 B–B4, B–B4 4 P–B3, N–B3 5 P–Q4, PxP 6 PxP, B–N5† 7 B–Q2, BxB† 8 QNxB, P–Q4 9 PxP, KNxP 10 Q–N3, N/3–K2 11 O–O, O–O 12 KR–K1, P–QB3

| | 9 | 10 | 11 |
|---|---|---|---|
| 13 | N–K4 | P–QR4 | – – |
| | Q–N3[1] | Q–N3 | Q–B2[7] |
| 14 | N–B3[2] | P–R5[4] | QR–B1 |
| | QxQ | QxQ | Q–B5[8] |
| 15 | BxQ | NxQ | N–K4 |
| | B–K3 | R–Q1[5] | B–B4 |
| 16 | N–KN5 | N–B5 | N–B5 |
| | B–Q2 | R–N1[6] | P–QN3 |
| 17 | R–K5[3] | = | N–Q3 |
| | ± | | BxN |
| 18 | | | BxB |
| | | | QR–Q1[9] |
| | | | = |

*Notes to practical variations 9–11:*

[1] For 13 . . . N–QN3, see Idea Var. 7.

[2] After 14 Q–R3, B–B4 15 N–B5, QR–Q1 16 N–K5, B–B1

17 QR–Q1, White has a slight superiority in space.

[3] Bogoljubov–Euwe, 7th Match Game 1941.

[4] After 14 Q–R3, B–K3 15 P–R5, Q–B2, Black is safe.

[5] For 15 . . . B–B4, see Idea Var. 6.

[6] Black has equality at least. He may soon proceed with . . . P–QN3.

[7] For 13 . . . P–QR4, see Game 3.

[8] On 14 . . . N–B5, there follows 15 N–N5, N/2–N3 16 R–K8! (Schiffers–Harmonist, Nuremberg 1887).

[9] Schlechter–Breyer, Baden 1914.

*Giuoco Piano Game 3*

*WHITE: Gligoric* *BLACK: H. Kramer*

*Amsterdam 1950*

| | WHITE | BLACK | | WHITE | BLACK |
|---|---|---|---|---|---|
| 1 | P–K4 | P–K4 | 34 | K–B3 | N/6–Q4 |
| 2 | N–KB3 | N–QB3 | 35 | N–B4 | R–KR1 |
| 3 | B–B4 | B–B4 | 36 | K–N3 | R–QB1 |
| 4 | P–B3 | N–B3 | 37 | B–B3 | R–Q1 |
| 5 | P–Q4 | PxP | 38 | P–B5 | PxP |
| 6 | PxP | B–N5† | 39 | PxP | R–KR1 |
| 7 | B–Q2 | BxB† | 40 | P–R5 | R–Q1 |
| 8 | QNxB | P–Q4 | 41 | P–R6 | PxP |
| 9 | PxP | KNxP | 42 | P–B6† | K–Q2 |
| 10 | Q–N3 | N/3–K2 | 43 | B–R5 | R–N1† |
| 11 | O–O | O–O | 44 | K–B3 | K–K3 |
| 12 | KR–K1 | P–QB3 | 45 | B–N4† | RxB |
| 13 | P–QR4 | P–QR4 | 46 | KxR | P–N4 |
| 14 | N–K4 | B–B4 | 47 | NxP | PxP |
| 15 | N–N3 | B–N3 | 48 | PxP | KxP |
| 16 | N–K5 | N–N5 | 49 | N–B4† | KxP |
| 17 | NxB | RPxN | 50 | R–KR2 | K–N3 |
| 18 | R–K5 | N/2–Q4 | 51 | N–K5† | K–N2 |
| 19 | R/1–K1 | Q–Q2 | 52 | K–B5 | P–B3 |
| 20 | N–K4 | QR–K1 | 53 | N–B4 | K–B2 |
| 21 | Q–N3 | P–N3 | 54 | RxP | N–K2† |
| 22 | P–R4 | RxR | 55 | K–K4 | K–K3 |
| 23 | PxR | Q–B4 | 56 | N–K3 | P–QB4 |
| 24 | N–Q6 | Q–B7 | 57 | R–R5 | P–B4† |
| 25 | P–N3 | Q–Q7 | 58 | NxP | N/2–Q4 |
| 26 | R–K2 | Q–B8† | 59 | N–N7† | K–Q3 |
| 27 | K–R2 | Q–B5 | 60 | R–R6† | K–B2 |
| 28 | QxQ | NxQ | 61 | N–K6† | K–N1 |
| 29 | R–Q2 | N/B–Q4 | 62 | NxP | K–R2 |
| 30 | P–N4 | R–Q1 | 63 | K–Q4 | N–B2 |
| 31 | K–N3 | K–B1 | 64 | R–R7 | K–N1 |
| 32 | P–B4 | N–K6 | 65 | K–B4 | N–B3 |
| 33 | B–K2 | K–K2 | 66 | R–R6 | Resigns |

## part 3—CENTER-HOLDING VARIATION

1 P–K4, P–K4
2 N–KB3, N–QB3
3 B–B4, B–B4
4 P–B3, Q–K2[A]
5 P–Q4, B–N3[B]
6 O–O[C], P–Q3
7 P–KR3[D], N–B3
8 R–K1, O–O[E]

KEY POSITION 3

### OBSERVATIONS ON KEY POSITION 3

[A] With this move Black intends to hold the center. Whether this set-up is ultimately satisfactory remains to be determined, but experience to date seems to justify Black's strategy. As was mentioned before, the variation can arise from a transposition of moves, i.e., 4 . . . B–N3 5 P–Q4, Q–K2.

[B] 5 . . . PxP is inconsistent. The game develops a wide-open character, and the position of Black's Queen becomes unsafe. White proceeds with 6 O–O, and now there are three plausible variations to consider:

1) 6 . . . P–Q6 7 P–K5, P–KR3 (7 . . . P–Q3? 8 B–KN5) 8 P–QN4, B–N3 9 P–QR4, P–QR4 10 B–R3, PxP 11 PxP, NxP 12 Q–N3, B–B4 13 N–B3 with advantage for White (Rossolimo–Evans, Hastings 1949–50).
2) 6 . . . PxP 7 NxP, P–Q3 8 N–Q5, Q–Q1 9 P–QN4 with good chances for White.
3) 6 . . . N–K4 7 NxN, QxN 8 P–B4, PxP† 9 K–R1, PxP? 10 PxQ, PxR(Q) 11 Q–Q5! with a winning attack.

[C] The interesting 6 P–Q5 is treated in Sup. Var. 4 and 5.

[D] 7 P–QR4, P–QR3 8 P–KR3 constitutes a transposition of moves. To allow Black to play . . . B–KN5 is not recommended for White: e.g., 7 P–QR4, P–QR3 8 P–QN4, N–B3 9 B–R3, B–N5 10 P–N5, N–R4 11 QN–Q2, NxP with a clear advantage for Black (Rossetto–Euwe, Buenos Aires 1947).

[E] 8 . . . P–KR3 with the idea of launching a Kingside attack with . . . P–KN4 is best answered by 9 P–QR4, P–QR3 10 B–K3: e.g., 10 . . . P–KN4 11 PxP, PxP 12 BxB, RPxB 13 N–R2, and White has the superior position.

Black has succeeded in maintaining the center, but White has a superiority in controlled space with chances of building an attacking position on the Kingside. Chances on the Queenside may also arise because of the somewhat precarious position of Black's King Bishop. A third possibility for White exists in the tentative opening of the diagonal QR3–KB8 by a timely PxKP. None of these plans constitutes an immediate danger in itself, but in combination they may become fatal for Black. A good strategy for Black consists in the strengthening of his center (after castling) by maneuvers such as . . . K–R1, . . . N–KN1 and . . . P–KB3.

### IDEA VARIATIONS 8–11:

(8) 9 N–R3, N–Q1 10 B–B1, N–K1? (10 . . . N–Q2) 11 N–B4, P–KB3 12 P–QR4, P–B3 13 NxB, PxN 14 Q–N3†, and White wins a Pawn. See Game 4.

(9) 9 N–R3, N–Q1 10 B–Q3, P–B3 11 N–B4, B–B2 12 PxP!, PxP 13 P–QN3!, P–QN4 14 B–R3, P–B4

15 N–K3 with a positional advantage for White.

(10) 9 P–QR4, P–QR3 10 P–QN4, K–R1 11 B–R3, N–KN1 12 P–N5, N–R4 13 NxP? P–KB3 14 BxN, PxN 15 B–R2, PxP 16 PxP, Q–B3, and Black has the superior game (Van Scheltinga–Euwe, Maastricht 1946).

(11) 9 P–QR4, P–QR3 10 P–QN4, P–R3 11 B–R3, N–Q2 12 P–N5, N–Q1 13 QN–Q2, Q–B3 14 N–B1 (or 14 B–N3) leads to an excellent game for White.

## PRACTICAL VARIATIONS 12-14:

1 P–K4, P–K4 2 N–KB3, N–QB3 3 B–B4, B–B4 4 P–B3, Q–K2 5 P–Q4, B–N3 6 O–O, P–Q3 7 P–KR3, N–B3 8 R–K1, O–O.

| | *12* | *13* | *14* |
|---|---|---|---|
| *9* | P–QR4 | – – | N–R3[7] |
| | P–QR3 | – – | K–R1[8] |
| *10* | B–K3[1] | N–R3 | N–B2[9] |
| | PxP[2] | K–R1 | N–Q1[10] |
| *11* | BxP[3] | N–B2 | P–QN3[11] |
| | NxB | N–KN1 | B–K3[12] |
| *12* | PxN | N–K3 | B–B1[13] |
| | B–K3 | B–R2 | N–N1 |
| *13* | QN–Q2 | N–Q5[5] | N–K3 |
| | N–R4[4] | Q–Q1[6] | P–KB3 |
| *14* | = | = | N–Q5 |
| | | | Q–B2 |
| *15* | | | P–B4 |
| | | | B–R4[14] |
| *16* | | | R–K2 |
| | | | N–B3[15] |
| | | | = |

*Notes to practical variations 12–14:*

[1] For 10 B–KN5, see Game 5.

[2] This exchange is basically not good for Black, but here it incidentally works because White is unable to profit from the situation on the Kingside.

[3] 11 PxP, QxP constitutes a dubious gambit.

[4] Christoffel–Smyslov, Groningen 1946.

[5] 13 N–B5 offers better chances.

[6] Black has a satisfactory game. See Game 6.

[7] The postponement of P–QR4 is considered an improvement. White aims to bring his Knight, via QB4 or QB2, to K3 and possibly to Q5 or KB5.

[8] For 9 . . . N–Q1, see Idea Var. 8 and 9.

[9] 10 B–B1, PxP 11 PxP, NxP is safe for Black. Or 10 B–N3, N–KN1 11 N–B4, N–R4!

[10] After 10 . . . N–KN1, White's 12 N–K3 has a good effect.

[11] With the threat of 12 B–R3.

[12] Now, on 13 B–R3, Black has 13 . . . BxB 14 PxB, P–B4.

[13] Rossolimo–Euwe, Gijon 1951, continued 12 B–Q3, N–N1 13 N–K3, P–KB3 14 N–Q5, Q–B2 with a good game for Black.

[14] Well worth considering is 15 . . . P–QB4.

[15] Bouwmeester–Euwe, Enschade 1952.

*Giuoco Piano Game 4*

*WHITE: Tartakover* *BLACK: Euwe*

*Venice 1948*

| | WHITE | BLACK | | WHITE | BLACK |
|---|---|---|---|---|---|
| 1 | P–K4 | P–K4 | 23 | PxN | B–R6† |
| 2 | N–KB3 | N–QB3 | 24 | K–N3 | KPxP† |
| 3 | B–B4 | B–B4 | 25 | BxP | Q–Q2 |
| 4 | P–B3 | B–N3 | 26 | N–R2 | PxB† |
| 5 | P–Q4 | Q–K2 | 27 | KxP | R–R5† |
| 6 | O–O | P–Q3 | 28 | K–K3 | B–N7 |
| 7 | P–KR3 | N–B3 | 29 | N–B3 | RxP† |
| 8 | R–K1 | O–O | 30 | KxR | N–Q3† |
| 9 | N–R3 | N–Q1 | 31 | K–Q3 | Q–B4† |
| 10 | B–B1 | N–K1? | 32 | K–Q4 | Q–B5† |
| 11 | N–B4 | P–KB3 | 33 | K–Q3 | QxB† |
| 12 | P–QR4 | P–B3 | 34 | K–B2 | BxN |
| 13 | NxB | PxN | 35 | P–N3? | B–K5† |
| 14 | Q–N3† | N–K3 | 36 | K–N2 | Q–Q6 |
| 15 | QxP | P–N4 | 37 | R–N1† | K–B2 |
| 16 | B–QB4 | P–R3 | 38 | QR–QB1 | Q–Q7† |
| 17 | P–R4 | K–R2 | 39 | K–R3 | N–B5† |
| 18 | RPxP? | RPxP | 40 | PxN | RxP† |
| 19 | PxP | QPxP | 41 | KxR | Q–R7† |
| 20 | B–K3 | R–R1 | 42 | K–N4 | Q–N7† |
| 21 | P–KN3? | K–N3 | | Resigns | |
| 22 | K–N2? | N–B5† | | | |

*Giuoco Piano Game 5*

*WHITE: Tarrasch* *BLACK: Alekhine*

*Baden–Baden 1925*

| | WHITE | BLACK | | WHITE | BLACK |
|---|---|---|---|---|---|
| 1 | P–K4 | P–K4 | 12 | B–Q3 | R–K1 |
| 2 | N–KB3 | N–QB3 | 13 | QN–Q2 | B–R2 |
| 3 | B–B4 | B–B4 | 14 | Q–B2 | PxP |
| 4 | P–B3 | B–N3 | 15 | NxP | N–K4 |
| 5 | P–Q4 | Q–K2 | 16 | B–B1 | P–Q4 |
| 6 | O–O | N–B3 | 17 | QR–B1 | P–B4 |
| 7 | R–K1 | P–Q3 | 18 | N–N3 | Q–B2 |
| 8 | P–QR4 | P–QR3 | 19 | B–KB4 | N–B6†! |
| 9 | P–R3 | O–O | 20 | NxN | QxB |
| 10 | B–KN5 | P–R3 | 21 | PxP? | B–KB4 |
| 11 | B–K3 | Q–Q1 | 22 | B–Q3 | BxP |

| | WHITE | BLACK | | WHITE | BLACK |
|---|---|---|---|---|---|
| 23 | PxB | QxN | 27 | K–R2 | N–N5† |
| 24 | RxR† | RxR | 28 | PxN | RxNP |
| 25 | B–B1 | R–K4 | | Resigns | |
| 26 | P–B4 | R–N4† | | | |

*Giuoco Piano Game 6*

*WHITE: Contedini* *BLACK: Euwe*

*Leipzig 1960*

| | WHITE | BLACK | | WHITE | BLACK |
|---|---|---|---|---|---|
| 1 | P–K4 | P–K4 | 16 | PxP | NxN |
| 2 | N–KB3 | N–QB3 | 17 | BxN | BxB |
| 3 | B–B4 | B–B4 | 18 | RxB | BPxP |
| 4 | P–B3 | B–N3 | 19 | B–N3 | Q–B3 |
| 5 | P–Q4 | Q–K2 | 20 | P–B4 | N–K2 |
| 6 | O–O | P–Q3 | 21 | P–B5 | PxP |
| 7 | P–QR4 | P–QR3 | 22 | PxP | N–N3 |
| 8 | P–KR3 | N–B3 | 23 | Q–Q5 | BxP! |
| 9 | R–K1 | O–O | 24 | PxB | N–R5 |
| 10 | N–R3 | K–R1 | 25 | NxN | QxP† |
| 11 | N–B2 | N–KN1 | 26 | K–R1 | QxR |
| 12 | N–K3 | B–R2 | 27 | N–B5 | QxRP† |
| 13 | N–Q5 | Q–Q1 | 28 | K–N1 | R–B3 |
| 14 | B–K3 | P–B3 | | Resigns | |
| 15 | P–QN4 | N/3–K2 | | | |

SUPPLEMENTARY VARIATIONS 1–10:

1 P–K4, P–K4 2 N–KB3, N–QB3 3 B–B4, B–B4.

The method given in Sup. Var. 1 constitutes an attempt to intensify the struggle. How good this strategy is for White remains to be seen.

The system adopted by Black in Sup. Var. 2 and 3 is somewhat meek; he abandons the center and acquiesces in advance to a cramped position.

Variations 4 and 5 involve interesting Pawn sacrifices, offering White considerable pressure.

Variations 6, 7, 8 and 9 illustrate quiet forms of the opening "Giuoco Pianissimo."

Finally, Sup. Var. 10 shows an unsuccessful attempt to force the Max Lange Variation of the Two Knights' Defense.

1 P–K4, P–K4 2 N–KB3, N–QB3 3 B–B4, B–B4

| | *1* | *2* | *3* | *4* | *5* |
|---|---|---|---|---|---|
| *4* | P–B3 | – – | – – | – – | – – |
| | N–B3 | P–Q3 | – – | Q–K2 | – – |
| *5* | P–Q4 | P–Q4 | – – | P–Q4 | – – |
| | PxP | PxP[4] | – – | B–N3 | – – |
| *6* | P–K5 | PxP | – – | P–Q5 | – – |
| | P–Q4![1] | B–N3[5] | – – | N–N1 | N–Q1! |
| *7* | B–QN5[2] | N–B3 | – – | P–Q6[14] | P–Q6[17] |
| | N–K5 | N–B3 | – – | QxP | QxQ |
| *8* | PxP | B–K3 | – – | QxQ | QxQ |
| | B–N3 | B–N5 | – – | PxQ | PxQ |
| *9* | N–B3 | B–N3[6] | – – | N–N5![15] | N–R3 |
| | O–O | O–O | – – | N–KR3 | N–K3 |
| *10* | B–K3 | Q–Q3 | – – | P–QR4 | B–Q5 |
| | P–B3 | R–K1 | – – | N–B3 | N–B3 |
| *11* | Q–N3 | O–O[7] | – – | P–QN4 | P–B4 |
| | NxN | B–KR4 | BxN | P–B3 | B–B2[18] |
| *12* | PxN | N–Q2 | PxB | N–B3 | = |
| | B–N5![3] | N–KN5[8] | N–KR4[10] | N–B2 | |
| *13* | = | N–Q5 | N–K2![11] | P–R5 | |
| | | NxB | Q–R5 | B–B2 | |
| *14* | | PxN | K–N2[12] | N–R3 | |
| | | R–KB1 | N–K2 | P–QR3 | |
| *15* | | R–B2[9] | R–KN1 | B–Q5 | |
| | | ± | N–N3[13] | N–K2[16] | |
| | | | ± | = | |

*Notes to supplementary variations 1–10:*

[1] Or 6 N–K5? 7 B–Q5!

[2] If 7 P–QN4, Black's best is 8 . . . N–K5!

[3] Black has equality at least.

[4] 5 . . . B–N3 costs Black a Pawn.

[5] 6 . . . B–N5† is supposed to be refuted by 7 K–B1, threatening 8 P–Q5; but after 7 . . . B–R4, Black has sufficient counterchances. Therefore 7 B–Q2 is actually stronger.

[6] The text move prevents 9 . . . NxKP.

[7] 11 O–O–O also deserves consideration. The possible doubling of White's King Bishop Pawn is no particular danger, as Black lacks the means to start an effective attack on the King-side.

[8] 12 . . . B–N3 is answered by 13 P–Q5, N–K4 14 Q–K2.

[9] White enjoys open lines.

[10] Threatening to win by 13 . . . BxP 14 BxB, N–B5!

[11] Not 13 N–Q5 because Black gains an important tempo with 13 . . . R–K3!

[12] Not 14 K–R1 because of 14 . . . Q–R6 15 N–N3?, NxP! 16 BxN?, N–B5!

[13] After 16 K–R1, White has the edge: e.g., 16 . . . N/3–B5 17 NxN, NxN 18 Q–B4 with numerous threats.

[14] An interesting Pawn sacrifice.

| 6 | 7 | 8 | 9 | 10 |
|---|---|---|---|---|
| N–B3[19] | – – | – – | – – | O–O |
| N–B3 | – – | – – | – – | N–B3 |
| P–Q3 | – – | – – | – – | P–Q4 |
| P–Q3[20] | – – | – – | – – | BxP[29] |
| B–K3 | B–KN5[21] | – – | – – | NxB |
| B–N3 | P–KR3 | N–QR4 | – – | NxN |
| Q–Q2 | BxN | BxN | – – | P–B4[30] |
| B–K3 | QxB | PxB | QxB! | P–Q3 |
| B–QN5 | N–Q5 | N–KR4 | N–Q5 | PxP |
| O–O | Q–Q1[22] | NxB | Q–Q1 | PxP |
| P–Q4 | P–B3 | PxN | P–QN4 | B–KN5 |
| PxP | P–R3[23] | P–B4 | P–QB3[26] | B–K3 |
| NxP | O–O | NxP | PxB | N–Q2 |
| NxN | O–O | BxN | NxB | Q–Q2 |
| BxN | P–QR4 | PxB | PxN | BxN |
| BxB | B–R2 | Q–R5 | PxN | PxB |
| QxB | Q–K2 | Q–B3 | QxP[27] | RxBP |
| P–Q4 | N–K2 | QxBP | Q–R4† | O–O[31] |
| = | N–K3 | QxP | K–B1[28] | ∓ |
| | N–N3 | K–Q2[24] | QxBP | |
| | = | Q–N3 | QxQ | |
| | | QxQ | PxQ | |
| | | RPxQ | NxP | |
| | | KR–KN1[25] | B–K3 | |
| | | ± | ± | |

[15] The text is stronger than the old-fashioned continuation 9 N–R3, N–KB3 10 B–Q5, NxB 11 PxN, P–B3 12 N–Q2, K–K2 13 N/2–B4, B–B2, after which Black safely emerges from the pressure.

[16] White's strong pressure compensates for the Pawn.

[17] 7 O–O, while Black's Queen Knight is inactively placed, merits consideration, but leads to no advantage after 7 . . . P–Q3 8 P–QR4, P–QR3. On 7 P–QR4, BxP† 8 KxB, Q–B4† 9 B–K3, QxB 10 QN–Q2, Q–R3 11 NxP, Q–B3†, Black has an equal game.

[18] Black is safe.

[19] 4 P–Q3, N–B3 5 N–B3 leads to the text column.

[20] The initial position of the Italian Four Knights' Game (the Giuoco Pianissimo).

[21] This sharp continuation breaks away from the ordinarily serene course of the Italian Four Knights' Game.

[22] 8 . . . Q–N3 9 NxP†, K–Q1 10 NxR, QxNP 11 R–KB1, B–KN5 is promising for Black, but White has better: 9 N–R4, Q–N4 10 P–KN3, B–N3 11 P–QB3, B–N5 12 P–B3, B–R6 13 P–QR4, O–O 14 P–QN4, and White has the edge (Blau-Porreca, Vevey 1953).

[23] Also plausible is 9 . . . N–K2 10 N–K3, O–O 11 O–O, B–N3 12 P–Q4, N–N3. For 10 . . . B–K3 in this line, see Game 7.

continued ▸

[24] Also favoring White is 13 . . . O–O 14 Q–K4, B–Q5 15 O–O–O.

[25] The ending favors White (Cortlever–Trifunovic, Utrecht 1950).

[26] Black can also reach this variation via 9 . . . NxB 10 PxB, P–B3!

[27] Critical for White is 12 PxP/6, PxKP (13 NxP? Q–R4†!). Or 12 BPxP/5, Q–R4† 13 Q–Q2, QxBP with a positional edge for Black.

[28] Not 13 K–K2 because of 13 . . . B–K3 (14 QxNP? or QxQP?, BxP†).

[29] 5 . . . PxP leads to the Max Lange Variation of the Two Knights' Defense.

[30] 7 B–N5 leads to Game 8.

[31] Van Scheltinga–Alexander, Maastricht 1946.

*Giuoco Piano Game 7*

*WHITE: Capablanca* *BLACK: Eliskases*

*Moscow 1936*

| | WHITE | BLACK | | WHITE | BLACK | | WHITE | BLACK |
|---|---|---|---|---|---|---|---|---|
| 1 | P–K4 | P–K4 | 19 | Q–B2 | P–B3 | 37 | PxP | RxP |
| 2 | N–KB3 | N–QB3 | 20 | P–K5 | R–B5 | 38 | R–N5 | Q–R2 |
| 3 | B–B4 | B–B4 | 21 | Q–Q1 | R/1–KB1 | 39 | Q–N3 | Q–R3 |
| 4 | N–B3 | N–B3 | 22 | P–B3 | Q–Q1 | 40 | Q–N4 | R–N2 |
| 5 | P–Q3 | P–Q3 | 23 | P–KN3 | R/5–B2 | 41 | R–N3 | K–R2 |
| 6 | B–N5 | P–KR3 | 24 | P–B4 | N–B4 | 42 | R–N2 | K–R1 |
| 7 | BxN | QxB | 25 | NxN | RxN | 43 | K–N3 | K–R2 |
| 8 | N–Q5 | Q–Q1 | 26 | P–KR4 | P–KN3 | 44 | R–R2 | R–K2 |
| 9 | P–B3 | N–K2 | 27 | K–N2 | Q–K2 | 45 | R–R3 | K–N2 |
| 10 | N–K3 | B–K3 | 28 | P–R3 | Q–N2 | 46 | RxR | QxR |
| 11 | BxB | PxB | 29 | R/3–B3 | Q–K2 | 47 | QxQ | PxQ |
| 12 | Q–N3 | Q–B1 | 30 | Q–B2 | K–N2 | 48 | P–B5! | PxP |
| 13 | P–Q4 | PxP | 31 | P–KN4 | R/4–B2 | 49 | K–B4 | R–K3 |
| 14 | NxP | BxN | 32 | K–R3 | Q–Q2 | 50 | KxP | R–N3 |
| 15 | PxB | O–O | 33 | P–N4 | R–KN1 | 51 | P–K6 | R–N5 |
| 16 | O–O | Q–Q2 | 34 | R–KN1 | K–R1 | 52 | K–K5 | R–K5† |
| 17 | QR–B1 | QR–N1 | 35 | Q–Q2 | R–R2 | 53 | K–Q6 | RxP |
| 18 | R–B3 | P–Q4 | 36 | Q–KB2 | P–KR4? | 54 | R–K3 | Resigns |

*Giuoco Piano Game 8*

*WHITE: Rosentreter* *BLACK: Hoefer*

*Berlin 1899*

| | WHITE | BLACK | | WHITE | BLACK |
|---|---|---|---|---|---|
| 1 | P–K4 | P–K4 | 8 | B–R4 | P–KN4? |
| 2 | N–KB3 | N–QB3 | 9 | P–B4!! | NPxP |
| 3 | B–B4 | B–B4 | 10 | RxP! | PxR |
| 4 | O–O | N–B3 | 11 | QxN | O–O |
| 5 | P–Q4 | BxP | 12 | BxN | Q–K1 |
| 6 | NxB | NxN | 13 | B–R8! | Resigns |
| 7 | B–KN5 | P–KR3 | | | |

# chapter 6—Unusual Openings

## Beginning with 1 P-K4, P-K4 2 N-KB3, N-QB3 3 B-B4

(The Evans Gambit, The Hungarian Defense and the Half Giuoco Game)

Apart from the Two Knights' Defense, some other openings arise after 1 P–K4, P–K4 2 N–KB3, N–QB3 3 B–B4; but these are so rarely played today that they hardly justify independent treatment.

Practical Variations 1–4 deal with the Evans Gambit, once the Queen but now the Cinderella of the openings, left behind by the steady progress of theory.

The gambit player aims at wild positions where he may take his opponent by surprise. A century ago such an objective was realistic and efficient. Sacrifices of all sorts could be justified if they produced complications which readily confused the defender. In modern times, however, the openings are too well known for such speculations to succeed. The informed defender knows how to handle typical gambit variations, so that they cannot be expected to pay adequate dividends.

Thus most gambits have practically disappeared from the scene, and with them the Evans. In this discussion of the Evans, therefore, we will make no attempt to dwell on large numbers of obsolete variations but rather restrict ourselves to those which still have a limited survival value. See especially Prac. Var. 3 which leads to quiet and reliable positions for Black.

For one old and one modern example of the Evans Gambit, see Games 1 and 2.

Prac. Var. 5 treats the Hungarian Defense, and Prac. Var. 6 the "Half" or "Lesser" Giuoco Piano. Both solid debuts.

## PRACTICAL VARIATIONS 1–6:

### 1 P–K4, P–K4 2 N–KB3, N–QB3 3 B–B4

| | 1 | 2 | 3 | 4 | 5 | 6 |
|---|---|---|---|---|---|---|
| 3 | — — | — — | — — | — — | — — | — — |
| | B–B4 | — — | — — | — — | B–K2[17] | P–Q3[22] |
| 4 | P–QN4[1] | — — | — — | — — | P–Q4 | P–Q4[23] |
| | BxP | — — | — — | B–N3[14] | P–Q3[18] | B–N5 |
| 5 | P–B3 | — — | — | P–QR4[15] | P–KR3![19] | P–B3 |
| | B–R4[2] | — — | B–K2![9] | P–QR3 | N–B3 | Q–Q2[24] |
| 6 | P–Q4 | — — | P–Q4 | B–N2 | N–B3 | P–Q5[25] |
| | P–Q3[3] | — — | N–R4[10] | P–Q3 | O–O[20] | ± |
| 7 | Q–N3[4] | — — | NxP[11] | P–N5 | O–O[21] | |
| | Q–Q2! | — — | NxB | PxP | ± | |
| 8 | PxP[5] | — — | NxN | PxP | | |
| | PxP | B–N3[7] | P–Q4 | RxR | | |
| 9 | O–O | PxP | PxP | BxR | | |
| | B–N3 | N–R4 | QxP | N–Q5 | | |
| 10 | R–Q1 | Q–N4 | N–K3 | NxN | | |
| | Q–K2 | NxB | Q–Q1[12] | PxN | | |
| 11 | B–R3 | QxN | O–O | P–QB3 | | |
| | Q–B3 | QxP[8] | N–B3 | N–B3 | | |
| 12 | QN–Q2 | = | P–QB4 | O–O | | |
| | KN–K2[6] | | O–O[13] | O–O | | |
| 13 | = | | = | P–Q3[16] | | |
| | | | | ± | | |

*Notes to practical variations 1–6:*

[1] This is the Evans' Gambit, named after the English Captain, W. Evans, who introduced this Pawn sacrifice in 1824. White sacrifices a Pawn with the obvious intention of accelerating the formation of a strong center by means of 5 P–B3 followed by 6 P–Q4.

[2] 5 . . . B–B4 assists White in achieving his aim, e.g., 6 P–Q4, PxP 7 PxP (or 7 O–O, PxP 8 NxP or 8 BxP†), B–N5† 8 K–B1! with good attacking chances for White.

[3] 6 . . . PxP 7 O–O offers White good attacking chances, e.g., 7 . . . PxP 8 Q–N3, Q–B3 9 P–K5, Q–N3 10 NxP, KN–K2 11 B–R3, O–O 12 QR–Q1 and White's edge in development is well worth the two Pawns. Black, however, may do better with Pachman's 7 . . . KN–K2.

[4] The recovery of the Pawn after 7 PxP leads to an even end game. Worth consideration is 7 B–KN5.

[5] With a Pawn down, White must open lines.

[6] Black proceeds with 13 . . . B–K3 with an even game.

[7] The most solid continuation.

[8] White has more freedom. Black has the two Bishops and the better Pawn structure.

[9] The safest, and at the same time Black's best chance for an opening advantage.

[10] The point of Black's preceding move.

[11] Alexander–Euwe (Maastricht 1946) continued: 7 B–Q3, P–Q3 8 Q–R4†, P–B3 9 B–R3 and White has attacking chances. Simpler is 7 . . . PxP 8 PxP, P–Q4.

[12] This is safer than 10 . . . Q–QR4 11 O–O, N–B3 12 R–K1 and Black will find it dangerous to play 12 . . . O–O because of 13 N–B4.

[13] Black has a sound Pawn formation and the two Bishops.

[14] The Evans Gambit Declined, which offers White fair chances for attack.

[15] Too ambitious is 5 P–N5, N–R4 6 NxP, N–R3 and White will have trouble meeting Black's 7 . . . P–Q3.

[16] Tartakover–Rubinstein, The Hague 1921.

[17] The Hungarian Defense where Black maintains his Pawn on K4. The exchange of this Pawn (. . . KPxQP) leads to a quiet variation of the Two Knights' Defense.

[18] Or 4 . . . PxP 5 P–B3! and now Black must not play 5 . . . PxP because of 6 Q–Q5! Black's best is 5 . . . N–R4.

[19] White obtains a slight edge by 5 PxP, PxP 6 QxQ†, BxQ 7 N–B3 (Rossolimo–Euwe, Beverwijk 1953).

[20] The alternative, 6 . . . NxKP 7 NxN, P–Q4, favors White because of 8 B–QN5, PxN 9 NxP!

[21] The reply 7 . . . NxKP still favors White because of 8 NxN, P–Q4 9 N–B3, PxB 10 P–Q5!

[22] The "Lesser" or "Half" Giuoco Piano, introduced by Alekhine. It does not seem quite sufficient for equality.

[23] Alekhine gave 4 P–B3, Q–K2 5 O–O, P–KN3 as satisfactory for Black.

[24] 5 . . . N–B3 courts danger because of 6 Q–N3.

[25] Or 6 B–QN5 and White has some superiority in space.

*Unusual Openings Game 1*

*WHITE: Sokolski* *BLACK: Schumacher*

*Postal Game 1954*

| | WHITE | BLACK | | WHITE | BLACK |
|---|---|---|---|---|---|
| 1 | P–K4 | P–K4 | 17 | P–B4 | N–B2 |
| 2 | N–KB3 | N–QB3 | 18 | NxB† | QRxN |
| 3 | B–B4 | B–B4 | 19 | R–Q5 | KR–Q1 |
| 4 | P–QN4 | BxP | 20 | Q–B2 | P–QR3 |
| 5 | P–B3 | B–R4 | 21 | N–R4 | K–B1 |
| 6 | P–Q4 | P–Q3 | 22 | N–B5 | RxR |
| 7 | Q–N3 | Q–Q2 | 23 | KPxR | Q–Q2 |
| 8 | PxP | B–N3 | 24 | P–B4 | B–Q1 |
| 9 | QN–Q2 | PxP | 25 | PxP | NxP |
| 10 | B–R3 | N–R4 | 26 | B–N2 | N–B2 |
| 11 | Q–N4 | P–QB4 | 27 | Q–B2 | P–QN4 |
| 12 | Q–N2 | NxB | 28 | Q–R4 | N–N4 |
| 13 | NxN | P–B3 | 29 | B–B1 | P–N3 |
| 14 | R–Q1 | Q–B3 | 30 | BxN | PxB |
| 15 | N–Q6† | K–K2 | 31 | Q–N4!! | Resigns |
| 16 | O–O | N–R3 | | | |

*Unusual Openings Game 2*

*WHITE: Tchigorin* *BLACK: Dorrer*

*1884*

| | WHITE | BLACK | | WHITE | BLACK |
|---|---|---|---|---|---|
| 1 | P–K4 | P–K4 | 16 | Q–B2! | R–B1 |
| 2 | N–KB3 | N–QB3 | 17 | P–QR4 | B–R4 |
| 3 | B–B4 | B–B4 | 18 | KR–N1 | N–K2 |
| 4 | P–QN4 | BxP | 19 | NxN | QxN |
| 5 | P–B3 | B–R4 | 20 | RxP | O–O |
| 6 | P–Q4 | PxP | 21 | RxRP | B–N3 |
| 7 | O–O | P–Q3 | 22 | R–R6 | R–R1 |
| 8 | PxP | B–N3 | 23 | P–R5! | RxR |
| 9 | N–B3! | N–R4 | 24 | Q–B4† | K–R1 |
| 10 | B–KN5 | P–KB3! | 25 | QxR | BxRP |
| 11 | B–B4 | NxB | 26 | QxB | QxP |
| 12 | Q–R4† | Q–Q2 | 27 | QxP | QxB |
| 13 | QxN | Q–B2 | 28 | QxB | R–QN1 |
| 14 | N–Q5 | B–K3 | 29 | Q–R7 | Resigns |
| 15 | Q–R4† | B–Q2 | | | |

# chapter 7—King's Gambit

The King's Gambit has definitely lost the pre-eminence that it had in the previous century. Yet, even today, it is still appealing because of its unparalleled wealth of variations and ideas. The adoption of this opening, however, requires profound theoretical knowledge as well as more than ordinary courage in view of the risks involved, which are greater than in any other opening.

In our time there are only a few players, such as Spasski, Bronstein and Robert Byrne, who now and then take a chance with the King's Gambit, often with success against prominent adversaries.

The King's Gambit is based on a strategic idea: after 1 P–K4, P–K4 2 P–KB4, PxP, White has obtained the Pawn majority in the center and is able to open the King Bishop file. The general idea of this debut finds its classical expression in the Kieseritzky Gambit after 3 N–KB3, P–KN4 4 P–KR4, P–N5 5 N–K5 (Part 1). A sharp struggle is thus initiated where, even today, White's chances, good or bad, are no more problematical than Black's.

With 3 . . . P–KN4, Black is definitely committed to the protection of the Gambit Pawn, which is a reason enough why most players prefer some more subtle system of development, possibly combined with the return of the Pawn. Apart from the Modern Defense 3 . . . P–Q4 (Part 4), the Reformed Cunningham Gambit, 3 . . . B–K2 4 B–B4, N–KB3! (Part 3), is also quite usual. Furthermore, Becker's idea 3 . . . P–KR3 is worth consideration (see Part 2 and Sup. Var. 3).

If Black wants to decline the gambit he has the choice between 2 . . . B–B4 (Part 5) and 2 . . . P–Q4 (the Falkbeer Counter Gambit, discussed in Part 6). Both lines are fully satisfactory but not stronger than the previously mentioned Modern Defense or Reformed Cunningham Gambit.

For White, the best form of this opening, according to present-day views, is the Knight's Gambit (1 P–K4, P–K4 2 P–KB4, PxP 3 N–KB3). Other variants, such as the Bishop's Gambit and Breyer's Gambit (Sup. Var. 6 and 8 respectively), are definitely weaker.

# part 1—KIESERITZKY GAMBIT

1 P–K4, P–K4
2 P–KB4, PxP
3 N–KB3, P–KN4
4 P–KR4, P–N5
5 N–K5[A]

KEY POSITION 1

OBSERVATIONS ON KEY POSITION 1

[A] 6 N–N5 is the Allgaier Gambit.

This is the most important position of the classical King's Gambit when Black plays 3 . . . P–KN4. White has disrupted the enemy Pawn chain by 4 P–KR4. If he now succeeds in recovering the weak Gambit Pawn, his advantage in the center is evident. Hence, Black must hasten to eliminate White's important King Pawn; this he can best do by adopting the Berlin Defense, 5 . . . N–KB3. Then the enticing attack on Black's KB7 by means of 6 B–B4 leads, after 6 . . . P–Q4, to advantage for Black. White must therefore treat the position strategically rather than tactically. His best answer to 5 . . . N–KB3 is 6 P–Q4. After 6 . . . P–Q3 7 N–Q3, NxP 8 BxP, White maintains sufficient material compensation for the Pawn.

At his fifth turn, Black has a great variety of continuations at his disposal, but none as good as 5 . . . N–KB3.

IDEA VARIATIONS 1–3:

(1) 5 . . . N–KB3 6 B–B4 (old-fashioned), P–Q4 7 PxP, B–N2 (Paulsen's move, which is stronger than Tchigorin's 7 . . . B–Q3) 8 P–Q4, N–R4 9 O–O, QxP 10 Q–K1, QxQ 11 RxQ, O–O 12 N–QB3, N–Q2 with a good game for Black (R. Byrne–Keres, USSR–USA, Moscow 1955; see Game 1). Black fares even better with 12 . . . P–QB4!

(2) 5 . . . N–KB3 6 P–Q4!, P–Q3 7 N–Q3, NxP 8 BxP, B–N2 (more usual is 8 . . . Q–K2; see the next Idea Var.) 9 N–B3?! (also possible is 9 P–B3 followed by N–Q2), NxN 10 PxN, P–QB4! 11 B–K2, PxP 12 O–O, N–B3! with chances for both sides (Spasski–Fischer, Mar del Plata 1960; see Game 2).

(3) 5 . . . N–KB3 6 P–Q4!, P–Q3 7 N–Q3, NxP 8 BxP, Q–K2 9 Q–K2, B–N2 10 P–B3, P–KR4 (Black does better with 10 . . . B–B4; see Prac. Var. 1) 11 N–Q2, NxN 12 KxN, QxQ† (else follows 13 Q–B2) 13 BxQ, and White has ample compensation for the Pawn (Stoltz-Saemisch, Swinemunde 1932; see Game 3). Black probably can still achieve equality with 13 . . . N–B3 14 QR–K1, B–K3.

### *King's Gambit Game 1*

*WHITE: R. Byrne* *BLACK: Keres*

*Moscow 1955*

| | WHITE | BLACK |
|---|---|---|
| 1 | P–K4 | P–K4 |
| 2 | P–KB4 | PxP |
| 3 | N–KB3 | P–KN4 |
| 4 | P–KR4 | P–N5 |
| 5 | N–K5 | N–KB3 |
| 6 | B–B4 | P–Q4 |
| 7 | PxP | B–N2 |
| 8 | P–Q4 | N–R4 |
| 9 | O–O | QxRP |
| 10 | Q–K1 | QxQ |
| 11 | RxQ | O–O |
| 12 | N–QB3 | N–Q2 |
| 13 | N–N5 | P–QB3 |
| 14 | N–B7? | PxP |
| 15 | NxR | PxB |
| 16 | B–Q2 | NxN |
| 17 | PxN | B–B4 |
| 18 | N–B7 | BxBP |
| 19 | QR–B1 | B–Q6 |
| 20 | N–Q5 | P–N4 |
| 21 | BxP | R–Q1 |
| 22 | N–K7† | K–B1 |
| 23 | B–N5 | R–K1 |
| 24 | N–B6 | N–N6 |
| 25 | R/B–Q1 | R–K3 |
| 26 | NxP | BxP |
| 27 | NxP | N–K7† |
| 28 | RxN | BxR |
| 29 | R–Q8† | R–K1 |
| 30 | RxR† | KxR |
| 31 | K–B2 | B–Q6 |
| 32 | N–B3 | K–Q2 |
| 33 | K–K3 | B–R7 |
| 34 | B–B4 | B–N8† |
| 35 | K–Q2 | P–R4 |
| 36 | P–KN3 | B–KB7 |
| 37 | N–Q1 | B–Q5 |
| 38 | N–B3 | K–B3? |
| 39 | P–N4 | B–B3 |
| 40 | P–N5†? | K–N2 |
| 41 | P–R4 | B–Q1 |
| 42 | N–Q5 | B–K5 |
| 43 | N–B3 | B–B6 |
| 44 | K–K3 | B–N3† |
| 45 | K–Q2 | P–B3 |
| 46 | B–Q6 | B–R4 |
| 47 | B–B4 | B–K5 |
| 48 | B–Q6 | B–Q6 |
| 49 | B–B4 | B–N5! |
| 50 | B–K3 | P–R5 |
| 51 | PxP | P–N6 |
| 52 | P–KR5 | P–N7 |
| 53 | P–R6 | P–B4 |
| 54 | B–B2 | P–B5 |
| 55 | B–N1 | B–R4 |
| 56 | B–R2 | B–N3 |
| 57 | P–R7 | BxP |
| 58 | K–K2 | P–N8/Q |
| 59 | BxQ | BxB |
| 60 | N–Q5 | B–Q5 |
| 61 | NxP | P–B6 |
| 62 | N–Q3 | BxN† |
| 63 | KxB | K–N3 |
| 64 | K–B2 | K–R4 |
| 65 | K–N3 | B–K4 |
| 66 | K–B2 | KxP |
| | Resigns | |

### *King's Gambit Game 2*

*WHITE: Spasski* *BLACK: Fischer*

*Mar del Plata 1960*

| | WHITE | BLACK |
|---|---|---|
| 1 | P–K4 | P–K4 |
| 2 | P–KB4 | PxP |
| 3 | N–KB3 | P–KN4 |
| 4 | P–KR4 | P–N5 |
| 5 | N–K5 | N–KB3 |
| 6 | P–Q4 | P–Q3 |
| 7 | N–Q3 | NxP |
| 8 | BxP | B–N2 |
| 9 | N–B3!? | NxN |
| 10 | PxN | P–QB4 |
| 11 | B–K2 | PxP |
| 12 | O–O | N–B3! |
| 13 | BxNP | O–O |
| 14 | BxB | RxB |
| 15 | Q–N4 | P–B4 |
| 16 | Q–N3 | PxP |
| 17 | QR–K1! | K–R1 |
| 18 | K–R1 | R–KN1 |
| 19 | BxP | B–B1? |
| 20 | B–K5† | NxB |
| 21 | QxN† | R–N2! |
| 22 | RxP | QxP† |
| 23 | K–N1 | Q–KN5 |
| 24 | R–B2 | B–K2 |
| 25 | R–K4 | Q–N4 |
| 26 | Q–Q4 | R–B1? |
| 27 | R–K5! | R–Q1 |
| 28 | Q–K4 | Q–R5 |
| 29 | R–B4 | Resigns |

*King's Gambit Game 3*

*WHITE: Stoltz* *BLACK: Saemisch*

*Swinemunde 1932*

| | WHITE | BLACK | | WHITE | BLACK |
|---|---|---|---|---|---|
| 1 | P–K4 | P–K4 | 11 | N–Q2 | NxN |
| 2 | P–KB4 | PxP | 12 | KxN | QxQ† |
| 3 | N–KB3 | P–KN4 | 13 | BxQ | B–B4 |
| 4 | P–KR4 | P–N5 | 14 | KR–KB1 | N–Q2? |
| 5 | N–K5 | N–KB3 | 15 | N–N4 | N–B3 |
| 6 | P–Q4 | P–Q3 | 16 | B–N5† | B–Q2 |
| 7 | N–Q3 | NxP | 17 | QR–K1† | K–Q1 |
| 8 | BxP | Q–K2 | 18 | B–N5! | BxB |
| 9 | Q–K2 | B–N2 | 19 | RxN | Resigns |
| 10 | P–B3 | P–KR4 | | | |

PRACTICAL VARIATIONS 1–5:

1 P–K4, P–K4 2 P–KB4, PxP 3 N–KB3, P–KN4 4 P–KR4, P–N5 5 N–K5

| | *1* | *2* | *3* | *4* | *5* |
|---|---|---|---|---|---|
| *5* | — — | — — | — — | — — | — — |
| | N–KB3 | B–N2 | P–Q4 | P–Q3 | P–KR4[11] |
| *6* | P–Q4 | P–Q4[3] | P–Q4 | NxNP | B–B4 |
| | P–Q3 | N–KB3[4] | N–KB3 | B–K2[8] | R–R2[12] |
| *7* | N–Q3 | N–QB3 | BxP | P–Q4 | P–Q4 |
| | NxP | P–Q3 | NxP | BxP† | B–Q3 |
| *8* | BxP | N–Q3 | N–Q2 | N–B2 | N–QB3 |
| | Q–K2 | O–O | NxN | Q–B3[9] | N–QB3 |
| *9* | Q–K2 | NxP | QxN | Q–B3 | BxP† |
| | B–N2 | NxP | B–Q3 | B–N6 | RxB |
| *10* | P–B3 | NxN | O–O–O | N–B3 | NxR |
| | B–B4 | R–K1 | B–K3 | QxP | KxN |
| *11* | N–Q2 | K–B2 | B–Q3 | BxP | BxP |
| | NxN | RxN | N–Q2[6] | BxN† | BxB |
| *12* | KxN[1] | P–B3 | QR–K1 | QxB | O–O |
| | QxQ† | Q–B3 | NxN | QxQ† | QxP |
| *13* | BxQ | P–KN3 | BxN | KxQ[10] | RxB†[13] |
| | N–Q2[2] | B–R3 | BxB | ± | ± |
| *14* | = | B–Q3 | RxB | | |
| | | BxN | Q–Q2 | | |
| *15* | | BxB[5] | Q–N5![7] | | |
| | | = | ± | | |

*Notes to practical variations 1–5:*

[1] White does better, according to Keres, with 12 QxQ†, KxQ 13 KxN.

[2] According to Pachman.

[3] According to Schlechter, 6 NxNP is also good: 6 . . . PxQ4 7 P–Q4!, PxP 8 BxP, QxP 9 QxQ, BxQ 10 P–B3, BxN 11 PxB, N–QB3 12 B–QN5, O–O–O 13 BxN, PxB 14 O–O.

[4] 6 . . . P–Q3 provokes a sacrifice which is very promising for White: e.g., 7 NxBP, KxN 8 B–B4†, K–K1 9 BxP.

[5] The sacrifice of the exchange is worked out in Bilguer's *Handbuch* as favorable for Black: 15 . . . RxB† 16 PxR, QxP† 7 K–N2? P–N4! Rubinstein, however, gave the following refutation: 17 K–K2!, P–N6 18 Q–Q2!

[6] After 11 . . . P–KB3? 12 QR–K1, White has an irresistible attack.

[7] The text move, according to Keres, leads to an advantage for White: e.g., 15 . . . Q–K2 16 B–B5, QxQ 17 PxQ. Instead, the older continuation 15 B–B5, O–O–O leads only to equality.

[8] Or 6 . . . P–KR4 7 N–B2, N–KB3 8 P–Q4, B–R3 9 N–B3, N–N5 10 NxN!, BxN (10 . . . PxN 11 N–Q5!) 11 Q–Q3.

[9] Or 8 . . . Q–N4 9 Q–B3, N–QB3 10 QxP, QxQ 11 BxQ, BxN† 12 KxB, NxP 13 B–Q3, and White has positional compensation for the Pawn.

[10] 13 . . . N–KB3 14 B–K2, QN–Q2 15 N–N5, K–Q1 16 B–B3 slightly favors White (Kostic–Tomovoc, Zagreb 1949).

[11] An obsolete defense. Insufficient also are:

1) 5 . . . B–K2 6 B–B4!, BxP† 7 K–B1, P–Q4 (7 . . . N–KR3 8 NxNP!) 8 BxP, N–KR3 9 P–Q4, B–N4 10 N–QB3!
2) 5 . . . Q–K2 6 P–Q4!, P–Q3 7 NxNP, P–KB4 (7 . . . QxP† 8 Q–K2) 8 N–B2, N–KB3 (8 . . . PxP 9 Q–R5†) 9 BxP, NxP (9 . . . PxP 10 P–Q5!) 10 Q–R5†.
3) 5 . . . N–QB3 6 P–Q4!, NxN 7 PxN, P–Q3 8 BxP, B–N2 (8 . . . Q–K2 9 B–N5†) 9 N–B3, PxP 10 QxQ†, KxQ 11 O–O–O†, B–Q2 12 B–K3.

[12] Or 6 . . . N–KR3 7 P–Q4, P–Q3 8 N–Q3, P–B6 9 PxP, PxP 10 QxP, B–N5 11 Q–B2, Q–K2 12 N–B3! with advantage for White.

[13] White has a very strong attack (Bronstein–Dubinin, Leningrad 1947). See Game 4.

## *King's Gambit Game 4*

*WHITE: Bronstein* — *BLACK: Dubinin*

*Leningrad 1947*

| | WHITE | BLACK | | WHITE | BLACK |
|---|---|---|---|---|---|
| 1 | P–K4 | P–K4 | 15 | QR–KB1 | N–Q1 |
| 2 | P–KB4 | PxP | 16 | N–Q5! | B–Q2 |
| 3 | N–KB3 | P–KN4 | 17 | P–K5! | PxP |
| 4 | P–KR4 | P–N5 | 18 | PxP | B–B3 |
| 5 | N–K5 | P–KR4 | 19 | P–K6! | BxN |
| 6 | B–B4 | R–R2 | 20 | R–B7†! | NxR |
| 7 | P–Q4 | B–R3 | 21 | RxN† | K–R1 |
| 8 | N–QB3 | N–QB3 | 22 | Q–B3† | N–B3 |
| 9 | NxBP! | RxN | 23 | RxN | QxR |
| 10 | BxR† | KxB | 24 | QxQ† | K–R2 |
| 11 | BxP! | BxB | 25 | Q–B5† | K–R3 |
| 12 | O–O | QxP? | 26 | QxB | K–N3 |
| 13 | RxB† | K–N2 | 27 | Q–Q7 | Resigns |
| 14 | Q–Q2 | P–Q3 | | | |

## part 2—PHILIDOR AND HANSTEIN GAMBITS

1 P–K4, P–K4
2 P–KB4, PxP
3 N–KB3, P–KN4
4 B–B4, B–N2

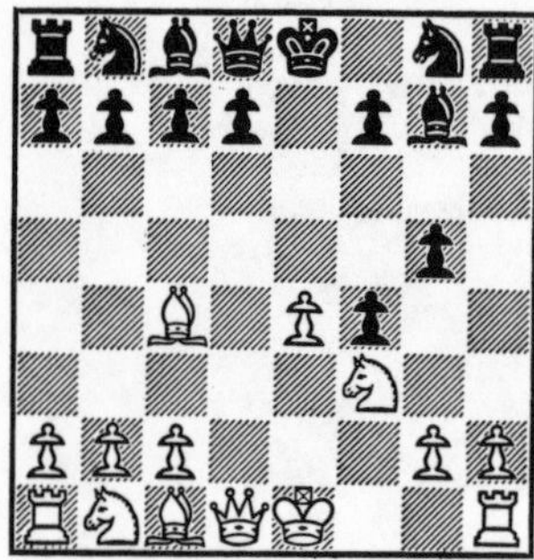

KEY POSITION 2

OBSERVATIONS ON KEY POSITION 2

In the last century the continuation 4 B–B4 was very usual. Today, however, 4 P–KR4 is preferred, so as to accentuate the weakening of Black's Kingside. The move 4 B–B4 allows Black to consolidate his Kingside by means of 4 . . . B–N2 and . . . P–KR3. 4 . . . P–N5, instead, has a weakening effect on Black's Pawn skeleton, enabling White to obtain fine attacking chances (see the Muzio Gambit, Sup. Var. 2).

Yet key position 2 has great theoretical significance even to-day, for it leads to variations which may also arise via Becker's Defense, 3 . . . P–KR3 (Sup. Var. 3).

The key position offers White the choice between two gambits, 5 P–KR4 (the Philidor) and 5 O–O (the Hanstein). 5 P–KR4 is a belated attempt to break up Black's Pawn chain on the Kingside. 5 O–O initiates an attempt by White to open up the KB file by means of P–KN3, possibly followed by a Knight sacrifice if Black counters . . . P–N5.

IDEA VARIATIONS 4–6:

(4) 5 P–KR4, P–N5 6 N–N5, N–KR3 7 P–Q4 favors White: e.g., 7 . . . N–QB3 (on 7 . . . P–KB3? White gets a strong attack with 8 BxP!) 8 P–B3, P–Q3 9 QBxP, N–R4 10 B–Q3, P–KB3 11 Q–Q2, N–N1 12 P–Q5.

(5) 5 P–KR4, P–KR3 6 P–Q4, P–Q3 (after 6 . . . P–N5? 7 QBxP, PxN 8 QxP, White has an ideal attacking position 7 P–B3, N–QB3 (7 . . . P–N5 8 N–N1!) 8 Q–N3, Q–K2 9 O–O. Bilguer's *Handbuch* now gives 9 . . . N–B3 (see Prac. Var. 6). It is an open question, however, whether this is Black's best. Black may also try 9 . . . P–N5, when it appears that White has no better than to sacrifice a piece with no clear compensation: 10 QBxP, PxN 11 RxP. Keres suggests for Black the quiet 9 . . . P–QR3, so as to proceed with . . . N–Q1, followed, after due preparation, by . . . P–QN4. The immediate 9 . . . N–Q1? fails because of 10 PxP, PxP 11 Q–N5† followed by QxKNP.

(6) 5 O–O, P–Q3 (or 5 . . . P–N5 6 N–K1) 6 P–Q4, N–QB3 7 P–B3, P–KR3 (so as to preclude the sacrificial possibility of NxP, followed by QBxP) 8 P–KN3, P–N5 9 N–R4, P–B6 10 N–Q2 (for other moves see Prac. Var. 9), B–B3 11 QNxP (a characteristic sacri-

fice), PxN 12 QxP, R–R2? 13 N–N6! and White has a tremendous attack (Spielmann–Grunfeld, Teplitz–Schoenau 1922; see Game 5). Grunfeld gives 12 . . . B–R6! as a refutation of White's attack. Spielmann contends, however, that, after 13 R–B2, followed by 14 P–K5, White has the better prospects. The last word is Panov's who claims that Black's defense remains sufficient after 13 . . . Q–Q2, threatening . . . O–O–O: e.g., 14 P–K5, PxP 15 PxP, BxN 16 BxP† (16 P–K6, BxKP 17 BxB, QxB 18 R–K2, QxR, 19 QxQ†, B–K2!), K–K2 17 P–K6, BxKP 18 BxB, QxB 19 R–K2, N–K4 20 QxP, N–KB3!

PRACTICAL VARIATIONS 6–10:

1 P–K4, P–K4 2 P–KB4, PxP 3 N–KB3, P–KN4 4 B–B4, B–N2

| | *6* | *7* | *8* | *9* | *10* |
|---|---|---|---|---|---|
| *5* | P–KR4 | – – | – – | O–O | – – |
| | P–KR3 | – – | – – | P–Q3 | – – |
| *6* | P–Q4 | – – | – – | P–Q4 | – – |
| | P–Q3 | – – | – – | P–KR3 | – – |
| *7* | P–B3 | Q–Q3 | N–B3 | P–B3 | – – |
| | N–QB3 | N–QB3 | N–QB3 | N–QB3 | – – |
| *8* | Q–N3 | PxP | N–K2 | P–KN3 | – – |
| | Q–K2 | PxP | Q–K2 | P–N5 | B–R6 |
| *9* | O–O | RxR | Q–Q3 | N–R4 | PxP |
| | N–B3 | BxR | B–Q2 | P–B6 | BxR |
| *10* | PxP | P–K5 | B–Q2 | Q–N3[5] | QxB |
| | PxP | B–N2[2] | O–O–O | Q–K2 | PxP |
| *11* | NxP | Q–R7 | O–O–O[4] | N–B5[6] | QBxP |
| | NxP | K–B1 | = | BxN | Q–B3 |
| *12* | NxN![1] | Q–R5 | | QxP![7] | B–N3 |
| | = | N–R3![3] | | = | O–O–O[8] |
| | | ∓ | | | = |

*Notes to practical variations 6–10:*

[1] 12 R–K1? fails against 12 . . . R–R8† 13 KxR, N–B7† 14 K–R2, QxR 15 BxP†, K–Q1 16 BxP, N–N5† with a winning attack for Black (Bilguer).

The text move has been recommended by Keres. 12 . . . QxN (12 . . . NxP? 13 Q–Q1) 13 QBxP and, according to Keres, the attacking chances belong to White. Panov, however, gives the following continuation as being favorable for Black: 13 . . . NxP 14 Q–Q1, N–B6† 15 QxN, QxKB! Therefore, Panov believes, White must replace 13 QBxP by 13 BxP†, K–Q1 14 RxP, after which Black must be content with a draw by perpetual check: 14 . . . Q–K8† 15 R–B1, Q–R5 16 Q–Q5, Q–R8† 17 K–B2, Q–R5† 18 K–N1, Q–R8†.

[2] 10 . . . P–Q4 11 Q–R7, K–B1 is unfavorable for Black: e. g., 12 B–N5! (not 12 QxB, PxB 13 P–B3, B–N5 [Bilguer])

continued ▸

B–N2 13 BxN, PxB 14 P–QN3! with a winning attack for White (Kmoch).

[3] 13 NxP, B–N5 14 Q–R4, NxP favors Black.

[4] Keres now considers White's position satisfactory, pointing out that Black's extra Pawn hardly matters: e.g., 11 . . . R–K1 12 KR–K1, QxP 13 Q–R3 or 13 QxQ, RxQ 14 PxP.

[5] On 10 N–R3 or 10 B–B4, there follows 10 . . . B–B3.

[6] On 11 B–B4, Black's best reply is 11 . . . N–B3: e.g., 12 N–Q2, N–KR4 13 N–B5, BxN 14 QxP, R–QN1 15 QxN†, Q–Q2. But not 11 . . . B–B3?, upon which 12 N–B5, BxN 13 QxP, R–N1 14 QxN†, Q–Q2 15 Q–R6, QBxP 16 N–Q2, B–N3 17 QxRP, RxP 18 B–N3 results in great advantage for White (Cortlever–Scholtens, Leeuwarden 1943).

[7] This complicated position offers about even chances. Weaker than the text move is 12 PxB, O–O–O! 13 BxP, Q–K7 14 Q–K6† (14 R–B2, NxP!), R–Q2! 15 R–B2, Q–Q8† 16 R–B1, Q–B7 with advantage for Black.

[8] 13 QN–Q2, KN–K2 14 Q–R3†, K–N1 15 R–KB1, Q–N3 16 N–R4, Q–N4 17 KN–B3, Q–N3 18 N–R4 and draws. If 18 . . . Q–R2? 19 P–QN4! and Black gets into trouble (Spielmann–Grunfeld, Carlsbad 1923).

*King's Gambit Game 5*

*WHITE: Spielmann* — *BLACK: Grunfeld*

*Teplitz–Schoenau 1922*

| | WHITE | BLACK | | WHITE | BLACK |
|---|---|---|---|---|---|
| 1 | P–K4 | P–K4 | 17 | N–R5 | R–R2 |
| 2 | P–KB4 | PxP | 18 | P–K5! | PxP |
| 3 | B–B4 | N–QB3 | 19 | Q–K4 | P–B4 |
| 4 | N–KB3 | P–KN4 | 20 | RxP | BxR |
| 5 | O–O | P–Q3 | 21 | QxB | R–K2 |
| 6 | P–Q4 | B–N2 | 22 | BxB | PxB |
| 7 | P–B3 | P–KR3 | 23 | R–KB1 | Q–Q3 |
| 8 | P–KN3 | P–N5 | 24 | BxN | PxP |
| 9 | N–R4 | P–B6 | 25 | Q–B8† | K–Q2 |
| 10 | QN–Q2 | B–B3 | 26 | QxR | Q–B4 |
| 11 | N/2xP | PxN | 27 | N–B6† | K–Q3 |
| 12 | QxP | R–R2? | 28 | Q–KB8 | Q–K4 |
| 13 | N–N6! | R–N2 | 29 | K–N2 | P–Q6 |
| 14 | N–B4 | B–N5 | 30 | R–B2 | Q–K8 |
| 15 | Q–N2 | B–N4 | 31 | Q–R6 | Resigns |
| 16 | P–KR3 | B–Q2 | | | |

1 P–K4, P–K4
2 P–KB4, PxP
3 N–KB3, B–K2
4 B–B4, N–KB3![A]

KEY POSITION 3

## part 3—CUNNINGHAM REFORMED GAMBIT

### OBSERVATIONS ON KEY POSITION 3

[A] After 4 . . . B–R5† 5 K–B1, B–B3, the strongest continuation for White is 6 P–Q4 (6 P–K5, B–K2 7 P–Q4, P–Q4 8

B–K2 offers Black good counterchances after 8 . . . P–KB3!; but not 8 . . . P–KN4 9 P–KR4, P–N5 10 N–R2, with advantage for White), P–KN4 7 P–KR4. Now 7 . . . P–N5 or 7 . . . P–KR3 is answered by 8 N–K5.

Cunningham's original idea was 4 . . . B–R5†. This check, however, is harmful only to Black. The modern continuation 4 . . . N–KB3, introduced by Schlechter and refined by Kmoch, offers Black a satisfactory game. The attack on the King Pawn practically forces 5 P–K5, after which Black plays 5 . . . N–N5, threatening to eliminate the hostile King Pawn by . . . P–Q3 or stabilize the center with . . . P–Q4. White can oppose these plans to a certain extent, but he cannot really prevent them. The protection of the White Pawn by 5 N–B3 is answered by 5 . . . NxP!, which is the main point of 4 . . . N–B3.

IDEA VARIATIONS 7–10:

(7) 5 P–K5, N–N5 6 P–KR3? B–R5† 7 K–B1, N–B7 8 Q–K1, NxR 9 QxB, QxQ 10 NxQ, N–N6†, and Black has won the exchange. White's blunder in this line is 6 P–KR3. Had this move been omitted, Black's Knight could not have escaped and White would have emerged with two pieces for a Rook.

(8) 5 P–K5, N–N5 6 P–Q4, P–Q4 7 B–N3? (7 PxP e.p., and if 7 . . . QxP 8 N–B3 or if 7 . . . BxP 8 Q–K2†, Q–K2 9 QxQ†, KxQ 10 O–O, and White still has a chance to recover the Pawn and obtain equality), B–R5† 8 K–B1, P–QN3 9 QBxP, B–R3† 10 P–B4, PxP 11 B–R4†, P–QN4 and Black won (Kramer–Euwe, 6th Match Game 1941).

(9) 5 P–K5, N–N5 6 O–O, P–Q4 (stronger is 6 . . . N–QB3!; see Prac. Var. 11) 7 PxP e.p., QxP (7 . . . BxP 8 R–K1†) 8 P–Q4, O–O 9 N–B3, N–K6 (better is 9 . . . P–QB3 10 N–K4, Q–KN3!) 10 BxN, PxB (Bronstein–Koblentz, USSR Championship 1945). Boleslavski points out that White gains the advantage as follows: 11 N–QN5!, Q–Q1 (or 11 . . . Q–QN3 12 N–K5, B–K3 13 BxB, PxB 14 RxR†, BxR 15 Q–B3!) 12 N–K5, B–K3 (or 12 . . . B–B3 13 NxKBP, RxN 14 Q–R5 with a winning attack for White) 13 BxB, PxB 14 RxR†, BxR 15 Q–N4!

(10) 5 N–B3? NxP! 6 NxN, P–Q4 7 B–Q3, PxN 8 BxP, P–KB4! with a clear advantage for Black (Stoltz–Reicher, Bucharest 1953. See Game 6). In this line only 6 N–K5 offers chances for White. See Prac. Var. 14. 6 BxP†, KxB 7 N–K5†, K–N1 8 NxN, P–Q4 favors Black.

*King's Gambit Game 6*

*WHITE: Stoltz* *BLACK: Reicher*

*Bucharest 1953*

| | WHITE | BLACK | | WHITE | BLACK |
|---|---|---|---|---|---|
| 1 | P–K4 | P–K4 | 15 | B–Q2 | P–KR4 |
| 2 | P–KB4 | PxP | 16 | P–KR4 | PxP |
| 3 | N–KB3 | B–K2 | 17 | N–K1 | KR–K1 |
| 4 | B–B4 | N–KB3 | 18 | Q–B3 | BxP†! |
| 5 | N–B3 | NxP | 19 | PxB | NxP |
| 6 | NxN | P–Q4 | 20 | Q–Q1 | N–K7† |
| 7 | B–Q3 | PxN | 21 | K–R1 | N–N6† |
| 8 | BxP | P–KB4 | 22 | K–N1 | Q–B4† |
| 9 | B–Q3 | Q–Q3 | 23 | R–B2 | N–K7† |
| 10 | Q–K2 | N–B3 | 24 | K–B1 | B–N4 |
| 11 | P–B3 | B–Q2 | 25 | P–R4 | N–N6† |
| 12 | B–B2 | O–O–O | 26 | K–N1 | R–K7 |
| 13 | O–O | P–KN4 | 27 | BxP† | NxB |
| 14 | P–Q4 | B–B3 | | Resigns | |

PRACTICAL VARIATIONS 11-15:

1 P–K4, P–K4 2 P–KB4, PxP 3 N–KB3, B–K2 4 B–B4, N–KB3

| | *11* | *12* | *13* | *14* | *15* |
|---|---|---|---|---|---|
| *5* | P–K5 | – – | – – | N–B3 | P–Q3[14] |
| | N–N5 | – – | – – | NxP | P–Q4 |
| *6* | O–O | N–B3! | – – | N–K5 | PxP |
| | N–QB3! | P–Q3 | P–Q4? | N–Q3[10] | NxP |
| *7* | P–Q4 | PxP[4] | BxP[8] | B–N3 | BxN |
| | P–Q4 | BxP[5] | B–R5† | B–R5†[11] | QxB |
| *8* | PxP e.p. | Q–K2† | K–B1 | P–N3! | BxP |
| | BxP | Q–K2 | N–QB3 | PxP | O–O |
| *9* | R–K1†[1] | QxQ† | BxN† | O–O! | O–O[15] |
| | N–K2 | KxQ[6] | PxB | PxP† | B–B3 |
| *10* | P–KR3 | N–Q5† | P–Q3 | K–R1 | P–Q4 |
| | N–B3[2] | K–Q1 | O–O | B–B3[12] | P–QB4[16] |
| *11* | N–K5[3] | P–Q4[7] | BxP[9] | P–Q4![13] | = |
| | = | = | = | ± | |

*Notes to practical variations 11–15:*

[1] Weaker is 9 N–B3, O–O 10 N–K2, N–K6 11 BxN, PxB 12 P–QR3 (better is 12 Q–Q3, Q–K2 13 QR–K1), Q–B3! (Keres–Alatortsev, USSR Championship 1950). On 13 N–K5, there follows 13 . . . Q–R3!

[2] Stronger is 10 . . . N–R3 (Black of course cannot play 10 . . . N–K6 because of 11 BxN, PxB 12 N–N5!): 11 N–K5, BxN 12 RxB, N/3–B4 13 P–B3, O–O. and now 14 QBxP fails

against 14 . . . N–N3 15 R–Q5 (or 15 R–K4? P–QN4! followed by 16 . . . B–N2), Q–R5 16 B–Q2, B–K3 17 R–QB5, Q–N6 with positional advantage for Black.

[3] White has practically equalized (A. R. B. Thomas–Euwe, Plymouth 1948).

[4] 7 P–Q4, PxP 8 PxP, QxQ† 9 NxQ, B–K3 leads to equality.

[5] The text move is safer than 7 . . . QxP 8 P–Q4, O–O 9 P–Q4, P–QB3 10 N–K4, Q–B2 11 P–KR3, whereupon White has good attacking prospects.

[6] 9 . . . BxQ 10 P–Q4, B–Q3 11 N–K4 is weaker (Bronstein–Lemoine, Munich 1958; see Game 7).

[7] White recovers the Pawn with approximate equality.

[8] 7 NxP, B–R5† 8 K–B1, P–QB3 9 N–B3 (9 NxP? N–K6†!), P–QN4 10 B–K2, B–B4 is promising for Black: e.g., 11 P–Q3, B–B7! 12 BxP, B–K6 13 B–N3, B–N3.

[9] White has a good game: 11 . . . P–B3 12 P–K6, P–KB4 13 NxB, QxN 14 Q–K1! (Panov).

[10] Black's best defense is 6 . . . N–N4! But 6 . . . NxN loses outright to 7 Q–R5! while 6 . . . B–R5† 7 P–KN3!, PxP 8 O–O offers promising prospects for White.

[11] Enticing, but dubious. Sound for Black is 7 . . . O–O 8 O–O, N–B3 9 P–Q4, NxN 10 PxN, N–K1.

[12] Black also faces difficult problems after 10 . . . O–O 11 P–Q4! (11 Q–R5, Q–N4!), B–B3: e.g., 12 Q–R5, N–B3 13 R–B3! with a winning attack for White.

[13] White has an attacking position of great promise (Podgorny–Stulik, Prague 1946; see Game 8).

[14] On 5 Q–K2, Black's best is 5 . . . P–Q4! (not 5 . . . O–O 6 P–K5, P–Q4 7 PxN, BxP 8 O–O!).

[15] If 9 BxP? R–K1, and White cannot castle because of 10 . . . Q–B4†.

[16] The game is even: 11 N–B3, BxP† (11 . . . Q–B4, B–Q6) 12 NxB, QxN† 13 QxQ, PxQ 14 N–N5, N–B3.

### *King's Gambit Game 7*

*WHITE: Bronstein* — *BLACK: Lemoine*

*Munich 1958*

| | WHITE | BLACK | | WHITE | BLACK |
|---|---|---|---|---|---|
| 1 | P–K4 | P–K4 | 14 | B–Q3 | P–Q4 |
| 2 | P–KB4 | PxP | 15 | O–O | O–O |
| 3 | N–KB3 | B–K2 | 16 | P–QN3 | N–B3 |
| 4 | B–B4 | N–KB3 | 17 | QR–K1 | B–N5 |
| 5 | P–K5 | N–N5 | 18 | R–K7 | N/N–Q2 |
| 6 | N–B3 | P–Q3 | 19 | B–K5 | P–QN3 |
| 7 | PxP | BxP | 20 | BxN | NxB |
| 8 | Q–K2† | Q–K2 | 21 | N–K5 | B–K3 |
| 9 | QxQ† | BxQ | 22 | B–R6 | B–B1 |
| 10 | P–Q4 | B–Q3 | 23 | B–N5 | P–QR3 |
| 11 | N–K4 | N–Q2 | 24 | B–B6 | R–N1 |
| 12 | NxB† | PxN | 25 | NxP! | B–N5 |
| 13 | BxP | N–N3 | 26 | RxN! | Resigns |

*King's Gambit Game 8*
*WHITE: Podgorny* *BLACK: Stulik*
*Czechoslovakian Championship 1956*

| | WHITE | BLACK | | WHITE | BLACK |
|---|---|---|---|---|---|
| 1 | P–K4 | P–K4 | 11 | P–Q4 | P–QN3 |
| 2 | P–KB4 | PxP | 12 | Q–R5 | B–N2† |
| 3 | N–KB3 | B–K2 | 13 | KxP | P–N3? |
| 4 | B–B4 | N–KB3 | 14 | Q–R6 | B–N2 |
| 5 | N–QB3 | NxP | 15 | NxKBP!! | BxQ |
| 6 | N–K5 | N–Q3 | 16 | NxN† | PxN |
| 7 | B–N3 | B–R5† | 17 | B–B7† | K–K2 |
| 8 | P–N3 | PxP | 18 | BxB | Q–N1 |
| 9 | O–O | PxP† | 19 | BxQ | Resigns |
| 10 | K–R1 | B–B3 | | | |

## part 4—MODERN VARIATION

1 P–K4, P–K4
2 P–KB4, PxP
3 N–KB3, P–Q4
4 PxP[A], N–KB3[B]

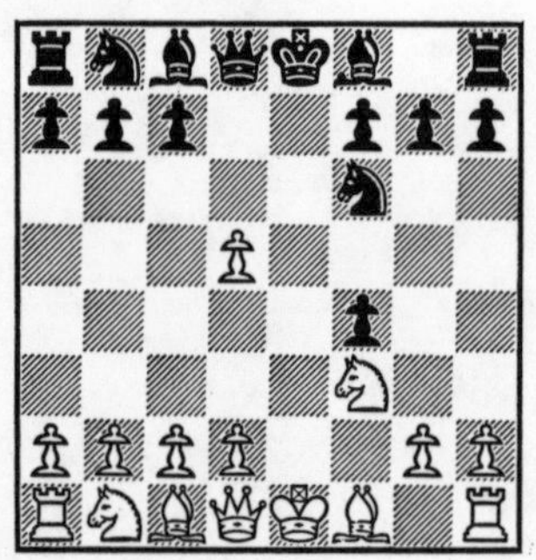

Key Position 4

### OBSERVATIONS ON KEY POSITION 4

[A] 4 P–K5 is weak because of 4 . . . P–KN4.

[B] 4 . . . QxP (4 . . . B–Q3 5 P–Q4, P–KN4 6 P–B4, P–QN3 7 B–Q3 favors White) 5 N–B3, Q–K3† 6 K–B2! results in advantage for White after 6 . . . Q–N3† 7 P–Q4, N–KB3 8 B–N5† P–B3 9 R–K1†, B–K2 10 B–B4.

This defense, which considerably restricts White's chances for attack, is often played in modern tournaments. Black abstains from protecting the Gambit Pawn, obtaining fine activity for his pieces instead, thanks to the open center files.

Although it is difficult for White to treat the position as aggressively as a gambiteer might wish, the chances, by and large, remain balanced. White's best possibilities are offered through 5 B–N5†, an old-fashioned continuation to which Russian masters have returned in recent years.

### IDEA VARIATIONS 11-13:

(11) 5 N–B3, NxP 6 NxN, QxN 7 P–Q4, B–K2! 8 P–QB4 (8 B–Q3, P–KN4!), Q–K5† 9 K–B2 (too ambitious; 9 B–K2, as in Prac. Var. 20, leads to equality), B–KB4 10 P–B5, N–B3! 11 B–N5, Q–Q4 (11 . . . O–O–O? costs a piece because of 12 R–K1, followed by 13 BxN) 12 BxP (or 12 R–K1, B–K5 13 Q–K2, P–B4), O–O–O with a good game for Black (Kieninger–Eliskases, Stuttgart 1939; see Game 9).

(12) 5 B–N5†, QN–Q2 6 O–O (6 P–B4 is not good because of 6 . . . P–QR3 7 B–R4, B–Q3 8 P–Q4, P–QN4 9 PxP, O–O!) NxP 7 P–B4, N–B3 (preferable is 7 . . . N–N3 8 R–K1†, B–K2 9 P–B5, P–QB3!) 8 P–Q4, B–K2 (8 . . . P–B3 9 B–R4, B–Q3 10 R–K1†, K–B1 11 N–B3 gives White sufficient positional compensation for the Pawn) 9 BxP. White has recovered the Pawn and retains a positional advantage. See Game 10. 5 . . . P–B3 is stronger than 5 . . . QN–Q2. See Prac. Var. 16–18. Also worthy of consideration is 5 . . . B–Q2 6 B–B4, B–Q3 7 O–O, O–O.

(13) 5 B–B4 (5 P–Q4 is weak because of 5 . . . NxP and an eventual . . . N–K6), B–Q3! (and not 5 . . . NxP 6 BxN, QxB 7 N–B3, as White gets a great lead in development) 6 O–O, O–O 7 P–Q4 with even chances.

*King's Gambit Game 9*

*WHITE: Kieninger* — *BLACK: Eliskases*

*Stuttgart 1939*

| | WHITE | BLACK | | WHITE | BLACK |
|---|---|---|---|---|---|
| 1 | P–K4 | P–K4 | 26 | P–QR4 | K–Q1 |
| 2 | P–KB4 | PxP | 27 | R–K4 | K–Q2 |
| 3 | N–KB3 | N–KB3 | 28 | P–N5 | PxP |
| 4 | N–B3 | P–Q4 | 29 | PxP | R–QR1 |
| 5 | PxP | NxP | 30 | R–Q4† | K–K3 |
| 6 | NxN | QxN | 31 | R–K4† | K–B3 |
| 7 | P–Q4 | B–K2 | 32 | R–Q4 | R–R6† |
| 8 | P–B4 | Q–K5† | 33 | K–K4 | R–QB6 |
| 9 | K–B2 | B–KB4 | 34 | K–Q5 | P–N4 |
| 10 | P–B5 | N–B3! | 35 | R–Q2 | P–N3 |
| 11 | B–N5 | Q–Q4! | 36 | PxP | PxP |
| 12 | BxP | O–O–O | 37 | K–Q6! | R–B4 |
| 13 | B–K3 | B–B3 | 38 | R–Q5! | R–B7 |
| 14 | Q–R4 | B–K5! | 39 | P–N4 | RxP |
| 15 | BxN | QxB | 40 | K–B6 | P–R4 |
| 16 | QxQ | BxQ | 41 | PxP | RxP |
| 17 | QR–Q1 | KR–K1 | 42 | KxP | K–K3 |
| 18 | KR–K1 | BxN! | 43 | K–B6 | P–B4 |
| 19 | KxB | BxP! | 44 | P–N6 | R–R1 |
| 20 | BxB | RxR | 45 | P–N7 | P–N5 |
| 21 | RxR | RxB | 46 | R–Q6† | K–K4 |
| 22 | R–K7 | R–Q2 | 47 | K–B7 | P–N6 |
| 23 | R–K8† | R–Q1 | 48 | R–Q8 | R–R2† |
| 24 | R–K7 | R–B1 | 49 | R–Q7 | R–R1 |
| 25 | P–QN4 | P–QR3 | 50 | R–Q8 | Draw |

*King's Gambit Game 10*

*WHITE: Bronstein* *BLACK: Ragozin*

*Saltsjobaden 1948*

| | WHITE | BLACK | | WHITE | BLACK | | WHITE | BLACK |
|---|---|---|---|---|---|---|---|---|
| 1 | P–K4 | P–K4 | 24 | B–N5! | BxB | 47 | N–B4† | K–K2 |
| 2 | P–KB4 | P–Q4 | 25 | NxB | N/4–B3 | 48 | N–N6 | N–N4† |
| 3 | PxQP | PxP | 26 | RxR† | RxR | 49 | K–N2 | B–B4 |
| 4 | N–KB3 | N–KB3 | 27 | QxP | QxQ | 50 | P–QR4 | N–R2 |
| 5 | B–N5† | QN–Q2 | 28 | NxQ | PxP | 51 | K–B3 | P–KR4 |
| 6 | O–O | NxP | 29 | PxP | R–K7 | 52 | K–Q4 | K–Q3 |
| 7 | P–B4 | N–B3 | 30 | B–B4 | R–QB7 | 53 | N–B4† | K–B2 |
| 8 | P–Q4 | B–K2 | 31 | B–N3 | R–K7 | 54 | K–B5 | B–Q2 |
| 9 | BxP | O–O | 32 | N–KB3 | N–K5 | 55 | N–Q6 | P–R5 |
| 10 | B–R4 | N–N3 | 33 | B–Q1 | R–K6 | 56 | B–K2 | P–B4 |
| 11 | B–N3 | B–N5 | 34 | K–N1! | N/5xP | 57 | P–N3 | PxP |
| 12 | N–B3 | P–B3 | 35 | NxN | NxN | 58 | PxP | N–B1 |
| 13 | Q–Q2 | P–QR4 | 36 | R–K1 | RxR† | 59 | NxN | BxN |
| 14 | P–QR3 | P–R5 | 37 | NxR | K–B1 | 60 | B–B3 | B–N2 |
| 15 | B–R2 | N/N–Q2 | 38 | K–B2 | K–K2 | 61 | P–R5 | P–N4 |
| 16 | QR–K1 | R–K1 | 39 | K–K3 | K–Q3 | 62 | B–K2 | P–B5 |
| 17 | N–KN5 | B–R4 | 40 | P–QN4 | N–R3 | 63 | PxP | PxP |
| 18 | K–R1 | B–N3 | 41 | B–K2 | N–B2 | 64 | B–B3 | B–R3 |
| 19 | N–B3 | N–R4 | 42 | N–B3 | N–Q4† | 65 | BxP | B–K7 |
| 20 | B–K3 | Q–B2 | 43 | K–Q4 | N–B5 | 66 | P–N5 | P–B6 |
| 21 | Q–Q1 | Q–R4 | 44 | B–B1 | P–B3 | 67 | P–R6 | Resigns |
| 22 | B–Q2 | Q–R2 | 45 | N–Q2 | N–K3† | | | |
| 23 | P–B5! | P–N3 | 46 | K–B3 | N–B2 | | | |

*King's Gambit Game 11*

*WHITE: Bronstein* *BLACK: Botvinnik*

*USSR Championship 1952*

| | WHITE | BLACK | | WHITE | BLACK |
|---|---|---|---|---|---|
| 1 | P–K4 | P–K4 | 14 | B–N3 | P–B4! |
| 2 | P–KB4 | PxP | 15 | P–B4? | Q–B3 |
| 3 | N–KB3 | P–Q4 | 16 | N–K5 | BxN |
| 4 | PxP | N–KB3 | 17 | PxB | QxP |
| 5 | B–N5† | P–B3 | 18 | BxP | Q–R4 |
| 6 | PxP | PxP | 19 | KR–K1 | KR–K1 |
| 7 | B–B4 | N–Q4 | 20 | P–R4 | B–K7! |
| 8 | P–Q4 | B–Q3 | 21 | Q–QB3 | N–Q2 |
| 9 | O–O | O–O | 22 | P–R5 | N–B3 |
| 10 | N–QB3 | NxN | 23 | B–R4 | R–K3 |
| 11 | PxN | B–KN5 | 24 | K–N2 | N–K5 |
| 12 | Q–Q3 | N–Q2 | 25 | Q–R3 | P–N4 |
| 13 | P–N3!? | N–N3! | | Resigns | |

PRACTICAL VARIATIONS 16–20:

1 P–K4, P–K4 2 P–KB4, PxP 3 N–KB3, P–Q4 4 PxP, N–KB3

| | *16* | *17* | *18* | *19* | *20* |
|---|---|---|---|---|---|
| *5* | B–N5† | – – | – – | P–B4 | N–B3 |
| | P–B3 | – – | – – | P–B3 | NxP |
| *6* | PxP | – – | – – | P–Q4 | NxN |
| | PxP | – – | – – | B–N5†[9] | QxN |
| *7* | B–B4 | – – | – – | N–B3 | P–Q4 |
| | B–Q3 | N–Q4! | – – | PxP | B–K2! |
| *8* | Q–K2† | P–Q4[3] | O–O! | BxP | P–B4 |
| | Q–K2 | B–Q3 | B–Q3[6] | O–O | Q–K5† |
| *9* | QxQ† | O–O | N–B3 | B–Q3 | B–K2 |
| | KxQ | O–O | B–K3[7] | R–K1† | N–B3 |
| *10* | O–O[1] | N–B3 | N–K4 | B–K5 | O–O |
| | B–K3 | NxN | B–K2 | N–B3[10] | B–KB4 |
| *11* | R–K1 | PxN | B–N3 | O–O | R–K1 |
| | QN–Q2 | B–KN5[4] | O–O | NxB | O–O–O |
| *12* | P–Q4[2] | Q–Q3 | P–Q4[8] | NxN | B–B1 |
| | ± | N–Q2[5] | | PxP | Q–B7[11] |
| *13* | | = | = | BxP | = |
| | | | | B–K3 | |
| | | | | = | |

*Notes to practical variations 16–20:*

[1] 10 P–Q4, B–KB4 11 N–K5 is also good (Nimzowitsch–Schweinburg, 1934).

[2] Bhend–Barcza, Zurich 1959.

[3] 8 Q–K2†, B–K3!

[4] Also good is 10 . . . N–Q2 11 B–Q3, P–QB4 (Bronstein–Lilienthal, Moscow 1953).

[5] Black has a good game (Bronstein–Botvinnik, USSR Championship 1952). See Game 11.

[6] Worthy of consideration is 8 . . . B–K3 in order to prevent 9 N–B3.

[7] 9 . . . NxN is answered by 10 R–K1†!

[8] 12 . . . N–Q2 13 Q–K2!, P–N4 14 P–B4, N/4–N3 15 P–KR4!, P–KR3 16 PxP, PxP 17 N/3xP!, BxN 18 BxP with a strong attack for the piece (Spasski–Lutikov, USSR Championship 1960).

[9] The immediate 6 . . . PxP allows 7 P–B5!

[10] 10 . . . B–K3 11 P–B5!, N–N5 12 O–O, BxN 13 PxB, N–K6 14 BxP†, K–R1 15 Q–Q2!, NxR 16 Q–R6, P–B3 17 Q–R5 with a winning attack (Reti–Duras, 1912).

[11] Spielmann–Milner-Barry, Margate 1938.

SUPPLEMENTARY VARIATIONS 1–5:
1 P–K4, P–K4 2 P–KB4, PxP 3 N–KB3

The Allgaier Gambit, 3 . . . P–KN4 4 P–KR4, P–N5 5 N–N5 (Sup. Var. 1), is not correct, according to present opinion. Black accepts the Knight sacrifice and is able to muster a sufficient defense.

The Muzio Gambit (Sup. Var. 2), which has been extensively analyzed in the course of time, offers White a strong attack for the piece, supposedly sufficient for a draw. Neither side can safely play for a win.

Becker's Defense (Sup. Var. 3), has basic significance. It aims at the set-up 4 . . . P–KN4 and 5 . . . B–N2, negating the sting of White's P–KR4. The column shows an independent variation on the part of White, which is sharp, rather obscure and so far insufficiently tested.

Sup. Var. 4 and 5 deal with 3 . . . N–KB3. Black avoids the classical defense 3 . . . P–KN4 and, as in the Modern Variation and the Cunningham Reformed, aims at a more positional treatment of the opening. The move 3 . . . N–KB3 must be considered satisfactory for Black.

| | *1* | *2* | *3* | *4* | *5* |
|---|---|---|---|---|---|
| *3* | – – | – – | – – | – – | – – |
| | P–KN4 | – – | P–KR3 | N–KB3 | – – |
| *4* | P–KR4 | B–B4 | P–Q4 | P–K5 | – – |
| | P–N5 | P–N5 | P–KN4 | N–R4 | – – |
| *5* | N–N5 | O–O! | P–KR4[4] | Q–K2!? | P–Q4 |
| | P–KR3 | PxN | B–N2 | B–K2 | P–Q3 |
| *6* | NxBP | QxP | P–KN3[5] | P–Q4 | N–B3 |
| | KxN | Q–B3 | P–N5 | O–O | B–N5[11] |
| *7* | B–B4†[1] | P–K5 | N–R2 | P–KN4 | B–B4 |
| | P–Q4 | QxP | PxP | PxP e.p. | N–QB3[12] |
| *8* | BxP† | P–Q3 | NxP[6] | Q–N2[8] | = |
| | K–N2 | B–R3 | P–Q3 | P–Q3 | |
| *9* | P–Q4 | N–B3 | P–B3 | RPxP | |
| | P–B6! | N–K2 | N–KB3 | B–N5 | |
| *10* | PxP | B–Q2 | NxN† | N–R2 | |
| | N–KB3! | QN–B3 | QxN | NxP! | |
| *11* | N–B3 | QR–K1 | B–K3[7] | R–N1[9] | |
| | B–QN5 | Q–KB4 | = | B–B4! | |
| *12* | B–QB4 | N–Q5 | | B–KB4[10] | |
| | PxP | K–Q1 | | B–K5! | |
| *13* | R–N1† | Q–K2! | | ∓ | |
| | N–N5[2] | Q–K3[3] | | | |
| | ∓ | = | | | |

*Notes to supplementary variations 1–5:*

[1] 7 P–Q4, P–B6 leads into the text line: 8 B–B4† (8 PxP, P–Q4), P–Q4. Weak is 7 QxP because of 7 . . . N–KB3 8 QxP, B–Q3!

[2] Consultation game, Marco–Schlechter, 1903: 14 QxP, QxP† 15 R–N3, R–B1 16 B–B4, but now 16 . . . B–K2! instead of 16 . . . Q–B3 as played.

[3] Bad for Black is 13 . . . NxN 14 BxN, QxB 15 B–B3. But 13 B–B3, R–K1 14 B–B6, B–N4 favors Black. After the text move, White has nothing better than a repetition of moves, e.g., 14 Q–B3, Q–B4 15 Q–K2, Q–K3.

[4] 5 B–B4 transposes into the Philidor and Hanstein Gambits (Part 2).

[5] After 6 PxP, PxP 7 RxR, BxR 8 P–KN3, Black has the active defense 8 . . . P–Q4!, e.g., 9 KPxP, Q–K2† or 9 NPxP, P–N5 10 N–N5, P–KB3.

[6] 8 QxP is insufficient because of 8 . . . PxN 9 QxB, QxP† 10 K–Q1, Q–B3.

[7] Stronger than 11 Q–K2, P–QB4! (Denk–Saemisch, Prague 1943). Pachman appraises this sharp position as approximately even.

[8] 8 N–B3, P–Q4 9 B–Q2, N–QB3 10 O–O–O, B–KN5 favors Black (Keres–Alekhine, Salzburg 1942).

[9] 11 NxB (11 QxN??, B–R5), NxR 12 QxN, B–R5† 13 K–Q1, N–B3 favors Black. The text move is supposedly an improvement, but is not sufficient either.

[10] Wade–Alexander, Centenary Tournament 1951.

[11] If 6 . . . PxP, then 7 Q–K2! (7 . . . N–QB3 8 P–Q5).

[12] Black has a satisfactory position and threatens 7 . . . PxP. The immediate 6 . . . PxP is bad because of 7 BxP†.

## SUPPLEMENTARY VARIATIONS 6–10:

1 P–K4, P–K4 2 P–KB4, PxP

The continuations other than 3 N–KB3 which White has at his disposal are all inferior to the Knight's Gambit and very rarely adopted.

The Bishop's Gambit with 3 B–B4 (Sup. Var. 6) has the drawback of exposing the Bishop to attack by . . . P–Q4

The lesser Bishop's Gambit with 3 B–K2 (Sup. Var. 7) fails to fit into the aggressive nature of the King's Gambit. Black easily obtains a good game, again, by means of . . . P–Q4.

Nor does the Breyer Gambit with 3 Q–B3 cause Black any difficulties (Sup. Var. 8).

Dangerous for White are the Mason Gambit with 3 N–QB3 and the Steinitz Gambit with 3 P–Q4. In these cases 3 . . . Q–R5† is, by way of exception, very effective, as White cannot reply K–B1.

1 P–K4, P–K4 2 P–KB4, PxP

| | 6 | 7 | 8 | 9 | 10 |
|---|---|---|---|---|---|
| 3 | B–B4 | B–K2 | Q–B3 | N–QB3 | P–Q4 |
| | N–KB3! | P–Q4! | N–QB3! | Q–R5† | Q–R5† |
| 4 | N–QB3[1] | PxP | P–B3[7] | K–K2 | K–K2 |
| | P–B3! | N–KB3! | N–B3 | P–Q4! | P–KB4! |
| 5 | B–N3[2] | P–B4[5] | P–Q4 | NxP | N–KB3 |
| | P–Q4 | P–B3 | P–Q4 | B–N5† | Q–R4 |
| 6 | PxP | P–Q4 | P–K5 | N–B3 | P–K5 |
| | PxP | B–N5† | N–K5 | B–Q3[10] | P–KN4 |
| 7 | P–Q4 | K–B1 | BxP | P–Q4 | P–KR4 |
| | B–Q3 | PxP | P–B3! | N–QB3 | N–QB3 |
| 8 | KN–K2 | BxP | B–QN5[8] | P–K5 | ∓ |
| | O–O | PxP![6] | B–K2 | O–O–O! | |
| 9 | O–O[3] | ∓ | PxP | BxP | |
| | P–KN4! | | BxP[9] | KN–K2 | |
| 10 | NxQP | | ∓ | P–B4[11] | |
| | N–B3[4] | | | ∓ | |
| | ∓ | | | | |

*Notes to supplementary variations 6–10:*

[1] 4 P–K5 is weak because of 4 . . . P–Q4! E.g., 5 B–N3, N–K5 6 N–KB3, B–KN5 7 O–O, N–QB3.

[2] Nor are other possibilities satisfactory:

1) 5 Q–B3, P–Q4! 6 PxP, B–Q3!
2) 5 Q–K2, P–Q4! 6 PxP†, B–K2!
3) 5 N–B3, P–QN4 6 B–N3, P–N5!
4) 5 P–Q4 or 5 P–Q3, B–N5!

[3] White has no time for 9 QBxP because of 9 . . . BxB 10 NxB, N–N5!

[4] Black clearly has the advantage due to his 4 to 2 Pawn majority on the Kingside (Spielmann–Boguljubow, Mahrisch-Ostrau 1923).

[5] Better is 5 N–QB3 or 5 N–KB3. 5 P–Q4, NxP 6 N–KB3, B–N5† 7 P–B3, B–K2 8 O–O, O–O 9 P–B4, N–K6 yields a slight edge for Black (Tartakover–Alekhine, New York 1924).

[6] 9 BxN? N–Q4 favors Black (Tartakover–Capablanca, New York 1924; see game 17). 9 BxP, O–O favors Black.

[7] Unsatisfactory is 4 N–K2, P–Q4! But 4 QxP offers chances for equality, e.g., 4 . . . P–Q4 5 PxP, N–N5 6 Q–K4†, Q–K2 7 QxQ†, BxQ 8 K–Q1, N–KB3 9 N–QB3.

[8] Or 8 B–Q3, PxP 9 BxN, PxKB 10 QxP, B–K2, and Black has sufficient compensation for the Pawn.

[9] Black has the advantage:

1) 10 N–K2, O–O 11 O–O, P–N4! (Spielmann–Tarrasch, Berlin 1919) with a winning attack for Black.
2) 10 N–Q2, NxN 11 KxN, O–O with a strong game for Black (Keres–Johansson, Correspondence Game 1937–39).

[10] The theoretical continuation is 6 . . . N–QB3! 7 NxP†, K–Q1 8 NxR, N–K4 9 Q–K1!, NxN 10 QxQ, NxQ† with advantage for Black.

[11] Spasski–Furman, Tallinn 1959. Black should now have played 10 . . . B–QN5; maintaining his advantage.

*King's Gambit Game 12*

*WHITE: Tartakover* *BLACK: Capablanca*

*New York 1924*

| | WHITE | BLACK | | WHITE | BLACK |
|---|---|---|---|---|---|
| 1 | P–K4 | P–K4 | 17 | PxB | N–K6 |
| 2 | P–KB4 | PxP | 18 | BxP† | K–R1 |
| 3 | B–K2 | P–Q4 | 19 | Q–Q3 | BxN |
| 4 | PxP | N–KB3 | 20 | PxB | N–Q4 |
| 5 | P–B4 | P–B3 | 21 | B–K4 | N–B5 |
| 6 | P–Q4 | B–N5† | 22 | Q–Q2 | Q–R5 |
| 7 | K–B1 | PxP | 23 | K–B1 | P–B4 |
| 8 | BxP | PxP | 24 | B–B6 | R–B3 |
| 9 | BxN | N–Q4! | 25 | P–Q5 | R–Q1 |
| 10 | K–B2 | RxB | 26 | R–Q1 | RxB |
| 11 | BxP | O–O | 27 | PxR | RxQ |
| 12 | N–KB3 | N–B3 | 28 | RxR | N–K3 |
| 13 | N–B3 | P–QN4 | 29 | R–Q6 | Q–B4† |
| 14 | B–Q3 | N–N5† | 30 | K–N2 | Q–K7† |
| 15 | K–N1 | B–N2 | | Resigns | |
| 16 | B–B5 | BxN | | | |

## part 5—KING'S GAMBIT DECLINED

### OBSERVATIONS ON KEY POSITION 5

1 P–K4, P–K4
2 P–KB4, B–B4
3 N–KB3, P–Q3

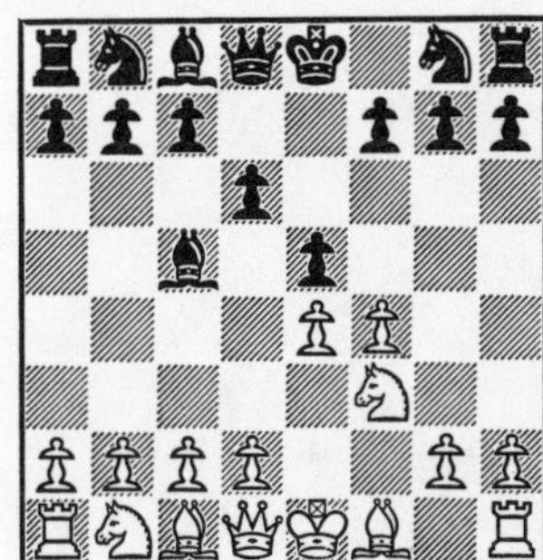

KEY POSITION 5

Declining the King's Gambit by 2 . . . B–B4 is based on the supposition that White's second move has weakened his Kingside. Black inhibits the enemy's castling and commits himself to the maintenance of his King Pawn. Consequently, White's main continuation is 4 P–B3, in order to neutralize the functions of the enemy Bishop and the King Pawn. Yet White's chance of obtaining an advantage in this way is very slight, because the exchange of center Pawns opens the position, leaving Black some advantage in development.

White's alternative is the classical 4 N–B3, followed by B–B4 and P–Q3. His aim is the elimination of the enemy Bishop by N–QR4. The upshot is lively play with pieces, offering even chances.

### IDEA VARIATIONS 14-18:

(14) 4 P–B3, N–KB3 (or 4 . . . N–QB3 5 B–N5! followed by P–Q4) 5 P–Q4, PxP 6 PxP, B–N3 (6 . . . B–N5† 7 B–Q2) 7 N–B3. Tartakover considered White's position as sound, but there is not enough experience to form a definitive conclusion.

(15) 4 P–B3, N–KB3 5 PxP, PxP 6 P–Q4 (the text is more enterprising than 6 NxP, for which see Prac. Var. 21), PxP 7 PxP. And now promising for White is 7 . . . B–N5† 8 B–Q2, BxB† (8 . . . Q–K2!) 9 QNxB, O–O 10 B–Q3, P–B4 11 P–Q5, B–N5 (11 . . . Q–K2 12 Q–K2!) 12 O–O, QN–Q2 13 Q–B2, R–K1 14 QR–K1! (Spielmann–Van Scheltinga, Amsterdam 1938). 7 . . . NxP leads to great complications, such as 8 PxB, QxQ† 9 KxQ, N–B7† 10 K–K1, NxR 11 P–KN3, O–O 12 B–N2, R–K1† 13 K–B1, NxP† 14 PxN, N–R3! Black emerges with a Rook and three Pawns for two minor pieces. Safest for Black is 7 . . . B–N3 with even chances.

(16) 4 N–B3, N–KB3 (4 . . . N–QB3 5 B–N5) 5 B–B4 (the win of a Pawn by 5 PxP, PxP 6 NxP, Q–Q5 7 N–Q3, B–N3 is too risky), N–QB3 6 P–Q3, N–KN5 (this enticing sortie is unfavorable) 7 N–KN5! (7 R–B1? NxP), O–O (7 . . . P–KR3? 8 P–B5!) 8 P–B5, B–B7† 9 K–B1, N–K6† 10 BxN, BxB 11 P–KR4, BxN 12 PxB, QxP 13 R–R5 with a clear advantage for White (Kamischow–Panov, Match 1944).

(17) 4 N–B3, N–KB3 5 B–B4, N–B3 6 P–Q3, O–O (castling at this point achieves nothing with respect to the central squares and is actually a loss of time) 7 N–QR4, B–KN5 8 NxB, PxN 9 P–B3 (or 9 O–O, PxP 10 BxP, N–QR4!, and Black has achieved equality), and White has the better game.

(18) 4 N–B3, N–KB3 5 B–B4, N–B3 6 P–Q3, P–QR3! 7 P–B5 (steadier is 7 PxP, PxP 8 B–KN5, P–KR3 9 BxN, QxB 10 N–Q5, Q–Q3 [Spielmann–Yates, Moscow 1925]), N–QR4 8 B–KN5, P–B3 9 Q–K2, P–N4 10 B–N3, Q–N3 11 N–Q1, R–R2 12 N–B2, P–KR3 with a good game for Black (Tchigorin–Janowski, Barmen 1905). 6 . . . P–QR3! is an old, safe continuation which opens a square of retreat for the Bishop, at the same time cancelling out the possibility of B–QN5. For the sharp 6 . . . B–KN5, which formerly was very usual, see Prac. Var. 24 and 25. A steady alternative is 6 . . . B–K3.

PRACTICAL VARIATIONS 21–25:

1 P–K4, P–K4 2 P–KB4, B–B4 3 N–KB3, P–Q3

| | 21 | 22 | 23 | 24 | 25 |
|---|---|---|---|---|---|
| 4 | P–B3 | – – | – – | N–B3 | – – |
| | N–KB3 | B–N5 | P–KB4 | N–KB3 | – – |
| 5 | PxP | PxP | PxKP! | B–B4 | – – |
| | PxP | PxP | QPxP | N–B3 | – – |

| | 21 | 22 | 23 | 24 | 25 |
|---|---|---|---|---|---|
| 6 | NxP | Q–R4† | P–Q4 | P–Q3 | – – |
| | Q–K2[1] | B–Q2[4] | PxQP | B–KN5 | – – |
| 7 | P–Q4 | Q–B2 | B–QB4! | P–KR3 | N–QR4 |
| | B–Q3 | N–QB3 | N–QB3[6] | BxN | N–Q5[14] |
| 8 | N–B3[2] | P–QN4 | P–QN4! | QxB | NxB |
| | NxP | B–Q3 | B–N3 | PxP![11] | PxN |
| 9 | B–K2 | B–QB4 | Q–N3 | B–N5[12] | P–B3 |
| | O–O | N–B3 | N–R3 | O–O | NxN† |
| 10 | O–O | P–Q3 | O–O[7] | BxN | PxN |
| | P–QB4 | Q–K2 | PxKP | PxB | B–R4 |
| 11 | QN–Q2 | O–O | B–KN5[8] | BxP[13] | Q–K2 |
| | NxN | O–O–O | Q–Q3 | = | Q–Q3[15] |
| 12 | BxN | P–QR4![5] | N–R3 | | PxP |
| | PxP | ± | B–KB4[9] | | QxP |
| 13 | PxP | | N–R4 | | P–B4[16] |
| | N–B3[3] | | B–N3[10] | | ± |
| | = | | = | | |

*Notes to practical variations 21–25:*

[1] 6 . . . O–O 7 P–Q4, B–Q3 8 N–B3, NxP 9 B–Q3, N–KB3 10 O–O slightly favors White (Keres–Kubanec, Prague 1943). See Game 13.

[2] 8 N–B4 is probably a little stronger.

[3] Choice is a matter of taste.

[4] 6 . . . Q–Q2 fails because of 7 B–N5, P–QB3 8 NxP! On 6 . . . N–B3 7 NxP, Q–R5† 8 P–N3, B–B7† 9 KxB, Q–B3† 10 K–N1, QxN 11 B–N2, Black has hardly sufficient compensation for the Pawn.

[5] Bronstein–Panov, Moscow 1947. See Game 14.

[6] Other moves are weaker:

1) 7 . . . N–KB3 8 P–K5, N–K5 9 PxP, B–N3 (9 . . . B–N5† 10 B–Q2) 10 N–B3, N–B3 11 B–K3, and White has the better of it.

2) 7 . . . PxKP 8 N–K5, N–KB3 9 N–B7, Q–K2 10 NxR, and Black has insufficient compensation.

[7] White's attacking chances are most likely better after 10 B–KN5, Q–Q3 11 QN–Q2! or 11 PxBP, according to Keres.

[8] Reti's continuation 11 NxP, NxN 12 B–B7† is surprisingly refuted by 12 . . . K–K2!: 13 B–N5†, K–B1 or 13 PxN, BxP† followed by 14 . . . BxR!

[9] 12 . . . PxP† 13 K–R1, QxP 14 QR–K1! offers White a stronger attack, the exchange of Queens notwithstanding.

[10] 14 QR–K1, P–Q6† 15 K–R1, P–Q7 16 R–K2, P–K6 with a rather obscure position (Fuderer–Rabar, Zagreb 1953).

[11] The text is simpler than 8 . . . N–Q5 9 Q–N3!, Q–K2 10 PxP, PxP 11 K–Q1, P–B3 12 P–QR4 and White for choice (Rubinstein–Hromadka, Mahrisch-Ostrau 1923). See Game 15. Black has better counterchances with 9 . . . PxP 10 QxNP, R–KB1; weak is 9 . . . NxP† 10 K–Q1, NxR 11 QxP, K–Q2 (11 . . . R–KB1 12 PxP, PxP 13 B–KN5, B–K2 14 R–B1!) 12 PxP, PxP 13 R–B1, B–K2 14 B–KN5.

continued ▸

[12] If 9 QBxP, Black, according to Alekhine, replies 9 . . . N–Q5 with a strong attack: e.g., 10 Q–Q1 (10 Q–N3?, N–R4!), P–B3 11 Q–Q2 (Mieses–Spielmann, Baden–Baden 1925), P–Q4 12 PxP, O–O!

[13] (analysis by Rubinstein).

[14] Or 7 . . . BxN 8 QxB, N–Q5 9 Q–N3!, and White obtains a winning attack, according to Keres: e.g., 9 . . . NxP† 10 K–Q1, NxR 11 QxP, R–KB1 12 NxB, PxN 13 PxP, NxP 14 R–B1, Q–K2 (14 . . . Q–Q2 15 BxP†) 15 B–R6! (15 . . . O–O–O 16 Q–N4†). Black's best is 7 . . . B–N3 or possibly 7 . . . Q–K2 followed by O–O–O.

[15] 11 . . . N–Q2 is a little better.

[16] 13 . . . Q–K2 14 Q–N2.

*King's Gambit Game 13*

*WHITE: Tartakover* *BLACK: Schlechter*

*St. Petersburg 1909*

| | WHITE | BLACK | | WHITE | BLACK | | WHITE | BLACK |
|---|---|---|---|---|---|---|---|---|
| 1 | P–K4 | P–K4 | 12 | N–B4 | P–B4 | 23 | R–KB1 | QxR† |
| 2 | P–KB4 | B–B4 | 13 | N/3–K5 | PxP | 24 | BxQ | N–Q2 |
| 3 | N–KB3 | P–Q3 | 14 | NxBP! | KxN | 25 | B–Q3 | N–B1 |
| 4 | PxP | PxP | 15 | Q–R5† | K–N1 | 26 | PxP | B–KB2 |
| 5 | P–B3 | N–KB3 | 16 | RxN | R–K8† | 27 | Q–B3 | N–K3 |
| 6 | NxP | O–O | 17 | R–B1 | RxR† | 28 | B–K3 | R–N1 |
| 7 | P–Q4 | B–Q3 | 18 | BxR | B–B1 | 29 | P–KN4 | P–KN4 |
| 8 | N–B3 | NxP | 19 | BxP! | Q–B3 | 30 | Q–B6 | B–B1 |
| 9 | B–Q3 | R–K1 | 20 | B–N5 | Q–B4 | 31 | B–R7† | KxB |
| 10 | O–O | P–KR3? | 21 | N–Q6! | BxN | 32 | QxB† | Resigns |
| 11 | QN–Q2 | N–KB3 | 22 | B–B4† | B–K3 | | | |

*King's Gambit Game 14*

*WHITE: Bronstein* *BLACK: Panov*

*Moscow 1947*

| | WHITE | BLACK | | WHITE | BLACK | | WHITE | BLACK |
|---|---|---|---|---|---|---|---|---|
| 1 | P–K4 | P–K4 | 12 | P–QR4 | P–QR4 | 23 | NxB† | PxN |
| 2 | P–KB4 | B–B4 | 13 | P–N5 | N–QN1 | 24 | N–Q2 | P–B3 |
| 3 | N–KB3 | P–Q3 | 14 | QN–Q2 | B–KN5 | 25 | N–B4 | K–N2 |
| 4 | P–B3 | B–KN5 | 15 | N–N3 | P–QN3 | 26 | BxP! | NxB |
| 5 | PxP | PxP | 16 | B–K3 | N/1–Q2 | 27 | NxRP† | K–B2 |
| 6 | Q–R4† | B–Q2 | 17 | QR–K1 | B–K3 | 28 | N–B6 | Q–K1 |
| 7 | Q–B2 | N–QB3 | 18 | BxB | QxB | 29 | P–R5 | N–Q2 |
| 8 | P–QN4 | B–Q3 | 19 | K–R1 | Q–K2 | 30 | P–N6†! | K–N2 |
| 9 | B–B4 | N–B3 | 20 | N/N–Q2 | N–N5 | 31 | P–R6†! | KxNP |
| 10 | P–Q3 | Q–K2 | 21 | B–N1 | P–R4 | 32 | R–N1† | Resigns |
| 11 | O–O | O–O–O | 22 | N–B4 | P–N4? | | | |

*King's Gambit Game 15*

*WHITE: Rubinstein* *BLACK: Hromadka*

*Mahrisch–Ostrau 1923*

| WHITE | BLACK | WHITE | BLACK |
|---|---|---|---|
| 1 P–K4 | P–K4 | 16 P–B3 | B–N3 |
| 2 P–KB4 | B–B4 | 17 P–R5 | B–B2 |
| 3 N–KB3 | P–Q3 | 18 B–K3 | K–N1 |
| 4 N–B3 | N–KB3 | 19 K–B2 | K–R1 |
| 5 B–B4 | N–B3 | 20 R–B3 | N–Q4 |
| 6 P–Q3 | B–N5 | 21 B–N1 | N–B5 |
| 7 P–KR3 | BxN | 22 Q–B2! | B–N1 |
| 8 QxB | N–Q5 | 23 P–KN3! | NxKRP |
| 9 Q–N3 | Q–K2 | 24 RxP | Q–Q3 |
| 10 PxP | PxP | 25 Q–N6! | R–Q2 |
| 11 K–Q1 | P–B3 | 26 B–B5!! | RxR |
| 12 P–QR4 | R–KN1 | 27 BxQ | R–B7† |
| 13 R–B1 | P–KR3 | 28 QxR | NxQ |
| 14 N–K2 | O–O–O | 29 B–B5 | Resigns |
| 15 NxN | BxN | | |

## part 6—FALKBEER COUNTER GAMBIT

### OBSERVATIONS ON KEY POSITION 6

1 P–K4, P–K4
2 P–KB4, P–Q4
3 PxQP[A], P–K5[B]

KEY POSITION 6

A Declining the gambit by 3 N–KB3 is convenient for Black: 3 . . . PxKP 4 NxP, N–Q2! 5 P–Q4, PxP e.p.

B The proper answer to 3 . . . P–QB3 is 4 N–QB3! Black can lead into the Modern Variation by 3 . . . PxP. But 3 . . . QxP is weak because of 4 N–QB3.

The Falkbeer Counter Gambit is based on a sound positional idea. Black counteracts both the opening of the King Bishop's file and the building up of a strong enemy center. The advance of White's King Bishop Pawn has lost significance, while Black's King Pawn exercises pressure, hampering the development of the enemy pieces.

White therefore must aim at the elimination of the enemy King Pawn by P–Q3, rather than try to hold his own Pawn on Q5. Having achieved this aim, however, White must quickly develop his pieces and not try to profit from the possible pin along the King file after PxP, NxP. Black, too, is better served by a rapid mobilization of his pieces than by the quick recovery of the White Pawn on his Q4; otherwise he may get into positive trouble.

Proper play on both sides keeps the chances balanced.

IDEA VARIATIONS 19–22:

(19) 4 N–QB3 (4 P–B4 is weak because of 4 . . . P–QB3!, but playable is 4 B–N5†, as illustrated in Prac. Var. 30), N–KB3 5 B–B4, B–QB4 6 KN–K2, O–O 7 P–Q4, PxP e.p. 8 QxP, and Black has now sufficient compensation for the Pawn: e.g., 8 . . . N–N5 9 N–Q1, R–K1 10 P–KR3, N–R3 11 N–K3, P–QB3. But less logical is 8 . . . R–K1 9 P–KR3, N–R4 10 Q–B3, Q–R5† 11 K–Q1 (Tchigorin–Marshall, Karlsbad 1907). Also good for Black is 8 . . . P–QB3. If 9 PxP, then 9 . . . Q–N3!

(20) 4 N–QB3, N–KB3 5 Q–K2, B–KB4 6 NxP, NxN 7 P–Q3. Rubinstein gives a continuation favorable for White: 7 . . . QxP 8 B–Q2, B–K2 9 PxN, QxKP 10 QxQ, BxQ 11 O–O–O! But Black has a finesse which offers him equality: 7 . . . Q–R5† 8 K–Q1 (8 P–N3?, Q–K2), Q–K2 9 PxN, BxP.

(21) 4 P–Q3, N–KB3 (4 . . . QxP 5 Q–K2! N–KB3 6 N–QB3 or 6 N–Q2 favors White) 5 PxP, NxP 6 N–KB3 (6 Q–K2, QxP 7 N–Q2, P–KB4 8 P–KN4, N–QB3! favors Black [Pillsbury]), B–QB4 7 Q–K2, B–B4! (7 . . . B–B7† 8 K–Q1, QxP† fails because of Alapin's 9 KN–Q2!) 8 P–KN4? (correct is 8 N–B3; see Prac. Var. 26), O–O! 9 PxB, R–K1, and Black has an irresistible attack for the piece (Spielmann–Tarrasch, Mahrisch–Ostrau 1923). See Game 16.

(22) 4 P–Q3, N–KB3 5 Q–K2, QxP? (good is 5 . . . B–KB4 or better B–KN5!, as in Prac. Var. 28) 6 N–QB3, B–QN5 7 B–Q2, BxN 8 BxB, B–N5 9 PxP, BxQ 10 PxQ, BxB 11 KxB, NxP 12 BxP with a better end game for White (Bronstein–Szabo, Moscow–Budapest 1949). See Game 17. 9 . . . QxKP 10 QxQ†, NxQ 11 BxP, R–N1 12 B–K5, N–QB3 13 B–Q3 also favors White (Reti–Tarrasch, Goteborg 1920).

PRACTICAL VARIATIONS 26–30:

1 P–K4, P–K4 2 P–KB4, P–Q4 3 PxQP, P–K5

| | *26* | *27* | *28* | *29* | *30* |
|---|---|---|---|---|---|
| *4* | P–Q3 | – – | – – | – – | B–N5† |
| | N–KB3 | – – | – – | – – | P–B3 |
| *5* | PxP | – – | Q–K2 | N–Q2 | PxP |
| | NxKP | – – | B–KN5! | PxP | NxP[8] |
| *6* | N–KB3 | B–K3 | N–KB3[4] | BxP | P–Q3 |
| | B–QB4 | B–Q3[2] | QxP | NxP | N–B3 |
| *7* | Q–K2 | N–KB3 | QN–Q2 | Q–K2†[6] | N–QB3 |
| | B–B4 | O–O | B–KB4 | B–K2 | B–QN5[9] |

| | *26* | *27* | *28* | *29* | *30* |
|---|---|---|---|---|---|
| *8* | N–B3 | B–B4 | N–R4 | N–K4[7] | B–Q2 |
| | Q–K2 | N–Q2 | B–KN5 | = | B–N5 |
| *9* | B–K3 | O–O | KN–B3 | | N–K2 |
| | BxB | R–K1 | B–KB4[5] | | O–O[10] |
| *10* | QxB | R–K1 | = | | = |
| | NxN | KN–B3 | | | |
| *11* | QxQ† | K–R1 | | | |
| | KxQ | N–N5 | | | |
| *12* | PxN | B–N1 | | | |
| | B–K5![1] | N–N3[3] | | | |
| | = | = | | | |

*Notes to practical variations 26–30:*

[1] The text move was suggested by Rabinowitsch. Inferior is 12 . . . BxP 13 K–Q2! (Wheatcroft–Keres, Margate 1939). After 13 P–B4, BxN 14 PxB, N–Q2 15 B–Q3, K–Q3, White has only equality at best, his extra Pawn notwithstanding.

[2] After 6 . . . Q–R5†, White may sacrifice the exchange, which is a fair try, e.g., 7 P–N3, NxP 8 PxN, QxR. The alternative 8 N–KB3, Q–R3 (8 . . . Q–K2 9 PxN, QxB†=) 9 R–N1, NxB 10 RxN, B–KN5 leads to equality.

[3] 13 B–N3, BxP 14 N–B3, RxR 15 QxR, B–B4 with even chances (Bronstein–Unzicker, Alekhine Memorial Tourney, Moscow 1956).

[4] 6 Q–K3 offers Black the choice of two promising continuations:

1) 6 . . . NxP 7 QxP†, B–K2 8 P–B5, N–KB3 9 QxP, QN–Q2, and Black has development for the Pawn (Pachman).
2) 6 . . . B–N5† 7 P–B3 (7 B–Q2, O–O! 8 BxB, NxP), O–O 8 PxB, NxP 9 Q–N3, PxP and Black has a dangerous attack for the sacrificed material (Persitz). Also, after 6 Q–K3, sufficient for equality is 6 . . . QxP 7 N–QB3, B–N5 8 B–Q2, BxN 9 BxB, QN–Q2.

[5] With a draw by repetition. White, of course, cannot play 9 Q–K3? because of 9 . . . B–B4!

[6] Weak is 7 N–K4? N–N5! 8 B–N5†, P–B3! 9 QxQ†, KxQ 10 B–R4, B–KB4 (Castaldi–Trifunovic, Hilversum 1947).

[7] Keres considers the chances approximately even. Vukovic mentions the interesting possibility 8 . . . N–N5 9 B–B4, B–N5 10 QxB, NxP† 11 K–K2, P–KN3! with obscure complications. Simple and good is 8 . . . O–O or 8 . . . QN–B3.

[8] More natural than the old-fashioned 5 . . . PxP 6 B–B4, N–B3, when 7 P–Q3 serves better than 7 P–Q4.

[9] Worthy of consideration is 7 . . . B–KB4.

[10] Black has sufficient compensation for the Pawn: e.g., 10 PxP, BxQN 11 BxB, NxP 12 QxQ, QRxQ 13 O–O, BxN 14 BxB, NxB 15 PxN, KR–K1 with an even end game (Fuderer–Pirc, Munich 1954).

*King's Gambit Game 16*

*WHITE: Spielmann* *BLACK: Tarrasch*

*Mahrisch–Ostrau 1923*

| | WHITE | BLACK | | WHITE | BLACK |
|---|---|---|---|---|---|
| 1 | P–K4 | P–K4 | 15 | NxB | NxN |
| 2 | P–KB4 | P–Q4 | 16 | PxP | Q–R5† |
| 3 | PxQP | P–K5 | 17 | K–B1 | R–KB1 |
| 4 | P–Q3 | N–KB3 | 18 | K–N1 | Q–Q5† |
| 5 | PxP | NxKP | 19 | B–K3 | QxKP |
| 6 | N–KB3 | B–QB4 | 20 | R–K1 | N–Q2 |
| 7 | Q–K2 | B–B4 | 21 | Q–B4 | K–R1 |
| 8 | P–KN4? | O–O! | 22 | B–K4 | QR–K1 |
| 9 | PxB | R–K1 | 23 | B–Q4 | Q–B5 |
| 10 | B–N2 | N–B7 | 24 | R–K2 | N–B3 |
| 11 | N–K5 | NxR | 25 | BxN | PxB |
| 12 | BxN | N–Q2! | 26 | P–KR3 | R–N1† |
| 13 | N–QB3 | P–KB3 | | Resigns | |
| 14 | N–K4 | PxN | | | |

*King's Gambit Game 17*

*WHITE: Bronstein* *BLACK: Szabo*

*Moscow vs. Budapest 1947*

| | WHITE | BLACK | | WHITE | BLACK |
|---|---|---|---|---|---|
| 1 | P–K4 | P–K4 | 24 | KxR | N–K1 |
| 2 | P–KB4 | P–Q4 | 25 | R–K1! | N–Q3 |
| 3 | PxQP | P–K5 | 26 | R–K7 | N–KB1 |
| 4 | P–Q3 | N–KB3 | 27 | B–K5! | N–N3 |
| 5 | Q–K2 | QxP? | 28 | BxN | NxR |
| 6 | N–QB3 | B–QN5 | 29 | BxN | K–Q4 |
| 7 | B–Q2 | BxN | 30 | K–B3 | K–K3 |
| 8 | BxB | B–N5 | 31 | B–N4 | R–Q1 |
| 9 | PxP | BxQ | 32 | K–K2 | K–B3 |
| 10 | PxQ | BxB | 33 | B–B3† | K–N4 |
| 11 | KxB | NxP | 34 | P–KR3 | R–K1† |
| 12 | BxP | R–N1 | 35 | K–B2 | R–Q1 |
| 13 | R–K1† | K–Q2 | 36 | N–B3† | K–R4 |
| 14 | R–Q1 | K–B3 | 37 | N–Q4 | K–N3 |
| 15 | B–Q4 | NxP | 38 | N–K6 | R–Q8 |
| 16 | N–B3 | N–Q2 | 39 | NxP | R–B8 |
| 17 | P–KN3 | N–K3 | 40 | K–B3 | RxP |
| 18 | B–K3 | P–N3 | 41 | N–N5 | P–QR3 |
| 19 | K–N2 | QR–K1 | 42 | N–B7 | P–QR4 |
| 20 | KR–KB1 | P–B4? | 43 | P–QR4 | R–B8 |
| 21 | N–R4 | N–N2 | 44 | N–Q5 | R–B8† |
| 22 | B–Q4 | R–K7† | 45 | K–N2 | Resigns |
| 23 | R–B2 | RxR† | | | |

# chapter 8—Petroff's Defense

This opening arises after 1 P–K4, P–K4 2 N–KB3 when Black, choosing not to defend his Pawn, counters with 2 . . . N–KB3. The Petroff has been known for centuries, but not until 1850 was it closely investigated by the Russian masters Petroff and Jaenisch, and in some countries it is known as the Russian Defense. Later on, the Americans Pillsbury and Marshall contributed substantially to our knowledge of this debut.

Considered from the standpoint of strategy, Black's counter may seem premature. Yet there is no such thing as a refutation if Black takes care not to exaggerate his aggressive attitude.

White is able to steer this opening into symmetrical channels, always to some extent making his initial tempo count; and this fact explains why the Petroff is so rarely adopted to-day. White's advantage however, apparently is no more than the edge of the first move.

Petroff's Defense is split into two main groups of variations beginning with (1) 3 NxP, P–Q3 4 N–B3, NxP 5 P–Q4, P–Q4 6 B–Q3 (Part 1) and (2) 3 P–Q4, PxP 4 P–K5, N–K5 5 QxP, P–Q4 6 PxP e.p., NxQP (Part 2). For a long time the move 3 NxP was considered White's best, although White achieves little more than slight superiority in controlled space. To-day, 3 P–Q4, strongly recommended by Steinitz, is preferred. This thrust offers White full activity for his pieces and chances to push an initiative.

In the first main variation, there are two important subvariations after Black's 4th move, ideas advocated respectively by Emanuel Lasker and Keres.

Lasker's line is 1 P–K4, P–K4 2 N–KB3, N–KB3 3 NxP, P–Q3 4 N–KB3, NxP 5 Q–K2, whereupon White, after an exchange of Queens, obtains a slight edge in development.

Keres' line varies from the above on White's 5th move. He plays 5 P–B4, making it more difficult for Black to maintain his Knight on its outpost than after the classical 5 P–Q4. In a number of games, Keres has demonstrated the full significance of 5 P–B4.

The protection of White's King Pawn by 3 N–B3 leads to the Three Knights' Game after 3 . . . B–N5. Black can also proceed with 3 . . . N–B3, transposing into the Four Knights' Game.

## part 1—CLASSICAL VARIATION

1 P–K4, P–K4
2 N–KB3, N–KB3
3 NxP, P–Q3[A]
4 N–KB3[B], NxP
5 P–Q4[C], P–Q4
6 B–Q3

KEY POSITION 1

OBSERVATIONS ON KEY POSITION 1

[A] 3 . . . NxP is bad because of 4 Q–K2, Q–K2 5 QxN, P–Q3 6 P–Q4, P–KB3 7 N–QB3, QPxN 8 N–Q5, Q–Q3 9 B–KB4, N–Q2 10 O–O–O with a big advantage for White. Or 4 . . . P–Q4 5 P–Q3, Q–K2 6 PxN, QxN 7 PxP, and White remains a Pawn plus. In the first line with 4 Q–K2, if 6 . . . N–Q2, then 7 N–QB3, PxN 8 N–Q5, N–B3 9 NxN†, PxN 10 B–N5†!

3 . . . Q–K2 is also weak because of 4 P–Q4, P–Q3 5 N–KB3, QxP† 6 B–K3, N–N5 7 Q–Q2, NxB 8 PxN, P–Q4 9 N–B3, Q–K3 10 B–Q3, P–KB4 11 N–K5, and White has the initiative (analysis by Loewenfisch).

[B] For 4 N–B4, see Sup. Var. 4.

[C] For 5 Q–K2, 5 N–B3 and 5 P–B4, see Sup. Var. 1, 2 and 3.

The pivotal point of this position is the maintenance or dislodgement of Black's centralized Knight. In this complicated struggle, White has the better chances, particularly if Black plays too sharply for an attack, though Marshall often successfully did so by continuing 6 . . . B–Q3.

But this continuation, designed to maintain the Knight on K5 and attempt a Kingside attack at the expense of a Pawn, is not quite sufficient. Modern experience has shown that White can stem the assault and hold the Pawn (Idea Var. 1). Black's best continuation in key position 1 today is considered to be 6 . . . B–K2, a move which was supposed to be inadequate until Maroczy in 1902 introduced an important improvement for Black (Idea Var. 2).

The best way for White to meet 6 . . . B–K2 is to undermine the enemy Knight by P–QB4, possibly combined with KR–K1. Black must then retreat his Knight, conceding to White superior freedom of movement.

IDEA VARIATIONS 1 and 2:

(1) 6 . . . B–Q3 7 O–O, O–O 8 P–B4, B–KN5 9 PxP, P–KB4 10 N–B3, N–Q2 (to maintain some chances, Black must sacrifice another Pawn) 11 P–KR3 (also good is 11 R–K1; Black must reply with 11 . . . QN–B3, not 11 . . . BxP†, because of 12 KxB, NxP 13 B–KN5!), B–R4 12 NxN, PxN 13 BxP, N–B3 14 B–B5, K–R1 15 P–KN4! (15 B–K6 is weak because of 15 . . . N–K5!

[Michell–Milner-Barry, Hastings 1934–35]) NxQP 16 B–K6! B–B2 17 N–N5! (Alexander's continuation which wins the exchange and refutes Black's system), BxB 18 NxB, Q–R5 19 Q–N3 (threatening to win the Queen with 20 B–N5), N–B5 20 BxN, BxB 21 NxR, and White won easily (Alexander–Mallison, Brighton 1938).

8 R–K1 instead of 8 P–B4 is more convenient for Black because of 8 . . . R–K1, in which case Black's Bishop is better placed on Q3 than on K2.

The offer of a Pawn at Black's 8th turn is consistent with his scheme of attack.

For variations on Black's 8th move, see Prac. Var. 1 and 2.

10 R–K1 fails because of 10 . . . BxP† 11 KxB, NxP 12 Q–K2, NxB 13 QxN, BxN 14 QxB, Q–R5† winning the Rook.

(2) 6 . . . B–K2 7 O–O, N–QB3 (this very old continuation recommended by Jaenisch serves to increase Black's pressure on the center) 8 R–K1, B–KN5 9 P–B3 (9 BxN, PxB 10 RxP achieves nothing because of 10 . . . BxN 11 QxB, NxP and 12 . . . N–K3), P–B4 10 P–B4 (until recently this peculiar continuation was considered the refutation of Black's deployment, since White intends to profit from the weakening of the QN3–KN8 diagonal incurred by Black's . . . P–KB4; however, the time wasted in making two moves with the Bishop Pawn enables Black to launch a dangerous attack, so that consistent and preferable is 10 Q–N3, as illustrated in Prac. Var. 3), B–R5! and now:

1) 11 PxP, BxP† 12 K–B1, BxR 13 PxN, BxN 14 PxB, QxP 15 Q–K2, O–O–O∓.

2) 11 BxN, QPxB 12 P–Q5, N–K4! 13 Q–R4†, P–N4! 14 QxP†, P–B3 15 PxP, NxN† 16 PxN, BxP† 17 KxB, Q–R5† 18 K–B1, O–O (after 19 PxB, Black can choose between drawing by perpetual check with 19 . . . Q–R6†, or continuing his assault by means of 19 . . . PxP† 20 K–K2, QR–Q1).

3) 11 B–K3, O–O 12 PxP, N–N5 13 P–Q6, NxB 14 QxN, BxN 15 PxB, and Black can proceed favorably with either 15 . . . P–B5 (16 QxN, Q–N4† 17 K–R1, QR–K1 18 QxNP, PxB) or simply 15 . . . NxQP.

## PRACTICAL VARIATIONS 1–8:

1 P–K4, P–K4 2 N–KB3, N–KB3 3 NxP, P–Q3 4 N–KB3, NxP 5 P–Q4, P–Q4 6 B–Q3

| | 1 | 2 | 3 | 4 | 5 | 6 | 7 | 8 |
|---|---|---|---|---|---|---|---|---|
| 6 | – – | – – | – – | – – | – – | – – | – – | – – |
| | B–Q3 | – – | B–K2 | – – | – – | – – | – – | – – |
| 7 | O–O | – – | O–O | – – | – – | – – | – – | – – |
| | O–O | – – | N–QB3 | – – | – – | – – | O–O | – – |
| 8 | P–B4 | – – | R–K1 | – – | P–B4[11] | – – | R–K1 | P–QB4! |
| | P–QB3 | B–K3 | B–KN5 | – – | B–KN5[12] | N–KB3 | N–Q3![18] | N–KB3 |
| 9 | Q–B2![1] | N–B3![4] | P–B3 | P–B4 | N–B3[13] | N–B3 | N–B3 | PxP |
| | N–KB3[2] | NxN | P–B4 | N–B3 | NxN[14] | O–O | P–QB3 | NxP |
| 10 | B–KN5 | PxN | Q–N3 | PxP | PxN | PxP | B–KB4 | N–QB3 |
| | P–KR3 | PxP | O–O | NxP/4 | O–O | N–QN5[16] | B–N5 | B–KN5[20] |
| 11 | B–R4 | B–K4 | QN–Q2[7] | N–B3 | R–N1 | B–QB4 | P–KR3 | B–K4 |
| | PxP | Q–B1 | K–R1 | O–O | PxP | QNxP | B–R4 | P–QB3 |
| 12 | BxP | R–N1 | QxNP | B–K4[9] | BxP | R–K1 | B–R2[19] | Q–N3[21] |
| | QN–Q2 | P–QB3 | R–B3 | B–K3[10] | N–R4 | P–B3 | = | ± |
| 13 | N–B3[3] | N–N5 | Q–N3 | = | B–Q3 | B–KN5 | | |
| | ± | B–KB4[5] | R–N3 | | P–QB4[15] | B–K3 | | |
| 14 | | BxB | B–KB1![8] | | ± | Q–N3[17] | | |
| | | QxB | ± | | | = | | |
| 15 | | RxP[6] | | | | | | |
| | | ± | | | | | | |

*Notes to practical variations 1–8:*

[1] If 9 N–B3, then not 9 . . . P–KB4? 10 Q–N3, but 9 . . . NxN 10 PxN, B–KN5! 11 P–KR3, B–R4 12 PxP, PxP 13 Q–N3, BxN 14 QxNP, N–Q2 15 PxB, N–N3, and Black has ample compensation for the Pawn (Capablanca–Marshall, Match 1909).

[2] Panov recommends the Pawn sacrifice 9 . . . N–R3 with these possibilities: 10 BxN, PxB 11 QxP, R–K1 12 Q–Q3, B–KN5 13 N–N5, P–KN3, or 10 P–QR3, P–KB4 11 N–B3, N–B2. The continuation 9 . . . P–KB4 is effectively countered by either 10 Q–N3 or 10 N–B3, and, after 9 . . . R–K1, White proceeds with 10 N–B3.

[3] Ilyin-Genevski–Polyak, Leningrad 1938.

[4] After 9 Q–B2, P–KB4 both 10 P–B5, B–K2 11 P–QN4 and 10 Q–N3, PxP! 11 QxNP, N–QB3! 12 BxN, PxB 13 N–N5, B–Q4 14 N–QB3, R–N1 15 Q–R6, N–N5 are satisfactory for Black.

[5] 13 . . . P–KR3 14 NxB, PxN 15 KR–K1 offers White sufficient compensation for the Pawn.

[6] White has a slight edge, according to Keres.

[7] 11 QxP is very risky because of 11 . . . R–B3 12 Q–N3, R–N1 13 Q–B2, R–KN3 14 B–K2, B–Q3, while 11 B–B4 is met by 11 . . . BxN 12 PxB, N–N4 13 K–N2, Q–Q2∓ (Lasker-Pillsbury, St. Petersburg 1895).

[8] It is questionable whether Black's attacking chances compensate for the Pawn; White's position is solid (Unzicker–Alexander, Biel 1960).

[9] 12 P–KR3, B–K3 13 N–K4 is a good alternative, since 12 . . . B–R4? fails against 13 BxP†! (see Game 1).

[10] Best. In the following cases, White's chances are greater than in the column: (a) 12 . . . NxN 13 PxN, Q–Q2 14 R–N1; (b) 12 . . . B–N5 13 NxN, BxR 14 QxB, P–KB4 15 B–KN5!; (c) 12 . . . N–B3 13 P–Q5, N–N5 14 P–QR3, NxB 15 RxN, BxN 16 QxB, N–R3 17 B–K3 (Keres).

[11] Sharp in appearance, but really no stronger than 8 R–K1.

[12] 8 . . . B–K3 is met by 9 R–K1.

[13] 9 R–K1 reverts to Prac. Var. 4.

[14] 9 . . . BxN 10 PxB, N–KB3 11 PxP, KNxP 12 B–K4 favors White.

[15] White's position is slightly more comfortable.

[16] 10 . . . NxP/4 11 R–K1, B–N5 is another transposition into Prac. Var. 4.

[17] Unzicker–Rabar, Munich 1954.

[18] A remarkable idea: Black prevents P–QB4.

[19] White has perhaps a microscopic advantage (see Game 2).

[20] 10 . . . N–QB3 is effectively met by 11 Q–N3, N/4–N5 12 B–K4.

[21] White has a very good game, e.g., 12 . . . N–N3 13 B–K3, QN–Q2 14 P–Q5! (Schlechter–Forgacs, Vienna 1910).

---

## part 2—STEINITZ VARIATION

1 P–K4, P–K4
2 N–KB3, N–KB3
3 P–Q4, PxP
4 P–K5[A], N–K5
5 QxP[B], P–Q4
6 PxP e.p., NxQP

KEY POSITION 2

### OBSERVATIONS ON KEY POSITION 2

[A] 4 B–B4 transposes into the Bishop's Opening.

[B] Steinitz's own intention was 5 Q–K2, when 5 . . . B–N5†! 6 K–Q1, P–Q4 7 PxP e.p., P–KB4 exposed him to a fierce attack (Steinitz–Pillsbury, St. Petersburg 1895). Fischer, ever undaunted, resuscitated the line in the 1962 Interzonal Tournament at Stockholm, and found his opponent unequal to the challenge (see Game 3).

White enjoys the better development as well as the control of more space. It is quite a problem, though, to make this slight advantage tell. For one thing, 7 B–KN5, which strongly suggests itself, leads to hardly more than equality.

Nonetheless, modern tournament play has produced two methods which offer White attacking chances. Soviet masters favor the enterprising 7 N–B3 soon to be followed by O–O–O, while in the West a quick development of the Kingside by means of 7 B–Q3 and O–O is preferred. As of this date the latter method, affording Black less counterplay, has proved the more reliable.

### *Petroff Defense Game 1*

*WHITE: Olafsson* *BLACK: Persitz*

*Hastings 1955*

| | WHITE | BLACK | | WHITE | BLACK |
|---|---|---|---|---|---|
| 1 | P–K4 | P–K4 | 15 | Q–Q3† | P–B4 |
| 2 | N–KB3 | N–KB3 | 16 | N–K6 | Q–Q3 |
| 3 | NxP | P–Q3 | 17 | NxN | K–R2 |
| 4 | N–KB3 | NxP | 18 | NxB | NxN |
| 5 | P–Q4 | P–Q4 | 19 | B–B4 | Q–Q2 |
| 6 | B–Q3 | B–K2 | 20 | N–B5 | Q–K1 |
| 7 | O–O | N–QB3 | 21 | B–N5 | R–B2 |
| 8 | R–K1 | B–KN5 | 22 | Q–KN3 | P–QN3 |
| 9 | P–B4 | N–B3 | 23 | N–Q3 | P–N3 |
| 10 | PxP | NxP/4 | 24 | Q–R4 | Q–N4 |
| 11 | N–B3 | O–O | 25 | N–K5 | R–N2 |
| 12 | P–KR3 | B–R4? | 26 | BxN | P–B5 |
| 13 | BxP†! | KxB | 27 | B–B6 | R/2–N1 |
| 14 | N–N5† | K–N3 | 28 | N–B3 | Resigns |

### *Petroff Defense Game 2*

*WHITE: Pilnik* *BLACK: Olafsson*

*Reykjavik 1955*

| | WHITE | BLACK | | WHITE | BLACK |
|---|---|---|---|---|---|
| 1 | P–K4 | P–K4 | 22 | R–K2 | B–Q3 |
| 2 | N–KB3 | N–KB3 | 23 | P–KN3? | N–N2 |
| 3 | NxP | P–Q3 | 24 | QR–K1 | Q–B3 |
| 4 | N–KB3 | NxP | 25 | K–N2 | N/2–K3 |
| 5 | P–Q4 | P–Q4 | 26 | B–N1 | QR–Q1 |
| 6 | B–Q3 | B–K2 | 27 | R–Q1 | R–R2 |
| 7 | O–O | O–O | 28 | P–QB4 | P–N5! |
| 8 | R–K1 | N–Q3 | 29 | BPxNP | BxP! |
| 9 | N–B3 | P–QB3 | 30 | NxB | RxP! |
| 10 | B–KB4 | B–N5 | 31 | PxBP? | N–B5† |
| 11 | P–KR3 | B–R4 | 32 | K–B3 | Q–R5 |
| 12 | B–R2 | P–KB4 | 33 | B–B2 | N–R2 |
| 13 | N–K2! | P–KN4 | 34 | R–KN1 | N–N4† |
| 14 | N–N3 | B–N3 | 35 | K–K3 | R–K1† |
| 15 | N–K5 | N–Q2 | 36 | K–Q2 | N–B6† |
| 16 | NxB | PxN | 37 | K–B3 | NxR† |
| 17 | Q–K2 | R–B2 | 38 | NxN | QxB |
| 18 | N–B1 | N–K5 | 39 | RxP† | K–R1 |
| 19 | P–KB3 | N–Q3 | 40 | Q–B1 | R–K6 |
| 20 | P–B3 | N–KB1 | 41 | N–B4 | R–K8 |
| 21 | Q–QB2 | N–K1 | | Resigns | |

*Petroff Defense Game 3*

*WHITE: Fischer* *BLACK: German*

*Stockholm 1962*

| | WHITE | BLACK | | WHITE | BLACK |
|---|---|---|---|---|---|
| 1 | P–K4 | P–K4 | 16 | P–B3 | B–K2 |
| 2 | N–KB3 | N–KB3 | 17 | P–B5 | P–B4 |
| 3 | P–Q4 | PxP | 18 | N–N5 | P–Q5 |
| 4 | P–K5 | N–K5 | 19 | B–KB4 | PxP |
| 5 | Q–K2 | N–B4? | 20 | NxP/3 | N–R5 |
| 6 | NxP | N–B3 | 21 | B–QN5! | RxB |
| 7 | NxN | NPxN | 22 | NxN | R–N5 |
| 8 | N–B3 | R–QN1 | 23 | N–B3 | B–N2 |
| 9 | P–B4 | B–K2 | 24 | KR–K1 | K–R1 |
| 10 | Q–B2! | P–Q4 | 25 | P–B6! | B–Q1 |
| 11 | B–K3 | N–Q2 | 26 | B–N5 | R–Q5 |
| 12 | O–O–O | O–O | 27 | PxP† | KxP |
| 13 | P–KN4 | B–N5 | 28 | B–B6† | K–N1 |
| 14 | N–K2 | N–N3 | 29 | Q–R4 | RxR† |
| 15 | N–Q4 | Q–K1 | 30 | NxR | Resigns |

IDEA VARIATIONS 3–6:

(3) 7 B–KN5, N–B3! 8 Q–B3, P–KB3 9 B–KB4, Q–K2† 10 B–K2, B–K3 11 QN–Q2, O–O–O 12 O–O=. 8 BxQ, NxQ 9 NxN, KxB gives Black the two Bishops, while 8 Q–K3†, B–K2 leads only to equality.

(4) 7 N–B3, N–B3 8 Q–KB4, P–KN3 (8 . . . B–B4 is weak because of 9 B–N5!, BxP 10 N–K5) 9 B–Q2, B–N2 10 O–O–O, O–O (it may be better to postpone 10 . . . O–O and play 10 . . . B–K3 instead, as in Prac. Var. 9–11) 11 P–KR4, P–KR3! (cumbersome are both 11 . . . Q–B3 because of 12 QxQ, BxQ 13 N–Q5, and 11 . . . B–K3 because of 12 P–R5, Q–B3 13 QxQ, BxQ 14 N–KN5; here 12 . . . R–K1 13 Q–R2! leads to Game 4) 12 B–Q3, B–K3 13 KR–K1, R–K1! 14 P–QR3, Q–B3 15 QxQ, BxQ 16 BxRP, BxN 17 PxB, B–N5, and Black has fair compensation for the Pawn (Boleslavski–Trifunovic, Zagreb 1958).

(5) 7 B–Q3, N–B3 8 Q–KB4, B–K2 9 O–O, B–K3 10 N–B3, B–B3 11 B–K3, O–O 12 QR–Q1, Q–B1 13 B–QB5, R–Q1 14 N–KN5!± (Unzicker–Keller, Lugano 1958).

(6) 7 B–Q3, N–B3 8 Q–KB4, P–KN3! 9 O–O, B–N2 10 R–K1†, B–K3 11 N–N5, O–O 12 NxB, PxN 13 Q–N4, B–Q5! 14 QxKP†, K–R1 15 R–K2, Q–R5, and

Black has good compensation for the Pawn. In the foregoing, 10 R–K1† is enticing but harmless. More effective is 10 N–B3 or 10 B–Q2 (see Prac. Var. 13 and 14). 16 P–KN3 is correctly met by 16 . . . Q–R4, not by 16 . . . RxP 17 RxR, BxR† 18 K–N2!

PRACTICAL VARIATIONS 9–16:

1 P–K4, P–K4 2 N–KB3, N–KB3 3 P–Q4, PxP 4 P–K5, N–K5 5 QxP, P–Q4 6 PxP e.p., NxQP

| | *9* | *10* | *11* | *12* | *13* | *14* | *15* | *16* |
|---|---|---|---|---|---|---|---|---|
| 7 | N–QB3 | – – | – – | – – | B–Q3 | – – | – – | – – |
| | N–B3 | – – | – – | – – | N–B3 | – – | – – | Q–K2† |
| 8 | Q–KB4 | – – | – – | – – | Q–KB4 | – – | – – | B–K3 |
| | P–KN3 | – – | – – | – – | P–KN3 | – – | Q–K2†? | B–B4[21] |
| 9 | B–Q2 | – – | – – | B–N5 | O–O | – – | B–K3 | N–B3 |
| | B–N2 | – – | – – | B–N2 | B–N2 | – – | P–KN3 | N–B3 |
| 10 | O–O–O | – – | – – | BxN† | N–B3 | B–Q2[16] | N–B3 | Q–QR4 |
| | B–K3 | – – | – – | PxB | O–O | Q–B3[17] | B–K3 | BxB |
| 11 | B–Q3 | N–KN5 | N–QN5[7] | O–O | B–K3 | QxQ | O–O[19] | PxB |
| | O–O | O–O | Q–K2[8] | O–O | B–K3[12] | BxQ | B–N2 | Q–Q2 |
| 12 | P–KR4 | P–KR4 | B–B3 | B–K3 | QR–Q1[13] | N–B3 | KR–K1 | P–Q4 |
| | Q–B3 | P–KR3 | BxB | P–QR4 | Q–B3 | B–K3 | O–O | B–K2 |
| 13 | Q–R2[1] | KN–K4 | NxB | B–Q4 | Q–QR4[14] | N–KN5[18] | B–B5! | P–Q5 |
| | N–K4 | Q–K2[5] | O–O–O | R–K1 | N–K4 | ± | P–N3 | N–N1 |
| 14 | B–KN5[2] | NxN | B–Q3 | BxB | NxN | | B–R3 | Q–N3 |
| | NxN | PxN | KR–K1 | KxB | QxN | | BxN | O–O |
| 15 | PxN[3] | B–QB4 | KR–K1 | KR–K1 | KR–K1 | | PxB | O–O |
| | QxP[4] | QR–B1 | P–B4[9] | RxR† | KR–K1 | | Q–Q2 | B–B3 |
| 16 | ∓ | B–N3[6] | N–KN5[10] | RxR[11] | B–KB4 | | QR–Q1[20] | QR–B1 |
| | | ± | ± | ± | Q–QB4[15] | | ± | P–QR4 |
| 17 | | | | | = | | | KR–Q1[22] |
| | | | | | | | | ± |

*Notes to practical variations 9–16:*

[1] 13 QxQ, BxQ 14 N–KN5 leads to nothing after 14 . . . N–N5!

[2] 14 NxN likewise offers no advantage.

[3] 15 BxQ, NxQ 16 BxB, KxB 17 RxN, leading to equality, is preferable.

[4] White lacks sufficient compensation for the Pawn: 16 P–R5, QxRP 17 QxQ, PxQ 18 RxP, P–KB4! 19 R/1–R1, R–B2∓ (Krogius–Cholmov, USSR Championship 1959). In this line 17 Q–B4 is met by 17 . . . Q–N5. White's best chance is probably 16 QR–N1.

[5] 13 . . . NxN 14 NxN, Q–K2 15 B–B3 leading to the exchange of Black's King Bishop favors White.

[6] 16 N–Q5? BxN! 17 BxB, N–Q5 leads to an excellent game for Black. After the text move, 16 . . . N–Q5 is best. The immediate threat is 17 . . . RxN followed by 18 . . . N–K7†.

[7] Bronstein's innovation.

[8] The critical continuation is 11 . . . P–QR3 12 B–B3, PxN 13 BxB, RxP 14 RxN, PxR; then 15 BxR, Q–R4 offers Black a strong attack for the piece, while 15 K–N1, Q–R4 16 P–QN3, R–KN1 leads to a wild position with approximately even chances.

[9] 15 . . . P–B3 is met by 16 N–Q5.

[10] Boleslavski–Tchoukayev, Spartakiade 1959.

[11] Bronstein–Maschlov, Spartakiade 1959.

[12] 12 . . . Q–B3 proves premature after 13 N–Q5! (Olafsson–Lopez Garcia, Bergen Dal 1950).

[13] 12 B–QB5! is extremely troublesome for Black, as the following examples show: (a) 12 . . . Q–B3 13 QxQ, BxQ 14 N–QN5! and White wins a Pawn (Unzicker–Jimenez, Leipzig 1960); (b) 12 . . . P–N3 13 B–R3, N–K2 14 QR–Q1, BxN? 15 PxB, N–Q4 16 Q–R6, Q–B3 17 N–N5, Q–N2 18 QxQ†, KxQ 19 B–K4!± (Yanofsky–German, Stockholm 1962).

[14] After 13 Q–N3, Black plays 13 . . . N–K4 with the same effect.

[15] Unzicker–Alexander, Hastings 1954.

[16] Duckstein's variation. White aims to exchange Black's effectively fianchettoed Bishop.

[17] 10 . . . BxP 11 B–B3, BxB 12 NxB favors White (see Game 5). Still worse for Black in this line is 11 . . . BxR 12 BxB, R–KN1 13 B–B6.

[18] White's edge is only slight.

[19] Equally good is 11 N–Q4, B–N2 12 NxN, PxN 13 Q–QR4± (Korchnoi–Averbach, USSR Championship 1958).

[20] See Game 6.

[21] 8 . . . N–B4 is weak because of 9 BxN, BxB 10 N–B3. 8 . . . N–B3 9 Q–KB4 reverts to Prac. Var. 15.

[22] Bronstein–Cholmov, USSR 1958.

## *Petroff Defense Game 4*

*WHITE: Zjilin* — *BLACK: Gusakov*

*USSR 1960*

| | WHITE | BLACK | | WHITE | BLACK |
|---|---|---|---|---|---|
| 1 | P–K4 | P–K4 | 11 | P–KR4 | B–K3 |
| 2 | N–KB3 | N–KB3 | 12 | P–R5 | R–K1 |
| 3 | P–Q4 | PxP | 13 | Q–R2 | B–B4 |
| 4 | P–K5 | N–K5 | 14 | PxP | RPxP |
| 5 | QxP | P–Q4 | 15 | B–KN5 | Q–Q2 |
| 6 | PxP e.p. | NxQP | 16 | Q–R7† | K–B1 |
| 7 | N–B3 | N–B3 | 17 | N–Q5 | P–B3 |
| 8 | Q–KB4 | P–KN3 | 18 | Q–R8†! | BxQ |
| 9 | B–Q2 | B–N2 | 19 | RxB† | K–B2 |
| 10 | O–O–O | O–O | 20 | R–R7† | Resigns |

## SUPPLEMENTARY VARIATIONS 1–8:
## 1 P–K4, P–K4 2 N–KB3, N–KB3

| | 1 | 2 | 3 | 4 | 5 | 6 | 7 | 8 |
|---|---|---|---|---|---|---|---|---|
| 3 | NxP | – – | – – | – – | P–Q4 | – – | N–B3 | – – |
| | P–Q3 | – – | – – | – – | NxP | – – | B–N5 | – – |
| 4 | N–KB3 | – – | – – | N–B4 | B–Q3 | – – | NxP | B–B4 |
| | NxP | – – | – – | NxP | P–Q4 | – – | O–O | O–O |
| 5 | Q–K2 | N–B3 | P–QB4 | N–B3[10] | NxP | – – | B–K2[20] | O–O |
| | Q–K2 | NxN | P–Q4[7] | NxN | B–Q3 | B–K2 | R–K1 | N–B3 |
| 6 | P–Q3 | QPxN | N–B3 | NPxN | O–O[14] | O–O | N–Q3 | P–Q3 |
| | N–KB3[1] | B–K2 | B–QB4[8] | P–KN3![11] | O–O | O–O | BxN | BxN |
| 7 | B–N5 | B–Q3 | P–Q4 | P–Q4[12] | P–QB4 | P–QB4 | QPxB | PxB |
| | QxQ†[2] | N–B3 | B–QN5 | B–N2 | P–QB3[15] | N–KB3 | NxP | P–Q4 |
| 8 | BxQ | B–K3[5] | B–Q2 | P–KR4 | N–QB3 | N–QB3 | O–O | PxP |
| | B–K2 | B–N5 | NxB | O–O | NxN | QN–Q2[18] | P–Q3 | NxP |
| 9 | N–QB3 | B–K4 | QxN | B–N5 | PxN | B–N5 | B–K3[21] | R–K1 |
| | B–Q2 | Q–Q2 | O–O | Q–K1† | BxN[16] | PxP | ± | B–N5[22] |
| 10 | O–O–O | Q–Q2 | PxP[9] | N–K3 | PxB | BxP | | ∓ |
| | N–B3 | O–O–O | = | P–QB4 | PxP | N–N3 | | |
| 11 | P–Q4 | O–O–O | | P–KR5 | BxP | B–N3 | | |
| | P–KR3[3] | KR–K1 | | N–B3 | QxQ | KN–Q4 | | |
| 12 | B–R4 | N–Q4 | | PxNP | RxQ | BxB | | |
| | O–O–O[4] | P–Q4[6] | | BPxP[13] | B–B4 | NxB | | |
| 13 | = | = | | ∓ | B–R3! | Q–B3[19] | | |
| | | | | | R–K1 | ± | | |
| 14 | | | | | P–KB4[17] | | | |
| | | | | | ± | | | |

*Notes to Supplementary Variations 1–8:*

[1] 6 . . . N–B4 7 N–B3!±

[2] In exchanging Queens, Black indeed loses a tempo, but this is of minor importance. At any rate, other moves are inferior. After (a) 7 . . . B–K3 8 N–B3, P–KR3, there are two possibilities. The first is 9 B–R4, in which case Black must not proceed with 9 . . . QN–Q2 as in Game 7, but with 9 . . . N–B3, e.g., 10 N–K4, P–KN4 or 10 P–Q4, P–KN4 11 B–N3, N–Q4! followed by . . . NxN and . . . P–KB4; the second possibility is 9 BxN, QxB 10 P–Q4, B–K2 11 Q–N5†, N–Q2 12 B–Q3, P–KN4 13 N–K4, Q–N2 14 P–KR3 followed by N–N3 with slightly better chances for White according to Keres. If (b) 7 . . . B–N5 8 BxN, Black must submit to a weakening of his Pawn formation, since 8 . . . BxN? loses a piece to 9 QxQ†, and if (c) 7 . . . N–B3, 8 N–B3!±.

[3] 11 . . . O–O–O is inaccurate because of 12 P–KR3! (12 B–K3, N–KN5!), P–KR3 13 B–K3, P–Q4 14 N–K5, B–K1 15 P–R3±.

[4] White has a slight pull, but Black has little difficulty in holding his own (Fine–Kashdan, New York 1934).

[5] Pachman suggests 8 B–KB4, B–K3 9 Q–Q2, Q–Q2 10 O–O–O, O–O with a minimal advantage for White.

[6] 13 NxN, QxN 14 BxP, Q–QR3 offers White no more than equality (Nimzowitsch–Marshall, St. Petersburg 1914).

[7] 5 . . . B–K2 6 P–Q4, O–O 7 B–Q3, P–Q4 8 O–O transposes into Prac. Var. 8.

[8] 6 . . . NxN 7 QPxN, P–QB3 8 Q–Q4, B–K3 9 N–N5! cedes White the two Bishops (Keres–Ribeiro, Leipzig 1960). Best according to Keres is 6 . . . N–KB3 7 P–Q4, B–KN5.

[9] Most accurate now is 10 . . . BxN. After 11 PxB, QxP as well as after 11 QxB, N–Q2 the position offers about even chances. For 10 . . . N–Q2? 11 P–QR3!, see Game 8.

[10] 5 P–Q3?! is a foxy psychological "gambit": after 5 . . . N–KB3 6 P–Q4, P–Q4 7 N–K5 Black finds himself on the White side of the Petroff!

[11] 6 . . . B–K2 7 P–Q4 favors White: (a) 7 . . . N–Q2 8 B–Q3, N–N3 9 N–K3, P–Q4 10 O–O, O–O 11 P–KB4 (Fuderer–Kostic, Ljubljana 1951); (b) 7 . . . N–B3 8 B–Q3, B–B3 9 O–O, O–O 10 N–K3, P–KN3 11 P–KB4, N–K2 12 P–B5 (Gligoric–Vidmar, Ljubljana 1951); (c) 7 . . . O–O 8 B–Q3, R–K1 9 O–O, N–Q2 10 P–B4, N–B1 11 Q–B3, P–KB4 12 N–K3, P–KN3 13 P–N4 (Matanovic–Paoli, Bad Pyrmont 1951).

[12] 7 B–K2, B–N2 8 O–O, O–O 9 P–Q4, N–Q2 10 N–K3, N–N3 11 P–QB4, B–K3 12 P–QB3, P–KB4∓ (Matanovic–Alexander, London 1951).

[13] The complications resulting from 13 B–B4†, B–K3 14 P–Q5, B–B2 most likely favor Black (Fuderer–Matanovic, Sarajevo 1951).

[14] 6 P–QB4! is a forceful alternative: (a) 6 . . . B–N5† 7 K–B1!; (b) 6 . . . N–QB3? 7 PxP, NxQP 8 Q–R4†, and White wins; (c) 6 . . . P–B3 7 O–O, O–O reverts to the column, but White has steered clear of the equalizing line suggested for Black in the following note.

[15] As the following variations indicate, 7 . . . N–QB3 is far more promising: (a) 8 PxP, NxQP 9 BxN, BxN 10 P–B4, B–B3 11 N–B3, B–B4 12 Q–Q3, BxB 13 NxB? (13 QxB=), QxP 14 NxB†, PxN∓ (Alekhine–Alexander, Hastings 1933). In this line 10 BxP† loses the exchange after 10 . . . KxB 11 Q–R5†, K–N1 12 QxB, N–B7. White's only chance to maintain the initiative is 9 N–B4. (b) After 8 P–B4, Black must not play 8 . . . NxQP because of 9 BxN, BxN 10 BxP†. Correct is 8 . . . BxN which leads to equality after 9 BPxB, NxQP as well as after 9 QPxB, P–B4. Lastly, (c) 8 NxN, PxN 9 P–B5, B–K2 10 N–Q2, B–B3! offers good counterplay to Black.

[16] 9 . . . B–K3 gives Black better chances.

[17] Analysis by Keres.

[18] 8 . . . B–K3 is effectively met by 9 P–B5! (Alekhine–Levitsky, St. Petersburg 1913). Other possibilities favoring White are 8 . . . PxP 9 BxP, N–B3 10 B–K3, B–Q3 11 P–B4, N–K2 12 Q–N3! and 8 . . . P–B3 9 Q–N3, Q–N3, 10 P–B5, QxQ 11 PxQ.

[19] Gligoric–Gudmundsson, Amsterdam 1950.

[20] For 5 P–Q3?, see Game 9.

[21] Tarrasch–Grunfeld, Vienna 1922.

[22] Bernstein–Alekhine, Match Game 1933.

*Petroff Defense Game 5*

*WHITE: Neumann* *BLACK: Spala*

*European Postal Championship 1958*

| | WHITE | BLACK | | WHITE | BLACK |
|---|---|---|---|---|---|
| 1 | P–K4 | P–K4 | 12 | NxB | B–K3 |
| 2 | N–KB3 | N–KB3 | 13 | KR–K1 | O–O |
| 3 | P–Q4 | PxP | 14 | N–KN5 | N–K1 |
| 4 | P–K5 | N–K5 | 15 | Q–KR4 | N–B3 |
| 5 | QxP | P–Q4 | 16 | Q–R6! | B–Q4 |
| 6 | PxP e.p. | NxQP | 17 | B–B4 | N–QN5 |
| 7 | B–Q3 | N–QB3 | 18 | BxB | N/5xB |
| 8 | Q–KB4 | P–KN3 | 19 | QR–Q1 | P–B3 |
| 9 | O–O | B–N2 | 20 | N/3–K4 | R–K1 |
| 10 | B–Q2 | BxP? | 21 | P–QB4 | Resigns |
| 11 | B–B3 | BxB | | | |

*Petroff Defense Game 6*

*WHITE: Matampvoc* *BLACK: Kieninger*

*Hamburg 1955*

| | WHITE | BLACK | | WHITE | BLACK |
|---|---|---|---|---|---|
| 1 | P–K4 | P–K4 | 14 | B–R3 | BxN? |
| 2 | N–KB3 | N–KB3 | 15 | PxB | Q–Q2 |
| 3 | P–Q4 | PxP | 16 | QR–Q1 | N–R4 |
| 4 | P–K5 | N–K5 | 17 | Q–R6! | P–KB3 |
| 5 | QxP | P–Q4 | 18 | BxP! | PxB |
| 6 | PxP e.p. | NxQP | 19 | QxP† | K–R1 |
| 7 | B–Q3 | N–B3 | 20 | BxN | PxB |
| 8 | Q–KB4 | Q–K2†? | 21 | RxB | QxR |
| 9 | B–K3 | P–KN3 | 22 | R–Q4 | Q–B5 |
| 10 | N–B3 | B–K3 | 23 | RxQ | NxR |
| 11 | O–O | B–N2 | 24 | Q–R5† | K–N1 |
| 12 | KR–K1 | O–O | 25 | Q–N4† | Resigns |
| 13 | B–QB5 | P–N3 | | | |

*Petroff Defense Game 7*

*WHITE: Lasker* *BLACK: Marshall*

*St. Petersburg 1914*

| | WHITE | BLACK | | WHITE | BLACK |
|---|---|---|---|---|---|
| 1 | P–K4 | P–K4 | 7 | B–KN5 | B–K3 |
| 2 | N–KB3 | N–KB3 | 8 | N–B3 | QN–Q2 |
| 3 | NxP | P–Q3 | 9 | O–O–O | P–KR3 |
| 4 | N–KB3 | NxP | 10 | B–R4 | P–KN4 |
| 5 | Q–K2 | Q–K2 | 11 | B–N3 | N–R4 |
| 6 | P–Q3 | N–KB3 | 12 | P–Q4 | NxB |

| | WHITE | BLACK | | WHITE | BLACK |
|---|---|---|---|---|---|
| 13 | RPxN | P–N5 | 22 | R–N3 | KR–K1 |
| 14 | N–KR4 | P–Q4? | 23 | P–R4 | B–KB4 |
| 15 | Q–N5 | O–O–O | 24 | N–R7 | B–Q2 |
| 16 | Q–R5 | P–R3 | 25 | P–R5 | Q–Q7 |
| 17 | BxP! | PxB | 26 | PxN | R–K8† |
| 18 | QxRP† | K–N1 | 27 | K–R2 | P–QB3 |
| 19 | N–N5 | N–N3 | 28 | N–N5 | PxN |
| 20 | R–Q3 | Q–N4†? | 29 | Q–R7† | Resigns |
| 21 | K–N1 | B–Q3 | | | |

*Petroff Defense Game 8*

*WHITE: Keres* *BLACK: Keller*

*Zurich 1959*

| | WHITE | BLACK | | WHITE | BLACK | | WHITE | BLACK |
|---|---|---|---|---|---|---|---|---|
| 1 | P–K4 | P–K4 | 14 | QR–B1 | B–KB4 | 27 | N–K3! | B–KB1 |
| 2 | N–KB3 | N–KB3 | 15 | KR–K1 | B–Q3 | 28 | NxB† | K–N1 |
| 3 | NxP | P–Q3 | 16 | B–N5 | RxR† | 29 | N–K3 | N–R5 |
| 4 | N–KB3 | NxP | 17 | RxR | Q–B3 | 30 | R–K2 | R–K1 |
| 5 | P–B4 | P–Q4 | 18 | N–K5 | P–QR3 | 31 | R–B2 | B–Q3 |
| 6 | N–B3 | B–QB4 | 19 | B–B1 | R–KB1 | 32 | K–B1 | P–N4 |
| 7 | P–Q4 | B–QN5 | 20 | Q–B4! | B–B1 | 33 | N–B5 | B–B1 |
| 8 | B–Q2 | NxB | 21 | QxQ | PxQ | 34 | P–N3 | N–N3 |
| 9 | QxN | O–O | 22 | N–Q3 | R–Q1 | 35 | RxP | BxP |
| 10 | PxP | N–Q2 | 23 | P–N3 | K–N2 | 36 | P–Q6 | B–N5 |
| 11 | P–QR3 | R–K1† | 24 | B–N2 | P–R3 | 37 | B–B3 | R–Q1 |
| 12 | B–K2 | B–B1 | 25 | N–Q1! | B–KB4 | 38 | R–N7 | N–Q2 |
| 13 | O–O | N–N3 | 26 | N–B5 | BxN | 39 | N–K7† | Resigns |

*Petroff Defense Game 9*

*WHITE: Lupi* *BLACK: Alekhine*

*Lisbon 1946*

| | WHITE | BLACK | | WHITE | BLACK |
|---|---|---|---|---|---|
| 1 | P–K4 | P–K4 | 13 | K–B1 | P–K6 |
| 2 | N–KB3 | N–KB3 | 14 | Q–K1 | QxP† |
| 3 | N–B3 | B–N5 | 15 | K–N1 | NxP! |
| 4 | NxP | O–O | 16 | PxN | QxP |
| 5 | P–Q3? | P–Q4! | 17 | R–N1 | QxN |
| 6 | P–QR3 | BxN† | 18 | B–N2 | Q–KB4 |
| 7 | PxB | R–K1 | 19 | R–Q1 | N–B3 |
| 8 | P–KB4 | PxP | 20 | R–Q5 | Q–B7 |
| 9 | P–Q4 | N–Q4! | 21 | B–R1 | B–B4 |
| 10 | P–B4 | N–K2 | 22 | B–Q1 | Q–N8 |
| 11 | B–K2 | N–B4 | | Resigns | |
| 12 | P–B3 | Q–R5† | | | |

# chapter 9—Ruy Lopez

The Ruy Lopez was named after a Spanish clergyman, Ruy Lopez of Safra, in Estramadura. About the middle of the sixteenth century, he edited a systematic work which presented the results of research into the openings. First noticed, however, by the writer of the Gottingen Ms. (1490), and later analyzed by other authors, including Lopez, it was seldom adopted in actual play until the middle of the last century. Credit for discovering its potency is due the Russian analyst, Jaenisch, who attempted a critical analysis during the years 1842–68.

It is currently and frequently in use in tournament practice as the "Old Reliable" because its inner logic is easy to comprehend, and it is rich in tactical threats combined with strategic goals, catering to the fertile imagination.

As in all openings, the battle in the Ruy is for control of the center, the squares K4, Q4, K5, and Q5. But the issue here is drawn quickly, directly, and to the point with White's inaugural third move, 3 B–N5. By a series of sharp plays, all engineered to undermine Black's hold on his K4, White aims to pre-empt the center. When, as, and if he succeeds in doing so, he has gained more than a moral victory. He is then well on his way to expanding his position at the expense of his opponent.

With full knowledge of the problems involved, Black has the onus of maintaining the center intact. It is he who must plan precisely to anticipate and thwart White's tactical and strategic designs.

To understand the simple mechanics of the initial action, setting forth the salient features and obvious overtones, let us examine the first few moves of the so-called Closed Defense.

| WHITE | BLACK |
|---|---|
| 1 P–K4 | . . . |

Striking at the central square Q5 and near-central square KB5.

| | |
|---|---|
| 1 . . . | P–K4 |

Following suit.

| | |
|---|---|
| 2 N–KB3 | . . . |

Still striking at the central squares, and particularly at Black's King Pawn.

| | |
|---|---|
| 2 . . . | N–QB3 |

Defending the King Pawn and maintaining Black's share of the center.

3 B–N5 . . .

Inaugurating the Ruy Lopez. White apparently strikes again at Black's King Pawn, only this time indirectly. He threatens to remove the defender.

3 . . . P–QR3

Ignoring White's threat, or treating it as an empty one.

4 B–R4 . . .

Why not, instead, 4 BxN, followed by 5 NxP? The gain or loss of a Pawn cannot be rated lightly. If, however, 4 BxN, QPxB 5 NxP, Q–Q5! Black simultaneously attacks Knight and King Pawn and assures himself of the recovery of the Pawn. Then Black remains with the "two Bishops," a minimal opening advantage.

If the above is valid, what, then, is the point of White's 3 B–N5? Observe that Black's counter-combination is possible only because White's King Pawn is undefended. The moment, however, that White's King Pawn is defended, White will be menacing Black's King Pawn. Hence, White retreats his Bishop, deferring the capture of the Knight until some such time as his threat is real.

4 . . . N–B3

Black now develops with pressure in the center and attacks White's King Pawn. As yet, he need not concern himself with White's latent threat of BxN, followed by NxP. For the situation has not changed any in that respect.

5 O–O . . .

Now White ignores the attack on his own King Pawn. Why? To begin with, he wishes to activate his King Rook and secure his King. Above all, however, is the technical fact that Black cannot gain a Pawn by 5 . . . NxP. For the counterattack 6 R–K1 or 6 P–Q4 not only retrieves White's Pawn, but also grants White an edge in position. Black's trouble would stem from his exposed King position. His King on K1 is on the same file as the Knight (after 5 . . . NxP). And he would be subject to an annoying pin. Hence

5 . . . B–K2

To intervene on the King file, while developing. Now 6 . . . NxP is a threat.

6 R–K1 . . .

Defending the King Pawn and reinstating or making real White's threat of BxN, followed by NxP, gaining a Pawn. Because the threat is real and Black no longer enjoys the counterattack to recover the Pawn, Black must parry.

At this stage, the alternatives of 6 Q–K2, 6 N–B3, or 6 P–Q3 compel Black to parry the threat of 7 BxN, followed by NxP.

| | |
|---|---|
| 6 . . . | P–QN4 |

Averting BxN.

| | |
|---|---|
| 7 B–N3 | P–Q3 |

Thus, in a small way, we have seen the patent, tactical implications of the initial phase of the opening. Black can successfully maintain his Pawn on K4 in the Closed Defense of the Ruy Lopez.

When Black cannot maintain his King Pawn and is compelled to swap it off, as in some variations, strategic advantages accrue to White. In the Steinitz Defense to the Ruy Lopez, for example, after the moves 1 P–K4, P–K4 2 N–KB3, N–QB3 3 B–N5, P–Q3 4 P–Q4, B–Q2 5 N–B3, N–B3 6 O–O, B–K2 7 R–K1, Black must acquiesce in 7 . . . PxP and surrender the center. Failure to do so will result in the loss of a Pawn. In Tarrasch–Marco, 1892, Black fell victim to a long-winded combination (afterward known as the Tarrasch trap) by playing 7 . . . O–O. There followed 8 BxN, BxB 9 PxP, PxP 10 QxQ, QRxQ 11 NxP, BxP 12 NxB, NxN 13 N–Q3, P–KB4 14 P–KB3, B–B4† 15 NxB, NxN 16 B–N5, R–Q4 17 B–K7, R–K1 18 P–QB4!, when White wins a piece. In this line, if 10 . . . KRxQ 11 NxP, BxP 12 NxB, NxN 13 N–Q3, P–KB4 14 P–KB3, B–B4† 15 K–B1, with a winning position for White.

Hence, in the above line, Black must play 7 . . . PxP and White recaptures with 8 NxP. White's Pawn at K4 then clearly exerts more pressure in the center than its counterpart, Black's Pawn at Black's Q3. White's King Bishop Pawn, moreover, being unopposed by Black's King Pawn, is free to advance and join the fray in an assault on Black's King.

These two examples provide a brief insight into the structure of the Ruy Lopez, whose long-lasting popularity has brought in its wake literally hundreds of thousands of games. Every so often, new ideas or modifications of older ones crop up. To facilitate the study of the Ruy Lopez, we have divided the opening into two groups:

[A] The systems without the move 3 . . . P–QR3, and

[B] The systems with the move 3 . . . P–QR3.

## (A) Systems Without the Move 3...P-QR3

It cannot be overemphasized that a cardinal strategic point for Black in the Ruy Lopez is to maintain his Pawn at K4. To exchange the King Pawn for White's Queen Pawn is a small but definite concession. Yet, in nearly all lines where Black omits 3 . . . P–QR3, he must sooner or later accede to this drawback. Hence, it is reasonably clear that there is a direct connection between that move and the retention of the King Pawn on its vital square. This stems from Black's ability (or inability) to drive White's King Bishop at the right moment from its attack on Black's Queen Knight, which supports Black's King Pawn. The fact that 3 . . . P–QR3 and its usual follow-up . . . P–QN4 somewhat loosen the Pawn structure on Black's Queenside cannot outweigh the importance of maintaining the center.

---

## part 1—BERLIN DEFENSE I

1 P–K4, P–K4
2 N–KB3, N–QB3
3 B–N5, N–B3
4 O–O[A], NxP[B]
5 P–Q4[C], B–K2![D]
6 Q–K2, N–Q3[E]
7 BxN, NPxB[F]
8 PxP[G], N–N2[H]

KEY POSITION 1

OBSERVATIONS ON KEY POSITION 1

[A] 4 P–Q4, studied by Barry, is inferior to 4 O–O. E.g., 4 P–Q4, PxP 5 O–O, B–K2 6 Q–K2, O–O 7 P–K5, N–K1 8 R–Q1, P–Q4 9 P–B3, B–KB4 10 PxP, N–N5 11 N–R3, P–QB3 12 B–R4=. In this line, easier for Black is 9 BxN, PxB 10 NxP, Q–Q2 11 N–QB3, P–QB4 12 N–N3, P–QB3 13 N–R4, P–B5= (Barry–Lasker, 1903). But not 9 . . . PxP (instead of 9 . . . B–KB4 above) 10 NxP, B–K3 11 B–QB4, N–N5 12 P–QR3, Q–B1 13 B–N3. White recovers the Pawn with a superior position.

[B] The first move of the Berlin Defense, popular in the second half of the nineteenth century. 4 . . . B–B4, treated with transposition of moves under key position 3 (Part 3) is currently in vogue.

[C] Weaker is 5 R–K1, N–Q3 6 NxP, B–K2 (see Game 4) 7 B–B1, O–O 8 P–Q4, N–B4 9 P–QB3, NxN 10 RxN, P–Q3 11 R–K1, P–Q4= (Ivkov–Wade, Belgrade 1954).

[D] For 5 . . . N–Q3, see key position 2, Part 2.

[E] Weaker is 6 . . . P–Q4 because of 7 NxP, B–Q2 8 BxN, PxB 9 R–K1. Black cannot castle. E.g., 9 . . . O–O 10 P–KB3 and 11 NxB. Difficult for Black is 6 . . . P–B4 7 PxP, O–O 8 N–B3, NxN 9 Q–B4†, K–R1 10 QxKN on account of his undeveloped Queenside.

[F] If 7 . . . QPxB 8 PxP, N–B4 9 R–Q1, B–Q2 10 P–K6!, PxP 11 N–K5, B–Q3 12 Q–R5†, P–N3 13 NxNP, N–N2 14 Q–R6, N–B4 15 Q–R3, R–KN1 16 QxP, R–N2 17 Q–R5, Q–B3 18 N–K5† (18 N–R4†, K–K2 19 NxN†, PxN 20 R–K1† gives Black sufficient chances for a counterattack), K–K2 19 N–N4, Q–N3 20 QxQ, RxQ 21 P–KR3, with clear advantage for White.

G White gets nothing by 8 NxP, O–O 9 N–Q2, R–K1 10 Q–Q3, P–B3 11 KN–B3, N–B2.

H 8 . . . N–B4 9 Q–K4, P–N3 leaves the Black squares KB3, KN2 and KR3 weak.

In this position, Black's development is somewhat retarded because he has spent four of his first eight moves on his King Knight. To boot, White's King Pawn hampers the free movement of Black's Queen Pawn, usurps the center and grants White superiority in space, which can be converted to an assault against the hostile King. A tiny compensation for Black is the "two Bishops," although this is more than offset by the awkward cluster of his Queenside Pawn group, QB2, QB3, Q2, which cannot advance without strategic disadvantages.

IDEA VARIATIONS 1–3:

(1) 9 N–B3, O–O 10 N–Q4, N–B4? 11 R–Q1, Q–K1 12 N–B5, P–B3? 13 B–R6!, N–K3 14 Q–N4 and wins. 14 . . . Q–B2 is met by 15 BxP!, NxB 16 N–R6†.

(2) 9 N–B3, P–Q4 10 PxP e.p., PxP 11 N–Q4, B–Q2 12 R–K1, N–B4 13 B–N5, P–B3 14 P–QN4, PxB 15 PxN, PxP 16 N–K6±. In this line 13 . . . N–K3 is insufficient on account of 14 BxB, QxB 15 N–B5.

(3) 9 N–B3, O–O 10 R–K1, N–B4 11 N–Q4, N–K3 12 B–K3, NxN 13 BxN, P–QB4 14 B–K3, P–Q4 15 PxP e.p., BxP 16 N–K4, B–N2 17 NxB (17 NxP?, BxN 18 BxB, Q–N4), PxN 18 QR–Q1, Q–B3 19 P–QB4, R–K1 20 Q–N4, R–K3=.

PRACTICAL VARIATIONS 1–5:

1 P–K4, P–K4 2 N–KB3, N–QB3 3 B–N5, N–B3 4 O–O, NxP 5 P–Q4, B–K2 6 Q–K2, N–Q3 7 BxN, NPxB 8 PxP, N–N2

| | 1 | 2 | 3 | 4 | 5 |
|---|---|---|---|---|---|
| 9 | N–B3 | – – | – – | N–Q4 | P–QN3 |
| | O–O[1] | – – | – – | O–O | O–O |
| 10 | R–K1[2] | N–Q4![8] | – – | R–Q1 | B–N2 |
| | N–B4[3] | B–B4[9] | – – | Q–K1 | P–Q4 |
| 11 | N–Q4 | R–Q1 | – – | N–B5 | PxP e.p. |
| | N–K3 | BxN | – – | P–Q4 | PxP |
| 12 | B–K3 | RxB | – – | PxP e.p. | QN–Q2 |
| | NxN | P–Q4 | – – | BxP | B–B3[13] |

| | 1 | 2 | 3 | 4 | 5 |
|---|---|---|---|---|---|
| 13 | BxN | PxP e.p. | — — | Q–B3 | BxB |
| | P–QB4[4] | PxP | — — | BxN | QxB |
| 14 | B–K3 | P–QN4! | — — | QxB | = |
| | P–Q4 | Q–B3 | R–K1 | Q–K4 | |
| 15 | PxP e.p. | B–K3 | B–K3 | = | |
| | BxP[5] | B–B4 | B–K3 | | |
| 16 | N–K4! | QR–Q1 | Q–B3[11] | | |
| | B–N2 | P–QR3 | Q–Q2! | | |
| 17 | NxB[6] | P–N4[10] | N–K4 | | |
| | PxN | ± | B–Q4![12] | | |
| 18 | QR–Q1 | | P–B4 | | |
| | Q–B3 | | BxN | | |
| 19 | P–QB4 | | RxB | | |
| | KR–K1 | | P–QR4! | | |
| 20 | Q–N4 | | = | | |
| | QxNP?[7] | | | | |
| | ∓ | | | | |

*Notes to practical variations 1–5:*

[1] Inferior is 9 . . . N–B4 because of 10 N–Q4, B–R3 11 Q–N4, BxR 12 QxNP, R–KB1 13 KxB, N–K3 14 NxN, BPxN 15 QxP±. 9 . . . P–Q4 leads to Idea Var. 2.

[2] Pillsbury's move which hinders the advance of Black's Queen Pawn. E.g., 10 . . . P–Q4 11 PxP e.p. when Black must recapture with his Bishop. Black then suffers from the doubled Pawns on the Queen Bishop file.

[3] 10 . . . P–B3, liquidating White's annoying King Pawn is promising. E.g., 11 B–B4, PxP 12 BxP, B–B4 13 B–Q4, BxB 14 NxB, N–Q3!= 14 Q–B4† in this line is profitable for Black: 14 . . . P–Q4 15 QxB, B–B4.

[4] This move derives from the Brazilian, Dr. Caldas Viana. From move 13 on, the line is known as the Rio de Janeiro Variation.

[5] If 15 . . . PxP? 16 BxP.

[6] 17 NxP? loses to . . . BxN 18 BxB, Q–N4. But 17 BxP BxB 18 NxB, BxP 19 KxB, Q–N4† 20 K–R1, QxN draws.

[7] Better is 20 . . . R–K3. See Idea Var. 3. After the text move Black loses: 21 R–N1, Q–B6 22 KR–QB1, Q–R6 23 B–R6, P–N3 24 Q–B4, with the double threat of 25 Q–B6 and 25 RxB. For 20 . . . B–B3? see Game 1.

[8] Suggested by Fine.

[9] 10 . . . N–B4 leads to Idea Var. 1.

[10] Schlechter–Reti, 1914.

[11] Inviting 16 . . . P–Q4 against which 17 P–N5 is strong. E.g., . . . PxP 18 NxQP. Or 17 . . . P–QB4 18 R–Q3, Q–N3 19 NxP, BxN 20 QxB, QxP? 21 R–N3 and White wins a piece.

[12] For 17 . . . B–B4? see Game 2.

[13] For 12 . . . R–K1! see Game 3.

*Lopez Game 1*

*WHITE: Tarrasch* *BLACK: Em. Lasker*

*Match, Munich 1908*

| | WHITE | BLACK | | WHITE | BLACK |
|---|---|---|---|---|---|
| 1 | P–K4 | P–K4 | 17 | NxB | PxN |
| 2 | N–KB3 | N–QB3 | 18 | QR–Q1 | Q–B3 |
| 3 | B–N5 | N–B3 | 19 | P–QB4 | KR–K1 |
| 4 | O–O | NxP | 20 | Q–N4 | B–B3? |
| 5 | P–Q4 | B–K2 | 21 | R–K2 | R–K5 |
| 6 | Q–K2 | N–Q3 | 22 | Q–N3 | Q–K3 |
| 7 | BxN | NPxB | 23 | P–KR3 | R–Q1 |
| 8 | PxP | N–N2 | 24 | KR–Q2 | R–K4 |
| 9 | N–B3 | O–O | 25 | B–R6 | Q–N3 |
| 10 | R–K1 | N–B4 | 26 | B–B4 | R–K3 |
| 11 | N–Q4 | N–K3 | 27 | BxP | Q–R4 |
| 12 | B–K3 | NxN | 28 | Q–N4 | QxQ |
| 13 | BxN | P–QB4 | 29 | PxQ | R–K5 |
| 14 | B–K3 | P–Q4 | 30 | BxP | RxR |
| 15 | PxP e.p. | BxP | 31 | RxR | P–KR4 |
| 16 | N–K4 | B–N2 | 32 | R–Q6 | Resigns |

*Lopez Game 2*

*WHITE: Keres* *BLACK: Unzicker*

*Match, Hamburg 1956*

| | WHITE | BLACK | | WHITE | BLACK |
|---|---|---|---|---|---|
| 1 | P–K4 | P–K4 | 15 | B–K3 | B–K3 |
| 2 | N–KB3 | N–QB3 | 16 | Q–B3 | Q–Q2 |
| 3 | B–N5 | N–B3 | 17 | N–K4 | B–B4? |
| 4 | O–O | NxP | 18 | N–N3 | BxP |
| 5 | P–Q4 | B–K2 | 19 | R–QB1 | B–R5 |
| 6 | Q–K2 | N–Q3 | 20 | N–R5 | P–KB4 |
| 7 | BxN | NPxB | 21 | R–KB4 | R–K2 |
| 8 | PxP | N–N2 | 22 | RxKBP | R–B2 |
| 9 | N–B3 | O–O | 23 | NxP! | RxN |
| 10 | N–Q4 | B–B4 | 24 | B–R6 | Q–K2 |
| 11 | R–Q1 | BxN | 25 | BxR | QxB |
| 12 | RxB | P–Q4 | 26 | P–R4 | P–KR3 |
| 13 | PxP e.p. | PxP | 27 | R–QB4 | Resigns |
| 14 | P–QN4! | R–K1 | | | |

*Lopez Game 3*

*WHITE: Porges* *BLACK: Em. Lasker*

*Nuremberg 1896*

| | WHITE | BLACK | | WHITE | BLACK |
|---|---|---|---|---|---|
| 1 | P–K4 | P–K4 | 18 | QxB | P–K5 |
| 2 | N–KB3 | N–QB3 | 19 | N–Q4 | Q–B3 |
| 3 | B–N5 | N–B3 | 20 | P–QB3 | R–KB1 |
| 4 | O–O | NxP | 21 | P–B3 | Q–N4 |
| 5 | P–Q4 | B–K2 | 22 | Q–B1 | N–B4 |
| 6 | Q–K2 | N–Q3 | 23 | N–B1 | Q–N3 |
| 7 | BxN | NPxB | 24 | R–K3 | N–Q6 |
| 8 | PxP | N–N2 | 25 | Q–Q1 | N–B5 |
| 9 | P–QN3 | O–O | 26 | N–N3 | P–KR4! |
| 10 | B–N2 | P–Q4 | 27 | N/4–K2 | NxP!! |
| 11 | PxP e.p? | PxP | 28 | KxN | PxP† |
| 12 | QN–Q2 | R–K1! | 29 | RxP | B–R6† |
| 13 | KR–K1 | B–Q2 | 30 | KxB | Q–N5† |
| 14 | N–K4? | P–Q4 | 31 | K–N2 | QxR† |
| 15 | N/4–Q2 | B–QR6 | 32 | K–N1 | P–R5 |
| 16 | B–K5 | P–B3 | 33 | N–R1 | Q–K6† |
| 17 | Q–R6 | PxB | | Resigns | |

*Lopez Game 4*

*WHITE: Neshmetdinov* *BLACK: Kotkov*

*Soviet Fed. Championship 1957*

| | WHITE | BLACK | | WHITE | BLACK |
|---|---|---|---|---|---|
| 1 | P–K4 | P–K4 | 14 | QR–K1 | N–B3 |
| 2 | N–KB3 | N–QB3 | 15 | P–R3 | N–Q2 |
| 3 | B–N5 | N–B3 | 16 | N–Q5! | P–KB4 |
| 4 | O–O | NxP | 17 | NxP | QxN |
| 5 | R–K1 | N–Q3 | 18 | Q–Q5† | K–R1 |
| 6 | NxP | B–K2 | 19 | R–K8 | N–B3 |
| 7 | B–Q3 | NxN | 20 | RxR† | BxR |
| 8 | RxN | O–O | 21 | B–N2 | B–N2 |
| 9 | N–B3 | B–B3 | 22 | B–B4!! | B–Q2 |
| 10 | R–K3 | P–KN3 | 23 | BxN | BxB |
| 11 | Q–B3 | B–N2 | 24 | Q–B7 | Q–Q1 |
| 12 | P–QN3 | N–K1 | 25 | R–K8† | Resigns |
| 13 | B–R3 | P–Q3 | | | |

## part 2—BERLIN DEFENSE II

1 P–K4, P–K4
2 N–KB3, N–QB3
3 B–N5, N–B3
4 O–O, NxP
5 P–Q4, N–Q3
6 BxN[A], QPxB[B]
7 PxP, N–B4

KEY POSITION 2

OBSERVATIONS ON KEY POSITION 2

[A] The temporary sacrifice of a piece by 6 PxP, NxB 7 P–QR4, P–Q3 8 PxN, NxP 9 R–K1, B–K2 leads to complete equality. In this line, if 7 . . . N/4–Q5 8 NxN, NxN 9 QxN, P–Q4 10 PxP e.p., QxP 11 Q–B3, B–K3 12 N–R3, P–QB3 13 B–K3, Q–N5 14 Q–K5, B–Q3! 15 QxP, O–O–O, Black enjoys chances for his Pawn minus. But not 14 . . . Q–Q3 as in Spasski–Sanguinetti, World Students' Team Championship, Varna 1958: 15 Q–KR5, Q–Q4 16 Q–K2, B–QB4 17 N–N5!, B–N3 18 KR–Q1, Q–K4 19 N–Q6†, K–K2 20 N–B4, BxN 21 B–N5†, K–K3 22 Q–N4†, Resigns.

[B] Not 6 . . . NPxB 7 PxP, N–B4 8 Q–Q3!, P–Q4 9 PxP e.p., PxP 10 R–K1†, B–K2 11 P–KN4±.

By suggesting the exchange of Queens, Black apparently is content to draw. The issue then is White's Kingside Pawn majority versus Black's Bishop-pair. Experience at the tournaments of Portoroz and Munich 1958, however, indicates a large plus factor for White.

IDEA VARIATIONS 4 and 5:

(4) 8 QxQ†, KxQ 9 N–B3, B–K2 (9 . . . K–K1!) 10 B–N5, P–KR4 11 QR–Q1†, K–K1 12 N–K2, B–K3 13 N–B4, P–B4 14 BxB, KxB 15 N–N5 (threatening N/5xB!), B–B5 16 KR–K1, N–Q5 17 P–K6!, NxKP 18 N/5xN, BxN 19 N–Q5† and wins (Schmid–Toran, Munich 1958).

(5) 8 QxQ†, KxQ 9 N–B3, K–K1 10 N–K2, B–K3 11 N–B4, B–Q4 12 NxB, PxN 13 P–KN4, N–K2 14 B–B4, P–QB4 15 QR–Q1, R–Q1 16 P–B3, N–B3 17 R–Q2, P–Q5 and Black has a satisfactory game (Gligoric–Sanguinetti, Portoroz 1958).

PRACTICAL VARIATIONS 6–8:

1 P–K4, P–K4 2 N–KB3, N–QB3 3 B–N5, N–B3 4 O–O, NxP 5 P–Q4, N–Q3 6 BxN[A], QPxB[B] 7 PxP, N–B4

| | 6 | 7 | 8 |
|---|---|---|---|
| 8 | Q–K2 | QxQ† | – – |
| | N–Q5 | KxQ | – – |
| 9 | NxN | N–B3 | – – |
| | QxN | K–K1[2] | – – |
| 10 | N–B3 | N–K2 | – – |
| | B–KN5 | B–K3 | – – |
| 11 | Q–K3 | N–B4 | – – |
| | QxQ | B–Q4 | – – |
| 12 | BxQ | NxB | – – |
| | B–N5 | PxN[3] | – – |
| 13 | N–K4 | P–KN4! | – – |
| | B–KB4 | N–K2 | – – |
| 14 | P–QB3 | B–B4 | – – |
| | BxN | N–N3 | P–QB4 |
| 15 | PxB | B–N3 | QR–Q1[5] |
| | P–QR4 | B–B4 | P–KR4[6] |
| 16 | PxP | K–N2 | P–KR3 |
| | RxP[1] | N–B1[4] | PxP |
| 17 | = | ± | PxP |
| | | | P–Q5[7] |
| | | | ± |

*Notes to practical variations 6–8:*

[1] Fischer–Neikirch, Interzonal, Portoroz 1958.

[2] 9 . . . P–KR3 10 B–Q2, B–K3 11 N–K2, P–B4 12 B–B3 (Tarrasch–Lasker, 1895) gives White a minimal plus. 9 . . . B–K2 leads to Idea Var. 4.

[3] Though Black undoubles his Pawns, he experiences difficulties in development because he cannot castle.

[4] See Game 5.

[5] Gligoric–Neikirch, Portoroz 1958, continued with 15 P–B3, N–B3 16 QR–Q1, R–Q1 17 KR–K1, B–K2 18 R–K2, P–KR4 19 P–N5, K–Q2 20 RxP†, K–K3 21 RxR, RxR 22 P–KR4, R–Q4? Instead, 22 . . . R–Q8† gives sufficient counterchances for the Pawn.

[6] Regarding 15 . . . QR–Q1, see Idea Var. 5.

[7] Continued 18 P–B3, N–B3 19 KR–K1, B–K2 20 PxP, PxP 21 P–QR3!, P–QR4 22 NxP, R–R5 23 B–N3, RxP 24 N–N5, R–Q1 25 N–Q6†, BxN 26 PxB†, K–Q2 27 R–Q5, P–B3 28 K–N2, P–KN4 29 R–QN5, R–QN1 30 R–KR1±. In this line, not 23 P–B3, NxN 24 RxN, B–B4.

### *Lopez Game 5*

*WHITE: Panno* — *BLACK: Benko*

*Interzonal Tournament, Portoroz 1958*

| | WHITE | BLACK | | WHITE | BLACK |
|---|---|---|---|---|---|
| 1 | P–K4 | P–K4 | 22 | QR–KB1 | R–N2 |
| 2 | N–KB3 | N–QB3 | 23 | K–B3 | B–K2 |
| 3 | B–N5 | N–B3 | 24 | R–Q1 | P–QB3 |
| 4 | O–O | NxP | 25 | P–B4 | PxP |
| 5 | P–Q4 | N–Q3 | 26 | RxQBP | R–Q1 |
| 6 | BxN | QPxB | 27 | RxR† | BxR |
| 7 | PxP | N–B4 | 28 | K–B4 | P–KR4 |
| 8 | QxQ† | KxQ | 29 | PxP | R–N4 |
| 9 | N–B3 | K–K1 | 30 | R–N4 | P–N3 |
| 10 | N–K2 | B–K3 | 31 | R–R4 | P–R4 |
| 11 | N–B4 | B–Q4 | 32 | R–Q4 | RxRP |
| 12 | NxB | PxN | 33 | R–Q6 | P–QB4 |
| 13 | P–KN4 | N–K2 | 34 | K–K4 | B–B2 |
| 14 | B–B4 | N–N3 | 35 | R–QB6 | K–Q2 |
| 15 | B–N3 | B–B4 | 36 | R–B6 | K–K2 |
| 16 | K–N2 | N–B1 | 37 | K–Q5 | B–Q1 |
| 17 | N–K1 | P–KN4 | 38 | P–QR4 | K–K1 |
| 18 | N–Q3 | N–K3 | 39 | R–B4 | P–B3 |
| 19 | P–KB4 | PxP | 40 | R–R4 | R–N4 |
| 20 | NxP | NxN | 41 | K–K6 | R–N1 |
| 21 | RxN | R–KN1 | 42 | PxP | Resigns |

## part 3—CORDEL DEFENSE

1 P–K4, P–K4
2 N–KB3, N–QB3
3 B–N5, B–B4
4 P–B3[A], N–B3[B]
5 O–O[C], O–O
6 P–Q4, B–N3!

KEY POSITION 3

OBSERVATIONS ON KEY POSITION 3

[A] 4 O–O averts the dangerous sally . . . P–B4. E.g., 5 PxP, N–B3 6 NxP, O–O 7 P–QB3, NxN 8 P–Q4±. If 4 O–O, KN–K2 5 P–B3, B–N3 6 P–Q4, PxP 7 PxP, P–Q4 8 PxP, NxP 9 R–K1†, B–K3 10 N–K5, N/4–K2! 11 B–K3, O–O 12 BxN, NxB 13 NxN, PxN 14 N–B3, Q–B3 15 Q–R4, B–Q4= (Evans-Fischer, Buenos Aires 1960). In this line, 4 . . . N–Q5 also equalizes.

[B] Another possibility is 4 . . . P–B4 5 BxN, QPxB 6 NxP, B–Q3 7 P–Q4, PxP 8 O–O!, N–B3 9 B–N5, Q–K2 10 N–Q2, B–KB4 11 R–K1, O–O–O 12 NxKP!±. If 12 . . . KBxN 13 N–N3! (Unzicker–Eisinger, German Championship 1953).

[C] Safer than 5 P–Q4, PxP 6 P–K5, N–K5 7 O–O, P–Q4! 8 PxP e.p., O–O 9 PxBP, QxP, with excellent prospects for the Pawn. If 7 . . . O–O? 8 PxP, B–N3 9 P–Q5, N–K2 10 B–Q3, P–KB4 11 QN–Q2, N–B4 12 P–Q6, N–N3 13 B–B4†± (Smyslov–Randviir, Parnu 1947). Or if 6 O–O (instead of 6 P–K5), NxP 7 PxP, B–N3! 8 Q–B2, N–B3 9 R–K1†, N–K2 10 B–N5, P–QB3, Black retains the extra Pawn with a tenable position.

This defense, popular in the Netherlands and in Belgium and sometimes referred to as the "Benelux System," is artificially contrived. It violates an important principle of opening theory, ignoring the battle for the center. Yet it still presents a formidable problem.

IDEA VARIATIONS 6 AND 7:

(6) 7 R–K1, P–Q3 8 P–QR4, P–QR3 9 ·BxN, PxB 10 PxP, PxP 11 QxQ, RxQ 12 B–N5, with a minimal plus for White.

(7) 7 B–N5, P–KR3 8 B–KR4, P–Q3 9 BxQN?, PxB 10 PxP, PxP 11 QxQ, RxQ 12 NxP, P–N4 13 B–N3, NxP 14 NxQBP, B–R3! 15 NxR, RxN with good prospects for Black. E.g., 16 N–R3, NxB 17 RPxN, R–Q7 18 P–B4, RxNP (analysis by Van Scheltinga).

PRACTICAL VARIATIONS 9-12:

1 P–K4, P–K4 2 N–KB3, N–QB3 3 B–N5, B–B4 4 P–B3, N–B3 5 O–O, O–O 6 P–Q4, B–N3!

| | *9* | *10* | *11* | *12* |
|---|---|---|---|---|
| 7 | R–K1 | – – | B–N5 | PxP |
| | P–Q3 | – – | P–KR3 | NxP |
| 8 | P–QR4 | P–KR3[4] | B–KR4 | Q–Q5 |
| | P–QR4[1] | Q–K2 | P–Q3 | N–B4 |
| 9 | P–R3 | B–N5[5] | P–R4[7] | B–N5 |
| | N–K2 | P–KR3 | P–QR4 | N–K2 |

| | *9* | *10* | *11* | *12* |
|---|---|---|---|---|
| *10* | QN–Q2 | QBxN | R–K1 | Q–Q1[9] |
| | P–B3 | QxB | B–N5 | N–K5 |
| *11* | B–Q3 | N–R3 | BxQN | B–KR4 |
| | N–N3 | N–K2 | PxB | P–Q4 |
| *12* | N–B1 | N–B4 | PxP | QN–Q2 |
| | N–R4 | N–N3 | PxP | P–QB3 |
| *13* | B–B2[2] | NxB | QxQ | B–Q3 |
| | N/4–B5 | RPxN[6] | QRxQ | P–KB4 |
| *14* | BxN | = | NxP | PxP e.p. |
| | PxB | | P–N4 | NxP/3 |
| *15* | Q–Q3 | | B–N3 | Q–B2 |
| | P–KB4 | | KR–K1 | P–N3 |
| *16* | P–K5 | | N–R3 | QR–K1 |
| | P–Q4 | | B–K3[8] | B–KB4 |
| *17* | Q–Q2 | | = | N–Q4[10] |
| | B–K3[3] | | | ± |
| | = | | | |

*Notes to practical variations 9–12:*

[1] 8 . . . P–QR3 leads to Idea Var. 6.

[2] 13 NxP?, PxN 14 QxN, PxP leaves Black better.

[3] Kupper–Duckstein, Zurich 1959.

[4] Weaker is 8 B–N5, PxP! 9 NxP, NxN 10 PxN, P–KR3 11 B–KR4, P–Q4 12 P–K5, P–KN4 13 B–N3, N–K5∓.

[5] For 9 N–R3, see Game 6.

[6] Blau–Van Scheltinga, Hilversum 1947.

[7] 9 BxQN? leads to Idea Var. 7.

[8] Averbach–Barcza, Saltsjobaden 1952.

[9] Or 10 Q–B4, P–B3 11 Q–KR4, R–K1 12 B–QB4, P–Q4 13 PxP e.p., QxP 14 B–B4, Q–N3 15 N–K5, N–B4! 16 Q–R3, RxN 17 BxR, N–Q5!= (Matanovic–Bobotzov, Amsterdam 1954).

[10] Bronstein–O'Kelly, Hastings 1953–54.

## *Lopez Game 6*

*WHITE: Bergama* *BLACK: Vlagsma*

*Team Matches, Netherlands 1953*

| WHITE | BLACK | WHITE | BLACK | WHITE | BLACK |
|---|---|---|---|---|---|
| 1 P–K4 | P–K4 | 12 BxN | PxB | 23 Q–K4 | P–KR4 |
| 2 N–KB3 | N–QB3 | 13 P–B3 | P–KR3! | 24 KR–B1 | PxP |
| 3 B–N5 | B–B4 | 14 NxN | PxN | 25 PxP | Q–B5 |
| 4 P–B3 | N–B3 | 15 PxP | Q–B3 | 26 QxQ | RxQ |
| 5 O–O | O–O | 16 B–K3 | Q–N3 | 27 B–K3 | RxP† |
| 6 P–Q4 | B–N3 | 17 Q–B3 | P–KB4 | 28 K–R2 | R–KB1 |
| 7 R–K1 | P–Q3 | 18 P–K5 | B–K3 | 29 R–KN1 | R–R5† |
| 8 P–KR3 | Q–K2 | 19 QxQBP | P–B5 | 30 K–N3 | R–R6† |
| 9 N–R3 | PxP | 20 B–B2 | P–B6 | Resigns | |
| 10 PxP? | NxKP | 21 P–KN4 | Q–B2 | | |
| 11 N–N5 | P–Q4 | 22 QR–Q1 | QR–Q1 | | |

## part 4—BIRD'S DEFENSE

1 P–K4, P–K4
2 N–KB3, N–QB3
3 B–N5, N–Q5
4 NxN, PxN
5 O–O, P–QB3[A]
6 B–B4, N–B3[B]
7 R–K1[C], P–Q3

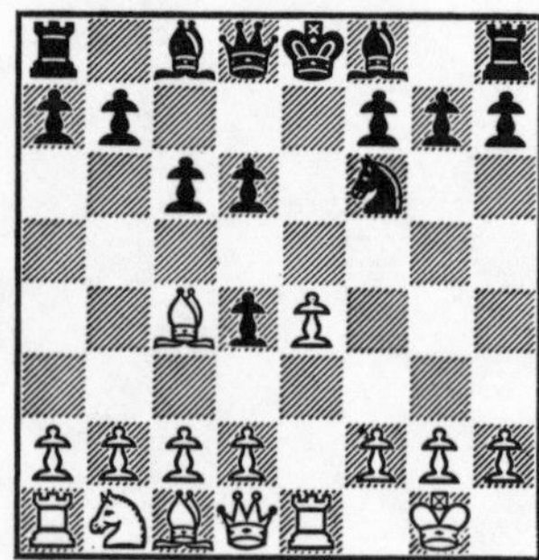

KEY POSITION 4

OBSERVATIONS ON KEY POSITION 4

[A] Another line is 5 . . . N–K2 6 P–QB4!, P–KN3 7 P–Q3, B–N2 8 B–B4, P–QB3 9 B–R4, P–Q3 10 Q–B1, O–O 11 B–R6, Q–R4?, as in Orbaan–Dr. Scholtens, Groningen 1953. 11 . . . P–KB4, however, gives Black more latitude.

[B] Weak is 6 . . . P–Q4 because of 7 PxP, PxP 8 R–K1†, B–K2 9 B–N5†, B–Q2 10 Q–N4±. For 6 . . . N–K2, see Game 7.

[C] Or 7 P–K5, P–Q4 8 PxN, PxB 9 PxP, BxP 10 P–Q3, PxP 11 PxP, B–K3 12 N–Q2, Q–B2 13 N–K4, O–O–O∓ (Kopylov–Tolush, 1950). Or 7 P–Q3, P–Q4 8 PxP, NxP 9 N–Q2, B–K3 10 N–K4, B–K2=. For 7 Q–K2, see Game 8.

Black's Pawn at Q5 is the issue. So long as it remains, it cramps White's mobility. The defense stands or falls on this point. Because few masters resort to the . . . N–Q5 sortie, it may be presumed that experience favors White.

IDEA VARIATIONS 8–11:

(8) 8 P–QB3!, PxP (better 8 . . . Q–N3) 9 Q–N3, Q–B2 10 P–QR4, PxQP 11 BxP, P–KN3 12 B–B3, B–N2 13 P–K5 wins. White's 9th is recommended by Keres, though 9 NxP or 9 PxP is also correct.

(9) 8 P–QB3, Q–N3 9 Q–N3, QxQ 10 BxQ, PxP 11 NPxP, B–K2 12 P–K5, PxP 13 RxP, N–Q2 14 R–K3, K–B1 15 P–Q4, N–N3 16 B–R3, BxB 17 NxB, B–Q2 18 P–QB4± (Lipnicky–Tolush, 1952).

(10) 8 P–QB3, N–N5?! 9 P–KR3, N–K4, 10 B–B1, P–Q6 11 P–KB4? (R–K3), Q–N3† 12 K–R1, P–KR4! 13 R–K3, N–B5 14 R–N3 14 B–N5, Q–K1, NxNP± (Milic–Nicolac, 1951). In this line if 13 PxN?, B–N5! 14 Q–N3, Q–B7. Or if 14 RxP? (instead of 14 R–N3), NxNP wins for Black.

(11) 8 Q–K2, B–K2 9 P–K5, PxP 10 QxP, P–QN4 11 B–N3, P–QR4 12 P–QR4, R–R2! 13 PxP, O–O 14 P–Q3, B–Q3! and Black has ample compensation for the sacrificed Pawn (Baturinsky–Lissitsin, 1948). In this line, 14 P–N6 leads to Game 8.

PRACTICAL VARIATIONS 13–16:

1 P–K4, P–K4 2 N–KB3, N–QB3 3 B–N5, N–Q5 4 NxN, PxN 5 O–O, P–QB3 6 B–B4, N–B3 7 R–K1, P–Q3

| | 13 | 14 | 15 | 16 |
|---|---|---|---|---|
| 8 | P–QB3 | – – | – – | P–Q3[8] |
| | Q–N3[1] | – – | N–N5?! | B–K2 |
| 9 | PxP[2] | Q–N3 | P–KR3[5] | N–Q2 |
| | QxQP | QxQ | N–K4 | O–O |

| | *13* | *14* | *15* | *16* |
|---|---|---|---|---|
| *10* | Q–N3 | BxQ | B–B1 | P–B4 |
| | NxP! | PxP | P–Q6 | P–Q4 |
| *11* | BxP† | QPxP | R–K3[6] | PxP |
| | K–Q1 | B–K2 | B–K2 | B–QN5[9] |
| *12* | R–K3 | N–R3 | P–KB4[7] | = |
| | K–B2[3] | O–O | N–B5 | |
| *13* | = | N–B2 | R–B3! | |
| | | R–K1 | Q–N3† | |
| *14* | | N–Q4 | K–R1 | |
| | | B–B1 | NxNP? | |
| *15* | | P–B3 | Q–N3! | |
| | | P–Q4[4] | ± | |
| | | = | | |

*Notes to practical variations 13-16:*

[1] For 8 . . . PxP, see Idea Var. 8. After 8 . . . B–K2, White obtains a tiny advantage by 9 PxP, P–Q4 10 PxP, NxP 11 N–B3, O–O 12 P–Q3, B–B3 13 B–K3 (Lipnicky–Bondarevsky, 1950).

[2] Too sharp. Better is 9 Q–N3. See Idea Var. 9.

[3] Chances for both sides.

[4] Tolush–Szabo, Bucharest 1953.

[5] If 9 PxP, Q–R5.

[6] For 11 P–KB4, see Idea Var. 10.

[7] Not 12 BxP, B–N4.

[8] 8 Q–K2 leads to Idea Var. 11.

[9] The threat is 12 . . . B–N5 (analysis by Nenarokov).

### *Lopez Game 7*

*WHITE: Alekhine* *BLACK: Grigoriev*

*Moscow 1919*

| | WHITE | BLACK | | WHITE | BLACK |
|---|---|---|---|---|---|
| 1 | P–K4 | P–K4 | 19 | R–B3 | R–Q1 |
| 2 | N–KB3 | N–QB3 | 20 | R/3–K3 | R–Q2 |
| 3 | B–N5 | N–Q5 | 21 | N–B4 | B–K3 |
| 4 | NxN | PxN | 22 | N–K5 | RxP |
| 5 | O–O | P–QB3 | 23 | NxKBP! | KxN |
| 6 | B–B4 | N–K2 | 24 | RxB | N–Q4 |
| 7 | P–Q3 | P–Q4 | 25 | R–K7† | K–B3 |
| 8 | B–N3 | PxP | 26 | R/1–K6† | K–B4 |
| 9 | PxP | N–N3 | 27 | B–B2† | KxP |
| 10 | P–QB3! | B–QB4 | 28 | RxKNP | R–KB1 |
| 11 | Q–R5 | Q–K2! | 29 | RxRP | N–K6 |
| 12 | B–N5 | QxP | 30 | R–R3 | N–B4 |
| 13 | N–Q2 | Q–N5 | 31 | R–B3† | K–N4 |
| 14 | QR–K1† | K–B1 | 32 | R–K5 | R–B5 |
| 15 | QxQ | BxQ | 33 | K–B2 | R–B3 |
| 16 | PxP | B–K2 | 34 | P–KR4† | K–N5 |
| 17 | P–B4 | B–KB4 | 35 | RxR† | KxR |
| 18 | BxB† | NxB | 36 | R–K4 mate | |

*Lopez Game 8*

*WHITE: Geller* *BLACK: Cholmov*

*17th Championship of USSR 1949*

| WHITE | BLACK | WHITE | BLACK |
|---|---|---|---|
| 1 P–K4 | P–K4 | 23 Q–R3 | Q–Q4 |
| 2 N–KB3 | N–QB3 | 24 P–QB3 | PxP |
| 3 B–N5 | N–Q5 | 25 PxP | B–K2 |
| 4 NxN | PxN | 26 P–KB4 | P–KB4 |
| 5 O–O | P–QB3 | 27 P–B4 | Q–Q5† |
| 6 B–B4 | N–B3 | 28 K–R1 | P–N3 |
| 7 Q–K2 | P–Q3 | 29 QR–N1 | P–R4 |
| 8 P–K5 | PxP | 30 R–N8† | K–B2 |
| 9 QxP† | B–K2 | 31 Q–N3 | PxN |
| 10 R–K1 | P–QN4 | 32 P–B5 | R–B3 |
| 11 B–N3 | P–QR4 | 33 R–KR8 | QxQP |
| 12 P–QR4 | R–R2 | 34 PxP† | K–N2 |
| 13 PxP | O–O | 35 R–R7† | K–N1 |
| 14 P–N6 | QxP | 36 QxQ | PxQ |
| 15 P–Q3 | B–QN5 | 37 RxR | BxR |
| 16 R–B1 | Q–Q1 | 38 RxR | B–Q5 |
| 17 B–N5 | R–K1 | 39 R–KB7 | P–Q7 |
| 18 Q–N3 | B–K3 | 40 R–B1 | B–N7 |
| 19 BxB | RxB | 41 K–N1 | P–QR5 |
| 20 N–Q2 | P–R3 | 42 K–B2 | P–R6 |
| 21 BxN | RxB | 43 K–K2 | P–R7 |
| 22 N–K4 | R–K3 | Resigns | |

---

## part 5—SCHLIEMANN DEFENSE

1 P–K4, P–K4
2 N–KB3, N–QB3
3 B–N5, P–B4
4 N–B3[A], PxP[B]
5 QNxP

KEY POSITION 5

### OBSERVATIONS ON KEY POSITION 5

[A] Analyzed and recommended by Dr. Dyckhoff. Weaker is 4 PxP, P–K5 5 Q–K2, Q–K2 6 BxN, QPxB! 7 N–Q4, Q–K4! 8 N–K6, BxN 9 PxB, B–Q3 10 N–B3, N–B3∓.

According to Bilguer's *Handbook,* Black is for choice after 4 BxN, QPxB 5 NxP, Q–Q5 6 Q–R5†, P–N3 7 NxNP, PxN 8 QxP†, K–Q1. The appraisal, however, is debatable.

4 P–Q4 loses a Pawn to . . . BPxP 5 NxP, NxN 6 PxN, P–B3 7 B–QB4?, Q–R4† (Cholmov–Bronstein, USSR Championship 1948). In this line 7 B–K2 is correct: . . . Q–R4† 8 B–Q2! QxKP 9 B–QB3, Q–KN4 10 B–R5†. After 10 . . . K–Q1 both sides have problems. See Game 9.

Solid is 4 P–Q3, but it gives no advantage. E.g., 4 . . . PxP 5 PxP, N–B3 6 O–O, P–Q3 7 Q–Q3, B–N5 8 B–N5, B–K2

9 QN–Q2, Q–Q2= (Wolf–Tarrasch, Monte Carlo 1903).

[B] If 4 . . . N–B3 5 PxP transposes into the King's Gambit Accepted with colors reversed: . . . B–B4 6 O–O, O–O 7 NxP, N–Q5 8 N–B3, P–B3 9 NxN, BxN 10 B–Q3, P–Q4 11 N–K2, B–K4 12 N–N3, N–K5 13 BxN, PxB 14 P–Q3, PxP 15 QxP, QxQ 16 PxQ, BxN 17 RPxB, BxP= (Tal–Spasski, 24th USSR Championship 1957). Black can hold the game because of Bishops of opposite colors.

In this line, for 7 R–K1? see Game 10. Equally good, however, is 10 B–R4, P–Q4 11 N–K2, B–N3? 12 P–Q4, BxBP± (Unzicker–Nievergelt, Zurich 1959). But 10 . . . B–N3 is weaker: 11 P–QN3, P–Q4 12 B–R3!± (Milic–Maric, 1956).

Black can obtain a superior development for a Pawn by 4 . . . N–Q5 5 B–R4, N–B3 6 PxP, B–B4 7 P–Q3, O–O 8 O–O P–Q4 9 NxKP, BxP 10 B–KN5, Q–Q3 (Boleslavsky–Tolush, 24th USSR Championship 1957). If 5 B–B4, P–Q3 6 P–Q3, N–B3 7 O–O, NxN† 8 QxN, P–B5 9 P–Q4, P–B3 10 Q–Q3, P–KN4∓ (Keres–Neshmetdinov, 24th USSR Championship 1957). For 5 . . . P–B3 instead of 5 . . . N–B3 above, see Game 11.

The Schliemann is a violent but not reckless Black attempt to seize an early initiative. Because it infringes upon sound principles of development, it is looked upon with disfavor by most of the leading masters. It crops up in master play, nonetheless, every so often. In the key position White leads in development. Black's center superiority and prospective open King Bishop file are a measure of compensation.

IDEA VARIATIONS 12–14:

(12) 5 . . . P–Q4 6 NxP, PxN 7 NxN, Q–Q4 8 P–QB4, Q–N4? (better 8 . . . Q–Q3) 9 P–Q4!, QxP 10 Q–R5†, P–N3 11 Q–K5†, K–B2 12 N–Q8 mate.

(13) 5 . . . N–B3 6 NxN†, PxN 7 P–Q4, P–K5 8 N–N5!, B–N5† 9 P–B3, PxN 10 Q–R5†, K–B1 11 BxP, B–K2 12 B–R6†, K–N1 13 B–B4†, and mate follows.

In this line, if 8 . . . PxN (instead of 8 . . . B–N5†) 9 Q–R5†, etc. Or if 9 . . . O–O (instead of 9 . . . PxN) 10 P–Q5±. Again, if 11 . . . Q–K1 (instead of 11 . . . B–K2) 12 Q–R6† and 13 B–B4†. Or if 11 . . . N–K2 12 B–QB4, P–Q4 13 BxP.

(14) 5 . . . P–Q4 6 N–N3?, B–KN5 7 P–KR3, BxN 8 QxB, N–B3 9 P–Q3, B–B4 and Black stands well.

PRACTICAL VARIATIONS 17–21:
1 P–K4, P–K4 2 N–KB3, N–QB3 3 B–N5, P–B4 4 N–B3, PxP 5 QNxP

| | 17 | 18 | 19 | 20 | 21 |
|---|---|---|---|---|---|
| 5 | — — | — — | — — | — — | — — |
| | N–B3 | B–K2 | P–Q4 | — — | — — |
| 6 | NxN | P–Q4 | NxP[7] | — — | — — |
| | PxN[1] | PxP | PxN | — — | — — |
| 7 | P–Q4 | O–O | NxN[8] | — — | — — |
| | P–Q3[2] | P–Q4[5] | PxN | Q–N4 | Q–Q4! |
| 8 | P–Q5[3] | N/4–N5 | BxP† | Q–K2 | P–QB4 |
| | P–QR3 | Q–Q3 | B–Q2 | N–B3 | Q–Q3![9] |
| 9 | B–K2 | QxP | Q–R5† | P–KB4 | NxP†[10] |
| | N–K2 | B–B3 | K–K2 | QxBP | K–Q1 |
| 10 | N–R4 | Q–QR4 | Q–K5† | N–K5† | NxB |
| | P–B3[4] | N–K2 | B–K3 | P–B3 | KxN |
| 11 | B–R5† | B–KB4 | BxR | P–Q4 | P–Q4 |
| | K–Q2 | Q–Q1 | QxB | PxP e.p. | PxP e.p. |
| 12 | PxP† | P–B4 | QxBP† | BxP | O–O |
| | PxP | O–O | B–Q2 | Q–N5† | ± |
| 13 | P–QB4 | PxP | ± | B–Q2 | |
| | ± | NxP | | Q–K2 | |
| 14 | | QR–Q1[6] | | O–O–O | |
| | | ± | | ± | |

*Notes to practical variations 17–21:*

[1] If 6 . . . QxN? 7 Q–K2 gains the KP.

[2] 7 . . . P–K5? leads to Idea Var. 13.

[3] If 8 PxP, QPxP!

[4] Weaker is 10 . . . N–N3 because of 11 B–R5, R–KN1 12 Q–Q3, K–B2 13 O–O, followed by 14 P–KB4 and the opening of the King Bishop file.

[5] For 7 . . . N–B3, see Game 12.

[6] Milic–Duckstein, Zagreb 1955.

[7] N–N3? leads to Idea Var. 14.

[8] 7 Q–R5†, P–N3 8 NxP, PxN 9 QxR, B–K3∓.

[9] 8 . . . Q–KN4? leads to Idea Var. 12.

[10] Interesting is 9 Q–R5†, P–N3 10 Q–K5†, QxQ 11 NxQ†, P–B3 12 B–R4, B–N2 13 P–Q4, PxP e.p. 14 NxQP, B–B4. If, in this line, 12 NxBP? (instead of 12 B–R4), P–QR3 13 B–R4, B–Q2! Or if 13 P–B4 (instead of 13 P–Q4), PxP e.p. 14 NxKBP, B–B4. Black's development compensates for his Pawn.

*Lopez Game 9*

*WHITE: Pedersen* *BLACK: Grynfeld*

*Olympics, Helsinki 1952*

| | WHITE | BLACK | | WHITE | BLACK |
|---|---|---|---|---|---|
| 1 | P–K4 | P–K4 | 26 | Q–N6 | P–K6 |
| 2 | N–KB3 | N–QB3 | 27 | P–QR4 | P–N5 |
| 3 | B–N5 | P–B4 | 28 | N–K4 | Q–K2 |
| 4 | P–Q4 | PxKP | 29 | BxP | R–Q5 |
| 5 | NxP | NxN | 30 | QR–B1 | K–N3 |
| 6 | PxN | P–B3 | 31 | NxN | PxN |
| 7 | B–K2! | Q–R4† | 32 | QxRP | B–N2 |
| 8 | B–Q2 | QxKP | 33 | KR–K1 | R–K1 |
| 9 | B–QB3 | Q–KN4 | 34 | P–QN3 | P–KB4 |
| 10 | B–R5† | K–Q1 | 35 | KR–Q1 | RxR† |
| 11 | O–O | P–Q4 | 36 | RxR | Q–K4 |
| 12 | B–Q2 | Q–B4 | 37 | P–R3 | Q–N6 |
| 13 | B–K3 | N–B3 | 38 | Q–B6 | P–K7 |
| 14 | B–K2 | B–Q3 | 39 | BxP | RxB |
| 15 | P–QB4 | K–B2 | 40 | Q–Q4† | P–B4 |
| 16 | N–B3 | PxP | 41 | Q–Q8† | Q–B2 |
| 17 | Q–R4 | P–QN4 | 42 | Q–Q3 | R–K4 |
| 18 | Q–R5† | K–N2 | 43 | Q–B4 | B–B3 |
| 19 | P–B3 | B–B4 | 44 | P–R4 | P–B5 |
| 20 | BxB | QxB† | 45 | K–R2 | R–R4 |
| 21 | K–R1 | Q–N3 | 46 | Q–K6 | RxP† |
| 22 | Q–N4 | P–QR4 | 47 | K–N1 | Q–KR2 |
| 23 | Q–Q6 | R–Q1 | 48 | K–B2 | Q–B7† |
| 24 | Q–N3 | Q–B2 | | Resigns | |
| 25 | Q–N5 | P–R3 | | | |

*Lopez Game 10*

*WHITE: Matanovic* *BLACK: Janosevic*

*Yugoslavian Championship 1953*

| | WHITE | BLACK | | WHITE | BLACK |
|---|---|---|---|---|---|
| 1 | P–K4 | P–K4 | 10 | BxN | PxB |
| 2 | N–KB3 | N–QB3 | 11 | N–R4 | P–N4! |
| 3 | B–N5 | P–B4 | 12 | PxP e.p. | N–N5 |
| 4 | N–B3 | N–B3 | 13 | PxP† | K–N2 |
| 5 | PxP | B–B4 | 14 | P–KN3 | Q–Q5 |
| 6 | O–O | O–O | 15 | Q–K2? | RxP |
| 7 | R–K1? | P–Q3 | 16 | QxP | R–B8† |
| 8 | N–QR4 | P–K5! | | Resigns | |
| 9 | NxB | QPxN | | | |

*Lopez Game 11*

*WHITE: Szabo* *BLACK: Minev*

*Olympics, Amsterdam 1954*

| | WHITE | BLACK | | WHITE | BLACK |
|---|---|---|---|---|---|
| 1 | P–K4 | P–K4 | 21 | PxP† | K–K1 |
| 2 | N–KB3 | N–QB3 | 22 | Q–R6 | BxR |
| 3 | B–N5 | P–B4 | 23 | RxB | PxB |
| 4 | N–B3 | N–Q5 | 24 | QxP† | K–Q1 |
| 5 | B–R4 | P–B3 | 25 | P–R4 | R/1–K1 |
| 6 | O–O | P–Q3 | 26 | Q–B6 | QxP |
| 7 | PxP | BxP | 27 | P–R5 | K–B2 |
| 8 | NxN | PxN | 28 | Q–R1 | R–KN1 |
| 9 | R–K1† | K–Q2 | 29 | P–N3 | K–Q2 |
| 10 | Q–B3 | N–R3 | 30 | Q–Q4 | K–B1 |
| 11 | P–Q3 | PxN | 31 | P–R6 | R/1–K1 |
| 12 | BxN | P–KN3 | 32 | Q–QN4 | R–QN2 |
| 13 | BxB | PxP | 33 | Q–N4† | Q–Q2 |
| 14 | QR–N1 | RxB | 34 | Q–B4† | K–N1 |
| 15 | RxP | Q–B2 | 35 | R–Q1 | Q–K3 |
| 16 | P–Q4 | QR–K1 | 36 | Q–B4 | Q–K4 |
| 17 | KR–N1 | P–QN4 | 37 | QxP | R–R1 |
| 18 | P–Q5 | BxP | 38 | Q–R4 | Q–K3 |
| 19 | Q–R3† | B–B4 | 39 | P–R7 | R/2xP |
| 20 | QxP† | R–K2 | | Resigns | |

*Lopez Game 12*

*WHITE: Trifunovic* *BLACK: Kostic*

*Rogaska Slatina 1930*

| | WHITE | BLACK | | WHITE | BLACK |
|---|---|---|---|---|---|
| 1 | P–K4 | P–K4 | 10 | N–N5 | O–O |
| 2 | N–KB3 | N–QB3 | 11 | NxP | KxN |
| 3 | B–N5 | P–B4 | 12 | Q–R5† | K–N1 |
| 4 | N–B3 | PxP | 13 | B–Q3 | R–K1 |
| 5 | QNxP | B–K2 | 14 | P–KN4 | P–Q3 |
| 6 | P–Q4 | PxP | 15 | P–N5 | B–K4 |
| 7 | O–O | N–B3 | 16 | B–R7† | K–B1 |
| 8 | NxN† | BxN | 17 | Q–B3† | Resigns |
| 9 | R–K1† | N–K2 | | | |

# part 6—STEINITZ DEFENSE I

1 P–K4, P–K4
2 N–KB3, N–QB3
3 B–N5, P–Q3
4 P–Q4[A], B–Q2[B]
5 N–B3[C], PxP[D]
6 NxP, N–B3[E]
7 O–O[F], B–K2[G]

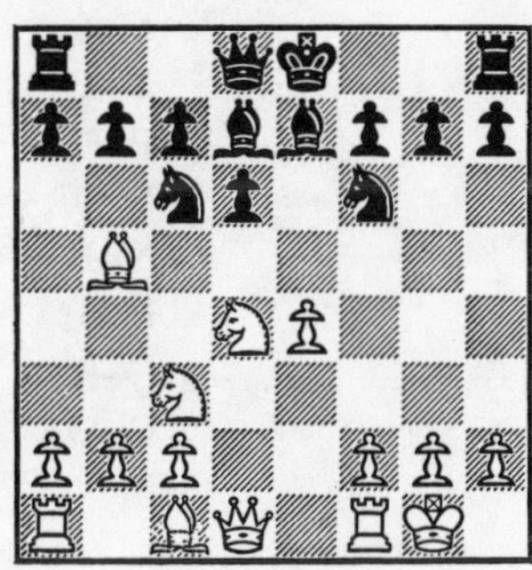

KEY POSITION 6

## OBSERVATIONS ON KEY POSITION 6

[A] Best! 4 P–B3, to prepare P–Q4, is weaker. E.g., 4 P–B3, P–B4! 5 P–Q4, BPxP 6 NxP, PxN 7 Q–R5†, K–K2 8 BxN, PxB 9 B–N5†, N–B3 10 PxP, Q–Q4 11 B–R4, B–R3 12 PxN†, PxP.

[B] For 4 . . . PxP see Game 13.

[C] 5 P–Q5, N–N1 6 B–Q3, B–K2 7 N–B3, KN–B3 8 N–K2, P–B3=.

[D] For 5 . . . N–B3 see key position 7, Part 7.

[E] Another possibility is 6 . . . NxN 7 QxN, BxB 8 NxB, N–K2 9 B–K3, etc. For 6 . . . P–KN3 see Game 14.

[F] An equally good continuation is 7 BxN, PxB 8 Q–B3, P–B4 9 N–B5, BxN 10 QxB, Q–Q2 11 Q–B3, Q–N5 12 QxQ, NxQ 13 N–Q5, K–Q2, with equal chances. In the above line Keres recommends 7 . . . BxB 8 NxB, PxN 9 Q–B3, N–Q2, and White's P–K5 has been prevented. Also, if 8 . . . B–K2? then 9 P–K5!, PxP 10 NxP, BxN 11 QxB†, N–Q2 12 O–O, O–O 13 R–Q1, B–Q3 14 N–N5 wins. Again, if 9 . . . P–N3? then 10 B–N5, PxN 11 P–K5, PxP 12 BxN, P–K5 13 NxP with great advantage for White. In a game Loewenfisch–Dubinin, 1934, 11 . . . R–QN1 12 O–O, B–K2 13 P–QN3 gave White a small advantage.

[G] Not so good is 7 . . . NxN 8 BxB†, QxB 9 QxN, B–K2 10 R–Q1, O–O 11 P–K5, N–K1 12 B–B4±.

3 . . . P–Q3 was introduced into master practice by Steinitz in 1889, and was later favored by Lasker and Capablanca. It fell into disuse about 1925. In the key position, while Black's Pawn structure is solid, White commands more space and greater mobility, which he may convert into a Kingside assault. Black is reduced to passivity and seeks to simplify by exchanging pieces or to free his game by the liberating . . . P–Q4.

## IDEA VARIATIONS 15 AND 16:

(15) 8 B–N5, O–O 9 BxQN, PxB 10 Q–Q3, R–K1 11 QR–K1, P–B4 12 N–N3, N–N5 13 BxB, RxB 14 P–B4, R–N1 15 P–KR3, N–R3 16 P–B5, P–KB3 17 N–Q5, R–K1 18 P–B4± (Lasker–Salwe, St. Petersburg 1909). Fine recommends 10 . . . P–KR3 11 B–R4, N–R4! Also strong is 16 P–N4 (instead of 16 P–B5).

(16) 8 P–QN3, NxN 9 QxN, BxB 10 NxB, N–Q2! 11 Q–B4, P–QB3 12 N–Q4, O–O 13 N–B5, B–B3 14 R–N1, P–Q4 15 PxP, N–K4 (15 . . . N–N3? 16 Q–KN4 and 17 B–R6!) 16 Q–K2, QxP 17 R–Q1, Q–K3 with equal chances. 18 N–Q6 is risky: 18 . . . QR–Q1 19 NxNP, RxR† 20 QxR, Q–K2! etc.

PRACTICAL VARIATIONS 22–24:

1 P–K4, P–K4 2 N–KB3, N–QB3 3 B–N5, P–Q3 4 P–Q4, B–Q2 5 N–B3, PxP 6 NxP, N–B3 7 O–O, B–K2

| | 22 | 23 | 24 |
|---|---|---|---|
| 8 | P–QN3[1] | KN–K2 | N–B5? |
| | NxN | O–O | BxN |
| 9 | QxN | N–N3 | PxB |
| | BxB | R–K1[5] | O–O |
| 10 | NxB | P–KR3 | R–K1 |
| | N–Q2! | P–KR3[6] | N–Q2 |
| 11 | B–R3[2] | B–K3 | N–Q5 |
| | P–QR3[3] | B–KB1 | B–B3 |
| 12 | N–B3 | Q–Q2 | P–QB3 |
| | B–B3 | K–R2 | N–N3 |
| 13 | Q–K3 | QR–K1 | NxB† |
| | O–O | P–KN3 | QxN |
| 14 | QR–Q1 | P–B4 | BxN |
| | BxN! | B–N2 | PxB |
| 15 | QxB | B–B4[7] | Q–B3 |
| | R–K1 | ± | KR–K1[8] |
| 16 | KR–K1 | | ∓ |
| | R–QB1 | | |
| 17 | Q–R3 | | |
| | N–K4 | | |
| 18 | B–N2 | | |
| | Q–N4[4] | | |
| | = | | |

*Notes to practical variations 22–24:*

[1] 8 BxN, PxB 9 P–QN3, O–O 10 B–N2, R–K1 11 Q–Q3, B–KB1 12 P–B4, P–N3 gives equal chances.

[2] 11 Q–B4 leads to Idea Var. 16.

[3] If 11 . . . B–B3 then 12 Q–B4!

[4] Lasker–Capablanca, 1924.

[5] 9 . . . N–K4? 10 BxB, QxB 11 P–N3, QR–Q1 12 B–N2, N–B3 13 N–B5± (Lasker–Walbrodt, 1895).

[6] Better is 10 . . . B–KB1 11 B–K3, P–KN3 and 12 . . . B–N2. In these variations the maneuver N–Q4–K2–N3 by White may be met by Black's . . . R–K1, . . . P–KN3 and . . . B–N2 preventing the occupation of KB5 by White's Knight.

[7] Yates–Gibson, 1931.

[8] Alekhine–Capablanca, 1914.

## part 7—STEINITZ DEFENSE II

1 P–K4, P–K4
2 N–KB3, N–QB3
3 B–N5, P–Q3
4 P–Q4, B–Q2
5 N–B3, N–B3
6 BxN[A], BxB
7 Q–Q3

KEY POSITION 7

OBSERVATIONS ON KEY POSITION 7

[A] For 6 O–O see key position 8, Part 8.

Keres considers 5 . . . N–B3 a weak move because it allows White to transpose to a favorable variation by playing 6 BxN! Keres recommends 1 P–K4, P–K4 2 N–KB3, N–QB3 3 B–N5, N–B3 4 O–O, P–Q3 5 P–Q4, B–Q2 6 N–B3, B–K2.

IDEA VARIATIONS 17 AND 18:

(17) 7 . . . PxP 8 NxP, B–Q2 9 B–N5, B–K2 10 O–O–O, O–O 11 P–B4, N–N5 12 BxB, QxB 13 R–Q2,

KR–K1 14 R–K2, P–QB3 15 P–KR3, N–B3 16 P–KN4, QR–Q1 17 Q–B3 (threatens to win a piece by 18 P–N5) 17 . . . B–B1 18 N–B5±.

(18) 7 . . . PxP 8 NxP, P–KN3 9 NxB (better 9 B–N5), PxN 10 Q–R6, Q–Q2 11 Q–N7, R–B1 12 QxRP, B–N2 13 O–O, O–O 14 Q–R6, KR–K1 15 Q–Q3, Q–K3 16 P–B3, N–Q2! Black has excellent play on the Queenside. (Nimzowitsch–Capablanca, St. Petersburg 1914).

PRACTICAL VARIATIONS 25–28:

1 P–K4, P–K4 2 N–KB3, N–QB3 3 B–N5, P–Q3 4 P–Q4, B–Q2 5 N–B3, N–B3 6 BxN, BxB 7 Q–Q3

| | *25* | *26* | *27* | *28* |
|---|---|---|---|---|
| 7 | – – | – – | – – | – – |
| | PxP | – – | N–Q2 | – – |
| 8 | NxP | – – | B–K3 | P–Q5 |
| | P–KN3 | B–Q2 | PxP[7] | N–B4 |
| 9 | B–N5![1] | B–N5 | BxP | Q–B4 |
| | B–N2 | B–K2 | N–B4 | B–Q2 |
| 10 | O–O–O | O–O–O | BxN | P–QN4 |
| | Q–Q2[2] | O–O[4] | PxB | N–R3 |
| 11 | P–KR3 | P–B4 | Q–K3! | B–K3 |
| | O–O | N–K1[5] | Q–B3 | B–K2 |
| 12 | KR–K1 | BxB | O–O–O | O–O |
| | K–R1 | QxB | B–K2 | O–O |
| 13 | Q–B3 | N–Q5 | N–Q5 | P–QR4 |
| | N–N1 | Q–Q1 | BxN | K–R1 |
| 14 | P–KN4 | P–KN4![6] | RxB[8] | N–QN5 |
| | QR–K1[3] | ± | ± | Q–B1 |
| 15 | = | | | P–B3[9] |
| | | | | ± |

*Notes to practical variations 25–28:*

[1] 9 NxB leads to Idea Var. 18.

[2] Alekhine recommends 10 . . . Q–B1 keeping Q2 for the Knight. Bad is 10 . . . O–O because of 11 NxB, PxN 12 P–K5, PxP 13 QxQ, QRxQ 14 RxR, RxR 15 N–K4. White wins the exchange.

[3] Black's position is tenable.

[4] Interesting is 10 . . . N–N5 11 BxB, QxB 12 Q–N3, N–B3 13 KR–K1, O–O–O=.

[5] 11 . . . N–N5 leads to Idea Var. 17.

[6] With a powerful attack (Spielmann–Maroczy, 1920): 14 . . . BxP? 15 QR–N1, B–Q2 16 R–N2, P–QB3 17 N–K3, P–KN3 18 P–KR4 etc.

[7] Black can no longer maintain the center because of the threat 9 P–Q5. If 8 . . . P–QN3 then 9 P–Q5, B–N2 and Black's Bishop has no future.

[8] White's mobile Pawn majority is more effective.

[9] Nimzowitsch–Breyer, 1920.

## part 8—STEINITZ DEFENSE III

1 P–K4, P–K4
2 N–KB3, N–QB3
3 B–N5, P–Q3
4 P–Q4, B–Q2
5 N–B3, N–B3
6 O–O, B–K2
7 R–K1, PxP[A]
8 NxP, O–O[B]

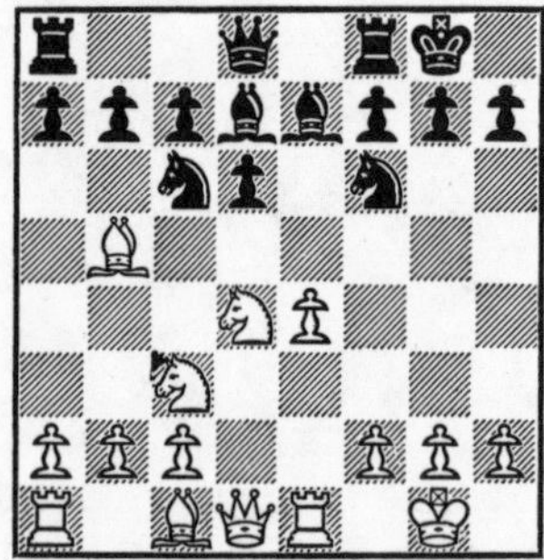

KEY POSITION 8

OBSERVATIONS ON KEY POSITION 8

[A] 7 . . . O–O? 8 BxN, BxB 9 PxP, PxP 10 QxQ, KRxQ 11 NxP, BxP 12 NxB, NxN 13 N–Q3!, P–KB4 14 P–KB3, B–B4† 15 K–B1±. White also wins after 7 . . . O–O? 8 BxN, BxB 9 PxP, PxP 10 QxQ, QRxQ 11 NxP, BxP 12 NxB, NxN 13 N–Q3, P–KB4 14 P–KB3, B–B4† 15 NxB (15 K–B1?, B–N3!) NxN 16 B–N5, R–Q4 17 B–K7, R–K1 18 P–QB4, winning a piece (Tarrasch–Marco, Dresden 1892). Compare discussion of the Tarrasch trap on page 84.

[B] For 8 . . . NxN see Game 16.

This key position is much the same as key position 6. White can try to use his greater mobility and command of space in several ways. See Part 6 for further characteristics and idea variations.

PRACTICAL VARIATIONS 29–32:

1 P–K4, P–K4 2 N–KB3, N–QB3 3 B–N5, P–Q3 4 P–Q4, B–Q2 5 N–B3, N–B3 6 O–O, B–K2 7 R–K1, PxP 8 NxP, O–O

| | 29 | 30 | 31 | 32 |
|---|---|---|---|---|
| 9 | BxN[1] | B–B1 | P–QN3[5] | B–N5 |
| | PxB[2] | R–K1 | NxN | P–KR3 |
| 10 | B–N5 | P–KR3 | QxN | B–R4 |
| | P–KR3 | B–B1 | BxB | N–R2 |
| 11 | B–R4 | B–KN5 | NxB | BxB |
| | R–K1 | P–KR3 | P–Q4! | QxB |
| 12 | Q–Q3 | B–R4 | PxP | N–Q5 |
| | N–R2 | P–KN4 | NxP | Q–Q1 |
| 13 | BxB | B–N3 | B–R3 | P–QB3 |
| | RxB | NxN | B–B3 | N–B3 |
| 14 | R–K3 | QxN | Q–Q3 | B–B1 |
| | Q–N1 | N–R4 | BxR | R–K1 |
| 15 | P–QN3 | B–R2 | BxR | Q–B3 |
| | Q–N3[3] | B–N2 | P–QR3 | KNxN |
| 16 | = | Q–Q1 | RxB | NxN |
| | | N–B5 | PxN[6] | BxN |
| 17 | | BxN | ∓ | PxN |
| | | PxB[4] | | B–Q2[7] |
| | | = | | = |

*Notes to practical variations 29–32:*

[1] For 9 NxN see Game 15.

[2] 9 . . . BxB? 10 NxB, PxN 11 N–K2, Q–Q2 12 N–N3, KR–K1 13 P–N3 and 14 B–N2± (Tarrasch–Lasker, 1908).

[3] Capablanca–Lasker, 1921.

[4] Kashdan–L. Steiner, 1930.

[5] Tarrasch's recommendation, the fianchetto of the Queen Bishop, is harmless.

[6] Tylor–Keres, Hastings 1937.

[7] Wolf–Maroczy, Teplitz-Schonau 1922.

### *Lopez Game 13*

*WHITE: Alekhine* *BLACK: Van Mindeno*

*Simultaneous Display, Amsterdam 1933*

| | WHITE | BLACK | | WHITE | BLACK | | WHITE | BLACK |
|---|---|---|---|---|---|---|---|---|
| 1 | P–K4 | P–K4 | 7 | N–B3 | N–B3 | 13 | PxP | NxP |
| 2 | N–KB3 | N–QB3 | 8 | B–N5 | B–K2 | 14 | R–R5 | Q–K3 |
| 3 | B–N5 | P–Q3 | 9 | O–O–O | O–O | 15 | QR–R1 | P–B4 |
| 4 | P–Q4 | PxP | 10 | P–KR4 | P–KR3 | 16 | N–K5!! | PxN |
| 5 | QxP | B–Q2 | 11 | N–Q5 | PxB | 17 | P–N6!! | Resigns |
| 6 | BxN | BxB | 12 | NxB† | QxN | | | |

### *Lopez Game 14*

*WHITE: Em. Lasker* *BLACK: Vidmar*

*St. Petersburg 1909*

| | WHITE | BLACK | | WHITE | BLACK | | WHITE | BLACK |
|---|---|---|---|---|---|---|---|---|
| 1 | P–K4 | P–K4 | 9 | P–B3 | O–O | 17 | PxP | BPxP |
| 2 | N–KB3 | N–QB3 | 10 | O–O–O | P–QR3 | 18 | N/4–K2 | R–B2 |
| 3 | B–N5 | P–Q3 | 11 | B–K2 | P–QN4 | 19 | QxP | Q–N3 |
| 4 | P–Q4 | B–Q2 | 12 | P–KR4 | N–K4 | 20 | Q–Q4 | P–B4 |
| 5 | N–B3 | PxP | 13 | B–R6 | N–B5 | 21 | N–Q5 | Q–N2 |
| 6 | NxP | P–KN3 | 14 | BxN | PxB | 22 | Q–B3 | QR–KB1 |
| 7 | B–K3 | B–N2 | 15 | P–R5 | P–B3 | 23 | NxN | RxN |
| 8 | Q–Q2 | N–B3 | 16 | BxB | KxB | 24 | R–Q6 | Resigns |

### *Lopez Game 15*

*WHITE: Tarrasch* *BLACK: Em. Lasker*

*Düsseldorf 1908*

| | WHITE | BLACK | | WHITE | BLACK | | WHITE | BLACK |
|---|---|---|---|---|---|---|---|---|
| 1 | P–K4 | P–K4 | 15 | BxP | NxBP! | 29 | R–Q1 | P–B5 |
| 2 | N–KB3 | N–QB3 | 16 | KxN | KxB | 30 | N–R1 | P–Q5 |
| 3 | B–N5 | N–B3 | 17 | N–B5† | K–R1 | 31 | N–B2 | Q–QR3 |
| 4 | O–O | P–Q3 | 18 | Q–Q4† | P–B3 | 32 | N–Q3 | R–KN4 |
| 5 | P–Q4 | B–Q2 | 19 | QxRP | B–B1 | 33 | R–R1 | Q–R3 |
| 6 | N–B3 | B–K2 | 20 | Q–Q4 | R–K4 | 34 | K–K1 | QxP |
| 7 | R–K1 | PxP | 21 | QR–Q1 | QR–K1 | 35 | K–Q1 | Q–N8† |
| 8 | NxP | O–O | 22 | Q–B3 | Q–B2 | 36 | N–K1 | R/4–K4 |
| 9 | NxN | BxN | 23 | N–N3 | B–R3 | 37 | Q–B6 | R/4–K3 |
| 10 | BxB | PxB | 24 | Q–B3 | P–Q4 | 38 | QxP | R/1–K2 |
| 11 | N–K2 | Q–Q2 | 25 | PxP | B–K6† | 39 | Q–Q8† | K–N2 |
| 12 | N–N3 | KR–K1 | 26 | K–B1 | PxP | 40 | P–R4 | P–B6! |
| 13 | P–N3 | QR–Q1 | 27 | R–Q3 | Q–K3 | 41 | PxP | B–N4 |
| 14 | B–N2 | N–N5 | 28 | R–K2 | P–KB4 | | Resigns | |

*Lopez Game 16*

*WHITE: Capablanca* *BLACK: Fonarov*

*New York 1918*

| | WHITE | BLACK | | WHITE | BLACK |
|---|---|---|---|---|---|
| 1 | P–K4 | P–K4 | 12 | N–Q4 | N–Q2 |
| 2 | N–KB3 | N–QB3 | 13 | N–B5 | B–B3 |
| 3 | P–Q4 | P–Q3 | 14 | Q–KN3 | N–K4 |
| 4 | N–B3 | N–B3 | 15 | B–B4 | Q–B2 |
| 5 | B–QN5 | B–Q2 | 16 | QR–Q1 | QR–Q1 |
| 6 | O–O | B–K2 | 17 | RxP! | RxR |
| 7 | R–K1 | PxP | 18 | BxN | R–Q8? |
| 8 | NxP | NxN | 19 | RxR | BxB |
| 9 | QxN | BxB | 20 | N–R6† | K–R1 |
| 10 | NxB | O–O | 21 | QxB | QxQ |
| 11 | Q–B3 | P–B3 | 22 | NxP† | Resigns |

SUPPLEMENTARY VARIATIONS 1–5:
1 P–K4, P–K4 2 N–KB3, N–QB3 3 B–N5

| | *1* | *2* | *3* | *4* | *5* |
|---|---|---|---|---|---|
| *3* | – – | – – | – – | – – | – – |
| | Q–B3[1] | P–B3[3] | KN–K2 | P–KN4[9] | P–KN3 |
| *4* | N–B3 | O–O | P–Q4 | P–Q4 | O–O |
| | KN–K2 | KN–K2 | PxP | NxP | B–N2 |
| *5* | P–Q3 | P–Q4 | NxP | NxN | P–B3 |
| | N–Q5 | N–N3 | P–KN3 | PxN | P–Q3 |
| *6* | NxN | P–QR3[4] | N–QB3[6] | QxP | P–Q4 |
| | PxN | B–K2 | B–N2 | Q–B3 | B–Q2 |
| *7* | N–K2 | B–QB4 | B–K3 | P–K5[10] | B–N5[11] |
| | P–B3 | P–Q3 | O–O | Q–KN3 | P–B3 |
| *8* | B–R4 | P–R3 | O–O[7] | N–B3 | B–K3 |
| | P–Q4 | B–Q2 | P–B4[8] | B–K2 | N–R3 |
| *9* | O–O | N–B3 | PxP | N–Q5 | B–QB4 |
| | P–KN3 | Q–B1 | NxP | B–Q1 | Q–K2 |
| *10* | P–QN4! | K–R2 | NxKN | O–O | PxP |
| | Q–Q3 | N–Q1 | RxN | P–QB3 | QPxP |
| *11* | P–QR3 | N–Q5[5] | B–B4† | B–Q3 | P–QN4 |
| | B–N2 | ± | K–R1 | Q–N2 | N–B2 |
| *12* | B–N2[2] | | Q–Q2 | N–K3 | Q–N3 |
| | ± | | ± | P–Q4 | P–N3 |
| *13* | | | | N–B5 | P–QR4 |
| | | | | BxN | O–O |
| *14* | | | | BxB | P–R5[12] |
| | | | | ± | ± |

*Notes to supplementary variations 1–5:*

[1] This move exposes the queen to danger and cannot be recommended.

[2] Bogoljubov–Ed. Lasker, 1924.

[3] Frequently played by Steinitz. However, this move weakens White's QR2–KN8 diagonal.

[4] This provides a retreat square for White's King Bishop.

[5] Tarrasch–Steinitz, 1896.

[6] For 6 B–N5 see Game 17.

[7] More energetic is 8 Q–Q2 and O–O–O.

[8] Better is 8 . . . P–Q3.

[9] An unnecessary weakening of the King's wing.

[10] White obtains an equally good game by means of 7 QxQ, NxQ.

[11] Better is first 7 PxP, PxP and then 8 B–N5. If Black replies 7 . . . NxP then 8 NxN, PxN 9 Q–N3± (Geller–Trifunovic, Belgrade 1956).

[12] Milic–Fuderer, 1952.

*Lopez Game 17*

*WHITE: Grigoriev* *BLACK: Alekhine*

*Moscow 1920*

| | WHITE | BLACK | | WHITE | BLACK |
|---|---|---|---|---|---|
| 1 | P–K4 | P–K4 | 14 | B–K5 | B–K3 |
| 2 | N–KB3 | N–QB3 | 15 | N–Q2 | P–B3 |
| 3 | B–N5 | KN–K2 | 16 | B–KN3 | Q–N3 |
| 4 | P–Q4 | PxP | 17 | R–K1 | KR–K1 |
| 5 | NxP | P–KN3 | 18 | N–K4? | P–KB4 |
| 6 | B–N5 | B–N2 | 19 | N–B5 | B–B2 |
| 7 | P–QB3 | P–KR3 | 20 | B–Q6 | QxP |
| 8 | B–KR4 | O–O | 21 | BxN | BxB |
| 9 | O–O | NxN | 22 | R–N1 | QxQP |
| 10 | PxN | P–QB3 | 23 | RxP | Q–KN5! |
| 11 | B–B4 | P–KN4 | 24 | P–B3 | B–Q5† |
| 12 | B–KN3 | P–Q4 | 25 | K–R1 | BxBP!! |
| 13 | PxP | NxP | | Resigns | |

## (B) Systems With the Move 3 . . . P-QR3

Introduced by Paul Morphy about a century ago, the move 3 . . . P–QR3 has retained its popularity to this day. It presages any one of a variety of actions, depending to a large extent upon White's parry. White can, for example, play 4 BxN, creating an imbalance in the Pawn structure and the material units. Or he can retire his Bishop to R4, waiting for a more propitious moment to effect the exchange. In the latter event, Black's . . . P–R3 may serve as a prop for . . . P–QN4, driving the Bishop and relieving the pressure against the Knight. It may, moreover, portend a general Queenside Pawn demonstration, with a consequent gain of space as against a weakening of the structure. All in all, the move is double-edged, apparently tactically correct and sufficiently flexible to introduce many versatile patterns.

---

## part 9—EXCHANGE VARIATION

1 P–K4, P–K4
2 N–KB3, N–QB3
3 B–N5, P–QR3!
4 BxN, QPxB[A]

KEY POSITION 9

OBSERVATIONS ON KEY POSITION 9

[A] Equally good is 4 . . . NPxB 5 P–Q4 (5 NxP, Q–N4!), PxP 6 QxP, Q–B3 7 P–K5, Q–N3 8 O–O, QxP 9 N–B3, N–K2 10 R–K1, Q–N3. It is not clear that White's plus in development is sufficient for his Pawn minus. Safer and stronger in this line, however, is 8 . . . B–N2 and 9 . . . P–QB4. After 8 . . . B–N2 9 P–K6!?, BPxP 10 N–K5, QxP† 11 KxQ, P–QB4†∓.

Black's doubled Queen Bishop Pawns are a chronic defect of sufficient import to guide the defender away from inane exchanges which will reduce the position to a Pawn skeleton. His two Bishops, however, compensate for the Pawn weakness.

IDEA VARIATIONS 19 AND 20:

(19) 5 N–B3, P–B3 6 P–Q4, PxP 7 QxP, QxQ 8 NxQ, B–Q3 9 B–K3, B–Q2 10 O–O–O, O–O–O 11 N–N3, B–QN5 (11 . . . P–QN3?, 12 BxP) 12 N–K2, N–K2 13 B–B5, BxB 16 NxB, N–N3 17 NxB, RxN 18 RxR, KxR±.

(20) 5 P–Q4, PxP 6 QxP, QxQ 7 NxQ, B–Q2 8 B–K3, O–O–O 9 N–Q2, P–KN3 10 O–O–O, B–N2 11 N–K2, N–K2 12 B–Q4, P–B3 (if possible Black should avoid the exchange of Bishops) 13 P–QB4?, KR–K1 14 P–B3, N–B4! 15 KR–K1, NxB 16 NxN, B–R3 17 P–KN3, B–N5∓ (Marco–Euwe, Pistyan 1922).

PRACTICAL VARIATIONS 33–37:

1 P–K4, P–K4 2 N–KB3, N–QB3 3 B–N5, P–QR3 4 BxN, QPxB

| | 33 | 34 | 35 | 36 | 37 |
|---|---|---|---|---|---|
| 5 | P–Q4 | – – | – – | N–B3[7] | O–O |
| | PxP[1] | – – | – – | P–B3[8] | B–KN5 |

| | 33 | 34 | 35 | 36 | 37 |
|---|---|---|---|---|---|
| 6 | QxP | – – | – – | P–Q4[9] | P–KR3 |
| | QxQ | – – | – – | PxP | P–KR4 |
| 7 | NxQ | – – | – – | QxP | P–Q3 |
| | B–Q2[2] | B–Q3 | P–QB4 | QxQ | Q–B3 |
| 8 | N–QB3[3] | N–QB3 | N–K2 | NxQ | R–K1 |
| | O–O–O | N–K2 | B–Q2 | B–Q2[10] | BxN |
| 9 | B–K3 | O–O | QN–B3 | B–K3 | QxB |
| | B–QN5 | O–O | O–O–O | O–O–O | QxQ |
| 10 | N–K2 | P–B4 | B–B4 | O–O–O | PxQ |
| | R–K1 | R–K1 | B–B3 | N–K2 | O–O–O |
| 11 | O–O–O | N–N3 | O–O | P–KR3 | P–KB4 |
| | P–KB4 | P–B3 | N–B3 | N–N3 | PxP |
| 12 | PxP | P–B5 | P–B3 | N–N3 | BxP |
| | BxP | P–QN3 | B–K2 | B–QN5 | N–K2 |
| 13 | P–QR3 | B–B4 | N–N3 | N–K2 | N–Q2 |
| | B–Q3 | B–N2?[4] | P–KN3 | KR–K1 | N–N3 |
| 14 | N–Q4 | BxB | KR–K1 | P–R3 | B–K3 |
| | B–Q2 | PxB | N–Q2 | B–B1 | B–Q3 |
| 15 | KR–K1 | N–Q4 | N–Q1 | N–B3 | N–B4 |
| | N–B3 | QR–Q1 | N–N3[6] | B–K3[11] | KR–B1[12] |
| 16 | = | N–K6[5] | ∓ | = | = |
| | | ± | | | |

*Notes to practical variations 33–37:*

[1] If 5 . . . B–KN5? 6 PxP, QxQ† 7 KxQ, O–O–O† 8 K–K1 (8 K–K2, P–B3!), B–QB4 9 P–KR3, B–R4 10 B–B4, P–B4 11 QN–Q2, N–K2 12 B–N5!± (Lasker–Marshall, New York 1924).

[2] For 7 . . . P–QB4, see Game 18 and column 35.

[3] B–K3 leads to Idea Var. 20.

[4] Better is 13 . . . BxB 14 RxB, P–B4 15 R–Q1, B–N2 16 R–B2, QR–Q1 17 RxR, RxR 18 R–Q2, RxR 19 NxR, N–B3= (Capablanca).

[5] Lasker–Capablanca, 1914.

[6] Lasker–Steinitz, 1894.

[7] This strong move forces Black to play P–B3 and blocks the King Knight's most natural square.

[8] If 5 . . . B–KN5 then 6 P–KR3, B–R4 7 P–KN4, B–N3 8 NxP, B–QB4 9 Q–K2, Q–B3 10 NxB, RPxN∓ (Rabinowitsch–Tolush, 1937). For 5 . . . B–QB4 see Game 19.

[9] Or 6 P–Q3, B–Q3 7 B–K3, P–QB4 8 N–K2, N–K2 9 N–N3, B–K3 10 P–B3, Q–Q2 11 O–O, O–O 12 Q–B2, N–B3= (Romanowski–Botvinnik, 1935).

[10] 8 . . . B–Q3 leads to Idea Var. 19.

[11] Bronstein–Smyslov, Zurich 1953.

[12] Ivkovic–Sokolov (14th Championship of Yugoslavia 1959).

*Lopez Game 18*

*WHITE: Werlinski* *BLACK: Alekhine*

*St. Petersburg 1909*

| | WHITE | BLACK | | WHITE | BLACK | | WHITE | BLACK |
|---|---|---|---|---|---|---|---|---|
| 1 | P–K4 | P–K4 | 11 | P–QB3? | O–O–O | 21 | N–Q4 | B–N6 |
| 2 | N–KB3 | N–QB3 | 12 | N–Q2 | B–B7 | 22 | K–K2 | RxP |
| 3 | B–N5 | P–QR3 | 13 | P–B3 | B–B4 | 23 | B–N2 | RxN† |
| 4 | BxN | QPxB | 14 | P–QR4 | N–B3 | 24 | KxR | N–K3 |
| 5 | P–Q4 | PxP | 15 | B–R3 | B–K6! | 25 | R–R3 | NxN |
| 6 | QxP | QxQ | 16 | N–KB1 | B–R2 | 26 | K–B4 | B–B4 |
| 7 | NxQ | P–QB4 | 17 | P–R5 | R–Q6 | 27 | KR–R1 | N–K7† |
| 8 | N–K2 | B–Q2 | 18 | P–B5 | KR–Q1 | 28 | K–N4 | B–K3† |
| 9 | P–QN3 | P–B5 | 19 | K–B2 | N–Q2 | | Resigns | |
| 10 | PxP | B–R5 | 20 | N–K3 | NxP | | | |

*Lopez Game 19*

*WHITE: Capablanca* *BLACK: Janowski*

*St. Petersburg 1914*

| | WHITE | BLACK | | WHITE | BLACK | | WHITE | BLACK |
|---|---|---|---|---|---|---|---|---|
| 1 | P–K4 | P–K4 | 12 | P–QN4 | N–B2 | 23 | R–B2 | PxP |
| 2 | N–KB3 | N–QB3 | 13 | P–QR4 | BxN | 24 | PxP | N–B5 |
| 3 | B–N5 | P–QR3 | 14 | RxB | P–QN3 | 25 | P–B5 | NxN |
| 4 | BxN | QPxB | 15 | P–N5 | BPxP | 26 | PxN | QxQP |
| 5 | N–B3 | B–QB4 | 16 | PxP | P–QR4 | 27 | P–B6† | K–N1 |
| 6 | P–Q3 | B–KN5 | 17 | N–Q5 | Q–B4 | 28 | PxR | QxP/2 |
| 7 | B–K3 | BxB | 18 | P–B4 | N–N4 | 29 | P–Q5 | R–K1 |
| 8 | PxB | Q–K2 | 19 | R–B2 | N–K3 | 30 | P–Q6 | PxP |
| 9 | O–O | O–O–O | 20 | Q–B3 | R–Q2 | 31 | Q–B6 | Resigns |
| 10 | Q–K1 | N–R3 | 21 | R–Q1 | K–N2 | | | |
| 11 | R–N1 | P–B3 | 22 | P–Q4 | Q–Q3 | | | |

---

1 P–K4, P–K4
2 N–KB3, N–QB3
3 B–N5, P–QR3
4 B–R4, P–QN4
5 B–N3, N–R4

## part 10—WING VARIATION

Key Position 10

### OBSERVATIONS ON KEY POSITION 10

In this line, Black seeks the advantage of the "two Bishops," particularly to swap off White's dangerous King Bishop. While the general idea is laudable, it consumes valuable time and impairs Black's Pawn structure.

### IDEA VARIATIONS 21 AND 22:

(21) 6 P–Q4, PxP 7 QxP, NxB 8 RPxN, N–K2 9 B–N5!, P–KB3 10 B–K3, N–B3 11 Q–Q5, B–K2 12 O–O, B–N2 13 P–B4±.

(22) 6 BxP†, KxB 7 NxP†, K–K2 8 N–QB3, B–N2 9 Q–B3, N–KB3 10 P–Q4, Q–K1 11 B–B4, K–Q1! 12 O–O–O, B–K2 13 N–N4, NxN 14 QxN, Q–N3 15 QxQ, PxQ∓ (Spasski–Taimanov, Moscow 1954).

PRACTICAL VARIATIONS 38–40:

1 P–K4, P–K4 2 N–KB3, N–QB3 3 B–N5, P–QR3 4 B–R4, P–QN4 5 B–N3, N–R4

| | *38* | *39* | *40* |
|---|---|---|---|
| 6 | BxP† | P–Q4[8] | O–O |
| | KxB | PxP | P–Q3 |
| 7 | NxP† | QxP | P–Q4 |
| | K–K2[1] | NxB | NxB |
| 8 | P–Q4[2] | RPxN | RPxN |
| | N–KB3[3] | N–K2 | P–KB3 |
| 9 | Q–B3[4] | O–O[9] | N–B3 |
| | B–N2 | N–B3 | B–N2 |
| 10 | P–QN4 | Q–Q5 | N–KR4 |
| | N–B5[5] | B–N2 | Q–Q2[12] |
| 11 | Q–K2 | P–B4 | P–B4 |
| | NxN | B–K2 | O–O–O |
| 12 | PxN | R–Q1[10] | N–B3[13] |
| | NxP | PxP | N–K2 |
| 13 | P–KB3 | PxP | QPxP |
| | K–K1 | P–Q3 | QPxP |
| 14 | O–O[6] | N–B3 | QxQ† |
| | N–N4 | O–O | RxQ |
| 15 | P–KB4 | B–B4 | PxP |
| | N–K5 | Q–B1 | P–N5 |
| 16 | N–Q2 | Q–KR5 | N–QR4[14] |
| | NxN | Q–K3 | N–N3[15] |
| 17 | BxN | N–Q5 | PxP |
| | Q–R5[7] | B–Q1[11] | BxP |
| 18 | ∓ | = | B–K3[16] |
| | | | PxP[17] |
| | | | = |

*Notes to practical variations 38–40:*

[1] After 7 . . . K–K1 8 Q–R5†, P–N3 (8 . . . K–K2 9 Q–B7†!) 9 NxNP. White gets a Rook and three Pawns for two minor pieces.

[2] 8 N–B3 leads to Idea Var. 22.

[3] 8 . . . P–Q3? 9 B–N5†, N–B3 10 N–Q3, K–B2 11 O–O, B–N2 12 N–B3, B–K2 13 P–K5, PxP 14 PxP, N–Q4 15 Q–B3†, K–N1 16 BxB, NxB 17 Q–N4, Q–KB1 18 P–QR4, P–KR4 19 Q–K6†, Q–B2 20 QxQ†, KxQ 21 PxP, PxP 22 NxP± (Neshmetdinov–Furman, 1954).

[4] Now 9 B–N5 is answered by 9 . . . Q–K1, followed by 10 . . . K–Q1.

[5] 10 . . . N–B3? 11 NxN†, BxN 12 P–Q5, B–N2 13 P–K5±. Also 10 . . . BxP is weak because of 11 Q–K2, P–Q3 12 N–N4±. White also gains the advantage after 10 . . . BxP? 11 Q–K2, N–N2 12 P–KB3, N–Q3 13 B–N5±.

[6] 14 PxN, Q–R5†∓.

[7] Rabar–Taimanov, 1956. The following moves were 18 QR–K1, K–Q1 19 P–B5, BxQNP 20 R–B4, B–B4† 21 K–R1, Q–K2∓.

[8] 6 NxP?, NxB 7 RPxN, Q–N4 8 P–Q4, QxNP 9 Q–B3, QxQ 10 NxQ, B–N2 11 QN–Q2, N–B3=.

[9] Better is 9 B–N5. See Idea Var. 21.

[10] 12 PxP, PxP 13 RxR, QxR 14 QxNP, O–O∓.

continued ▸

[11] Smyslov–Furman, 1955.

[12] For 10 . . . N–K2?, see Game 20.

[13] After 12 QPxP, QPxP 13 QxQ†, RxQ 14 PxP comes first 14 . . . B–B4† and 15 . . . PxP.

[14] After 16 PxP, PxN 17 PxN, KBxP 18 PxP, B–B4† 19 K–R1, BxP 20 RxP, K–N2 21 R–R2, R–KB1 and 22 . . . QR–B2 Black has sufficient compensation for the sacrificed material.

[15] If 16 . . . BxP? 17 N–B5.

[16] Black gets dangerous counterchances after 18 PxP, BxNP 19 N–B5, BxN 20 NxR, B–Q5† 21 K–R1, B–QB3, with the double threat of 22 . . . BxN and 22 . . . N–R5.

[17] Unzicker–Taimanov, Alekhine Memorial Tournament, Moscow 1956.

*Lopez Game 20*

*WHITE: Spasski* — *BLACK: Taimanov*

| | WHITE | BLACK | | WHITE | BLACK |
|---|---|---|---|---|---|
| 1 | P–K4 | P–K4 | 21 | P–B3 | P–R6 |
| 2 | N–KB3 | N–QB3 | 22 | P–N3 | K–K1 |
| 3 | B–N5 | P–QR3 | 23 | QxP | R–N3 |
| 4 | B–R4 | P–QN4 | 24 | QxP† | B–B3 |
| 5 | B–N3 | N–R4 | 25 | Q–N8† | K–B2 |
| 6 | O–O | P–Q3 | 26 | QxP | R–B3 |
| 7 | P–Q4 | NxB | 27 | B–N5 | R–K3 |
| 8 | RPxN | P–KB3 | 28 | P–QN4 | K–N1 |
| 9 | N–B3 | B–N2 | 29 | Q–N8 | N–N3 |
| 10 | N–KR4 | N–K2? | 30 | K–B2 | N–K4 |
| 11 | PxP | QPxP | 31 | P–N5 | B–K1 |
| 12 | Q–B3 | Q–Q2 | 32 | B–K3 | B–Q3 |
| 13 | R–Q1 | Q–K3 | 33 | Q–B8 | K–B2 |
| 14 | B–K3 | P–N4 | 34 | P–N6 | R–B3 |
| 15 | NxP! | PxN | 35 | B–B4 | B–Q2 |
| 16 | Q–R5† | Q–B2 | 36 | P–N7! | B–K3 |
| 17 | RxR† | BxR | 37 | BxN | BxB |
| 18 | R–Q8† | KxR | 38 | P–N8(Q) | BxQ/B |
| 19 | QxQ | PxN | 39 | QxB | Resigns |
| 20 | QxBP | R–N1 | | | |

1 P–K4, P–K4
2 N–KB3, N–QB3
3 B–N5, P–QR3
4 B–R4, P–QN4
5 B–N3, B–B4

KEY POSITION 11

## part 11—GRAZ VARIATION

### OBSERVATIONS ON KEY POSITION 11

This variation derives from the Austrian chessmaster A. Fink of Graz. Its basic idea is to steer into lines similar to the Giuoco Piano. From a theoretical point of view, all that can be said in its favor is that it is little analyzed and may surprise an unwary opponent.

IDEA VARIATIONS 23 AND 24:

(23) 6 P–B3, P–Q3 7 P–Q4, PxP 8 PxP, B–N3 9 B–K3, B–N5 10 B–Q5 (10 O–O, Q–B3!), Q–Q2 11 BxN, QxB 12 P–Q5, Q–Q2 13 BxB, PxB 14 O–O, N–K2 15 QN–Q2, O–O 16 Q–N3±.

(24) 6 NxP?, Q–N4 7 NxBP? (better is 7 BxP†), QxP 8 R–B1, N–Q5 9 P–Q3, N–B6† 10 K–K2, P–Q4 11 BxP, B–KN5∓. Or 8 . . . QxP† 9 Q–K2, QxQ† 10 KxQ, N–Q5† 11 K–Q1, NxB 12 NxR, NxR and wins.

PRACTICAL VARIATIONS 41–49:

1 P–K4, P–K4 2 N–KB3, N–QB3 3 B–N5, P–QR3 4 B–R4, P–QN4 5 B–N3, B–B4

| | 41 | 42 | 43 | 44 | 45 | 46 | 47 | 48 | 49 |
|---|---|---|---|---|---|---|---|---|---|
| 6 | NxP | – – | – – | – – | – – | O–O | – – | – – | P–B3 |
| | Q–N4[1] | – – | – – | – – | – – | P–Q3 | – – | – – | P–Q3 |
| 7 | BxP†[2] | – – | – – | – – | N–N4 | P–B3 | – – | B–Q5 | P–Q4[20] |
| | K–B1 | – – | – – | – – | P–Q3 | B–N5 | – – | KN–K2 | PxP |
| 8 | BxN | – – | – – | – – | P–Q4 | B–Q5 | – – | P–B3 | PxP |
| | KxB[3] | – – | – – | – – | B–N5† | Q–Q2[13] | – – | NxB | B–N3 |
| 9 | N–N4[4] | – – | – – | – – | P–B3 | BxN | – – | PxN | P–QR4[21] |
| | P–Q4 | – – | – – | – – | QxN | QxB | – – | N–K2 | R–N1 |
| 10 | P–Q4 | – – | P–KR3 | – – | QxQ | NxP | – – | P–Q4 | N–B3 |
| | B–N5† | – – | Q–N3! | – – | BxQ | PxN | – – | B–N3 | P–N5 |
| 11 | P–B3 | – – | PxP | – – | P–Q5 | QxB | – – | PxP | N–Q5 |
| | QxN | – – | N–N5 | – – | B–QB4[10] | N–B3 | – – | PxP | N–R4 |
| 12 | QxQ | – – | P–Q3 | – – | PxN | Q–K2[14] | – – | B–K3 | NxB |
| | BxQ | – – | P–KR4 | – – | N–K2 | QxP | – – | BxB | NxB |
| 13 | PxB | – – | P–R3 | B–K3 | P–B3[11] | R–K1 | QxQ | PxB | QxN |
| | NxNP | NxQP! | BxN | B–Q3 | B–K3 | QxQ | NxQ | QxP | RxN |
| 14 | P–B3 | N–R3 | PxB | P–R3 | K–K2 | RxQ | P–Q4? | QxQ | B–K3 |
| | B–R4 | PxP | R–K1† | NxBP† | NxP | O–O–O | PxP | NxQ | N–K2 |
| 15 | K–Q2! | B–Q2[6] | K–B1 | QxN | B–K3 | P–QN4[15] | R–K1 | NxP | P–Q5 |
| | B–N3 | R–Q1 | R–KB1 | PxN | BxB | B–N3 | P–B4 | NxKP![19] | R–QN1 |
| 16 | P–QR3 | R–QB1 | P–Q4 | N–B3 | KxB[12] | P–QR4 | P–B3 | ∓ | O–O |
| | N–B3 | B–B6[7] | BxP | PxP | = | K–N2 | PxP† | | O–O |
| 17 | K–K3 | ∓ | QxB | PxP | | N–R3 | K–B1[17] | | N–Q4 |
| | K–B2 | | NxBP | RxP | | R–Q4[16] | O–O![18] | | K–R1 |
| 18 | P–K5 | | Q–Q1 | RxR | | ∓ | ∓ | | N–B6! |
| | N–R4[5] | | NxR[8] | BxR[9] | | | | | ± |
| | = | | ∓ | = | | | | | |

*Notes to practical variations 41–49:*

[1] If 6 . . . BxP† 7 KxB, NxN 8 P–Q4, Q–B3† 9 K–N1, N–B3 10 B–K3, KN–K2 11 N–B3, O–O 12 Q–Q2, P–Q3 13 R–KB1±. Or in this line if 8 . . . N–N3 9 R–B1!, N/1–K2 10 K–N1±. 6 . . . NxN is not good because of 7 P–Q4.

continued ▸

[2] 7 NxBP leads to Idea Var. 24.

[3] If 8 . . . QxNP? 9 Q–B3†, White retains the sacrificed Pawn with a good position. Also if 8 . . . NxN 9 O–O, Q–N3 10 P–Q4, BxP 11 P–B3± (Schuch–Fink, 1954).

[4] If 9 N–KB3, QxNP 10 R–B1, P–Q4!, threatening 11 . . . B–KR6 or 11 . . . B–KN5.

[5] With the continuation 19 N–Q2, N–B5† 20 NxN, NPxN 21 B–Q2, K–K3. Though White is a Pawn up, the game is even. Black has chances through the open Queen Knight file. Bishops of opposite colors tend toward a draw (Duckstein–Fink, 1955).

[6] 15 B–K3, N–K3 16 R–QB1, K–B2 17 O–O, KR–Q1∓.

[7] Not 16 . . . R–Q2 as in Dr. Hein-Fink, 1955.

[8] With the continuation 19 N–B3, PxP 20 RxR†, KxR 21 B–K3, N–B7 22 B–B5, R–K1∓ (Sedlacek–Mugenschnabel, 1957).

[9] After 19 O–O–O, P–N5 Black's chances are fair because of White's doubled Pawns. Black's Bishop-pair give some compensation for the Pawn.

[10] If 11 . . . N–K4? 12 PxB, N–Q6† 13 K–Q2, NxBP 14 R–K1, N–B3 15 N–B3, B–R4 16 P–KR3, O–O 17 P–K5, PxP 18 K–K3±. Also if 17 K–K3, N/7xKP 18 NxN, NxN 19 KxN, KR–K1†.

[11] 13 B–Q5?, B–K3 14 P–QB4, PxP 15 N–B3, B–QN5∓.

[12] Liedtke–Nowak, 1958.

[13] After 8 . . . KN–K2? comes 9 BxP†, KxB 10 N–N5†, K–N1 11 QxB.

[14] Dangerous for White is 12 QxNP, R–KN1 13 Q–R6, QxP 14 Q–R3, R–Q1! etc.

[15] If 15 RxP then 15 . . . BxP† 16 KxB, N–N5†.

[16] Regina–Fink, 1954.

[17] If 17 K–R1 then 17 . . . B–B7 18 R–B1 (18 R–K2, O–O–O), B–Q5! etc.

[18] White cannot play 18 PxN because of mate in three: 18 . . . PxP† 19 K–K2, R–B7† 20 K–Q1, P–B7 mate.

[19] Playable too is 15 . . . O–O!

[20] For 7 P–KR3 see Game 21.

[21] 9 B–K3 leads to Idea Var. 23.

## *Lopez Game 21*

*WHITE: Weghofer* *BLACK: Fink*

*Graz 1953*

| WHITE | BLACK | WHITE | BLACK |
|---|---|---|---|
| 1 P–K4 | P–K4 | 4 B–R4 | P–QN4 |
| 2 N–KB3 | N–QB3 | 5 B–N3 | B–B4 |
| 3 B–N5 | P–QR3 | 6 P–B3 | P–Q3 |

| WHITE | BLACK | WHITE | BLACK |
|---|---|---|---|
| 7 P–KR3 | Q–B3! | 19 Q–B1 | NxP† |
| 8 P–Q3 | P–R3 | 20 PxN | RxN |
| 9 O–O | KN–K2 | 21 Q–N2 | RxNP |
| 10 B–K3 | O–O | 22 R–Q3 | B–K3 |
| 11 P–Q4 | B–N3 | 23 R–B3 | Q–K2 |
| 12 PxP | PxP | 24 R–N3 | P–N3 |
| 13 BxB | PxB | 25 K–R1 | K–R2 |
| 14 Q–K2 | N–R4 | 26 N–B3 | BxNP |
| 15 QN–Q2 | NxB | 27 P–R4 | R–Q1 |
| 16 PxN | N–N3 | 28 P–R5 | R–Q8† |
| 17 N–R2 | R–Q1 | Resigns | |
| 18 KR–Q1 | N–B5 | | |

## part 12—SCHLIEMANN DEFENSE DEFERRED

1 P–K4, P–K4
2 N–KB3, N–QB3
3 B–N5, P–QR3
4 B–R4, P–B4

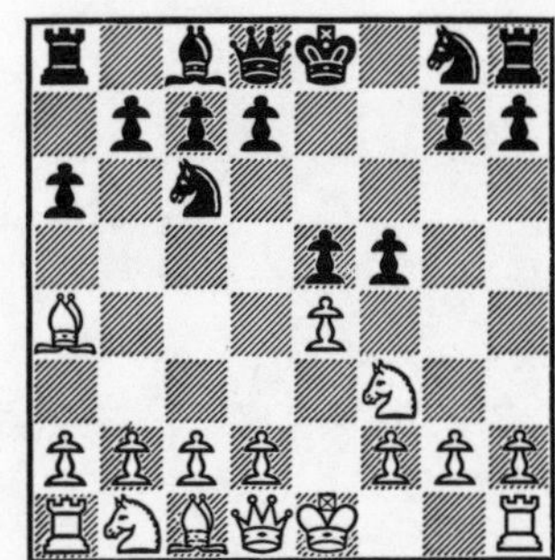

KEY POSITION 12

### OBSERVATIONS ON KEY POSITION 12

This gambit, though similar in appearance to key position 5, is completely independent. The moves 3 . . . P–QR3 and 4 B–R4 introduce brand new tactics.

Until recently, practice has not evoked a substantial refutation. Now, however, 5 N–B3, formerly thought to be inexpedient, has been reinforced by a grand gambit — the sacrifice of a piece. Compare columns 57 and 59 and Games 23 and 24. After more than fifty years, the empirical principle that Black dare not unwarrantedly seize the opening initiative has been confirmed.

### IDEA VARIATIONS 25 AND 26:

(25) 5 P–Q4, PxQP 6 NxP, NxN 7 QxN, P–B4 8 Q–K5†, Q–K2 9 QxQ†, BxQ 10 B–N3, PxP 11 N–B3, N–B3 12 N–Q5, B–Q1 13 O–O, P–QN4 14 NxN†, BxN 15 B–Q5, R–R2 16 P–QB3, B–N2 17 R–Q1± (17 . . . K–K2 18 B–KB4).

(26) 5 P–Q4, PxQP 6 P–K5, B–B4 7 P–B3, PxP 8 NxP, KN–K2 9 B–N3, P–Q4 10 PxP e.p., QxP 11 Q–K2, N–R4 12 O–O, NxB 13 PxN, O–O∓.

## PRACTICAL VARIATIONS 50–59:

1 P–K4, P–K4 2 N–KB3, N–QB3 3 B–N5, P–QR3 4 B–R4, P–B4

| | *50* | *51* | *52* | *53* | *54* |
|---|---|---|---|---|---|
| *5* | PxP | P–Q3[4] | – – | P–Q4 | – – |
| | P–K5 | P–Q3 | PxP | KPxP[7] | – – |
| *6* | Q–K2 | PxP | PxP | NxP | P–K5 |
| | Q–K2 | BxP | N–B3 | NxN | B–B4 |
| *7* | BxN | P–Q4 | BxN | QxN | P–B3 |
| | QPxB[1] | P–K5 | NPxB | P–B4![8] | PxP |
| *8* | N–Q4 | P–Q5 | NxP | Q–K5† | NxP |
| | Q–K4 | PxN | Q–K2 | Q–K2 | KN–K2 |
| *9* | N–K6[2] | PxN | N–KB3 | QxQ†[9] | B–N3 |
| | BxN | P–QN4 | QxP† | BxQ | P–Q4! |
| *10* | PxB | B–N3[5] | B–K3 | P–QB4[10] | NxP[12] |
| | B–Q3 | PxP | B–N5† | PxP | NxN |
| *11* | P–Q3 | R–N1 | P–B3 | N–B3 | BxN |
| | PxP | Q–R5 | B–B4 | P–QN3[11] | N–N5 |
| *12* | QxQ | Q–K2† | QN–Q2 | NxP | B–QB4 |
| | BxQ | Q–K5 | Q–K2 | B–N2 | QxQ† |
| *13* | PxP | N–B3 | O–O | P–B3 | KxQ |
| | K–K2 | QxQ† | O–O | O–O–O | P–QN4[13] |
| *14* | P–B4 | KxQ | R–K1 | B–B4 | B–N3 |
| | B–Q5 | N–K2 | BxB | P–Q4 | B–N2 |
| *15* | P–B5 | = | RxB | = | = |
| | R–KB1 | | Q–Q1 | | |
| *16* | R–B1 | | Q–K2 | | |
| | N–R3![3] | | P–Q3 | | |
| *17* | ∓ | | R–K1 | | |
| | | | B–Q2[6] | | |
| | | | = | | |

*Notes to practical variations 50–59:*

[1] Weaker is 7 . . . NPxB 8 N–Q4, N–B3 9 O–O, Q–K4 10 N–N3, P–Q3 11 P–KB3, B–K2 12 PxP, QxP 13 QxQ, NxQ 14 P–Q3, N–B3 and White is a Pawn up. If 9 . . . P–B4? 10 N–N3, P–Q4 11 P–KB3!, BxP 12 N–B3, Black experiences difficulty in castling.

[2] If 9 N–N3, BxP 10 P–KB3, or 10 P–Q3, B–Q3!=.

[3] White's Pawns at KB5 and K6 cannot be held. If 17 BxN, BxP!

[4] If 5 BxN, QPxB 6 NxP, Q–Q5 7 Q–R5†, P–N3 8 NxNP, PxN 9 QxP†, K–Q1, White's three Pawns do not add up to Black's piece plus his superior development.

[5] If 10 QxBP, Q–K2† 11 K–Q1!, B–K5 12 Q–KR3!, PxB 13 R–K1, White regains his piece in a position of wild complications. But not 11 B–K3, B–K5!

[6] Black is able to swap all the major pieces on the King file.

[7] Faulty is 5 . . . BPxP 6 NxP, N–B3 7 B–KN5, B–K2 8 N–B3. Black is out of good moves, e.g., 8 . . . O–O 9 B–N3† or 8 . . . P–N4 9 B–N3, P–N5 10 N–B7±.

| *55* | *56* | *57* | *58* | *59* |
|---|---|---|---|---|
| – – | – – | N–B3 | – – | – – |
| – – | – – | P–QN4 | – – | – – |
| – – | – – | B–N3 | – – | – – |
| – – | – – | P–N5 | – – | – – |
| – – | O–O | N–QN1?[17] | – – | N–Q5[19] |
| – – | KN–K2 | N–B3 | PxP | PxP |
| – – | B–N3 | P–Q3 | NxP | P–Q4[20] |
| – – | N–R4[15] | PxP | Q–N4![18] | PxN[21] |
| – – | P–B3 | PxP | NxN | QxP[22] |
| – – | NxB | N–QR4 | PxN | B–K2[23] |
| O–O | QxN | NxP | P–Q3 | NxP†[24] |
| B–K3 | P–Q4 | Q–K2 | QxP | QxN |
| N–KN5 | PxP e.p. | N–KB3 | Q–R5† | Q–B7† |
| B–N1 | QxP | QxP† | P–N3 | K–Q1 |
| P–K6[14] | PxP | B–K3 | Q–K5† | QxP |
| N–Q5 | B–N3 | NxB | N–K2 | P–Q4 |
| Q–R5† | R–K1 | RPxN | QxKP | QxR |
| K–B1 | P–R3 | B–B4 | QxQ | B–K3 |
| N–B7 | N–B3 | QN–Q2 | PxQ | PxP |
| Q–K1 | K–B1 | Q–K2 | = | QxP† |
| ∓ | B–B4[16] | O–O | | QxQ |
| | ± | O–O | | NxQ |
| | | R–K1 | | B–KB4 |
| | | B–N2 | | N–N3 |
| | | = | | B–N3 |
| | | | | ± |

[8] With the threat of . . . P–QN4 and . . . P–B5.

[9] Other Queen moves are bad.

[10] Better is 10 B–N3 which leads to Idea Var. 25.

[11] If 11 . . . N–B3 12 B–KN5, O–O 13 O–O–O±. If 12 B–B2, P–QN3 13 NxP, B–N2=.

[12] 10 PxP e.p. leads to Idea Var. 26. For 10 B–N5, see Game 22.

[13] If 13 . . . BxP 14 P–QR3, N–B3 15 R–B1, B–B4 16 P–K6!±.

[14] If 12 Q–R5†, P–N3 13 Q–R6, NxP 14 N–K2! (Q–N7, B–Q5!), N/2–B3 15 Q–N7, Q–K2 16 QxR, O–O–O 17 B–Q2, P–B5! 18 P–KR4, P–B6 19 PxP, B–K3 20 QxP, QxQ 21 NxQ, NxP† 22 K–N2, NxB 23 KR–Q1, NxB 24 PxN, P–Q5!, the position is double-edged. In this line, if 18 BxBP, N–Q6 or 18 NxBP, B–Q5 or 18 N–R3, B–K3.

[15] No better is 8 . . . P–Q4 9 PxP e.p., QxP 10 R–K1, P–R3 11 QN–Q2, P–QN4 12 P–QR4, QR–N1 13 PxP, PxP±.

[16] Not 15 . . . QxB 16 RxN, KxR 17 N–Q5†, etc. (Fuderer–O'Kelly, 1951).

continued ▸

[17] See column 59 and note 19 below. If 7 N–Q5, PxP 8 N–N1?, Q–N4 9 P–KN3, B–Q3 10 Q–K2, Q–N3∓. Also 9 NxP†, K–Q1 10 NxR, QxP∓.

[18] Not 8 . . . NxN? 9 Q–R5†, N–N3 10 Q–Q5, with threats of mate and win of Rook.

[19] Stronger than 7 N–QN1 because of White's new eighth move.

[20] A genial conception in harmony with the position.

[21] If 8 . . . P–Q3 9 B–N5, B–K2 10 BxB, KNxB 11 N–N5, NxP 12 Q–R5†, K–Q2 13 N–B7, Q–K1 14 B–R4† wins.

[22] Threatens 10 NxP†, etc.

[23] If 9 . . . N–B3? 10 PxP, NxN 11 BxN, NxP 12 Q–R5†, N–N3 13 O–O!, P–B3 14 R–K1†, B–K2 15 B–N5, PxB 16 BxB, QxB 17 RxQ†, KxR 18 QxQP, R–QN1 19 R–K1†, etc. Or 13 . . . B–K2 14 R–K1, K–B1 15 RxB!, QxR 16 B–N5, Q–K4 17 Q–B3†, etc.

[24] White recovers all his material. Other moves have been tried here without success — so far! A powerful bind for the piece, which Black can hardly shake, is reached for example, after 10 B–N5, N–B3 11 PxP.

*Lopez Game 22*

*WHITE: Pachman* — *BLACK: Castaldi*

*Hilversum 1947*

| | WHITE | BLACK | | WHITE | BLACK |
|---|---|---|---|---|---|
| 1 | P–K4 | P–K4 | 24 | P–QN4 | K–N1 |
| 2 | N–KB3 | N–QB3 | 25 | Q–Q1 | P–B5 |
| 3 | B–N5 | P–QR3 | 26 | Q–K2 | Q–K3 |
| 4 | B–R4 | P–B4 | 27 | KR–K1 | R–Q4 |
| 5 | P–Q4 | KPxP | 28 | K–R1 | R–K1 |
| 6 | P–K5 | B–B4 | 29 | P–N3! | PxP |
| 7 | P–B3 | PxP | 30 | BPxP | K–R2 |
| 8 | NxP | KN–K2 | 31 | Q–KB2 | R–Q2 |
| 9 | B–N3 | P–Q4! | 32 | R–B1 | Q–Q4† |
| 10 | B–N5 | B–K3 | 33 | Q–N2 | R–K3? |
| 11 | BxN | NxB | 34 | QxQ | RxQ |
| 12 | N–KN5 | Q–Q2 | 35 | K–N2 | B–B2 |
| 13 | O–O | P–B3 | 36 | QR–K1 | P–QR4 |
| 14 | R–B1 | B–R2 | 37 | R–B7 | B–Q1 |
| 15 | N–K2 | B–KN1 | 38 | P–QR3 | R–K2 |
| 16 | N–B4 | O–O–O | 39 | RxR | BxR |
| 17 | N–Q3 | P–R3 | 40 | K–B3 | PxP |
| 18 | N–B3 | P–Q5? | 41 | PxP | K–N3 |
| 19 | BxB | KRxB | 42 | K–K4 | K–B2 |
| 20 | N–Q2 | N–Q4 | 43 | R–KB1 | K–Q2 |
| 21 | Q–R4 | P–KN4 | 44 | R–B7 | K–K1 |
| 22 | N–QB4 | N–N3 | 45 | R–R7 | R–N4 |
| 23 | NxN† | BxN | 46 | P–K6 | K–Q1 |

| | WHITE | BLACK | | WHITE | BLACK |
|---|---|---|---|---|---|
| 47 | RxP | BxP | 61 | Q–Q5† | K–R5 |
| 48 | NxB | RxN | 62 | Q–Q4† | K–N6 |
| 49 | K–B5 | P–Q6 | 63 | Q–Q5† | K–B6 |
| 50 | R–R8†? | K–B2 | 64 | Q–QB5† | K–Q7 |
| 51 | P–K7 | P–Q7 | 65 | P–R4 | Q–N5† |
| 52 | R–B8† | K–N3 | 66 | K–K7 | K–K7 |
| 53 | R–Q8 | R–N4† | 67 | Q–QN5 | Q–K5† |
| 54 | K–K6 | R–Q4 | 68 | K–Q8 | Q–Q5† |
| 55 | RxR | PxR | 69 | K–B8 | K–B7 |
| 56 | P–K8(Q) | P–Q8(Q) | 70 | Q–B5† | K–N7 |
| 57 | Q–Q8† | K–R3 | 71 | P–R5 | P–Q7 |
| 58 | QxNP | P–Q5 | 72 | Q–B2 | Q–N5† |
| 59 | Q–Q5? | P–Q6 | 73 | K–N8 | Q–K7 |
| 60 | Q–R2† | K–N4 | | Resigns | |

*Lopez Game 23*

*WHITE: Blau* *BLACK: O'Kelly*

*Hilversum 1947*

| | WHITE | BLACK | | WHITE | BLACK |
|---|---|---|---|---|---|
| 1 | P–K4 | P–K4 | 26 | P–R4 | B–R3 |
| 2 | N–KB3 | N–QB3 | 27 | NxP! | K–Q3 |
| 3 | B–N5 | P–QR3 | 28 | N–K5 | P–B4 |
| 4 | B–R4 | P–B4 | 29 | P–B3 | BPxP |
| 5 | N–B3 | P–QN4 | 30 | BPxQP | R–B1 |
| 6 | B–N3 | P–N5 | 31 | R–B1 | R–QB2 |
| 7 | N–QN1 | PxP | 32 | RxR | KxR |
| 8 | NxP | Q–N4! | 33 | N–B4 | B–KB1 |
| 9 | P–Q4 | QxP | 34 | K–B1 | K–Q1 |
| 10 | Q–R5† | P–N3 | 35 | B–Q1 | B–K3 |
| 11 | B–B7† | K–Q1 | 36 | B–K2 | B–Q4 |
| 12 | Q–N5† | QxQ | 37 | R–B1 | RxR |
| 13 | BxQ† | B–K2 | 38 | BxR | B–R3 |
| 14 | NxN† | PxN | 39 | K–B2 | K–K2 |
| 15 | B–K3 | N–B3 | 40 | N–K5 | P–N4 |
| 16 | N–Q2 | B–KB4 | 41 | PxP | BxNP |
| 17 | N–B4 | N–N5 | 42 | BxP | BxP |
| 18 | N–R5 | K–Q2 | 43 | N–B6† | K–Q3 |
| 19 | B–N3 | B–R5 | 44 | NxP | B–K3 |
| 20 | O–O | NxB | 45 | B–N7 | B–R5† |
| 21 | PxN | B–N4 | 46 | K–N2 | B–N4 |
| 22 | QR–K1 | QR–KB1 | 47 | BxP | BxP |
| 23 | K–N2! | R–B3 | 48 | N–B2 | B–B8 |
| 24 | B–R4 | KR–KB1 | 49 | P–N4 | B–N6 |
| 25 | K–N3! | P–R4 | | Draw | |

*Lopez Game 24*

*WHITE: Lombardy* *BLACK: Sherwin*

*U. S. Championship, New York 1958-59*

| | WHITE | BLACK | | WHITE | BLACK | | WHITE | BLACK |
|---|---|---|---|---|---|---|---|---|
| 1 | P–K4 | P–K4 | 14 | QxR | Q–B5 | 27 | RxP | Q–R6 |
| 2 | N–KB3 | N–QB3 | 15 | RPxN | Q–K3 | 28 | Q–B2 | B–KR5 |
| 3 | B–N5 | P–QR3 | 16 | R–R5 | B–B3 | 29 | Q–Q2 | B–KN4 |
| 4 | B–R4 | P–B4 | 17 | QxP | B–QN2 | 30 | PxQ | BxQ† |
| 5 | N–B3 | P–QN4 | 18 | B–K3 | N–K2 | 31 | K–B2 | B–B5 |
| 6 | B–N3 | P–N5 | 19 | R–B5 | B–B3 | 32 | P–N4 | R–KR1 |
| 7 | N–Q5 | PxP | 20 | P–KB3 | K–B2 | 33 | K–N2 | R–N1† |
| 8 | P–Q4 | PxN | 21 | Q–Q3 | N–Q4 | 34 | K–B2 | R–KR1 |
| 9 | QxP | B–K2 | 22 | R–Q1 | NxB | 35 | K–N2 | R–N1† |
| 10 | O–O | NxP | 23 | QxN | R–KN1 | 36 | K–B2 | R–KR1 |
| 11 | NxP† | QxN | 24 | R–B4 | K–Q1 | | Draw | |
| 12 | Q–B7† | K–Q1 | 25 | RxP | K–K2 | | | |
| 13 | QxP | NxB | 26 | R–N6 | K–B2 | | | |

---

## part 13—NEO-STEINITZ DEFENSE

1 P–K4, P–K4
2 N–KB3, N–QB3
3 B–N5, P–QR3
4 B–R4, P–Q3

KEY POSITION 13

OBSERVATIONS ON KEY POSITION 13

This system is distinguished from the Steinitz Defense by the interpolation of the moves 3 . . . P–QR3 and 4 B–R4. Because Black is ready for an immediate . . . P–QN4, driving the Bishop and relieving the indirect pressure on his King Pawn, he is not compelled to abandon the center by the exchange . . . PxP. Hence, Black's chances are enhanced.

Under the circumstances it is difficult for White to maintain the initiative. Usual moves like O–O or N–B3 or P–Q4 are ineffectual. To strengthen the pressure against Black's center, White often relies on KBxQN, but this involves giving up a Bishop for a Knight. Otherwise White may play his King Bishop to QN3 or QB2. In the latter case, he must provide a retreat for his Bishop by first playing P–QB3 or P–QB4.

IDEA VARIATIONS 27–29:

(27) 5 P–B3, B–Q2 6 P–Q4, KN–K2 7 B–N3, P–R3 8 QN–Q2, N–N3 9 N–B4, B–K2 10 O–O, O–O 11 N–K3, B–B3 (better is 11 . . . R–K1) 12 N–Q5, R–K1 13 PxP, BxP 14 NxB, PxN 15 Q–B3± (Smyslov–Reshevsky, Moscow 1948). If in the above line 13 . . . KNxP, then 14 NxN, NxN 15 P–KB4. For 5 P–B3, B–Q2 6 P–Q4, N–B3 see Part 14.

(28) 5 BxN†, PxB 6 P–Q4, P–B3 7 B–K3, P–KN3 8 Q–Q2, B–KN2 9 N–B3, N–K2 10 O–O–O, O–O 11 P–KR3, B–K3 12 P–KN4, Q–B1 13 B–R6, Q–N2 14 BxB, KxB=.

(29) 5 O–O, B–N5 6 P–B3 (6 P–KR3 can be answered by 6 . . . P–KR4), Q–B3 7 P–Q3, KN–K2 8 B–K3, BxN 9 QxB, QxQ 10 PxQ, P–KN4 11 N–Q2, P–R3=.

PRACTICAL VARIATIONS 60-67:

1 P–K4, P–K4 2 N–KB3, N–QB3 3 B–N5, P–QR3 4 B–R4, P–Q3

| | *60* | *61* | *62* | *63* | *64* | *65* | *66* | *67* |
|---|---|---|---|---|---|---|---|---|
| 5 | P–B3[1] | – – | – – | – – | P–B4[19] | – – | BxN† | – – |
| | P–B4 | – – | B–Q2[9] | – – | B–N5 | B–Q2 | PxB | – – |
| 6 | PxP[2] | – – | P–Q4 | – – | N–B3[20] | N–B3 | P–Q4 | – – |
| | BxP | – – | P–KN3 | KN–K2[14] | N–K2 | P–KN3 | P–B3[25] | – – |
| 7 | O–O | P–Q4 | O–O[10] | B–N3![15] | P–KR3 | P–Q4 | P–B4[26] | B–K3 |
| | B–Q6[3] | P–K5 | B–N2 | P–R3 | BxN | PxP[22] | N–K2[27] | N–K2 |
| 8 | R–K1 | N–N5 | PxP | QN–Q2[16] | QxB | NxP | B–K3 | N–B3 |
| | B–K2[4] | P–Q4 | PxP[11] | N–N3 | N–N3 | B–N2 | N–N3 | N–N3[30] |
| 9 | R–K3 | P–B3 | B–KN5 | N–B4 | N–Q5 | B–K3[23] | N–B3 | Q–Q2[31] |
| | P–K5 | P–K6[5] | KN–K2 | B–K2 | R–QN1 | KN–K2 | B–K2 | B–K2[32] |
| 10 | N–K1 | P–KB4[6] | Q–Q3 | O–O | N–N4 | O–O | P–B5[28] | P–KR4 |
| | BxN | B–Q3[7] | P–R3 | O–O | N–K2 | O–O | B–Q2 | P–KR4[33] |
| 11 | RxB | Q–R5†[8] | B–K3 | N–K3 | N–B2 | R–B1 | N–Q2 | O–O–O |
| | N–B3 | P–N3 | N–R4[12] | R–K1[17] | Q–Q2 | NxN | PxBP | B–K3 |
| 12 | P–Q3 | Q–B3 | BxB† | R–K1 | P–Q3 | BxN | PxBP | PxP[34] |
| | P–Q4 | Q–B3 | QxB | B–KB1 | N–B1 | QBxB | O–O | BPxP |
| 13 | R–R3 | QxP† | QxQ† | B–B2 | B–Q2 | NxB | O–O | N–KN5 |
| | ± | N–K2 | KxQ | N–R5 | B–K2 | BxB | P–QR4[29] | BxN |
| 14 | | O–O | N–R3 | NxN | Q–N3 | QxB | ± | BxB |
| | | O–O | K–K3[13] | QxN | B–B3[21] | N–B3[24] | | Q–N1 |
| 15 | | ± | = | N–Q5 | = | = | | P–QN3 |
| | | | | QR–B1 | | | | Q–N5 |
| 16 | | | | R–B1 | | | | P–B3 |
| | | | | N–K2 | | | | P–R4 |
| 17 | | | | N–K3 | | | | N–R4 |
| | | | | N–N3[18] | | | | P–B4[35] |
| | | | | = | | | | ∓ |

*Notes to practical variations 60–67:*

[1] 5 N–B3, B–Q2 6 O–O, P–KN3 7 P–Q4, B–N2=. For 5 P–Q4 see Game 25 and for 5 O–O see Idea Var. 29.

[2] 6 P–Q4?, PxKP 7 NxP, PxN 8 Q–R5†, K–K2 9 BxN, PxB 10 B–N5†, N–B3 11 PxP, Q–Q4! 12 B–R4, K–K3 13 BxN, PxB 14 Q–K8†, K–B4 15 Q–R5† draws by perpetual check (Foltys–Kottnauer, Amsterdam 1950).

continued ▸

[3] Or 7 . . . B–K2 8 P–Q4, P–K5 9 P–Q5, PxN 10 PxN, P–QN4 11 B–N3, PxP 12 R–K1± (Panov–Loewenfisch, 1948).

[4] Or 8 . . . KN–K2 9 R–K3, P–K5 10 N–K1, N–B4 11 R–R3± (Boleslavski–Ragozin, 1949).

[5] 9 . . . PxP? 10 O–O!± (Keres).

[6] 10 BxP?, P–R3 11 N–KR3, BxKN 12 PxB, Q–B3 13 Q–Q3, B–Q3 14 N–Q2, N–K2 15 B–QB2, Q–R5† 16 B–B2, QxRP∓ (Ragozin–Tolush, 1945).

[7] Or 10 . . . N–B3 11 N–B3, B–KN5 12 BxN†, PxB 13 O–O±.

[8] To deprive Black of his KN3 later on.

[9] For 5 . . . N–B3 see Game 26.

[10] 7 B–KN5 leads to Game 27.

[11] 8 . . . NxP? 9 NxN, PxN 10 P–KB4, KN–K2 11 P–B5, P–KB3 12 B–K3, BxB 13 QxB†, Q–Q2 14 QxQ†, KxQ 15 P–B4± (Keres–Goldenov, 1952).

[12] 11 . . . B–N5? 12 Q–K2, O–O 13 B–B5± (Alekhine).

[13] Wade–Bronstein, Amsterdam 1954.

[14] 6 . . . N–B3 7 O–O leads to the Russian Defense (see Part 14).

[15] Or 7 P–KR4, P–R3 8 B–K3, PxP 9 PxP, P–Q4 10 P–K5, P–QN4 11 B–B2, N–R4 12 N–B3, B–N5 13 P–R4, P–QB3= (Euwe–Reshevsky, 1948).

[16] 8 N–R4, N–B1 9 N–B5, P–KN3 10 N–N3, B–N2 11 O–O, PxP 12 P–KB4, PxP 13 NxP, N–N3 14 P–B5 with sharp play for both sides (Geller–Keres, 1950).

[17] 11 . . . B–B3 leads to Idea Var. 27.

[18] 18 P–KN3, Q–R6 19 P–KB4, PxBP 20 PxP, P–KB4!= (Bronstein–Keres, 1948).

[19] The Duras Variation. The move prevents . . . P–QN4 and . . . P–Q4.

[20] Another possibility is 6 P–Q3, N–B3 7 N–B3, N–Q2 8 P–KR3, BxN 9 QxB, B–K2 10 O–O, O–O 11 N–K2, N–B4 12 BxN, PxB 13 N–N3, B–N4= (Prins–Rossolimo, Venice 1949).

[21] Keres–Reshevsky, 1948.

[22] 7 . . . B–N2 8 PxP, PxP 9 N–Q5, N–B3 10 B–KN5± (Fine).

[23] Or 9 NxN, PxN 10 O–O, N–K2 (10 . . . N–B3!) 11 P–B5± (Boleslavski–Fine, 1945).

[24] Analysis by Keres.

[25] Another possibility is 6 . . . PxP 7 NxP, P–QB4 8 N–KB3, N–B3 9 O–O, B–N2 10 R–K1, B–K2 11 N–B3, O–O 12 B–B4, R–K1 13 Q–Q3, N–Q2 (Milic–Keres, Belgrade 1956).

[26] For 7 B–K3 see Idea Var. 28. Compare also Game 28.

[27] 7 . . . B–K3? 8 Q–R4, B–Q2 9 P–B5, PxQP 10 QxQP, PxP 11 Q–B3, B–Q3 12 B–K3, Q–N1 13 O–O, Q–N5 14 KR–B1± (Trifunovic–Milic, 1954).

[28] For 10 P–KR4 see Game 29.

[29] Bertok–Filip, 1955.

[30] Or 8 . . . R–QN1 9 Q–Q2!, N–N3 10 O–O–O, B–K2 11 P–KR4± (Szily–Sliwa, 1952). If after 8 . . . R–QN1 9 Q–Q2!, RxP? 10 O–O–O, R–QN1 11 PxP, BPxP 12 NxP, B–K3 13 N–Q3, Q–B1 14 N–B4, Q–N2 15 Q–Q3±.

[31] White can also play 9 Q–Q3, B–K2 10 P–KR4, P–KR4 11 O–O–O, B–N5 12 QR–N1, Q–Q2 13 N–Q2, PxP 14 BxP, N–K4 15 Q–B1± (Matanovic–Poulsen, Moscow 1956).

[32] Another possibility is 9 . . . P–QR4 10 P–KR4, P–KR4 11 O–O–O, B–K2 12 N–K2, B–K3 13 Q–B3, R–R3 14 PxP, BPxP 15 N–KN5, B–N1 16 P–KN3, Q–N1=.

[33] 10 . . . O–O? 11 P–R5, N–R1 12 O–O–O, B–N5 13 QR–N1, Q–K1 14 N–KR4, BxP 15 P–KN4, B–N3 16 P–B4± (Lilienthal–Bondarevski, Parnu 1947).

[34] 12 P–Q5?, PxP 13 NxQP, Q–Q2 14 Q–R5, B–Q1∓.

[35] Ivkov–Smyslov, Belgrade 1956.

*Lopez Game 25*

*WHITE: Stoltz* *BLACK: Alekhine*

*Bled 1931*

| | WHITE | BLACK | | WHITE | BLACK | | WHITE | BLACK |
|---|---|---|---|---|---|---|---|---|
| 1 | P–K4 | P–K4 | 15 | Q–Q3 | P–N5 | 29 | K–R3 | B–K6 |
| 2 | N–KB3 | N–QB3 | 16 | N–K2 | Q–B3 | 30 | R–B1 | R–Q4! |
| 3 | B–N5 | P–QR3 | 17 | P–KB3 | P–Q4! | 31 | N–B4 | Q–Q2† |
| 4 | B–R4 | P–Q3 | 18 | PxP | NxP | 32 | P–N4 | R–Q5 |
| 5 | P–Q4 | P–QN4 | 19 | QR–K1 | B–B3 | 33 | Q–KN2 | P–QB3 |
| 6 | B–N3 | NxP | 20 | P–QB4 | Q–B4† | 34 | N–R5 | B–N4 |
| 7 | NxN | PxN | 21 | R–B2 | N–K6 | 35 | Q–K2 | P–N3 |
| 8 | B–Q5 | R–N1 | 22 | P–QN3 | QR–Q1 | 36 | N–N3 | P–KR4 |
| 9 | B–B6† | B–Q2 | 23 | BxN | RxB | 37 | N–K4 | QxP†! |
| 10 | BxB† | QxB | 24 | Q–B2 | B–R5 | 38 | QxQ | PxQ† |
| 11 | QxP | N–B3 | 25 | P–N3 | RxBP | 39 | KxP | RxN† |
| 12 | N–B3 | B–K2 | 26 | QR–KB1 | B–N4 | 40 | KxB | K–N2 |
| 13 | O–O | O–O | 27 | K–N2 | RxR† | | Resigns | |
| 14 | B–Q2 | KR–K1 | 28 | RxR | Q–B3† | | | |

*Lopez Game 26*

*WHITE: Tal* *BLACK: Averbach*

*26th Championship of USSR, Tbilisi 1959*

| | WHITE | BLACK | | WHITE | BLACK | | WHITE | BLACK |
|---|---|---|---|---|---|---|---|---|
| 1 | P–K4 | P–K4 | 18 | N–Q2 | P–Q4 | 35 | P–R5 | N–Q4 |
| 2 | N–KB3 | N–QB3 | 19 | PxP | NxP | 36 | P–R6 | N–N3 |
| 3 | B–N5 | P–QR3 | 20 | B–B5 | B–K2 | 37 | R–R5 | P–B3 |
| 4 | B–R4 | P–Q3 | 21 | N–K4 | BxB | 38 | P–R7 | R–R7† |
| 5 | P–B3 | N–B3 | 22 | NxB | N–B5 | 39 | K–N3 | R–QN7 |
| 6 | P–Q4 | N–Q2 | 23 | QxQ | KRxQ | 40 | R–N5 | N–R1 |
| 7 | P–QR3 | B–K2 | 24 | BxP | BxP | 41 | N–Q6 | K–R2 |
| 8 | P–QN4 | O–O | 25 | KR–Q1 | B–B6 | 42 | R–N8 | N–B2 |
| 9 | O–O | B–B3 | 26 | RxR† | RxR | 43 | R–QB8 | P–R5† |
| 10 | B–K3 | P–QN4 | 27 | B–N7 | N–R6† | 44 | KxP | RxP† |
| 11 | P–Q5 | N–K2 | 28 | K–B1 | BxB | 45 | K–N3 | R–N6† |
| 12 | B–N3 | N–QN3 | 29 | NxB | R–Q7 | 46 | K–B2 | R–N7† |
| 13 | QN–Q2 | B–N2 | 30 | P–R4 | RxP† | 47 | K–K1 | R–N8† |
| 14 | P–B4 | PxP | 31 | K–K1 | RxP | 48 | K–Q2 | R–N3 |
| 15 | NxBP | NxN | 32 | R–R3 | R–R8† | 49 | N–K8 | Resigns |
| 16 | BxN | P–B3 | 33 | K–K2 | N–B5† | | | |
| 17 | PxP | BxP | 34 | K–B2 | P–R4 | | | |

*Lopez Game 27*

*WHITE: Bogoljubov* *BLACK: Alekhine*

*Match, Amsterdam 1929*

| WHITE | BLACK | WHITE | BLACK | WHITE | BLACK |
|---|---|---|---|---|---|
| 1 P–K4 | P–K4 | 15 B–K3 | Q–K2 | 29 PxQ | R–Q6 |
| 2 N–KB3 | N–QB3 | 16 Q–K2 | N–Q1 | 30 R–R1 | N–Q3 |
| 3 B–N5 | P–QR3 | 17 B–Q5 | B–B3 | 31 R–R6 | R–N1 |
| 4 B–R4 | P–Q3 | 18 P–B4 | BxB | 32 B–B3 | NxKP! |
| 5 P–B3 | B–Q2 | 19 BPxB | P–KB4 | 33 BxP | BxB |
| 6 P–Q4 | P–KN3 | 20 N–B4 | N–N2 | 34 NxB | R–Q8† |
| 7 B–KN5 | P–B3 | 21 QR–B1 | QR–Q1! | 35 K–R2 | N–Q7 |
| 8 B–K3 | N–R3 | 22 P–Q6 | QNxP | 36 P–R4 | R–K1 |
| 9 O–O | B–N2 | 23 NxN | RxN | 37 N–B3 | NxN† |
| 10 P–KR3 | N–B2 | 24 QxP | Q–Q2! | 38 PxN | R/1–K8 |
| 11 QN–Q2 | O–O | 25 R–B2 | P–B4 | 39 K–R3 | P–R4 |
| 12 PxP | QPxP | 26 P–QR4 | P–KB5! | Resigns | |
| 13 B–B5 | R–K1 | 27 B–Q2 | P–KN4! | | |
| 14 B–N3 | P–N3 | 28 Q–N5 | QxQ | | |

*Lopez Game 28*

*WHITE: Matanovic* *BLACK: Sliwa*

*Zonal Tournament, Sofia 1957*

| WHITE | BLACK | WHITE | BLACK | WHITE | BLACK |
|---|---|---|---|---|---|
| 1 P–K4 | P–K4 | 21 Q–K6 | QxQ | 41 N–B4 | R–N6† |
| 2 N–KB3 | N–QB3 | 22 PxQ | N–Q1 | 42 K–B2 | R–N5 |
| 3 B–N5 | P–QR3 | 23 P–B5 | P–B3 | 43 K–B3 | RxP |
| 4 B–R4 | P–Q3 | 24 B–B4 | N–N2 | 44 N–Q5† | K–B1 |
| 5 BxN† | PxB | 25 PxP | PxP | 45 NxP | N–Q3 |
| 6 P–Q4 | P–B3 | 26 N–R4 | K–R1 | 46 K–N3 | R–Q5 |
| 7 B–K3 | R–N1 | 27 P–B4 | R–N1 | 47 N–Q7† | K–K2 |
| 8 P–QN3 | N–K2 | 28 N–N6 | R–N5 | 48 NxP | K–B3 |
| 9 N–B3 | N–N3 | 29 B–Q2 | QR–N1 | 49 N–Q7† | K–K2 |
| 10 Q–Q3 | B–K2 | 30 B–B3 | R–B5 | 50 N–K5 | K–B3 |
| 11 O–O–O! | P–QR4 | 31 QR–B1 | RxR† | 51 N–N4† | K–N4 |
| 12 P–KR4 | PxP | 32 RxR | R–N6 | 52 N–K3 | P–R4 |
| 13 NxP | N–K4 | 33 N–B8 | RxB† | 53 K–B3 | R–B5† |
| 14 Q–K2 | B–Q2 | 34 K–Q2 | R–N6 | 54 K–K2 | RxR |
| 15 P–B4 | N–B2 | 35 NxB | P–Q4 | 55 KxR | K–B3 |
| 16 P–KN4 | O–O | 36 PxP | PxP | 56 P–R3 | N–K5 |
| 17 P–N5 | P–QB4 | 37 NxP | K–N2 | 57 P–N4 | PxP |
| 18 N–B5 | BxN | 38 N–B4 | K–B1 | 58 PxP | N–N4 |
| 19 PxB | Q–Q2 | 39 N–R5 | R–N7† | 59 P–N5 | P–R5 and Resigns |
| 20 B–Q2 | KR–K1 | 40 K–K3 | K–K2 | | |

### *Lopez Game 29*

*WHITE: Walther* — *BLACK: Keres*

*Zurich 1959*

| | WHITE | BLACK | | WHITE | BLACK |
|---|---|---|---|---|---|
| 1 | P–K4 | P–K4 | 22 | BxB | NxB |
| 2 | N–KB3 | N–QB3 | 23 | N–B4 | Q–N6 |
| 3 | B–N5 | P–QR3 | 24 | N–K3 | P–Q4 |
| 4 | B–R4 | P–Q3 | 25 | PxP | PxP |
| 5 | BxN† | PxB | 26 | N–B2 | P–Q5 |
| 6 | P–Q4 | P–B3 | 27 | N–N5 | R–QN1 |
| 7 | P–B4 | N–K2 | 28 | P–R4 | O–O |
| 8 | B–K3 | N–N3 | 29 | QxP | N–B3 |
| 9 | N–B3 | B–K2 | 30 | QxBP | KR–B1 |
| 10 | P–KR4 | P–KR4 | 31 | Q–B4 | N–N5 |
| 11 | Q–R4 | B–Q2 | 32 | N/2xP | RxP† |
| 12 | P–B5 | Q–N1 | 33 | K–Q2 | QxP† |
| 13 | O–O–O | P–R4 | 34 | K–K1 | R–K1 |
| 14 | PxKP | BPxP | 35 | Q–Q2 | B–R6† |
| 15 | N–Q2 | R–QR3 | 36 | K–B2 | N–Q6† |
| 16 | Q–B4 | B–QB1 | 37 | K–N1 | R–K8† |
| 17 | P–KN3 | Q–N5 | 38 | K–R2 | RxR† |
| 18 | Q–K2 | R–R1 | 39 | KxR | N–B7† |
| 19 | P–R3 | Q–N1 | 40 | K–R2 | NxR |
| 20 | B–N5 | B–N5 | 41 | QxQ | NxQ |
| 21 | P–B3 | B–K3 | | Resigns | |

SUPPLEMENTARY VARIATIONS 6–8:

1 P–K4, P–K4 2 N–KB3, N–QB3 3 B–N5, P–QR3 4 B–R4

| | 6 | 7 | 8 |
|---|---|---|---|
| 4 | – – | – – | – – |
| | P–KN3 | – – | KN–K2[3] |
| 5 | P–Q4 | – – | P–Q4 |
| | NxP[1] | PxP | PxP |
| 6 | NxN | NxP | NxP |
| | PxN | B–N2 | NxN |
| 7 | QxP | B–K3 | QxN |
| | Q–B3 | KN–K2 | N–B3 |
| 8 | P–K5[2] | N–QB3 | Q–Q3 |
| | ± | ± | ± |

*Notes to supplementary variations 6–8:*

[1] Weaker here than without 3 . . . P–QR3.

[2] Black lacks the reply 8 . . . Q–N3 which now leads to a shattered Pawn formation.

[3] Recommended by Steinitz.

SUPPLEMENTARY VARIATIONS 9–14:

1 P–K4, P–K4 2 N–KB3, N–QB3 3 B–N5, P–QR3 4 B–R4, N–B3.

Many of these variations arise from the Closed Defense (5 O–O, B–K2; see Parts 20–25), especially after 5 P–Q3 or 5 Q–K2 (see Sup. Var. 11 and 12).

| | 9 | 10 | 11 | 12 | 13 | 14 |
|---|---|---|---|---|---|---|
| 5 | P–Q4[1] | – – | Q–K2 | P–Q3[13] | N–B3[17] | BxN[24] |
| | PxP[2] | – – | P–QN4 | P–Q3 | B–K2 | QPxB |
| 6 | O–O | – – | B–N3 | P–B4[14] | O–O[18] | N–B3 |
| | B–K2 | – – | B–B4[10] | B–N5![15] | P–QN4[19] | B–Q3 |
| 7 | P–K5[3] | – – | P–QR4[11] | P–KR3 | B–N3 | P–Q3[25] |
| | N–K5 | – – | QR–N1[12] | BxN | P–Q3 | P–B4! |
| 8 | R–K1 | NxP | PxP | QxB | N–Q5 | P–KR3 |
| | N–B4 | NxN[8] | PxP | N–Q2 | O–O[20] | B–K3 |
| 9 | BxN | QxN | P–Q3 | BxN | P–B3[21] | B–K3 |
| | QPxB | N–B4 | O–O | PxB | NxP | P–R3[26] |
| 10 | NxP | N–B3 | O–O | N–B3 | P–Q4 | = |
| | O–O! | O–O | P–Q3 | P–N3[16] | B–N2 | |
| 11 | QN–B3 | B–K3 | B–K3 | = | R–K1 | |
| | P–B4![4] | NxB | B–KN5 | | N–B3 | |
| 12 | QN–K2[5] | QxN | P–R3 | | NxB†[22] | |
| | N–K3 | P–Q4 | BxN | | QxN | |
| 13 | NxN | PxPe.p. | QxB | | B–N5 | |
| | QxQ | BxP | N–Q5 | | P–R3 | |
| 14 | RxQ | QR–Q1[9] | = | | B–R4 | |
| | BxN | ± | | | P–K5 | |
| 15 | N–Q4![6] | | | | BxN! | |
| | B–B1[7] | | | | QxB | |
| 16 | ∓ | | | | RxP[23] | |
| | | | | | = | |

*Notes to supplementary variations 9–14:*

[1] Prematurely snaps the center tension.

[2] If 5 . . . NxKP 6 O–O transposes into the Open Defense. Weaker is 5 . . . NxQP 6 NxN, PxN 7 P–K5, N–K5 8 QxP, N–B4 9 N–B3, B–K2 10 Q–KN4, K–B1± (Szabo–Pachman, 1948).

[3] 7 R–K1 is harmless after . . . P–QN4 8 P–K5, NxP. E.g., 9 RxN, P–Q3! 10 R–N5, PxB 11 RxP, N–R4∓ (Reshevsky–Euwe, Dubrovnik 1950). In this line if 10 RxB†, QxR 11 B–N3, P–B4∓.

[4] Customary here was 11 . . . R–K1 12 B–K3, B–B1 13 P–B4, P–B3! 14 PxP, QxP 15 Q–B3, B–B4!= (Alekhine–Keres, 1937). In this line, however, 13 Q–R5!, P–KN3 14 Q–N5, QxQ 15 BxQ, P–R3 16 B–B6± (Teschner–Keres, Helsinki 1952). The text move prevents N–B5.

[5] Weaker is 12 P–B4?, N–K3 13 B–K3, NxN 14 QxN, QxQ 15 BxQ, B–K3∓.

[6] Weaker is 15 N–B4?, QR–Q1 16 B–K3, B–B1 17 N–Q3 (17 N–K2, P–B4), P–QN3 18 P–QN4?, P–B5∓ (Vesely–Pachman, 1951).

[7] 15 . . . R–Q1? 16 B–N5! (analysis by Pachman).

[8] . . . O–O leads to Games 30 and 31. 8 . . . N–B4 9 N–B5, O–O 10 Q–N4, P–KN3 11 BxN, QPxB 12 NxB†, QxN 13 Q–N5, R–K1 14 QxQ, RxQ 15 P–KB4, B–B4 16 N–R3, P–B3 17 PxP, R–K3 18 R–B2, R–K8† 19 R–B1, R–K7= (O'Kelly–Smyslov, 1955).

[9] Lombardy–Horowitz, New York 1955–56.

[10] . . . B–K2 occurs in the English Variation. See Part 24, key position 24.

[11] 7 P–B3 leads to Game 32.

[12] Weaker is 7 . . . P–N5? 8 BxP†, KxB 9 Q–B4†, P–Q4 10 QxB±.

[13] Favored by Andersen and later Steinitz to avoid the Open Defense. 5 P–Q3 slackens the pace and can be parried easily with . . . P–QN4 or . . . P–Q3. Lines with 5 . . . P–QN4 will be found in the Pilnik Variation, Part 22, key position 22.

[14] 6 P–B3, B–K2 7 O–O, O–O transposes into Game 33. The text move leads to the Duras system.

[15] If 6 . . . B–K2 7 N–B3, O–O 8 P–Q4.

[16] White is a bit more active.

[17] 5 N–B3 is one of the oldest lines, favored by Tarrasch, Alekhine, and now Keres.

[18] If 6 BxN, QPxB 7 NxKP, NxP! 8 NxN, Q–Q5, etc.

[19] 6 . . . P–Q3 leads to Game 34.

[20] 8 . . . NxP 9 P–Q4, B–N2 10 R–K1, N–R4 11 PxP, NxB 12 RPxN, PxP 13 P–B4, N–B3 14 NxB, QxQ 15 RxQ, BxN 16 PxB, KxN 17 P–B4, P–K5∓ (Karaklaic–Keres, 1956). 8 . . . N–QR4 leads to Game 35.

[21] Recommended by Alekhine.

[22] Not 12 PxP?, NxP 13 KNxN, PxN 14 RxP, NxN 15 BxN, B–B3 16 R–B5 (16 B–N5, P–B3!), Q–Q2! 17 RxB, PxR 18 B–B3, QR–Q1∓ (Keres–Barcza, 1957).

[23] Analysis by Barcza.

[24] The Delayed Exchange Variation without . . . P–KB3, which hardly matters.

[25] 7 P–Q4, the original point of the system, is met by . . . B–QN5!

[26] In a match game, Bogoljubov–Alekhine, 1934, Black cleverly continued with N–Q2–N1–B3–Q5!

*Lopez Game 30*

*WHITE: Sanguinetti* *BLACK: Matanovic*

*Interzonal Tournament, Portoroz 1958*

| | WHITE | BLACK | | WHITE | BLACK |
|---|---|---|---|---|---|
| 1 | P–K4 | P–K4 | 27 | R–KB1 | P–KN3 |
| 2 | N–KB3 | N–QB3 | 28 | B–N5? | P–R3 |
| 3 | B–N5 | P–QR3 | 29 | RxN | RxR |
| 4 | B–R4 | N–B3 | 30 | R–K1 | QR–K1 |
| 5 | O–O | B–K2 | 31 | BxP | K–B3 |
| 6 | P–Q4 | PxP | 32 | BxR | RxB |
| 7 | P–K5 | N–K5 | 33 | B–N5† | K–B2 |
| 8 | NxP | O–O | 34 | RxR | KxR |
| 9 | P–QB3!? | NxKP | 35 | K–B2 | K–Q4 |
| 10 | R–K1 | P–Q4 | 36 | K–K3 | B–R7 |
| 11 | P–B3 | P–QB4 | 37 | B–B6 | P–QN4 |
| 12 | PxN | PxN | 38 | K–B3 | K–K3 |
| 13 | BPxP | B–KN5 | 39 | B–N5 | B–Q3 |
| 14 | Q–Q2 | N–N3 | 40 | P–KN4 | PxP |
| 15 | P–K5 | P–B3 | 41 | KxP | B–B1 |
| 16 | P–K6 | Q–Q3 | 42 | B–Q8 | B–R3 |
| 17 | B–Q7 | KR–Q1 | 43 | B–B7 | B–K6 |
| 18 | P–KR3 | B–B4 | 44 | B–K5 | K–Q4 |
| 19 | N–B3 | N–B1 | 45 | P–QN3 | K–K5 |
| 20 | Q–B4 | B–K5 | 46 | B–B7 | B–Q7 |
| 21 | QxQ | BxQ | 47 | P–Q5 | KxP |
| 22 | NxB | PxN | 48 | B–B4 | B–K8 |
| 23 | B–R4 | NxP | 49 | K–N5 | K–Q5 |
| 24 | B–N3 | K–B2 | 50 | KxP | K–B6 |
| 25 | RxP | R–K1 | 51 | B–K5† | K–B7 |
| 26 | B–Q2 | P–B4 | 52 | B–B6 | Draw |

*Lopez Game 31*

*WHITE: Gufeld* *BLACK: Keres*

*Championship of USSR, Tbilisi 1959*

| | WHITE | BLACK | | WHITE | BLACK |
|---|---|---|---|---|---|
| 1 | P–K4 | P–K4 | 11 | PxB | QxP |
| 2 | N–KB3 | N–QB3 | 12 | BxN | PxB |
| 3 | B–N5 | P–QR3 | 13 | Q–B3 | Q–B3 |
| 4 | B–R4 | N–B3 | 14 | N–R3 | Q–N3 |
| 5 | O–O | B–K2 | 15 | B–B4 | N–Q3 |
| 6 | P–Q4 | PxP | 16 | P–B3 | KR–K1 |
| 7 | P–K5 | N–K5 | 17 | KR–K1 | R–K5 |
| 8 | NxP | O–O | 18 | RxR | BxR |
| 9 | N–B5 | P–Q4 | 19 | Q–N3 | Draw |
| 10 | PxP e.p. | BxN | | | |

*Lopez Game 32*

*WHITE: Aronson* *BLACK: Neshmetdinov*

*24th Championship of USSR 1957*

| | WHITE | BLACK | | WHITE | BLACK |
|---|---|---|---|---|---|
| 1 | P–K4 | P–K4 | 16 | BxN | QxB |
| 2 | N–KB3 | N–QB3 | 17 | QN–Q2 | N–K2 |
| 3 | B–N5 | P–QR3 | 18 | N–B1 | N–N3 |
| 4 | B–R4 | N–B3 | 19 | P–KN3 | Q–K3 |
| 5 | Q–K2 | P–QN4 | 20 | N–K3 | QxKRP |
| 6 | B–N3 | B–B4 | 21 | RxP | B–B4 |
| 7 | P–B3 | P–Q3 | 22 | RxN? | PxR |
| 8 | O–O | O–O | 23 | NxP | K–R2 |
| 9 | KR–Q1 | Q–K2 | 24 | R–Q1 | RxP!! |
| 10 | P–KR3 | B–N3 | 25 | KxR | Q–R7† |
| 11 | P–Q4 | B–N2 | 26 | K–K1 | QxP† |
| 12 | P–Q5 | N–QR4 | 27 | K–Q2 | QxN/4 |
| 13 | B–B2 | P–B3! | 28 | N–Q5 | Q–N4† |
| 14 | PxP | QNxP | | Resigns | |
| 15 | B–N5 | P–R3 | | | |

*Lopez Game 33*

*WHITE: Pilnik* *BLACK: Geller*

*Candidates' Tournament, Amsterdam 1956*

| | WHITE | BLACK | | WHITE | BLACK | | WHITE | BLACK |
|---|---|---|---|---|---|---|---|---|
| 1 | P–K4 | P–K4 | 22 | Q–R5 | P–R3 | 43 | R–K5 | R–Q5 |
| 2 | N–KB3 | N–QB3 | 23 | R–N3 | R–K3 | 44 | R–B5 | RxP |
| 3 | B–N5 | P–QR3 | 24 | B–B4? | Q–K1 | 45 | R–B3 | P–QR4 |
| 4 | B–R4 | N–B3 | 25 | QxQ | R/3xQ | 46 | K–Q2 | K–K3 |
| 5 | O–O | B–K2 | 26 | BxBP | R–B2 | 47 | R–Q3 | P–R5 |
| 6 | P–Q3 | P–Q3 | 27 | B–N6 | R–B3 | 48 | K–B2 | K–K4 |
| 7 | P–B3 | O–O | 28 | R–K3 | N–N5 | 49 | PxP | PxP |
| 8 | R–K1 | P–QN4 | 29 | PxN | RxB | 50 | R–Q8 | R–N3 |
| 9 | B–B2 | P–Q4 | 30 | R–QB3 | R–Q3 | 51 | R–Q7 | R–B3† |
| 10 | PxP | QxP | 31 | R–Q1 | KR–Q1 | 52 | K–Q2 | R–QN3 |
| 11 | QN–Q2 | B–N2 | 32 | R–B7 | B–Q4 | 53 | K–B2 | R–B3† |
| 12 | N–K4 | QR–K1 | 33 | K–B1 | R/1–Q2 | 54 | K–Q2 | R–R3 |
| 13 | B–K3 | K–R1 | 34 | RxR | RxR | 55 | R–Q3 | P–R4 |
| 14 | N/3–N5 | Q–Q1 | 35 | B–N3 | BxB | 56 | PxP | R–R3 |
| 15 | NxN | BxN | 36 | PxB | P–N4 | 57 | R–R3 | RxP |
| 16 | Q–R5 | BxN | 37 | K–K2 | P–B5 | 58 | RxP | RxP† |
| 17 | BxB | Q–Q4 | 38 | P–Q5 | K–N2 | 59 | K–K1! | RxP |
| 18 | P–Q4 | P–K5 | 39 | R–Q4 | K–B3 | 60 | R–R5† | K–Q5 |
| 19 | Q–R4 | P–B3 | 40 | RxP | RxP | 61 | K–B1 | P–N5 |
| 20 | B–Q2 | P–B4 | 41 | P–N4 | R–Q1 | 62 | R–R4† | Draw |
| 21 | R–K3 | Q–Q1 | 42 | P–B3 | K–B2 | | | |

*Lopez Game 34*

*WHITE: Keres* *BLACK: Smyslov*

*Candidates' Tournament, Amsterdam 1956*

| | WHITE | BLACK | | WHITE | BLACK |
|---|---|---|---|---|---|
| 1 | P–K4 | P–K4 | 11 | B–K3 | B–Q3 |
| 2 | N–KB3 | N–QB3 | 12 | P–B4 | Q–K2 |
| 3 | B–N5 | P–QR3 | 13 | R–B1 | Q–K3 |
| 4 | B–R4 | N–B3 | 14 | Q–B2 | R–K1 |
| 5 | O–O | B–K2 | 15 | KR–Q1 | N–B1 |
| 6 | N–B3 | P–Q3 | 16 | Q–B3 | P–QR4 |
| 7 | BxN† | PxB | 17 | B–B5 | BxB |
| 8 | P–Q4 | N–Q2 | 18 | NxB | Q–K2 |
| 9 | PxP | PxP | 19 | Q–K3 | B–N5 |
| 10 | N–QR4 | O–O | | Draw | |

*Lopez Game 35*

*WHITE: H. Wolf* *BLACK: Przepiorka*

*Pistyan 1922*

| | WHITE | BLACK | | WHITE | BLACK |
|---|---|---|---|---|---|
| 1 | P–K4 | P–K4 | 18 | PxP | R–K3 |
| 2 | N–KB3 | N–QB3 | 19 | QR–Q1 | B–N2 |
| 3 | B–N5 | P–QR3 | 20 | KR–K1 | P–B5 |
| 4 | B–R4 | N–B3 | 21 | N/4–B5 | R–B1 |
| 5 | O–O | B–K2 | 22 | PxP | PxP |
| 6 | N–B3 | P–QN4 | 23 | R–K2 | P–QR4 |
| 7 | B–N3 | P–Q3 | 24 | P–B3 | N–Q2 |
| 8 | P–Q3 | N–QR4 | 25 | KR–Q2 | N–B4 |
| 9 | N–K2 | NxB | 26 | R–Q8 | R–K1 |
| 10 | RPxN | P–B4 | 27 | R/8–Q6 | BxR |
| 11 | B–Q2 | O–O | 28 | RxB | Q–B2 |
| 12 | N–N3 | Q–B2 | 29 | B–B6 | R–K3 |
| 13 | Q–K2 | R–K1 | 30 | Q–N4 | P–N3 |
| 14 | P–R3 | B–B1 | 31 | Q–N5 | RxB |
| 15 | N–R4 | P–Q4 | 32 | QxR | N–K3 |
| 16 | B–N5 | Q–B3 | | White mates in five. | |
| 17 | Q–B3 | PxP | | | |

# part 14—RUSSIAN DEFENSE

1 P–K4, P–K4
2 N–KB3, N–QB3
3 B–N5, P–QR3
4 B–R4, N–B3
5 O–O, P–Q3

KEY POSITION 14

## OBSERVATIONS ON KEY POSITION 14

More popular than 5 . . . P–Q3 are 5 . . . NxP (the Open Variation) and 5 . . . B–K2 (the Closed Variation). The great distinction between the Russian defense and some others is the location of Black's King Knight. At KB3 it pre-empts . . . P–KB3 and consequently Black is unable to support his center. White's chances as a result of this deployment, however, are not enhanced. Black, for example, can neutralize White's majority in some cases by . . . NxP. Or he may obtain relief by . . . P–QN4 as in the Neo-Steinitz. Also the natural . . . B–Q2, eventually followed by . . . N–QN5, may solve the greater part of Black's problems.

## IDEA VARIATIONS 30–32:

(30) 6 P–B3, B–Q2 7 P–Q4, B–K2 8 R–K1, O–O 9 QN–Q2, PxP (without this exchange, Black's position remains very cramped, as can be seen from Prac. Var. 68. The text — in connection with the next move — attempts to liberate the position) 10 PxP, N–QN5 11 BxB, QxB 12 N–B1, P–B4 13 P–QR3, N–B3 14 P–Q5, N–K4 15 NxN, PxN 16 N–K3 (Bronstein's recommendation).

Black has some difficulties, although it is doubtful whether White can maintain his advantage after 16 . . . NxKP! 17 N–B4, Q–B4 18 Q–B2, N–Q3 19 QxQ, NxQ 20 RxP, N–Q3!

(31) 6 BxN†, PxB 7 P–Q4, NxP 8 R–K1, P–KB4 9 PxP, P–Q4 10 N–Q4, B–B4 11 B–K3 (preferable is 11 P–QB3), P–B5! 12 NxP (12 . . . PxB! 13 NxQ, PxP† 14 K–B1, PxR(Q)† 15 KxQ, B–B7† and Black can at least draw).

(32) 6 P–Q4, P–QN4 7 B–N3 (7 PxP, PxP leads to a drawish game), NxQP 8 NxN, PxN 9 B–Q5, NxB 10 PxN, B–K2 11 QxP, O–O. Black stands well. 9 P–B3 is a gambit of doubtful value.

PRACTICAL VARIATIONS 68–74:
1 P–K4, P–K4 2 N–KB3, N–QB3 3 B–N5, P–QR3 4 B–R4, N–B3 5 O–O, P–Q3

| | 68 | 69 | 70 | 71 | 72 | 73 | 74 |
|---|---|---|---|---|---|---|---|
| 6 | P–B3[1] | – – | – – | – – | BxN† | – – | R–K1[27] |
| | B–Q2 | – – | NxP | – – | PxB | – – | P–QN4 |
| 7 | P–Q4 | – – | P–Q4 | – – | P–Q4 | – – | B–N3 |
| | B–K2[2] | – – | B–Q2 | – – | NxP | B–N5!? | N–QR4 |
| 8 | R–K1 | – – | R–K1 | – – | R–K1[20] | PxP | P–Q4 |
| | O–O | – – | N–B3! | – – | P–KB4 | NxP | NxB |
| 9 | QN–Q2 | – – | PxP | – – | PxP | PxP | RPxN |
| | B–K1[3] | PxP | PxP[10] | – – | P–Q4 | BxP | B–N2[28] |
| 10 | B–N3 | PxP | NxP | BxN[14] | N–Q4 | P–KR3 | B–N5[29] |
| | N–Q2 | N–QN5 | NxN | BxB | B–B4[21] | B–KB4 | P–R3 |
| 11 | N–B1 | BxB[5] | RxN† | QxQ† | P–QB3[22] | N–Q4 | B–R4 |
| | B–B3 | QxB | B–K2 | RxQ[15] | O–O[23] | Q–B3 | B–K2[30] |
| 12 | N–K3 | N–B1[6] | B–KN5[11] | NxP | P–B3 | Q–Q3 | N–B3! |
| | N–K2 | P–Q4[7] | BxB | B–K5 | N–N4 | R–Q1 | P–N5 |
| 13 | N–N4 | N–K5 | QxB† | QN–Q2[16] | K–R1 | NxB[25] | BxN |
| | N–N3 | Q–K1 | Q–Q2 | B–K2 | BxN | QxN | BxB |
| 14 | P–N3 | P–QR3 | QxQ† | NxB | BxN | QxP | N–Q5 |
| | B–K2 | N–B3 | KxQ | NxN | QxB | O–O | P–QR4 |
| 15 | P–KR4[4] | NxN | N–Q2 | B–R6![17] | PxB[24] | QxP | NxB† |
| | ± | QxN | QR–K1 | NxQBP[18] | ± | B–B4 | QxN |
| 16 | | P–K5 | R–Q1[12] | BxP | | B–K3 | PxP |
| | | N–K5 | K–B1 | R–KN1 | | R–Q3![26] | PxP |
| 17 | | P–B3[8] | QR–K1 | N–B6 | | ∓ | Q–Q3! |
| | | N–N4 | B–Q3 | PxN | | | O–O |
| 18 | | P–B4 | RxR† | BxN | | | Q–N5 |
| | | N–K5 | RxR | R–N3 | | | Q–QN3[31] |
| 19 | | P–B5[9] | RxR† | R–K4[19] | | | ± |
| | | = | NxR | ± | | | |
| 20 | | | N–K4 | | | | |
| | | | B–B1[13] | | | | |
| | | | = | | | | |

*Notes to practical variations 68–74:*

[1] To meet . . . P–QN4, . . . N–QR4 and . . . NxB, which, however, is not very serious. Compare Prac. Var. 74. Bad is 6 P–B4, NxP! 7 P–Q4, B–Q2 8 Q–K2, P–B4 9 BxN, PxB 10 PxP, B–K2 and Black is a little better (Spielmann–Rubinstein, Meran 1924).

[2] Inferior is 7 . . . NxKP because of 8 R–K1, N–B3 9 BxN, BxB 10 PxP, PxP 11 QxQ†, RxQ 12 NxP, B–K5 13 B–N5!, B–K2 14 N–Q2, B–Q4 15 QN–B3, O–O 16 N–Q4, KR–K1 17 N–B5, B–K3 18 NxB†, RxN 19 N–N4 (Neshmetdinov–Sliwa, Bucharest 1954). If 13 P–B3?, B–B4† 14 K–B1, BxN! 15 N–B6†, K–Q2 16 NxR, B–Q6†.

[3] To make room for the KN. Better is 9 . . . R–K1 and now:

1) 10 BxN, BxB 11 PxP, PxP 12 NxP, BxP 13 NxP, KxN 14 NxB, QxQ 15 N–N5†, K–N1 16 RxQ, B–B4 and Black has compensation for the sacrificed Pawn.
2) 10 B–N3, P–R3 11 N–B1, B–KB1 12 N–N3, N–QR4 13 B–B2, P–KN3 14 N–Q2, P–B4 and Black holds his own (Neshmetdinov–Szabo, Bucharest 1954).
3) 10 P–QR3 leads to Game 36.

[4] Black has a cramped game (Smyslov–Ljubinski, Moscow 1949)

[5] 11 B–N3 is not bad: 11 . . . P–B4 12 N–B1, B–N4 13 N–N3, P–Q4 14 P–K5, N–K1! with chances for both sides.

[6] 12 P–Q5 has to be considered.

[7] 12 . . . P–B4 leads to Idea Var. 30.

[8] 17 N–K3 leads to Game 37.

[9] 19 . . . KR–Q1 (Hans Muller) seems to guarantee an equal game.

[10] Or 9 . . . NxP 10 B–B4!, BxB 11 QxB†, Q–Q2 12 Q–Q4, B–K2 13 BxN, PxB 14 QxP, K–B1 15 QN–Q2 (Pilnik–Averbach, 1952).

[11] After 12 BxB†, QxB 13 Q–K2, O–O–O! 14 RxB? QxR∓.

[12] Somewhat stronger seems 16 N–QB4.

[13] Boleslavski–Bronstein, 1949.

[14] Recommended by Geller.

[15] Better is 11 . . . KxQ 12 NxP, B–Q4.

[16] Or 13 P–B3, B–B4† 14 K–B1 (14 K–R1, B–B7!), B–B4 15 N–N6†, K–Q2 16 NxR, B–Q6†∓.

[17] Geller, 1954.

[18] If 15 . . . PxB 16 RxN±.

[19] Boleslavski–Sliwa, 1955.

[20] The alternative 8 Q–K2, P–KB4 9 QN–Q2, NxN 10 BxN, B–K2 11 PxP, O–O! gives Black counterchances (12 Q–B4†, K–R1 13 QxBP, R–QN1).

[21] 10 . . . P–B4? is bad. E.g., 11 N–K2, B–K3? 12 N–B4, Q–Q2 13 NxB, QxN 14 P–KB3 and wins.

[22] 11 B–K3 leads to Idea Var. 31. To be considered is 11 P–KB3, N–N4 12 K–R1, BxN 13 BxN, QxB 14 QxB. After 11 P–KB3, Q–R5?! 12 P–B3, N–B7 13 P–KN3, Q–R4 14 Q–K2 the position becomes very wild—probably, however, in White's favor.

[23] 11 . . . Q–R5 leads to the position described in the preceding note.

[24] Smyslov–Loewenfisch, Moscow 1938).

[25] Or 13 R–K1, B–K4! 14 P–QB3, BxN 15 PxB, RxP 16 QxRP, O–O=.

[26] With good attacking chances for Black.

[27] The solid continuation 6 P–Q4 leads to Idea Var. 32.

[28] 9 . . . PxP 10 NxP is better for White.

[29] 10 PxP is another attempt to obtain an advantage. One example: 10 . . . NxP 11 PxP, BxP 12 Q–Q4, Q–K2! 13 N–B3!, P–KB4 14 B–N5 and the result is uncertain.

[30] 11 . . . P–N4 12 B–N3, NxP 13 NxKP!, PxN 14 BxP, P–KB3 15 Q–R5† is enterprising and speculative for White.

[31] With the continuation 19 QxQ, PxQ 20 NxKP, KR–K1 21 N–B4, R–K3 22 P–KB3± (Unzicker–Lehmann, 1953).

## SUPPLEMENTARY VARIATIONS 15–17:

1 P–K4, P–K4 2 N–KB3, N–QB3 3 B–N5, P–QR3 4 B–R4, N–B3 5 O–O

| | *15* | *16* | *17* |
|---|---|---|---|
| *5* | – – | – – | – – |
| | P–QN4 | – – | B–B4[7] |
| *6* | B–N3 | – – | P–B3 |
| | P–Q3 | – – | B–R2 |
| *7* | N–N5 | P–B3 | P–Q4 |
| | P–Q4! | B–K2 | NxKP |
| *8* | PxP | P–Q4 | R–K1 |
| | N–Q5 | B–N5 | P–B4 |
| *9* | P–QB3[1] | P–KR3[4] | QN–Q2![8] |
| | NxB | BxN | O–O |
| *10* | QxN | QxB | NxN |
| | NxP[2] | PxP | PxN |
| *11* | R–K1 | Q–N3 | B–N5 |
| | P–KB3[3] | N–KR4[5] | Q–K1 |
| *12* | = | Q–Q3 | RxP |
| | | PxP | P–Q3 |
| *13* | | NxP[6] | PxP |
| | | = | B–B4 |
| *14* | | | R–K1 |
| | | | $\pm$ |

*Notes to supplementary variations 15–17:*

[1] 9 R–K1, B–QB4! 10 RxP†, K–B1$\mp$ (11 P–QB3, N–N5!).

[2] 10 . . . QxP 11 R–K1! brings Black into difficulties.

[3] Black can hold his own. An interesting variation is: 12 P–Q4, PxN 13 RxP†, N–K2 14 BxP, P–R3 15 BxN, BxB 16 N–Q2, K–B1 with complications.

[4] 9 B–K3 is also possible. 9 R–K1 leads to a variation of the Closed Defense.

[5] 11 . . . P–N3 12 B–Q5! gives White a good game. 11 . . . O–O 12 B–R6$\pm$.

[6] White has sufficient counterchances for the Pawn sacrificed. 13 BxP†, KxB 14 Q–Q5† is also good.

[7] Moller's defense is not quite satisfactory.

[8] Capablanca's recommendation.

### *Lopez Game 36*

*WHITE: Tal* *BLACK: Gligoric*

*Zurich 1959*

| WHITE | BLACK | WHITE | BLACK | WHITE | BLACK |
|---|---|---|---|---|---|
| 1 P–K4 | P–K4 | 16 Q–N3 | P–QN4 | 31 BxB | QxB |
| 2 N–KB3 | N–QB3 | 17 B–B4 | R–B1 | 32 N–B4 | B–B2 |
| 3 B–N5 | P–QR3 | 18 P–B3 | PxP | 33 Q–Q2 | R–K2 |
| 4 B–R4 | P–Q3 | 19 N–N4 | K–R1 | 34 QR–KN1 | QR–K1 |
| 5 P–B3 | N–B3 | 20 PxP | P–KB3 | 35 Q–Q3 | P–N3 |
| 6 P–Q4 | B–Q2 | 21 P–KR4 | Q–Q2 | 36 Q–B5 | K–B1 |
| 7 O–O | B–K2 | 22 N–K3 | B–B2 | 37 Q–N4 | P–N4 |
| 8 QN–Q2 | O–O | 23 K–B2 | P–B3 | 38 N–Q3 | R–K7† |
| 9 R–K1 | R–K1 | 24 P–R5 | BxRP | 39 K–B1 | B–N3 |
| 10 P–QR3 | B–KB1 | 25 R–R1 | Q–KB2 | 40 N–B2 | Q–K2 |
| 11 P–QN4 | P–Q4 | 26 Q–R3 | B–N3 | 41 Q–N3 | P–KR4 |
| 12 BxN | BxB | 27 Q–N4 | K–N1 | 42 K–N2 | P–R5 |
| 13 NxP | NxP | 28 Q–N1 | Q–K3 | Resigns | |
| 14 NxN | PxN | 29 Q–QB1 | B–Q3 | | |
| 15 Q–N4 | B–Q4 | 30 N–N2 | QR–Q1 | | |

*Lopez Game 37*

*WHITE: Szabo* *BLACK: Euwe*

*Budapest 1940*

| | WHITE | BLACK | | WHITE | BLACK | | WHITE | BLACK |
|---|---|---|---|---|---|---|---|---|
| 1 | P–K4 | P–K4 | 15 | NxN | QxN | 29 | PxP | BxP |
| 2 | N–KB3 | N–QB3 | 16 | P–K5 | N–K5 | 30 | N–B5 | K–R1 |
| 3 | B–N5 | P–QR3 | 17 | N–K3 | Q–Q2 | 31 | Q–R5 | R–KN1 |
| 4 | B–R4 | N–B3 | 18 | P–B3 | N–N4 | 32 | R–B3 | B–N4 |
| 5 | O–O | P–Q3 | 19 | P–B4 | N–K5 | 33 | QR–KB1 | QR–KB1 |
| 6 | R–K1 | B–Q2 | 20 | P–B5 | KR–K1 | 34 | N–R6 | BxB† |
| 7 | P–B3 | B–K2 | 21 | Q–B3 | P–QB3 | 35 | RxB | RxR† |
| 8 | P–Q4 | O–O | 22 | P–B6! | B–B1 | 36 | KxR | Q–B3† |
| 9 | QN–Q2 | PxP | 23 | PxP | BxNP | 37 | N–B5 | R–KB1 |
| 10 | PxP | N–QN5 | 24 | N–B5 | Q–K3 | 38 | P–KN4 | QxP |
| 11 | BxB | QxB | 25 | B–K3 | Q–N3 | 39 | QxP†?? | KxQ |
| 12 | N–B1 | P–Q4 | 26 | QR–Q1 | P–B3! | | Resigns | |
| 13 | N–K5 | Q–K1 | 27 | N–R4 | Q–B2 | | | |
| 14 | P–QR3 | N–B3 | 28 | R–KB1 | Q–K3 | | | |

---

## part 15—OPEN DEFENSE I

OBSERVATIONS ON KEY POSITION 15

1 P–K4, P–K4
2 N–KB3, N–QB3
3 B–N5, P–QR3
4 B–R4, N–B3
5 O–O, NxP
6 P–Q4, P–QN4
7 B–N3[A], P–Q4
8 NxP[B], NxN
9 PxN

KEY POSITION 15

[A] Less good is 7 P–Q5, PxB! 8 PxN, P–Q3 9 R–K1, N–B3 10 P–QB4, B–K3 11 QxRP, B–K2 12 N–B3, O–O 13 B–N5, N–R4 14 BxB, QxB 15 N–Q5, BxN 16 PxB, KR–N1 (Zellner–Johner, 1938).

[B] According to Keres 8 NxP, NxN 9 PxN, B–N2 or 9 . . . P–QB3 is good for Black, but he must not play 9 . . . B–K3 because of P–KB4–5.

In this position White can maneuver more easily on the Kingside because his KBP is not blocked by a Knight. The absence of Black's Queen Knight facilitates the development of his other pieces making it easier for Black to equalize.

IDEA VARIATIONS 33 AND 34:

(33) 9 . . . P–QB3 10 P–QB3, B–KB4 11 B–B2, Q–Q2 12 P–QR4, R–B1? (preferable is 12 . . . P–N5) 13 PxP, RPxP 14 B–K3, N–B4 15 N–Q2, BxB 16 QxB, B–K2 17 P–KB4, O–O 18 P–B5, KR–K1 19 B–Q4±. Bronstein–Pachman, Portoroz 1958, continued 19 . . . B–B1 20 R–B3, N–K5 21 NxN, PxN 22 QxP, P–B4 23 B–B2, B–Q3 24 R–Q1, Q–K2 25 P–K6, PxP 26 B–R4, Q–QB2 27 P–B6!

(34) 9 . . . B–N2 10 P–QB3, B–B4 11 N–Q2, Q–K2 12 NxN, PxN 13 P–K6, P–KB3 14 B–KB4, R–Q1 15 Q–N4, B–Q3 16 QR–Q1, O–O 17 P–KR4, BxB 18 QxB, P–QB4= (Darga–Milev, Munich 1957).

PRACTICAL VARIATIONS 75-78:

1 P–K4, P–K4 2 N–KB3, N–QB3 3 B–N5, P–QR3 4 B–R4, N–B3 5 O–O, NxP 6 P–Q4, P–QN4 7 B–N3, P–Q4 8 NxP, NxN 9 PxN

| | 75 | 76 | 77 | 78 |
|---|---|---|---|---|
| 9 | – – | – – | – – | – – |
| | B–K3? | – – | P–QB3[5] | – – |
| 10 | B–K3 | P–QR4 | P–QB3[6] | – – |
| | B–QB4 | N–B4 | B–KB4? | B–K2 |
| 11 | BxB | N–Q2 | B–B2 | B–K3 |
| | NxB | B–K2 | B–B4[7] | O–O |
| 12 | P–KB4 | Q–K2 | Q–K2[8] | N–Q2 |
| | P–KN3 | P–QB3 | O–O | NxN |
| 13 | N–Q2 | P–QB3 | B–K3 | QxN |
| | O–O | NxB[2] | BxB | B–KB4 |

| | 75 | 76 | 77 | 78 |
|---|---|---|---|---|
| 14 | N–B3 | NxN | QxB | KR–K1 |
| | NxB | PxP | N–N6! | Q–Q2 |
| 15 | RPxN | N–Q4 | = | QR–Q1 |
| | P–QB4 | B–Q2 | | Q–K3 |
| 16 | Q–Q2 | P–K6 | | B–N5 |
| | P–N5 | PxP | | B–B4[9] |
| 17 | Q–B2 | RxRP! | | = |
| | Q–N3 | Q–B1[3] | | |
| 18 | Q–R4[1] | R–K1 | | |
| | ± | K–B2[4] | | |
| | | ± | | |

*Notes to practical variations 75-78:*

[1] Kieninger–Bogoljubov, 1951.

[2] Somewhat better is 13 . . . O–O or 13 . . . B–KB4=.

[3] After 17 . . . P–QB4? 18 NxP, BxN 19 QxB Black has no defense against threats like 20 RxRP or 20 R–Q1.

[4] Alekhine–Borochow, 1932. Better is 18 . . . O–O 19 NxP, BxN 20 QxB†, QxQ 21 RxQ, B–B4! 22 B–B4, R–B3 23 RxR, PxR=.

[5] 9 . . . B–N2 leads to Idea Var. 34.

[6] For 10 B–K3 see Game 38.

[7] 11 . . . Q–Q2 leads to Idea Var. 33.

[8] Stronger is 12 Q–B3.

[9] Trifunovic–Donner, Wageningen 1957.

1 P–K4, P–K4
2 N–KB3, N–QB3
3 B–N5, P–QR3
4 B–R4, N–B3
5 O–O, NxP
6 P–Q4, P–QN4
7 B–N3, P–Q4
8 PxP, B–K3
9 P–B3, B–K2[A]

KEY POSITION 16

## part 16—OPEN DEFENSE II

### OBSERVATIONS ON KEY POSITION 16

[A] If 9 . . . N–B4, 10 N–Q4 gives White a positional plus as indicated. This is superior to 10 B–B2; see Games 43 and 44.

1) 10 . . . NxP 11 P–KB4, N–B5 12 R–K1, N–K5 13 P–B5, B–Q2 14 BxN, NPxB 15 N–Q2, etc.
2) 10 . . . NxN 11 PxN, NxB 12 QxN, P–QB4 13 PxP, BxP 14 Q–KN3!, etc.
3) 10 . . . NxB 11 NxQN, Q–Q2 12 PxN, QxN 13 P–QN4±.
4) 10 . . . Q–Q2 11 B–B2, B–K2 12 P–KB4 with good attacking chances.

The Pawn formation is a clue to the subsequent play. White enjoys a Pawn majority on the Kingside; Black on the Queenside. Each must assert himself. White must try to dislodge Black's forward Knight, poise his men in the direction of Black's King for attack with such moves as B–B2 and N–Q4, and finally advance his King Bishop Pawn and possibly his King Knight Pawn to establish a Pawn-rolling demonstration. Black's scope is limited to an eventual . . . P–QB4 and possibly counterplay in the center. Typical for Black is . . . N–R4, . . . P–QB4 and . . . P–Q5, and possibly . . . P–Q5 even without . . . P–QB4. Each side, too, will attempt to contain his adversary. White may resort to such maneuvers as B–K3 and QN–Q2–N3, while Black may meet the assault with a propitious . . . P–KB3 or . . . P–KB4.

IDEA VARIATIONS 35–37:

(35) 10 QN–Q2, O–O 11 B–B2, N–B4? (better . . . P–B4) 12 N–Q4, NxP 13 Q–R5!, N–N3 14 P–B4, B–Q2 15 P–B5, N–R1 16 P–B6 and wins a piece.

(36) 10 QN–Q2, O–O 11 R–K1, N–B4 12 B–B2, P–Q5! 13 PxP, NxQP 14 NxN, QxN 15 Q–K2, QR–Q1 16 N–B3, Q–QB5 17 QxQ, BxQ. Black's Queenside Pawn majority is an important factor. In this line, if 12 N–Q4, NxN 13 PxN, N–Q6 14 R–K3, N–B5 15 B–B2, P–QB4 is also satisfactory for Black. 12 N–B1 leads to Game 42.

(37) 10 QN–Q2, NxN 11 QxN, N–R4 12 B–B2, P–QB4 13 P–QR4, N–B3 14 PxP, PxP 15 RxR, QxR 16 N–N5, BxN 17 QxB, O–O 18 Q–R4, P–N3 19 B–R6 wins. (If 19 . . . Q–Q1 20 B–N5, Q–B2 21 B–B6.)

*Lopez Game 38*

*WHITE: Kieninger* *BLACK: Karaklaic*

*Ljubljana 1955*

| | WHITE | BLACK | | WHITE | BLACK | | WHITE | BLACK |
|---|---|---|---|---|---|---|---|---|
| 1 | P–K4 | P–K4 | 15 | Q–Q4 | Q–K2 | 29 | P–N4 | B–Q2 |
| 2 | N–KB3 | N–QB3 | 16 | B–B2 | P–N3 | 30 | P–N5 | K–K3 |
| 3 | B–N5 | P–QR3 | 17 | QR–K1 | B–K3 | 31 | P–R4 | K–B2 |
| 4 | B–R4 | N–B3 | 18 | P–KB4 | P–KB4 | 32 | P–R5 | K–N2 |
| 5 | O–O | NxP | 19 | PxP e.p. | QxP | 33 | P–R6† | K–B2 |
| 6 | P–Q4 | P–QN4 | 20 | R–K5 | QR–K1 | 34 | K–K3 | B–N5 |
| 7 | B–N3 | P–Q4 | 21 | KR–K1 | P–QR4 | 35 | B–Q3 | B–B1 |
| 8 | NxP | NxN | 22 | P–KN3 | B–Q2 | 36 | K–Q2 | B–N5 |
| 9 | PxN | P–QB3 | 23 | RxR | QxQ† | 37 | K–B2 | B–B6 |
| 10 | B–K3 | B–QB4 | 24 | PxQ | RxR | 38 | K–N3 | B–K5 |
| 11 | N–Q2 | NxN | 25 | RxR† | BxR | 39 | B–R6 | K–K2 |
| 12 | QxN | Q–N3 | 26 | P–QR3 | P–N5 | 40 | KxP | K–Q3 |
| 13 | BxB | QxB | 27 | PxP | PxP | 41 | B–B8 | Resigns |
| 14 | P–B3 | O–O | 28 | K–B2 | K–B2 | | | |

PRACTICAL VARIATIONS 79–85:

1 P–K4, P–K4 2 N–KB3, N–QB3 3 B–N5, P–QR3 4 B–R4, N–B3 5 O–O, NxP 6 P–Q4, P–QN4 7 B–N3, P–Q4 8 PxP, B–K3 9 P–B3, B–K2.

| | 79 | 80 | 81 | 82 | 83 | 84 | 85 |
|---|---|---|---|---|---|---|---|
| 10 | QN–Q2 | – – | – – | – – | – – | Q–K2 | R–K1 |
| | N–B4? | O–O[4] | – – | – – | – – | O–O[15] | O–O |
| 11 | B–B2 | B–B2[5] | – – | Q–K2[9] | – – | B–B2[16] | N–Q4[19] |
| | B–KN5[1] | P–B4[6] | – – | N–B4 | NxN | Q–Q2! | NxKP[20] |
| 12 | R–K1 | PxP e.p. | N–N3 | N–Q4[10] | BxN | R–Q1[17] | P–B3 |
| | Q–Q2 | NxP/3 | Q–Q2 | NxN?[11] | N–R4 | P–B4 | B–Q3 |
| 13 | N–B1 | N–N3 | KN–Q4 | PxN | B–B2 | PxP e.p. | PxN |
| | R–Q1 | B–KN5 | QR–Q1 | NxB | P–QB4 | NxP/3 | B–KN5 |
| 14 | N–K3 | Q–Q3 | NxN | NxN | Q–Q3 | N–N5 | Q–QB2[21] |
| | B–R4[2] | B–R4 | QxN | P–QB3 | P–N3 | B–KN5 | P–QB4 |
| 15 | N–B5 | QN–Q4 | N–Q4 | B–K3 | B–R6 | P–B3 | BxP |
| | N–K3 | NxN | Q–Q2 | P–QR4 | R–K1 | B–B4† | PxN |
| 16 | P–QR4[3] | NxN | P–B3 | KR–B1 | Q–Q2?[13] | K–R1 | BxR |
| | ± | B–N3[7] | N–N4 | P–R5 | N–B5 | QR–K1[18] | Q–R5 |
| 17 | | = | P–QN4 | N–B5[12] | Q–B4 | ∓ | R–B1 |
| | | | N–B2 | ± | NxNP | | P–Q6 |
| 18 | | | P–KB4 | | B–N5 | | Q–B2 |
| | | | P–QB4 | | P–Q5 | | QxQ† |
| 19 | | | PxP | | PxP | | RxQ |
| | | | BxP | | PxP | | RxB |
| 20 | | | K–R1 | | B–K4 | | B–B4 |
| | | | BxN | | B–Q4[14] | | P–B3![22] |
| 21 | | | PxB | | ∓ | | P–N4 |
| | | | P–QR4[8] | | | | P–QR4![23] |
| | | | ± | | | | ∓ |

*Notes to practical variations 79–85:*

[1] 11 . . . P–Q5? 12 N–K4, PxP 13 NxN, QxQ 14 RxQ, BxN 15 B–K4, B–Q2 16 PxP±.

[2] Romanowsky recommends 14 . . . O–O 15 NxB, QxN 16 BxP†, KxB 17 N–N5†, QxN 18 BxQ, BxB. Instead of 16 BxP† Fuderer recommends 16 B–K3 followed by 17 N–Q4.

[3] Bronstein–Makagonov, 1944.

[4] 10 . . . NxN leads to Idea Var. 37.

[5] 11 NxN, PxN 12 BxB, PxB favors Black.

[6] For 11 . . . N–B4 see Idea Var. 35.

[7] Boleslavski–Euwe, Groningen 1946.

[8] White has a slight advantage because of his Pawn at K5 and the Bishop pair. Black aims at the open QB file and has a Pawn majority on the Queenside.

[9] 11 Q–K1 leads to Game 39.

[10] If 12 B–B2, 12 . . . P–Q5 is very strong.

[11] Preferable is 12 . . . NxB, and if:

1) 13 QNxN, Q–Q2 14 NxN, QxN 15 B–K3, B–KB4 16 KR–Q1, Q–KN3 (16 . . . KR–Q1 leads to Game 41) 17 P–B3, P–QB3=.
2) 13 NxQN, NxB! 14 KRxN, Q–Q2 15 NxB†, QxN 16 P–QN4, P–QB4=.

[12] White has considerable pressure on the QB file.

[13] Better is 16 P–QN3.

[14] Tal–Korchnoi, 1955.

[15] To be considered is also 10 . . . N–B4 with the following possibilities:

1) 11 R–Q1, NxB 12 PxN, O–O 13 P–QN4, P–B3! 14 PxP, RxP=.
2) 11 QN–Q2, P–Q5 12 PxP, NxQP 13 NxN, QxN 14 BxB, PxB 15 N–B3, Q–Q6=.
3) 11 B–B2, P–Q5 12 R–Q1, B–B5 13 Q–K1, P–Q6 14 N–R3, Q–B1 15 B–N1, B–Q4 16 BxP, BxN 17 PxB, NxB 18 RxN, Q–B4∓.

[16] Equally playable is 11 N–Q4 after which Black is compelled to defend himself very prudently. For instance:

1) 11 . . . NxN? 12 PxN, P–R3 (White threatens to win a piece by 13 P–B3, N–N4 14 P–KR4) 13 P–B3, N–N4 14 P–B4 and 15 P–B5±.
2) 11 . . . Q–Q2 12 B–B2, P–B4! 13 PxP e.p., BxP=.
3) 11 . . . NxP 12 P–B3! and Black loses a piece without sufficient compensation. For instance: 12 . . . B–Q3 13 PxN, B–KN5 14 Q–K3, Q–R5 15 Q–N5, etc.

[17] If 12 BxN, PxB 13 QxKP, B–Q4, and now:

1) 14 Q–K3, BxN 15 PxB, Q–B4 16 P–KB4, P–B3 with attacking chances for Black.
2) 14 R–Q1, BxQ 15 RxQ, KR–Q1 16 RxR, RxR 17 QN–Q2, Black regains the Pawn with advantage.

[18] 17 Q–Q3 with the double threat 18 PxB or NxP is refuted by 17 . . . N–K4 18 Q–B1, B–B4, etc.

[19] Other possibilities are:

1) 11 QN–Q2, N–B4 12 N–Q4 (12 B–B2, P–Q5 leads to Idea Var. 36), NxN 13 PxN, N–Q6 14 R–K3, NxB 15 RxN, P–QB4 16 PxP, R–B1 17 P–B6, Q–N3 with equal chances (18 KR–QB3, B–QN5).
2) 11 B–B2, B–KN5!∓. 12 BxN, PxB 13 QxQ, QRxQ 14 RxP? is refuted by 14 . . . R–Q8† 15 R–K1, BxN, etc.

[20] The so-called Breslau Variation. Black sacrifices a piece for a strong attack. Other possibilities are favorable to White:

1) 11 . . . Q–Q2? 12 NxB! winning a piece (the famous Tarrasch trap).
2) 11 . . . NxN 12 PxN, P–R3 13 P–B3, N–N4 14 N–B3±.
3) 11 . . . N–R4 12 B–B2, P–QB4 13 NxB, PxN 14 BxN, PxB 15 Q–N4±.

[21] 14 Q–Q2 leads to Game 40.

[22] After 20 . . . R–K1 21 P–N4! is very strong (21 . . . B–B2 22 P–QR4!).

[23] Black has sufficient compensation for the exchange.

*Lopez Game 39*

*WHITE: Keres* *BLACK: Euwe*

*Second Match Game 1939*

| | WHITE | BLACK | | WHITE | BLACK |
|---|---|---|---|---|---|
| 1 | P–K4 | P–K4 | 22 | QxB | N–B5 |
| 2 | N–KB3 | N–QB3 | 23 | P–KN3 | QR–KB1 |
| 3 | B–N5 | P–QR3 | 24 | P–B3 | N–R4 |
| 4 | B–R4 | N–B3 | 25 | Q–K3 | N–N2 |
| 5 | O–O | NxP | 26 | P–B4 | R–K1 |
| 6 | P–Q4 | P–QN4 | 27 | Q–Q2 | R/2–K2 |
| 7 | B–N3 | P–Q4 | 28 | RxR | RxR |
| 8 | PxP | B–K3 | 29 | P–B5! | PxP |
| 9 | P–B3 | B–K2 | 30 | Q–N5 | R–K4 |
| 10 | QN–Q2 | O–O | 31 | Q–B6 | Q–K1 |
| 11 | Q–K1 | N–B4 | 32 | BxP | NxB |
| 12 | N–Q4 | Q–Q2 | 33 | RxN | RxR |
| 13 | B–B2 | P–B3 | 34 | QxR | Q–K6† |
| 14 | NxB | NxN | 35 | K–N2 | P–B3 |
| 15 | N–B3 | PxP | 36 | K–R3 | Q–R3† |
| 16 | NxP | NxN | 37 | K–N2 | Q–Q7† |
| 17 | QxN | B–Q3 | 38 | Q–B2 | Q–Q6 |
| 18 | Q–R5 | P–N3 | 39 | K–R3 | Q–B5 |
| 19 | Q–R3 | R–B2 | 40 | Q–B6 | QxRP |
| 20 | B–R6 | B–B5 | 41 | QxP | Draw |
| 21 | QR–K1 | BxB | | | |

*Lopez Game 40*

*WHITE: Wolf* *BLACK: Tarrasch*

*Karlsbad 1923*

| | WHITE | BLACK | | WHITE | BLACK |
|---|---|---|---|---|---|
| 1 | P–K4 | P–K4 | 14 | Q–Q2 | Q–R5 |
| 2 | N–KB3 | N–QB3 | 15 | P–KR3 | P–QB4 |
| 3 | B–N5 | P–QR3 | 16 | PxB | PxN |
| 4 | B–R4 | N–B3 | 17 | Q–KB2 | QxP |
| 5 | O–O | NxP | 18 | B–Q1 | Q–N3 |
| 6 | P–Q4 | P–QN4 | 19 | QxP | B–B2! |
| 7 | B–N3 | P–Q4 | 20 | B–K3 | PxP |
| 8 | PxP | B–K3 | 21 | N–Q2 | P–B4 |
| 9 | P–B3 | B–K2 | 22 | Q–B5 | QR–B1 |
| 10 | R–K1 | O–O | 23 | R–KB1 | N–Q6 |
| 11 | N–Q4 | NxKP! | 24 | Q–Q5† | K–R1 |
| 12 | P–B3 | B–Q3 | 25 | R–B2 | NxR |
| 13 | PxN | B–KN5 | 26 | BxN | KR–Q1 |

| WHITE | BLACK | WHITE | BLACK |
|---|---|---|---|
| 27 Q–N7 | Q–Q3 | 40 Q–Q6 | P–N4 |
| 28 N–B1 | R–R1 | 41 P–N4?! | PxP† |
| 29 B–QN3 | KR–QN1 | 42 K–K1 | R–K2 |
| 30 Q–Q5 | R–KB1 | 43 B–Q5 | K–N3 |
| 31 B–B5? | Q–R3 | 44 K–Q1 | P–K6 |
| 32 BxR? | RxB | 45 N–B8† | K–N2 |
| 33 R–Q1 | B–N3† | 46 N–K6† | K–N3 |
| 34 R–Q4 | Q–KB3 | 47 N–B8† | K–B4 |
| 35 N–K3 | P–N3 | 48 Q–Q8 | Q–K4 |
| 36 N–B2 | K–N2 | 49 Q–B8† | K–B5 |
| 37 K–B1 | BxR | 50 Q–QB5 | K–N6 |
| 38 NxB | K–R3 | 51 K–B1 | K–R5! |
| 39 N–K6 | R–K1 | Resigns | |

*Lopez Game 41*

*WHITE: Botvinnik* *BLACK: Euwe*

*Leningrad 1940*

| WHITE | BLACK | WHITE | BLACK |
|---|---|---|---|
| 1 P–K4 | P–K4 | 26 RxB | P–Q5 |
| 2 N–KB3 | N–QB3 | 27 B–N5 | R–Q4 |
| 3 B–N5 | P–QR3 | 28 P–B4 | P–R5 |
| 4 B–R4 | N–B3 | 29 Q–B3 | PxP |
| 5 O–O | NxP | 30 PxP | R–Q2 |
| 6 P–Q4 | P–QN4 | 31 P–B5 | R/2–R2 |
| 7 B–N3 | P–Q4 | 32 Q–N3 | R–R8 |
| 8 PxP | B–K3 | 33 R/2–B1 | RxR |
| 9 P–B3 | B–K2 | 34 RxR | K–R1 |
| 10 QN–Q2 | O–O | 35 R–B1 | R–R3 |
| 11 Q–K2 | N–B4 | 36 P–R3 | Q–R1 |
| 12 N–Q4 | NxB | 37 K–R2 | Q–K1 |
| 13 QNxN | Q–Q2 | 38 R–B3 | B–R4 |
| 14 NxN | QxN | 39 B–B4 | B–B2 |
| 15 B–K3 | B–KB4 | 40 R–B1 | R–R1 |
| 16 KR–Q1 | KR–Q1 | 41 R–K1 | Q–B3 |
| 17 P–B3 | B–KB1 | 42 P–K6 | BxB |
| 18 Q–B2 | P–QR4 | 43 QxB | PxP |
| 19 R–Q2 | P–N5 | 44 PxP | R–K1 |
| 20 R–QB1 | Q–R5 | 45 P–K7 | P–R3 |
| 21 N–Q4 | B–N3 | 46 Q–B5 | Q–Q3† |
| 22 P–QN3 | Q–K1 | 47 K–R1 | K–N1 |
| 23 PxP | BxP | 48 R–K6 | Q–Q2 |
| 24 R/2–Q1 | P–QB4 | 49 Q–K5 | Draw |
| 25 N–B2 | BxN | | |

### *Lopez Game 42*

*WHITE: Olland* — *BLACK: Euwe*

*Göteborg 1920*

| | WHITE | BLACK | | WHITE | BLACK |
|---|---|---|---|---|---|
| 1 | P–K4 | P–K4 | 21 | N–N5† | K–N3 |
| 2 | N–KB3 | N–QB3 | 22 | R–K3 | PxP |
| 3 | B–N5 | P–QR3 | 23 | PxP | B–KN5 |
| 4 | B–R4 | N–B3 | 24 | P–R4 | R–R1 |
| 5 | O–O | NxP | 25 | QxP | N–Q1 |
| 6 | P–Q4 | P–QN4 | 26 | Q–Q4 | Q–B1 |
| 7 | B–N3 | P–Q4 | 27 | P–K6 | RxB |
| 8 | PxP | B–K3 | 28 | PxP | N–B3 |
| 9 | P–B3 | B–K2 | 29 | Q–K4† | K–N2 |
| 10 | R–K1 | O–O | 30 | R–R5 | R–N3 |
| 11 | QN–Q2 | N–B4 | 31 | P–R5! | BxP |
| 12 | N–B1 | NxB | 32 | R–N3 | K–R3 |
| 13 | PxN | P–N5! | 33 | P–B8(Q)† | BxQ |
| 14 | Q–Q3 | Q–B1 | 34 | N–B7† | K–N2 |
| 15 | N–N3 | P–R3 | 35 | RxB | RxR |
| 16 | B–B4 | Q–N2? | 36 | PxR | N–K2 |
| 17 | N–R5 | K–R1 | 37 | N–K5 | Q–K3 |
| 18 | Q–Q2 | K–R2 | 38 | R–N5† | K–B3 |
| 19 | NxP! | KxN | 39 | N–N4† | K–B2 |
| 20 | BxP† | K–R2 | 40 | Q–B3† | Resigns |

### *Lopez Game 43*

*WHITE: Unzicker* — *BLACK: Lehmann*

*Championship of Western Germany 1955*

| | WHITE | BLACK | | WHITE | BLACK |
|---|---|---|---|---|---|
| 1 | P–K4 | P–K4 | 17 | BxP† | PxB |
| 2 | N–KB3 | N–QB3 | 18 | QxR | N–B7! |
| 3 | B–N5 | P–QR3 | 19 | B–R6 | Q–K2 |
| 4 | B–R4 | N–B3 | 20 | BxB | QxB |
| 5 | O–O | NxP | 21 | QxQ† | KxQ |
| 6 | P–Q4 | P–QN4 | 22 | R–QB1 | NxR |
| 7 | B–N3 | P–Q4 | 23 | RxN | R–Q1 |
| 8 | PxP | B–K3 | 24 | N–R3 | R–Q7 |
| 9 | P–B3 | N–B4 | 25 | R–B1 | RxNP |
| 10 | B–B2 | B–N5 | 26 | RxN | P–B4 |
| 11 | R–K1 | P–Q5 | 27 | R–QB1 | RxRP |
| 12 | P–KR3 | B–R4 | 28 | NxP | PxN |
| 13 | P–K6 | BPxP | 29 | RxP | P–N5 |
| 14 | PxP | BxN | 30 | R–QN5 | R–N7 |
| 15 | QxB | NxP | 31 | R–N7 | Draw |
| 16 | Q–R5† | P–N3 | | | |

### *Lopez Game 44*

*WHITE: Pilnik* *BLACK: Spasski*

*FIDE Candidates' Tournament, Amsterdam 1956*

| | WHITE | BLACK | | WHITE | BLACK | | WHITE | BLACK |
|---|---|---|---|---|---|---|---|---|
| 1 | P–K4 | P–K4 | 17 | B–K3 | N–B3 | 33 | NxB | RxN |
| 2 | N–KB3 | N–QB3 | 18 | P–KN4 | B–N3 | 34 | N–K3 | KR–Q1 |
| 3 | B–N5 | P–QR3 | 19 | KR–K1 | P–N5 | 35 | R–B1 | R–Q7 |
| 4 | B–R4 | N–B3 | 20 | P–B4 | P–KR4 | 36 | R–QR1 | R–KB1 |
| 5 | O–O | NxP | 21 | K–N2 | P–R4 | 37 | N–Q1 | K–Q2 |
| 6 | P–Q4 | P–QN4 | 22 | P–N3 | O–O–O | 38 | K–N3 | P–R5 |
| 7 | B–N3 | P–Q4 | 23 | QR–B1 | PxP | 39 | PxP | R–QR1 |
| 8 | PxP | B–K3 | 24 | PxP | P–B4! | 40 | N–K3 | RxP/5 |
| 9 | P–B3 | N–B4 | 25 | PxP e.p. | BxP | 41 | R–KR1 | R/5xP |
| 10 | B–B2 | B–N5 | 26 | R–K2 | R–Q8! | 42 | R–R7 | P–N6 |
| 11 | P–KR3 | B–R4 | 27 | RxP | BxR | 43 | RxP† | Game was adjourned and White resigned without resuming play. |
| 12 | B–B4 | B–K2 | 28 | RxB | N–Q5 | | | |
| 13 | QN–Q2 | P–Q5 | 29 | BxN | BxB | | | |
| 14 | N–K4 | P–Q6 | 30 | N–K6 | B–B6 | | | |
| 15 | NxN | PxB | 31 | N–B4 | R–K1 | | | |
| 16 | QxQ† | NxQ | 32 | N–Q5 | B–Q5 | | | |

SUPPLEMENTARY VARIATIONS 18–21:

1 P–K4, P–K4 2 N–KB3, N–QB3 3 B–N5, P–QR3 4 B–R4, N–B3 5 O–O, NxP 6 P–Q4, P–QN4 7 B–N3, P–Q4 8 PxP, B–K3 9 P–B3, B–K2

| | *18* | *19* | *20* | *21* |
|---|---|---|---|---|
| *10* | B–KB4[1] | – – | P–QR4 | N–Q4 |
| | P–N4 | O–O | P–N5 | NxKP |
| *11* | B–K3 | N–Q4 | N–Q4 | P–B3 |
| | P–N5 | N–R4 | NxKP | N–B4 |
| *12* | KN–Q2 | P–B3 | P–B4 | B–B2 |
| | N–N4[2] | N–B4 | B–N5 | B–Q2 |
| *13* | = | B–B2 | Q–B2 | P–QN4 |
| | | N–Q2 | P–QB4 | N–R5 |
| *14* | | P–QN4 | PxN | R–K1 |
| | | N–B5 | PxN | N–B5 |
| *15* | | Q–Q3 | PxQP | Q–K2 |
| | | P–N3 | O–O[4] | K–B1[5] |
| *16* | | N–B6 | = | ∓ |
| | | Q–K1 | | |
| *17* | | B–R6 | | |
| | | N/2xP | | |
| *18* | | NxN | | |
| | | NxN[3] | | |
| | | = | | |

*Notes to supplementary variations 18-21:*

[1] To fortify K5. But the move is easily repulsed.

[2] With chances for both sides. See Game 45.

[3] Black has sufficient compensation for the exchange.

[4] The continuation 16 Q–B6, B–K3 leads to nothing, as 17 N–Q2 fails against 17 . . . R–B1 and 18 . . . RxB.

[5] Black keeps the Pawn without danger.

*Lopez Game 45*

*WHITE: Averbach* *BLACK: Korchnoi*

*25th Championship of USSR 1958*

| | WHITE | BLACK | | WHITE | BLACK |
|---|---|---|---|---|---|
| 1 | P–K4 | P–K4 | 22 | R–KB1 | N–K4 |
| 2 | N–KB3 | N–QB3 | 23 | N–N3 | K–N3 |
| 3 | B–N5 | P–QR3 | 24 | B–Q4 | QR–K1 |
| 4 | B–R4 | N–B3 | 25 | N–B5 | Q–B1 |
| 5 | O–O | NxP | 26 | Q–KB2 | KR–B1 |
| 6 | P–Q4 | P–QN4 | 27 | Q–R4 | N–B3 |
| 7 | B–N3 | P–Q4 | 28 | R–B4 | NxB |
| 8 | PxP | B–K3 | 29 | PxN | K–N2 |
| 9 | P–B3 | B–K2 | 30 | QR–KB1 | B–N3 |
| 10 | B–B4 | P–N4 | 31 | RxBP | Q–Q1 |
| 11 | B–K3 | P–N5 | 32 | RxB† | KxR |
| 12 | KN–Q2 | N–B4 | 33 | QxNP† | K–R3 |
| 13 | Q–K2 | Q–Q2 | 34 | RxR | RxR |
| 14 | R–Q1 | NxB | 35 | N–K6 | Q–K2 |
| 15 | NxN | NxP | 36 | Q–R3† | K–N3 |
| 16 | QN–Q2 | B–Q3 | 37 | Q–N3† | K–B2 |
| 17 | B–Q4 | P–KB3 | 38 | NxR | KxN |
| 18 | N–B5 | BxN | 39 | Q–B4† | K–N2 |
| 19 | BxB | K–B2 | 40 | P–KR4 | P–B3 |
| 20 | P–KB4 | N–N3 | 41 | K–R2 | Q–K3 |
| 21 | P–B5 | BxP | | Draw | |

1 P–K4, P–K4
2 N–KB3, N–QB3
3 B–N5, P–QR3
4 B–R4, N–B3
5 O–O, NxP
6 P–Q4, P–QN4
7 B–N3, P–Q4
8 PxP, B–K3
9 P–B3, B–K2
10 B–K3

KEY POSITION 17

## part 17—OPEN DEFENSE III

### OBSERVATIONS ON KEY POSITION 17

There is a great similarity between key positions 16 and 17. White's last move, however, accents restraint rather than assault. First he inhibits . . . P–QB4. Then he will try to dislodge Black's King Knight.

### IDEA VARIATIONS 38 AND 39:

(38) 10 . . . O–O 11 QN–Q2, Q–Q2 12 NxN, PxN 13 QxQ, BxQ 14 N–Q2, NxP 15 NxP, N–N5 16 B–B5. White controls QB5.

(39) 10 . . . O–O 11 QN–Q2, N–B4 12 B–B2, N–Q2 13 N–Q4, QNxP 14 P–KB4, N–N5 15 NxB, NxB 16 BxP†!, K–R1 17 Q–R5 wins.

### PRACTICAL VARIATIONS 86–93:

1 P–K4, P–K4 2 N–KB3, N–QB3 3 B–N5, P–QR3 4 B–R4, N–B3 5 O–O, NxP 6 P–Q4, P–QN4 7 B–N3, P–Q4 8 PxP, B–K3 9 P–B3, B–K2 10 B–K3

| | 86 | 87 | 88 | 89 | 90 | 91 | 92 | 93 |
|---|---|---|---|---|---|---|---|---|
| 10 | – – | – – | – – | – – | – – | – – | – – | – – |
| | O–O | – – | – – | – – | – – | – – | N–R4[17] | – – |
| 11 | QN–Q2 | – – | – – | – – | – – | – – | N–Q4! | – – |
| | B–KN5[1] | – – | P–B4[6] | NxN | – – | N–R4[15] | O–O[18] | NxB |
| 12 | NxN | – – | PxP e.p. | QxN | – – | NxN | N–Q2[19] | PxN |
| | PxN | – – | NxP/3 | N–R4 | Q–Q2[12] | NxB! | NxN | P–QB4?[22] |
| 13 | Q–Q5! | – – | N–N5 | B–B2[9] | B–B2[13] | N–B6† | QxN | NxB |
| | PxN | QxQ | B–B2[7] | N–B5 | N–R4 | BxN | N–B5[20] | PxN |
| 14 | QxN | BxQ | NxB | Q–Q3 | P–QN3 | PxN | BxN | Q–N4†[23] |
| | PxP | PxN | RxN | P–N3 | P–QB4 | B–K2 | QPxB | ± |
| 15 | QxKNP | BxN | N–B3[8] | B–R6 | N–N5 | P–QN4 | P–B4 | |
| | Q–Q2 | PxP | ± | R–K1[10] | P–N3[14] | B–N5[16] | B–Q2 | |
| 16 | B–R6![2] | KR–B1! | | Q–Q4 | ± | = | P–B5 | |
| | PxB | QR–Q1 | | NxNP | | | P–B4 | |
| 17 | P–B3 | P–QR4 | | Q–KB4[11] | | | N–B2[21] | |
| | B–B4† | PxP[4] | | ± | | | ± | |
| 18 | K–R1 | RxP | | | | | | |
| | QR–K1 | B–B1 | | | | | | |
| 19 | QR–K1[3] | BxP | | | | | | |
| | ± | P–KB3[5] | | | | | | |
| | | ± | | | | | | |

*Notes to practical variations 86–93:*

[1] This attempt to maintain the Knight in its position fails because Black weakens his Q4.

[2] An excellent suggestion by Fine.

[3] 19 . . . P–KR4 20 PxB, PxP (. . . QxP? 21 Q–Q5) 21 Q–K4, K–R1 22 P–K6!

[4] If 17 . . . P–N5 then 18 PxP, BxP 19 R–B4.

[5] White stands better after 20 R–QB4.

[6] This move in general is doubtful as long as White's King Bishop is on N3.

[7] After other moves QN–K4 will be very strong, e.g., 13 . . . B–KN5 14 P–B3, B–KB4 15 QN–K4! etc.

[8] White's two Bishops give him positional advantage.

[9] For 13 N–Q4 see Game 47.

[10] 15 . . . NxNP transposes to the text after 16 Q–Q4, and 16 Q–K3 leads to Game 48.

[11] White has a very strong attack for only one Pawn, e.g., 17 . . . N–B5 (17 . . . N–R5 is probably better) 18 N–N5, Q–Q2 19 QR–Q1 (threatens 20 N–K4), Q–B3 20 P–N4 with all kinds of possibilities.

[12] This move may lead to the same kinds of positions as in Prac. Var. 88, only White now can avoid the sacrifice of his Queen Knight Pawn and still obtain good attacking chances.

[13] For 13 B–N5 see Game 46.

[14] White and Black have both realized their aims, but White stands better.

[15] 11 . . . Q–Q2 leads to Idea Var. 38 and 11 . . . N–B4 leads to Idea Var. 39.

continued ▸

[16] Black is all right as he contains White through the pin on the Knight.

[17] 10 . . . N–B4 11 B–B2, B–N5 leads to game 48.

[18] 11 . . . P–QB4? 12 NxB, PxN 13 Q–N4.

[19] Still stronger seems Keres' suggestion: 12 P–B3, N–B4 13 B–B2, N–B5 14 B–B1, NxKP 15 P–QN4, N–N2 16 P–KB4, N–B5 17 Q–Q3, P–N3 18 P–B5 and White's attack is overwhelming. Inferior, however, would be 13 P–KB4, N/B4xB 14 NxN, N–B5 15 B–Q4, B–KB4∓ (Keres–Euwe 1937).

[20] 13 . . . NxB 14 NxN means positional disadvantage for Black, as White controls square B5. After 13 . . . P–QB4 14 NxB, PxN 15 B–B2, N–B5 16 Q–Q3, P–N3 17 B–R6, R–B2 18 P–QN3!, NxP 19 Q–N3 White obtains a winning attack. The Black Knight cannot move on account of BxP, so 19 . . . B–B3 is forced: 20 QR–K1, N–Q2 ( . . . Q–B2 21 B–B4) 21 RxP.

[21] White has a clear advantage because he is poised for a powerful assault.

[22] Not good, but after other moves White will control QB5 with 13 P–QN4.

[23] With clear advantage: 14 . . . K–B2 15 P–B3.

*Lopez Game 46*

*WHITE: Keres* — *BLACK: Unzicker*

*Zurich 1959*

| | WHITE | BLACK | | WHITE | BLACK |
|---|---|---|---|---|---|
| 1 | P–K4 | P–K4 | 19 | NxB | P–KR4 |
| 2 | N–KB3 | N–QB3 | 20 | P–QN3 | N–N3 |
| 3 | B–N5 | P–QR3 | 21 | QR–Q1 | Q–K2 |
| 4 | B–R4 | N–B3 | 22 | P–KR3 | K–N2 |
| 5 | O–O | NxP | 23 | P–KB4 | N–Q2 |
| 6 | P–Q4 | P–QN4 | 24 | P–B5! | PxP |
| 7 | B–N3 | P–Q4 | 25 | R–Q3 | K–R3 |
| 8 | PxP | B–K3 | 26 | R–N3 | R–KN1 |
| 9 | P–B3 | B–K2 | 27 | Q–B4! | RxN |
| 10 | B–K3 | O–O | 28 | P–KR4 | R–KN1 |
| 11 | QN–Q2 | NxN | 29 | R/1–K3 | N–B1 |
| 12 | QxN | Q–Q2 | 30 | RxR | RxR |
| 13 | B–N5 | QR–Q1 | 31 | R–N3 | N–R2 |
| 14 | KR–K1 | N–R4 | 32 | PxR† | NxP |
| 15 | B–B2 | N–B5 | 33 | BxP | BxB |
| 16 | Q–Q3 | P–N3 | 34 | QxB | P–R5 |
| 17 | Q–Q4! | KR–K1 | 35 | R–N4 | Resigns |
| 18 | Q–R4 | BxB | | | |

### *Lopez Game 47*

*WHITE: Clarke* *BLACK: Cortlever*

*Netherlands–England, Vlissingen 1958*

| | WHITE | BLACK | | WHITE | BLACK |
|---|---|---|---|---|---|
| 1 | P–K4 | P–K4 | 22 | B–N6 | R–QN1 |
| 2 | N–KB3 | N–QB3 | 23 | Q–K3 | N–N5 |
| 3 | B–N5 | P–QR3 | 24 | B–B5 | BxB |
| 4 | B–R4 | N–B3 | 25 | QxB | P–QR4 |
| 5 | O–O | NxP | 26 | P–QR3 | N–R3 |
| 6 | P–Q4 | P–QN4 | 27 | Q–K3 | QR–Q1 |
| 7 | B–N3 | P–Q4 | 28 | R–B3 | Q–B3 |
| 8 | PxP | B–K3 | 29 | RxP | RxR |
| 9 | P–B3 | B–K2 | 30 | QxR | N–B4 |
| 10 | B–K3 | O–O | 31 | Q–Q6 | QxQ |
| 11 | QN–Q2 | NxN | 32 | PxQ | R–Q1 |
| 12 | QxN | N–R4 | 33 | R–B3 | N–K5 |
| 13 | N–Q4 | P–QB4 | 34 | R–B6 | P–N3 |
| 14 | NxB | PxN | 35 | BxP | RxP |
| 15 | B–B2 | N–B3 | 36 | RxR | NxR |
| 16 | P–KB4 | P–Q5 | 37 | K–B2 | K–N2 |
| 17 | PxP | PxP | 38 | K–K3 | K–B3 |
| 18 | B–B2 | P–Q6 | 39 | B–Q5 | P–N4 |
| 19 | B–QN3 | Q–Q2 | 40 | PxP† | KxP |
| 20 | QR–Q1 | K–R1 | 41 | K–Q4 | Resigns |
| 21 | B–K3 | QR–Q1 | | | |

### *Lopez Game 48*

*WHITE: Averbach* *BLACK: Zak*

*Moscow 1948*

| | WHITE | BLACK | | WHITE | BLACK |
|---|---|---|---|---|---|
| 1 | P–K4 | P–K4 | 14 | Q–Q3 | P–N3 |
| 2 | N–KB3 | N–QB3 | 15 | B–R6 | NxNP |
| 3 | B–N5 | P–QR3 | 16 | Q–K3 | KR–K1 |
| 4 | B–R4 | N–B3 | 17 | N–Q4 | Q–Q2 |
| 5 | O–O | NxP | 18 | P–KB4 | N–B5 |
| 6 | P–Q4 | P–QN4 | 19 | Q–N3 | P–QB4 |
| 7 | B–N3 | P–Q4 | 20 | P–B5 | PxN |
| 8 | PxP | B–K3 | 21 | KBPxP | RPxP |
| 9 | P–B3 | B–K2 | 22 | BxP | K–R1 |
| 10 | B–K3 | O–O | 23 | B–N7† | KxB |
| 11 | QN–Q2 | NxN | 24 | BxP† | K–R1 |
| 12 | QxN | N–R4 | 25 | Q–N6 | B–B1 |
| 13 | B–B2 | N–B5 | 26 | Q–N8 mate | |

*Lopez Game 49*

*WHITE: Gligoric* *BLACK: Szabo*

*Zurich 1953*

| WHITE | BLACK | WHITE | BLACK | WHITE | BLACK |
|---|---|---|---|---|---|
| 1 P–K4 | P–K4 | 15 P–R5 | B–N3 | 29 R–R1 | R–N4 |
| 2 N–KB3 | N–QB3 | 16 N–N3 | PxP | 30 R–R4 | QR–N1 |
| 3 B–N5 | P–QR3 | 17 PxP | Q–N1 | 31 KR–R1 | B–B6 |
| 4 B–R4 | N–B3 | 18 Q–R2 | O–O | 32 R–QB1 | R–N8 |
| 5 O–O | NxP | 19 BxB | RPxP | 33 RxR | RxR† |
| 6 P–Q4 | P–QN4 | 20 QR–N1? | Q–N4 | 34 K–B2 | R–QR8 |
| 7 B–N3 | P–Q4 | 21 Q–B2 | Q–B5 | 35 RxR | BxR |
| 8 PxP | B–K3 | 22 KN–Q2 | Q–KN5 | 36 K–K2 | B–B6 |
| 9 P–B3 | B–K2 | 23 P–KB4 | Q–B4 | 37 K–Q3 | BxRP |
| 10 B–K3 | N–B4 | 24 QxQ | PxQ | 38 P–R3 | B–K8 |
| 11 B–B2 | B–N5 | 25 N–B3 | KR–N1 | 39 P–N4 | P–N3 |
| 12 QN–Q2 | N–K3 | 26 KN–Q4 | N/B3xN | 40 K–B2 | K–B1 |
| 13 Q–N1 | B–R4 | 27 NxN | NxN | 41 K–Q1 | B–N6 |
| 14 P–QR4 | P–N5 | 28 PxN | B–N5 | Resigns | |

---

## part 18—OPEN DEFENSE, ITALIAN VARIATION

1 P–K4, P–K4
2 N–KB3, N–QB3
3 B–N5, P–QR3
4 B–R4, N–B3
5 O–O, NxP
6 P–Q4, P–QN4
7 B–N3, P–Q4
8 PxP, B–K3
9 P–B3, B–QB4

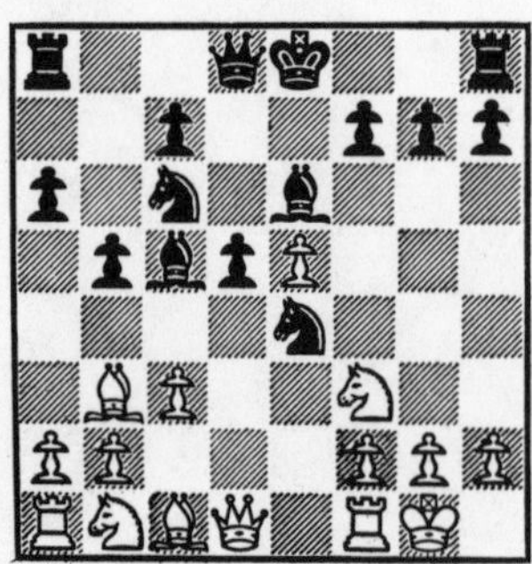

KEY POSITION 18

OBSERVATIONS ON KEY POSITION 18

In key position 18, Black's King Bishop is on B4 instead of K2; thus, tactics come to the foreground. While the move . . . P–QB4 is now more difficult to carry out, Black's King Bishop and King Knight coordinate against White's KB2.

White now must take measures to lessen the force of Black's pieces, e.g., by playing B–K3 after some preparation. After this he can continue his attack against the hostile King.

Black may try to strengthen his pressure by moves like . . . P–B3 (opening the KB file), . . . P–B4 (giving the Knight extra support) or even the explosive . . . NxKBP.

IDEA VARIATIONS 40 AND 41:

(40) 10 Q–Q3, O–O 11 B–K3, BxB 12 QxB, N–K2 13 QN–Q2, N–KB4 14 Q–K2, NxN 15 QxN, P–B4 16 QR–Q1, Q–N3 (preferable is 16 . . . Q–B2) 17 Q–B4, QR–Q1 18 B–B2, N–K2 19 BxP†, winning a Pawn (Euwe–Vlagsma, Maastricht 1946).

(41) 10 Q–Q3, O–O 11 B–K3, P–B4 12 PxP e.p., QxP 13 BxP, QR–Q1 14 BxB†, QxB 15 Q–K2, NxKBP! 16 KxN, N–K4! 17 BxB, N–N5† 18 K–K1, QxQ† and wins. In the above variation 15 N–Q4 is preferable. After 15 Q–B2 Black wins by 15 . . . RxN! 16 PxR, Q–N3† 17 K–R1, N–N6†, etc.

PRACTICAL VARIATIONS 94-98:

1 P–K4, P–K4 2 N–KB3, N–QB3 3 B–N5, P–QR3 4 B–R4, N–B3 5 O–O, NxP 6 P–Q4, P–QN4 7 B–N3, P–Q4 8 PxP, B–K3 9 P–B3, B–QB4

| | 94 | 95 | 96 | 97 | 98 |
|---|---|---|---|---|---|
| 10 | Q–Q3[1] | – – | QN–Q2 | – – | – – |
| | O–O | – – | O–O | – – | – – |
| 11 | B–K3[2] | – – | B–B2 | – – | – – |
| | P–B4 | BxB | P–B4[7] | – – | – – |
| 12 | PxP e.p. | QxB | N–N3 | – – | – – |
| | BxB[3] | N–K2 | B–N3 | B–R2! | – – |
| 13 | QxB | B–B2[5] | P–QR4[8] | QN–Q4 | – – |
| | QxP | N–N3 | P–N5 | NxN | – – |
| 14 | QN–Q2 | R–K1 | P–R5 | NxN | – – |
| | NxN | P–KB4 | B–R2 | BxN | – – |
| 15 | QxN | PxP e.p. | KN–Q4 | PxB[11] | – – |
| | QR–Q1 | QxP | NxN | P–B5 | – – |
| 16 | N–Q4 | BxN | NxN | P–B3 | – – |
| | B–B2 | PxB | BxN | N–N6 | – – |
| 17 | B–B2 | N–N5 | PxB | R–B2 | PxN |
| | N–K4 | N–B5 | P–B5 | Q–R5 | PxP |
| 18 | P–KB4 | NxKP | P–B3 | Q–Q3 | Q–Q3 |
| | N–B5 | Q–N3 | N–N6[9] | R–B4 | B–B4 |
| 19 | Q–Q3 | Q–N3 | R–B2 | BxP | QxB |
| | Q–R3 | Q–R4 | Q–R5 | RxB | RxQ |
| 20 | N–B5 | P–B3 | R–R4[10] | Q–B3[12] | BxR |
| | Q–N3† | B–B5[6] | ± | ± | Q–R5 |
| 21 | K–R1 | = | | | B–R3 |
| | P–N3[4] | | | | QxP†[13] |
| | ± | | | | = |

*Notes to practical variations 94-98:*

[1] The Motzko Variation. Equally good is 10 Q–K2, O–O 11 B–K3, Q–K2 12 BxB, NxB 13 QN–Q2, NxB 14 PxN, B–N5 15 KR–K1, P–B3 16 Q–Q3± (Matanovic–Karaklaic, 1955).

[2] For 11 QN–Q2 see Game 52.

[3] For 12 . . . QxP see Idea Var. 41.

[4] See Game 50.

continued ▸

[5] For 13 QN–Q2 see Idea Var. 40.

[6] Gligoric–Trifunovic, London 1951.

[7] For 11 . . . NxN see Game 53. 11 . . . NxKBP is the Dilworth Variation. A reasonable continuation for White is 12 RxN, P–B3 13 PxP, QxP 14 N–B1, BxR† 15 KxB, N–K4 16 K–N1, QR–K1 17 B–K3, NxN† 18 QxN, QxQ 19 PxQ, RxP 20 B–B2±. White can avoid all these complications by 10 Q–Q3 or 10 Q–K2.

[8] For 13 QN–Q4 see Game 51.

[9] Fleissing–Mackenzie, Vienna 1882. The soundness of this sacrifice is still an unsettled question. Safe and good is 18 . . . N–N4 19 P–R4, N–B2 20 BxP, QxP∓.

[10] Boleslavski–Szabo, Groningen 1946.

[11] The game Averbach–Szabo, Zurich 1953, continued: 15 QxB, P–B4 16 Q–Q1, P–KB5 17 P–B3, N–N4 18 P–QR4, P–N5 19 P–R4, N–R6† 20 PxN, QxP 21 R–B2, BxP 22 R–R2, QR–K1 23 QxP†, K–R1 24 B–Q2, RxP 25 QxR, Q–N6†=.

[12] Analysis by Pachman. The threat is 21 Q–B6!

[13] With the continuation 22 K–R1, QxKP 23 B–Q2, P–B4 (for 23 . . . QxP see Game 51.) 23 QR–K1, QxP 25 B–B4, P–Q5 26 BxP, P–Q6= (Boleslavski–Botvinnik, 1943).

*Lopez Game 50*

*WHITE: Ivkov* *BLACK: Geller*

*Zagreb 1955*

| | WHITE | BLACK | | WHITE | BLACK |
|---|---|---|---|---|---|
| 1 | P–K4 | P–K4 | 22 | N–K7† | K–N2 |
| 2 | N–KB3 | N–QB3 | 23 | QR–K1 | Q–KB3 |
| 3 | B–N5 | P–QR3 | 24 | P–QN3 | N–R6 |
| 4 | B–R4 | N–B3 | 25 | B–Q1 | KR–K1? |
| 5 | O–O | NxP | 26 | P–B5 | P–N4 |
| 6 | P–Q4 | P–QN4 | 27 | R–K6 | BxR |
| 7 | B–N3 | P–Q4 | 28 | PxB | QxR†? |
| 8 | PxP | B–K3 | 29 | QxQ | RxN |
| 9 | P–B3 | B–QB4 | 30 | Q–B5 | R–KB1 |
| 10 | Q–Q3 | O–O | 31 | QxNP† | K–R1 |
| 11 | B–K3 | P–B4 | 32 | Q–K5† | K–N1 |
| 12 | PxP e.p. | BxB | 33 | B–B3 | P–N5 |
| 13 | QxB | QxP | 34 | PxP | N–N4 |
| 14 | QN–Q2 | NxN | 35 | P–QR4 | N–Q3 |
| 15 | QxN | QR–Q1 | 36 | QxP | R–B4 |
| 16 | N–Q4 | B–B2 | 37 | Q–R8† | K–N2 |
| 17 | B–B2 | N–K4 | 38 | QxP | RxP |
| 18 | P–B4 | N–B5 | 39 | P–R3 | R/4–K4 |
| 19 | Q–Q3 | Q–R3 | 40 | K–R2 | N–B2 |
| 20 | N–B5 | Q–N3† | 41 | Q–N7 | Resigns |
| 21 | K–R1 | P–N3 | | | |

*Lopez Game 51*

*WHITE: Smyslov* *BLACK: Reshevsky*

*Radio Match USA–USSR 1945*

| | WHITE | BLACK | | WHITE | BLACK | | WHITE | BLACK |
|---|---|---|---|---|---|---|---|---|
| 1 | P–K4 | P–K4 | 15 | PxB | P–B5 | 29 | B–K5 | P–N5 |
| 2 | N–KB3 | N–QB3 | 16 | P–B3 | N–N6 | 30 | B–QN3 | R–Q7 |
| 3 | B–N5 | P–QR3 | 17 | PxN | PxP | 31 | P–B4 | P–KR4 |
| 4 | B–R4 | N–B3 | 18 | Q–Q3 | B–B4 | 32 | R–QN1 | R–KB7 |
| 5 | O–O | NxP | 19 | QxB | RxQ | 33 | KR–K1 | Q–Q7 |
| 6 | P–Q4 | P–QN4 | 20 | BxR | Q–R5 | 34 | QR–Q1 | Q–N7 |
| 7 | B–N3 | P–Q4 | 21 | B–R3 | QxP† | 35 | R–Q8† | K–R2 |
| 8 | PxP | B–K3 | 22 | K–R1 | QxKP | 36 | B–N8† | K–N3 |
| 9 | P–B3 | B–QB4 | 23 | B–Q2 | QxP? | 37 | R–Q6† | K–B4 |
| 10 | QN–Q2 | O–O | 24 | B–B4 | P–B4 | 38 | B–K6† | K–N3 |
| 11 | B–B2 | P–B4 | 25 | B–K6† | K–R1 | 39 | B–Q5† | K–R2 |
| 12 | N–N3 | B–N3 | 26 | BxQP | R–Q1 | 40 | B–K4† | K–N1 |
| 13 | QN–Q4 | NxN | 27 | QR–Q1 | P–B5 | 41 | B–N6 | Resigns |
| 14 | NxN | BxN | 28 | BxNP | P–B6 | | | |

*Lopez Game 52*

*WHITE: Blau* *BLACK: Trifunovic*

*Zonal Tournament, Hilversum 1947*

| | WHITE | BLACK | | WHITE | BLACK | | WHITE | BLACK |
|---|---|---|---|---|---|---|---|---|
| 1 | P–K4 | P–K4 | 20 | PxP | NxQBP | 39 | R–Q4 | RxR |
| 2 | N–KB3 | N–QB3 | 21 | B–B2? | P–Q5 | 40 | BxR | NxP |
| 3 | B–N5 | P–QR3 | 22 | R–Q1 | QR–Q1 | 41 | BxN | R–K7† |
| 4 | B–R4 | N–B3 | 23 | B–N5 | R–Q2 | 42 | K–N1 | RxB |
| 5 | O–O | NxP | 24 | P–B3 | P–Q6 | 43 | RxP | P–QR4 |
| 6 | P–Q4 | P–QN4 | 25 | B–N1 | B–B4 | 44 | R–Q5 | P–R5 |
| 7 | B–N3 | P–Q4 | 26 | P–R3 | R–K1 | 45 | K–R2 | R–N6 |
| 8 | PxP | B–K3 | 27 | B–R2† | B–K3 | 46 | P–B4 | K–B2 |
| 9 | P–B3 | B–QB4 | 28 | BxB† | RxB | 47 | R–K5 | P–N3 |
| 10 | Q–Q3 | O–O | 29 | QR–B1 | R–Q4 | 48 | P–N4 | P–R3 |
| 11 | QN–Q2 | P–B4 | 30 | B–Q2 | R–K7 | 49 | P–N3 | P–N4 |
| 12 | PxP e.p. | NxP/3 | 31 | R–B3 | N–R5 | 50 | PxP | PxP |
| 13 | N–N5 | N–K4 | 32 | R–N3 | K–B2 | 51 | RxKNP | RxRP |
| 14 | Q–N3 | Q–Q3 | 33 | K–B1 | R–K2 | 52 | RxP | K–N3 |
| 15 | QN–B3 | NxN† | 34 | B–R5 | R/K–Q2 | 53 | K–R3 | R–R8 |
| 16 | NxN | QxQ | 35 | K–B2 | N–B4 | 54 | P–N5 | K–R4 |
| 17 | RPxQ | N–K5 | 36 | R–N4? | R–K2? | 55 | P–N6† | KxP |
| 18 | N–Q4 | BxN | 37 | R–B4† | K–N1 | | Draw | |
| 19 | PxB | P–B4 | 38 | B–B3 | N–R5 | | | |

*Lopez Game 53*

*WHITE: Em. Lasker* *BLACK: Rubinstein*

*St. Petersburg 1914*

| | WHITE | BLACK | | WHITE | BLACK | | WHITE | BLACK |
|---|---|---|---|---|---|---|---|---|
| 1 | P–K4 | P–K4 | 23 | P–R3 | R–K5 | 45 | K–K2 | K–K2 |
| 2 | N–KB3 | N–QB3 | 24 | Q–Q2 | R/1–K3 | 46 | K–Q3 | R–N3 |
| 3 | B–N5 | P–QR3 | 25 | R–B6 | Q–Q2 | 47 | P–KN3 | R–B3 |
| 4 | B–R4 | N–B3 | 26 | RxR | QxR | 48 | P–B4 | K–Q2 |
| 5 | O–O | NxP | 27 | Q–Q3 | Q–K1 | 49 | R–K1 | R–B1 |
| 6 | P–Q4 | P–QN4 | 28 | Q–B3 | K–B2 | 50 | R–R1 | P–R4 |
| 7 | B–N3 | P–Q4 | 29 | Q–Q3 | K–N1 | 51 | B–K3 | P–N3 |
| 8 | PxP | B–K3 | 30 | Q–B3 | Q–K3 | 52 | R–KB1! | K–Q3 |
| 9 | P–B3 | B–QB4 | 31 | R–R1 | Q–K1 | 53 | P–KN4 | PxP |
| 10 | QN–Q2 | O–O | 32 | K–B1 | P–R3 | 54 | PxP | P–B4 |
| 11 | B–B2 | NxN | 33 | Q–Q3 | K–B2 | 55 | PxP† | BxP |
| 12 | QxN | P–B3 | 34 | R–B1 | K–N1 | 56 | BxB† | KxB |
| 13 | PxP | RxP | 35 | Q–N3 | Q–B2 | 57 | P–B5 | PxP |
| 14 | N–Q4 | NxN | 36 | R–Q1 | P–B3 | 58 | PxP | R–B3 |
| 15 | PxN | B–N3? | 37 | P–B3 | Q–B3 | 59 | R–B4 | P–N5 |
| 16 | P–QR4 | R–N1 | 38 | Q–Q3 | R–K2 | 60 | P–N3 | R–B2 |
| 17 | PxP | PxP | 39 | B–B2 | Q–Q3 | 61 | P–B6 | K–Q3 |
| 18 | Q–B3 | Q–Q3 | 40 | Q–B2 | K–B2 | 62 | K–Q4 | K–K3 |
| 19 | B–K3 | B–KB4 | 41 | R–B1 | R–K3 | 63 | R–B2 | K–Q3 |
| 20 | KR–B1 | BxB | 42 | Q–B5† | R–B3 | 64 | R–QR2 | R–B2 |
| 21 | RxB | R–K1 | 43 | Q–K5 | R–K3 | 65 | R–R6† | K–Q2 |
| 22 | QR–QB1 | R/B–K3 | 44 | QxQ | RxQ | 66 | R–N6 | Resigns |

---

1 P–K4, P–K4
2 N–KB3, N–QB3
3 B–N5, P–QR3
4 B–R4, N–B3
5 O–O, NxP
6 P–Q4, P–QN4
7 B–N3, P–Q4
8 PxP, B–K3
9 Q–K2[A]

KEY POSITION 19

## part 19—OPEN DEFENSE, KERES VARIATION

### OBSERVATIONS ON KEY POSITION 19

[A] Other moves than 9 Q–K2 and 9 P–B3 are seldom played. One example: 9 QN–Q2, N–B4 10 P–B3, P–Q5 (. . . B–K2 11 B–B2 leads to Idea Var. 35) 11 PxP, NxQP 12 NxN, QxN 13 BxB, NxB 14 Q–B3, R–Q1 15 P–QR4, B–N5!

In this variation White conducts a very tricky attack against Black's weakened Queenside. Often White prepares P–QB4 by playing R–Q1 (sometimes even sacrificing a Pawn to attain this bayonet-like charge).

Black's defense is not easy, and in some cases he must push his QP as a reaction to P–QB4; in other cases Black works with moves like . . . N–R4 and . . . P–QB3. It should be noted that the exchange . . . NxB in general does not bring any relief.

IDEA VARIATIONS 42–44:

(42) 9 . . . N–B4 10 R–Q1, NxB 11 RPxN, Q–B1 12 P–B4! QPxP (a little better is 12 . . . N–N5) 13 PxP, BxP 14 Q–K4, N–K2 (14 . . . Q–N2 15 B–N5±) 15 N–R3, P–QB3 16 NxB, PxN 17 QxBP± (Smyslov–Euwe, Moscow 1948).

(43) 9 . . . N–R4? 10 N–Q4, P–QB4 11 NxB, PxN 12 P–QB3, NxB 13 PxN, P–B5 (White threatened 14 RxP) 14 P–QN4, and not only is the Black Knight in danger but White has a better Pawn position: e.g., 14 . . . B–K2 15 Q–N4.

(44) 9 . . . B–K2 10 R–Q1, N–B4 11 P–B4, P–Q5! 12 PxP, P–Q6 13 Q–B1, N–Q5 14 NxN, QxN 15 BxB, PxB 16 PxP, O–O and Black has a splendid game for the sacrificed Pawns.

PRACTICAL VARIATIONS 99–104:

1 P–K4, P–K4 2 N–KB3, N–QB3 3 B–N5, P–QR3 4 B–R4, N–B3 5 O–O, NxP 6 P–Q4, P–QN4 7 B–N3, P–Q4 8 PxP, B–K3 9 Q–K2

| | *99* | *100* | *101* | *102* | *103* | *104* |
|---|---|---|---|---|---|---|
| *9* | – – | – – | – – | – – | – – | – – |
| | N–B4[1] | B–QB4 | B–K2[9] | – – | – – | – – |
| *10* | R–Q1 | B–K3 | R–Q1 | – – | – – | – – |
| | NxB[2] | Q–K2[7] | O–O | N–B4 | – – | – – |
| *11* | RPxN | P–QR4 | P–B4 | B–K3[12] | BxP | P–B4 |
| | Q–B1[3] | P–N5 | NPxP | NxB[13] | BxB | P–Q5 |
| *12* | P–B4[4] | R–Q1 | BxP | RPxN' | N–B3 | PxP |
| | QPxP | BxB | B–QB4[10] | Q–B1 | B–B5 | P–Q6 |
| *13* | PxP | QxB | B–K3 | N–B3 | RxQ† | Q–K3[17] |
| | BxP | R–Q1 | BxB | N–N5 | RxR | NxB |
| *14* | Q–K4 | QN–Q2 | QxB | B–N5 | Q–K3 | RPxN |
| | N–N5[5] | N–B4 | Q–N1 | P–R3[14] | P–N5 | N–N5 |
| *15* | B–N5 | N–Q4 | B–N3 | BxB | P–QN3 | N–Q4 |
| | P–QB3 | NxN | N–R4 | KxB | B–K3 | B–N5[18] |
| *16* | R–Q8† | QxN[8] | QN–Q2 | N–N1 | N–K4 | ∓ |
| | QxR | ± | NxN | P–QB4 | R–Q8† | |
| *17* | BxQ | | RxN | P–B3 | N–K1 | |
| | RxB[6] | | NxB | N–B3 | N–Q5 | |
| *18* | ± | | PxN | Q–K3 | B–N2 | |
| | | | R–B1 | N–N1 | NxBP | |
| *19* | | | R–QB1[11] | P–QN4[15] | Q–K2 | |
| | | | ± | ± | RxR | |
| *20* | | | | | BxR | |
| | | | | | NxB[16] | |
| | | | | | ± | |

*Notes to practical variations 99-104:*

[1] For 9 . . . N–R4 see Idea Var. 43.

[2] Equally insufficient is 10 . . . P–N5 11 B–K3, NxB 12 RPxN, Q–B1 13 P–B4, QPxP 14 PxP, P–R3 15 QN–Q2, B–K2 16 N–N3, O–O 17 B–B5± (Smyslov–Reshevsky, 1948).

[3] 11 . . . B–K2 12 P–B4, O–O 13 N–B3, N–N5! 14 B–K3!, P–QB3 15 QR–B1, Q–N1 16 B–N5± (Keres–Alexander, London 1947).

[4] Weaker is 12 B–N5, P–R3 13 B–R4, B–QB4 14 N–B3, P–N4 15 B–N3, Q–N2 16 NxQP, O–O–O∓ (Keres–Reshevsky, 1948).

[5] For 14 . . . N–K2 see Idea Var. 42.

[6] White stands better, but his task is not easy.

[7] The grouping . . . B–QB4 and . . . Q–K2 is a suggestion by the Soviet grandmasters Bronstein and Boleslavski. The point is to meet 11 R–Q1 with . . . R–Q1. Despite this, White stands better.

[8] White has a sounder Pawn structure and a Kingside Pawn majority.

[9] In combination with N–B4 the best continuation.

[10] Also 12 . . . PxB! 13 RxQ, QRxR 14 N–B3, NxN 15 PxN, R–Q4, with sharp play for both sides (Aronin–Ragosin, 1949).

[11] Keres–Euwe, 1948.

[12] Recommended by Smyslov.

[13] For 11 . . . O–O see Game 54.

[14] Better 14 . . . B–QB4.

[15] Matanovic–Rabar, 1951.

[16] With the continuation 21 NxN, BxN 22 N–Q3, B–N3 23 NxP, O–O 24 N–B6, P–B3 25 P–KR4 (for 25 . . . PxP! see Games 55 and 56), K–R1. 26 K–R2, B–Q2 27 PxP± (Boleslavski–Karaklaic, 1957).

[17] For 13 Q–B1 see Idea Var. 44.

[18] 16 P–B3?, B–QB4 (Mross–Euwe, Berlin 1950).

## *Lopez Game 54*

*WHITE: Donner* *BLACK: Euwe*

*Match, The Hague 1955*

| | WHITE | BLACK | | WHITE | BLACK | | WHITE | BLACK |
|---|---|---|---|---|---|---|---|---|
| 1 | P–K4 | P–K4 | 13 | BxP | N–R4 | 25 | R/2–Q2 | N–B5! |
| 2 | N–KB3 | N–QB3 | 14 | P–QN4? | NxB | 26 | Q–K3 | QxQ |
| 3 | B–N5 | P–QR3 | 15 | BxN | BxB | 27 | PxQ | N–K3 |
| 4 | B–R4 | N–B3 | 16 | PxB | Q–K2 | 28 | R–R1 | R–N1 |
| 5 | O–O | NxP | 17 | P–B6 | Q–B4 | 29 | RxRP | P–N4 |
| 6 | P–Q4 | P–QN4 | 18 | N–B3 | QR–N1 | 30 | R–N2 | R–N5 |
| 7 | B–N3 | P–Q4 | 19 | N–Q4? | N–N7! | 31 | P–R3 | P–R4 |
| 8 | PxP | B–K3 | 20 | N–N3 | RxN! | 32 | R–R1 | R–N3 |
| 9 | Q–K2 | B–K2 | 21 | PxR | QxN | 33 | R–QB1 | N–Q1 |
| 10 | R–Q1 | N–B4 | 22 | R/Q–QB1 | Q–Q5 | | Resigns | |
| 11 | B–K3 | O–O | 23 | R–R2 | N–Q6 | | | |
| 12 | P–B4 | NPxP | 24 | R–Q1 | B–B4 | | | |

*Lopez Game 55*

*WHITE: Suetin* *BLACK: Geller*

*25th Championship of USSR, Riga 1958*

| | WHITE | BLACK | | WHITE | BLACK |
|---|---|---|---|---|---|
| 1 | P–K4 | P–K4 | 24 | N–B6 | P–B3 |
| 2 | N–KB3 | N–QB3 | 25 | P–KR4 | PxP |
| 3 | B–N5 | P–QR3 | 26 | QxKP | R–B3 |
| 4 | B–R4 | N–B3 | 27 | P–KN4 | BxP† |
| 5 | O–O | NxP | 28 | K–R1 | BxRP |
| 6 | P–Q4 | P–QN4 | 29 | N–K7† | K–B1 |
| 7 | B–N3 | P–Q4 | 30 | N–B5 | BxN |
| 8 | PxP | B–K3 | 31 | PxB | NxP |
| 9 | Q–K2 | B–K2 | 32 | PxN | R–Q3 |
| 10 | R–Q1 | N–B4 | 33 | Q–B5 | B–Q1 |
| 11 | BxP | BxB | 34 | K–N2 | P–N3 |
| 12 | N–B3 | B–B5 | 35 | PxP | PxP |
| 13 | RxQ† | RxR | 36 | Q–B3 | K–K1 |
| 14 | Q–K3 | P–N5 | 37 | Q–N7 | B–K2 |
| 15 | P–QN3 | B–K3 | 38 | K–B3 | K–Q2 |
| 16 | N–K4 | R–Q8† | 39 | K–K4 | R–K3† |
| 17 | N–K1 | N–Q5 | 40 | K–Q5 | R–Q3† |
| 18 | B–N2 | NxBP | 41 | K–K4 | P–N4 |
| 19 | Q–K2 | RxR | 42 | Q–N8 | B–Q1 |
| 20 | BxR | NxB | 43 | Q–B7† | K–B1 |
| 21 | NxN | BxN | 44 | Q–N8 | K–N2 |
| 22 | N–Q3 | B–N3 | 45 | K–B5 | P–B3 |
| 23 | NxP | O–O | | Draw | |

*Lopez Game 56*

*WHITE: Suetin* *BLACK: Boleslavski*

*25th Championship of USSR, Riga 1958*

| | WHITE | BLACK | | WHITE | BLACK | | WHITE | BLACK |
|---|---|---|---|---|---|---|---|---|
| 1 | P–K4 | P–K4 | 14 | Q–K3 | P–N5 | 27 | N–Q4 | B–B2 |
| 2 | N–KB3 | N–QB3 | 15 | P–QN3 | B–K3 | 28 | N–B3 | N–B7 |
| 3 | B–N5 | P–QR3 | 16 | N–K4 | R–Q8† | 29 | Q–K4 | B–N3 |
| 4 | B–R4 | N–B3 | 17 | N–K1 | N–Q5 | 30 | Q–Q5† | K–B1 |
| 5 | O–O | NxP | 18 | B–N2 | NxBP | 31 | P–R5 | B–K1 |
| 6 | P–Q4 | P–QN4 | 19 | Q–K2 | RxR | 32 | Q–K4 | BxP |
| 7 | B–N3 | P–Q4 | 20 | BxR | NxB | 33 | QxN | BxN |
| 8 | PxP | B–K3 | 21 | NxN | BxN | 34 | PxB | RxP |
| 9 | Q–K2 | B–K2 | 22 | N–Q3 | B–N3 | 35 | QxRP | RxBP |
| 10 | R–Q1 | N–B4 | 23 | NxP | O–O | 36 | P–R4 | R–B3† |
| 11 | BxP | BxB | 24 | N–B6 | P–B3 | 37 | K–N2 | P–R4 |
| 12 | N–B3 | B–B5 | 25 | P–KR4 | PxP | | Draw | |
| 13 | RxQ† | RxR | 26 | QxKP | R–B3 | | | |

SUPPLEMENTARY VARIATIONS 22–26:

1 P–K4, P–K4 2 N–KB3, N–QB3 3 B–N5, P–QR3 4 B–R4, N–B3 5 O–O, NxP

| | *22* | *23* | *24* | *25* | *26* |
|---|---|---|---|---|---|
| *6* | Q–K2 | R–K1 | – – | P–Q4 | – – |
| | N–B4 | N–B4 | – – | PxP[8] | – – |
| *7* | BxN | N–B3 | BxN | R–K1 | – – |
| | QPxB | NxB | QPxB | P–Q4[9] | – – |
| *8* | P–Q4 | NxP! | P–Q4 | NxP | B–KN5[12] |
| | N–K3 | B–K2[3] | N–K3 | B–Q3 | B–K2 |
| *9* | PxP | N–Q5 | NxP | NxN | BxB |
| | N–Q5[1] | O–O | B–K2 | BxP† | QxB[13] |
| *10* | NxN | NxN | P–QB3[6] | K–R1[10] | NxP |
| | QxN | QPxN | O–O | Q–R5 | O–O |
| *11* | P–KR3[2] | NxB† | P–KB4 | RxN† | BxN |
| | B–K2 | K–R1 | P–B3 | PxR | PxB |
| *12* | = | Q–R5 | N–B3 | Q–Q8† | P–KB3 |
| | | N–N3[4] | Q–Q4 | QxQ | P–QB4 |
| *13* | | R–K4 | P–B4[7] | NxQ† | N–B6 |
| | | Q–Q3 | = | KxN | Q–Q3 |
| *14* | | P–QN3 | | KxB | QxP |
| | | P–R3 | | B–K3 | N–B3 |
| *15* | | B–N2 | | B–K3 | QxQ |
| | | N–Q4 | | P–KB4 | PxQ |
| *16* | | B–K5![5] | | N–QB3 | = |
| | | ± | | K–K2[11] | |
| | | | | ± | |

*Notes to supplementary variations 22–26:*

[1] If 9 . . . B–QB4, then 10 R–Q1, Q–K2 11 N–B3, O–O 12 N–K4, B–N3 13 N–N3±.

[2] Similar to Fischer–Neikirch, Portoroz 1958. After 11 R–Q1 comes of course 11 . . . B–KN5!

[3] After 8 . . . NxKN comes 9 RxN†, B–K2 10 N–Q5, O–O 11 NxB†, K–R1 12 Q–R5 (threatening 13 QxRP†, KxQ 14 R–R5 mate), P–KN3 13 Q–R6, P–Q3 14 R–KR5!, PxR 15 Q–B6 mate. The move 8 . . . NxQN is not too good because of 9 NxN†, B–K2 10 NxB!!, NxQ 11 N–N6†, Q–K2 12 NxQ! and Black's Knight at Q8 is lost.

[4] Keres recommends 12 . . . B–K3 13 RxB, PxR 14 N–N6†, K–N1 15 NxR, QxN 16 Q–N4, N–N3 17 QxKP†, K–R1. However, after 18 Q–N4, R–K1 19 Q–Q1, Q–K2 20 P–KN3 Black's possibilities for attack seem to be exhausted.

[5] Yates–Conde, Hastings 1923.

[6] For 10 B–K3 see Game 57.

[7] Played in a match game, Cambridge–Hastings, 1921.

[8] The so-called Riga Variation.

[9] Much weaker is 7 . . . P–B4.

[10] After 10 KxB, Q–R5† 11 K–N1, QxP† the game is drawn because of perpetual check.

[11] 17 P–KN4, P–KN3 18 K–N3± (Capablanca–Ed. Lasker, 1915).

[12] A recommendation by Berger (1909), trying to refute the Riga Variation. This attempt, however, was not convincing.

[13] Krause recommends 9 . . . KxB 10 P–B4, PxP e.p. 11 NxP, B–K3 12 BxN, PxB 13 N–Q4, NxN! 14 PxN, Q–Q2 15 Q–N4. Krause is of the opinion that this position favors Black. Keres, on the contrary, gives the best chances to White!

*Lopez Game 57*

*WHITE: Cipalis* *BLACK: Averbach*

*Championship of USSR 1958*

| WHITE | BLACK | WHITE | BLACK |
|---|---|---|---|
| 1 P–K4 | P–K4 | 28 R–N3 | P–QR4 |
| 2 N–KB3 | N–QB3 | 29 R–N5 | RxP |
| 3 B–N5 | P–QR3 | 30 RxP | R–B8† |
| 4 B–R4 | N–B3 | 31 K–B2 | R–B7† |
| 5 O–O | NxP | 32 K–N1 | R–B8† |
| 6 R–K1 | N–B4 | 33 K–B2 | R–B7† |
| 7 BxN | QPxB | 34 K–N1 | K–B2 |
| 8 NxP | B–K2 | 35 R–B5† | K–K3 |
| 9 P–Q4 | N–K3 | 36 RxP | P–B4 |
| 10 B–K3 | O–O | 37 R–KN4 | P–N3 |
| 11 P–QB4 | P–B3 | 38 R–N5 | K–Q3 |
| 12 N–KB3 | P–KB4 | 39 K–B1 | RxRP |
| 13 B–Q2 | P–B5 | 40 K–K1 | P–B5 |
| 14 B–B3 | N–N4 | 41 K–Q1 | K–K3 |
| 15 NxN | BxN | 42 P–R4 | P–B6 |
| 16 P–B3 | B–B4 | 43 P–R5 | R–Q7† |
| 17 N–R3 | Q–Q2 | 44 K–B1 | R–Q4 |
| 18 Q–Q2 | QR–K1 | 45 RxR | KxR |
| 19 N–B2 | B–B3 | 46 PxP | PxP |
| 20 RxR | RxR | 47 K–B2 | K–Q5 |
| 21 R–Q1 | P–B4 | 48 P–B4 | K–K6 |
| 22 PxP | QxQ | 49 KxP | KxP |
| 23 RxQ | BxB | 50 K–Q3 | P–N4 |
| 24 PxB | BxN | 51 K–K2 | K–N6 |
| 25 RxB | R–K4 | 52 K–B1 | K–R7 |
| 26 R–N2 | RxP | 53 P–N4! | Draw |
| 27 RxP | RxP | | |

# part 20—CLOSED DEFENSE, CLASSICAL VARIATION

1 P–K4, P–K4
2 N–KB3, N–QB3
3 B–N5, P–QR3
4 B–R4, N–B3
5 O–O, B–K2
6 R–K1, P–QN4
7 B–N3, P–Q3
8 P–B3, O–O[A]
9 P–KR3[B], N–QR4
10 B–B2, P–B4
11 P–Q4, Q–B2
12 QN–Q2[C]

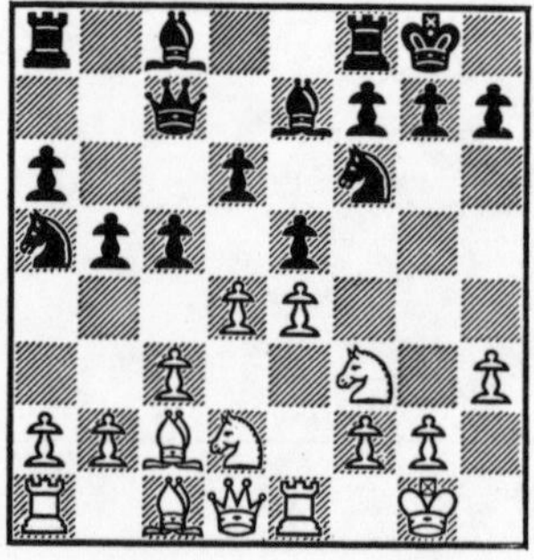

KEY POSITION 20

## OBSERVATIONS ON KEY POSITION 20

[A] Not good is 8 . . . B–N5 because of 9 P–Q3. Inferior is 9 P–KR3, B–R4 10 P–Q3, Q–Q2 when Black may strike at the Pawn at R3. However, after 8 . . . B–N5 9 P–Q3, O–O 10 QN–Q2 White eventually wins a tempo with the maneuver QN–Q2–B1–K3, or QN–Q2–B1–N3 followed by P–KR3. Black defers . . . B–N5 until White has played P–Q4, for then he exercises considerable pressure on the center.

[B] Preparing for P–Q4. If 9 P–Q4 then . . . B–N5 is feasible.

[C] Most frequently played by far. True, there are other systems—characterized by the exchange 12 PxP or 12 P–Q5, but White can follow them later under better conditions. E.g., 12 P–Q5 wins a tempo if played after . . . N–QB3. Here it only facilitates Black's counterplay: 12 . . . B–Q2 13 QN–Q2, P–B5 14 N–B1, N–N2 15 B–K3, N–B4 16 KN–Q2, P–N3 17 P–B4, PxP 18 BxP, N–R4 19 B–R6, N–KN2 ∓ (Mikenas–Keres, Tallinn 1938). The exchange 12 PxP is premature; White discloses his plans too early. Nor can 12 P–QR4 be recommended. In a game Fine–Reshevsky (AVRO Tournament 1938) the follow-up was 12 . . . B–Q2! 13 QN–Q2, BPxP 14 BPxP, KR–B1 15 B–Q3, NPxP∓. The modern move 12 P–QN4, on the contrary, must be considered as a promising attempt to steer the game into new channels. After 12 . . . PxNP 13 PxNP Black has the choice between:

1) 13 . . . N–B3 14 B–N2 (14 P–R3, PxP is easy for Black), NxNP 15 B–N3, N–B3 16 N–B3 and White has sufficient compensation for the Pawn.
2) 13 . . . N–B5 14 QN–Q2, B–N2 15 NxN, PxN 16 P–Q5, P–QR4 17 P–N5, P–R5 18 BxP, Q–R4 19 B–B2, QxNP=.

Paradoxically, the Closed Defense is fraught with tension which may be resolved in various ways of White's or Black's choosing. Courses of action to be pursued, among others, are: (1) closing of the center with P–Q5 — this facilitates Pawn storming on both wings by either side; usually White attacks on the Kingside; (2) the exchange of Pawns by White — in doing so, he still retains attacking chances against the enemy King which may be augmented by maneuvering toward and occupying Q5; (3) the exchange of Pawns by Black (. . . BPxP) —

Black hopes to use the open QB-file to divert some of White's pressure from other directions; if White can be induced later to lock the center with P–Q5 or to simplify by exchanging the other center Pawn, Black has enhanced his prospects over (1) and (2); (4) failure to persuade White into such action still leaves open to Black the plan for complete liquidation of the center by . . . P–Q4; the resultant opening of lines — diagonals and files — should be viewed with caution, however, as these may accrue to White.

IDEA VARIATIONS 45–50:

(45) 12 . . . B–N2 13 P–Q5, B–B1 14 N–B1, R–K1 15 K–R2, P–N3 16 N–K3, B–B1 17 P–KN4, with good attacking chances for White. See Game 58.

(46) 12 . . . N–B3 13 P–Q5, N–Q1 14 P–QR4, R–N1 15 PxP, PxP 16 P–B4, P–N5 17 N–B1, N–K1 18 P–N4, P–N3 19 N–N3, N–KN2 20 K–R1, P–B3 21 N–R2, N–B2 22 R–KN1, B–Q2 23 B–K3, R–R1 24 Q–Q2, RxR 25 RxR, Q–N2 26 P–N3, R–R1 27 Q–B1, R–R3= (Johansson–Grunfeld, correspondence game 1935).

(47) 12 . . . N–B3 13 PxBP, PxP 14 N–B1, B–K3 15 N–K3, QR–Q1 16 Q–K2, P–N3 17 N–N5, B–B1 18 B–Q2, K–N2 19 QR–Q1, P–R3 20 N–B3, B–K3 21 P–QR4, Q–N1 22 B–B1, RxR 23 RxR, R–Q1 24 RxR, BxR 25 PxP, PxP 26 N–Q5±. See Game 59.

(48) 12 . . . BPxP 13 PxP, N–B3 14 N–N3, P–QR4 15 B–K3, P–R5 16 QN–Q2, N–QN5 17 B–N1, B–Q2 18 P–R3, N–B3 19 B–Q3, Q–N1 20 P–QN4± (Boleslavski–Goldenov, Leningrad 1947).

(49) 12 . . . BPxP 13 PxP, B–N2 14 N–B1, QR–B1 15 B–Q3, P–Q4 16 PxQP, P–K5 17 BxP, NxB 18 RxN, BxP 19 R–K1, Q–N2 and Black has sufficient compensation for the Pawn. See Game 62.

(50) 12 . . . BPxP 13 PxP, B–N2 14 P–Q5, B–B1 15 N–B1, B–Q2 16 KN–R2, KR–B1 17 B–Q3, N–N2 18 P–QN4, P–QR4 19 B–Q2, PxP 20 QBxP, N–B4 21 P–R3, Q–R2 22 N–N3, B–Q1∓ (Bronstein–Keres, Moscow 1951).

PRACTICAL VARIATIONS 105–114:

1 P–K4, P–K4 2 N–KB3, N–QB3 3 B–N5, P–QR3 4 B–R4, N–B3 5 O–O, B–K2 6 R–K1, P–QN4 7 B–N3, P–Q3 8 P–B3, O–O 9 P–KR3, N–QR4 10 B–B2, P–B4 11 P–Q4, Q–B2 12 QN–Q2

| | 105 | 106 | 107 | 108 | 109 |
|---|---|---|---|---|---|
| 12 | – – | – – | – – | – – | – – |
| | N–B3 | – – | – – | BPxP | B–Q2[15] |
| 13 | PxBP | – – | P–Q5 | PxP | N–B1 |
| | PxP | – – | N–QR4[7] | B–N2[10] | KR–K1 |
| 14 | P–QR4 | N–B1 | P–QN3[8] | P–Q5[11] | N–K3[16] |
| | R–N1 | B–Q3[3] | B–Q2 | B–B1[12] | P–N3 |
| 15 | PxP | N–R4 | N–B1 | R–N1![13] | PxBP |
| | PxP | N–K2[4] | N–N2 | P–N5 | PxP |
| 16 | N–B1 | Q–B3 | P–B4 | N–B1 | N–R2 |
| | B–Q3[1] | B–K3[5] | KR–N1 | N–N2 | B–K3 |
| 17 | B–N5 | N–N3 | N–K3 | B–K3 | Q–B3 |
| | N–K1 | Q–B3 | PxP | B–Q2 | QR–Q1 |
| 18 | N–K3 | KN–B5 | NxBP | R–B1 | KN–N4[17] |
| | P–B3 | NxN | B–KB1 | KR–B1 | NxN |
| 19 | N–Q5 | NxN | P–QR4 | Q–Q2 | PxN |
| | Q–B2 | BxN | N–QR4 | Q–R4 | Q–B3 |
| 20 | B–K3 | QxB | KN–Q2 | B–N1 | Q–N3[18] |
| | N–K2 | N–K1[6] | P–N3[9] | B–Q1 | P–B3 |
| 21 | R–R7 | = | = | N–N3 | P–N5 |
| | R–N2 | | | RxR | K–R1 |
| 22 | R–R8 | | | RxR | P–N3 |
| | B–K3 | | | R–B1 | R–KB1 |
| 23 | NxN† | | | RxR | N–Q5 |
| | BxN | | | BxR | BxN |
| 24 | Q–R1 | | | Q–B1[14] | PxB |
| | N–B2 | | | = | QxP[19] |
| 25 | RxR† | | | | = |
| | QxR[2] | | | | |
| | = | | | | |

*Notes to practical variations 105-114:*

[1] This maneuver is known since the game Lipnitzky–Botvinnik, 1952. If White plays 17 N–K3, there follows 17 . . . N–K2 protecting the important squares Q4 and KB4.

[2] Smyslov–Bolbochan, 1956.

[3] 14 . . . B–K3 leads to Idea Var. 47.

[4] In the sixteenth match game Smyslov–Botvinnik, 1957, Black played less exactly 15 . . . P–N3 16 B–R6, R–Q1 17 Q–B3, N–K1 18 N–K3, P–B3 19 N–Q5, Q–B2 20 N–N6 and White obtained the two Bishops.

[5] 16 . . . R–Q1 leads to Game 60.

[6] Tal–Filip, Reykjavik 1957.

| 110 | 111 | 112 | 113 | 114 |
|---|---|---|---|---|
| — — | — — | — — | — — | — — |
| — — | — — | R–K1 | B–N2 | R–Q1 |
| — — | — — | N–B1 | N–B1[28] | N–B1 |
| — — | — — | N–B5[26] | BPxP | P–Q4 |
| — — | — — | P–QN3 | PxP | N–N3[35] |
| — — | — — | N–N3 | QR–B1 | PxKP |
| P–QN4 | — — | N–N3 | B–Q3[29] | KNxP |
| PxNP | — — | P–N3 | P–Q4[30] | PxP |
| PxNP | — — | B–K3 | QPxP[31] | PxP |
| N–B5 | — — | B–N2 | NxP | B–Q3[36] |
| NxN | — — | Q–Q2 | N–N3 | Q–K2 |
| PxN | — — | QN–Q2 | P–B4[32] | BxN |
| B–Q2 | — — | QR–Q1 | PxP e.p. | PxB |
| P–B6 | — — | QR–Q1 | BxP | QxP |
| B–R6[20] | — — | B–R6 | NxN | NxP |
| QR–N1[21] | P–R4 | P–Q4[27] | PxN | B–B4 |
| B–N3 | PxRP | ∓ | BxKP | B–N5 |
| B–KB1[22] | QxP | | KR–Q1 | BxN |
| BxB | B–N3 | | Q–K2 | BxN |
| RxB | B–R5 | | R–K1 | QxB[37] |
| PxP | N–N5 | | N–Q2[33] | = |
| PxP | BxB | | Q–Q2 | |
| R–QB1 | QxB | | Q–B1 | |
| RxP | P–Q4 | | N–B3 | |
| Q–Q3 | QPxP | | N–B3 | |
| B–R5[23] | NxP | | N–Q5 | |
| RxP | NxN | | BxB | |
| Q–R4[24] | PxN[25] | | QxB[34] | |
| = | = | | = | |

[7] In Rossolimo–Foltys, 1949, the continuation was: 13 . . . N–Q1 14 N–B1, N–K1 15 P–KN4, P–B3 16 K–R2, N–B2 17 N–N3, P–N3 18 R–KN1, N–N2 19 B–K3, B–Q2 20 Q–K2, P–QR4 21 R–N2, K–R1 22 QR–KN1, KR–QN1 23 K–R1, P–R5=.

[8] 14 N–B1 leads to Idea Var. 45.

[9] Keres–Alexander, 1937-38.

[10] 13 . . . N–B3 leads to Idea Var. 48 and Game 61.

[11] For 14 N–B1 see Prac. Var. 113.

[12] Best. On other moves the Bishop remains out of play. For example: 14 . . . KR–B1 15 B–Q3, N–Q2 16 N–B1, N–B4 17 N–K3, NxB 18 QxN, N–B5 19 N–B5, B–B1 20 P–QN3,

continued ▸

N–N3 21 B–Q2± (Aronin–Tolush, 1950).

[13] 15 N–B1 leads to Idea Var. 50.

[14] Gligoric–Reshevsky, 1952.

[15] At present the usual and most elastic system is 12 . . . B–Q2 and 13 . . . KR–K1. Thus Black continues his development and keeps the tension in the center. But if 12 . . . R–K1, White is for choice after 13 P–QN4, PxNP 14 PxNP, N–B3 15 B–N2, NxNP 16 B–N3. Now . . . N–Q6 fails against BxP† (Tahl–Gurgenidze, Baku 1961).

[16] 14 B–N5 leads to Game 63; 14 P–QR4 leads to Game 65. If 14 N–N3, P–N3 15 B–N5, K–N2 16 P–QR4, B–K3 17 Q–K2, P–R3=.

[17] White exchanges Black's Knight in order to weaken Black's hold on Q4. The game revolves around the struggle for the control of this central square.

[18] Preferable is 20 P–KN5. See Game 64.

[19] With the continuation: 25 PxP, BxP 26 B–R6, KR–K1 27 B–K4, Q–K3 28 Q–B3, Q–K2 29 QR–Q1, B–N2 30 B–K3, R–KB1 31 Q–R3, K–N1 32 Q–N4 and White's two Bishops compensate for his Pawn (Boleslavski–Tal, 1957).

[20] The maneuver B–Q2–R6 first occurred in Bronstein–Gligoric, 1956. Black's Bishop Pawn in advancing opens the White diagonal QR2–KN8 for use of his King Bishop. 19 B–N5 seems stronger. E.g., . . . P–QR4 20 PxRP, RxP 21 B–N3± (Gufeld–Bannik, Kiev 1960). Because of this, Black's best try in the column is 18 . . . B–KB1 after which 19 B–B3, B–R3! and 19 R–QB1, PxP 20 NxP, P–Q4! are satisfactory for Black.

[21] Analyzed and recommended by Rabar.

[22] This is slower than 20 . . . KR–QB1 (21 N–N5 is met by 21 . . . B–K1) 21 R–QB1, RxP 22 R–K3 (Szabo–Gligoric, Hastings 1957).

[23] The troublesome Bishop is eliminated.

[24] Bogdanovic–Rabar, Sombor 1957, and Blatny–Rabar, Wenen 1957.

[25] The passed QBP completely compensates for his material disadvantage (Szabo–Geller, 1957).

[26] 13 . . . P–N3 leads to Game 66.

[27] Reinhardt–Donner, Buenos Aires 1955.

[28] After 13 P–Q5 Black continues with 13 . . . B–B1 and then much as in Prac. Var. 107.

[29] Niephaus–Trifunovic, Wageningen 1957, continued: 15 B–N1, P–Q4 16 KPxP, PxP 17 B–N5, KR–K1 18 NxP, NxP 19 BxB, RxB=. If 17 . . . P–R3? 18 BxP, PxB 19 Q–Q2, KR–Q1 20 QxP, RxP 21 R–K4±. Besides 15 B–Q3 and B–N1 White has a third possibility: 15 R–K2, KR–K1 16 N–N3, P–N3 17 P–N3, N–QB3 18 B–N2± (Matanovic–Keres, Wenen 1957).

[30] 15 . . . N–Q2 leads to Game 67 and 15 . . . N–B3 leads to Game 68.

[31] 16 PxQP leads to Idea Var. 49.

[32] In a game Petrosian–Trifunovic, 1958, the continuation was: 17 . . . B–N5!? 18 R–K2, P–B4 19 PxP e.p., NxN 20 PxN, QxP 21 B–B5, P–Q5 22 B–K6†, K–R1 23 BxR, BxN 24 Q–Q3, RxB 25 QxB, QxQ 26 PxP†±.

[33] If 22 Q–Q3 then 22 . . . RxB! 23 RxR, R–Q1.

[34] With the continuation 26 NxN, BxN, and the strong

Bishop on Q5 compensates for the sacrificed Pawn (Geller–Keres, Amsterdam 1956).

[35] Or 14 PxKP, PxKP 15 PxN, RxQ 16 PxB, B–K3!∓. For 14 PxQP see Game 69.

[36] Weaker is 16 . . . B–K3 17 NxKP, QR–B1 18 R–K2, N–B5 19 N–KB3, B–Q4 20 NxN†, BxN 21 B–K4 (Gligoric–Milic, 1953).

[37] Nilsson–Keres, Amsterdam 1954.

*Lopez Game 58*

*WHITE: Alexander* *BLACK: Pachman*

*Zonal Tournament, Hilversum 1957*

| | WHITE | BLACK | | WHITE | BLACK | | WHITE | BLACK |
|---|---|---|---|---|---|---|---|---|
| 1 | P–K4 | P–K4 | 15 | K–R2 | P–N3 | 29 | Q–R5† | N–N3 |
| 2 | N–KB3 | N–QB3 | 16 | N–K3 | B–B1 | 30 | PxN† | K–N1 |
| 3 | B–N5 | P–QR3 | 17 | P–KN4 | B–N2 | 31 | Q–B5 | Q–K2 |
| 4 | B–R4 | N–B3 | 18 | R–KN1 | K–R1 | 32 | R–KN1 | N–B5 |
| 5 | O–O | B–K2 | 19 | N–N5! | R–B1 | 33 | B–B1 | B–Q2 |
| 6 | R–K1 | P–QN4 | 20 | P–KR4 | N–N1 | 34 | Q–B3 | R–KB1 |
| 7 | B–N3 | P–Q3 | 21 | Q–K2 | B–Q2 | 35 | P–N3 | N–N3 |
| 8 | P–B3 | O–O | 22 | B–Q2 | N–K2? | 36 | P–R5 | P–B4 |
| 9 | P–KR3 | N–QR4 | 23 | N–B5! | PxN | 37 | B–N5 | PxP |
| 10 | B–B2 | P–B4 | 24 | NPxP | P–B3 | 38 | Q–K2 | Q–K1 |
| 11 | P–Q4 | Q–B2 | 25 | NxP | B–K1 | 39 | BxP | B–B4 |
| 12 | QN–Q2 | B–N2 | 26 | RxB | KxR | 40 | B–R6 | R–B3 |
| 13 | P–Q5 | B–B1 | 27 | NxR | KxN | 41 | Q–B3 | Resigns |
| 14 | N–B1 | R–K1 | 28 | B–R6† | K–B2 | | | |

*Lopez Game 59*

*WHITE: Euwe* *BLACK: Smyslov*

*World Championship, The Hague 1948*

| | WHITE | BLACK | | WHITE | BLACK | | WHITE | BLACK |
|---|---|---|---|---|---|---|---|---|
| 1 | P–K4 | P–K4 | 16 | Q–K2 | P–N3 | 31 | B–Q4 | K–R2 |
| 2 | N–KB3 | N–QB3 | 17 | N–N5 | B–B1 | 32 | N–KB4 | B–B5 |
| 3 | B–N5 | P–QR3 | 18 | B–Q2 | K–N2 | 33 | N/5xNP | PxN |
| 4 | B–R4 | N–B3 | 19 | QR–Q1 | P–R3 | 34 | NxP? | KxN |
| 5 | O–O | B–K2 | 20 | N–B3 | B–K3 | 35 | P–K5† | K–B2 |
| 6 | R–K1 | P–QN4 | 21 | P–QR4 | Q–N1 | 36 | Q–R5† | K–B1 |
| 7 | B–N3 | O–O | 22 | B–B1 | RxR | 37 | P–B4 | B–N3 |
| 8 | P–B3 | P–Q3 | 23 | RxR | R–Q1 | 38 | Q–B5† | K–K2 |
| 9 | P–KR3 | N–QR4 | 24 | RxR | BxR | 39 | Q–R7† | K–Q1 |
| 10 | B–B2 | P–B4 | 25 | PxP | PxP | 40 | BxB† | QxB† |
| 11 | P–Q4 | Q–B2 | 26 | N–Q5! | N–N1 | 41 | K–R2 | Q–K6 |
| 12 | QN–Q2 | N–B3 | 27 | B–K3 | P–B5 | 42 | Q–B5 | N–QB3 |
| 13 | PxBP | PxP | 28 | P–QN3 | N–R4? | | Resigns | |
| 14 | N–B1 | B–K3 | 29 | NxP | PxP | | | |
| 15 | N–K3 | QR–Q1 | 30 | B–N1 | Q–N2 | | | |

### *Lopez Game 60*

*WHITE: Tal* — *BLACK: Filip*

*Interzonal Tournament, Portoroz 1958*

| | WHITE | BLACK | | WHITE | BLACK |
|---|---|---|---|---|---|
| 1 | P–K4 | P–K4 | 20 | NxN | BxN |
| 2 | N–KB3 | N–QB3 | 21 | NPxB | K–R1 |
| 3 | B–N5 | P–QR3 | 22 | K–R2? | P–R3 |
| 4 | B–R4 | N–B3 | 23 | R–KN1 | Q–K2 |
| 5 | O–O | B–K2 | 24 | B–Q2 | B–B4 |
| 6 | R–K1 | P–QN4 | 25 | QR–Q1 | R–Q2 |
| 7 | B–N3 | P–Q3 | 26 | Q–N3 | Q–B1 |
| 8 | P–B3 | O–O | 27 | K–R1 | QR–Q1 |
| 9 | P–KR3 | N–QR4 | 28 | BxP | PxB |
| 10 | B–B2 | P–B4 | 29 | QxP | B–K2? |
| 11 | P–Q4 | Q–B2 | 30 | R–Q4 | RxR |
| 12 | QN–Q2 | N–B3 | 31 | PxR | K–R2 |
| 13 | PxBP | PxP | 32 | R–Q1 | N–K1 |
| 14 | N–B1 | B–Q3 | 33 | P–B6 | NxP |
| 15 | N–R4 | N–K2 | 34 | Q–B5† | K–R1 |
| 16 | Q–B3 | R–Q1 | 35 | P–K5 | Q–N2 |
| 17 | N–K3 | Q–N2 | 36 | PxN | BxP |
| 18 | P–KN4 | P–B5 | 37 | R–KN1 | B–N4 |
| 19 | N/4–B5 | NxN | 38 | P–B4 | Resigns |

### *Lopez Game 61*

*WHITE: Unzicker* — *BLACK: Keres*

*Alekhine Memorial Tournament, Moscow 1956*

| | WHITE | BLACK | | WHITE | BLACK |
|---|---|---|---|---|---|
| 1 | P–K4 | P–K4 | 21 | R–B2 | Q–Q1 |
| 2 | N–KB3 | N–QB3 | 22 | N–R5 | RxR |
| 3 | B–N5 | P–QR3 | 23 | NxB | Q–B2 |
| 4 | B–R4 | N–B3 | 24 | QxR!! | QxN |
| 5 | O–O | B–K2 | 25 | BxB | R–B1 |
| 6 | R–K1 | P–QN4 | 26 | BxP | RxQ |
| 7 | B–N3 | P–Q3 | 27 | BxR | P–B3 |
| 8 | P–B3 | O–O | 28 | B–N3 | N–B5 |
| 9 | P–KR3 | N–QR4 | 29 | R–Q1 | N–Q2 |
| 10 | B–B2 | P–B4 | 30 | R–Q2 | N–QN3! |
| 11 | P–Q4 | Q–B2 | 31 | B–B7 | N–B5 |
| 12 | QN–Q2 | BPxP | 32 | P–Q6 | N–K3 |
| 13 | PxP | N–B3 | 33 | B–R5! | N–B4? |
| 14 | N–N3 | B–N2 | 34 | B–N4 | N–Q2 |
| 15 | B–N5 | P–R3 | 35 | R–B2 | P–QR4 |
| 16 | B–R4 | N–QN5 | 36 | BxP | QxP |
| 17 | B–N1 | QR–B1 | 37 | N–Q2! | Q–Q6 |
| 18 | R–K2 | N–R4 | 38 | RxN | K–R2 |
| 19 | P–R3! | N–B3 | 39 | B–B2 | Resigns |
| 20 | P–Q5 | N–N1 | | | |

*Lopez Game 62*

*WHITE: Unzicker* *BLACK: Euwe*

*Germany–Netherland, Düsseldorf 1950*

| | WHITE | BLACK | | WHITE | BLACK |
|---|---|---|---|---|---|
| 1 | P–K4 | P–K4 | 22 | PxQ | N–B3 |
| 2 | N–KB3 | N–QB3 | 23 | N–Q5 | B–R5 |
| 3 | B–N5 | P–QR3 | 24 | R–K4 | QR–Q1 |
| 4 | B–R4 | N–B3 | 25 | N–B7 | NxP |
| 5 | O–O | B–K2 | 26 | K–N2 | B–B3 |
| 6 | R–K1 | P–QN4 | 27 | B–B4 | N–K3 |
| 7 | B–N3 | P–Q3 | 28 | NxN | PxN |
| 8 | P–B3 | O–O | 29 | B–K5 | R–Q2 |
| 9 | P–KR3 | N–QR4 | 30 | BxB | RxB |
| 10 | B–B2 | P–B4 | 31 | P–N4 | R–Q6 |
| 11 | P–Q4 | BPxP | 32 | R–QB1 | R/6xP |
| 12 | PxP | Q–B2 | 33 | R–B8† | K–B2 |
| 13 | QN–Q2 | B–N2 | 34 | R–B7† | K–B1 |
| 14 | N–B1 | QR–B1 | 35 | R–K2 | P–R3 |
| 15 | B–Q3 | P–Q4 | 36 | R–Q2 | K–N1 |
| 16 | KPxP | P–K5 | 37 | R–Q8† | K–R2 |
| 17 | BxKP | NxB | 38 | R/8–Q7 | RxP† |
| 18 | RxN | BxP | 39 | K–N3 | R/3–B6† |
| 19 | R–K1 | Q–N2 | 40 | K–N4 | P–R4† |
| 20 | N–K3 | BxN | 41 | KxP | R–KN7 |
| 21 | QxB | QxQ | | Resigns | |

*Lopez Game 63*

*WHITE: Schmid* *BLACK: Ivkov*

*Europa Cup, Wenew 1957*

| | WHITE | BLACK | | WHITE | BLACK | | WHITE | BLACK |
|---|---|---|---|---|---|---|---|---|
| 1 | P–K4 | P–K4 | 16 | P–QN3 | N–R6 | 31 | RxR | PxR |
| 2 | N–KB3 | N–QB3 | 17 | B–Q3 | P–B5 | 32 | Q–B3 | P–Q4 |
| 3 | B–N5 | P–QR3 | 18 | B–K2 | KPxP | 33 | QxP | P–Q5? |
| 4 | B–R4 | N–B3 | 19 | NxP | NxP | 34 | N–N4 | N–B5 |
| 5 | O–O | B–K2 | 20 | BxB | RxB | 35 | Q–N6! | K–R1 |
| 6 | R–K1 | P–QN4 | 21 | B–B3 | QR–K1 | 36 | Q–K8† | K–R2 |
| 7 | B–N3 | P–Q3 | 22 | BxN | RxB | 37 | QxKP | QxP |
| 8 | P–B3 | O–O | 23 | RxR | RxR | 38 | Q–K4† | K–R1 |
| 9 | P–KR3 | N–QR4 | 24 | P–QN4 | P–QR4 | 39 | K–R2! | Q–N6 |
| 10 | B–B2 | P–B4 | 25 | N–K3 | B–K3 | 40 | Q–K8† | K–R2 |
| 11 | P–Q4 | Q–B2 | 26 | R–B1 | PxP | 41 | Q–B7 | K–R1 |
| 12 | QN–Q2 | B–Q2 | 27 | PxP | Q–R2! | 42 | N–K5! | K–R2 |
| 13 | N–B1 | KR–K1 | 28 | NxB | PxN | 43 | N–Q7 | Resigns |
| 14 | B–N5 | P–R3 | 29 | R–B3 | R–Q5 | | | |
| 15 | B–KR4 | N–B5 | 30 | Q–QB1 | R–Q6 | | | |

*Lopez Game 64*

*WHITE: Fischer* *BLACK: Unzicker*

*Zurich 1959*

| | WHITE | BLACK | | WHITE | BLACK |
|---|---|---|---|---|---|
| 1 | P–K4 | P–K4 | 34 | R–R7 | Q–Q3 |
| 2 | N–KB3 | N–QB3 | 35 | B–K2 | R–K2 |
| 3 | B–N5 | P–QR3 | 36 | RxR | QxR |
| 4 | B–R4 | N–B3 | 37 | BxP | K–N2 |
| 5 | O–O | B–K2 | 38 | B–K2 | Q–QB2 |
| 6 | R–K1 | P–QN4 | 39 | Q–K3 | Q–R4 |
| 7 | B–N3 | P–Q3 | 40 | P–N3 | Q–R6 |
| 8 | P–B3 | O–O | 41 | K–N2 | Q–R4 |
| 9 | P–KR3 | N–QR4 | 42 | Q–Q3 | Q–N3 |
| 10 | B–B2 | P–B4 | 43 | Q–B4 | Q–B3 |
| 11 | P–Q4 | Q–B2 | 44 | B–Q3 | Q–N3 |
| 12 | QN–Q2 | B–Q2 | 45 | P–QN4 | PxP |
| 13 | N–B1 | KR–K1 | 46 | PxP | N–N5 |
| 14 | N–K3 | P–N3 | 47 | Q–B5 | QxQ |
| 15 | PxKP | PxP | 48 | PxQ | K–B2 |
| 16 | N–R2 | QR–Q1 | 49 | P–B4 | K–K2 |
| 17 | Q–B3 | B–K3 | 50 | K–B3 | N–B3 |
| 18 | N/2–N4 | NxN | 51 | B–N5 | K–K3 |
| 19 | PxN | Q–B3 | 52 | B–B4† | K–K2 |
| 20 | P–N5! | N–B5 | 53 | P–B6 | N–K1 |
| 21 | N–N4 | BxN | 54 | PxP | P–R3 |
| 22 | QxB | P–B3 | 55 | K–K3 | N–B2 |
| 23 | PxP | BxP | 56 | K–Q4 | P–R4 |
| 24 | P–R4 | N–N3 | 57 | K–K3 | P–N4 |
| 25 | PxP | PxP | 58 | B–K2 | P–R5 |
| 26 | B–K3 | R–R1 | 59 | PxP | PxP |
| 27 | KR–Q1 | K–R1 | 60 | B–B4 | N–K1 |
| 28 | P–QN3 | B–N2 | 61 | K–B4 | K–Q1 |
| 29 | Q–R4 | B–B3 | 62 | K–N4 | K–B2 |
| 30 | B–N5 | BxB | 63 | B–B7 | N–N2 |
| 31 | QxB | RxR | 64 | KxP | KxP |
| 32 | RxR | N–Q2 | 65 | K–N5 | Resigns |
| 33 | B–Q1 | N–B3 | | | |

*Lopez Game 65*

*WHITE: Keres* *BLACK: Gligoric*

*Zagreb 1959*

| | WHITE | BLACK | | WHITE | BLACK |
|---|---|---|---|---|---|
| 1 | P–K4 | P–K4 | 3 | B–N5 | P–QR3 |
| 2 | N–KB3 | N–QB3 | 4 | B–R4 | N–B3 |

| WHITE | BLACK | WHITE | BLACK |
|---|---|---|---|
| 5 O–O | P–QN4 | 26 R–KN3! | R–R3? |
| 6 B–N3 | B–K2 | 27 RxP† | BxR |
| 7 R–K1 | P–Q3 | 28 Q–N4 | QxN |
| 8 P–B3 | O–O | 29 QxQ | R–QB3 |
| 9 P–KR3 | N–QR4 | 30 Q–Q7 | R/3–K3 |
| 10 B–B2 | P–B4 | 31 R–K3 | PxP |
| 11 P–Q4 | Q–B2 | 32 R–KN3 | R–R1 |
| 12 QN–Q2 | B–Q2 | 33 Q–Q4 | R–KN3 |
| 13 N–B1 | KR–K1 | 34 QxP | R–QB1 |
| 14 P–QR4 | BPxP | 35 P–N3 | N–B3 |
| 15 BPxP | N–B3 | 36 R–Q3 | R–K3 |
| 16 N–K3 | N–N5 | 37 Q–B4 | R/3–K1 |
| 17 B–N3 | NPxP | 38 R–N3 | R–K3 |
| 18 BxP | BxB | 39 B–R6! | R–N3 |
| 19 RxB | P–QR4 | 40 BxB | KxB |
| 20 N–B5 | B–B1 | 41 Q–B3† | K–N1 |
| 21 B–N5 | N–Q2 | 42 P–R4 | N–K2 |
| 22 R–R3 | P–Q4 | 43 RxR† | RPxP |
| 23 QPxP | NxP | 44 QxP | R–B8† |
| 24 B–B4 | NxN† | 45 K–R2 | Resigns |
| 25 RxN | Q–Q2 | | |

*Lopez Game 66*

*WHITE: Toran* *BLACK: Donner*

*Beverwijk 1957*

| WHITE | BLACK | WHITE | BLACK |
|---|---|---|---|
| 1 P–K4 | P–K4 | 16 PxNP | N–B3 |
| 2 N–KB3 | N–QB3 | 17 B–N2 | B–QN2 |
| 3 B–N5 | P–QR3 | 18 B–N3 | B–N2 |
| 4 B–R4 | N–B3 | 19 R–B1 | Q–Q1 |
| 5 O–O | B–K2 | 20 PxP | QNxKP |
| 6 R–K1 | P–QN4 | 21 BxN | PxB |
| 7 B–N3 | P–Q3 | 22 QxQ | QRxQ |
| 8 P–B3 | O–O | 23 R–B7 | R–Q2 |
| 9 P–KR3 | N–QR4 | 24 RxR | NxR |
| 10 B–B2 | P–B4 | 25 N–N5 | R–K2 |
| 11 P–Q4 | Q–B2 | 26 R–QB1 | B–KR3 |
| 12 QN–Q2 | R–K1 | 27 NxBP | BxN |
| 13 N–B1 | P–N3 | 28 PxB | K–N2 |
| 14 N–K3 | B–B1 | 29 R–B7 | BxP |
| 15 P–QN4! | PxNP | 30 N–Q6 | Resigns |

### *Lopez Game 67*

*WHITE: Smyslov* *BLACK: Keres*

*Candidates' Tournament, Bled 1959*

| | WHITE | BLACK | | WHITE | BLACK | | WHITE | BLACK |
|---|---|---|---|---|---|---|---|---|
| 1 | P–K4 | P–K4 | 21 | N/6–N4 | P–R4 | 41 | N–K6 | K–B2 |
| 2 | N–KB3 | N–QB3 | 22 | N/4–R2 | N–B4 | 42 | P–KR4 | K–B3 |
| 3 | B–N5 | P–QR3 | 23 | N–Q5 | BxN | 43 | K–K2 | N–B4 |
| 4 | B–R4 | N–B3 | 24 | PxB | NxB | 44 | NxN | RxN |
| 5 | O–O | B–K2 | 25 | QxN | Q–B7 | 45 | K–B3 | P–N4 |
| 6 | R–K1 | P–QN4 | 26 | R–Q1 | KR–K1 | 46 | PxP† | KxP |
| 7 | B–N3 | P–Q3 | 27 | QxQ | RxQ | 47 | R–Q3 | P–N5 |
| 8 | P–B3 | O–O | 28 | N–B1 | N–B5 | 48 | R–Q2 | R–B6† |
| 9 | P–KR3 | N–QR4 | 29 | P–QN3 | N–N7 | 49 | K–B2 | P–R5 |
| 10 | B–B2 | P–B4 | 30 | R–Q2 | RxR | 50 | K–N1 | K–B5 |
| 11 | P–Q4 | Q–B2 | 31 | BxR | N–Q6 | 51 | K–R2 | K–K4 |
| 12 | QN–Q2 | BPxP | 32 | N–K3 | P–B4 | 52 | R–Q1 | P–R4 |
| 13 | PxP | B–N2 | 33 | K–B1 | B–Q5 | 53 | R–Q2 | P–B5 |
| 14 | N–B1 | QR–B1 | 34 | N–B2 | BxP | 54 | R–KB2 | R–Q6 |
| 15 | B–Q3 | N–Q2 | 35 | B–B3† | K–N1 | 55 | R–B2 | KxP |
| 16 | N–K3 | PxP | 36 | R–Q1 | N–B4 | 56 | R–B8 | P–B6 |
| 17 | NxP | B–KB3 | 37 | B–Q4 | BxB | 57 | R–B8 | PxP |
| 18 | N/4–B5 | P–N3 | 38 | NxB | R–K6 | 58 | R–B5† | K–K5 |
| 19 | N–R6† | K–R1 | 39 | N–K6 | R–B6 | 59 | RxP | P–R6 |
| 20 | R–N1 | B–N2 | 40 | N–N5 | N–Q6 | | Resigns | |

### *Lopez Game 68*

*WHITE: Fischer* *BLACK: Keres*

*Zurich 1959*

| | WHITE | BLACK | | WHITE | BLACK |
|---|---|---|---|---|---|
| 1 | P–K4 | P–K4 | 18 | B–N5 | N–Q2 |
| 2 | N–KB3 | N–QB3 | 19 | R–QB1 | Q–N1 |
| 3 | B–N5 | P–QR3 | 20 | B–N1 | NxP |
| 4 | B–R4 | N–B3 | 21 | N/3xN | RxR |
| 5 | O–O | B–K2 | 22 | BxR | PxN |
| 6 | R–K1 | P–QN4 | 23 | N–R6† | PxN |
| 7 | B–N3 | P–Q3 | 24 | Q–N4† | K–R1 |
| 8 | P–B3 | O–O | 25 | QxN | B–Q4 |
| 9 | P–KR3 | N–QR4 | 26 | Q–B5 | R–K4 |
| 10 | B–B2 | P–B4 | 27 | Q–B3 | P–B4 |
| 11 | P–Q4 | Q–B2 | 28 | B–B4 | R–K1 |
| 12 | QN–Q2 | BPxP | 29 | Q–R5 | BxKP |
| 13 | PxP | B–N2 | 30 | P–B3 | B–B3 |
| 14 | N–B1 | QR–B1 | 31 | R–QB1 | B–Q2 |
| 15 | B–Q3 | N–B3 | 32 | BxRP | R–K3 |
| 16 | N–K3 | KR–K1 | 33 | BxB | QxB |
| 17 | N–B5 | B–B1 | 34 | Q–R4 | Q–B3 |

| WHITE | BLACK | WHITE | BLACK |
|---|---|---|---|
| 35 QxQ† | RxQ | 59 K–K4 | R–N4 |
| 36 K–B2 | K–N2 | 60 B–R6 | B–B2 |
| 37 R–B7 | R–B2 | 61 B–B8 | R–N3 |
| 38 K–K2 | P–B5 | 62 R–R7 | K–B1 |
| 39 R–R7 | K–B3 | 63 B–N4 | R–N2 |
| 40 RxP | R–K2† | 64 R–R6 | R–N3 |
| 41 K–B2 | B–K3 | 65 RxR | BxR† |
| 42 RxP | K–K4 | 66 KxP | K–N2 |
| 43 R–B6 | B–Q4 | 67 K–N5 | B–Q6 |
| 44 R–KR6 | R–QB2 | 68 P–B4 | B–K5 |
| 45 R–R5† | K–Q3 | 69 P–R4 | B–Q6 |
| 46 R–R6† | K–K4 | 70 P–R5 | B–K5 |
| 47 R–R5† | K–Q3 | 71 P–R6† | K–R1 |
| 48 R–B5 | R–B8 | 72 B–B5 | B–Q4 |
| 49 B–Q3 | R–Q8 | 73 B–N6 | B–K3 |
| 50 K–K2 | R–KN8 | 74 K–B6 | B–B5 |
| 51 K–B2 | R–Q8 | 75 K–N5 | B–K3 |
| 52 K–K2 | R–KN8 | 76 B–R5 | K–R2 |
| 53 R–N5 | BxP | 77 B–N4 | B–B5 |
| 54 BxNP | R–N8 | 78 P–B5 | B–B2 |
| 55 K–Q3 | P–R3 | 79 B–R5 | B–B5 |
| 56 R–R5 | RxP | 80 B–N6† | K–N1 |
| 57 KxP | RxP | 81 P–B6 | Resigns |
| 58 RxP† | K–K2 | | |

*Lopez Game 69*

*WHITE: Boleslavski* *BLACK: Keres*

*Zurich 1953*

| WHITE | BLACK | WHITE | BLACK |
|---|---|---|---|
| 1 P–K4 | P–K4 | 18 NxP? | P–N3 |
| 2 N–KB3 | N–QB3 | 19 B–R6 | B–B3 |
| 3 B–N5 | P–QR3 | 20 N–N3 | N–QB5 |
| 4 B–R4 | N–B3 | 21 N–K4 | BxP |
| 5 O–O | B–K2 | 22 N/3–B5 | BxR |
| 6 R–K1 | P–QN4 | 23 RxB | P–B4 |
| 7 B–N3 | O–O | 24 NxB | QxN |
| 8 P–B3 | P–Q3 | 25 N–B5 | Q–B3 |
| 9 P–KR3 | N–QR4 | 26 N–Q3 | N–B6! |
| 10 B–B2 | P–B4 | 27 Q–K1 | Q–B3 |
| 11 P–Q4 | Q–B2 | 28 P–B4 | N–K5 |
| 12 QN–Q2 | R–Q1 | 29 K–R2 | Q–B6 |
| 13 N–B1 | P–Q4 | 30 Q–N1 | N/B–Q7 |
| 14 KPxP | KPxP | 31 Q–QB1 | RxN |
| 15 PxP | NxP | 32 BxR | QxB |
| 16 Q–K2 | B–N2 | 33 Q–B7 | N–B6† |
| 17 N–N3 | PxP | Resigns | |

SUPPLEMENTARY VARIATIONS 27–31:

1 P–K4, P–K4 2 N–KB3, N–QB3 3 B–N5, P–QR3 4 B–R4, N–B3 5 O–O, B–K2 6 R–K1, P–QN4 7 B–N3, P–Q3 8 P–B3, O–O 9 P–KR3

| | 27 | 28 | 29 | 30 | 31 |
|---|---|---|---|---|---|
| 9 | – – | – – | – – | – – | – – |
| | B–N2 | P–QR4[6] | N–Q2 | N–N1 | Q–Q2[14] |
| 10 | P–Q4 | P–Q3 | P–Q4 | P–Q4 | P–Q4 |
| | PxP | P–R5 | N–N3[8] | QN–Q2 | R–K1 |
| 11 | PxP | B–B2 | B–K3 | P–B4 | P–QR4 |
| | P–Q4 | N–Q2 | B–B3[9] | P–N5 | B–N2 |
| 12 | P–K5[1] | QN–Q2 | QN–Q2 | P–B5 | QPxP |
| | N–K5 | N–N3 | N–R4 | B–N2 | QNxP |
| 13 | N–B3[2] | N–B1 | PxP | Q–B2 | PxP |
| | N–R4 | P–B4 | PxP[10] | KPxP | NxN† |
| 14 | B–B2 | B–K3! | BxN | P–B6 | QxN |
| | P–KB4 | R–N1 | PxB | P–Q6 | PxP |
| 15 | PxP e.p. | BxN | B–Q5 | Q–B4 | RxR |
| | BxP[3] | RxB | B–N2 | N–N3 | BxR |
| 16 | NxN | N–K3 | P–QN4 | PxB | QN–Q2 |
| | PxN | P–B5 | N–B3[11] | NxQ | B–B1 |
| 17 | BxP | N–Q5 | P–B4 | PxR (Q) | R–K3 |
| | BxB | R–N1 | Q–N1 | QxQ | P–B4 |
| 18 | RxB | P–B4[7] | QR–B1 | BxN | B–B2 |
| | P–B4 | ± | NxP | NxP | Q–R2 |
| 19 | P–Q5[4] | | BxB | BxQP | Q–K2 |
| | N–B5 | | QxB | P–Q4 | P–B5 |
| 20 | R–N1 | | Q–N3 | P–R3! | P–QN3 |
| | Q–Q2[5] | | N–B3[12] | N–B4[13] | Q–R8[15] |
| | = | | ± | ± | ∓ |

*Notes to supplementary variations 27–31:*

[1] 12 PxP, N–QR4 13 B–B2, NxP 14 N–B3, NxN 15 PxN, B–KB3=.

[2] Weaker is 13 QN–Q2, N–R4 14 BxP?, NxP 15 KxN, BxB∓ (Bouwmeester–Van Scheltinga, Beverwijk 1956).

[3] Black offers a Pawn for the initiative, since on 15 . . . NxP/3 16 N–N5!

[4] In the game Unzicker–Euwe (Clare Benedict Tournament 1956) White played 19 B–Q2, N–B5 20 B–B3, Q–Q4 21 Q–B2, P–N5 22 B–K1, PxP 23 R–Q1 (23 BxP, KR–B1 and if 23 NxP?, N–Q3!) QR–B1 24 R/4xP, BxR 25 RxB, N–K4! 26 RxQ, NxN† 27 PxN, RxQ 28 BxP=.

[5] The continuation was 21 P–QN3, Q–B4 22 Q–B2, N–Q3? (better is 22 . . . N–N3! 23 P–Q6, N–Q4!) 23 R–K2, QxQP 24 B–R3!± (Lowenfisch–Flohr, 1946).

[6] The idea of 9 . . . P–QR4 is to exchange White's King

Bishop by 10 P–Q4, PxP 11 PxP, P–R5 12 B–B2, N–N5. White's best answer to 9 . . . P–QR4 is probably 10 P–Q3.

[7] Vasiukov–Suetin, 1954.

[8] Better than 10 . . . B–B3, after which White can undertake strong action against Black's Queenside by 11 P–QR4, B–N2 12 PxNP, PxNP 13 RxR, BxR 14 P–Q5 and 15 N–R3.

[9] Tal–Antoshin, 1957, continued 11 . . . PxP? 12 PxP, P–Q4 13 N–QB3! PxP 14 NxKP, B–KB4 15 P–Q5! N–R4 16 P–Q6!±.

[10] Better is 13 . . . NxB.

[11] 16 . . . BxB 17 PxB, N–N2 18 N–K4!

[12] There followed 21 PxP, N–R4 22 Q–N2, KR–B1 23 P–QR4± (Aronin–Furman, 1957).

[13] Shamkowitsch–Ragosin, 1957. After both 21 RxB, NxB 22 B–Q2, R–K1 23 R–K3 and 21 B–B1, N–N6 22 RxB, NxR 23 PxP, White maintains a minimal initiative. Attempts by Black to veer from the column also favor White. See Chess Review, April 1961, page 115.

[14] Smyslov's idea to make Q1 available to Black's Queen Knight.

[15] Keres–Smyslov, Bled 1959.

---

## part 21—CLOSED DEFENSE, CENTER COUNTERATTACK VARIATION

1 P–K4, P–K4
2 N–KB3, N–QB3
3 B–N5, P–QR3
4 B–R4, N–B3
5 O–O, B–K2
6 R–K1, P–QN4
7 B–N3, P–Q3
8 P–B3, O–O
9 P–Q4, B–N5[A]

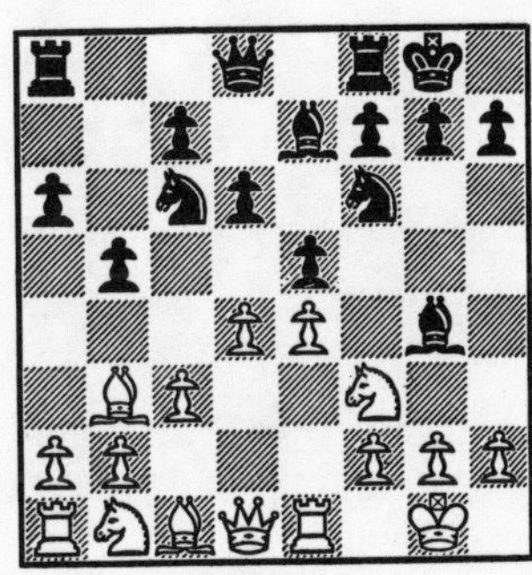

KEY POSITION 21

### OBSERVATIONS ON KEY POSITION 21

[A] The right reaction to White's somewhat premature advance in the center. After 9 . . . PxP 10 PxP, B–N5 White continues by 11 N–B3!

Black is threatening . . . BxN which would force White to weaken his Kingside, as QxB would cost a Pawn. White can either strengthen his center (by B–K3), neutralize the tension (by P–Q5), or finally neglect the threat and offer a Pawn sacrifice by P–KR3.

As in key position 24 the second method seems to be the best.

### IDEA VARIATIONS 51–53:

(51) 10 B–K3, NxKP 11 B–Q5, Q–Q2 12 BxKN, P–Q4 13 B–Q3, P–K5 14 B–K2, PxN 15 BxBP=.

(52) 10 P–Q5, N–R4 11 B–B2, P–B3 12 PxP, NxBP 13 P–KR3, B–R4 14 QN–Q2, R–B1 15 N–B1, P–N5=.

(53) 10 P–KR3, BxN 11 QxB, PxP 12 Q–Q1, PxP 13 NxP, N–QR4 14 B–B2, P–B4 15 N–K2, N–B3 16 N–N3, N–Q5 17 B–K3, NxB 18 QxN, R–K1, and White has insufficient compensation for the Pawn (19 N–B5, P–N3 20 NxB†, QxN 21 B–N5, Q–K4 22 P–B4, Q–Q5† etc., as in Pytlakowski–Tarnowski, Salzbrunnen 1950). In this line, however, 12 Q–N3 seems sharper.

PRACTICAL VARIATIONS 115–119:

1 P–K4, P–K4 2 N–KB3, N–QB3 3 B–N5, P–QR3 4 B–R4, N–B3 5 O–O, B–K2 6 R–K1, P–QN4 7 B–N3, P–Q3 8 P–B3, O–O 9 P–Q4, B–N5

| | *115* | *116* | *117* | *118* | *119* |
|---|---|---|---|---|---|
| *10* | B–K3 | – – | P–Q5[7] | P–KR3 | – – |
| | NxKP[1] | – – | N–QR4 | BxN | – – |
| *11* | B–Q5 | – – | B–B2 | QxB | – – |
| | Q–Q2 | – – | P–B3 | PxP | – – |
| *12* | BxKN | PxP | PxP | Q–Q1 | – – |
| | P–Q4 | N–B4[6] | NxBP | PxP | – – |
| *13* | B–B2[2] | = | QN–Q2[8] | NxP | – – |
| | P–K5 | | P–N5[9] | N–QR4 | – – |
| *14* | P–KR3 | | B–R4 | B–B2 | – – |
| | BxN! | | R–B1 | R–K1 | P–B4 |
| *15* | PxB | | BxN | P–B4 | N–K2 |
| | QxP | | PxP! | P–N5 | N–B3 |
| *16* | PxP[3] | | B–N7 | N–Q5 | N–N3 |
| | P–B4! | | PxN | NxN | N–Q5 |
| *17* | PxQP[4] | | BxQP | QxN | B–K3 |
| | B–Q3 | | R–N1 | P–B3 | NxB |
| *18* | PxN[5] | | BxP | Q–Q3 | QxN |
| | R–B3 | | P–Q4[10] | P–N3[11] | P–N3[12] |
| | ∓ | | = | = | ∓ |

*Notes to practical variations 115–119:*

[1] 10 . . . PxP 11 PxP, N–QR4 12 B–B2, N–B5 13 B–B1, P–B4 also gives Black a satisfactory game. See Game 70. Fischer, however, advocates 14 P–QN3, N–QR4 15 P–Q5±. See Chess Review, May 1962.

[2] 13 B–Q3 leads to Idea Var. 51.

[3] 16 P–B4 is answered by 16 . . . P–KB4 followed by 17 . . . R–B3.

[4] If 17 P–K5 then 17 . . . P–B5; and if 17 PxBP then 17 . . . B–Q3.

[5] Or 18 P–KB4, R–B3.

[6] Not 12 . . . N–N4 13 QBxN, BxB 14 P–KR3. See Game 71.

[7] 10 P–QR4 is answered by 10 . . . Q–Q2.

[8] 13 P–KR3 leads to Idea Var. 52.

[9] 13 . . . R–B1 is simpler.

[10] The position is complicated, but White cannot attain more than equality. Compare Game 72.

[11] Bronstein–Keres, Budapest 1950. The continuation was; 19 K–R1, B–B1 20 R–B1, B–N2 (20 . . . P–Q4!) 21 B–Q2, P–B4? (21 . . . P–Q4!) 22 B–R4±. See Game 73.

[12] 18 . . . R–K1! leads to Idea Var. 53. After the text White has play for the Pawn, e.g., 19 QR–Q1, Q–B2 20 B–N5 (Simagin–Pogats, Salzbrunnen 1950).

*Lopez Game 70*

*WHITE: Geller* *BLACK: Panno*

*Candidates' Tournament, Amsterdam 1956*

| | WHITE | BLACK | | WHITE | BLACK |
|---|---|---|---|---|---|
| 1 | P–K4 | P–K4 | 18 | B–N3 | R–B4 |
| 2 | N–KB3 | N–QB3 | 19 | B–B4 | Q–B1 |
| 3 | B–N5 | P–QR3 | 20 | QR–Q1 | N–R4 |
| 4 | B–R4 | N–B3 | 21 | B–N3 | Q–R6 |
| 5 | O–O | B–K2 | 22 | B–Q5 | NxB? |
| 6 | R–K1 | P–QN4 | 23 | RPxN | Q–B1 |
| 7 | B–N3 | O–O | 24 | P–QN4 | R–B6 |
| 8 | P–Q4 | P–Q3 | 25 | P–B4 | Q–B2 |
| 9 | P–B3 | B–N5 | 26 | K–N2 | R–Q1 |
| 10 | B–K3 | PxP | 27 | R–KR1 | P–R3 |
| 11 | PxP | N–QR4 | 28 | R–R5 | B–B3 |
| 12 | B–B2 | N–B5 | 29 | P–K5 | PxP |
| 13 | B–B1 | P–B4 | 30 | PxP | B–K2 |
| 14 | QN–Q2 | NxN | 31 | Q–K4 | R–B5? |
| 15 | QxN | BxN | 32 | BxR | RxR |
| 16 | PxB | PxP | 33 | BxP† | Resigns |
| 17 | QxP | R–B1 | | | |

*Lopez Game 71*

*WHITE: Johner* *BLACK: Bernstein*

*Zurich 1934*

| | WHITE | BLACK | | WHITE | BLACK |
|---|---|---|---|---|---|
| 1 | P–K4 | P–K4 | 22 | NxP | BxN |
| 2 | N–KB3 | N–QB3 | 23 | QxB | QxP |
| 3 | B–N5 | P–QR3 | 24 | R–Q1 | P–R3 |
| 4 | B–R4 | N–B3 | 25 | Q–B6 | Q–N1 |
| 5 | O–O | B–K2 | 26 | R–Q7 | R–R2 |
| 6 | R–K1 | P–QN4 | 27 | Q–Q5 | Q–N8† |
| 7 | B–N3 | P–Q3 | 28 | K–R2 | Q–KN3 |
| 8 | P–B3 | O–O | 29 | R–K7 | Q–KB3 |
| 9 | P–Q4 | B–N5 | 30 | Q–K4 | P–N3 |
| 10 | B–K3 | KNxP | 31 | R–Q7 | K–N2 |
| 11 | B–Q5 | Q–Q2 | 32 | K–N1 | Q–R8† |
| 12 | PxP | N–B4 | 33 | K–R2 | Q–B3 |
| 13 | P–KR3 | B–K3 | 34 | K–N1 | P–QR4 |
| 14 | PxP | BxQP | 35 | P–N3 | P–R5 |
| 15 | B/3xN | B/KxB | 36 | Q–K8 | P–R4 |
| 16 | BxB | QxB | 37 | R–Q8 | K–R3 |
| 17 | QN–Q2 | KR–K1 | 38 | Q–K3† | K–N2 |
| 18 | Q–B2 | N–K4 | 39 | Q–K8 | K–R3 |
| 19 | NxN | RxN | 40 | Q–K3† | K–N2 |
| 20 | RxR | QxR | 41 | Q–K8 | Draw |
| 21 | P–QB4! | PxP | | | |

*Lopez Game 72*

*WHITE: Euwe* *BLACK: Keres*

*Second Match Game 1939–40*

| | WHITE | BLACK | | WHITE | BLACK |
|---|---|---|---|---|---|
| 1 | P–K4 | P–K4 | 16 | B–N7 | PxN |
| 2 | N–KB3 | N–QB3 | 17 | QBxP | R–N1 |
| 3 | B–N5 | P–QR3 | 18 | BxP | P–Q4! |
| 4 | B–R4 | N–B3 | 19 | B–K2 | BxN! |
| 5 | O–O | B–K2 | 20 | PxB | B–B4 |
| 6 | R–K1 | P–QN4 | 21 | R–N1 | PxP |
| 7 | B–N3 | P–Q3 | 22 | B–K3 | B–Q5 |
| 8 | P–B3 | O–O | 23 | BxB | PxB |
| 9 | P–Q4 | B–N5 | 24 | B–B1 | Q–Q4 |
| 10 | P–Q5 | N–QR4 | 25 | PxP | NxP |
| 11 | B–B2 | P–B3 | 26 | Q–B3 | P–B4 |
| 12 | PxP | NxBP | 27 | P–N3 | Q–R1 |
| 13 | QN–Q2 | P–N5 | 28 | P–QR4 | R–N3 |
| 14 | B–R4 | R–B1 | 29 | QR–Q1 | Q–R4?? |
| 15 | BxN | PxP | 30 | B–B4† | Resigns |

*Lopez Game 73*

*WHITE: Bronstein* *BLACK: Keres*

*Candidates' Tournament, Budapest 1950*

| | WHITE | BLACK | | WHITE | BLACK |
|---|---|---|---|---|---|
| 1 | P–K4 | P–K4 | 18 | Q–Q3 | P–N3 |
| 2 | N–KB3 | N–QB3 | 19 | K–R1 | B–B1 |
| 3 | B–N5 | P–QR3 | 20 | R–B1 | B–N2 |
| 4 | B–R4 | N–B3 | 21 | B–Q2 | P–QB4 |
| 5 | O–O | B–K2 | 22 | B–R4 | R–KB1 |
| 6 | R–K1 | P–QN4 | 23 | QR–N1 | Q–N3 |
| 7 | B–N3 | O–O | 24 | P–B5 | B–Q5 |
| 8 | P–Q4 | P–Q3 | 25 | Q–KN3! | N–B5 |
| 9 | P–B3 | B–N5 | 26 | B–R6 | B–N2? |
| 10 | P–KR3 | BxN | 27 | BxB | KxB |
| 11 | QxB | PxP | 28 | P–B6† | K–R1 |
| 12 | Q–Q1! | PxP | 29 | Q–N5 | P–N6 |
| 13 | NxP | N–QR4 | 30 | PxP | Q–N5 |
| 14 | B–B2 | R–K1 | 31 | PxN | QxB |
| 15 | P–B4 | P–N5? | 32 | R–B4 | Q–B7 |
| 16 | N–Q5 | NxN | 33 | Q–R6! | Resigns |
| 17 | QxN | P–B3 | | | |

# part 22—CLOSED DEFENSE, PILNIK VARIATION

1 P–K4, P–K4
2 N–KB3, N–QB3
3 B–N5, P–QR3
4 B–R4, N–B3
5 O–O, B–K2
6 R–K1, P–QN4
7 B–N3, P–Q3
8 P–B3, O–O
9 P–Q3[A], N–QR4[B]
10 B–B2, P–B4
11 QN–Q2, N–B3
12 N–B1[C]

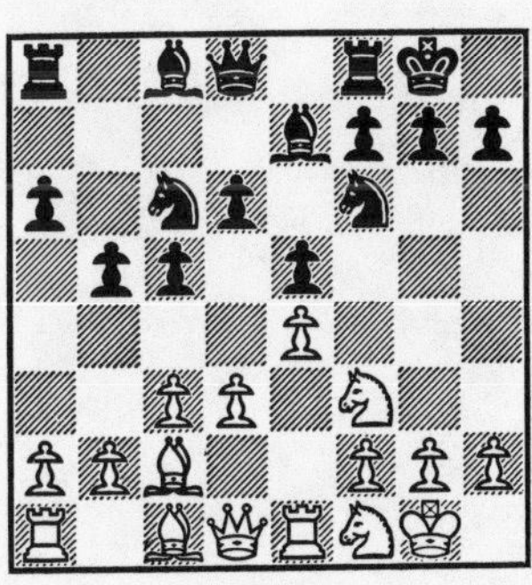

KEY POSITION 22

OBSERVATIONS ON KEY POSITION 22

[A] This variation, preferred by the Argentine Grandmaster H. Pilnik, can arise by transposition as follows: 5 P–Q3 (instead of 5 O–O), P–QN4 6 B–N3, B–K2 7 O–O, P–Q3 8 P–B3, O–O 9 R–K1.

[B] 9 . . . B–N5 does not suit Black's strategy.

[C] 12 P–KR3, P–Q4 is all right for Black.

In the Closed Defense, White's Queen Knight usually operates on the Kingside via the time-consuming maneuver QN–Q2–B1–N3 (or K3), readying for an assault in that direction. By avoiding an early P–Q4 and its consequent tension, White can execute this plan without disturbance. The onus then falls upon Black to counterattack in the center with . . . P–Q4. Prematurely timed, however, the move will meet with a technical refutation.

IDEA VARIATIONS 54–56:

(54) 12 . . . R–K1 13 N–K3, P–Q4? 14 PxP, NxP 15 NxN, QxN 16 P–Q4!, KPxP 17 B–K4, Q–Q2 18 PxP, B–B3 19 B–N5±. See Game 75.

(55) 12 . . . P–Q4? 13 PxP, QxP 14 Q–K2, B–N2 (hoping for 15 NxP??, NxN and 16 . . . QxNP mate) 15 B–N5, KR–K1 16 B–KR4, QR–Q1 17 B–QN3, QxP 18 QxQ, RxQ 19 NxP, NxN 20 RxN±. See Game 74.

(56) 12 . . . B–K3 13 N–K3, P–Q4 14 PxP, NxP 15 NxN, QxN 16 P–Q4, KPxP 17 B–K4, Q–Q3 18 PxP, PxP 19 BxN, QxB 20 NxP, Q–Q4 21 NxB, QxQ 22 RxQ, PxN= (Black's isolated Pawn is compensated by possibilities on both wings: B–B3 and B–B4).

PRACTICAL VARIATIONS 120–123:

1 P–K4, P–K4 2 N–KB3, N–QB3 3 B–N5, P–QR3 4 B–R4, N–B3 5 O–O, B–K2 6 R–K1, P–QN4 7 B–N3, P–Q3 8 P–B3, O–O 9 P–Q3, N–QR4 10 B–B2, P–B4 11 QN–Q2, N–B3 12 N–B1

| | *120* | *121* | *122* | *123* |
|---|---|---|---|---|
| *12* | – – | – – | – – | – – |
| | P–Q4 | R–K1 | Q–B2 | B–K3 |
| *13* | PxP | N–K3 | N–K3 | N–K3 |
| | QxP | B–B1[4] | B–K3[6] | P–Q4[8] |

continued ▸

| | 120 | 121 | 122 | 123 |
|---|---|---|---|---|
| 14 | Q–K2 | N–Q5 | N–N5 | PxP |
| | B–N2 | NxN | P–Q4 | NxP |
| 15 | B–N3[1] | PxN | PxP | NxN |
| | Q–Q2 | N–K2 | NxP | QxN |
| 16 | NxP? | P–Q4 | NxB | P–Q4! |
| | NxN | KPxP | PxN | KPxP |
| 17 | QxN | PxP | Q–N4[7] | B–K4 |
| | B–Q3 | P–B5[5] | ± | Q–Q3 |
| 18 | Q–N5 | ± | | PxP |
| | KR–K1 | | | QR–Q1[9] |
| 19 | B–KB4[2] | | | N–N5[10] |
| | P–R3 | | | ± |
| 20 | Q–R4 | | | |
| | BxB[3] | | | |
| | ∓ | | | |

*Notes to practical variations 120–123:*

[1] Stronger is 15 B–N5 which leads to Idea Var. 55.

[2] If 19 B–K3 then 19 . . . R–K4!

[3] 21 QxB is answered by 21 . . . QxP 22 QR–Q1, Q–N3.

[4] 13 . . . P–Q4 leads to Idea Var. 54 and 13 . . . B–K3 is answered by 14 P–Q4±.

[5] This variation, recommended by Alekhine as "almost sufficient for equality" is not very convincing. White can start a murderous attack by 18 BxP†, KxB 19 N–N5† and now:

1) 19 . . . K–N1 20 Q–R5, B–B4 21 QxP†, K–R1 22 R–K3 threatening 23 R–R3† etc.

2) 19 . . . K–N3 20 P–R4, P–B4 (practically forced) 21 P–R5†, K–B3 22 Q–K2 with overwhelming threats.

[6] 13 . . . B–N2 leads to Game 76.

[7] Black has some troubles (Keres).

[8] Perhaps better is first . . . P–R3, . . . Q–B2, and . . . QR–Q1.

[9] Better is 18 . . . PxP which leads to Idea Var. 56.

[10] Smyslov–Benko, Budapest 1952.

### *Lopez Game 74*

*WHITE: Pilnik* *BLACK: H. Kramer*

*Amsterdam 1950*

| | WHITE | BLACK | | WHITE | BLACK |
|---|---|---|---|---|---|
| 1 | P–K4 | P–K4 | 6 | R–K1 | P–QN4 |
| 2 | N–KB3 | N–QB3 | 7 | B–N3 | O–O |
| 3 | B–N5 | P–QR3 | 8 | P–Q3 | P–Q3 |
| 4 | B–R4 | N–B3 | 9 | P–B3 | N–QR4 |
| 5 | O–O | B–K2 | 10 | B–B2 | P–B4 |

| WHITE | BLACK | WHITE | BLACK |
|---|---|---|---|
| 11 QN–Q2 | N–B3 | 36 K–B3 | P–B4 |
| 12 N–B1 | P–Q4 | 37 P–KN4 | PxP† |
| 13 PxP | QxP | 38 NxP | BxN† |
| 14 Q–K2 | B–N2 | 39 KxB | K–B2 |
| 15 B–N5! | KR–K1 | 40 B–K5 | B–B1 |
| 16 B–KR4 | QR–Q1 | 41 P–KR4 | B–K2 |
| 17 B–QN3! | QxP | 42 P–R3 | N–B4 |
| 18 QxQ | RxQ | 43 BxN | PxB† |
| 19 NxP | NxN | 44 KxP | BxKRP |
| 20 RxN | P–B5 | 45 K–K4 | K–K3 |
| 21 B–B2 | R/6–Q1? | 46 P–B5† | K–Q2 |
| 22 QR–K1 | K–B1? | 47 K–Q5 | B–N4 |
| 23 BxP! | B–Q3 | 48 P–B6 | B–R5 |
| 24 RxR† | RxR | 49 K–B5 | K–K3 |
| 25 RxR† | NxR | 50 B–Q4 | B–N4 |
| 26 B–B2 | B–K4 | 51 K–N6 | B–B8 |
| 27 N–K3 | N–Q3 | 52 KxP | BxP |
| 28 P–B3 | K–K1 | 53 KxP | BxRP |
| 29 B–B2 | B–B5 | 54 KxP | B–B8 |
| 30 N–Q1 | B–Q4 | 55 K–N4 | B–N7 |
| 31 B–Q4 | P–N3 | 56 K–N3 | B–B8 |
| 32 P–KN3 | B–R3 | 57 P–B4 | B–R3 |
| 33 K–B2 | K–Q2 | 58 K–N4 | B–N4 |
| 34 N–K3 | B–K3 | 59 K–N5 | Resigns |
| 35 P–B4 | K–K2 | | |

*Lopez Game 75*

*WHITE: Alekhine* *BLACK: Eliskases*

*Podebrad 1936*

| WHITE | BLACK | WHITE | BLACK |
|---|---|---|---|
| 1 P–K4 | P–K4 | 14 PxP | NxP |
| 2 N–KB3 | N–QB3 | 15 NxN | QxN |
| 3 B–N5 | P–QR3 | 16 P–Q4! | KPxP |
| 4 B–R4 | N–B3 | 17 B–K4 | Q–Q2 |
| 5 O–O | B–K2 | 18 PxP | B–B3 |
| 6 R–K1 | P–QN4 | 19 B–N5! | RxB |
| 7 B–N3 | P–Q3 | 20 RxR | BxP |
| 8 P–B3 | N–QR4 | 21 NxB | NxN |
| 9 B–B2 | P–B4 | 22 Q–R5! | B–N2 |
| 10 P–Q3 | N–B3 | 23 R–R4 | Q–B4 |
| 11 QN–Q2 | O–O | 24 B–K3! | R–Q1 |
| 12 N–B1 | R–K1 | 25 RxN! | Resigns |
| 13 N–K3 | P–Q4 | | |

*Lopez Game 76*

*WHITE: Teichmann* *BLACK: Schlechter*

*Karlsbad 1911*

| WHITE | BLACK | WHITE | BLACK |
|---|---|---|---|
| 1 P–K4 | P–K4 | 14 N–B5! | KR–K1 |
| 2 N–KB3 | N–QB3 | 15 B–N5 | N–Q2 |
| 3 B–N5 | P–QR3 | 16 B–N3 | N–B1 |
| 4 B–R4 | N–B3 | 17 B–Q5! | N–N3 |
| 5 O–O | B–K2 | 18 BxB | N/NxB |
| 6 R–K1 | P–QN4 | 19 BxP† | KxB |
| 7 B–N3 | P–Q3 | 20 N–N5† | K–N1 |
| 8 P–B3 | O–O | 21 Q–R5 | NxN |
| 9 P–Q3 | N–QR4 | 22 QxP† | K–B1 |
| 10 B–B2 | P–B4 | 23 QxN† | K–N1 |
| 11 QN–Q2 | Q–B2 | 24 Q–N6! | Q–Q2 |
| 12 N–B1 | N–QB3 | 25 R–K3 | Resigns |
| 13 N–K3 | B–N2? | | |

SUPPLEMENTARY VARIATIONS 32–33:

1 P–K4, P–K4 2 N–KB3, N–QB3 3 B–N5, P–QR3 4 B–R4, N–B3 5 O–O, B–K2 6 R–K1, P–QN4 7 B–N3, P–Q3 8 P–B3

| | *32* | *33* | | *32* | *33* |
|---|---|---|---|---|---|
| *8* | – – | – – | *14* | QN–Q2[3] | QN–Q2 |
| | N–QR4[1] | – – | | N–B3 | B–K3[5] |
| *9* | B–B2 | – – | *15* | N–B1 | N–B1 |
| | P–B4 | – – | | O–O | KR–B1 |
| *10* | P–Q4 | – – | *16* | N–K3 | N–K3 |
| | Q–B2 | – – | | B–K3 | P–N3 |
| *11* | P–QR4[2] | – – | *17* | N–N5 | P–QN3 |
| | R–QN1 | P–N5 | | QR–Q1 | N–R4 |
| *12* | PxNP | PxNP | *18* | Q–K2±[4] | B–N2 |
| | PxNP | PxNP | | ± | B–B3[6] |
| *13* | PxKP | P–R3 | | | ± |
| | PxP | O–O | | | |

*Notes to supplementary variations 32–33:*

[1] This leads in most cases to transposition to key positions, but gives White a little more choice.

[2] More energetic than 11 QN–Q2 or 11 P–KR3.

[3] Not 14 NxP, QxN 15 RxN, N–N5 16 P–KN3, Q–R4 17

P–R4, BxP 18 PxB, QxP 19 Q–B3, Q–R7† 20 K–B1, N–K4 21 Q–N3, Q–R8† 22 K–K2, Q–R4† and Black has an overwhelming attack. If 23 P–B3, NxP!

[4] Loewenfisch–Lilienthal, Moscow 1939.

[5] 14 . . . B–N2 is to be considered. Black intends to play . . . QR–B1 and . . . P–Q4.

[6] 19 R–QB1 with a superior game for White (Keres–Reshevsky, Stockholm 1937).

---

## part 23—CLOSED DEFENSE, MARSHALL GAMBIT

1 P–K4, P–K4
2 N–KB3, N–QB3
3 B–N5, P–QR3
4 B–R4, N–B3
5 O–O, B–K2
6 R–K1, P–QN4
7 B–N3, O–O
8 P–B3, P–Q4

KEY POSITION 23

OBSERVATIONS ON KEY POSITION 23

Black offers a Pawn in return for the opening of lines (the long diagonal from Black's QN2 to KN7, the diagonals Q3–KR7 and Q1–KR5, the open King file which he hopes to use), the liquidation of White's King Knight, momentarily White's only defensive unit, and his superiority of development. To decline the offer leaves White in a passive position.

IDEA VARIATIONS 57–60:

(57) 9 PxP, NxP 10 NxP, NxN 11 RxN, N–B3 12 P–Q4!, B–Q3 13 R–K1, N–N5 14 P–KR3, Q–R5 15 Q–B3, NxP 16 QxN? (B–Q2!), B–R7† (not . . . B–N6 17 QxP†!) 17 K–B1, B–N6±. Now if 18 QxP†, RxQ†!

(58) 9 PxP, NxP 10 NxP, NxN 11 RxN, N–B3 12 P–KR3, B–Q3 13 R–K1, N–N5 14 PxN, Q–R5 15 Q–B3, Q–R7† (. . . B–R7†!) 16 K–B1, BxP 17 QxB, Q–R8† 18 K–K2, QR–K1† 19 B–K6!±.

(59) 9 PxP, P–K5 10 PxN, PxN 11 QxP, B–N5 12 Q–N3, B–Q3 13 P–B4? (13 Q–R4!) 13 . . . R–K1 14 R–K5, BxR 15 PxB, N–R4 16 QxB, RxP 17 N–R3, R–K8† 18 K–B2, N–B3. See Game 77.

(60) 9 PxP, NxP 10 NxP, NxN 11 RxN, P–QB3 12 P–Q4, B–Q3 13 R–K1, Q–R5 14 P–N3, Q–R6 15 B–K3, B–KN5 16 Q–Q3, P–KB4 17 P–B4, K–R1 18 BxN, PxB 19 N–Q2, R–KN1 20 Q–B1, Q–R4 21 P–QR4 and Black has too little compensation for the Pawn (Euwe–Donner, Amsterdam 1950).

In this line 15 R–K4 fails, e.g., . . . P–N4 16 N–Q2, B–KB4 17 B–B2, K–R1 18 R–K2, BxB 19 QxB, N–B5 20 PxN, PxP 21 P–B3, R–N1† 22 K–R1, R–N2 23 R–B2, QR–KN1 24 Q–Q1, R–N7, Resigns (Neal – – McLellan, Omaha, 1962).

## PRACTICAL VARIATIONS 124–138:

1 P–K4, P–K4 2 N–KB3, N–QB3 3 B–N5, P–QR3 4 B–R4, N–B3 5 O–O, B–K2 6 R–K1, P–QN4 7 B–N3, O–O 8 P–B3, P–Q4

| | *124* | *125* | *126* | *127* | *128* | *129* | *130* | *131* |
|---|---|---|---|---|---|---|---|---|
| *9* | PxP | – – | – – | – – | – – | – – | – – | – – |
| | P–K5[1] | – – | – – | – – | – – | NxP | – – | – – |
| *10* | PxN | – – | – – | N–N5[10] | – – | NxP | – – | – – |
| | PxN | – – | – – | B–KN5 | – – | NxN | – – | – – |
| *11* | QxP | P–Q4 | – – | P–B3 | Q–B2 | RxN | – – | – – |
| | B–KN5 | PxP | B–Q3 | PxP | N–K4 | N–B3[14] | – – | – – |
| *12* | Q–N3 | B–N5 | B–N5[8] | PxP[11] | NxKP | P–Q4[15] | – – | – – |
| | R–K1[2] | Q–Q3 | BxP† | NxP | NxN | B–Q3 | – – | – – |
| *13* | P–Q4[3] | Q–B3 | KxB | NxRP[12] | QxN | R–K1[16] | – – | – – |
| | B–Q3 | N–N5 | N–N5† | B–Q3 | B–Q3 | N–N5 | – – | – – |
| *14* | P–KB4[4] | B–KB4 | K–N1 | BxN | P–Q4 | P–KR3 | – – | – – |
| | N–R4 | Q–B3 | QxB | BxRP† | P–KB4 | Q–R5 | – – | – – |
| *15* | RxR† | N–Q2 | QxP | KxB | Q–B2 | Q–B3 | – – | – – |
| | QxR | B–Q3 | B–B4 | Q–R5†[13] | N–B6† | NxP | – – | P–KR4 |
| *16* | Q–B2 | R–K4 | N–Q2[9] | = | PxN | R–K2[17] | – – | N–Q2 |
| | QxP | BxB | ± | | Q–R5 | N–N5[18] | – – | B–N2 |
| *17* | P–KR3 | RxB[7] | | | R–K5 | B–KB4[19] | R–K8 | N–K4 |
| | B–QB1[5] | ± | | | B–KR6 | B–N2 | N–B3 | QR–K1 |
| *18* | B–Q1 | | | | ∓ | QxB | RxR† | B–N5 |
| | N–B3[6] | | | | | BxB | KxR | BxN |
| *19* | B–B3 | | | | | ∓ | N–Q2 | RxB |
| | ± | | | | | | R–N1 | B–R7† |
| *20* | | | | | | | N–B1[21] | K–B1[22] |
| | | | | | | | = | ± |
| *21* | | | | | | | | |
| *22* | | | | | | | | |
| *23* | | | | | | | | |
| *24* | | | | | | | | |
| *25* | | | | | | | | |

---

*Notes to practical variations 124–138:*

[1] A sharp continuation, which, however, White can refute.

[2] 12 . . . B–Q3 leads to Idea Var. 59.

[3] After 13 P–B3, Q–Q6 14 PxB, B–B4† 15 R–K3 Black has good chances.

[4] Another way is 14 RxR†, QxR 15 Q–K3, QxP 16 P–B3, R–K1 17 Q–B2, etc.

| *132* | *133* | *134* | *135* | *136* | *137* | *138* |
|---|---|---|---|---|---|---|
| — — | — — | — — | — — | — — | — — | — — |
| — — | — — | — — | — — | — — | — — | — — |
| — — | — — | — — | — — | — — | — — | — — |
| — — | — — | — — | — — | — — | — — | — — |
| — — | — — | — — | — — | — — | — — | — — |
| — — | N–N3 | P–QB3[25] | — — | — — | — — | — — |
| — — | P–Q4 | P–Q4 | — — | — — | BxN | — — |
| — — | B–Q3 | B–Q3 | — — | — — | PxB | — — |
| — — | B–N5 | R–K1 | — — | — — | P–Q4 | — — |
| — — | Q–Q2 | Q–R5 | — — | — — | B–Q3 | — — |
| — — | R–K1 | P–N3 | — — | — — | R–K3 | — — |
| — — | B–N2 | Q–R6 | — — | — — | P–B4 | Q–R5 |
| B–K3 | N–Q2 | B–K3! | Q–Q3 | — — | N–Q2 | P–KR3 |
| B–R7† | QR–K1 | B–KN5[26] | B–KB4 | — — | P–B5[32] | B–K3[35] |
| K–B1 | P–B3 | Q–Q3 | Q–B1 | — — | R–K1 | N–Q2 |
| B–B5 | Q–B4 | P–KB4 | Q–R4 | — — | P–B6[33] | QR–K1 |
| Q–Q2 | B–KR4 | P–KB4 | B–K3 | — — | NxP | N–B3 |
| NxB† | P–B4 | P–N4[27] | B–R6 | QR–K1 | B–KN5 | Q–R4 |
| PxN | N–B1 | Q–B1 | B–Q1 | N–Q2 | R–K3 | B–Q2 |
| B–N6 | PxP | Q–R4 | Q–B4 | R–K3 | R–R2[34] | P–B3 |
| R–B1 | PxP | N–Q2 | Q–K2 | B–Q1 | P–KR3! | P–QR4![36] |
| B–N2 | N–Q4 | K–R1 | QR–K1 | B–N5 | ± | ± |
| N–R3 | B–N3 | BxN[28] | N–Q2 | BxB | | |
| QR–K1 | N–B5 | PxB | P–B4 | QxB | | |
| K–N1 | Q–Q2 | PxP | N–B3 | P–B3 | | |
| B–Q3[23] | R–Q1[24] | P–B5 | N–B5 | Q–N3 | | |
| ∓ | = | BxP | Q–B2 | B–B2[31] | | |
| | | R–B4 | N–Q6 | ± | | |
| | | Q–N2 | N–R4 | | | |
| | | BxB | NxR | | | |
| | | PxB | QxQ | | | |
| | | RxBP | BxQ | | | |
| | | QxP![29] | NxB[30] | | | |
| | | ± | ± | | | |

[5] 17 . . . B–K3 leads to Game 79.

[6] Foltys–Pirc, 1947.

[7] Gilman–Estrin, 1949.

[8] Also possible is 12 QxP, R–K1 13 Q–Q1, B–KN5 14 P–B3, N–K5 15 P–N3± (Stulik–Dobias, 1946).

[9] Kofman–Kopajev, 1948.

[10] This looks more solid, but is not as good as 10 PxN.

*continued* ▸

[11] If 12 NxP/3, NxP 13 P–Q4=.

[12] 13 NxBP, RxN 14 PxB, Q–Q6 gives Black good attacking chances.

[13] Drawn by perpetual check (Pulevic–Suravlev, Kalinin 1949).

[14] This move constitutes the Classical Variation of the Marshall Gambit.

[15] 12 P–KR3 leads to Idea Var. 58.

[16] 13 R–K2, N–R4! gives White more difficult problems to solve.

[17] 16 QxN? leads to Idea Var. 57. Best is 16 B–Q2, BxP 17 PxB, NxP† 18 K–B1 and Black does not seem to have sufficient attack.

[18] 16 . . . B–KN5 leads to Game 78.

[19] If 17 PxN then 17 . . . BxP∓.

[20] If 18 QxN, QxQ 19 PxQ, BxB∓.

[21] The variations 129 and 130, deriving from the late Dr. Tartakover, have not been refuted as yet.

[22] Boleslavski–Schamkowitsch, 1956.

[23] Tolush–Szabo, 1958.

[24] Nedeljkovic–Geller, 1957.

[25] This looks more promising than 11 . . . N–B3, but is just a bit weaker.

[26] Another continuation is 15 . . . R–R2 16 BxN, PxB 17 Q–B3!, R–K2 18 N–Q2, KR–K1 19 P–R4, P–N5 20 P–B4, PxP 21 NxP, B–N1 22 B–Q2!± (Unzicker–Rossolimo, 1951).

[27] 17 . . . K–R1 leads to Idea Var. 60.

[28] This is the point on which White's defensive system is based: White's Q Bishop is exchanged for the Knight only after Black has lost a tempo by moving his King out of the Bishop's diagonal.

[29] Analysis by Yanofsky.

[30] Boleslavski–Saigin, 1951.

[31] Aronin–Suetin, 1949.

[32] If 15 . . . R–R2 16 Q–N3! (L. Schmid–Eidenfeldt).

[33] Black is forced to sacrifice a second Pawn to keep his attack alive. In a game Nilsson–Nyman, Black tried 16 . . . P–N4 17 Q–R5, Q–B3 18 P–KR4, P–R3 19 N–B3, R–R2 20 B–Q2, R–KN2 21 R–K8±.

[34] Incorrect is 18 . . . B–B5 19 R–Q3, B–B4 20 BxB, BxR 21 B–N5 and 22 QxB.

[35] If 15 . . . B–B5? 16 P–KN3, Q–N4 17 R–K5!

[36] Nilsson–Ahman, 1954.

*Lopez Game 77*

*WHITE: Van den Berg* *BLACK: L. Szabo*

*Tel Aviv 1958*

| | WHITE | BLACK | | WHITE | BLACK |
|---|---|---|---|---|---|
| 1 | P–K4 | P–K4 | 6 | R–K1 | P–QN4 |
| 2 | N–KB3 | N–QB3 | 7 | B–N3 | O–O |
| 3 | B–N5 | P–QR3 | 8 | P–B3 | P–Q4 |
| 4 | B–R4 | N–B3 | 9 | PxP | P–K5 |
| 5 | O–O | B–K2 | 10 | PxN | PxN |

| WHITE | BLACK | WHITE | BLACK |
|---|---|---|---|
| 11 QxP | B–KN5 | 19 Q–KB4 | Q–K2 |
| 12 Q–N3 | B–Q3 | 20 Q–B3 | R–R8 |
| 13 P–KB4 | R–K1 | 21 N–B2 | N–K5† |
| 14 R–K5 | BxR | 22 K–K2 | NxBP†† |
| 15 PxB | N–R4 | 23 K–Q3 | R–Q1† |
| 16 QxB | RxP | 24 N–Q4 | N–K7 |
| 17 N–R3 | R–K8† | Resigns | |
| 18 K–B2 | N–B3 | | |

*Lopez Game 78*

*WHITE: Capablanca BLACK: Marshall*

*New York 1918*

| WHITE | BLACK | WHITE | BLACK | WHITE | BLACK |
|---|---|---|---|---|---|
| 1 P–K4 | P–K4 | 14 Q–B3 | Q–R5 | 27 PxP | BxP |
| 2 N–KB3 | N–QB3 | 15 P–Q4 | NxP | 28 P–N4 | B–Q3 |
| 3 B–N5 | P–QR3 | 16 R–K2 | B–KN5 | 29 P–R4 | P–QR4 |
| 4 B–R4 | N–B3 | 17 PxB | B–R7† | 30 RPxP | RPxP |
| 5 O–O | B–K2 | 18 K–B1 | B–N6 | 31 R–R6 | PxP |
| 6 R–K1 | P–QN4 | 19 RxN | Q–R8† | 32 NxP | B–N5 |
| 7 B–N3 | O–O | 20 K–K2 | BxR | 33 P–N6 | BxN |
| 8 P–B3 | P–Q4 | 21 B–Q2 | B–R5 | 34 BxB | P–R3 |
| 9 PxP | NxP | 22 Q–R3 | QR–K1† | 35 P–N7 | R–K6 |
| 10 NxP | NxN | 23 K–Q3 | Q–KB8† | 36 BxP† | RxB |
| 11 RxN | N–B3 | 24 K–B2 | B–B7 | 37 P–N8(Q)† | K–R2 |
| 12 R–K1 | B–Q3 | 25 Q–B3 | Q–N8 | 38 RxP† | Resigns |
| 13 P–KR3 | N–N5 | 26 B–Q5 | P–QB4 | | |

*Lopez Game 79*

*WHITE: Hakanen (Finland) BLACK: Estrin (USSR)*

*4th World Correspondence Championship*

| WHITE | BLACK | WHITE | BLACK |
|---|---|---|---|
| 1 P–K4 | P–K4 | 15 RxR† | QxR |
| 2 N–KB3 | N–QB3 | 16 Q–B2 | QxP |
| 3 B–N5 | P–QR3 | 17 P–KR3 | B–K3 |
| 4 B–R4 | N–B3 | 18 P–N4 | N–B3 |
| 5 O–O | B–K2 | 19 BxB | PxB |
| 6 R–K1 | P–QN4 | 20 Q–N2 | N–Q4! |
| 7 B–N3 | O–O | 21 N–Q2 | BxP |
| 8 P–B3 | P–Q4 | 22 N–K4 | P–K4 |
| 9 PxP | P–K5 | 23 PxP | R–KB1 |
| 10 PxN | PxN | 24 N–B2 | Q–B4 |
| 11 QxP | B–KN5 | 25 P–N4 | Q–B5 |
| 12 Q–N3 | R–K1 | 26 Q–K4 | B–R7† |
| 13 P–Q4 | B–Q3 | Resigns | |
| 14 P–KB4 | N–R4 | | |

# part 24—CLOSED DEFENSE, ENGLISH VARIATION

1 P–K4, P–K4
2 N–KB3, N–QB3
3 B–N5, P–QR3
4 B–R4, N–B3
5 O–O, B–K2
6 Q–K2, P–QN4
7 B–N3, P–Q3[A]
8 P–B3[B], O–O
9 P–Q4, B–N5

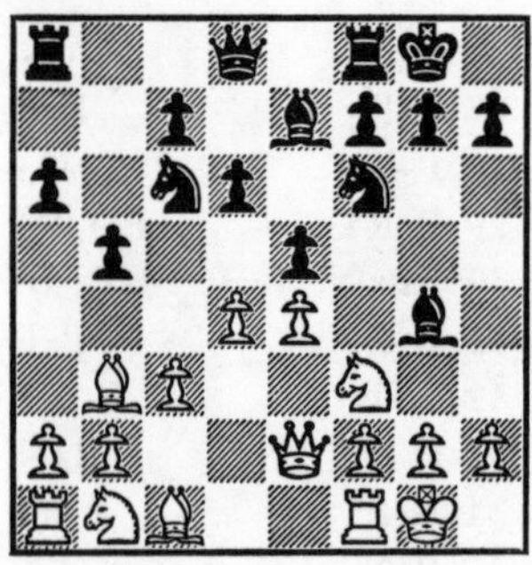

KEY POSITION 24

## OBSERVATIONS ON KEY POSITION 24

[A] 7 . . . O–O 8 P–B3, P–Q4 leads to key position 25.
[B] For 8 P–QR4 see supplementary variations 34–38.

Generally speaking, . . . B–N5 in this variation is effective after White has advanced his QP to Q4, because Black's Queen Bishop exercises pressure on White's center. As long as White's Queen Pawn remains in its initial position, White can consolidate his center by P–Q3, and eventually start a Kingside attack by P–KR3 and P–N4 (after . . . B–R4). This may lead to positions similar to those discussed in the Pilnik Variation, Part 22.

In key position 24, Black's . . . B–N5 is strong. White can either defend his center (by R–Q1) or resolve the tension by advancing his QP to Q5. In the first case Black maintains the balance in the center by . . . PxP and . . . P–Q4. In the second case Black has to seek counter-chances on the Queenside (. . . N–QR4 and . . . P–B3).

White's chances to obtain an advantage are about equal to those in the main variation after 6 R–K1 (see Part 21).

## IDEA VARIATIONS 61 AND 62:

(61) 10 R–Q1, PxP 11 PxP, P–Q4 12 P–K5, N–K5 13 N–B3, NxN 14 PxN, N–R4 15 B–B2, Q–Q2 with equal chances.

(62) 10 P–Q5, N–QR4 11 B–B2, P–B3 12 PxP, NxBP 13 P–KR3, B–K3, and Black will soon be able to free his game by . . . P–Q4.

## PRACTICAL VARIATIONS 139–141:

1 P–K4, P–K4 2 N–KB3, N–QB3 3 B–N5, P–QR3 4 B–R4, N–B3 5 O–O, B–K2 6 Q–K2, P–QN4 7 B–N3, P–Q3 8 P–B3, O–O 9 P–Q4, B–N5

| | 139 | 140 | 141 | | 139 | 140 | 141 |
|---|---|---|---|---|---|---|---|
| 10 | R–Q1 | – – | P–Q5 | 14 | PxN | B–Q5[6] | P–KR3 |
| | PxP | Q–B1[4] | N–QR4 | | Q–Q2[2] | ± | B–R4 |
| 11 | PxP | P–KR3 | B–B2 | 15 | P–QR4 | | B–N5[8] |
| | P–Q4 | B–R4 | P–B3 | | N–R4 | | R–Q1 |
| 12 | P–K5 | B–N5![5] | PxP | 16 | B–B2 | | QN–Q2 |
| | N–K5 | R–K1 | NxBP | | N–B5 | | P–N5![9] |
| 13 | N–B3[1] | BxN | R–Q1[7] | 17 | Q–Q3 | | ∓ |
| | NxN | BxB | Q–B1 | | P–N3[3] | | |
| | | | | | = | | |

*Notes to practical variations 139–141:*

[1] 13 P–QR4 is answered by 13 . . . P–N5, and 13 B–B2 by 13 . . . P–B4!

[2] 14 . . . N–R4 leads to Idea Var. 61. See Game 80 for the results of the weak 14 . . . P–B3.

[3] Brinckmann–Vajda, Budapest 1929.

[4] An interesting but unsatisfactory attempt to maintain the center.

[5] 12 P–N4 is refuted by 12 . . . NxNP.

[6] The pin is disturbing.

[7] 13 P–KR3 leads to Idea Var. 62.

[8] 15 P–N4 is refuted by 15 . . . NxNP.

[9] Black has the initiative.

*Lopez Game 80*

*WHITE: Em. Lasker* *BLACK: Teichmann*

*St. Petersburg 1909*

| | WHITE | BLACK | | WHITE | BLACK | | WHITE | BLACK |
|---|---|---|---|---|---|---|---|---|
| 1 | P–K4 | P–K4 | 11 | R–Q1! | P–Q4 | 21 | K–R1! | B–Q3 |
| 2 | N–KB3 | N–QB3 | 12 | P–K5 | N–K5 | 22 | PxP | Q–R5 |
| 3 | B–N5 | P–QR3 | 13 | N–B3 | NxN | 23 | Q–B3 | PxP |
| 4 | B–R4 | N–B3 | 14 | PxN | P–B3? | 24 | R–KN1 | P–B5 |
| 5 | O–O | B–K2 | 15 | P–KR3 | B–R4 | 25 | R–N4 | Q–R3 |
| 6 | Q–K2 | P–QN4 | 16 | P–N4 | B–B2 | 26 | P–K7! | BxP |
| 7 | B–N3 | P–Q3 | 17 | P–K6 | B–N3 | 27 | BxP | Q–K3 and Resigns |
| 8 | P–B3 | O–O | 18 | N–R4 | N–R4 | | | |
| 9 | P–Q4 | PxP | 19 | NxB | PxN | | | |
| 10 | PxP | B–N5 | 20 | B–B2 | P–KB4 | | | |

---

# part 25—CLOSED DEFENSE, ENGLISH VARIATION OF MARSHALL GAMBIT

1 P–K4, P–K4
2 N–KB3, N–QB3
3 B–N5, P–QR3
4 B–R4, N–B3
5 O–O, B–K2
6 Q–K2, P–QN4
7 B–N3, O–O
8 P–B3[A], P–Q4

KEY POSITION 25

## OBSERVATIONS ON KEY POSITION 25

[A] After 8 P–QR4 both 8 . . . R–N1 and 8 . . . P–N5 are satisfactory (even 8 . . . B–N2 is playable). One example: 8 P–QR4, R–N1 9 PxP, PxP 10 N–B3 (better 10 P–B3), P–Q3 11 NxNP?, B–N5! 12 B–B4, RxN 13 BxR, N–Q5 14 Q–B4, BxN 15 PxB, Q–B1 etc. (16 K–R1, NxKBP).

Comparing key position 25 with key position 23, in which White has played 6 R–K1 instead of 6 Q–K2, it is clear that White runs greater risks by accepting the gambit with his Queen on K2 than when it is less exposed.

White therefore generally prefers the quiet move 9 P–Q3, which, however, does not give him much opportunity for a strong initiative.

IDEA VARIATIONS 63 AND 64:

(63) 9 PxP, NxP 10 NxP, N–B5! 11 Q–K4, NxN 12 QxR?, Q–Q6! 13 R–K1, N–K7† 14 K–R1, P–QB3 and wins (15 N–R3, N–N5).

(64) 9 P–Q3, P–Q5 10 PxP, NxQP 11 NxN, QxN 12 B–K3, Q–Q3 13 N–B3, B–K3 14 BxB, PxB 15 P–QR4, P–B3 16 KR–Q1, KR–Q1 17 P–R3±.

PRACTICAL VARIATIONS 142–146:

1 P–K4, P–K4 2 N–KB3, N–QB3 3 B–N5, P–QR3 4 B–R4, N–B3 5 O–O, B–K2 6 Q–K2, P–QN4 7 B–N3, O–O 8 P–B3, P–Q4

| | *142* | *143* | *144* | *145* | *146* |
|---|---|---|---|---|---|
| 9 | PxP | – – | P–Q3 | – – | – – |
| | NxP | B–N5[4] | P–Q5 | R–K1 | – – |
| *10* | NxP | P–KR3[5] | PxP | PxP | R–K1 |
| | N–B5 | BxN | NxQP | NxP | B–N2 |
| *11* | Q–K4 | QxB | NxN | NxP | QN–Q2 |
| | NxN | N–QR4 | QxN | NxN | Q–Q2 |
| *12* | P–Q4[1] | B–B2 | B–K3 | QxN | N–B1 |
| | B–N2! | QxP | Q–Q3 | B–N2 | QR–Q1 |
| *13* | QxB[2] | QxQ | N–B3 | P–Q4 | B–N5[11] |
| | N–K7† | NxQ | B–K3 | N–B3 | N–QR4 |
| *14* | K–R1 | B–K4 | BxB | B–N5 | B–B2 |
| | NxB | QR–Q1[6] | PxB[7] | Q–Q2[10] | PxP |
| *15* | RxN | = | P–B4[8] | ∓ | PxP |
| | N–Q6 | | PxP | | N–B5 |
| *16* | R–B1 | | BxP | | N–K3 |
| | P–QB4[3] | | P–K4[9] | | NxN[12] |
| *17* | = | | ∓ | | QxN |
| | | | | | N–N5[13] |
| | | | | | = |

*Notes to practical variations 142–146:*

[1] 12 QxR? leads to Idea Var. 63; 12 QxN/K5 or QxN/B4 is answered by 12 . . . B–Q3 with strong attacking chances.

[2] After 13 QxN/4, N–Q6 14 Q–N4, NxB 15 RxN, K–R1 16 N–Q2, P–KB4, Black gets tactical chances.

[3] Black can recover his Pawn at will.

[4] The sharpest continuation.

[5] 10 PxN leads to Game 81.

[6] Superior development compensates for White's "Bishop pair."

[7] After 14 . . . QxB the advance 15 P–B4 is more effective than in the text.

[8] 15 P–QR4 leads to Idea Var. 64.

[9] See Game 82.

[10] Black has a strong attack.

[11] 13 N–N3 is perhaps better.
[12] For 16 . . . NxNP see Game 83.
[13] Exchanges quickly level the position.

*Lopez Game 81*

*WHITE: Foltys* *BLACK: Keres*

*Salzburg 1943*

| | WHITE | BLACK | | WHITE | BLACK |
|---|---|---|---|---|---|
| 1 | P–K4 | P–K4 | 17 | N–K4 | N–B5 |
| 2 | N–KB3 | N–QB3 | 18 | Q–K3 | Q–R5 |
| 3 | B–N5 | P–QR3 | 19 | N–N3 | P–N4 |
| 4 | B–R4 | N–B3 | 20 | NxB | QxN |
| 5 | O–O | B–K2 | 21 | P–K6! | Q–R6? |
| 6 | Q–K2 | P–QN4 | 22 | PxP† | K–N2 |
| 7 | B–N3 | O–O | 23 | Q–Q4† | R–K4! |
| 8 | P–B3 | P–Q4 | 24 | QxR† | K–N3 |
| 9 | PxP | B–N5! | 25 | QxN | PxQ |
| 10 | PxN | P–K5 | 26 | KR–K1 | R–KB1 |
| 11 | P–Q4 | PxN | 27 | R–K7 | QxBP |
| 12 | PxP | B–R4 | 28 | QR–K1 | Q–N5† |
| 13 | B–KB4 | R–K1 | 29 | K–R1 | Q–B6† |
| 14 | B–K5 | B–Q3 | 30 | K–N1 | Q–N5† |
| 15 | N–Q2 | BxB | | Draw | |
| 16 | PxB | N–Q4 | | | |

*Lopez Game 82*

*WHITE: Keres* *BLACK: Euwe*

*World Championship, The Hague 1948*

| | WHITE | BLACK | | WHITE | BLACK |
|---|---|---|---|---|---|
| 1 | P–K4 | P–K4 | 18 | QR–Q1 | Q–K3 |
| 2 | N–KB3 | N–QB3 | 19 | R–B5 | B–B4† |
| 3 | B–N5 | P–QR3 | 20 | K–R1 | B–Q5 |
| 4 | B–R4 | N–B3 | 21 | B–R4 | R–Q2 |
| 5 | O–O | B–K2 | 22 | R–QB1 | R/2–B2 |
| 6 | Q–K2 | P–QN4 | 23 | P–QR3 | BxN |
| 7 | B–N3 | O–O | 24 | PxB | N–Q2 |
| 8 | P–B3 | P–Q4 | 25 | RxR | RxR |
| 9 | P–Q3 | P–Q5 | 26 | B–N3 | Q–N6 |
| 10 | PxP | NxQP | 27 | P–Q4 | QxRP |
| 11 | NxN | QxN | 28 | Q–Q1 | N–B3 |
| 12 | B–K3 | Q–Q3 | 29 | R–R1 | Q–B1 |
| 13 | N–B3 | B–K3 | 30 | PxP | NxP |
| 14 | BxB | PxB | 31 | Q–Q3 | N–B4 |
| 15 | P–B4 | PxP | 32 | Q–K2 | N–K3 |
| 16 | BxP | P–K4 | 33 | P–KR3 | Q–B1 |
| 17 | B–N3 | QR–Q1 | 34 | Q–R2 | Draw |

*Lopez Game 83*

*WHITE: Keres* *BLACK: Geller*

*Maroczy Memorial Tournament, Budapest 1952*

| | WHITE | BLACK | | WHITE | BLACK | | WHITE | BLACK |
|---|---|---|---|---|---|---|---|---|
| 1 | P–K4 | P–K4 | 15 | PxP | N–B5 | 29 | B–B1 | B–N6 |
| 2 | N–KB3 | N–QB3 | 16 | N–K3 | NxNP | 30 | R–Q7† | K–B1 |
| 3 | B–N5 | P–QR3 | 17 | NxP | Q–K3 | 31 | RxBP | R–K4 |
| 4 | B–R4 | N–B3 | 18 | NxP! | QxN | 32 | R–B6 | RxP |
| 5 | O–O | B–K2 | 19 | B–N3 | N–B5 | 33 | R–QN6! | B–B7 |
| 6 | Q–K2 | P–N4 | 20 | NxN | PxN | 34 | RxP | R–QB4 |
| 7 | B–N3 | O–O | 21 | BxP | N–Q4 | 35 | R–R3 | R–Q4 |
| 8 | P–B3 | P–Q4 | 22 | BxB | QxB | 36 | P–B3 | R–Q8 |
| 9 | P–Q3 | R–K1 | 23 | PxN | QxQ | 37 | K–B2 | R–B8 |
| 10 | R–K1 | B–N2 | 24 | RxQ | RxR | 38 | P–R4 | B–N3 |
| 11 | QN–Q2 | Q–Q2 | 25 | BxR | BxP | 39 | B–B4 | K–K2 |
| 12 | N–B1 | QR–Q1 | 26 | P–QR4! | R–Q3 | 40 | P–N4 | P–R3 |
| 13 | B–N5 | N–QR4 | 27 | R–Q1 | K–B2 | 41 | B–Q5 | Resigns |
| 14 | B–B2 | PxP | 28 | P–R5! | R–K3 | | | |

SUPPLEMENTARY VARIATIONS 34–38:

1 P–K4, P–K4 2 N–KB3, N–QB3 3 B–N5, P–QR3 4 B–R4, N–B3 5 O–O, B–K2

| | *34* | *35* | *36* | *37* | *38* |
|---|---|---|---|---|---|
| *6* | BxN[1] | N–B3 | P–Q3[8] | Q–K2 | – – |
| | QPxB[2] | P–QN4 | P–QN4 | P–QN4 | – – |
| *7* | P–Q3[3] | B–N3 | B–N3 | B–N3 | – – |
| | N–Q2! | P–Q3 | O–O[9] | P–Q3[13] | – – |
| *8* | QN–Q2 | N–Q5 | B–Q5 | P–QR4[14] | – – |
| | O–O | N–QR4![5] | NxB | B–N5![15] | – – |
| *9* | N–B4 | NxB | PxN | P–B3 | – – |
| | B–B3 | QxN | N–N5 | O–O | – – |
| *10* | P–QN3 | P–Q4 | P–B4 | PxP? | P–R3 |
| | R–K1 | O–O[6] | PxP | PxP | N–QR4![18] |
| *11* | B–N2 | PxP | PxP | RxR | B–B2[19] |
| | P–B4 | PxP | P–K5 | QxR | B–K3 |
| *12* | P–QR4 | B–N5 | N–K1 | QxP?[16] | PxP |
| | P–KN3 | B–N2 | P–QR4[10] | N–R2! | PxP |
| *13* | K–R1 | Q–K1 | N–QB3 | Q–R6 | P–Q4 |
| | B–N2 | NxB | B–Q3[11] | QxP | B–B5 |
| *14* | Q–K1 | RPxN | P–B4[12] | QxN | B–Q3 |
| | Q–K2 | P–R3 | ± | BxN | BxB |
| *15* | N–N1 | BxN | | PxB | QxB |
| | P–KB3 | QxB | | QxN | N–B5 |

| | 34 | 35 | 36 | 37 | 38 |
|---|---|---|---|---|---|
| *16* | P–B4 | Q–K3 | | QxP | RxR |
| | N–N1 | Q–B3 | | Q–N3† | QxR |
| *17* | PxP | KR–K1 | | K–R1 | P–QN3 |
| | PxP | P–B3[7] | | Q–Q6[17] | Q–R7[20] |
| *18* | N–B3 | = | | ∓ | ± |
| | N–B3[4] | | | | |
| | = | | | | |

*Notes to supplementary variations 34–38:*

[1] The idea of this exchange is to place obstacles in the path of Black's normal development by forcing him to protect his King Pawn unnaturally.

[2] Weaker is 6 . . . NPxB 7 NxP, NxP 8 Q–N4.

[3] In recent years 7 Q–K1 has often been played. Its aim is threefold: to protect White's King Pawn while attacking Black's King Pawn, to avoid a pin on the King Knight by . . . B–KN5, and to be able to play P–Q4 at a later stage without having wasted time with P–Q3. In spite of all these factors, the variation fails to give White an advantage. In the game Karaklaic–O'Kelly, 1955, the continuation was: 7 Q–K1, N–Q2 8 P–Q4, PxP 9 NxP, O–O 10 QN–B3, N–N3 11 B–K3, N–B5 12 R–Q1, Q–K1 13 P–QN3, NxB 14 QxN, B–QN5 15 QN–K2, Q–K2=. If 10 . . . N–K4? 11 KN–Q2, P–KB4 12 P–KB4, N–N3 13 P–K5, B–B4† 14 K–R1, B–K3 15 Q–N3 with B–K3 to follow gives White a positional edge.

[4] Gligoric–Reshevsky match, 1952.

[5] After 8 . . . NxP 9 P–Q4!, O–O 10 R–K1 White regains the Pawn with a good game because of his two Bishops.

[6] 10 . . . B–N2 leads to Game 85.

[7] Keres–Euwe, 1940.

[8] Anderssen's recommendation, if played a move earlier, avoids the Open Defense.

[9] For 7 . . . P–Q3 8 P–QR4 see Game 87.

[10] White threatened 13 P–QR3.

[11] Not 13 . . . P–KB4 14 P–QR3, N–R3 15 P–Q6!

[12] See Game 88.

[13] 7 . . . O–O leads to key position 25.

[14] 8 P–B3 leads to key position 24.

[15] If 8 . . . P–N5? 9 Q–B4! The alternative 8 . . . R–QN1 gives White a slight advantage after 9 PxP, PxP 10 P–B3, B–N5 11 P–R3, B–R4 12 P–Q3.

[16] Preferable is 12 P–Q3 or R–Q1.

[17] Black has at least a draw.

[18] Stronger than 10 . . . B–R4 11 P–N4, B–N3 12 P–Q3.

[19] 11 BxP†, RxB 12 PxB, NxNP 13 PxP, PxP 14 QxP, B–R5! leads to perpetual check (15 RxN, RxR 16 QxR, RxN 17 PxR, Q–N4 etc.).

[20] White's position is slightly superior: 18 PxN, PxBP 19 Q–K3, QxN 20 PxP, NxP ( . . . PxP? 21 B–R3) 21 R–K1!, N–B4 22 B–R3, Q–N3 23 Q–Q4! or 22 . . . Q–Q6 23 PxP!, QxQ 24 PxB! Compare Game 86 in which White continued 18 QN–Q2.

*Lopez Game 84*

*WHITE: Blau* *BLACK: Keres*

*Zurich 1959*

| | WHITE | BLACK | | WHITE | BLACK |
|---|---|---|---|---|---|
| 1 | P–K4 | P–K4 | 31 | P–N3 | Q–QB1 |
| 2 | N–KB3 | N–QB3 | 32 | Q–B1 | B–R3 |
| 3 | B–N5 | P–QR3 | 33 | Q–N2 | B–Q2 |
| 4 | B–R4 | N–B3 | 34 | R–K2 | Q–B2 |
| 5 | O–O | B–K2 | 35 | R/1–K1 | R–K3 |
| 6 | BxN | QPxB | 36 | Q–B3 | K–N2 |
| 7 | Q–K1 | B–K3! | 37 | R–B2 | B–R5 |
| 8 | P–Q3 | N–Q2 | 38 | R–N2 | R–N3 |
| 9 | P–QN3 | P–QB4 | 39 | R/1–K2 | R–N5 |
| 10 | B–N2 | P–KB3 | 40 | Q–N2 | P–QN4 |
| 11 | QN–Q2 | O–O | 41 | PxP | B/3xN |
| 12 | Q–K3 | N–N1 | 42 | NxB | R–B6 |
| 13 | KR–Q1 | N–B3 | 43 | Q–B1 | BxP |
| 14 | P–B3 | Q–K1 | 44 | R/K–B2 | B–R5 |
| 15 | QR–B1 | R–Q1 | 45 | N–N3 | Q–N3 |
| 16 | N–B1 | R–B2 | 46 | Q–B1 | BxN |
| 17 | N–N3 | B–KB1 | 47 | PxB | R/5xP |
| 18 | R–Q2 | R/2–Q2 | 48 | R–R2 | RxP |
| 19 | R/1–Q1 | P–QR4 | 49 | RxP | R/Q–QB6 |
| 20 | N–K2 | P–R5 | 50 | RxR | PxR |
| 21 | PxP | R–R1 | 51 | R–B2 | R–N7 |
| 22 | N–B1 | RxRP | 52 | K–N2 | P–N4 |
| 23 | P–B4 | N–Q5 | 53 | P–R4 | Q–N2 |
| 24 | P–KR3 | P–KN3 | 54 | RxP | QxP† |
| 25 | BxN | BPxB | 55 | R–B3 | R–N6 |
| 26 | Q–K2 | Q–R1 | 56 | Q–Q1 | QxR† |
| 27 | R–B2 | R–Q3 | 57 | QxQ | RxQ |
| 28 | N–Q2 | R–N3 | 58 | KxR | PxP |
| 29 | N/2–N3 | R–R6 | 59 | PxP and Resigns | |
| 30 | K–R2 | P–QB4 | | | |

*Lopez Game 85*

*WHITE: Keres* *BLACK: Spasski*

*Amsterdam 1956*

| | WHITE | BLACK | | WHITE | BLACK |
|---|---|---|---|---|---|
| 1 | P–K4 | P–K4 | 3 | B–N5 | P–QR3 |
| 2 | N–KB3 | N–QB3 | 4 | B–R4 | N–B3 |

| WHITE | BLACK | WHITE | BLACK |
|---|---|---|---|
| 5 O–O | B–K2 | 18 R–B4 | Q–N3 |
| 6 N–B3 | P–QN4 | 19 Q–B3† | K–N3 |
| 7 B–N3 | P–Q3 | 20 RxP | QxBP! |
| 8 N–Q5 | N–QR4! | 21 Q–B4 | Q–QB4 |
| 9 NxB | QxN | 22 RxNP | QR–Q1 |
| 10 P–Q4 | B–N2 | 23 R–B7 | R–Q3 |
| 11 B–N5 | NxB | 24 R–QB1 | R–K1! |
| 12 RPxN | BxP? | 25 P–R4 | Q–K4 |
| 13 NxP! | PxN | 26 QxQ | RxQ |
| 14 R–K1 | PxP | 27 K–B1 | P–B4 |
| 15 BxN | QxB | 28 R–K1 | R/4–Q4 |
| 16 RxB† | K–Q2 | 29 R–R1 | Draw |
| 17 Q–N4†? | K–B3! | | |

*Lopez Game 86*

*WHITE: Keres* *BLACK: Szabo*

*Amsterdam 1956*

| WHITE | BLACK | WHITE | BLACK |
|---|---|---|---|
| 1 P–K4 | P–K4 | 22 B–N5? | P–R3 |
| 2 N–KB3 | N–QB3 | 23 BxN | BxB |
| 3 B–N5 | P–QR3 | 24 RxP | R–Q1 |
| 4 B–R4 | N–KB3 | 25 Q–K2 | Q–R8† |
| 5 Q–K2 | B–K2 | 26 K–R2 | QxP |
| 6 O–O | P–QN4 | 27 R–N2 | Q–Q6 |
| 7 B–N3 | P–Q3 | 28 QxQ | RxQ |
| 8 P–QR4 | B–N5 | 29 R–N5 | R–Q2 |
| 9 P–B3 | O–O | 30 NxP | R–K2 |
| 10 P–R3 | N–QR4 | 31 P–B4 | BxN |
| 11 B–B2 | B–K3 | 32 PxB | K–B1 |
| 12 PxP | PxP | 33 K–N3 | P–QB3 |
| 13 P–Q4 | B–B5 | 34 R–B5 | R–B2 |
| 14 B–Q3 | BxB | 35 K–B4 | K–K2 |
| 15 QxB | N–B5 | 36 P–R4 | P–N3 |
| 16 RxR | QxR | 37 K–K3 | K–Q2 |
| 17 P–QN3 | Q–R7 | 38 K–Q4 | R–R2 |
| 18 QN–Q2 | NxN | 39 R–B2 | R–R5† |
| 19 BxN | QxP | 40 K–K3 | R–R6† |
| 20 PxP | PxP | 41 K–B4 | R–R4 |
| 21 R–N1 | Q–R5 | Draw | |

*Lopez Game 87*

*WHITE: Pilnik* *BLACK: Filip*

*Amsterdam 1956*

| | WHITE | BLACK | | WHITE | BLACK |
|---|---|---|---|---|---|
| 1 | P–K4 | P–K4 | 30 | P–R4 | P–R3 |
| 2 | N–KB3 | N–QB3 | 31 | PxP | RPxP |
| 3 | B–N5 | P–QR3 | 32 | R–R3 | QR–K1 |
| 4 | B–R4 | N–B3 | 33 | Q–KN3 | R–KR1 |
| 5 | O–O | B–K2 | 34 | RxR | KxR |
| 6 | P–Q3 | P–QN4 | 35 | R–B1 | Q–K2 |
| 7 | B–N3 | P–Q3 | 36 | Q–QB3 | R–K6 |
| 8 | P–QR4 | B–N2 | 37 | Q–Q2 | Q–K5 |
| 9 | N–B3 | P–N5 | 38 | R–B4 | Q–K4 |
| 10 | N–Q5 | N–QR4 | 39 | RxP | R–K8† |
| 11 | B–R2 | NxN | 40 | K–B2 | R–QN8 |
| 12 | PxN | P–N6! | 41 | R–B8† | K–N2 |
| 13 | PxP | BxP | 42 | R–B7† | K–R3 |
| 14 | P–QN4 | BxB | 43 | R–B3 | P–Q4 |
| 15 | RxB | N–B3 | 44 | P–N5 | PxP |
| 16 | B–Q2 | Q–Q2 | 45 | PxP | QxP† |
| 17 | Q–B2 | N–Q1 | 46 | R–B3 | Q–K4 |
| 18 | P–Q4 | PxP | 47 | R–QN3 | Q–K5 |
| 19 | NxP | O–O | 48 | R–R3† | K–N2 |
| 20 | R–R3 | B–B3 | 49 | Q–QB3 | Q–B5† |
| 21 | R–R3 | P–N3 | 50 | R–B3 | Q–R5† |
| 22 | B–B3 | R–K1 | 51 | K–K2 | Q–K5† |
| 23 | N–B5! | BxB | 52 | K–B2 | P–Q5 |
| 24 | N–R6† | K–N2 | 53 | Q–Q2 | Q–R5† |
| 25 | QxB† | P–KB3 | 54 | R–N3 | Q–R8 |
| 26 | P–B4 | N–B2 | 55 | RxP† | K–B2 |
| 27 | NxN | QxN | 56 | R–N4! | Q–N8† |
| 28 | P–B5 | P–N4 | 57 | K–N3 | Draw |
| 29 | R–N3 | R–K4 | | | |

*Lopez Game 88*

*WHITE: Neikirch* *BLACK: Pfeiffer*

*Zonal Tournament, Sofia 1957*

| | WHITE | BLACK | | WHITE | BLACK |
|---|---|---|---|---|---|
| 1 | P–K4 | P–K4 | 30 | PxP | RxP/4 |
| 2 | N–KB3 | N–QB3 | 31 | N–B4 | N–K4 |
| 3 | B–N5 | P–QR3 | 32 | P–B5 | N–N5 |
| 4 | B–R4 | N–B3 | 33 | Q–N3 | P–K6 |
| 5 | O–O | B–K2 | 34 | K–N1 | N–B7 |
| 6 | P–Q3 | P–QN4 | 35 | QxP | NxR |
| 7 | B–N3 | O–O | 36 | RxN | R–N5 |
| 8 | B–Q5 | NxB | 37 | P–N3 | Q–B3 |
| 9 | PxN | N–N5 | 38 | P–B6 | Q–K4 |
| 10 | P–B4 | PxP | 39 | R–K1 | R–K1 |
| 11 | PxP | P–K5 | 40 | K–B2 | K–B2 |
| 12 | N–K1 | P–QR4 | 41 | Q–Q2 | QxR† |
| 13 | N–QB3 | B–Q3 | 42 | QxQ | RxQ |
| 14 | P–B4 | B–B4† | 43 | KxR | R–KN1 |
| 15 | K–R1 | P–B4 | 44 | P–N5 | P–R4 |
| 16 | P–QR3 | N–R3 | 45 | P–QR4 | P–R5 |
| 17 | N–B2 | R–N1 | 46 | P–R5 | PxP |
| 18 | N–R4 | Q–B3 | 47 | PxP | RxP |
| 19 | B–Q2 | R–N6 | 48 | K–Q2 | R–N1 |
| 20 | BxP | R–Q6 | 49 | P–R6 | BxP |
| 21 | Q–K2 | B–R2 | 50 | PxB | R–QR1 |
| 22 | QR–Q1 | R–KN6 | 51 | N–K6 | RxP |
| 23 | B–B3 | Q–R3 | 52 | NxP | R–R4 |
| 24 | B–Q4 | BxB | 53 | N/7–N5 | K–K2 |
| 25 | NxB | P–Q3 | 54 | N–Q4 | K–Q1 |
| 26 | Q–KB2 | R–N5 | 55 | NxP | K–B2 |
| 27 | P–N4 | P–N4 | 56 | N–Q4 | R–B4? |
| 28 | N–K2 | N–N1 | 57 | N–K6† | Resigns |
| 29 | N/4–B3 | N–Q2 | | | |

# chapter 10 – Scotch Opening

This old opening is not particularly risky, and therefore, unlike, say, the Evans Gambit, is better fit for survival than other old openings.

White's aim is rather simple: to eliminate the enemy's King Pawn, thus obtaining mastery in the center. This he will not enjoy for long, since Black can soon regain the balance by means of . . . P–Q4. Apart from the Scotch Game proper there are also the gambits arising from 4 B–QB4 (the Scotch Gambit) and 4 P–B3 (the Goring Gambit, Part 2).

---

## part 1—SCOTCH FOUR KNIGHTS' GAME

1 P–K4, P–K4
2 N–KB3, N–QB3
3 P–Q4, PxP
4 NxP, N–B3[A]
5 N–QB3[B], B–N5[C]
6 NxN, NPxN
7 B–Q3, P–Q4[D]
8 PxP[E], PxP[F]
9 O–O, O–O
10 B–KN5

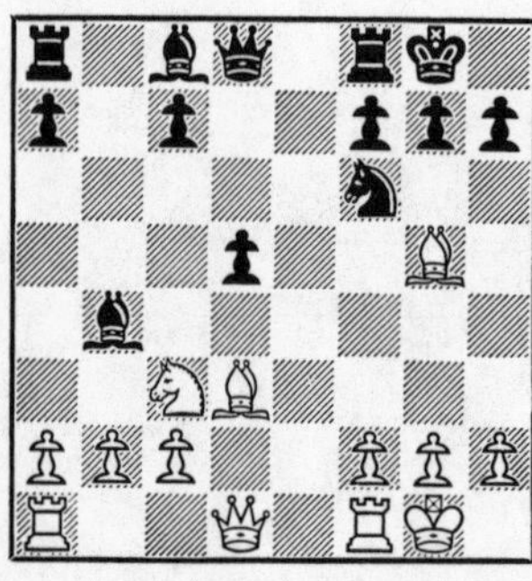

KEY POSITION 1

OBSERVATIONS ON KEY POSITION 1

[A] 4 . . . Q–R5 is too risky because of 5 N–N5!, QxKP† 6 B–K2, B–N5† 7 B–Q2, K–Q1 8 O–O, BxB 9 NxB with advantage for White. For 4 . . . B–B4, see Sup. Var. 13 and 14.

[B] For 5 NxN, see Sup. Var. 10–12.

[C] Lothar Schmidt's 5 . . . NxP is flashy, but it leads to a clear advantage for White after 6 NxN/4, Q–K2 7 P–KB3, P–Q4 8 B–QN5, B–Q2 9 O–O, PxN 10 BxN, PxB 11 R–K1, P–KB4 12 PxP, PxP 13 Q–K2 (Cortlever–Barendregt, Amsterdam 1954).

[D] Thus Black restores the balance in the center.

[E] Inferior is 8 P–K5 because of 8 . . . N–N5 9 O–O, O–O 10 B–KB4, P–B3!

[F] For 8 . . . Q–K2†, see Sup. Var. 8.

White's pieces are well developed and he has some chances for a Kingside attack. However, Black has counterchances, thanks to the center Pawn he maintains and his control of the half-open QN file.

The situation is not particularly dangerous for Black, but he must strive for active counterplay. Great caution is indicated concerning . . . P–KR3. The possible doubling of Black's King Bishop Pawns, in conjunction with the exchange of Queens, is not necessarily an achievement for White.

IDEA VARIATIONS 1–3:

(1) 10 . . . P–B3 11 Q–B3, B–K2 12 QR–K1, P–KR3 13 BxP (a promising sacrifice), PxB 14 Q–K3, P–Q5 15 QxRP, Q–Q3 16 Q–N5†, K–R1 17 P–B4, PxN (better is 17 . . . N–N1; see Prac. Var. 2) 18 Q–R6†, K–N1 19

R–B3, B–N5 20 R–N3, Q–B4† 21 K–B1, Q–KR4 22 QxQ, NxQ 23 RxB†, N–N2 24 RxB, PxP 25 R–K1±.

(2) 10 . . . P–B3 11 Q–B3, B–Q3 12 BxN, QxB 13 QxQ, PxQ 14 N–K2, P–QB4 15 P–QB4 (better is 15 P–QN3), PxP 16 BxP, B–K4 17 N–B3, R–N1∓. (Gligoric–Alexander, Hastings 1956–57).

(3) 10 . . . B–K3 11 N–K2, B–K2 (11 . . . P–KR3 is superior; see Prac. Var. 6) 12 N–B4, Q–Q3 13 R–K1, QR–K1 14 P–QB3 (or 14 P–QB4, PxP? 15 NxB!), P–B4 15 Q–B2, P–KR3 16 NxB, PxN 17 B–R4±.

PRACTICAL VARIATIONS 1–7:

1 P–K4, P–K4 2 N–KB3, N–QB3 3 P–Q4, PxP 4 NxP, N–B3 5 QN–B3, B–N5 6 NxN, NPxN 7 B–Q3, P–Q4 8 PxP, PxP 9 O–O, O–O 10 B–KN5

| | *1* | *2* | *3* | *4* | *5* | *6* | *7* |
|---|---|---|---|---|---|---|---|
| *10* | – – | – – | – – | – – | – – | – – | – – |
| | P–B3[1] | – – | – – | – – | B–K3 | – – | – – |
| *11* | Q–B3 | – – | – – | – – | Q–B3 | N–K2[17] | – – |
| | B–K2 | – – | – – | B–Q3 | B–K2 | P–KR3[18] | – – |
| *12* | QR–K1 | – – | KR–K1 | BxN[10] | QR–K1 | B–R4 | – – |
| | R–N1 | P–KR3 | R–N1 | QxB | R–N1[14] | B–Q3[19] | – – |
| *13* | N–Q1 | BxP | QR–N1 | QxQ | N–Q1 | P–KB4 | N–Q4 |
| | R–K1 | PxB | P–KR3 | PxQ | P–B4[15] | B–B4† | P–B4 |
| *14* | P–KR3 | Q–K3 | BxP | N–K2 | B–B5 | K–R1 | N–B5 |
| | B–K3 | P–Q5 | PxB | P–QB4[11] | Q–Q2 | B–KN5 | BxN |
| *15* | R–K2 | QxRP | Q–K3 | P–QN3[12] | BxB | P–KR3 | BxB |
| | P–B4 | Q–Q3[3] | B–Q3 | B–N2 | PxB | BxN | B–K4 |
| *16* | R/1–K1 | Q–N5†[4] | QxKRP | P–QB4 | Q–K3 | QxB | P–QB3 |
| | P–Q5 | K–R1 | R–N5[9] | P–Q5[13] | R–N3[16] | R–K1 | R–N1 |
| *17* | B–B5 | P–B4[5] | = | ∓ | = | Q–B3 | P–KB4 |
| | B–B5 | N–N1[6] | | | | R–K6 | B–B2 |
| *18* | R–K5[2] | RxB | | | | BxN | P–QN3 |
| | = | PxN[7] | | | | RxQ | Q–Q3 |
| *19* | | R–K3 | | | | BxQ | Q–B3 |
| | | Q–B3 | | | | RxR† | KR–K1 |
| *20* | | Q–QB5[8] | | | | RxR | QR–Q1 |
| | | = | | | | RxB[20] | P–Q5[21] |
| | | | | | | = | = |

*Notes to practical variations 1–7:*

[1] Not 10 . . . B–K2? because of 11 BxN, BxB 12 Q–R5, P–KR3 13 QxQP, QxQ 14 NxQ, BxP 15 QR–N1, B–K4 16 KR–K1, B–Q3 17 N–K7†, BxN (17 . . . K–R1? 18 B–K4) 18 RxB with an edge for White. 10 . . . BxN 11 PxB, P–KR3 12 B–R4, R–K1 13 P–QB4, PxP 14 BxP likewise yields a White plus.

continued ▸

[2] White has chances for attack (Spielmann–Yates, Semmering 1926).

[3] A complicated position which most likely should end in a draw.

[4] Not 16 P–B4 because of 16 . . . N–K5!

[5] Safer is 17 Q–R6† with a draw.

[6] For 17 . . . PxN, see Idea Var. 1.

[7] If 18 . . . QxR or 18 . . . NxR 19 Q–R5†!

[8] The issue is in the balance. After 20 . . . B–N5 21 P–KR3, B–K3 22 R–K5 there are problems for both sides.

[9] White has nothing better than a draw (Romanovski–Capablanca, Moscow 1925).

[10] Simpler is 12 B–B5, BxB 13 QxB, Q–Q2 with even chances (Alexander–Unzicker, Amsterdam 1954).

[11] For 14 . . . B–K3, see Game 1.

[12] For 15 P–QB4, see Idea Var. 2.

[13] If 17 N–N3, BxN.

[14] After 12 . . . P–KR3 13 BxP, PxB, White obtains a draw by perpetual check: 14 RxB, PxR 15 Q–N3†, K–R1 16 Q–N6 (Alekhine–Lasker, Moscow 1914).

[15] For 13 . . . P–Q5? see Game 2.

[16] Black's King Pawn is weak, indeed, but his pieces are very active.

[17] Recommended by Czerniak.

[18] Stronger than 11 . . . B–K2. See Idea Var. 3.

[19] Black obtains equality.

[20] Black's Pawn structure is more promising, but Bishops of opposite colors tend to produce a draw.

[21] There are chances for both sides.

### *Scotch Opening Game 1*

*WHITE: Czerniak* — *BLACK: W. Unzicker*

*Team Tournament, Moscow 1956*

| | WHITE | BLACK | | WHITE | BLACK |
|---|---|---|---|---|---|
| 1 | P–K4 | P–K4 | 18 | P–KB4 | P–B5 |
| 2 | N–KB3 | N–QB3 | 19 | PxP | PxP |
| 3 | N–B3 | N–B3 | 20 | B–K4 | B–B4† |
| 4 | P–Q4 | PxP | 21 | K–R1 | QR–N1 |
| 5 | NxP | B–N5 | 22 | P–B5 | RxR |
| 6 | NxN | NPxN | 23 | RxR | B–Q2 |
| 7 | B–Q3 | P–Q4 | 24 | N–B3 | B–K1 |
| 8 | PxP | PxP | 25 | P–N4 | B–N5 |
| 9 | O–O | O–O | 26 | N–Q5 | K–N2 |
| 10 | B–KN5 | P–B3 | 27 | R–Q4 | BxP |
| 11 | Q–B3 | B–Q3 | 28 | RxP | B–N4 |
| 12 | BxN | QxB | 29 | R–B7 | B–Q3 |
| 13 | QxQ | PxQ | 30 | R–R7 | P–R5 |
| 14 | N–K2 | B–K3 | 31 | P–N5 | PxP |
| 15 | P–QN3 | P–QR4 | 32 | P–B6† | K–B1 |
| 16 | P–QR4 | P–QB4 | 33 | N–B3 | B–K1 |
| 17 | QR–Q1 | KR–Q1 | 34 | B–Q5 | B–B4 |

| WHITE | BLACK | WHITE | BLACK |
|---|---|---|---|
| 35 R–R6 | R–Q1 | 47 NxP | R–Q8† |
| 36 B–B4 | B–Q5 | 48 K–N2 | B–N6 |
| 37 N–K4 | R–B1 | 49 N–Q6 | P–R6 |
| 38 B–Q5 | RxP | 50 N–B5 | B–Q4† |
| 39 R–R8 | P–N5 | 51 K–N3 | B–K4† |
| 40 P–R3 | P–N6 | 52 K–B2 | P–R7 |
| 41 NxP | BxP | 53 N–K3 | R–Q7† |
| 42 N–B5 | R–Q7 | 54 K–K1 | B–QB6 |
| 43 B–K4 | R–Q1 | 55 N–Q1 | R–K7† |
| 44 R–R6 | B–N7 | 56 KxR | B–B5† |
| 45 N–Q6 | B–Q2 | Resigns | |
| 46 BxP | B–K3 | | |

*Scotch Opening Game 2*

*WHITE: F. Ekstrom* *BLACK: Dr. M. Euwe*

*Hastings 1945–46*

| WHITE | BLACK | WHITE | BLACK |
|---|---|---|---|
| 1 P–K4 | P–K4 | 18 R–QB5 | P–QB3 |
| 2 N–KB3 | N–QB3 | 19 N–N2 | R–Q3 |
| 3 N–B3 | N–B3 | 20 R–K1 | K–B1 |
| 4 P–Q4 | PxP | 21 R–QR5 | R–Q2 |
| 5 NxP | B–N5 | 22 N–R4 | N–N3 |
| 6 NxN | NPxN | 23 N–B5 | R–K2 |
| 7 B–Q3 | P–Q4 | 24 R–R4 | R–Q1 |
| 8 PxP | PxP | 25 R–K4 | R–Q4 |
| 9 O–O | O–O | 26 NxB† | PxN |
| 10 B–KN5 | B–K3 | 27 KRxQP | P–K4 |
| 11 Q–B3 | B–K2 | 28 R/Q–Q4 | R/2–Q2 |
| 12 QR–K1 | R–N1 | 29 P–N3 | K–K2 |
| 13 N–Q1 | P–Q5 | 30 B–K4 | R–Q8† |
| 14 P–QN3 | Q–Q4 | 31 K–N2 | K–Q3 |
| 15 QxQ | NxQ | 32 BxN | PxB |
| 16 BxB | NxB | White won | |
| 17 R–K5 | KR–Q1 | | |

SUPPLEMENTARY VARIATIONS 1–7:

1 P–K4, P–K4 2 N–KB3, N–QB3 3 P–Q4, PxP 4 NxP

Sup. Var. 8 and 9 illustrate Black's desire to exchange Queens and restrict White's chances for attack.

Sup. Var. 10, 11 and 12 are examples of the Mieses Variation where White tries to intensify the character of the struggle. This set-up is not dangerous for Black.

Sup. Var. 13 and 14 give the old-fashioned treatment of the Scotch Game. Black easily obtains equality.

| | *1* | *2* | *3* | *4* | *5* | *6* | *7* |
|---|---|---|---|---|---|---|---|
| *4* | – – | – – | – – | – – | – – | – – | – – |
| | N–B3 | – – | – – | – – | – – | B–B4 | – – |
| *5* | N–QB3 | – – | NxN | – – | – – | B–K3[10] | – – |
| | B–N5 | – – | NPxN[5] | – – | – – | Q–B3[11] | – – |
| *6* | NxN | – – | P–K5 | N–Q2 | B–Q3 | P–QB3 | N–N5[13] |
| | NPxN | – – | Q–K2 | B–B4 | P–Q4 | KN–K2 | BxB |
| *7* | B–Q3 | – – | Q–K2 | P–K5 | N–Q2[8] | N–B2 | PxB |
| | P–Q4 | – – | N–Q4 | Q–K2 | B–QB4 | BxB | Q–R5† |
| *8* | PxP | – – | N–Q2 | Q–K2 | O–O | NxB | P–N3 |
| | Q–K2†[1] | – – | B–N2 | N–Q4 | O–O | O–O | Q–Q1[14] |
| *9* | Q–K2 | – – | N–N3 | N–N3 | Q–B3 | B–K2 | Q–N4 |
| | NxP[2] | PxP | O–O–O | B–N3 | N–N5 | P–Q3 | K–B1! |
| *10* | QxQ† | O–O | P–QB4 | B–Q2 | PxP | O–O | Q–B4 |
| | KxQ | QxQ | N–N3[6] | P–QR4 | Q–Q3 | B–K3 | P–Q3[15] |
| *11* | P–QR3 | NxQ | = | P–QR4 | Q–N3 | N–Q2 | ∓ |
| | B–R4 | P–B4 | | O–O | QxQ | P–Q4[12] | |
| *12* | P–QN4[3] | P–QB3 | | O–O–O | PxQ | = | |
| | ± | B–R4 | | R–K1[7] | PxP[9] | | |
| *13* | | B–KB4 | | ∓ | ∓ | | |
| | | B–N3[4] | | | | | |
| | | ± | | | | | |

*Notes to supplementary variations 1–7:*

[1] The move is playable, provided Black does not expect too much from the position.

[2] For 9 . . . QxQ† 10 KxQ see Game 3.

[3] 12 . . . NxN 13 PxB, N–Q4 14 O–O and White has the advantage. Or 12 . . . BxP 13 PxB, NxN 14 B–N2, N–Q4 15 BxNP, R–KN1 16 B–Q4 and White's two Bishops give him the advantage (Czerniak–Rellstab, Reggio Emilia 1951).

[4] White has only a tiny edge (Spielmann–Bogoljubov, Pistyan 1922).

[5] The unbalancing of the Pawn structure creates chances for both sides.

[6] Match game, Mieses–Tarrasch, 1916.

[7] Continuing with 13 . . . P–Q3.

[8] 7 P–K5 is not commendable because of 7 . . . N–N5 8 B–KB4, B–QB4 9 O–O, P–N4 10 B–Q2 (10 B–N3, P–KR4!), Q–K2 11 B–B3, B–K3 with advantage for Black. Instead, 7 PxP quickly leads to a draw.

[9] Black has the center, superior development and an advantage in space.

[10] After 5 NxN, Black's best is 5 . . . Q–B3.

[11] This deployment is pointed and tricky.

[12] Black has equalized.

[13] Blumenfeld's variation, though apparently dangerous for Black, only compromises White's game.

[14] 8 . . . QxKP is also playable. Then after 9 NxP†, K–Q1 10 NxR, N–B3 11 Q–Q6, QxR 12 N–Q2, attack and counterattack are in the balance.

[15] Collijn *Larobok.*

*Scotch Opening Game 3*

*WHITE: R. Spielmann BLACK: Dr. Emanuel Lasker*

*Moscow 1935*

| | WHITE | BLACK | | WHITE | BLACK |
|---|---|---|---|---|---|
| 1 | P–K4 | P–K4 | 22 | BxN | RxB |
| 2 | N–KB3 | N–QB3 | 23 | N–Q8† | K–R3 |
| 3 | P–Q4 | PxP | 24 | BxP | B–K3 |
| 4 | NxP | N–B3 | 25 | N–B6 | B–N2 |
| 5 | N–QB3 | B–N5 | 26 | QR–B1 | R–B5 |
| 6 | NxN | NPxN | 27 | B–K3 | K–N4 |
| 7 | B–Q3 | P–Q4 | 28 | N–R7† | KxP |
| 8 | PxP | Q–K2† | 29 | B–N6 | R–B6 |
| 9 | Q–K2 | QxQ† | 30 | R–N1† | R–N6 |
| 10 | KxQ | PxP | 31 | N–B6† | K–R5 |
| 11 | N–N5 | K–Q1 | 32 | B–Q4 | RxR |
| 12 | R–Q1 | P–B3 | 33 | RxR | BxB |
| 13 | P–QB3 | R–K1† | 34 | NxB | R–R3 |
| 14 | K–B1 | B–B1 | 35 | R–R1† | K–N5 |
| 15 | N–Q4 | K–B2 | 36 | K–K2 | B–Q2 |
| 16 | B–B4† | K–N3 | 37 | N–B2† | K–B6 |
| 17 | P–QR4 | P–QR4 | 38 | N–K3 | B–N4† |
| 18 | P–QN4 | PxP | 39 | K–K1 | P–Q5 |
| 19 | P–R5† | K–N2 | 40 | R–B1† | K–Q6 |
| 20 | PxP | N–K5 | 41 | R–Q1† | Draw |
| 21 | NxP | P–N4 | | | |

---

## part 2—**GORING GAMBIT**

1 P–K4, P–K4
2 N–KB3, N–QB3
3 P–Q4, PxP
4 P–B3[A], PxP[B]
5 NxP, B–N5[C]
6 B–QB4, N–B3[D]
7 O–O, BxN
8 PxB, P–Q3
9 P–K5

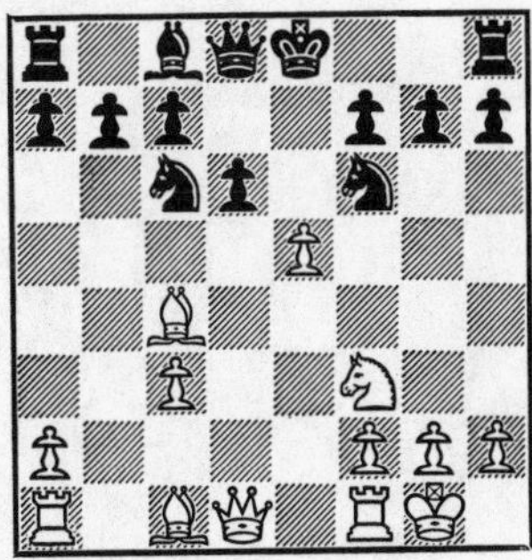

KEY POSITION 2

### OBSERVATIONS ON KEY POSITION 2

[A] 4 B–QB4 leads to the Scotch Gambit, which in turn leads to the Two Knights' Defense after 4 . . . N–B3. However, Black can also safely proceed with 4 . . . B–B4; e.g., 5 P–B3!, P–Q6 (also playable is 5 . . . PxP 6 BxP†, KxB 7 Q–Q5†, K–B1 8 QxB†, Q–K2) 6 P–QN4, B–N3 7 P–QR4, P–QR3 8 P–R5, B–R2 9 Q–N3, Q–K2 10 O–O, N–B3! (but not 10 . . . P–Q3 because of 11 P–N5, PxP 12 BxNP, B–Q2 13 P–R6!) 11 QN–Q2, O–O with even chances.

[B] 4 . . . P–Q4 leads to the Danish Gambit. An alternative, offering Black a steady game, is 4 . . . P–Q6 5 BxP, B–B4 6 O–O, P–Q3 7 QN–Q2, P–QR4 8 R–K1, KN–K2 (Penrose–Keres, Moscow 1956).

[C] Also playable is 5 . . . P–Q3, and it appears that Black will be able to withstand the attack; e.g., 6 B–QB4, B–K3 7 BxB, PxB 8 Q–N3, Q–B1 9 N–KN5, N–Q1 10 P–B4 (according to

Emanuel Lasker, preferable is 10 P–K5), B–K2 11 O–O, BxN 12 PxB, N–K2 13 N–N5, P–K4 14 Q–B4, N/2–B3 and it is Black for choice (Marco–Spielmann, Goteborg 1920).

D Smyslov recommends 6 . . . P–Q3, when 7 O–O, BxN 8 PxB, N–B3 9 P–K5 leads to key position 2. But if White varies on his 9th turn with 9 B–R3, the continuation favors Black, as in 9 . . . B–N5 10 B–N5, O–O 11 BxN, PxB 12 P–K5, N–Q4 (Penrose–Smyslov, Munich 1958).

This is a tense position where the activity of White's pieces compensates for the Pawn. Black will normally be able to withstand the attack by a timely return of the extra Pawn, and obtain a satisfactory end game.

## IDEA VARIATIONS 4 AND 5:

(4) 9 . . . PxP 10 N–N5, O–O (10 . . . B–K3!) 11 B–R3, QxQ 12 QRxQ, B–B4 13 BxR, RxB 14 KR–K1, P–KR3 15 N–B3, B–N5 16 B–N5 (for 16 R–N1 see Game 4), P–K5 17 BxN, PxB 18 P–KR3, B–R4 19 P–N4, NxP 20 PxN, BxP 21 N–K5, BxR 22 RxB, with advantage for White.

(5) 9 . . . NxP 10 NxN, PxN 11 QxQ†, KxQ 12 BxP, K–K2 13 B–N3, B–K3 14 P–QB4, QR–Q1 15 R–K1, P–K5 16 P–B3, KR–K1 17 PxP, K–B2 with even chances.

*Scotch Opening Game 4*

*WHITE: B. Juchtman* *BLACK: M. Tal*

*Moscow 1959*

| | WHITE | BLACK | | WHITE | BLACK |
|---|---|---|---|---|---|
| 1 | P–K4 | P–K4 | 21 | PxB | NxP† |
| 2 | P–Q4 | PxP | 22 | K–B2 | N–N5† |
| 3 | P–QB3 | PxP | 23 | K–N3 | NxR |
| 4 | NxP | N–QB3 | 24 | RxN | P–B4 |
| 5 | N–B3 | B–N5 | 25 | BxP† | K–R2 |
| 6 | B–QB4 | N–B3 | 26 | B–K2 | N–K4 |
| 7 | O–O | BxN | 27 | K–B4 | N–N3† |
| 8 | PxB | P–Q3 | 28 | K–K3 | P–B5† |
| 9 | P–K5 | PxP | 29 | K–Q4 | K–R1 |
| 10 | N–N5 | O–O | 30 | R–KN1 | N–R5 |
| 11 | B–R3 | QxQ | 31 | KxP | R–K1† |
| 12 | QRxQ | B–B4 | 32 | K–Q3 | P–B6 |
| 13 | BxR | RxB | 33 | B–Q1 | N–N7 |
| 14 | KR–K1 | P–KR3 | 34 | K–Q2 | N–R5 |
| 15 | N–B3 | B–N5 | 35 | N–Q4 | R–Q1 |
| 16 | R–N1 | P–K5 | 36 | R–B1 | R–Q4 |
| 17 | N–Q4 | N–K4 | 37 | K–Q3 | R–QR4 |
| 18 | B–B1 | P–B4 | 38 | B–N3 | P–KN4 |
| 19 | N–N5 | P–B5 | 39 | NxP | |
| 20 | P–B3 | BxP | | White won | |

PRACTICAL VARIATIONS 8–10:

1 P–K4, P–K4 2 N–KB3, N–QB3 3 P–Q4, PxP 4 P–B3, PxP 5 NxP, B–N5 6 B–QB4, N–B3 7 O–O, BxN 8 PxB, P–Q3 9 P–K5

| | 8 | 9 | 10 |
|---|---|---|---|
| 9 | – – | – – | – – |
| | PxP | – – | NxP |
| 10 | N–N5! | – – | NxN |
| | B–K3![1] | – – | PxN |
| 11 | BxB | NxB | Q–N3[4] |
| | PxB | PxN | Q–K2 |
| 12 | Q–N3 | BxP | B–R3 |
| | Q–Q4 | QxQ† | P–B4 |
| 13 | NxKP | RxQ | Q–N5† |
| | QxQ | K–K2 | N–Q2[5] |
| 14 | PxQ | B–N3 | $\mp$ |
| | K–B2 | KR–Q1[3] | |
| 15 | NxBP | $\mp$ | |
| | QR–Q1[2] | | |
| | $\mp$ | | |

*Notes to practical variations 8–10:*

[1] For 10 . . . O–O see Idea Var. 4 and Game 4. Inferior is 10 . . . QxQ because of 11 BxP†, K–B1 12 RxQ, P–KN3 13 B–N3 and White has ample compensation for the Pawn.

[2] Black has an easier game (Aronin).

[3] Black is a Pawn ahead.

[4] For 11 QxQ†, see Idea Var. 5.

[5] White has some pressure for the two Pawns, but this is probably insufficient compensation.

---

## part 3—SCOTCH FOUR KNIGHTS' GAMBIT

1 P–K4, P–K4
2 N–KB3, N–QB3
3 N–B3, N–B3
4 P–Q4, PxP
5 N–Q5

KEY POSITION 3

OBSERVATIONS ON KEY POSITION 3

This is an idea of revivifying the well analyzed and almost monotonous Scotch Four Knights' Game. It may arise from the Four Knights' Game or the Scotch by transpositions. It is tricky and perilous for one unaware of its intricacies.

IDEA VARIATION 6:

5 . . . NxN (not quite satisfactory) 6 PxN, B–N5† (6 . . . N–N5 7 B–QB4, Q–K2† 8 K–Q2!) 7 B–Q2, Q–K2† 8 Q–K2, BxB† 9 KxB, QxQ† 10 BxQ, N–K2 11 P–Q6$\pm$.

PRACTICAL VARIATIONS 11-13:

1 P–K4, P–K4 2 N–KB3, N–QB3 3 N–B3, N–B3 4 P–Q4, PxP 5 N–Q5

| | 1 | 2 | 3 |
|---|---|---|---|
| 5 | – – | – – | – – |
| | NxP[1] | – – | B–K2 |
| 6 | Q–K2 | – – | B–KB4[7] |
| | P–B4 | – – | P–Q3 |
| 7 | N–N5 | – – | NxP |
| | P–Q6![2] | – – | KNxN[8] |
| 8 | PxP | – – | PxN |
| | N–Q5 | – – | NxN |
| 9 | Q–R5† | – – | QxN |
| | P–N3 | – – | B–B3 |
| 10 | Q–R4 | – – | Q–K4† |
| | P–B3![3] | – – | Q–K2 |
| 11 | PxN | – – | QxQ† |
| | PxN | – – | KxQ |
| 12 | PxQP | PxBP | O–O–O |
| | B–N2[4] | NxP | ± |
| 13 | K–Q1 | Q–KN4 | |
| | P–KR3 | B–B4[6] | |
| 14 | N–B3 | ∓ | |
| | NxN | | |
| 15 | QxQ† | | |
| | KxQ | | |
| 16 | PxN | | |
| | P–KN4[5] | | |
| | = | | |

*Notes to practical variations 11-13:*

[1] Leads to difficult complications.

[2] 7 . . . B–K2 8 NxN±.

[3] 10 . . . N–B7† 11 K–Q1, NxR 12 PxN±.

[4] 12 . . . N–B7† 13 K–Q1, NxR 14 Q–Q4, R–KN1 15 P–Q6±, but 12 . . . Q–R4† 13 K–Q1, QxQP deserves consideration. Thus 14 B–QB4!, QxB 15 R–K1† leads to a draw.

[5] If 17 R–KN1, B–Q5.

[6] Or 13 . . . Q–K2†∓.

[7] 6 B–QN5, P–Q3 7 NxP, B–Q2 8 O–O, NxN leads to equality.

[8] 7 . . . NxP 8 B–QN5, B–Q2 9 O–O is risky for Black.

[9] 14 B–QB4!, QxB 15 R–K1† leads to a draw.

# chapter 11—Two Knights' Defense

The Two Knights' Defense arises after 1 P–K4, P–K4 2 N–KB3, N–QB3 3 B–B4, N–B3. It is one of the most difficult and extensively analyzed openings, already known to Greco in 1630. The first to investigate it thoroughly was the Berlin master Von Bilguer, who devoted a considerable part of his famous *Handbuch* to this opening. In our time The Two Knights' Defense has appealed particularly to American masters who have enriched its theory with new variations.

After 3 . . . N–B3 there are two great groups of variations: one beginning with 4 P–Q4, the other with 4 N–N5. The consequences of these two moves are entirely different.

With 4 P–Q4, PxP 5 O–O White aims at quick development. Black's best answer is 5 . . . NxP, which, indeed, opens lines, but also has the merit of eliminating White's last center Pawn (Part 1). Unusual to-day is 5 . . . B–B4, which, after 6 P–K5, P–Q4 leads to the very complicated Max Lange Attack (Sup. Var. 3–6).

The attack on Black's KB2 by 4 N–N5 wins a Pawn almost by force, but at the expense of development. The assessment of 4 N–N5 has repeatedly and rapidly changed during the course of time. Tarrasch called it a "duffer's" move, but present-day opinion considers that 4 N–N5 makes matters more difficult for Black than 4 P–Q4.

The main variation after 4 N–N5 is 4 . . . P–Q4 5 PxP, N–QR4 6 B–N5†, P–B3 7 PxP, PxP 8 B–K2, P–KR3 9 N–KB3, P–K5 10 N–K5 (Part 2). Stemming from the above line, the continuation 6 P–Q3 (Part 3) popular in Morphy's time, is rarely adopted to-day. Again, in connection with 6 B–N5†, P–B3 7 PxP, PxP, the old-fashioned move 8 Q–B3 (Sup. Var. 15) has retired to the archives. Other interesting offshoots at Black's disposal are 5 . . . N–Q5 (the Fritz Variation, Sup. Var. 13), 5 . . . P–N4 (the Ulvestad Variation, Sup. Var. 14) and 4 . . . B–B4 (the Wilkes–Barre Variation, Sup. Var. 11).

---

## part 1—P-Q4 VARIATION

1 P–K4, P–K4
2 N–KB3, N–QB3
3 B–B4, N–B3
4 P–Q4, PxP
5 O–O[A], NxP[B]
6 R–K1, P–Q4
7 BxP[C], QxB
8 N–B3, Q–QR4[D]
9 NxN[E], B–K3

KEY POSITION 1

OBSERVATIONS ON KEY POSITION 1

[A] For 5 P–K5 and 5 N–N5 see Sup. Var. 1 and 2 respectively. Inferior for White is: 5 NxP, NxP 6 BxP†, KxB 7 Q–R5†, P–N3 8 Q–Q5†, K–N2 9 NxN, NPxN 10 QxN, Q–K1! 11 QxQ, B–N5†!

[B] For 5 . . . B–B4 (Max Lange) and 5 . . . P–Q3 see, respectively, Sup. Var. 3–6 and Sup. Var. 7.

C The text move is Canal's original idea. 7 N–B3?! instead leads to Black's advantage after 7 . . . PxN 8 BxP, B–K3! 9 BxN (if 9 RxN? N–K2!), B–QN5. The only chance for White to complicate matters is 10 Q–K2?!

D For 8 . . . Q–KR4 and 8 . . . Q–Q1 see Sup. Var. 8 and Sup. Var. 9 respectively. Inferior for Black is 8 . . . Q–QB5 9 N–Q2!, Q–R3 10 N–Q5, Q–R4 11 P–QB4! Also weak for Black is 8 . . . Q–KB4 9 NxN, B–K2 10 B–N5.

E Inferior for White is 9 RxN† B–K3 10 NxP, O–O–O. White may experiment with 9 NxP, NxN 10 QxN, P–KB4 11 B–Q2, Q–N3 12 Q–Q3! For a detailed analysis of White's chances, see CHESS REVIEW, September, 1958.

The classical continuation in this position is 10 N/4–N5, whereby White recovers the Pawn by force. Then, however, after 10 . . . O–O–O 11 NxB, PxN 12 RxP, Black obtains a good position with the modern continuation 12 . . . B–Q3. Other moves on Black's 12th turn leave White with good chances, as has been demonstrated by games in the past.

Instead of 10 N/4–N5, however, White may try to counteract Black's deployment by 10 B–N5 or 10 B–Q2. After 10 B–N5, Black, if he still aims at . . . O–O–O by driving off the enemy Bishop, takes risky chances because of the so-called Jordansky Attack: 10 . . . P–KR3 11 B–R4, P–KN4?! 12 N–B6†! The safe line for Black, leading to a fully satisfactory game, is . . . B–QN5, possibly preceded by . . . P–KR3 and followed by . . . O–O.

But White has a more precise move, according to present opinion, in 10 B–Q2. If Black answers with 10 . . . B–QN5?!, the continuation leads to complications requiring meticulous play on Black's part: 11 NxP!, NxN 12 P–QB3! Therefore it is considered safer for Black to answer 10 B–Q2 with 10 . . . Q–KB4.

IDEA VARIATIONS 1–3:

(1) 10 N/4–N5, O–O–O 11 NxB, PxN 12 RxP, B–Q3 (for other possibilities see Prac. Var. 1–3) 13 Q–K2 (13 B–KN5 is followed by 13 . . . QR–B1 14 Q–K2, K–Q2!), Q–R4 (threatening 14 . . . P–Q6! 15 PxP, N–Q5!) 14 P–KR3, QR–K1 (not 14 . . . KR–K1 15 B–N5!) 15 B–Q2, N–K4 16 RxR†, RxR 17 NxP, QxQ 18 NxQ, N–B5! 19 B–K3, NxP and the end game slightly favors Black according to Euwe.

(2) 10 B–N5, P–KR3, (for 10 . . . B–QN5 see Prac. Var. 4) 11 B–R4, P–KN4?! (risky; here, too, 11 B–QN5

is best) 12 N–B6†!, K–K2 13 P–QN4! Q–KB4 (13 . . . NxP 14 B–N3!) 14 P–N5! with a strong White attack according to Keres: 14 . . . QxNP 15 P–B4, QxP 16 R–QB1±, or 14 . . . PxB 15 PxN, QxN 16 PxP, R–QN1 17 N–K5! But insufficient for White is 14 B–N3, KxN 15 P–N5, QxNP 16 NxP, Q–Q4 17 NxN, QxQ 18 B–K5†, K–N3 19 QRxQ, B–N2 (Sanguinetti–Guimard, Zonal Tournament 1954).

(3) 10 B–Q2, B–QN5 (for 10 . . . Q–KB4, see Prac. Var. 5) 11 NxP! NxN 12 P–QB3, Q–Q4 (stronger for Black is 12 . . . B–K2 13 PxN, Q–Q4 14 B–N4, BxB 15 Q–R4†, Q–B3 16 QxB, O–O–O with even chances) 13 PxB, O–O 14 R–QB1, QR–Q1 (better is 14 . . . P–QN3 15 RxP, QR–Q1) 15 R–B5!, QxP (15 . . . Q–Q2!) 16 B–B3!, N–N4? 17 N–B6†, PxN 18 BxP, R–Q4 19 Q–Q2!, and mate is inevitable (Konzel–Duckstein, Vienna 1959).

*Two Knights' Defense Game 1*

*WHITE: Tartakover* *BLACK: Steiner*

*Budapest 1921*

| | WHITE | BLACK | | WHITE | BLACK |
|---|---|---|---|---|---|
| 1 | P–K4 | P–K4 | 14 | B–B4 | P–KN4 |
| 2 | B–B4 | N–KB3 | 15 | B–N3 | P–Q6 |
| 3 | P–Q4 | PxP | 16 | PxP | P–N5 |
| 4 | N–KB3 | N–B3 | 17 | RxN! | PxR |
| 5 | O–O | NxP | 18 | N–K5 | P–KR4 |
| 6 | R–K1 | P–Q4 | 19 | P–Q4 | K–N2 |
| 7 | BxP | QxB | 20 | R–QB1 | R–K1 |
| 8 | N–B3 | Q–QR4 | 21 | R–B3 | QxP |
| 9 | NxN | B–K3 | 22 | R–N3† | K–R1 |
| 10 | N/4–N5 | O–O–O | 23 | NxBP | Q–Q2 |
| 11 | NxB | PxN | 24 | N–K5 | B–N2? |
| 12 | RxP | Q–Q4 | 25 | Q–K4†! | P–B3 |
| 13 | Q–K2 | P–KR3 | 26 | R–N8† | Resigns |

PRACTICAL VARIATIONS 1–5:

1 P–K4, P–K4 2 N–KB3, N–QB3 3 B–B4, N–B3 4 P–Q4, PxP 5 O–O, NxP 6 R–K1, P–Q4 7 BxP, QxB 8 N–B3, Q–QR4 9 NxN, B–K3

| | *1* | *2* | *3* | *4* | *5* |
|---|---|---|---|---|---|
| *10* | N/4–N5 | – – | – – | B–N5 | B–Q2 |
| | O–O–O | – – | – – | B–QN5 | Q–KB4! |
| *11* | NxB | – – | – – | R–K2 | B–N5 |
| | PxN | – – | – – | O–O![9] | P–KR3![12] |
| *12* | RxP | – – | – – | P–QR3[10] | B–R4[13] |
| | Q–KB4 | Q–Q4 | B–K2 | B–Q3! | B–B4 |
| *13* | Q–K2 | Q–K2 | N–K5![6] | NxB | P–QN4 |
| | P–KR3 | P–KR3 | NxN | PxN | BxNP |
| *14* | B–Q2! | B–B4 | RxB | B–B4 | NxP |
| | QxP | P–KN4 | R–Q2 | B–N5[11] | NxN |
| *15* | R–QB1 | B–N3 | RxR | ∓ | QxN |
| | QxP | P–Q6 | NxR | | BxR |
| *16* | R/6xN | PxP | B–B4 | | QxNP |
| | PxR | P–N5[3] | R–K1 | | K–Q2 |
| *17* | Q–K6†[1] | RxN | P–KR3 | | RxB |
| | K–N1 | PxR[4] | Q–KB4[7] | | P–QN4![14] |
| *18* | Q–K4 | N–K5 | B–N3[8] | | = |
| | P–Q6 | P–KR4 | ± | | |
| *19* | N–K5 | P–Q4![5] | | | |
| | K–R1 | ± | | | |
| *20* | NxBP | | | | |
| | Q–N2[2] | | | | |
| | ± | | | | |

*Notes to practical variations 1–5:*

[1] 17 N–K5 is insufficient because of 17 . . . R–K1 18 Q–R6†, Q–N2 (Kostich–Vidmar, Bled 1931.

[2] The correct continuation is 21 R–B3, B–B4 22 RxB, KR–K1 23 Q–QB4, Q–N8† 24 Q–B1, QxQ 25 RxQ, and Black must fight for a draw. The alternative, 21 Q–QR4, R–K1 22 P–N3, R–K7 23 R–B3, is surprisingly refuted by 23 . . . B–N5! 24 R–N3, RxB 24 RxB, RxRP!

[3] 16 . . . QxQP 17 QxQ, RxQ 18 N–K5 favors White.

[4] 17 . . . QxR 18 N–K5, Q–K3 19 Q–K3, K–N1 20 R–QB1± (Tartakover).

[5] White has a very strong attack. See Game 1.

[6] Otherwise Black gets a good position with 13 . . . B–B3.

[7] On 17 . . . Q–N5 (Bernstein–Vidmar, Groningen 1946) White gets a good initiative with 18 Q–R5!, R–K8† 19 K–R2! (Keres).

[8] See Game 2.

[9] After 11 . . . P–KR3, a promising continuation for White is 12 P–QR3! PxB 13 PxB, QxP 14 P–B3!

[10] Or 12 NxP, B–B5 13 R–K3, P–B4!

[11] See Game 3.

[12] An important finesse. The immediate 11 . . . B–B4 costs a piece: 12 N–R4, Q–Q4 13 P–QB4!, QxP 14 R–QB1.

[13] Or 12 Q–Q3, Q–R4 (12 . . . PxB? 13 N–Q6†) 13 B–R4, B–QN5 14 R–K2, P–KN4!

[14] Tinnesand–Matzl, Correspondence Game 1959.

*Two Knights' Defense Game 2*

*WHITE: Tartakover* *BLACK: Tarrasch*

*Göteborg 1920*

| | WHITE | BLACK | | WHITE | BLACK |
|---|---|---|---|---|---|
| 1 | P–K4 | P–K4 | 17 | P–KR3 | Q–KB4 |
| 2 | N–KB3 | N–QB3 | 18 | B–N3 | Q–K5 |
| 3 | B–B4 | N–B3 | 19 | Q–Q2 | P–QN3 |
| 4 | P–Q4 | PxP | 20 | P–N4 | N–B3 |
| 5 | O–O | NxP | 21 | R–Q1 | K–N2 |
| 6 | R–K1 | P–Q4 | 22 | P–QR4 | Q–K7 |
| 7 | BxP | QxB | 23 | QxP | QxP |
| 8 | N–B3 | Q–QR4 | 24 | P–R5 | R–K5 |
| 9 | NxN | B–K3 | 25 | Q–R1 | Q–K7? |
| 10 | N/4–N5 | O–O–O | 26 | R–QB1 | R–B5 |
| 11 | NxB | PxN | 27 | PxP | RPxP |
| 12 | RxP | B–K2 | 28 | P–N5! | K–N1? |
| 13 | N–K5 | NxN | 29 | R–K1 | Q–B7 |
| 14 | RxB | R–Q2 | 30 | Q–R6 | R–K5 |
| 15 | RxR | NxR | 31 | R–R1 | Resigns |
| 16 | B–B4 | R–K1 | | | |

*Two Knights' Defense Game 3*

*WHITE: Cortlever* *BLACK: Euwe*

*Dutch Championship 1938*

| | WHITE | BLACK | | WHITE | BLACK |
|---|---|---|---|---|---|
| 1 | P–K4 | P–K4 | 18 | QxP | QR–N1 |
| 2 | N–KB3 | N–QB3 | 19 | Q–K7 | RxP |
| 3 | P–Q4 | PxP | 20 | RxP! | Q–R5! |
| 4 | B–B4 | N–B3 | 21 | R/1–K1 | RxP |
| 5 | O–O | NxP | 22 | R–KN5 | P–N3 |
| 6 | R–K1 | P–Q4 | 23 | R–N3 | Q–B5 |
| 7 | BxP | QxB | 24 | Q–K4 | R–B8 |
| 8 | N–B3 | Q–QR4 | 25 | P–KR4 | RxR† |
| 9 | NxN | B–K3 | 26 | QxR | P–Q6 |
| 10 | B–N5 | B–QN5 | 27 | Q–Q2 | R–Q1 |
| 11 | R–K2 | O–O | 28 | P–R5 | Q–B7 |
| 12 | P–QR3 | B–Q3 | 29 | Q–N5 | R–QB1 |
| 13 | NxB | PxN | 30 | K–R2 | P–Q7 |
| 14 | B–B4 | B–N5! | 31 | P–R6 | P–Q8/Q |
| 15 | Q–Q3 | N–K4! | 32 | Q–B6 | Q–R5† |
| 16 | BxN | BxN! | 33 | R–R3 | Q–QB6 |
| 17 | QxB | PxB | | Resigns | |

SUPPLEMENTARY VARIATIONS 1-9:

1 P–K4, P–K4 2 N–KB3, N–QB3 3 B–B4, N–B3 4 P–Q4, PxP

| | 1 | 2 | 3 | 4 | 5 | 6 | 7 | 8 | 9 |
|---|---|---|---|---|---|---|---|---|---|
| 5 | P–K5 | N–N5 | O–O | — — | — — | — — | — — | — — | — — |
| | N–K5[1] | P–Q4 | B–B4 | — — | — — | — — | P–Q3 | NxP | — — |
| 6 | O–O[2] | PxP | P–K5 | — — | — — | — — | NxP | R–K1 | — — |
| | P–Q4 | Q–K2† | P–Q4 | — — | — — | N–N5 | B–K2 | P–Q4 | — — |
| 7 | B–QN5 | K–B1[4] | PxN[6] | — — | — — | B–B4![15] | N–B3 | BxP | — — |
| | B–KN5 | N–K4 | PxB | — — | — — | P–Q3[16] | O–O | QxB | — — |
| 8 | P–KR3 | QxP | R–K1†[7] | — — | — — | PxP | P–QN3[20] | N–B3 | — — |
| | BxN | NxB | B–K3 | — — | — — | BxP | B–Q2 | Q–KR4 | Q–Q1 |
| 9 | QxB | QxN | N–N5 | — — | — — | R–K1† | B–N2 | NxN | RxN†[24] |
| | P–QR3 | P–KR3 | Q–Q4 | — — | — — | K–B1[17] | R–K1 | B–K3 | B–K2! |
| 10 | BxN† | N–KB3 | N–QB3 | — — | — — | BxB† | Q–Q2 | B–N5 | NxP |
| | PxB | Q–B4[5] | Q–B4 | — — | — — | QxB | N–K4 | B–QN5![22] | P–B4 |
| 11 | N–Q2 | = | QN–K4[8] | — — | — — | P–B3! | B–K2 | NxP | R–B4[25] |
| | N–N4 | | O–O–O! | B–B1 | B–N3 | B–B4[18] | P–B3 | QxQ | O–O |
| 12 | Q–Q3 | | N/5xB | NxBP | PxP | PxP | P–B4 | KRxQ | NxN |
| | N–K3 | | PxN | KxN | R–KN1 | R–Q1 | N–N3 | NxN | QxQ† |
| 13 | P–B4 | | P–KN4 | N–N5† | P–KN4 | B–N5! | QR–K1[21] | RxN | NxQ |
| | P–N3 | | Q–K4 | K–N1[11] | Q–N3 | P–KN3 | ± | B–K2[23] | PxN |
| 14 | P–B5 | | PxP | P–KN4! | NxB | BxN | | = | R–B4 |
| | PxP | | KR–N1 | Q–N3 | PxN | QxB | | | B–Q3 |
| 15 | QxBP | | B–R6! | RxB[12] | B–N5! | N–B3[19] | | | B–K3 |
| | Q–Q2[3] | | P–Q6! | PxP | RxP | ± | | | P–B5[26] |
| 16 | ∓ | | P–QB3 | Q–B3 | Q–B3![14] | | | | = |
| | | | P–Q7[9] | K–N2 | ± | | | | |
| 17 | | | R–K2 | B–B4![13] | | | | | |
| | | | R–Q6[10] | ± | | | | | |
| | | | = | | | | | | |

*Notes to supplementary variations 1–9:*

[1] Also satisfactory is 5 . . . P–Q4 6 B–QN5, N–K5 7 NxP, B–Q2.

[2] Better is 6 B–Q5, N–B4 7 O–O (Janosevic–Gligoric, Yugoslavian Championship 1960).

[3] Black succeeded in bringing his King into safety on the Queenside, maintaining his Pawn (Pachman–Gligoric, Olympiade, Leipzig 1960).

[4] 7 Q–K2 is effectively met by 7 . . . N–QN5!

[5] Black has sufficient compensation for the Pawn. Also good is 10 . . . B–Q2 followed by . . . O–O–O.

[6] After 7 B–QN5, N–K5 8 NxP, Black has the choice between 8 . . . B–Q2 and 8 . . . O–O!

[7] 8 PxP, R–KN1 9 B–N5, B–K2 10 BxB, KxB 11 R–K1†,

B–K3 12 R–K4, P–Q6 13 N–N5, PxP 14 QxP, Q–Q6 15 QxQ, PxQ 16 NxB, PxN 17 N–B3, QR–Q1 18 QR–Q1, RxP 19 R–K3, P–Q7 20 N–K4 and White's ending is superior (analysis in CHESS REVIEW, August, 1957, and July, 1958).

[8] The characteristic position in the Max Lange Attack.

[9] Weaker is 16 . . . B–Q3 17 P–B4, Q–Q4 18 Q–B3, B–K2 19 P–N5 (Marshall–Tarrasch, Hamburg 1910). A good alternative for Black, however, is 16 . . . B–K2 17 Q–B3 (after 17 P–B4, there may follow 17 . . . Q–Q4 18 Q–Q2, R–Q2 and eventually . . . N–Q1–B2), Q–Q4 18 Q–B7, B–R5 19 QR–Q1, N–K4 20 Q–B4, N–N3 21 Q–B7, N–K4 with repetition of moves.

[10] Black has sufficient counterchances, according to Seibold's investigations. Keres gives the following line as offering even chances: 18 NxB (or 18 K–N2, Q–Q4! 19 P–B3, N–K4 20 RxQP, NxNP), QxN 19 RxQP, N–K4 20 RxR, PxR 21 K–N2, Q–Q4† 22 K–N3. Marshall–Leonhardt continued: 18 Q–KB1, B–N3 19 R–Q1, N–Q1 20 P–N5, N–B2 with equality.

[11] After 13 . . . K–N3, White obtains a strong attack with Maroczy's suggestion: 14 PxP, BxP 15 RxB†, B–B3 16 P–KN4, Q–Q4 17 N–R3!

[12] On 15 PxP, Black proceeds successfully with 15 . . . B–Q4.

[13] The text move was suggested by Estrin and confronts Black with difficult problems. In previous analysis, Tartakover had considered only 17 P–KR4, P–KR3! Or 17 N–K4, B–K2 or 17 . . . N–K4.

[14] This strong move is also the answer to 15 . . . P–KR3. Black has no longer a satisfactory defense. See Game 4.

[15] 7 P–B3!, P–Q4 8 B–QN5, PxP 9 P–KR3, PxP 10 BxP, N–R3 11 Q–B2 (analysis in CHESS REVIEW, August, 1957).

[16] Or 7 . . . O–O 8 P–KR3, N–R3 9 BxN, PxB 10 P–B3, P–Q4 (not 10 . . . PxP because of 11 NxP and if then 11 . . . P–Q3 12 N–K4) 11 B–N3!, PxP 12 NxP, P–Q5 13 N–Q5, B–K2 14 B–B2, threatening 15 Q–Q3 (analysis by Euwe).

[17] After 9 . . . N–K2 White proceeds 10 BxB, QxB 11 Q–K2!

[18] 11 . . . PxP 12 NxP is promising for White.

[19] See Game 5. In the column 8 . . . PxP is Steinitz's suggestion. After 9 R–K1†, K–B1 10 P–KR3, N–B3 11 QN–Q2, B–B4 12 N–N3, Q–N3, White can claim no advantage.

[20] Or 8 P–KR3, NxN 9 QxN, B–K3 10 BxB, PxB 11 P–K5, N–Q2! 12 PxP, PxP, and White has only a slight edge (Tarrasch–Taubenhaus, Ostende 1905).

[21] See Game 6.

[22] 10 . . . P–KR3 is followed by 11 B–B6!, Q–R4 12 NxP, PxB 13 NxP†, K–K2 14 P–QN4! and wins. Or 11 . . . Q–Q4 12 P–B3!, P–Q6 13 N–Q4.

[23] White has an infinitesimal lead, which will soon disappear.

[24] Keres recommends 9 NxN, B–K2 10 B–N5, B–K3 11 BxB, KxB 12 N/4–N5, Q–Q4 13 Q–Q2. See CHESS REVIEW, October, 1958, for the complications resulting from 9 B–N5!, P–B3 10 RxN†!, K–B2 11 Q–Q3!!

[25] Interesting is 11 B–R6?, PxR 12 BxP, NxN 13 Q–R5†, K–Q2 14 R–Q1, B–B3 15 Q–Q5†, K–K1 16 Q–R5† with perpetual check (analysis by Dr. Hartlaub).

[26] Ragosin–Botvinnik, Leningrad 1930.

*Two Knights' Defense Game 4*

*WHITE: Tchigorin* *BLACK: Teichmann*

*London 1899*

| | WHITE | BLACK | | WHITE | BLACK | | WHITE | BLACK |
|---|---|---|---|---|---|---|---|---|
| 1 | P–K4 | P–K4 | 11 | N/3–K4 | B–N3 | 21 | B–B6 | R/2–N1 |
| 2 | N–KB3 | N–QB3 | 12 | PxP | R–KN1 | 22 | Q–B5† | K–Q4 |
| 3 | B–B4 | N–B3 | 13 | P–KN4 | Q–N3 | 23 | P–N3 | RxP† |
| 4 | P–Q4 | PxP | 14 | NxB | PxN | 24 | QxR | R–KN1 |
| 5 | O–O | B–B4 | 15 | B–N5 | RxP | 25 | PxP† | KxP |
| 6 | P–K5 | P–Q4 | 16 | Q–B3 | P–K4 | 26 | B–N5 | PxB |
| 7 | PxN | PxB | 17 | N–B6† | K–B2 | 27 | Q–N3 | N–R4 |
| 8 | R–K1† | B–K3 | 18 | P–KR4 | P–KR3 | 28 | QxKP | Resigns |
| 9 | N–N5 | Q–Q4 | 19 | N–K4† | K–K3 | | | |
| 10 | N–QB3 | Q–B4 | 20 | P–R5 | Q–B2 | | | |

*Two Knights' Defense Game 5*

*WHITE: Rossolimo* *BLACK: O'Kelly*

*Trentschin, Teplitz 1949*

| | WHITE | BLACK | | WHITE | BLACK | | WHITE | BLACK |
|---|---|---|---|---|---|---|---|---|
| 1 | P–K4 | P–K4 | 18 | N–B5 | Q–N3 | 35 | N–Q2 | NxN |
| 2 | N–KB3 | N–QB3 | 19 | Q–Q2 | K–N2 | 36 | KxN | K–K4 |
| 3 | B–B4 | N–B3 | 20 | R–K3 | R–QN1 | 37 | K–B3 | B–B8 |
| 4 | P–Q4 | PxP | 21 | R–N3 | Q–B3 | 38 | P–N3 | K–Q4 |
| 5 | O–O | B–B4 | 22 | NxP | Q–R3 | 39 | P–R4 | P–R4 |
| 6 | P–K5 | N–KN5 | 23 | Q–R5 | QxQ | 40 | N–B3! | B–K7 |
| 7 | B–B4 | P–Q3 | 24 | NxQ | B–K3 | 41 | N–N5 | P–B3 |
| 8 | PxP | BxP | 25 | RxR | RxR | 42 | N–R3 | K–K5 |
| 9 | R–K1† | K–B1 | 26 | P–QN3 | R–N4 | 43 | N–B4 | B–N5 |
| 10 | BxB† | QxB | 27 | N–B6 | P–QR4 | 44 | P–N5 | K–B6 |
| 11 | P–B3 | B–B4 | 28 | R–B5 | RxR | 45 | P–N6 | PxP |
| 12 | PxP | R–Q1 | 29 | PxR | P–R5 | 46 | PxP | B–B1 |
| 13 | B–N5 | P–KN3 | 30 | N/6–Q4 | PxP | 47 | NxNP | KxP |
| 14 | BxN | QxB | 31 | PxP | B–Q4 | 48 | P–N4! | PxP |
| 15 | N–B3 | N–B3 | 32 | K–B1 | N–K5 | 49 | P–R5 | Resigns |
| 16 | R–B1 | Q–N3? | 33 | P–QN4 | B–B5† | | | |
| 17 | N–R4 | Q–Q3 | 34 | K–K1 | K–B3 | | | |

*Two Knights' Defense Game 6*

*WHITE: Euwe* *BLACK: Gens*

*Scheveningen 1925*

| | WHITE | BLACK | | WHITE | BLACK |
|---|---|---|---|---|---|
| 1 | P–K4 | P–K4 | 6 | NxP | B–Q2 |
| 2 | N–KB3 | N–QB3 | 7 | N–QB3 | B–K2 |
| 3 | B–B4 | N–B3 | 8 | P–QN3 | O–O |
| 4 | P–Q4 | PxP | 9 | B–N2 | R–K1 |
| 5 | O–O | P–Q3 | 10 | Q–Q2 | N–K4 |

| | WHITE | BLACK | | WHITE | BLACK |
|---|---|---|---|---|---|
| 11 | B–K2 | P–B3 | 25 | N–Q4 | QR–Q1 |
| 12 | P–B4 | N–N3 | 26 | B–K4 | Q–R2 |
| 13 | QR–K1 | B–KB1 | 27 | Q–N2 | N–K4 |
| 14 | B–Q3 | Q–N3 | 28 | N–B3 | B–Q3 |
| 15 | N–R4 | Q–B2 | 29 | BxN | PxB |
| 16 | N–KB3 | B–K2 | 30 | N–N5 | P–B4 |
| 17 | P–B4 | P–N4 | 31 | B–Q5† | K–N2 |
| 18 | PxP | PxP | 32 | N–B7 | Q–N1 |
| 19 | N–B3 | P–QR3 | 33 | Q–KB2 | P–KR3 |
| 20 | K–R1 | Q–N2 | 34 | Q–R4 | R–R1 |
| 21 | P–K5 | PxP | 35 | NxKP | BxN |
| 22 | PxP | P–N5 | 36 | Q–K7† | K–N3 |
| 23 | PxN | PxN | 37 | B–B7† | K–R2 |
| 24 | BxBP | PxP | 38 | RxB | Resigns |

---

## part 2—N-N5 VARIATION WITH 6 B-N5

### OBSERVATIONS ON KEY POSITION 2

1 P–K4, P–K4
2 N–KB3, N–QB3
3 B–B4, N–B3
4 N–N5[A], P–Q4[B]
5 PxP, N–QR4[C]
6 B–N5†[D], P–B3[E]
7 PxP, PxP
8 B–K2[F], P–KR3
9 N–KB3, P–K5
10 N–K5

KEY POSITION 2

[A] After 4 N–B3, Black has the choice between 4 . . . B–B4, the Italian Four Knights' Game, and 4 . . . NxP, the Prussian Four Knights' Game.

[B] For 4 . . . B–B4, the Wilkes–Barre Variation, see Sup. Var. 11.

[C] Insufficient is 5 . . . NxP; see Sup. Var. 12. Interesting possibilities are 5 . . . N–Q5, the Fritz Variation, and 5 . . . P–N4, the Ulvestad Variation; see Sup. Var. 13 and 14 respectively.

[D] For 6 P–Q3 (the Morphy Variation) see Part 3.

[E] 6 . . . B–Q2 is unsatisfactory because of 7 Q–K2, B–Q3 8 BxB†, QxB 9 O–O, O–O 10 N–QB3.

[F] For 8 Q–B3 and 8 B–Q3, see Sup. Var. 15 and 16 respectively.

This is the most important position of the Two Knights' Defense with 4 N–N5. As compensation for his Pawn, Black has a lead in development and some superiority in freedom of movement. Consequently, Black has attacking chances which, however, should not be overestimated. White has no weaknesses and is able to return the Pawn with a good game. The latter point has been demonstrated by Fine and other American masters.

Starting from key position 2, Black can develop his game in several ways. Most usual is 10 . . . B–Q3, when 11 P–KB4 serves better than 11 P–Q4. Well worth consideration, however, are 10 . . . Q–B2 (Tenner) and 10 . . . B–QB4 (Steiner) tending to make castling more difficult for White after P–KB4. The old continuation of Steinitz, 10 . . . Q–Q5, is still considered to be insufficient, although interesting attempts at its rehabilitation have been made by Geller.

IDEA VARIATIONS 4–7:

(4) 10 . . . B–Q3 11 P–KB4, Q–B2 12 P–Q4 (for 12 O–O! see Idea Var. 5) O–O 13 O–O (stronger is 13 P–QB4! so as to meet 13 . . . P–B4 with 14 N–R3), P–B4! And Black has an excellent game for the Pawn. See Game 7.

(5) 10 . . . B–Q3 11 P–KB4, Q–B2 (for 11 . . . PxP e.p., see Prac. Var. 6) 12 O–O! O–O (or 12 . . . BxN 13 PxB, QxP 14 P–Q4, Q–K2 15 P–QN3! with an edge for White [Seidman–Finkelstein, New York 1945]) 13 N–QB3!, BxN 14 PxB, QxP 15 P–Q4, PxP e.p. 16 QxP with a positional advantage for White. Fine–Reshevsky, USA Championship 1940, continued 16 . . . N–N5 17 R–B4! Q–B4† 18 Q–Q4!

(6) 10 . . . Q–B2 11 N–N4? (for 11 P–KB4, B–QB4!, see Prac. Var. 8; the continuation 11 P–Q4, PxP e.p. 12 NxP, B–Q3 transposes into Prac. Var. 7), BxN 12 BxB, B–B4 13 B–K2 (13 O–O, P–KR4 14 B–K2, N–N5 15 P–KN3, NxBP 16 RxN, P–R5! offers Black an irresistible attack), R–Q1! with a favorable game for Black. See Game 8.

(7) 10 . . . B–QB4 11 P–QB3, Q–B2 12 P–KB4 (for 12 P–Q4, see Prac. Var. 9), N–N2 13 P–Q4, PxP e.p. 14 QxP, O–O 15 N–Q2, N–Q3 16 B–B3, B–B4 17 Q–K2, N–Q4 and Black's attacking chances amply compensate for the Pawn.

*Two Knights' Defense Game 7*

*WHITE: Arnold* — *BLACK: Tchigorin*

*St. Petersburg 1885*

| | WHITE | BLACK | | WHITE | BLACK | | WHITE | BLACK |
|---|---|---|---|---|---|---|---|---|
| 1 | P–K4 | P–K4 | 12 | P–Q4 | O–O | 23 | Q–R4 | B–K7 |
| 2 | N–KB3 | N–QB3 | 13 | O–O | P–B4 | 24 | R–K1 | N–N5 |
| 3 | B–B4 | N–B3 | 14 | P–B3 | R–N1 | 25 | P–R3 | Q–B7 |
| 4 | N–N5 | P–Q4 | 15 | N–R3 | PxP! | 26 | B–Q2 | B–B4 |
| 5 | PxP | N–QR4 | 16 | N–N5 | RxN! | 27 | BxP† | RxB |
| 6 | B–N5† | P–B3 | 17 | BxN | Q–N3 | 28 | Q–K8† | K–R2 |
| 7 | PxP | PxP | 18 | P–QR4 | P–Q6† | 29 | QxR | QxP†! |
| 8 | B–K2 | P–KR3 | 19 | K–R1 | P–R3 | 30 | KxQ | B–B6† |
| 9 | N–KB3 | P–K5 | 20 | N–B4 | NxN | 31 | K–B1 | N–R7 mate |
| 10 | N–K5 | Q–B2 | 21 | BxN | B–KN5 | | | |
| 11 | P–KB4 | B–Q3 | 22 | P–R5 | Q–R2 | | | |

*Two Knights' Defense Game 8*

*WHITE: Ciocaltea* *BLACK: Neshmetdinov*

*Bucharest 1954*

| | WHITE | BLACK | | WHITE | BLACK |
|---|---|---|---|---|---|
| 1 | P–K4 | P–K4 | 15 | O–O | P–KR4! |
| 2 | N–KB3 | N–QB3 | 16 | P–Q4 | PxP e.p. |
| 3 | B–B4 | N–B3 | 17 | BxP | N–N5 |
| 4 | N–N5 | P–Q4 | 18 | Q–K2† | K–B1 |
| 5 | PxP | N–QR4 | 19 | P–KN3 | Q–Q2 |
| 6 | B–N5† | P–B3 | 20 | B–K4 | P–R5! |
| 7 | PxP | PxP | 21 | B–B4 | NxRP! |
| 8 | B–K2 | P–KR3 | 22 | R–K1 | N–N5 |
| 9 | N–KB3 | P–K5 | 23 | B–B3 | NxP |
| 10 | N–K5 | Q–B2 | 24 | B–K3 | PxP |
| 11 | N–N4 | BxN | 25 | BxB† | NxB |
| 12 | BxB | B–B4 | 26 | BxP | N–R6† |
| 13 | B–K2 | R–Q1 | 27 | K–B1 | Q–B4† |
| 14 | P–QB3 | N–N2 | | Resigns | |

PRACTICAL VARIATIONS 6–10:

1 P–K4, P–K4 2 N–KB3, N–QB3 3 B–B4, N–B3 4 N–N5, P–Q4 5 PxP, N–QR4 6 B–N5†, P–B3 7 PxP, PxP 8 B–K2, P–KR3 9 N–KB3, P–K5 10 N–K5

| | *6* | *7* | *8* | *9* | *10* |
|---|---|---|---|---|---|
| *10* | – – | – – | – – | – – | – – |
| | B–Q3 | – – | Q–B2 | B–QB4 | Q–Q5 |
| *11* | P–KB4 | P–Q4 | P–KB4 | P–QB3[9] | P–KB4 |
| | PxP e.p. | PxP e.p. | B–QB4[6] | Q–B2 | B–QB4 |
| *12* | NxP | NxP | P–B3[7] | P–Q4[10] | R–B1 |
| | Q–B2 | Q–B2 | N–N2 | PxP e.p. | Q–Q1 |
| *13* | O–O | P–KR3[3] | P–QN4 | NxP | P–B3[12] |
| | O–O[1] | O–O | B–Q3 | B–Q3 | N–Q4 |
| *14* | P–Q4 | O–O | P–Q4 | P–QN4 | Q–R4 |
| | P–B4 | R–QN1[4] | PxP e.p. | N–N2 | O–O |
| *15* | N–B3 | N–B3 | QxP | P–KR3 | P–QN4 |
| | P–QR3 | P–B4[5] | O–O | O–O | Q–R5† |
| *16* | K–R1 | ∓ | O–O | O–O | K–Q1![13] |
| | B–N2[2] | | P–QR4[8] | B–K3[11] | ∓ |
| | = | | = | = | |

*Notes to practical variations 6–10:*

[1] An interesting but dubious bid for attack is 13 . . . N–N5 14 P–KR3, B–R7† 15 K–R1, P–R4 16 P–Q4, B–N6 17 B–Q3, B–K3 18 Q–K2, O–O–O 19 P–N4, N–N2, and now not 20 B–K3?, QR–K1! (Leonhardt–Von Holzhausen) but 20 P–B4!

[2] Black has sufficient compensation for the Pawn (Spasski–Geller, Goteborg 1955).

[3] Other continuations are inferior: 13 N–Q2, O–O 14 P–QN4, N–Q4 15 B–N2, NxP 16 NxN, BxN 17 O–O, R–Q1 18 B–Q3, Q–B5 (Spielmann–Cohn, Stockholm 1909). Or 13 N–R3 B–R3 14 P–KN3, O–O 15 O–O, QR–Q1 (Spielmann–Eliskases, 7th Match Game 1936).

[4] The text is more accurate than 14 . . . P–B4 15 P–QB4!, NxP 16 N–B3, B–R3 17 Q–R4, N–QR4 18 B–K3 with an edge for White (Ragosin–Gligoric, Moscow 1947).

[5] White might have done better with 15 P–QN3 or 15 N–Q2 than with the text move.

[6] Tenner's continuation. 11 . . . PxP e.p. leads to Prac. Var. 6.

[7] Pinkus recommends 12 P–Q4, PxP e.p. 13 PxP!, O–O 14 B–Q2, N–N2 15 Q–R4, followed by N–B3 and O–O–O.

[8] 17 B–B3, BxN 18 PxB, QxP 19 BxBP, PxP 20 Q–N5, QxQ 21 BxQ, N–B4 with even chances (Mednis–Spasski, Brussels 1955).

[9] Inferior is 11 O–O? because of 11 . . . Q–Q3 12 N–N4, BxN 13 BxB, P–R4 14 B–K2, N–N5! Compare with Idea Var. 6.

[10] 12 P–KB4 leads, after 12 . . . N–N2, to Prac. Var. 8.

[11] Black has sufficient compensation for the Pawn (Weisz–Redisch, Correspondence Game 1956).

[12] Or 13 P–Q4, B–N3! 14 B–K3, N–Q4 15 B–N1, O–O 16 P–B4, N–N5 17 Q–Q2, N–Q6†! 18 BxN, PxB 19 QxP, R–K1 with good attacking chances for Black (Ragosin–Geller, USSR Championship 1949).

[13] Bad for White is 16 P–N3?, QxRP 17 PxB, QxP† 18 K–Q1, R–Q1! with numerous threats. After the text move, however, Black's attack comes to a standstill: 16 . . . R–Q1 17 K–B2, B–B4 18 PxB.

---

## part 3—MORPHY VARIATION

1 P–K4, P–K4
2 N–KB3, N–QB3
3 B–B4, N–B3
4 N–N5, P–Q4
5 PxP, N–QR4
6 P–Q3, P–KR3
7 N–KB3, P–K5
8 Q–K2[A], NxB
9 PxN, B–QB4[B]

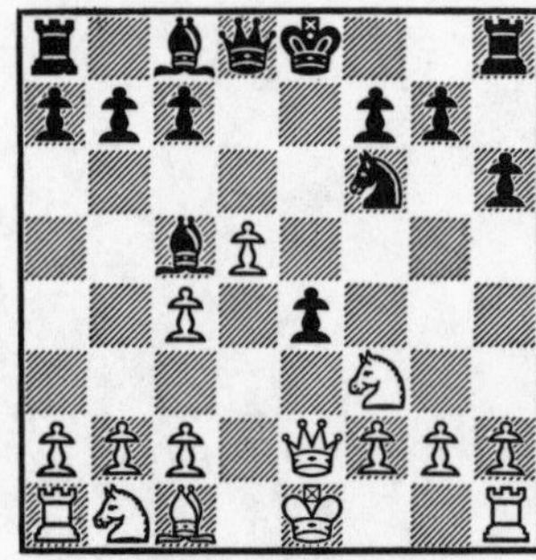

KEY POSITION 3

### OBSERVATIONS ON KEY POSITION 3

[A] Bronstein, in his game with Rojahn at the Moscow Olympics 1956, essayed 8 PxP?! NxB 9 Q–Q4, N–N3 10 P–B4, P–B4? 11 Q–Q3, B–N5 12 QN–Q2, obtaining full compensation for the piece. See Game 9. In this line, however, after 10 . . . B–N5† 11 QN–Q2, O–O 12 O–O, R–K1 13 P–QR3, B–B1, White's compensation is insufficient.

[B] Inferior is 9 . . . B–K2 (Maroczy) because of 10 N–Q4, P–B3 11 N–QB3, O–O 12 O–O, PxP 13 PxP, B–KN5 14 Q–N5!, when, according to Keres, Black's compensation for the Pawn is problematic.

Black's last move has the essential effect of denying to White's Knight the square Q4. White consequently faces considerable difficulty in his development. It is particularly difficult for him to bring his King into safety Black always obtains good chances for attack that compensate for the Pawn.

An important trump in Black's hand is the break-up of the enemy's center by . . . P–QB3 or . . . P–QN4. The opening of lines naturally favors the attacker.

*Two Knights' Defense Game 9*
*WHITE: Bronstein* *BLACK: Rojahn*
*Moscow 1956*

| WHITE | BLACK | WHITE | BLACK | WHITE | BLACK |
|---|---|---|---|---|---|
| 1 P–K4 | P–K4 | 14 N–K5 | B–R4 | 27 Q–N3 | P–B3 |
| 2 N–KB3 | N–QB3 | 15 P–QN3 | N/B–Q2 | 28 P–K6 | N–K4 |
| 3 B–B4 | N–B3 | 16 B–N2 | NxN | 29 P–KR4 | K–R1 |
| 4 N–N5 | P–Q4 | 17 BxN | N–Q2 | 30 P–N5 | QR–B1 |
| 5 PxP | N–QR4 | 18 B–B3 | B–B3 | 31 K–R1 | Q–Q1 |
| 6 P–Q3 | P–KR3 | 19 QR–K1 | BxB | 32 P–N6 | BxP |
| 7 N–KB3 | P–K5 | 20 QxB | Q–B3? | 33 PxB | P–N4 |
| 8 PxP | NxB | 21 P–K5 | Q–B4 | 34 P–Q6 | Q–N3 |
| 9 Q–Q4 | N–N3 | 22 P–B4 | B–N3 | 35 P–Q7 | NxP |
| 10 P–B4 | P–B4? | 23 N–K4 | QR–N1 | 36 PxN | QR–Q1 |
| 11 Q–Q3 | B–N5 | 24 Q–B3 | B–R2 | 37 NxP | Q–B3† |
| 12 QN–Q2 | B–K2 | 25 P–KN4 | Q–N3 | 38 Q–N2 | QxQ† |
| 13 O–O | O–O | 26 P–B5 | Q–N3 | 39 KxQ | Resigns |

IDEA VARIATIONS 8 AND 9:

(8) 10 O–O, O–O 11 KN–Q2, B–KN5 12 Q–K1, Q–Q2! 13 N–N3, B–B6! 14 B–B4, Q–N5 15 B–N3, N–R4! 16 NxB, N–B5 17 NxP, Q–R6!! and mate is inevitable. Or 16 K–R1, BxP† 17 KxB, Q–B6† 18 K–N1, NxB 19 PxN, QxP† 20 K–R1, Q–R6† 21 K–N1, B–Q3 22 P–B4, PxP e.p. with an overwhelming onslaught. Also yielding a winning attack for Black is 16 PxB, PxP 17 K–R1, QR–K1! Black's advanced King Pawn is an outpost that makes White's 10 O–O too dangerous.

(9) 10 KN–Q2, O–O 11 N–N3, B–N5 12 Q–B1, B–N5† (so as to provoke P–QB3 which weakens White's Q3) 13 N–B3 (nevertheless, White is better off if he does play 13 P–B3; see Prac. Var. 11) P–B3 14 P–KR3, B–KR4 15 P–N4, B–N3 16 PxP, PxP 17 B–Q2? (B–K3!), P–K6! 18 PxP, BxN 19 PxB, BxP 20 N–Q4, N–K5 and

Black won quickly (Luckis–Keres, Buenos Aires 1939). 11 P–KR3? with the idea of preventing 11 . . . B–KN5 is effectively countered by 11 . . . P–K6 12 PxP, BxKP.

PRACTICAL VARIATIONS 11–13:

1 P–K4, P–K4 2 N–KB3, N–QB3 3 B–B4, N–B3 4 N–N5, P–Q4 5 PxP, N–QR4 6 P–Q3, P–KR3 7 N–KB3, P–K5 8 Q–K2, NxB 9 PxN, B–QB4

| | *11* | *12* | *13* |
|---|---|---|---|
| *10* | KN–Q2 | P–KR3 | P–B3 |
| | O–O | O–O | P–QN4! |
| *11* | N–N3 | N–R2 | P–QN4 |
| | B–N5 | P–K6[5] | B–K2 |
| *12* | Q–B1 | BxP | KN–Q2 |
| | B–N5† | BxB | B–N5 |
| *13* | P–B3 | PxB | P–B3 |
| | B–K2 | N–K5 | PxP/6 |
| *14* | P–KR3 | N–B1[6] | PxBP |
| | B–R4 | Q–R5† | B–R4 |
| *15* | B–K3 | P–N3 | PxP |
| | N–Q2! | Q–B3 | O–O |
| *16* | P–KN4 | P–B3 | O–O |
| | B–N3 | B–B4 | R–K1 |
| *17* | N/1–Q2 | Q–B3 | Q–B4 |
| | N–K4 | N–N4 | B–Q3[8] |
| *18* | O–O–O | Q–B4[7] | ∓ |
| | P–N4![1] | ∓ | |
| *19* | PxP | | |
| | N–Q6† | | |
| *20* | K–N1 | | |
| | QxP[2] | | |
| *21* | K–R1[3] | | |
| | QxP[4] | | |
| | ∓ | | |

*Notes to practical variations 11–13:*

[1] This old continuation is stronger than 18 . . . N–Q6† 19 K–N1, B–N4 20 N–Q4, Q–B3 21 P–KR4! (Boguljubow–Eliskases, 10th Match Game 1939).

[2] According to Keres, 20 . . . P–R3! in order to open more lines against White's King is even stronger.

[3] Eliskases gives 21 P–QB4 as a better defense. However, according to Keres, Black still maintains a strong attack with 21 . . . Q–K3 22 N–Q4, Q–K4 followed by an eventual . . . P–QR3.

[4] Black has fine attacking chances. See Game 10.

[5] Inferior is 11 . . . R–K1 12 B–K3, BxB 13 PxB, Q–Q3

14 N–QB3, P–R3 15 O–O–O (Korchnoi–Geller, Moscow 1952). Meriting consideration, however, is 11 . . . P–QN4 (Grob–Euwe, Zurich 1934).

[6] Steinitz recommended 14 O–O, N–N6 15 Q–B3, NxR 16 NxN, a sacrifice of the exchange which offers about even chances.

[7] Black should now have played 18 . . . NxP, since 19 QxBP fails against 19 . . . B–Q6! (Korchnoi–Sliwa, Bucharest 1954).

[8] Black has a winning attack. See Game 11.

### *Two Knights' Defense Game 10*

*WHITE: Salwe* — *BLACK: Marshall*

*Vienna 1908*

| | WHITE | BLACK | | WHITE | BLACK |
|---|---|---|---|---|---|
| 1 | P–K4 | P–K4 | 20 | K–N1 | QxP |
| 2 | N–KB3 | N–QB3 | 21 | K–R1 | QxP |
| 3 | B–B4 | N–B3 | 22 | P–KB4 | P–QR4 |
| 4 | N–N5 | P–Q4 | 23 | R–QN1 | P–KB4 |
| 5 | PxP | N–QR4 | 24 | N–Q4 | Q–R5 |
| 6 | P–Q3 | P–KR3 | 25 | P–N3 | Q–Q2 |
| 7 | N–KB3 | P–K5 | 26 | PxP | BxP |
| 8 | Q–K2 | NxB | 27 | Q–N2 | P–B4 |
| 9 | PxN | B–QB4 | 28 | NxB | QxN |
| 10 | KN–Q2 | O–O | 29 | QxP | B–B3! |
| 11 | N–N3 | B–KN5 | 30 | Q–B4† | K–R1 |
| 12 | Q–B1 | B–N5† | 31 | N–K4 | QR–K1 |
| 13 | P–B3 | B–K2 | 32 | NxB | RxN |
| 14 | P–KR3 | B–R4 | 33 | B–B1 | R/3–K3 |
| 15 | P–N4 | B–N3 | 34 | B–R3 | R–K7 |
| 16 | B–K3 | N–Q2 | 35 | KR–Q1 | N–K8 |
| 17 | N/1–Q2 | N–K4 | 36 | BxP | N–B7† |
| 18 | O–O–O | P–N4 | 37 | K–N2 | N–N5† |
| 19 | PxP | N–Q6† | | Resigns | |

### *Two Knights' Defense Game 11*

*WHITE: Grob* — *BLACK: Keres*

*Dresden 1936*

| | WHITE | BLACK | | WHITE | BLACK | | WHITE | BLACK |
|---|---|---|---|---|---|---|---|---|
| 1 | P–K4 | P–K4 | 11 | P–QN4 | B–K2 | 21 | R–B1 | RxR† |
| 2 | N–KB3 | N–QB3 | 12 | KN–Q2 | B–N5 | 22 | KxR | QxP† |
| 3 | B–B4 | N–B3 | 13 | P–B3 | KPxP | 23 | K–B2 | NxN† |
| 4 | N–N5 | P–Q4 | 14 | NPxP | B–R4 | 24 | QxN | R–K1 |
| 5 | PxP | N–QR4 | 15 | PxP | O–O | 25 | N–R3 | Q–Q2 |
| 6 | P–Q3 | P–KR3 | 16 | O–O | R–K1 | 26 | Q–R4 | Q–B4 |
| 7 | N–KB3 | P–K5 | 17 | Q–B4 | B–Q3 | 27 | P–KB4 | R–K7† |
| 8 | Q–K2 | NxB | 18 | Q–R4 | R–K7 | 28 | K–N1 | Q–K5 |
| 9 | PxN | B–QB4 | 19 | R–B2 | Q–K1 | | Resigns | |
| 10 | P–QB3 | P–QN4 | 20 | N–K4 | R–K8† | | | |

## SUPPLEMENTARY VARIATIONS 10–16:

### 1 P–K4, P–K4 2 N–KB3, N–QB3 3 B–B4, N–B3

| | *10* | *11* | *12* | *13* | *14* | *15* | *16* |
|---|---|---|---|---|---|---|---|
| *4* | N–B3 | N–N5 | – – | – – | – – | – – | – – |
| | NxP! | B–B4[4] | P–Q4 | – – | – – | – – | – – |
| *5* | NxN[1] | NxBP[5] | PxP | – – | – – | – – | – – |
| | P–Q4 | BxP† | NxP | N–Q5 | P–N4 | N–QR4 | – – |
| *6* | B–Q3 | KxB[6] | P–Q4! | P–QB3[10] | B–B1![15] | B–N5† | – – |
| | PxN | NxP† | B–N5†[8] | P–N4 | NxP[16] | P–B3 | – – |
| *7* | BxP | K–N1 | P–B3 | B–B1[11] | BxP | PxP | – – |
| | B–Q3 | Q–R5 | B–K2 | NxP | B–N2 | PxP | – – |
| *8* | P–Q4 | P–KN3 | NxBP! | N–K4[12] | P–Q4 | Q–B3 | B–Q3 |
| | PxP | NxNP | KxN | Q–R5[13] | PxP[17] | R–QN1![19] | N–Q4 |
| *9* | BxN†[2] | PxN | Q–B3† | N–N3 | O–O! | B–Q3[20] | N–K4 |
| | PxB | QxP† | K–K3 | B–KN5 | B–K2 | P–KR3 | P–KB4 |
| *10* | QxP | K–B1 | Q–K4![9] | P–B3 | N–KB3 | N–K4 | N–N3 |
| | O–O | R–B1 | ± | N–B4 | O–O | N–Q4 | N–B5 |
| *11* | O–O | Q–R5 | | BxP† | BxN | N–N3 | B–B1 |
| | P–QB4 | P–Q3 | | K–Q1 | BxB | P–N3 | B–B4 |
| *12* | Q–B3 | N–B3 | | O–O | NxP | O–O | P–QB3 |
| | B–N2 | B–N5 | | B–B4† | B–N2 | B–KN2[21] | B–N3 |
| *13* | P–QN3 | Q–R2 | | P–Q4 | P–QB3[18] | ∓ | P–Q4 |
| | Q–Q2 | Q–B6† | | PxP | ± | | N–N3 |
| *14* | B–N2 | K–N1 | | N–K4![14] | | | B–Q3 |
| | P–KB3[3] | N–Q5[7] | | ± | | | O–O[22] |
| | = | = | | | | | ∓ |

*Notes to supplementary variations 10–16:*

[1] 5 BxP†, KxB 6 NxN, P–Q4! is weak for White. The old-fashioned Pawn sacrifice 5 O–O is insufficient: 5 . . . NxN 6 QPxN, P–B3 7 N–R4, P–KN3 8 P–B4, P–B4 9 N–B3, B–B4† 10 K–R1, P–K5 11 N–N5, Q–K2 12 P–QN4, B–N3 13 P–QR4, P–QR4 (Ursell–Pachman, Southsea 1949).

[2] 9 NxP is inferior because of 9 . . . O–O 10 NxN, Q–R5! If 10 B–K3, Q–R5! (Tarrasch–Lasker, 1906).

[3] Tartakover–Bogoljubow, Pistyan 1922. Black has an easy game. His Bishops amply compensate for the weakness of his Pawn formation.

[4] Known as the Wilkes-Barre Variation.

[5] 5 BxP†, K–K2 6 B–N3 (for 6 P–Q4 see Game 12; according to Neustadt, 6 B–Q5! is stronger), R–B1 7 O–O, P–KR3 8 N–KB3, P–Q3 9 P–KR3, Q–K1! gives Black good attacking chances for the Pawn. Or 5 P–Q4, P–Q4! 6 BxP, NxB 7 PxB, N–B3! 8 QxQ†, NxQ, and White's extra Pawn is of little significance because of the Bishops of opposite colors. In the above line an interesting try for Black is 6 . . . NxQP 7 NxBP, Q–K2 8 NxR, B–N5 with attacking chances.

[6] K–B1 may be White's best move to refute Black's counter: 6 . . . Q–K2 7 NxR, P–Q4 8 PxP, N–Q5 9 P–KR3!, N–K5 10 N–B3, N–N6† 11 KxB, Q–R5 12 K–N1, NxR 13 Q–B1!

[7] 15 B–Q5, N–K7† 16 QxN, Q–N6† 17 Q–N2, Q–K8† 18 Q–B1, Q–N6† with perpetual check (Foltys–Rossolimo, Amsterdam 1950). Or 15 Q–B2, P–QN4 16 B–Q5, N–K7† 17 K–B1, N–N6† 18 K–K1, QxQ† 19 KxQ, NxR† 20 BxN, RxN† 21 K–N3, O–O–O 22 KxB, QR–B1 (analysis by Keres). White, hampered by his lack of development, cannot profit from his material advantage.

[8] Nor are other possibilities satisfactory for Black:

1) 6 . . . PxP 7 O–O!, B–K2 (7 . . . B–K3 8 R–K1, Q–Q2 9 NxBP!) 8 NxBP, KxN 9 Q–R5†, P–N3 10 BxN†, K–K1 11 Q–B3.
2) 6 . . . B–K2 7 NxBP, KxN 8 Q–B3†, K–K3 9 N–B3, N–N5 10 Q–K4, P–B3 11 P–QR3.

[9] White has an irresistible attack (Barden–Adams, Hastings 1951–52).

[10] Or 6 P–Q6, QxP 7 BxP†, K–K2 8 B–N3, NxB 9 RPxN, P–KR3 10 N–KB3, P–K5 11 N–N1, K–B2, and Black probably has just enough compensation for the Pawn (Bogoljubov–Rubinstein, Stockholm 1919).

[11] PxN, PxB 8 PxP, QxP is good for Black.

[12] 8 PxN, QxN 9 BxP†, K–Q1 10 O–O, B–N2 and Black has sufficient counterchances. 8 NxBP, KxN 9 PxN, PxP 10 BxP (for 10 Q–B3† N–B3!, see Game 13) Q–K2† 11 Q–K2, QxQ† 12 BxQ, N–N5 13 B–B4†, B–K3 14 BxB†, KxB gives Black enough compensation for the Pawn.

[13] Safer is 8 . . . N–K3 9 BxP†, B–Q2 10 Q–R4, when Black gets adequate compensation for the Pawn with either 10 . . . N/4–B5 (Estrin) or 10 . . . B–B4 (Grunfeld).

[14] Not 14 . . . PxB? 15 P–Q6† and Black wins (Rubinov–Steiner, USA Championship 1950). The complications after the text move favor White. If 14 . . . N/Q4–K6, then 15 Q–N3! In the column, 11 Q–K2 also favors White.

[15] 6 BxP, QxP and Black has attacking chances: 7 BxN†, QxB 8 Q–B3, P–K5! 9 Q–QN3, B–QB4 10 QxP†, K–Q1 (Van Scheltinga–Prins, Rotterdam 1946).

[16] 6 . . . N–Q5 is preferable (Sup. Var. 13).

[17] After 8 . . . P–B3, White proceeds simply and effectively with 9 N–KB3, followed by 10 O–O.

[18] Black's compensation for the Pawn is not quite sufficient (Keres).

[19] Sharper than 8 . . . PxB and leading to a speculative exchange sacrifice.

[20] After 9 BxP†, NxB 10 QxN†, N–Q2 Black obtains a tremendous lead in development for his Pawns.

[21] Black has adequate positional compensation for the Pawn: 13 N–B3, O–O 14 B–K2, R–N5 15 NxN, PxN 16 Q–R3, N–B3 17 P–Q3, P–KR4 (Estrin–Ragosin, Moscow 1955).

[22] Castaldi–Keres, 1937.

*Two Knights' Defense Game 12*

*WHITE: Paoli* *BLACK: Rossolimo*

*Trentschin–Teplitz 1949*

| | WHITE | BLACK | | WHITE | BLACK |
|---|---|---|---|---|---|
| 1 | P–K4 | P–K4 | 14 | B–B2 | B–K3 |
| 2 | N–KB3 | N–QB3 | 15 | O–O–O | N–Q2 |
| 3 | B–B4 | N–B3 | 16 | P–KR3 | QR–QN1 |
| 4 | N–N5 | B–B4 | 17 | N–R4 | Q–B2 |
| 5 | BxP† | K–K2 | 18 | N–B5† | BxN |
| 6 | P–Q4 | NxQP | 19 | PxB | QxRP |
| 7 | P–QB3 | N–B3 | 20 | P–QN4? | Q–R6† |
| 8 | B–N3 | R–B1 | 21 | K–N1 | P–QN3! |
| 9 | B–K3 | BxB | 22 | Q–Q3 | N–B4! |
| 10 | PxB | P–Q3 | 23 | Q–Q5 | QxP |
| 11 | N–Q2 | Q–K1 | 24 | PxN/B | PxP† |
| 12 | Q–K2 | Q–N3 | 25 | N–N3 | N–B5! |
| 13 | N/5–B3 | N–QR4 | | Resigns | |

*Two Knights' Defense Game 13*

*WHITE: Semenenko* *BLACK: Deriljev*

*Postal Game 1947*

| | WHITE | BLACK | | WHITE | BLACK |
|---|---|---|---|---|---|
| 1 | P–K4 | P–K4 | 11 | QxR | B–QB4 |
| 2 | N–KB3 | N–QB3 | 12 | BxP | R–K1†! |
| 3 | B–B4 | N–B3 | 13 | K–B1 | B–R3 |
| 4 | N–N5 | P–Q4 | 14 | Q–B6 | Q–K2 |
| 5 | PxP | N–Q5 | 15 | P–KN3 | BxB† |
| 6 | P–QB3 | P–N4 | 16 | QxB | Q–K5 |
| 7 | B–B1 | NxP | 17 | Q–B4† | K–N3 |
| 8 | NxBP | KxN | 18 | K–N1 | Q–B6 |
| 9 | PxN | PxP | 19 | Q–B1 | P–Q6 |
| 10 | Q–B3† | N–B3! | | Resigns | |

# chapter 12—Vienna Game

1 P–K4, P–K4
2 N–QB3

KEY POSITION

## OBSERVATIONS ON KEY POSITION

The Vienna has practically disappeared from modern tournament play. The move 2 N–QB3 has the enterprising purpose of serving as a preparation for P–KB4 in the spirit of the King's Gambit. Black, however, proceeds with 2 . . . N–KB3! 3 P–KB4, P–Q4, in analogy with the Falkbeer Gambit, but without the sacrifice of a Pawn. He easily achieves equality.

White can meet 2 . . . N–KB3 with 3 B–B4, but then Black can play 3 . . . NxP, which leads to equality after 4 NxN, P–Q4. Alternatively, White can play the speculative 4 Q–R5!?, N–Q3 5 B–N3!? giving rise to interesting and risky complications. Instead of 5 B–N3 White may play 5 QxP† with prospects of a tame draw.

## IDEA VARIATIONS 1–4:

(1) 2 . . . N–KB3 3 P–B4, PxP? 4 P–K5, Q–K2 6 Q–K2 with a clear advantage for White. Nor is 3 . . . P–Q3 satisfactory, since it concedes to White a superiority in space. The only good move is 3 . . . P–Q4!

(2) 2 . . . N–KB3 3 P–B4, P–Q4! 4 PxQP. Black can now transpose into variations of the King's Gambit in two ways: (1) 4 . . . P–K5, the Falkbeer, or (2) 4 . . . PxP, the Modern Defense. Besides, he can simply and satisfactorily proceed with 4 . . . NxP 5 NxN, QxN 6 PxP, N–B3 7 N–B3, B–KN5.

(3) 2 . . . N–KB3 3 P–B4, P–Q4 4 PxKP, NxP. Now the best move for White is 5 N–KB3 (Prac. Var. 1), but it leads to no advantage. Consistent would be 5 Q–B3 (Steinitz) so as to dislodge the enemy Knight. But this continuation has been discarded because of the strong reply 5 . . . N–QB3. White cannot then play 6 NxN, because of 6 . . . N–Q5 7 Q–B4, PxN 8 B–B4, B–KB4 9 P–QB3, P–KN4 which wins for Black (Borosch–Lilienthal, Budapest 1933).

(4) 2 . . . N–KB3 3 B–B4, NxP! 4 Q–R5 (4 NxN, P–Q4! or 4 BxP†, KxB 5 NxN, P–Q4! favors Black), N–Q3 5 B–N3!? Black can now play 5 . . . N–B3 (see Prac. Var. 2) which leads to an old sacrifice of the exchange, still considered promising for Black. Or Black can proceed more modestly with 5 . . . B–K2 6 N–B3,

N–B3 7 NxP. Alekhine now gives 7 . . . O–O! as leading to equality: 8 N–Q5, N–Q5 9 O–O, NxB 10 RPxN. Instead, 7 . . . NxN 8 QxN, O–O 9 N–Q5, R–K1 10 O–O offers White good chances.

PRACTICAL VARIATIONS 1–5:
1 P–K4, P–K4 2 N–QB3

| | *1* | *2* | *3* | *4* | *5* |
|---|---|---|---|---|---|
| *2* | — — | — — | — — | — — | — — |
| | N–KB3 | — — | N–QB3 | — — | B–B4 |
| *3* | P–B4 | B–B4 | P–B4 | B–B4 | N–B3 |
| | P–Q4 | NxP | PxP | N–B3 | P–Q3 |
| *4* | PxKP | Q–R5 | N–B3 | P–Q3 | P–Q4 |
| | NxP | N–Q3 | P–KN4[7] | B–N5 | PxP |
| *5* | N–B3[1] | B–N3[4] | P–Q4 | B–KN5[10] | NxP |
| | B–K2 | N–B3 | P–N5[8] | P–KR3 | N–KB3 |
| *6* | P–Q4 | N–N5[5] | B–B4 | BxN | B–N5 |
| | O–O | P–KN3 | PxN | BxN† | P–KR3 |
| *7* | B–Q3 | Q–B3 | QxP[9] | PxB | B–R4 |
| | P–KB4 | P–B4 | ± | QxB | N–B3 |
| *8* | PxP e.p. | Q–Q5 | | N–K2 | NxN |
| | BxP[2] | Q–K2 | | P–Q3 | PxN |
| *9* | O–O | NxP† | | O–O | B–Q3 |
| | N–QB3[3] | K–Q1 | | P–KN4 | Q–K2 |
| *10* | = | NxR | | P–Q4 | O–O[12] |
| | | P–N3[6] | | N–K2[11] | ± |
| | | ∓ | | = | |

*Notes to practical variations 1–5:*

[1] Good for Black is 5 Q–B3, N–QB3! 6 B–N5 (6 NxN is inferior because of 6 . . . N–Q5!; see Idea Var. 3), NxN 7 QPxN, Q–R5† 8 P–N3, Q–K5† 9 QxQ, PxQ 10 BxN†, PxB 11 N–K2, B–K2 12 R–B1, O–O 13 R–B4, P–B3! (Hromadka–Spielmann, Trentschin–Teplitz 1928). Or 5 P–Q3, after which Black obtains a good game: 5 . . . NxN 6 PxN, P–Q5!, but not 5 . . . Q–R5†? 6 P–N3, NxP 7 N–B3, Q–R4 8 NxP!, B–N5 9 B–N2, NxR 10 NxP†, K–Q2 11 NxR, N–B3 with White for choice.

[2] Not 8 . . . NxP? 9 O–O, N–B3 10 B–KN5, B–KN5 11 Q–K1! and White has good prospects for an attack (Euwe–Reti, 1922). The text move is based on 9 NxN? PxN 10 BxP, R–K1.

[3] 10 NxN (10 N–K2, N–N5), PxN 11 BxP, NxP 12 N–N5, B–B4! (Konstantinopolsky–Keres, USSR Championship 1940). See Game 1.

[4] 5 QxKP†, Q–K2 6 QxQ†, BxQ 7 B–N3, N–B4 8 N–B3, P–QB3 9 O–O, P–Q4 leads to an equal game (Saemisch–Rubinstein, Hanover 1926).

[5] The American master, Weaver Adams, suggests 6 P–Q4 which involves the sacrifice of a Pawn or two. Up to date the idea has not been professionally accepted.

[6] Black proceeds with . . . B–QN2 and . . . N–Q5, obtaining fine compensation for the exchange: 11 N–B3, B–QN2 12 P–Q4, NxP 13 B–N5, NxN† 14 QxN, QxB 15 B–Q5, P–K5 or 15 . . . B–QR3 (see Game 3). In the above line if 12 P–Q3 or 12 P–KR4, then 12 . . . P–B5.

[7] 4 . . . N–B3 5 B–B4 transposes into a form of the Bishop's Gambit, favorable for White: 5 . . . B–N5 (5 . . . NxP? 6 Q–K2) 6 N–Q5!, NxP 7 O–O, O–O 8 P–Q4 (Spielmann).

[8] 5 . . . B–N2 6 P–Q5, N–K4 7 P–Q6! favors White. Also good for White is 5 . . . P–Q3 6 P–Q5, N–K4 7 B–N5†.

[9] 7 O–O is answered by 7 . . . P–Q4! 8 KPxP, B–KN5! White's text move transposes favorably into the obsolete Muzio-MacDonnell Gambit.

[10] Or 5 N–K2, P–Q4 6 PxP, NxP 7 BxN, QxB 8 O–O, Q–R4! with even chances (Spielmann–Reti, Dortmund 1928).

[11] Black has a satisfactory game, according to Alekhine. He plays . . . N–N3, preventing P–KB4.

[12] Horowitz–Kupchik, Syracuse 1934.

*Vienna Game 1*

*WHITE: Konstantinopolsky* *BLACK: Keres*

*USSR Championship 1940*

| | WHITE | BLACK | | WHITE | BLACK | | WHITE | BLACK |
|---|---|---|---|---|---|---|---|---|
| 1 | P–K4 | P–K4 | 13 | BxB | NxB | 25 | R–QN3 | B–Q5† |
| 2 | N–QB3 | N–KB3 | 14 | N–K6? | QxQ | 26 | K–N2? | P–QN3 |
| 3 | P–B4 | P–Q4 | 15 | RxQ | KR–K1! | 27 | P–QR3 | B–B4 |
| 4 | PxKP | NxP | 16 | NxBP | QR–Q1 | 28 | B–B1 | RxP† |
| 5 | N–B3 | B–K2 | 17 | B–B4 | R–K7 | 29 | R–N3 | RxR† |
| 6 | P–Q4 | O–O | 18 | RxR† | BxR | 30 | PxR | N–Q5 |
| 7 | B–Q3 | P–KB4 | 19 | R–Q1 | B–B3 | 31 | P–B4 | N–N6 |
| 8 | PxP e.p. | BxP | 20 | R–Q2 | R–K5 | 32 | B–B4 | N–R4 |
| 9 | O–O | N–B3 | 21 | N–Q5 | BxP | 33 | P–QR4 | NxP |
| 10 | NxN | PxN | 22 | R–Q3 | R–R5 | | | and Black won. |
| 11 | BxP | NxP | 23 | P–N4 | N–Q5 | | | |
| 12 | N–N5 | B–B4 | 24 | R–K3 | N–B3 | | | |

*Vienna Game 2*

*WHITE: Koch* *BLACK: Sefc*

*Prague 1958*

| | WHITE | BLACK | | WHITE | BLACK | | WHITE | BLACK |
|---|---|---|---|---|---|---|---|---|
| 1 | P–K4 | P–K4 | 10 | NxR | P–N3 | 19 | R–R4 | B–N2 |
| 2 | B–B4 | N–KB3 | 11 | N–B3 | B–QN2 | 20 | RxRP | BxB |
| 3 | N–QB3 | NxP | 12 | P–Q4 | NxP | 21 | NxP† | K–N1 |
| 4 | Q–R5 | N–Q3 | 13 | B–N5 | NxN† | 22 | R–R4 | BxKNP |
| 5 | B–N3 | N–B3 | 14 | QxN | QxB | 23 | R–N1 | B–QB3 |
| 6 | N–N5 | P–KN3 | 15 | B–Q5 | B–QR3 | 24 | R–QN4 | K–B2 |
| 7 | Q–B3 | P–B4 | 16 | R–Q1 | Q–B5! | 25 | R–QN3 | N–K5 |
| 8 | Q–Q5 | Q–K2 | 17 | QxQ | PxQ | 26 | N–B4 | B–Q4 |
| 9 | NxP† | K–Q1 | 18 | R–Q4 | K–B1 | | Resigns | |

# chapter 13—Unusual King Pawn Games

This section includes a diversity of double King Pawn Openings seldom encountered in serious tournament chess.

PONZIANI'S OPENING (PRAC. VAR. 1 AND 2)

1 P–K4, P–K4 2 N–KB3, N–QB3 3 P–B3

White obviously intends to form a strong center with P–Q4. But, since this advance cannot be made with a tempo, as for example in the Giuoco Piano, Black experiences little difficulty maintaining the balance. He may, in fact, strive for even more by offering a Pawn sacrifice, but this line of play leads only to complications of a rather obscure nature.

PHILIDOR'S DEFENSE (PRAC. VAR. 3 AND 4)

1 P–K4, P–K4 2 N–KB3, P–Q3

This defense is designed to maintain Black's King Pawn on K4. In developing consistently with . . . QN–Q2, . . . P–QB3 and . . . Q–B2, Black achieves a steady though cramped position. The older and incongruous continuation, . . . PxQP, however, concedes White a distinct advantage.

GRECO COUNTER GAMBIT (PRAC. VAR. 5)

1 P–K4, P–K4 2 N–KB3, P–KB4

Black's early attempt to seize the initiative is reckless, but not easily refutable. With best play, though, White can stem Black's intentions on the one hand, and obtain a clear positional edge on the other.

QUEEN PAWN COUNTER GAMBIT (PRAC. VAR. 6)

1 P–K4, P–K4 2 N–KB3, P–Q4

This gambit is similar in design to the Greco, but far less dangerous.

DAMIANO'S DEFENSE (PRAC. VAR. 7)

1 P–K4, P–K4 2 N–KB3, P–KB3

This naive defense is a mere compendium curiosity, not having been employed in tournament chess for many decades. Black's unnatural way of protecting his King Pawn fails not only against the tactical 3 NxP, but also against the positional 3 B–B4.

PRACTICAL VARIATIONS 1–7:

1 P–K4, P–K4 2 N–KB3

| | *1* | *2* | *3* | *4* | *5* | *6* | *7* |
|---|---|---|---|---|---|---|---|
| 2 | — — | | — — | — — | — — | — — | — — |
| | N–QB3 | — — | P–Q3 | — — | P–KB4 | P–Q4 | P–KB3 |
| 3 | P–B3[1] | — — | P–Q4 | — — | NxP[22] | PxP[28] | NxP[31] |
| | P–Q4[2] | N–B3[7] | N–KB3 | N–Q2[14] | Q–B3 | P–K5 | Q–K2[32] |
| 4 | Q–R4![3] | P–Q4 | PxP[10] | B–QB4![15] | P–Q4 | Q–K2 | KN–B3 |
| | P–B3[4] | NxKP[8] | NxP | P–QB3[16] | P–Q3[23] | N–KB3[29] | QxP† |
| 5 | B–N5 | P–Q5 | QN–Q2![11] | O–O[17] | N–B4 | N–B3 | B–K2 |
| | KN–K2 | N–N1 | NxN | B–K2 | PxP | B–K2 | N–B3 |
| 6 | PxP | B–Q3 | BxN | N–B3[18] | N–B3 | NxP | O–O[33] |
| | QxP | N–B4 | P–Q4[12] | KN–B3 | Q–N3[24] | NxP | ± |
| 7 | P–Q4 | NxP | B–Q3 | P–QR4[19] | N–K3[25] | N–B3 | |
| | B–Q2 | NxB† | B–K2 | O–O[20] | N–KB3 | N–N3 | |
| 8 | O–O | NxN | O–O | Q–K2 | KN–Q5 | P–Q3[30] | |
| | PxP[5] | P–Q3 | O–O[13] | P–KR3 | NxN | ± | |
| 9 | PxP | O–O | ± | B–N3 | NxN | | |
| | N–K4 | B–K2 | | Q–B2 | Q–B2 | | |
| 10 | BxB† | Q–B3 | | P–KR3[21] | B–QB4 | | |
| | QxB[6] | O–O[9] | | ± | P–B3 | | |
| 11 | = | = | | | N–K3[26] | | |
| | | | | | P–Q4 | | |
| 12 | | | | | B–N3 | | |
| | | | | | B–K3 | | |
| 13 | | | | | O–O | | |
| | | | | | B–Q3 | | |
| 14 | | | | | P–KB4[27] | | |
| | | | | | ± | | |

*Notes to practical variations 1–7:*

[1] Ponziani's Opening.

[2] The continuation which strongly suggests itself, since 4 PxP, QxP does not expose Black's Queen to attack by 5 N–QB3.

[3] Sharpest and best.

[4] Introduced by Steinitz. More or less questionable alternatives are: (1) 4 . . . PxP? 5 NxP, Q–Q4 6 NxN, PxN 7 B–B4, Q–Q2 8 P–Q3, PxP 9 O–O, B–Q3 10 BxP, N–K2 11 R–K1 and Black lacks any compensation for his weakened Pawn structure; (2) 4 . . . B–Q2 5 PxP, N–Q5 6 Q–Q1, NxN† 7 QxN, P–KB4 8 P–Q4, P–K5 9 Q–Q1, B–Q3 10 P–QB4 and Black's compensation for the Pawn is nebulous; (3) 4 . . . N–B3 5 NxP, B–Q3 6 NxN, PxN 7 P–Q3, O–O 8 B–KN5, P–KR3 9 BxN, QxB with snowballing complexities difficult to assess.

[5] For 8 . . . P–K5, see Game 1.

[6] After 11 Q–N3, NxN† 12 QxN, Black is out of danger. continued ▶

[7] The most solid continuation.

[8] 4 . . . P–Q4 is effectively met by 5 B–QN5.

[9] White controls more terrain, but Black has the two Bishops.

[10] If 4 N–B3, QN–Q2 5 B–QB4, then 5 . . . P–B3 leads to Prac. Var. 4, but 5 . . . B–K2 invites the sacrificial continuation 6 N–N5!, O–O 7 BxP†, RxB 8 N–K6, Q–K1 9 NxBP, Q–Q1 10 NxR±. Now 10 . . . P–QN3 is effectively met by 11 PxP! Interestingly enough, 6 BxP† (instead of 6 N–N5!) favors Black; e.g., 6 . . . KxB 7 N–N5†, K–N1 8 N–K6, Q–K1 9 NxBP, Q–N3 10 NxR, QxP 11 R–B1, PxP 12 QxP, N–K4 13 P–B4, N/3–N5!

[11] This line, suggested by Sokolski, is the simplest way to obtain a small but clear advantage. Also playable, however, is 5 Q–Q5, N–B4 6 B–N5, B–K2 7 PxP, QxP 8 N–B3.

[12] 6 . . . PxP 7 B–QB4!, B–K2 8 NxP, O–O 9 Q–R5 offers White a strong initiative.

[13] Both 10 P–KR3, P–KB3 11 Q–K2 and 10 Q–K2, B–KN5 11 P–KR3, B–R4 12 P–KN4, B–N3 13 BxB, RPxB 14 P–K6! favor White.

[14] The Hanham Variation, long favored by Nimzowitsch. For 3 . . . B–N5? see Game 2. As for 3 . . . PxP, this concedes the center to White unnecessarily.

[15] Also playable is 4 N–B3, but the text is sharper.

[16] Black must be wary. 4 . . . KN–B3? loses at least a Pawn because of 5 PxP, PxP 6 N–N5. Similar consequences result from 4 . . . B–K2?, e.g., 5 PxP, NxP 6 NxN, PxN 7 Q–R5 or, still worse, 5 . . . PxP 6 Q–Q5!

[17] The continuation 5 N–N5, N–R3 6 O–O is only a trap in that 6 . . . B–K2 loses because of 7 N–K6! Black, however, can hold his own with 6 . . . N–N3! Another trap at White's disposal after 5 N–N5, N–R3 is 6 P–QR4, after which 6 . . . B–K2 loses to 7 BxP†!

[18] White can also maintain an edge with 6 PxP. See Game 3.

[19] Further constricting Black's position by preventing . . . P–QN4.

[20] 7 . . . P–KR3, hoping to obtain an aggressive position by means of . . . N–KB1, . . . P–KN4, and . . . N–N3 is too presumptuous, e.g., 8 P–QN3, Q–B2 9 B–N2, N–B1? 10 PxP, PxP 11 NxP!, QxN 12 N–Q5, and White wins.

[21] Black's position is cramped, but White has no immediate breakthrough.

[22] Other continuations are less convincing: (1) 3 B–B4, PxP 4 NxP, Q–N4 5 P–Q4, QxP 6 Q–R5†, P–N3 7 NxNP with obscure complications offering approximately even chances; (2) 3 P–Q4, PxKP 4 NxP, N–KB3 5 N–QB3, P–Q3=; (3) 3 PxP, P–K5 4 N–K5, N–KB3 5 B–K2, P–Q3 6 B–R5†, K–K2 7 N–B7, Q–K1 8 NxR, QxB 9 QxQ, NxQ 10 P–KN4, N–KB3 11 R–N1, and the situation is unclear.

[23] Not 4 . . . PxP because of 5 B–QB4.

[24] 6 . . . P–B3 is refuted by 7 NxKP, Q–K3 8 Q–K2, P–Q4 9 N/K–Q6†, K–Q2 10 N–B7!

[25] 7 P–B3 and 7 B–B4 also offer White an advantage.

[26] A fair alternative is 11 N–N6, P–Q4 12 NxR, PxB 13 Q–K2.

[27] White has a great advantage; see Game 4. In addition to the column, White has the option of Nimzowitsch's 4 N–B4, PxP 5 N–B3, Q–N3 6 P–Q3!±.

[28] Also good is 3 NxP; after 3 . . . PxP, however, White must not play 4 B–B4 because of 4 . . . Q–N4!, but 4 P–Q4 threatening 5 B–QB4.

[29] 4 . . . Q–K2 is met by 5 N–Q4, N–KB3 6 N–QB3, Q–K4 7 N–B3, Q–K2 8 N–KN5±.

[30] White has a strong extra Pawn.

[31] Simple and potent is 3 B–B4, P–Q3 4 P–Q4, N–B3 5 P–B3, after which Black chokes to death.

[32] 3 . . . PxN? fails against the elementary 4 Q–R5†: 4 . . . K–K2 5 QxP†, K–B2 6 B–B4†, P–Q4! 7 BxP†, K–N3 8 P–KR4, P–KR4, 9 BxP!! (9 . . . B–Q3 10 Q–R5).

[33] White enjoys a substantial advance in development.

*Ponziani's Opening Game 1*

*WHITE: Euwe* *BLACK: Speyer*

*Exhibition Game, Gouda 1921*

| | WHITE | BLACK | | WHITE | BLACK |
|---|---|---|---|---|---|
| 1 | P–K4 | P–K4 | 21 | BxP | B–B3 |
| 2 | N–KB3 | N–QB3 | 22 | Q–N3 | Q–B2 |
| 3 | P–B3 | P–Q4 | 23 | P–B4 | P–KN4 |
| 4 | Q–R4 | P–B3 | 24 | BxKNP | Q–N2 |
| 5 | B–N5 | N–K2 | 25 | P–Q5 | BxP |
| 6 | PxP | QxP | 26 | PxB | QxB |
| 7 | O–O | B–Q2 | 27 | BxP† | N/1xB |
| 8 | P–Q4 | P–K5 | 28 | NxN | R–N1 |
| 9 | KN–Q2 | P–QR3 | 29 | NxN† | K–Q2 |
| 10 | N–R3 | N–B1 | 30 | Q–N5† | K–K2 |
| 11 | B–B4 | Q–KB4 | 31 | NxP† | QxN |
| 12 | Q–B2 | BxN | 32 | P–Q6† | K–B3 |
| 13 | PxB | N–Q3 | 33 | QxQ† | KxQ |
| 14 | R–K1 | O–O–O | 34 | PxP | R–N2 |
| 15 | B–B1 | QR–K1 | 35 | R–N5† | K–B3 |
| 16 | N–N3 | Q–N3 | 36 | R–N8 | R/2–N1 |
| 17 | B–K3 | P–B4 | 37 | P–N3 | RxR |
| 18 | N–B5 | KR–B1 | 38 | PxR/Q | RxQ |
| 19 | B–KB4 | Q–B3 | 39 | RxP | Resigns |
| 20 | QR–N1 | N–Q1 | | | |

*Philidor's Defense Game 2*

*WHITE: Morphy* *BLACK: Duke of Brunswick and Count Isouard*

*Paris 1858*

| | WHITE | BLACK | | WHITE | BLACK |
|---|---|---|---|---|---|
| 1 | P–K4 | P–K4 | 10 | NxP! | PxN |
| 2 | N–KB3 | P–Q3 | 11 | BxNP† | QN–Q2 |
| 3 | P–Q4 | B–N5? | 12 | O–O–O | R–Q1 |
| 4 | PxP | BxN | 13 | RxN | RxR |
| 5 | QxB | PxP | 14 | R–Q1 | Q–K3 |
| 6 | B–QB4 | N–B3 | 15 | BxR† | NxB |
| 7 | Q–QN3 | Q–K2 | 16 | Q–N8† | NxQ |
| 8 | N–B3 | P–B3 | 17 | R–Q8 Mate | |
| 9 | B–KN5 | P–N4 | | | |

*Philidor's Defense Game 3*

*WHITE: A. Steiner* *BLACK: Brinckmann*

*Budapest 1929*

| | WHITE | BLACK | | WHITE | BLACK |
|---|---|---|---|---|---|
| 1 | P–K4 | P–K4 | 26 | R–K1 | P–B5 |
| 2 | N–KB3 | P–Q3 | 27 | KR–N1 | P–N5 |
| 3 | B–B4 | P–QB3 | 28 | R–N2 | P–R4 |
| 4 | P–Q4 | N–Q2 | 29 | B–N4 | P–N3 |
| 5 | PxP | PxP | 30 | BxN | KxB |
| 6 | O–O | B–K2 | 31 | RxP | R/2–R2 |
| 7 | N–N5 | BxN | 32 | P–R6 | K–Q3 |
| 8 | Q–R5 | P–KN3 | 33 | R–R5 | P–R5 |
| 9 | QxB | QxQ | 34 | P–B5† | K–B2 |
| 10 | BxQ | P–KR3 | 35 | R–R3 | R–QN1 |
| 11 | B–Q2 | P–KN4 | 36 | RxR | KxR |
| 12 | B–B3 | P–B3 | 37 | R–Q3 | B–B5 |
| 13 | N–Q2 | N–N3 | 38 | R–QR3 | BxB |
| 14 | B–N3 | N–K2 | 39 | KxB | R–Q2 |
| 15 | P–QR4 | P–QR4 | 40 | P–R3 | P–N6 |
| 16 | KR–Q1 | N–N3 | 41 | PxP | BPxP |
| 17 | N–B4 | NxN | 42 | K–K2 | K–R2 |
| 18 | BxN | K–K2 | 43 | R–KB3 | R–Q5 |
| 19 | P–QN4! | B–K3 | 44 | K–K3 | R–R5 |
| 20 | B–B1 | PxP | 45 | R–B5 | R–R6† |
| 21 | BxP† | K–B2 | 46 | K–K2 | KxP |
| 22 | B–B5 | KR–Q1 | 47 | RxP | K–N4 |
| 23 | KR–N1 | R–Q2 | 48 | R–R5 | K–B5 |
| 24 | P–R5 | N–K2 | 49 | RxP | KxP |
| 25 | P–QB4 | P–B4 | 50 | R–R6 | K–Q5 |

| WHITE | BLACK | WHITE | BLACK |
|---|---|---|---|
| 51 RxP | KxP | 57 R–R3 | R–N2 |
| 52 R–B5† | K–B4? | 58 R–R5† | K–B3 |
| 53 R–Q4! | R–R7† | 59 K–B4 | R–N1 |
| 54 R–Q2 | R–R1 | 60 R–B5† | K–K3 |
| 55 R–Q3 | R–KN1 | 61 R–KN5 | Resigns |
| 56 K–B3 | K–K4 | | |

*Greco Counter Gambit Game 4*

*WHITE: A. Steiner* *BLACK: Apscheneek*

*The Hague 1928*

| WHITE | BLACK | WHITE | BLACK |
|---|---|---|---|
| 1 P–K4 | P–K4 | 14 P–KB4 | Q–B2 |
| 2 N–KB3 | P–KB4 | 15 P–B4! | BxP |
| 3 NxP | Q–B3 | 16 PxP | BxN† |
| 4 P–Q4 | P–Q3 | 17 BxB | PxP |
| 5 N–B4 | PxP | 18 Q–R5† | P–N3 |
| 6 N–B3 | Q–N3 | 19 Q–N5! | R–N1 |
| 7 N–K3 | N–KB3 | 20 R–B6 | B–B1 |
| 8 N/K–Q5 | NxN | 21 QxP | R–N2 |
| 9 NxN | Q–B2 | 22 R/1–KB1 | B–B4 |
| 10 B–QB4 | P–B3 | 23 R/1xB | PxR |
| 11 N–K3 | P–Q4 | 24 Q–K6† | R–K2 |
| 12 B–N3 | B–K3 | 25 R–B8† | Resigns |
| 13 O–O | B–Q3 | | |

# chapter 14—Alekhine's Defense

This opening arises after 1 P–K4, N–KB3. Alekhine's Defense is a typical product of the hypermodern idea which prevailed in international chess during the period immediately following the end of the first World War.

White is lured into the formation of a broad Pawn center which may become vulnerable. Although this center is not as weak as was originally thought, its proper maintenance demands precise play. Extreme accuracy is particularly required in handling the Four Pawn Attack (Part 1), the sharpest line at White's disposal.

Many players who are satisfied with a more modest center formation prefer the Exchange Variation (Part 2) or the Modern Variation (Part 3). Both methods, in fact, offer White a lasting positional advantage. Another interesting line is the Two Pawn Attack (Part 4), much favored by aggressive players with a flair for speculative sacrifices.

Attempts to refute Black's defense with moves other than 2 P–K5 are doomed to failure. Black can easily equalize against 2 N–QB3 and 2 P–Q3 by simply transposing into a double King Pawn game by means of 2 . . . P–K4. An independent variation which does yield White some attacking chances, however, is 2 N–QB3, P–Q4 (Part 5).

## part 1—FOUR PAWN ATTACK

1 P–K4, N–KB3
2 P–K5, N–Q4
3 P–Q4, P–Q3
4 P–QB4, N–N3
5 P–B4, PxP[A]
6 BPxP, N–B3[B]
7 B–K3[C], B–B4
8 N–QB3, P–K3
9 N–B3[D]

KEY POSITION 1

### OBSERVATIONS ON KEY POSITION 1

[A] Trifunovic suggests 5 . . . B–B4 6 B–K3, P–K3 7 N–QB3, N–R3 with the idea of demolishing White's center with . . . P–QB4, e.g., 8 N–B3, P–B4 9 R–B1, PxKP 10 BPxP, PxP 11 NxP, B–B4 with a good game for Black (Medina–Trifunovic, Montevideo 1953). 9 P–Q5 in this line is met by 9 . . . N–N5 10 R–B1, PxKP 11 NxP, P–B3! Consequently, White's best course is to steer clear of a possible . . . P–QB4 by means of 8 PxP! There might then follow 8 . . . PxP 9 N–B3, B–K2 10 B–K2, O–O 11 QR–B1!, R–B1 12 P–QN3, and White has an edge. 11 R–QB1 in this variation is important; 11 O–O permits 11 . . . P–Q4! and if 12 P–B5, then 12 . . . N–B5!

[B] 6 . . . B–B4, postponing the development of the Queen Knight, is also playable; but after 7 N–QB3, P–K3 8 N–B3, B–K2 9 B–K2, O–O 10 10 O–O, Black must continue with 10 . . . P–KB3, not with 10 . . . N–B3, which fails against 11 P–Q5!, e.g., 11 . . . PxP 12 PxP, N–N5 13 N–K1, B–N3 14 B–B3±. After 10 . . . P–KB3, however, White has nothing better than 11 PxP, BxP 12 B–K3, N–B3 13 Q–Q2, which transposes into one of the main variations. Weaker is 11 B–B4?,

N–B3 12 PxP, BxP 13 P–Q5, N–R4! (Geller-Korchnoi, USSR Championship 1960).

An entirely different idea is 6 . . . P–B4, but this early attempt to smash the White center proves premature: 7 P–Q5!, P–K3 8 N–QB3, PxP 9 PxP, Q–R5† 10 P–N3, Q–Q5 11 B–N5†, B–Q2 12 Q–K2, and now 12 . . . NxP as well as 12 . . . P–QR3 are effectively countered by 13 P–K6! In this line 7 . . . NxBP? loses to 8 Q–R4†!

C The following line analyzed by Loewenfisch is interesting: 7 N–KB3!?, B–N5 8 P–K6!, PxP 9 P–B5, and now not 9 . . . P–K4 10 PxN, P–K5 11 P–Q5!±, but 9 . . . N–Q4! 10 B–QN5, Q–Q2 11 QN–Q2, P–KN3 12 Q–R4, B–N2 13 N–K5, BxN 14 PxB, N–K6 16 Q–K4, Q–Q5! with equal chances. As a possible improvement for White, 9 B–K2 deserves consideration; most likely Black's best is then 9 . . . Q–Q2.

D Some analysts prefer 9 B–K2 in order to avoid the pin by 9 . . . B–KN5 (see Prac. Var. 5).

White has an advantage in space. His center, however, is subject to attack, and attack Black can — in several different ways.

There is first of all the possibility of playing . . . Q–Q2 followed by . . . O–O–O combined with . . . P–KB3. This set-up, designed to increase the pressure on White's Queen Pawn, is in itself entirely logical, but it has the drawback of exposing Black's King to a dangerous assault. It is for this reason that the line has virtually vanished from today's tournament scene.

Another method consists in . . . N–QN5 followed by . . . P–QB4. This line, at any rate, leads to the exchange of White's Queen Pawn. The ensuing complications, however, enable White to maintain the initiative.

The third method, that of quickly mobilizing the Kingside by . . . B–K2 and . . . O–O, then attacking the enemy center by . . . P–KB3, poses many problems for White. It is this system which offers Black his best chance to achieve an equal position.

IDEA VARIATIONS 1–6:

(1) 9 . . . Q–Q2 10 B–K2, O–O–O 11 Q–Q2, P–B3 12 PxP, PxP 13 O–O, R–N1 14 KR–Q1, Q–N2 15 B–B1, N–K4 with a good game for Black (see Game 1). In this line 15 . . . B–KN5 is even stronger for Black.

(2) 9 . . . Q–Q2 10 B–K2, O–O–O 11 O–O, B–KN5 12 P–B5!, N–Q4 (12 . . . BxN 13 PxN!±) 13 NxN, QxN 14 N–N5!, BxB 15 QxB, NxQP 16 BxN, QxB† 17 K–R1, and although Black has won a Pawn, his position is far from enviable.

(3) 9 . . . Q–Q2 10 B–K2, O–O–O 11 O–O, P–B3 12 P–Q5! (12 PxP, PxP 13 P–Q5, Q–N2! favors Black

in view of the open King Knight file), NxKP 13 NxN, PxN 14 P–QR4! (Weaver Adams' idea, far stronger than Mikenas' 14 Q–N3, when Black can hold his own with 14 . . . PxP 15 PxP, B–KN5!), P–QR4 15 N–N5, B–QN5 16 P–Q6!, P–B4 17 B–Q2± Black's King position is extremely shaky.

(4) 9 . . . N–N5 10 R–B1, P–B4 11 P–QR3 (premature), PxP 12 NxP (or 12 B–N5, PxN!∓, as in the game (Znosko-–Borovsky–Alekhine, Paris 1925), N–B3 13 NxB, PxN 14 Q–B3, and numerous analysts assess this position in White's favor. The truth is that after 14 . . . B–K2! 15 QxP, O–O Black has excellent counterchances owing to his lead in development and the vulnerability of White's King Pawn.

(5) 9 . . . N–N5 10 R–B1, P–B4 11 B–K2, PxP (Black does better to postpone this capture until White plays P–QR3; see Prac. Var. 1) 12 NxP, N–B3 (12 . . . B–N3 13 P–QR3, N–B3 14 NxN, PxN 15 QxQ†, KxQ 16 BxN†, PxB 17 B–B3, R–B1 18 N–K4!± [Tartakover]) 13 NxB, QxQ† 14 RxQ, PxN 15 O–O! (both 15 . . . NxKP and 15 . . . P–N3 are effectively answered by 16 N–N5!)±. See Game 2.

(6) 9 . . . B–K2 10 B–K2 (interesting but speculative is 10 P–Q5, PxP 11 PxP, N–N5 12 N–Q4, B–N3 13 B–N5†, K–B1 14 O–O, K–N1 15 Q–N4, N/5xQP 16 N–K6, NxB 17 RxP!!±), O–O 11 O–O, P–B3 12 PxP, BxP 13 Q–Q2, R–B2 14 QR–Q1 (Mikenas, who originated 13 . . . R–B2, gives only the line 14 P–Q5, PxP 15 N–KN5, BxN 16 BxB, Q–Q2 17 PxP, N–K4 18 Q–Q4, R–K1; the text considerably improves White's chances), R–Q2 15 P–B5!, N–Q4 16 NxN, PxN 17 N–K5, BxN 18 RxB, B–B3 19 B–N5± (Lutikov–Bagirov, USSR Championship 1960).

PRACTICAL VARIATIONS 1–5:

1 P–K4, N–KB3 2 P–K5, N–Q4 3 P–Q4, P–Q3 4 P–QB4, N–N3 5 P–B4, PxP 6 BPxP, N–B3 7 B–K3, B–B4 8 N–QB3, P–K3 9 N–B3

| | *1* | *2* | *3* | *4* | *5* |
|---|---|---|---|---|---|
| *9* | — — | — — | — — | — — | — — |
| | N–N5 | — — | B–K2 | — — | B–KN5 |
| *10* | R–B1 | — — | B–K2 | — — | B–K2[13] |
| | P–B4 | — — | O–O | — — | BxN |
| *11* | B–K2[1] | — — | O–O | — — | PxB |
| | B–K2[2] | — — | P–B3 | — — | Q–R5† |
| *12* | O–O | P–QR3 | PxP | N–KR4 | B–B2 |
| | O–O | PxP | BxP | PxP | Q–B5 |

| | 1 | 2 | 3 | 4 | 5 |
|---|---|---|---|---|---|
| 13 | P–QR3 | NxP | Q–Q2 | NxB | Q–B1 |
| | PxP | N–B3 | Q–K2[7] | PxN | QxQ† |
| 14 | NxP | NxB | QR–Q1 | P–Q5 | RxQ |
| | N–B3 | PxN[4] | QR–Q1 | N–Q5! | O–O–O |
| 15 | NxB | Q–B2[5] | Q–B1![8] | BxN | R–Q1 |
| | PxN | B–N4 | B–N3 | PxB | B–N5 |
| 16 | RxP | R–Q1 | K–R1[9] | QxP | P–R3 |
| | P–N3 | BxB! | ± | N–Q2 | BxN† |
| 17 | R–B1 | RxQ† | | K–R1![10] | PxB |
| | B–N4! | RxR | | B–B4 | N–R4 |
| 18 | B–B5! | QxP | | Q–Q2[11] | P–B5 |
| | R–K1 | O–O | | Q–R5[12] | N–Q4[14] |
| 19 | QxQ | R–B1 | | = | = |
| | QRxQ | P–N3[6] | | | |
| 20 | QR–Q1 | = | | | |
| | NxKP[3] | | | | |
| | ± | | | | |

*Notes to practical variations 1–5:*

[1] Another possibility is 11 P–Q5!?, PxP 12 PxP, N/5xQP 13 B–KN5, B–K2 14 B–N5†, K–B1! For 11 P–QR3, see Idea Var. 4.

[2] For 11 . . . PxP, see Idea Var. 5.

[3] Less commendable is 20 . . . R–Q7 21 RxR, BxR 22 B–Q6, BxN 23 PxB, when White's Bishops come to play a significant role (Petrov–Fine, Kemeri 1937). The text move leaves White with only a tiny edge after 21 N–K4, RxR 22 BxR!, B–K2 23 P–QN3, BxB† 24 NxB, R–K2 25 B–B2, P–B4 (Keres–Sajtar, Prague 1943).

[4] 14 . . . QxQ† 15 RxQ, PxN 16 O–O clearly favors White.

[5] A simple, safe, and sound alternative is 15 O–O, possibly followed by N–Q5.

[6] The situation is somewhat obscure, but analyst Pachman concludes that Black seems to have sufficient compensation for the Queen.

[7] After 13 . . . Q–K1 14 QR–Q1, R–Q1 15 Q–B1, Q–N3 16 K–R1, B–N5, White successfully defends his center by 17 B–Q3!, Q–R4 18 N–K2! (Suetin–Korchnoi, USSR Championship 1952). For 13 . . . R–B2, see Idea Var. 6.

[8] 15 Q–K1, N–N5 16 P–QR3!, N–B7 17 Q–B2, NxB 18 QxN (Rouzer–Fine, Leningrad 1937), 18 . . . P–B3!

[9] See Game 3.

[10] 17 N–R4, P–QN4! 18 PxP, B–Q3 is promising for Black (Spielmann–Colle, Dortmund 1928).

[11] For the inferior 18 Q–Q3, see Game 4.

[12] Znosko-Borovsky–Colle, Paris 1929.

[13] More enterprising is 10 Q–Q2!, B–K2 11 O–O–O, O–O 12 N–K4, B–KB4 13 N–B5 (Bronstein–Kopylov, USSR Championship 1952). In this line White has the simple option of 12 P–KR3, and if 12 . . . B–R4 or 12 . . . B–B4, then 13 P–KN4.

[14] 19 K–Q2, P–B3! 20 B–N3!, R–KB1 offers equal chances (Prins–Tartakover, Hastings 1945).

*Alekhine's Defense Game 1*

*WHITE: Naegeli* *BLACK: Euwe*

| | WHITE | BLACK | | WHITE | BLACK |
|---|---|---|---|---|---|
| 1 | P–K4 | N–KB3 | 17 | Q–KB2 | B–KN5 |
| 2 | P–K5 | N–Q4 | 18 | R–Q2 | PxP |
| 3 | P–Q4 | P–Q3 | 19 | BxP? | RxB |
| 4 | P–QB4 | N–N3 | 20 | RxR | B–QB4 |
| 5 | P–B4 | B–B4 | 21 | R–Q8† | RxR |
| 6 | N–KB3 | PxP | 22 | QxB | R–Q7 |
| 7 | BPxP | P–K3 | 23 | N–K4 | RxQNP |
| 8 | N–B3 | N–B3 | 24 | N–Q6† | K–Q2 |
| 9 | B–K3 | Q–Q2 | 25 | N–N5 | K–B1 |
| 10 | B–K2 | O–O–O | 26 | R–K1 | K–N1 |
| 11 | Q–Q2 | P–B3 | 27 | R–K5 | B–B4 |
| 12 | PxP | PxP | 28 | Q–Q4 | R–Q7! |
| 13 | O–O | R–N1 | 29 | Q–K3 | R–Q1 |
| 14 | KR–Q1 | Q–N2 | 30 | K–B2 | Q–B3 |
| 15 | B–B1 | N–K4 | 31 | B–K2 | B–K5† |
| 16 | NxN | PxN | | Resigns | |

*Alekhine's Defense Game 2*

*WHITE: Bronstein* *BLACK: Mikenas*

*USSR Championship 1945*

| | WHITE | BLACK | | WHITE | BLACK |
|---|---|---|---|---|---|
| 1 | P–K4 | N–KB3 | 15 | O–O! | B–K2 |
| 2 | P–K5 | N–Q4 | 16 | RxP | P–N3 |
| 3 | P–Q4 | P–Q3 | 17 | R–B4 | NxKP |
| 4 | P–QB4 | N–N3 | 18 | R–K4 | P–B3 |
| 5 | P–B4 | PxP | 19 | P–B5 | N–Q2 |
| 6 | BPxP | N–B3 | 20 | N–Q5 | K–B1 |
| 7 | B–K3 | B–B4 | 21 | N–B7! | R–Q1 |
| 8 | N–QB3 | P–K3 | 22 | N–K6† | K–B2 |
| 9 | B–K2 | N–N5 | 23 | NxR† | RxN |
| 10 | R–B1 | P–QB4 | 24 | R/K–Q4 | K–K3 |
| 11 | N–B3 | PxP | 25 | P–QN4 | B–B1 |
| 12 | NxP | N–B3 | 26 | B–QN5 | P–B4 |
| 13 | NxB | QxQ† | 27 | B–KB4 | Resigns |
| 14 | RxQ | PxN | | | |

*Alekhine's Defense Game 3*

*WHITE: Bronstein* *BLACK: Rudakovski*

*USSR Championship 1945*

| | WHITE | BLACK | | WHITE | BLACK |
|---|---|---|---|---|---|
| 1 | P–K4 | N–KB3 | 17 | P–Q5! | N–N5 |
| 2 | P–K5 | N–Q4 | 18 | P–QR3 | N–R3 |
| 3 | P–Q4 | P–Q3 | 19 | P–QN4 | KR–Q1 |
| 4 | P–QB4 | N–N3 | 20 | B–Q4 | P–QB4 |
| 5 | P–B4 | PxP | 21 | BxB | PxB |
| 6 | BPxP | N–B3 | 22 | N–KR4 | PxQP |
| 7 | B–K3 | B–B4 | 23 | B–N4 | PxNP |
| 8 | N–QB3 | P–K3 | 24 | RPxP | R–B2 |
| 9 | B–K2 | B–K2 | 25 | P–B5 | NxBP |
| 10 | N–B3 | O–O | 26 | PxN | QxP |
| 11 | O–O | P–B3 | 27 | NxB | QxN |
| 12 | PxP | BxP | 28 | Q–R6! | Q–QB3 |
| 13 | Q–Q2 | Q–K2 | 29 | QR–K1 | P–B4 |
| 14 | QR–Q1 | QR–Q1 | 30 | BxP | R–B2 |
| 15 | Q–B1 | B–N3 | 31 | N–K7† | RxN |
| 16 | K–R1 | R–Q2? | 32 | Q–N5† | Resigns |

*Alekhine's Defense Game 4*

*WHITE:* *BLACK:*
*Deschna Chess Club* *Lenin Chess Club*

*Radio Match, USSR 1960*

| | WHITE | BLACK | | WHITE | BLACK |
|---|---|---|---|---|---|
| 1 | P–K4 | N–KB3 | 15 | BxN | PxB |
| 2 | P–K5 | N–Q4 | 16 | QxP | N–Q2 |
| 3 | P–QB4 | N–N3 | 17 | K–R1 | B–B4 |
| 4 | P–Q4 | P–Q3 | 18 | Q–Q3 | Q–N4! |
| 5 | P–B4 | PxP | 19 | N–N5 | QR–K1! |
| 6 | BPxP | N–B3 | 20 | B–B3 | R–K6 |
| 7 | B–K3 | B–B4 | 21 | Q–Q2 | R–B3 |
| 8 | N–QB3 | P–K3 | 22 | P–QN4 | B–K2 |
| 9 | B–K2 | B–K2 | 23 | NxBP | R–R3 |
| 10 | N–B3 | O–O | 24 | N–K6 | Q–N6 |
| 11 | O–O | P–B3 | 25 | P–KR3 | B–Q3 |
| 12 | N–KR4 | PxP | 26 | K–N1 | RxP! |
| 13 | NxB | PxN | | Resigns | |
| 14 | P–Q5 | N–Q5 | | | |

## part 2—EXCHANGE VARIATION

1 P–K4, N–KB3
2 P–K5, N–Q4
3 P–Q4, P–Q3
4 P–QB4, N–N3
5 PxP, KPxP[A]
6 N–QB3[B]

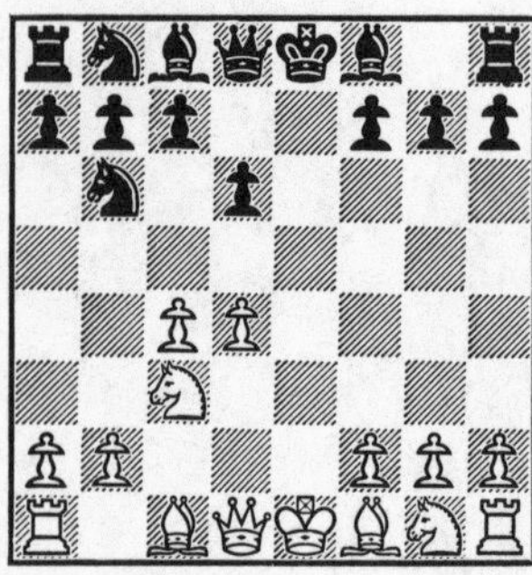

KEY POSITION 2

OBSERVATIONS ON KEY POSITION 2

[A] The recapture with the King Pawn is reputed to be Black's best bid for equality, but 5 . . . BPxP is not really bad, e.g., 6 B–K3, P–N3 7 N–QB3, B–N2 8 N–B3 and now, not 8 . . . N–B3 9 P–KR3!, O–O 10 Q–Q2± (Yates–Alekhine, Dresden 1926), but 8 . . . B–N5! (see Game 5). As for 5 . . . QxP, this is weak because of 6 P–B5. If 6 . . . Q–K3† 7 B–K2, N–Q4 8 N–QB3.

[B] After 6 B–K3, Black proceeds logically with 6 . . . P–N3 7 N–KB3, B–N2, e.g., 8 QN–Q2, N–B3 9 B–K2, O–O 10 O–O, B–N5 11 R–B1, P–Q4 12 P–B5, N–B1 followed by . . . N–K2 and . . . N–B4.

An interesting plan is to defer the development of the Queen Knight and eventually play it to QR3, with maneuver B2–K3 in mind. For full details, see CHESS REVIEW, November, 1950.

Although White has abandoned his spearhead at K5, he still retains some advantage in space, an advantage which may easily become a factor of major significance. Theoretically, Black's most active counterplay is in . . . P–KN3 followed by . . . B–N2. In this way, Black increases the pressure on White's Queen Pawn. Unfortunately for Black, experience has shown that against 6 N–QB3, this line of play fails to produce its desired effect. The realization of this fact has created renewed interest in the complexities of the Exchange Variation.

Black, if he is not to fianchetto his King Bishop, must content himself with . . . B–K2 and, if possible, . . . B–KB3. Black can also attempt to increase the pressure on White's Queen Pawn by means of . . . B–KN5, but White can easily circumvent this tactic, developing his King Knight at K2.

IDEA VARIATIONS 7–9:

(7) 6 . . . P–N3 7 N–KB3, B–N2 8 B–N5!, P–KB3 9 B–K3, O–O (9 . . . N–B3 is better, e.g., 10 B–K2, O–O 11 O–O, B–N5) 10 P–B5!, PxP 11 PxP, N/3–Q2 (11 . . . QxQ† is met by 12 RxQ followed by 13 N–Q5) 12 Q–Q5†, K–R1 13 O–O–O, N–B3 14 P–KR4! with good attacking chances for White (Rouzer–Mazel, Leningrad 1936). Black can try to anticipate 8 B–KN5 in this variation by 7 . . . B–KN5, but then 8 Q–K2†! is disturbing (8 . . . Q–K2 9 N–K4! or 8 . . . B–K2 9 B–R6!).

(8) 6 . . . N–B3 7 B–K3, P–N3 8 B–Q3, B–N2 9

KN–K2, O–O 10 P–QN3, P–Q4! 11 P–B5, N–Q2 12 NxP, NxBP! and Black has good counterplay.

(9) 6 . . . B–K2 7 B–Q3, N–B3 8 KN–K2, B–N5 9 P–B3, B–R5† (9 . . . B–R4 is more accurate) 10 N–N3! (10 P–N3?, BxP! 11 O–O, BxN 12 QxB†, B–K2∓), B–R4 11 O–O, BxN 12 PxB, O–O (13 P–KN4!; for 12 . . . B–N3 13 R–K1†, which also favors White, see Game 6) 13 P–N3, R–K1 14 P–KN4, B–N3 15 BxB, RPxB 16 P–Q5 with an advantage in space for White (Panov–Mikenas, Moscow 1942).

PRACTICAL VARIATIONS 6–10:

1 P–K4, N–KB3 2 P–K5, N–Q4 3 P–Q4, P–Q3 4 P–QB4, N–N3 5 PxP, KPxP 6 N–QB3

| | *6* | *7* | *8* | *9* | *10* |
|---|---|---|---|---|---|
| *6* | – – | – – | – – | – – | – – |
| | N–B3 | – – | – – | – – | – – |
| 7 | B–K3 | – – | – – | – – | – – |
| | B–K2[1] | – – | – – | B–B4 | P–Q4? |
| 8 | B–Q3 | – – | – – | N–B3 | P–B5 |
| | O–O | – – | – – | B–K2 | N–B5 |
| *9* | KN–K2[2] | – – | – – | P–Q5! | BxN |
| | B–N5 | – – | N–N5! | N–N1 | PxB |
| *10* | O–O | – – | O–O | N–Q4 | Q–R4 |
| | N–N5 | B–B3 | NxB | B–N3 | B–K3 |
| *11* | R–B1 | P–B3 | QxN | B–K2 | KN–K2[7] |
| | NxB | B–R4 | P–Q4 | N/1–Q2 | ± |
| *12* | QxN[3] | P–QN3[4] | P–B5 | O–O[6] | |
| | ± | ± | N–B5[5] | ± | |
| | | | = | | |

*Notes to practical variations 6–10:*

[1] Here, too, 7 . . . P–N3 has its drawbacks, e.g., 8 Q–K2!, Q–K2 9 P–B5, PxP 10 PxP, N–Q2 11 N–Q5. For 8 B–Q3, which lets Black escape, see Idea Var. 8.

[2] Better than 9 N–B3, which permits 9 . . . B–N5 with greater effect than in the column.

[3] White's advantage in space outweighs Black's pair of Bishops (Lissitzin–Lilienthal, Moscow 1937).

[4] 12 . . . R–K1 13 Q–Q2, B–N3 14 QR–K1 offers White a slight superiority (Ilyin–Genevsky–Rabinovitch, USSR Championship 1937).

[5] 13 B–B1, P–QN3 14 P–QN3, N–R4 15 N–B4, B–N2 (Ilyin–Genevsky–Nenarokov, Moscow 1926).

[6] Ilyin–Genevsky–Gruenfeld, Moscow 1925.

[7] The threat of 12 P–Q5! will net White at least a Pawn. The immediate 11 P–Q5 is premature because of 11 . . . BxQP 12 O–O–O, BxNP!

*Alekhine's Defense Game 5*

*WHITE: Toran* *BLACK: Korchnoi*

*Uppsala 1956*

| | WHITE | BLACK | | WHITE | BLACK |
|---|---|---|---|---|---|
| 1 | P–K4 | N–KB3 | 21 | P–QR4 | P–N3 |
| 2 | P–K5 | N–Q4 | 22 | PxP | QxNP |
| 3 | P–Q4 | P–Q3 | 23 | KR–Q1 | R–R4 |
| 4 | P–QB4 | N–N3 | 24 | Q–B3 | KR–R1 |
| 5 | PxP | BPxP | 25 | QR–B1 | NxP! |
| 6 | B–K3 | P–KN3 | 26 | RxN | RxN |
| 7 | N–QB3 | B–N2 | 27 | PxR | BxR |
| 8 | N–B3 | B–N5 | 28 | Q–Q2 | R–Q1 |
| 9 | B–K2 | N–B3 | 29 | B–Q1 | P–K4 |
| 10 | O–O | O–O | 30 | Q–K2 | R–N1 |
| 11 | P–QN3 | P–Q4 | 31 | R–N1 | Q–B4 |
| 12 | P–B5 | N–B1 | 32 | P–N3 | R–N3 |
| 13 | P–KR3? | BxN | 33 | K–N2 | K–N2 |
| 14 | BxB | P–K3 | 34 | R–N3 | P–K5 |
| 15 | P–QN4 | P–QR3 | 35 | Q–R2 | Q–Q3 |
| 16 | P–N5 | PxP | 36 | Q–Q2 | B–B4 |
| 17 | NxNP | N/1–K2 | 37 | B–B2 | Q–K4 |
| 18 | B–N5 | Q–R4 | 38 | Q–K2 | R–KB3 |
| 19 | BxN | NxB | | Resigns | |
| 20 | Q–Q3 | N–B3 | | | |

*Alekhine's Defense Game 6*

*WHITE: Boleslavski* *BLACK: Kopylov*

*USSR Championship 1949*

| | WHITE | BLACK | | WHITE | BLACK |
|---|---|---|---|---|---|
| 1 | P–K4 | N–KB3 | 14 | P–N3 | Q–B3 |
| 2 | P–K5 | N–Q4 | 15 | B–K3 | R–K1 |
| 3 | P–Q4 | P–Q3 | 16 | Q–Q2 | BxB |
| 4 | P–QB4 | N–N3 | 17 | QxB | Q–N3 |
| 5 | PxP | KPxP | 18 | Q–Q2 | QxP |
| 6 | N–QB3 | B–K2 | 19 | P–B5! | N–Q2 |
| 7 | B–Q3 | N–B3 | 20 | B–B4 | Q–N3 |
| 8 | KN–K2 | B–N5 | 21 | N–N5 | PxP |
| 9 | P–KB3 | B–R5† | 22 | NxBP | R–Q1 |
| 10 | N–N3 | B–R4 | 23 | PxP | Q–B4 |
| 11 | O–O | BxN | 24 | QR–Q1 | N/3–N1 |
| 12 | PxB | B–N3 | 25 | Q–Q6† | Resigns |
| 13 | R–K1† | K–B1 | | | |

# part 3—MODERN VARIATION

1 P–K4, N–KB3
2 P–K5, N–Q4
3 P–Q4, P–Q3
4 N–KB3, B–N5[A]
5 B–K2[B]

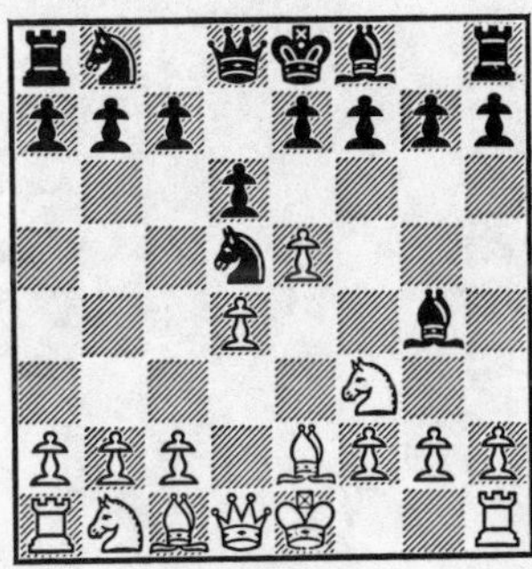

KEY POSITION 3

## OBSERVATIONS ON KEY POSITION 3

[A] Other moves are inferior. For example:

1) 4 . . . N–QB3 5 P–B4, N–N3 6 P–K6!, PxP and now 7 N–B3±. After Keres' 7 N–N5, Kevitz gives 7 . . . P–K4 8 P–Q5, N–Q5. 9 B–K3, P–K3 10 B–Q3, PxP! as assuring Black equality.
2) 4 . . . PxP 5 NxP!±.
3) 4 . . . B–B4 5 B–Q3!±.
4) 4 . . . P–KN3 5 N–N5!±.

[B] After 5 P–KR3, BxN 6 QxB, PxP 7 PxP, P–K3 followed by . . . QN–Q2, White's two-Bishop advantage is offset by the vulnerability of his King Pawn. Alekhine often tried 5 P–B4, N–N3 6 B–K2, when 6 . . . PxP offers these possibilities:

1) 7 P–B5!, P–K5! 8 PxN, PxN 9 BxP, BxB 10 QxB, N–B3! 11 O–O, NxP! 12 QxP, RPxP 13 B–K3, R–QN1 14 Q–K4, N–N4 followed by . . . N–Q3, and White, according to Fine, lacks sufficient compensation for the Pawn.
2) 7 NxP, BxB 8 QxB, QxP 9 O–O, QN–Q2 10 NxN, QxN! 11 R–Q1, Q–B3 12 P–QN3, P–K3 13 B–N2, B–Q3! and again White has no compensation for the Pawn. Far weaker for Black in this line is 10 . . . NxN? 11 N–B3, P–QB3 12 B–K3, Q–K4 13 QR–Q1, P–K3 14 Q–B3!, O–O–O 15 BxP!± (Alekhine–Reshevsky, Kemeri 1937).

The Modern Variation is considered White's most reliable method of meeting Alekhine's Defense. Instead of forming a broad center, White restricts himself to maintaining his Pawn on K5. As is shown by the Idea Variations, Black is unable effectively to increase the pressure on this Pawn. Black has only two reasonable continuations at his disposal, 5 . . . P–QB3 and 5 . . . P–K3.

5 . . . P–QB3 actually represents an involved focus on the King Pawn, but White still can maintain his center by means of 6 N–N5! It can be stated as a general rule that in positions of this type White's King Knight serves better than his King Bishop in the struggle for the center.

Taking all factors into account, the continuation 5 . . . P–K3 is probably Black's best. In this line, White is unable to avoid KPxQP for very long; even so, however, he retains a slight superiority in space.

## IDEA VARIATIONS 10–16:

(10) 5 . . . PxP 6 NxP, BxB 7 QxB, N–N3 (if 7 . . . P–QB3, there follows 8 Q–B3, N–B3 9 Q–N3!) 8 O–O (8 Q–B3 is now met by 8 . . . Q–Q4), QN–Q2 (8 . . . QxP? 9 R–Q1 and White obtains a crushing attack) 9 R–Q1 with an excellent position for White.

(11) 5 . . . N–QB3 6 P–K6!, PxP 7 N–N5, BxB 8 QxB, P–K4 9 Q–B4± (Kupper–Nievergelt, Zurich 1954).

(12) 5 . . . N–Q2 6 P–KR3!, B–R4 (6 . . . BxN is imperative) 7 N–N5!, B–N3 (7 . . . BxB 8 P–K6!) 8 P–K6!, N/2–B3 9 B–Q3± (Maroczy–Vukovic, London 1927).

(13) 5 . . . BxN 6 BxB, P–B3 (6 . . . PxP? 7 P–B4!) 7 PxP!, QxP 8 O–O with White for choice.

(14) 5 . . . P–QB3 6 O–O, BxN! 7 BxB, PxP 8 PxP, P–K3 9 Q–K2 (the alternative of 9 P–B4, N–K2 10 QxQ†, KxQ 11 B–B4, N–Q2 12 R–K1, K–B2 13 N–B3, N–KN3 14 B–N3, B–N5 15 QR–B1 holds no terror for Black thanks to his control of the open Queen file [Zarachov–Kopylov, Leningrad 1954], Q–B2 10 P–B4, N–K2! 11 B–N4, N–Q2 12 P–B4, P–KR4! 13 B–R3, O–O–O∓. See Game 7.

(15) 5 . . . P–QB3 6 N–N5!, BxB 7 QxB, PxP 8 PxP, P–K3 9 O–O, N–Q2 10 P–QB4, N–K2 11 N–QB3, Q–B2 12 R–K1, N–KB4 13 N–B3, B–N5 14 B–Q2, and White enjoys an advantage in space. See Game 8.

(16) 5 . . . P–K3 6 O–O, B–K2 7 P–KR3, B–R4 8 P–B4, N–N3 9 N–B3, QN–Q2 (the Knight may be better placed here than on QB3; cf. Practical Variations) 10 PxP, PxP 11 P–QN3, O–O 12 P–QR4, P–QR4 13 B–B4, N–N1 14 R–K1 (with 14 N–K1! followed by N–QB2, aimed against . . . N–QN5, White can maintain an edge), N–R3 15 N–QN5, N–N5= (Boleslavski–Bronstein, Moscow 1950).

PRACTICAL VARIATIONS 11–15:

1 P–K4, N–KB3 2 P–K5, N–Q4 3 P–Q4, P–Q3 4 N–KB3, B–N5 5 B–K2

| | *11* | *12* | *13* | *14* | *15* |
|---|---|---|---|---|---|
| 5 | — — | — — | — — | — — | — — |
| | P–QB3 | — — | — — | P–K3 | — — |
| 6 | N–N5! | — — | — — | O–O | — — |
| | B–B4 | — — | — — | B–K2 | QN–B3 |
| 7 | B–Q3 | P–K6! | — — | P–B4 | P–B4 |
| | BxB | BxKP | PxP | N–N3 | N/4–K2[9] |
| 8 | QxB | NxB | P–N4 | PxP | PxP |
| | PxP | PxN | B–N3 | PxP | QxP |
| 9 | PxP | B–N4 | B–Q3![5] | N–B3 | N–B3 |
| | P–KR3 | N–B2 | BxB | N–B3 | BxN[10] |

| | 11 | 12 | 13 | 14 | 15 |
|---|---|---|---|---|---|
| 10 | N–KB3[1] | O–O | QxB | P–QN3 | BxB |
| | P–K3 | N–Q2 | P–KN3! | B–B3 | O–O–O[11] |
| 11 | O–O | R–K1 | O–O![6] | B–K3![7] | P–Q5! |
| | N–Q2 | P–K4! | ± | P–Q4 | N–K4 |
| 12 | R–Q1 | BxN† | | P–B5 | B–B4[12] |
| | Q–B2 | QxB | | N–Q2 | ± |
| 13 | P–B4 | PxP | | P–QN4! | |
| | N–K2![2] | O–O–O | | NxNP | |
| 14 | B–B4 | Q–K2![4] | | R–N1 | |
| | N–KN3 | ± | | N–B3 | |
| 15 | B–N3 | | | RxP[8] | |
| | O–O–O[3] | | | ± | |
| | = | | | | |

*Notes to practical variations 11–15:*

[1] 10 N–K4, P–K3 and now both 11 O–O, N–Q2 12 P–KB4, N–B4 and 11 P–KB4, N–Q2 12 P–B4, N–N5 13 Q–K2, N–B4 offer Black equality.

[2] 13 . . . N/4–N3 14 Q–K2 favors White (Book-Reshevsky, Kemeri 1937).

[3] Black has a satisfactory game, e.g., 16 N–B3, B–N5! 17 Q–K3, BxN 18 QxB, N–B4.

[4] 14 . . . P–K3 15 PxP, BxP 16 N–Q2 favors White (Pachman–Seimeanes, Bucharest 1949). White also has the edge after 14 . . . Q–K3 15 N–Q2, P–Q4 16 N–B3.

[5] Keres' own improvement on 9 NxKP, Q–Q2 10 N–B4, B–B2 (Turn–Keres, Talinn 1943).

[6] White maintains the initiative: 11 . . . Q–Q2 12 R–K1± or 11 . . . B–R3 12 NxKP, Q–Q2 13 Q–K2±.

[7] In this variation the Bishop almost invariably serves better on K3 than N2. An example of the latter: 11 B–N2, P–Q4! 12 P–B5, N–Q2 13 N–QN5, NxBP 14 B–R3, N–K5 15 N–Q2!, BxB! 16 QxB, B–K2! 17 BxB, QxB 18 NxN, PxN 19 QxP, O–O∓ (Alexander–Pachman, London 1947).

[8] This position supposedly favors White, e.g., 15 . . . NxBP 16 PxN, BxN 17 Q–R4, Q–B1 18 B–QN5 and wins; or 15 . . . BxN 16 BxB, NxBP, when 17 NxP! is a crusher (Nedelkovic–Janosevic, Yugoslavian Championship 1948). In this latter line, however, Black obtains sufficient tactical counterplay, according to Mikenas, with 16 . . . O–O, and if 17 Q–R4, simply 17 . . . Q–B1. Even so, 18 R–N3 keeps some initiative.

[9] 7 . . . N–N3 is effectively countered by 8 PxP, PxP 9 P–Q5!, PxP 10 PxP, BxN 11 PxB!, N–K4 12 B–N5†, N/4–K2 13 Q–Q4! For the inferior 9 P–QN3 in this variation, see Game 9.

[10] For 9 . . . N–N3, see Game 10.

[11] 10 . . . QxP 11 QxQ, NxQ 12 BxP, R–QN1 13 B–K4 slightly favors White.

[12] White has good attacking chances (Unzicker–Pomar, Bad Pyrmont 1951).

## part 4—TWO PAWN ATTACK

1 P–K4, N–KB3
2 P–K5, N–Q4
3 P–QB4, N–N3
4 P–B5, N–Q4
5 B–B4[A], P–K3
6 N–QB3

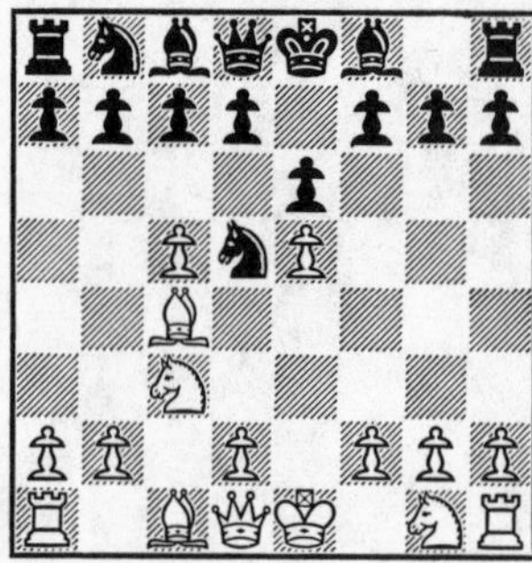

KEY POSITION 4

OBSERVATIONS ON KEY POSITION 4

[A] After 5 N–QB3, Black easily equalizes with 5 . . . NxN 6 QPxN, P–Q3 7 B–QB4, P–Q4! 8 QxP, QxQ 9 BxQ, P–K3 10 B–K4, BxP (Alekhine–Fine, Pasadena 1932). In this line both 7 . . . PxBP? and 7 . . . PxKP? cost Black a Queen after 8 BxP†.

This interesting continuation has received increased attention of late. White sacrifices his Queen Bishop Pawn in return for a speculative attack against the enemy King-side, often aided by Q–KN4. Black, on his part, may accept the sacrifice immediately, or first play . . . NxN; in either event, his task is none too simple.

IDEA VARIATIONS 17–19:

(17) 6 . . . BxP 7 P–Q4, B–N5 8 BxN, PxB 9 Q–N4, K–B1. This immediate acceptance of the sacrifice is recommended by Pachman. He offers the following variation as proof of Black's defensive resources: 10 N–B3, P–Q3 11 Q–N3, N–B3 12 B–N5, Q–Q2 13 O–O, Q–N5, when White lacks sufficient compensation for the Pawn. However, White does have better; by playing 12 O–O (rather than 12 B–N5) he maintains good attacking chances.

(18) 6 . . . NxN 7 QPxN, BxP 8 Q–N4, K–B1 (8 . . . O–O? loses the exchange to 9 B–R6, while 8 . . . P–KN3 causes a serious weakening of the black squares, of which White can take immediate advantage by 9 B–KN5) 9 B–B4, P–Q4 10 O–O–O, B–Q2 (10 . . . BxP is very risky because of 11 N–R3, but better defensive possibilities are offered by 10 . . . N–Q2 followed by . . . B–K2 and . . . N–B4; an alternative system worth trying is 10 . . . N–B3 followed by . . . N–K2) 11 B–Q3, B–K2 12 P–KR4 and White has excellent attacking prospects. See Game 11.

(19) 6 . . . P–Q3 7 NxN, PxN 8 BxP, P–QB3 (otherwise 9 Q–N3) 9 BxP†, KxB 10 BPxP, Q–K1! (10 . . . B–K3 11 N–R3±) 11 Q–B3†, K–N1 12 Q–K3, B–K3 13 N–K2, N–Q2; sharpest now is 14 P–Q4. For the less accurate 14 O–O, see Game 12.

*Alekhine's Defense Game 7*

*WHITE: Botvinnik* *BLACK: Flohr*

*Nottingham 1936*

| | WHITE | BLACK | | WHITE | BLACK |
|---|---|---|---|---|---|
| 1 | P–K4 | N–KB3 | 20 | P–B5 | N–Q4 |
| 2 | P–K5 | N–Q4 | 21 | N–B4 | RxR† |
| 3 | P–Q4 | P–Q3 | 22 | RxR | Q–R5 |
| 4 | N–KB3 | B–N5 | 23 | R–QB1 | P–R5! |
| 5 | B–K2 | P–QB3 | 24 | P–QN4 | P–R6 |
| 6 | O–O | BxN | 25 | P–N3 | R–Q1 |
| 7 | BxB | PxP | 26 | Q–B2 | QxQ |
| 8 | PxP | P–K3 | 27 | RxQ | K–Q2 |
| 9 | Q–K2 | Q–B2 | 28 | K–B2 | K–K3 |
| 10 | P–B4 | N–K2 | 29 | B–B1 | P–KN3 |
| 11 | B–N4 | N–Q2 | 30 | B–N2 | R–QR1 |
| 12 | P–B4 | P–KR4 | 31 | N–R5 | R–QN1 |
| 13 | B–R3 | O–O–O | 32 | K–B3 | B–Q1 |
| 14 | B–K3 | N–KB4 | 33 | N–N3 | K–Q2 |
| 15 | BxN | PxB | 34 | N–Q4 | R–R1 |
| 16 | Q–KB2 | Q–R4 | 35 | R–K2 | B–K2 |
| 17 | N–Q2 | N–N3 | 36 | N–N3 | B–B1 |
| 18 | P–QR3 | R–Q6 | 37 | N–Q4 | Draw |
| 19 | KR–Q1 | B–K2 | | | |

*Alekhine's Defense Game 8*

*WHITE: Unzicker* *BLACK: Schmid*

*Nuremberg 1959*

| | WHITE | BLACK | | WHITE | BLACK |
|---|---|---|---|---|---|
| 1 | P–K4 | N–KB3 | 13 | N–B3 | B–N5 |
| 2 | P–K5 | N–Q4 | 14 | B–Q2 | P–QR4 |
| 3 | P–Q4 | P–Q3 | 15 | P–QR3 | BxN |
| 4 | N–KB3 | B–N5 | 16 | BxB | O–O |
| 5 | B–K2 | P–QB3 | 17 | KR–Q1 | KR–Q1? |
| 6 | N–N5 | BxB | 18 | P–KN4! | N–K2 |
| 7 | QxB | PxP | 19 | R–Q6! | N–QB1 |
| 8 | PxP | P–K3 | 20 | R–Q2 | N–B4 |
| 9 | O–O | N–Q2 | 21 | R/1–Q1 | RxR |
| 10 | P–QB4 | N–K2 | 22 | QxR | N–K2? |
| 11 | N–QB3 | Q–B2 | 23 | BxP! | P–QN3 |
| 12 | R–K1 | N–KB4 | 24 | Q–Q6! | Resigns |

*Alekhine's Defense Game 9*

*WHITE: Witkowski* *BLACK: Mikenas*

*Riga 1959*

| | WHITE | BLACK | | WHITE | BLACK | | WHITE | BLACK |
|---|---|---|---|---|---|---|---|---|
| 1 | P–K4 | N–KB3 | 11 | BxB | B–B3 | 21 | QxN | NxP |
| 2 | P–K5 | N–Q4 | 12 | B–K3 | P–Q4 | 22 | QxN | BxQ |
| 3 | P–Q4 | P–Q3 | 13 | P–B5 | N–Q2 | 23 | NxB | QR–N1! |
| 4 | N–KB3 | B–N5 | 14 | N–R3 | O–O | 24 | R–R1 | Q–R6 |
| 5 | B–K2 | P–K3 | 15 | N–B2 | P–QN3 | 25 | B–B4 | R–N3 |
| 6 | O–O | N–QB3 | 16 | P–QN4 | PxP | 26 | KR–B1 | R–K1 |
| 7 | P–B4 | N–N3 | 17 | NPxP | Q–R4 | 27 | N–B6? | Q–R5 |
| 8 | PxP | PxP | 18 | Q–K1 | Q–R5 | 28 | N–K7† | RxN |
| 9 | P–QN3 | B–K2 | 19 | Q–B3 | KR–B1 | | Resigns | |
| 10 | P–KR3? | BxN | 20 | QR–N1 | NxBP | | | |

*Alekhine's Defense Game 10*

*WHITE: Aronin* *BLACK: Mikenas*

*Semi-finals, USSR Championship 1951*

| | WHITE | BLACK | | WHITE | BLACK |
|---|---|---|---|---|---|
| 1 | P–K4 | N–KB3 | 10 | P–Q5! | PxP |
| 2 | P–K5 | N–Q4 | 11 | PxP | BxN |
| 3 | P–Q4 | P–Q3 | 12 | PxB! | N/B–K4 |
| 4 | N–KB3 | B–N5 | 13 | N–N5 | Q–Q2 |
| 5 | B–K2 | P–K3 | 14 | P–B4 | N–R5 |
| 6 | O–O | N–QB3 | 15 | PxN! | Q–R6 |
| 7 | P–B4 | N/4–K2 | 16 | NxP† | K–Q1 |
| 8 | PxP | QxP | 17 | N–K6†! | Resigns |
| 9 | N–B3 | N–N3? | | | |

*Alekhine's Defense Game 11*

*WHITE: Ravinski* *BLACK: Friedstein*

| | WHITE | BLACK | | WHITE | BLACK |
|---|---|---|---|---|---|
| 1 | P–K4 | N–KB3 | 12 | P–KR4 | P–QB4 |
| 2 | P–K5 | N–Q4 | 13 | P–R5 | B–QR5 |
| 3 | P–QB4 | N–N3 | 14 | R–Q2 | P–B5 |
| 4 | P–B5 | N–Q4 | 15 | B–N1! | N–Q2 |
| 5 | B–B4 | P–K3 | 16 | R–R3 | P–B4 |
| 6 | N–QB3 | NxN | 17 | PxP e.p. | NxP |
| 7 | QPxN | BxP | 18 | Q–K2 | K–B2 |
| 8 | Q–N4 | K–B1 | 19 | N–B3 | N–Q2 |
| 9 | B–B4 | P–Q4 | 20 | B–N6†! | K–B1 |
| 10 | O–O–O | B–Q2 | 21 | QxKP | PxB |
| 11 | B–Q3 | B–K2 | 22 | PxP | Resigns |

*Alekhine's Defense Game 12*
*WHITE: Vasiukov* *BLACK: Spasski*
*USSR Championship 1959*

| WHITE | BLACK | WHITE | BLACK | WHITE | BLACK |
|---|---|---|---|---|---|
| 1 P–K4 | N–KB3 | 14 O–O | NxP! | 27 K–K3 | K–K3 |
| 2 P–K5 | N–Q4 | 15 QxN | B–B5 | 28 K–K4 | P–KN3 |
| 3 P–QB4 | N–N3 | 16 QxQ | RxQ | 29 P–QN4 | P–KR4 |
| 4 P–B5 | N–Q4 | 17 P–Q3! | B/5xQP | 30 P–N3 | K–B3 |
| 5 B–B4 | P–K3 | 18 R–Q1! | BxN! | 31 P–KR3 | K–K3 |
| 6 N–QB3 | P–Q3 | 19 P–Q7 | R–Q1 | 32 P–N4 | P–N3 |
| 7 NxN | PxN | 20 B–N5 | BxR | 33 K–Q4 | K–B3 |
| 8 BxP | P–QB3 | 21 RxB | B–K2! | 34 P–QR4 | K–K3 |
| 9 BxP† | KxB | 22 BxB | K–B2 | 35 K–K4 | K–Q3 |
| 10 BPxP | Q–K1 | 23 BxR | RxB | 36 P–R5 | K–K3 |
| 11 Q–B3† | K–N1 | 24 P–B4 | K–K2 | Draw | |
| 12 Q–K3 | B–K3 | 25 K–B2 | RxP | | |
| 13 N–K2 | N–Q2 | 26 RxR† | KxR | | |

PRACTICAL VARIATIONS 16–20:

1 P–K4, N–KB3 2 P–K5, N–Q4 3 P–QB4, N–N3 4 P–B5, N–Q4 5 B–B4, P–K3 6 N–QB3

| | *16* | *17* | *18* | *19* | *20* |
|---|---|---|---|---|---|
| *6* | — — | — — | — — | — — | — — |
| | NxN | — — | — — | — — | — — |
| 7 | QPxN | — — | — — | NPxP | — — |
| | N–B3 | — — | — — | BxP | P–Q4 |
| *8* | B–B4[1] | — — | — — | Q–N4! | BPxP e.p. |
| | BxP | — — | P–Q3 | K–B1 | PxP |
| *9* | Q–N4 | — — | BPxP | P–Q4 | PxP |
| | P–KN4! | — — | PxP | B–K2 | BxP |
| *10* | BxNP[2] | — — | N–B3[6] | P–KR4[7] | P–Q4 |
| | R–KN1[3] | — — | ± | = | O–O |
| *11* | N–R3 | — — | | | N–B3 |
| | B–K2 | — — | | | Q–B2! |
| *12* | P–B4 | BxB | | | Q–Q3! |
| | NxP | RxQ | | | N–Q2 |
| *13* | PxN | BxQ | | | O–O |
| | BxB | KxB | | | P–QN3 |
| *14* | Q–R5[4] | P–B4[5] | | | B–N3! |
| | = | = | | | B–N2[8] |
| | | | | | = |

*Notes to practical variations 16–20:*

[1] 8 P–B4 fails against 8 . . . NxP!, while 8 N–B3, BxP holds no prospects for White.

[2] 10 QxP, QxQ 11 BxQ, NxP 12 B–B6 is met by 12 . . . BxP†!

[3] 10 . . . NxP? is refuted by 11 Q–R5.

continued ▸

[4] Vasiukov–Korchnoi, Minsk 1953, continued with 14 . . . P–N4!? 15 QxP, R–B1 16 O–O, PxB 17 RxP, B–K6† 18 K–R1, RxR 19 Q–R8†, ending in perpetual check. In this line, however, 16 B–Q3, B–N2 17 B–K4 offers White excellent attacking chances — reason enough why Black does better to play 14 . . . P–KR3!, and if 15 O–O, simply 15 . . . R–N2. It is then even questionable if White has sufficient compensation for the Pawn, though his practical chances remain good enough.

[5] 14 . . . P–N3 15 B–K2, RxNP 16 B–B3, R–KN1 17 O–O–O, B–N2 18 N–N5! favors White (Kaufman–Santasiere, New Orleans 1954). After 14 . . . RxNP 15 O–O–O, however, Black may be safe enough.

[6] Best. The text is stronger than 10 PxP, which permits 10 . . . P–K4.

[7] White has good attacking chances. The column was introduced by Lasker in the course of a simultaneous exhibition given in 1923.

[8] 15 P–KR3, P–K4! with sharp play (Sergeant–Tartakover, Hastings 1945).

## SUPPLEMENTARY VARIATIONS 1–5:
### 1 P–K4, N–KB3 2 P–K5, N–Q4

Sup. Var. 1 and 2 deal with a pet variation of Canal's. Black faces few problems according to the theoreticians, but in practice his task is none too easy.

Sup. Var. 3 and 4 illustrate an old-fashioned line which, for all its innocent appearance, requires accurate defense.

Sup. Var. 5 is is without any danger for Black. White's early development of his King Bishop is less effective in this case than in Sup. Var. 1 and 2.

| | 1 | 2 | 3 | 4 | 5 |
|---|---|---|---|---|---|
| 3 | P–Q4 | – – | N–QB3 | – – | B–B4 |
| | P–Q3 | – – | NxN | – – | N–N3 |
| 4 | B–QB4 | – – | QPxN | NPxP | B–N3 |
| | N–N3[1] | – – | P–Q3[5] | P–Q3 | P–QB4 |
| 5 | B–N3 | – – | B–KB4[6] | P–KB4 | Q–K2 |
| | PxP[2] | – – | N–B3[7] | PxP | N–QB3 |
| 6 | Q–B3 | Q–R5! | N–B3 | PxP | N–KB3 |
| | P–K3 | P–K3 | B–N5[8] | B–B4[10] | P–Q4 |
| 7 | PxP | PxP | B–QN5! | Q–B3 | PxP e.p. |
| | N–B3 | P–B4 | P–QR3 | Q–B1 | P–K3 |
| 8 | Q–N3 | P–QB3 | B–R4 | N–K2 | N–B3 |
| | N–Q5! | N–B3 | P–K3 | P–K3[11] | BxP[13] |
| 9 | N–KB3 | Q–K2 | P–B4[9] | P–Q3 | = |
| | NxN† | B–K2 | ± | N–B3 | |
| 10 | QxN | N–B3[4] | | B–B4 | |
| | Q–Q5![3] | ± | | B–K2[12] | |
| | = | | | = | |

*Notes to supplementary variations 1–5:*

[1] The continuation 4 . . . P–K3 has been held in low esteem since Canal–Gruenfeld, Karlsbad 1929, which continued 5 N–KB3, B–K2 6 O–O, N–QB3 7 R–K1, O–O 8 N–B3, NxN 9 PxN, P–Q4 10 B–Q3, N–R4 11 N–Q2 with White for choice. But 9 . . . PxP gives Black a satisfactory game. The advantage of 4 . . . P–K3 is that it permits Black's Knight to maintain its centralized position.

[2] In combination with Black's preceding move, this is the usual continuation. In view of Canal's improvement (Sup. Var. 2), however, 5 . . . N–QB3 is preferable.

[3] The continuation 11 Q–N3, N–Q2 12 P–KB4, Q–K5† 13 B–K3, B–B4 leads to an end game fully satisfactory for Black (Goglidge–Mikenas, Tiflis 1945).

[4] See Game 13.

[5] Another good continuation is 4 . . . P–Q4, e.g., 5 N–KB3, P–QB4 6 B–KB4, N–B3 7 Q–Q2, B–N5 8 O–O–O, P–K3 (Yates–Capablanca, Moscow 1925). 5 P–QB4 is worth consideration.

[6] 5 PxP, QxP 6 QxQ, BPxQ, leads to an end game favoring Black (Maroczy–Euwe, Karlsbad 1929). Also satisfactory for Black is 5 N–KB3, PxP 6 QxQ†, KxQ 7 NxP, K–K1 8 B–QB4, P–K3 9 B–B4, B–Q3 (Tarrasch–Reti, Baden–Baden 1925).

[7] The alternative of 5 . . . PxP 6 QxQ†, KxQ 7 O–O–O† is uncomfortable for Black.

[8] 6 . . . PxP is now satisfactory.

[9] See Game 14.

[10] Tartakover's 6 . . . Q–Q4 favors White after 7 N–B3, N–B3 8 P–Q4, Q–K5† 9 K–B2! (not 9 B–K2, B–B4!), B–N5 10 B–Q3, Q–Q4 11 Q–K2, P–K3 12 B–K4, Q–Q2 13 R–QN1 (Mattison–Gruenfeld, Karlsbad 1929).

[11] 8 . . . BxP is risky because of 9 N–Q4, B–N3 10 P–K6.

[12] White has a freer game, though hardly significant.

[13] Black has an easy game.

---

## part 5—SCANDINAVIAN VARIATION

### OBSERVATIONS ON KEY POSITION 5

1 P–K4, N–KB3
2 N–QB3[A], P–Q4

KEY POSITION 5

[A] 2 P–Q3, P–K4 3 P–KB4, N–B3 4 N–KB3, P–Q4 5 PxQP, NxP 6 PxP, B–N5 7 B–K2, BxN 8 BxB, Q–R5† 9 P–N3, Q–Q5 10 Q–K2, O–O–O 11 P–B3, QxKP=. In this line 9 K–B1?, O–O–O 10 N–B3, B–B4 11 N–K4, N–K6† strongly favors Black (Maroczy–Alekhine, New York 1924). 2 B–B4 is met by 2 . . . NxP, when 3 BxP†, KxB 4 Q–R5†, K–N1 5 Q–Q5†, P–K3 6 QxN, P–Q4 7 Q–K2, P–B4 gives Black the edge.

White has the choice between 3 PxP and 3 P–K5.

After 3 PxP, NxP 4 B–B4, Black has several ways to achieve equality. Curiously, only the continuation 4 . . . N–N3 5 B–N3, P–B4, strongly recommended by theory, has its drawbacks (see Idea Var. 20).

Better chances for initiative are offered White by 3 P–K5, to meet 3 . . . KN–Q2 by Spielmann's sacrifice 4

P–K6. In thus hampering the development of the enemy pieces, White obtains chances for attack. The variations of this gambit have been but partially investigated to this day.

IDEA VARIATIONS 20 AND 21:

(20) 3 PxP, NxP 4 B–B4, N–N3 5 B–N3, P–QB4 (this is the usual continuation, but the weakest! Black, proceeding logically, may encounter insurmountable difficulties. 5 . . . P–QB4 is a loss of time since 6 . . . P–B5 is not a genuine threat. Correct is 5 . . . N–B3!, which offers Black an easy game) 6 Q–R5!, P–K3 (6 . . . P–B5? 7 BxP, NxB 8 Q–N5†±) 7 P–Q3, N–B3 8 N–B3, B–K2 (better is 8 . . . P–N3 followed by 9 . . . B–N2) 9 N–N5!, BxN (for 9 . . . P–N3, see Game 15) 10 BxB, Q–B2 11 B–K3!± (Van den Bosch–De Jong, Baarn 1941).

(21) 3 P–K5, KN–Q2 4 P–K6!?, PxP 5 P–Q4, P–B4 6 N–B3, N–QB3 7 PxP, P–KN3 8 P–KR4, B–N2 (Black must prevent 9 P–R5 by playing 8 . . . N–B3! Pachman then gives 9 B–QN5, B–Q2 10 B–K3, B–N2, assessing the chances as about even. Meriting further scrutiny is the sharp continuation 10 P–R5!?, PxP! 11 N–N5. In this latter line 10 . . . NxP is bad because of 11 RxN, PxR 12 BxN, BxB 13 N–K5±) 9 P–R5, Q–R4 10 B–Q2, QxBP 11 PxP, PxP 12 RxR†, BxR 13 N–KR4! with White for choice (see Game 16).

PRACTICAL VARIATIONS 21-25:

1 P–K4, N–KB3 2 N–QB3, P–Q4

| | 21 | 22 | 23 | 24 | 25 |
|---|---|---|---|---|---|
| 3 | PxP | – – | P–K5 | – – | – – |
| | NxP | – – | KN–Q2[5] | – – | – – |
| 4 | B–B4 | – – | P–Q4[6] | P–B4 | P–K6!? |
| | P–K3 | P–QB3[3] | P–QB4[7] | P–K3 | PxP |
| 5 | N–B3[1] | Q–B3 | B–QN5[8] | N–B3[11] | P–Q4 |
| | NxN | B–K3 | N–QB3 | P–QB4 | P–K4!? |
| 6 | NPxN | KN–K2 | N–B3 | P–KN3 | NxP[13] |
| | B–K2 | N–B2 | P–QR3[9] | N–QB3 | PxP |
| 7 | O–O | B–N3 | BxN | B–N2 | B–QB4[14] |
| | N–Q2 | N–Q2 | PxB | B–K2 | P–K4 |
| 8 | P–Q4 | P–Q4 | P–K6! | O–O | B–Q3 |
| | O–O | P–KN3[4] | PxP | O–O | B–Q3 |
| 9 | Q–K2 | = | O–O[10] | P–Q3[12] | Q–R5† |
| | P–QB4[2] | | = | ∓ | K–B1 |
| 10 | = | | | | B–KN5 |
| | | | | | Q–K1[15] |
| | | | | | ∓ |

*Notes to practical variations 21–25:*

[1] 5 Q–B3 causes Black no difficulty after 5 . . . N–N5 6 B–N3, P–QB4 followed by . . . N/5–B3–Q5 or . . . N/1–B3–Q5. Nor does 5 Q–N4, N–KB3 6 Q–N3 hold any terror for Black, e.g., 6 . . . B–B4! 7 QxNP, R–N1 8 Q–R6, BxP† !

[2] Wolf–Gruenfeld, Carlsbad 1923.

[3] Another continuation sufficient for equality is 4 . . . NxN 5 Q–B3, P–K3 6 QxN, Q–B3.

[4] Spielmann–Sacconi, Meran 1928.

[5] Unusual is 3 . . . P–Q5, when 4 QN–K2, N–N5 as well as 4 PxN, PxN 5 PxNP, PxP† 6 QxP, QxQ† yields Black equality. But White may play 6 BxP, BxP 7 Q–R5! with fair prospects.

[6] 4 NxP, NxP 5 N–K3, P–QB4 6 N–B3, NxN† 7 QxN, N–B3 8 B–N5, B–Q2 is comfortable for Black.

[7] 4 . . . P–K3 transposes into the Steinitz Variation of the French Defense.

[8] 5 NxP is met by 5 . . . P–K3!, e.g., 6 N–B4, PxP 7 N–B3, NxP!

[9] 6 . . . P–K3 is safer.

[10] White has good attacking chances in return for the Pawn (Bogoljubov–Alekhine, Carlsbad 1923).

[11] 5 P–Q4 again transposes into the French.

[12] Nimzowitsch–Alekhine, Semmering 1926. Black proceeded with 9 . . . N–N3, but should have played 9 . . . P–B3! instead. After 10 PxP, BxP Black stands well.

[13] 6 PxP!, P–K3 7 B–Q3 is promising for White.

[14] Here, too, 7 B–Q3 offers attacking chances. Faulty, however, is 7 QxP? because of 7 . . . N–N3.

[15] Bronstein–Mikenas, Baku 1944.

### *Alekhine's Defense Game 13*

*WHITE: Canal* *BLACK: Perez*

*Madrid 1951*

| | WHITE | BLACK | | WHITE | BLACK |
|---|---|---|---|---|---|
| 1 | P–K4 | N–KB3 | 16 | N–K4 | N–N3 |
| 2 | P–K5 | N–Q4 | 17 | RxR† | NxR |
| 3 | P–Q4 | P–Q3 | 18 | B–N3 | B–N2 |
| 4 | B–QB4 | N–N3 | 19 | R–Q1 | N–B3 |
| 5 | B–N3 | PxP | 20 | N–B6†! | PxN |
| 6 | Q–R5! | P–K3 | 21 | PxP | N–B5 |
| 7 | PxP | P–QB4 | 22 | Q–Q2 | BxP |
| 8 | P–QB3 | N–B3 | 23 | BxN | N–K4 |
| 9 | Q–K2 | B–K2 | 24 | NxN | BxN |
| 10 | N–B3 | Q–B2 | 25 | B–N3! | BxB |
| 11 | O–O | N–Q2 | 26 | Q–N5† | K–R1 |
| 12 | R–K1 | O–O | 27 | Q–B6† | K–N1 |
| 13 | B–KB4 | R–Q1 | 28 | RPxB | B–K5 |
| 14 | QN–Q2 | N–B1 | 29 | BxP! | Resigns |
| 15 | QR–Q1 | P–QN3 | | | |

*Alekhine's Defense Game 14*

*WHITE: Kamenetski* *BLACK: Breitman*

*Minsk 1954*

| | WHITE | BLACK | | WHITE | BLACK |
|---|---|---|---|---|---|
| 1 | P–K4 | N–KB3 | 22 | P–QN4 | P–KB4 |
| 2 | P–K5 | N–Q4 | 23 | P–QR4 | P–B5 |
| 3 | N–QB3 | NxN | 24 | B–Q2 | P–K5 |
| 4 | QPxN | P–Q3 | 25 | B–K2 | B–B3 |
| 5 | B–KB4 | N–B3 | 26 | K–Q1 | P–B6 |
| 6 | N–B3 | B–N5 | 27 | PxP | PxP |
| 7 | B–QN5 | P–QR3 | 28 | BxP | RxP |
| 8 | B–R4 | P–K3 | 29 | P–R5 | R/3–R1 |
| 9 | P–B4 | B–K2 | 30 | B–K4 | B–K4 |
| 10 | P–KR3 | BxN | 31 | K–B2 | B–B5 |
| 11 | QxB | Q–Q2 | 32 | B–K1 | P–N5 |
| 12 | R–Q1 | R–Q1 | 33 | P–B4 | QR–Q1 |
| 13 | Q–N3 | P–KN4 | 34 | B–QB3 | KR–B1 |
| 14 | B–K3 | P–N4 | 35 | P–N5 | P–B4 |
| 15 | PxP | NxP | 36 | P–N6† | K–Q3 |
| 16 | QxN! | PxQ | 37 | R–Q1† | K–K2 |
| 17 | RxQ | KxR | 38 | RxR | RxR |
| 18 | PxP† | P–B3 | 39 | P–R6 | P–N6 |
| 19 | B–N3 | K–B2 | 40 | PxP | BxP |
| 20 | B–QB4 | P–R4 | 41 | P–R7 | Resigns |
| 21 | P–QB3 | R–R1 | | | |

*Alekhine's Defense Game 15*

*WHITE: Visser* *BLACK: Spanjaard*

*Utrecht 1948*

| | WHITE | BLACK | | WHITE | BLACK |
|---|---|---|---|---|---|
| 1 | P–K4 | N–KB3 | 10 | Q–R6 | B–B1 |
| 2 | N–QB3 | P–Q4 | 11 | Q–R3 | B–N2 |
| 3 | PxP | NxP | 12 | N/5–K4 | N–Q4 |
| 4 | B–B4 | N–N3 | 13 | B–R6! | P–K4 |
| 5 | B–N3 | P–QB4 | 14 | BxB! | BxQ |
| 6 | Q–R5 | P–K3 | 15 | NxN | Q–R4† |
| 7 | P–Q3 | N–B3 | 16 | K–B1 | O–O–O |
| 8 | N–B3 | B–K2 | 17 | BxR | RxB |
| 9 | N–KB5 | P–N3 | 18 | PxB and White soon won. | |

*Alekhine's Defense Game 16*

*WHITE: E. Steiner* *BLACK: Hansen*

*Munich 1936*

| | WHITE | BLACK | | WHITE | BLACK |
|---|---|---|---|---|---|
| 1 | P–K4 | N–KB3 | 15 | B–Q3 | N/B–K4 |
| 2 | N–QB3 | P–Q4 | 16 | BxN† | NxB |
| 3 | P–K5 | KN–Q2 | 17 | Q–R5 | K–B2 |
| 4 | P–K6 | PxP | 18 | N–K4 | QxP |
| 5 | P–Q4 | P–B4 | 19 | Q–R7† | B–N2 |
| 6 | N–B3 | N–QB3 | 20 | N–N5† | K–B1 |
| 7 | PxP | P–KN3 | 21 | R–B1 | Q–KB4 |
| 8 | P–KR4 | B–N2 | 22 | P–KN4! | Q–K4† |
| 9 | P–R5 | Q–R4 | 23 | K–B1 | N–B5? |
| 10 | B–Q2 | QxBP | 24 | BxN | Q–B3 |
| 11 | PxP | PxP | 25 | Q–R5 | K–N1 |
| 12 | RxR† | BxR | 26 | B–K5! | QxB |
| 13 | N–KR4 | N–B1 | 27 | Q–B7† | K–R1 |
| 14 | NxNP! | NxN | 28 | Q–K8† | Resigns |

# chapter 15—Center Counter Game

The Center Counter Game, 1 P–K4, P–Q4, is one of the oldest openings. It is also known as the Scandinavian Defense because it was Scandinavian analysts, particularly Collijn, who succeeded in pointing out that the tempo White wins after 2 PxP, QxP 3 N–QB3 has less significance than was formerly assumed. Among masters, Mieses frequently adopted this defense and contributed greatly to its theory.

According to present opinion, however, the Center Counter does not fully comply with the requirements of sound opening strategy. White's advance in development is small, indeed, but it still offers him an initiative.

In recent years Russian masters have tried to rehabilitate the Marshall Gambit (1 P–K4, P–Q4 2 PxP, N–KB3!?). White then cannot comfortably maintain the extra Pawn. He is better off proceeding positionally. It is far from easy, though, for White to obtain an opening advantage after 2 . . . N–KB3 3 P–Q4, NxP.

The two forms of the Center Counter Game are treated separately in Parts 1 and 2.

---

1 P–K4, P–Q4
2 PxP, QxP
3 N–QB3, Q–QR4[A]
4 P–Q4

KEY POSITION 1

## part 1—ANDERSSEN VARIATION

### OBSERVATIONS ON KEY POSITION 1

[A] Obsolete is 3 . . . Q–Q1. For example: 4 P–Q4, N–KB3 5 B–QB4, P–K3 6 N–B3, B–K2 7 O–O, O–O 8 Q–K2, QN–Q2 9 R–K1, N–N3 10 B–N3, and White has the edge (Alekhine–Schlechter, Carlsbad 1911). Or 4 P–Q4, N–KB3 5 B–QB4, B–N5? 6 P–B3, B–B1 (if 6 . . . B–B4 7 P–KN4, B–N3 8 KN–K2) 7 B–N5, P–K3 8 P–B4!, QN–Q2 9 N–B3, N–N3 10 B–N3, P–QR4 11 P–QR4, B–K2 12 O–O, O–O 13 Q–K2, P–B3 14 QR–Q1, QN–Q4 15 N–K5, and White has a fine attacking position (Fuderer–Bronstein, Yugoslavia vs. USSR, Kiev 1959).

After 4 P–Q4, Black has a choice of two systems: 4 . . . P–K4 (Anderssen) or 4 . . . N–KB3 (Mieses).

The first method is an attempt to restore the balance in the center without delay; but the opening of lines only increases the small advance in development which White originally has, provided he does not try to refute 4 . . . P–K4 with 5 Q–R5?.

The second method keeps the position closed, but concedes superiority to White in the center. Consequently, Black must proceed eventually with QB–N5, and in order not to lose any tempos exchanges this Bishop for the Knight. This routine concedes to White not only a slight superiority in space, but also the pair of Bishops.

IDEA VARIATIONS 1–3:

(1) 4 . . . P–K4 5 Q–R5?, N–QB3 6 B–QN5, B–Q2 7 BxN, BxB 8 P–Q5, B–N5! 9 PxB, BxN† 10 K–B1, B–Q5 11 N–K2, N–B3 12 PxP, R–Q1 and Black has excellent attacking chances.

(2) 4 . . . P–K4 5 PxP (another continuation is 5 N–B3; see Prac. Var. 1–3), B–QN5 (the "book" move). Known examples of this variation proceed with 6 B–Q2, N–QB3 7 N–B3, B–N5 8 P–QR3, and now Black obtains good chances with 8 . . . N–Q5! Wherefore White on his 7th turn should have played 7 P–QR3!, in which case 7 . . . N–Q5 fails against 8 KN–K2, or 7 . . . QxP† 8 B–K2! Preferable to 5 . . . B–QN5 is 5 . . . QxP†, although the continuation is slightly in White's favor: 6 Q–K2 (if 6 B–K2, then 6 . . . B–QN5), QxQ† 7 BxQ, B–QN5 8 B–Q2, N–KB3 9 O–O–O.

(3) 4 . . . N–KB3 5 N–B3, B–N5 6 P–KR3! (the text is Lasker's idea; or 6 B–K2, N–B3 7 B–K3, O–O–O 8 N–Q2, BxB 9 QxB, which nets nothing as Black continues 9 . . . Q–KB4, to be followed eventually by . . . P–K4), B–R4 (Black's best is 6 . . . BxN; see Prac. Var. 4 and 5) 7 P–KN4, B–N3 8 N–K5, P–B3 9 N–B4, Q–B2? 10 Q–B3!, BxP? 11 B–B4, Q–Q1 12 Q–K2, B–N3 13 N–Q6† and wins (Horowitz–Kibberman, Warsaw 1935). Also good in the line above is 9 P–KR4, QN–Q2 (if 9 . . . N–K5, then 10 B–Q2) 10 N–B4, Q–B2 11 P–R5, B–K5 12 NxB, NxN 13 Q–B3 to be followed by 14 B–B4.

PRACTICAL VARIATIONS 1–5:

1 P–K4, P–Q4 2 PxP, QxP 3 N–QB3, Q–QR4 4 P–Q4

| | *1* | *2* | *3* | *4* | *5* |
|---|---|---|---|---|---|
| *4* | – – | – – | – – | – – | – – |
| | P–K4 | – – | – – | N–KB3 | – – |
| *5* | N–B3 | – – | – – | N–B3 | – – |
| | B–KN5 | – – | B–QN5 | B–N5[12] | – – |
| *6* | B–K2 | B–N5†[6] | B–Q2 | P–KR3! | – – |
| | N–QB3![1] | P–QB3 | B–KN5 | BxN | – – |
| *7* | NxP[2] | B–K2 | B–K2 | QxB | – – |
| | BxB | B–N5 | PxP[10] | P–B3 | – – |
| *8* | QxB[3] | O–O | NxP | B–Q2 | B–QB4 |
| | NxP | BxKN[7] | Q–K4 | QN–Q2 | P–K3 |
| *9* | Q–K4 | BxB | N/3–N5! | O–O–O | O–O |
| | NxP† | N–K2[8] | BxB | P–K3 | QN–Q2 |
| *10* | K–Q1 | PxP | QxB | B–QB4 | B–B4 |
| | N–B3 | O–O | BxB† | Q–B2 | B–K2 |
| *11* | QxNP[4] | B–Q2 | KxB | KR–K1[13] | KR–K1[14] |
| | R–Q1† | QxKP | QxQ† | ± | ± |
| *12* | KxN | R–K1[9] | KxQ[11] | | |
| | QxN[5] | ± | ± | | |
| | = | | | | |

*Notes to practical variations 1–5:*

[1] 6 . . . B–QN5, B–Q2 leads to Prac. Var. 3.

[2] 7 O–O is answered by 7 . . . O–O–O 8 NxP, BxB 9 NxN, BxQ 10 NxQ, BxP.

[3] 8 NxN? loses a piece by 8 . . . QxN†.

[4] Or 11 QxN?, QxN 12 R–K1, and Black favorably escapes with 12 . . . O–O–O†.

[5] White has nothing better than perpetual check by 13 Q–B6†, R–Q2 14 Q–R8†, R–Q1 etc. (analysis by Collijn).

[6] A finesse designed to cancel out . . . N–QB3.

[7] Or 8 . . . BxQN 9 PxB, QxP 10 NxP±.

[8] Instead 9 . . . BxN 10 PxB, QxP 11 R–N1 offers White fine compensation for the Pawn.

[9] A correspondence game Lyskov–Persitz, 1955, continued 12 . . . Q–B2 13 N–N5!, PxN 14 BxB, R–K1 15 RxN, RxR 16 BxR, QxB 17 BxP!, Resigns.

[10] Or 7 . . . N–QB3 8 P–QR3!

[11] White has the superior development. See Game 1.

[12] If 5 . . . B–B4 6 N–K5! On 5 . . . N–B3 6 B–QN5!

[13] Rubinstein–Bernstein, San Sebastian 1911.

[14] White has the pair of Bishops and superiority in space. See Game 2.

### Center Counter Game 1

*WHITE: Tarrasch* *BLACK: Mieses*

*Göteborg 1920*

| | WHITE | BLACK | | WHITE | BLACK | | WHITE | BLACK |
|---|---|---|---|---|---|---|---|---|
| 1 | P–K4 | P–Q4 | 15 | N/7–B6† | PxN | 29 | P–R5 | K–Q2 |
| 2 | PxP | QxP | 16 | NxP† | K–B1 | 30 | P–R6 | N–Q4 |
| 3 | N–QB3 | Q–QR4 | 17 | NxR | KxN | 31 | R–QR1 | N–R2 |
| 4 | P–Q4 | P–K4 | 18 | QR–Q1† | K–K1 | 32 | P–N3 | P–B3 |
| 5 | N–B3 | B–QN5 | 19 | K–Q3† | N–K2 | 33 | R–R4 | N–N3 |
| 6 | B–Q2 | B–N5 | 20 | K–B4 | P–R4 | 34 | R–R5 | P–N3 |
| 7 | B–K2 | PxP | 21 | R–Q3 | N–N1 | 35 | P–B4 | N/3–B1 |
| 8 | NxP | Q–K4 | 22 | R/3–K3 | N–B3 | 36 | R–R1 | N–Q3 |
| 9 | N/3–N5! | BxB | 23 | P–QN4 | P–B3 | 37 | K–Q4 | N/3–B1 |
| 10 | QxB | BxB† | 24 | P–B4 | K–B2 | 38 | K–B5 | K–B2 |
| 11 | KxB | QxQ† | 25 | P–QR4 | R–QN1 | 39 | R–K1 | N–N3 |
| 12 | KxQ | N–QR3 | 26 | P–B3 | R–Q1 | 40 | R–K7† | N–Q2† |
| 13 | KR–K1 | O–O–O | 27 | R–Q3 | RxR | 41 | RxN†! | Resigns |
| 14 | NxP† | K–N1 | 28 | KxR | K–K1 | | | |

### Center Counter Game 2

*WHITE: Botvinnik* *BLACK: Konstantinopolski*

*USSR Championship 1952*

| | WHITE | BLACK | | WHITE | BLACK | | WHITE | BLACK |
|---|---|---|---|---|---|---|---|---|
| 1 | P–K4 | P–Q4 | 19 | QxB | R–Q2 | 37 | B–Q3 | PxP |
| 2 | PxP | QxP | 20 | P–QB3 | Q–B2 | 38 | QxP† | K–B1 |
| 3 | N–QB3 | Q–QR4 | 21 | Q–N5 | Q–Q1 | 39 | Q–B8† | K–N2 |
| 4 | N–B3 | N–KB3 | 22 | Q–R5 | Q–B3 | 40 | Q–N4† | K–B1 |
| 5 | P–Q4 | B–N5 | 23 | P–QR4 | P–QN3 | 41 | Q–N4† | K–N1 |
| 6 | P–KR3 | BxN | 24 | R/1–K1 | R/1–Q1 | 42 | K–N2 | P–KR4 |
| 7 | QxB | P–B3 | 25 | P–B4 | R–N2 | 43 | P–R4 | Q–B3† |
| 8 | B–QB4 | P–K3 | 26 | Q–B3 | R–B2 | 44 | Q–K4 | Q–B3 |
| 9 | O–O | QN–Q2 | 27 | P–N4 | P–N3 | 45 | K–N3 | K–B1 |
| 10 | B–B4 | B–K2 | 28 | R–K5 | K–N2 | 46 | Q–N4† | K–N2 |
| 11 | KR–K1 | O–O | 29 | Q–N3 | P–B4 | 47 | B–B2 | P–R3 |
| 12 | P–QR3 | KR–K1 | 30 | NPxP | PxP | 48 | Q–B5 | Q–B8 |
| 13 | B–KN3 | Q–N3 | 31 | P–B5? | KPxP | 49 | QxP† | |
| 14 | Q–Q3 | QR–Q1 | 32 | RxKBP | PxR | | and White won. | |
| 15 | P–N4 | N–B1 | 33 | QxR | PxQP? | | | |
| 16 | QR–Q1 | B–Q3 | 34 | R–K7! | R–Q2 | | | |
| 17 | N–K4 | NxN | 35 | RxR | NxR | | | |
| 18 | RxN | BxB | 36 | QxN | PxBP | | | |

## part 2—MARSHALL GAMBIT

1 P–K4, P–Q4
2 PxP, N–KB3

KEY POSITION 2

OBSERVATIONS ON KEY POSITION 2

The continuation 2 . . . N–KB3 is today considered more promising than 2 . . . QxP. Black intends to recapture the Pawn with his Knight, thereby avoiding the loss of a tempo. True, the Pawn can now be held with 3 P–QB4, but this leads to a gambit which offers Black good chances. Nor is the temporary maintenance of the Pawn by 3 B–N5† so effective as was formerly thought. Best is 3 P–Q4. Then, after 3 . . . NxP 4 P–QB4 with some advantage in space for White.

All in all, Black has fair chances for equality; he must fianchetto his King Bishop so as to exercise pressure on his Q5.

IDEA VARIATIONS 4–6:

(4) 3 P–QB4, P–B3 4 PxP (4 P–Q4, PxP 5 N–QB3 transposes into the Panov Attack of the Caro-Kann), NxP 5 P–Q3, P–K4 6 N–QB3, B–KB4 7 N–B3, Q–Q2 8 B–K2, R–Q1 9 O–O, BxP 10 BxB, QxB 11 Q–R4. Although White has returned the Gambit Pawn, Lasker holds that he has a good game. According to Mieses, however, Black can improve on the above line by playing 6 . . . B–QB4 7 B–K3, BxB 8 PxB, Q–N3 9 Q–Q2, B–K3 10 P–K4, N–KN5! with the possibility of . . . N–K6 and . . . P–B4. Lasker had considered only 10 . . . R–Q1, which is met effectively by 11 N–Q5!

(5) 3 B–N5†, B–Q2 4 B–B4, B–N5 5 P–KB3, B–B4 6 N–K2 (probably 6 N–QB3 is a little better; see Prac. Var. 6), NxP 7 N–N3, B–N3 8 O–O, P–K3 9 P–KB4. This position is supposed to favor White; it stems from Mieses–Marshall, Carlsbad 1907, which continued 9 . . . N–N3 10 B–N3, B–B4† 11 K–R1, O–O 12 N–B3, N–B3 13 QN–K4. In Bergraser–Lothar Schmidt, 1955, Black found a sharper line to counter the potential P–KB5. Thus, Black varied with 9 . . . N–QB3 10 P–Q4 (or 10 P–KB5, PxP 11 NxP, BxP 12 RxB, B–B4† 13 K–R1, QN–K2, followed by 14 . . . O–O), N/3–K2 11 B–N3, P–KR4 12 Q–K2, P–R5 13 N–K4, BxN 14 QxB and obtained even chances.

(6) 3 P–Q4, NxP 4 P–QB4, N–N3 5 N–KB3, P–KN3 6 N–B3, B–N2 7 P–KR3, O–O 8 B–K2, N–B3 9 B–K3, P–K4 10 P–Q5, N–K2 with even chances. See Game 3.

PRACTICAL VARIATIONS 6–10:

1 P–K4, P–Q4 2 PxP, N–KB3

| | 6 | 7 | 8 | 9 | 10 |
|---|---|---|---|---|---|
| 3 | B–N5† | – – | P–Q4 | – – | – – |
| | B–Q2 | – – | NxP | – – | – – |
| 4 | B–B4 | B–K2 | P–QB4 | – – | N–KB3 |
| | B–N5 | NxP | N–N3 | N–KB3[6] | P–KN3 |
| 5 | P–KB3 | P–Q4 | N–KB3 | N–KB3 | B–K2 |
| | B–B4 | P–KN3 | P–KN3 | P–B3 | B–N2 |
| 6 | N–QB3 | P–QB4 | B–K2 | N–B3 | O–O |
| | QN–Q2 | N–N3 | B–N2 | B–N5 | O–O |
| 7 | N–K2[1] | N–QB3 | O–O | B–K3 | R–K1 |
| | N–N3 | B–N2 | O–O | P–K3 | N–N3[9] |
| 8 | B–N3 | P–B5 | B–K3 | Q–N3[7] | P–B3 |
| | QNxP | N–B1 | B–N5 | Q–N3 | N–B3 |
| 9 | NxN | P–Q5[3] | QN–Q2 | N–K5 | B–KB4 |
| | NxN | P–B3 | N–Q2 | QxQ | N–Q4 |
| 10 | N–N3 | Q–N3 | P–KR3 | PxQ | B–N3 |
| | B–N3 | P–N3 | BxN | QN–Q2 | P–QR3 |
| 11 | O–O | B–B3 | BxB | B–Q3 | QN–Q2 |
| | P–K3 | O–O[4] | R–N1 | NxN | B–B4 |
| 12 | P–KB4[2] | = | P–B5 | PxN | N–B1[10] |
| | ± | | N–B1[5] | N–Q2[8] | ± |
| | | | = | = | |

*Notes to practical variations 6–10:*

[1] Or 7 Q–K2, N–N3 8 B–N3, Q–Q2! 9 P–Q3, QNxP with even chances (Bogatirtschuk–Torre, Moscow 1925).

[2] The potential P–B5 rules in White's favor.

[3] Safer is 9 B–KB4, O–O 10 B–B3, N–B3 11 KN–K2, P–K4 with equality (Sultin–Lustikov, USSR Championship 1960).

[4] In this sharp position Black's chances are adequate. See Game 4.

[5] 13 N–B4, P–K3 14 Q–N3, N–K2 with even chances (Matanovic–Bronstein, Olympiad, Munich 1958).

[6] Or 4 . . . N–N5?, the so-called Kiel Variation, which offers Black chances only in case of 5 Q–R4†? (5 P–QR3±) QN–B3 6 P–Q5?, P–QN4!

[7] 8 B–K2 offers better chances for the initiative.

[8] 13 P–B4, B–QB4 14 K–B2, P–B3 with equality (Reti–Tartakover, Match 1920).

[9] 7 . . . N–QB3 is better, although after 8 P–B3, Black must abstain from 8 . . . P–K4 because of 9 PxP, NxP? 10 NxN, BxN 11 B–B3 winning a piece. After 8 . . . R–K1, Black's . . . P–K4 is still prevented by 9 B–QN5.

[10] See Game 5.

*Center Counter Game 3*

*WHITE: Tal* *BLACK: Gurgenidze*

*Club Competition 1959*

| | | | WHITE | BLACK | | WHITE | BLACK |
|---|---|---|---|---|---|---|---|
| 1 | P–K4 | P–Q4 | 9 | B–K3 | P–K4 | 17 PxP | RxR |
| 2 | PxP | N–KB3 | 10 | P–Q5 | N–K2 | 18 RxR | P–K5 |
| 3 | P–Q4 | NxP | 11 | O–O | P–KR3 | 19 N–Q4 | Q–R5 |
| 4 | P–QB4 | N–N3 | 12 | Q–Q2 | N–B4 | 20 P–B6 | PxP |
| 5 | N–KB3 | P–N3 | 13 | P–B5 | NxB | 21 PxP | N–K4 |
| 6 | N–B3 | B–N2 | 14 | PxN/3 | N–Q2 | 22 R–KB1 | BxP |
| 7 | P–KR3 | O–O | 15 | P–QN4 | P–QR4 | 23 PxB | Draw |
| 8 | B–K2 | N–B3 | 16 | P–R3 | PxP | | |

*Center Counter Game 4*

*WHITE: Bronstein* *BLACK: Lutikov*

*USSR Championship 1960*

| WHITE | BLACK | WHITE | BLACK | WHITE | BLACK |
|---|---|---|---|---|---|
| 1 P–K4 | P–Q4 | 11 B–B3 | O–O | 21 NxP | PxP |
| 2 PxP | N–KB3 | 12 B–K3 | PxQP | 22 B–R6 | P–B5 |
| 3 B–N5† | B–Q2 | 13 BxP | N–B3 | 23 QxQ | R/1xQ |
| 4 B–K2 | NxP | 14 R–Q1 | Q–B2 | 24 NxR | RxN |
| 5 P–Q4 | P–KN3 | 15 N–N5 | Q–N2 | 25 RxN | BxP |
| 6 P–QB4 | N–N3 | 16 N–Q4 | R–N1? | 26 R–N1 | B–N2 |
| 7 N–QB3 | B–N2 | 17 N/1–B3 | P–K4? | 27 RxB† | RxR |
| 8 P–B5 | N–B1 | 18 BxP† | RxB | 28 BxR | KxB |
| 9 P–Q5 | P–QB3 | 19 NxN | BxN | 29 R–N5 | Resigns |
| 10 Q–N3 | P–N3 | 20 R–Q8† | B–B1 | | |

*Center Counter Game 5*

*WHITE: Rabar* *BLACK: Milic*

*Yugoslavian Championship 1954*

| WHITE | BLACK | WHITE | BLACK | | |
|---|---|---|---|---|---|
| 1 P–K4 | P–Q4 | 7 R–K1 | N–N3 | 13 B–QB4 | B–K3 |
| 2 PxP | N–KB3 | 8 P–B3 | N–B3 | 14 Q–K2! | P–QN4? |
| 3 P–Q4 | NxP | 9 B–KB4 | N–Q4 | 15 B–N3 | R–K1 |
| 4 N–KB3 | P–KN3 | 10 B–N3 | P–QR3 | 16 Q–K4 | N–R4 |
| 5 B–K2 | B–N2 | 11 QN–Q2 | B–B4 | 17 Q–R4! | K–N2 |
| 6 O–O | O–O | 12 N–B1 | B–R3? | 18 RxB! and White won. | |

# chapter 16 – Caro-Kann Defense

Polerio mentioned 1 . . . P–QB3 in response to 1 P–K4 as far back as 1590. The opening owes its name, however, to M. Kann, a Viennese, who introduced it about 1880, and to H. Caro, a Berlin chessmaster, who shortly thereafter recommended it very highly.

Close to a half century passed before the Caro-Kann gained a measure of respectable recognition. The defense achieved its peak popularity in the 1920's when Capablanca, Nimzowitsch, and Tartakover were its chief exponents. In the 1930's the Caro-Kann found favor with Flohr, who was almost its sole advocate until the late 1950's. Today the defense is experiencing a remarkable revival. Led by Botvinnik and his countryman Petrosian, chessplayers around the globe are once again placing their faith in the Caro–Kann, probably the most solid of Black's defenses.

The Caro–Kann, though similar to the French Defense in its fundamental idea of challenging White's command of the center with 2 . . . P–Q4, has the advantage of allowing Black to develop his Queen Bishop. As in the Sicilian Defense, Black hopes to create an imbalance in the center and thus avoid the drawing possibilities which are implicit in symmetrical positions. White, on the other hand, maintains freedom of action in the center, and Black must guard constantly against bold strokes.

It follows that unless Black is completely sure of his ground, the Caro–Kann can bring more than the usual share of problems which normally confront the chessplayer.

---

## part 1—CLASSICAL VARIATION

### OBSERVATIONS ON KEY POSITION 1

A 2 P–Q3, P–Q4 3 N–Q2, P–K4 4 KN–B3, N–Q2 5 P–Q4, PxKP 6 QNxP, PxP 7 QxP (Tal–Smyslov, Bled 1959). Better in this variation is 3 . . . P–KN3, e.g., 4 P–KN3, B–N2 5 B–N2, P–K4 6 N–K2, N–B3 (Alexander–Bouwmeester, Cheltenham 1959).

B Alternatives are weak: 3 . . . N–B3 4 P–K5, KN–Q2 5 P–K6!, PxP 6 N–B3 with good chances for White.

C 4 P–B3, P–K4! 5 QPxP, QxQ† 6 NxQ, PxP and Black stands well.

1 P–K4, P–QB3
2 P–Q4[A], P–Q4
3 N–QB3, PxP[B]
4 NxP[C], B–B4

KEY POSITION 1

Black has abandoned his Pawn center in order to free his position. If Black now fails to deploy his forces to their maximum advantage, White's superiority in the center will become overwhelming. Black must keep ever alert, build up a solid defense, and, when the time is ripe, counter with . . . P–QB4. Only by taking these measures will he succeed in loosening White's grip on the game.

IDEA VARIATIONS 1 AND 2:

(1) 5 N–N3, B–N3 6 N–R3, P–KR3? 7 N–B4, B–R2 8 B–B4, N–B3 9 O–O, P–K3 10 R–K1, N–Q4 11 Q–R5, NxN 12 BxN, B–N3 (12 . . . B–K2 13 BxKP, O–O yields White a solid Pawn plus) 13 RxP†, and White has a winning attack. 6 N–R3 is a novelty which sets Black some difficult problems. The apparently obvious reply, 6 . . . P–KR3, proves too cautious. Correct is 6 . . . N–Q2, followed if possible by 7 . . . P–K4. 10 R–K1 threatens to destroy Black's position by 11 BxP! If 10 . . . B–K2 instead of 10 . . . N–Q4, then 11 BxP! PxB 12 NxP, Q moves 13 NxP†, and White obtains a powerful attack.

(2) 5 N–N3, B–N3 (though White does not threaten to win the Bishop — if 6 NxB, Q–R4†! — Black is not inclined to permit the exchange of this piece) 6 P–KR4 (sharpest), P–KR3 (6 . . . P–KR4 would greatly weaken Black's KN4) 7 N–B3, N–Q2 (played to prevent 8 N–K5) 8 B–Q3 (8 B–QB4 is a worthwhile alternative), BxB 9 QxB, Q–B2 (most exact: 9 . . . P–K3 10 B–B4 gives White very strong chances) 10 B–Q2 (both players, aware of their threatened Kingsides, prepare for Queenside castling), P–K3 11 O–O–O, KN–B3 12 K–N1, O–O–O 13 P–B4, P–B4 (the characteristic liberating move; Black's position is passive but solid, and the chances are about equal) 14 B–B3, PxP 15 NxP, P–R3 (see Game 1).

PRACTICAL VARIATIONS 1–4:

1 P–K4, P–QB3 2 P–Q4, P–Q4 3 N–QB3, PxP 4 NxP, B–B4 5 N–N3, B–N3

| | *1* | *2* | *3* | *4* |
|---|---|---|---|---|
| 6 | P–KR4 | N–B3 | N–R3 | B–QB4[9] |
| | P–KR3 | N–Q2 | N–Q2[5] | P–K3[10] |
| 7 | N–B3[1] | B–Q3 | B–QB4[6] | N/1–K2 |
| | N–Q2 | KN–B3 | KN–B3 | B–Q3[11] |

| | 1 | 2 | 3 | 4 |
|---|---|---|---|---|
| 8 | B–Q3 | O–O | N–B4 | P–KR4 |
| | BxB | P–K3 | P–K4[7] | P–KR3 |
| 9 | QxB | R–K1 | PxP | B–B4[12] |
| | KN–B3 | B–K2 | Q–R4† | Q–B2 |
| 10 | B–Q2 | P–B4 | B–Q2 | Q–Q2 |
| | P–K3 | O–O | QxP† | N–B3[13] |
| 11 | O–O–O | BxB | N3–K2 | O–O–O |
| | Q–B2 | RPxB | B–QB4 | QN–Q2 |
| 12 | N–K4[2] | B–B4 | O–O | BxB |
| | O–O–O | R–K1![4] | O–O–O[8] | QxB |
| 13 | P–B4 | = | = | N–B4 |
| | P–B4 | | | B–R2 |
| 14 | NxN | | | N/3–R5 |
| | NxN | | | NxN |
| 15 | B–B3 | | | NxN |
| | Q–B5†[3] | | | B–N3[14] |
| | ∓ | | | = |

*Notes to practical variations 1–4:*

[1] If 7 N–R3, P–K4!

[2] Better is 12 K–N1 which leads to Idea Var. 2.

[3] The game Penrose–Euwe, Cheltenham 1959, continued as follows: 16 Q–Q2, QxQ† 17 RxQ, N–K5 18 R–K2, NxB 19 PxN, B–Q3 20 R–Q1, PxP 21 PxP, R–Q2 22 K–B2, KR–Q1 23 R–K4, R–B2 24 K–Q3, P–KN3 25 R–Q2, B–K2 26 N–K5, B–B3 27 R/2–K2, BxN 28 RxB, R/2–Q2 29 R/5–K4, R–Q3 30 K–B3, R–R3 31 R/4–K3, R/1–Q3 32 R–N2, R–R5 33 R/3–K2, R/3–R3 34 P–Q5, PxP 35 PxP, RxKRP 36 R–K7, R–QR6† 37 K–B2, P–N3 38 RxBP, R–Q5 39 R–B6, RxQP 40 RxKNP, P–KR4 *Drawn.*

[4] Najdorf–Kotov, Zurich 1953.

[5] For 6 . . . P–KR3? see Idea Var. 1.

[6] After 7 N–B4, P–K4! is good.

[7] The liberating move. Otherwise White's game is freer.

[8] Equal, but perilous for both sides.

[9] This move gives chances, as Keres has shown several times.

[10] After 6 . . . N–Q2 White has the strong move 7 P–B4! preventing 7 . . . P–K4.

[11] Best in Keres' opinion. For 7 . . . N–B3 see Game 2.

[12] Interesting is 9 N–B4, B–R2 10 Q–N4, BxP 11 QxP, Q–B3 with a reasonable game for Black. But not 9 N–B4, B–R2 10 Q–N4, BxN? because of 11 BxB, QxQP 12 R–Q1!, QxKB 13 B–KN5!!

[13] And not 10 . . . BxB 11 NxB, BxP? because of 12 NxP!

[14] This move is recommended by Keres. Now 16 NxP† fails because of 16 . . . K–B1 17 P–R5, B–K5, and 16 N–B4 is answered by 16 . . . B–K5. After the text move (15 . . . B–N3) Black has a satisfactory game.

*Caro-Kann Defense Game 1*

*WHITE: Smyslov* *BLACK: Botvinnik*

*Third Match Game 1958*

| | WHITE | BLACK | | WHITE | BLACK |
|---|---|---|---|---|---|
| 1 | P–K4 | P–QB3 | 35 | K–B2 | P–KR4 |
| 2 | P–Q4 | P–Q4 | 36 | P–QN4 | K–N2 |
| 3 | N–QB3 | PxP | 37 | K–N3 | B–Q3 |
| 4 | NxP | B–B4 | 38 | P–R3 | B–B2 |
| 5 | N–N3 | B–N3 | 39 | R–B2 | B–N3 |
| 6 | P–KR4 | P–KR3 | 40 | K–B4 | N–B5 |
| 7 | N–B3 | N–Q2 | 41 | P–N3 | N–R6 |
| 8 | B–Q3 | BxB | 42 | P–B3 | N–N8 |
| 9 | QxB | Q–B2 | 43 | P–B4 | N–B6 |
| 10 | B–Q2 | KN–B3 | 44 | P–R4 | N–Q5 |
| 11 | O–O–O | P–K3 | 45 | R–Q2 | N–B4 |
| 12 | K–N1 | O–O–O | 46 | P–R5 | B–K6 |
| 13 | P–B4 | P–B4 | 47 | R–Q8 | B–B7 |
| 14 | B–B3 | PxP | 48 | P–N5 | K–B2 |
| 15 | NxP | P–R3 | 49 | R–KN8 | PxP† |
| 16 | Q–K2 | B–Q3 | 50 | KxP | BxP |
| 17 | N–K4 | NxN | 51 | P–R6 | B–B7 |
| 18 | QxN | N–B3 | 52 | K–R5 | P–N3 |
| 19 | Q–K2 | R–Q2 | 53 | R–QR8 | B–K8† |
| 20 | R–QB1 | Q–B4 | 54 | K–N5 | N–Q3† |
| 21 | N–N3 | Q–B4† | 55 | K–R4 | N–B1 |
| 22 | R–B2 | B–B2 | 56 | K–N5 | B–B7 |
| 23 | P–B5 | R–Q4! | 57 | K–R5 | B–R2 |
| 24 | P–B6 | B–N3! | 58 | K–N5 | P–B3 |
| 25 | N–Q2 | Q–Q6 | 59 | K–N4 | P–K4 |
| 26 | N–B4 | B–B2 | 60 | PxP | PxP |
| 27 | QxQ | RxQ | 61 | K–B3 | B–N1 |
| 28 | N–K5? | RxB! | 62 | K–Q3 | N–N3 |
| 29 | PxP† | KxP | 63 | P–R7 | NxR |
| 30 | RxR | BxN | 64 | PxB (Q) † | KxQ |
| 31 | R–N3† | K–R2 | 65 | K–K4 | N–N3 |
| 32 | R–QB1 | R–QN1 | 66 | KxP | N–Q2† |
| 33 | RxR | KxR | | Resigns | |
| 34 | R–B4 | N–Q4 | | | |

*Caro-Kann Defense Game 2*

*WHITE: Keres* *BLACK: Golombek*

*Alekhine Memorial Tournament, Moscow 1956*

| | WHITE | BLACK | | WHITE | BLACK |
|---|---|---|---|---|---|
| 1 | P–K4 | P–QB3 | 3 | N–QB3 | PxP |
| 2 | P–Q4 | P–Q4 | 4 | NxP | B–B4 |

| WHITE | BLACK | WHITE | BLACK |
|---|---|---|---|
| 5 N–N3 | B–N3 | 26 BxP | R–N3 |
| 6 B–QB4 | P–K3 | 27 BxR | PxB |
| 7 N/1–K2 | N–B3 | 28 N–N3 | R–K1 |
| 8 O–O | B–Q3 | 29 B–B4 | K–N2 |
| 9 P–B4 | Q–B2 | 30 N–K4 | P–KN4 |
| 10 P–B5 | PxP | 31 N–Q6 | R–K3 |
| 11 NxP | BxP† | 32 B–N3 | P–N3 |
| 12 K–R1 | O–O? | 33 R–K1 | RxR |
| 13 P–KN3 | BxN | 34 BxR | K–N3 |
| 14 RxB | BxP | 35 N–B8 | P–QB4 |
| 15 RxN! | Q–K2 | 36 PxP | NxP |
| 16 Q–B1! | Q–K5† | 37 NxRP | P–B4 |
| 17 Q–B3 | Q–R5† | 38 B–B2 | N–Q2 |
| 18 K–N2 | Q–R7† | 39 B–Q4 | K–R4 |
| 19 K–B1 | Q–R6† | 40 N–B8 | N–B1 |
| 20 Q–N2 | QxQ† | 41 N–K7 | P–B5 |
| 21 KxQ | PxR | 42 N–B5 | N–N3 |
| 22 NxB | N–Q2 | 43 N–N7† | K–R3 |
| 23 B–KR6 | KR–K1 | 44 K–N4 | N–B1 |
| 24 K–B3 | K–R1 | 45 N–B5† | Resigns |
| 25 N–R5 | R–KN1 | | |

---

## part 2—**KNIGHT VARIATION**

1 P–K4, P–QB3
2 P–Q4, P–Q4
3 N–QB3, PxP
4 NxP, N–B3
5 NxN†[A], NPxN[B]

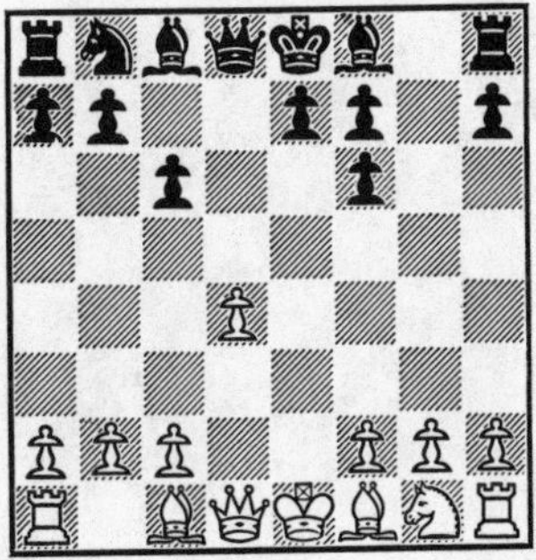

KEY POSITION 2

### OBSERVATIONS ON KEY POSITION 2

A White's best chance for maintaining the initiative. For 5 N–N3 see Sup. Var. 4.

B By far the most important move. After 5 . . . KPxN White's Queenside Pawn majority is of telling significance. See Sup. Var. 5.)

Today this variation is considered to be one of the most important in the Caro-Kann Defense. Black's Pawn formation may be weakened, but in practice it is very difficult for White to profit from this circumstance. In fact, under certain conditions Black's broken line of Pawns may prove an asset: in many lines White castles Kingside and Black may then unleash an attack on the open King Knight file. Attack or no, however, Black must exercise caution in the development of his Queen Bishop. Careless play may result in this piece being locked out of action on the Kingside.

White controls more space and therefore usually maintains a slight initiative, but the chances seem approximately equal.

An important factor is that many of the positions which arise in this variation call for tactical blows; an inaccuracy on the part of either player may prove fatal.

IDEA VARIATIONS 3 AND 4:

(3) 6 N–K2, B–N5 (6 . . . P–KR4 or 6 . . . B–B4 [see Game 3] are more advisable) 7 Q–Q3!, B–R4 8 Q–QN3!, BxN 9 BxB, Q–B2? (9 . . . Q–N3 is necessary) 10 B–R5!, Q–R4† (10 . . . P–K3 11 QxP†! and wins) 11 B–Q2, QxB 12 QxP and White wins.

(4) 6 B–K3, B–B4 7 N–K2, P–KR4 (7 . . . P–K4 8 N–N3, B–K3 9 B–K2 and White has the edge) 8 P–KR4, N–Q2 9 N–N3, B–N3 10 B–Q3 (or 10 B–K2, Q–R4† 11 P–B3, O–O–O∓) BxB 11 QxB, Q–R4† 12 P–B3, O–O–O 13 O–O, P–K3 14 P–N4, Q–B2 (Black's position is very solid; he is able to ward off White's coming attack and initiate one of his own) 15 P–N5, PxP 16 QxP, P–B4! and Black has forceful counterplay (Clarke–Donner, Wageningen 1957).

PRACTICAL VARIATIONS 5–8:

1 P–K4, P–QB3 2 P–Q4, P–Q4 3 N–QB3, PxP 4 NxP, N–B3 5 NxN†, NPxN

| | 5 | 6 | 7 | 8 |
|---|---|---|---|---|
| 6 | P–QB3[1] | – – | N–B3 | B–QB4[13] |
| | B–B4 | – – | B–N5 | B–B4 |
| 7 | B–QB4[2] | N–K2 | B–K2[9] | N–B3 |
| | P–K3 | P–KR4 | Q–B2[10] | P–K3 |
| 8 | N–K2 | N–N3[5] | P–B4[11] | B–B4 |
| | B–Q3[3] | B–KN5 | N–Q2 | B–Q3[14] |
| 9 | B–B4 | B–K2[6] | O–O | Q–Q2 |
| | Q–B2 | BxB | O–O–O | Q–B2[15] |
| 10 | BxB | QxB | Q–R4 | = |
| | QxB | Q–Q4[7] | K–N1[12] | |
| 11 | N–N3 | O–O | = | |
| | B–N3 | N–Q2 | | |
| 12 | P–KR4 | B–K3 | | |
| | P–KR4 | N–N3[8] | | |
| 13 | Q–B3 | = | | |
| | N–Q2 | | | |
| 14 | O–O | | | |
| | O–O–O | | | |
| 15 | P–N4 | | | |
| | P–KB4 | | | |
| 16 | N–K2 | | | |
| | QR–N1[4] | | | |
| | = | | | |

*Notes to practical variations 5–8:*

[1] For 6 N–K2 and 6 B–K3 see Idea Var. 3 and 4 respectively.

[2] If 7 Q–N3, Q–B2 8 B–KB4?, QxB 9 QxP, B–R3! 10 N–B3, O–O 11 QxR, Q–B2 12 P–Q5, Q–N3 13 B–B4, B–B1 14 PxP, NxP 15 O–O, B–KN5∓ (Fuderer–Szabo, Goteborg 1955).

[3] For 8 . . . P–KR4 see Game 4 (Ciocaltea–Pachman).

[4] With a difficult game and chances for both players.

[5] Or 8 P–KR4, N–Q2 9 N–N3, B–N5 10 B–K2, BxB 11 QxB, Q–R4 with about equal play (Averbach–Sokolski, USSR Championship 1950).

[6] After 9 P–B3, B–K3 is safest. On the other hand 9 . . . P–KR5 10 PxB, PxN 11 P–KR4, P–K4 12 PxP, QxQ† 13 KxQ seems favorable for White.

[7] Centralizing and paving the way for Queenside castling.

[8] With sufficient counterplay for Black.

[9] Black has nothing to fear from 7 P–B3, N–Q2 8 B–QB4, P–K3 9 P–KR3, B–R4 10 Q–K2, N–N3 11 B–N3, P–QR4 with a good game (Niephaus–Donner, Wageningen 1957).

[10] Black has the choice of several good moves, e.g., 7 . . . N–Q2 8 O–O, P–K3 9 B–KB4, N–N3 10 B–N3, P–KR4 11 B–R4, N–Q4, etc.

[11] For 8 P–KR3, B–R4 9 N–R4 see the interesting Game 5 (Najdorf–Panno).

[12] The chances are about counterbalanced.

[13] Recommended by Boleslavski. By postponing the move N–KB3 White avoids the pin of this piece by . . . B–KN5.

[14] It is important to challenge the Bishop to cut down White's attacking chances.

[15] Black can maintain himself.

### *Caro–Kann Defense Game 3*

*WHITE: Horowitz* — *BLACK: Flohr*

*First Radio Match, USA–USSR 1945*

| WHITE | BLACK | WHITE | BLACK | WHITE | BLACK |
|---|---|---|---|---|---|
| 1 P–K4 | P–QB3 | 15 B–B4! | B–N6 | 29 RxR† | K–K2 |
| 2 P–Q4 | P–Q4 | 16 B–Q3 | P–K4 | 30 Q–N3 | N–Q2 |
| 3 N–QB3 | PxP | 17 B–K3 | B–Q4 | 31 B–B7 | Q–Q4 |
| 4 NxP | N–B3 | 18 B–K4 | Q–N6 | 32 P–QB4 | Q–KN4 |
| 5 NxN† | NPxN | 19 PxP | PxP | 33 QxQ | PxQ |
| 6 N–K2 | B–B4 | 20 QR–Q1 | BxB | 34 R–R8 | K–K3 |
| 7 N–N3 | B–N3 | 21 QxB | Q–K3 | 35 BxP | P–KB4 |
| 8 P–KR4 | P–KR3 | 22 R–Q2 | N–B3 | 36 B–B3 | P–B5 |
| 9 P–KR5 | B–R2 | 23 Q–B3 | R–KN1 | 37 P–R5 | P–N5 |
| 10 P–QB3 | Q–N3 | 24 KR–Q1 | R–N5 | 38 P–N4 | P–B6 |
| 11 B–QB4 | N–Q2 | 25 N–B5! | P–K5 | 39 B–Q2 | K–B2 |
| 12 P–R4 | P–R4 | 26 B–N6 | RxP† | 40 R–R7 | P–N6 |
| 13 Q–B3 | P–K3 | 27 QxR! | QxN | 41 RxP | Resigns |
| 14 O–O | B–B7 | 28 R–Q8† | RxR | | |

### *Caro–Kann Defense Game 4*

*WHITE: Ciocaltea* *BLACK: Pachman*

*Alekhine Memorial Tournament, Moscow 1956*

| | WHITE | BLACK | | WHITE | BLACK |
|---|---|---|---|---|---|
| 1 | P–K4 | P–QB3 | 22 | K–N1 | BxB |
| 2 | N–QB3 | P–Q4 | 23 | QxB | N–B5 |
| 3 | P–Q4 | PxP | 24 | B–B1 | P–K4 |
| 4 | NxP | N–B3 | 25 | B–Q3 | K–N1 |
| 5 | NxN† | NPxN | 26 | B–K4 | BPxP |
| 6 | B–QB4 | B–B4 | 27 | PxP | RxP |
| 7 | P–QB3 | P–K3 | 28 | Q–K3 | Q–N3 |
| 8 | N–K2 | P–KR4 | 29 | R–QB1 | KR–Q1 |
| 9 | N–N3 | B–N3 | 30 | KR–N1 | N–K7 |
| 10 | Q–K2 | N–Q2 | 31 | QxN | R–Q7 |
| 11 | P–B4 | P–KB4 | 32 | QxR | RxQ |
| 12 | N–B1 | P–R5 | 33 | R–N8† | R–Q1 |
| 13 | N–Q2 | N–B3 | 34 | R–N5 | P–R3 |
| 14 | N–B3 | B–R4 | 35 | RxP | R–Q7 |
| 15 | B–Q2 | B–Q3 | 36 | R–K8† | K–R2 |
| 16 | B–Q3 | Q–B2 | 37 | B–B2 | RxP |
| 17 | BxP | BxN | 38 | R–K7 | Q–KB3 |
| 18 | PxB | O–O–O | 39 | R–K3 | R–B7 |
| 19 | B–R3 | BxP | 40 | R–N3 | RxP |
| 20 | O–O–O | N–Q4 | 41 | B–Q3 | R–K6 |
| 21 | QR–N1 | P–QB4 | | Resigns | |

### *Caro–Kann Defense Game 5*

*WHITE: Najdorf* *BLACK: Panno*

*Zonal Tournament, Buenos Aires 1957*

| | WHITE | BLACK | | WHITE | BLACK |
|---|---|---|---|---|---|
| 1 | P–K4 | P–QB3 | 15 | Q–B3 | Q–B3 |
| 2 | N–KB3 | P–Q4 | 16 | P–Q5 | Q–R3 |
| 3 | N–B3 | PxP | 17 | P–R3 | B–R4 |
| 4 | NxP | N–B3 | 18 | B–B4 | B–B2 |
| 5 | NxN† | NPxN | 19 | BxB | KxB |
| 6 | P–Q4 | B–N5 | 20 | KR–Q1 | KR–K1 |
| 7 | B–K2 | Q–B2 | 21 | Q–B4† | K–B1 |
| 8 | P–KR3 | B–R4 | 22 | N–B3! | P–K4 |
| 9 | N–R4 | BxB | 23 | Q–K4 | P–B4 |
| 10 | QxB | N–Q2 | 24 | QxBP | QxBP |
| 11 | O–O | P–K3 | 25 | N–N5! | P–B3 |
| 12 | P–QB4 | O–O–O | 26 | N–B7? | Q–R3 |
| 13 | P–QN4! | BxP | 27 | NxR | RxN |
| 14 | R–N1 | P–QB4 | 28 | QxRP | P–N4 |

| WHITE | BLACK | WHITE | BLACK |
|---|---|---|---|
| 29 Q–K4 | Q–N2 | 39 R/1–N1 | P–N5 |
| 30 P–KR4 | R–R1 | 40 Q–B4! | K–N2 |
| 31 P–N3 | P–R3 | 41 R–R1 | QxP |
| 32 Q–B5 | Q–N3 | 42 Q–K4† | K–N3 |
| 33 Q–K6 | K–B2 | 43 R/2–R2 | N–N1 |
| 34 P–Q6† | K–B1 | 44 Q–R8 | R–Q1 |
| 35 KR–QB1 | Q–B3 | 45 P–R5! | Q–Q6 |
| 36 P–R4 | K–N2 | 46 Q–R5† | K–B3 |
| 37 R–N2 | K–N3 | 47 R–QB1! | Q–Q4 |
| 38 PxP | PxP | 48 Q–R8† | Resigns |

## part 3—KNIGHT VARIATION DEFERRED

1 P–K4, P–QB3
2 P–Q4, P–Q4
3 N–QB3, PxP
4 NxP, N–Q2

KEY POSITION 3

OBSERVATIONS ON KEY POSITION 3

This artificial system has acquired increasing popularity in recent years. Black wishes to play the Knight Variation without weakening his Pawn structure. The drawback, however, is that Black's Queen Bishop must normally be developed arduously via QN2, a time-consuming maneuver which gives White the opportunity to obtain an important advantage in space. As in most variations of the Caro-Kann, however, Black's position proves tough to crack, and in many lines he obtains sufficient counterchances.

IDEA VARIATIONS 5 AND 6:

(5) 5 B–QB4, KN–B3 6 N–N5 (6 NxN†, NxN! and Black avoids the weakening of his Pawn structure), P–K3 (for 6 . . . N–Q4 see Game 6) 7 Q–K2, N–N3 8 B–N3, QxP (dangerous; correct is 8 . . . P–KR3 9 N/5–B3, B–Q3, etc.) 9 KN–B3, Q–B4 (equally insufficient is 9 . . . B–N5† 10 P–B3, BxP† 11 K–B1!±) 10 N–K5 with great advantage for White.

(6) 5 N–KB3, KN–B3 (5 . . . QN–B3 has been tried but found wanting: 6 N–N3, B–N5 7 B–K2, P–K3 8 O–O, N–K2 9 R–K1, N–N3 10 B–KN5, B–K2 11 N–K5± [Rabar–Trifunovich, Yugoslav Championship 1948]) 6 N–N3, P–K3 7 B–Q3 (experience has shown this move to be better than 7 B–QB4), B–K2 8 O–O, O–O 9 Q–K2, P–B4 10 R–Q1 (for 10 P–B3, see Game 7), Q–B2 11 P–B4, R–K1, and although White's development is preferable, Black may just be able to equalize.

PRACTICAL VARIATIONS 9–11:

1 P–K4, P–QB3 2 P–Q4, P–Q4 3 N–QB3, PxP 4 NxP, N–Q2

| | 9 | 10 | 11 |
|---|---|---|---|
| 5 | B–QB4 | N–KB3 | – – |
| | KN–B3[1] | KN–B3 | – – |
| 6 | N–N5 | NxN†[5] | – – |
| | P–K3 | NxN | – – |
| 7 | Q–K2 | B–QB4 | – – |
| | N–N3[2] | B–B4 | P–KN3 |
| 8 | B–N3 | N–K5 | N–K5 |
| | P–KR3[3] | P–K3 | N–Q4 |
| 9 | N/5–B3 | P–KN4[6] | Q–B3 |
| | B–Q3 | B–K5 | B–K3 |
| 10 | N–K5 | P–KB3 | O–O |
| | Q–K2 | B–Q4 | B–N2 |
| 11 | KN–B3 | B–K2 | R–Q1 |
| | B–Q2 | P–QN4! | O–O |
| 12 | B–KB4[4] | P–QR4 | B–N3 |
| | ± | N–Q2![7] | Q–B1[8] |
| | | ∓ | = |

*Notes to practical variations 9–11:*

[1] Not to be ruled out is 5 . . . QN–B3 in conjunction with a later fianchetto, e.g., 6 N–N3, P–KN3 7 N–B3, N–R3 8 N–K5, N–Q4 9 Q–B3, N–B4 with a reasonable game for Black.

[2] The threat was 8 NxBP!

[3] For 8 . . . QxP see Idea Var. 5.

[4] White enjoys more space.

[5] For 6 N–N3 see Idea Var. 6.

[6] Probably 9 P–QB3 is even better.

[7] White has somewhat overextended himself.

[8] Black has a satisfactory position. In a game Gligoric–Van Scheltinga, Amsterdam 1950, Black was in command after 13 P–KR3?, P–QR4 14 P–B3, P–R5! 15 B–B4, N–N3 16 B–B1, B–Q4 17 Q–K2, P–B3 18 N–N4, R–K1 19 Q–B2, Q–K3. Better for White is 13 Q–K2.

### *Caro–Kann Defense Game 6*

*WHITE: Duckstein* — *BLACK: Kramer*

*Chess Olympics, Moscow 1956*

| | WHITE | BLACK | | WHITE | BLACK |
|---|---|---|---|---|---|
| 1 | P–K4 | P–QB3 | 17 | Q–Q2 | P–KN4 |
| 2 | P–Q4 | P–Q4 | 18 | P–KR4 | PxQP |
| 3 | N–QB3 | PxP | 19 | NxQP | N–B4 |
| 4 | NxP | N–Q2 | 20 | NxN | PxN |
| 5 | B–QB4 | KN–B3 | 21 | N–B5 | QR–Q1 |
| 6 | N–N5 | N–Q4 | 22 | BxN | PxB |
| 7 | Q–R5 | P–KN3 | 23 | Q–K2 | P–K3 |
| 8 | Q–K2 | B–N2 | 24 | B–R4 | R–KB1 |
| 9 | KN–B3 | O–O | 25 | NxB | KxN |
| 10 | O–O | P–KR3 | 26 | Q–N4† | K–R2 |
| 11 | N–K4 | Q–B2 | 27 | B–B2† | K–R1 |
| 12 | B–N3 | P–N3 | 28 | Q–R5 | K–N2 |
| 13 | P–B4 | B–R3 | 29 | R–K5! | R–KN1 |
| 14 | R–K1 | KR–K1 | 30 | R/1–K1 | R–Q7 |
| 15 | Q–B2 | N–B5 | 31 | RxKP | PxR |
| 16 | B–K3 | P–QB4 | 32 | RxP | Resigns |

## *Caro–Kann Defense Game 7*

*WHITE: Jevsejev* *BLACK: Flohr*

| | WHITE | BLACK | | WHITE | BLACK | | WHITE | BLACK |
|---|---|---|---|---|---|---|---|---|
| 1 | P–K4 | P–QB3 | 10 | P–B3 | P–QN3 | 19 | Q–R3 | R–KR1 |
| 2 | P–Q4 | P–Q4 | 11 | N–K5 | B–N2 | 20 | N–B6† | K–N2 |
| 3 | N–QB3 | PxP | 12 | P–KB4 | PxP | 21 | Q–K3 | R–B7 |
| 4 | NxP | N–Q2 | 13 | PxP | NxN | 22 | Q–KN3 | Q–Q6! |
| 5 | N–KB3 | KN–B3 | 14 | QPxN | N–N5! | 23 | QxQ | RxKNP |
| 6 | N–N3 | P–K3 | 15 | BxP† | KxB | 24 | N–N4 | R/7xP†! |
| 7 | B–Q3 | B–K2 | 16 | QxN | Q–Q5† | | Resigns | |
| 8 | O–O | O–O | 17 | K–R1 | QR–B1 | | | |
| 9 | Q–K2 | P–B4 | 18 | N–R5? | P–N3 | | | |

SUPPLEMENTARY VARIATIONS 1–5:

1 P–K4, P–QB3 2 P–Q4, P–Q4 3 N–QB3, PxP 4 NxP

| | *1* | *2* | *3* | *4* | *5* |
|---|---|---|---|---|---|
| *4* | – – | – – | – – | – – | – – |
| | P–K4 | B–B4 | N–B3 | – – | – – |
| *5* | PxP | Q–B3 | Q–Q3 | N–N3 | NxN† |
| | Q–R4† | P–K3! | P–K4[3] | P–K4[6] | KPxN |
| *6* | B–Q2 | P–B3 | PxP | N–B3 | B–QB4[9] |
| | QxKP | N–Q2 | Q–R4† | PxP | B–Q3 |
| *7* | Q–K2[1] | B–KB4 | B–Q2 | NxP | Q–K2† |
| | ± | QN–B3! | QxKP[4] | B–K2![7] | B–K2[10] |
| *8* | | N–Q2 | O–O–O! | B–K2 | N–B3[11] |
| | | N–K2[2] | NxN? | O–O | B–KN5[12] |
| *9* | | = | Q–Q8†[5] | O–O | P–B3 |
| | | | ± | B–QB4 | N–Q2 |
| *10* | | | | N/4–B5[8] | P–KR3! |
| | | | | ± | B–R4 |
| *11* | | | | | P–KN4! |
| | | | | | B–N3 |
| *12* | | | | | N–R4 |
| | | | | | N–N3 |
| *13* | | | | | B–N3 |
| | | | | | N–Q4 |
| *14* | | | | | B–Q2[13] |
| | | | | | ± |

*Notes to supplementary variations 1–5:*

[1] Superior development favors White.

[2] Black enjoys an easy development.

[3] Better is 5 . . . NxN 6 QxN, N–Q2 with equality.

[4] Black's apparent plus is an illusion.

[5] Mate in two (Reti–Tartakover, 1910).

[6] After 5 . . . QN–Q2 we have transposed into Idea Var. 6. A good move is 5 . . . P–QB4, e.g., 6 PxP., Q–R4† 7 B–Q2, QxBP with equality.

continued ▶

[7] Less good is 7 . . . B–QB4 8 Q–K2†, B–K2 9 B–K3, O–O 10 O–O–O, and White has the better chances. 7 . . . B–QB4 8 Q–K2†, Q–K2? 9 QxQ†, BxQ 10 N/4–B5!±.

[8] White has a slight initiative.

[9] 6 P–QB3, too, is good, for instance, 6 . . . B–Q3 7 B–Q3, O–O 8 Q–R5, P–KN3 9 Q–R6, and White has good attacking chances.

[10] The end game after 7 . . . Q–K2 8 QxQ† favors White because of his Queenside Pawn majority.

[11] Interesting is 8 Q–R5, after which might follow 8 . . . O–O 9 N–K2, P–KN3 10 Q–B3, and now not 10 . . . N–Q2? because of 11 B–R6, R–K1 12 BxP†, KxB 13 Q–QN3 mate.

[12] In a game Nimzowitsch–Reti the sequel was 8 . . . O–O 9 O–O, B–Q3 10 R–K1, P–QN4 11 B–Q3, N–R3 12 P–QR4, N–N5 13 PxP, NxB 14 QxN, PxP 15 QxP, Q–B2 16 Q–Q3, B–N2, and White could have maintained the better chances by playing 17 P–QB4!

[13] Bogoljubov–Alekhine, 1942.

---

## part 4—**EXCHANGE VARIATION**

1 P–K4, P–QB3
2 P–Q4, P–Q4
3 PxP, PxP
4 B–Q3[A]

KEY POSITION 4

OBSERVATIONS ON KEY POSITION 4

[A] The most important variation at this stage is 4 P–QB4, the Panov Attack. This line is treated separately in Part 5.

The Exchange Variation offers White a sound but lifeless game with but little chance for the initiative. The Pawn formation resulting from the opening allows each side a minority attack; White's chances are on the Kingside: Black's on the Queen.

With correct play the game develops at a quiet pace and the chances remain balanced. An early draw is often the consequence.

IDEA VARIATIONS 7-9:

(7) 4 . . . N–QB3 5 P–QB3, N–B3 6 P–KR3 (preventing a later pin of White's King Knight) P–K3 (too passive; far better is 6 . . . P–K4! and after 7 PxP, NxP Black's open position is full compensation for his isolated Queen Pawn) 7 N–B3, B–K2 8 O–O, O–O 9 Q–K2, P–QR3 10 P–QR4, P–QN3 11 N–K5, B–N2 12 P–B4 with an excellent game for White.

5 P–QB3 is a temporizing move; 5 N–KB3 would permit 5 . . . B–N5. The text also anticipates the possibility of a later . . . N–QN5.

(8) 4 . . . N–QB3 5 P–QB3, N–B3 6 B–KB4, B–N5 7 P–B3 (for 7 N–K2, see Prac. Var. 14), B–R4 8 N–K2, B–N3 9 O–O, P–K3 10 BxB, RPxB 11 N–Q2, P–QN4!

(initiating the minority attack!) 12 P–QR3, B–Q3 13 BxB, QxB 14 N–N3, P–QR4 and White is completely on the defensive.

(9) 4 . . . N–QB3 5 P–QB3, N–B3 6 B–KB4, B–N5 7 Q–N3, N–QR4 (7 . . . Q–B1 is also playable, though the text move is simpler) 8 Q–R4†, B–Q2 9 Q–B2, Q–N3 10 N–Q2, P–K3 11 KN–B3, B–N4! (a characteristic maneuver — Black exchanges his "bad" Bishop for White's "good" one) 12 O–O, BxB 13 QxB, R–B1 (better than 13 . . . QxNP 14 KR–N1, Q–R6 15 Q–N5†, etc.) 14 QR–N1, B–K2 and the game is about equal (see Game 8).

PRACTICAL VARIATIONS 12–15:

1 P–K4, P–QB3 2 P–Q4, P–Q4 3 PxP, PxP 4 B–Q3

| | *12* | *13* | *14* | *15* |
|---|---|---|---|---|
| *4* | – – | – – | – – | – – |
| | N–QB3 | – – | – – | – – |
| *5* | P–QB3 | – – | – – | – – |
| | N–B3 | – – | – – | – – |
| *6* | P–KR3 | – – | B–KB4 | B–KN5 |
| | P–K4 | P–KN3[3] | B–N5[6] | B–N5 |
| *7* | PxP | N–B3 | N–K2[7] | N–K2 |
| | NxP | B–B4[4] | Q–Q2[8] | P–K3 |
| *8* | N–B3[1] | BxB | Q–N3[9] | Q–N3 |
| | NxB† | PxB | B–R4 | Q–Q2 |
| *9* | QxN[2] | Q–Q3 | = | N–N3 |
| | = | Q–B1 | | N–KR4[10] |
| *10* | | B–B4 | | = |
| | | B–N2[5] | | |
| | | = | | |

*Notes to practical variations 12–15:*

[1] After 8 Q–K2, Q–K2 9 B–N5†, B–Q2 10 B–K3, BxB 11 QxB†, Q–Q2 12 Q–K2, O–O–O! Black has a good game (Wagner–Nimzowitsch, 1925).

[2] White has the better Pawn structure and Black has the two Bishops.

[3] This move is seldom played, but it is quite satisfactory for Black.

[4] Less good is 7 . . . B–N2 8 B–KB4, O–O 9 O–O, P–QR3 10 R–K1, etc.

[5] Black has a tenable game despite his doubled Pawns.

[6] Here, too, 6 . . . P–KN3 is possible.

[7] For 7 P–B3 and 7 Q–N3 see Idea Var. 8 and 9.

[8] A small finesse! After 7 . . . P–K3 8 Q–N3! Black is in trouble. For instance, 8 . . . Q–Q2 9 N–N3, N–KR4 10 B–K3 and White has the better chances.

[9] After 8 P–KR3, B–B4 is a good reply (Alekhine).

[10] Van den Bosch–Capablanca, 1929.

*Caro–Kann Defense Game 8*

*WHITE: Maroczy* — *BLACK: Capablanca*

*Lake Hopatcong 1926*

| | WHITE | BLACK | | WHITE | BLACK |
|---|---|---|---|---|---|
| 1 | P–K4 | P–QB3 | 26 | R–K2 | Q–R5 |
| 2 | P–Q4 | P–Q4 | 27 | K–R2 | R–N3 |
| 3 | PxP | PxP | 28 | P–KN3 | Q–B3 |
| 4 | B–Q3 | N–QB3 | 29 | R–N1 | K–N2 |
| 5 | P–QB3 | N–B3 | 30 | Q–Q3 | P–QR3! |
| 6 | B–KB4 | B–N5 | 31 | R–QB1 | P–KR4 |
| 7 | Q–N3 | N–QR4 | 32 | P–KR4 | K–R3 |
| 8 | Q–R4† | B–Q2 | 33 | P–B4 | PxP |
| 9 | Q–B2 | Q–N3 | 34 | RxP | RxP! |
| 10 | N–B3 | P–K3 | 35 | QxR | RxR |
| 11 | O–O | B–N4 | 36 | R–Q2 | Q–N3 |
| 12 | QN–Q2 | BxB | 37 | Q–N5† | QxQ |
| 13 | QxB | R–B1 | 38 | RPxQ† | K–N3 |
| 14 | QR–N1 | B–K2 | 39 | K–N3 | R–B3! |
| 15 | P–KR3 | O–O | 40 | K–B3 | R–Q3 |
| 16 | KR–K1 | N–B5 | 41 | K–N3 | P–B3 |
| 17 | NxN | RxN | 42 | PxP | KxP |
| 18 | N–K5 | QR–B1 | 43 | K–B3 | P–R5 |
| 19 | B–N5 | Q–Q1 | 44 | R–R2 | RxP |
| 20 | BxN | PxB! | 45 | RxP | P–N4 |
| 21 | N–N4 | K–R1 | 46 | R–R6† | K–K2 |
| 22 | P–KB4 | P–B4 | 47 | R–R7† | K–Q3 |
| 23 | N–K5 | B–Q3 | 48 | R–R7 | R–R5 |
| 24 | Q–B3 | BxN | 49 | P–R3 | K–Q4 |
| 25 | RxB | R–KN1 | | Resigns | |

## part 5—MODERN VARIATION

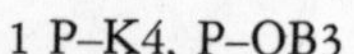

1 P–K4, P–QB3
2 P–QB4[A], P–Q4[B]
3 KPxP[C], PxP

KEY POSITION 5

### OBSERVATIONS ON KEY POSITION 5

[A] This system was very much in evidence in the thirties. It was at first believed to be the refutation of the Caro–Kann, but this judgment has proved to be too optimistic. Today the variation is not much in vogue.

[B] At this stage Black may vary, transposing into other openings: 2 . . . P–K4 3 N–KB3, P–Q3 4 P–Q4, N–Q2 (Old Indian Defense) or 2 . . . P–K3 3 P–Q4, P–Q4 4 BPxP, BPxP 5 P–K5 (French Defense).

[C] 3 BPxP, PxP 4 P–K5, N–QB3 5 P–Q4, B–B4 gives White no advantage.

White must choose between two important systems. He can play 4 P–Q4, exerting more pressure on the center, or 4 PxP, hoping to gain from the disappearance of Black's Queen Pawn.

4 P–Q4 leads to the famous Panov Attack, a weapon which Botvinnik has wielded with considerable success throughout the years. White's development is both quick and harmonious. With a timely P–QB5, White can obtain a promising Queenside pawn majority. Black must counter this stratagem with . . . P–K4 at the right moment or his game will crumble. Needless to say, this type of play is highly combinative and both players must keep constantly alert or suffer dire consequences.

With 4 PxP, White relies on the consideration that Black must sacrifice some time in recapturing his Pawn. Black's best policy, therefore, is first to complete his development and then to direct his forces against the hostile Queen Pawn. No definite opinion has yet been established on this difficult line, but in most variations Black emerges in satisfactory fashion.

IDEA VARIATIONS 10–13:

(10) 4 P–Q4, N–KB3 5 N–QB3, N–B3 6 B–N5 (this was thought at one time to demolish Black's entire defense), Q–R4!? 7 Q–Q2, P–K4! (7 . . . PxP 8 BxP, P–K4 9 P–Q5, N–Q5 10 P–B4 favors White) 8 BxN (after 8 PxKP, N–K5! 9 NxN, B–QN5! 10 N–QB3, P–Q5 Black has good attacking chances), PxB 9 NxP, QxQ† 10 KxQ, B–R3† 11 K–Q1! (11 K–K1, NxP! or if 11 K–B3 then 11 . . . PxP† 12 K–N3, O–O! and Black has more than adequate compensation for his Pawn offer), O–O! 12 NxP†, K–N2 13 PxP, NxP 14 N–Q5, R–Q1 15 K–K1, P–N4 (allowing White no opportunity to consolidate his position) 16 N–B7, B–K3 (shades of Morphy!) 17 NxR (if 17 NxB†, PxN 18 PxP, R–Q7! 19 N–B3, NxN† 20 PxN, R/1–Q1, White has no more than a draw), B–Q7† 18 K–Q1, B–N4† 19 K–K1 (best; after 19 K–B2, B–B4† 20 K–N3, PxP† 21 BxP, R–N1† 22 K–B3, R–QB1, White is in serious trouble), B–Q7† with a draw by perpetual check. This beautiful line is only a sample of the swashbuckling tactics to be anticipated when this variation is essayed!

6 . . . Q–R4!? initiates a little-known line leading to great complications. 7 BxN is stronger than 7 Q–Q2, e.g., 7 . . . KPxB 8 PxP, B–QN5 9 Q–Q2, BxN 10 PxB, QxQP 11 N–B3, B–R6 12 P–B4±.

(11) 4 P–Q4, N–KB3 5 N–QB3, N–B3 6 B–N5, P–K3 7 P–B5 (after 7 N–B3, PxP is satisfactory for Black; the position is similar to the Queen's Gambit Accepted), B–K2 (if 7 . . . P–QN3, best is 8 P–QN4!, PxP 9

NPxP, etc.) 8 B–N5 (directed against a later . . . P–K4), O–O 9 N–B3, N–K5! (initiating a fine freeing maneuver) 10 BxB, QxB (after 10 . . . NxB 11 R–QB1, N–N3 12 O–O, B–Q2 13 B–Q3, P–B4 14 P–QN4!, as played in the Botvinnik–Kmoch game, Leningrad 1934, White's Queenside Pawn majority becomes dangerously active) 11 Q–B2, N–N4! (eliminating White's King Knight and preparing for . . . P–K4) 12 NxN, QxN 13 BxN, PxB (13 . . . QxP 14 BxQP, PxB 15 O–O–O±) 14 O–O, P–K4! and the chances are about equal (Keres–Alekhine, 1938).

(12) 4 PxP, QxP 5 N–QB3, Q–QR4 (more modest but not too bad is 5 . . . Q–Q1) 6 B–B4, N–KB3 7 N–B3, P–K3 (7 . . . P–K4 would open the position to White's advantage) 8 O–O, B–K2 9 P–Q4, O–O 10 Q–K2 and White, owing to his advantage in space and mobility, has a clear edge. This line indicates the drawbacks of 4 . . . QxP.

(13) 4 PxP, N–KB3 (4 . . . P–QR3 to prevent 5 B–N5† is another possibility; see Prac. Var. 23) 5 B–N5†, QN–Q2 6 N–QB3, P–KN3 (a key move in this system) 7 N–B3 (7 P–Q4 is best answered by 7 . . . P–QR3! and not by 7 . . . B–N2, which is met by 8 P–Q6!; and if then 8 . . . PxP, simply 9 B–KB4), B–N2 8 O–O, O–O 9 Q–N3, N–N3 and Black has an excellent position.

PRACTICAL VARIATIONS 16-19:

1 P–K4, P–QB3 2 P–QB4, P–Q4 3 KPxP, PxP

| | 16 | 17 | 18 | 19 |
|---|---|---|---|---|
| 4 | P–Q4 | – – | – – | – – |
| | N–KB3[1] | – – | – – | – – |
| 5 | N–QB3 | – – | – – | – – |
| | P–K3 | – – | N–B3 | – – |
| 6 | N–B3 | – – | B–N5 | – – |
| | B–K2[2] | – – | PxP | Q–N3[14] |
| 7 | P–B5 | B–N5 | P–Q5! | PxP |
| | O–O[3] | N–B3[8] | N–QR4[11] | NxP/Q5[15] |
| 8 | B–Q3[4] | R–B1[9] | P–QN4! | KN–K2[16] |
| | P–QN3 | O–O | PxP e.p. | N–B4 |
| 9 | P–QN4 | B–Q3 | PxP | Q–Q2 |
| | P–QR4 | P–QN3 | P–QN3[12] | N–Q3 |
| 10 | N–QR4 | O–O | P–QN4 | N–N3[17] |
| | KN–Q2[5] | N–QN5[10] | N–N2 | ± |
| 11 | P–N5 | = | B–N5† | |
| | PxP | | B–Q2 | |
| 12 | PxP | | N–B3[13] | |
| | P–K4![6] | | ± | |
| 13 | P–B6 | | | |
| | P–K5[7] | | | |
| | = | | | |

*Notes to practical variations 16–19:*

[1] Best : 4 . . . PxP 5 BxP, P–K3 6 N–KB3 transposes into a variation of the Queen's Gambit Accepted which favors White. If 4 . . . N–QB3?, 5 PxP, QxP 6 N–KB3, P–K4 7 N–B3!.

[2] Now if 6 . . . N–B3 7 P–B5!, N–K5 8 B–QN5, NxN 9 PxN, with advantage for White.

[3] After 7 . . . P–QN3 8 P–QN4, P–QR4 9 N–QR4, KN–Q2 10 B–QN5, Black is at a disadvantage (Euwe–Kramer, 1941).

[4] 8 B–KN5 accomplishes little after 8 . . . P–QN3 9 P–QN4, N–K5!

[5] Perhaps 10 . . . QN–Q2 is also good, e.g., 11 B–KB4, PxNP! 12 P–B6, N–B4, etc.

[6] Each side has achieved his goal.

[7] With a difficult game for both sides.

[8] Equally playable is 7 . . . O–O. See Game 9.

[9] After 8 P–B5 the position is similar to Idea Var. 11.

[10] Keres–Taimanov, Zurich 1953.

[11] Very favorable for White is 7 . . . N–K4 8 Q–Q4, N–Q6† 9 BxN, PxB 10 N–B3.

[12] If 9 . . . P–K3 or 9 . . . P–K4 then 10 B–N5† is strong.

[13] White has more than sufficient compensation for his Pawn.

[14] For 6 . . . Q–R4 and 6 . . . P–K3 see Idea Var. 10 and 11.

[15] A well-known mistake is 7 . . . QxNP? 8 R–B1, N–QN5 9 N–R4, QxRP 10 B–QB4, B–N5 11 N–KB3 and wins (Botvinnik–Spielmann, 1935).

[16] Recommended by Fine. If 8 B–K3?, P–K4 9 PxP e.p., B–B4 10 PxP†, K–K2 and Black has sufficient counterchances for the material sacrificed.

[17] White has the superior development.

## PRACTICAL VARIATIONS 20–23:

1 P–K4, P–QB3 2 P–QB4, P–Q4 3 KPxP, PxP

| | 20 | 21 | 22 | 23 |
|---|---|---|---|---|
| 4 | P–Q4 | – – | PxP | – – |
| | N–KB3 | – – | N–KB3 | P–QR3 |
| 5 | N–QB3 | – – | Q–R4†[12] | N–QB3 |
| | N–B3 | P–KN3 | B–Q2[13] | N–KB3 |
| 6 | N–B3[1] | Q–N3[5] | Q–N3 | Q–R4†[20] |
| | B–N5 | B–N2! | N–R3 | QN–Q2 |
| 7 | PxP[2] | PxP | P–Q4[14] | N–B3 |
| | KNxP | O–O | Q–N3 | P–KN3 |
| 8 | Q–N3[3] | B–K2[6] | B–QB4[15] | P–Q4 |
| | BxN | QN–Q2[7] | R–B1 | B–N2 |
| 9 | PxB | B–B3 | N–K2[16] | P–Q6 |
| | N–N3 | N–N3 | Q–N5† | PxP[21] |

| | 20 | 21 | 22 | 23 |
|---|---|---|---|---|
| 10 | P–Q5 | B–N5[8] | N–Q2 | = |
| | N–Q5 | B–N5[9] | P–QN4[17] | |
| 11 | Q–Q1 | BxN | P–QR3 | |
| | N–B4 | QBxB | PxB | |
| 12 | B–N5† | NxB | QxQ[18] | |
| | N–Q2 | PxB[10] | NxQ | |
| 13 | B–KB4 | O–O | PxN | |
| | P–QR3 | Q–Q2[11] | NxP | |
| 14 | B–Q3 | = | RxP | |
| | P–KN3[4] | | P–K3 | |
| 15 | = | | N–K4 | |
| | | | NxP[19] | |
| | | | ∓ | |

*Notes to practical variations 20–23:*

[1] At one time recommended by Dr. Krause. The move gives practically no chance for advantage.

[2] After 7 B–K2 safest is 7 . . . P–K3.

[3] Sharpest. After 8 B–QN5, R–B1! 9 P–KR3, BxN 10 QxB, P–K3 the game is equal.

[4] The positions are equal: 15 BxN, PxB 16 Q–Q3, B–N2! 17 QxBP, BxN† 18 PxB, Q–R4!, etc.

[5] This forces the sacrifice of a Pawn. Other moves lead to nothing.

[6] After 8 B–QB4, QN–Q2 9 KN–K2, N–N3 10 O–O, NxB 11 QxN, P–N3 12 B–N5, B–N2, Black has a good game,

continued ▶

though the situation is far from simple (Alekhine–Euwe, Zurich 1934).

[7] Most frequently played. Perhaps also to be considered is 8 . . . N–K1 followed by 9 . . . N–Q3.

[8] If 10 KN–K2 then 10 . . . B–B4 is good.

[9] Now 10 . . . B–B4 is met by 11 R–Q1. Again 10 . . . N–K1 is a possibility.

[10] Less good is 12 . . . BxB 13 O–O, R–B1 14 KR–K1, Q–B2 15 N–K5 and White has the advantage (Euwe–Van der Hoek, 1942).

[11] White's extra Pawn has little significance. See Game 10.

[12] For 5 B–N5† see Idea Var. 13.

[13] Probably 5 . . . QN–Q2 is stronger as well as simpler. For instance: 6 N–QB3, P–KN3 7 P–KN3, B–N2 8 B–N2, O–O 9 KN–K2, N–N3 10 Q–N3, B–B4! with an excellent game for Black (Sefc–Bouwmeester, 1955).

[14] Nothing results from 7 BxN, PxB 8 N–QB3 on account of 8 . . . R–QN1 9 Q–Q1, B–N4, and if 7 QxP, N–B4 8 Q–N4, P–K3 is even dangerous for White.

[15] The threat was 8 . . . QxQ and 9 . . . N–QN5.

[16] 9 N–QB3 can best answered by 9 . . . N–QN5 (threatening 10 . . . RxB).

[17] White's defense of the Queen Pawn is repulsed.

[18] Or 12 PxQ, PxQ 13 RxN, R–B2 and Black has a satisfactory position.

[19] Black has a slightly better end game (Szabo–Sliwa, 1957).

[20] For 6 Q–N3 see Game 10.

[21] Randviir–Kotov, 1947.

*Caro–Kann Defense Game 9*

*WHITE: Botvinnik* *BLACK: Konstantinopolski*

*Sverdlovsk 1943*

| WHITE | BLACK | WHITE | BLACK | WHITE | BLACK |
|---|---|---|---|---|---|
| 1 P–K4 | P–QB3 | 19 PxQ | RxP | 37 PxP | PxP |
| 2 P–Q4 | P–Q4 | 20 P–B4 | R–K2 | 38 NxP | R–N8 |
| 3 PxP | PxP | 21 KR–K1 | KR–K1 | 39 N–B3! | K–B2 |
| 4 P–QB4 | N–KB3 | 22 RxR | RxR | 40 R–QN2 | R–KB8 |
| 5 N–QB3 | P–K3 | 23 K–B2 | K–B2 | 41 N–K2! | R–K8 |
| 6 N–B3 | B–K2 | 24 R–Q1! | R–K1 | 42 K–K5! | P–Q5 |
| 7 B–N5 | O–O | 25 R–Q2 | P–KR3 | 43 KxP | K–N3 |
| 8 R–B1 | N–B3 | 26 R–K2 | R–QN1 | 44 N–B3 | K–R4 |
| 9 P–B5 | N–K5 | 27 K–K3 | R–N6 | 45 R–K2 | RxR |
| 10 BxB | QxB | 28 K–Q4 | K–B3 | 46 NxR | K–N5 |
| 11 B–K2 | B–Q2 | 29 N–R2 | R–N1 | 47 K–K5 | B–B1 |
| 12 P–QR3 | P–B4? | 30 P–QN4 | P–N4 | 48 N–Q4 | P–R4 |
| 13 B–N5 | N–N4 | 31 P–N3 | PxP | 49 NxP! | B–Q2 |
| 14 BxN | NxN† | 32 PxP | P–R3 | 50 N–N7 | B–R5 |
| 15 QxN | PxB | 33 N–B3 | R–N1 | 51 P–B5 | K–N4 |
| 16 Q–B4! | QR–K1 | 34 P–QR4 | R–N5 | 52 N–K6† | Resigns |
| 17 O–O | P–K4 | 35 R–KB2 | B–K3 | | |
| 18 QxP | QxQ | 36 P–N5! | RPxP | | |

*Caro–Kann Defense Game 10*

*WHITE: L. Steiner* *BLACK: Flohr*

*Hastings 1946–47*

| | WHITE | BLACK | | WHITE | BLACK | | WHITE | BLACK |
|---|---|---|---|---|---|---|---|---|
| 1 | P–K4 | P–QB3 | 19 | B–B3 | P–B4 | 37 | K–R2 | R–K3 |
| 2 | P–QB4 | P–Q4 | 20 | R–Q1 | KR–K1 | 38 | N–K3 | Q–Q3† |
| 3 | KPxP | PxP | 21 | P–N3 | R–K2 | 39 | QxQ | RxQ |
| 4 | PxP | P–QR3 | 22 | N–B3 | QR–K1 | 40 | N–B4 | R–QB3 |
| 5 | Q–N3 | N–KB3 | 23 | R–K2 | B–KB3 | 41 | N–K5 | R–B6 |
| 6 | N–QB3 | QN–Q2 | 24 | RxR | RxR | 42 | N–Q7 | R–QN6 |
| 7 | B–K2 | P–KN3 | 25 | N–R2 | P–QR4 | 43 | P–N5 | P–B4 |
| 8 | P–Q4 | B–N2 | 26 | Q–N5 | P–R4 | 44 | N–B6† | K–B2 |
| 9 | P–QR4 | O–O | 27 | P–QN4? | P–R5! | 45 | N–Q5 | K–K3 |
| 10 | B–B3 | N–K1 | 28 | B–N2 | PxP | 46 | N–B4† | K–Q3 |
| 11 | KN–K2 | N–Q3 | 29 | RPxP | P–B5 | 47 | NxP | R–N5 |
| 12 | O–O | P–N3 | 30 | P–N4 | P–B6! | 48 | K–N3 | R–N5† |
| 13 | N–K4 | NxN | 31 | BxP | Q–B5 | 49 | K–B3 | RxP |
| 14 | BxN | B–N2 | 32 | Q–Q3 | KBxP | 50 | N–B4 | R–N8 |
| 15 | B–N5! | N–B3 | 33 | QxB | QxB | 51 | N–Q3 | R–QR8 |
| 16 | BxN | PxB | 34 | N–B3 | PxP | 52 | N–N2 | K–Q4 |
| 17 | QR–B1 | Q–Q3 | 35 | QxP/4 | BxP! | 53 | K–B4 | K–Q5 |
| 18 | R–B2 | QR–Q1 | 36 | NxB | QxR† | | Resigns | |

## part 6—TWO KNIGHTS' VARIATION

OBSERVATIONS ON KEY POSITION 6

By postponing — or even abandoning — P–Q4 White gains time for the swift development of his minor pieces. Failure on Black's part to react accurately may spell his sudden death, but if Black maintains a closed position while soundly completing his development he need have nothing to fear.

In recent years the Two Knights' Variation has proved rather popular despite disappointing results. It can safely be assumed that unless improvements for White are found, the variation may soon disappear from tournament practice.

1 P–K4, P–QB3
2 N–QB3, P–Q4
3 N–B3

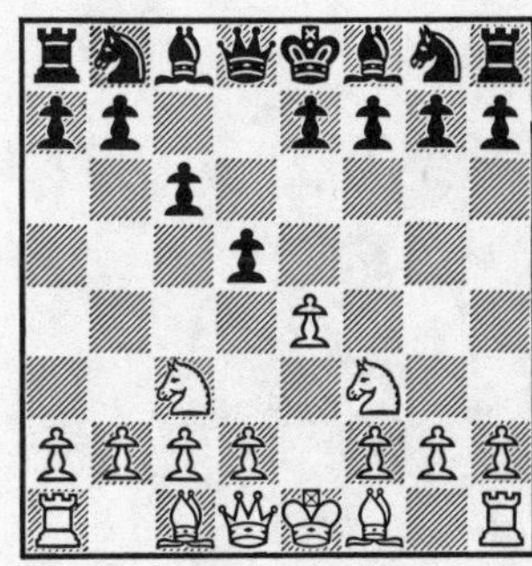

KEY POSITION 6

IDEA VARIATIONS 14–17:

(14) 3 . . . PxP 4 NxP, B–B4 5 N–N3, B–N3? 6 P–KR4, P–KR3 7 N–K5, B–R2 (relatively best is 7 . . . Q–Q3, e.g., 8 NxB, QxN 9 P–Q4, N–KB3 10 B–Q3, Q–N5 and though Black's position is bad, he can still

carry on the struggle) 8 Q–R5, P–KN3 9 B–B4! (gaining an important tempo), P–K3 10 Q–K2, N–B3? (disastrous, but 10 . . . Q–B2 would stave off only immediate defeat; Black's position is hopelessly lost) 11 NxKBP!, KxN 12 QxP† with mate to follow (Alekhine–Bruce, Plymouth 1938).

4 . . . B–B4 is an instructive error. Black believes he can transpose into the Classical Variation, but sadly learns otherwise. With 5 . . . B–N3? he blindly rushes to his doom. Better is 5 . . . B–N5, but White would then still keep an advantage after 6 B–B4, P–K3 7 P–B3, N–Q2 8 P–Q4.

(15) 3 . . . PxP 4 NxP, N–Q2 (here 4 . . . B–N5 is playable, e.g., 5 N–N3, N–B3 6 B–K2, P–K3 with approximately equal chances) 5 B–B4, KN–B3 6 N/4–N5!, P–K3 7 Q–K2 (threatening to obtain an irresistible attack by 8 NxBP), N–Q4 8 P–Q4, P–KR3 (this weakening move cannot be avoided forever) 9 N–K4, B–K2 10 O–O, Q–B2 11 B–N3, O–O 12 P–B4 with advantage to White because of his greater mobility (Smyslov–Golombek, Venice 1950).

(16) 3 . . . B–N5 (best, according to contemporary practice) 4 P–KR3, B–R4 (better is 4 . . . BxN, but the text move, when treated correctly, is probably a playable alternative) 5 PxP, PxP 6 P–KN4, B–N3 7 N–K5, P–QR3? (7 . . . N–QB3 is the right move; see Game 11) 8 P–KR4!, P–Q5 9 P–R5!, PxN 10 PxB and White has a winning attack (Noteboom–Van Mindeno, 1937).

(17) 3 . . . B–N5 4 P–KR3, BxN 5 QxB, N–B3! (this innovation of Van Scheltinga gives White more trouble than the passive 5 . . . P–K3) 6 P–Q3 (6 P–Q4, PxP 7 NxP, QxP 8 B–Q3, QN–Q2 9 B–K3, Q–QR5 is dubious for White), P–K3 7 P–KN3 (played by Fischer on several occasions without success in the Candidates' Tournament of 1959; 7 P–R3, preventing the forthcoming pin, is stronger), B–N5 8 B–Q2, P–Q5 9 N–N1, Q–N3! 10 P–N3, P–QR4 (even stronger perhaps is 10 . . . QN–Q2, e.g., 11 B–N2, P–QR4 12 P–R3, BxB† 13 NxB, Q–B4 14 Q–Q1, P–R4, and it is evident that Black's position leaves nothing to be desired) 11 P–R3, B–K2! 12 B–N2, P–R5! and Black soon obtained a decisive advantage. See Game 12.

This line provides an excellent example of Black's chances in this variation. White's two Bishops are of no significance because Black has kept his position closed.

PRACTICAL VARIATIONS 24–27:

1 P–K4, P–QB3 2 N–QB3, P–Q4 3 N–B3

| | 24 | 25 | 26 | 27 |
|---|---|---|---|---|
| 3 | — — | — — | — — | — — |
| | B–N5 | PxP | N–B3 | P–Q5[15] |
| 4 | P–KR3 | NxP | P–K5 | N–K2 |
| | BxN | N–B3 | N–K5 | P–QB4 |
| 5 | QxB | NxN† | NxN[10] | N–N3 |
| | N–B3 | NPxN | PxN | N–QB3 |
| 6 | P–Q3 | B–B4 | N–N5 | B–B4 |
| | P–K3 | B–N2[7] | Q–Q4 | P–K4 |
| 7 | P–R3[1] | P–KR3 | P–Q4[11] | P–Q3 |
| | QN–Q2[2] | B–KB4 | PxP e.p. | B–K2 |
| 8 | P–KN4 | O–O | BxP | O–O |
| | P–KN3[3] | P–K3 | QxP†[12] | N–B3 |
| 9 | Q–N3[4] | R–K1[8] | B–K3 | N–N5 |
| | P–KR4 | O–O | P–KR3[13] | O–O |
| 10 | B–N2 | P–Q4 | N–B3 | P–B4[16] |
| | Q–N3 | N–Q2 | Q–B2 | ± |
| 11 | P–N3[5] | B–B4[9] | Q–Q2 | |
| | PxNP | = | P–K4 | |
| 12 | PxNP | | O–O–O[14] | |
| | RxR | | ± | |
| 13 | BxR | | | |
| | Q–R4 | | | |
| 14 | B–Q2 | | | |
| | B–N5[6] | | | |
| | ∓ | | | |

*Notes to practical variations 24–27:*

[1] Less good is 7 B–K2, QN–Q2 8 Q–N3, P–KN3! 9 O–O, B–N2 10 B–B4, Q–N3! and Black has a good game (Smyslov–Botvinnik, 1st Match Game 1958). After 7 B–Q2, 7 . . . B–N5 can be answered immediately by 8 P–R3.

[2] For 7 . . . B–K2 8 P–KN4! see Game 13.

[3] Thus making possible the answer 9 . . . N–R4 to 9 P–N5.

[4] If 9 B–N2, B–N2 10 O–O, Q–N3=.

[5] Suddenly White is in trouble. After 11 P–N5, P–Q5 12 PxN, PxN 13 PxP, NxP he has weaknesses on both wings.

[6] Black has the initiative.

[7] There are many possibilities hereabouts for transposing into variations discussed in Part 2.

[8] To proceed after 9 . . . Q–B2 or 9 . . . N–Q2 very strongly with 10 N–Q4!

[9] Smyslov–Botvinnik, 17th Match Game 1958.

[10] This amounts to an interesting Pawn sacrifice. Safer is 5 N–K2 but then 5 . . . B–B4! is adequate.

[11] The point. White gets nice chances for the Pawn.

[12] 8 . . . QxNP 9 B–K4, Q–N5 10 Q–Q3 also gives White chances.

[13] Dangerous is 9 . . . P–KN3? on account of 10 B–B4!, P–K3 11 Q–Q8†, etc.

[14] Gligoric–Muller, Vienna 1949.

[15] This move is not recommended.

[16] White has a sound initiative.

---

## part 7—3 **P-K5 VARIATION**

### OBSERVATIONS ON KEY POSITION 7

Played by Tal with disastrous results in his 1961 match against Botvinnik, this variation still remains the theoretician's problem child. On the surface White's 3 P–K5 is senseless. Unlike its analogue in the French De-

1 P–K4, P–QB3
2 P–Q4, P–Q4
3 P–K5, B–B4

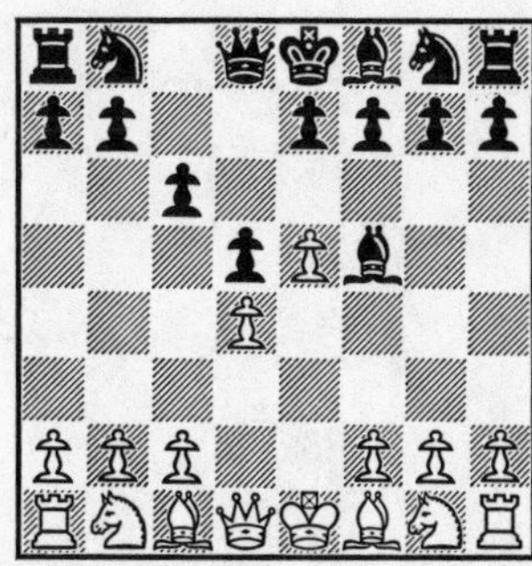

KEY POSITION 7

fense, the move has no constrictive effect on Black's Queen Bishop; but in spite of this, Black must play with caution. Only further investigation will finally determine its role in tournaments of the future.

PRACTICAL VARIATIONS 28–30:

1 P–K4, P–QB3 2 P–Q4, P–Q4 3 P–K5, B–B4

| | 28 | 29 | 30 |
|---|---|---|---|
| 4 | B–Q3 | P–KN4!? | P–QB4 |
| | BxB[1] | B–N3[4] | P–K3[7] |
| 5 | QxB | P–KR4[5] | N–QB3 |
| | P–K3 | P–KR4 | PxP[8] |
| 6 | N–QB3 | P–K6 | BxP |
| | Q–N3 | Q–Q3[6] | N–K2 |
| 7 | KN–K2 | ∓ | KN–K2 |
| | P–QB4[2] | | N–Q2 |
| 8 | PxP | | O–O |
| | BxP | | N–QN3 |

| | 28 | 29 | 30 |
|---|---|---|---|
| 9 | O–O | | B–N3 |
| | N–K2 | | Q–Q2 |
| 10 | N–R4 | | P–QR4 |
| | Q–B3 | | P–QR4 |
| 11 | NxB | | N–N3 |
| | QxN[3] | | B–N3 |
| 12 | = | | B–B2 |
| | | | BxB |
| 13 | | | QxB[9] |
| | | | N–B4[10] |
| | | | = |

*Notes to practical variations 28–30:*

[1] Weak is 4 . . . B–N3 5 BxB! (less clear is 5 P–K6, Q–Q3!), RPxB 6 P–K6!, etc.

[2] The characteristic sally in the center.

[3] Nimzowitsch–Capablanca, New York 1927.

[4] Also safe and good is 4 . . . B–Q2.

[5] Again 5 P–K6 can be met by 5 . . . Q–Q3!

[6] White's Kingside Pawn structure is punctured.

[7] Too bold is 4 . . . BxN 5 RxB, Q–R4† 6 B–Q2, QxP 7 P–B5!, etc.

[8] 5 . . . B–QN5, too, is possible.

[9] White's plus in space is counterbalanced by Black's sounder Pawn position.

[10] A difficult game. For 13 . . . KN–Q4? see Game 14.

*Caro–Kann Defense Game 14*

*WHITE: Tal* *BLACK: Golombek*

*Chess Olympics, Munich 1958*

| WHITE | BLACK | WHITE | BLACK |
|---|---|---|---|
| 1 P–K4 | P–QB3 | 8 O–O | N–QN3 |
| 2 P–Q4 | P–Q4 | 9 B–N3 | Q–Q2 |
| 3 P–K5 | B–B4 | 10 P–QR4 | P–QR4 |
| 4 P–QB4 | P–K3 | 11 N–N3 | B–N3 |
| 5 N–QB3 | PxP | 12 B–B2 | BxB |
| 6 BxP | N–K2 | 13 QxB | KN–Q4? |
| 7 KN–K2! | N–Q2 | 14 QN–K4 | N–N5 |

| | WHITE | BLACK | | WHITE | BLACK |
|---|---|---|---|---|---|
| 15 | Q–K2 | N/3–Q4 | 26 | N–B5 | Q–B1 |
| 16 | P–B4 | P–KN3 | 27 | P–B5 | NPxP |
| 17 | R–R3 | B–K2 | 28 | Q–K3 | P–N3 |
| 18 | B–Q2 | N–B7 | 29 | Q–N5 | R–R2 |
| 19 | R–Q3 | N/4–N5 | 30 | R–B4! | PxN |
| 20 | BxN | NxN | 31 | RxP | RxR |
| 21 | QR–Q1 | R–Q1 | 32 | Q–N7† | K–K1 |
| 22 | K–R1 | P–R4 | 33 | Q–N8† | K–Q2 |
| 23 | N–B6† | BxN | 34 | QxP† | K–Q3 |
| 24 | PxB | K–B1 | 35 | Q–K7† | Resigns |
| 25 | N–K4 | P–R5 | | | |

## part 8—GAMBIT VARIATION

OBSERVATIONS ON KEY POSITION 8

Although White's third move does not constitute the sacrifice of a Pawn, White should not play this move if he is not prepared to continue in true gambit style. Black does best to refuse the gambit, in which case he frequently obtains a positional advantage.

1 P–K4, P–QB3
2 P–Q4, P–Q4
3 P–KB3

KEY POSITION 8

PRACTICAL VARIATIONS 31–33:

1 P–K4, P–QB3 2 P–Q4, P–Q4 3 P–KB3

| | 31 | 32 | 33 |
|---|---|---|---|
| 3 | – – | – – | – – |
| | PxP | P–K3 | – – |
| 4 | PxP | B–K3 | N–B3 |
| | P–K4 | N–B3![3] | N–B3 |
| 5 | N–KB3 | B–Q3[4] | B–KN5[6] |
| | B–K3![1] | P–B4! | P–KR3 |
| 6 | N–B3 | P–B3 | B–KB4 |
| | B–QN5[2] | BPxP | Q–N3 |
| 7 | = | BPxP | P–QR3 |
| | | PxP | P–B4[7] |
| 8 | | PxP | KN–K2 |
| | | NxP![5] | N–B3 |
| 9 | | ∓ | PxBP |
| | | | BxP[8] |
| | | | ∓ |

*Notes to practical variations 31–33:*

[1] A risky continuation is 5 . . . PxP 6 B–QB4, N–B3! 7 O–O, B–QB4! 8 N–N5, O–O 9 NxBP, Q–K2! with troublesome complications.

continued ▸

[2] Difficult and requiring sharp play by both sides.

[3] Dangerous is 4 . . . PxP, e.g., 5 N–Q2, PxP 6 KNxP, N–B3 7 N–B4, with attacking chances (Smyslov–Gereben, 1949).

[4] Better is 5 N–B3. After 5 . . . Q–N3 6 Q–Q2, QxNP 7 R–N1, Q–R6, White has sufficient compensation for the Pawn.

[5] Tartakover–Sultan Khan, 1931. If 9 BxN then 9 . . . Q–R5†.

[6] After 5 P–K5, KN–Q2 6 P–B4, P–QB4 the game has transposed remarkably into the Steinitz Variation of the French Defense.

[7] Energetic and correct.

[8] Smyslov–Botvinnik, 15th Match Game 1958.

## UNUSUAL VARIATIONS 1–4:
1 P–K4, P–QB3

| | *1* | *2* | *3* | *4* |
|---|---|---|---|---|
| *2* | N–KB3<br>P–Q4 | Q–K2<br>P–Q4 | P–KB4<br>P–Q4 | P–QN3<br>P–Q4 |
| *3* | P–K5<br>B–B4 | P–Q3<br>PxP | P–K5<br>P–KR4 | PxP<br>PxP |
| *4* | N–Q4<br>B–N3 | PxP<br>P–K4 | B–K2<br>P–KN3 | B–N2<br>N–QB3 |
| *5* | P–K6<br>Q–N3! | N–KB3<br>B–KN5 | N–KB3<br>B–N5 | P–KN3<br>P–K4 |
| *6* | Q–N4<br>P–QB4! | P–KR3<br>B–R4 | P–B3<br>P–K3 | B–N2<br>N–B3![4] |
| *7* | PxP†<br>KxP | B–Q2<br>N–Q2 | P–Q3<br>N–KR3[3] | = |
| *8* | N–KB3<br>N–KB3 | P–B3<br>P–B3[2] | = | |
| *9* | Q–B8<br>Q–K3†[1] | = | | |
| | ∓ | | | |

*Notes to unusual variations 1–4:*

[1] Tolush–Kotov, 1944.

[2] Niephaus–Rodl, 1947.

[3] The pattern is sound but unappetizing.

[4] Less good is 6 . . . B–K3 7 Q–K2! as played in a game Euwe–Reti, 1920.

*Caro–Kann Defense Game 11*

*WHITE: Fischer* *BLACK: Smyslov*

*Candidates' Tournament 1959, 7th Round*

| | WHITE | BLACK | | WHITE | BLACK |
|---|---|---|---|---|---|
| 1 | P–K4 | P–QB3 | 5 | PxP | PxP |
| 2 | N–QB3 | P–Q4 | 6 | B–N5† | N–B3 |
| 3 | N–B3 | B–N5 | 7 | P–KN4 | B–N3 |
| 4 | P–KR3 | B–R4 | 8 | N–K5 | R–B1! |

| | WHITE | BLACK | | WHITE | BLACK |
|---|---|---|---|---|---|
| 9 | P–KR4 | P–B3 | 32 | NxP | QR–Q6† |
| 10 | NxB | PxN | 33 | K–B1 | RxQP |
| 11 | P–Q4 | P–K3 | 34 | N–K3 | NxN |
| 12 | Q–Q3 | K–B2 | 35 | PxN | RxNP |
| 13 | P–R5 | PxP | 36 | K–Q2 | P–N5 |
| 14 | PxP | KN–K2 | 37 | R–QB1 | R–N2 |
| 15 | B–K3 | N–B4 | 38 | R–KN1 | R–Q2† |
| 16 | BxN | RxB | 39 | K–B2 | P–B4 |
| 17 | N–K2 | Q–R4† | 40 | P–K4 | K–B3 |
| 18 | P–B3 | Q–R3 | 41 | PxP | P–N6 |
| 19 | Q–B2 | B–Q3 | 42 | R–K8 | R–KN2 |
| 20 | B–B4 | BxB | 43 | R–B8† | K–K2 |
| 21 | NxB | R–R3 | 44 | R–QR8 | K–Q3 |
| 22 | Q–K2 | QxQ† | 45 | R–KB8 | R–B7† |
| 23 | KxQ | R–R1 | 46 | K–Q3 | P–N7 |
| 24 | K–Q3 | P–QN4 | 47 | P–B6 | R–N6† |
| 25 | KR–K1 | P–N5 | 48 | K–B4 | K–K3 |
| 26 | PxP | R–B5 | 49 | R–K1† | K–B4 |
| 27 | NxKP | RxRP | 50 | P–B7 | R–N2 |
| 28 | P–N3 | R–R6† | 51 | R–KN1 | K–B3 |
| 29 | K–Q2 | QR–B6 | 52 | P–R4 | RxP |
| 30 | N–B4 | KR–B6 | | Draw | |
| 31 | R–K2 | P–N4 | | | |

*Caro–Kann Defense Game 12*

*WHITE: Fischer* *BLACK: Keres*

*Candidates' Tournament 1959*

| | WHITE | BLACK | | WHITE | BLACK |
|---|---|---|---|---|---|
| 1 | P–K4 | P–QB3 | 17 | Q–K2 | P–K4 |
| 2 | N–QB3 | P–Q4 | 18 | P–KB4 | KR–B1 |
| 3 | N–B3 | B–N5 | 19 | P–R4 | R–B3 |
| 4 | P–KR3 | BxN | 20 | B–R3 | Q–B2 |
| 5 | QxB | N–B3! | 21 | PxP | QNxP |
| 6 | P–Q3 | P–K3 | 22 | B–B4 | B–Q3 |
| 7 | P–KN3 | B–N5 | 23 | P–R5 | R–R4 |
| 8 | B–Q2 | P–Q5 | 24 | P–R6 | N–N3 |
| 9 | N–N1 | Q–N3 | 25 | Q–B3 | R–R4 |
| 10 | P–N3 | P–QR4 | 26 | B–N4 | N/NxB |
| 11 | P–R3 | B–K2! | 27 | BxR | N/5xB |
| 12 | B–N2 | P–R5! | 28 | P–N4 | B–R7† |
| 13 | P–QN4 | QN–Q2 | 29 | K–N2 | NxNP |
| 14 | O–O | P–B4 | 30 | N–Q2 | N–K6† |
| 15 | R–R2 | O–O | | Resigns | |
| 16 | PxP | BxP | | | |

*Caro–Kann Defense Game 13*

*WHITE: Smyslov* *BLACK: Botvinnik*

*Nineteenth Match Game 1958*

| | WHITE | BLACK | | WHITE | BLACK | | WHITE | BLACK |
|---|---|---|---|---|---|---|---|---|
| 1 | P–K4 | P–QB3 | 13 | O–O–O | Q–N1 | 25 | Q–N3 | P–R5 |
| 2 | N–QB3 | P–Q4 | 14 | P–B4 | PxP | 26 | Q–N4 | PxP |
| 3 | N–B3 | B–N5 | 15 | NxP | N–B3 | 27 | BxP | K–B1 |
| 4 | P–KR3 | BxN | 16 | NxN† | BxN | 28 | B–K4 | Q–R7 |
| 5 | QxB | N–B3 | 17 | Q–B2 | B–R5 | 29 | P–B3 | R–Q1 |
| 6 | P–Q3 | P–K3 | 18 | Q–B3 | N–K2 | 30 | R–B1! | N–Q4 |
| 7 | P–R3 | B–K2 | 19 | B–Q3 | P–KN3 | 31 | B–Q2 | R–Q3 |
| 8 | P–KN4 | KN–Q2 | 20 | P–B5! | KPxP | 32 | Q–B8† | K–K2 |
| 9 | P–Q4 | N–B1 | 21 | B–KB4 | Q–Q1 | 33 | QxP† | R–Q2 |
| 10 | B–K3 | N–N3 | 22 | PxP | Q–Q4 | 34 | QR–K1! | Q–R8† |
| 11 | Q–N3 | B–R5 | 23 | Q–N4 | B–B3 | 35 | B–N1† | Resigns |
| 12 | Q–R2 | N–Q2 | 24 | KR–K1 | P–KR4 | | | |

*Caro–Kann Defense Game 14*

*WHITE: Fischer* *BLACK: Portisch*

*Stockholm Interzonal 1962*

| | WHITE | BLACK | | WHITE | BLACK | | WHITE | BLACK |
|---|---|---|---|---|---|---|---|---|
| 1 | P–K4 | P–QB3 | 24 | B–R4 | QR–Q1 | 47 | K–K5 | R–Q7 |
| 2 | N–QB3 | P–Q4 | 25 | KR–Q1 | RxR | 48 | R–QB3 | P–N3 |
| 3 | N–B3 | PxP | 26 | RxR | P–KN4 | 49 | P–B5 | R–Q8 |
| 4 | NxP | N–Q2 | 27 | B–Q1 | B–B3 | 50 | R–R3 | P–N4 |
| 5 | B–B4 | KN–B3 | 28 | R–Q6 | R–B1 | 51 | R–R7† | K–N1 |
| 6 | N/4–N5 | N–Q4 | 29 | K–B2 | K–B1 | 52 | R–N7 | PxP |
| 7 | P–Q4 | P–KR3 | 30 | B–B3 | BxB | 53 | PxP | R–Q5 |
| 8 | N–K4 | N/2–N3 | 31 | PxB | PxP | 54 | K–K6 | R–K5† |
| 9 | B–N3 | B–B4 | 32 | PxP | K–K2 | 55 | K–Q5 | R–B5 |
| 10 | N–N3 | B–R2 | 33 | P–B5 | PxP | 56 | KxP | RxKBP† |
| 11 | O–O | P–K3 | 34 | RxP | R–Q1 | 57 | K–Q6 | R–B3† |
| 12 | N–K5 | N–Q2 | 35 | K–K2 | R–KN1 | 58 | K–K5 | R–B2 |
| 13 | P–QB4 | N/4–B3 | 36 | K–B2 | R–Q1 | 59 | R–N6 | R–B2 |
| 14 | B–B4 | NxN | 37 | K–K3 | R–Q8 | 60 | K–Q5 | R–B2 |
| 15 | BxN | B–Q3 | 38 | P–N3 | R–K8† | 61 | RxP | R–B2 |
| 16 | Q–K2 | O–O | 39 | K–B4 | R–K7 | 62 | R–N6† | K–B1 |
| 17 | QR–Q1 | Q–K2 | 40 | KxP | RxP | 63 | R–Q6 | K–K2 |
| 18 | BxB | QxB | 41 | P–B4 | R–K7 | 64 | P–B5 | R–B1 |
| 19 | P–B4 | P–B4 | 42 | R–R3 | R–K8 | 65 | P–B6 | R–B2 |
| 20 | Q–K5 | QxQ | 43 | R–Q3 | R–QN8 | 66 | R–R6 | K–Q1 |
| 21 | QPxQ | N–K5 | 44 | R–K3 | R–N7 | 67 | R–R8† | K–K2 |
| 22 | R–Q7 | NxN | 45 | P–K6 | P–R3 | 68 | R–R8 | Resigns |
| 23 | PxN | B–K5 | 46 | PxP† | KxP | | | |

# chapter 17—French Defense

The reply 1 . . . P–K3 to 1 P–K4 is very old and already mentioned in Lucena's work of 1497. But the name "French Defense" became generally accepted only after 1834, when a correspondence game between London and Paris, in which the French replied with 1 . . . P–K3 to 1 P–K4, was won by Black. Later, the Russian master Jaenisch published an extensive analysis in 1842 of the variations springing from 1 . . . P–K3. But only toward the end of the nineteenth century did this debut become popular, in which connection the name of Maroczy deserves special mention.

The French Defense is based on the idea of attacking White's King Pawn so that White will be forced to decide upon an immediate course of action. After 1 P–K4, P–K3 2 P–Q4, P–Q4, White may protect his Pawn with a piece: 3 N–QB3 or 3 N–Q2. Or he may exchange Pawns by 3 PxP, PxP. Or he may advance the Pawn: 3 P–K5. The Exchange Variation, 3 PxP, has disappeared from the scene, while the "push," 3 P–K5, is rarely played. The exchange line leads to a symmetrical position with strong drawish tendencies. The Pawn advance with its relief of tension in the center allows Black to mount an early attack on White's Pawn center.

The main continuation after 3 N–QB3 is 3 . . . N–KB3 4 B–N5, B–K2 5 P–K5, KN–Q2 6 BxB, QxB. This is the so-called Classical Variation (Part 1), in which Black obtains a sound but somewhat passive position. White, however, may increase the impetus of the struggle by playing 6 P–KR4, the Alekhine–Chatard attack, offering a Pawn (Part 2). Though many players fear this attack, there is no proof that 6 P–KR4 is stronger than 6 BxB.

To avoid the classical line, Black may vary at his fourth move and play 4 . . . B–N5 or 4 . . . PxP. The former increases the pressure on White's King Pawn and leads to the interesting MacCutcheon Variation (Part 4). This line offers good tactical possibilities for Black but has some strategic drawbacks.

The move 4 . . . PxP, the Burn Variation, is safe enough but White has a slight superiority in the center. See Part 5.

To-day, Black's most frequent reply to 3 N–QB3 is 3 . . . B–N5, a continuation popularized by the Russian masters, led by Botvinnik. This effective pin strengthens Black's pressure on White's King Pawn. White can react in several ways: advance, exchange, protect, or sacrifice. White's usual procedure is 4 P–K5, and Black attacks the center with 4 . . . P–QB4, when follows 5 P–QR3, BxN† 6 PxB, leading to very complicated positions (Parts 7–9). If White wishes to avoid this complex Nimzo–Variation, he can play 3 N–Q2, the so-called Tarrasch Variation (Parts 11–15), but since this lifts the pressure on Black's Q4, Black can immediately react with 3 . . . P–QB4. White then replies 4 P–K5 and maintains a slight edge, but the chances for a draw are great.

With this we have summed up those systems of the French Defense considered today to be the most important. The ensuing complete treatment of the French Defense contains, however, some variations which, though out of date, are sometimes used: for instance, the Anderssen Attack (Part 3) and the Steinitz Variation (Part 6).

---

## part 1—CLASSICAL VARIATION, RUBINSTEIN SYSTEM

1 P–K4, P–K3
2 P–Q4, P–Q4
3 N–QB3, N–KB3
4 B–N5, B–K2
5 P–K5, KN–Q2
6 BxB, QxB
7 Q–Q2, O–O[A]
8 P–B4[B], P–QB4[C]
9 N–B3[D], N–QB3

KEY POSITION 1

### OBSERVATIONS ON KEY POSITION 1

[A] Bad is 7 . . . P–QB4, since the entailed offer of the Exchange, 8 N–N5, O–O 9 N–B7, offers no chances for Black. Possible is 7 . . . P–QR3, which after 8 P–B4, P–QB4 9 N–B3, N–QB3 10 PxP transposes to Sup. Var. 2.

[B] Maroczy's move, 8 N–N5, is well met by 8 . . . P–QR3, and if White grabs the Pawn (9 NxP?) there follows 9 . . . R–R2 10 P–QB4, PxP 11 P–Q5, Q–B4! To try to build up a center by 8 N–Q1 followed by 9 P–QB3 is too clumsy: 8 N–Q1, P–QB4 9 P–QB3, P–B3 10 P–KB4, N–QB3 11 N–B3, PxQP 12 PxQP, PxP 13 BPxP, RxN! 14 PxR, Q–R5†, with very good play for Black. If White now plays 15 Q–B2, Black answers 15 . . . NxQP! (Gottschall–Tarrasch, Frankfurt 1887).

In the above line beginning with 8 N–Q1, if White varies on his 13th move with 13 QPxP, Black gets the better of it with 13 . . . N–B4! Playable is 8 QN–K2, P–QB4 9 P–QB3, P–B3 10 P–KB4, PxQP 11 PxQP, PxP 12 BPxP, N–QB3 13 N–KB3, N–N3 14 N–N3, B–Q2 or 14 . . . Q–N5 with equality (analysis by Tartakover).

[C] Also possible is 8 . . . P–KB3 which, after 9 PxP, QxP 10 P–KN3 transposes into the main variation. In the above line White should not play 9 N–B3 because he runs into difficulties in the center after 9 . . . PxP 10 BPxP, P–B4.

D Less consistent is 9 N–N5, P–QR3! 10 N–Q6, PxP 11 N–B3, N–QB3 12 B–Q3, P–B3 and White's center falls (Asztalos–Spielmann, Bad–Vedes 1931). If White varies in the above line with 12 NxQP, Black counters with 12 . . . N/2xP 13 PxN, Q–R5†!

The most important point in the Classical Variation is the set-up starting with 7 Q–Q2, introduced by Rubinstein. White intends to castle on the Queenside with P–KN3 and B–KN2 to follow. He also may start with the Kingside fianchetto and castle later on that side.

In both cases White intends to meet the attack on his center with KPxBP combined with QPxQBP. White, with his center Pawns gone, nonetheless still controls his Q4 and K5 with his pieces, blockading Black's center Pawns. Black, whose Queen Bishop is blockaded by his own Pawns, must be careful not to drift into an end game where White's Knight is placed in an unassailable position on Q4 or K5. Counterchances in the middle game are Black's best bet. He may play for attack against the King if White castles on the Queenside. In all cases, Black must try to create tactical complications. White's best strategy to restrict his opponent's chances is the immediate Pawn exchange on his QB5 (Prac. Var. 4 and 5).

IDEA VARIATIONS 1–3:

(1) 10 O–O–O, P–B3. By this move Black allows White to carry out his strategy in full. 11 KPxP, QxP 12 P–KN3, P–QR3 13 B–N2, N–N3 14 KR–K1, N–B5 15 Q–B2, P–QN4 16 PxP, NxP 17 KxN, P–N5 18 N–Q4 brings about a complicated position with chances for both sides (Rubinstein–Loewenfisch, Carlsbad 1911). In the above line, if 12 . . . PxP 13 KNxP, N–B4 14 B–N2, B–Q2 15 KR–K1 White has the better of it (Stahlberg–Keres, Kemeri 1937).

(2) 10 O–O–O, P–B5 (still better is 10 . . . N–N3) 11 P–KN4, R–N1 12 B–R3, P–QN4 13 P–B5, P–N5 14 N–K2, P–N6, and Black's attack is the more dangerous. However, in this line White can vary at move 12 with 12 P–B5! P–QN4 13 Q–N5, QxQ 14 NxQ with good chances (L. Steiner–Purdy, Adelaide 1947).

(3) 10 P–KN3, P–QR3 11 B–KN2, P–QN4 (stronger is 11 . . . N–N3) 12 O–O, PxP 13 KNxP, NxN 14 QxN, Q–B4 15 QxQ, NxQ 16 N–K2 with the occupation of Q4 and a clear end game advantage for White.

PRACTICAL VARIATIONS 1–5:

1 P–K4, P–K3 2 P–Q4, P–Q4 3 N–QB3, N–KB3 4 B–N5, B–K2 5 P–K5, KN–Q2 6 BxB, QxB 7 Q–Q2, O–O 8 P–B4, P–QB4 9 N–B3, N–QB3

| | *1* | *2* | *3* | *4* | *5* |
|---|---|---|---|---|---|
| *10* | O–O–O | P–KN3 | – – | PxP! | – – |
| | N–N3![1] | P–QR3 | P–B3 | NxBP | QxP |
| *11* | P–KR4 | B–N2 | KPxP | O–O–O[9] | O–O–O |
| | B–Q2 | N–N3![3] | NxBP | P–QR3 | P–B3 |
| *12* | R–R3 | P–N3 | O–O–O[6] | B–Q3 | PxP |
| | NxQP | B–Q2 | PxP[7] | P–QN4 | NxP |
| *13* | NxN | N–K2 | KNxP | N–K2 | B–Q3 |
| | PxN | PxP | P–K4 | B–Q2 | B–Q2 |
| *14* | N–K2 | QNxP[4] | PxP | KN–Q4 | K–N1 |
| | P–B3 | Q–B4 | QxP | NxN | QR–QN1 |
| *15* | NxP | O–O | B–N2[8] | NxN[10] | QR–K1 |
| | PxP | N–B1 | B–N5 | ± | P–QN4 |
| *16* | PxP | K–R1 | N–B3 | | N–K2[11] |
| | QR–B1[2] | N/1–K2[5] | Q–R4 | | ± |
| | = | = | ∓ | | |

*Notes to practical variations 1–5:*

[1] Less good is 10 . . . P–B3 or 10 . . . P–B5 (see Idea Var. 1 and 2). But to be considered is 10 . . . P–QR3 to be followed by . . . P–QN4.

[2] (Wade–Eliskases, Stockholm 1952).

[3] Weaker for Black is 11 . . . P–QN4 12 O–O. See Idea Var. 3.

[4] Or 14 KNxP, P–B3 15 PxP, PxP 16 O–O, P–K4 with good play for Black (Kostisch–Maroczy, Bad Veldes 1931).

[5] (L. Steiner–Yanofsky, Karlsbad 1948).

[6] The White King dare not remain in the center in view of an imminent . . . P–K4 on Black's part. For instance, 12 B–N2, PxP 13 KNxP, P–K4! 14 NxP, KNxN 15 BxN†, K–R1 16 N–K2, B–N5 17 O–O–O, QR–Q1 18 P–B4, N–N5 with an overwhelming position for Black. (L. Steiner–Stahlberg, Budapest 1934). Or 12 PxP, P–K4! 13 NxQP, NxN 14 QxN†, B–K3 and White is in trouble.

[7] Black must free his position. After 12 . . . B–Q2 13 R–K1, PxP 14 KNxP, Q–B4 15 N–N3 White has the edge.

[8] A little stronger is 15 B–K2. After the text move Black obtains a good position.

[9] If 11 B–Q3, P–B3 12 PxP, QxP 13 P–KN3, Black's correct continuation, according to Alekhine, is 13 . . . NxB† 14 PxN, P–K4! 15 O–O, B–R6 16 KR–K1, QR–K1, with the better game for Black. In the above line if White plays 14 QxN, the Queen later on becomes a target for the Black Bishop, which develops with tempos via Q2, K1, and KN3. Also, in this line, if White plays 15 QNxP, then 15 . . . Q–B2 presents Black with important tempos. Continuing the main line, if White now plays 17 NxQP, Black plays . . . Q–B2 with all his pieces poised for attack. However, in the above line if Black varies with 13

. . . B–Q2, there follows 14 O–O, NxB 15 PxN, B–K1 16 QR–K1, B–N3 (so far this is Capablanca–Reti, New York 1924) and White gets the better game with 17 N–K5.

[10] Gligoric–Stahlberg, 7th Match Game 1949.

[11] If 16 . . . P–N5 17 QN–Q4, NxN 18 NxN with a positional edge for White (Sterner–Czerniak, Chess Olympics, Munich 1958). Somewhat better is 16 . . . K–R1.

## SUPPLEMENTARY VARIATIONS 1–5:

1 P–K4, P–K3 2 P–Q4, P–Q4 3 N–QB3, N–KB3 4 B–N5, B–K2 5 P–K5, KN–Q2 6 BxB, QxB

Apart from 7 Q–Q2 (the Rubinstein system, Part 1), there are a number of other continuations at White's disposal. Most important is 7 P–B4 (Steinitz, Sup. Var. 1 and 2), much in conformity with the Rubinstein system. 7 B–Q3 (Tarrasch, Sup. Var. 3) is slightly inferior strategically to 7 Q–Q2 and 7 P–B4. True, with 7 B–Q3 White develops a piece, but neglects to strengthen his center. This drawback shows up even more distinctly after 7 Q–N4? (Pollack, Sup. Var. 4). Finally, White may proceed with 7 N–N5 (Alapin, Sup. Var. 5) in order to support his center with P–QB3, but this idea costs too much time.

| | *1* | *2* | *3* | *4* | *5* |
|---|---|---|---|---|---|
| 7 | P–B4 | – – | B–Q3 | Q–N4 | N–N5 |
| | O–O | P–QR3[7] | O–O[11] | O–O | N–N3 |
| 8 | N–B3 | N–B3 | QN–K2[12] | N–B3 | P–QB3 |
| | P–QB4 | P–QB4 | P–QB4[13] | P–QB4 | P–QR3 |
| *9* | B–Q3[1] | PxP | P–QB3 | B–Q3 | N–QR3 |
| | P–B3[2] | N–QB3[8] | P–B3 | P–B4[17] | P–QB4[19] |
| *10* | QPxP[3] | P–QR3[9] | P–KB4 | PxP e.p. | P–KB4 |
| | N–B3[4] | QxP | PxKP | RxP | N–B3 |
| *11* | PxP | Q–Q2 | BPxP[14] | Q–R4 | N–B2 |
| | QxP/3 | P–QN4 | PxP | N–B1 | N–R5 |
| *12* | P–KN3 | Q–B2 | NxP | PxP | R–N1 |
| | NxP | B–N2 | Q–N4[15] | QxP | P–QN4 |
| *13* | O–O | QxQ | KN–B3 | O–O | N–B3 |
| | B–Q2[5] | NxQ[10] | QxNP | N–B3[18] | B–Q2[20] |
| *14* | Q–Q2 | ± | R–KN1 | ∓ | = |
| | B–K1 | | QxNP | | |
| *15* | QR–K1 | | NxP | | |
| | R–Q1 | | QxP†[16] | | |
| *16* | N–K5[6] | | = | | |
| | ± | | | | |

*Notes to supplementary variations 1–5:*

[1] With 9 Q–Q2 White can transpose into the main line. After 9 N–QN5 Black has Bronstein's strong suggestion at his disposal: 9 . . . PxP 10 N–B7, NxP 11 NxR, NxN† 12 QxN, Q–N5†!

continued ▸

[2] White threatened a Bishop sacrifice at KR7. Also good for Black is 9 . . . P–B4. If White takes the Pawn *en passant,* this leads to note 5. But if White closes the center, Black obtains a strong point at his K5 as follows: 9 . . . P–B4 10 O–O, P–QR3 11 PxP, NxBP 12 N–K2, N–B3 13 P–B3, B–Q2. See Game 1.

[3] In Bronstein–Yanofsky (Saltsjobaden) White obtained the edge after 10 KPxP, RxP 11 Q–Q2, N–B3 12 PxP, NxP 13 O–O, NxB 14 PxN, Q–QB2 15 N–K2, B–Q2 16 Q–K3. Less clear are the consequences stemming from 10 . . . QxP. Bronstein gave 11 N–KN5 as the right continuation, but Gusev pointed out that Black can afford 11 . . . QxBP 12 BxP†, K–R1 13 Q–R5, Q–B7† 14 K–Q1, N–KB3. Worth closer investigation in the above line is 10 . . . QxP 11 P–KN3, PxP 12 NxP. Or 11 . . . N–B3 12 PxP.

[4] Or 10 . . . . QxP 11 N–Q4, Q–N3 12 Q–R5, P–B4 13 QN–K2, N–B4 (Corte–Stahlberg, Parana 1946) and now 14 O–O–O with a sharp position offering chances to both sides (Keres). White may vary with 12 N–R4, Q–R4† 13 P–B3, threatening 14 P–QN4! Or 10 . . . PxP 11 PxP, QxP and White simply plays 12 Q–Q2 because Black's . . . Q–N5 no longer involves a simultaneous attack on two Pawns.

[5] 13 . . . NxB 14 PxN, B–Q2 15 Q–Q2, P–K4 16 QR–K1 favors White (Alekhine). In the above line Black may vary with 15 . . . B–K1 16 KR–K1 and White has the edge. (Capablanca–Reti, New York 1924). See note 9, Prac. Var. 4, Part 1.

[6] White controls the center and Black's Pawns are fixed.

[7] Black keeps his King in the center for the time being, aiming for a quick . . . P–QB4, but first he must make the preliminary text move. The immediate 7 . . . P–QB4 is dubious because of 8 N–N5, O–O 9 N–B7, PxP 10 NxR, P–B3 11 N–B3, PxP 12 PxP, N–QB3 13 B–Q3, N/2xP 14 O–O, N–KN5 15 N–Q2! (Loewenfisch–Fahrni, Carlsbad 1911).

[8] 9 . . . QxP favors White because of his control of Q4 after 10 Q–Q4!, QxQ 11 NxQ, N–QB3 12 N/3–K2, NxN 13 NxN, N–N1 14 K–B2!, N–B3 15 K–K3, NxN 16 KxN. If Black varies with 10 . . . N–QB3 11 QxQ, NxQ 12 B–Q3, followed by N–K2, White has a slight edge (Konstantinopolsky–Lilienthal, Moscow 1936).

[9] 10 B–Q3, QxP 11 Q–Q2, P–QN4 12 Q–B2, B–N2 13 QxQ, NxQ 14 N–K2, P–Q5! 15 N/2xP, O–O–O and Black favorably recovers the Pawn (Stahlberg–Alekhine, Warsaw 1935).

[10] 14 N–K2, P–B3 15 QN–Q4, NxN 16 NxN, PxP 17 PxP, K–K2 and Black has sufficient counterplay because of the vulnerability of White's KP. Stronger, according to Keres, is 14 O–O–O followed by B–Q3 and QR–K1, and only later, if possible, N–K2–Q4.

[11] 7 . . . P–QB4? is bad because of 8 N–N5; but 7 . . . P–QR3 (Maroczy) is a steady continuation. Too risky is 7 . . . Q–N5 (Schlechter) 8 N–B3, QxNP 9 QN–K2, P–QB4 10 P–QB3 with a strong attack for White (Keres).

[12] 8 P–B4! P–QB4 9 N–B3 transposes into Sup. Var. 1.

[13] 8 . . . Q–N5† 9 P–B3, QxNP 10 P–KB4 followed by N–KB3 offers White good attacking chances.

[14] 11 QPxKP, P–KN4 proves unpleasant for White.

[15] Also possible is 12 . . . NxP 13 BxP†, KxB 14 Q–R5†, K–N1 15 QxN, N–B3 (Keres).

[16] 16 K–K2, Q–N7† 17 K–K1, Q–B6† with perpetual check (analysis by Euwe).

[17] Alekhine recommends 9 . . . PxP. And now the sacrifice 10 BxP†, KxB 11 Q–R5†, K–N1 12 N–KN5 leads after 12 . . . QxN 13 QxQ, PxN to a position where Black, having three pieces for the Queen, is not badly off.

[18] 14 QR–K1, B–Q2 15 N–K5, NxN 16 RxN, Q–N3 with a good game for Black (Bernstein–Lasker, Zurich 1934).

[19] 9 . . . P–KB3 is best met, according to Panov, by 10 PxP!, QxP 11 Q–R5†, Q–B2 12 Q–R4 followed by N–B3, B–Q3, and O–O. In the above line Black may vary: 11 . . . P–N3 12 Q–R6, P–K4 13 PxP, QxP† 14 K–Q2!

[20] Black has sufficient counterplay on the Queenside (Lasker–Lilienthal, Moscow 1936).

*French Defense Game 1*

*WHITE: Bondarevski* *BLACK: Lilienthal*

*Saltsjobaden 1948*

| | WHITE | BLACK | | WHITE | BLACK | | WHITE | BLACK |
|---|---|---|---|---|---|---|---|---|
| 1 | P–K4 | P–K3 | 25 | P–N4 | Q–R5 | 49 | Q–B3 | N–B5 |
| 2 | P–Q4 | P–Q4 | 26 | QR–B1 | P–B6 | 50 | QxP | QxQ |
| 3 | N–QB3 | N–KB3 | 27 | PxQBP | RxBP | 51 | RxQ | NxB |
| 4 | B–N5 | B–K2 | 28 | RxR | PxR | 52 | RxP | N–K6 |
| 5 | P–K5 | KN–Q2 | 29 | Q–K3 | P–B7 | 53 | R–N5 | R–N3 |
| 6 | BxB | QxB | 30 | K–N2 | R–QB1 | 54 | P–QR4 | N–B5 |
| 7 | P–B4 | O–O | 31 | R–QB1 | R–B6 | 55 | R–N4 | N–R4 |
| 8 | N–B3 | P–QB4 | 32 | Q–B4 | Q–R6† | 56 | P–R3 | K–N2 |
| 9 | B–Q3 | P–B4 | 33 | K–N1 | R–B1 | 57 | K–R2 | K–B2 |
| 10 | O–O | P–QR3 | 34 | B–B3 | R–KN1 | 58 | P–R4 | K–K2 |
| 11 | PxP | NxBP | 35 | RxP | Q–R5 | 59 | K–R3 | R–QB3 |
| 12 | N–K2 | N–B3 | 36 | Q–B1 | N–N4 | 60 | R–N5 | N–N2 |
| 13 | P–B3 | B–Q2 | 37 | B–N2 | QxP | 61 | R–KR5 | P–R3 |
| 14 | N/2–Q4 | QR–B1 | 38 | K–R1 | N–K5 | 62 | R–K5† | K–B3 |
| 15 | B–B2 | N–K5 | 39 | Q–B1 | Q–R5 | 63 | R–K8 | N–Q3 |
| 16 | Q–K2 | K–R1 | 40 | K–N1 | Q–N5 | 64 | R–K3 | R–B5 |
| 17 | K–R1 | NxN | 41 | K–R1 | Q–R5 | 65 | R–QN3 | N–B1 |
| 18 | NxN | P–KN4 | 42 | K–N1 | P–N3 | 66 | R–B3† | K–N3 |
| 19 | Q–K3 | PxP | 43 | Q–K2 | Q–B5 | 67 | R–B8 | N–K2 |
| 20 | QxP | R–KN1 | 44 | K–R1 | QxP | 68 | R–QN8 | R–QN5 |
| 21 | B–Q1 | B–N4 | 45 | Q–Q1 | N–B4 | 69 | K–N3 | N–B4† |
| 22 | NxB | PxN | 46 | R–K2 | Q–B3 | 70 | K–B3 | NxP† |
| 23 | B–K2 | P–N5 | 47 | Q–QN1 | P–K4 | | Resigns | |
| 24 | P–B4 | PxP | 48 | Q–N2 | N–Q6 | | | |

# part 2—ALBIN—CHATARD—ALEKHINE ATTACK

1 P–K4, P–K3
2 P–Q4, P–Q4
3 N–QB3, N–KB3
4 B–N5, B–K2
5 P–K5, KN–Q2
6 P–KR4

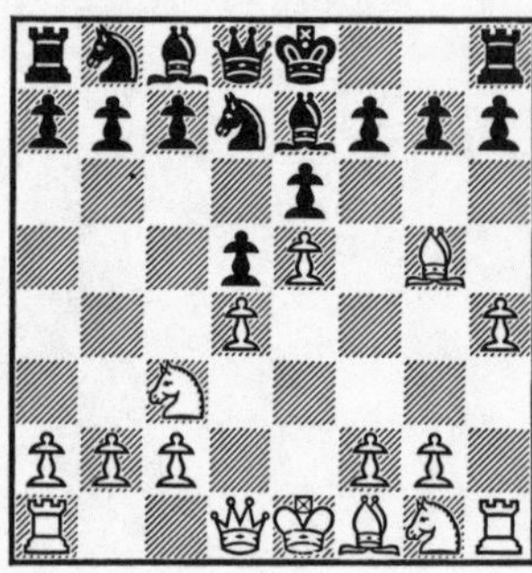

KEY POSITION 2

OBSERVATIONS ON KEY POSITION 2

This interesting continuation was first tested in the game Albin–Csank, Vienna 1897. Later, the move was investigated by the Parisian, Chatard, but it gained popularity only after Alekhine's repeated adoption. Today this line is as important as the Classical Variation, but the struggle becomes more pitted.

There is no doubt that after the acceptance of the Pawn sacrifice White gets an attack. Nor is 6 . . . O–O safe as White retains a strong initiative. The best defense consists of placing White's Queen Pawn under fire by . . . P–QB4, possibly preceded by . . . P–QR3.

IDEA VARIATIONS 4 AND 5:

(4) . . . BxB 7 PxB, QxP 8 N–R3, Q–K2 (after 8 . . . Q–R3 9 N–QN5, N–R3 10 P–KB4, Black has great difficulties in mobilizing) 9 N–B4, P–QR3 (bad for Black is 9 . . . N–B1 10 Q–N4, P–KB4 11 PxP e.p., PxP 12 O–O–O) 10 Q–N4, K–B1 11 Q–B3, K–N1 (the threat was 12 N–N6†) 12 B–Q3, P–QB4 (necessary was 12 . . . P–KR3) 13 BxP†, RxB 14 RxR, KxR 15 O–O–O, P–B4 16 R–R1†, K–N1 17 R–R8†, and Black resigned (Keres–Wade, USSR–England 1954). If, after 10 . . . P–KN3 in the foregoing main line, then 11 Q–N3, intending to meet 11 . . . P–QB4 with 12 N/3xP, PxN 13 NxP, Q–Q1 14 P–K6! Again, 10 . . . P–KN3, 11 O–O–O, P–QB4 12 Q–N3, N–N3 13 PxP, QxP 14 B–Q3, Q–B1 15 B–K4! (Bogoljubov–Spielmann, Stockholm 1919).

(5) 6 . . . O–O? 7 B–Q3, P–QB4 8 N–R3, (threatening the Bishop sacrifice at R7) R–K1 (8 . . . P–KR3 is bad because of 9 BxP! PxB 10 Q–N4†, K–R1 11 N–KN5 with an overwhelming attack) 9 N–N5 and the threat 10 N–Q6 poses insurmountable problems (Bogoljubov–Spielmann, Vienna 1922).

PRACTICAL VARIATIONS 6–10:

1 P–K4, P–K3 2 P–Q4, P–Q4 3 N–QB3, N–KB3 4 B–N5, B–K2 5 P–K5, KN–Q2 6 P–KR4

| | 6 | 7 | 8 | 9 | 10 |
|---|---|---|---|---|---|
| 6 | — — | — — | — — | — — | — — |
| | P–KB3 | P–KR3 | P–QR3 | P–QB4 | — — |
| 7 | Q–R5†[1] | B–K3[7] | Q–N4 | BxB[14] | — — |
| | K–B1[2] | P–QB4 | K–B1[10] | KxB![15] | — — |

| | 6 | 7 | 8 | 9 | 10 |
|---|---|---|---|---|---|
| 8 | PxP | Q–N4 | P–B4[11] | Q–N4 | P–B4 |
| | NxP | K–B1 | P–QB4 | K–B1 | PxP[21] |
| 9 | Q–B3[3] | N–B3 | N–B3 | N–B3[16] | QxP |
| | P–B4 | N–QB3 | N–QB3 | PxP[17] | N–QB3 |
| 10 | PxP | O–O–O | O–O–O | QxP | Q–Q2 |
| | QN–Q2[4] | PxP | P–N4 | Q–N3[18] | P–QR3[22] |
| 11 | O–O–O | BxQP | BxB†[12] | QxQ[19] | O–O–O |
| | NxP | Q–R4[8] | NxB | PxQ[20] | P–QN4 |
| 12 | N–R3 | R–R3[9] | P–R5[13] | = | N–B3 |
| | B–Q2 | ± | ± | | N–N3[23] |
| 13 | Q–K3[5] | | | | ± |
| | R–B1[6] | | | | |
| | ± | | | | |

*Notes to practical variations 6–10:*

[1] The modern reply. Insufficient is the old sacrificial line 7 B–Q3, P–QB4 8 Q–R5†, K–B1 9 NxP!?, PxB 10 R–R3, P–N5 11 N–B4, NxP 12 PxN, PxR 13 KNxP, K–N1 14 B–B4, P–KN3 15 Q–N4. Now Black's best move is 15 . . . N–B3! 16 BxP†, BxB 17 QxB†, K–N2 18 R–Q1, Q–R4† 18 P–B3, KR–Q1. In this line 9 KPxP is simpler and better. Also 9 . . . PxN 10 P–K6, Q–K1 achieves equality. Again, in the above line beginning with 7 B–Q3, 10 PxNP offers better chances.

[2] The forfeiture of castling is less serious than the weakening of the Kingside after 7 . . . P–N3 8 PxP, NxP 9 Q–K2, O–O 10 O–O–O, P–B4 11 N–B3, N–B3, after which White obtains the advantage by 12 PxP followed by P–KN3 and B–R3. Of course, in the above line if 8 . . . PxQ, then 9 PxP!

[3] 9 Q–K2, P–B4 10 PxP, N–R3 11 N–B3, NxP 12 O–O–O, P–N4 13 NxNP, R–QN1 14 QN–Q4, Q–R4! and Black has strong attacking possibilities for the Pawn (Spasski–Guimard, Goteberg, 1955). However, according to Boleslavski, everything is under control with 13 Q–K3.

[4] 10 . . . P–QN3?! 11 P–R5, PxP 12 P–R6! P–N3 13 O–O–O, QN–Q2 14 R–K1, Q–N3 15 B–N5!, K–B2 16 N–R3 and White won quickly (Unzicker–Stahlberg, Stockholm 1960). In this line 11 . . . P–KR3 is better.

[5] Czerniak gives 13 N–B4 followed by P–R5 as more energetic.

[6] Alexander–Tylor, Brighton 1938. White now can maintain a slight edge by 14 P–B3, according to Fine.

[7] 7 BxB, QxB gives the position the character of the main line with P–KR4 and . . . P–KR3. The continuation 7 B–B4 followed by O–O–O is probably stronger than the text move. On 7 Q–R5, P–QR3 8 O–O–O, P–QB4 9 PxP, NxP 10 N–B3, White has the edge (Keres).

[8] Much better is 11 . . . NxB 12 QxN, B–B4 13 Q–Q2, Q–R4.

[9] Dubinin–Rabinowitsch, Leningrad 1934. The Black Kingside is hard to defend: 12 . . . NxB 13 RxN, B–B4 14 R–KB4! In the game cited White got the edge with 12 . . . N–B4 13 R–N3, P–KN3 14 Q–B4, K–K1 15 N–Q2.

continued ▸

[10] 7 . . . P–KB4 8 Q–R5†, P–N3 9 Q–R6, BxB 10 PxB, K–B2 11 KN–K2, P–B4 12 N–B4! with a strong attack. See Game 2. In the above line only 11 . . . N–B1 followed by . . . R–N1–N2 offers Black fair chances.

[11] White may also support the Pawn on K5 by 8 N–B3 or 8 Q–B4. Also deserving consideration is 8 R–R3; if 8 . . . P–KR4 9 Q–B4.

[12] A typical mistake is 11 R–R3?, P–KR4 12 BxB†, NxB 13 Q–N3, Q–R4 14 K–N1, P–N5 15 N–K2, P–B5 with excellent attacking chances.

[13] White controls the necessary space for an attack on the Kingside. If 12 . . . N–B4 13 Q–R3 preparing P–KN4 and an eventual threat of NxQP.

[14] Or 7 N–N5, P–B3! 8 B–Q3, P–QR3! 9 Q–R5†, K–B1 10 R–R3, PxN 11 B–R6!, Q–R4† 12 B–Q2, Q–B2 13 R–N3, PxP 14 N–B3, NxP 15 RxP, P–R3 16 B–R7, KxR 17 QxP†, K–B2 18 Q–R5†, with perpetual check (Rossetto–Stahlberg, Vina del Mar 1947). In the above line if 10 N–KR3, PxQP! 11 N–B4, NxP 12 QNxP, Q–N3! (Ragosin–Yanofsky, Saltsjobaden 1948).

[15] The sacrifice of the exchange is incorrect, but accurate play on White's part is required: 7 . . . QxB? 8 N–N5, O–O 9 N–B7, PxP 10 NxR, P–B3 11 QxP, N–B3 12 Q–Q2, PxP 13 O–O–O, N–B3 14 P–KB3, Q–Q3 15 N–K2, B–Q2 16 N–B3, RxN 17 N–K4! (Bronstein–Stahlberg, Budapest 1950). Kashdan suggests 11 N–B7, PxP 12 N–N5, P–QR3 13 N–R7!, Q–N5† Q–Q2. However, Stahlberg gives Black a better defense with 12 . . . N–KB3, threatening 13 . . . N–K5. Another suggestion by Stahlberg: 10 . . . N–QB3 11 N–B3, P–B3 12 NxP, PxP 13 NxP!, QxN 14 N–B7 followed by 15 QxP(†).

[16] Or 9 PxP, NxKP 10 Q–N3, KN–Q2 11 O–O–O, N–QB3 12 P–B4, N–K2 13 P–R5, NxP 14 P–R6, P–KN3 15 N–B3. White has good attacking chances.

[17] 9 . . . N–QB3, though seldom played, is as good as the text: 10 PxP, N/2xKP 11 NxN, NxN 12 Q–N3, N–B3 (Ostman–Fine, Detroit 1933) or 12 . . . P–B3.

[18] Or 10 . . . N–QB3 11 Q–B4, P–QR3 12 P–R5, P–R3 13 O–O–O, Q–B2 14 R–K1, P–B3 15 N–KR4, N/2xP 16 N–N6†, K–K1 17 Q–N3!

[19] If White wants to keep Queens on the board he must sacrifice a Pawn: 11 Q–Q2, QxP 12 R–QN1, Q–R6 13 N–QN5, QxRP 14 Q–N4†, K–N1 15 N–B3 (Spielmann–Opocensky, Vienna 1923). The position is complicated but White's compensation for the Pawn is questionable. Or 11 Q–KB4, QxP 12 K–Q2!, N–QB3! 13 R–QN1, Q–R6 14 B–N5. White exercises pressure for the Pawn (correspondence game, Geoffrey–Baumann 1954–56). In the above line if 12 . . . QxR? 13 N–KN5 with a devastating attack.

[20] Now the chances are even: 12 B–N5, N–QB3 13 BxN, PxB 14 K–Q2, K–K2. Inferior is 11 . . . NxQ 12 N–Q2! N–B3 13 P–B4, B–Q2 14 O–O–O, R–B1 15 N–N3 (Bogolyubov–Spielmann, Baden–Baden 1925). White has gained time to support his Pawn on K5.

[21] Or 8 . . . Q–N3 9 N–B3, N–QB3? 10 N–QR4, Q–R4† 11 P–B3, PxP 12 P–QN4, Q–B2 13 NxP, P–QR3 14 R–R3, and

White has the edge (Gligoric–Yanofsky, Saltsjobaden 1946). If 9 . . . QxP 10 N–QN5, Q–N5† 11 K–B2!, N–QB3 12 P–B4! Or 10 . . . P–QR3 11 N–B7, Q–N5† 12 K–B2, R–R2 13 P–B4! In either case White has a promising game.

[22] 10 . . . Q–R4 11 N–B3, R–Q1 12 R–R3, K–B1 13 B–Q3, N–N3 14 N–QN5. White has a slight edge.

[23] (Correspondence Game, Amersfoort–Fredericksholm).

*French Defense Game 2*

*WHITE: Unzicker* *BLACK: Czerniak*

*Amsterdam 1954*

| | WHITE | BLACK | | WHITE | BLACK |
|---|---|---|---|---|---|
| 1 | P–K4 | P–K3 | 15 | B–K2 | Q–B2 |
| 2 | P–Q4 | P–Q4 | 16 | PxP | N–B6† |
| 3 | N–QB3 | N–KB3 | 17 | BxN | QxN |
| 4 | B–N5 | B–K2 | 18 | P–B6! | R–N1 |
| 5 | P–K5 | KN–Q2 | 19 | R–R3 | B–Q2 |
| 6 | P–KR4 | P–QR3 | 20 | NxP! | Q–K4† |
| 7 | Q–N4 | P–KB4 | 21 | N–K3 | QxQNP |
| 8 | Q–R5† | P–N3 | 22 | QR–Q1 | R–Q1 |
| 9 | Q–R6 | BxB | 23 | P–B6! | PxP |
| 10 | PxB | K–B2 | 24 | K–B1 | P–B4 |
| 11 | KN–K2! | P–B4 | 25 | N–B4 | B–N4 |
| 12 | N–B4 | N–B1 | 26 | QxRP†! | NxQ |
| 13 | PxP! | N–B3 | 27 | RxP† | K–B1 |
| 14 | P–KN4! | NxP | 28 | RxR† | Resigns |

---

## part 3—ANDERSSEN ATTACK

1 P–K4, P–K3
2 P–Q4, P–Q4
3 N–QB3, N–KB3
4 B–KN5, B–K2
5 BxN, BxB
6 P–K5[A], B–K2
7 Q–N4, O–O

KEY POSITION 3

### OBSERVATIONS ON KEY POSITION 3

[A] 6 N–B3, O–O 7 B–Q3, P–QB4 8 P–K5, B–K2 9 PxP, N–Q2 is a very satisfactory continuation for Black (Foltys–Keres, Prague 1937). Keres mentions an interesting attacking possibility in 9 P–KR4, PxP 10 BxP†, KxB 11 N–N5†, K–R3 12 Q–Q3, P–KN3 13 P–R5, BxN 14 PxNP†, B–R5 15 Q–N3, PxNP 16 RxB†, K–N2 17 R–N4 with a winning attack. In the above line, 9 . . . P–KB4 10 PxP e.p., NPxP 11 N–KN5 also gives White attacking chances.

Anderssen's Attack is aimed at direct action against the Black King, quite in the aggressive style of the last century. Today it is the German master Kurt Richter, famous for his attacking virtuosity, who handles Anderssen's weapon with virtuosity. Black must combine careful defense with steps to organize and attack on the Queenside. On his 8th move White has two choices: 8 B–Q3 and 8 O–O–O

IDEA VARIATIONS 6–8:

(6) 8 B–Q3, P–QB4 9 PxP, N–Q2 (correct is 9 . . . N–B3; see Prac. Var. 11) 10 N–B3 (also good is 10 Q–N3, P–KR3 11 P–B4, NxBP 12 O–O–O, P–B4 13 N–B3=, as in Showalter–Albin, 1895), NxBP 11 O–O–O, Q–R4 (better is 11 . . . NxB† although White maintains the edge) 12 BxP†! KxB 13 Q–R5† K–N1 14 P–KR4 with a winning attack (Richter–Darga, Berlin 1950).

(7) 8 B–Q3, P–QB4 9 Q–R3 (at this point inefficient), P–KN3 10 PxP, N–B3 11 P–KB4? BxP 12 N–B3, P–B3 13 Q–R6 (13 O–O–O fails against 13 . . . B–K6†), R–B2 14 PxP (14 O–O–O? B–K6† 15 K–N1, PxP), QxP: Black for choice (Charousek–Maroczy, 1897).

(8) 8 O–O–O, P–KB4 9 Q–R3, P–QB4 10 PxP, N–Q2 (stronger than 10 . . . N–B3; see Prac. Var. 15) 11 P–B4, NxBP 12 B–Q3 (or 12 N–B3, N–K5), P–QN4! 13 NxNP, Q–R4 14 N–Q4, B–Q2 15 P–KN4, NxB† 16 QxN, QxP 17 PxP, B–N5 18 P–B3, BxP! and Black won (Richter–Koch, Bad–Oyenhausen 1938).

PRACTICAL VARIATIONS 11–15:

1 P–K4, P–K3 2 P–Q4, P–Q4 3 N–QB3, N–KB3 4 B–N5, B–K2 5 BxN, BxB 6 P–K5, B–K2 7 Q–N4, O–O

| | *11* | *12* | *13* | *14* | *15* |
|---|---|---|---|---|---|
| *8* | B–Q3 | – – | – – | O–O–O | – – |
| | P–QB4 | – – | – – | P–KB4 | – – |
| *9* | PxP | – – | – – | Q–R3 | – – |
| | N–B3 | – – | – – | P–QB4 | – – |
| *10* | P–B4 | – – | – – | PxP | – |
| | P–B4 | – – | – – | N–B3 | N–Q2 |
| *11* | Q–R3 | – – | – – | P–B4 | P–B4 |
| | P–QN3 | BxP | Q–R4! | BxP[5] | NxBP |
| *12* | O–O–O[1] | O–O–O | O–O–O | P–KN4 | B–Q3[7] |
| | PxBP | Q–R4 | P–Q5 | PxNP | P–QN4 |
| *13* | P–KN4 | K–N1 | N–N1 | Q–N3[6] | N–B3[8] |
| | P–B5 | P–Q5 | N–N5[4] | ± | P–N5[9] |
| *14* | BxQBP | QN–K2[3] | = | | N–K2 |
| | PxNP | ± | | | NxB† |
| *15* | Q–N2[2] | | | | RxN[10] |
| | | | | | B–R3[11] |
| | ∓ | | | | |
| | | | | | = |

*Notes to practical variations 11–15:*

[1] 12 PxP, QxP is too dangerous.

[2] Naturally not 15 QxNP, RxP! In Pilnik–Stahlberg, Mar del Plata 1942, the text move was met by 15 . . . N–R4? and White won with 16 RxP! Correct is 15 . . . RxP 16 B–N3, N–Q5 17 KN–K2, NxB† 18 RPxN, R–B2 with a slight edge for Black.

[3] Black's attack is at a standstill so White has good prospects (Tarrasch–Walbrodt, 6th Match Game 1894).

[4] The text is stronger than 13 . . . QxP 14 P–KN4. If 14 B–B4, Black has the choice between 14 . . . NxP† and 14 . . . QxBP.

[5] Black must strive for counterattack with 11 . . . Q–R4 12 K–N1, P–QN3 or directly 11 . . . P–QN3.

[6] White threatens 13 P–KR3. His attack is the more dangerous (Richter–Stahlberg, Podebrad 1936).

[7] Or 12 P–KN4, PxNP 13 Q–N3, RxP!

[8] 13 BxNP, R–N1 or 13 NxNP, Q–R4 gives Black good attacking chances. Better for White is 13 QN–K2 in order to meet 13 . . . P–N5 with 14 P–KN4, NxB† 15 RxN, B–R3 16 R–KN3! However, Black can proceed better by 13 . . . N–K5.

[9] After 13 . . . Q–R4 14 N–Q4, White maintains the edge. See Game 3. If 14 . . . P–N5, then 15 N–B6.

[10] The recapture with the Bishop Pawn also deserves consideration.

[11] 16 R–Q2, BxN, 17 RxB, Q–R4 with a satisfactory game for Black (Richter–Koch, Berlin 1951).

*French Defense Game 3*

*WHITE: Richter* *BLACK: Lieb*

*Berlin 1957*

| | WHITE | BLACK | | WHITE | BLACK |
|---|---|---|---|---|---|
| 1 | P–K4 | P–K3 | 16 | QxN | QR–N1 |
| 2 | P–Q4 | P–Q4 | 17 | P–KN4 | P–N3 |
| 3 | N–QB3 | N–KB3 | 18 | PxP | NPxP |
| 4 | B–N5 | B–K2 | 19 | NxQP | PxN |
| 5 | BxN | BxB | 20 | P–K6 | B–K1 |
| 6 | P–K5 | B–K2 | 21 | NxBP | RxN |
| 7 | Q–N4 | O–O | 22 | QxR | Q–B2 |
| 8 | B–Q3 | P–KB4 | 23 | KR–N1† | K–R1 |
| 9 | Q–R3 | P–B4 | 24 | Q–N4 | B–N3 |
| 10 | PxP | N–Q2 | 25 | P–B5 | B–B3 |
| 11 | P–B4 | NxBP | 26 | PxB | Q–K4 |
| 12 | O–O–O | P–QN4 | 27 | P–B3 | P–N5 |
| 13 | N–B3 | Q–R4 | 28 | QR–K1 | Q–Q3 |
| 14 | N–Q4 | B–Q2 | 29 | PxRP | Resigns |
| 15 | K–N1 | NxB | | | |

## part 4—MAC CUTCHEON VARIATION

1 P–K4, P–K3
2 P–Q4, P–Q4
3 N–QB3, N–KB3
4 B–N5, B–N5
5 P–K5, P–KR3
6 B–Q2[A], BxN
7 PxB, N–K5
8 Q–N4, P–KN3[B]

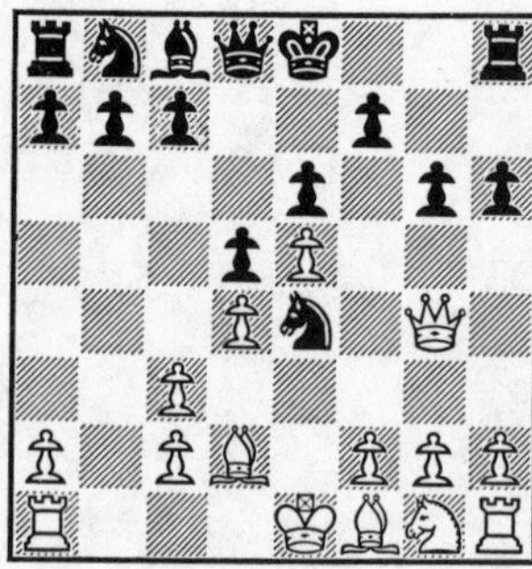

KEY POSITION 4

### OBSERVATIONS ON KEY POSITION 4

[A] White has other continuations but they all give Black the edge and are considered obsolete:

(1) 6 PxN (Tchigorin), PxB 7 PxP, R–N1 8 P–KR4, PxP 9 Q–R5 or Q–N4, Q–B3! (2) 6 B–R4 (Bernstein), P–KN4 7 B–N3, N–K5 8 N–K2, P–QB4 9 P–QR3, BxN† 10 NxN, Q–R4! (3) 6 B–K3 (Janowski), N–K5 7 Q–N4, K–B1 8 B–Q3, NxN 9 P–QR3, N–R5† (4) 6 B–B1 (Olland), N–K5 7 Q–N4, K–B1 8 N–K2, P–QB4 9 P–QR3, B–R4 10 P–QN4, NxN!

[B] Black can avoid the weakening of his Pawn position by 8 . . . K–B1, at the obvious expense, however, of abandoning the possibility of castling. White's best is then the immediate mobilization of his heavy pieces by 9 P–KR4, P–QB4 10 R–R3, Q–R4 11 B–Q3, NxB, 12 R–N3! (a strong interpolative move, delaying the recapture of the Knight), P–KN3 13 KxN, PxP 14 QxP, N–B3 15 Q–KB4, P–Q5 16 N–B3, QxP† 17 K–K2, N–K2 18 QxQP with a positional advantage for White (Sachsenmeier–Keres, 1936). In this line 12 . . . R–KN1 is worth testing. Again, in the above line 14 BxP? fails against 14 . . . R–KN1, but 14 R–B3 offers good chances, according to Keres. Finally, 17 . . . QxR loses, according to Maroczy, by 18 Q–B6, R–KN1 19 P–R5. In this main line beginning with 8 . . . K–B1, Black may vary with 10 . . . NxB 11 KxN, P–B5? 12 R–N3, R–R2 13 R–B3, threatening 14 Q–N6 (Euwe–Cawi, Berlin, 1950). Black may also vary with 10 . . . P–KB4 11 PxP, e.p., NxP 12 Q–B4! (Keres). But White maintains a positional edge in each instance.

This is the most important position in the MacCutcheon Variation. White has the choice between two continuations, 9 B–Q3 (old-fashioned) or 9 B–B1 (modern). The idea of 9 B–B1 is to retain this Bishop to profit from the weakness of the Black squares in the enemy camp. Experience with this modern continuation had been very good at the beginning, but essential improvements for Black have been found, so that attention has been refocused on 9 B–Q3. The original idea of 9 B–Q3 was a brisk attack, possibly culminating in the sacrifice of the Bishop on KN6. These immediate threats are, however, easily parried, and to-day 9 B–Q3 is played as one of the corner-stones of a sound, more conservative position.

### IDEA VARIATIONS 9–11:

(9) 9 B–Q3, NxB 10 KxN, P–QB4 (not 10 . . . Q–N4† 11 QxQ, PxQ 12 P–N4!) 11 P–KR4, Q–R4? (correct is 11 . . . N–B3; see Idea Var. 10) 12 R–R3, PxP 13 BxP!, Q–B2 14 R–B3, R–N1 15 RxP with a winning position for White (Euwe–Maroczy, 1921).

(10) 9 B–Q3, NxB 10 KxN, P–QB4 11 P–KR4 (best is 11 Q–B4, as seen in Prac. Var. 18; 11 PxP is followed

by 11 . . . N–Q2), N–B3 12 R–R3 (12 N–B3 is usually preferred to-day; see Prac. Var. 17), PxP 13 PxP, B–Q2 14 N–B3, Q–N3 15 Q–B4 (see also Prac. Var. 16), O–O–O 16 P–KN4, Q–N5† (still stronger is 16 . . . P–KN4) 17 K–K3 and not 17 K–K2 which fails against 17 . . . P–B3 (Lilienthal–Bondarevski, Moscow 1937).

(11) 9 B–B1, NxQBP 10 B–Q3, B–Q2 (indicated is 10 . . . P–QB4 which transposes into Prac. Var. 19 and 20) 11 BxP, Q–K2 12 B–Q3, N–B3 (Yanofsky–Muller, Karlsbad 1948) and now White should have played 13 B–Q2! maintaining his advantage: 13 . . . N–R5 14 N–K2, O–O–O 15 O–O, P–KB4 16 Q–B3, QR–N1 17 Q–K3, Q–N2 18 N–B4 and White has good chances on the Queenside (Woronesch–Makarov, Championship of Ukraine 1956).

PRACTICAL VARIATIONS 16–20:

1 P–K4, P–K3 2 P–Q4, P–Q4 3 N–QB3, N–KB3 4 B–N5, B–N5 5 P–K5, P–KR3 6 B–Q2, BxN 7 PxB, N–K5 8 Q–N4, P–KN3

| | *16* | *17* | *18* | *19* | *20* |
|---|---|---|---|---|---|
| *9* | B–Q3 | – – | – – | B–B1 | – – |
| | NxB | – – | – – | P–QB4 | – – |
| *10* | KxN | – – | – – | B–Q3[8] | – – |
| | P–QB4 | – – | – – | NxQBP[9] | – – |
| *11* | P–KR4 | – – | Q–B4 | PxP | – – |
| | N–B3 | – – | N–B3[6] | N–B3[10] | Q–R4! |
| *12* | R–R3 | N–B3 | N–B3 | N–B3 | B–Q2 |
| | PxP | Q–B2 | B–Q2 | Q–R4 | Q–R5 |
| *13* | PxP | PxP[4] | QR–QN1 | O–O | QxQ |
| | B–Q2 | NxKP | P–B5 | Q–R5[11] | NxQ |
| *14* | N–B3[1] | NxN | B–K2 | QxQ | B–N4 |
| | Q–N3 | QxN | P–QN3 | NxQ | B–Q2 |
| *15* | R/3–R1[2] | QR–QN1[5] | P–KR4[7] | B–K3[12] | P–KB4 |
| | O–O–O[3] | ± | ± | ± | B–B3[13] |
| | ∓ | | | | = |

*Notes to practical variations 16–20:*

[1] Or 14 R–B3, Q–N3 15 Q–B4, QxP 16 QxP†, K–Q1 with a good game for Black (Yates–Kmoch, Kecskemet 1927). 14 BxP fails against 14 . . . Q–R4†. Other possibilities are 14 P–QB3, Q–K2 15 Q–Q1, N–R4 16 Q–N1, R–QB1 17 N–K2 with equality (Capablanca–Torre, Moscow 1925), and 14 N–K2, Q–K2 15 QR–QN1, N–R4 16 R–B3, O–O–O and Black has sufficient counterplay (Yates–Torre, Moscow 1925).

[2] It is rather difficult for White to develop his game (cf. Idea Var. 10). In retreating with his Rook, he admits his action on the Kingside has failed. The maneuver can better be omitted, as in Prac. Var. Var. 17 and 18.

continued ▸

[3] 16 KR–QN1, Q–R4† 17 K–K2 with an excellent game for Black. See Game 4. In the above line White may improve his play by 16 QR–QN1 and 17 P–B3.

[4] Or 13 Q–B4, P–B4!, an important finesse which explains why in Prac. Var. 18 White plays Q–B4 at his 11th turn.

[5] With the continuation 15 . . . Q–B3 16 Q–Q4, QxQ 17 PxQ with the better end game for White. See Game 5.

[6] Barden recommends here 11 . . . PxP 12 PxP, Q–R4† 13 P–B3, Q–R6 14 N–K2, N–Q2 to prevent Q–B6, but White plays 15 KR–QN1 with a good position.

[7] 15 . . . Q–K2 16 P–KR5, PxP 17 RxP favors White (Uusi–Schistjakov, Moscow 1956).

[8] Or 10 N–K2, PxP! 11 P–KB3, P–KR4! 12 Q–R3, NxP 13 NxP, N–B3 and Black has a sound extra Pawn (Penrose–O'Kelly, Hastings 1950–51). In the above line if 11 PxP, then 11 . . . Q–R4†.

[9] Weaker is 10 . . . PxP 11 N–K2, Q–R4 12 O–O, PxP 13 BxN, PxB 14 N–N3. If 14 . . . QxKP 15 B–B4, Q–N2 16 N–R5, Q–Q5 17 Q–N3, N–B3 18 QR–Q1, Q–B5 19 B–Q6!, PxN 20 Q–N7 and White wins, as Black is helpless on the black squares. He must always look out for this danger in the MacCutcheon. In the above line if Black plays 11 . . . NxQBP, then 12 NxP. But 11 . . . N–B3 is better for Black.

[10] 11 . . . N–Q2 is preferable. Black need not fear 12 BxP, NxKP 13 Q–Q4, NxB 14 QxN, P–Q5, in view of which White would have done better with 12 N–B3, Q–B2 13 O–O.

[11] 13 . . . QxBP 14 Q–KR4, N–K2 15 Q–B6, R–R2 16 P–QR4, Q–B2 17 B–R3 is favorable for White (Smyslov–Donner, Venice 1950).

[12] 15 . . . B–Q2 16 QR–QN1, O–O–O 17 R–N3 with a distinct edge for White (Barden–Donner, England–Holland 1950) In the above line, if 15 . . . N–B6, then 16 P–QR4 followed by 17 R–QR3.

[13] Black has a fully satisfactory game. He even won a Pawn by 16 N–K2, N–Q2, but to no avail (Lombardy–Minev, Olympiad, Munich 1958).

*French Defense Game 4*

*WHITE: Euwe* — *BLACK: Castaldi*

*Venice 1948*

| | WHITE | BLACK | | WHITE | BLACK |
|---|---|---|---|---|---|
| 1 | P–K4 | P–K3 | 12 | R–R3 | PxP |
| 2 | P–Q4 | P–Q4 | 13 | PxP | Q–N3 |
| 3 | N–QB3 | N–KB3 | 14 | N–B3 | B–Q2 |
| 4 | B–N5 | B–N5 | 15 | R/3–R1 | O–O–O |
| 5 | P–K5 | P–KR3 | 16 | KR–QN1 | Q–R4† |
| 6 | B–Q2 | BxN | 17 | K–K2 | P–B4 |
| 7 | PxB | N–K5 | 18 | Q–B4 | Q–B6 |
| 8 | Q–N4 | P–KN3 | 19 | R–R1 | P–KN4 |
| 9 | P–KR4 | P–QB4 | 20 | PxP | PxP |
| 10 | B–Q3 | NxB | 21 | QxNP | KR–N1 |
| 11 | KxN | N–B3 | 22 | Q–K3 | P–B5 |

| | WHITE | BLACK | | WHITE | BLACK |
|---|---|---|---|---|---|
| 23 | Q–Q2 | NxP† | 37 | QxP† | K–K1 |
| 24 | NxN | QxN | 38 | Q–N8† | K–B2 |
| 25 | QR–QN1 | RxP | 39 | Q–B7 | Q–K5† |
| 26 | K–B3 | R/1–N1 | 40 | K–Q1 | Q–R5 |
| 27 | R–N4 | RxP† | 41 | Q–Q8 | K-N3 |
| 28 | QxR | R–N6† | 42 | Q–B6† | K–R4 |
| 29 | K–K2 | QxR | 43 | Q–B7† | K–N5 |
| 30 | QxRP | R–K6† | 44 | Q–N6† | K–R4 |
| 31 | K–Q1 | K–B2 | 45 | Q–R6† | K–N6 |
| 32 | B–K2 | Q–N8† | 46 | Q–N5† | K–B7 |
| 33 | K–Q2 | RxB† | 47 | Q–R4† | K–K6 |
| 34 | KxR | QxR | 48 | Q–K1† | K–Q5 |
| 35 | Q–R5† | P–N3 | | Resigns | |
| 36 | Q–R7† | K–Q1 | | | |

*French Defense Game 5*

*WHITE: Neshmetdinov* *BLACK: Stahlberg*

*Bucharest 1954*

| | WHITE | BLACK | | WHITE | BLACK |
|---|---|---|---|---|---|
| 1 | P–K4 | P–K3 | 27 | R–KB1 | BxP |
| 2 | P–Q4 | P–Q4 | 28 | R–B6 | K–Q2 |
| 3 | N–QB3 | N–KB3 | 29 | B–B5† | K–K2 |
| 4 | B–N5 | B–N5 | 30 | R–Q6 | R–QN1 |
| 5 | P–K5 | P–KR3 | 31 | RxRP | B–B6 |
| 6 | B–Q2 | BxN | 32 | R–Q6 | B–K5 |
| 7 | PxB | N–K5 | 33 | BxB | PxB |
| 8 | Q–N4 | P–KN3 | 34 | KxP | R–KR1 |
| 9 | B–Q3 | NxB | 35 | P–B6 | PxP |
| 10 | KxN | P–QB4 | 36 | RxP | R–R5† |
| 11 | N–KB3 | N–QB3 | 37 | K–Q5 | R–R5 |
| 12 | P–KR4 | Q–B2 | 38 | R–B7† | K–K1 |
| 13 | PxP | NxP | 39 | P–B4 | RxRP |
| 14 | NxN | QxN | 40 | P–B5 | R–Q7† |
| 15 | QR–N1 | Q–B3 | 41 | K–B6 | R–K7 |
| 16 | Q–Q4 | QxQ | 42 | RxRP | RxP |
| 17 | PxQ | K–Q1 | 43 | R–QN7 | R–K6† |
| 18 | P–N4 | K–B2 | 44 | K–B7 | P–B4 |
| 19 | P–R5 | P–KN4 | 45 | P–B6 | K–K2 |
| 20 | P–KB4 | PxP | 46 | R–N5 | K–B3 |
| 21 | QR–KB1 | P–K4 | 47 | K–N7 | K–N4 |
| 22 | PxP | BxP | 48 | P–B7 | R–K1 |
| 23 | RxP | B–K3 | 49 | K–B6 | R–QB1 |
| 24 | K–B3 | QR–KN1 | 50 | R–N8 | RxP† |
| 25 | K–Q4 | R–N5 | 51 | KxR | K–B5 |
| 26 | RxR | BxR | 52 | K–Q6 | Resigns |

SUPPLEMENTARY VARIATIONS 6–10:

1 P–K4, P–K3 2 P–Q4, P–Q4 3 N–QB3, N–KB3 4 B–N5, B–N5

If White wants to avoid the advance of his King Pawn, he must either protect or exchange it. The protection by 5 B–Q3 causes Black no difficulty. The indirect protection by 5 N–K2 is better, but still not particularly inconvenient for Black. The best chance for White to gain some opening advantage is by the exchange of Pawns. Formerly this exchange was popular because of the then prevailing opinion that White could take advantage of the too aggressive position of Black's King Bishop. Black, it was thought, had to exchange this Bishop, which might be needed later for defense, or lose time retreating it. But experience has shown that Black has compensations insofar as the release in the center facilitates his counterplay.

| | *6* | *7* | *8* | *9* | *10* |
|---|---|---|---|---|---|
| *5* | B–Q3 | N–K2 | PxP | – – | P–B3? |
| | PxP | PxP[5] | QxP | PxP | P–KR3 |
| *6* | BxP | P–QR3 | BxN | B–Q3[11] | BxN |
| | P–QB4 | B–K2 | PxB[8] | O–O | QxB |
| *7* | PxP[1] | BxN | Q–Q2 | N–K2 | N–K2 |
| | QxQ†[2] | PxB | Q–R4 | B–K3 | PxP |
| *8* | RxQ | NxP | N–K2 | P–QR3 | PxP |
| | QN–Q2 | P–QN3[6] | N–Q2 | B–K2 | P–K4![13] |
| *9* | BxN[3] | N/2–B3 | P–QR3[9] | Q–Q2 | ∓ |
| | NxB | B–N2 | N–N3 | QN–Q2 | |
| *10* | B–B3 | Q–B3 | R–Q1 | O–O[12] | |
| | BxP[4] | P–QB3[7] | B–K2[10] | ± | |
| | ∓ | = | ∓ | | |

*Notes to supplementary variations 6–10:*

[1] Alapin suggested 7 N–K2, PxP 8 BxN, QxB 9 QxP with equality.

[2] Weaker is 7 . . . BxN† 8 PxB, Q–R4 9 BxN, PxB 10 Q–Q4 (Lasker–Tarrasch, 7th Match game 1908).

[3] Black also has a very good game after 9 B–B3, BxN† 10 PxB, NxP 11 B–K3, QN–K5.

[4] The end game favors Black in view of his two Bishops (Lasker–Tarrasch, 9th Match game 1908).

[5] Or 5 . . . P–KR3 6 BxN, QxB 7 P–QR3, BxN† 8 NxB, O–O 9 PxP, R–K1 10 B–K2, Q–N4 11 Q–Q2! with advantage for White (Marshall–Levy, New York 1941).

[6] Premature is 8 . . . P–KB4 9 N/4–B3, B–Q2 10 Q–Q2, B–Q3 11 O–O–O and White has the edge (Lasker–Reti, New York 1924).

[7] Continued 11 O–O–O, P–KB4 — at the right moment —

12 N–N3, N–Q2 13 B–B4, Q–B2. Black has a satisfactory game (Te Kolste–Torre, Baden-Baden 1925). In this line, if 11 . . . N–Q2, then 12 Q–N3, threatening 13 N–Q6†.

[8] The continuation 6 . . . BxN† 7 PxB, PxB only increases White's chances.

[9] 9 N–B1, N–N3 10 N–N3, Q–KN4! favors Black (Capablanca–Bogoljubov, New York 1924).

[10] 11 N–N3, B–Q2 is good for Black.

[11] Another good continuation is 6 Q–B3 (Olland–Pillsbury, Hanover 1902).

[12] On 10 . . . P–QB4 11 PxP, NxP (Alekhine–Opocensky, Prague 1943), White has a slight edge if he plays 12 KR–K1.

[13] Black clearly has the initiative.

## part 5—BURN VARIATION

1 P–K4, P–K3
2 P–Q4, P–Q4
3 N–QB3, N–KB3
4 B–N5, PxP
5 NxP[A], B–K2
6 BxN[B], BxB[C]
7 N–KB3, N–Q2

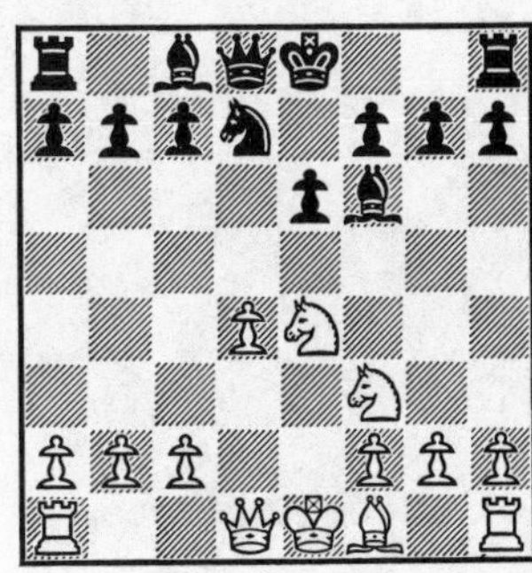

KEY POSITION 5

### OBSERVATIONS ON KEY POSITION 5

[A] Or 5 BxN, best answered by 5 . . . PxB 6 NxP, P–KB4 7 N–QB3, B–N2 8 N–B3, O–O 9 Q–Q2, P–B4 10 PxP, Q–R4 11 N–QN5, QxQ† 12 NxQ, N–R3 13 P–QB3, NxP 14 N–N3, NxN 15 PxN, P–QR3 with equality (Alekhine–Tartakover, Vienna 1922). If 7 N–N3, 7 . . . P–QB4! follows, but if 7 . . . P–QB4 in answer to 7 N–QB3, then 8 P–Q5! Again, in the above line 8 . . . P–QB4 is more active than the text: 9 B–N5†, B–Q2 (Najdorf–Guimard, Mar del Plata 1945). Or 5 BxN, QxB 6 NxP with superiority in space for White: 6 . . . Q–Q1 7 N–B3, N–Q2 8 B–Q3, B–K2 9 Q–K2 (Maroczy–Tartakover, Goteborg 1920). Instead of the retreat 6 . . . Q–Q1, Black may vary: 6 . . . Q–N3 7 N–N3, B–Q3 8 N–B3, O–O 9 B–Q3, still with a slight edge for White.

[B] Avoiding an exchange of pieces by 6 N–QB3 or 6 N–N3 costs too much time: 6 N–QB3, O–O 7 N–B3, P–QN3 8 Q–Q2, B–N2 9 B–K2, QN–Q2 and Black has a satisfactory game (Tarrasch–Tartakover, Mahrisch-Ostrau 1923). The alternative 6 NxN† is comfortable for Black: 6 . . . BxN 7 BxB, QxB 8 N–B3, O–O 9 P–QB3, N–Q2 10 B–K2, P–K4 11 PxP, NxP 12 NxN, QxN 13 O–O, B–K3 with a drawish position (Capablanca–Alekhine, New York 1927).

[C] Here the recapture with the Pawn is inferior: 6 . . . PxB 7 P–KN3, P–KB4 8 N–QB3, P–QB3 9 B–N2, P–N3 10 P–Q5!, B–N2 11 PxKP, QxQ† 12 RxQ, PxP 13 N–N5, N–R3 14 N–Q4, B–B3 15 NxKP, B–N2 16 N–K2 with advantage for White (Estrin–Nikitin, Moscow 1957).

This is the characteristic position of the Burn Variation. The exchange 4 . . . PxP leads to simpler positions than after 4 . . . B–K2 or 4 . . . B–N5. Black has abandoned the center, but he intends to proceed with either . . . P–QB4 or . . . P–K4, restoring the balance. Black may also obtain sufficient control of the central squares by the fianchetto of his Queen Bishop. He has, at any rate, fair chances for equality. Yet, if White proceeds accurately, he maintains a slight superiority in space.

IDEA VARIATIONS 12 AND 13:

(12) 8 B–Q3, O–O (for 8 . . . P–QB4 see Prac. Var. 24) 9 Q–K2, P–QB4 10 NxB†, NxN 11 PxP, Q–R4† 12 P–B3, QxP/4 13 O–O, P–QN3 14 KR–K1, B–N2 15 N–K5, QR–Q1 16 QR–Q1, P–N3 17 N–N4, NxN 18 QxN, R–Q4. Black, having his pieces well centralized, has the edge.

(13) 8 B–B4, O–O (if 8 . . . P–QB4, then P–Q5!) 9 Q–K2, N–N3 (or 9 . . . P–QB4 10 O–O–O or 9 . . . P–QN3 10 P–Q5) 10 B–N3, B–Q2 11 O–O, B–QR5? (a premature attempt to exchange pieces; for 11 . . . Q–K2 see Prac. Var. 23) 12 NxB†, PxN (if 12 . . . QxN 13 BxB, NxB 14 Q–B4, and White wins a Pawn) 13 P–QB4, BxB 14 PxB, P–B3 15 Q–K3, K–R1 16 N–Q2! with a clear advantage for White (Smyslov–Stahlberg, Budapest 1950).

PRACTICAL VARIATIONS 21–25:

1 P–K4, P–K3 2 P–Q4, P–Q4 3 N–QB3, N–KB3 4 B–N5, PxP 5 NxP, B–K2 6 BxN, BxB 7 N–B3, N–Q2

| | 21 | 22 | 23 | 24 | 25 |
|---|---|---|---|---|---|
| 8 | Q–Q2 | – – | B–B4 | B–Q3 | P–QB3 |
| | P–QN3[1] | – – | O–O | P–QB4 | P–QN3 |
| 9 | B–N5 | O–O–O | Q–K2 | PxP | NxB† |
| | B–N2 | B–N2 | N–N3 | NxP | PxN[11] |
| 10 | NxB† | Q–B4 | B–N3 | B–N5†[8] | B–Q3 |
| | PxN[2] | O–O[4] | B–Q2 | K–K2 | B–N2 |
| 11 | Q–B3 | B–Q3 | O–O | QxQ† | Q–K2 |
| | Q–K2 | P–KN3 | Q–K2[6] | RxQ | P–QB4 |
| 12 | QxBP | P–KR4 | KR–K1 | NxN[9] | O–O–O[12] |
| | Q–N5† | B–N2 | QR–Q1 | R–Q4 | Q–B2 |
| 13 | P–QB3 | P–R5[5] | QR–Q1 | N–R6 | P–KN3 |
| | QxB | ± | B–QR5 | BxP | PxP |
| 14 | QxB | | BxB | R–QN1 | B–N5 |
| | QxNP | | NxB | RxB | P–QR3[13] |
| 15 | O–O[3] | | Q–N5[7] | N–B7 | = |
| | ± | | ± | B–B6†[10] | |
| | | | | = | |

*Notes to practical variations 21–25:*

[1] After 8 . . . O–O 9 O–O–O, Q–K2 10 P–KN4! White obtains a Kingside attack.

[2] Of course, Black cannot take with the Queen because of 11 N–K5.

[3] 15 . . . R–Q1 16 P–B4, Q–R3 17 KR–K1, O–O 18 P–Q5! with an edge for White (L. Steiner–Stahlberg, Saltsjobaden 1948).

[4] Safer is 10 . . . Q–K2, followed by O–O–O.

[5] White has good chances for a Kingside attack (Tolush–Bondarevski, USSR Championship 1939).

[6] Weak is 11 . . . B–QR5? See Idea Var. 13. Best is 11 . . . B–B3 12 NxB†, QxN 13 N–K5, B–K1. Or 11 . . . P–KN3 and, if possible, 12 . . . B–N2.

[7] 15 . . . N–N3 16 P–B4 with a positional advantage for White.

[8] Or 10 NxN, Q–R4†. Also good for Black is 10 NxB† QxN (Yates–Alekhine, Kecskemet 1927).

[9] After 12 NxB, KxN, the end game slightly favors Black (Alekhine–Averbach, Bern 1925, and L. Steiner–Alekhine, Bradley Beach 1929).

[10] 16 K–K2, RxR 17 RxR, R–N1 18 N–R6, R–R1 19 N–B7 and drawn by repetition (analysis by Averbach).

[11] Weak is 9 . . . QxN? 10 B–N5. Or 9 . . . NxN? 10 N–K5 and, if 10 . . . Q–Q4, then 11 B–K2!

[12] 12 PxP, NxP 13 B–N5†, K–K2 is comfortable for Black (Alekhine).

[13] 14 . . . O–O–O 15 RxP, N–K4 16 B–R6, BxB 17 QxB†, K–N1 18 Q–K2 with advantage for White. But after the text move Black has a satisfactory game, according to Alekhine: 15 BxN†, QxB 16 RxP, Q–N4 17 Q–K3, K–K2.

---

## part 6—STEINITZ VARIATION

### OBSERVATIONS ON KEY POSITION 6

1 P–K4, P–K3
2 P–Q4, P–Q4
3 N–QB3, N–KB3
4 P–K5, KN–Q2
5 P–KB4[A], P–QB4
6 PxP[B], N–QB3[C]

KEY POSITION 6

[A] Obsolete is the maintenance of the broad center by 5 N/3–K2, P–QB4 6 P–QB3, N–QB3 7 P–KB4, P–KB3 8 N–B3, Q–N3. Yet White has no bad game after 9 P–QR3, B–K2 10 P–QN4! (Enevoldsen–Koch, Helsinki 1952). Here 9 . . . P–QR4 deserves consideration. In the above line 9 P–KN3 is also possible. The aggressive continuation 5 Q–N4 (Gledhill) is harmless because of 5 . . . P–QB4 6 N–B3, N–B3 7 PxP, P–B4!

[B] 6 N–B3, N–B3 7 B–K3, PxP 8 KNxP, B–B4 9 B–N5, O–O! 10 NxN, PxN 11 BxB, NxB 12 Q–Q4, Q–N3 13 P–QN4, PxB 14 PxN (Boleslavski–Guimard, USSR–Argentina 1954), and now Black should have played 14 . . . Q–R4 with a good game. 12 BxP (instead of 12 Q–Q4), R–N1 favors Black.

[C] This is the usual continuation, although there is no objection to 6 . . . BxP. If 6 . . . NxBP, White gets control of his Q4 by 7 N–B3, N–B3 8 B–K3.

This is the most important position of the Steinitz Variation. White has supported his King Pawn with his Bishop Pawn and interrupts the counterattack of . . . P–QB4 by simply taking the Pawn.

It is White's general idea to obtain a Kingside attack based on the advanced position of his King Pawn. However, it is easy for Black to obtain counterplay by centralizing his pieces. Formerly, it was usual for White to proceed with 7 P–QR3 (Pillsbury). Today, however, 7 N–B3 is preferred.

IDEA VARIATIONS 14–16:

(14) 7 P–QR3, NxBP 8 P–QN4, N–Q2 9 B–Q3, P–QR4 10 P–N5, N/3–N1 11 N–B3, N–B4 12 B–K3, N/1–Q2 13 O–O with advantage for White. This is the famous Pillsbury–Lasker game. Lasker showed, however, that Black can obtain an edge with 8 . . . P–Q5 9 QN–K2, P–Q6! Therefore White is better advised to play 8 N–B3, P–B4 9 PxP e.p., QxP 10 B–K3, P–QR3 11 Q–Q2, B–Q3 12 O–O–O, O–O 13 P–KN3 with a good game (Platz–Donner, Helsinki 1952). In the above line, 8 . . . B–K2 is well met by P–QN4, N–Q2 10 B–Q3.

(15) An unusual but safe continuation is 7 P–QR3, BxP 8 Q–N4, P–KN3 (for 8 . . . O–O see Prac. Var. 26) 9 N–B3, P–QR3 10 B–Q3, P–QN4 11 P–QN4, B–R2 12 P–KR4, P–KR4 13 Q–N3, Q–K2 14 P–B5? (correct is 14 N–K2, N–N3), B–N1! 15 PxNP, N/2xP with advantage for Black (Spielmann–Keres, Nordwik 1938).

(16) 7 N–B3, BxP 8 B–Q3, N–N5 — the exchange of White's King Bishop serves no good purpose (for other continuations see Prac. Var. 28, 29, and 30) — 9 P–QR3, NxB† 10 QxN, and now 10 . . . O–O fails because of 11 N–KN5, while 10 . . . P–B3 11 B–K3, according to Boleslavski, leaves White with the better game.

PRACTICAL VARIATIONS 26–30:

1 P–K4, P–K3 2 P–Q4, P–Q4 3 N–QB3, N–KB3 4 P–K5, KN–Q2 5 P–KB4, P–QB4 6 PxP, N–QB3

| | *26* | *27* | *28* | *29* | *30* |
|---|---|---|---|---|---|
| 7 | P–QR3 | – – | N–B3 | – – | – – |
| | BxP | – – | BxP | – – | – – |
| 8 | Q–N4 | – – | B–Q3 | – – | – – |
| | O–O | – – | P–QR3 | P–KB3 | – – |
| 9 | N–B3 | – – | Q–K2 | PxP | – – |
| | N–Q5 | P–B4 | N–Q5[6] | NxP | – – |
| 10 | B–Q3 | Q–R3 | NxN | Q–K2 | – – |
| | P–B4 | B–K2[4] | BxN | O–O | – – |
| 11 | Q–R3 | B–K3 | B–K3 | B–Q2 | – – |
| | P–QR3[1] | N–B4 | BxB | P–K4?! | B–Q2[9] |
| 12 | NxN[2] | N–Q4 | QxB | PxP | O–O–O |
| | BxN | B–Q2 | Q–N3 | B–N5 | K–R1 |
| 13 | N–K2 | B–K2 | QxQ | O–O–O | QR–K1 |
| | B–R2 | QR–B1 | NxQ | N–Q5 | P–QN4 |
| 14 | B–K3 | QR–Q1 | N–K2 | Q–K1 | BxNP |
| | N–B4 | NxN | B–Q2 | N–R4 | QR–N1[10] |
| 15 | O–O–O[3] | BxN | N–Q4[7] | B–K2[8] | ∓ |
| | ± | N–R5[5] | ± | ± | |
| | | ∓ | | | |

*Notes to practical variations 26–30:*

[1] Simpler is 11 . . . NxN† 12 QxN, B–N3, followed by . . . N–B4 (Tarrasch–Spielmann, Nuremburg 1906).

[2] Stronger than 12 B–Q2, P–QN4 13 O–O–O, NxN 14 QxN, B–N2 15 N–K2, Q–B2! (Tarrasch–Marshall, Match 1905).

[3] 15 . . . B–Q2 16 BxN, BxB 17 P–KN4 and White has good attacking chances.

[4] 10 . . . N–Q5 11 NxN, BxN 12 N–N5, followed by 13 B–K3 leads to a good position for White.

[5] Black has a good game (Klavintsj–Schistjakov, Semi-finals, USSR Championship 1957).

[6] After 9 . . . N–N5 10 B–K3, White controls Q4. Another inferior continuation is 9 . . . Q–B2 10 B–Q2, P–QN4 11 P–QR3, R–QN1 12 N–Q1! (Boleslavski–Pachman, Saltsjobaden 1948).

[7] White has a slight but distinct advantage (Korchnoi–Stahlberg, Bucharest 1954). To be considered is 11 . . . BxN† 12 PxB, Q–B2 13 Q–Q2, N–N3.

[8] The complications eventually are resolved in White's favor (Neshmetdinov–Wade, Bucharest 1954).

[9] Keres recommends 11 . . . N–Q5 12 NxN, BxN with a satisfactory game for Black.

[10] Black has good attacking chances for the Pawn. See Game 6.

## *French Defense Game 6*

*WHITE: Tringov* — *BLACK: Fuchs*

*Kienbaum 1958*

| | WHITE | BLACK | | WHITE | BLACK |
|---|---|---|---|---|---|
| 1 | P–K4 | P–K3 | 21 | Q–R5 | P–Q6 |
| 2 | P–Q4 | P–Q4 | 22 | B–B3 | PxP† |
| 3 | N–QB3 | N–KB3 | 23 | K–R1 | B–Q6 |
| 4 | P–K5 | KN–Q2 | 24 | Q–K5 | R–N2 |
| 5 | P–B4 | P–QB4 | 25 | N–N5 | B–KB4 |
| 6 | N–KB3 | N–QB3 | 26 | P–KN4 | BxP |
| 7 | PxP | BxP | 27 | KR–N1 | B–Q3 |
| 8 | B–Q3 | P–B4 | 28 | Q–K4 | B–B4 |
| 9 | PxP e.p. | NxP | 29 | Q–B3 | B–QN5 |
| 10 | Q–K2 | O–O | 30 | B–N2 | BxR |
| 11 | B–Q2 | B–Q2 | 31 | RxB | R–Q2 |
| 12 | O–O–O | K–R1 | 32 | P–QR4 | R–Q6 |
| 13 | QR–K1 | P–QN4 | 33 | QxR | BxR |
| 14 | BxP | R–QN1 | 34 | K–R2 | P–KR3 |
| 15 | BxN | BxB | 35 | NxP | R–B2 |
| 16 | N–KN5 | Q–N3 | 36 | N–Q4 | K–R2 |
| 17 | P–QN3 | P–Q5 | 37 | P–B5 | BxP |
| 18 | N/3–K4 | B–R6† | 38 | R–K5 | P–B8(Q) |
| 19 | K–N1 | NxN | | Resigns | |
| 20 | NxN | B–N4 | | | |

SUPPLEMENTARY VARIATIONS 11–15:
1 P–K4, P–K3 2 P–Q4, P–Q4 3 N–QB3, N–KB3

Sup. Var. 11 and 12 are concerned with Tartakover's subvariations of the Classical Variation, where Black at his 5th turn plays 5 . . . N–K5 instead of 5 . . . KN–Q2. This continuation offers tactical chances but is positionally inferior if properly met. Still less commendable is 5 . . . N–N1, a retreat once tried by Tarrasch.

Sup. Var. 14 and 15 show subvariations arising from the exchange of Pawns on White's Q5. If this exchange is carried out on White's 4th move, it leads to the so-called Svenonius Variation. On White's 5th turn, this exchange is even less usual and the variation has no specific name. In both cases, equality for Black is easily obtained.

| | *11* | *12* | *13* | *14* | *15* |
|---|---|---|---|---|---|
| *4* | B–KN5 | – – | – – | B–KN5 | PxP |
| | B–K2 | – – | – – | B–K2 | PxP[11] |
| *5* | P–K5 | – – | – – | PxP | B–KN5 |
| | N–K5 | – – | N–N1 | NxP | B–K2 |
| *6* | BxB | NxN | BxB[7] | BxB | B–Q3 |
| | QxB[1] | BxB[4] | NxB | QxB | N–B3 |
| *7* | NxN | NxB | Q–N4 | Q–Q2 | KN–K2 |
| | PxN | QxN | N–N3[8] | Q–N5 | B–K3 |
| *8* | Q–K2 | P–KN3 | P–KR4 | NxN | O–O |
| | N–Q2[2] | P–QB4[5] | P–KR4 | QxQ† | P–KR3 |
| *9* | O–O–O | P–QB3 | Q–N3 | KxQ | BxN |
| | P–KB4 | N–B3 | N–Q2 | PxN | BxB |
| *10* | PxP e.p. | P–B4 | B–Q3 | QR–K1†[10] | B–N5 |
| | NxP | Q–K2 | QN–B1 | = | Q–Q3 |
| *11* | P–KB3![3] | N–B3 | N–B3[9] | | BxN† |
| | ± | B–Q2 | ± | | QxB |
| *12* | | Q–Q2[6] | | | N–B4 |
| | | ± | | | O–O–O[12] |
| | | | | | = |

*Notes to supplementary variations 11–15:*

[1] Interesting is 6 . . . NxN 7 Q–N4, QxB 8 QxNP, Q–N5! 9 QxR†, K–Q2 with sufficient counterplay for Black according to an analysis by Haberditz. But after 10 B–Q3!, QxNP 11 R–Q1, NxR 12 KxN, QxQP 13 QxP, White's King Rook Pawn may become dangerous.

[2] Also favorable for White is 8 . . . P–QN3 9 O–O–O, B–N2 10 P–KN3, P–QB4 11 B–N2 (Flohr–Alekhine, Bled 1931).

[3] But 11 P–KN3, O–O 12 B–N2, P–K4! offers Black good counterplay (Spielmann–Van den Bosch, 1935). The text move

enables White to bring the enemy King Pawn under fire after 11 . . . PxP 12 NxP, O–O 13 P–KN3, B–Q2 14 B–R3.

[4] If 6 . . . PxN White has good play with 7 BxB, QxB 8 Q–K2! transposing into Sup. Var. 11. Or 7 B–K3, P–QB4 8 PxP, Q–B2 9 Q–Q4, N–Q2 10 QxP, NxKP 11 N–B3 with White for choice (Milner–Barry–Penrose, Championship of England 1955).

[5] 8 . . . B–Q2 9 P–KB4, Q–K2 10 P–B3, N–B3 11 N–B3, O–O–O offers Black sufficient counterchances, according to Lasker, but there have been no practical examples of the line.

[6] White has the edge (Forgacs–Tartakover, St. Petersburg 1909).

[7] Also worth considering is 6 B–K3 which Black can meet by 6 . . . P–QB4 or 6 . . . P–QN3.

[8] Better is 7 . . . N–B4.

[9] White has the edge (Tarrasch vs. Allies in consultation, Nuremburg 1888).

[10] Black can obtain equality as follows: 10 . . . K–B1 11 B–Q3, N–B3 12 P–QB3, B–Q2 13 N–K2, R–K1.

[11] 4 . . . NxP 5 N–K4 makes things more difficult for Black: 5 . . . N–Q2 6 N–KB3, B–K2 7 B–Q3, P–QN3 8 O–O, N–N5 9 B–QB4, B–N2 10 Q–K2, O–O 11 P–QR3, N–Q4 12 R–Q1 (Alekhine–Nimzowitsch, Kecskemet 1927).

[12] Spielmann–Alekhine, San Remo 1930.

---

## part 7—NIMZOWITSCH VARIATION I

1 P–K4, P–K3
2 P–Q4, P–Q4
3 N–QB3, B–N5
4 P–K5, P–QB4
5 P–QR3[A], BxN†[B]
6 PxB, N–K2[C]
7 Q–N4, PxP[D]
8 QxNP[E], R–KN1
9 QxRP, Q–B2[F]
10 N–K2[G], QN–B3
11 P–KB4, B–Q2
12 Q–Q3[H], PxP

KEY POSITION 7

### OBSERVATIONS ON KEY POSITION 7

[A] The former usual continuation, 5 B–Q2, has disappeared from tournament play. After 5 . . . N–K2 6 N–N5, BxB† 7 QxB, O–O, Black easily obtains an even game.

[B] The retreat 5 . . . B–R4 is risky because of 6 P–QN4, PxQP 7 Q–N4! See Game 7. Another example is Unzicker–Botvinnik, Olympics, Amsterdam 1954. In the above line if 6 . . . PxNP, then 7 N–N5! PxP† 8 P–B3 with advantage for White. If Black plays 5 . . . PxP, White obtains good chances with Rauzer's Pawn sacrifice: 6 PxB, PxN 7 N–B3!

[C] By playing 6 . . . Q–B2, Black can meet 7 Q–N4 with 7 . . . P–B4. However, White maintains an edge with 8 Q–N3, PxP 9 PxP, N–K2 10 B–Q2, O–O 11 B–Q3, P–QN3 12 N–K2, B–R3 13 N–B4! (Reshevsky–Botvinnik, The Hague–Moscow 1948). Or 8 . . . N–K2 9 QxP, R–N1 10 QxP, PxP 11 K–Q1! with advantage for White (Tal–Botvinnik, 1st Match Game 1960).

[D] The most important continuation. It leads to key position 7 almost by force. See also the supplementary variations.

[E] White must proceed consistently, since 8 PxP is followed effectively by 8 . . . Q–B2!, the only plausible alternative to the text move is 8 B–Q3 (Bontsch–Osmolowski), Q–B2 9 N–K2, PxP 10 QxNP, R–N1 11 QxRP, QxKP 12 B–KB4, Q–B3 13 P–KR4! and the King Rook Pawn becomes very strong (Geller–

Sokolski, USSR Championship 1950). Correct, according to Konstantinopolsky, is 8 . . . Q–R4! 9 N–K2, O–O. However, Keres considers the situation anything but clear after 10 O–O, PxP 11 N–N3.

[F] Weak is 9 . . . Q–R4? 10 R–N1, QxP† 11 B–Q2, Q–B2 12 P–B4, QN–B3 13 N–B3, B–Q2 14 N–N5! (Alexander–Botvinnik, Radio Match, England–USSR 1946).

[G] Too venturesome here is 10 K–Q1, because of 10 . . . N–Q2, after which 11 P–KB4 is met by . . . N–QB4 and . . . N–K5.

[H] Also good is 12 R–N1, O–O–O 13 Q–Q3, PxP 14 NxP, transposing into Idea Var. 18. Or 12 . . . PxP 13 Q–Q3 or 13 B–K3.

This is a crucial position. White has a passed Pawn on the King Rook file and would even have an extra Pawn after the fall of Black's advanced Queen Bishop Pawn. But White is wise not to rush the win of this weakling, because Black then may get dangerous play along the Queen Bishop file by . . . QR–B1. White does better to wait until Black plays . . . O–O–O, but even then he must proceed cautiously. Black has a lead in development, and the position of White's King in the center is not exactly safe.

IDEA VARIATIONS 17 AND 18:

(17) 13 NxP, P–QR3 14 B–Q2, R–QB1 15 N–K2, N–B4 16 P–KN4?, NxP 17 BPxN, QxKP 18 B–B3, RxB! 19 QxR, P–Q5, and Black has a tremendous attack. White does better with 16 P–B3, preparing 17 N–Q4. In the main line, another good reply to 16 P–KN4? is 16 . . . RxP 17 B–R3, NxP!

(18) 13 R–QN1, O–O–O (for other moves see Prac. Var. 31–33) 14 NxP, N–R4 15 N–N5, BxN 16 RxB, and White has chances to make his extra Pawn tell (Tscherbakov–Kreschnov, Semi-finals, USSR Championship 1959).

PRACTICAL VARIATIONS 31–33:

1 P–K4, P–K3 2 P–Q4, P–Q4 3 N–QB3, B–N5 4 P–K5, P–QB4 5 P–QR3, BxN† 6 PxB, N–K2 7 Q–N4, PxP 8 QxNP, R–N1 9 QxRP, Q–B2 10 N–K2, QN–B3 11 P–KB4, B–Q2 12 Q–Q3, PxP

| | *31* | *32* | *33* |
|---|---|---|---|
| *13* | R–QN1 | – – | B–K3 |
| | N–B4 | P–Q5 | N–B4 |

| | *31* | *32* | *33* |
|---|---|---|---|
| *14* | P–KR4[1] | N–N3[4] | N–Q4 |
| | P–QR3 | O–O–O | N/4xN |
| *15* | P–R5 | B–K2[5] | BxN |
| | O–O–O | ± | O–O–O |
| *16* | R–R3 | | P–KN3[6] |
| | P–Q5 | | P–B3![7] |
| *17* | N–N3 | | ∓ |
| | QN–K2[2] | | |
| *18* | N–K4![3] | | |
| | ± | | |

*Notes to practical variations 31–33:*

[1] Simpler is 14 P–KN3, followed by B–KN2 and O–O.

[2] The sacrifice 17 . . . NxP is worth trying.

[3] White has the edge (Chistjakov–Benavenetz, Moscow 1937).

[4] The acceptance of the Pawn offer is playable, according to Keres: 14 NxQP, NxN 15 QxN, N–B4 16 Q–B2, and Black has difficulty strengthening his attack.

[5] White proceeds with 16 O–O and eventually N–N3–K4 with a good game. Instead of the text, 15 N–K4 is premature: 15 . . . NxP! 16 PxN, QxP 17 Q–K2, B–B3 18 N–N3, Q–Q4, and Black obtains a very strong attack (Tarasov–Haiduk, Leningrad 1951).

[6] White must try 16 O–O–O in order to bring his King to safety.

[7] The text is much stronger than 16 . . . K–N1 17 B–K2 (Barden–Sterner, Hastings 1957–58). In opening the center at the expense of some Pawns, Black gets a very strong attack against the White King. See Game 8.

## SUPPLEMENTARY VARIATIONS 16–20:

1 P–K4, P–K3 2 P–Q4, P–Q4 3 N–QB3, B–N5 4 P–K5, P–QB4 5 P–QR3, BxN† 6 PxB, N–K2 7 Q–N4

There are two ways for Black to protect his King Knight Pawn: 7 . . . N–B4 and 7 . . . O–O. 7 . . . N–B4 was the usual move for quite some time. However, White after 8 B–Q3, P–KR4 9 Q–R3, eventually can play P–KN4, dislodging the Knight and creating complications not unfavorable to him. The quieter continuations Sup. Var. 16, 17, and 18 also offer White chances for an initiative.

The protection of Black's King Knight Pawn by . . . O–O is reputedly too risky in view of White's chances for a Kingside attack. According to some recent experiences, however, Black seems able to hold his own. See Sup. Var. 19 and 20. Final judgment is yet to be passed.

1 P–K4, P–K3 2 P–Q4, P–Q4 3 N–QB3, B–N5 4 P–K5, P–QB4 5 P–QR3, BxN† 6 PxB, N–K2 7 Q–N4

| | *16* | *17* | *18* | *19* | *20* |
|---|---|---|---|---|---|
| 7 | – – | – – | – – | – – | – – |
| | N–B4 | – – | – – | O–O | – – |
| *8* | B–Q3 | – – | – – | N–B3[9] | – – |
| | P–KR4 | – – | – – | QN–B3 | Q–R4 |
| *9* | Q–B4 | Q–R3 | Q–B3 | B–Q3 | B–Q2 |
| | Q–R5[1] | PxP | PxP | P–B4[10] | Q–R5 |
| *10* | N–K2! | N–B3 | BxN | PxP e.p. | B–Q3 |
| | QxQ | Q–B2[5] | PxB | RxP | P–B5 |
| *11* | NxQ | R–QN1 | PxP[7] | B–KN5 | BxP† |
| | N–K2[2] | PxP | N–B3 | R–B2[11] | KxB |
| *12* | B–K2 | P–KN4 | N–K2 | BxN | Q–R4† |
| | P–R5[3] | N–K2 | B–K3 | RxB | K–N1 |
| *13* | N–R5 | PxP | Q–N3[8] | Q–R4 | QxN |
| | K–B1 | QN–B3 | ± | P–KN3 | N–B3 |
| *14* | B–KN5 | B–KB4 | | O–O | Q–R4 |
| | PxP | N–N3 | | P–B5 | QxBP |
| *15* | PxP | B–N3 | | B–K2 | O–O |
| | P–QN3 | N/N3xP[6] | | B–Q2 | B–Q2 |
| *16* | P–N4![4] | ± | | KR–K1 | KR–K1 |
| | ± | | | Q–R4[12] | P–B3 |
| | | | | = | = |

*Notes to supplementary variations 16–20:*

[1] Safer is first 9 . . . PxP 10 PxP, and only then 10 . . . Q–R5. However, White can transpose into Sup. Var. 18 by 10 BxN, PxB 11 PxP or 11 Q–N3.

[2] Now 11 . . . PxP is not playable because of 12 BxN, PxB 13 NxQP!

[3] Better is 12 . . . P–KN3.

[4] White for choice. See Game 9.

[5] Weaker is 10 . . . N–B3 11 P–N4, KN–K2 12 PxRP, Q–B2 13 B–KB4, N–N3 14 Q–N4 (Tal–Petrosian, USSR Championship 1957 and Kupper–Durao, Chess Olympics, Munich 1958).

[6] 16 NxN, NxN 17 K–B1, B–Q2, and now White ought to proceed 18 R–K1, P–B3 19 B–N6†. Instead in Tal–Korchnoi, USSR Championship 1958, White played 18 Q–R4, and now Black could have obtained the edge by 18 . . . N–B6! In the above line, a good alternative for White is 16 K–B1, while 17 K–Q1 fails because of 17 . . . NxB!

[7] Also plausible is 11 Q–N3 and, if 11 . . . P–KN3, then White can take advantage of the weakening of his opponent's black squares. Black is therefore advised to play 11 . . . K–B1.

[8] White has the edge (Karaklaic–Wade, Belgrade 1954).

[9] 8 B–KN5 is parried by 8 . . . Q–R4, and 8 B–KR6 by 8 . . . N–B4.

[10] White threatens BxP†.

[11] Bad is 11 . . . P–K4? because of 12 BxP†!, KxB 13 Q–R5†, K–N1 14 BxR, PxB 15 PxKP, NxP 16 NxN, PxN 17 Q–N5†, K–B2 18 O–O!

[12] This sharp position offers even chances.

### *French Defense Game 7*

*WHITE: Smyslov* *BLACK: Botvinnik*

*Ninth Match Game 1954*

| | WHITE | BLACK | | WHITE | BLACK |
|---|---|---|---|---|---|
| 1 | P–K4 | P–K3 | 14 | B–N5 | R–B1 |
| 2 | P–Q4 | P–Q4 | 15 | N–Q4 | N–B4 |
| 3 | N–QB3 | B–N5 | 16 | R–QN1! | R–B5 |
| 4 | P–K5 | P–QB4 | 17 | NxN | PxN |
| 5 | P–QR3 | B–R4 | 18 | RxP | R–K5† |
| 6 | P–QN4 | PxQP | 19 | QxR! | QPxQ |
| 7 | Q–N4 | N–K2 | 20 | R–N8† | B–B1 |
| 8 | PxB | PxN | 21 | B–N5† | QxB |
| 9 | QxNP | R–N1 | 22 | RxQ | N–K3 |
| 10 | QxP | N–Q2 | 23 | B–B6 | RxP |
| 11 | N–B3 | N–B1 | 24 | P–R5 | B–R3 |
| 12 | Q–Q3 | QxP | 25 | P–R6! | Resigns |
| 13 | P–KR4! | B–Q2 | | | |

### *French Defense Game 8*

*WHITE: Padevski* *BLACK: Bertholdt*

*Kienbaum 1958*

| | WHITE | BLACK | | WHITE | BLACK |
|---|---|---|---|---|---|
| 1 | P–K4 | P–K3 | 18 | PxP | R–N5 |
| 2 | P–Q4 | P–Q4 | 19 | B–K3 | QxKP |
| 3 | N–QB3 | B–N5 | 20 | B–R3 | P–Q5 |
| 4 | P–K5 | P–QB4 | 21 | O–O | PxB |
| 5 | P–QR3 | BxN† | 22 | BxR | BxB |
| 6 | PxN | N–K2 | 23 | P–B7 | R–B1 |
| 7 | Q–N4 | PxP | 24 | QR–K1 | P–K7 |
| 8 | QxNP | R–N1 | 25 | R–B4 | Q–B4† |
| 9 | QxP | Q–B2 | 26 | K–N2 | N–K4 |
| 10 | N–K2 | QN–B3 | 27 | Q–K4 | B–Q2 |
| 11 | P–KB4 | PxP | 28 | QxP | B–B3† |
| 12 | Q–Q3 | B–Q2 | 29 | K–R3 | NxP |
| 13 | B–K3 | N–B4 | 30 | P–N4 | N–N4† |
| 14 | N–Q4 | N/4xN | 31 | K–N3 | N–K5† |
| 15 | BxN | O–O–O | 32 | RxN | BxR |
| 16 | P–N3 | P–B3! | 33 | R–KB1 | Q–K4† |
| 17 | PxP | P–K4! | | Resigns | |

*French Defense Game 9*

*WHITE: Gligoric* *BLACK: Pachman*

*Munich 1958*

| WHITE | BLACK | WHITE | BLACK | WHITE | BLACK |
|---|---|---|---|---|---|
| 1 P–K4 | P–K3 | 17 BPxP | B–R3 | 33 B–N5 | N–R6 |
| 2 P–Q4 | P–Q4 | 18 P–N4 | BxB | 34 B–B1 | N–N8? |
| 3 N–QB3 | B–N5 | 19 KxB | QN–B3 | 35 B–N2 | K–R2 |
| 4 P–K5 | N–K2 | 20 P–B3 | R–B1 | 36 RxP | R/1–QB1 |
| 5 P–QR3 | BxN† | 21 P–KR4 | K–N1 | 37 P–N5 | NxP |
| 6 PxB | P–QB4 | 22 KR–KB1! | N–N3 | 38 BxN | RxR |
| 7 Q–N4 | N–B4 | 23 R–B3 | R–B2 | 39 RxR | RxB† |
| 8 B–Q3 | P–KR4 | 24 QR–KB1 | R–R2 | 40 K–N4! | R–B5 |
| 9 Q–B4 | Q–R5 | 25 K–B2 | N–R4 | 41 K–R5 | RxQP |
| 10 N–K2! | QxQ | 26 K–N3 | N–QB5 | 42 RxP | R–KB5 |
| 11 NxQ | N–K2 | 27 P–R4 | N–B1 | 43 R–K7 | P–Q5 |
| 12 B–K2 | P–R5 | 28 R/1–B2 | N–N3 | 44 P–N6† | K–N1 |
| 13 N–R5 | K–B1 | 29 N–B4 | NxN | 45 RxKP | K–B1 |
| 14 B–KN5 | PxP | 30 BxN | R–R1 | 46 K–N5 | R–B6 |
| 15 PxP | P–QN3 | 31 B–B1 | N–R4 | 47 RxP | Resigns |
| 16 P–N4! | PxP e.p. | 32 B–Q2 | N–B5 | | |

## part 8—**NIMZOWITSCH VARIATION II**

1 P–K4, P–K3
2 P–Q4, P–Q4
3 N–QB3, B–N5
4 P–K5, P–QB4
5 P–QR3, BxN†
6 PxB, N–K2
7 N–B3, Q–R4
8 B–Q2[A], P–B5
9 P–QR4[B]

KEY POSITION 8

### OBSERVATIONS ON KEY POSITION 8

A After 8 Q–Q2, Black can blockade White's Queenside with 8 . . . Q–R5, but this is not necessarily a serious disadvantage (Keres–Boleslavski and Bondarevski–Boleslavski, USSR Championship 1941).

B The usual continuation. White forestalls the occupation of his QR4 by an enemy piece. It remains to be seen whether this precautionary move is necessary. Instead of the anticipatory 9 P–QR4, White may play 9 N–N5, P–KR3 10 N–R3, N–Q2 11 N–B4, P–KN3 12 P–KR4, N–N3 13 P–R5, P–KN4 14 N–R3, B–Q2 15 B–K2, N–R5 16 B–N4, with a positional edge for White (Skold–Kaila, Chess Olympics, Helsinki 1952). Another plausible plan for White is 9 P–KN3, followed by B–R3, N–R4, P–B4 and P–B5.

On White's 7th move, apart from 7 Q–N4 (Part 7), he has two worth-while alternatives: 7 N–B3 or 7 P–QR4. Both continuations may lead to the same position, but they still require separate treatment because of their respective main lines.

In this part we shall consider 7 N–B3, which usually leads to key position 8. The point is quite interesting, since Black can win the Queen Rook Pawn by force, playing, after 7 . . . Q–R4, eventually . . . N–Q2, . . . N–N3, and . . . NxP or . . . B–Q2 and . . . BxP. White's counterchances are on the Kingside. He must aim at creating a weakness there and subsequently at breaking through by a Pawn storm. Playing with proper consistency, White usually gets sufficient compensation for the sacrificed Queen Rook Pawn. Black's defense is hampered by the pin subsequent upon the capture of the Pawn. The chances for both White and Black are demonstrated by Idea Var. 19–21. Black may postpone the capture of the Queen Rook Pawn and instead complete his development by QN–B3, B–Q2, and O–O–O. For this safer system see Prac. Var. 34–37.

IDEA VARIATIONS 19–21:

(19) 9 . . . N–Q2 10 B–K2, N–QN3 11 O–O, NxP 12 N–R4?, N–KN3 13 NxN, RPxN 14 R–K1, B–Q2 15 B–KB1, P–QN4 16 Q–B3, R–QN1 with advantage for Black. White's maneuver N–B3, N–R4, NxN has only strengthened Black's control of his KB4, so that White's attacking chances have evaporated. White ought to play 12 N–N5! P–KR3 13 N–R3 followed by P–B4 and P–B5 with sufficient chances for attack. In this line, if 13 . . . N–KN3, then 14 B–R5. Even stronger, however, is the immediate 10 N–N5! as in Idea Var. 20.

(20) 9 . . . N–Q2 10 N–N5, P–KR3 11 N–R3, N–QN3 12 N–B4, P–N3 (a weakening of Black's Kingside; however, 12 . . . B–Q2 13 N–R5, R–KN1 leaves White's Knight dominantly placed, and he can strongly proceed with B–K2 and O–O and then advance his King Bishop Pawn and King Knight Pawn) 13 P–R4, B–Q2 14 P–R5, P–N4 15 N–K2, O–O–O 16 P–N4, QR–N1 17 B–R3, NxP 18 P–B4, PxP 19 O–O. White has a clear advantage on the Kingside because of the vulnerability of Black's King Rook Pawn. In the above line, if 11 . . . N–KN3, then 12 B–K2 followed by B–R5.

(21) 9 . . . B–Q2 10 P–N3 (10 N–N5 is also a good plan for White), B–B3 (more consistent is the immediate 10 . . . BxP, although White obtains a good position with 11 B–R3, QN–B3 12 O–O) 11 B–R3, N–Q2 12 O–O, N–QN3 13 N–R4, NxP (if 13 . . . N–KN3, then 14 N–N2 followed by P–B4) 14 P–B4, P–KN3 15 P–B5!, KPxP 16 P–N4 with an edge for White (Lilienthal–Ragosin, 1944).

PRACTICAL VARIATIONS 34–37:

1 P–K4, P–K3 2 P–Q4, P–Q4 3 N–QB3, B–N5 4 P–K5, P–QB4 5 P–QR3, BxN† 6 PxB, N–K2 7 N–B3, Q–R4 8 B–Q2, P–B5 9 P–QR4

| | 34 | 35 | 36 | 37 |
|---|---|---|---|---|
| 9 | – – | – – | – – | – – |
| | QN–B3 | – – | – – | – – |
| 10 | N–N5 | B–K2 | – – | P–N3 |
| | P–KR3 | B–Q2 | – – | B–Q2 |
| 11 | N–R3 | O–O | – – | B–N2[7] |
| | N–KN3 | N–Q1 | N–B4 | O–O–O |
| 12 | Q–B3[1] | N–N5 | Q–K1[4] | O–O |
| | B–Q2 | P–KR3 | O–O–O | P–B4 |

| | 34 | 35 | 36 | 37 |
|---|---|---|---|---|
| 13 | N–B4 | N–R3 | B–QB1 | PxP e.p. |
| | NxN | BxP[3] | P–B3 | PxP |
| 14 | QxN | = | P–N4?[5] | KR–K1 |
| | N–K2! | | N/4–K2 | N–N3 |
| 15 | P–KR4 | | B–QR3 | B–R6 |
| | BxP[2] | | N–N3[6] | KR–KN1[8] |
| | ∓ | | ∓ | = |

*Notes to practical variations 34–37:*

[1] Stronger is 12 B–K2, B–Q2 13 B–R5 with attacking chances on the Kingside.

[2] Black has captured a Pawn under favorable circumstances.

[3] White ought to continue 14 N–B4 followed by 15 N–R5. Good for Black is 14 P–B4, P–QN4 15 P–N4, P–N3 16 Q–K1, Q–N3 17 B–Q1, N/1–B3 18 Q–R4, O–O–O (Neshmetdinov–Ljublinski, Semi-finals, USSR Championship 1950).

[4] Again, 12 N–N5 is stronger.

[5] This move only weakens the Kingside. White ought to play 14 B–QR3.

[6] Black has the edge (Ljublinski–Sokolski, USSR Championship 1950).

[7] Also worth trying is 11 B–KR3, possibly followed by P–KB4 and P–B5.

[8] Boleslavski–Barcza, Bucharest 1953.

1 P–K4, P–K3
2 P–Q4, P–Q4
3 N–QB3, B–N5
4 P–K5, P–QB4
5 P–QR3, BxN†
6 PxB, N–K2
7 P–QR4, Q–R4[A]
8 Q–Q2[B], QN–B3[C]
9 N–B3

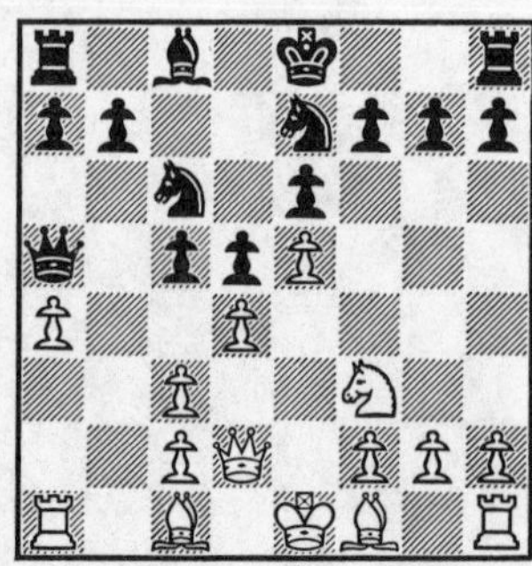

KEY POSITION 9

## part 9—NIMZOWITSCH VARIATION III

### OBSERVATIONS ON KEY POSITION 9

[A] Black may also proceed 7 . . . QN–B3 8 N–B3, Q–R4. If then 9 Q–Q2, the ensuing continuation is treated in this section, while a transposition into 9 B–Q2 has been discussed in Part 8, Prac. Var. 34–37.

[B] Also worth consideration is 8 B–Q2, when 8 . . . P–B5 or 8 . . . QN–B3 is countered by the aggressive 9 Q–N4. The latter case differs from Part 8 in that the White Knight is here still on N1.

[C] A new idea is 8 . . . B–Q2. Schamkowitsch–Petrosian, USSR Championship 1960, continued: 9 B–R3, PxP 10 PxP, QxQ† 11 KxQ, N–B4 12 N–B3, N–B3 13 B–N2, N–R4 14 B–B3, N–B5† 15 BxN, PxB 16 B–N4, B–B3, and the active position of Black's Bishop compensates for the weakness of his Queen Bishop Pawn.

The continuation 7 P–QR4 serves to prevent the blockade of White's Queenside by an enemy piece on his QR4. Besides, White intends to develop his Queen Bishop via QR3. The attack on the Queen Bishop Pawn by Black's Queen is answered by Q–Q2.

Key position 9 offers Black the possibility of transposing into the end game through exchanges on his Q5 and Q7. This liquidation is not quite satisfactory for Black long as White is able to recapture on his Q2 with the Queen Bishop, so that Black is then unable to proceed with . . . N–QR4 and . . . N–QB5. Therefore, White must not play B–QR3 too early, which would commit him to the capture of the Black Queen with his King.

IDEA VARIATIONS 22 AND 23:

(22) 9 . . . PxP 10 PxP, QxQ† 11 BxQ! N–B4 12 B–B3! (not 12 P–QB3? because of 12 . . . N–R4), B–Q2 13 B–Q3, R–B1 14 K–Q2, O–O 15 P–R5 with an edge for White. See Game 10.

(23) 9 . . . B–Q2 10 B–R3, PxP 11 PxP, QxQ† 12 KxQ, N–B4 13 R–QN1, P–QN3 14 P–B3, N–R4 15 B–N5, N–B5† 16 BxN, PxB 17 P–R5, B–B3 with a good end game for Black (Kan–Botvinnik, Sverdlovsk 1943). Correct is 10 B–Q3. See the practical variations below.

PRACTICAL VARIATIONS 38–40:

1 P–K4, P–K3 2 P–Q4, P–Q4 3 N–QB3, B–N5 4 P–K5, P–QB4 5 P–QR3, BxN† 6 PxB, N–K2 7 P–QR4, Q–R4 8 Q–Q2, QN–B3 9 N–B3

| | *38* | *39* | *40* |
|---|---|---|---|
| *9* | – – | – – | – – |
| | B–Q2 | – – | P–B5[5] |
| *10* | B–Q3 | – – | P–N3 |
| | P–B5 | R–QB1[2] | O–O |
| *11* | B–K2 | B–R3!?[3] | B–N2 |
| | O–O–O | PxP | P–B3 |
| *12* | B–R3 | Q–N5! | PxP |
| | P–B3 | QxP† | RxP |
| *13* | O–O | K–K2[4] | O–O |
| | N–B4 | = | B–Q2 |
| *14* | P–KN4 | | B–QR3[6] |
| | N/4–K2 | | ± |
| *15* | KR–QN1[1] | | |
| | ± | | |

*Notes to practical variations 38–40:*

[1] Rabinowitsch–Botvinnik, USSR Championship 1939, continued 15 . . . Q–R3? (better at once 15 . . . QR–B1) 16 P–R5! QR–B1, and now White should have played 17 B–Q6, maintaining his advantage. Instead White played 17 N–K1?! — initiating an interesting but dubious combination. See Game 11.

continued ▸

[2] 10 . . . PxP 11 PxP, QxQ† 12 BxQ, N–B4 13 B–B3! leads to Game 10 from Idea Var. 22.

[3] White may also proceed simply with 11 O–O.

[4] White has attacking chances for the Pawns (Schifferdecker–Unzicker, Pyrmont 1950). Black ought to continue 13 . . . K–B1 instead of 13 . . . N–N5 14 BxN, QxB 15 KR–QN1 followed by 16 QxP.

[5] Black can better postpone this advance until White has played B–Q3. See Prac. Var. 38.

[6] Smyslov–Boleslavski, USSR Championship 1941.

## SUPPLEMENTARY VARIATIONS 21–25:

1 P–K4, P–K3 2 P–Q4, P–Q4 3 N–QB3, B–N5

The most usual continuation after 3 . . . B–N5 is 4 P–K5, extensively treated in the preceding pages. There now remains for discussion a number of continuations in which White aims at maintaining the tension in the center. Some of these variations involve the temporary or permanent sacrifice of White's King Pawn.

Most important are the continuations arising from 4 P–QR3 (Sup. Var. 24), where White aims at retaining his pair of Bishops, and those stemming from 4 B–Q2, where White's aim is quick development.

| | *21* | *22* | *23* | *24* | *25* |
|---|---|---|---|---|---|
| *4* | B–Q3[1] | N–K2 | Q–N4 | P–QR3 | B–Q2 |
| | PxP | PxP | N–KB3 | BxN† | PxP |
| *5* | BxP | P–QR3 | QxP | PxB | Q–N4 |
| | N–KB3 | B–K2![4] | R–N1 | PxP | N–KB3[13] |
| *6* | B–B3[2] | NxP | Q–R6 | Q–N4 | QxNP |
| | P–QB4 | N–QB3 | P–QB4![8] | N–KB3 | R–N1 |
| *7* | N–K2 | B–K3[5] | P–QR3 | QxNP | Q–R6 |
| | PxP | N–B3 | R–N3 | R–N1 | QxP[14] |
| *8* | QxP | N/1–B3 | Q–K3 | Q–R6 | O–O–O |
| | QxQ | NxN[6] | B–R4 | P–B4 | B–B1 |
| *9* | NxQ[3] | NxN | B–Q2 | N–K2 | Q–R4 |
| | ± | P–K4 | BPxP | R–N3[10] | R–N5 |
| *10* | | P–Q5 | QxP | Q–K3[11] | Q–R3 |
| | | N–Q5[7] | N–B3[9] | N–B3[12] | QxP[15] |
| | | ∓ | ∓ | ± | ± |

*Notes to supplementary variations 21–25:*

[1] The exchange on Q5 is obsolete and leads to nothing: 4 PxP, PxP 5 B–Q3, N–QB3 6 N–K2, N–K2! 7 O–O, B–KB4! with equality (Capablanca–Alekhine, 1st Match Game 1927).

[2] Stronger than 6 B–Q3, P–QB4 7 P–QR3, BxN† 8 PxB, QN–Q2 9 N–B3, Q–B2 10 O–O, P–B5 11 B–K2, N–Q4 with a good game for Black (Lilienthal–Boleslavski, Leningrad–Moscow 1941).

[3] White has a slight edge.

[4] Or 5 . . . BxN† 6 NxB, N–QB3 7 B–QN5, N–K2 8 B–N5, P–B3 9 B–K3, O–O 10 Q–Q2, P–B4 11 P–B3! White obtains good chances for the Pawn: 11 . . . PxP 12 PxP, N–Q4 13 BxN, NxB 14 QxN, Q–R5† 15 Q–B2, QxQ† 16 KxQ, PxB (Pilnik–Donner, Beverwijk 1951) and now White ought to play 17 KR–K1 with a promising end game. Too risky is 6 . . . P–B4 7 P–B3, PxP 8 QxP (Alekhine–Nimzowitsch, Bled 1931).

[5] To 7 P–KN4 (Alekhine–Euwe, 7th Match Game 1935) the strongest reply is 7 . . . P–K4! If 8 P–Q5, then 8 . . . N–Q5 9 NxN? QxP!

[6] This is more comfortable than 8 . . . O–O 9 N–N3, P–QN3 10 B–K2, B–N2 11 O–O, Q–Q2 12 Q–Q2, QR–Q1 13 KR–Q1, Q–B1 (Alekhine–Euwe, 3rd Match Game 1935).

[7] Black has a fully satisfactory game. On 11 BxN, he plays 11 . . . QxP!

[8] Or 6 . . . R–N3 7 Q–K3, NxP 8 B–Q3, P–KB4 9 N–K2, P–QB4 10 BxN (Alekhine–Euwe, 9th Match Game 1935), and now Black can get sufficient counterchances by 10 . . . QPxB 11 PxP, N–Q2. Black played instead 10 . . . BPxB and White replied strongly with 11 Q–R3!

[9] Black has the better chances. The answer to 11 B–QN5 is 11 . . . B–N3, while, after 11 Q–Q3, Black, according to Keres, has the choice of 11 . . . N–K4 or 11 . . . P–Q5.

[10] Or 9 . . . QN–Q2 10 N–N3, R–N3 11 Q–K3, N–Q4 12 QxP, NxP 13 Q–Q3, N–Q4 14 B–K2, Q–B3 15 P–QB3, with an edge for White (Alekhine–Euwe, 3rd Match Game 1935). In the above line, according to Alekhine, Black can play better on his 10th turn: 10 . . . Q–R4 11 B–Q2, Q–R5.

[11] It is difficult to decide whether the Queen ought to return to Q2 or K3. If 10 Q–Q2, QN–Q2 11 B–N2, P–N3 (Smyslov–Botvinnik, 21st Match Game 1954), White obtains a good game with 12 N–B4, followed by 13 P–Q5 (Keres) or 13 B–QN5 (Bronstein). Botvinnik thinks it more accurate for Black to play first 11 . . . Q–B2, followed by P–QN3.

[12] 11 PxP, N–KN5 12 QxP, Q–Q8† 13 KxQ, NxP† 14 K–K1, NxQ 15 N–B4, R–N1 16 B–Q3 with an end game favoring White (Smyslov–Botvinnik, 7th Match Game 1954). Stronger is 11 . . . P–K4! (see Game 12) or 11 . . . Q–R4. Again, in the above line, 12 . . . P–K4 is better than the text move.

[13] 5 . . . QxP 6 O–O–O, P–KB4 7 Q–N3, B–Q3 8 B–KB4, BxB† 9 QxB, Q–B4 10 P–B3!, N–K2 11 PxP, O–O 12 N–B3 offers sufficient positional compensation for the Pawn (Keres–Loewenfisch, USSR Championship 1948). A new idea is 6 . . . P–KR4 7 Q–N5, B–K2 8 Q–N3, B–Q3 9 B–KB4, P–R5 10 Q–N4, N–KB3! (Chitescu–Bertholdt, Bucharest 1959). The point is that 11 QxNP fails against 11 . . . BxB† 12 K–N1, R–R2! Also, 6 KN–K2 gives White chances.

[14] Or 7 . . . N–B3 8 O–O–O, R–N3 9 Q–R4, BxN 10 BxB, Q–Q4 11 P–QN3, N–K2 12 P–B3! with sharp play and even chances (Keres–Botvinnik, The Hague and Moscow 1948).

[15] 11 B–K2!, R–R5 12 QxR, QxQ 13 P–KN3, and White recovers the Queen, emerging with the exchange for two Pawns and some advantage: 13 . . . P–K6 14 PxQ, PxB† 15 K–N1!

*continued* ▶

Or 13 . . . Q–R3 14 BxQ, BxB† 15 K–N1. In the above line, after 11 . . . R–N3, White proceeds strongly with 12 P–KN4 (threatening to trap the Black Queen), Q–B4 13 B–K3, Q–QR4 14 P–N5, RxP 15 Q–R4! Bad for White is 11 N–N5?, N–R3 12 K–N1, B–Q2 13 B–K3, Q–B4, and Black quickly obtained a winning advantage (Boleslavski–Bronstein, 14th and decisive game of their 1950 match).

*French Defense Game 10*

*WHITE: Smyslov* *BLACK: Letelier*

*Venice 1950*

| | WHITE | BLACK | | WHITE | BLACK | | WHITE | BLACK |
|---|---|---|---|---|---|---|---|---|
| 1 | P–K4 | P–K3 | 15 | P–R5! | R–B2 | 29 | RxR | N–B3 |
| 2 | P–Q4 | P–Q4 | 16 | KR–K1 | P–B3 | 30 | P–R6! | PxP |
| 3 | N–QB3 | B–N5 | 17 | BxN! | PxB | 31 | R–B7† | K–N3 |
| 4 | P–K5 | P–QB4 | 18 | PxP | RxP | 32 | R–Q7 | N–K2 |
| 5 | P–QR3 | BxN† | 19 | QR–N1 | P–KR3 | 33 | B–N4 | N–B4 |
| 6 | PxB | N–K2 | 20 | R–N5 | B–K3 | 34 | RxQP | N–K6 |
| 7 | P–QR4 | Q–R4 | 21 | R/1–QN1 | R/3–B2 | 35 | R–Q8 | NxNP |
| 8 | Q–Q2 | QN–B3 | 22 | N–K1 | P–B5 | 36 | P–Q5 | R–N3 |
| 9 | N–B3 | PxP | 23 | P–B3 | P–KN4 | 37 | B–B5 | R–N2 |
| 10 | PxP | QxQ† | 24 | N–Q3 | K–R2 | 38 | R–QB8 | N–R5 |
| 11 | BxQ | N–B4 | 25 | R–K1 | R–B3 | 39 | K–K2 | N–B4 |
| 12 | B–B3! | B–Q2 | 26 | R–B5! | R–QB1 | 40 | R–B6† | K–R4 |
| 13 | B–Q3 | R–QB1 | 27 | N–N4! | NxN | 41 | P–Q6 | R–Q2 |
| 14 | K–Q2 | O–O | 28 | RxB! | R/3xR | 42 | R–B7 | Resigns |

*French Defense Game 11*

*WHITE: Rabinowitsch* *BLACK: Botvinnik*

*USSR Championship 1939*

| | WHITE | BLACK | | WHITE | BLACK |
|---|---|---|---|---|---|
| 1 | P–K4 | P–K3 | 18 | N–Q3? | PxN |
| 2 | P–Q4 | P–Q4 | 19 | BxP | QxP |
| 3 | N–QB3 | B–N5 | 20 | BxN | Q–B2 |
| 4 | P–K5 | P–QB4 | 21 | BxR | RxB |
| 5 | P–QR3 | BxN† | 22 | B–N5? | R–B5! |
| 6 | PxB | N–K2 | 23 | P–KR3 | P–QR3! |
| 7 | N–B3 | QN–B3 | 24 | BxN | BxB |
| 8 | B–Q3 | Q–R4 | 25 | R–K1 | P–K5 |
| 9 | Q–Q2! | P–B5 | 26 | R–K3 | B–N4 |
| 10 | B–K2 | B–Q2 | 27 | R–N3 | P–KN4 |
| 11 | P–QR4 | P–B3 | 28 | K–N2 | Q–B2 |
| 12 | B–R3 | O–O–O | 29 | Q–K3 | Q–B3 |
| 13 | O–O | N–B4 | 30 | R–K1 | B–K1 |
| 14 | P–N4 | N/4–K2 | 31 | Q–K2 | K–N1 |
| 15 | KR–N1 | Q–R3? | 32 | R–QN1 | B–N4 |
| 16 | P–R5! | QR–B1 | 33 | Q–K3 | B–K1 |
| 17 | N–K1? | PxP | 34 | Q–K2 | K–B2 |

| | WHITE | BLACK | | WHITE | BLACK |
|---|---|---|---|---|---|
| 35 | R–KR1 | B–N3 | 52 | K–N1 | K–N3 |
| 36 | R–K1 | B–K1 | 53 | R–R2 | R–B2 |
| 37 | R–KR1 | P–KR4! | 54 | R–N2 | R–B6 |
| 38 | K–N1 | B–N4 | 55 | K–R1 | R–B1 |
| 39 | Q–K1 | P–R5 | 56 | K–N1 | R–B3 |
| 40 | R–K3 | B–B5 | 57 | R–R2 | K–B3 |
| 41 | R–R2 | P–N3 | 58 | R–N2 | R–B6 |
| 42 | Q–R1 | Q–B1 | 59 | K–R1 | B–B8! |
| 43 | R–N2 | P–R4 | 60 | RxR | PxR! |
| 44 | Q–R4 | Q–K2 | 61 | R–R2 | P–R5 |
| 45 | Q–R1 | K–N2 | 62 | K–N1 | P–R6 |
| 46 | Q–R4 | R–B1 | 63 | Q–B1 | B–B5 |
| 47 | R–K1 | Q–Q3 | 64 | QxNP | P–R7 |
| 48 | Q–R1 | K–R3 | 65 | Q–B1 | P–K4 |
| 49 | R–K3 | P–N4 | 66 | PxP | QxP |
| 50 | Q–N2 | R–B6! | 67 | Q–R1 | Q–K7 |
| 51 | K–R1 | R–B3 | | Resigns | |

*French Defense Game 12*

*WHITE: Fichtl* *BLACK: Winiwarter*

*Salzburg 1957*

| | WHITE | BLACK | | WHITE | BLACK |
|---|---|---|---|---|---|
| 1 | P–K4 | P–K3 | 12 | N–N3 | B–N5 |
| 2 | P–Q4 | P–Q4 | 13 | B–N2 | Q–R4 |
| 3 | N–QB3 | B–N5 | 14 | NxP? | NxN |
| 4 | P–QR3 | BxN† | 15 | QxN | N–Q5! |
| 5 | PxB | PxP | 16 | B–Q3 | O–O–O |
| 6 | Q–N4 | N–KB3 | 17 | Q–K3 | P–K5 |
| 7 | QxP | R–N1 | 18 | BxP | P–B4 |
| 8 | Q–R6 | P–B4 | 19 | BxNP† | KxB |
| 9 | N–K2 | R–N3 | 20 | Q–K7† | K–B1 |
| 10 | Q–K3 | N–B3 | 21 | O–O | B–B6 |
| 11 | PxP | P–K4 | | Resigns | |

## part 10—RUBINSTEIN VARIATION

### OBSERVATIONS ON KEY POSITION 10

[A] After 4 . . . N–KB3 5 NxN†, QxN 6 N–B3, B–Q2 (better is 6 . . . P–KR3) 7 B–KN5, Q–N3 8 B–Q3, White has a clear advantage (Tarrasch–Lasker, 6th Match Game 1908). Black has developed his Queen prematurely. In this line he does better to accept the weakening of his Pawn formation and play on his 5th turn 5 . . . PxN, but even so, White maintains the edge: 6 N–B3, P–N3 7 B–KB4, B–QN2 8 P–B3, B–Q3 9 B–N3, N–Q2 10 Q–R4, P–QR3 11 B–Q3 (Aronin–Ufimzew, USSR Championship 1947).

1 P–K4, P–K3
2 P–Q4, P–Q4
3 N–QB3, PxP
4 NxP, N–Q2[A]
5 N–KB3, KN–B3[B]
6 NxN†, NxN
7 B–Q3[C]

KEY POSITION 10

[B] Another possibility is 5 . . . B–K2, so as to recapture on KB3 with the Bishop. This, however, entails the postponement of . . . P–QB4 and . . . P–QN3, making the development of the Queen Bishop more difficult. An example is Keres–Pavey, USSR–USA, New York 1954: 5 . . . B–K2 6 B–Q3, KN–B3 7 Q–K2!, NxN (if 7 . . . P–QB4, then NxP!) 8 BxN, P–QB4 (if 8 . . . N–B3, then 9 BxNP!) 9 B–K3 (also good is 9 P–Q5, as in Unzicker–Donner, Goteborg 1955), O–O 10 O–O–O, N–B3 (better immediately 10 . . . Q–B2) 11 B–Q3, Q–B2 12 PxP with an edge for White. In the above line if Black varies with 8 . . . O–O, then 9 O–O, N–B3 10 B–Q3, leading to positions in the Practical Variations.

[C] Capablanca's continuation 7 N–K5 is still interesting: 7 . . . Q–Q4 (the theoretical reply) 8 B–K2! QxNP 9 B–B3, Q–R6 10 Q–Q3, and White has sufficient compensation for the sacrificed Pawn. Inferior for White are both 8 P–QB4, B–N5†! and 8 P–QR3, B–Q3. But in favor of White is 7 . . . B–Q3 8 Q–B3 as played by Capablanca against Blanca, Havana 1913. 7 . . . B–K2 deserves consideration.

This position offers Black a choice between two different systems of development. He can either quickly play . . . P–QB4 or postpone this advance and play . . . P–QN3 followed by . . . B–QN2. The latter method, for which Rubinstein showed a preference, offers Black a sound if somewhat restricted development of his pieces. Attempts by White to profit from Black's . . . P–QN3 by playing N–K5 have led to no favorable results. White does better to continue his own development; then Black has difficulty playing . . . P–QB4, and continues to struggle with a deficiency in space. All things taken into consideration, Black should adopt the system stemming from an early . . . P–QB4. White then exchanges on Black's QB4, obtaining an initiative which he must try to hold by preventing the smooth development of Black's Queen Bishop.

IDEA VARIATIONS 24–26:

(24) 7 . . . P–QN3 8 N–K5. This enticing attempt to take advantage of Black's . . . P–QN3 is premature (for other moves, see Prac. Var. 41–43): 8 . . . B–N2 9 B–N5†? P–B3! Stemming from Black's 9th move are three plausible continuations, all of which favor Black:

1) 10 BxP† BxB 11 NxB, Q–Q4 12 N–K5, QxNP 13 Q–B3, QxQ with a better endgame for Black (Schlechter–Rubinstein, San Sebastian 1912).
2) 10 NxP, Q–Q4! 11 P–QB4! QxNP 12 N–K5†, K–Q1 13 R–B1, B–N5† 14 B–Q2, Q–K5† 15 Q–K2, BxB† 16 KxB, and now not 16 . . .

QxP†? 17 K–K1, K–K2 18 B–B6!, but 16 . . . K–K2! with a better game for Black.

3) 10 Q–B3, Q–Q4! 11 QxQ, NxQ 12 BxP†, (if 12 NxP? then 12 . . . P–QR3!), BxB 13 NxB, R–B1 14 NxP, RxP 15 O–O, B–K2 16 P–QN3, N–B6, and Black has positional compensation for the sacrificed Pawn.

(25) 7 . . . P–QB4 8 PxP, BxP 9 B–KN5, B–Q2 10 O–O, B–B3 11 Q–K2, P–KR3 12 B–R4, Q–Q4 13 QR–Q1, Q–R4 14 BxN, PxB 15 B–K4 with an edge for White (Euwe–Eliskases, Buenos Aires 1947). If 9 O–O instead of 9 B–KN5, then Black gets a satisfactory game with 9 . . . O–O 10 B–KN5, P–QN3 11 Q–K2, B–N2 12 QR–Q1, Q–B2! Again, in the main line above, if Black plays 9 . . . B–K2, White builds an attacking position: 10 Q–K2, O–O 11 O–O–O.

(26) 7 . . . B–K2 8 Q–K2, O–O 9 B–KN5, P–QB4 and not 9 . . . P–QN3? because White wins a Rook by 10 BxN, BxB 11 Q–K4!

PRACTICAL VARIATIONS 41–45:

1 P–K4, P–K3 2 P–Q4, P–Q4 3 N–QB3, PxP 4 NxP, N–Q2 5 N–KB3, KN–B3 6 NxN†, NxN 7 B–Q3

| | *41* | *42* | *43* | *44* | *45* |
|---|---|---|---|---|---|
| 7 | – – | – – | – – | – – | – – |
| | P–QN3 | – – | – – | B–K2 | – – |
| *8* | Q–K2 | – – | O–O | Q–K2 | – – |
| | B–N2 | – – | B–N2 | O–O | – – |
| *9* | B–KN5 | – – | P–B3 | B–KN5 | O–O |
| | B–K2 | – – | B–K2 | P–QB4 | P–QN3[10] |
| *10* | O–O–O | O–O | Q–K2 | PxP | P–B4 |
| | O–O | O–O | O–O | Q–R4† | B–N2 |
| *11* | P–KR4 | QR–Q1 | B–KB4[6] | P–B3 | KR–Q1[11] |
| | Q–Q4[1] | BxN[3] | P–QB4 | QxBP | ± |
| *12* | K–N1 | QxB | PxP | O–O[8] | |
| | KR–Q1 | Q–Q4 | PxP | R–Q1 | |
| *13* | P–B4 | QxQ[4] | KR–Q1 | N–K5[9] | |
| | Q–Q3 | NxQ | Q–N3 | ± | |
| *14* | KR–K1[2] | B–Q2[5] | N–K5[7] | | |
| | ± | ± | ± | | |

*Notes to practical variations 41–45:*

[1] Or 11 . . . P–B4 12 K–N1, Q–B2 13 R–R3, KR–Q1 14 R–K1, QR–B1 15 N–K5, and White obtained a dangerous attack (Milner-Barry–Wade, British Championship 1946). After 12

continued ▶

PxP, Black gets counterchances: 12 . . . Q–B2 13 PxP, PxP. If, on the other hand, White plays 12 BxN, contemplating a follow-up sacrifice of the King Bishop on KR7, then Black interpolates the move 12 . . . BxN!

[2] White has the edge because of superiority in space: 14 . . . P–KR3 15 B–B1, B–KB1 16 N–K5, N–Q2 17 P–KN4, NxN 18 PxN ± (Bronstein–Kan, Moscow Championship 1947).

[3] Black's best line may be 11 . . . P–QB3, followed by . . . Q–B2 and . . . QR–Q1 as a preparation for the liberating move . . . P–QB4.

[4] White may also keep the Queens on the board with 13 Q–K3 (cf. Game 13), and then 13 . . . N–N5? is bad for Black because of 14 Q–R3! If Black plays the plausible 13 . . . QxRP, White has the choice of winning the exchange by 14 R–R1, Q–Q4 (14 . . . QxP? 15 KR–N1!) 15 BxN, BxB 16 B–K4 or of keeping his attack rolling by 14 P–QB4.

[5] The end game favors White because of his two Bishops (Pachman–Doerner, Hilversum 1947).

[6] Keres also mentions 11 B–KN5 so as to provoke 11 . . . P–KR3; then after 12 B–KB4, Black's Kingside is weakened.

[7] White has a slight superiority in space (Keres–Foltys, Salzbrunn 1950).

[8] Well worth considering is 12 O–O–O, R–Q1 13 N–K5 to anticipate Black's maneuver . . . B–Q2 and . . . B–K1.

[9] Now Black cannot proceed 13 . . . RxB because of 14 P–QN4!, Q–Q4 15 P–QB4, Q–K5 16 QxQ, NxQ 17 BxB, R–Q7 18 QR–Q1, with a superior end game for White (see Game 14). Also 13 . . . B–Q2 is faulty because of 14 BxN, BxB 15 BxP†! and White wins at least a Pawn. It is therefore necessary for Black to play first 13 . . . P–KR3 14 B–R4, B–Q2, although 15 QR–Q1 or 15 KR–K1 gives White an edge. The weakening effect of . . . P–KR3 may become serious.

[10] After 9 . . . P–QB4 10 PxP, Q–R4 11 B–KN5, White has gained a tempo over his play in Prac. Var. 44, since he has saved the move P–QB3.

[11] White stands well (Najdorf–Stahlberg, Budapest 1950).

*French Defense Game 13*

*WHITE: Tarrasch* *BLACK: Mieses*

*Ninth Match Game 1916*

| WHITE | BLACK | WHITE | BLACK |
|---|---|---|---|
| 1 P–K4 | P–K3 | 9 Q–K2 | B–N2 |
| 2 P–Q4 | P–Q4 | 10 B–N5 | B–K2 |
| 3 N–QB3 | PxP | 11 O–O | O–O |
| 4 NxP | N–Q2 | 12 QR–Q1 | BxN |
| 5 N–KB3 | KN–B3 | 13 QxB | Q–Q4 |
| 6 B–Q3 | NxN | 14 Q–K3 | QR–Q1 |
| 7 BxN | N–B3 | 15 P–QB4 | Q–Q2 |
| 8 B–Q3 | P–QN3 | 16 KR–K1 | P–N3 |

| WHITE | BLACK | WHITE | BLACK |
|---|---|---|---|
| 17 B–B2 | N–R4 | 30 BxR | RxB |
| 18 B–R6 | KR–K1 | 31 PxN | R–K8† |
| 19 P–KN4 | N–B3 | 32 QxR | BxQ |
| 20 P–KR3 | B–B1 | 33 B–N3 | K–B3 |
| 21 B–N5 | B–K2 | 34 BxP | K–K2 |
| 22 Q–K5 | K–N2 | 35 K–N2 | B–N5 |
| 23 P–Q5 | P–KR3 | 36 K–B3 | B–B4 |
| 24 B–R4 | PxP | 37 B–N3 | B–Q5 |
| 25 RxP | Q–K3 | 38 P–N3 | K–Q2 |
| 26 Q–B3 | QxR† | 39 K–K4 | B–B3 |
| 27 QxQ | NxR | 40 B–K5 | B–K2 |
| 28 B–R4 | B–N5 | 41 K–B5 | Resigns |
| 29 Q–B1 | P–KN4 | | |

## *French Defense Game 14*

*WHITE: Euwe* — *BLACK: Landau*

*Netherlands Championship 1939*

| WHITE | BLACK | WHITE | BLACK |
|---|---|---|---|
| 1 P–K4 | P–K3 | 22 B–Q6 | B–Q2 |
| 2 P–Q4 | P–Q4 | 23 BxP | B–K1 |
| 3 N–Q2 | PxP | 24 R–Q4 | P–KN3 |
| 4 NxP | N–Q2 | 25 P–KR4 | R–B1 |
| 5 KN–B3 | KN–B3 | 26 P–N4 | P–KR4 |
| 6 NxN† | NxN | 27 P–B3 | P–R3 |
| 7 B–Q3 | B–K2 | 28 K–B2 | B–B3 |
| 8 Q–K2 | O–O | 29 K–K3 | R–KN1 |
| 9 B–KN5 | P–B4 | 30 K–B4 | K–K2 |
| 10 PxP | Q–R4† | 31 P–KN5 | R–QB1 |
| 11 P–B3 | QxP/4 | 32 B–Q6† | K–B2 |
| 12 O–O | R–Q1 | 33 K–K5 | K–N2 |
| 13 N–K5 | RxB | 34 R–B4 | R–K1 |
| 14 P–QN4! | Q–Q4 | 35 R–B6 | P–N4 |
| 15 P–B4 | Q–K5 | 36 P–B5 | B–Q4 |
| 16 QxQ | NxQ | 37 P–R3 | R–Q1 |
| 17 BxB | R–Q7 | 38 RxKP | BxR |
| 18 QR–Q1! | P–B3 | 39 KxB | R–QR1 |
| 19 RxR | NxR | 40 P–B6 | R–K1† |
| 20 R–Q1 | PxN | 41 K–Q7 | K–B2 |
| 21 RxN | K–B2 | 42 P–B7 | Resigns |

## part 11—TARRASCH VARIATION I

1 P–K4, P–K3
2 P–Q4, P–Q4
3 N–Q2, P–QB4
4 PxQP[A], QxP[B]
5 KN–B3, PxP[C]
6 B–B4

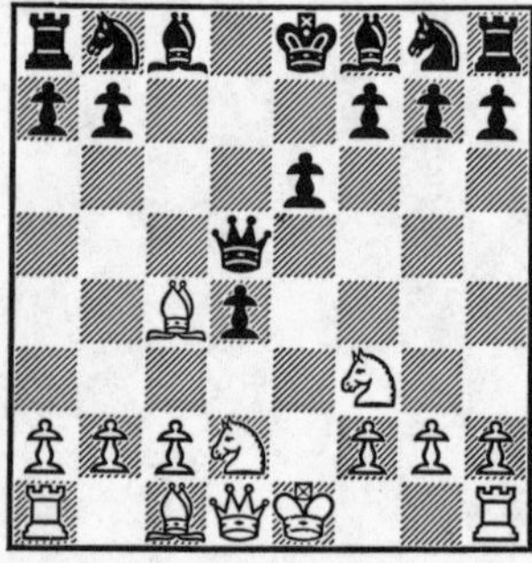

KEY POSITION 11

OBSERVATIONS ON KEY POSITION 11

[A] If 4 KN–B3, the best answer is 4 . . . N–KB3, so as to meet 5 PxQP by 5 . . . NxP 6 N–N3, PxP (6 . . . N–Q2 also deserves consideration) 7 QNxP, B–K2 8 P–KN3, O–O 9 B–N2, B–B3 10 O–O, N–QB3 (Keres–Stahlberg, Budapest 1952). Obsolete is 4 PxBP, BxP 5 B–Q3 (Spielmann). A good reply is 5 . . . N–QB3 6 PxP (or 6 KN–B3, KN–K2), QxP! (Alekhine). On 7 Q–N4, Black proceeds with 7 . . . N–K4! 8 QxP, B–Q5 9 Q–N3, N–KB3! In the above line, 5 N–N3, B–N3 6 PxP, PxP gives Black equal chances despite his isolated Pawn.

[B] Faulty is 4 . . . BPxP because of 5 B–N5†, B–Q2 6 PxP! and if 6 . . . BxB, then 7 PxP†, KxP 8 Q–R5†!

[C] After 5 . . . N–QB3, White has a promising Pawn sacrifice at his disposal: 6 P–B4, Q–R4 7 P–Q5!, PxP 8 PxP, QxQP 9 B–B4! (Skalicka).

If 5 . . . N–KB3, then 6 B–B4, Q–B3 (other moves lead to well-known positions) 7 P–QR4, P–QR3 8 B–N5 leads to liquidations not yet finally appraised: 8 . . . PxB 9 PxP, QxN 10 RxR (not 10 Q or NxQ?, RxR), QxNP 11 Q–B3, QxQ 12 NxQ, KN–Q2 13 N–K5, PxP 14 NxN, KxN 15 RxN, B–Q3 16 R–R8, R–K1, and Black has hardly sufficient compensation for the exchange (Boleslavski–Chistjakov, Semi-finals, USSR Championship 1957).

By recapturing the Pawn on Q4 with his Queen, Black has avoided the isolation of his Queen Pawn. However, his Queen is thus somewhat prematurely deployed, allowing White to obtain a lead in development. In the key position White develops his King Bishop with a tempo, and Black must decide where to retreat his Queen. The most important continuations are 6 . . . Q–Q1 and 6 . . . Q–Q3. The latter is somewhat more active, as Black may get a chance to protect his Queen Pawn by . . . P–K4. Normally, however, it is impossible to maintain this Pawn, as demonstrated in Idea Var. 27 and 28 and Prac. Var. 49 and 50.

IDEA VARIATIONS 27–29:

(27) 6 . . . Q–KR4 7 O–O, N–QB3 8 N–N3, P–K4? 9 NxKP, QxQ 10 RxQ, NxN 11 R–K1, P–B3 12 P–B4, B–QN5 13 B–Q2, BxB 14 NxB, B–B4 15 PxN, O–O–O 16 B–Q3 with advantage for White (Tarrasch–Thorold, Manchester 1890).

(28) 6 . . . Q–QB4 7 O–O, N–KB3 8 Q–K2, N–B3 9 N–N3, Q–N3 10 R–Q1, B–B4 11 P–QR4, P–QR4 12 NxB, QxN 13 P–QN3, N–Q4 14 B–R3, N/4–N5 15 B–N2, O–O with an edge for White (Keres–Stahlberg, Buenos Aires 1939).

(29) 6 . . . Q–Q3 7 O–O, N–KB3 8 N–N3, N–B3 9 Q–K2? (correct is 9 QNxP or 9 R–K1; see Prac. Var. 49 and 50), B–K2 10 R–Q1, P–K4! 11 B–QN5, B–N5 12 N–R5, O–O 13 NxP, Q–B2 with Black for choice (Medina–Eliskases, Mar del Plata 1953).

PRACTICAL VARIATIONS 46–50:

1 P–K4, P–K3 2 P–Q4, P–Q4 3 N–Q2, P–QB4 4 PxQP, QxP 5 KN–B3, PxP 6 B–B4

| | *46* | *47* | *48* | *49* | *50* |
|---|---|---|---|---|---|
| *6* | – – | – – | – – | – – | – – |
| | Q–Q1 | – – | – – | Q–Q3 | – – |
| 7 | O–O | – – | – – | O–O | – – |
| | N–QB3 | – – | – – | N–KB3 | – – |
| *8* | N–N3 | – – | – – | N–N3 | – – |
| | N–B3 | – – | B–K2[5] | N–B3 | – – |
| *9* | Q–K2[1] | – – | Q–K2[6] | QNxP | R–K1 |
| | B–K2[2] | – – | B–B3 | NxN | P–QR3 |
| *10* | R–Q1 | – – | R–Q1 | NxN | P–QR4 |
| | O–O | – – | P–QR3[7] | P–QR3 | B–K2 |
| *11* | QNxP | – – | QNxP | P–QN3[9] | KNxP |
| | Q–B2 | NxN | BxN | Q–B2 | NxN |
| *12* | NxN | RxN | B–K3 | Q–K2[10] | QxN |
| | PxN | Q–N3 | N–K2 | = | B–Q2 |
| *13* | B–KN5 | P–QB3 | BxB | | B–KB4 |
| | B–N2 | B–Q2 | NxB | | QxQ |
| *14* | Q–K5[3] | N–K5[4] | RxN[8] | | NxQ[11] |
| | ± | ± | ± | | ± |

*Notes to practical variations 46–50:*

[1] Also good is 9 QNxP, NxN 10 NxN or 10 QxN. But the set-up Q–K2 and R–Q1 is more energetic.

[2] After 9 . . . P–QR3, White's best is 10 R–Q1. Kamyschow–Tschistjakov, Moscow Championship 1946, continued: 10 . . . P–QN4 11 QNxP, NxN 12 RxN, Q–N3 13 B–Q3, B–B4 14 R–KR4, B–N2 15 P–QN4 with a clear advantage for White. 10 P–QR4 is inexact: 10 . . . B–Q3 11 R–Q1, Q–B2, and Black is no longer exposed to N–QN5.

[3] White gets a favorable end game. See Game 15. Also strong is 14 N–K5 because 14 . . . N–Q4? loses a Pawn: 15 BxB, QxB 16 NxQBP! BxN 17 BxN! (Pachman–Van Helden, Hilversum 1947).

[4] White has the advantage (Foltys–Rossolimo, Czechoslovakia–France 1947).

[5] Stahlberg's continuation. Black intends to proceed with . . . B–B3 followed by . . . N–K2, but this method costs too much time.

[6] White gets a good position also after the immediate 9 QNxP, NxN 10 NxN or 10 QxN.

continued ▸

[7] 10 . . . KN–K2 led to a satisfactory game for Black (Rossolimo–Stahlberg): 11 P–QB3, P–QR3 12 B–K3, O–O 13 KNxP, Q–B2. However, White has a stronger follow-up in this line at his 11th turn: 11 KNxP!, BxN 12 B–K3, N–B4 (or 12 . . . P–K4 13 P–QB3) 13 NxB, KNxN 14 BxN, NxB 15 Q–K3, and White recovers the Pawn favorably. In the preceding line, if Black varies with 11 . . . NxN, then 12 NxN, BxN 13 B–K3.

[8] 14 . . . Q–B2 15 QR–Q1, O–O 16 Q–K5 and, when Queens were exchanged, White obtained pressure in the end game (Averbach–Stahlberg, Stockholm 1952).

[9] Other good continuations are 11 B–K3 and 11 B–N3.

[10] Black ought to continue with 12 . . . P–QN4 because the sacrificial continuation 13 BxKP is insufficient for White: 13 . . . PxB 14 NxKP, BxN 15 QxB†, B–K2 16 B–R3, Q–Q2 17 KR–K1, QxQ 18 RxQ, R–R2 19 QR–K1, N–N1! After 12 . . . P–QN4 13 B–Q3, B–Q3 Black has a satisfactory game. In Geller–Stahlberg, Goteborg 1955, Black played directly 12 . . . B–Q3 and White replied with 13 N–B5, creating promising complications.

[11] White has an edge (Auerbach–Stahlberg, Zurich 1953).

*French Defense Game 15*

*WHITE: Keres* — *BLACK: Eliskases*

*Norway 1938*

| | WHITE | BLACK | | WHITE | BLACK |
|---|---|---|---|---|---|
| 1 | P–K4 | P–K3 | 24 | P–N3 | B–K3 |
| 2 | P–Q4 | P–Q4 | 25 | P–KB4 | R–Q5 |
| 3 | N–Q2 | P–QB4 | 26 | PxP† | KxP |
| 4 | PxQP | QxP | 27 | RxR | PxR† |
| 5 | KN–B3 | PxP | 28 | K–Q2 | B–Q4 |
| 6 | B–B4 | Q–Q1 | 29 | B–B4! | R–QB1 |
| 7 | O–O | N–QB3 | 30 | BxB | KxB |
| 8 | N–N3 | N–B3 | 31 | R–K1 | K–Q3 |
| 9 | Q–K2 | B–K2 | 32 | R–K2 | R–B6 |
| 10 | R–Q1 | O–O | 33 | R–K8 | R–B6! |
| 11 | N/NxP | Q–B2 | 34 | K–K2 | R–B6 |
| 12 | NxN | PxN | 35 | K–Q1 | R–B6 |
| 13 | B–N5 | B–N2 | 36 | R–Q8† | K–K4 |
| 14 | Q–K5 | QxQ | 37 | R–Q7 | R–B7! |
| 15 | NxQ | KR–Q1 | 38 | RxRP | RxRP |
| 16 | N–Q7! | P–B4 | 39 | P–R4 | R–N7 |
| 17 | NxN† | BxN | 40 | RxP | RxP |
| 18 | BxB | PxB | 41 | RxP | P–B5 |
| 19 | P–KB3 | P–B4 | 42 | P–R5 | P–B6 |
| 20 | K–B2 | K–N2 | 43 | K–K1 | K–B5 |
| 21 | K–K3 | K–B3 | 44 | K–Q2 | R–N8 |
| 22 | B–K2 | P–K4 | 45 | R–B7† | K–K5 |
| 23 | P–KN3 | B–Q4 | 46 | P–R6 | R–N7† |

| WHITE | BLACK | WHITE | BLACK |
|---|---|---|---|
| 47 K–B1 | P–Q6! | 53 P–R7 | R–QR7 |
| 48 PxP† | K–K6 | 54 P–N6 | K–B6! |
| 49 P–N4 | R–QR2 | 55 K–N1 | R–R3!! |
| 50 P–N5 | P–B7 | 56 P–N7 | R–N3† |
| 51 P–Q4 | KxP!! | 57 K–B1 | R–KR3! |
| 52 RxP | RxR | Draw | |

---

## part 12—TARRASCH VARIATION II

1 P–K4, P–K3
2 P–Q4, P–Q4
3 N–Q2, P–QB4
4 PxQP, KPxP
5 KN–B3

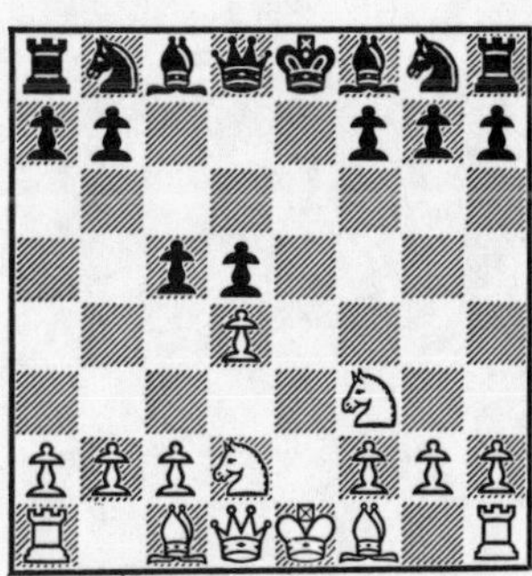

KEY POSITION 12

### OBSERVATIONS ON KEY POSITION 12

Black's recapture with the Pawn on his Q4 offers him an active development. Essentially, his Queen Bishop obtains an open diagonal. White can meet 4 . . . KPxP in two different ways. He can try to profit from the isolated Pawn, either in the middle game or the end game. In the former case he must proceed with 5 KN–B3, which is discussed in this section. In the latter case White proceeds with 5 B–N5† which is the subject of Part 13.

In the key position after 5 KN–B3, Black has several developing systems at his disposal. He can anticipate White's B–N5† by 5 . . . P–QR3, a line favored by Botvinnik. Or he can play 5 . . . N–KB3 or 5 . . . N–QB3. After 5 . . . N–QB3, the move 6 B–N5 gains in significance because of the pin. On 5 . . . N–KB3, the reply 6 B–N5†, B–Q2 is somewhat uncomfortable for Black.

### IDEA VARIATIONS 30–32:

(30) 5 . . . N–QB3 6 B–N5, Q–K2† (for other moves, see Prac. Var. 51 and 52) 7 B–K2! (no loss of time, since Black's Queen cannot long remain on K2), PxP 8 O–O, Q–B2 9 N–N3, B–Q3 10 QNxP, P–QR3 11 P–QN3! followed by 12 B–N2 with a good game for White.

(31) 5 . . . N–KB3 6 B–N5†, N–B3 (safer is 6 . . . B–Q2; see Prac. Var. 53) 7 O–O, B–K3 (if 7 . . . B–K2 8 PxP, or 7 . . . PxP 8 R–K1†) 8 R–K1, B–Q3 (better is 8 . . . Q–N3) 9 PxP, BxP 10 N–N3 with an edge for White.

(32) 5 . . . P–QR3 6 PxP (more enterprising is 6 P–B4, and also deserving consideration is 6 B–K2; see Prac. Var. 54 and 55), BxP 7 N–N3, B–R2 8 B–KN5, N–KB3 9 QN–Q4, O–O 10 B–K2, Q–Q3 11 O–O, N–K5 with an even game (Keres–Botvinnik, The Hague and Moscow 1948). A little stronger than 8 B–KN5

is 8 B–Q3, N–KB3 9 Q–K2†. If 8 . . . Q–K2†, 9 B–K2. After 9 Q–K2† instead of 9 QN–Q4 Black ought not to play 9 . . . Q–K2 because of 10 BxN! Correct is 9 . . . B–K3 10 QN–Q4, Q–K2 followed by . . . N–B3.

PRACTICAL VARIATIONS 51–55:

1 P–K4, P–K3 2 P–Q4, P–Q4 3 N–Q2, P–QB4 4 PxQP, KPxQP 5 KN–B3

| | *51* | *52* | *53* | *54* | *55* |
|---|---|---|---|---|---|
| *5* | – – | – – | – – | – – | – – |
| | N–QB3 | – – | N–KB3 | P–QR3 | P–B5 |
| *6* | B–N5 | – – | B–N5† | P–B4 | B–K2[12] |
| | B–Q3 | P–B5 | B–Q2 | N–KB3 | N–QB3 |
| *7* | O–O | O–O | BxB†[7] | B–K2[10] | O–O |
| | N–K2 | B–Q3 | QNxB | N–B3 | B–Q3 |
| *8* | PxP | P–QN3 | O–O | PxQP | P–QN3 |
| | BxP | PxP | B–K2 | NxP/4 | PxP |
| *9* | N–N3 | RPxP[5] | PxP | O–O | P–B4 |
| | B–N3[1] | N–K2 | NxP | PxP | KN–K2 |
| *10* | B–K3[2] | R–K1 | N–Q4 | N–N3 | P–B5 |
| | BxB | O–O | O–O[8] | B–K2 | B–B2 |
| *11* | BxN† | N–B1 | N–B5 | KNxP | NxP |
| | PxB[3] | B–KN5 | R–K1 | O–O | O–O[13] |
| *12* | PxB | P–B3 | N–N3[9] | B–B3 | = |
| | O–O | Q–B2 | ± | B–B3 | |
| *13* | Q–Q2 | B–R3[6] | | N–B2 | |
| | Q–N3 | ± | | N/4–K2 | |
| *14* | Q–B3[4] | | | N–K3 | |
| | ± | | | Q–B2 | |
| *15* | | | | Q–B2 | |
| | | | | B–K4[11] | |
| | | | | = | |

*Notes to practical variations 51–55:*

[1] The most important, though probably not the best, reply. Meriting consideration is 9 . . . B–Q3 10 QN–Q4, O–O 11 P–QN3, B–KN5 12 B–N2, Q–B2! (Panov).

[2] Botvinnik's method. White submits to the isolation of his King Pawn in order to control his Q4 and QB5. Also worthwhile is 10 P–B4, O–O 11 B–N5, P–B3 (better is 11 . . . PxP) 12 B–B4, P–QR3 13 BxN, PxB 14 P–B5 with an edge for White (Consultation Stahlberg–Allies in consultation, Parana 1941).

[3] After 11 . . . NxB, White gains a slight positional advantage with 12 R–K1 followed by 13 RxB.

[4] According to an analysis by Filip, Black can obtain equality by 14 . . . P–QR4! 15 P–QR4, B–R3 16 KR–K1, B–B5. Inferior is 14 . . . R–N1 15 QR–N1, R–K1 16 KR–K1, N–N3 17 N–B5, B–N5 18 N–Q4 with a positional edge for White.

[5] More energetic is 9 P–B4!, PxBP 10 R–K1†, N–K2 (if 10

. . . B–K2, then 11 N–K5) 11 P–Q5, P–QR3 12 PxP, R–QN1 13 B–R4, P–QN4 14 PxN with advantage for White (analysis by Keres).

[6] (Keres–Stahlberg, Buenos Aires 1939).

[7] Q–K2†, B–K2 8 PxP leads by transposition into Prac. Var. 56 and 57. See Part 13.

[8] Or 10 . . . Q–Q2 11 N/2–B3, O–O 12 N–K5, Q–B1 13 B–N5, R–K1 14 N–Q3, NxN 15 QxN, and White still gains KB5 for his Knight (Botvinnik–Bronstein, 15th Match Game 1951).

[9] Geller–Stahlberg, Zurich 1953.

[10] On 7 PxQP Black's best reply is 7 . . . NxP and not 7 . . . PxP because of 8 B–B4!

[11] Black has a fully satisfactory position (Szily–Botvinnik, Budapest 1952).

[12] Bondarevski recommends 6 P–QN3! PxP 7 B–N5†, B–Q2 (if 7 . . . N–B3, then 8 N–K5) 8 Q–K2†.

[13] Black has a satisfactory game (Geller–Mikenas, USSR Championship 1949).

---

## part 13—TARRASCH VARIATION III

1 P–K4, P–K3
2 P–Q4, P–Q4
3 N–Q2, P–QB4
4 PxQP, KPxP
5 B–N5†

KEY POSITION 13

### OBSERVATIONS ON KEY POSITION 13

The idea of 5 B–N5† is to follow up with Q–K2†, exchange Queens after . . . Q–K2 and try to take advantage of Black's isolated Pawn in the end game, which procedure indeed slightly favors White. Some difficulties notwithstanding, however, Black ought to be able to hold his own in the end game. Many players prefer to avoid exchanging Queens and answer White's 6 Q–K2† with 6 . . . B–K2. This continuation often leads to the loss of Black's Queen Bishop's Pawn, but Black gets active counterplay with good prospects for recovering the Pawn at a later stage.

### IDEA VARIATIONS 33 AND 34:

(33) 5 . . . N–B3 6 Q–K2† (6 KN–B3 leads by transposition into Part 12), Q–K2 (better is 6 . . . B–K2; see Prac. Var. 56) 7 PxP, QxQ† 8 NxQ, BxP 9 N–QN3, B–N3 10 P–QR4!, N–K2 (if 10 . . . P–QR4, then 11 B–K3) 11 P–R5, B–B2 12 B–KB4, BxB 13 NxB, P–QR3 14 BxN†, PxB 15 N–B5 with a positional end game edge for White. Less strong than 10 P–QR4! in the foregoing sequence is 10 B–Q2, N–K2 11 B–N4, P–QR3 12 B–B5, B–B2 (Euwe–Botvinnik, The Hague and Moscow 1948).

(34) 5 . . . B–Q2 6 Q–K2†, Q–K2 (here, too, Black does better to avoid exchanging Queens by playing 6 . . . B–K2; see Prac. Var. 58 and 59) 7 BxB†, NxB 8 PxP, NxP 9 N–N3 (a little stronger is 9 QN–B3, threat-

ening B–K3), QxQ† 10 NxQ, NxN 11 RPxN, B–B4 12 B–Q2 (other good continuations are 12 O–O and 12 N–B4), N–K2 13 B–B3, and Black ought to continue 13 . . . O–O with fair chances for equality. In the game Euwe–Botvinnik, The Hague and Moscow 1948, Black played 13 . . . N–B3, and White could have maintained an advantage with 14 R–Q1.

PRACTICAL VARIATIONS 56–59:

1 P–K4, P–K3 2 P–Q4, P–Q4 3 N–Q2, P–QB4 4 PxQP, KPxP 5 B–N5†

| | *56* | *57* | *58* | *59* |
|---|---|---|---|---|
| *5* | – – | – – | – – | – – |
| | N–QB3 | – – | B–Q2 | – – |
| *6* | Q–K2† | – – | Q–K2† | – – |
| | B–K2 | – – | B–K2 | – – |
| *7* | PxP | – – | PxP | – – |
| | N–B3 | – – | N–KB3 | – – |
| *8* | N–N3 | – – | KN–B3 | N–N3 |
| | O–O | – – | O–O | O–O |
| *9* | N–B3 | B–K3 | N–N3 | B–K3 |
| | R–K1 | N–KN5[2] | R–K1[4] | R–K1 |
| *10* | B–K3 | O–O–O | B–K3 | O–O–O |
| | N–K5 | NxB | BxP | P–QR3 |
| *11* | O–O | QxN | KBxB | B–Q3[6] |
| | NxP | R–K1 | QNxB | P–QR4 |
| *12* | Q–Q1 | N–B3[3] | NxB | N–B3 |
| | N–K5[1] | ± | NxN | P–R5 |
| *13* | = | | Q–N5![5] | QN–Q4 |
| | | | ± | BxP[7] |
| | | | | ∓ |

*Notes to practical variations 56–59:*

[1] The activity of Black's pieces compensates for the isolation of his Queen Pawn (Gerstenfeld–Boleslavski, USSR Championship 1940).

[2] Here, and at Black's next turn, . . . R–K1 is stronger.

[3] Peljak–Sokolski, Semi-finals, USSR Championship 1951.

[4] 9 . . . BxP 10 BxB, QNxB 11 NxB, NxN 12 B–K3 leads into approximately the same set up.

[5] This strong move assures White an advantage, as is evident from the following continuations:

1) 13 . . . QN–K5 14 O–O, Q–B2 15 P–B3, N–N5 16 KR–K1 (Castaldi–Foerder, Hilversum 1947).

2) 13 . . . N–K3 14 O–O, Q–B2 15 P–B3, P–QR3 16 Q–N3 (Keres–Bondarevski, USSR Championship 1948).

[6] Nor can White maintain the extra Pawn after 11 BxB, QNxB. The set-up with the Pawn on B5 is not commendable (See Game 16).

[7] Black has favorably recovered the Pawn (Makarov–Konstantinopolsky, Semi-finals, USSR Championship 1951).

*French Defense Game 16*

*WHITE: Rabar* *BLACK: Matulovic*

*Yugoslav Championship 1957*

| | WHITE | BLACK | | WHITE | BLACK |
|---|---|---|---|---|---|
| 1 | P–K4 | P–K3 | 12 | Q–B3 | P–QR4 |
| 2 | P–Q4 | P–Q4 | 13 | P–QR4? | Q–B2 |
| 3 | N–Q2 | P–QB4 | 14 | KN–K2 | BxP |
| 4 | PxQP | KPxP | 15 | NxB | NxN |
| 5 | B–N5† | B–Q2 | 16 | N–B3 | QR–B1 |
| 6 | Q–K2† | B–K2 | 17 | Q–B4 | QxQ |
| 7 | PxP | N–KB3 | 18 | BxQ | P–Q5! |
| 8 | N–N3 | O–O | 19 | N–N5 | P–Q6 |
| 9 | B–K3 | R–K1 | 20 | N–B3 | N–Q4! |
| 10 | O–O–O | P–QR3 | 21 | B–Q2 | N–N5! |
| 11 | BxB | QNxB | | Resigns | |

---

## part 14—TARRASCH VARIATION IV

1 P–K4, P–K3
2 P–Q4, P–Q4
3 N–Q2, N–KB3[A]
4 P–K5, KN–Q2
5 B–Q3, P–QB4
6 P–QB3, N–QB3[B]
7 N–K2

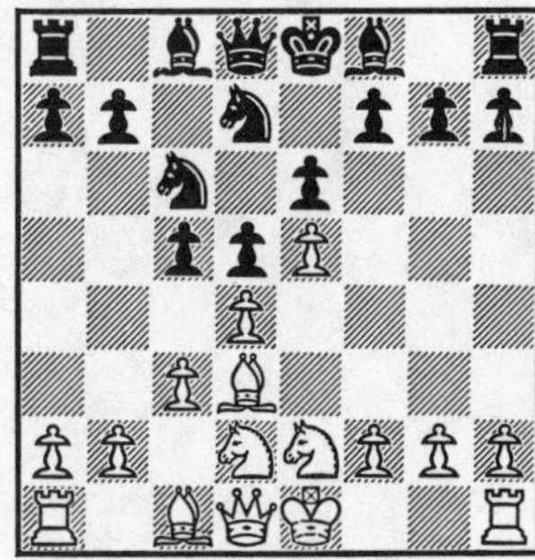

KEY POSITION 14

### OBSERVATIONS ON KEY POSITION 14

[A] Some years ago, 3 . . . P–QR3 (Bogoljubov) was rather usual. This was in preparation for an early . . . P–QB4, canceling out White's probable B–N5† (Parts 12 and 13). Experience has shown, however, that White can then play 4 P–K5 (cf. Part 16) with practically a gain of a tempo, since in this case 3 . . . P–QR3 has little significance: 4 P–K5, P–QB4 5 P–QB3, N–QB3 6 QN–KB3, B–Q2 7 B–Q3, R–B1 8 N–K2, PxP 9 N/2xP (equally good is 9 PxP, N–N5 10 B–N1), KN–K2 10 Q–K2 with a positional advantage for White (Aronin–Schamkowitsch, Tula 1952). 3 . . . P–KB4 (Haberditz) also leads to an opening advantage for White after 4 PxBP, PxP 5 B–Q3 (or 5 QN–B3 or 5 Q–R5†), B–Q3 6 QN–B3, N–KB3 7 N–K2, O–O 8 O–O, P–QB3 9 B–KB4, K–R1 10 P–B4 (Rossolimo–Gudmundsson, Amsterdam 1950).

[B] Playing for the exchange of White's King Bishop is too slow: e.g., 6 . . . P–QN3 7 N–K2, B–R3 8 BxB, NxB 9 O–O, B–K2 10 N–KN3, O–O 11 Q–N4, P–B4 12 PxP e.p., RxP 13 N–R5, R–N3 14 Q–K2, N–B2 15 N–B3 with a positional edge for White (Kotov–Keres, USSR Championship 1948).

The attack on White's King Pawn by 3 . . . N–KB3 in the Tarrasch Variation has its strategical drawbacks. It is different from the Classical Variation (3 N–QB3, N–KB3) in that White, after P–K5, has no difficulty defending his Queen Pawn, since now he has at his disposal P–QB3. Consequently, Black does not achieve enough by attacking White's center with . . . P–QB4 alone. He must also (if he persists in a center attack) play . . . P–KB3, which exposes him to critical situations, as White has chances for a Kingside attack by N–KB4 and Q–R5†.

However, White must not overreach himself. There are variations in which Black by sacrificing his King Rook for Knight obtains promising compensation. It is wise on White's part first to fulfill the strategical requirements of the position, that is, the defense of the center. Then, as opportunity arises, he may operate with tactical threats against the King.

IDEA VARIATIONS 35–38:

(35) 7 . . . Q–N3 8 N–B3, PxP 9 PxP, B–N5† 10 K–B1?! (simple and good is 10 B–Q2), P–B3! (10 . . . B–K2? 11 P–QR3, N–B1 12 P–QN4 offers White a great superiority in space) 11 N–B4 (11 PxP, NxBP is satisfactory for Black), PxP 12 NxP/6 (12 PxP, N/2xP transposes into Idea Var. 36). Now the sacrifice of the Queen by 12 . . . P–K5 is insufficient: 13 B–KB4, PxN 14 B–B7, N–B3 (Spielmann–Stoltz, Match 1930) 15 BxQ!, BxN 16 B–B5, BxB 17 PxB, PxP† 18 KxP, O–O 19 R–K1. But, according to Keres, Black gains the upper hand with 12 . . . N–B3!: 13 NxP† (if 13 PxP, then 13 . . . N–N5!), K–B1! (not 13 . . . K–B2 because of 14 N–R5!) 14 B–R6, K–N1! and now Black has a trio of threats: 15 . . . P–K5, 15 . . . N–N5, and 15 . . . B–B1.

(36) 7 . . . Q–N3 8 N–B3, PxP 9 PxP, P–B3 10 N–B4 (best is 10 PxP; see Prac. Var. 61), PxP 11 PxP (on 11 NxP/6, Black proceeds well with 11 . . . P–K5!; see Game 17), B–N5† 12 K–B1, N/2xP 13 NxN, NxN 14 Q–R5†, N–B2 15 BxP, Q–Q5 16 B–K3, QxP 17 R–B1, Q–K4, and Black maintains the edge (Menke–Wilde, Correspondence Game 1957).

(37) 7 . . . P–B3 8 N–KB4 (the text move is good here; 8 PxKBP, NxBP 9 N–B3, B–Q3 is satisfactory for Black), Q–K2! 9 N–B3 (here White must play 9 KPxP, as in Prac. Var. 62; weak is 9 Q–R5†, Q–B2! 10 B–N6, PxB), PxQP 10 PxQP, PxP 11 N–N6, PxN 12 BxP†, K–Q1 13 B–N5, N–B3 14 PxP, Q–N5† 15 K–B1, B–K2 16 PxN, PxP with uncertain complications (Euwe–Kramer, 3rd Match Game 1940).

(38) 7 . . . PxP 8 PxP, P–B3 9 N–KB4 dubious at this point; safer is 9 PxP), NxQP!? (again, 9 . . . Q–K2 is possible) 10 Q–R5†, K–K2 11 N–N6†, PxN 12 PxP†, NxP 13 QxR, K–B2 14 O–O, P–K4, and Black has good compensation for the exchange (Hinne–Weise, West German Championship, Nuremburg 1959).

## PRACTICAL VARIATIONS 60–64:

1 P–K4, P–K3 2 P–Q4, P–Q4 3 N–Q2, N–KB3 4 P–K5, KN–Q2 5 B–Q3, P–QB4 6 P–QB3, N–QB3 7 N–K2

| | *60* | *61* | *62* | *63* | *64* |
|---|---|---|---|---|---|
| 7 | – – | – – | – – | – – | – – |
| | Q–N3 | – – | P–B3 | PxP | PxP |
| *8* | N–B3 | – – | N–B4 | PxP | PxP |
| | PxP | – – | Q–K2 | P–B3 | N–N3[8] |
| *9* | PxP | | KPxP | PxP | O–O |
| | B–N5† | P–B3 | QxP[4] | QxP | B–Q2 |
| *10* | B–Q2! | PxP | N–B3 | N–B3 | N–KB3[9] |
| | BxB† | NxBP | B–Q3[5] | B–N5† | B–K2[10] |
| *11* | QxB | O–O | N–R5 | B–Q2 | N–B4 |
| | Q–N5 | B–Q3 | Q–K2 | BxB† | P–QR4[11] |
| *12* | R–B1 | N–B3![12] | O–O | QxB | N–R5 |
| | QxQ† | O–O | P–KN3 | O–O | P–KN3[12] |
| *13* | KxQ | B–K3 | PxP[6] | O–O | N–B6†[13] |
| | N–N3 | K–R1 | = | P–K4 | ± |
| *14* | P–QN3[1] | R–B1[3] | | PxP | |
| | ± | ± | | N/2xP[7] | |
| | | | | ± | |

*Notes to practical variations 60–64:*

[1] White's advantage in the end game is slight but distinct (Keres–Flores, Buenos Aires 1939).

[2] After 12 N–B4, O–O 13 R–K1, Black obtains good chances with Lothar Schmid's Pawn sacrifice: 13 . . . B–Q2! 14 NxKP, KR–K1 15 B–B5, B–N5! 16 B–Q2 (if 16 R–K3, then 16 . . . N–QR4!), BxB 17 QxB, N–K2! with sharp advantage for Black (analysis by H. Heemsoth). On 18 B–R3, then 18 . . . N–K5! Apart from the text set up of Prac. Var. 61, also worthwhile is the continuation 12 B–Q2, O–O 13 B–B3 (Pilnik–Teschner, Chess Olympics, Moscow 1956).

[3] With an edge for White. See Game 18.

[4] 9 . . . NxBP 10 N–B3, P–K4 11 PxKP, NxP 12 O–O, NxN† 13 QxN, B–N5 14 B–N5† favors White (Euwe–Kramer, 1st Match Game 1940).

[5] If 10 . . . PxP, White has the promising reply 11 O–O! (11 PxP, B–Q3 leads to an equal game), N/2–K4 12 NxN, NxN 13 B–N5†, B–Q2 14 BxB†, KxB 15 R–K1, R–K1 (Keres–Czerniak, Helsinki 1952). According to Keres, White gets a dangerous attack by 16 P–B4!

[6] Black must now play 13 . . . BxP with an equal game: 14 N–B4, O–O 15 P–B4, P–Q5 or 15 R–K1, N–B3. Insufficient is 13 . . . B–B2? 14 N–N3! (14 N–B4, O–O!), NxP 15 P–B4! O–O 16 B–R6 (Szabo–Balonel, Marienbad 1951).

continued ▸

[7] 15 NxN, NxN (also good is 15 . . . QxN) 16 N–Q4. White has only a minute edge (Trifunovic–Matanovic, Belgrade 1954).

[8] The so-called Leningrad System. Black abstains from attacking the center, aiming, rather, for a Queenside attack; but White, thanks to an advantage in space, has better chances of succeeding with an attack on the Kingside than Black has on the opposite wing.

[9] Another possibility is 10 P–B4, P–N3 11 N–KB3, P–KR4 12 B–Q2, N–N5 13 B–N1, N–B5 14 B–B1, P–R4 15 P–QN3, N–N3 16 P–QR3, N–B3 (Aronin–Furman, USSR Championship, 1948). And now White can play 17 PQR4! with a fine game. Instead, he played 17 B–Q3, and Black countered 17 . . . P–R5!, giving him good counterplay on the Queenside.

[10] After 10 . . . N–N5, White plays 11 B–N1 or, following Donner's idea, 11 P–QN3, NxB 12 QxN, R–B1 13 P–QR4. In this set up, Black's pieces on the Queenside interfere with each other. Hence, after 11 P–QN3, Black does better with 11 . . . R–B1 12 P–QR4, B–K2! (Pachman–Fichtl, Prague 1954).

[11] Safer is 11 . . . P–KN3.

[12] On 12 . . . O–O, White plays 13 Q–Q2, threatening to sacrifice on KN7.

[13] 13 . . . BxN 14 PxB, QxP 15 B–N5 and White's superiority on the black squares amply compensates for the Pawn (Mjassojedov–Furman, Leningrad Championship 1949).

*French Defense Game 17*

*WHITE: Barden* *BLACK: Wade*

*Hastings 1958*

| | WHITE | BLACK | | WHITE | BLACK |
|---|---|---|---|---|---|
| 1 | P–K4 | P–K3 | 13 | PxN | BxN |
| 2 | P–Q4 | P–Q4 | 14 | N–N5 | B–N5† |
| 3 | N–Q2 | N–KB3 | 15 | K–B1 | B–KB4 |
| 4 | P–K5 | KN–Q2 | 16 | B–K2 | R–Q1 |
| 5 | B–Q3 | P–QB4 | 17 | B–N4 | O–O |
| 6 | P–QB3 | N–QB3 | 18 | P–K6 | N–Q5 |
| 7 | N–K2 | Q–N3 | 19 | B–B7 | QxB |
| 8 | N–B3 | PxP | 20 | QxN | B–B4 |
| 9 | PxP | P–B3 | 21 | R–QB1 | BxQ |
| 10 | N–B4? | PxP | 22 | RxQ | BxB |
| 11 | NxP/6 | P–K5 | 23 | P–B3 | B–K6 |
| 12 | B–KB4 | N/2–K4! | | Resigns | |

*French Defense Game 18*

*WHITE: Trifunovic* *BLACK: Schmid*

*Munich 1958*

| | WHITE | BLACK | | WHITE | BLACK |
|---|---|---|---|---|---|
| 1 | P–K4 | P–K3 | 4 | P–K5 | KN–Q2 |
| 2 | P–Q4 | P–Q4 | 5 | B–Q3 | P–QB4 |
| 3 | N–Q2 | N–KB3 | 6 | P–QB3 | N–QB3 |

| WHITE | BLACK | WHITE | BLACK |
|---|---|---|---|
| 7 N–K2 | Q–N3 | 25 BxN | BxB |
| 8 N–B3 | PxP | 26 B–Q4! | B–N4 |
| 9 PxP | P–B3 | 27 N–K5 | R–K2? |
| 10 PxP | NxBP | 28 P–QR4 | B–R3 |
| 11 O–O | B–Q3 | 29 Q–Q2! | N–Q3 |
| 12 N–B3 | O–O | 30 Q–N4! | R–K3 |
| 13 B–K3 | K–R1 | 31 R–B7 | P–KR3? |
| 14 R–B1 | B–Q2 | 32 N–B7†! | K–R2 |
| 15 N–QR4 | Q–B2 | 33 NxN | Q–N8† |
| 16 P–KR3 | QR–K1 | 34 K–R2 | R–N3 |
| 17 N–B5 | B–B1 | 35 RxP† | RxR |
| 18 B–QN5! | P–K4 | 36 BxR | KxB |
| 19 PxP | BxP | 37 Q–Q4† | K–R2 |
| 20 NxB | QxN | 38 N–K8 | Q–N3 |
| 21 N–Q3 | Q–B4 | 39 N–B6† | K–N2 |
| 22 B–B5! | R–B2 | 40 NxP† | K–B2 |
| 23 R–K1 | B–Q2 | 41 Q–B4† | Resigns |
| 24 RxR† | NxR | | |

---

## part 15—TARRASCH VARIATION V (GUIMARD SUBVARIATION)

1 P–K4, P–K3
2 P–Q4, P–Q4
3 N–Q2, N–QB3
4 KN–B3[A], N–B3[B]
5 P–K5, N–Q2

KEY POSITION 15

### OBSERVATIONS ON KEY POSITION 15

[A] On 4 P–QB3, Black may play 4 . . . P–K4, but the consequences are somewhat obscure after 5 PxQP, QxP 6 KN–B3, with three plausible continuations: (1) 6 . . . B–KN5? 7 B–B4, BxN 8 Q–N3! N–R4 9 Q–R4†, Q–Q2 10 BxP†, K–Q1 11 QxQ†, KxQ 12 NxB, and White has a sound extra Pawn (Keres–Botvinnik, USSR Championship 1955). Or 8 . . . Q–Q2 9 NxB, PxP (9 . . . N–R4? 10 BxP†) 10 O–O with a strong game for White. (2) 6 . . . PxP 7 B–B4, Q–KR4 8 O–O, B–K3 (if 8 . . . PxP, then 9 N–K4!) 9 BxB, PxB 10 Q–N3, O–O–O 11 QxKP†, K–N1 12 PxP, B–Q3 13 N–N3, N–B3, and Black has sufficient compensation for the Pawn (Averbach–Owetschlin, USSR 1944). Keres points out, however, that White can gain the edge by 11 PxP, N–B3 (if 11 . . . Q–Q4, then 12 R–K1) 12 N–K4! Q–Q4 13 N/4–N5 and Black is at a disadvantage because of the weakness of his isolated Pawn. (3) 6 . . . P–K5 7 B–B4! Q–KB4, 8 Q–K2.

[B] Bronstein has experimented with 4 . . . P–KN3 5 P–QB3, B–N2 6 B–Q3, N–R3, giving rise to these two major possibilities: (1) 7 P–K5, P–B3 8 PxP, QxP 9 N–B1, N–B2 10 N–K3, B–Q2 11 Q–K2, Q–K2 12 B–Q2, O–O–O 13 O–O–O, KR–K1 14 N–N4, P–K4! with equality (Lipnitzky–Bronstein, USSR Championship 1952); (2) 7 O–O, O–O 8 R–K1, P–B3 9 P–QN4, P–QR3 10 P–QR4, R–K1 11 Q–N3 with an edge for White (Sokolski–Kortchnoi, USSR Championship 1954). A line similar to Bronstein's, sometimes played by Russian masters, is 4 . . . N–R3, to which a good answer is 5 B–N5 (Lothar Schmid).

There is an anomalous strategical idea behind the Guimard Subvariation. Black abstains from the thematic . . . P–QB4 and concentrates instead on a possible . . . P–KB3 and a possible . . . P–K4. White can oppose this plan in several ways. After . . . P–KB3 he may try to refute Black's strategy by means of a Kingside attack. This does not offer much chance for success as it requires the disappearance of his King Pawn, which is the bulwark of his position, exercising pressure and restricting Black's development. It seems, therefore, that White's best strategy is the maintenance of the King Pawn in the key position, later proceeding with KPxP, provided he is ready to counter Black's impending . . . P–K4.

IDEA VARIATIONS 39–42:

(39) 6 P–B3, P–B3 7 N–R4 (this tactical sortie is too rash; for other moves see Prac. Var. 69), Q–K2 8 B–Q3, PxP! 9 Q–R5†, Q–B2 10 B–N6, PxB 11 QxR, P–K5, and Black has ample compensation for the exchange. The threat is . . . P–KN4. See Game 19.

(40) 6 B–Q3, and now 6 . . . P–B3? is a surprising mistake because of 7 N–N5! (Luckis–Stahlberg, Mar del Plata 1942). Correct for Black is 6 . . . N–N5 7 B–K2, P–QB4 8 P–QB3, N–QB3 9 O–O. Even now Black must not play directly 9 . . . P–B3, whereupon follows 10 KPxP, QxP 11 P–B4! (Burgalat–Marini, Buenos Aires 1942). Black obtains a satisfactory position with 9 . . . PxP, 10 PxP, and now 10 . . . P–KB3!

(41) 6 N–N3, P–B3 7 B–QN5 (not 7 PxP? QxP 8 B–KN5, Q–B2 9 B–N5, B–Q3 10 O–O, O–O, as Black can successfully play . . . P–K4), P–QR3 (provoking the ensuing exchange with the idea of attacking White's center with . . . P–QB4; for a steadier line see Prac. Var. 65) 8 BxN, PxB 9 O–O, P–QB4 10 P–QB4! This is Bronstein's continuation, White profiting from his advance in development by opening lines against the Black. See Game 20.

(42) 6 B–K2, P–B3 7 PxP, QxP (better is . . . NxBP; see Prac. Var. 68) 8 N–B1!, P–K4 (consistent, but dubious; safer is 8 . . . B–Q3) 9 N–K3, P–K5 10 NxP, Q–Q3 11 P–B4, PxN 12 B–B4, and White has a tremendous attack for the piece:. 12 . . . PxB (12 . . . PxP 13 R–KN1, QxB B–R5†!) 13 QxP†, N/2–K4 (better is 13 . . . K–Q1) 14 PxN, Q–Q1 15 O–O–O and White won quickly (Kortchmar–Aratowski, Saratov 1948).

*French Defense Game 19*

*WHITE: Rowner* *BLACK: Tolush*

*Leningrad 1946*

| | WHITE | BLACK | | WHITE | BLACK |
|---|---|---|---|---|---|
| 1 | P–K4 | P–K3 | 21 | BxN | P–K4 |
| 2 | P–Q4 | P–Q4 | 22 | Q–N2 | Q–R4 |
| 3 | N–Q2 | N–QB3 | 23 | PxP | B–R6 |
| 4 | KN–B3 | N–B3 | 24 | Q–KB2 | BxP |
| 5 | P–K5 | N–Q2 | 25 | KR–K1 | B–N5 |
| 6 | P–B3 | P–B3 | 26 | B–Q4 | B–B6 |
| 7 | N–R4 | Q–K2 | 27 | BxB | N–N5 |
| 8 | B–Q3 | PxP | 28 | Q–B2 | R–R1 |
| 9 | Q–R5† | Q–B2 | 29 | N–Q4 | NxP |
| 10 | B–N6 | PxB | 30 | RxP | BxR |
| 11 | QxR | P–K5 | 31 | QxB | N–N5 |
| 12 | N–N3 | N–B3 | 32 | Q–N2 | NxB |
| 13 | P–B3 | B–Q2 | 33 | R–K1 | P–N5 |
| 14 | PxP | PxP | 34 | R–K3 | P–B4 |
| 15 | O–O | O–O–O | 35 | N–N5 | N–B6† |
| 16 | P–N3 | B–Q3 | 36 | K–B2 | Q–Q4 |
| 17 | Q–R7 | N–K2 | 37 | P–B4 | Q–Q7† |
| 18 | N–N2 | P–KN4 | 38 | R–K2 | Q–B8 |
| 19 | N–K3 | N–B4 | | Resigns | |
| 20 | Q–R3 | NxN | | | |

*French Defense Game 20*

*WHITE: Bronstein* *BLACK: Szabo*

*Saltsjobaden 1948*

| | WHITE | BLACK | | WHITE | BLACK | | WHITE | BLACK |
|---|---|---|---|---|---|---|---|---|
| 1 | P–K4 | P–K3 | 14 | B–N5 | QxP | 27 | B–K3 | R–QR4 |
| 2 | P–Q4 | P–Q4 | 15 | Q–Q8† | K–B2 | 28 | RxP | RxP |
| 3 | N–Q2 | N–QB3 | 16 | QR–Q1 | B–N2 | 29 | B–B5 | R–R4 |
| 4 | KN–B3 | N–B3 | 17 | NxB | RxQ | 30 | P–QN4 | R–R5 |
| 5 | P–K5 | N–Q2 | 18 | NxQ | R–Q4 | 31 | P–N3 | P–QR4 |
| 6 | N–N3 | P–B3 | 19 | N–K4 | B–Q3 | 32 | P–N5 | R–Q1 |
| 7 | B–QN5 | P–QR3 | 20 | N–B3 | R–R4 | 33 | K–N2 | R–R7 |
| 8 | BxN | PxB | 21 | B–B1 | P–KR3 | 34 | BxB | PxB |
| 9 | O–O | P–QB4 | 22 | KR–K1 | N–R5 | 35 | R–B7† | K–B3 |
| 10 | P–B4! | PxBP | 23 | NxN | RxN | 36 | N–Q4 | R–K1 |
| 11 | N–R5 | N–N3 | 24 | P–QR3 | P–B6 | 37 | P–N6 | P–K4 |
| 12 | KPxP | QxP | 25 | P–QN3 | R–R4 | 38 | P–N7 | Resigns |
| 13 | PxP | Q–B4 | 26 | R–Q3 | R–QB4 | | | |

PRACTICAL VARIATIONS 65–69:

1 P–K4, P–K3 2 P–Q4, P–Q4 3 N–Q2, N–QB3 4 KN–B3, N–B3 5 P–K5, N–Q2

| | *65* | *66* | *67* | *68* | *69* |
|---|---|---|---|---|---|
| *6* | N–N3 | P–QN3 | P–B4 | B–K2 | P–B3 |
| | P–B3[1] | P–B3[5] | P–B3[8] | P–B3 | P–B3 |
| *7* | B–QN5 | B–N2 | PxQP | PxP | PxP[11] |
| | B–K2[2] | PxP | PxQP | NxBP | QxP |
| *8* | B–KB4 | PxP | B–N5 | O–O | B–N5 |
| | O–O | B–B4[6] | P–QR3 | B–Q3 | B–Q3 |
| *9* | PxP | B–Q3 | B–R4 | P–B4 | N–B1 |
| | PxP | Q–K2 | PxP | O–O | P–QR3 |
| *10* | O–O | P–QR3 | NxP | R–K1 | B–R4 |
| | N–N3[3] | P–QR4 | N/2xN | B–Q2 | P–K4![12] |
| *11* | R–K1 | P–B4![7] | PxN | P–B5 | = |
| | B–Q3 | ± | P–QN4 | B–B5 | |
| *12* | B–N3[4] | | B–N3[9] | N–B1 | |
| | ± | | = | N–K5[10] | |
| | | | | ∓ | |

*Notes to practical variations 65–69:*

[1] After 6 . . . B–K2, a good continuation for White is 7 P–QB3, O–O 8 B–Q3, P–B3 9 Q–K2. Instead of the above (after 6 . . . B–K2) 7 B–QN5, O–O 8 O–O offers Black an interesting possibility: 8 . . . N/3–N1 9 B–Q3, P–QN3 10 P–B3, B–R3 11 BxB, NxB 12 Q–K2, Q–B1. Black has a satisfactory position (Reinhardt–Guimard, Buenos Aires 1955).

[2] After 7 . . . PxP 8 PxP, B–K2 White proceeds effectively with 9 QN–Q4, N/2–N1, 10 N–N5!, BxN 11 Q–R5†, P–N3 12 QxB, QxQ 14 BxQ, and White's two Bishops are a distinct advantage (Estrin–Bagirov, Baku 1958).

[3] Better is 10 . . . P–QR3.

[4] White has a slight edge (Botvinnik–Boleslavski, USSR Championship 1944).

[5] A remarkable idea is 6 . . . P–QR4 7 B–N2, B–K2 8 P–QR3, P–R5 9 B–Q3, O–O 10 O–O, P–B4 11 PxP e.p., BxP 12 P–QN4, N–K2 with a satisfactory game for Black (Trifunovic–Guimard, Buenos Aires 1955).

[6] Better is 8 . . . B–K2. Not 8 . . . P–KN3 because White obtains a dangerous attack after 9 B–Q3, B–N2 10 Q–K2, N–N5 11 P–KR4 (Pogats–Szabo, Budapest 1950).

[7] Trifunovic–Bondarevski (Game 21).

[8] Preferable is 6 . . . PxP 7 NxP, N–N3! 8 NxN, RPxN 9 B–Q3, N–N5! 10 B–K4, B–Q2 11 BxNP, R–R2 with equality (Pachman). In the above line, if 7 BxBP, then 7 . . . N–N3 8 B–QN5, Q–Q4!

[9] 12 . . . N–Q5 13 O–O with sharp play and chances for both sides (Trifunovic–Szabo, Hilversum 1947).

[10] 13 B–QN5, P–K4 14 PxP, B–KN5 with a good game for Black (Liberson–Gusev, Moscow Championship 1957).

[11] Or 7 B–Q3, PxP 8 PxP, N/2xP 9 NxN, NxN 10 Q–R5†, N–B2 11 BxP, B–K2 (also good is 11 . . . B–Q2 or 11 . . .

Q–B3) 12 N–B3, B–B3 13 P–KR4, P–K4. This is sharp position, not unfavorable to Black (Prins–Yanofsky, Karlsbad 1948).

[12] Tartakover–Guimard, Groningen 1946.

*French Defense Game 21*

*WHITE: Trifunovic* *BLACK: Bondarevski*

*Saltsjobaden 1948*

| WHITE | BLACK | WHITE | BLACK | WHITE | BLACK |
|---|---|---|---|---|---|
| 1 P–Q4 | P–K3 | 12 PxP | P–QN3 | 23 N–K4 | Q–K2 |
| 2 P–K4 | P–Q4 | 13 B–K4 | B–N2 | 24 QxN | QxQ |
| 3 N–Q2 | N–QB3 | 14 Q–R4 | N–Q1 | 25 RxQ | K–B2 |
| 4 KN–B3 | N–B3 | 15 O–O | BxB | 26 P–QR4 | B–N2 |
| 5 P–K5 | N–Q2 | 16 NxB | O–O | 27 P–KB4 | K–K2 |
| 6 P–QN3 | P–B3 | 17 QR–Q1 | N–N1 | 28 R/1–Q1 | P–QB4 |
| 7 B–N2 | PxP | 18 N/3–N5! | P–KR3 | 29 R/1–Q6 | B–Q5† |
| 8 PxP | B–B4 | 19 N–B6†! | PxN | 30 K–B1 | B–K6 |
| 9 B–Q3 | Q–K2 | 20 PxP | RxP | 31 P–N3 | B–Q5 |
| 10 P–QR3 | P–QR4 | 21 BxR | QxB | 32 R–QB8 | Resigns |
| 11 P–B4! | PxP | 22 Q–K8† | B–B1 | | |

## part 16—"EARLY" P-K5 VARIATION

### OBSERVATIONS ON KEY POSITION 16

1 P–K4, P–K3
2 P–Q4, P–Q4
3 P–K5, P–QB4
4 P–QB3, N–QB3[A]
5 N–B3[B], Q–N3

KEY POSITION 16

[A] Remarkable is Wade's idea 4 . . . Q–N3, already preparing to exchange his "bad" Bishop by 5 N–B3, B–Q2! 6 B–K2, B–N4 7 O–O, BxB 8 QxB, Q–R3 9 Q–Q1, N–Q2 10 B–K3 with equality (Alexander–Wade, Hastings 1953–54). In the above line, Black should not play 7 . . . N–QB3? because of 8 BxB, QxB 9 P–QR4, Q–N3 10 PxP, BxP 11 P–QN4 with an edge for White. Black should also avoid 9 . . . N–QB3? in answer to 9 Q–Q1 because of 10 PxP, BxP 11 P–QN4!

[B] Further support of White's King Pawn by P–KB4 is bad: 5 P–KB4? Q–N3 6 N–B3, N–R3 followed by . . . N–B4. Also weak for White is 5 Q–N4, PxP 6 PxP, N–R3! 7 Q–B4, N–B4 (Weiss–Haberditz, Correspondence Game 1933).

The position shows the theme of the King Pawn advance in its most characteristic shape. White meets the attack on his Queen Pawn by P–QB3, with which he means to maintain his center in full. Black, on the other hand, increases the pressure on White's Queen Pawn by . . . Q–N3 and . . . KN–K2, followed by . . . N–B4. Occasionally, Black may attack White's center by . . . P–KB3. It is, however, a general strategic rule that a Pawn chain can better be attacked at its base than at its peak. Hence, for Black, pressure on White's Q4 is indicated all the more because of the restrictive effect it has on the White pieces.

It follows, then, that 6 B–Q3 is almost a blunder. White must content himself with the modest 6 B–K2. Black for his part must meet 6 B–K2 with 6 . . . PxP followed by . . . KN–K2. The immediate 6 . . . KN–K2 is inaccurate because of 7 PxP. The continuation 6 P–QR3 as a preparation for 7 P–QN4 was popular some years ago, but is no longer played to-day. Black takes the edge off this thrust by 6 . . . P–B5, obtaining good play on the Queenside.

IDEA VARIATIONS 43–46:

(43) 6 B–Q3, B–Q2? 7 PxP!, BxP 8 O–O, P–B3 9 P–QN4!, B–K2 10 B–KB4 with an edge for White. See Game 22. 8 P–QN4, BxP† 9 K–K2, planning to trap Black's Bishop, fails tactically by reason of 9 . . . P–KB3. 8 . . . P–QR4 in reply to 8 O–O is bad because it leaves a hole for White's Queen Knight after 9 P–QR4, followed eventually by N–QR3–N5.

(44) 6 B–Q3, PxP 7 PxP, B–Q2 8 B–K2, KN–K2 9 P–QN3, N–B4 10 B–N2, B–N5† 11 K–B1, O–O (also good is 11 . . . B–K2 or 11 . . . P–KR4; playing 11 . . . O–O, Black aims at the characteristic sacrifice of the exchange) 12 P–N4, N–R3 13 R–N1, P–B3! 14 PxP, RxP 15 P–N5, RxN! 16 BxR, N–B4 with complications favoring Black. 7 . . . NxP? 8 NxN, QxN fails because of 9 B–N5†, but after 7 . . . B–Q2 White's Queen Pawn is really loose. Now 8 B–K2 represents a serious loss of time. To try to justify 6 B–Q3, White must sacrifice a Pawn by playing 8 O–O (see Prac. Var. 72). Weak is 8 B–B2 because of 8 . . . N–N5 9 B–N3, Q–R3!

(45) 6 B–K2, KN–K2 (the theoretical move, but 6 . . . PxP is preferable; See Idea Var. 46) 7 PxP, Q–B2 (7 . . . QxP? 8 B–K3) 8 N–Q4! (a new idea — 8 B–KB4, N–N3 and 8 B–QN5, B–Q2 favor Black), QxP (8 . . . NxP? 9 N–N5, QxP 10 Q–Q4! wins the exchange for White, as in Euwe–Kramer, Zaandam 1946) 9 O–O! followed by 10 P–QN4 with a good position for White. But not 9 P–KB4?, Q–B3 10 N–N5, because of 10 . . . N–B4! 11 N–B7†, K–Q1 12 NxR, Q–R5†, and Black has a tremendous attack.

(46) 6 B–K2, PxP 7 PxP, KN–K2 (well worth consideration is 7 . . . N–R3, so as to anticipate White's next move; 8 BxN is not correct because of 8 . . . QxNP, so White must transpose into Prac. Var. 70 or 71 by playing 8 P–QN3 or 8 N–B3) 8 N–R3 (following present-

day practice of defending the Queen Pawn by N–B2; otherwise 8 P–QN3 or 8 N–B3 again leads to Prac. Var. 70 or 71), N–B4 9 N–B2, B–N5† 10 K–B1 (10 NxB? costs a Pawn by 10 . . . QxN†), B–K2 11 P–QN4! (a recommendation of Dr. Claparede), B–Q2 (the capture of this Pawn loses a piece to QR–N1) 12 P–QR3. White has some superiority in freedom of movement: 12 . . . P–KR4 13 P–KR4, R–QB1 14 B–KN5, BxB 15 PxB, K–K2 16 Q–Q2 (Antoschin–Batugin, Moscow 1954). Also good is 12 R–QN1, but not 12 P–N4, N–R5 13 NxN, BxN 14 B–K3, P–B3!

PRACTICAL VARIATIONS 70–74:

1 P–K4, P–K3 2 P–Q4, P–Q4 3 P–K5, P–QB4 4 P–QB3, N–QB3 5 N–B3, Q–N3

| | 70 | 71 | 72 | 73 | 74 |
|---|---|---|---|---|---|
| 6 | B–K2 | – – | B–Q3 | P–QR3 | – – |
| | PxP | – – | PxP | B–Q2 | P–B5[12] |
| 7 | PxP | – – | PxP | P–QN4 | P–KN3 |
| | KN–K2 | – – | B–Q2 | PxQP | B–Q2 |
| 8 | P–QN3 | N–B3 | O–O | PxP | B–N2 |
| | N–B4 | N–B4 | NxQP | KN–K2 | O–O–O |
| 9 | B–N2 | N–QR4 | NxN | N–B3 | O–O |
| | B–N5† | Q–R4† | QxN | N–B4 | N–R4 |
| 10 | K–B1 | B–Q2[4] | Q–K2[8] | N–QR4 | N–Q2 |
| | P–KR4[1] | B–N5 | N–K2 | Q–Q1 | P–KR3 |
| 11 | N–B3[2] | B–B3 | N–B3 | B–K2[10] | R–K1 |
| | BxN | BxB†[5] | N–B3![9] | N–R5 | KN–K2 |
| 12 | BxB | NxB | ∓ | NxN | N–B1 |
| | B–Q2 | Q–N3[6] | | QxN | N–B4[13] |
| 13 | Q–Q2 | B–QN5[7] | | B–K3[11] | ∓ |
| | P–QR4[3] | = | | ± | |
| | ∓ | | | | |

*Notes to practical variations 70–74:*

[1] Here, too, Black can bring off a promising sacrifice of the exchange: 10 . . . O–O 11 P–N4, N–R3 (11 . . . KN–K2? 12 P–QR3), 12 R–N1, P–B3! 13 PxP, RxP 14 P–N5, RxN. Compare Idea Var. 44. But the text move 10 . . . P–KR4 is safe and good.

[2] Better than 11 P–KR4, B–Q2 12 N–B3, BxN (if 12 . . . N/3xQP, then 13 NxQP!) 13 BxB, R–QB1. See Game 23.

[3] 14 P–N3 (stronger is first 14 P–KR4), P–KR5 15 P–KN4, KN–K2 with a good position for Black (Cholmov–Petrosian, USSR Championship1949).

[4] Interesting is 10 K–B1!?, P–QN4! 11 N–B3, P–N5 12 B–QN5!, B–Q2 13 BxN, BxB 14 N–K2 (Bigot–Schmid, Cor-

continued ▸

respondence Game 1954–56). Black's best now is the exchange of White's Knight on K2 by 14 . . . B–N4.

[5] If 11 . . . P–QN4 or 11 . . . B–Q2, then 12 P–QR3!

[6] After 12 . . . Q–N5, Black still cannot capture the Queen Knight Pawn: 13 P–QR3, QxNP? 14 N–R4!

[7] Nimzowitsch–Stahlberg, Match 1934.

[8] After 10 N–B3, QxKP 11 R–K1, Q–Q3 12 N–N5, BxN 13 BxB†, K–Q1, the Black King is perfectly safe behind its strong center Pawns.

[9] Stronger than 11 . . . P–QR3 12 R–Q1, N–B3 13 BxQRP!, QxP 14 QxQ, NxQ 15 BxP, R–R2 16 BxP, PxB 17 R–K1, and White recovers the piece with about even chances (Ulvestad–Rothman, USA Championship 1946). The point of 11 . . . N–B3 is that 12 N–N5 fails because of 12 . . . QxKP! Nor did White obtain sufficient compensation for the Pawn in a correspondence game between Sturm and L. Schmid that continued 12 B–K3, QxP 13 P–B4, Q–Q3 14 N–N5, Q–N1 15 P–B5, P–K4 16 Q–R5, P–QR3!

[10] Also good is 11 B–N2.

[11] White has a slight superiority in space (Unzicker–Gligoric, Stockholm 1952).

[12] Another way to counter White's P–QN4 is 6 . . . P–QR4. Also, the immediate attack on White's center by 6 . . . P–B3 deserves consideration.

[13] Black has a good game. See Game 24.

*French Defense Game 22*

*WHITE: Nimzowitsch* *BLACK: Salve*

*Carlsbad 1911*

| | WHITE | BLACK | | WHITE | BLACK |
|---|---|---|---|---|---|
| 1 | P–K4 | P–K3 | 21 | Q–B2 | R–KB2 |
| 2 | P–Q4 | P–Q4 | 22 | R–K3 | P–QN3 |
| 3 | P–K5 | P–QB4 | 23 | R–N3 | K–R1 |
| 4 | P–QB3 | N–QB3 | 24 | BxRP | P–K4! |
| 5 | N–KB3 | Q–N3 | 25 | B–N6 | R–K2 |
| 6 | B–Q3 | B–Q2? | 26 | R–K1 | Q–Q3 |
| 7 | PxP | BxP | 27 | B–K3 | P–Q5 |
| 8 | O–O | P–B3 | 28 | B–N5 | RxP |
| 9 | P–QN4 | B–K2 | 29 | RxR | PxR |
| 10 | B–KB4 | PxP | 30 | QxP | K–N1 |
| 11 | NxP | NxN | 31 | P–QR3 | K–B1 |
| 12 | BxN | N–B3 | 32 | B–R4 | B–K1 |
| 13 | N–Q2 | O–O | 33 | B–B5 | Q–Q5 |
| 14 | N–B3 | B–Q3 | 34 | QxQ | PxQ |
| 15 | Q–K2 | QR–B1 | 35 | RxR | KxR |
| 16 | B–Q4 | Q–B2 | 36 | B–Q3 | K–Q3 |
| 17 | N–K5 | B–K1 | 37 | BxN | PxB |
| 18 | QR–K1 | BxN | 38 | K–B1 | B–B3 |
| 19 | BxB | Q–B3 | 39 | P–KR4 | Resigns |
| 20 | B–Q4 | B–Q2 | | | |

### French Defense Game 23

*WHITE: Aitken* *BLACK: Bondarevsky*

*Radio Match, England–USSR 1946*

| | WHITE | BLACK | | WHITE | BLACK |
|---|---|---|---|---|---|
| 1 | P–K4 | P–K3 | 18 | R–K1 | P–B3! |
| 2 | P–Q4 | P–Q4 | 19 | PxP | RxP |
| 3 | P–K5 | P–QB4 | 20 | BxB | QxB† |
| 4 | P–QB3 | N–QB3 | 21 | N–K2 | N/3xP |
| 5 | N–B3 | Q–N3 | 22 | P–R4 | Q–R3 |
| 6 | B–K2 | PxP | 23 | B–N4 | R–N3 |
| 7 | PxP | KN–K2 | 24 | QxP | R–R3 |
| 8 | P–QN3 | N–B4 | 25 | Q–N4 | R–B7 |
| 9 | B–N2 | B–N5† | 26 | P–N3 | N–K6† |
| 10 | K–B1 | P–KR4 | 27 | PxN | R–B3† |
| 11 | P–KR4 | B–Q2 | 28 | Q–B4 | RxQ† |
| 12 | N–B3 | BxN | 29 | NPxR | N–B4 |
| 13 | BxB | R–QB1 | 30 | K–B2 | Q–Q6 |
| 14 | R–R3 | QN–K2 | 31 | R–B3 | R–R7 |
| 15 | Q–Q2 | B–N4 | 32 | P–R5 | P–QN3 |
| 16 | N–N1 | N–N3 | 33 | PxP | PxP |
| 17 | Q–N5 | O–O | | Resigns | |

### French Defense Game 24

*WHITE: Clarke* *BLACK: Petrosian*

*Munich 1958*

| | WHITE | BLACK | | WHITE | BLACK |
|---|---|---|---|---|---|
| 1 | P–K4 | P–K3 | 22 | N–R2 | QR–KN1 |
| 2 | P–Q4 | P–Q4 | 23 | P–KN4 | Q–N3 |
| 3 | P–K5 | P–QB4 | 24 | B–B3 | PxP |
| 4 | P–QB3 | N–QB3 | 25 | BxP/4 | N–B3 |
| 5 | N–KB3 | Q–N3 | 26 | P–B3 | B–Q1 |
| 6 | P–QR3 | P–B5 | 27 | B–B2 | N–K2 |
| 7 | P–KN3 | B–Q2 | 28 | R–K1 | R–R3 |
| 8 | B–N2 | O–O–O | 29 | N–B1 | R/1–R1 |
| 9 | O–O | N–R4 | 30 | B–N3 | RxP |
| 10 | QN–Q2 | P–KR3 | 31 | BxR | RxB |
| 11 | R–K1 | N–K2 | 32 | Q–N2 | Q–R2 |
| 12 | N–B1 | N–B4 | 33 | N–K3 | N–N3 |
| 13 | N–K3 | NxN | 34 | N–N4 | N–B5 |
| 14 | RxN | B–K2 | 35 | BxN | PxB |
| 15 | R–K1 | Q–N6 | 36 | K–B1 | R–N6 |
| 16 | Q–K2 | B–R5 | 37 | Q–B2 | Q–R6† |
| 17 | B–K3 | K–N1 | 38 | K–K2 | R–N7 |
| 18 | QR–Q1 | Q–B7 | 39 | R–N1 | RxQ† |
| 19 | R–Q2 | Q–B4 | 40 | NxR | Q–R7 |
| 20 | R–KB1 | P–KN4 | 41 | R–KR1 | Q–N6 |
| 21 | P–R3 | P–R4 | | Resigns | |

SUPPLEMENTARY VARIATIONS 26–30:

1 P–K4, P–K3 2 P–Q4, P–Q4 3 P–K5, P–QB4

White can also treat the "Early" P–K5 Variation by confining himself to an attempt at maintenance of the King Pawn alone, not extending his center by means of P–QB3. His Queen Pawn then disappears, either by QPxP or by . . . QBPxP. The former method (Sup. Var. 26 and 27) was recommended by Steinitz. In this case, Black's best procedure is an attack on White's King Pawn by . . . P–KB3. White is unable to maintain his outpost on K5.

The latter method (Sup. Var. 28–30) was preferred by Nimzowitsch. It usually involves the sacrifice of the Queen Pawn. In this line, also Black has sufficient chances for counterplay.

| | *26* | *27* | *28* | *29* | *30* |
|---|---|---|---|---|---|
| *4* | PxP | – – | N–KB3 | Q–N4 | – – |
| | N–QB3[1] | – – | PxP | PxP | N–QB3! |
| *5* | N–KB3 | – – | B–Q3[6] | N–KB3 | N–KB3 |
| | BxP | – – | N–QB3 | N–QB3 | KN–K2 |
| *6* | B–Q3 | | O–O | B–Q3 | P–B3?[11] |
| | P–B4[2] | KN–K2 | P–B3[7] | KN–K2[9] | N–B4 |
| *7* | P–B3 | B–KB4[4] | B–QN5 | O–O | B–Q3 |
| | P–QR3 | Q–N3 | B–Q2 | N–N3 | PxP![12] |
| *8* | QN–Q2 | O–O | BxN | R–K1 | ∓ |
| | KN–K2 | QxP | PxB | B–K2[10] | |
| *9* | N–N3 | N–Q2 | QxP[8] | = | |
| | B–R2 | Q–N3 | = | | |
| *10* | O–O | P–B4[5] | | | |
| | O–O[3] | ± | | | |
| | = | | | | |

*Notes to supplementary variations 26–30:*

[1] Also possible is 4 . . . BxP; for, after 5 Q–N4, N–K2! 6 QxNP, N–N3, Black either recovers the Pawn or forces a repetition of moves by B–B1–K2.

[2] Somewhat better is 6 . . . P–B3 7 Q–K2 (7 PxP, NxP is good for Black), Q–B2! 8 B–KB4, P–KN4 9 B–N3, P–N5 10 KN–Q2, NxP, and it is doubtful if White has sufficient compensation for the Pawn (Keres).

[3] Tarrasch–Lasker, St. Petersburg 1914.

[4] The text initiates a promising gambit for White. On 7 O–O, N–N3 8 R–K1, B–Q2 9 P–B3, B–N3 10 N–R3, P–QR3 11 N–B2, B–B2 12 BxN, RPxB, the position is satisfactory for Black (Nimzowitsch–Alekhine, St. Petersburg 1914).

[5] White has good attacking chances. See Game 25. Another possibility is 10 N–N3, N–N3 11 B–N3, B–K2 12 P–KR4 (Nimzowitsch–Spielmann, San Sebastian 1912).

[6] 5 NxP, N–QB3 or 5 QxP, N–QB3 6 Q–KB4, P–B4 is comfortable for Black See Game 26.

[7] Or 6 . . . B–B4 7 B–KB4!, KN–K2 8 N–Q2, N–N3 9 B–N3 with equality. Inferior for White is 7 P–QR3, KN–K2 8 QN–Q2, N–N3 9 N–N3, B–N3 10 R–K1, B–Q2. See Game 27.

[8] Black ought to play 9 . . . Q–N3 with a fully satisfactory game. Instead, 9 . . . PxP 10 QxP, N–B3 11 B–B4, B–B4 12 N–B3, O–O 13 B–N3 offers White some positional advantage (Alekhine–Euwe, Nottingham 1936).

[9] Well worth consideration is 6 . . . Q–B2 7 Q–N3, P–B3 8 B–KB4, P–KN4! (Araiza–Fine, Syracuse 1934). In the above line if 7 B–KB4, then 7 . . . N–N5. But a better continuation for White is 7 O–O, P–B3 8 B–KB4, PxP 9 NxP, NxN 10 Q–R5†.

[10] To prevent . . . P–KR4. According to Nimzowitsch the chances are even. Weaker is 8 . . . Q–N3 9 Q–N3, B–B4 10 P–KR4 (Nimzowitsch–Szekeley, Kecskemet 1927). An interesting idea is 8 . . . Q–B2 9 Q–N3 (stronger is 9 Q–R5), P–B3 10 BxN†, PxB 11 QxP†, Q–B2 13 Q–N3, R–R4 with advantage for Black (Maric–Antoschin, Upsala 1956).

[11] Correct is 6 B–Q3, but Black plays 6 . . . NxQP with a satisfactory game.

[12] Black wins a Pawn, since 8 PxP fails against 8 . . . N–N5! (Canepa–Alekhine, Montevideo 1938).

## *French Defense Game 25*

*WHITE: Keres* *BLACK: Alexandrescu*

*Munich 1936*

| | WHITE | BLACK | | WHITE | BLACK | | WHITE | BLACK |
|---|---|---|---|---|---|---|---|---|
| 1 | P–K4 | P–K3 | 9 | QN–Q2 | Q–N3 | 17 | P–K6! | PxP |
| 2 | P–Q4 | P–Q4 | 10 | P–B4 | P–KR3 | 18 | N–K5 | NxB |
| 3 | P–K5 | P–QB4 | 11 | Q–B1 | N–N5 | 19 | RPxN | Q–B2 |
| 4 | PxP | N–QB3 | 12 | B–K2 | B–Q2 | 20 | NxB | KxN |
| 5 | N–KB3 | BxP | 13 | P–QR3 | N–R3 | 21 | Q–N2 | B–N3 |
| 6 | B–Q3 | KN–K2 | 14 | R–N1 | Q–B3 | 22 | QxP† | K–Q3 |
| 7 | B–KB4 | Q–N3 | 15 | B–N3 | N–B4 | 23 | N–B4† | PxN |
| 8 | O–O | QxP | 16 | PxP | PxP | 24 | KR–Q1† | Resigns |

## *French Defense Game 26*

*WHITE: Keres* *BLACK: Euwe*

*Zandvoort 1936*

| | WHITE | BLACK | | WHITE | BLACK | | WHITE | BLACK |
|---|---|---|---|---|---|---|---|---|
| 1 | P–K4 | P–K3 | 12 | QN–Q2 | P–QR4 | 23 | B–Q2 | P–Q6 |
| 2 | P–Q4 | P–Q4 | 13 | N–N3 | N–R3 | 24 | P–QN3 | P–B5 |
| 3 | P–K5 | P–QB4 | 14 | P–QR4 | N–N5 | 25 | R–K4 | R–B4 |
| 4 | N–KB3 | PxP | 15 | N/B–Q4 | B–Q2 | 26 | R/1–K1 | R–R4 |
| 5 | QxP | N–QB3 | 16 | B–QN5 | N–B3 | 27 | P–R3 | R–N4 |
| 6 | Q–KB4 | P–B4 | 17 | P–QB4 | NxN | 28 | N–Q6 | QxP |
| 7 | B–Q3 | KN–K2 | 18 | NxN | B–B4! | 29 | BxP | NxB |
| 8 | O–O | N–N3 | 19 | Q–Q3 | BxB | 30 | RxN | Q–N6! |
| 9 | Q–N3 | B–K2 | 20 | NxB | Q–R5! | 31 | R/B–K4 | R–R4 |
| 10 | R–K1 | O–O | 21 | Q–B1 | QR–Q1 | | Resigns | |
| 11 | P–QR3 | N–N1 | 22 | B–K3 | P–Q5 | | | |

*French Defense Game 27*

*WHITE: Bondarevski* *BLACK: Botvinnik*

*USSR Championship 1941*

| | WHITE | BLACK | | WHITE | BLACK |
|---|---|---|---|---|---|
| 1 | P–K4 | P–K3 | 16 | B–N4 | P–N4 |
| 2 | P–Q4 | P–Q4 | 17 | QxQ | RxQ |
| 3 | P–K5 | P–QB4 | 18 | PxBP | PxBP |
| 4 | N–KB3 | N–QB3 | 19 | PxNP | P–K4 |
| 5 | B–Q3 | PxP | 20 | PxP | KxP |
| 6 | O–O | B–B4 | 21 | B–Q6 | R–K1 |
| 7 | P–QR3 | KN–K2 | 22 | N–R4 | R–KN1 |
| 8 | QN–Q2 | N–N3 | 23 | K–R2 | B–KB4 |
| 9 | N–N3 | B–N3 | 24 | R–K2 | P–Q6 |
| 10 | R–K1 | B–Q2 | 25 | R–Q2 | PxP |
| 11 | P–KN3 | P–B3 | 26 | P–B4 | B–K6 |
| 12 | BxN† | PxB | 27 | BxP† | NxB |
| 13 | Q–Q3 | K–B2 | 28 | PxN† | K–K2 |
| 14 | P–KR4 | Q–KN1! | 29 | R–KB1 | P–B8 (Q) |
| 15 | B–Q2 | Q–R2 | | Resigns | |

## part 17—UNUSUAL VARIATIONS

This part comprises a round-up of several unusual variations of the French Defense, diverging after 1 P–K4, P–K3 and widely different in character.

### OBSERVATIONS ON UNUSUAL VARIATIONS 1–5

Var. 1 shows the Marshall Variation which, though sharp, is regarded as unsatisfactory for Black.

Var. 2 is the so-called Exchange Variation, usually considered drawish.

Var. 3 is Tchigorin's pet line, now and then used even to-day. White actually plays a type of Indian Defense in reverse. The same is true of Var. 4, where White builds his position with P–Q3, followed by P–KN3 and B–N2.

Var. 5 shows an original method of development which Reti once adopted.

### UNUSUAL VARIATIONS 1–5:

1 P–K4, P–K3

| | *1* | *2* | *3* | *4* | *5* |
|---|---|---|---|---|---|
| *2* | P–Q4 | – – | Q–K2 | P–Q3 | P–QN3 |
| | P–Q4 | – – | P–QB4[6] | P–QB4[12] | P–Q4[15] |
| *3* | N–QB3 | PxP | P–KN3[7] | N–Q2 | B–N2 |
| | P–QB4 | PxP | N–QB3 | N–QB3 | PxP |

| | *1* | *2* | *3* | *4* | *5* |
|---|---|---|---|---|---|
| *4* | KPxP | B–Q3 | B–N2 | P–KN3 | N–QB3 |
| | KPxP | N–QB3 | KN–K2[8] | P–KN3 | N–KB3 |
| *5* | PxP | N–KB3[4] | N–QB3 | B–N2 | Q–K2 |
| | P–Q5[1] | B–KN5 | P–KN3 | B–N2 | B–K2 |
| *6* | B–N5† | P–B3 | P–Q3 | KN–B3 | O–O–O |
| | N–B3 | Q–Q2 | B–N2 | KN–K2 | N–B3![16] |
| *7* | BxN† | O–O | B–K3?[9] | O–O | NxP |
| | PxB | O–O–O | P–Q4! | O–O | N–Q5[17] |
| *8* | QN–K2 | R–K1 | PxP[10] | P–B3 | ∓ |
| | BxP | B–Q3 | N–Q5 | P–Q3[13] | |
| *9* | N–KB3 | QN–Q2 | Q–Q2 | P–QR4 | |
| | Q–R4†[2] | KN–K2 | PxP[11] | P–B4 | |
| *10* | B–Q2 | P–QN4 | ∓ | Q–N3 | |
| | Q–N3 | QR–K1![5] | | P–Q4 | |
| *11* | O–O[3] | = | | PxQP | |
| | ± | | | PxP[14] | |
| | | | | = | |

*Notes to unusual variations 1–5:*

[1] On 5 . . . N–KB3, White can well proceed with 6 B–K3.

[2] The Black Queen Pawn is hard to defend. To 9 . . . B–KN5, White replies with 10 N/3xP, and 9 . . . B–N5† 10 B–Q2, BxB† 11 QxB, P–QB4 12 O–O–O gives White a substantial positional advantage. Also favoring White is 9 . . . Q–Q4 10 O–O, B–KN5 11 N/3xP, KBxN 12 QxB, BxN 13 QxQ, PxQ 14 R–K1! Or 11 . . . O–O–O 12 P–QB3, KBxN 13 PxB, BxN 14 QxB, QxQP 15 Q–R6† with an overwhelming attack.

[3] The threat is 12 P–QN4. If Black now plays 11 . . . QxP then 12 R–K1, N–K2 13 N/2xP! BxN 14 NxB, QxN? 15 RxN†, and White wins. Or 11 . . . P–QR4 12 R–K1, N–K2 (if 12 . . . B–K3, then 13 N–B4, or 12 . . . P–Q6 13 N–B4†) 13 N/3xP! BxN 14 NxB, QxN? 15 RxN†, and White wins.

[4] Or 5 N–K2, B–Q3 6 QN–B3, N–B3 7 B–KB4, B–KN5 with equality. But 5 P–QB3, B–Q3 6 N–K2 allows Alekhine's line 6 . . . Q–R5! 7 N–Q2, B–KN5 8 Q–B2, O–O–O 9 N–B1, P–KN3 10 B–K3, KN–K2 11 O–O–O, B–KB4 12 N/1–N3, BxB 13 QxB, P–KR3 with a positional edge for Black. See Game 28.

[5] So as to meet P–N5 with . . . N–Q1. The chances are even: 11 N–N3, P–B3 12 N–B5, BxN 13 NPxB, N–Q1.

[6] Another steady continuation is 2 . . . B–K2, still intending . . . P–Q4 (if immediately 2 . . . P–Q4? then 3 PxP, QxP 4 N–QB3, and White has the edge in development), 3 P–Q3, P–Q4 4 P–KN3. Or 3 P–QN3, P–Q4 4 B–N2, B–B3 5 P–K5, B–K2 6 Q–N4, B–B1 7 N–KB3, P–QB4 (Tchigorin–Tarrasch, 14th Match Game 1893). Black's superiority in the center compensates for White's edge in development.

[7] The immediate 3 P–KB4 is playable: 3 . . . N–QB3 4 N–KB3, B–K2 5 N–B3, P–Q4 6 P–Q3, P–Q5 7 N–Q1, N–B3 8 P–KN3, P–QN4 9 B–N2 (see Game 29), Black's closing of the center by . . . P–Q5 is generally not to be recommended, for it enables White to prepare comfortably for an attack on the

continued ▸

Kingside. Black does better in the above variation with 6 . . . N–B3, but his best plan is to vary with 4 . . . KN–K2 5 P–KN3, P–KN3 6 B–N2, B–N2 with a set-up similar to Stoltz–Botvinnik in the main text.

[8] Here 4 . . . N–Q5 is a waste of time because of 5 Q–Q1 followed by P–QB3 and P–Q4.

[9] Correct is 7 P–KB4, O–O 8 N–B3, N–Q5 with an even position.

[10] If 8 BxP, then 8 . . . Q–R4.

[11] Stoltz–Botvinnik, Groningen 1946.

[12] Also good is 2 . . . P–Q4 3 N–Q2, N–KB3 4 P–KN3, PxP 5 PxP, B–B4 6 B–N2, N–B3 7 P–KR3, P–K4 8 KN–B3, B–K3 9 O–O,Q–Q2 10 N–N5, O–O–O 11 NxB, PxN 12 P–QB3, P–KR4 (Kasparian–Tolush, USSR Championship 1946).

[13] The immediate 8 . . . P–Q4 is playable. It leads to a position of the King's Indian with colors reversed in which White has an extra tempo.

[14] 12 R–K1, P–KB5! 13 N–B1, B–N5! 14 PxP, BxN 15 BxB, K–R1, and Black has sufficient compensation for the Pawn. See Game 30. In the above line, Botvinnik suggests 12 N–N1 in preparation for 13 B–B4.

[15] Here or on the following move . . . P–QB4 is good.

[16] After 6 . . . QN–Q2 7 P–KN4, P–KR3 8 B–N2, P–QB3 9 P–KR4, White obtains a dangerous attack (Reti–Maroczy, Goteborg 1920).

[17] The Black position is quite satisfactory according to Keres.

### *French Defense Game 28*

*WHITE: Winter* *BLACK: Alekhine*

*Nottingham 1936*

| | WHITE | BLACK | | WHITE | BLACK |
|---|---|---|---|---|---|
| 1 | P–Q4 | P–K3 | 21 | B–Q2 | R–K3 |
| 2 | P–K4 | P–Q4 | 22 | N–N4 | R/1–K1 |
| 3 | PxP | PxP | 23 | QR–K1 | R/1–K2 |
| 4 | B–Q3 | N–QB3 | 24 | K–Q1 | Q–K1 |
| 5 | N–K2 | B–Q3 | 25 | Q–B3 | N–R4 |
| 6 | P–QB3 | Q–R5 | 26 | P–QN3 | N–B5! |
| 7 | N–Q2 | B–KN5 | 27 | B–B1 | N/5–Q6† |
| 8 | Q–B2 | O–O–O | 28 | BxN | NxB† |
| 9 | N–B1 | P–KN3 | 29 | NxN | RxN |
| 10 | B–K3 | KN–K2 | 30 | Q–B2 | Q–N4! |
| 11 | O–O–O | B–KB4 | 31 | N–B1 | RxBP |
| 12 | N/1–N3 | BxB | 32 | RxR | BxR |
| 13 | QxB | P–KR3 | 33 | Q–K1 | K–Q2 |
| 14 | P–KB4 | Q–N5 | 34 | P–B5 | R–K6 |
| 15 | P–KR3 | Q–Q2 | 35 | Q–B2 | P–N4 |
| 16 | KR–B1 | P–KR4! | 36 | R–K1 | R–K5 |
| 17 | N–N1 | P–R5 | 37 | RxR | PxR |
| 18 | N/3–K2 | N–B4 | 38 | K–Q2 | B–Q3 |
| 19 | N–B3 | P–B3 | 39 | K–B3 | B–B5 |
| 20 | N–R2 | QR–K1 | | Resigns | |

### *French Defense Game 29*

*WHITE: Tchigorin* *BLACK: Von Gottschall*

*Barmewi 1905*

| | WHITE | BLACK | | WHITE | BLACK |
|---|---|---|---|---|---|
| 1 | P–K4 | P–K3 | 26 | R–R5! | N–N1 |
| 2 | Q–K2 | P–QB4 | 27 | N–K5 | N/1–Q2 |
| 3 | P–KB4 | N–QB3 | 28 | N–B4! | Q–R3 |
| 4 | N–KB3 | B–K2 | 29 | R–N1 | N–B3 |
| 5 | N–B3 | P–Q4 | 30 | R–R3 | N/4–Q2 |
| 6 | P–Q3 | P–Q5 | 31 | N–B3 | Q–R2 |
| 7 | N–Q1 | N–B3 | 32 | Q–K2 | N–B4 |
| 8 | P–KN3 | P–QN4 | 33 | N/3–K5 | N/4–Q2 |
| 9 | B–N2 | B–R3 | 34 | K–R1 | NxN |
| 10 | O–O | R–QB1 | 35 | PxN | N–K1 |
| 11 | P–N3 | P–B5 | 36 | R–N1 | R/2–B2 |
| 12 | N–K1 | PxQP | 37 | Q–R5 | P–N3 |
| 13 | PxP | O–O | 38 | B–KB3! | R–N2 |
| 14 | B–Q2 | Q–N3 | 39 | Q–N4 | B–B1 |
| 15 | N–B2 | N–QN5 | 40 | B–R6 | Q–K2 |
| 16 | Q–Q1 | B–N2 | 41 | B–K2 | B–B2 |
| 17 | P–QR3 | N–B3 | 42 | BxR | QxB |
| 18 | P–KN4 | P–QR4 | 43 | Q–N5 | B–Q2 |
| 19 | P–N5 | N–Q2 | 44 | R/3–N3 | R–B2 |
| 20 | N–N4 | P–N5 | 45 | P–R4! | K–R1 |
| 21 | P–QR4 | N–B4 | 46 | P–R5 | PxP |
| 22 | R–B3 | P–B4 | 47 | BxP | QxQ |
| 23 | PxP e.p. | BxP | 48 | RxQ | R–B1 |
| 24 | R–KR3 | B–Q1 | 49 | B–B7 | Resigns |
| 25 | R–B1 | R–QB2 | | | |

### *French Defense Game 30*

*WHITE: Smyslov* *BLACK: Botvinnik*

*Twenty-fourth Match Game, Moscow 1954*

| | WHITE | BLACK | | WHITE | BLACK |
|---|---|---|---|---|---|
| 1 | P–K4 | P–K3 | 15 | BxB | K–R1 |
| 2 | P–Q3 | P–QB4 | 16 | B–Q2 | B–R3 |
| 3 | N–Q2 | N–QB3 | 17 | R–K6 | BxP |
| 4 | P–KN3 | P–KN3 | 18 | R/1–K1 | BxB? |
| 5 | B–N2 | B–N2 | 19 | NxB | N–B4 |
| 6 | KN–B3 | KN–K2 | 20 | B–N2! | N/R5 |
| 7 | O–O | O–O | 21 | QxQP | NxB |
| 8 | P–B3 | P–Q3 | 22 | QxN/2 | QxP |
| 9 | P–QR4 | P–B4 | 23 | N–K4 | R–B4? |
| 10 | Q–N3! | P–Q4 | 24 | N–Q6 | R–B6 |
| 11 | PxP | PxP | 25 | NxP | R/1–KB1 |
| 12 | R–K1 | P–KB5 | 26 | NxP | Q–B4 |
| 13 | N–B1 | B–N5 | 27 | R–K8 | K–N1 |
| 14 | PxP | BxN | 28 | RxR† | Resigns |

# chapter 18—Nimzowitsch Defense

1 P–K4, N–QB3
2 P–Q4

KEY POSITION

Black's novel intention is to proceed with 2 . . . P–Q4 so as to exert pressure on White's Queen Pawn after 3 PxP, QxP. Of course White can avoid the exchange and obtain some advantage in space by playing 3 P–K5 instead; the position then resembles the Advance Variation of the French Defense, with two important differences: Black lacks the rejoinder . . . P–QB4, but does have an open diagonal for his Queen Bishop. The former of these two factors, however, is strategically the more important. That this defense never found favor in the eyes of anyone but its originator is an emphatic testimonial to its numerous drawbacks.

## OBSERVATIONS ON KEY POSITION

The American master, Alex Kevitz, also combines 1 . . . N–QB3 with another and better plan; he proceeds with 2 . . . P–K4, concluding that after 3 PxP, NxP the centralized Knight is satisfactorily placed. Indeed, the customary "refutation" 4 P–KB4 offers White very little in the way of an advantage. White, therefore, is well advised to ignore the Knight for the moment, and concentrate instead on the quick mobilization of his pieces.

Still another idea for Black in the diagrammed position is to build his center by means of . . . P–Q3 and then . . . P–K4, but very little is known concerning the theory of this line, as few tournament examples exist.

## IDEA VARIATIONS 1–5:

(1) 2 . . . P–Q4 3 PxP, QxP 4 N–KB3, P–K4 5 PxP? (5 N–B3 is correct; see Prac. Var. 1), QxQ† 6 KxQ, B–QB4 7 K–K1, B–B4 8 P–B3, O–O–O 9 B–K2, P–B3, and Black has excellent attacking chances in return for his Pawn (Loewenberg–Nimzowitsch, Copenhagen 1925).

(2) 2 . . . P–Q4 3 P–K5, B–B4 4 N–K2, P–B3 5 P–KB4, P–K3 6 N–N3, PxP 7 BPxP, Q–Q2 (7 . . . B–N3 8 B–Q3±) 8 NxB, PxN 9 B–QN5 (Alekhine considered 9 P–B3 followed by B–Q3 stronger), P–QR3 10 B–K2, P–KN3 11 O–O, B–R3 12 BxB, NxB 13 Q–Q2, Q–N2 14 N–B3 with a slight edge for White (Te Kolste-Nimzowitsch, Baden–Baden 1925).

(3) 2 . . . P–K3 3 N–KB3 (more accurate than 3 N–QB3, B–N5 4 N–B3, P–Q3!), P–Q4 4 P–K5, P–QN3 5 P–B3, QN–K2 6 B–Q3, P–QR4 7 Q–K2! with a positional advantage for White (Spielmann–Nimzowitsch, New York 1927).

(4) 2 . . . P–K4 3 PxP, NxP 4 P–KB4, N–N3 5

B–K3 (5 B–B4, B–B4? fails against 6 BxP†; correct, according to Kevitz, is 5 . . . B–N5† 6 P–B3, B–Q3, 7 P–K5, Q–K2 8 Q–K2, B–B4), B–N5† 6 P–B3, B–R4 7 Q–B3 (or 7 N–Q2, N–B3 8 B–Q3, Q–K2, when both 9 Q–B3, P–Q4! 10 P–K5, N–N5 and 9 N–B4, B–N3 10 NxB, RPxN 11 Q–B2 [if 11 P–K5, N–Q4], N–N5 12 B–Q2, Q–B4 are satisfactory for Black), P–Q4! 8 PxP, N–B3 9 B–QB4, O–O with very good counterplay for Black.

(5) 2 . . . P–K4 3 PxP, NxP 4 N–KB3, Q–B3 (4 . . . B–N5† 5 P–B3, B–Q3, as suggested by Kevitz, is slightly better than the text) 5 B–K2, B–N5† 6 QN–Q2, NxN† 7 BxN, N–K2 8 O–O, O–O 9 N–N3, N–B3 10 P–KN3, R–K1 11 B–N2, B–B1 12 P–QB3, P–Q3 13 P–B4 with White for choice (Keres–Kevitz, New York 1954).

PRACTICAL VARIATIONS 1–5:

1 P–K4, N–QB3 2 P–Q4

Perfectly practical is 2 N–KB3 with probable transposition into regular openings.

| | *1* | *2* | *3* | *4* | *5* |
|---|---|---|---|---|---|
| *2* | — — | — — | — — | — — | — — |
| | P–Q4 | — — | P–K3 | P–K4 | P–Q3 |
| *3* | PxP | N–QB3 | N–QB3[9] | PxP | N–KB3 |
| | QxP | PxP[4] | B–N5[10] | NxP | B–N5 |
| *4* | N–KB3 | P–Q5 | N–B3[11] | N–QB3 | B–QN5[16] |
| | P–K4[1] | N–N1[5] | P–Q3![12] | B–B4[14] | P–QR3 |
| *5* | N–B3 | B–QB4[6] | B–KB4 | P–B4 | B–R4 |
| | B–QN5 | N–KB3 | KN–K2 | N–N3 | P–QN4 |
| *6* | B–K3[2] | B–B4 | B–K2 | N–B3 | B–N3 |
| | B–N5[3] | P–B3 | BxN† | P–Q3 | N–B3 |
| *7* | B–K2 | KN–K2 | PxB | B–B4 | P–B3 |
| | O–O–O | PxP[7] | O–O | B–K3 | P–K3 |
| *8* | O–O | NxQP | O–O | Q–K2 | Q–K2 |
| | Q–R4 | NxN | N–KN3 | BxB | B–K2 |
| *9* | NxP | BxKN | B–K3 | QxB | O–O |
| | BxB | P–K3 | Q–K2 | Q–Q2 | O–O |
| *10* | QxB | BxP/4 | R–K1 | P–B5[15] | QN–Q2[17] |
| | NxN | QxQ† | B–Q2 | ± | ± |
| *11* | PxN | RxQ[8] | Q–B1 | | |
| | N–R3 | ± | P–N3 | | |
| *12* | N–N5! | | N–Q2 | | |
| | ± | | P–K4[13] | | |
| | | | = | | |

*Notes to practical variations 1–5:*

[1] Characteristic, but probably not best; 4 . . . B–N5 5 B–K2, O–O–O 6 B–K3, N–B3 7 N–B3, Q–QR4 is a variation of the Center Counter Defense in which Black has little difficulty, if any.

continued ▸

[2] Also good is 6 B–Q2, BxN 7 BxB, PxP 8 NxP, NxN 9 QxN, QxQ 10 BxQ± or 7 . . . P–K5 8 N–K5, NxN 9 PxN, QxQ† 10 RxQ±.

[3] The immediate 6 . . . Q–QR4 is better. Compare column with Game 1.

[4] Or 3 . . . P–K3 4 N–B3±.

[5] 4 . . . N–K4 is less commendable, e.g., 5 B–KB4 (not 5 Q–Q4? P–KB3), N–N3 6 B–N3, P–QR3 7 B–QB4, N–B3 8 Q–Q4±.

[6] Both 5 P–B3 and 5 Q–Q4 are best met by 5 . . . P–K3.

[7] Not 7 . . . P–QN4? 8 PxP!

[8] White has recovered the Pawn and has a great advantage in development (analysis by Panov).

[9] 3 N–KB3 squelches Black's counterplay; see Idea Var. 3.

[10] 3 . . . P–Q4 is effectively met by 4 N–B3; e.g. 4 . . . B–N5 5 P–K5. The immediate 4 P–K5 is not so good because of 4 . . . KN–K2!, e.g., 5 N–B3, P–QN3 6 N–K2, B–R3 7 P–B3, Q–Q2 8 N–N3, BxB 9 NxB, P–KR4 (Vajda–Nimzowitsch, Kecskemet 1927). In this line, however, the simple 6 B–K2 offers White a good game.

[11] 4 N–K2, P–Q4 5 P–K5, P–KR4 6 N–B4, P–KN3 7 B–K3, BxN† 8 PxB, N–R4 9 B–Q3, N–K2 10 N–R3, P–QB4 11 B–KN5 definitely favors White (Kmoch–Nimzowitsch, Niendorf 1927), but Pachman suggests the thematic 4 . . . P–Q3! as an improvement; he offers the following analysis: 5 B–K3, KN–K2 6 P–QR3, BxN† 7 NxB, O–O 8 B–K2, P–B4!

[12] 4 . . . P–Q4 5 P–K5, KN–K2 6 P–QR3, BxN† 7 PxB leads to a position similar to the Winawer Variation of the French. Here, however, White's chances are definitely better, since Black's . . . P–QB4 cannot be played without difficulty.

[13] Maroczy–Nimzowitsch, San Remo 1930.

[14] 4 . . . B–N5 followed by . . . N–B3 and possibly . . . P–Q4 may be better.

[15] Keres–Mikenas, Tiflis 1946. See Game 2.

[16] 4 P–Q5 sets an astonishing trap: 4 . . . N–K4? (4 . . . BxN equalizes), 5 NxN!, BxQ 6 B–N5†, P–B3 7 PxP, Q–R4† 8 N–B3, O–O–O 9 N–B4! with complications all in White's favor.

[17] Fine–Mikenas, Hastings 1938.

### *Nimzowitsch Defense Game 1*

*WHITE: Mieses* *BLACK: Schenk*

*Oxford 1947*

| | WHITE | BLACK | | WHITE | BLACK |
|---|---|---|---|---|---|
| 1 | P–K4 | N–QB3 | 15 | KR–N1 | P–QB3 |
| 2 | P–Q4 | P–Q4 | 16 | P–QB3! | RPxN |
| 3 | PxP | QxP | 17 | PxB | Q–R3 |
| 4 | N–KB3 | P–K4 | 18 | P–R5 | N–B4 |
| 5 | N–B3 | B–QN5 | 19 | B–N6 | R–Q4 |
| 6 | B–K3 | B–N5 | 20 | R–Q1 | N–K2 |
| 7 | B–K2 | O–O–O | 21 | Q–N4† | K–N1 |
| 8 | O–O | Q–QR4 | 22 | QxP | R–QB1 |
| 9 | NxP | BxB | 23 | Q–B6 | RxR† |
| 10 | QxB | NxN | 24 | RxR | N–Q4 |
| 11 | PxN | N–R3 | 25 | Q–Q6† | K–R1 |
| 12 | N–N5! | P–QR3 | 26 | RxN | PxR |
| 13 | P–QR4 | B–K2 | 27 | P–N3 | Resigns |
| 14 | P–QN4! | BxP | | | |

### *Nimzowitsch Defense Game 2*

*WHITE: Keres* *BLACK: Mikenas*

*Tiflis 1946*

| | WHITE | BLACK | | WHITE | BLACK |
|---|---|---|---|---|---|
| 1 | P–K4 | N–QB3 | 16 | P–KR3 | Q–R2 |
| 2 | P–Q4 | P–K4 | 17 | R–R2 | B–K6† |
| 3 | PxP | NxP | 18 | K–N1 | P–R5 |
| 4 | N–QB3 | B–B4 | 19 | B–B2 | BxB |
| 5 | P–B4 | N–N3 | 20 | RxB | R–Q2 |
| 6 | N–B3 | P–Q3 | 21 | N–Q4 | NxN |
| 7 | B–B4 | B–K3 | 22 | QxN | P–N3 |
| 8 | Q–K2 | BxB | 23 | N–Q5 | Q–B2 |
| 9 | QxB | Q–Q2 | 24 | Q–R4 | K–N2 |
| 10 | P–B5 | N/3–K2 | 25 | R–B3 | N–R3 |
| 11 | B–N5 | P–KB3 | 26 | N–N4 | P–R4 |
| 12 | B–B4 | N–B3 | 27 | Q–B6† | K–N1 |
| 13 | O–O–O | O–O–O | 28 | N–R6† | K–R2 |
| 14 | P–KN4 | P–KN4 | 29 | N–B5 | Resigns |
| 15 | B–N3 | P–KR4 | | | |

# chapter 19—Pirc Defense

1 P–K4, P–Q3
2 P–Q4, N–KB3
3 N–QB3, P–KN3
4 P–B4, B–N2
5 N–B3, O–O[A]

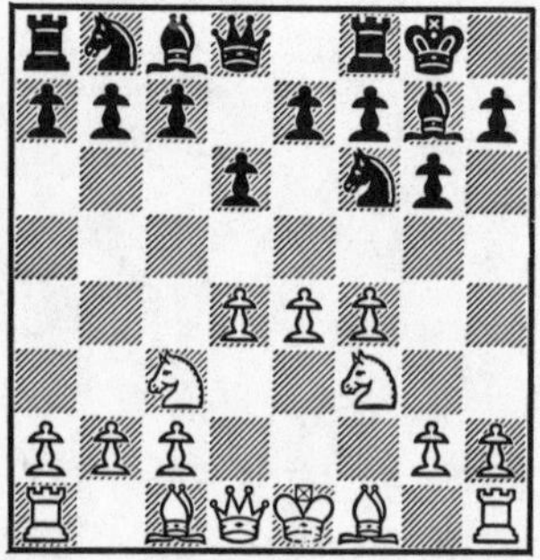

KEY POSITION 1

The Pirc Defense is brought about after 1 P–K4, P–Q3 2 P–Q4, N–KB3 3 N–QB3, when Black fianchettoes his King Bishop with 3 . . . P–KN3. The increased popularity of this debut is directly attributable to the efforts of the Yugoslavian Grandmaster, Vasja Pirc, its most ardent advocate of the past decade. Curiously, at the same time Pirc was introducing the defense in over-the-board play, the Russian analyst Ufimzev was championing its cause in numerous chess journals; hence, its alternate name, the Ufimzev Defense.

Black's strategic aim is to provide free diagonals for both his Bishops. The Pirc Defense resembles the Yugoslav Variation of the King's Indian in its thematic idea: Black intends to strike at the enemy center by means of . . . P–QB4. In some cases, however, Black must forego . . . P–QB4 in favor of . . . P–K4, and there are even times when neither of these moves is executed, and Black operates with . . . P–QB3 and . . . P–QN4.

One striking advantage of the defense is that Black can adjust his center policy to whatever method of development White chooses. Ironically, this is at the same time its most serious drawback, because White has much greater freedom in the center all the way through. As a result, if White plays aggressively, Black must spend so much time opposing White's schemes, he is afforded but little scope to further his own.

Most promising for White is the attacking system 4 P–KB4, B–N2 5 N–B3. This is the line which must be considered as the main variation. Moves other than 4 P–B4 make it easier for Black to achieve equality, although Unzicker's 4 B–KN5 does pose some problems for the second player. Of little promise are both 4 P–B3 and 4 N–B3 which lead to a game with even chances.

---

## part 1—THREE PAWN ATTACK

### OBSERVATIONS ON KEY POSITION 1

[A] 5 . . . P–B4 is dubious because of 6 B–N5†, B–Q2 7 P–K5, N–N5 8 P–K6! (Krogious–Polugayevsky, USSR Championship 1958).

White has obtained maximum control of the center, and for the time being Black must be content to play a waiting game.

In the diagrammed position, White's most usual continuation is 6 B–K2 followed soon by O–O. True, Black can counter by . . . P–QB4, but then QPxBP assures White a secure, if slight, advantage.

Although but limited attention has been paid thus far to 6 B–Q3, it does appear that this line of play is less solid than 6 B–K2. Another option at White's fingertips is 6 P–K5, but this sharp variation actually causes Black no trouble. Black also need not fear 6 B–B4 against which 6 . . . NxP more than equalizes.

IDEA VARIATIONS 1–5:

(1) 6 P–K5, KN–Q2 (6 . . . PxP is safer; see Prac. Var. 1) 7 P–KR4 (an interesting but risky bid for the attack; more prudent is 7 B–B4, for which see Prac. Var. 2), P–QB4 8 P–R5, PxQP 9 QxP, PxKP 10 Q–B2!, PxBP (10 . . . P–K3! to parry Q–R4 is correct; after 11 PxKP, N–QB3 12 PxP, BPxP, White cannot play 13 B–KN5 because of 13 . . . RxN!) 11 PxP, RPxP±, (not 11 . . . BPxP, which fails against 12 B–B4†, K–R1 13 RxP†!, KxR 14 N–N5†, K–R1 15 Q–R4†, B–R3 16 QxB mate) and White has a powerful attack (Bronstein–Palmiotto, Munich 1958; see Game 1).

(2) 6 B–K2, P–B4 7 P–Q5, P–K3 8 PxP, PxP! 9 O–O, N–B3∓ (Trott–Bouwmeester, Beverwijk 1953; see Game 2).

(3) 6 B–K2, P–B4 (O'Kelly has suggested 6 . . . P–B3) 7 PxP, Q–R4 8 O–O (8 PxP?, NxP∓) QxP† 9 K–R1, N–N5? (9 . . . N–B3 is called for; see Prac. Var. 3) 10 N–Q5!, N–B7†? 11 RxN, QxR 12 B–K3±, and Black's Queen is trapped.

(4) 6 B–Q3, QN–Q2 (also playable is 6 . . . B–N5 7 O–O, N–B3; the text was suggested by Bouwmeester, and is probably better than the usual 6 . . . P–B4 [see Prac. Var. 5]) 7 O–O, P–K4! 8 BPxP, PxP 9 PxP, NxP/4! 10 NxN, Q–Q5† 11 K–R1, QxN/4 12 B–KB4, Q–QB4∓.

(5) 6 B–B4, NxP! 7 BxP†, RxB 8 NxN, R–B1 9 O–O, P–KR3 10 N–N3, P–K3∓ (Staute–Vidmar, Jr., Dubrovnik 1950).

*Pirc Defense Game 1*

*WHITE: Bronstein* *BLACK: Palmiotto*

*Munich 1958*

| | WHITE | BLACK | | WHITE | BLACK |
|---|---|---|---|---|---|
| 1 | P–K4 | P–Q3 | 16 | O–O | B–R4 |
| 2 | P–Q4 | N–KB3 | 17 | QR–K1 | P–K4 |
| 3 | N–QB3 | P–KN3 | 18 | B–Q2 | Q–B4† |
| 4 | P–B4 | B–N2 | 19 | B–K3 | Q–B3 |
| 5 | N–B3 | O–O | 20 | B–N5 | Q–B2 |
| 6 | P–K5 | KN–Q2 | 21 | B–K2 | BxB |
| 7 | P–KR4 | P–QB4 | 22 | RxB | KR–B1 |
| 8 | P–R5 | PxQP | 23 | N/3–K4 | K–B1 |
| 9 | QxP | PxKP | 24 | NxN | NxN |
| 10 | Q–B2 | PxBP | 25 | RxN | BxR |
| 11 | PxP | RPxP | 26 | N–R7† | K–K2 |
| 12 | BxP | N–KB3 | 27 | QxB† | K–K1 |
| 13 | Q–R4 | Q–R4 | 28 | R–Q2 | P–R4 |
| 14 | N–KN5 | B–N5 | 29 | Q–N7 | Resigns |
| 15 | B–Q3 | QN–Q2 | | | |

PRACTICAL VARIATIONS 1–5:

1 P–K4, P–Q3 2 P–Q4, N–KB3 3 N–QB3, P–KN3 4 P–B4, B–N2 5 N–B3, O–O

| | *1* | *2* | *3* | *4* | *5* |
|---|---|---|---|---|---|
| *6* | P–K5 | – – | B–K2 | – – | B–Q3 |
| | PxP | KN–Q2 | P–B4 | – – | P–B4 |
| 7 | BPxP[1] | B–B4 | PxP | – – | PxP[11] |
| | N–Q4 | P–QB4 | Q–R4 | PxP | PxP |
| *8* | N–K4[2] | P–K6 | O–O | QxQ | B–K3 |
| | B–B4 | N–N3 | QxP† | RxQ | Q–R4 |
| *9* | N–KN3 | PxBP† | K–R1 | P–K5 | B–Q2 |
| | B–N5 | K–R1 | N–B3 | N–K1[9] | B–N5 |
| *10* | P–QB4 | B–N5![4] | N–Q2![6] | B–K3 | P–K5 |
| | N–N3 | PxP | B–K3[7] | P–N3 | KN–Q2 |
| *11* | B–K3 | NxP | N–N3 | R–Q1! | P–KR3 |
| | P–QB4! | P–K4 | Q–N3 | RxR† | BxN |
| *12* | PxBP | N–B3 | P–KN4[8] | KxR | QxB |
| | N/3–Q2 | N–B3[5] | ± | N–QB3 | N–QB3 |
| *13* | B–K2 | = | | K–B1[10] | P–KR4[12] |
| | N–QB3[3] | | | ± | ± |
| | ∓ | | | | |

*Notes to practical variations 1–5:*

[1] 7 QPxP, QxQ† 8 KxQ, R–Q1† followed by 9 . . . N–Q4 is comfortable for Black, as is 8 NxQ, N–Q4.

[2] Or 8 NxN, QxN 9 B–K2, P–QB4 10 P–B4, Q–K5∓.

[3] Black recovers the Pawn with a good game (Bertok–Sandor, Bratislava 1957).

[4] Stronger than 10 B–K2, PxP 11 NxP, N–B3 12 B–K3, RxP (Horne–Matanovic, Hastings 1953).

[5] Black has just enough counterplay.

[6] Transferring the King Knight to QN3 brings about a favorable transposition into the Sicilian Defense.

[7] 10 . . . N–Q5 11 N–N3, NxN 12 RPxN, P–QN4? 13 P–K5!, PxP 14 PxP, QxP 15 B–KB4, and White wins the exchange. In this line 12 . . . B–Q2 is better, but White still maintains a strong initiative. For 10 . . . P–QR4 11 N–N3, Q–N3 12 P–QR4, N–QN5 (probably Black's best), see Game 3. In this game, White miscalculated with 13 P–N4. Correct is 13 P–B5 with a very sharp game and obscure complications.

[8] White has an attacking position of considerable promise: e.g., 12 . . . QR–B1 13 P–B5, BxN 14 RPxB, N–QN5 15 B–QB4, Q–B3 16 Q–B3, NxBP 17 P–N5, NxR 18 PxN, KPxP 19 PxP, RPxP 20 R–KN1, P–N4 21 BxP! (Estrin–Zugovitszky, Semi-finals, USSR Championship 1958).

[9] 9 . . . N–Q4 10 NxN, RxN 11 B–B4, R–Q1 12 B–K3, P–N3 13 N–N5 also favors White (De Moura–Matanovic, Bad Pyrmont 1951).

[10] The end game favors White thanks to his superiority in space (Boleslavski–Pirc, Helsinki 1952).

[11] 7 P–Q5, P–K3 8 PxP, PxP is satisfactory for Black, but 8 . . . BxP leads to a clear advantage for White after 9 P–B5!, B–B1 10 O–O, N–B3 11 K–R1, N–KN5 12 N–Q5 (Matanovic–Vidmar, Jr., Yugoslavian Championship 1951).

[12] Spasski–Gadia, Mar del Plata 1960. If 13 . . . P–KR4, then 14 P–K6!

## *Pirc Defense Game 2*

*WHITE: Trott* *BLACK: Bouwmeester*

*Hoogoven 1953*

| | WHITE | BLACK | | WHITE | BLACK | | WHITE | BLACK |
|---|---|---|---|---|---|---|---|---|
| 1 | P–K4 | P–Q3 | 15 | B–K3 | P–N5 | 29 | N–R2 | K–R2 |
| 2 | P–Q4 | N–KB3 | 16 | Q–B2 | PxP | 30 | N–N4 | Q–K3 |
| 3 | N–QB3 | P–KN3 | 17 | PxP | R–N1 | 31 | R–Q2 | P–Q4 |
| 4 | P–B4 | B–N2 | 18 | QR–Q1 | B–QR3 | 32 | BxBP | PxP |
| 5 | N–B3 | O–O | 19 | Q–R4 | B–N4 | 33 | N/4xB | NxN |
| 6 | B–K2 | P–B4 | 20 | Q–R3 | P–K4 | 34 | NxN | R–B1 |
| 7 | P–Q5 | P–K3 | 21 | P–B5 | B–KR3 | 35 | BxR | QxB† |
| 8 | PxP | PxP | 22 | Q–B1 | B–B5 | 36 | K–R1 | KxN |
| 9 | O–O | N–B3 | 23 | PxP | PxP | 37 | R/1–Q1 | B–Q6 |
| 10 | P–KR3 | N–KR4 | 24 | P–KR4 | R–N3 | 38 | R–N2 | Q–KB3 |
| 11 | N–KN5 | N–N6 | 25 | N–N3 | N–Q1 | 39 | Q–K3 | KxP? |
| 12 | R–K1 | NxB† | 26 | P–R5 | N–B2 | 40 | Q–R3† | Resigns |
| 13 | NxN | P–QN4 | 27 | N–B3 | P–N4 | | | |
| 14 | P–QB3 | Q–K2 | 28 | N–B5 | Q–B3 | | | |

*Pirc Defense Game 3*

*WHITE: Fischer* — *BLACK: Korchnoi*

*Curacao 1962*

| | WHITE | BLACK | | WHITE | BLACK |
|---|---|---|---|---|---|
| 1 | P–K4 | P–Q3 | 18 | P–B5 | Q–B5 |
| 2 | P–Q4 | N–KB3 | 19 | Q–B3 | QxRP |
| 3 | N–QB3 | P–KN3 | 20 | N–B7 | QR–K1! |
| 4 | P–B4 | B–N2 | 21 | N–Q5 | QxN |
| 5 | N–B3 | O–O | 22 | B–N5 | QxP |
| 6 | B–K2 | P–B4 | 23 | BxP | B–K4! |
| 7 | PxP | Q–R4 | 24 | R–B2 | Q–B8† |
| 8 | O–O | QxP† | 25 | R–B1 | Q–R3! |
| 9 | K–R1 | N–B3 | 26 | P–R3 | PxP! |
| 10 | N–Q2 | P–QR4! | 27 | BxR | RxB |
| 11 | N–N3 | Q–N3 | 28 | N–K7† | K–R1 |
| 12 | P–QR4 | N–QN5 | 29 | NxP | Q–K3! |
| 13 | P–KN4? | BxP! | 30 | R–KN1 | P–R5 |
| 14 | BxB | NxB | 31 | R–N4 | Q–N6 |
| 15 | QxN | NxP | 32 | Q–B1 | P–R6 |
| 16 | N–N5 | NxR | 33 | R–N3 | QxR |
| 17 | NxN | Q–B3 | | Resigns | |

SUPPLEMENTARY VARIATIONS 1–5:

1 P–K4, P–Q3 2 P–Q4, N–KB3 3 N–QB3, P–KN3

| | *1* | *2* | *3* | *4* | *5* |
|---|---|---|---|---|---|
| *4* | N–KB3 | – – | – – | P–KB3 | B–KN5[13] |
| | B–KN2 | – – | – – | P–B3 | P–KR3[14] |
| *5* | B–K2 | B–QB4 | P–KR3 | B–K3 | B–R4 |
| | O–O | P–B3 | O–O | Q–N3[11] | B–KN2 |
| *6* | O–O[1] | O–O[4] | B–K3 | Q–B1 | B–K2[15] |
| | B–N5![2] | P–Q4 | QN–Q2[7] | B–KN2 | P–B4 |
| *7* | B–K3 | B–Q3 | Q–Q2 | KN–K2 | P–K5 |
| | KN–Q2 | B–N5 | P–QB4 | O–O | N–R4[16] |
| *8* | Q–Q2 | B–K3[5] | PxP[8] | N–B4 | PxBP |
| | N–QB3 | PxP | NxP | Q–R4 | N–B5 |
| *9* | P–Q5 | NxP | P–K5 | B–K2 | B–N3 |
| | BxN | NxN | N/3–K5 | P–K4 | PxKP |
| *10* | BxB | BxN | NxN | PxP | QxQ† |
| | N–K4 | N–Q2 | NxN | PxP | KxQ |
| *11* | B–K2 | P–KR3 | Q–Q5 | N–Q3 | O–O–O† |
| | N–N3 | N–KB3! | N–B4 | QN–Q2 | B–Q2 |
| *12* | P–QN3 | B–Q3 | P–B3[9] | O–O | B–B3 |
| | P–QB3 | BxN | B–K3 | R–K1 | N–B3 |
| *13* | P–KB4 | QxB | Q–Q1 | P–QR4 | BxN/5 |
| | N/3–Q2[3] | N–Q4[6] | R–B1[10] | N–B1[12] | PxB[17] |
| | = | = | = | = | = |

*Notes to supplementary variations 1–5:*

[1] White's line is too tame.

[2] But 6 . . . P–QR3 7 B–KB4, P–QN4 8 P–K5, KN–Q2 9 P–QR4!, PxRP 10 R–K1 favors White (Najdorf–Stahlberg, Amsterdam 1950).

[3] Cueller–Robatsch, Moscow 1956.

[4] 6 P–K5 is met by 6 . . . N–Q4!, e.g., 7 BxN, PxB 8 NxP, Q–R4† 9 N–B3, PxP.

[5] 8 P–K5, KN–Q2 leaves White's center open to attack by . . . P–QB4; see Game 4.

[6] Lundquist–O'Kelly, Third World Postal Championship 1958-60.

[7] For 6 . . . P–B3, see Game 5.

[8] Or 8 B–R6, PxP 9 NxP, N–B4 10 BxB, KxB 11 B–Q3, P–K4 12 N–N3, NxN 13 RPxN, P–Q4 with equality (Eliskases–Pirc, Mar del Plata 1950).

[9] 12 BxN is bad because of 12 . . . B–K3; e.g., 13 QxNP, PxB, and White is threatened by . . . Q–R4† followed by . . . KR–N1. Black's lead in development is too great.

[10] On 14 PxP (Toran–Pirc, Munich 1954), 14 . . . QxP! gives equality.

[11] 5 . . . QN–Q2 6 Q–Q2, Q–R4 7 B–QB4, N–N3 8 B–N3, B–K3 leads to a comfortable game for Black. Stronger, however, is 7 KN–K2 followed by N–QB1–N3.

[12] Lipnitzky–Bronstein, USSR Championship 1951.

[13] Unzicker's recommendation.

[14] After 4 . . . B–N2, White can continue along lines similar to this column with 5 B–K2, or else try 5 P–B4 with the following possibilities:

1) 5 . . . O–O 6 P–K5, N–K1 7 N–B3, N–Q2 8 B–QB4, N–N3 9 B–N3, P–Q4 10 O–O± (Unzicker–Pirc, Opatija 1953).

2) 5 . . . P–B4 6 P–K5!, PxQP? 7 PxN, PxP 8 QxP, Q–K2†, and now not 9 K–B2?, N–B3 10 B–N5, O–O 11 BxN, BPxB 12 Q–K4, Q–Q1! 13 B–R4, Q–N3† 14 K–B3, B–N5† as Black wins (Payne–Van Deene, *Chess Review* Postal Tournament 1958), but simply 9 QN–K2! enabling White to maintain his extra piece (9 . . . N–B3 10 Q–B3).

3) 5 . . . P–KR3! 6 B–R4, P–B4! See note 15.

[15] White has two inferior alternatives: 6 P–K5 is premature because of 6 . . . PxP 7 PxP, N–N5!, e.g., 8 QxQ†, KxQ 9 O–O–O†, B–Q2 10 P–B4, P–KN4∓, while 6 P–B4 is effectively met by 6 . . . P–B4; e.g., 7 P–K5!?, N–R4! 8 N–Q5, PxQP 9 B–N5†, B–Q2 10 BxP, Q–R4† 11 P–N4, QxB 12 N–B7†, KxB 13 NxQ, BxN∓ (Minev–Kratkowsky, Bulgarian Championship 1956).

[16] Provoking 8 BxN which is met by 8 . . . PxQP!, whereupon 9 BxNP, PxN and 9 N–Q5, Q–R4† favor Black.

[17] After 14 KN–K2, P–KR4, Black achieves a tenuous equality (Unzicker–Botvinnik, Alekhine Memorial Tournament 1956).

*Pirc Defense Game 4*

*WHITE: Van Scheltinga* *BLACK: Botvinnik*

*Wageningen 1958*

| | WHITE | BLACK | | WHITE | BLACK | | WHITE | BLACK |
|---|---|---|---|---|---|---|---|---|
| 1 | P–Q4 | P–KN3 | 12 | P–B3 | N–QB3 | 23 | BxB | QxB |
| 2 | P–K4 | B–N2 | 13 | B–K3? | BxP! | 24 | Q–Q4 | QxQ |
| 3 | N–KB3 | P–Q3 | 14 | PxP | B–N2 | 25 | PxQ | QR–N1 |
| 4 | B–B4 | P–QB3 | 15 | Q–N3 | O–O | 26 | P–QN3 | R–N5 |
| 5 | O–O | N–B3 | 16 | P–KB4 | Q–K2 | 27 | BxN | QPxB |
| 6 | N–B3 | P–Q4 | 17 | Q–B2 | P–B4 | 28 | KR–Q1 | R–Q1 |
| 7 | B–Q3 | B–N5 | 18 | N–Q4 | N–B3 | 29 | P–Q5 | PxP |
| 8 | P–K5 | KN–Q2 | 19 | NxN | PxN | 30 | P–B6 | P–Q5 |
| 9 | P–KR3 | BxN | 20 | B–Q4 | N–K5 | 31 | QR–B1 | P–Q6 |
| 10 | QxB | P–K3 | 21 | Q–K3 | P–K4 | 32 | R–B5 | R/5–Q5 |
| 11 | N–K2 | P–QB4 | 22 | PxP | BxP | | Resigns | |

*Pirc Defense Game 5*

*WHITE: Prins* *BLACK: Kramer*

*Beverwijk 1954*

| | WHITE | BLACK | | WHITE | BLACK | | WHITE | BLACK |
|---|---|---|---|---|---|---|---|---|
| 1 | N–KB3 | N–KB3 | 12 | PxP | PxP | 23 | RxR | R–Q1 |
| 2 | P–Q4 | P–KN3 | 13 | N–R2! | P–N5 | 24 | R–R1 | R–Q5 |
| 3 | N–B3 | B–N2 | 14 | N–N1 | N–B4 | 25 | PxP | RxB |
| 4 | P–K4 | P–Q3 | 15 | Q–K3 | B–K3 | 26 | PxRP† | NxP |
| 5 | P–KR3 | O–O | 16 | N–N4! | BxN | 27 | QxN† | K–B1 |
| 6 | B–K3 | P–B3 | 17 | PxB | NxNP | 28 | Q–R8† | K–K2 |
| 7 | Q–Q2 | Q–R4 | 18 | Q–N5 | N–B3 | 29 | QxP† | K–Q2 |
| 8 | B–KR6 | P–K4 | 19 | P–KB4 | KR–K1; | 30 | R–Q1† | K–B1 |
| 9 | O–O–O | P–QN4 | 20 | Q–R6† | K–N1 | 31 | Q–K8† | K–N2 |
| 10 | BxB | KxB | 21 | P–B5 | QR–Q1! | 32 | QxKBP† | Resigns |
| 11 | B–Q3 | QN–Q2 | 22 | B–B4! | RxR† | | | |

*Pirc Defense (by transposition) Game 6*

US Championship 1963-4

*WHITE: Fischer* *BLACK: Benko*

| | WHITE | BLACK | | WHITE | BLACK | | WHITE | BLACK |
|---|---|---|---|---|---|---|---|---|
| 1 | P–K4 | P–KN3 | 8 | QxB | N–B3 | 15 | Q–N3 | K–R1 |
| 2 | P–Q4 | B–N2 | 9 | B–K3 | P–K4 | 16 | Q–N4 | P–QB3 |
| 3 | N–QB3 | P–Q3 | 10 | QPxP | PxP | 17 | Q–R5 | Q–K1 |
| 4 | P–B4 | N–KB3 | 11 | P–B5 | PxP? | 18 | BxN | PxB |
| 5 | N–B3 | O–O | 12 | QxP | N–Q5 | 19 | R–B6! | K–N1 |
| 6 | B–Q3 | B–N5 | 13 | Q–B2 | N–K1 | 20 | P–K5 | P–KR3 |
| 7 | P–KR3 | BxN | 14 | O–O | N–Q3 | 21 | N–K2 | Resigns |

# chapter 20—Sicilian Defense

The Sicilian Defense has been the subject of uninterrupted acclaim since its introduction by Polerio in 1594. As it is rich in complications and gives rise to involved positions without much chance for early simplification, its continued popularity is not surprising.

The initial moves for both sides determine the character of the coming struggle. Unless White abandons his chance for the initiative, he must play P–Q4; and after Black replies . . . PxP, an asymmetrical position results. Black has the half-open Queen Bishop file; White, the half-open Queen file. White's superiority in terrain is balanced by Black's center Pawn majority. Strategically, White must play for a Kingside attack; Black, for Queenside counterplay, possibly aiming at a favorable endgame. 1 . . . P–QB4 is a dynamic defense with new patterns of procedure evolving almost daily. The Herculean task of passing final judgment on the seemingly inexhaustible complexities of this debut belongs to the distant future.

---

## part 1—CLASSICAL DRAGON

### OBSERVATIONS ON KEY POSITION 1

[A] According to theory 5 . . . P–KN3 is weak because of 6 NxN, QPxN (6 . . . NPxN 7 P–K5) 7 QxQ†, but in the 21st game of the 1958 Smyslov–Botvinnik match, Black achieved clear equality after 7 . . . KxQ 8 B–QB4, K–K1 9 P–QR4, P–K4 10 P–B4, B–K3! 11 BxB, PxB 12 R–B1, B–R3. White has a better chance for gaining the initiative by 8 B–KB4 followed by O–O–O.

[B] In Spielmann–Alekhine, Margate 1938, Black gained equality as follows: 9 . . . P–QR4 10 P–QR4, B–K3 11 N–Q4, P–Q4! 12 PxP, BxP 13 NxB, NxN/4 14 NxN, PxN 15 B–Q4, P–K4. An improvement for White in this line seems to be 12 NxB!, PxN 13 PxP, PxP 14 N–N5 followed by 15 P–QB3 and possibly Q–N3.

In this position the action centers on Black's struggle to free his game by means of . . . P–Q4. White's 10 P–B4 is played with the intention of meeting 10 . . . P–Q4? by 11 P–B5. Accordingly, Black must now make a crucial choice between the two systems at his disposal:

1 P–K4, P–QB4
2 N–KB3, N–QB3
3 P–Q4, PxP
4 NxP, N–B3
5 N–QB3, P–Q3[A]
6 B–K2, P–KN3
7 B–K3, B–N2
8 O–O, O–O
9 N–N3, B–K3[B]
10 P–B4

KEY POSITION 1

10 . . . N–QR4 (Maroczy) and 10 . . . Q–B1 (Tartakover). The latter system definitely offers Black his sharpest counterchances. 10 . . . Q–B1 serves a dual purpose; it prevents 11 P–B5 and clears Q1 for the use of Black's King Rook. Black can then operate with the disconcerting threat of . . . P–Q4.

IDEA VARIATIONS 1–3:

(1) 10 . . . P–Q4? 11 P–B5!, PxBP 12 PxBP, B–B1 13 P–N4 and White is for choice. In this line 11 . . . B–B1 costs Black a Pawn, e.g., 12 PxQP, N–QN5 13 PxP, RPxP 14 B–B3, B–B4 15 N–Q4!

(2) 10 . . . N–QR4 11 NxN, QxN 12 B–B3, B–B5 13 R–K1, KR–Q1 14 Q–Q2, Q–B2 15 QR–B1, P–K4! 16 P–QN3, P–Q4! with complications favoring Black (Rouzer–Botvinnik, Leningrad 1939). After 17 PxQP there followed 17 . . . P–K5! 18 PxB, PxB 19 P–QB5, Q–R4 20 KR–Q1 (20 Q–Q3!), N–N5! 21 B–Q4, P–B7† 22 K–B1, Q–R3† 23 Q–K2, BxB 24 RxB, Q–KB3! and Black soon won.

(3) 10 . . . N–QR4 11 P–B5, B–B5 12 B–Q3, P–Q4? 13 P–K5, N–K1 14 P–B6, PxP 15 B–B5 and White wins the exchange (Ragosin–Taimanov, Leningrad 1945). This was the interesting follow-up: 15 . . . PxP 16 BxR, BxB 17 NxN, QxN 18 BxB, PxB 19 Q–B3, N–Q3 20 QR–Q1, Q–N3† 21 K–R1, QxP 22 RxN!, BxR 23 N–K4!, B–B1 24 QxP†, K–R1 25 N–B6!, B–N2 26 N–K8! and Black resigned.

12 . . . P–Q4? is premature. For the correct procedure against 12 B–Q3, see Prac. Var. 1.

PRACTICAL VARIATIONS 1–5:

1 P–K4, P–QB4 2 N–KB3, N–QB3 3 P–Q4, PxP 4 NxP, N–B3 5 N–QB3, P–Q3 6 B–K2, P–KN3 7 B–K3, B–N2 8 O–O, O–O 9 N–N3, B–K3 10 P–B4

| | *1* | *2* | *3* | *4* | *5* |
|---|---|---|---|---|---|
| *10* | – – | – – | – – | – – | – – |
| | N–QR4 | – – | Q–B1 | – – | – – |
| *11* | P–B5 | – – | P–KR3[8] | – – | Q–K1 |
| | B–B5 | – – | R–Q1 | P–QR4 | P–QR4[19] |
| *12* | B–Q3 | NxN[3] | B–B3[9] | N–Q4[15] | P–QR4 |
| | BxB | BxB | B–B5[10] | NxN | N–QN5 |
| *13* | PxB | QxB | R–K1[11] | BxN | N–Q4 |
| | NxN | QxN | P–QR4[12] | B–B5 | B–B5 |

| | 1 | 2 | 3 | 4 | 5 |
|---|---|---|---|---|---|
| 14 | PxN | P–KN4[4] | N–Q5[13] | B–Q3 | P–B5 |
| | P–Q4 | N–Q2[5] | NxN | P–K4 | N–Q2[20] |
| 15 | B–Q4 | N–Q5 | PxN | PxP[16] | ± |
| | PxKP | QR–K1[6] | N–N5 | PxP | |
| 16 | PxKP | P–N5 | P–R3 | B–K3[17] | |
| | P–QR3[1] | P–K3 | BxN![14] | Q–B3[18] | |
| 17 | P–K5 | N–K7†![7] | = | = | |
| | N–K1 | = | | | |
| 18 | P–QN4 | | | | |
| | N–B2[2] | | | | |
| | = | | | | |

*Notes to practical variations 1–5:*

[1] According to Spielmann 16 . . . Q–B2 17 P–K5, QR–Q1 18 PxN, BxP (Spielmann–Petrov, Riga 1934) is questionable for Black, e.g., 19 R–R4!, P–QN4 20 NxP, Q–Q2 21 Q–K2, P–QR3 22 BxB, PxN 23 BxP, PxR 24 BxKR, KxB and Black is minus a Pawn without compensation.

[2] 19 P–B6, PxP 20 PxP, B–R3 21 B–N6, Q–B1! with a difficult but tenable position for Black.

[3] An immediate 12 P–N4 also comes into consideration, e.g., 12 . . . N–Q2 13 NxN, BxB 14 QxB, QxN 15 N–Q5, KR–K1 16 Q–B2, N–K4 17 PxP, RPxP 18 B–Q4± (Milner-Barry–Foltys, Buenos Aires 1939). In this line 12 . . . R–B1 is worth a try, e.g., 13 BxP, BxB 14 QxB, N–B5!

[4] Milner-Barry's aggressive innovation, introduced in his game against Capablanca at Margate 1939.

[5] Inferior is 14 . . . Q–N5 15 P–N5, N–Q2 16 P–QR3!, QxNP 17 N–Q5, QR–K1 18 QR–N1, Q–K4 19 R–N4! with the powerful threat of 20 B–B4. In this variation 15 . . . NxP is answered by 16 N–Q5. If 18 . . . QxRP, then either 19 P–B6! or 19 RxP gives White an edge.

14 . . . P–KR3 also favors White, e.g., 15 K–R1!, QR–B1 16 P–N5, PxP 17 BxNP, KR–K1 18 Q–N2!, N–R2 19 PxP, PxP 20 N–Q5. Worth investigating, however, is 14 . . . QR–B1. Pachman suggests the following continuation: 15 P–N5, N–Q2 16 N–Q5, KR–K1 17 Q–B2, N–K4 and Black has good defensive chances.

[6] 15 . . . P–K3 is met by 16 N–K7†!, K–R1 17 P–N5, KPxP 18 PxP, BxP 19 R–N1, Q–K4 20 RxB, QxR 21 R–Q1, N–K4 22 B–Q4, Q–N5 23 PxP with a strong attack (Ilyin–Genevsky–Wolk, Leningrad 1940).

[7] 17 . . . RxN 18 P–B6, R/2–K1 19 PxB, KxP 20 QR–Q1 with full compensation for the sacrificed Pawn. Unsatisfactory for White is 17 N–B6†, NxN 18 PxN, BxP 19 B–R6, KPxP! 20 BxR, RxP 21 Q–B3, KxB 22 P–B3, Q–K4 (Nazarov–Ajuarvlev, USSR 1951).

[8] Played to prevent a later . . . N–KN5 or . . . B–KN5, but somewhat artificial and even unnecessary. 11 K–R1 was tested in Alekhine–Golombek, Montevideo 1939. There followed: 11 . . . P–QR4 12 P–QR4, N–KN5? 13 B–N1, R–Q1? 14 N–Q5!±. 12 . . . N–QN5! was correct.

*continued* ▶

[9] Or 12 N–Q4, NxN 13 BxN, B–B5 14 P–B5!, P–Q4! 15 P–K5, N–K5 16 P–B6, PxP 17 PxP= (Geller–Lipnitzky, USSR 1951). Weak is 12 K–R2?, P–Q4 13 P–K5, N–K5 14 N–N5, P–N4!∓ (A. Thomas–Flohr, Bournemouth 1939).

[10] After 12 . . . P–Q4 13 P–K5!, N–K5 14 N–K2! White stands well.

[11] Better is 13 R–B2, e.g., 13 . . . P–Q4 14 PxP, NxP 15 NxN, BxN 16 BxB, P–K3 17 R–Q2!, RxB 18 RxR, PxR 19 P–B3! with a slight positional advantage. 14 P–K5 is met by 14 . . . BxN! and if 15 RPxB, then 15 . . . P–Q5! etc. Black's best answer to 13 R–B2 is probably 13 . . . P–K4! with about equal chances.

[12] 13 . . . P–Q4 can be played in this position. Compare note 11.

[13] This favors White, but 14 N–R4 also deserves investigation.

[14] 17 PxN and now 17 . . . QxP! is most precise. See Game 1 for 17 . . . BxBP.

[15] Inferior for White is 12 N–Q5?, BxN 13 PxB, N–QN5 14 P–B4, P–R5 15 N–Q4, P–R6! Equally ineffective is 12 N–R4 because of 12 . . . BxN 13 RPxB and now not 13 . . . NxP? 14 N–N6, Q–K3 15 B–B4! (15 NxR?, N–N6!), but 13 . . . Q–K3! 12 P–QR4, N–QN5 13 N–Q4, B–B5 leads to an equal game.

[16] After 15 B–K3, PxP 16 BxP, P–Q4! the position is also equal. (Cortlever–Silva Rocha and O'Hanlon–Cortlever, Buenos Aires 1939).

[17] 15 BxP?, Q–B4† 16 K–R1, BxB costs White the exchange.

[18] 17 B–N5, N–R4= (Alexander–Euwe, The Hague 1939).

[19] For the inferior alternatives 11 . . . N–KN5 and 11 . . . R–Q1, see Games 2 and 3.

[20] White's advantage is minimal.

## *Sicilian Game 1*

*WHITE: Cortlever* *BLACK: Euwe*

*Leiden 1946*

| | WHITE | BLACK | | WHITE | BLACK | | WHITE | BLACK |
|---|---|---|---|---|---|---|---|---|
| 1 | P–K4 | P–QB4 | 14 | N–Q5 | NxN | 27 | P–B5 | Q–R4 |
| 2 | N–KB3 | N–QB3 | 15 | PxN | N–N5 | 28 | QxQ | RxQ |
| 3 | P–Q4 | PxP | 16 | P–R3 | BxN | 29 | B–N6 | R/1–R1 |
| 4 | NxP | N–B3 | 17 | PxN | BxBP | 30 | BxR | RxB |
| 5 | N–QB3 | P–Q3 | 18 | Q–Q2 | BxP | 31 | PxP | RPxP |
| 6 | B–K2 | P–KN3 | 19 | QR–B1 | B–B6 | 32 | B–B2 | P–R6 |
| 7 | O–O | B–N2 | 20 | QxB/2 | BxR | 33 | R–R1 | P–QN4 |
| 8 | B–K3 | O–O | 21 | Q–N3 | P–R5 | 34 | B–N3 | P–N5 |
| 9 | N–N3 | B–K3 | 22 | Q–R3 | BxP | 35 | K–B2 | R–B4 |
| 10 | P–B4 | Q–B1 | 23 | QxB | Q–KB4 | 36 | K–K1 | R–B6 |
| 11 | P–KR3 | R–Q1 | 24 | R–R1 | Q–B7 | | Resigns | |
| 12 | B–B3 | B–B5 | 25 | B–K4 | Q–K7 | | | |
| 13 | R–K1 | P–QR4 | 26 | R–K1 | Q–R3 | | | |

*Sicilian Game 2*

*WHITE: Ragosin* *BLACK: Veresov*

*USSR Championship 1945*

| | WHITE | BLACK | | WHITE | BLACK |
|---|---|---|---|---|---|
| 1 | P–K4 | P–QB4 | 19 | P–B3 | KR–K1? |
| 2 | N–KB3 | N–QB3 | 20 | R–N4 | P–N4 |
| 3 | P–Q4 | PxP | 21 | N–Q4 | NxN |
| 4 | NxP | N–KB3 | 22 | BxN | R–B5 |
| 5 | N–QB3 | P–Q3 | 23 | BxB | KxB |
| 6 | B–K2 | P–KN3 | 24 | RxB† | BPxR |
| 7 | O–O | B–N2 | 25 | R–B7† | KxR |
| 8 | B–K3 | O–O | 26 | QxRP† | K–K3 |
| 9 | N–N3 | B–K3 | 27 | QxNP† | K–K4 |
| 10 | P–B4 | Q–B1 | 28 | Q–N7† | KxP |
| 11 | Q–K1 | N–KN5 | 29 | N–B6† | PxN |
| 12 | BxN | BxB | 30 | QxQ | R–K4 |
| 13 | P–B5! | PxP | 31 | QxQP | K–B4 |
| 14 | P–KR3 | P–B5 | 32 | Q–Q7† | K–N3 |
| 15 | RxP | B–R4 | 33 | QxRP† | R–K7 |
| 16 | N–Q5 | Q–Q2 | 34 | Q–R3 | R–B5 |
| 17 | Q–R4 | B–N3 | 35 | Q–Q6 | Resigns |
| 18 | QR–KB1 | QR–B1 | | | |

*Sicilian Game 3*

*WHITE: Bergquist* *BLACK: Nilsson*

*Stockholm 1950*

| | WHITE | BLACK | | WHITE | BLACK |
|---|---|---|---|---|---|
| 1 | P–K4 | P–QB4 | 14 | P–QR3 | BxB |
| 2 | N–KB3 | N–QB3 | 15 | QxB | N–B3 |
| 3 | P–Q4 | PxP | 16 | NxN | QxN? |
| 4 | NxP | N–KB3 | 17 | N–Q5 | R–Q2 |
| 5 | N–QB3 | P–Q3 | 18 | B–Q4 | N–K1? |
| 6 | B–K2 | P–KN3 | 19 | BxB | NxB |
| 7 | O–O | B–N2 | 20 | P–B5! | N–K1 |
| 8 | B–K3 | O–O | 21 | Q–B3 | N–B3 |
| 9 | N–N3 | B–K3 | 22 | PxP | RPxP |
| 10 | P–B4 | Q–B1 | 23 | P–K5! | NxN |
| 11 | Q–K1 | R–Q1 | 24 | QxP† | K–R1 |
| 12 | R–Q1 | N–QN5 | 25 | R–B3 | Resigns |
| 13 | N–Q4 | B–B5 | | | |

SUPPLEMENTARY VARIATIONS 1–5:

1 P–K4, P–QB4 2 N–KB3, N–QB3 3 P–Q4, PxP 4 NxP, N–B3 5 N–QB3, P–Q3 6 B–K2, P–KN3

In the main line of the Dragon (Part 1) White develops his game with B–K3, O–O, and N–N3. The variations treated in this supplementary section possess one common feature: White omits one of these three moves.

In Sup. Var. 1 Black obtains excellent counterplay along the QN3–KN8 diagonal, illustrating the prematurity of 9 P–B4.

In Sup. Var. 2 White allows the exchange of his King Bishop by means of 9 . . . N–KN5, but maintains superiority in space with some attacking chances. This system is quite popular nowadays.

Sup. Var. 3 is the famous Nottingham Variation (Alekhine–Botvinnik, 1936); White plays B–K3 and N–N3 but postpones castling in order to begin a Pawn-storming demonstration with P–KN4.

In Sup. Var. 4 White plays N–N3, postponing B–K3, but preparing P–KB4 by means of K–R1. This line was also favored by Alekhine.

In Sup. Var. 5 White supports his King Pawn with P–KB3, preparing to play N–Q5. This positional variation was introduced by Euwe.

| | 1 | 2 | 3 | 4 | 5 |
|---|---|---|---|---|---|
| 7 | B–K3 | – – | – – | O–O | – – |
| | B–N2 | – – | – – | B–N2 | – – |
| 8 | O–O | – – | N–N3 | N–N3 | – – |
| | O–O | – – | O–O | O–O [17] | – – |
| 9 | P–B4 | Q–Q2[6] | P–B4 | K–R1[18] | P–B3 |
| | Q–N3![1] | N–KN5[7] | B–K3[12] | B–K3[19] | B–K3 |
| 10 | Q–Q3[2] | BxN | P–N4 | P–B4 | N–Q5[21] |
| | N–KN5![3] | BxB | P–Q4 | N–QR4 | ± |
| 11 | N–Q5 | P–B4[8] | P–B5 | B–B3 | |
| | BxN! | B–Q2[9] | B–B1 | B–B5 | |
| 12 | BxN![4] | QR–Q1 | PxQP[13] | R–KN1[20] | |
| | BxB† | R–B1 | N–QN5[14] | ± | |
| 13 | QxB | N–Q5[10] | P–Q6[15] | | |
| | QxQ† | NxN | QxP | | |
| 14 | NxQ | BxN | B–B5 | | |
| | BxB | BxB | Q–B5! | | |
| 15 | NxB[5] | QxB | R–KB1 | | |
| | = | RxP[11] | QxRP[16] | | |
| | | = | = | | |

*Notes to supplementary variations 1–5:*

[1] After 9 . . . N–KN5? 10 BxN, BxN 11 B/3xB, BxB 12 Q–Q2 White has an excellent game; 13 P–B5 is a threat (Lasker–Golmayo, Match 1893). If 9 . . . P–Q4?, then 10 P–K5!±.

[2] 10 N–R4 invites a draw by repetition, e.g., 10 . . . Q–Q1 or 10 . . . Q–R4 11 N–QB3 and Black's best is again 11 . . . Q–N3. For 10 P–K5!?, see Game 4.

[3] 10 . . . QxP? 11 QR–N1, Q–R6 12 NxN, PxN 13 N–Q5!, QxQ 14 NxP†, K–R1 15 PxQ±.

[4] 12 NxQ, BxB† 13 K–R1, BxQ 14 BxN, BxB favors Black. White cannot profit from the awkward position of Black's Queen Bishop, e.g., 15 P–B5, B–KR4 16 QR–K1, N–K4 17 Q–KR3, P–B3 18 Q–R4, B–N5! (Horowitz–Reshevsky, New York 1951). Equally good for Black in this line is 15 . . . PxP 16 PxP, N–K4.

[5] The ending offers equal chances.

[6] If 9 K–R1 or 9 P–KR3, Black frees his game with 9 . . . P–Q4!, e.g., 10 PxP, NxP 11 N/3xN, QxN 12 B–B3, Q–QR4! 13 NxN, PxN 14 BxBP, R–N1 and Black has sufficient compensation for his sacrificed Pawn.

[7] 9 . . . P–Q4 is inferior here, e.g., 10 PxP, NxP 11 N/4xN, PxN 12 QR–Q1, B–B4 13 NxN, and after either 13 . . . QxN or 13 . . . PxN, then 14 P–QB4!±. Also good for White is 10 NxN, PxN 11 P–K5.

[8] Interesting is 11 N–Q5, R–B1 12 P–QB4!, NxN 13 BxN, RxP 14 BxB, KxB 15 N–K3!, RxP 16 P–B3± (Kok–Spanjaard, Utrecht 1948). Better for Black is 11 . . . B–Q2 12 QR–Q1, R–B1 13 P–KB4 transposing into the column. If White tries for more with 12 P–QB4, Black achieves active counterplay with 12 . . . N–K4 13 P–QN3, P–K3.

[9] The alternative 11 . . . NxN merits serious consideration, e.g.; 12 BxN, P–K4! 13 B–K3, PxP 14 RxP, B–K3 15 R–B2, B–K4 16 B–Q4, Q–K2 17 R–Q1, KR–Q1= (Matanovic–Trifunovic, Yugoslavia 1952). Or in the line 14 BxBP, Q–N3† 15 K–R1, QxP 16 N–Q5. White has attacking chances for the Pawn.

[10] 13 P–B5!? is sharper (see Game 5). 13 R–B2 (protecting the QBP) is a conservative try which deserves investigation.

[11] 16 P–B5, B–B3 17 N–K3, R–K7! 18 N–N4, P–KR4 19 N–R6†, K–R2 20 NxP!, Q–N3! (Richter–Petrov, Hamburg 1938). Black has sufficient counterplay.

[12] Allowing White a powerful Kingside assault. More forceful is 9 . . . P–QR4!, e.g., 10 P–QR4, B–K3 11 B–B3, N–QN5 12 O–O, N–Q2 13 N–Q4, B–B5 14 R–B2, P–K4! and Black has no problems (Bronstein–Korchnoi, Spartakiade 1959). In this variation 11 N–Q4 is met by 11 . . . Q–N3! 12 NxB, QxB 13 NxR, N–KN5!

[13] After 12 PxNP, RPxP 13 PxP, N–QN5 14 B–B3, BxP 15 BxB, NxB 16 QxN, NxP† 17 K–B2!, NxR 18 RxN, Black obtains counterchances with 18 . . . R–B1! 19 B–Q4, R–B5 followed by . . . P–QN4–5 (not, however, 18 . . . BxN 19 PxB, QxP 20 B–Q4!±).

[14] White must now react vigorously to maintain the initiative.

continued ▸

[15] 13 B–B3! is more promising, e.g., 13 . . . PxP 14 P–QR3, PxP 15 PxN, PxB 16 QxP, B–N5 17 Q–N2, B–R4 18 B–Q4, B–N3 19 O–O–O± (Pachman), or 15 B–N2, N–R3 16 Q–K2±.

[16] 16 BxN, NxP! 17 BxN, Q–N6† 18 R–B2, Q–N8† 19 R–B1, Q–N6† with a draw by perpetual check (Alekhine–Botvinnik, Nottingham 1936).

[17] For 8 . . . B–K3? see Game 6.

[18] Preparing for P–B4. If immediately 9 P–B4, then 9 . . . P–QN4! with the following possibilities:

1) 10 NxP, NxP.
2) 10 BxP, Q–N3† 11 K–R1, NxP!
3) 10 B–B3, B–N2 11 B–K3, P–QR3.

[19] After 9 . . . P–QR3 10 P–B4, Q–B2 11 P–N4, P–K3 12 P–B5, R–K1 13 B–KB4, N–K4 White has attacking chances (Alekhine–Foltys, Munich 1942). 9 . . . P–QR4 is an active defense, but after 10 P–QR4, B–K3 11 P–B4, Q–N3 12 P–B5, BxN 13 PxB, Q–Q5 (Enevoldsen–Minev, Munich 1958) or 13 . . . Q–N5 (Van den Berg–Larsen, Beverwijk 1959). White maintains the advantage.

[20] White's attack is ready to roll (Konig–A. Thomas, Bournemouth 1939).

[21] White stands well, e.g., 10 . . . R–B1 11 P–QB4, N–K4 12 N–Q2. If 10 . . . P–QR4 or 10 . . . P–QN4, then 11 P–QR4 (Euwe–Landau, Holland 1939).

---

## part 2—RICHTER—ROUZER ATTACK

1 P–K4, P–QB4
2 N–KB3, N–QB3
3 P–Q4, PxP
4 NxP, N–B3
5 N–QB3, P–Q3
6 B–KN5, P–K3[A]
7 Q–Q2

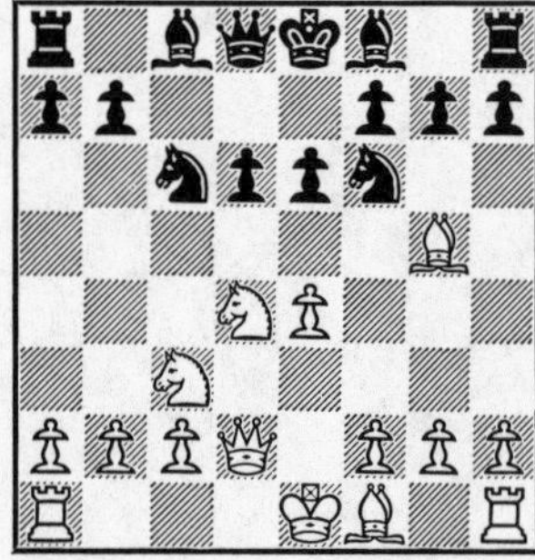

Key Position 2

### OBSERVATIONS ON KEY POSITION 2

[A] Other moves are weaker: (1) 6 . . . Q–R4 7 BxN, NPxB 8 B–N5, B–Q2 9 O–O, O–O–O 10 N–N3, Q–N3 11 P–QR4± (Alekhine–Frentz, Paris 1933) or (2) 6 . . . B–Q2 7 BxN, NPxB 8 N–B5, Q–B1 9 N–Q5! BxN 10 PxB, R–QN1 11 B–Q3± (Balogh–Van Kol, Correspondence Game 1934).

With 6 B–KN5, introduced by the German master, Kurt Richter, White effectively prevents Black from playing the Classical Dragon as well as the Boleslavski system (Part 6). Unless 6 . . . P–K3 is played, Black's King Bishop Pawn becomes doubled.

Originally 6 B–KN5 was intended as the prelude to an interesting Pawn sacrifice, but this variation proved to be too ambitious, and today is out of favor. See Sup. Var. 6.

The great popularity that 6 B–KN5 enjoys can be directly attributed to Rouzer's continuation 7 Q–Q2. Here White's idea is to castle on the Queenside and exercise pressure along the Queen file. White also reserves the possibility of P–KB4 to initiate an attack with P–K5.

Black's best according to present-day opinion is to counter with quick development starting with 7 . . . B–K2; Black's Queen Pawn may fall, but Black is then guaranteed sufficient counterplay.

Other important continuations are 7 . . . P–QR3 and 7 . . . P–KR3 (Prac. Var. 8, 9, and10).

*Sicilian Defense Game 4*

*WHITE: Samarian* *BLACK: Roele*

*Munich 1942*

| | WHITE | BLACK | | WHITE | BLACK |
|---|---|---|---|---|---|
| 1 | P–K4 | P–QB4 | 14 | B–Q4 | Q–N5 |
| 2 | N–KB3 | N–QB3 | 15 | NxB | R–Q1! |
| 3 | P–Q4 | PxP | 16 | N–N5 | QRxN |
| 4 | NxP | N–B3 | 17 | P–B3 | Q–K2 |
| 5 | N–QB3 | P–Q3 | 18 | NxP | RxP |
| 6 | B–K2 | P–KN3 | 19 | N–N5 | N–K5! |
| 7 | O–O | B–N2 | 20 | Q–R4 | R/6–B1 |
| 8 | B–K3 | O–O | 21 | B–N6 | N–B5! |
| 9 | P–B4 | Q–N3 | 22 | BxN? | BxR |
| 10 | P–K5 | PxP | 23 | RxB | Q–B3 |
| 11 | PxP | NxP | 24 | B–Q4 | RxB |
| 12 | N–B5 | QxP | | Resigns | |
| 13 | NxP† | K–R1 | | | |

*Sicilian Defense Game 5*

*WHITE: Unzicker* *BLACK: Giustolosi*

*Luzano 1959*

| | WHITE | BLACK | | WHITE | BLACK | | WHITE | BLACK |
|---|---|---|---|---|---|---|---|---|
| 1 | P–K4 | P–QB4 | 16 | BxB | NxR | 31 | K–N1 | K–N2 |
| 2 | N–KB3 | N–QB3 | 17 | Q–R6 | NxN | 32 | QxP | R–Q8† |
| 3 | P–Q4 | PxP | 18 | P–B6 | Q–N3 | 33 | K–B2 | R–Q7† |
| 4 | NxP | N–B3 | 19 | BxR | QxN† | 34 | K–K1 | R–K7† |
| 5 | N–QB3 | P–Q3 | 20 | K–R1 | QxBP | 35 | K–B1 | RxBP |
| 6 | B–K2 | P–KN3 | 21 | RxQ | RxB | 36 | Q–N7† | K–R3 |
| 7 | O–O | B–N2 | 22 | R–B4 | P–B3 | 37 | QxP | K–N4 |
| 8 | B–K3 | O–O | 23 | P–K5! | N–Q4 | 38 | P–QR4 | K–B5 |
| 9 | Q–Q2 | N–KN5 | 24 | R–KR4 | R–B2 | 39 | Q–N8† | K–K5 |
| 10 | BxN | BxB | 25 | PxQP | PxP | 40 | Q–N1 | K–B5 |
| 11 | P–B4 | B–Q2 | 26 | Q–Q2 | B–B3 | 41 | K–N1 | N–K6 |
| 12 | QR–Q1 | R–B1 | 27 | R–Q4 | N–K2 | 42 | P–R5 | RxP† |
| 13 | P–B5!? | N–K4 | 28 | RxP | N–B4 | 43 | K–R1 | Resigns |
| 14 | B–R6! | N–B5 | 29 | RxB | PxR | | | |
| 15 | Q–B1 | NxP | 30 | Q–B3 | R–Q2 | | | |

*Sicilian Defense Game 6*

*WHITE: Gusew* *BLACK: Averbach*

*Moscow 1951*

| | WHITE | BLACK | | WHITE | BLACK |
|---|---|---|---|---|---|
| 1 | P–K4 | P–QB4 | 20 | PxN | BxP |
| 2 | N–KB3 | N–QB3 | 21 | B–R6† | K–N1 |
| 3 | P–Q4 | PxP | 22 | RxB!† | PxR |
| 4 | NxP | N–B3 | 23 | QxP | R–B3 |
| 5 | N–QB3 | P–KN3 | 24 | QxN! | PxQ |
| 6 | B–K2 | P–Q3 | 25 | R–KB1 | R–B1 |
| 7 | N–N3 | B–N2 | 26 | B–Q1! | R–B5 |
| 8 | O–O | B–K3? | 27 | B–N3 | P–QN4 |
| 9 | P–B4 | QR–B1? | 28 | BxR | PxB |
| 10 | P–B5 | B–Q2 | 29 | P–N3 | P–R4 |
| 11 | P–KN4! | N–K4 | 30 | PxP | Q–K2 |
| 12 | P–N5 | N–N1 | 31 | K–N2 | Q–R6 |
| 13 | N–Q5 | P–B3 | 32 | R–B2 | Q–K2 |
| 14 | B–K3 | P–N3 | 33 | R–B1 | P–N4 |
| 15 | N–Q4 | K–B2 | 34 | R–B5 | P–N5 |
| 16 | P–B3 | Q–K1 | 35 | P–B5 | Q–Q1 |
| 17 | N–K6! | BxN | 36 | P–B6 | Q–K2 |
| 18 | PxB† | K–B1 | 37 | P–B7 | Resigns |
| 19 | NxBP! | NxN | | | |

IDEA VARIATIONS 4–6:

(4) 7 . . . B–K2 8 BxN, BxB 9 N/4–N5, O–O 10 NxQP, Q–R4 and Black's edge in development fully compensates for the Pawn, e.g., 11 N–B4, Q–QB4 12 Q–Q6, Q–KN4 13 P–B4, Q–R3 14 Q–Q2, R–Q1 15 B–Q3, B–R5† 16 K–B1, P–QN3 17 Q–K3, B–R3 (Fuderer–Gligoric, Yugoslavian Championship 1956).

(5) 7 . . . B–K2 8 O–O–O, O–O 9 BxN, BxB 10 NxN, PxN 11 QxP, Q–R4 12 Q–N3, BxN 13 QxB, QxP 14 B–B4, Q–R5 15 K–N1, and though Black has recaptured his Pawn, White definitely enjoys the advantage. More in the spirit of Black's defense is 11 . . . Q–N3! with sharp counterplay for the Pawn, e.g., 12 Q–N3, R–N1.

(6) 7 . . . B–K2 8 O–O–O, O–O 9 P–B4, NxN 10 QxN, Q–R4 11 P–K5, PxP 12 QxP, and in this position 12 . . . QxQ is correct. 12 . . . Q–N3? costs Black the Queen, e.g., 13 N–R4, Q–N5 14 R–Q4 or 13 . . . Q–B7 14 R–Q2.

PRACTICAL VARIATIONS 6–10:

1 P–K4, P–QB4 2 N–KB3, N–QB3 3 P–Q4, PxP 4 NxP, N–B3 5 N–QB3, P–Q3 6 B–KN5, P–K3 7 Q–Q2

| | 6 | 7 | 8 | 9 | 10 |
|---|---|---|---|---|---|
| 7 | – – | – – | – – | – – | – – |
| | B–K2 | – – | P–QR3 | – – | P–KR3 |
| 8 | O–O–O | – – | O–O–O | – – | BxN |
| | O–O[1] | – – | P–R3 | B–Q2 | PxB[20] |
| 9 | P–B4[2] | – – | B–KB4[13] | P–B4 | O–O–O |
| | NxN[3] | – – | B–Q2 | B–K2[17] | P–R3 |
| 10 | QxN | – – | NxN[14] | N–B3 | P–B4 |
| | P–KR3[4] | – – | BxN | P–N4 | B–Q2 |
| 11 | B–R4[5] | – – | P–B3 | P–K5[18] | B–K2 |
| | Q–R4[6] | – – | P–Q4[15] | P–N5! | P–KR4[21] |
| 12 | P–K5 | B–B4 | Q–K1 | PxN | K–N1 |
| | PxP | P–K4[9] | B–K2 | PxN | Q–N3 |
| 13 | QxKP | PxP | PxP | QxBP | N–N3![22] |
| | QxQ | PxP | PxP | PxP | O–O–O |
| 14 | PxQ | Q–Q3 | N–K2! | B–R4 | KR–B1 |
| | N–Q4 | Q–B4[10] | O–O | P–Q4 | N–R4 |
| 15 | BxB | BxN[11] | N–Q4 | K–N1 | R–B3 |
| | NxB | BxB | B–Q3 | N–N5 | NxN |
| 16 | B–Q3[7] | K–N1 | Q–Q2[16] | N–Q4 | RPxN |
| | P–QN3 | B–K3[12] | ± | R–QB1 | K–N1 |
| 17 | B–K4 | ± | | Q–K3 | N–R4[23] |
| | R–N1 | | | Q–N3 | ± |
| 18 | KR–K1 | | | P–QR3 | |
| | B–N2[8] | | | N–B3[19] | |
| | = | | | = | |

*Notes to practical variations 6–10:*

[1] 8 . . . NxN 9 QxN, O–O 10 P–B4 transposes into the column, but Black's inversion of moves permits 10 P–K5!, PxP 11 QxKP, Q–N3 12 B–K3, N–N5 13 BxQ, NxQ 14 B–B7, N–N5 15 B–N3± (Vasjukov–Boleslavski, USSR 1957). In this line 11 . . . B–Q2 offers more promise.

[2] Attempts to increase the pressure on Black's Queen Pawn come to naught:

1) 9 N–N3, Q–N3! 10 BxN, BxB and 11 QxP is simply answered by 11 . . . QxP. After 11 N–R4, Q–B2 Black's Queen Pawn is poison: 12 QxP?, B–N4†! 13 K–N1, R–Q1. For 9 . . . P–QR4, see Game 7.

2) 9 N/4–N5, Q–R4 10 BxN, BxB 11 NxQP, R–Q1 12 P–B4, P–K4 13 Q–Q5, Q–B2 14 P–B5, N–Q5 15 N/6–N5, Q–R4 16 Q–B4, BxP! and in this exciting position (Korchnoi–Boleslavski, USSR 1952) the game terminated in a draw! An interesting continuation would have been 17 PxB, QR–B1 18 Q–R4, QxQ 19 NxQ, N–N6† 20 PxN, B–N4† 21 R–Q2!, BxR† 22

continued ▸

K–N1, P–QR3 23 N/5–B3, BxN 24 NxB, RxN! 25 PxR, R–Q8† 26 K–N2, P–K5 and Black will recover his piece. 17 P–QN4 in this variation is answered by 17 . . . Q–R3.

[3] The general liquidation resulting from 9 . . . P–KR3 10 B–R4, NxP?! 11 BxB, NxQ 12 BxQ, NxKB 13 NxN, PxN 14 B–K7, R–K1 15 KRxN, RxB 16 RxP, B–N2 17 P–KN3! favors White (Unzicker–Stahlberg, Alekhine Memorial Tournament 1956). Also inferior is 9 . . . P–K4 10 N–B5!, BxN 11 PxB, R–B1 12 K–N1± (Rabar–Geller, Goteborg 1955). For the passive 9 . . . P–QR3, see Game 9.

[4] A useful precautionary interpolation. After 10 . . . Q–R4 11 B–B4, P–KR3 Pachman–Barcza, Stockholm 1952, continued successfully with 12 P–KR4!? after which there followed: 12 . . . P–K4 13 Q–N1!, PxP 14 BxBP, B–N5 15 R–Q3, N–R4? (15 . . . Q–B2 is better) 16 BxQP, BxB 17 RxB, N–N6 18 Q–Q4!±.

The acceptance of the sacrifice is extremely dangerous, e.g., 12 . . . PxB 13 RPxP, N–N5 14 R–R4, N–R3 15 QR–R1, P–K4 16 Q–B2, PxP 17 PxN!, BxR 18 QxB, P–KN4 19 P–R7†, K–R1 20 Q–R6, Q–Q1 21 R–R5, P–B3 22 Q–N6 followed by 23 Q–N8† (M. Salm, *Chess World*). Undoubtedly Black's best reply to 12 P–KR4 is 12 . . . R–Q1! and White must play 13 BxN.

[5] 11 BxN, BxB 12 QxQP, Q–R4= (13 P–K5, R–Q1). On 11 P–KR4!?, the reply 11 . . . Q–R4! is correct, and if 12 B–B4, then 12 . . . R–Q1! (cf. note 4), or if 12 B–K2, then 12 . . . P–K4! 11 . . . PxB is risky. Michel–Aguilar, Mar del Plata 1957, continued: 12 RPxP, N–R2 13 P–K5, BxP 14 PxB, QxP† 15 K–N1, PxP 16 Q–Q6!, N–B3 17 R–R8†, KxR 18 QxR†, K–R2 19 B–Q3†, P–K5 20 NxP, NxN 21 QxP, QxP 22 BxN†, QxB 23 Q–R5†, K–N1 24 R–Q8 mate.

[6] 10 . . . B–Q2!? is an interesting but rarely tried alternative, e.g., 11 BxN, BxB 12 P–K5, B–K2 13 PxP, B–KB3 and Black has attacking chances for the Pawn. Similarly, Black has an attack after 12 QxQP, BxN 13 QxB (cf. Game 8).

[7] Keres' once popular novelty, 16 B–N5, has been shorn of its terrors by 16 . . . P–QR3 17 B–Q3, P–QN4 18 B–K4, R–N1! 19 P–QR3, P–QR4 20 P–QN4, PxP 21 PxP, B–N2 22 KR–K1, KR–B1 23 K–N2, R–B5! (Schmid–Eliskases, Munich 1958).

[8] The end game offers even chances e.g., 19 R–Q7, BxB 20 RxB, N–B3 21 N–N5, KR–Q1 22 R–B7, QR–B1 (Gligoric–Benko, Candidates' Tournament 1959).

[9] 12 . . . R–Q1 is probably stronger; thus, 13 P–K5, PxP 14 QxQP, Q–N5 15 B–N3, B–Q2 16 R–Q4 (Pachman–Illivitzky, Match 1956) 16 . . . Q–N3!=.

[10] Not 14 . . . R–Q1? because of 15 N–Q5! 14 . . . B–KN5 is risky because of 15 BxN, BxB 16 QR–B1, QR–B1 17 RxB, PxR 18 N–Q5, and according to Czech analysts White has a strong, most likely a winning, attack.

[11] This exchange is not urgent. 15 B–N3 may offer even better chances.

[12] 17 BxB, PxB 18 Q–Q6, Q–B5 19 Q–Q3, QxQ 20 RxQ (Gligoric–Taimanov, Stockholm 1952), and although the game was drawn in this position, White still retains a slight advantage.

[13] 9 B–R4, NxP 10 Q–B4, N–N4! constitutes a dubious Pawn sacrifice. Smyslov in his 1957 match with Botvinnik was successful with 9 B–K3. The best reply for Black is simply 9 . . . B–Q2 and if 10 P–B4 then 10 . . . B–K2.

[14] Black threatens 10 . . . NxN 11 QxN, P–K4. In the game Duckstein–Botvinnik, Munich 1958, White parried with 10 B–N3; the continuation was 10 . . . B–K2 11 P–B3, N–K4 12 P–B4, N–R4 13 B–K2, NxB 14 RPxN, N–B3 15 K–N1, Q–N3 16 N–N3, O–O–O and White's advantage in space proved superior to Black's two Bishops. A preferable system for Black in this line is 11 . . . R–QB1 to meet the threatened 12 NxN with 12 . . . RxN when the Queen Pawn remains protected. Sharp tactics are required to meet 10 N–N3, e.g., 10 . . . P–QN4! 11 BxQP, P–N5 12 N–Q5!, PxN 13 PxP, N–K5! with complications favoring Black (Mednis–Hearst, New York 1956). White recovers the piece and even wins a Pawn by means of 14 R–K1, BxB 15 PxN, BxP 16 P–KB3, but Black emerges with a superior game after 16 . . . Q–B3 17 K–N1, O–O 18 PxN, B–K4, possibly followed by P–QR4–5.

[15] Freeing the position—at the expense, however, of isolating the Queen Pawn. An alternative worth noting is 11 . . . Q–N3: Tal–Djurasevic, Warna 1958, continued 12 B–B4, O–O–O 13 B–K3, Q–B2 14 Q–B2, N–Q2 15 P–B4, P–QN4 16 B–K2, Q–N2 17 P–QR3. Here Black should play 17 . . . N–B3, answering 18 P–K5 with 18 . . . N–Q4. In this variation 12 BxQP is simply met by 12 . . . O–O–O, e.g., 13 P–K5, N–K1.

[16] Having firmly blockaded Black's isolated Pawn, White clearly has the edge (Keres–Cuellar and Keres–Wexler, Mar del Plata 1959).

[17] Some years ago the following continuation was usual. 9 . . . P–R3 10 B–R4, NxP 11 Q–K1, N–B3 12 N–B5, Q–R4 13 NxQP†, BxN 14 RxB, Q–B2. It has been abandoned because of the forceful Pawn sacrifice 15 R–Q2! In Gligoric–Barden, Bognor Regis 1957, there followed 15 . . . QxP 16 B–K2!, N–K5 17 NxN, QxN 18 Q–B2, N–K4 19 KR–Q1, R–QB1 20 B–R5 and White won quickly. After 18 . . . P–K4, correct is 19 B–B3, Q–R5 20 KR–Q1, N–Q5 21 RxN! with a winning game. Relatively better for Black but still unsatisfactory is 16 . . . O–O–O 17 R–B1, Q–K4 18 Q–B2±.

The aggressive continuation 9 . . . R–B1 10 N–B3, Q–R4 11 K–N1, P–N4 is interesting but insufficient because of 12 P–K5!, P–N5 13 PxN, PxN 14 PxNP, BxP 15 QxQP, R–B2 16 N–K5± (Yanofsky–Olafsson, Dallas 1957). 14 . . . R–QN1 is met adequately by 15 P–QN3!

The Russians have lavished analysis on an attempt to strengthen this line with 9 . . . P–KR3: 10 B–R4, R–B1 11 N–B3, Q–R4 12 K–N1, P–QN4 13 P–K5, P–N5 14 PxN, PxN 15 PxNP, PxQ 16 PxR (Q), N–N5 17 P–QR3, NxP — the point of Black's 9th move; if White's Queen Bishop were now on N5, this attack would fail against 18 B–R6. But even in this position, White's resources are more than ample: 18 NxP!, NxP† 19 PxN, P–K4 20 N–B4!, B–B4† 21 K–R2, B–K3 22 RxP!, Q–B6 23 RxB†!, PxR 24 N–Q6†, K–Q2 25 Q–R7† and wins. In this line, 22 . . . RxN fails to 23 R–Q8†.

continued ▸

An immediate 9 . . . P–QN4 is dubious because of 10 BxN!, and now:

1) 10 . . . QxB 11 BxP!, PxB 12 N/4xNP, Q–Q1 13 NxP†, BxN 14 QxB, N–K2 15 P–B5! and White has a strong attack (Bonch-Osmolovsky–Geller, USSR 1957). 14 . . . Q–K2 offers Black better defensive chances.

2) 10 . . . PxB 11 P–B5!, NxN 12 QxN, B–R3† 13 K–N1, B–B5 14 N–K2, B–K4 15 Q–Q2, Q–B2 16 P–KN3, R–QB1 17 B–R3, Q–B4 18 N–B4! with a promising attack (Tal–Malich, Warna 1958).

[18] Recent experience has shown 11 BxN, PxB 12 P–B5! to be preferable. Black's best chance for counterplay then is 12 . . . Q–N3 13 K–N1, P–N5 14 N–K2, Q–B7!.

[19] Matanovic–Perez, Munich 1958.

[20] 8 . . . QxB? costs a Pawn because of 9 N/4–N5, Q–Q1 10 O–O–O.

[21] 12 B–R5 must be prevented, e.g., 11 . . . Q–N3 12 B–R5, QxN 13 QxQ, NxQ 14 RxN, R–KN1 15 P–KN3, B–K2 16 KR–B1, possibly followed by P–B5± (Bondarevsky–Botvinnik, USSR 1951).

[22] An improvement on 13 KR–B1, e.g., 13 . . . QxN 14 QxQ, NxQ 15 RxN, P–R5 16 P–B5, R–B1 17 R–Q3, R–B4 18 PxP, PxP 19 RxBP, R–KN4 20 R–B2, KR–N1=. Black's pressure is just enough to compensate for the Pawn (Keres–Petrosian, Amsterdam 1956).

[23] Keres–Botvinnik, Alekhine Memorial Tournament 1956, continued 17 . . . Q–R2 18 P–B5, B–K2 19 PxP, PxP 20 RxP! Correct is 17 . . . BxN, when White enjoys only a slight advantage.

*Sicilian Defense Game 7*

*WHITE: Alexander* *BLACK: Gligoric*

*Staunton Centenary Tournament 1951*

| | WHITE | BLACK | | WHITE | BLACK |
|---|---|---|---|---|---|
| 1 | P–K4 | P–QB4 | 16 | RxNP | BxR |
| 2 | N–KB3 | N–QB3 | 17 | PxB | R–Q1 |
| 3 | P–Q4 | PxP | 18 | N–K4 | P–K4 |
| 4 | NxP | N–B3 | 19 | B–Q3 | B–B4? |
| 5 | N–QB3 | P–Q3 | 20 | N–B6†! | PxN |
| 6 | B–KN5 | P–K3 | 21 | PxP | Q–KB5 |
| 7 | Q–Q2 | B–K2 | 22 | QxQ | PxQ |
| 8 | O–O–O | O–O | 23 | BxB | R–Q3 |
| 9 | N–N3 | P–QR4 | 24 | B–R7† | K–B1 |
| 10 | P–QR4 | Q–N3 | 25 | B–K4 | K–N1 |
| 11 | Q–K3 | Q–N5 | 26 | B–R7† | K–B1 |
| 12 | P–B3 | P–R3 | 27 | N–B5 | R–K1 |
| 13 | P–R4! | P–Q4 | 28 | N–Q7† | RxN |
| 14 | PxP | NxP | 29 | B–B5 | R–K8† |
| 15 | RxN! | PxB | 30 | RxR | R–Q3 |

| | WHITE | BLACK | | WHITE | BLACK |
|---|---|---|---|---|---|
| 31 | R–K4 | N–Q5 | 37 | RxR | NxR |
| 32 | B–B8 | P–N3 | 38 | K–Q2 | N–Q2 |
| 33 | B–R6 | N–K3 | 39 | K–K3 | N–K4 |
| 34 | B–B4 | N–B4 | 40 | B–K2 | K–K2 |
| 35 | RxP | N–Q2 | 41 | K–K4 | Resigns |
| 36 | P–KN4 | RxP | | | |

*Sicilian Defense Game 8*

*WHITE: Lehmann* *BLACK: Muhring*

*Utrecht 1954*

| | WHITE | BLACK | | WHITE | BLACK |
|---|---|---|---|---|---|
| 1 | P–K4 | P–QB4 | 18 | Q–N3 | B–Q7 |
| 2 | N–KB3 | N–QB3 | 19 | KR–B1 | R–N3 |
| 3 | P–Q4 | PxP | 20 | Q–B4 | R–N5 |
| 4 | NxP | N–B3 | 21 | Q–B7 | RxP†! |
| 5 | N–QB3 | P–Q3 | 22 | KxR | Q–Q5† |
| 6 | B–KN5 | P–K3 | 23 | P–B3 | QxB |
| 7 | Q–Q2 | B–K2 | 24 | K–N3 | P–QR4 |
| 8 | O–O–O | NxN | 25 | P–QR4 | P–QN4! |
| 9 | QxN | O–O | 26 | PxP | P–R5† |
| 10 | P–B4 | P–KR3 | 27 | K–N4 | R–Q1 |
| 11 | B–R4 | B–Q2!? | 28 | RxB | QxR/7 |
| 12 | BxN | BxB | 29 | R–B2 | R–Q5† |
| 13 | QxQP | BxN | 30 | K–R5 | QxR |
| 14 | QxB | Q–N3 | 31 | PxR | P–R6! |
| 15 | Q–N5 | Q–K6† | 32 | P–N6 | P–R7 |
| 16 | K–N1 | QR–Q1 | | Resigns | |
| 17 | B–Q3 | R–Q3 | | | |

*Sicilian Defense Game 9*

*WHITE: Keres* *BLACK: Szabo*

*USSR–Hungary 1955*

| | WHITE | BLACK | | WHITE | BLACK |
|---|---|---|---|---|---|
| 1 | P–K4 | P–QB4 | 13 | P–KR4! | R–N1 |
| 2 | N–KB3 | P–Q3 | 14 | Q–K3 | R–K1 |
| 3 | P–Q4 | PxP | 15 | R–R3 | Q–R4 |
| 4 | NxP | N–KB3 | 16 | BxB | RxB |
| 5 | N–QB3 | N–B3 | 17 | R–N3 | R–K1 |
| 6 | B–KN5 | P–K3 | 18 | RxN! | BxR |
| 7 | Q–Q2 | B–K2 | 19 | B–Q3! | P–R3 |
| 8 | O–O–O | O–O | 20 | Q–B4 | K–B1 |
| 9 | P–B4 | P–QR3 | 21 | RxP! | KxR |
| 10 | P–K5 | PxP | 22 | Q–B6† | K–B1 |
| 11 | NxN | PxN | 23 | B–N6! | Resigns |
| 12 | PxP | N–Q2 | | | |

SUPPLEMENTARY VARIATIONS 6–10:

1 P–K4, P–QB4 2 N–KB3, N–QB3 3 P–Q4, PxP 4 NxP, N–B3 5 N–QB3, P–Q3 6 B–KN5, P–K3

Richter's original continuation (Sup. Var. 6), if met properly, offers White insufficient chances for attack.

The continuation in Sup. Var. 7 was repeatedly adopted by Alekhine until Foltys found the correct defense.

Sup. Var. 8 is also an idea of Alekhine's. White aims at increased pressure on the hostile Queen Pawn, but Black's defense is easy.

In Sup. Var. 9 White omits O–O–O; he proceeds quietly, trying, however, to double Black's King Bishop Pawn.

The most important of these subsidiary lines is Sup. Var. 10 with Keres' continuation 7 Q–Q3. White intends to use his Queen on the Kingside, but if Black plays accurately he has little to fear.

| | *6* | *7* | *8* | *9* | *10* |
|---|---|---|---|---|---|
| 7 | NxN | B–N5 | N–N3 | B–K2 | Q–Q3 |
| | PxN | B–Q2 | B–K2 | B–K2 | B–K2[11] |
| *8* | P–K5 | O–O[4] | Q–Q2 | O–O | R–Q1[12] |
| | Q–R4[1] | P–KR3 | P–KR3 | O–O | O–O |
| *9* | B–N5 | B–KR4[5] | B–K3[7] | N/4–N5[9] | B–K2 |
| | PxB | P–R3 | O–O[8] | P–QR3 | P–Q4!? |
| *10* | PxN | B–K2 | = | BxN | PxP |
| | P–N5 | B–K2 | | PxB | N–QN5 |
| *11* | N–K4[2] | N–N3 | | N–Q4 | Q–N3 |
| | Q–K4 | Q–B2 | | K–R1 | N/5xQP |
| *12* | P–KB3 | P–B4 | | K–R1 | NxN[13] |
| | P–Q4 | P–KN4![6] | | R–KN1 | NxN |
| *13* | Q–Q2 | ∓ | | P–B4 | BxB |
| | P–KR3![3] | | | B–Q2[10] | QxB[14] |
| | ∓ | | | ∓ | = |

*Notes to supplementary variations 6–10:*

[1] The older 8 . . . PxP 9 Q–B3 also favors Black if he returns his extra Pawn with 9 . . . B–K2!, e.g., 10 BxN, BxB 11 QxP†, B–Q2 12 Q–B3, O–O∓ or 10 QxP†?, B–Q2 11 Q–B3, P–K5!∓. The miserly 9 . . . B–Q2, on the other hand, offers White a promising game: 10 O–O–O, B–K2 11 BxN, BxB 12 N–K4 and in this position Black cannot play 12 . . . O–O because of 13 RxB!, QxR 14 QxB!.

[2] If 11 Q–B3, then not 11 . . . PxN?, Q–B6!†, but simply 11 . . . Q–K4†!∓.

[3] Not 13 . . . PxN because of 14 O–O–O, Q–Q4 15 Q–B4 when White wins. The text move, however, favors Black: 13 B–R4, P–N4! 14 B–N3, QxNP 15 R–Q1, B–R3∓ (Nilsson–Geller, Stockholm 1954). If White veers from this line, he fares even worse, e.g., 14 B–B2, PxN 15 O–O–O, Q–B2∓, or 15 O–O, PxN 16 QR–Q1, B–B4†∓.

[4] A new plan here is 8 KBxN, PxB 9 Q–B3, P–B4 10 P–K5!, PxN 11 PxN, P–N3 12 N–K2, R–QN1 13 NxP, RxP 14 O–O, Q–B1 15 KR–N1! and White won quickly (Mrs. Eretova–Mrs. Rubtsova, Plovdiv 1959; even the women contribute to chess theory today!). In this variation 9 . . . P–K4 is correct. Of interest, too, is Rossolimo's 8 B–QR4, e.g., 8 . . . P–QR3? 9 NxN, BxN 10 BxB†, PxB 11 P–K5!, Q–R4 12 BxN, PxB 13 PxQP, Q–K4† 14 K–B1!± (Rossolimo–Marchand, Milwaukee 1953). Black's best answer to the Bishop's retreat is probably 8 . . . NxN.

[5] 9 B–K3 is preferable; thus, 9 . . . P–R3 10 B–K2, Q–B2 11 N–N3, B–K2=.

[6] 13 B–N3, PxP 14 RxP, N–K4∓ (Alekhine–Foltys, Margate 1937). After 13 PxP?, PxP 14 BxP, P–Q4 15 P–KR3, RxP Black, according to Alekhine, has a winning attack.

[7] After 8 B–R4, O–O White faces the unpleasant threat of 9 . . . NxP!

[8] Black's game is satisfactory (Alekhine).

[9] Played with the intention of weakening Black's Pawn formation; a preferable plan, however, is 9 Q–Q2 followed by QR–Q1.

[10] Thanks to his strong center and two Bishops, Black has a fine position.

[11] Also good is 7 . . . P–QR3, e.g., 8 R–Q1, B–Q2 9 B–K2, B–K2 10 O–O, O–O 11 Q–N3, Q–B2 12 N–N3, K–R1 13 B–KB4, N–K4 14 B–B1, B–N4! (Keres–Stahlberg, Budapest 1950). For 8 . . . B–K2 in this system, see Game 10.

[12] The text move, in addition to bringing additional pressure to bear on the Queen file, prepares a safe retreat for the Queen Bishop on B1, a retreat which otherwise would lock in the Queen Rook, as in Keres–Bronstein, Budapest 1950: 8 B–K2, O–O 9 O–O, P–KR3! 10 B–B1, NxN 11 QxN, B–Q2 13 P–K5, PxP 14 QxKP, B–B3 15 R–Q1, Q–N1 with a very satisfactory game for Black. Returning the Bishop to B1 in this game was a necessary evil; the otherwise convenient 10 B–R4 is met by 10 . . . NxN 11 QxN, NxP!, while after 10 B–K3, White's Queen is cut off from the Kingside.

[13] Keres' suggestion 12 B–KR6, N–K1 13 N–B5, B–B3 14 N–K4, BxP 15 P–QB3 leads to wild complications.

[14] Keres–Aronin, USSR Championship 1951.

*Sicilian Defense Game 10*

*WHITE: Platz* *BLACK: Szily*

*Helsinki 1952*

| WHITE | BLACK | WHITE | BLACK |
|---|---|---|---|
| 1 P–K4 | P–QB4 | 11 N–N3 | N–K4 |
| 2 N–KB3 | N–QB3 | 12 Q–Q2 | O–O |
| 3 P–Q4 | PxP | 13 P–B4 | N–B3 |
| 4 NxP | N–B3 | 14 P–K5! | PxP |
| 5 N–QB3 | P–Q3 | 15 PxP | N–Q4 |
| 6 B–KN5 | P–K3 | 16 NxN | PxN |
| 7 Q–Q3 | P–QR3 | 17 B–B6! | PxB |
| 8 R–Q1 | B–K2 | 18 PxP | Q–K4 |
| 9 B–K2 | B–Q2 | 19 Q–R6 | Resigns |
| 10 O–O | Q–B2 | | |

## part 3—SOZIN ATTACK

1 P–K4, P–QB4
2 N–KB3, N–QB3
3 P–Q4, PxP
4 NxP, N–B3
5 N–QB3, P–Q3
6 B–QB4

KEY POSITION 3

OBSERVATIONS ON KEY POSITION 3

The Russian master, Sozin, experimented with 6 B–QB4 in the 1930's; the move gained in importance, however, only after 1945 when its preventative effect against both the Boleslavski and Dragon systems was realized (see Idea Var. 7 and 8).

Black's safest procedure against the Sozin Attack is an immediate 6 . . . P–K3, but even then White still maintains an initiative as has been repeatedly demonstrated, especially by Bobby Fischer.

IDEA VARIATIONS 7 AND 8:

(7) 6 . . . P–K4 7 N–B5 (of equal merit are the alternatives 7 N/4–K2 and 7 N–B3), BxN 8 PxB, B–K2 9 O–O, Q–Q2 10 P–KN4!, P–KR3 11 P–B4, PxP 12 BxP, O–O 13 N–Q5 with excellent prospects for White (Sokolski–Mokovski, Correspondence Game 1954).

(8) 6 . . . P–KN3 7 NxN, PxN 8 P–K5!, N–N5 (or 8 . . . N–Q2 9 PxP, PxP 10 O–O followed by 11 R–K1) 9 B–B4 (9 P–K6, P–KB4 10 O–O, B–N2 11 B–B4 is also promising for White; on 9 PxP, Black's best is 9 . . . QxP), Q–N3 (also insufficient but perhaps an improvement on the text is 9 . . . P–Q4 10 NxP!, B–KN2) 10 Q–B3, B–B4 11 PxP, PxP 12 O–O, O–O–O 13 KR–K1, P–Q4 14 P–KR3 and White has the better game (Lipnitzky).

## PRACTICAL VARIATIONS 11-15:

1 P–K4, P–QB4 2 N–KB3, N–QB3 3 P–Q4, PxP 4 NxP, N–B3 5 N–QB3, P–Q3 6 B–QB4

| | *11* | *12* | *13* | *14* | *15* |
|---|---|---|---|---|---|
| *6* | – – | – – | – – | – – | – – |
| | P–K3 | – – | – – | B–Q2 | Q–N3 |
| *7* | O–O | – – | – – | B–N3![14] | N/4–K2![17] |
| | P–QR3 | B–K2 | – – | P–KN3 | P–K3 |
| *8* | B–N3 | B–N3 | – – | P–B3[15] | O–O |
| | Q–B2[1] | O–O[6] | – – | N–QR4 | B–K2 |
| *9* | B–K3 | B–K3 | – – | B–N5 | B–N3 |
| | N–QR4 | B–Q2 | N–QR4 | B–N2 | O–O |
| *10* | P–B4 | P–B4 | P–B4 | Q–Q2 | K–R1 |
| | B–K2[2] | NxN | P–QN3[9] | P–KR3 | N–QR4 |
| *11* | Q–B3 | BxN | P–K5![10] | B–K3 | B–N5 |
| | P–QN4 | B–B3 | N–K1[11] | R–QB1 | Q–B4 |
| *12* | P–K5 | Q–K2 | P–B5! | O–O–O | P–B4 |
| | B–N2 | P–QN4 | QPxP[12] | N–B5 | P–N4 |
| *13* | Q–N3 | NxP | PxP | Q–K2! | N–N3 |
| | PxP | BxN[7] | P–B3 | NxB | P–N5[18] |
| *14* | PxP | QxB | N–B5![13] | QxN | P–K5![19] |
| | N–R4 | NxP | ± | O–O | ± |
| *15* | Q–R3[3] | P–B5 | | P–N4 | |
| | NxB[4] | B–B3![8] | | Q–R4 | |
| *16* | NxN | = | | P–KR4[16] | |
| | QxP | | | ± | |
| *17* | N–R5 | | | | |
| | P–N5![5] | | | | |
| | = | | | | |

*Notes to practical variations 11–15:*

[1] Pitksaar–Krogius, USSR 1958, resulted in a quick draw after: 8 . . . N–QR4 9 P–B4, P–QN4 10 P–K5, PxP 11 PxP, B–B4! 12 B–K3, NxB 13 RPxN, N–Q4 14 Q–B3!, O–O 15 NxN, QxN 16 QxQ. White, however, can obtain a more lasting initiative with 10 P–B5.

[2] This is safer than 10 . . . P–QN4 11 P–B5, NxB 12 BPxN!, B–K2 13 R–B1, Q–Q2 and now:

1) 14 PxP, PxP 15 P–QN4, O–O 16 Q–N3, K–R1 17 P–KR3, P–K4 18 N–B5, B–N2 with approximate equality (Keres–Taimanov, Zurich 1953).
2) 14 Q–B3, O–O 15 P–K5, B–N2 16 PxN, BxQ 17 BPxB, QxP 18 RxB (Suetin). White has three minor pieces for Queen and Pawn, but, in addition, has good attacking chances: 18 . . . P–K4?, e.g., fails against 19 P–B6!, PxP 20 N–B5 with an easy win. Black cannot conveniently evade this line, e.g., 15 . . . QPxP 16 PxP, PxP 17 NxKP!±.

continued ▸

[3] The position is extremely complex. Chenkin, the Moscow analyst, makes mention of the following Queen sacrifice: 15 BxP!?, NxQ 16 BxP†, K–Q2 17 B–K6†, K–K1! 18 B–B7† with a draw by perpetual check. If 17 . . . K–Q1, then 18 QR–Q1. Inferior for Black, though more daring, are both 15 . . . PxB 16 Q–R3, QxP 17 NxP± and 15 . . . O–O 16 RxP±.

[4] 15 . . . QxP 16 BxP!± (Averbach–Taimanov, Zurich 1953).

[5] The next few moves, leading to a general liquidation, are now practically forced: 18 N–B4, Q–B2 19 QxN, P–KN3 20 Q–K5, QxQ 21 NxQ. Smaillogovic–Dantar, Yugoslavia 1957, resulted in a draw after 21 . . . PxN 22 RxP, PxP 23 R–N1, B–Q4 24 P–B4!, B–Q3! 25 PxB, BxN 26 PxP, R–KB1 27 QR–KB1, B–Q3 28 B–R6, B–B4† 29 K–R1, RxR 30 PxR†, K–Q2. As an alternative to 21 . . . PxN, Black can seriously consider 21 . . . P–B3, but its consequences are not clear.

[6] Boleslavski's suggestion 8 . . . NxN 9 QxN, O–O 10 K–R1, P–QN3 also merits attention. Fischer–Kupper, Zurich 1959, continued: 11 P–B4, B–N2 12 P–B5, P–K4 13 Q–Q3, P–KR3 14 R–B3, R–B1 15 R–R3, K–R2 16 B–K3, Q–Q2 17 N–Q5, BxN 18 BxB, NxB 19 PxN, B–B3? 20 BxRP! and White had a winning attack. This game, however, cannot constitute a refutation of Boleslavski's system. Black missed the chance to obtain strong counterplay with 15 . . . RxN! followed by either 16 . . . BxP or 16 . . . NxP. Another interesting possibility for Black is 11 . . . B–R3, e.g., 12 R–K1, P–Q4, when 13 PxP is met with 13 . . . N–N5.

[7] 13 . . . NxP is inferior because of 14 P–B4!, when 14 . . . BxN is met with 15 QxN, while 13 . . . P–K4?! fails against 14 PxP!, PxP 15 B–K3, P–QR3 16 N–B3, NxP 17 RxP!, RxR 18 BxR†, White winning a Pawn (Fischer–Nievergelt, Zurich 1959). In this line 15 . . . BxP or 15 . . . NxP is simply answered by 16 NxP.

[8] In Yudowitsch–Geller, Gorki 1954, there followed: 16 QR–Q1, BxB† 17 RxB, P–Q4 18 PxP, PxP 19 R/4–Q1, Q–N4 20 Q–K2 with about even chances. White does better to play 16 Q–Q3!

[9] A risky continuation. Steadier is 10 . . . NxB 11 BPxN, P–K4 (Ciocaltea–Filip, Bucharest 1953), or still better 11 . . . N–Q2 (Boleslavski).

[10] White must play for a sharp attack. For 11 Q–B3, see Game 11.

[11] 11 . . . PxP 12 PxP, N–Q4 is indicated for Black, but not 12 . . . N–Q2? because of 13 RxP!.

[12] If 12 . . . NxB then 13 N–B6!

[13] White has a tremendous attack (Geller–Vasjukov, USSR 1951).

[14] Other continuations make matters more comfortable for Black:

1) 7 P–B4, P–KN3 8 NxN, BxN! 9 P–K5, PxP 10 QxQ†, RxQ 11 PxP, N–N5 12 P–K6, P–B4 (Lipnitzky–Boleslavski, USSR 1950). White's King Pawn proves to be untenable.

2) 7 B–KN5, Q–R4 8 BxN, NPxB 9 N–N3, Q–KN4!

Black has good counterchances (Geller–Averbach, Zurich 1953).

[15] An excellent idea; White adopts the modern system against the Dragon. Black's best is now 8 . . . B–N2 9 B–K3, R–QB1.

[16] White has splendid attacking chances (Fischer–Gligoric, Candidates' Tournament 1959).

[17] An improvement on 7 N–N3, P–K3 8 O–O, B–K2 9 B–K3, Q–B2 10 P–B4, O–O 11 P–N4?, P–Q4! when Black seizes the initiative (Cardoso–Benko, Portoroz 1958). In this line 11 B–K2 may keep the position balanced.

[18] Better is 13 . . . NxB or 13 . . . B–N2. The text move concedes White a strong attack.

[19] 14 . . . PxP 15 BxN!, PxB 16 N/B–K4, Q–Q5 17 Q–R5, NxB 18 Q–R6! and White soon won (Fischer–Benko, Candidates' Tournament 1959).

*Sicilian Defense Game 11*

*WHITE: Padevski* *BLACK: Botvinnik*

*Alekhine Tournament, Moscow 1956*

| WHITE | BLACK | WHITE | BLACK |
|---|---|---|---|
| 1 P–K4 | P–QB4 | 14 PxR | NxP |
| 2 N–KB3 | N–QB3 | 15 Q–N4 | Q–B1 |
| 3 P–Q4 | PxP | 16 R–B3 | NxB |
| 4 NxP | N–B3 | 17 RPxN | P–B4 |
| 5 N–QB3 | P–Q3 | 18 Q–R4 | P–K4 |
| 6 B–QB4 | P–K3 | 19 R–KR3 | P–KR3 |
| 7 O–O | B–K2 | 20 Q–R5 | QxP |
| 8 B–K3 | O–O | 21 R–Q1 | PxN |
| 9 B–N3 | N–QR4 | 22 B–Q2 | Q–B3 |
| 10 P–B4 | P–QN3 | 23 PxP | N–N4 |
| 11 Q–B3 | B–N2 | 24 R–N3 | Q–R8† |
| 12 P–N4 | R–B1 | 25 K–B2 | N–K5† |
| 13 P–N5 | RxN | Resigns | |

---

## part 4—ACCELERATED FIANCHETTO

1 P–K4, P–QB4
2 N–KB3, N–QB3
3 P–Q4, PxP
4 NxP, P–KN3
5 P–QB4[A], B–N2
6 B–K3[B], N–B3[C]
7 N–QB3, N–KN5[D]
8 QxN, NxN
9 Q–Q1

KEY POSITION 4

### OBSERVATIONS ON KEY POSITION 4

[A] White can also continue his mobilization with 5 N–QB3, e.g., 5 . . . B–N2 6 B–K3, N–B3 7 NxN, NPxN 8 P–K5, N–N1 9 B–Q4, P–QB4 10 BxP, Q–B2 11 B–Q4, BxP 12 B–K2, N–B3 13 BxB, QxB 14 O–O, O–O 15 B–B3, R–N1 16 R–K1 with a positional advantage for White (Ivkov–Pachman, Buenos Aires 1955). In this variation Black can improve with 12 . . . B–QN2, obtaining approximate equality. 6 . . . P–Q3 transposes into the ordinary Dragon.

Another interesting possibility occurs if White abstains from 7 NxN and plays instead 7 B–QB4, e.g., 7 . . . O–O 8 B–N3, N–QR4? 9 P–K5! N–K1 10 BxP†!, KxB 11 N–K6!, as in the famous Fischer–Reshevsky game, New York 1958. This miniature had occurred before in the preliminaries of the 1958 USSR Championship (Bastrikov–Schamkowitsch). Reshevsky has since improved Black's chances with 8 . . . N–KN5: 9 QxN, NxN 10 Q–Q1, NxB 11 RPxN, P–N3 12 Q–Q5, BxN†! 13 PxB, Q–B2! 14 O–O–O, QxBP! 15 B–Q4, Q–B3 16 Q–K5, P–B3 17 QxKP, B–N2 18 P–KB3, P–QR4 with sharp play and only the slightest edge for White (Fischer–Reshevsky, 4th Match Game, New York 1961).

B After 6 N–B2, P–Q3 7 B–K2 Black obtains sufficient counterplay with 7 . . . P–B4!, e.g., 8 PxP, BxBP 9 O–O, N–R3 10 N–Q2, O–O 11 N–B3 (Alexander–Botvinnik, Amsterdam 1954). Most accurate now is 11 . . . K–R1 so as to continue after 12 N–K3, B–K3 13 N–N5 with 13 . . . B–N1.

C Striving for . . . P–B4 is less to the point: 6 . . . N–R3 7 N–QB3, O–O 8 B–K2, P–B4 9 PxP, BxN 10 BxN!, RxP 11 B–K3, BxB 12 PxB, P–Q3 13 Q–Q2, B–K3 14 B–N4, R–K5 15 BxB†, RxB 16 O–O with some positional advantage for White (Pachman–Sanguinetti, Portoroz 1958). Black fares slightly better perhaps with 13 . . . Q–R4.

D After 7 . . . P–Q3 8 B–K2, O–O 9 O–O, B–Q2 10 P–B3 White's advantage in space is significant (Rubinstein–Marotti, London 1922).

The Accelerated Fianchetto owes its recent popularity to a finer appreciation of the merits of 7 . . . N–KN5. After this move, White can hardly avoid the exchange of minor pieces which eases Black's game considerably.

The attempt to maintain the centralized Knight in the diagrammed position by means of 9 . . . P–K4 is frustrated by Pachman's 10 N–N5!, when the weakness of Black's position is clearly seen, although White still must surmount some tactical hurdles to bring home his advantage.

Undoubtedly from the positional point of view, Black's soundest line is 9 . . . N–K3, a strategical withdrawal which leads to approximate equality.

IDEA VARIATIONS 9 AND 10:

(9) 9 . . . P–K4 10 Q–Q2, O–O 11 BxN? (11 N–N5!), PxB 12 N–N5 (or 12 N–K2, R–K1 13 P–B3, P–Q4!, 14 BPxP, P–B4 15 N–N3, QxP, when White's position comes apart at the seams), P–QR3! 13 NxP (13 N–Q6, Q–N3∓), R–K1 14 P–B3, P–Q4! 15 O–O–O, PxKP 16 PxP, B–N5! and Black quickly obtained a winning advantage (Hoerberg–Nilsson, Stockholm 1957).

(10) 9 . . . P–K4 10 N–N5!, O–O 11 NxN (for the correct reply 11 Q–Q2!, see Prac. Var. 17), PxN 12 BxP, Q–R4† 13 K–K2, R–K1 14 P–B3, P–Q4! 15 PxP, RxP†! 16 PxR, B–N5†, winning the Queen (analysis by Penrose).

PRACTICAL VARIATIONS 16-20:

1 P–K4, P–QB4 2 N–KB3, N–QB3 3 P–Q4, PxP 4 NxP, P–KN3 5 P–QB4, B–N2 6 B–K3, N–B3 7 N–QB3, N–KN5 8 QxN, NxN 9 Q–Q1

| | *16* | *17* | *18* | *19* | *20* |
|---|---|---|---|---|---|
| *9* | – – | – – | – – | – – | – – |
| | P–K4?! | – – | N–K3 | – – | N–B3 |
| *10* | B–Q3 | N–N5! | Q–Q2 | R–B1 | Q–Q2 |
| | P–Q3[1] | O–O | P–Q3[6] | P–Q3[8] | Q–R4 |
| *11* | O–O | Q–Q2! | B–K2 | B–K2 | R–B1 |
| | O–O | Q–R5[4] | B–Q2 | O–O | P–N3 |
| *12* | R–B1 | B–Q3 | O–O | O–O | B–K2 |
| | B–K3 | P–Q4 | O–O | P–N3 | B–N2 |
| *13* | P–QN3 | B–N5! | QR–B1 | P–B4! | O–O |
| | P–QR3 | Q–N5 | B–QB3 | B–N2 | P–Q3 |
| *14* | B–N1 | P–B3 | KR–Q1 | B–B3 | KR–Q1[10] |
| | R–N1 | Q–Q2 | N–B4 | R–B1 | = |
| *15* | K–R1[2] | NxN[5] | P–B3[7] | P–N3[9] | |
| | P–QN4[3] | ± | = | ± | |
| | = | | | | |

*Notes to practical variations 16–20:*

[1] More consistent in Botvinnik's opinion is 10 . . . P–QR3, to be followed by . . . R–QN1 and . . . P–QN4.

[2] After 15 N–K2!, NxN† 16 QxN, P–B4 17 P–B3 White stands slightly better.

[3] Black's position is satisfactory (see Game 12).

[4] After 11 . . . NxN 12 PxN, P–Q3 13 B–B4 White has a slight but distinct advantage.

[5] 15 . . . PxKP 16 BxP, QxN 17 QxQ, PxQ 18 P–QN3, P–QR4 19 O–O, P–R5 (Barcza–Szabo, Hungary 1959), and best is now 20 P–QN4!±. A wiser policy for Black is to avoid an end game with 16 . . . PxN.

[6] Larsen, an expert in this defense, prefers the following remarkable blockading strategy: 10 . . . Q–R4 11 R–B1, P–N3 12 B–K2, B–N2 13 P–B3, P–KN4 followed by . . . B–K4 and . . . B–B5, as in Gligoric–Larsen, Dallas 1957, and Cardoso–Larsen, Portoroz 1958.

[7] White's superiority in space is without significance (see Game 13).

[8] On 10 . . . Q–R4, White can choose between the steady 11 P–QR3 and the speculative 11 B–K2 (see Game 14).

[9] After 15 . . . N–B4 16 P–B5!, with a promising game for White (Karaklaic–Pirc, Zagreb 1955). If . . . BxN 17 RxB, NxKP 18 BxN, BxB 19 B–R6, R–K1 20 Q–Q4.

[10] White controls more terrain, but the chances are about even (Trifunovic–Stoltz, Prague 1946).

*Sicilian Defense Game 12*

*WHITE: Smyslov* *BLACK: Botvinnik*

*Alekhine Tournament, Moscow 1956*

| | WHITE | BLACK | | WHITE | BLACK |
|---|---|---|---|---|---|
| 1 | P–K4 | P–QB4 | 24 | Q–N4 | P–B4 |
| 2 | N–KB3 | N–QB3 | 25 | Q–R3 | QxQP |
| 3 | P–Q4 | PxP | 26 | B–K3 | N–N4 |
| 4 | NxP | P–KN3 | 27 | KR–Q1 | Q–B2 |
| 5 | P–QB4 | B–N2 | 28 | B–Q2 | P–Q4 |
| 6 | B–K3 | N–B3 | 29 | B–Q3 | P–K5 |
| 7 | N–QB3 | N–KN5 | 30 | BxN | RxB |
| 8 | QxN | NxN | 31 | B–B4 | R–Q1 |
| 9 | Q–Q1 | P–K4 | 32 | R–B7 | R–Q2 |
| 10 | B–Q3 | P–Q3 | 33 | R–B8 | R–B4 |
| 11 | O–O | O–O | 34 | R–R8 | R–R2 |
| 12 | R–B1 | B–K3 | 35 | R–N8 | R–N2 |
| 13 | P–QN3 | P–QR3 | 36 | R–R8 | R–R2 |
| 14 | B–N1 | R–N1 | 37 | R–N8 | R–N2 |
| 15 | K–R1 | P–QN4 | 38 | R–R8 | Q–Q2 |
| 16 | PxP | PxP | 39 | Q–K3 | R–B1 |
| 17 | Q–Q3 | P–N5 | 40 | RxR | QxR |
| 18 | N–Q5 | BxN | 41 | RxP | B–K2! |
| 19 | PxB | Q–R4 | 42 | P–KR3 | Q–B6 |
| 20 | Q–B4 | R–N4 | 43 | Q–K2 | Q–QB3 |
| 21 | B–Q2 | KR–N1 | 44 | R–R5 | R–Q2 |
| 22 | Q–B8† | B–B1 | 45 | Q–B4† | QxQ |
| 23 | Q–Q7! | R/4–N2 | 46 | PxQ | Draw |

*Sicilian Defense Game 13*

*WHITE: Keres* *BLACK: Petrosian*

*Candidates' Tournament 1959*

| | WHITE | BLACK | | WHITE | BLACK |
|---|---|---|---|---|---|
| 1 | P–K4 | P–QB4 | 14 | KR–Q1 | N–B4 |
| 2 | N–KB3 | N–QB3 | 15 | P–B3 | P–QR4 |
| 3 | P–Q4 | PxP | 16 | P–QN3 | Q–N3 |
| 4 | NxP | P–KN3 | 17 | N–N5 | KR–B1 |
| 5 | P–QB4 | B–N2 | 18 | B–B1 | Q–Q1 |
| 6 | B–K3 | N–B3 | 19 | Q–KB2 | Q–K1 |
| 7 | N–QB3 | N–KN5 | 20 | N–B3 | P–N3 |
| 8 | QxN | NxN | 21 | R–B2 | Q–B1 |
| 9 | Q–Q1 | N–K3 | 22 | Q–Q2 | B–Q2 |
| 10 | Q–Q2 | P–Q3 | 23 | N–Q5 | QR–N1 |
| 11 | B–K2 | B–Q2 | 24 | B–N5 | R–K1 |
| 12 | O–O | O–O | 25 | R–K1 | R–N2 |
| 13 | QR–B1 | B–QB3 | 26 | Q–B2 | B–QB3 |

| | WHITE | BLACK | | WHITE | BLACK |
|---|---|---|---|---|---|
| 27 | Q–R4 | P–B3 | 40 | N–K2 | R/2–KN2 |
| 28 | B–K3 | P–K3 | 41 | N–Q4 | B–Q2 |
| 29 | N–B3 | R–Q2 | 42 | P–QR3 | Q–R1 |
| 30 | B–Q4 | P–B4 | 43 | K–N1 | P–R4 |
| 31 | PxP | NPxP | 44 | R–N1 | P–KR5 |
| 32 | R–Q2 | BxB† | 45 | R/1–N2 | R–N5 |
| 33 | RxB | R–KN2 | 46 | R–KB2 | Q–Q1 |
| 34 | K–R1 | R–N3 | 47 | P–N4 | R–N6 |
| 35 | R–Q2 | R–Q1 | 48 | PxR | PxP |
| 36 | R/1–Q1 | R–Q2 | 49 | R/B–Q2 | Q–R5 |
| 37 | Q–B2 | Q–Q1 | 50 | B–K2 | R–R2 |
| 38 | Q–K3 | P–K4 | 51 | K–B1 | QxP† |
| 39 | P–B4 | P–K5 | | Resigns | |

### *Sicilian Defense Game 14*

*WHITE: Bolanel* *BLACK: Sziligyl*

*Ploesti 1956*

| | WHITE | BLACK | | WHITE | BLACK |
|---|---|---|---|---|---|
| 1 | P–K4 | P–QB4 | 21 | R–Q4 | PxP |
| 2 | N–KB3 | N–QB3 | 22 | PxP | BxP |
| 3 | P–Q4 | PxP | 23 | K–B2 | BxB? |
| 4 | NxP | P–KN3 | 24 | KxB | N–B3 |
| 5 | P–QB4 | B–N2 | 25 | R–Q5! | P–N4? |
| 6 | B–K3 | N–B3 | 26 | RxNP | Q–Q3 |
| 7 | N–QB3 | N–KN5 | 27 | Q–K2 | O–O–O |
| 8 | QxN | NxN | 28 | Q–B3! | P–K4 |
| 9 | Q–Q1 | N–K3 | 29 | RxRP | Q–Q6† |
| 10 | R–B1 | Q–R4 | 30 | K–B2 | Q–B7† |
| 11 | B–K2 | BxN† | 31 | K–K1 | P–K5 |
| 12 | RxB | QxP | 32 | R–R8† | K–B2 |
| 13 | Q–B1 | Q–R4 | 33 | B–N6† | K–N2 |
| 14 | O–O | P–N3 | 34 | B–B5† | K–B2 |
| 15 | R–R3 | Q–N5 | 35 | B–Q6† | KxB |
| 16 | P–B4 | B–N2 | 36 | Q–R3† | K–B2 |
| 17 | P–B5 | N–Q1 | 37 | R–R7† | NxR |
| 18 | Q–B2 | R–KN1 | 38 | QxN† | K–Q3 |
| 19 | R–Q1 | B–B3 | 39 | Q–B5 mate | |
| 20 | B–KB1 | P–B3 | | | |

SUPPLEMENTARY VARIATIONS 11-15:

1 P–K4, P–QB4 2 N–KB3, N–QB3 3 P–Q4, PxP 4 NxP

Sup. Var. 11–13 treat Nimzowitsch's bold 4 . . . P–Q4. If White replies with the enticing 5 B–QN5 (Sup. Var. 11), Black obtains distinct tactical counterchances, but by proceeding with either 5 PxP (Sup. Var. 12) or 5 NxN (Sup. Var. 13), White obtains a slight positional advantage.

4 . . . Q–B2 is an antiquated line once considered passe, but repeatedly adopted of late. If White proceeds with 5 P–QB4 (Sup. Var. 14), he is forced to sacrifice a Pawn with no convincing compensation; but 5 N/4–N5, the supposed "refutation," also is of little promise, improvements for Black having recently been found. White, in reality, has nothing better than to allow Black to transpose into the Scheveningen (Part 9) or to the Modern Variation (Parts 10 and 11).

| | *11* | *12* | *13* | *14* | *15* |
|---|---|---|---|---|---|
| *4* | – – | – – | – – | – – | – – |
| | P–Q4!? | – – | – – | Q–B2 | – – |
| *5* | B–QN5 | PxP | NxN[5] | P–QB4 | N–N5 |
| | PxP | QxP | PxN | N–B3[6] | Q–N1[9] |
| *6* | NxN | B–K3 | PxP | N–QB3 | P–QB4 |
| | QxQ† | P–K3[3] | QxP | NxP! | N–B3 |
| *7* | KxQ | N–QB3 | N–Q2 | NxKN[7] | QN–B3 |
| | P–QR3 | B–N5 | N–B3 | Q–K4 | P–K3 |
| *8* | N–Q4†[1] | N–N5 | B–K2 | N–N5 | B–K3 |
| | PxB | Q–K4 | P–K3 | QxN† | P–QN3![10] |
| *9* | NxP | P–QR3[4] | O–O | B–K2 | Q–Q2 |
| | B–N5† | ± | B–K2 | Q–K4 | B–N5[11] |
| *10* | K–K1 | | B–B3 | P–B4 | B–Q3 |
| | O–O–O![2] | | ± | Q–N1 | N–K4[12] |
| *11* | ∓ | | | P–B5![8] | ± |
| | | | | ± | |

*Notes to supplementary variations 11–15:*

[1] White does better to proceed with 8 B–R4!, B–Q2 9 N–B3, e.g., 9 . . . BxN 10 BxB†, PxB 11 NxP, P–K4 12 K–K2, P–B4 13 N–Q2, N–B3 14 N–B4 with an endgame slightly in White's favor. But an attempt to win a Pawn with 9 NxP? results in the loss of material: 9 . . . BxB 10 N–B3, R–Q1† 11 B–Q2, BxN 12 NxB, B–N4!

[2] 11 QN–B3, P–K4 12 P–KR3, B–R4 13 P–KN4, B–N3 14 B–K3, N–K2 with good play for Black (Fink–Sandrin, U. S. Championship 1946).

[3] 6 . . . NxN is powerfully met by 7 N–B3!, and if 7 . . . N–B6† then 8 PxN ± (L. Steiner–Goldstein, Sydney 1943).

[4] (Rubinstein–Nimzowitsch, Karlsbad 1923). If now 9 . . . BxN†, best is 10 NxB.

[5] Emanuel Lasker's suggestion.

[6] The immediate 5 . . . Q–K4 forces the win of a Pawn: 6 N–KB3, QxP† 7 B–K2, P–Q3 8 N–B3, Q–B4 9 O–O, N–B3 10 N–Q5, Q–Q2. White has some pressure, but Black's position is solid (Matanovic–Benko, Portoroz 1958). An alternative worth trying is 6 N–N5, QxP† 7 B–K2. After the text move White can save the Pawn, but without obtaining an advantage — hence the speculative sacrifice.

[7] Sharpest is 7 N/4–N5! (see Game 15).

[8] 11 . . . P–KN3 12 O–O, P–QR3 13 N–B3, B–N2 14 N–Q5, B–K4 15 K–R1! offers White good chances for the Pawn (Witkowski–Gromek, Poland 1959). 12 . . . B–N2 in this line fails to 13 P–B6! Black's correct defense is 11 . . . P–K3!, e.g., 12 O–O, P–QR3 13 N–B3, B–Q3.

[9] After 5 . . . Q–K4 6 QN–B3, P–QR3 7 P–B4, Q–N1 8 N–Q4 White has a good game.

[10] An improvement on 8 . . . B–K2 9 B–K2, O–O 10 O–O, R–Q1 11 P–QR3, P–QN3 12 P–QN4, B–N2 13 P–B4, P–Q3 14 R–R2± (Kan–Flohr, Moscow 1936). The text move prepares a possible . . . B–B4.

[11] Equally good is 9 . . . B–B4 (if 10 B–B4, then 10 . . . N–K4).

[12] 11 P–QR3, B–B4 12 P–QN4, BxB 13 QxB and now not 13 . . . O–O 14 B–K2!± (Matanovic–Fuester, Portoroz 1958), but 13 . . . NxB†.

### *Sicilian Defense Game 15*

*WHITE: Bronstein* — *BLACK: Krogius*

*USSR Championship 1959*

| | WHITE | BLACK | | WHITE | BLACK |
|---|---|---|---|---|---|
| 1 | P–K4 | P–QB4 | 14 | O–O! | PxN |
| 2 | N–KB3 | N–QB3 | 15 | PxP | B–N5 |
| 3 | P–Q4 | PxP | 16 | QR–B1 | N–K2 |
| 4 | NxP | Q–B2 | 17 | Q–B4 | BxN |
| 5 | P–QB4 | N–B3 | 18 | QxR | NxP |
| 6 | N–QB3 | NxP | 19 | B–B3 | N–N3 |
| 7 | N/4–N5 | Q–R4 | 20 | Q–B4 | P–B3 |
| 8 | P–QN4 | QxNP | 21 | Q–N3 | P–N4 |
| 9 | B–Q2 | NxB | 22 | B–R5 | B–K4 |
| 10 | N–B7† | K–Q1 | 23 | P–B4 | PxP? |
| 11 | QxN | R–QN1 | 24 | Q–N7 | P–B4 |
| 12 | N/7–Q5 | Q–R4 | 25 | Q–N5† | Resigns |
| 13 | B–K2 | P–K3 | | | |

# part 5—MODERN DRAGON VARIATION (2 . . . P-Q3)

1 P–K4, P–QB4
2 N–KB3, P–Q3[A]
3 P–Q4, PxP[B]
4 NxP, N–KB3
5 N–QB3[C], P–KN3
6 P–B3, B–N2
7 B–K3, O–O
8 Q–Q2, N–B3[D]
9 O–O–O[E]

KEY POSITION 5

## OBSERVATIONS ON KEY POSITION 5

[A] The most usual way of aiming for the Dragon Variation. Black avoids the Richter–Rouzer Attack.

[B] 3 . . . N–KB3 is dubious because of 4 PxP, NxP 5 PxP and now:

1) 5 . . . NxQP 6 B–KB4!, P–K3 7 N–B3, N–B3 8 Q–Q2, P–B3 9 O–O–O, P–K4 10 N–QN5! with decisive advantage for White (Cortlever–Euwe, Beverwijk 1941).
2) 5 . . . Q–N3 (Stolz) 6 Q–Q4, QxQ 7 NxQ, NxQP 8 N–QB3, B–Q2 9 N–Q5!, K–Q1 10 B–KB4, P–K3 11 N–QB3, P–B3 12 NxP†!, BxN 13 O–O–O±. White recovers his piece and emerges with an extra Pawn.
3) 5 . . . P–K3 6 B–Q3, NxQP 7 B–KB4±.

[C] 5 P–KB3, threatening to continue in Maroczy Bind fashion with 6 P–QB4, avoids the Dragon, but is otherwise of little promise (see Sup. Var. 20).

[D] 8 . . . P–Q4 is premature; after 9 P–K5, N–K1 10 P–B4, P–B3 11 O–O–O!, PxP 12 PxP, N–QB3 13 N–B3, P–K3 14 B–KR6! White enjoys a positional advantage. In this line 11 . . . BxP is simply met by 12 N–B3±.

[E] Very common at this point is 9 B–QB4, which transposes into Prac. Var. 21 after 9 . . . NxN 10 BxN, B–K3 11 B–N3, Q–R4 12 O–O–O. Attempts to deviate from this line rebound to White's favor, e.g., 9 . . . B–Q2 10 B–N3, R–B1 11 P–KR4, N–K4 12 P–R5!, N–B5 13 BxN, RxB 14 O-O-O, Q–R4 15 N–N3, Q–B2 16 B–R6 with a powerful attack (Djurasevic–Averbach, Wenen 1957).

This build-up which combines the comforts of a solid position with the advantages of an attacking formation is presently the most popular method of meeting the Dragon Variation.

White's attack if met indifferently may easily become decisive, but Black, by taking forceful counter-measures, can emerge from the opening with approximately even chances.

## IDEA VARIATIONS 11–13:

(11) 9 . . . B–Q2 (too passive) 10 P–KN4, NxN 11 BxN, B–B3 12 P–KR4, Q–R4 13 P–R5, KR–Q1 14 PxP, RPxP 15 K–N1, P–K4 16 B–K3, P–Q4 17 B–KR6!, PxP 18 BxB!, NxP 19 PxN, P–K6 20 B–B6! and Black resigned (Beni–Dorn, Wenen 1959). 20 . . . BxR is answered by 21 Q–R2!

(12) 9 . . . NxN 10 BxN, Q–R4 11 K–N1, P–K4 12 B–K3, B–K3 13 B–K2, KR–B1 14 P–KN4, RxN! 15 QxR, QxP† 16 K–B1, P–Q4! and Black has ample com-

pensation for the exchange (Ivkov–Panno, Copenhagen 1953). Correct is 14 P–QR3.

(13) 9 . . . NxN 10 BxN, B–K3 11 K–N1, Q–B2 12 P–KN4, KR–B1 13 P–KR4, Q–R4 14 P–R3, QR–N1 15 P–R5, P–QN4 16 PxP, RPxP 17 Q–N5, Q–B2! 18 P–K5, N–K5! 19 PxN, PxP 20 B–B2, P–N5 21 PxP, RxP 22 R–R3, RxP and Black has full compensation for the sacrificed piece (Janosevic–Bertok, Vinkovci 1958). As Vukovic has demonstrated, 17 . . . P–QR3 instead of 17 . . . Q–B2 would lose quickly, e.g., 18 R–Q2, Q–B2 19 R/2–R2, P–N5 20 Q–R6!! (20 Q–R4 is met by 20 . . . N–R4). White's best chance of maintaining the initiative consists not in 16 PxP, as played, but in 16 P–R6!, e.g., 16 . . . B–R1 17 BxN, BxB 18 N–Q5! White succeeds in demolishing the enemy Pawn formation.

PRACTICAL VARIATIONS 21–25:

1 P–K4, P–QB4 2 N–KB3, P–Q3 3 P–Q4, PxP 4 NxP, N–KB3 5 N–QB3, P–KN3 6 P–B3, B–N2 7 B–K3, O–O 8 Q–Q2, N–B3 9 O–O–O

| | 21 | 22 | 23 | 24 | 25 |
|---|---|---|---|---|---|
| 9 | – – | – – | – – | – – | – – |
| | NxN | – – | B–K3 | P–Q4! | – – |
| 10 | BxN | – – | K–N1! | PxP | – – |
| | Q–R4[1] | – – | R–B1 | NxP | – – |
| 11 | B–B4 | K–N1 | NxB[8] | N/4xN | – – |
| | B–K3 | P–K4 | PxN | PxN | – – |
| 12 | B–N3 | B–K3 | B–QB4 | NxN | B–Q4 |
| | P–QN4[2] | B–K3 | Q–Q2 | PxN | P–K4 |
| 13 | K–N1 | P–QR3[5] | B–N3[9] | QxP | B–B5 |
| | P–N5 | QR–Q1[6] | ± | Q–B2[10] | B–K3! |
| 14 | N–Q5 | P–KN4[7] | | QxR[11] | N–K4[13] |
| | BxN | ± | | B–B4 | R–K1 |
| 15 | PxB[3] | | | QxR† | B–R6[14] |
| | Q–N4 | | | KxQ | Q–B2[15] |
| 16 | KR–K1 | | | R–Q2 | = |
| | P–QR4 | | | P–KR4[12] | |
| 17 | Q–K2 | | | ∓ | |
| | QxQ | | | | |
| 18 | RxQ[4] | | | | |
| | ± | | | | |

*Notes to practical variations 21–25:*

[1] 10 . . . B–K3 is answered by 11 K–N1! which prevents 11 . . . Q–R4 because of the well-known twist 12 N–Q5! The game Bronstein–Denker, New York 1954, continued after 11 K–N1! as follows: 11 . . . P–QR3 12 P–KR4, P–KR4 13 N–Q5!, BxN

continued ▸

14 PxB, N–Q2 15 BxB, KxB 16 Q–Q4†, P–B3 17 P–KN4!, Q–N3 18 QxQ, NxQ 19 PxP, PxP 20 B–R3 with a clear advantage for White.

[2] 12 . . . BxB only strengthens White's position, e.g., 13 BPxB!, KR–Q1 14 K–N1, R–Q2 15 P–KR4, QR–Q1 16 Q–KB2!, P–QN4 17 P–R5, P–K4 18 B–K3, P–Q4 19 P–R6, P–N5? 20 PxB, PxN 21 B–N5, PxKP 22 RxR, RxR 23 BxN! and White won quickly (Sjianovski–Gufeld, Ukrainian Championship 1958). After 23 . . . R–Q7 White wins with 24 RxP! but not with 24 Q–R4, P–R4 25 QxRP, when 25 . . . P–B7† followed by 26 . . . R–Q8† saves the day.

As an alternative to the text's 12 . . . P–QN4, Averbach's 12 . . . KR–B1 is commendable.

[3] If 15 BxB Black forces equality with 15 . . . NxB, e.g., 16 BxB, N–B6†! 17 BxN, PxB 18 QxBP, QxQ 19 PxQ, KR–B1= (Filtsjer–Brasilsky, Moscow 1958). 17 PxN in this line is answered by 17 . . . QR–N1! with the following possibility: 18 PxP, QxP†! 19 QxQ, RxQ† 20 B–N2, R/1–N1. 15 . . . QR–B1? in reply to 15 BxB is inferior (see Game 16).

[4] The ensuing end game slightly favors White, e.g., 18 . . . P–R5 19 B–B4, KR–B1 20 P–QN3! but not 20 B–N5, R–R5! 21 BxN, BxB 22 B–B6, P–R6 with Bishops of opposite colors (Tal–Larsen, Zurich 1959).

[5] If 13 QxP?, KR–Q1.

[6] 13 . . . KR–Q1 14 N–N5! favors White (Boleslavski–Lissitzin, USSR Championship). After 14 . . . QxQ 15 RxQ the natural 15 . . . P–Q4 is strongly answered by 16 N–B7.

[7] This is now more promising than 14 N–N5, QxQ 15 RxQ, when Black can safely play 15 . . . P–Q4, e.g., 16 PxP, NxP 17 BxP?, N–B6†! 18 K–B1, B–R3∓.

[8] For the inferior 11 P–KN4, see Game 17.

[9] Matanovic–Larsen, Portoroz 1958.

[10] After 13 . . . R–N1 14 P–QN3! Black's attack is at a standstill.

[11] Preferable, according to Botvinnik, is 14 Q–QB5, Q–N2 15 Q–R3, B–B4 16 B–R6, but Black then achieves equality with 16 . . . Q–B2!, e.g., 17 Q–B5, Q–N3! 18 QxQ, PxQ 19 B–QB4, KR–B1 20 B–N3, RxP! 21 R–Q8†, RxR 22 BxR, B–Q5 (Averbach). In this line 17 B–Q3 is answered by 17 . . . Q–K4.

[12] Black's Queen is stronger than White's two Rooks in view of Black's attacking chances.

[13] After 14 BxR, QxB Black has ample compensation for the exchange. In addition to the text move, however, 14 B–B4 is important: 14 . . . NxN 15 QxN, Q–N4† 16 B–K3, QxP 17 BxB, PxB 18 QxBP, QR–B1 19 Q–K4, RxP 20 KR–B1, R–B7 21 QxQ, R/1xP† 22 K–N1, RxP† with a draw by perpetual check (Trifunovic–Averbach, Zagreb 1956).

[14] After 15 P–QB4, Q–B2! White, according to Chenkin, has nothing better than 16 B–Q6, Q–N3 17 B–B5, Q–B2 18 B–Q6 with a draw by repetition. If Black deviates with 17 . . . Q–B1 White has the strong answer 18 B–R3, while if White tries 17 P–B5 Black replies 17 . . . Q–N2 with a strong attack.

[15] Keres–Averbach, Tiflis 1959, resulted in a draw after 16 P–KN4, KR–Q1 17 Q–K1, N–B3 18 RxR†, RxR 19 P–N5, NxN 20 PxN, B–KB1 21 BxB, KxB.

### *Sicilian Defense Game 16*

*WHITE: Fischer* *BLACK: Larsen*

*Portoroz 1958*

| WHITE | BLACK | WHITE | BLACK |
|---|---|---|---|
| 1 P–K4 | P–QB4 | 17 P–KR4 | Q–QN4 |
| 2 N–KB3 | P–Q3 | 18 P–R5 | KR–B1 |
| 3 P–Q4 | PxP | 19 PxP | PxP |
| 4 NxP | N–KB3 | 20 P–N4 | P–R4 |
| 5 N–QB3 | P–KN3 | 21 P–N5 | N–R4 |
| 6 B–K3 | B–N2 | 22 RxN | PxR |
| 7 P–B3 | O–O | 23 P–N6 | P–K4 |
| 8 Q–Q2 | N–B3 | 24 PxP† | K–B1 |
| 9 B–QB4 | NxN | 25 B–K3 | P–Q4 |
| 10 BxN | B–K3 | 26 PxP | RxP/2 |
| 11 B–N3 | Q–R4 | 27 P–Q6 | R–KB3 |
| 12 O–O–O | P–N4 | 28 B–N5 | Q–N2 |
| 13 K–N1 | P–N5 | 29 BxR | BxB |
| 14 N–Q5 | BxN | 30 P–Q7 | R–Q1 |
| 15 BxB | QR–B1? | 31 Q–Q6† | Resigns |
| 16 B–N3 | R–B2 | | |

### *Sicilian Defense Game 17*

*WHITE: Geller* *BLACK: Byrne*

*USA–USSR, Moscow 1955*

| WHITE | BLACK | WHITE | BLACK |
|---|---|---|---|
| 1 P–K4 | P–QB4 | 23 Q–N2 | P–N5 |
| 2 N–KB3 | P–Q3 | 24 N–K2 | Q–B4 |
| 3 P–Q4 | PxP | 25 Q–R3 | R–B6 |
| 4 NxP | N–KB3 | 26 RxR | RxR |
| 5 N–QB3 | P–KN3 | 27 Q–N4 | RxB |
| 6 B–K3 | N–B3 | 28 R–QB1 | R–Q8 |
| 7 P–B3 | B–N2 | 29 P–B3 | RxR† |
| 8 Q–Q2 | O–O | 30 KxR | NxN† |
| 9 O–O–O | B–K3 | 31 QxN | PxP |
| 10 K–N1 | R–B1 | 32 Q–N2 | PxP† |
| 11 P–KN4 | Q–R4 | 33 KxP | Q–N5† |
| 12 NxB | PxN | 34 K–B2 | P–R4 |
| 13 B–QB4 | N–Q1 | 35 Q–N4 | Q–B4 |
| 14 B–K2 | N–Q2 | 36 K–N3 | Q–N3† |
| 15 B–Q4 | N–K4? | 37 K–B3 | P–R5 |
| 16 P–B4 | N/1–B3 | 38 P–R4 | Q–Q5† |
| 17 BxN? | PxB | 39 K–B2 | Q–B7† |
| 18 P–B5 | N–Q5 | 40 K–Q3 | QxQRP |
| 19 PxNP | PxP | 41 P–R5 | Q–N6† |
| 20 KR–B1 | R–KB5 | 42 K–Q2 | PxP |
| 21 P–N5 | P–N4 | Resigns | |
| 22 B–Q3 | QR–B1 | | |

SUPPLEMENTARY VARIATIONS 16–20:

1 P–K4, P–QB4 2 N–KB3, P–Q3 3 P–Q4, PxP 4 NxP, N–KB3

Loewenfisch's aggressive 6 P–B4 (Sup. Var. 16 and 17) was considered for quite some time White's strongest weapon against the modern Dragon. Today, however the line holds no terrors for Black.

Sup. Var. 18 (6 P–KR3) is an old-fashioned attempt to play for a quick attack. The modern system with 6 P–B3 (Part 5) offers White a more lasting initiative.

6 P–KN3 (Sup. Var. 19) is of little promise. Black obtains a fine game with Reshevsky's 6 . . . N–B3! followed by 7 . . . NxN!

In Sup. Var. 20 White delays the development of his Queen Knight, protecting his attacked King Pawn with 5 P–KB3. White aims for a Maroczy Bind with 6 P–QB4; Black, however, easily thwarts this plan and emerges from the opening with the initiative.

| | *16* | *17* | *18* | *19* | *20* |
|---|---|---|---|---|---|
| *5* | N–QB3 | – – | – – | – – | P–KB3 |
| | P–KN3 | – – | – – | – – | P–K4![14] |
| *6* | P–B4 | – – | P–KR3 | P–KN3 | B–N5†[15] |
| | N–B3![1] | – – | B–N2 | N–B3![11] | QN–Q2 |
| *7* | NxN | B–N5 | B–K3 | B–N2 | N–B5 |
| | PxN | B–Q2 | N–B3 | NxN! | P–Q4! |
| *8* | P–K5 | BxN | Q–Q2[8] | QxN | PxP |
| | N–Q2[2] | BxB[6] | O–O | B–N2 | P–QR3 |
| *9* | PxP[3] | P–K5 | O–O–O | O–O[12] | BxN† |
| | PxP | PxP | NxN | O–O | QxB |
| *10* | B–K3 | PxP | BxN | Q–Q3 | N–K3 |
| | Q–K2[4] | N–K5 | Q–R4[9] | B–K3 | P–QN4[16] |
| *11* | Q–Q4 | NxN | K–N1 | N–Q5 | ═ |
| | B–N2 | BxN | P–K4 | R–B1 | |
| *12* | QxB | O–O | B–K3 | P–QB3 | |
| | QxB[5]† | B–N2[7] | B–K3[10] | R–K1[13] | |
| | ═ | ═ | ═ | ═ | |

*Notes to supplementary variations 16–20:*

[1] Weak for Black is 6 . . . B–N2? 7 P–K5, PxP 8 PxP:

1) 8 . . . N–N1 9 B–N5†, N–B3 10 NxN, QxQ† 11 NxQ, P–QR3 12 B–R4, B–Q2 13 P–R3, N–R3 14 NxP, White winning a Pawn (Pilnick–Kashdan, New York 1949).

2) 8 . . . KN–Q2 9 P–K6, N–K4 10 B–N5†, QN–B3 11 PxP†, KxP 12 O–O† with White for choice (Kamyschov–Averbach, Moscow 1948).

3) 8 . . . N–Q4? 9 B–N5†, K–B1 10 O–O, BxP? 11 B–R6†, K–N1 12 NxN, QxN 13 N–B5!, Q–B4† 14

B–K3, Q–B2 15 N–R6†, K–B1 16 RxP mate.

6 . . . QN–Q2 parries the threat of 7 P–K5 but is somewhat passive, e.g., 7 B–K2, B–N2 8 B–K3, O–O 9 O–O, P–QR3 10 B–B3, Q–B2 11 K–R1, R–N1 12 P–QR4, P–N3 13 P–K5!, PxP 14 N–B6± (Horowitz–Reshevsky, rapid transit, New York 1944).

[2] 8 . . . PxP 9 QxQ†, KxQ 10 PxP favors White:

1) 10 . . . N–N5 11 B–KB4, B–KN2 12 O–O–O†, K–K1? 13 N–N5!± (Clarke–Dake, San Francisco 1943). Black's 12th move is open to criticism, but even if Black plays the superior 12 . . . K–B2 or 12 . . . B–Q2 it is still White for choice.
2) 10 . . . N–Q2 11 B–KB4, B–KN2 12 O–O–O, K–K1 13 R–K1, N–B4 14 B–K2, B–Q2 15 B–B3± (Fine).
3) 10 . . . N–Q4 11 NxN, PxN 12 B–KN5!, P–KR3 13 B–R4, P–N4 14 B–B2, B–KN2 15 O–O–O, B–N2? 16 B–Q4, P–K3 17 B–K2 and the weakness of Black's Pawn structure soon proved fatal (Donner-Spanjaard, Veenendaal 1953). Instead of 15 . . . B–N2? in this line, Black should play 15 . . . BxP, answering 16 RxP† with 16 . . . B–Q3. Because of this possibility, White does better to play 15 B–Q4 in lieu of 15 O–O–O.

[3] Interesting but dubious for White is 9 Q–B3, B–KN2! 10 B–N5, O–O! 11 QxP, R–N1 12 B–K3, P–QR3 13 B–R4, PxP 14 O–O–O, Q–R4, when Black has promising counterplay (Bronstein–Vasiukov, Tiflis 1959). Another inferior try for White is 9 B–B4, e.g., 9 . . . N–N3!, and if 10 Q–Q4? then 10 . . . B–KN2∓ (Averbach–Lissitzin, USSR 1948).

[4] An idea of Eliskases. 10 . . . B–K2 11 Q–Q2, O–O 12 O–O–O, N–B3 13 P–KR3, B–K3 14 P–KN4 favors White (Fuderer–Trifunovic, Yugoslavia 1953), but Black fares much better in this variation with 12 . . . Q–R4, e.g., 13 K–N1, P–Q4 with active counterplay.

[5] The chances are about even:

1) 13 B–K2, R–B1 14 R–KB1, B–R3 15 R–B3, Q–N8† =.
2) 13 N–K2, R–B1 14 R–Q1, B–R3 15 RxP, BxN 16 BxB, QxP 17 Q–Q4, QxQ 18 RxQ, O–O–O =.

[6] Less clear for Black is 8 . . . PxB 9 P–K5, PxP 10 PxP, N–N5 11 P–K6!?, BxP 12 Q–B3!, Q–Q2 13 B–B4 followed by 14 O–O–O, as suggested by Neshmetdinov.

[7] The game Penrose–Barden, Hastings 1958, continued 13 R–K1, Q–Q4 14 P–B3, QxP 15 B–B4!, QxB 16 Q–R4†, B–B3? 17 RxP†!, K–B1 18 N–K6†! and White won. Correct for Black in this complicated variation is 16 . . . P–N4!, e.g., 17 NxP, O–O 18 RxB, Q–N4. If Black wants to avoid these fireworks, however, he can safely answer White's 13 R–K1 with 13 . . . B–Q4 or 13 . . . B–QB3.

[8] For the supersharp 8 P–KN4, see Game 18. Even though White won this game, Black can improve his play with 12 . . . B–N5!

[9] 10 . . . B–K3 11 K–N1!, Q–B2 12 P–KN4, KR–B1 13 B–N2, P–QN4 14 P–R3, QR–N1 15 N–Q5 favors White (Adams–Reshevsky, Hollywood 1945).

[10] Black has sufficient counterplay. His task is easier here than in an analogous system with White playing P–KR3.

continued ▶

[11] If Black fails to increase his influence in the center immediately, White gains the upper hand. Two examples follow:

1) 6 . . . B–N2 7 B–N2, O–O 8 P–KR3, N–B3 9 N/4–K2!, P–QR3 10 O–O, N–K4 11 K–R2, B–Q2 12 P–B4, N–B5 13 P–N3, N–QR4 14 B–K3, R–B1 15 Q–Q2, P–QN4 16 P–R3, Q–B2 17 QR–Q1± (Bronstein–Saitar, Moscow 1948).
2) 6 . . . B–N5 7 Q–Q3, Q–B1 8 B–N2, B–N2 9 P–KR3!± (Adams–Suesman, Boston 1944).

[12] After 9 B–K3, O–O 10 Q–Q2, N–N5 Black has the advantage (see Game 19).

[13] 13 B–K3, Q–R4 14 P–KR3, Q–R5! 15 KR–K1, P–QN4 and Black has the initiative (Teschner–Tal, Baden 1957). Correct for White in this line is 14 P–QR4!, nipping Black's Queenside play in the bud.

[14] Otherwise White obtains the Maroczy Bind with 6 P–QB4, e.g., 5 . . . N–B3 6 P–QB4, P–K3 7 N–B3, B–K2 8 N–N3, O–O 9 B–K2, Q–B2 10 O–O, R–Q1 11 B–B4, and White has an advantage in space (Euwe–Winter, Amsterdam 1937).

[15] Other possibilities:

1) 6 N–N5, P–QR3 7 N/5–B3, B–K3 8 N–Q5, NxN 9 PxN, B–B1! 10 B–K3, B–K2 11 Q–Q2, P–B4∓ (Smyslov–Bondarevski, Leningrad–Moscow 1941). In this line of play 8 B–N5 is simply answered by 8 . . . QN–Q2.
2) 6 N–N3, P–Q4! 7 B–N5, B–K3! 8 PxP, QxP= (Evans and Prins–Reshevsky and Horowitz, New York 1951).

[16] Black has sufficient compensation for the Pawn (see Game 20).

*Sicilian Defense Game 18*

*WHITE: Lasker* — *BLACK: Napier*

*Cambridge Springs 1904*

| | WHITE | BLACK | | WHITE | BLACK |
|---|---|---|---|---|---|
| 1 | P–K4 | P–QB4 | 19 | B–B5 | NPxP |
| 2 | N–KB3 | P–Q3 | 20 | B–B4 | PxP |
| 3 | P–Q4 | PxP | 21 | BxBP | N–K5 |
| 4 | NxP | N–KB3 | 22 | BxR | BxP |
| 5 | N–QB3 | P–KN3 | 23 | QR–N1 | B–B6† |
| 6 | P–KR3 | B–N2 | 24 | K–B1 | B–KN5 |
| 7 | B–K3 | N–QB3 | 25 | BxKRP | BxB |
| 8 | P–KN4 | O–O | 26 | RxB | N–N6† |
| 9 | P–N5 | N–K1 | 27 | K–N2 | NxR |
| 10 | P–KR4 | N–B2 | 28 | RxP | P–R4 |
| 11 | P–B4 | P–K4! | 29 | R–N3 | B–N2 |
| 12 | N/4–K2 | P–Q4? | 30 | R–KR3 | N–N6 |
| 13 | KPxP | N–Q5 | 31 | K–B3 | R–R3 |
| 14 | NxN | NxP | 32 | KxP | N–K7† |
| 15 | N–B5!! | NxN | 33 | K–B5 | N–B6 |
| 16 | QxQ | RxQ | 34 | P–R3 | N–R5 |
| 17 | N–K7† | K–R1! | 35 | B–K3 | Resigns |
| 18 | P–R5!! | R–K1 | | | |

*Sicilian Defense Game 19*

*WHITE: Evans* *BLACK: Reshevsky*

*Havana 1952*

| | WHITE | BLACK | | WHITE | BLACK |
|---|---|---|---|---|---|
| 1 | P–K4 | P–QB4 | 27 | Q–KR4 | R–N8 |
| 2 | N–KB3 | P–Q3 | 28 | Q–B6† | B–N2 |
| 3 | P–Q4 | PxP | 29 | Q–B3 | RxR† |
| 4 | NxP | N–KB3 | 30 | QxR | BxP |
| 5 | N–QB3 | P–KN3 | 31 | N–B6 | B–B6 |
| 6 | P–KN3 | N–B3 | 32 | P–R3 | K–N2 |
| 7 | B–N2 | NxN | 33 | Q–Q3 | B–B3 |
| 8 | QxN | B–N2 | 34 | K–R2 | B–B5 |
| 9 | B–K3 | O–O | 35 | Q–KB3 | Q–QB7 |
| 10 | Q–Q2 | N–N5 | 36 | N–N4 | Q–Q7 |
| 11 | O–O? | NxB | 37 | N–Q5 | B–Q5 |
| 12 | QxN | B–K3 | 38 | P–R4 | Q–K8 |
| 13 | N–Q5 | P–QR4 | 39 | N–B4 | B–N8† |
| 14 | P–QB3 | R–N1 | 40 | K–R3 | B–N4 |
| 15 | QR–Q1 | P–QN4 | 41 | Q–Q5 | Q–K1! |
| 16 | P–KB4 | P–N5 | 42 | P–N4 | P–R4 |
| 17 | PxP | PxP | 43 | NxP† | PxN |
| 18 | P–K5 | K–R1 | 44 | Q–N5† | K–B1 |
| 19 | P–N3 | Q–Q2 | 45 | Q–R6† | K–K2 |
| 20 | K–R1 | KR–Q1 | 46 | QxP | Q–QN1 |
| 21 | R–Q4 | PxP | 47 | Q–N5† | P–B3 |
| 22 | PxP | Q–R2 | 48 | Q–N7† | K–K3 |
| 23 | RxNP! | QxP | 49 | P–N5 | Q–R7† |
| 24 | RxR | RxR | 50 | K–N4 | B–K7† |
| 25 | NxP | RxP | 51 | B–B3 | Q–N7† |
| 26 | Q–Q4 | B–KB1 | | Resigns | |

*Sicilian Defense Game 20*

*WHITE: Klaeger* *BLACK: Kottnauer*

*Beverwijk 1954*

| | WHITE | BLACK | | WHITE | BLACK |
|---|---|---|---|---|---|
| 1 | P–K4 | P–QB4 | 13 | N–K4? | NxN |
| 2 | N–KB3 | P–Q3 | 14 | PxN | P–B4 |
| 3 | P–Q4 | PxP | 15 | KPxP | Q–R2 |
| 4 | NxP | N–KB3 | 16 | Q–K2 | BxP |
| 5 | P–KB3 | P–K4! | 17 | PxP | B–Q2 |
| 6 | B–N5† | QN–Q2 | 18 | P–QR4 | R–B5 |
| 7 | N–B5 | P–Q4! | 19 | R–B1 | R–K5 |
| 8 | PxP | P–QR3 | 20 | R–R3 | BxR |
| 9 | BxN† | QxB | 21 | PxB | PxP |
| 10 | N–K3 | P–QN4 | 22 | PxP | Q–B4 |
| 11 | P–QB4 | B–B4 | | Resigns | |
| 12 | N–B3 | O–O! | | | |

# part 6—BOLESLAVSKI SYSTEM

1 P–K4, P–QB4
2 N–KB3, N–QB3
3 P–Q4, PxP
4 NxP, N–B3
5 N–QB3, P–Q3
6 B–K2[A], P–K4
7 N–N3[B], B–K2
8 O–O[C], O–O

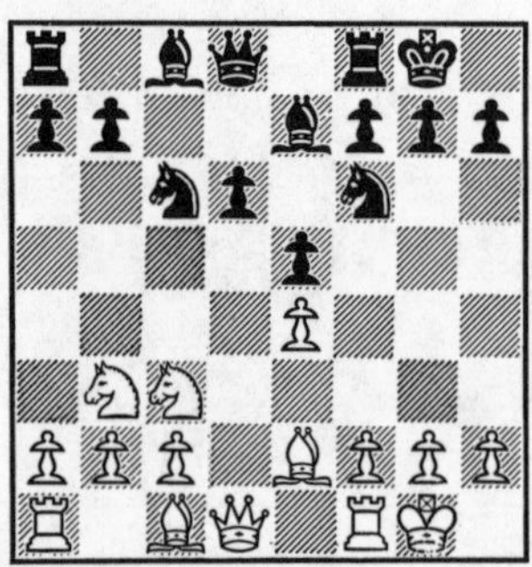

KEY POSITION 6

## OBSERVATIONS ON KEY POSITION 6

[A] White can definitely avoid the Boleslavski with either 6 B–KN5 (Richter–Rouzer) or 6 B–QB4 (Sozin). In addition, 6 B–K3 may also prove a deterrent to Black's plans, e.g., 6 . . . P–K4 7 N/4–N5!, P–QR3 8 N–R3, P–QN4 9 N–Q5!, NxN 10 PxN, N–N1 11 P–QB4, PxP 12 NxP, N–Q2 13 Q–R4 with a promising game for White (Ragosin–Lebedew, Moscow 1956). In this line, however, Feuerstein's suggestion of 8 . . . P–Q4!? leads to a very sharp and intense struggle apparently not unfavorable to Black. An unclear situation results if Black abstains from the Boleslavski and answers 6 B–K3 with 6 . . . N–KN5, e.g., 7 B–QN5, NxB 8 PxN, B–Q2 9 O–O, P–K3! 10 BxN, PxB 11 P–K5, P–Q4 12 Q–B3, Q–K2 13 P–QN4, P–N3 14 P–N5, P–QB4 15 P–K4! B–N2 16 PxP, O–O! (Karaklaic–Averbach, Belgrade 1956). This complicated game ended in a draw. In this variation Black must not play the faulty 9 . . . N–K4 which is powerfully met by 10 N–B3! (Ivkov–Taimanov, Hastings 1955).

[B] 7 NxN and 7 N–B3 are of little promise:

1) 7 NxN, PxN 8 O–O, B–K2 9 P–B4, N–Q2! and now both 10 P–B5, O–O 11 Q–Q3, N–N3! and 10 Q–Q3, PxP 11 BxP, N–K4! prove satisfactory for Black. See Game 21 for the inferior 9 . . . PxP.

2) 7 N–B3, P–KR3 (White threatens 8 B–KN5) 8 O–O, B–K2, when White has a choice of three continuations: 9 R–K1, O–O 10 P–KR3, B–K3 11 B–B1, Q–R4! 12 B–Q2, Q–Q1 13 B–B1, Q–R4! with a draw by repetition (Bouwmeester–Matanovic, Beverwijk 1960); 9 P–QN3, O–O 10 B–N2, B–N5 (10 . . . B–K3!) 11 R–K1, R–B1 12 P–KR3, BxN 13 BxB, N–Q5 14 Q–Q3, P–QN4 15 B–Q1!, P–N5 16 N–K2 with a positional advantage for White (Smyslov–Ciocaltea, Alekhine Memorial Tournament, Moscow 1956); or 9 B–K3, O–O 10 Q–Q?, B–K3 11 QR–Q1, Q–Q2! 12 P–KR3, KR–Q1 followed by . . . P–Q4 with equality (Euwe–Martin, Correspondence Game 1959).

[C] After 8 B–KN5 Black has a choice between liquidating with 8 . . . NxP 9 BxB, NxN 10 BxQ, NxQ 11 RxN, KxB 12 RxP†, K–K2= (Book–Bronstein, Saltsjobaden 1948) or ignoring White's positional "threat" of 9 BxN with 8 . . . O–O, as demonstrated in Game 22.

That Black can play . . . P–K4 with impunity in many variations of the Sicilian Defense was one of the important positional discoveries made immediately after World War II. Prior to that time, the prevailing opinion — strongly influenced by the writings of Dr. Tarrasch — was that . . . P–K4 causes an irreparable weakening of Black's Q4. Boleslavski, however, succeeded in demonstrating that this weakness is more than offset by the activity of Black's pieces.

In this variation one essential strategic point must be underscored: Black must not hesitate to exchange Bishop for Knight if White plays N–Q5. If White then recaptures with a Pawn, Black's weakness on Q4 vanishes. White may emerge with a Queenside Pawn majority, but in most cases this is of little import if properly countered.

White, on his part, must not play passively. If Black succeeds in playing . . . P–Q4 effectively, he normally obtains the advantage.

IDEA VARIATIONS 14-16:

(14) 9 P–B3, P–QR4! 10 B–K3 (better is 10 P–QR4; see Prac. Var. 30), P–R5 11 N–B1 (11 N–Q2, P–R6), Q–R4 (11 . . . P–R6 12 P–QN3, N–N5 13 N–Q3), 12 Q–Q2, N–Q5 13 B–Q3 (13 BxN, PxB 14 QxP, P–Q4! 15 N–Q3, PxP 16 NxKP, R–Q1 with sufficient compensation for the Pawn), B–K3 14 P–QR3 (Pachman–Bronstein, Helsinki 1952) and 14 . . . P–Q4! now gives Black the edge.

(15) 9 P–B3, B–K3? (for 9 . . . Q–N3†, see Prac. Var. 30, note 11) 10 N–Q5!, BxN 11 PxB, N–QN5 12 P–QB4, P–QR4 13 B–K3, N–R4 14 Q–Q2, N–B5 15 B–Q1, P–QN4? (15 . . . P–QN3 is indicated) 16 P–QR3, PxP 17 PxN, PxN 18 PxP, Q–N1 19 R–R3 with a clear advantage for White (Geller–Barcza, Stockholm 1952).

(16) 9 B–K3, B–K3 10 B–B3, P–QR4 11 N–Q5, BxN 12 PxB, N–N1! 13 P–QR4 (13 Q–Q3! keeping the Queenside Pawn structure flexible is more effective; see Prac. Var. 27), QN–Q2 14 B–K2, N–N3 15 P–QB4, QN–Q2 16 N–Q2, N–K1 17 K–R1, B–N4 with a positional advantage for Black (Pilnik–Petrosian, Buenos Aires 1954).

PRACTICAL VARIATIONS 26–30:

1 P–K4, P–QB4 2 N–KB3, N–QB3 3 P–Q4, PxP 4 NxP, N–B3 5 N–QB3, P–Q3 6 B–K2, P–K4 7 N–N3, B–K2 8 O–O, O–O

| | *26* | *27* | *28* | *29* | *30* |
|---|---|---|---|---|---|
| *9* | B–K3 | – – | – – | P–B4 | P–B3 |
| | B–K3 | – – | P–QR4 | P–QR4![8] | P–QR4![11] |
| *10* | B–B3 | – – | B–B3[5] | P–QR4 | P–QR4[12] |
| | N–QR4 | P–QR4 | P–R5 | N–QN5 | N–QN5 |
| *11* | NxN | N–Q5 | N–Q2 | B–B3 | B–KN5 |
| | QxN | BxN | P–R6 | B–K3 | B–K3 |
| *12* | Q–Q2 | PxB | PxP[6] | K–R1[9] | BxN |
| | KR–B1! | N–N1 | Q–R4 | R–B1 | BxB[13] |
| *13* | KR–Q1![1] | Q–Q3![3] | N–Q5 | P–B5 | = |
| | Q–N5 | KN–Q2 | NxN | B–B5 | |
| *14* | QR–N1 | B–N4 | PxN | R–K1 | |
| | P–KR3 | Q–B2 | N–Q5 | N–Q2 | |
| *15* | P–QR3 | P–QR4 | BxN | N–Q2 | |
| | Q–B5 | N–N3 | PxB | B–R3 | |
| *16* | QR–B1 | N–Q2 | N–N3 | N–B1 | |
| | P–R3 | N/3–Q2 | QxRP | BxN! | |
| *17* | B–K2 | BxN | NxP | RxB | |
| | Q–B2 | NxB[4] | B–B3 | N–N3 | |
| *18* | P–B3 | ± | Q–Q2 | Q–K2 | |
| | N–Q2[2] | | Q–N7[7] | B–N4[10] | |
| | = | | = | ∓ | |

*Notes to practical variations 26–30:*

[1] After 13 N–Q5, QxQ 14 NxB†, K–B1 15 BxQ, RxP! 16 B–B3, KxN 17 B–Q1, RxB 18 PxR, NxP Black has ample compensation for the exchange.

[2] Boleslavski–Euwe, Zurich 1953.

[3] An important improvement on the immediate 13 P–QR4. See Idea Var. 16.

[4] Pilnik–Smyslov, Amsterdam 1956. A good plan for White in this position is 18 P–QB3, and if 18 . . . N–B4 then 19 Q–N5 followed by N–QB4 and P–QN4. White's chances are excellent if he maintains a mobile Queenside.

[5] Pilnik's suggestion of 10 N–Q2! followed by 11 N–B4 merits serious consideration.

[6] 12 P–QN3 is a plausible alternative.

[7] Matanovic–Gligoric, Stockholm 1952. Black has sufficient counterchances.

[8] 9 . . . PxP is weaker by far. The game Botvinnik–Boleslavski, Sverdlovsk 1943, continued 10 BxP, B–K3 11 B–Q3, N–K4 12 K–R1, Q–N3 13 Q–K2, NxB? 14 PxN, BxN? 15 B–K3, Q–N5 16 PxB, QxNP 17 R–B5, when White has a powerful initiative in return for his sacrificed Pawn.

[9] A common mistake is 12 P–B5, B–B5 13 R–K1?, when 13 . . . NxBP 14 QxN, Q–N3† nets Black a Pawn.

[10] Guldin–Boleslavski, USSR Championship 1949. Black has Queenside pressure.

[11] 9 . . . B–K3? is weak (see Idea Var. 12). 9 . . . Q–N3†, however, is a good alternative, e.g., 10 K–R1, B–K3 11 N–Q5, BxN 12 PxB, N–QN5 13 P–QB4, P–QR4 14 B–Q2, P–R5 15 N–B1, N–R3 16 R–QN1, N–B4 17 B–B3 and White has only a slight edge (Bisguier–Milic, Helsinki 1952). Even better for Black in this variation is 10 . . . R–Q1 which equalizes.

[12] The text move is steadier than 10 B–K3. See Idea Var. 14.

[13] After 13 N–Q5, BxN 14 PxB, B–N4 the chances are even.

*Sicilian Defense Game 21*

*WHITE: N. Bergquist* — *BLACK: Chr. Poulsen*

*Radio Match, Stockholm–Copenhagen 1952*

| WHITE | BLACK | WHITE | BLACK |
|---|---|---|---|
| 1 P–K4 | P–QB4 | 12 Q–Q3 | Q–N5 |
| 2 N–KB3 | N–QB3 | 13 QR–N1 | Q–B4 |
| 3 P–Q4 | PxP | 14 N–R4 | Q–QR4 |
| 4 NxP | N–KB3 | 15 BxP! | QxN |
| 5 N–QB3 | P–Q3 | 16 BxB | KxB |
| 6 B–K2 | P–K4 | 17 P–K5 | N–K1 |
| 7 NxN | PxN | 18 Q–QB3! | N–B2 |
| 8 O–O | B–K2 | 19 Q–B5† | K–K1 |
| 9 P–B4 | PxP? | 20 Q–Q6 | N–Q4 |
| 10 BxP | Q–N3† | 21 B–N5! | PxB |
| 11 K–R1 | QxP? | 22 QxN | Resigns |

*Sicilian Defense Game 22*

*WHITE: Reicher* — BLACK: *Boleslavski*

*Bucharest 1953*

| WHITE | BLACK | WHITE | BLACK |
|---|---|---|---|
| 1 P–K4 | P–QB4 | 15 P–QB3 | N–K2 |
| 2 N–KB3 | N–QB3 | 16 R–Q1 | N–N3 |
| 3 P–Q4 | PxP | 17 P–R5 | N–R5 |
| 4 NxP | N–B3 | 18 B–Q3 | Q–N4 |
| 5 N–QB3 | P–Q3 | 19 P–B3 | B–N6† |
| 6 B–K2 | P–K4 | 20 K–B1 | P–B4! |
| 7 N–N3 | B–K2 | 21 R–KN1 | NxP! |
| 8 B–KN5 | O–O | 22 RxB | PxKP |
| 9 BxN | BxB | 23 K–N2 | PxB |
| 10 N–Q5 | B–N4 | 24 RxP | BxN |
| 11 B–B4 | B–K3 | 25 RxB | Q–R5 |
| 12 P–KR4 | B–R3 | 26 RxN | QxP† |
| 13 P–N4 | B–B5 | Resigns | |
| 14 Q–K2 | R–B1 | | |

## part 7—NAJDORF SYSTEM WITH 6 B-K2

1 P–K4, P–QB4
2 N–KB3, P–Q3
3 P–Q4, PxP
4 NxP, N–KB3
5 N–QB3, P–QR3
6 B–K2, P–K4
7 N–N3[A], B–K2[B]
8 O–O, O–O

KEY POSITION 7

OBSERVATIONS ON KEY POSITION 7

[A] 7 N–B3 is countered simply with 7 . . . B–K2. Black, with QN–Q2 at his disposal, need not fear 8 B–KN5 as in the analogous position in the Boleslavski (cf. Part 6, note B of the introductory moves).

[B] 7 . . . B–K3 is inferior, e.g., 8 O–O, QN–Q2 9 P–B4!, Q–B2 10 P–B5, B–B5 11 P–QR4!, R–B1 12 B–K3, B–K2 13 P–R5, P–R4 14 BxB, QxB 15 R–R4, Q–B2 16 P–R3 with a clear positional advantage for White. 13 . . . O–O in this line is met strongly by 14 P–N4.

The Pawn formation of the Najdorf Variation is similar to that of the Boleslavski; in both systems Black plays . . . P–K4, but in the Najdorf 5 N–QB3 is replaced by 5 . . . P–QR3. This latter move offers Black a wider choice in his later development. Black may proceed with . . . QN–Q2 and possibly fianchetto his Queen Bishop.

The set-up with . . . QN–Q2 and . . . B–QN2 is particularly harmonious in those cases in which White plays for attack by means of P–KB4. Black's Queen Bishop then exercises strong pressure on White's KP which may lack adequate support. Because of this, White often abstains from an attack and continues his development along purely positional lines: supporting his King Pawn with P–KB3 or B–KB3 and exercising pressure on the Queen file. Black's struggle to achieve . . . P–Q4 plays an important role in the course of the game.

IDEA VARIATIONS 17–19:

(17) 9 P–B4, QN–Q2 10 Q–K1, P–QN4 11 P–QR3, B–N2 12 B–B3, R–B1 13 K–R1, R–K1 14 Q–B2, B–B1 15 B–Q2, P–Q4!∓ (Novotelnov–Petrosian, USSR Championship 1951). Now 16 PxQP is met by 16 . . . P–K5!, while 16 PxKP fails to 16 . . . PxP!

(18) 9 B–K3, Q–B2 10 P–QR4, B–K3? 11 P–R5, Q–B3 12 B–B3, QN–Q2 13 N–Q5, BxN 14 PxB, Q–N4 15 Q–Q3! KR–B1 16 KR–B1, QxQ 17 PxQ, P–KR3 18 R–B3!± (Smyslov–Tal, Candidates' Tournament 1959). 10 . . . B–K3? enables White to freeze Black's Queenside play. Correct is 10 . . . P–QN3 as played in Idea Var. 19.

(19) 9 B–K3, Q–B2 10 P–QR4, P–QN3 11 Q–Q2, B–K3 12 KR–Q1 (correct is 12 N–Q5), R–B1! 13 Q–K1, Q–N2 14 R–Q2, QN–Q2 15 P–B3, P–Q4! 16 PxP, NxP 17 NxN, BxN∓. Black's pieces enjoy the greater

mobility as a result of his enterprising and original strategy (Unzicker–Bronstein, Goteborg 1955). Note that 11 . . . B–K3 leaves QN2 open for the Queen, so that Black's Q4 can be controlled with the maximum number of pieces.

PRACTICAL VARIATIONS 31–35:

1 P–K4, P–QB4 2 N–KB3, P–Q3 3 P–Q4, PxP 4 NxP, N–KB3 5 N–QB3, P–QR3 6 B–K2, P–K4 7 N–N3, B–K2 8 O–O, O–O

| | *31* | *32* | *33* | *34* | *35* |
|---|---|---|---|---|---|
| *9* | B–K3 | – – | – – | B–KN5 | – – |
| | QN–Q2 | Q–B2 | B–K3 | QN–Q2[10] | B–K3! |
| *10* | P–B3 | P–B3[4] | P–B4[8] | P–QR4 | BxN |
| | Q–B2[1] | B–K3[5] | PxP | P–QN3 | BxB |
| *11* | P–QR4[2] | N–Q5 | BxP | B–QB4 | N–Q5 |
| | P–QN3 | BxN | N–B3 | B–N2 | N–Q2 |
| *12* | Q–Q2 | PxB | K–R1! | Q–K2 | Q–Q3 |
| | B–N2 | QN–Q2[6] | Q–N3 | Q–B2 | R–B1 |
| *13* | KR–Q1 | P–QB4 | Q–Q2 | KR–Q1 | P–QB3 |
| | KR–Q1 | P–QN3 | QR–B1 | KR–B1 | B–N4 |
| *14* | Q–K1 | N–Q2 | B–K3 | N–Q2 | QR–Q1 |
| | P–Q4!? | P–QR4 | Q–B2 | P–R3 | K–R1 |
| *15* | PxP | N–N1! | N–Q4 | BxN | B–B3 |
| | B–N5 | N–K1 | NxN | NxB | P–QN3[12] |
| *16* | R–Q3[3] | N–B3[7] | BxN[9] | B–N3[11] | = |
| | ± | ± | ± | ± | |

*Notes to practical variations 31–35:*

[1] 10 . . . P–QN4 is premature owing to 11 P–QR4, P–N5 12 N–Q5, NxN 13 QxN, R–N1 14 QR–B1, B–N2 15 Q–R5± (Bisguier–Udovic, Zagreb 1955). Here if 13 . . . N–N3 14 Q–R5!.

[2] It is essential to prevent . . . P–QN4–5, thus: 11 Q–K1, P–QN4 12 P–QR3, N–N3 13 Q–B2, R–N1 14 QR–N1, B–K3 15 K–R1, N–B5∓ (Smyslov–Kotov, Zurich 1953).

[3] Black hardly has sufficient compensation for the Pawn: 16 . . . N–B4 17 NxN, PxN 18 Q–B2, P–B5 19 B–N6!, Q–B1 20 R–K3, R–Q3 21 P–R5, NxP 22 NxN, RxN 23 R–R4! (Bisguier–Gligoric, Zagreb 1955). According to H. Muller, Black's best is 16 . . . BxN 17 RxB, Q–N1. But after 18 B–N5, P–R3 19 B–R4 White is better, thus: 19 . . . P–N4? 20 B–N3, NxP 21 R–Q3. Or 19 . . . BxP 20 R–Q1.

[4] Bisguier's pet line. More accurate, however, is 10 P–QR4 to prevent . . . P–QN4–5. See Idea Var. 18 and 19.

[5] 10 . . . P–QN4 has never been played, though it may well be the most promising move.

[6] Stronger is 6 . . . P–QR4, followed by . . . N–R3.

[7] 16 . . . Q–Q1 17 P–QR3, when White obtained a strong Queenside initiative by an eventual P–QN4 (Bisguier–Barcza, Zagreb 1955). See Game 28.

continued ▸

[8] This advance offers better chances than in the analogous line of the Boleslavski system.

[9] White controls greater space.

[10] 9 . . . NxP 10 BxB, NxN 11 BxQ, NxQ 12 B–K7, R–K1 13 QRxN, RxB 14 RxP leads to an end game favorable to White.

[11] Black has not satisfactorily solved the problem of his backward Queen Pawn (Larsen–Gligoric, Moscow 1956).

[12] Black's chances are a hairline better (Averbach–Petrosian, USSR Championship, Tiflis 1959).

*Sicilian Defense Game 23*

*WHITE: Bisguier* *BLACK: Barcza*

*Zagreb 1955*

| | WHITE | BLACK | | WHITE | BLACK |
|---|---|---|---|---|---|
| 1 | P–K4 | P–QB4 | 32 | B–Q4 | B–K6†! |
| 2 | N–KB3 | P–Q3 | 33 | QxB | PxB |
| 3 | P–Q4 | PxP | 34 | QxQP | QxQ† |
| 4 | NxP | N–KB3 | 35 | R/1xQ | PxP |
| 5 | N–QB3 | P–QR3 | 36 | PxP | R–Q1 |
| 6 | B–K2 | P–K4 | 37 | B–R4! | R–R1 |
| 7 | N–N3 | B–K2 | 38 | R–N5 | R–R2 |
| 8 | O–O | O–O | 39 | R/4–Q5 | N–B3 |
| 9 | B–K3 | K–B2 | 40 | R/Q–B5 | R–R3 |
| 10 | P–B3 | B–K3 | 41 | P–Q7! | NxP |
| 11 | N–Q5! | BxN | 42 | R–B7 | R–Q3 |
| 12 | PxB | QN–Q2 | 43 | RxRP | R–Q6 |
| 13 | P–QB4 | P–QN3 | 44 | B–B6 | N–K4 |
| 14 | N–Q2 | P–QR4 | 45 | R–B8† | K–N2 |
| 15 | N–N1! | N–K1 | 46 | RxN | RxRP |
| 16 | N–B3 | Q–Q1 | 47 | K–B2 | R–B6 |
| 17 | P–QR3 | B–N4 | 48 | B–N7 | RxR |
| 18 | B–B2 | P–B4 | 49 | BxR | R–B2 |
| 19 | Q–B2 | Q–B3 | 50 | B–R6 | K–B3 |
| 20 | B–Q3 | P–N3 | 51 | R–Q5 | R–B7† |
| 21 | N–R4 | Q–Q1 | 52 | K–N3 | P–B5† |
| 22 | P–QN4 | N/1–B3 | 53 | K–R3 | R–B7 |
| 23 | P–B5! | NPxP | 54 | R–Q3 | P–R4 |
| 24 | PxP | NxBP | 55 | B–N7 | P–N4 |
| 25 | NxN | PxN | 56 | R–Q6†! | K–N2 |
| 26 | QR–Q1 | N–Q2 | 57 | R–Q7† | K–R1 |
| 27 | B–N5 | R–B1 | 58 | B–K4! | P–N5† |
| 28 | P–Q6! | K–R1 | 59 | PxP | PxP† |
| 29 | R–Q5 | R–KB2 | 60 | KxP | RxP |
| 30 | KR–Q1 | Q–B3 | 61 | K–N5 | P–B6 |
| 31 | Q–B3 | P–K5 | 62 | K–B6 | Resigns |

## part 8—NAJDORF SYSTEM WITH 6 B-N5

1 P–K4, P–QB4
2 N–KB3, P–Q3
3 P–Q4, PxP
4 NxP, N–KB3
5 N–QB3, P–QR3
6 B–N5

KEY POSITION 8

OBSERVATIONS ON KEY POSITION 8

As of today this is one of the most important parries to the Najdorf system. White employs Rouzer's method of attack, and Black can choose from among a number of defensive deployments. Final judgment on its merits is still an open question. Fischer definitely prefers the system with Black's Queen Knight on Q2 rather than on B3. Theory and practice, however, evoke new ideas daily and the last word is yet to be spoken. One thing is certain. Having played . . . QN–Q2 and permitted White's King Bishop unchallenging access to QB4, Black faces imminent danger. He must constantly guard against the sacrifice of that Bishop on White's K6.

IDEA VARIATIONS 20–22:

(20) 6 . . . P–K3 7 P–B4, B–K2 8 Q–B3, QN–Q2 (correct is first 8 . . . Q–B2; see Prac. Var. 36) 9 B–B4, P–R3 10 BxN, BxB 11 O–O–O, O–O 12 B–N3, Q–N3? (if 12 . . . N–B4? 13 P–K5!, but 12 . . . Q–K2 or 12 . . . Q–B2 is better) 13 N/4–K2, N–B4 14 P–N4!, B–R5? 15 K–N1, B–Q2 16 KR–N1, NxB 17 RPxN, QR–B1 18 P–N5, PxP 19 PxP, P–N3 20 R–N4, B–B7 21 Q–B6, B–N4 22 NxB, PxN 23 R–Q3, Resigns (Keres–Benko, Candidates' Tournament 1959).

(21) 6 . . . QN–Q2 7 B–QB4, P–K3 (correct is 7 . . . Q–R4; see Idea Var. 22) 8 O–O, Q–B2? 9 BxKP!, PxB 10 NxP, Q–B5 11 N–Q5!, K–B2 12 BxN, KxN (if 12 . . . NxB 13 P–QN3!, or 12 . . . PxB 13 Q–R5†) 13 B–B3, N–B3 14 BxN, PxB 15 N–N6 and White won quickly (Keres–Saitar, Amsterdam Olympics 1954).

(22) 6 . . . QN–Q2 7 B–QB4, Q–R4 8 Q–Q2, P–K3 9 O–O (not 9 O–O–O, P–N4 10 B–N3, B–N2, when Black's Queenside initiative is dangerous; e.g., see Matanovic–Tal, Portoroz 1958), P–R3 (if 9 . . . P–N4 10 B–Q5!, PxB 11 N–B6, Q–N3 12 PxP, followed by 13 R–K1†) 10 B–R4, P–KN4 11 B–KN3, N–R4 12 BxKP!?, PxB 13 NxP, NxB! 14 BPxN, N–K4 15 RxB† (if 15 NxB?, Q–B4†), RxR 16 QxQP, R–B3 (if 16 . . . BxN 17 QxB†, K–Q1 18 R–Q1†; or 16 . . . R–B2 17 P–QN4!) 17 N–B7†, (if 17 N–Q5, RxN 18 N–B7†, QxN! 19 QxQ,

R–K2) K–B2 18 R–KB1, RxR† 19 KxR, N–B5! (if 19 . . . R–N1 20 N/7–Q5 wins) 20 QxKRP, Q–QB4 21 NxR, N–Q7† 22 K–K2, B–N5† 23 K–Q3, Q–B5† 24 K–K3, Q–B4†. Draw by perpetual check; see Tal–Petrosian, Candidates' Tournament 1959.

PRACTICAL VARIATIONS 36–40:

1 P–K4, P–QB4 2 N–KB3, P–Q3 3 P–Q4, PxP 4 NxP, N–KB3 5 N–QB3, P–QR3 6 B–N5

| | *36* | *37* | *38* | *39* | *40* |
|---|---|---|---|---|---|
| *6* | – – | – – | – – | – – | – – |
| | P–K3 | – – | – – | – – | – – |
| *7* | P–B4 | – – | – – | – – | – – |
| | B–K2 | – – | – – | P–R3[12] | P–QN4 |
| *8* | Q–B3 | – – | – – | B–R4 | P–K5[16] |
| | Q–B2 | – – | P–R3 | Q–N3 | PxP |
| *9* | O–O–O | – – | B–R4 | P–QR3[13] | PxP |
| | QN–Q2 | N–B3[6] | P–KN4!? | N–B3[14] | Q–B2 |
| *10* | P–KN4[1] | NxN | PxP | B–B2 | PxN |
| | P–N4 | PxN[7] | KN–Q2 | Q–B2 | Q–K4† |
| *11* | BxN | P–K5 | NxP?[9] | Q–B3 | B–K2 |
| | NxB[2] | PxP | PxN | B–K2 | QxB |
| *12* | P–N5 | PxP | Q–R5† | O–O–O | O–O |
| | N–Q2 | N–Q4 | K–B1 | B–Q2 | R–R2 |
| *13* | P–QR3[3] | BxB | B–N5 | P–KN4 | Q–Q3 |
| | B–N2 | NxB | R–KR2[10] | P–KN4 | R–Q2 |
| *14* | B–R3 | N–K4 | O–O†[11] | NxN | N–K4[17] |
| | O–O–O[4] | O–O | = | BxN[15] | = |
| *15* | P–B5![5] | Q–B3[8] | | ± | |
| | ± | ± | | | |

*Notes to practical variations 36–40:*

[1] The most enterprising and common continuation. Two other possibilities are:

1) 10 B–K2, P–N4 11 BxN, NxB 12 P–K5, B–N2 13 PxN!?, BxQ 14 BxB, BxP 15 BxR, P–Q4 16 BxP, BxN 17 RxB, PxB 18 NxQP, Q–B4 19 R–K1†, K–B1 20 P–B3, P–KR4 with compensation for the Queen (Keres–Fischer, Candidates' Tournament 1959). To be considered in this line is 10 . . . O–O (Tal–Petrosian, Beverwijk 1960).

2) 10 Q–N3, P–R3 11 B–R4, R–KN1 12 B–K2, P–KN4 13 PxP, N–K4 14 P–N6, NxNP! 15 KR–B1, NxB 16 QxN, R–N3 17 B–Q3, N–N5 with even chances (Tal–Fischer, Zurich 1959). In this line 14 . . . NxNP is an improvement over 14 . . . RxP 15 Q–R3 (Bannik–Petrosian, USSR Championship 1957).

[2] 11 . . . BxB is faulty because of 12 BxP!, etc. But 11

. . . PxB is tenable (Gligoric–Fischer, Zurich 1959, and Candidates' Tournament, Belgrade 1959).

[3] A necessary precautionary measure. 13 B–R3, P–N5 14 N/3–K2, B–N2 15 K–N1, N–B4 16 N–N3, P–Q4! (Smyslov–Fischer, Candidates' Tournament 1959).

[4] The threat is 15 BxP. 14 . . . O–O is experimental.

[5] An attacking system essayed by Gligoric, the consequences of which are hazy. In Gligoric–Fischer, Candidates' Tournament 1959, follows 15 . . . BxP† 16 K–N1, P–K4 17 N/4xP, PxN 18 NxP, Q–B4 19 NxP†, K–N1 20 NxP, Q–K2 21 NxKR, RxN 22 KR–K1 and White's task is not so easy. Suggested alternatives or improvements on the play are 15 . . . P–K4 16 P–B6! or 15 . . . PxP 16 QxP. Fischer recommends 18 . . . Q–N3 as better than 18 . . . Q–B4, whereas Gligoric gives 20 Q–QN3 as superior to 20 NxP. All in all, White's chances are better.

[6] After 9 . . . O–O 10 B–Q3, N–B3, Black experiences greater difficulties: 11 NxN, PxN 12 P–K5!, PxP 13 Q–R3, P–R3 14 QBxP!, PxB 15 QxRP, P–K5 16 NxP, NxN 17 BxN, P–B4 18 Q–N6†, K–R1 19 R–Q3, QxP† 20 K–N1, PxB 21 Q–R5†, K–N2 22 R–N3†, winning (analysis by Hans Muller).

[7] Stronger is 10 . . . QxN. E.g., 11 P–K5!?, QxQ 12 PxQ, PxP 13 PxP, N–R4!

[8] Keres–Stahlberg, Alekhine Memorial, Moscow 1956.

[9] This sacrifice is not quite sufficient. Better seems 11 Q–R5, N–K4 12 B–N3, BxP 13 N–B3.

[10] The rehabilitation of the famous Argentine line. Insufficient is 13 . . . N–K4 14 B–N3! or 13 . . . K–N2 14 O–O, N–K4 15 B–N3.

[11] This insures perpetual check after 14 . . . K–N1 15 P–N6, R–N2 16 R–B7, BxB 17 QxP, RxR 18 PxR†, KxP 19 Q–R7†, K–B1. White dare not play for a win by 20 P–K5, because of 20 . . . PxP 21 Q–R8†, K–K2! 22 QxB†, N–B3. Or 21 BxN, BxB 22 Q–R8†, K–B2 23 R–B1†, K–N3.

In Gligoric–Fischer, Portoroz 1958, there followed 14 Q–N6, R–B2 15 QxP†, K–N1 16 Q–N6†, R–N2 17 QxP†, K–R1 18 BxN, NxB 19 O–O–O. The game ended in a draw, but Black's piece is worth more than White's extra Pawns. After 19 . . . N–K4 20 Q–Q5, B–N5 21 QR–B1, Black should play 21 . . . R–B1 instead of 21 . . . BxP†.

[12] The immediate 7 . . . Q–N3 is met by 8 N–N3, Q–K6† 9 Q–K2, QxQ† 10 BxQ, QN–Q2 11 O–O–O (Keres–Van den Berg, Munich Olympics 1958). White's advantage in development is significant, the exchange of Queens notwithstanding. But after 7 . . . Q–N3 the well-known Pawn sacrifice 8 Q–Q2 is dubious, thus: 8 . . . QxP 9 R–QN1, Q–R6 10 P–K5, PxP 11 PxP, KN–Q2 12 B–QB4, B–N5! Or 12 N–K4, P–R3! or 12 B–K2, Q–B4!

[13] At this point the Pawn sacrifice is correct: 9 Q–Q3!, QxP 10 R–QN1, Q–R6 11 P–K5, N–Q4 12 NxN, QxQ 13 BxQ, PxN 14 P–K6, N–B3 15 NxN, PxN 16 PxP†, KxP 17 R–N6, with excellent compensation for the Pawn (Mikenas–Tal, Riga 1959). In this line if 11 . . . PxP 12 PxP, KN–Q2? 13 NxP! Or later if 14 . . . PxP 15 B–N6†, K–Q2 16 P–B5, P–K4 17 N–K6!

[14] Of course not 9 . . . QxP 10 N–R4. To be considered,

continued ▶

however, and threatening . . . QxP is 9 . . . B–Q2. White then lacks the opportunity of proceeding aggressively with Q–B3. After 10 Q–Q2, N–B3 11 B–B2, White still has the lead.

[15] 15 PxP, PxP 16 B–Q4, R–R3 17 P–KR4, B–Q2 18 P–R5, Q–R4 with an initiative for White, though Black's control of his K4 slows down the proceedings (Tal–Olafsson, Candidates' Tournament 1959). This line is stronger than 15 P–KR4, PxBP 16 QxP, O–O–O (Smyslov–Benko, Candidates' Tournament 1959).

[16] White must play aggressively. After 8 Q–B3?, B–N2 9 B–Q3, B–K2 10 O–O–O, Q–N3 11 KR–K1, QN–Q2, Black stands well (Kupper–Tal, Zurich 1959; see Game 32). This line is an improved version of Prac. Var. 36, with the Queen on . . . N3 instead of . . . B2.

[17] 14 . . . Q–K4! 15 N–KB3, QxNP 16 Q–K3, B–N2 17 QR–Q1, BxN 18 QxB, and the position is unclear.

## *Sicilian Defense Game 24*

*WHITE: Kupper* — *BLACK: Tal*

*Zurich 1959*

| | WHITE | BLACK | | WHITE | BLACK |
|---|---|---|---|---|---|
| 1 | P–K4 | P–QB4 | 13 | BxN | BxB |
| 2 | N–KB3 | P–Q3 | 14 | P–KN4 | N–R5 |
| 3 | P–Q4 | PxP | 15 | P–B3 | P–N5 |
| 4 | NxP | N–KB3 | 16 | B–B2 | NxNP!? |
| 5 | N–QB3 | P–QR3 | 17 | KxN | PxP† |
| 6 | B–N5 | P–K3 | 18 | KxP | O–O |
| 7 | P–B4 | P–N4 | 19 | R–QN1 | Q–R4† |
| 8 | Q–B3 | B–N2 | 20 | K–Q3 | QR–B1 |
| 9 | B–Q3 | B–K2 | 21 | Q–B2 | B–R1 |
| 10 | O–O–O | Q–N3 | 22 | R–N3? | P–K4! |
| 11 | KR–K1 | QN–Q2 | 23 | P–N5 | PxN |
| 12 | N/3–K2 | N–B4 | | Resigns | |

## *Sicilian Defense Game 25*

*WHITE: Keres* — *BLACK: Fuderer*

*Göteborg 1955*

| | WHITE | BLACK | | WHITE | BLACK |
|---|---|---|---|---|---|
| 1 | P–K4 | P–QB4 | 10 | P–K5 | KN–Q2? |
| 2 | N–KB3 | P–Q3 | 11 | P–B5! | NxP |
| 3 | P–Q4 | PxP | 12 | PxP | PxP |
| 4 | NxP | N–KB3 | 13 | B–K2 | N/1–B3 |
| 5 | N–QB3 | P–QR3 | 14 | NxN | PxN |
| 6 | B–N5 | P–K3 | 15 | N–K4! | P–Q4 |
| 7 | P–B4 | Q–N3 | 16 | O–O | Q–R5 |
| 8 | Q–Q2 | QxP | 17 | B–R5† | K–Q2 |
| 9 | R–QN1 | Q–R6 | 18 | RxB | Resigns |

*Sicilian Defense Game*

*WHITE: Bilek* *BLACK: Fischer*

*Stockholm Interzonal 1962*

| | WHITE | BLACK | | WHITE | BLACK | | WHITE | BLACK |
|---|---|---|---|---|---|---|---|---|
| 1 | P–K4 | P–QB4 | 11 | PxP | KN–Q2 | 21 | RxN | B–Q2 |
| 2 | N–KB3 | P–Q3 | 12 | B–QB4 | B–K2 | 22 | N–B3 | Q–K6† |
| 3 | P–Q4 | PxP | 13 | BxP | O–O | 23 | K–R1 | Q–B8† |
| 4 | NxP | N–KB3 | 14 | O–O | BxB | 24 | N–N1 | QxP |
| 5 | N–QB3 | P–QR3 | 15 | QxB | P–R3 | 25 | R–N8 | Q–B7 |
| 6 | B–N5 | P–K3 | 16 | Q–R4 | QxN | 26 | R–B8 | QxP |
| 7 | P–B4 | Q–N3 | 17 | RxBP | RxR | 27 | R–B3 | K–R2 |
| 8 | Q–Q2 | QxP | 18 | Q–Q8† | N–B1 | | Resigns | |
| 9 | R–QN1 | Q–R6 | 19 | BxR† | KxB | | | |
| 10 | P–K5 | PxP | 20 | R–B1† | K–N3 | | | |

*Sicilian Defense Game*

*WHITE: Fischer* *BLACK: Olafsson*

*Stockholm Interzonal 1962*

| | WHITE | BLACK | | WHITE | BLACK | | WHITE | BLACK |
|---|---|---|---|---|---|---|---|---|
| 1 | P–K4 | P–QB4 | 12 | PxP | N–Q2 | 23 | RxQ | KR–Q1 |
| 2 | N–KB3 | P–Q3 | 13 | O–O | P–N5 | 24 | QRxP | QR–B1 |
| 3 | P–Q4 | PxP | 14 | N–K4 | B–N2 | 25 | R–B2 | P–QR4 |
| 4 | NxP | N–KB3 | 15 | N–Q6 | BxN | 26 | R/2–Q2 | P–B3 |
| 5 | N–QB3 | N–B3 | 16 | PxB | Q–N4 | 27 | R–QB4 | K–B2 |
| 6 | B–QB4 | P–K3 | 17 | Q–K2 | B–Q4 | 28 | R–B7† | K–N3 |
| 7 | B–N3 | B–K2 | 18 | QR–Q1 | BxB | 29 | R–K7 | P–R4 |
| 8 | P–B4 | O–O | 19 | RPxB | P–K4 | 30 | P–Q7 | R–B2 |
| 9 | B–K3 | NxN | 20 | Q–N5 | P–QR3 | 31 | P–B4 | K–R2 |
| 10 | BxN | P–QN4 | 21 | QxN | PxB | 32 | P–R4 | K–N3 |
| 11 | P–K5 | PxP | 22 | Q–B5 | QxQ | 33 | R–Q5 | Resigns |

SUPPLEMENTARY VARIATIONS 21–25:

1 P–K4, P–QB4 2 N–KB3, P–Q3 3 P–Q4, PxP 4 NxP, N–KB3 5 N–QB3, P–QR3

The fianchetto of Sup. Var. 21 was originally intended as a preventative measure against . . . P–K4. White's B–KN2 is well placed in respect to Black's weak Q4; yet experience has shown that this set-up is not stronger than the set-up with B–K2.

The attacking set-up with P–B4 (Sup. Var. 22 and 23) for quite a time was considered to be strong, but Black is well able to hold his own. Accurate play is called for, however, as has been proved in several recent games. See Game 26.

Sup. Var. 24 and 25 illustrate the set-up of B–QB4 (Cf. the Sosin Attack, Part 3). In the Candidates' Tournament of 1959, Fischer continuously experimented with this system but with little success. Black has not yet played . . . QN–B3 (in contrast to Part 3). Here the set-up . . . QN–Q2 . . . P–QN4 and . . . B–N2 is sufficient.

| | *21* | *22* | *23* | *24* | *25* |
|---|---|---|---|---|---|
| *6* | P–KN3 | P–B4 | – – | B–QB4 | – – |
| | P–K4[1] | P–K4[4] | – – | P–K3 | – – |
| *7* | N–N3[2] | N–B3 | – – | O–O | B–N3[13] |
| | P–QN4 | Q–B2 | QN–Q2 | P–QN4 | B–K2[14] |
| *8* | B–N2 | B–Q3 | B–B4[7] | B–N3 | P–KB4 |
| | B–N2 | B–K2 | B–K2 | P–QN5[10] | O–O |
| *9* | P–QR4 | O–O | P–QR4 | N–R4 | Q–B3 |
| | P–N5 | O–O | O–O | NxP | Q–B2 |
| *10* | N–Q5 | Q–K1 | Q–K2 | R–K1 | O–O |
| | BxN | B–K3[5] | P–QN3[8] | N–KB3[11] | P–QN4! |
| *11* | PxB | K–R1 | O–O | B–N5[12] | P–B5 |
| | P–QR4 | QN–Q2 | B–QN2 | ± | P–N5 |
| *12* | B–Q2 | N–KR4[6] | PxP | | N–R4 |
| | KN–Q2 | ± | PxP | | P–K4 |
| *13* | P–QB3[3] | | B–KN5[9] | | N–K2 |
| | ± | | ± | | B–N2[15] |
| | | | | | ∓ |

*Notes to supplementary variations 21–25:*

[1] Or 6 . . . P–QN4 7 B–N2, B–N2 8 O–O, P–K3 9 Q–K2!, QN–Q2 10 P–QR3, Q–B2 11 P–B4!, R–B1 12 P–KR3 followed eventually by P–KN4, which offers White a promising attack (Fine–Najdorf, New York 1949).

[2] According to present opinion this line is sharper than 7 N/4–K2, P–QN4! E.g., 8 B–N2, B–N2 9 P–KR3, B–K2 10 O–O, QN–Q2 11 N–Q5, NxN 12 PxN, O–O 13 P–KB4, R–B1 14 PxP, NxP 15 P–N3, B–N4 with a good game for Black (Donner–Pachman, Goteborg 1955). Najdorf's 7 . . . B–K3 8 B–N2, P–QN4 is effectively parried by H. Kramer's 9 N–B4!

[3] For 13 . . . N–R3 14 PxP, PxP 15 O–O, B–K2 16 Q–N4!? see Fuderer–Kotov (Game 27).

[4] Najdorf–Reshevsky, 9th Match Game 1952, continued 6 . . . Q–B2 7 B–Q3, P–KN3 (7 . . . P–K4 is the text move) 8 O–O, B–N2 9 K–R1!, O–O 10 Q–K1, P–QN4 11 P–QR3, B–N2 12 N–B3, QN–Q2 13 Q–R4, P–K3 14 B–K3, P–Q4 15 P–K5, N–K1 16 N–N5, P–R3 17 NxKP, PxN 18 BxKNP with a strong attack for the piece.

[5] White also maintains the initiative after 10 . . . P–QN4 11 N–KR4, P–N5 12 N–Q1, P–Q4 13 BPxP, NxP 14 BxN, PxB 15 QxP, B–N2 16 Q–KN4, QxKP 17 N–B5 (Pilnik–Donner, Beverwijk 1958).

[6] Najdorf–Reshevsky, 11th Match Game, continued 12 . . . QR–Q1 13 PxP, PxP 14 N–B5, BxN 15 RxB, N–B4 16 R–B3, P–R3 17 B–Q2 with the better game for White.

[7] White attempts to profit by Black's omission of . . . Q–B2. But after 8 B–Q3, B–K2 9 O–O, O–O 10 P–QR4, P–QN3 11 Q–K1, B–N2 12 K–R1, R–K1 (Flores–Pachman, Mar del Plata 1955) Black's task is easier than in the text line of Prac. Var. 23 because White cannot effect the characteristic maneuver N–KR4–B5, e.g., 13 N–KR4? NxP!

[8] Also deserving consideration is 10 . . . PxP 11 BxBP, N–B4 12 O–O, B–K3.

[9] Clarke–Toran, Hastings 1956-57, continued: 13 . . . N–R4? 14 QR–Q1! B–B4† 15 K–R1, Q–B2 16 RxN and White won quickly.

[10] This plan to win a Pawn is very risky. Safe and sound is 8 . . . B–K2: e.g., 9 P–B4, O–O 10 P–B5, P–N5 11 N/3–K2, P–K4 12 N–KB3, B–N2 13 N–N3, NxP 14 NxN, BxN 15 Q–K1, BxN 16 RxB, N–B3 and White has insufficient compensation for the Pawn (Fischer–Smyslov, Candidates' Tournament 1959).

[11] To meet 10 . . . P–Q4 the Moscow theoretician Chenkin gives 11 B–KB4, B–N2 12 Q–R5! On 12 . . . Q–B3 there follows 13 RxN, PxR 14 NxP! Weak is 10 . . . N–B4 11 NxN, PxN 12 Q–B3, R–R2 13 B–KB4, B–N2 14 B–R4†, N–Q2 15 NxP! and White won quickly in the game Dezje–Vasiljevic, Tuzla 1958.

[12] White has a very strong attack for the Pawn. 11 . . . B–K2 12 N–B5! (Yovcic–Slaten, Yugoslavia 1957). If 12 . . . PxN, then 13 BxN, PxB 14 Q–Q5!

[13] Better is 7 P–QR3, B–K2 8 O–O, O–O 9 B–R2, P–QN4 10 P–B4, B–N2 11 P–B5, P–K4 12 N/4–K2, QN–Q2 13 N–N3, R–B1 14 B–N5, N–N3 15 N–R5 and now Black should have played 15 . . . NxN instead of 15 . . . RxN? (Olafsson–Fischer, Candidates' Tournament 1959). 12 . . . NxP 13 NxN, BxN 14 N–N3, B–N2 15 N–R5 is dangerous for Black.

[14] Very daring is 7 . . . P–QN4 8 P–B4, P–N5 9 N–R4, NxP 10 O–O, P–KN3 (better is 10 . . . B–K2 or 10 . . . N–KB3) 11 P–B5, NPxP 12 NxBP, R–N1 13 B–Q5! R–R2 14 BxN, PxN (Fischer–Tal, Candidates' Tournament 1959). And now White should have played 15 B–Q5, convincingly maintaining his advantage.

[15] Fischer–Tal, Candidates' Tournament 1959. See Game 28.

## *Sicilian Defense Game 26*

*WHITE: Kupper* *BLACK: Olafsson*

*Zurich 1959*

| | WHITE | BLACK | | WHITE | BLACK | | WHITE | BLACK |
|---|---|---|---|---|---|---|---|---|
| 1 | P–K4 | P–QB4 | 8 | B–Q3 | QN–Q2 | 15 | N–KN5 | N–R4? |
| 2 | N–KB3 | P–Q3 | 9 | P–QR4 | P–QN3 | 16 | BxB | KxB |
| 3 | P–Q4 | PxP | 10 | O–O | B–N2 | 17 | RxP†! | K–N1 |
| 4 | NxP | N–KB3 | 11 | Q–K1 | P–N3? | 18 | R–N7† | K–R1 |
| 5 | N–QB3 | P–QR3 | 12 | Q–R4 | B–N2 | 19 | RxP† | K–N1 |
| 6 | P–B4 | P–K4 | 13 | PxP | PxP | 20 | R–N7† | Resigns |
| 7 | N–B3 | Q–B2 | 14 | B–R6 | O–O | | | |

### *Sicilian Defense Game 27*

*WHITE: Fuderer* *BLACK: Kotov*

*Zagreb 1958*

| | WHITE | BLACK | | WHITE | BLACK | | WHITE | BLACK |
|---|---|---|---|---|---|---|---|---|
| 1 | P–K4 | P–QB4 | 18 | Q–QB4 | NxB | 35 | B–B1 | Q–B7 |
| 2 | N–KB3 | P–Q3 | 19 | QxN | R–N1 | 36 | BxN | PxB |
| 3 | P–Q4 | PxP | 20 | Q–B3 | B–B3 | 37 | R–KB1 | P–Q7 |
| 4 | NxP | N–KB3 | 21 | P–R5 | P–K5 | 38 | Q–K6† | K–N2 |
| 5 | N–QB3 | P–QR3 | 22 | Q–B2 | Q–B1 | 39 | Q–K7† | R–B2 |
| 6 | P–KN3 | P–QN4 | 23 | Q–Q1 | Q–N2 | 40 | Q–K2 | R–B1 |
| 7 | B–N2 | B–N2 | 24 | N–Q2 | BxP | 41 | N–N8 | Q–R5 |
| 8 | P–QR4 | P–K4 | 25 | P–R6 | Q–R2? | 42 | QxP | B–B3 |
| 9 | N–N3 | P–N5 | 26 | R–R2 | N–K4 | 43 | N–B6 | R–B2 |
| 10 | N–Q5 | BxN | 27 | Q–K2 | N–Q6 | 44 | Q–B4 | Q–R6 |
| 11 | PxB | P–QR4 | 28 | N–B4! | B–Q5 | 45 | R–N1 | Q–R7 |
| 12 | B–Q2 | KN–Q2 | 29 | N–R5! | R–N7 | 46 | R–N8 | B–K4 |
| 13 | P–QB3 | N–R3 | 30 | RxR | BxR | 47 | P–R8/Q | QxQ |
| 14 | PxP | PxP | 31 | N–B6 | Q–QB2 | 48 | RxQ | BxQ |
| 15 | O–O | B–K2 | 32 | R–N1 | Q–N3 | 49 | PxB | Resigns |
| 16 | Q–N4 | O–O | 33 | P–R7 | P–N3 | | | |
| 17 | BxP | P–B4 | 34 | Q–K3 | Q–N6 | | | |

### *Sicilian Defense Game 28*

*WHITE: Fischer* *BLACK: Tal*

*Zurich 1959*

| | WHITE | BLACK | | WHITE | BLACK | | WHITE | BLACK |
|---|---|---|---|---|---|---|---|---|
| 1 | P–K4 | P–QB4 | 13 | N–K2 | B–N2 | 25 | BxN | BxB |
| 2 | N–KB3 | P–Q3 | 14 | N–N3 | QN–Q2 | 26 | NxB | Q–QB2 |
| 3 | P–Q4 | PxP | 15 | B–K3 | B–B3 | 27 | Q–K3 | QR–K1 |
| 4 | NxP | N–KB3 | 16 | B–B2 | Q–N2 | 28 | R–K2 | NxR† |
| 5 | N–QB3 | P–QR3 | 17 | KR–K1 | P–Q4! | 29 | QxN | BxP! |
| 6 | B–QB4 | P–K3 | 18 | PxP | NxP | 30 | NxP | Q–R2† |
| 7 | B–N3 | B–K2 | 19 | N–K4 | N–B5 | 31 | KxB | R–N1† |
| 8 | P–B4 | O–O | 20 | P–B4 | P–N3! | 32 | K–R3 | Q–N2 |
| 9 | Q–B3 | Q–B2 | 21 | PxP | P–B4! | 33 | B–Q1 | R–K3 |
| 10 | O–O | P–QN4 | 22 | P–N7 | KxP | | Resigns | |
| 11 | P–B5? | P–N5! | 23 | Q–N3† | K–R1 | | | |
| 12 | N–R4 | P–K4 | 24 | N/K–B5 | NxN | | | |

SUPPLEMENTARY VARIATIONS 26–30:

1 P–K4, P–QB4 2 N–KB3

Sup. Var. 26 and 27 show an old-fashioned ancestor of the Boleslavski system. Sup. Var. 26 was rehabilitated by Pelikan's Pawn sacrifice 9 . . . P–Q4! It was later discovered that White should have postponed the exchange on KB6 (Sup. Var. 27). Then Black is left with no chance to free his game by means of . . . P–Q4.

Sup. Var. 28 shows a modern system wherein Black's P–K4 is played on his 4th turn. The interesting complications of this system are not yet sufficiently investigated.

Sup. Var. 29 and 30 demonstrate a system worked out by O'Kelly. Black plays 2 . . . P–QR3, preventing N–QN5 in answer to . . . P–K4. The conservative 3 P–Q4 allows Black to carry out his idea quite satisfactorily; he has not yet played . . . P–Q3 and can consequently develop his King's Bishop on QN5. The correct way to meet this is by 3 P–QB4, gaining an advantage in space. But the last word on this system awaits investigation (see note 22, Sup. Var. 30).

| | *26* | *27* | *28* | *29* | *30* |
|---|---|---|---|---|---|
| 2 | – – | – – | – – | – – | – – |
| | N–QB3 | – – | – – | P–QR3 | – – |
| 3 | P–Q4 | – – | – – | P–Q4 | P–B4[21] |
| | PxP | – – | – – | PxP | N–QB3 |
| 4 | NxP | – – | – – | NxP | P–Q4 |
| | N–B3 | – – | P–K4 | N–KB3 | PxP |
| 5 | N–QB3 | – – | N–N5[10] | N–QB3 | NxP |
| | P–K4 | – – | P–QR3[11] | P–K4 | N–KB3[22] |
| 6 | N/4–N5[1] | – – | N–Q6† | N–B3 | N–QB3 |
| | P–Q3[2] | – – | BxN | B–N5 | P–K4[23] |
| 7 | B–N5 | – – | QxB | B–QB4[18] | N–KB5![24] |
| | P–QR3[3] | – – | Q–B3 | Q–B2 | P–Q4 |
| 8 | BxN | N–R3! | Q–Q1[12] | B–N3 | BPxP |
| | PxB | B–K3[7] | Q–KN3[13] | O–O[19] | BxN |
| 9 | N–QR3 | N–B4 | N–QB3 | O–O | PxB |
| | P–Q4! | N–Q5 | KN–K2 | BxN | N–Q5 |
| 10 | NxP[4] | BxN! | P–KR4[14] | PxB | B–Q3 |
| | BxN | PxN[8] | P–KR4 | NxP | NxQP |
| 11 | PxB | N–K3 | B–KN5 | R–K1![20] | O–O |
| | B–K3 | R–B1 | P–Q4 | = | B–N5 |
| 12 | N–K3[5] | B–Q3 | PxP[15] | | B–K4![25] |
| | Q–R4† | P–KR4 | N–N5[16] | | ± |
| 13 | Q–Q2 | O–O[9] | R–B1 | | |
| | QxP | ± | B–B4 | | |
| 14 | B–Q3 | | P–Q6[17] | | |
| | O–O–O | | ± | | |
| 15 | O–O[6] | | | | |
| | = | | | | |

*Notes to supplementary variations 26–30:*

[1] All other Knight moves give Black a favorable game:

1) 6 NxN, NPxN 7 B–KN5, R–QN1! (Malmgren–Alekhine, Oerebro, 1935).
2) 6 N–N3, B–N5 7 B–Q3, P–Q4 (Schlechter–Lasker, 9th Match Game 1910).

continued ▸

3) 6 N–B5, P–Q4!

4) 6 N–B3, B–N5.

5) 6 N/4–K2, B–N5! 7 P–QR3, B–R4 8 P–QN4, B–N3 9 N–N3, B–Q5 followed by . . . P–Q4.

[2] Weaker is 6 . . . B–B4 7 B–K3!, BxB 8 N–Q6†, K–B1 9 PxB. Also weak for Black is 6 . . . P–KR3 (Haberditz) 7 N–Q6†, BxN 8 QxB, Q–K2 9 QxQ†, KxQ 10 P–QN3, R–Q1 11 B–R3†, P–Q3 12 O–O–O, N–Q5 13 P–B4, K–K1 14 BxP!

[3] This Queenside advance with a tempo cannot be bad.

[4] 10 QxP, B–K3! 11 QxQ†, RxQ 12 N–B4, B–QN5 is satisfactory for Black, as is 10 PxP, BxN 11 PxN, BxP 12 QxQ†, KxQ 13 R–Q1†, K–B2. If, in the latter sequence, 11 PxB, Q–R4 12 Q–Q2, N–Q5 with the edge for Black.

[5] Or 12 B–B4, Q–R4† 13 Q–Q2, O–O–O 14 QxQ (also deserving consideration is 14 R–Q1, QxP 15 O–O), NxQ 15 B–N3, NxB 16 RPxN, BxN 17 PxB, RxP with a drawish end game (Chasin–Spasski, USSR 1956). After 13 . . . QxQ† 14 KxQ, O–O–O, Muller recommends 15 QR–Q1 instead of 15 K–K3.

[6] The text is Geller–Pilnik, Amsterdam 1956. So far Black has a satisfactory game, but he can do even better with 15 . . . KR–N1 or 15 . . . R–Q5 instead of 15 . . . K–N1 (as played).

[7] Now the advance 8 . . . P–Q4 lacks its proper effect: e.g., 9 NxP, BxN 10 PxB, Q–R4† 11 B–Q2 or 11 Q–Q2 and White obtains a fine game with his two Bishops. If 8 . . . P–QN4, naturally 9 N–Q5!

[8] After 10 . . . QxB 11 N–K3, B–K2 12 B–Q3, O-O 13 O–O, White dominates Q5.

[9] White controls the position (Bronstein–Pilnik, Olympiad, Moscow 1956).

[10] The text is the only chance for the initiative. Morphy–Lowenthal, Paris 1858, continued: 5 NxN, NPxN 6 B–QB4, N–B3 7 O-O, P–Q4 8 PxP, PxP 9 B–N5†, B–Q2 10 BxB†, QxB 11 R–K1 and Black got into difficulties. Lowenthal later suggested 6 . . . B–R3 (7 BxB, Q–R4†). Premature, at any rate, is 7 . . . P–Q4. However, 7 . . . B–K2 8 N–B3, P–Q3 followed by 9 . . . O–O gives Black a satisfactory game. The position shows great similarity to the Boleslavski system, but a century ago the correct strategical procedure was unknown.

[11] In a game Matanovic–Larsen, Beverwijk 1960, Black tried 5 . . . P–Q3 6 N/1–B3, P–QR3 7 N–R3, B–K3, but White obtained a positional advantage after 8 N–B4, R–B1 9 N–Q5!, BxN 10 PxB, N–N1 11 B–K2, N–Q2 12 O–O, N/1–B3 14 P–QR4.

[12] Well worth notice is 8 Q–B7, KN–K2 9 N–B3, N–N5 10 B–Q3, P–Q4 11 O–O, P–Q5 12 N–K2, NxB 13 PxN eventually followed by P–B4 (Neshmetdinov–Zacharov, Leningrad 1957).

[13] Gligoric–Benko, Dublin 1957, played 8 . . . KN–K2 9 N–B3, O–O 10 B–K3, P–QN4 11 Q–Q2, Q–N3 12 P–KB3, P–Q3 13 O–O–O, R–Q1 14 K–N1, B–N2 15 P–KN4. P–B3 16 N–Q5 with a positional edge for White.

[14] An enterprising move which threatens P–R5, practically forcing . . . P–KR4, after which White's N5 becomes a safe square for his Bishop. If White plays 10 B–K3, the Pawn sacrifice 10 . . . P–Q4 is strong for Black. A steady continuation for White is 10 P–B3.

[15] 12 BxN is answered shrewdly by 12 . . . P–Q5.

[16] Meriting further investigation is 12 . . . N–Q5! 13 B–Q3, B–B4 (14 BxB, N/2xB), Black has sufficient compensation for the Pawn.

[17] This strong move leads to White's advantage by force, e.g., 14 . . . NxP† 15 RxN, BxR 16 Q–Q2, N–B3 17 P–Q7†, K–B1 18 P–Q8(Q)†! (Romanevsky–Lentsjinner, Odessa 1959).

[18] Keres–Olafsson, Candidates' Tournament 1959, continued 7 NxP, O–O! 8 B Q3, P–Q4 9 O–O, BxN 10 PxB, PxP 11 B–K2, Q–B2 with a good game for Black. See Game 29. 7 . . . Q–K2 8 N–B4, NxP 9 B–K2!, NxN 10 PxN, BxP† 11 K–B1, BxR 12 B–R3! is good for White.

[19] After 8 . . . BxN† 9 PxB, QxP† 10 B–Q2, Taimanov gives 10 . . . Q–B2, but 10 . . . Q–B4 is stronger.

[20] White has sufficient compensation for the Pawn (Geller–Taimanov, Moscow 1958).

[21] Also plausible is 3 P–B3 which reduces the significance of 2 . . . P–QR3 to almost a loss of time: e.g., 3 . . . P–Q4 4 PxP, QxP 5 P–Q4, P–K3 6 B–Q3, N–KB3 7 O–O, B–K2 8 Q–K2, O–O 9 PxP, QxP 10 QN–Q2 and White is slightly superior in regard to space (Pachman–Muller, Venice 1950).

[22] Possibly stronger is 5 . . . P–K4 directly (6 N–B5, P–Q4!).

[23] The thematic move, but 6 . . . P–K3 to prepare . . . P–Q4 is to be considered to avoid having the backward Queen Pawn.

[24] The only chance to retain the initiative, but a good one. Pilnik–Euwe, New York 1948, continued 7 N–B2, B–B4 8 B–K3, P–Q3 9 B–K2, O–O 10 Q–Q2, B–K3 11 O–O, R–B1 12 QR–N1, N–QN5 with a satisfactory game for Black.

[25] White now has excellent chances for the Pawn, e.g., 12 . . . NxN 13 PxN, BxP 14 R–N1, O–O 15 Q–N4, Q–Q3 16 R–Q1, QR–Q1 17 R–Q3, B–N5 18 P–B6! (Kupper–Tordian, Switzerland 1956). If 16 . . . QR–B1 17 R–Q3, R–B5 18 P–KR4!

## *Sicilian Defense Game 29*

*WHITE: Keres* *BLACK: Olafsson*

*Candidates' Tournament 1959*

| WHITE | BLACK | WHITE | BLACK | WHITE | BLACK |
|---|---|---|---|---|---|
| 1 P–K4 | P–QB4 | 15 KRxR | N–B3 | 29 R–KB1 | N–N4 |
| 2 N–KB3 | P–QR3 | 16 NxR | B–N5 | 30 R–B4 | Q–R6 |
| 3 P–Q4 | PxP | 17 BxB | NxB | 31 R–QB2 | Q–Q3 |
| 4 NxP | N–KB3 | 18 N–B7? | Q–B4 | 32 P–B4 | P–N4 |
| 5 N–QB3 | P–K4 | 19 B–N3 | P–K6! | 33 P–KR4 | PxP |
| 6 N–B3 | B–N5 | 20 PxP | NxKP | 34 R–Q4 | Q–K4 |
| 7 NxP | O–O | 21 B–B2 | Q–KN4 | 35 R/2xP | N–K3 |
| 8 B–Q3 | P–Q4 | 22 BxN | QxB† | 36 R–Q1 | Q–K7 |
| 9 O–O | BxN | 23 K–R1 | QxP | 37 R/1–QB1 | QxP |
| 10 PxB | PxP | 24 N–Q5 | Q–B4! | 38 N–B4 | N–B1 |
| 11 B–K2 | Q–B2 | 25 R–Q2 | P–R3 | 39 R–B7 | Q–Q7 |
| 12 N–B4 | R–Q1 | 26 R–K1 | N–Q5 | 40 R–B1 | N–Q2 |
| 13 B–B4 | Q–K2 | 27 P–B3 | N–K3 | 41 R–R7 | . . . |
| 14 N–N6 | RxQ | 28 P–KR3 | K–R2 | Resigns | |

## part 9—SCHEVENINGEN VARIATION

1 P–K4, P–QB4
2 N–KB3, P–K3
3 P–Q4, PxP[A]
4 NxP, N–KB3
5 N–QB3[B], P–Q3
6 B–K2[C], B–K2[D]
7 O–O, N–B3

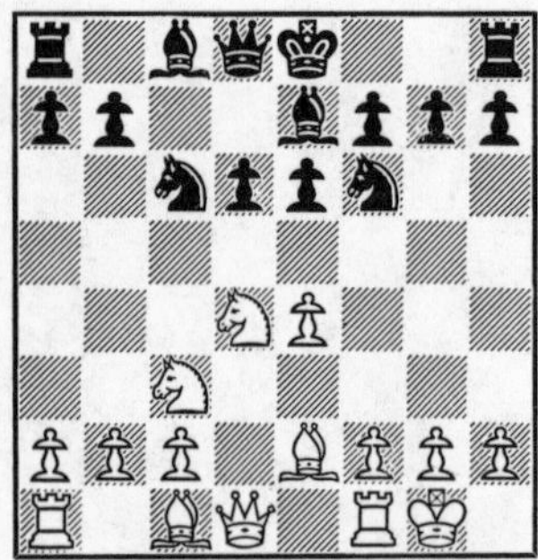

KEY POSITION 9

### OBSERVATIONS ON KEY POSITION 9

[A] Marshall had a liking for 3 . . . P–Q4, which gives the opening the character of a French Defense. A good way of meeting this is 4 PxQP, KPxP 5 B–N5†, N–B3 6 O–O, N–B3 7 N–K5, B–Q2 8 BxN, PxB 9 R–K1, B–K2 10 PxP, O–O 11 B–N5 (Keres–Konstantinopolsky, USSR Championship 1950).

[B] Morphy's old move 5 B–Q3 leads to equality after 5 . . . N–B3 6 NxN, QPxN! 7 N–Q2, P–K4! 8 N–B4, B–QB4 9 B–K3, BxB 10 NxB, B–K3 11 O–O, O–O (Spielmann–Alekhine, New York 1927).

[C] The sharp 6 P–KN4!?, attributed to Keres, is best met, according to Panov, as follows: 6 . . . P–KR3 7 B–N2, N–B3! 8 N–N3 (8 NxN, PxN 9 P–K5, N–Q4), P–K4 9 P–KR3 (9 P–N5, PxP 10 BxP, B–K2 11 BxN, BxB 12 N–Q5, B–N4 followed by . . . N–K2), P–QR4 with active counterplay for Black, who actually plays a kind of Boleslavski system, which cannot be bad.

Steadiest for White is 6 P–KN3, P–QR3 7 B–N2, Q–B2 8 O–O, N–B3 9 N/4–K2, B–K2 10 P–KR3, P–QN4 11 P–QR3, B–N2 12 B–K3, O–O with chances for both sides. Black's Queen Bishop is better placed at N2 than Q2. Compare Game 30.

[D] After 6 . . . P–QR3 7 O–O, N–B3 8 B–K3, Q–B2 9 P–B4, Black must proceed with 9 . . . B–K2. The time for 9 . . . N–QR4? is not yet come: e.g., 10 P–B5, N–B5? (necessary is 10 . . . B–K2! 11 Q–Q3, N–B3!) 11 BxN, QxB 12 PxP, PxP? 13 RxN, PxR 14 Q–R5†, K–Q1 15 Q–B7 with a winning attack (Lasker–Pirc, Moscow 1935).

White's superiority in freedom of movement tends to culminate in a Kingside attack. Black, thanks to the control of the half-open Queen Bishop file is able to operate on the Queenside. His strategic threat is the maneuver . . . Q–B2, . . . P–QR3, . . . P–QN4, and . . . N–QR4–QB5. This threat White must meet accurately or face disadvantages. There are two well-established methods open to White: 8 K–R1 (Maroczy) and 8 B–K3. The continuation 8 B–K3 has been especially popularized by Russian players. Less usual but satisfactory is 8 P–QN3, protecting QB4.

### IDEA VARIATIONS 23–25:

(23) 8 N–N3, O–O 9 P–B4, P–QN4! with a good game for Black, e.g., 10 BxP, Q–N3† 11 K–R1, NxP.

Or 10 B–B3, B–N2. This variation explains the significance of 8 K–R1.

(24) 8 K–R1, O–O 9 P–B4, Q–B2 10 N–N3, P–QR3 11 B–B3, P–QN4 12 Q–K1, B–N2 13 B–K3, N–Q2 with a good game for Black. White must not allow 11 . . . P–QN4 and must play 11 P–QR4. See Prac. Var. 41.

(25) 8 B–K3, P–QR3 9 P–B4, Q–B2 10 Q–K1, N–QR4? 11 R–Q1, N–B5 12 B–B1! Black's maneuver . . . N–QR4, . . . QB5 is a waste of time against White's set-up. Correct is 10 . . . O–O. See Prac. Var. 43.

PRACTICAL VARIATIONS 41–45:

1 P–K4, P–QB4; 2 N–KB3, P–K3; 3 P–Q4, PxP; 4 NxP, N–KB3; 5 N–QB3, P–Q3; 6 B–K2, B–K2; 7 O–O, N–QB3

| | *41* | *42* | *43* | *44* | *45* |
|---|---|---|---|---|---|
| *8* | K–R1 | – – | B–K3 | – – | P–QN3 |
| | O–O | – – | P–QR3 | – – | O–O |
| *9* | P–B4 | – – | P–B4 | – – | B–N2 |
| | Q–B2 | – – | Q–B2 | – – | Q–R4[12] |
| *10* | N–N3 | – – | Q–K1 | – – | Q–Q2 |
| | P–QR3 | – – | O–O[7] | – – | R–Q1 |
| *11* | P–QR4 | – – | Q–N3 | R–Q1 | QR–Q1 |
| | P–QN3 | N–QR4![14] | NxN[8] | NxN | NxN |
| *12* | B–B3 | NxN | BxN | BxN | QxN[13] |
| | B–N2 | QxN | P–QN4 | P–QN4 | = |
| *13* | B–K3 | Q–K1 | P–QR3 | P–K5[10] | |
| | KR–Q1[1] | Q–B2[5] | B–N2 | PxP | |
| *14* | Q–K1 | B–B3 | K–R1 | BxP | |
| | N–Q2 | B–Q2 | KR–Q1 | Q–N3† | |
| *15* | R–Q1[2] | B–K3 | B–Q3 | K–R1 | |
| | QR–B1 | B–B3 | N–K1 | B–N2[11] | |
| *16* | Q–B2 | P–R5 | QR–K1 | = | |
| | B–R1[3] | N–Q2[6] | B–KB1[9] | | |
| | = | = | = | | |

*Notes to practical variations 41–45:*

[1] The text move is a suggestion by Pachman which is an improvement on 13 . . . N–QN5.

[2] Premature is 15 P–N4, QR–N1 16 R–Q1, N–B4! 17 NxN, NPxN with an edge for Black (Pachman).

[3] White has a superiority in space, yet according to Pachman, the position is level.

continued ▶

[4] Stahlberg's maneuver 11 . . . B–Q2 12 B–B3, N–QN5 is best met by 13 B–K3, followed by 14 P–R5. But 13 P–K5? is unfavorable for White because of 13 . . . KN–Q4 (Euwe–Stahlberg, Buenos Aires 1949).

[5] Capablanca recommended 13 . . . K–R1 to render the threat N–Q5 harmless.

[6] Leonhard–Hilse, Magdeburg 1927. White's slight superiority in terrain has little significance.

[7] Less accurate is 10 . . . NxN 11 BxN:

1) 11 . . . P–K4? 12 PxP, PxP 13 Q–N3!, B–QB4 14 BxB, QxB† 15 K–R1, K–B1 16 N–Q5! and White wins (Boleslavski–Book, Saltsjobaden 1948).
2) 11 . . . B–Q2 12 B–B3, B–B3 13 Q–N3, O–O 14 QR–Q1, P–QN4 15 P–K5!, N–K1 16 P–B5! and White has a strong attack (Boleslavski–Stahlberg, Saltsjobaden 1948).
3) 11 . . . P–QN4 12 P–K5! (12 Q–N3, O–O leads to Prac. Var. 43), PxP 13 PxP, N–Q2 14 N–K4, B–N2 (Aronin–Kotov) 15 N–Q6†, BxN 16 PxB, QxP 17 R–Q1, Q–B2 18 Q–B2! with a strong attack for White according to Tolush: e.g., 18 . . . O–O 19 QBxP! KxB 20 RxN, QxR 21 Q–B6†, K–N1 22 R–B4.

[8] O'Kelly strongly recommends 11 . . . P–Q4. If 12 P–K5, NxN 13 BxN, B–B4 14 BxB (14 Q–Q3, N–Q2), QxB† 15 K–R1, N–K5 16 NxN, PxN 17 P–B3, B–Q2 and White cannot profit from Black's isolated Pawn on his K5. White's best chance to keep the initiative after 11 . . . P–Q4 is 12 PxP, PxP 13 K–R1.

[9] Black's last two moves constitute the backbone of a defensive set-up which Kotov has repeatedly adopted:

1) 17 Q–R3, B–B3 18 P–K5, P–N3 19 N–K4, BxN 20 BxB, QR–B1 with equality (Smyslov–Kotov, Budapest 1950).
2) 17 P–K5, P–N3 18 N–K4, BxN 19 BxB, QR–N1 20 P–B5, KPxP 21 BxP, PxP 22 QBxP, B–Q3, and White's attack is repulsed (Smyslov–Kotov, USSR Championship 1951).
3) 17 Q–R4, Q–K2 18 Q–R3.

[10] 13 B–B3, P–K4! 14 PxP, PxP 15 B–K3, B–QB4! with equality (Kotov).

[11] According to Kotov, Black has a satisfactory game.

[12] After 9 . . . P–QR3 10 K–R1, B–Q2 11 P–B4, Q–R4 12 B–B3, KR–Q1 13 P–KN4! White has good chances for attack (Taimanov–Panov, Baku 1944).

[13] The 9th game of the Alekhine–Euwe 1927 match continued: 12 . . . N–K1 (safer is 12 . . . B–Q2) 13 Q–K3 (13 P–QN4, Q–B2 14 N–N5 favors White, according to Becker), B–Q2 14 P–QR3, B–KB3 15 P–B4, QR–B1 16 R–B3, when Black could have obtained an even game by 16 . . . Q–QB4.

*Sicilian Defense Game 30*

*WHITE: Tolush* *BLACK: Kotov*

*USSR Championship 1945*

| | WHITE | BLACK | | WHITE | BLACK |
|---|---|---|---|---|---|
| 1 | P–K4 | P–QB4 | 22 | NxNP! | BxN |
| 2 | N–KB3 | P–K3 | 23 | QxB | KxN |
| 3 | P–Q4 | PxP | 24 | BxP | N–Q4 |
| 4 | NxP | N–KB3 | 25 | Q–R5 | KR–Q1 |
| 5 | N–QB3 | P–Q3 | 26 | R–KN1 | B–B4 |
| 6 | P–KN3 | N–B3 | 27 | PxP† | K–B1 |
| 7 | B–N2 | B–Q2 | 28 | RxN† | KxR |
| 8 | N/4–K2 | P–QR3 | 29 | BxP† | K–B1 |
| 9 | O–O | P–QN4 | 30 | Q–N6 | NxP/3 |
| 10 | P–QR3 | Q–B2 | 31 | QxN† | Q–B2 |
| 11 | P–R3 | B–K2 | 32 | Q–R6† | K–K2 |
| 12 | K–R1 | O–O | 33 | Q–N5† | K–Q2 |
| 13 | P–KN4 | K–R1 | 34 | QxB | QxB |
| 14 | N–N3 | P–N5 | 35 | R–Q1† | K–K1 |
| 15 | PxP? | QNxP | 36 | Q–B6† | K–B1 |
| 16 | P–N5 | N–N1 | 37 | B–N4† | K–B2 |
| 17 | P–B4 | B–QB3? | 38 | Q–B7† | K–N3 |
| 18 | QN–K2! | B–N4 | 39 | P–B5† | K–R3 |
| 19 | B–Q2 | P–Q4 | 40 | Q–B4† | K–N2 |
| 20 | B–QB3 | PxP | 41 | Q–N5† | Resigns |
| 21 | N–R5 | P–B3 | | | |

SUPPLEMENTARY VARIATIONS 31–35:

1 P–K4, P–QB4 2 N–KB3, P–K3 3 P–Q4, PxP 4 NxP, N–KB3 5 N–QB3

Sup. Var.. 31 and 32 illustrate the Paulsen Variation which differs from the Scheveningen Variation in that Black aims for an early . . . P–QN4 and plays . . . QN–Q2 instead of . . . QN–B3, keeping the Queen Bishop fianchetto diagonal open. This set-up was considered risky for Black in view of the attack which White obtains by the advance P–K5 (Sup. Var. 31). In the Candidates' Tournament of 1959, however, Smyslov found a way to operate against this White advance.

The old-fashioned Four Knights' Variation is treated in Sup. Var. 33 and 34. This steady method of defense is still fairly popular in tournaments.

The Pin Variation (Sup. Var. 35) is too ambitious. Not Black but White gets the attack.

1 P–K4, P–QB4 2 N–KB3, P–K3 3 P–Q4, PxP 4 NxP, N–KB3 5 N–QB3

| | 31 | 32 | 33 | 34 | 35 |
|---|---|---|---|---|---|
| 5 | – – | – – | – – | – – | – – |
| | P–Q3 | – – | N–B3 | – – | B–N5 |
| 6 | B–K2[1] | – – | N/4–N5 | B–K2!?[19] | P–K5[23] |
| | P–QR3 | – – | B–N5 | B–N5 | N–Q4[24] |
| 7 | O–O[2] | – – | P–QR3[12] | O–O | B–Q2[25] |
| | Q–B2[3] | QN–Q2! | BxN† | BxN | NxN[26] |
| 8 | P–B4[4] | P–B4 | NxB | PxB | PxN |
| | P–QN4[5] | P–QN4 | P–Q4 | NxP | B–K2 |
| 9 | B–B3 | B–B3 | PxP | B–Q3[20] | Q–N4 |
| | B–N2 | B–N2 | PxP[13] | P–Q4[21] | K–B1 |
| 10 | P–K5[6] | P–QR3[9] | B–Q3 | B–R3 | B–Q3 |
| | PxP | Q–B2 | O–O[14] | NxN | P–Q3 |
| 11 | PxP | Q–K1 | O–O | PxN | P–KB4 |
| | KN–Q2 | B–K2 | P–KR3[15] | Q–R4 | N–B3[27] |
| 12 | B–B4[7] | K–R1[10] | B–KB4 | Q–B1 | O–O[28] |
| | B–B4 | QR–N1! | P–Q5 | B–Q2 | ± |
| 13 | K–R1[8] | P–QN3 | N–N5[16] | R–N1 | |
| | ± | O–O | N–Q4[17] | B–QB3 | |
| 14 | | B–N2 | B–N3[18] | B–N4 | |
| | | KR–K1[11] | ± | Q–B2[22] | |
| | | = | | = | |

*Notes to supplementary variations 31–35:*

[1] Here Keres tried against Smyslov (Candidates' Tournament 1959): 6 P–B4, P–QR3 7 Q–B3. There followed 7 . . . Q–N3 8 N–N3, N–B3 9 B–Q3, B–K2 10 B–K3, Q–B2 11 O–O, O–O 12 QR–K1 (if 12 P–QR3, then 12 . . . P–QN4 followed by . . . P–N5), N–QN5 13 P–QR3, NxB 14 PxN, B–Q2 15 R–B1, Q–N1! 16 N–R5 (more promising is 16 P–KN4), B–Q1! with good play for Black.

[2] 7 B–K3 is also good.

[3] 7 . . . P–QN4? is premature. Thus, 8 B–B3! R–R2 (8 . . . B–N2? 9 P–K5!) 9 Q–K2, R–B2 10 QR–Q1, QN–Q2 11 P–QR4 with a superior game for White (Smyslov–Kottnauer, Groningen 1946).

[4] White must either attack on the Kingside or take countermeasures against Black's plans on the Queenside. The continuation 8 K–R1, P–QN4 9 P–QR3, B–N2 10 Q–K1, QN–Q2 leads to the ideal form of the Paulsen Variation (Vajda–Alekhine, Kecskemet 1927). 8 P–QR4, N–B3 9 K–R1, B–K2 10 N–N3 leads into the Maroczy Variation of the Scheveningen system.

[5] 8 . . . B–K2 9 B–K3, O–O 10 Q–K1, P–QN4 11 B–B3, B–N2 12 P–K5! offers White good chances (Unzicker–Golombek, Olympiad, Moscow 1956).

[6] Or 10 Q–K1, QN–Q2 11 K–R1, P–N5 12 N–Q1 (Pachman–Foltys, Prague 1946). Black can fearlessly proceed with 12 . . . P–K4, followed by 13 . . . QxP.

[7] 12 BxB, QxB 13 Q–R5 is sharp, but unconvincing: 13 . . . P–N3 14 Q–R4, B–B4 15 K–R1, BxN 16 QxB, N–QB3 17 Q–KR4!, O–O 18 B–R6 and Black, threatened by 19 N–K4, is forced to abandon the exchange (Bolbochan–Ujtelky, Trentschin Teplitz 1949). However, 13 . . . N–B4 offers Black sufficient defense.

[8] White has a slight edge.

[9] Now 10 P–K5 loses its proper effect because of 10 . . . BxB 11 NxB, PxP 12 PxP, N–N5 13 Q–K2, Q–N3† 14 K–R1, P–N5 15 N–Q1, Q–N4!

[10] After 12 P–K5, PxP 13 BxB, QxB 14 PxP, Black plays 14 . . . B–B4!

[11] 15 Q–N3, B–KB1 16 QR–K1, P–K4! and Black stands well (Tal–Smyslov, Candidates' Tournament 1959). Better chances for a White attack are offered by a Pawn storm, beginning with 15 P–KN4.

[12] Two other possibilities, neither of lasting promise, are:

1) 7 B–KB4, NxP 8 N–B7†, an old-fashioned continuation which creates complications without offering a real chance for advantage. After 8 . . . K–K2! 9 Q–B3, P–Q4 10 O–O–O, BxN 11 PxB (11 NxR, Q–R4!), P–KN4! 12 QxN, Black has two plausible continuations: 12 . . . QxN 13 BxP†, P–B3 14 RxP, and White's attack guarantees a draw (Pilnik–Villegas, Mar del Plata 1944); 12 . . . PxQ 13 BxP†, P–B3 14 RxQ, RxR 15 BxP†, KxB 16 NxR, R–Q2, and White's Knight is in trouble.
2) 7 N–Q6†, K–K2, and White has two plausible possibilities: 8 NxB†, RxN 9 B–Q3, P–Q4 10 PxP, QxP 11 O–O, Q–KR4 with equality (Keres–Trifunovic, Tchigorin Tournament, Moscow 1947); 8 B–KB4, P–K4 9 N–B5†, K–B1 10 B–KN5, P–Q4! 11 BxN, QxB 12 QxP, QBxN 13 PxB, R–Q1! 14 Q–K4, R–Q5 15 Q–K3, QxP 16 B–Q3, P–K5 17 B–K2, P–KN3 with an edge for Black.

[13] Less usual but playable is 9 . . . NxP 10 NxN, PxN 11 B–K2, O–O 12 O–O, B–B4 13 B–B3, P–Q5 14 P–QN4, P–Q6 with equality (Najdorf–Trifunovic, Match 1949). A deviation worth considering is 10 B–Q2.

[14] Safest; for . . . B–N5, see Note 15.

[15] 11 . . . B–N5 12 P–B3, B–K3 13 B–KN5, Q–N3† 14 K–R1, N–Q2 (14 . . . QxNP? 15 BxN, PxB 16 Q–Q2 etc.) 15 P–B4! favors White: e.g., 15 . . . P–B3 16 Q–R5, P–B4 17 Q–B3, Q–B4 18 P–QN4! (18 . . . QxN 19 BxP, QxQ 20 BxB† followed by 21 RxQ) (Donner–Orbaan, Wageningen 1957).

[16] Panov's suggestion, which is most usual to-day. If 13 N–K4, Black's best is 13 . . . NxN 14 BxN, Q–B3 followed by 15 . . . B–B4, but not 13 . . . B–B4? because of 14 B–B7! and Black cannot prevent the doubling of his King Bishop Pawns (14 . . . Q–K2? 15 B–Q6!). After 13 N–K2, Q–Q4 14 N–N3, B–N5 15 P–B3, B–K3, Black gains equality.

[17] 13 . . . P–QR3 is met by 14 N–Q6. The text move prevents 14 B–Q6? because Black, with 14 . . . P–QR3, wins two pieces for a Rook.

[18] 14 . . . B–K3 15 R–K1, Q–Q2 16 P–KR3, QR–Q1 17 continued ▸

Q–B3 with a good game for White (Krogius–Tal, USSR Championship, Tiflis 1959). For 16 . . . P–R3 17 N–Q6 see Game 31.

[19] This old gambit line was revived by Geller. Other continuations make it easy for Black:

6 NxN, NPxN 7 P–K5, N–Q4 8 N–K4, P–KB4 (also good is 8 . . . Q–B2 or 8 . . . Q–R4† 9 B–Q2, N–N5) 9 PxP e.p., NxP 10 N–Q6†, BxN 11 QxB (so far, Yates–Lasker, New York 1924), Q–N3! 12 B–Q3, P–B4 13 B–KB4, B–N2! 14 O–O, R–QB1 with a satisfactory game for Black (analysis by Alekhine); 6 B–K3, B–N5 7 B–Q3, P–Q4 8 NxN, NPxN 9 P–K5, N–Q2 10 Q–N4, B–B1! 11 P–B4, R–QN1 12 N–Q1, B–R3 (13 BxB, Q–R4†) with a good game for Black (Spielmann–Janowski, Semmering 1926); 6 P–KN3, B–N5 7 B–N2, O–O 8 O–O, P–QR3 9 B–K3, Q–B2 10 N–R4, P–QN4 11 NxN, PxN 12 P–QB3, B–K2 13 N–B5, P–K4 14 P–KR3, N–Q2 with a satisfactory game for Black (Steiner–Gilg, Kecskemet 1927).

[20] If 9 B–B3, Geller's improvement 9 . . . P–Q4! compels White to play for a draw by 10 NxN, PxN 11 BxN, PxB 12 QxQ†, relying on Bishops of opposite colors.

[21] On 9 . . . NxQBP (if 9 . . . N–B3, then 10 N–N5, and if 9 . . . NxN, then 10 BxN, N–B3 11 B–R3) 10 Q–N4, O–O 11 B–N2, P–B4! 12 NxBP, PxN 13 Q–B4†, P–Q4, Black maintains his extra Pawn under favorable circumstances (Trifunovic). Hence, White must try 11 NxN or 12 NxN.

[22] So far Geller–Trifunovic, Zagreb 1955. O'Kelly now gives 15 R–N3! as offering White sufficient attacking chances for the Pawn.

[23] The text is the most enterprising. Other continuations are:

1) 6 N–N5, P–Q4! 7 PxP (safer is 7 P–K5, N/3–Q2 8 Q–N4, B–B1 9 B–N5, Q–N3! 10 B–K3, Q–B3), P–QR3! 8 Q–Q4, B–K2 9 P–Q6, PxN 10 NxP, N–B3 11 Q–Q1, B–B1 (12 N–B7†, K–Q2 13 NxR, Q–R4†!) and White lacks clear compensation for the piece (Szabo–Dake, Warsaw 1935).
2) 6 B–Q3, N–B3 7 NxN, QPxN 8 P–K5, N–Q2 9 Q–N4, Q–R4 10 O–O, BxN 11 PxB, QxKP 12 B–KB4, and White's advance in development compensates for the Pawn (Spielmann–Tartakover, Mahrisch-Ostrau 1923).

[24] Other moves are bad:

1) 6 . . . N–K5 7 Q–N4, NxN (7 . . . Q–R4 8 QxN!, BxN† 9 PxB, QxP† 10 K–Q1, QxR 11 N–N5, P–Q4 12 Q–N4, QxKP 13 P–B4!; or 11 . . . K–Q1 12 P–QB3!) 8 QxNP, R–B1 9 P–QR3, N–N4† 10 PxB, NxN 11 B–KN5!, Q–N3 12 B–R6, QxP† 13 P–B3, N–B4 14 PxQ, NxQ 15 BxN, R–N1 16 B–B6 with a superior game for White (Szabo–Mikenas, Kemeri 1937).
2) 6 . . . Q–R4 7 PxN, BxN† 8 PxB, QxP† 9 Q–Q2, QxR 10 P–QB3! and White has a winning attack (Oskam–Muhring, Rotterdam 1933).

[25] Less clear is 7 Q–N4, P–KN3 8 P–QR3, BxN† 9 PxB, Q–B2 10 Q–N3, QxBP† 11 QxQ, NxQ 12 B–Q2, N–K5! 13 B–R6, P–R3.

[26] 7 . . . BxN 8 PxB, Q–B2 9 P–KB4, P–QR3 (9 . . . NxP 10 Q–B3, N–Q4 11 N–N5) 10 P–B4, N–K2 11 B–Q3 favors White. See Game 32.

[27] Weaker for Black is 11 . . . N–Q2 12 O–O, N–B4 (12 . . . PxKP 13 NxP†) 13 P–B5, PxKP 14 PxP, B–B3 15 RxB, QxR 16 B–KN5, and White won quickly (Richter–Koch, Berlin 1950).

[28] White has good attacking chances.

## *Sicilian Defense Game 31*

*WHITE: Tal* *BLACK: Olafsson*

*Zurich 1959*

| | WHITE | BLACK | | WHITE | BLACK |
|---|---|---|---|---|---|
| 1 | P–K4 | P–QB4 | 33 | K–R2 | R–Q1 |
| 2 | N–KB3 | P–K3 | 34 | Q–B5† | K–R1 |
| 3 | P–Q4 | PxP | 35 | R–K6 | Q–B2† |
| 4 | NxP | N–KB3 | 36 | P–N3 | Q–Q2 |
| 5 | N–QB3 | N–B3 | 37 | Q–K5 | Q–Q7 |
| 6 | N/4–N5 | B–N5 | 38 | K–N2 | R–KB1 |
| 7 | P–QR3 | BxN† | 39 | Q–K2 | Q–Q4† |
| 8 | NxB | P–Q4 | 40 | K–N1 | R–B1 |
| 9 | PxP | PxP | 41 | Q–K4 | Q–Q7 |
| 10 | B–Q3 | O–O | 42 | Q–K5 | R–B1 |
| 11 | O–O | P–KR3 | 43 | Q–K2 | Q–B8† |
| 12 | B–KB4 | P–Q5 | 44 | K–N2 | Q–B1 |
| 13 | N–N5 | N–Q4 | 45 | P–QN4 | Q–N2† |
| 14 | B–N3 | B–K3 | 46 | K–N1 | Q–B1 |
| 15 | R–K1 | Q–Q2 | 47 | Q–K3 | K–N1 |
| 16 | P–R3 | P–R3 | 48 | P–KR4 | K–R1 |
| 17 | N–Q6 | N–B3 | 49 | R–K7 | Q–N5 |
| 18 | Q–B3 | K–R1 | 50 | K–N2 | Q–B4 |
| 19 | QR–Q1 | N–KR2 | 51 | Q–Q4 | Q–B6† |
| 20 | BxN | KxB | 52 | K–N1 | R–B2 |
| 21 | P–B3 | PxP | 53 | R–K6 | K–N1 |
| 22 | N–K4 | Q–B1 | 54 | RxQRP | R–K2 |
| 23 | QxQBP | N–K2 | 55 | Q–Q8† | K–B2 |
| 24 | N–B5 | N–B4 | 56 | Q–Q2 | K–N1 |
| 25 | B–B7! | P–QN4! | 57 | R–Q6 | Q–B1 |
| 26 | NxB | PxN | 58 | R–Q5 | R–K1 |
| 27 | Q–B6 | N–K2 | 59 | RxP | Q–B3 |
| 28 | QxKP | QxB | 60 | R–QR5 | K–R1 |
| 29 | QxN | Q–N3 | 61 | Q–Q5 | R–KB1 |
| 30 | R–K3 | QR–Q1 | 62 | Q–Q2 | Q–KB6 |
| 31 | R–Q7 | RxR | 63 | R–Q5 | QxP |
| 32 | QxR/8 | R–Q8† | 64 | R–Q8 | Resigns |

*Sicilian Defense Game 32*

*WHITE: Olafsson* *BLACK: Cardoso*

*Portoroz 1958*

| WHITE | BLACK | WHITE | BLACK |
|---|---|---|---|
| 1 P–K4 | P–QB4 | 15 NxN | PxN |
| 2 N–KB3 | P–K3 | 16 QR–K1 | P–QB4 |
| 3 P–Q4 | PxP | 17 P–KR4 | O–O |
| 4 NxP | N–KB3 | 18 Q–N5 | Q–Q1 |
| 5 N–QB3 | B–N5 | 19 P–R5 | N–R1 |
| 6 P–K5 | N–Q4 | 20 Q–N3 | P–B4 |
| 7 B–Q2 | BxN | 21 PxP e.p. | RxP |
| 8 PxB | Q–B2 | 22 B–B3 | RxR† |
| 9 P–KB4 | P–QR3 | 23 RxR | Q–K2 |
| 10 P–B4 | N–K2 | 24 P–R6 | P–K4 |
| 11 B–Q3 | P–Q3 | 25 BxP | N–N3 |
| 12 O–O | PxP | 26 B–Q6 | Q–Q2 |
| 13 PxP | N–N3 | 27 BxN | PxB |
| 14 Q–N4 | N–B3 | 28 P–R7† | Resigns |

---

## part 10—MODERN VARIATION WITH 5 P-QB4

1 P–K4, P–QB4
2 N–KB3, P–K3
3 P–Q4, PxP
4 NxP, P–QR3
5 P–QB4, N–KB3
6 N–QB3[A], B–N5

KEY POSITION 10

### OBSERVATIONS ON KEY POSITION 10

[A] Benko versus Smyslov, in the Candidates' Tournament 1959, played 6 B–Q3, avoiding the pin on his Queen Knight by . . . B–N5. The game continued 6 . . . N–B3 7 NxN, QPxN 8 O–O, P–K4 9 Q–B2, B–QB4 10 N–Q2, B–K3 with a balanced position.

In vogue to-day is the set-up with 2 . . . P–K3 and 4 . . . P–QR3, which we call the Modern Variation. White may try to establish a strong center with 5 P–QB4, but then Black obtains active counterplay with 5 . . . N–KB3 and 6 . . . B–N5.

Black may also open the position with . . . P–Q4. At any rate it is difficult for White to consolidate his position in the center.

### IDEA VARIATIONS 26–28:

(26) 7 B–Q3 (7 P–K5? Q–R4!), N–B3 8 NxN, QPxN 9 P–K5!? (9 O–O, P–K4), Q–R4! 10 PxN, BxN† 11 PxB, QxP† 12 Q–Q2 (12 B–Q2, QxB 13 PxP, R–N1), QxR, and White's compensation for the exchange is not quite sufficient (Nievergelt–Kupper, 2nd Match Game 1957).

(27) 7 Q–B3, N–B3 8 N–B2, P–Q4! 9 KPxP, PxP 10 PxP (10 B–KN5!), NxP 11 B–Q2, BxN 12 PxB, O–O 13 B–K2, R–K1, and White faces serious difficulties.

He cannot castle because of 14 . . . N–B3! If then 15 B–KN5, Black still plays 15 . . . B–N5! (Matanovic-Van Scheltinga, Beverwijk 1958).

(28) 7 B–Q2, O–O 8 P–K5, N–K1 9 N–B2, B–K2 10 B–Q3 with a good game for White (Stoliar–Tal, USSR Championship 1957). Stronger is 8 . . . BxN 9 BxB, N–K5 10 Q–B2, P–Q4. Or 10 B–N4, P–Q3. See Prac. Var. 48, note 5.

PRACTICAL VARIATIONS 46–50:

1 P–K4, P–QB4 2 N–KB3, P–K3 3 P–Q4, PxP 4 NxP, P–QR3 5 P–QB4, N–KB3 6 N–QB3, B–N5

| | 46 | 47 | 48 | 49 | 50 |
|---|---|---|---|---|---|
| 7 | B–Q3 | – – | B–Q2 | Q–B3 | N–B2!? |
| | N–B3 | – – | O–O | Q–B2[7] | BxN† |
| 8 | N–B2[1] | B–B2!? | P–K5 | N–B2 | PxB |
| | BxN† | Q–B2 | BxN | B–Q3 | NxP |
| 9 | PxB | O–O | BxB | B–K2 | Q–N4 |
| | P–Q4 | NxN | N–K5 | N–B3 | P–B4 |
| 10 | KPxP | QxN | Q–B2[5] | Q–K3 | QxNP |
| | PxP | N–N5 | P–Q4 | P–QN3 | Q–B3 |
| 11 | B–R3 | P–K5 | PxP e.p. | B–Q2 | QxQ |
| | B–K3 | NxKP[3] | NxB | O–O | NxQ |
| 12 | Q–K2 | B–B4 | QxN | P–KN4[8] | P–B3![9] |
| | Q–B2[2] | P–KB3[4] | QxP[6] | ± | = |
| | = | ± | = | | |

*Notes to practical variations 46–50:*

[1] A new idea is 8 N–K2, Q–B2 9 O–O, N–K4 10 P–B4! NxP (10 . . . NxB!) 11 K–R1! B–K2 12 P–QN3, N–N3 13 P–K5, KN–Q4 14 N–K4, P–B4 15 PxP e.p. NxP/3 16 N/2–N3, QN–Q4 17 B–N2! and White has ample compensation for the Pawn (Olafsson–Tal, Candidates' Tournament 1959).

[2] Better than 12 . . . Q–R4 (Nievergelt–Kupper, match for Swiss championship) 13 B–N4!, NxB 14 PxN, Q–B2 15 P–B5. After the text move the chances are even, e.g., 13 O–O, O–O–O (13 . . . Q–K4 14 N–K3).

[3] Black must accept the Pawn sacrifice. The continuation 11 . . . P–KR4 12 B–B4, B–B4 13 Q–Q2 clearly favors White (Bronstein–Boleslavski, USSR Championship, Riga 1958). See Game 33.

[4] Not 12 . . . P–Q3 13 N–K4, P–QN3, 14 P–QR3, B–B4 15 Q–B3. After the text move, according to Boleslavski, Black's game is tenable: e.g., 13 N–K4 (or 13 KR–K1, B–B4 14 Q–K4, P–Q3), P–QN3 (13 . . . N–B6†? 14 PxN, QxB 15 P–B5!)14 B–KN3, B–N2 15 QR–Q1, O–O–O.

[5] Or 10 B–N4, P–Q3 11 Q–K2 (11 PxP, Q–N3), Q–N3 12 N–B2, N–QB3 13 P–QR3, P–Q4 14 P–B3 (14 BxR, QxP, threatening 15 . . . N–Q5), N–B4 15 Q–K3, P–Q5 with even chances (Korchnoi–Furman, Leningrad 1957).

continued ▸

[6] Black has a satisfactory game: 13 O–O–O, Q–B5† 14 Q–K3, QxQ† 15 PxQ, N–Q2 16 B–K2, N–K4 17 P–QN3, R–K1 18 R–Q2, P–B4! (Boleslavski–Kotov, Semi-finals, USSR Championship 1957). Or 13 R–Q1, P–K4! (Unzicker–Tal, Zurich, 1959). See Game 34.

[7] Well worth consideration is 7 . . . P–Q4! This unusual push is even stronger than 7 . . . N–B3 8 N–B2, P–Q4! (Idea Var. 27).

[8] 12 . . . B–B4 13 Q–N3, P–Q3 14 P–N5, N–Q2 15 P–KR4, B–N2 16 P–R5, N–Q5 17 NxN, BxN 18 O–O–O with a good game for White (Smyslov–Olafsson, Candidates' Tournament 1959).

[9] In order to meet 12 . . . N–B3 with 13 P–B5. Therefore 12 . . . P–Q3 is Black's best. Weaker is 12 . . . P–Q4 13 PxP, NxP 14 P–B4, N–KB3 15 R–QN1, QN–Q2 16 B–K3 (Nilsson–Hultquist, Stockholm 1959).

*Sicilian Defense Game 33*

*WHITE: Bronstein* *BLACK: Boleslavski*

*USSR Championship, Riga 1958*

| | WHITE | BLACK | | WHITE | BLACK | | WHITE | BLACK |
|---|---|---|---|---|---|---|---|---|
| 1 | P–K4 | P–QB4 | 15 | B–B4 | Q–Q5 | 29 | R–KN3 | R–KR1 |
| 2 | N–KB3 | P–K3 | 16 | QxQ | BxQ | 30 | P–R4 | K–B3 |
| 3 | P–Q4 | PxP | 17 | P–KR3 | N–R3 | 31 | P–B4 | K–B2 |
| 4 | NxP | P–QR3 | 18 | KR–K1! | K–B1 | 32 | R–N5 | N–K2 |
| 5 | P–QB4 | N–KB3 | 19 | B–Q6† | K–N1 | 33 | R–Q3 | N–N1 |
| 6 | N–QB3 | B–N5 | 20 | QR–Q1 | BxN | 34 | R/Q–KN3 | N–B3 |
| 7 | B–Q3 | N–B3 | 21 | PxB | P–B4 | 35 | R–N7† | K–K1 |
| 8 | B–B2 | Q–B2 | 22 | P–B5 | R–KR2 | 36 | R/3–N6 | N–K5 |
| 9 | O–O | NxN | 23 | P–QB4 | N–B2 | 37 | RxP† | K–Q1 |
| 10 | QxN | N–N5 | 24 | B–B4 | P–R4 | 38 | RxN | PxR |
| 11 | P–K5!? | P–KR4 | 25 | B–R4 | N–Q1 | 39 | P–B5 | P–K6 |
| 12 | B–B4 | B–B4 | 26 | B–Q6 | N–B3 | 40 | P–B6 | P–K7 |
| 13 | Q–Q2 | P–KN4 | 27 | R–K3 | K–B2 | 41 | K–B2 | R–K1 |
| 14 | BxP | QxP | 28 | P–R3 | R–QR3 | 42 | K–K1 | Resigns |

*Sicilian Defense Game 34*

*WHITE: Unzicker* *BLACK: Tal*

*Zurich 1959*

| | WHITE | BLACK | | WHITE | BLACK |
|---|---|---|---|---|---|
| 1 | P–K4 | P–QB4 | 10 | Q–B2 | P–Q4 |
| 2 | N–KB3 | P–K3 | 11 | PxP e.p. | NxB |
| 3 | P–Q4 | PxP | 12 | QxN | QxP |
| 4 | NxP | P–QR3 | 13 | R–Q1 | P–K4! |
| 5 | P–QB4 | N–KB3 | 14 | N–B3 | Q–KN3 |
| 6 | N–QB3 | B–N5 | 15 | B–Q3 | P–K5 |
| 7 | B–Q2 | O–O | 16 | B–N1 | P–B4 |
| 8 | P–K5 | BxN | 17 | N–R4 | Q–K3 |
| 9 | BxB | N–K5 | 18 | P–KN3 | N–B3 |

| WHITE | BLACK | WHITE | BLACK |
|---|---|---|---|
| 19 R–Q5 | Q–B2 | 29 R–Q6 | N–B6† |
| 20 O–O | B–K3 | 30 K–R1 | R–QB1! |
| 21 R–Q6 | BxP | 31 B–Q1 | R–B8 |
| 22 R/1–Q1 | B–K3 | 32 R–Q8† | K–N2 |
| 23 B–B2 | QR–K1 | 33 K–N2 | N–K8† |
| 24 N–N2 | Q–B3 | 34 K–R3 | N–Q6 |
| 25 QxQ? | RxQ | 35 B–K2 | NxN† |
| 26 P–QR3 | N–K4 | 36 PxN | R–B7 |
| 27 N–B4 | B–B2 | Resigns | |
| 28 RxR | PxR | | |

---

## part 11—MODERN VARIATION WITH 5 N-QB3

1 P–K4, P–QB4
2 N–KB3, P–K3
3 P–Q4, PxP
4 NxP, P–QR3
5 N–QB3[A], Q–B2

KEY POSITION 11

### OBSERVATIONS ON KEY POSITION 11

[A] The continuation 5 B–Q3, N–QB3 6 NxN, in the trend of Morphy, was adopted in some games of the 1959 Candidates' Tournament. Recapture with the Knight Pawn was played in the game Smyslov–Tal, but White obtained a positional advantage after 6 . . . NPxN 7 O–O, P–Q4 8 N–Q2, N–B3 9 Q–K2, B–K2 10 R–K1, O–O 11 P–QN3, P–QR4 12 B–N2, P–R5 13 P–QR3, RPxP 14 BPxP, Q–N3 15 PxP, BPxP 16 P–QN4, N–Q2 17 N–N3. In his game versus Keres, however, Tal played 6 . . . QPxN, obtaining an almost even position after 7 O–O, P–K4 8 N–Q2, Q–B2 9 P–QR4, N–B3 10 Q–B3, B–QB4 11 N–B4, O–O 12 N–K3, R–K1 13 B–QB4, B–K3 14 BxB, RxB.

Since Black obtains active counterplay after 5 P–QB4 (Part 10), the simple developing move 5 N–QB3 has become increasingly popular. Then, with 5 . . . Q–B2, Black threatens 6 . . . B–N5. This threat, however, is easily parried, and Black therefore must complete his development in some other way.

Black should proceed with the quick mobilization of his Queenside with . . . P–QN4 and . . . B–N2, in which set-up 5 . . . Q–B2 is a useful link. Both sides have plenty of choice and the theory of this young variation is still in its evolutionary stages.

### IDEA VARIATIONS 29-31:

(29) 6 B–K2 (only this move makes Black's pin of the Queen Knight effective), B–N5 7 O–O, N–KB3 (7 . . . BxN 8 PxB, QxP 9 R–N1 is too risky for Black) 8 Q–Q3 (White must not sacrifice the Pawn at K4) N–B3 9 P–QR3 (also plausible is 9 B–Q2) BxN 10 PxB, O–O 11 P–KB4, P–Q4 12 P–K5, N–K5 13 B–B3, N–B4 with a satisfactory game for Black (Keres–Chasin, USSR Championship 1957).

(30) 6 P–KN3, B–N5 (this move is now ineffective, in view of the possibility of 7 N–K2) 7 N–K2, N–KB3 8 B–N2, N–B3 (so far, Darga–Portisch, Hastings 1957-58) 9 B–B4! and White gets the edge: e.g., 9 . . . P–K4 10 B–N5! or 9 . . . P–Q3 10 P–QR3!

(31) 6 P–B4, P–QN4 7 P–QR3, B–N2 8 B–Q3 (Mikenas–Furman, USSR Championship 1957). Now Black could have proceeded effectively with 8 . . . B–B4! 9 B–K3, Q–N3.

PRACTICAL VARIATIONS 51–55:

1 P–K4, P–QB4 2 N–KB3, P–K3 3 P–Q4, PxP 4 NxP, P–QR3 5 N–QB3, Q–B2

| | *51* | *52* | *53* | *54* | *55* |
|---|---|---|---|---|---|
| *6* | B–Q3 | – – | P–KN3 | – – | P–QR3 |
| | P–QN4 | N–QB3 | B–N5 | N–KB3 | N–QB3 |
| *7* | O–O | B–K3[4] | N–K2 | B–N2 | B–K3 |
| | B–N2 | N–B3 | P–KR4?! | N–B3 | N–B3 |
| *8* | R–K1[1] | Q–K2[5] | P–KR3 | O–O | B–K2[10] |
| | N–KB3[2] | B–Q3[6] | N–KB3 | B–K2 | P–QN4[11] |
| *9* | P–K5 | P–KR3 | B–N2 | K–R1 | P–B4 |
| | N–Q4 | P–QN4 | N–B3 | O–O | B–N2 |
| *10* | B–Q2 | N–N3 | B–B4! | P–B4 | B–B3 |
| | NxN | O–O | P–K4 | P–Q3[9] | P–Q3 |
| *11* | BxN | O–O | B–N5 | = | O–O |
| | N–B3 | B–B5[7] | P–Q3[8] | | B–K2 |
| *12* | NxN | = | ± | | Q–K1 |
| | BxN[3] | | | | O–O[12] |
| | ± | | | | = |

*Notes to practical variations 51-55:*

[1] This move offers better chances than 8 Q–K2, N–KB3! 9 B–Q2, N–B3 10 NxN, QxN 11 P–QR3, B–B4 with an even game (Boleslavski–Kotov, USSR Championship, Riga 1958).

[2] Or 8 . . . N–QB3 9 NxN, QxN 10 P–QR4, P–N5 11 N–Q5! This variation reveals why the Rook on K1 serves well (Tal–Gipslis, Riga 1958). See Game 35.

[3] Durasevic–Taimanov, Yugoslavia–USSR, Zagreb 1958. The game was called a draw at this point, but 13 Q–N4 still offers White an advantage in space.

[4] Or 7 N/4–K2, N–B3 8 O–O, P–QN4 9 P–QR3, B–N2 10 B–KB4, P–Q3 11 P–QN4, B–K2 12 Q–K1, O–O, and Black has a satisfactory game (Blau–Gligoric, Zurich 1959). As for 7 NxN, this only strengthens Black's center: e.g., 7 . . . NPxN 8 O–O, N–B3 9 P–B4, P–Q4 10 Q–B3, B–N2 (Walther–Tal). See Game 36.

[5] 8 O–O enables Black to simplify by 8 . . . NxN 9 BxN, B–B4. After the text move, however, the continuation 8 . . . NxN 9 BxN, B–B4 is not good for Black because of 10 BxB, QxB 11 P–K5!

[6] The Bishop maneuver . . . B–Q3–B5 is characteristic of this variation.

[7] The chances are equal: e.g., 12 QR–K1, BxB 13 QxB, P–Q3 (Durasevic–Taimanov, Zagreb 1958).

[8] Donner–Keres, Zurich 1959. White has a good game, but the continuation he chose was not the best: 12 P–QR3, B–QB4 13 BxN, PxB 14 N–Q5, Q–Q1 15 P–QN4, B–R2. Instead, he should have played 12 O–O! threatening 13 BxN, followed by N–Q5 or directly 13 N–Q5.

[9] The game is now similar to the Scheveningen–Fianchetto Variation. Inferior is 10 . . . R–Q1 11 P–K5! See Bronstein–Filip, Game 37.

[10] Another plan of mobilization is 8 P–B4, followed by Q–B3, B–Q3, and O–O.

[11] The text is better than 8 . . . B–Q3 9 Q–Q2, B–K4 10 P–B4!, BxN 11 BxB, NxB 12 QxN, QxP 13 P–KN3, Q–B2 14 P–K5, as White has sufficient positional compensation for the Pawn (Neshmetdinov–Tal, USSR Championship, Tiflis 1959).

[12] Keres–Olafsson, Candidates' Tournament 1959.

### *Sicilian Defense Game 35*

*WHITE: Tal* — *BLACK: Gipslis*

*Riga 1958*

| | WHITE | BLACK | | WHITE | BLACK | | WHITE | BLACK |
|---|---|---|---|---|---|---|---|---|
| 1 | P–K4 | P–QB4 | 10 | P–QR4 | P–N5 | 19 | QR–Q1 | B–K2 |
| 2 | N–KB3 | P–K3 | 11 | N–Q5! | N–B3 | 20 | P–KN4! | R–B1 |
| 3 | P–Q4 | PxP | 12 | B–Q2 | NxN | 21 | PxP | K–N1 |
| 4 | NxP | P–QR3 | 13 | PxN | Q–B4 | 22 | Q–N2! | B–B3 |
| 5 | N–QB3 | P–QN4 | 14 | B–K4! | P–B4 | 23 | BxB | RxB |
| 6 | B–Q3 | B–N2 | 15 | B–KB3 | BxP | 24 | RxQP! | QxR |
| 7 | O–O | Q–B2 | 16 | BxP | BxB | 25 | QxR† | R–B1 |
| 8 | R–K1 | N–QB3 | 17 | QxB | Q–B1 | 26 | QxP | Resigns |
| 9 | NxN | QxN | 18 | B–B3! | K–B2 | | | |

### *Sicilian Defense Game 36*

*WHITE: Walther* — *BLACK: Tal*

*Zurich 1959*

| | WHITE | BLACK | | WHITE | BLACK | | WHITE | BLACK |
|---|---|---|---|---|---|---|---|---|
| 1 | P–K4 | P–QB4 | 12 | PxP | P–B5 | 23 | PxP | PxP |
| 2 | N–KB3 | P–K3 | 13 | B–K4 | PxP | 24 | RxP | Q–N3 |
| 3 | N–B3 | P–QR3 | 14 | B–B5 | B–B4† | 25 | B–K3 | Q–N8† |
| 4 | P–Q4 | PxP | 15 | K–R1 | P–N3! | 26 | B–N1 | B–K5! |
| 5 | NxP | Q–B2 | 16 | QR–K1† | K–B1 | 27 | BxB | NxB |
| 6 | B–Q3 | N–QB3 | 17 | N–R4 | P–Q5 | 28 | R–B3 | QR–Q1 |
| 7 | NxN | NPxN | 18 | Q–R3 | K–N2 | 29 | P–N3 | RxR |
| 8 | O–O | N–B3 | 19 | NxB | QxN | 30 | PxR | Q–N2! |
| 9 | P–B4 | P–Q4 | 20 | R–K5 | Q–B3 | | Resigns | |
| 10 | Q–B3 | B–N2 | 21 | R–B3 | KR–K1 | | | |
| 11 | B–Q2 | P–B4 | 22 | R–N3 | P–B6! | | | |

*Sicilian Defense Game 37*

*WHITE: Bronstein* *BLACK: Filip*

*Moscow 1959*

| WHITE | BLACK | WHITE | BLACK | WHITE | BLACK |
|---|---|---|---|---|---|
| 1 P–K4 | P–QB4 | 12 NxN | NPxN | 23 Q–R5 | P–Q5 |
| 2 N–KB3 | P–K3 | 13 Q–B3 | B–N2 | 24 Q–QB5 | QxQ |
| 3 P–Q4 | PxP | 14 B–K3 | P–Q4 | 25 NxQ | B–B4 |
| 4 NxP | P–QR3 | 15 P–B5! | QxP? | 26 BxR | RxB |
| 5 N–QB3 | Q–B2 | 16 PxP | QxKP | 27 N–N7 | BxP |
| 6 P–KN3 | N–KB3 | 17 B–N6 | B–B3 | 28 NxN | K–B1 |
| 7 B–N2 | N–B3 | 18 QR–K1! | Q–Q3 | 29 N–K4 | B–K2 |
| 8 O–O | B–K2 | 19 N–R4 | Q–N5 | 30 P–QN4 | P–QR4 |
| 9 K–R1 | O–O | 20 P–N3 | N–Q3 | 31 N–B5 | PxP |
| 10 P–B4 | R–Q1 | 21 P–QR3! | Q–N4 | 32 N–K6† | Resigns |
| 11 P–K5! | N–K1 | 22 Q–N4 | B–B1 | | |

---

## part 12—ROSSOLIMO VARIATION

1 P–K4, P–QB4
2 N–KB3, N–QB3
3 B–N5[A]

KEY POSITION 12

OBSERVATIONS ON KEY POSITION 12

[A] 3 P–QB3 leads by transposition, via 3 . . . P–Q4 or 3 . . . N–KB3, to Sup. Var. 40.

3 B–N5 in the Sicilian Defense is actually an idea of Nimzowitsch, who called it one of his little jokes in the opening. The move was popularized only after 1945 after Rossolimo had repeatedly adopted it with remarkable success. At present 3 B–N5 is employed mostly by Russian masters.

The main purpose of 3 B–N5 is quick development, building a strong center with P–QB3 and P–Q4. The struggle for White's Q4 depends a good deal on tactics, as is demonstrated in the Idea Variations. Black must be careful about capturing on White's Q4, or White will obtain a great lead in development.

IDEA VARIATIONS 32 AND 33:

(32) 3 . . . P–K3 4 P–B3, P–KN3 5 P–Q4, PxP 6 PxP, B–N2 7 O–O, Q–N3? (7 . . . P–Q4) 8 N–R3! NxP? 9 N–B4! NxN† 10 QxN, Q–B2 11 B–B4, P–K4 12 NxP (also strong is 12 KR–Q1, PxB 13 N–Q6†), BxN 13 QR–B1, Q–N1 (13 . . . Q–Q3 is better, but not 13 . . . BxB 14 RxQ, BxR 15 Q–B3!) 14 RxB!, and White won quickly (Rossolimo–O'Kelly, Oldenburg 1949).

(33) 3 . . . N–B3 4 N–B3 (4 P–K5 is stronger; See Prac. Var. 60) N–Q5! 5 B–R4, Q–R4! 6 P–K5, N–K5!

and Black has excellent counterplay after 7 BxP†, BxB 8 NxN, Q–R5! recovering the Pawn (Visser–Euwe, Utrecht 1952).

PRACTICAL VARIATIONS 56–60:

1 P–K4, P–QB4 2 N–KB3, N–QB3 3 B–N5

| | 56 | 57 | 58 | 59 | 60 |
|---|---|---|---|---|---|
| 3 | – – | – – | – – | – – | – – |
| | P–KN3 | – – | – – | Q–N3[12] | N–B3 |
| 4 | O–O | P–B3 | – – | BxN[13] | P–K5[15] |
| | B–N2 | B–N2[4] | N–KB3! | QPxB | N–Q4[16] |
| 5 | P–B3[1] | P–Q4 | P–K5[9] | P–Q3 | O–O |
| | Q–N3[2] | Q–N3[5] | N–Q4 | N–B3 | P–K3[17] |
| 6 | N–R3 | P–QR4! | O–O | Q–K2 | BxN |
| | N–B3 | PxP | B–N2 | P–N3 | NPxB |
| 7 | P–K5 | O–O![6] | P–Q4 | O–O | P–B4 |
| | N–Q4 | P–QR3 | PxP | B–N2 | N–N5 |
| 8 | B–B4 | BxN | PxP | R–K1 | P–Q4 |
| | N–B2 | QxB[7] | O–O | O–O | PxP |
| 9 | R–K1 | PxP | N–B3[10] | N–B3 | P–QR3 |
| | O–O | QxKP | N–B2! | R–Q1 | N–R3 |
| 10 | B–N3 | N–B3[8] | B–QB4 | P–KR3 | QxP[18] |
| | N–R4[3] | = | P–Q3[11] | N–Q2[14] | ± |
| | = | | = | = | |

*Notes to practical variations 56–60:*

[1] The usual continuation. For 5 R–K1 see Game 38.

[2] 5 . . . P–Q4? is premature: e.g., 6 Q–R4!, PxP 7 BxN†, PxB 8 QxP†, B–Q2 9 QxKP, N–B3 10 Q–KR4, O–O (Tartakover–Boleslavski, Groningen 1946), and now White should have played 11 P–Q4, simply maintaining his advantage.

[3] Nimzowitsch–Stolz, Match 1934, continued 11 P–Q4, PxP 12 NxP, NxB 13 PxN, P–Q4 with approximate equality.

[4] Also meriting consideration is 4 . . . Q–N3. Here 5 N–R3 leads to Prac. Var. 56. 5 P–QR4 is answered by 5. . . . P–QR3.

[5] An improvement for Black is 5 . . . Q–R4! 6 BxN, QPxB (6 . . . NPxB is also good) 7 PxP, QxP 8 B–K3, Q–QN4 9 Q–B2, N–B3 (Winiwarter–Pirc, Vienna 1956–57). Here, too, the gambit line 6 P–QR4, PxP 7 O–O! is well worth investigation.

[6] A promising gambit.

[7] Better is 8 . . . QPxB 8 PxP, B–N5.

[8] 10 . . . Q–B4 11 R–K1, P–Q4 (11 . . . P–Q3 12 N–K4) 12 P–R5, B–Q2 (12 . . . N–B3 13 N–QR4) 13 Q–N3, and White's lead in development fully compensates for the Pawn (Bronstein–Geller, Goteborg 1955).

[9] More comfortable for Black is 5 Q–K2, B–N2 6 O–O, O–O 7 P–Q4, PxP 8 NxP, Q–B2 9 N–Q2, P–Q4 (Szabo–Boleslavski, Bucharest 1953).

[10] 9 BxN, QPxB leaves White's Queen Pawn backward.

[11] After 10 . . . P–Q4 White has a strong center. The text continued ▶

move aims to undermine the White Pawn on K5: e.g., 11 Q–K2, B–N5 12 R–Q1, PxP 13 PxP, Q–B1 with even chances (if 14 B–B4, then 14 . . . Q–B4) (Neshmetdinov–Boleslavski, Spartakiade 1959).

[12] Inferior is 3 . . . Q–B2 4 O–O, N–B3 5 N–B3, as in the continuation 5 . . . P–K3 6 R–K1, P–Q3 7 P–Q4, PxP 8 N–Q5!, Q–Q1 9 NxQP, B–Q2 10 B–N5!, B–K2 11 NxB, NxN/5 12 BxB†, QxB 13 BxN, PxB 14 N–Q5! and White wins (Richter–Grohmann, Berlin 1950).

[13] Pachman recommends 4 P–QR4, P–K3 5 O–O, P–QR3 6 BxN, QPxB 7 N–B3 with a slight edge for White.

[14] 11 P–K5, N–B1 12 B–B4, N–K3 with even chances (Henneberger–Flohr, Zurich 1934).

[15] 4 N–B3 is effectively met by 4 . . . N–Q5! See Idea Var. 33.

[16] Weaker is 4 . . . N–KN5 5 BxN, QPxB 6 O–O. See Cholmov–Keres, Game 39.

[17] Correct is 5 . . . N–B2 so that, after 6 BxN, QPxB, the diagonal for Black's Queen Bishop is left open.

[18] 10 . . . P–Q4 11 Q–B4, B–K2 12 Q–N4!, K–B1 13 N–B3, B–N2 14 P–KR4, N–B2 15 R–Q1, and White exercises heavy pressure (Bronstein–Zacharov, Spartakiade 1959).

*Sicilian Defense Game 38*

*WHITE: Rossolimo* *BLACK: Romanenko*

*Bad Gastein 1948*

| WHITE | BLACK | WHITE | BLACK | WHITE | BLACK |
|---|---|---|---|---|---|
| 1 P–K4 | P–QB4 | 7 P–K5 | N–N1 | 13 R–K8†! | KxR |
| 2 N–KB3 | N–QB3 | 8 P–Q3 | NxB | 14 Q–K2† | K–B1 |
| 3 B–N5 | P–KN3 | 9 NxN | P–QR3 | 15 B–K7† | K–K1 |
| 4 O–O | B–N2 | 10 N–Q6†! | PxN? | 16 B–Q8†! | KxB |
| 5 R–K1 | N–B3 | 11 B–N5! | Q–R4 | 17 N–N5 | Resigns |
| 6 N–B3 | N–Q5 | 12 PxP† | K–B1 | | |

*Sicilian Defense Game 39*

*WHITE: Cholmov* *BLACK: Keres*

*USSR Championship 1959*

| WHITE | BLACK | WHITE | BLACK | WHITE | BLACK |
|---|---|---|---|---|---|
| 1 P–K4 | P–QB4 | 11 NxP | P–B4? | 21 RxQ† | BxR |
| 2 N–KB3 | N–QB3 | 12 N–B6! | Q–Q2 | 22 RxB | K–B2 |
| 3 B–N5 | N–B3 | 13 NxKP! | KxN | 23 R–K7 | QR–Q1 |
| 4 P–K5 | N–KN5 | 14 BxN | BxB | 24 P–QR4 | P–KN4 |
| 5 BxN | QPxB | 15 Q–B3! | B–KN2 | 25 Q–Q5 | KR–K1 |
| 6 O–O | P–KN3 | 16 N–Q5†! | K–Q1 | 26 RxP | P–N5 |
| 7 R–K1 | B–N2 | 17 QR–Q1 | B–N2 | 27 P–R5 | PxKRP |
| 8 P–KR3 | N–R3 | 18 Q–QN3! | B–QB3 | 28 PxP† | KxP |
| 9 N–B3 | P–N3 | 19 NxP | PxN | 29 RxB | Resigns |
| 10 P–Q4 | PxP | 20 QxBP | BxKP | | |

## SUPPLEMENTARY VARIATIONS 36–40:

1 P–K4, P–QB4 2 N–KB3, P–Q3

Sup. Var. 36, 37, and 38 illustrate 3 B–N5† after 2 . . . P–Q3. The Bishop move here is less effective than after 2 . . . N–QB3 in Part 12. The best answer is 3 . . . B–Q2. White, then, achieves nothing but simplification in an even position.

Sup. Var. 39 illustrates a variant of the Wing Gambit which offers better chances than the original 2 P–QN4, although it is still doubtful whether White can obtain sufficient compensation for the Pawn.

In Sup. Var. 40 White tries to form a strong center with 3 P–QB3 followed by 4 P–Q4, but here the idea is less effective than the direct 2 P–QB3. Compare Sup. Var. 42 following Part 14.

| | *36* | *37* | *38* | *39* | *40* |
|---|---|---|---|---|---|
| *3* | B–N5† | – – | – – | P–QN4 | P–QB3 |
| | B–Q2 | N–B3 | N–Q2 | PxP[8] | N–KB3 |
| *4* | BxB† | O–O | P–Q4 | P–Q4 | P–K5[12] |
| | QxB | P–QR3 | P–K3[6] | N–KB3 | PxP |
| *5* | O–O[1] | BxN† | O–O | B–Q3 | NxP |
| | N–KB3 | PxB | N–K2 | P–Q4 | N–B3?[13] |
| *6* | R–K1[2] | P–Q4 | PxP | QN–Q2[9] | NxN |
| | N–B3 | PxP | PxP | P–K3[10] | PxN |
| *7* | P–B3 | QxP | N–R3 | O–O | B–B4 |
| | P–K3 | P–K4 | N–N3 | N–B3 | B–B4 |
| *8* | P–Q4 | Q–Q3 | N–B4 | R–K1 | P–Q3 |
| | PxP | N–B3 | Q–B2 | B–K2 | P–K3 |
| *9* | PxP | R–Q1 | P–KR4 | P–K5 | Q–B3 |
| | P–Q4 | B–K2 | P–KR4 | N–Q2 | Q–Q2 |
| *10* | P–K5 | B–N5 | P–K5[7] | N–B1 | P–KR3[14] |
| | N–K5[3] | O–O | ± | N–N3[11] | ± |
| *11* | N–B3 | QN–Q2[5] | | = | |
| | NxN | ± | | | |
| *12* | PxN | | | | |
| | B–K2[4] | | | | |
| | = | | | | |

*Notes to supplementary variations 36–40:*

[1] After 5 P–B4 Black plays too riskily if he tries to win a Pawn by 5 . . . Q–N5: e.g., 6 O–O, QxP 7 P–Q4, and White has more than sufficient development for the Pawn. But 5 . . . N–QB3 leads to equality: 6 O–O, P–KN3 7 P–Q4, PxP 8 NxP, B–N2 9 B–K3, N–B3 10 P–B3, O–O 11 N–B3, QR–B1 12 P–QN3, P–K3 13 R–B1, KR–Q1 14 Q–Q2, P–Q4! (Blau–Fischer, Zurich 1959).

continued ▸

[2] 6 P–K5 is met by 6 . . . N–Q4! 7 PxP, P–K3!

[3] Virtually forced, but good.

[4] The game is approximately even: e.g., 13 N–N5, BxN 14 BxB, N–K2 15 R–N1, N–N3 16 Q–N4, R–QB1 17 P–KR4, P–KR4 18 Q–N3, P–N3 (Boleslavski–Najdorf, Budapest 1950). For 13 . . . P–KR3, see Game 40.

[5] 11 . . . Q–B2 12 N–B4, R–Q1 13 N–K3, B–K3 14 P–B4 with a positional edge for White (see Game 41). Or 11 . . . R–R2 12 N–B4, R–Q2 13 N–K3, and White has a margin (Sokolski–Botvinnik, Tchigorin Tournament 1947).

[6] 4 . . . PxP 5 QxP, N–B3 6 O–O, P–K3 7 B–N5, B–K2 8 N–B3, O–O 9 QR–Q1 leads to a good game for White (Barendregt–Donner, Beverwijk 1960).

[7] White has some superiority in space (Gligoric–Reshevsky, Helsinki 1952).

[8] Black may also decline the gambit, with about even chances: e.g., 3 . . . N–KB3 4 PxP, NxP 5 PxP, P–K3!

[9] Or 9 P–K5, KN–Q2 10 P–K6, N–KB3, and Black is all right.

[10] Black must maintain the center. After 6 . . . PxP 7 NxP, QN–Q2, White has chances for attack as in 8 O–O! NxN 9 BxN, P–KN3 10 R–N1, N–B3 11 B–Q3, N–Q4 12 N–K5 with a fine game for White (Spielmann–De Haas, Amsterdam 1938). For 8 N/4–N5!? see Game 42.

[11] Black has a steady position. White has no real compensation for the Pawn.

[12] Other possibilities are:

1) 4 B–Q3, N–B3 5 O–O, P–KN3 6 B–B2, B–N5 7 P–KR3,. BxN 8 QxB, B–N2 9 Q–K2, O–O 10 P–Q3, P–QN4 11 B–K3, R–B1 with even chances (Czerniak–Stahlberg, Mar del Plata 1943).

2) 4 Q–B2, Q–B2 5 B–B4, P–K3 6 P–Q4, QN–Q2 7 P–Q5, P–K4 8 N–R4, P–KN3 9 P–KB4, PxP 10 BxP, B–N2 11 O–O, O–O 12 B–K2, R–K1 with an edge for Black (Lundin–Najdorf, Helsinki 1952).

[13] This move involves an unnecessary weakening of the Pawn formation. Instead, 5 . . . QN–Q2 leads to equality.

[14] 10 . . . B–K2 11 O–O, R–Q1 12 R–Q1 favors White (Alekhine–Zvetkov, Buenos Aires 1939).

### *Sicilian Defense Game 40*

*WHITE: Szabo* — *BLACK: Tal*

*Portoroz 1958*

| | WHITE | BLACK | | WHITE | BLACK |
|---|---|---|---|---|---|
| 1 | P–K4 | P–QB4 | 7 | R–K1 | P–K3 |
| 2 | N–KB3 | P–Q3 | 8 | P–Q4 | PxP |
| 3 | B–N5† | B–Q2 | 9 | PxP | P–Q4 |
| 4 | BxB† | QxB | 10 | P–K5 | N–K5 |
| 5 | O–O | N–QB3 | 11 | N–QB3 | NxN |
| 6 | P–B3 | N–B3 | 12 | PxN | B–K2 |

| | WHITE | BLACK | | WHITE | BLACK |
|---|---|---|---|---|---|
| 13 | N–N5 | P–KR3 | 32 | Q–B8 | R–N2 |
| 14 | Q–R5 | BxN | 33 | K–B2? | Q–B5! |
| 15 | BxB | N–K2 | 34 | R–N2 | N–R2 |
| 16 | B–Q2 | O–O | 35 | R–N6 | N–B3 |
| 17 | P–QR4? | P–B4 | 36 | K–K1 | Q–Q6 |
| 18 | P–KB4? | QR–B1 | 37 | P–N5 | PxP |
| 19 | KR–N1 | R–B5 | 38 | PxP | NxRP |
| 20 | Q–Q1 | R/1–B1 | 39 | RxKP | N–B5 |
| 21 | P–R5 | N–B3 | 40 | B–B1 | QxP† |
| 22 | Q–N3 | R–B2 | 41 | K–Q1 | QxP† |
| 23 | R–N2 | K–R2 | 42 | K–K2 | Q–K5† |
| 24 | P–R3 | P–R3 | 43 | K–Q1 | Q–B6† |
| 25 | Q–N6 | N–K2 | 44 | K–B2 | Q–K7† |
| 26 | Q–Q6 | Q–K1 | 45 | K–B3 | P–Q5† |
| 27 | R–N6 | R/5–B3 | 46 | K–N4 | P–R4† |
| 28 | RxR | QxR | 47 | K–B5 | R–B2† |
| 29 | R–N1 | R–Q2 | 48 | K–N5 | NxP† |
| 30 | Q–N4 | N–B1 | 49 | K–N6 | R–B3† |
| 31 | P–N4 | P–KN3 | | Resigns | |

*Sicilian Defense Game 41*

*WHITE: Sokolski* *BLACK: Kotov*

*Moscow 1949*

| | WHITE | BLACK | | WHITE | BLACK |
|---|---|---|---|---|---|
| 1 | P–K4 | P–QB4 | 21 | N–K1 | N–B4 |
| 2 | N–KB3 | P–Q3 | 22 | N–Q3 | Q–R2 |
| 3 | B–N5† | N–B3 | 23 | NxN | QxN |
| 4 | O–O | P–QR3 | 24 | Q–K2 | B–KB1 |
| 5 | BxN† | PxB | 25 | Q–R5 | K–R2 |
| 6 | P–Q4 | PxP | 26 | N–N4 | B–N2 |
| 7 | QxP | P–K4 | 27 | N–K3 | P–R4 |
| 8 | Q–Q3 | N–B3 | 28 | Q–B3 | P–R5 |
| 9 | R–Q1 | B–K2 | 29 | PxRP | R–QR1 |
| 10 | B–N5 | O–O | 30 | N–B5 | B–KB1 |
| 11 | QN–Q2 | Q–B2 | 31 | R–N1 | R–KB2 |
| 12 | N–B4 | R–Q1 | 32 | P–R5! | RxP |
| 13 | N–K3 | B–K3 | 33 | R–N8 | P–Q4 |
| 14 | P–B4 | QR–N1 | 34 | Q–R5 | P–Q5 |
| 15 | Q–B2 | R–N2 | 35 | R/1–N1 | R–Q2 |
| 16 | QR–B1 | Q–N1 | 36 | NxP! | BxN |
| 17 | P–QN3 | P–KR3 | 37 | R–R8† | KxR |
| 18 | B–R4 | P–N4 | 38 | QxB† | R–R2 |
| 19 | B–N3 | N–Q2 | 39 | QxP† | R–N2 |
| 20 | P–KR4 | P–B3 | 40 | R–N7 | Resigns |

*Sicilian Defense Game 42*

*WHITE: Keres* *BLACK: Eliskases*

*Semmering 1937*

| | WHITE | BLACK | | WHITE | BLACK |
|---|---|---|---|---|---|
| 1 | P–K4 | P–QB4 | 18 | R–K1 | P–N5 |
| 2 | N–KB3 | P–Q3 | 19 | N–R4 | N–N3 |
| 3 | P–QN4 | PxP | 20 | R–N1 | B–Q2 |
| 4 | P–Q4 | N–KB3 | 21 | R–K4 | KR–K1 |
| 5 | B–Q3 | P–Q4 | 22 | R–B4 | Q–Q3 |
| 6 | QN–Q2 | PxP | 23 | B–Q2 | N–Q4 |
| 7 | NxP | QN–Q2 | 24 | RxKNP | BxR? |
| 8 | N/4–N5!? | Q–B2? | 25 | QxB | Q–KB3 |
| 9 | P–B4! | P–KR3 | 26 | N–B5 | K–B1 |
| 10 | N–R3 | P–KN4 | 27 | NxB | QxN |
| 11 | N/R–N1 | B–N2 | 28 | Q–R5! | N–B3 |
| 12 | N–K2 | P–K4 | 29 | Q–R4 | P–KR4 |
| 13 | N–N3 | O–O | 30 | RxP | QR–B1 |
| 14 | O–O | P–K5 | 31 | P–KR3 | R–B2 |
| 15 | NxKP | NxN | 32 | R–N5 | R/1–K3 |
| 16 | BxN | QxP | 33 | RxRP! | Resigns |
| 17 | B–Q3 | Q–Q4 | | | |

---

## part 13—NIMZOWITSCH VARIATION

1 P–K4, P–QB4
2 N–KB3, N–KB3

KEY POSITION 13

### OBSERVATIONS ON KEY POSITION 13

This concept of Nimzowitsch is a predecessor of the Alekhine Defense. Black wants to provoke P–K5 and subsequently place this advanced Pawn under fire. According to present opinion it is rather difficult for White to obtain any opening advantage by this Pawn push. The critical case is Prac. Var. 63 where Black obtains a very active position at the expense of a Pawn. This idea was originally advanced by Dr. Krause, and Larsen dug it up in a game against Gligoric (Zurich 1959). See Game 43.

After 3 P–K5, N–Q4 White achieves nothing by chasing the Knight with 4 P–B4; nor does 4 P–Q4 advance his game, instead only weakening his center, as is evident from the Idea Variations. The best White can do is to exchange the centralized enemy Knight by 4 N–B3 as shown in Prac. Var. 61, 62, and 63.

Of course, White can omit 3 P–K5 and proceed simply 3 N–KB3, but then Black can safely play 3 . . . P–Q4 or better 3 . . . N–B3 4 P–Q4, P–Q4!

IDEA VARIATIONS 34 AND 35:

(34) 3 P–K5, N–Q4 4 P–B4, N–B2 5 P–Q4, PxP 6 QxP, N–B3 7 Q–K4, P–Q4 8 PxP e.p., QxP 9 N–B3, Q–N3! 10 QxQ, RPxQ 11 B–B4, N–K3 12 B–N3, B–Q2! 13 O–O–O, P–KN4 with even chances (O'Hanlon–Kostic, Hastings 1921).

(35) 3 P–K5, N–Q4 4 P–Q4, PxP 5 QxP, P–K3 6 B–QB4 (6 P–B4, N–QB3 7 Q–K4, P–B4!), N–QB3 (but Black here obtains a satisfactory game by adopting a finesse: 6 . . . P–Q3! followed by 7 BxN, PxP or 7 PxP, N–QB3) 7 Q–K4, N–N3 8 B–N3, P–Q4 9 PxP e.p., BxP 10 N–B3, Q–B3 (10 . . . N–Q2!) 11 B–N5, Q–N3 12 O–O–O, B–K2 13 QxQ, RPxQ 14 B–K3 with White for choice (Panov–Alatortzev, USSR Championship 1937).

PRACTICAL VARIATIONS 61–65:

1 P–K4, P–QB4 2 N–KB3, N–KB3

| | *61* | *62* | *63* | *64* | *65* |
|---|---|---|---|---|---|
| *3* | P–K5 | – – | – – | N–B3 | – – |
| | N–Q4 | – – | – – | P–Q4 | N–B3 |
| *4* | N–B3 | – – | – – | PxP | P–Q4 |
| | NxN! | P–K3 | – – | NxP | P–Q4[19] |
| *5* | QPxN! | NxN[4] | – – | B–N5†[15] | PxQP |
| | P–Q4[1] | PxN | – – | N–B3[16] | KNxP |
| *6* | PxP e.p. | P–Q4 | – – | N–K5 | NxN |
| | QxP | P–Q3 | N–B3! | NxN | QxN |
| *7* | QxQ | B–N5†[5] | PxP | QPxN[17] | B–K3[20] |
| | PxQ | N–B3[6] | BxP | QxQ† | PxP |
| *8* | B–KB4 | O–O | QxP | KxQ | NxP |
| | P–Q4[2] | B–K2 | Q–N3[9] | B–Q2 | Q–R4†[21] |
| *9* | O–O–O | P–B4 | B–QB4[10] | BxN | P–B3 |
| | B–K3 | PxBP[7] | BxP† | BxB | B–Q2 |
| *10* | B–N5† | P–Q5 | K–K2 | NxB | B–K2 |
| | N–B3 | P–QR3 | O–O | PxN | NxN |
| *11* | N–K5 | B–R4 | R–B1[11] | P–QB4[18] | BxN |
| | B–Q3 | P–QN4 | B–B4 | ± | P–K4[22] |
| *12* | B–N3[3] | PxN | N–N5 | | = |
| | ± | PxB | N–Q5†[12] | | |
| *13* | | PxQP[8] | K–Q1[13] | | |
| | | ± | N–K3[14] | | |
| | | | = | | |

*Notes to practical variations 61–65:*

[1] Best, according to Nimzowitsch. The continuation 5 . . . N–B3 6 B–QB4, P–Q3 7 B–B4, PxP 8 NxP, QxQ† 9 RxQ, NxN 10 BxN, P–QR3 11 B–B7, B–N5 12 P–B3, R–B1 13 B–N6, B–B4 14 B–N3 favors White (Alapin–Rubinstein, Vienna 1912).

continued ▸

[2] Black may try to play for a draw with 8 . . . B–N5 9 O–O–O, N–Q2! 10 BxP, BxB 11 RxB, BxN 12 PxB, O–O–O.

[3] White has the edge.

[4] A new idea is 5 N–K4: e.g., 5 . . . N–B3 6 P–QN3, P–B3 7 B–N2!, PxP 8 NxP, NxN 9 BxN, P–Q3? 10 Q–R5†, P–N3 11 B–N5†, B–Q2 12 Q–R3 and White won quickly (Lipnitzky–Lazarov, Kiev 1959). Black must play . . . P–B4! on his 5th or 6th move.

[5] The gambit line 7 B–N5, Q–R4† 8 P–B3, PxP 9 B–Q3, PxP 10 O–O is dubious because of 10 . . . N–B3! 11 R–K1, B–K3 12 NPxP, PxP 13 NxP, NxN 14 RxN, B–Q3 15 R–K3, P–Q5! 16 RxB†, PxR 17 Q–R5†, P–N3! 18 BxP†, K–Q2 (Keller–Witkowski, Belgrade 1956). But if Black plays 10 . . . PxNP, White initiates an overwhelming attack with 11 R–N1. See Game 44.

[6] Safer is 7 . . . B–Q2 8 BxB†, QxB 9 O–O, N–B3, although White clearly holds the edge: e.g., 10 PxQP, BxP 11 R–K1†, N–K2 12 PxP, BxP 13 P–QN3, O–O 14 B–N2.

[7] Or 9 . . . B–K3 10 B–K3!, Q–N3 11 P–QR4, P–QR3 (11 . . . O–O–O 12 P–R5, NxRP 13 P–QN4) 12 KPxP, BxP (12 . . . PxB 13 PxBP) 13 PxQP, PxB 14 PxB, PxKP 15 RPxP, RxR 16 QxR, QxP 17 PxP, BxP 18 Q–R8†, N–Q1 19 B–N5 with a substantial advantage for White (Fichtl–Kopriva, Czechoslovakian Championship 1957).

[8] 13 . . . QxP 14 QxP favors White (Prins–Wotkowski, Munich 1958).

[9] Still sharper is 8 . . . P–Q3 9 PxP (9 B–QB4 is safer), Q–N3: e.g. 10 B–QB4, BxP† 11 K–B1 (also meriting consideration is 11 K–K2 followed by 12 R–Q1), O–O 12 Q–K4, B–Q2 13 B–KN5 (another possibility is 13 N–N5), B–QB4 14 B–Q3, P–N3 15 B–B6, N–N5 16 Q–R4, QxP (16 . . . N–Q4 sets difficult problems for White) 17 B–K5, Q–K2 18 B–B6, Q–Q3 with a draw by repetition (Tal–Gipslis, Riga 1959).

[10] 9 Q–Q2, O–O 10 B–Q3, P–Q3! offers Black excellent chances for the Pawn.

[11] 11 N–N5 is answered by 11 . . . P–Q3, after which 12 NxBP? fails against 12 . . . B–K3 (13 QxB??, N–Q5† or 13 N–R6†, K–R1!), or 12 PxP?, R–K1†.

[12] Now 12 . . . P–Q3 will not do because of 13 RxP.

[13] Risky is 13 K–Q3, Q–N3† 14 Q–K4, P–Q4! See Game 43.

[14] Auerbach–Kudratsjov, Spartakiade 1959, continued 14 B–Q3, NxN 15 BxN, Q–QB3 16 B–K4, P–KR3 17 B–R4, Q–K3 18 QxQ, QPxQ 19 P–B3 with a better end game for White. The consequences are not clear, however, if Black plays 15 . . . QxP or 15 . . . P–Q3. The proper answer to 14 N–K4 is not 14 . . . B–K2 15 P–B3, but 14 . . . P–Q3! 15 PxP, R–Q1.

[15] L. Steiner's 5 N–K5, threatening 6 Q–B3, is made harmless by 5 . . . Q–B2! 6 B–N5†, N–Q2 7 NxQN, BxN 8 NxN, Q–K4†, recovering the piece.

[16] Weaker is 5 . . . B–Q2 6 N–K5!, BxB (6 . . . NxN? 7 Q–B3!, but relatively best for Black is 6 . . . P–K3 7 Q–B3, Q–K2) 7 Q–B3, P–B3 (7 . . . N–KB3 8 QxP, B–R3 9 QxR, Q–B2 fails against 10 N–B6!) 8 NxB, N–R3 (8 . . . PxN 9 QxN!) 9 Q–R5†, P–N3 10 NxNP, PxN 11 QxR, Q–Q2 12 N–B3, Q–K3† 13 K–B1, N/3–N5 14 Q–R3, QxQ 15 PxQ, N–B2!

(Sozin–Kyrillof, Moscow 1931). White has won the exchange, but the win is problematic because of White's weak Pawn formation which remains after . . . NxBP.

[17] 7 NPxN, Q–Q4 is fully satisfactory for Black.

[18] The end game slightly favors White (analysis by Rabar).

[19] Of course Black can transpose into regular variations with 4 . . . PxP 5 NxP.

[20] Inferior is 7 P–QB4 because of 7 . . . Q–K5† 8 B–K3, PxP 9 NxP, P–K4 and, if 10 N–N5, then 10 . . . B–N5†.

[21] Now, if 8 . . . P–K4, then 9 N–N5 is strong. The end game after 8 NxN 9 QxN, QxQ 10 BxQ favors White.

[22] 12 B–K3, B–R5 13 Q–B1, B–B3 14 O–O, B–K2 offers even chances (Llado–Bouwmeester, Spain–Holland 1958).

### *Sicilian Defense Game 43*

*WHITE: Gligoric* — *BLACK: Larsen*

*Zurich 1959*

| | WHITE | BLACK | | WHITE | BLACK |
|---|---|---|---|---|---|
| 1 | P–K4 | P–QB4 | 21 | B–B4 | R–Q2 |
| 2 | N–KB3 | N–KB3 | 22 | P–QN3 | Q–KB3 |
| 3 | P–K5 | N–Q4 | 23 | N–K6 | Q–B6†? |
| 4 | N–B3 | P–K3 | 24 | K–K2 | R/1xP |
| 5 | NxN | PxN | 25 | P–N4 | N–Q3 |
| 6 | P–Q4 | N–B3 | 26 | Q–Q3 | Q–B3 |
| 7 | PxP | BxP | 27 | P–N5 | Q–K2? |
| 8 | QxP | Q–N3 | 28 | R–KB1 | Q–K1 |
| 9 | B–QB4 | BxP† | 29 | Q–R3! | R–B4 |
| 10 | K–K2 | O–O | 30 | BxN | RxR |
| 11 | R–B1 | B–B4 | 31 | BxB | R–QR8 |
| 12 | N–N5 | N–Q5† | 32 | B–QB3 | RxP† |
| 13 | K–Q3 | Q–N3† | 33 | K–K3 | PxP |
| 14 | Q–K4 | P–Q4! | 34 | B–K4 | Q–N1 |
| 15 | BxP | B–B4 | 35 | P–N6 | PxP |
| 16 | RxB | NxB | 36 | N–N5 | R–QB7 |
| 17 | P–K6 | QR–Q1 | 37 | QxR | RxB† |
| 18 | PxP† | K–R1 | 38 | K–Q2 | Q–QB8 |
| 19 | P–B4 | P–N4 | 39 | N–B7† | Resigns |
| 20 | R–QN1 | B–N5 | | | |

*Sicilian Defense Game 44*

*WHITE: Keres* *BLACK: Winter*

*Warsaw 1935*

| WHITE | BLACK | WHITE | BLACK |
|---|---|---|---|
| 1 P–K4 | P–QB4 | 11 R–N1 | PxP |
| 2 N–KB3 | N–KB3 | 12 NxP | B–Q3 |
| 3 P–K5 | N–Q4 | 13 NxP! | KxN |
| 4 N–B3 | P–K3 | 14 Q–R5† | P–N3 |
| 5 NxN | PxN | 15 BxP†! | PxB |
| 6 P–Q4 | P–Q3 | 16 QxR | B–KB4 |
| 7 B–KN5 | Q–R4† | 17 QR–K1 | B–K5 |
| 8 P–B3 | PxQP | 18 RxB! | PxR |
| 9 B–Q3! | PxBP | 19 Q–B6† | Resigns |
| 10 O–O | PxNP | | |

---

## part 14—**CLOSED SICILIAN**

1 P–K4, P–QB4
2 N–QB3, N–QB3
3 P–KN3, P–KN3
4 B–N2, B–N2
5 P–Q3

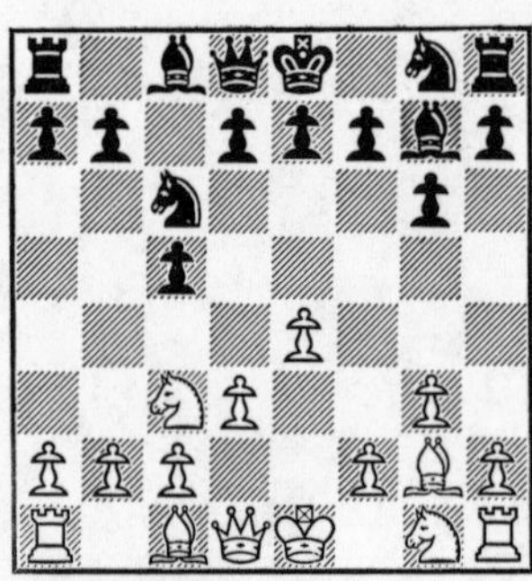

KEY POSITION 14

OBSERVATIONS ON KEY POSITION 14

The Closed Sicilian has an entirely different character from the variations we have treated so far. White omits P–Q4, denying Black the chance of obtaining counterplay along the half-open Queen Bishop file. The center of gravity, however, remains on the Queenside. Black must increase the activity of his fianchettoed King Bishop by means of . . . R–QN1 and . . . P–QN4 . . . P–QN5, exercising pressure on his Q5. This latter square is primarily suited for occupation by Black's Knight. Tactical finesses are involved, as Smyslov, a great expert on this system, has repeatedly demonstrated.

IDEA VARIATIONS 36 AND 37:

(36) 5 . . . P–Q3 6 KN–K2, R–N1 7 O–O (premature; correct is 7 B–K3 in order to meet . . . P–QN4 . . . P–N5 with Q–Q2 and N–Q1, as in Prac. Var. 67), P–QN4 8 N–Q5 (now it is too late for 8 B–K3 because of 8 . . . P–QN5 9 N–R4, Q–R4 10 P–QB3, B–Q2), P–K3 9 N–K3, KN–K2 10 P–QB3, P–N5 11 B–Q2, O–O 12 Q–B1, PxP 13 PxP, B–R3 14 Q–B2, Q–R4 with advantage for Black (Nilsson–Euwe, The Hague 1928).

(37) 5 . . . P–K3 6 B–K3!, N–Q5? (correct is first 6 . . . P–Q3; see Prac. Var. 66) 7 QN–K2 (an idea of Smyslov's), NxN 8 NxN, BxP? 9 R–QN1, Q–R4†? 10 B–Q2, QxP 11 RxB!, QxR 12 B–B3, and White wins.

PRACTICAL VARIATIONS 66-70:

1 P–K4, P–QB4 2 N–QB3, N–QB3 3 P–KN3, P–KN3 4 B–N2, B–N2 5 P–Q3

| | 66 | 67 | 68 | 69 | 70 |
|---|---|---|---|---|---|
| 5 | – – | – – | – – | – – | – – |
| | P–K3 | P–Q3 | – – | – – | P–N3 |
| 6 | B–K3 | KN–K2 | – – | P–B4 | P–B4[9] |
| | P–Q3[1] | R–N1 | P–K4 | N–B3[7] | B–N2 |
| 7 | KN–K2 | B–K3 | N–Q5[5] | N–B3 | N–B3 |
| | N–Q5 | P–QN4 | KN–K2 | O–O | P–K3 |
| 8 | O–O | Q–Q2[3] | P–QB3 | O–O | O–O |
| | N–K2 | N–Q5 | NxN | N–K1 | KN–K2 |
| 9 | P–B4 | P–B3 | PxN | P–KR3 | B–Q2 |
| | R–QN1 | P–K3 | N–K2 | N–B2 | P–QR3 |
| 10 | R–N1 | N–Q1 | O–O | B–K3 | R–N1 |
| | KN–B3 | P–N5 | O–O | P–N3 | P–Q4 |
| 11 | P–QR3 | O–O | P–KB4 | Q–Q2 | P–K5 |
| | Q–R4?! | N–K2 | B–Q2 | B–N2 | P–QN4 |
| 12 | B–Q2[2] | NxN | P–KR3 | P–B5[8] | N–K2 |
| | = | PxN[4] | Q–B2[6] | ± | Q–N3[10] |
| | | = | ∓ | | = |

*Notes to practical variations 66-70:*

[1] Other ways to protect the Pawn are inferior:

1) 6 . . . N–Q5? 7 QN–K2!, P–Q3 (7 . . . NxN 8 NxN, BxP? leads to Idea Var. 37) 8 P–QB3, N–QB3 (8 . . . NxN!) 9 P–Q4, PxP 10 NxP, NxN 11 BxN with clear advantage for White. See Game 45.

2) 6 . . . Q–R4 7 KN–K2, N–Q5 8 O–O, KN–K2 9 K–R1, O–O 10 P–QR3! N/5–B3 11 R–QN1, P–Q3 12 P–QN4! and White has good chances (Smyslov–Boleslavski, Moscow 1935).

[2] 12 . . . Q–B2 13 P–QN4, P–N3 14 K–R1, B–N2 15 PxP, NPxP? (15 . . . QPxP!) 16 P–B5!, NPxP 17 PxP, NxP 18 N–K4, and White has good chances for the Pawn (Smyslov–Opocensky, Moscow–Prague 1946).

[3] With an eye to B–R6 and BxB when feasible, and also to permit (. . . P–QN5) N–Q1.

[4] 13 B–R6, O–O 14 BxB, KxB 15 N–B2, P–K4 16 P–KB4, P–B3 with even chances (Thomas–Eckstrom, Zaandam 1946).

[5] Or 7 O–O, KN–K2 8 P–KB4, O–O followed by . . . P–B4 with even chances.

[6] 13 B–K3, QR–K1 14 Q–Q2, N–B4 15 B–B2, P–KR4 16 QR–K1, Q–Q1! and Black has the edge (Smyslov–Botvinnik, Match 1954).

[7] Inferior is 6 . . . R–N1 7 N–B3, P–K3 8 O–O, KN–K2 9 P–K5!, PxP 10 PxP, NxP 11 B–B4, NxN† 12 QxN, R–R1 13 B–K3! (Bronstein–Keres, Zurich 1953). For 6 . . . P–B4 7 N–B3, N–B3 8 O–O, O–O, see Game 46.

continued ▸

Black's best set-up against P–KB4 and N–B3 is 6 . . . P–K3 7 B–K3, KN–K2 8 N–B3, N–Q5 9 B–B2, N/2–B3 (Smyslov–Kottnauer, Moscow 1947).

[8] 12 . . . P–Q4 13 B–R6, PxP 14 NxP, N–Q5 15 N–R4! favors White (Smyslov–Lipnitzky, USSR Championship 1952).

[9] After 6 KN–K2, P–Q3 7 O–O, B–N2 8 P–B4, P–B4! 9 P–KN4?!, PxNP 10 P–B5, Q–Q2, White failed to obtain compensation for the Pawn (Smyslov–Botvinnik, 13th Match Game 1954).

[10] 13 P–B3, P–N5 14 Q–K1, P–QR4 15 P–B4, R–Q1 16 Q–B2, PxP 17 PxP, and now Black should play 17 . . . N–B4, maintaining a good position (Smyslov–Kotov, Tchigorin Tournament, Moscow 1947).

### *Sicilian Defense Game 45*

*WHITE: Smyslov* — *BLACK: Denker*

*USSR-USA 1946*

| | WHITE | BLACK | | WHITE | BLACK |
|---|---|---|---|---|---|
| 1 | P–K4 | P–QB4 | 27 | R–Q3 | R–B2 |
| 2 | N–QB3 | N–QB3 | 28 | R/1–Q1 | R–B2 |
| 3 | P–KN3 | P–KN3 | 29 | N–K4 | B–B1 |
| 4 | B–N2 | B–N2 | 30 | R–Q5 | Q–N5 |
| 5 | P–Q3 | P–K3 | 31 | R/1–Q3 | B–K2 |
| 6 | B–K3 | N–Q5 | 32 | NxP | BxN |
| 7 | QN–K2! | P–Q3 | 33 | RxB | R/1–KB1 |
| 8 | P–QB3 | N–QB3 | 34 | QxKP | RxP |
| 9 | P–Q4 | PxP | 35 | R–Q7† | R/1–B2 |
| 10 | NxP | NxN | 36 | RxR† | RxR |
| 11 | BxN | P–K4 | 37 | R–Q8! | R–N2 |
| 12 | B–K3 | N–K2 | 38 | Q–K8 | P–KN4 |
| 13 | N–K2 | O–O | 39 | Q–R8† | K–N3 |
| 14 | O–O | B–K3 | 40 | R–Q6† | K–B2 |
| 15 | Q–Q2 | Q–B2 | 41 | QxP | Q–B4 |
| 16 | KR–QB1! | P–B4 | 42 | R–Q1! | Q–B4† |
| 17 | P–QB4 | PxP | 43 | K–N2 | Q–K2 |
| 18 | N–B3 | N–B4 | 44 | R–B1† | K–N1 |
| 19 | NxP | NxB | 45 | Q–B6 | Q–K1 |
| 20 | QxN | P–KR3 | 46 | Q–B5 | P–N5 |
| 21 | R–Q1 | KR–Q1 | 47 | R–B2 | Q–K2 |
| 22 | QR–B1 | QR–B1 | 48 | Q–Q3 | R–N4 |
| 23 | P–N3 | P–N3 | 49 | R–K2 | Q–B1 |
| 24 | N–B3! | Q–K2 | 50 | Q–K4 | R–N2 |
| 25 | B–Q5 | K–R2 | 51 | Q–Q5† | Q–B2 |
| 26 | BxB | QxB | 52 | R–K6! | Resigns |

*Sicilian Defense Game 46*

*WHITE: Smyslov* *BLACK: Larsen*

*Munich 1958*

| | WHITE | BLACK | | WHITE | BLACK |
|---|---|---|---|---|---|
| 1 | P–K4 | P–QB4 | 20 | P–B5 | N–K4 |
| 2 | N–QB3 | N–QB3 | 21 | NxP | NxN |
| 3 | P–KN3 | P–KN3 | 22 | QxN | N–B2 |
| 4 | B–N2 | B–N2 | 23 | B–Q5 | Q–R3 |
| 5 | P–Q3 | P–Q3 | 24 | R–QB2?? | K–R1 |
| 6 | P–B4 | P–B4 | 25 | R–N2 | B–R3 |
| 7 | N–B3 | N–B3 | 26 | Q–R3 | B–B3 |
| 8 | O–O | O–O | 27 | P–B4 | BxB |
| 9 | K–R1 | B–Q2 | 28 | PxB | N–N4 |
| 10 | B–K3 | R–N1 | 29 | N–N6† | K–N2 |
| 11 | Q–K2 | P–QN4 | 30 | N–B4 | R–B3 |
| 12 | B–N1 | P–N5 | 31 | N–K6† | K–R1 |
| 13 | N–Q1 | N–K1 | 32 | NxN | BxN |
| 14 | P–B3 | N–B2 | 33 | RxB | QxRP |
| 15 | R–B1 | N–K3 | 34 | Q–N2 | R–B2 |
| 16 | N–K3 | Q–R4 | 35 | B–Q4† | PxB |
| 17 | PxBP | PxKBP | 36 | R–KN1 | R/2–B1 |
| 18 | N–R4 | N/K–Q1 | 37 | R–N7 | Resigns |
| 19 | P–N4 | PxNP | | | |

---

## part 15—UNUSUAL VARIATIONS

### OBSERVATIONS ON UNUSUAL VARIATIONS 1–5

After the moves 1 P–K4, P–QB4; Var. 1 illustrates Keres pet line: 2 N–K2. White prepares both P–Q4 and the possible fianchetto of the King Bishop by P–KN3, the latter while the diagonal remains free. Black may either transpose into regular variations by 2 . . . N–QB3 or give the game an independent character by 2 . . . N–KB3 3 QN–B3, P–Q4.

The continuation 2 P–QB3 of Var. 2 and 3 was preferred by Alekhine in his later years. Black has the choice of 2 . . . P–Q4 or 2 . . . N–KB3. Both lines are satisfactory but 2 . . . N–KB3 is more subtle.

Var. 4 and 5 illustrates the Morra Gambit, in which there has been some increased interest in recent years. Black may accept the gambit, but should not try hard to retain the Pawn.

UNUSUAL VARIATIONS 1–5:
1 P–K4, P–QB4

| | 1 | 2 | 3 | 4 | 5 |
|---|---|---|---|---|---|
| 2 | N–K2 | P–QB3 | – – | P–Q4[13] | – – |
| | N–KB3[1] | P–Q4 | N–KB3 | PxP | – – |
| 3 | QN–B3 | PxP | P–K5 | P–QB3 | – – |
| | P–Q4 | QxP | N–Q4 | PxP | N–KB3 |
| 4 | PxP | P–Q4 | P–Q4 | NxP | P–K5 |
| | NxP | PxP[6] | PxP[10] | N–QB3 | N–Q4 |
| 5 | NxN | PxP | PxP | N–B3 | B–QB4[17] |
| | QxN | N–QB3 | P–Q3 | P–Q3 | Q–B2! |
| 6 | P–Q4![2] | N–KB3 | N–KB3 | B–QB4 | Q–K2 |
| | P–K4[3] | B–N5 | N–QB3 | P–K3[14] | N–N3 |
| 7 | N–B3!? | B–K2[7] | PxP[11] | O–O | B–N3[18] |
| | QxP | P–K3 | QxP | N–B3 | P–Q6 |
| 8 | B–N5†[4] | N–B3 | N–B3 | Q–K2 | Q–K4 |
| | B–Q2 | Q–Q2[8] | B–N5 | B–K2[15] | N–R3 |
| 9 | Q–K2 | B–K3 | B–K2 | R–Q1 | B–K3 |
| | N–B3 | B–Q3 | P–K3 | P–K4! | P–K3 |
| 10 | O–O | O–O | O–O | P–KR3 | N–B3 |
| | O–O–O[5] | N–B3[9] | B–K2[12] | O–O[16] | N–B4[19] |
| | ∓ | = | = | = | = |

*Notes to unusual variations 1-5:*

[1] After 2 . . . N–QB3, White actually has nothing better than to transpose into the regular variation 3 P–Q4, PxP 4 NxP. The point is that 3 P–KN3 leads to a good game for Black after 3 . . . P–Q4! Even after 2 . . . P–Q3, if White plays 3 P–KN3, Black must react with 3 . . . P–Q4! (O'Kelly–Denker, Groningen 1946). In the above line, however, if Black plays 3 . . . N–QB3, White obtains a superior position by 4 B–N2, P–KN3 5 P–QB3, B–N2 6 P–Q4! Examples are: Capablanca–Wheatcroft (Margate 1939), Tartakower–Broadbent (London 1946), and Keres–Pilnik (Amsterdam 1956).

[2] Else 6 . . . P–K4 gives Black the edge.

[3] 6 . . . PxP 7 QxP, QxQ 8 NxQ, P–QR3 9 B–K3 definitely favors White because of his lead in development, the exchange of Queens notwithstanding.

[4] Offering better chances for White is 8 B–K3, QxQ† 9 RxQ, B–K3 10 N–K4!

[5] 11 R–Q1, Q–KN5 12 BxN, QxQ 13 BxP†, KxB 14 NxQ, B–K2 15 B–K3, B–B4 with a slight end-game edge for Black (Keres–Filip, Helsinki 1952).

[6] After 4 . . . N–QB3 5 PxP!, QxBP 6 B–K3, Q–QR4 7 P–QN4, Q–B2 8 N–QR3, White has a lead in development (Canal–Euwe, Zurich 1954). Safest is 4 . . . P–K3!: e.g., 5 N–KB3, N–QB3 6 B–K2, N–B3 7 O–O, PxP 8 PxP, B–K2 9 N–B3, Q–QR4 10 B–QN5, O–O 11 N–K5, B–N5 (Tartakower–Gligoric, Amsterdam 1950).

[7] 7 N–B3! BxN 8 PxB, QxQP 9 QxQ, NxQ 10 N–N5! offers White a winning attack for the Pawn.

[8] Weaker is 8 . . . B–N5 9 O–O: e.g., 9 . . . Q–QR4 10 P–QR3! N–B3? 11 P–Q5! PxP 12 PxB, QxR 13 N–Q2! (Alekhine–Podgorny, Prague 1943). Or 9 . . . Q–Q2 10 P–Q5! (Heidenfeld–Spanjaard, Utrecht 1954).

[9] 11 Q–Q2, O–O with equality (Perlis–Rubinstein, Vienna 1908).

[10] Inferior is 4 . . . P–K3: 5 N–B3, PxP 6 PxP, P–Q3 7 N–B3, NxN 8 PxN, N–B3 9 PxP, BxP 10 B–Q3, Q–R4 11 B–Q2, and White has the initiative (Zita–Alster, Czechoslovakian Championship 1953).

[11] Or 7 N–B3, PxP! 8 PxP, NxN with a satisfactory game for Black. But not 7 . . . NxN? 8 PxN, PxP 9 P–Q5, P–K5 10 N–N5 with advantage for White. For 7 Q–N3, P–K3 8 B–QN5, B–Q2 9 N–B3, see Game 61.

[12] 11 Q–N3, O–O! leads to a fully satisfactory game for Black (Unzicker–Geller, Goteborg 1955).

[13] The old-fashioned Wing Gambit 2 P–QN4, PxP 3 P–QR3 (3 P–Q4, P–Q4!) is no longer played because of 3 . . . P–Q4! 4 PxQP, QxP 5 N–KB3, P–K4 6 PxP, BxP 7 N–R3, N–KB3 8 N–QN5, O–O! 9 N–B7, Q–B4 10 NxR, P–K5 with complications favoring Black (Rossetto–Iliesco, Mar del Plata 1944). If 7 B–R3, BxB 8 RxB, N–QB3 9 N–B3, Q–Q3! 10 N–QN5, Q–K2 11 Q–R1, N–B3 12 B–B4 (12 NxRP, P–K5!), O–O 13 O–O, B–N5 with Black for choice (Podgorny–Pachman, Czechoslovakian Championship 1953).

[14] Faulty is 6 . . . N–KB3 because of 7 P–K5!, e.g., 7 . . . PxP 8 QxQ†, KxQ (8 . . . NxQ 9 N–QN5, R–QN1 10 NxKP!) 9 N–KN5, K–B2 10 NxBP, R–KN1 11 N–N5†, K–N1 12 NxKP, NxN 13 B–B4, and White won quickly (Matulovic–Vincenti, Sirmione 1954).

[15] Too risky for Black is 8 . . . P–QR3 9 R–Q1, Q–B2 10 B–B4, P–K4 11 N–Q5! with a substantial advantage for White (11 . . . NxN 12 PxN, N–R4 13 QR–B1).

Preferable is 10 . . . B–K2, but, after 11 QR–B1, O–O 12 B–N3, White stands better (Waligora–Mohrlock, Stuttgart 1955).

[16] Black has a tenable game: e.g., 11 B–KN5, B–K3 12 BxN, BxB 13 N–QN5, B–K2 14 BxB, PxB 15 Q–Q3, Q–Q2 16 R–Q2, QR–Q1 17 R/1–Q1, Q–B1 18 Q–N3, P–QR3 19 NxP, BxN 20 RxB, N–Q5! with equality (Lokvenc–Bolbochan, 1950).

[17] 5 PxP, P–Q3 leads to Var. 3.

[18] Another possibility is 7 B–Q3.

[19] 11 BxN, BxB 12 QxQP, P–Q3 with equality (Milner-Barry–Van den Berg, England-Holland, Cheltenham 1959).

*Sicilian Defense Game 47*

*WHITE: Mineo* *BLACK: Najdorf*

*Amsterdam 1954*

| | WHITE | BLACK | | WHITE | BLACK |
|---|---|---|---|---|---|
| 1 | P–K4 | P–QB4 | 22 | P–QR3 | P–KR4 |
| 2 | P–QB3 | N–KB3 | 23 | R/1–QN1 | P–R4 |
| 3 | P–K5 | N–Q4 | 24 | RxR | RxR |
| 4 | P–Q4 | PxP | 25 | R–N5 | R–KR5 |
| 5 | PxP | P–Q3 | 26 | P–KR3 | R–R5 |
| 6 | N–KB3 | N–QB3 | 27 | R–N2 | P–N5 |
| 7 | Q–N3 | P–K3 | 28 | K–K3 | P–B5† |
| 8 | B–QN5 | B–Q2 | 29 | K–K2 | PxP† |
| 9 | N–B3 | NxN | 30 | PxP | K–B3 |
| 10 | PxN | PxP | 31 | P–R4 | P–N4 |
| 11 | BxN | BxB | 32 | R–N1 | R–QB5 |
| 12 | NxP | Q–Q4 | 33 | R–QB1 | K–Q2 |
| 13 | P–B3? | B–Q3 | 34 | B–B8 | K–K1 |
| 14 | B–R3 | BxN | 35 | B–Q6 | K–B2 |
| 15 | QxQ | BxQ | 36 | R–B2 | R–B1 |
| 16 | PxB | R–QB1 | 37 | K–Q3 | R–KN1 |
| 17 | K–Q2 | K–Q2 | 38 | R–B2? | R–N6 |
| 18 | B–Q6 | R–B5 | 39 | B–B7 | P–R5 |
| 19 | QR–QN1 | KR–QB1 | 40 | B–Q8 | K–N3 |
| 20 | KR–QB1 | P–KN4 | 41 | K–Q4 | RxP |
| 21 | R–N4 | P–B4! | | Resigns | |

# Section Two:

# QUEEN'S PAWN OPENINGS

# chapter 21—Queen's Gambit Accepted

This opening arises after 1 P–Q4, P–Q4 2 P–QB4, PxP. Black abandons the center but intends to restore the balance by proceeding soon with . . . . P–QB4. His counteraction will be facilitated by the fianchetto of his Queen Bishop. White on his part must try to make his Pawn majority in the center count. The struggle leads to sharp positions requiring tactical alertness.

Formerly the acceptance of the Queen's Gambit was considered inferior and rarely adopted. Today it is a fully reliable line and played frequently.

---

## part 1—MODERN VARIATION

1 P–Q4, P–Q4
2 P–QB4, PxP
3 N–KB3[A], N–KB3[B]
4 P–K3[C], P–K3[D]
5 BxP, P–B4[E]
6 O–O[F], P–QR3[G]
7 Q–K2[H], N–B3[I]
8 N–B3[J]

Key Position 1

### OBSERVATIONS ON KEY POSITION 1

[A] For 3 P–K3 and 3 P–K4, see Sup. Var. 23 and 24 respectively.

[B] For 3 . . . P–QR3, see Part 3. For 3 . . . B–N5 see Sup. Var. 21. 3 . . . P–QB4 is best met by 4 P–K3, which may lead to transposition of moves. Less commendable for White is 4 P–Q5, P–K3 5 P–K4, PxP 6 PxP, N–KB3 7 BxP, B–Q3 8 O–O. Black has a comfortable game.

[C] For 4 Q–R4†, see Sup. Var. 17-20.

[D] For 4 . . . P–KN3, see Sup. Var. 14 and 15.

[E] With this move Black restores the balance in the center.

[F] 6 N–B3, P–QR3 7 O–O, P–B4 8 B–Q3 transposes into the Meran Defense.

[G] For 6 . . . PxP, see Sup. Var. 8. 6 . . . N–B3 usually leads to transposition of moves. After 7 N–B3, Black can play 7 . . . P–QR3, which leads to variations of Part 1, or 7 . . . B–K2?, which is inferior because of 8 PxP, QxQ 9 RxQ, BxP 10 P–QR3, P–QR3 11 P–QN4, B–K2 12 B–N2, with a fine game for White.

[H] For 7 P–QR4, see Sup. Var. 11, and for 7 P–K4, see Sup. Var. 12 and 13. The move 7 PxP leads to an even game after the exchange of Queens.

[I] For 7 . . . P–QN4, see Part 2.

[J] 8 R–Q1, which was formerly considered to be the main variation of this opening, is treated in Sup. Var. 1-6. 8 PxP is treated in Sup. Var. 9.

By vacating QN1 White has anticipated the possible exchange of his King Bishop for a Knight, because after

8 . . . P–QN4 there follows 9 B–Q3, N–QN5, or 9 B–N3, P–B5 10 B–B2, N–QN5. Preserving the White King Bishop is motivated by the important role it plays in this opening. Besides, White's Queen Knight observes those central squares which White may need for a possible breakthrough by P–Q5 or P–K4.

Black's counterpressure on White's Queen Pawn is of little effect because a possible . . . BPxQP only opens more lines for White, speeding his development. Nor is it good for Black to proceed after . . . P–QN4 with . . . P–B5, as this gives White a free hand in the center.

IDEA VARIATIONS 1–3:

(1) 8 . . . PxP 9 PxP (also strong is 9 R–Q1, with the immediate recovery of the Pawn), NxP 10 NxN, QxN 11 R–Q1, Q–N5 (a little better is 11 . . . Q–N3, although 12 B–K3 still leads to a fine game for White) 12 N–Q5, QxQ 13 N–B7†, K–K2 14 BxQ, R–N1 15 B–KB4 with a winning advantage for White.

(2) 8 . . . P–QN4 9 B–N3, B–N2 10 R–Q1, Q–N3 (somewhat better is 10 . . . Q–B2) 11 P–Q5, PxP 12 P–K4, PxP 13 NxKP, NxN 14 QxN†, and White has a winning attack. See Game 1.

(3) 8 . . . P–QN4 9 B–N3, B–N2 10 R–Q1, P–B5 11 B–B2, N–QN5 12 B–N1, QN–Q4 13 P–K4, NxN 14 PxN±.

*Queen's Gambit Accepted Game 1*

*WHITE: Reshevsky* *BLACK: Vidmar*

*Nottingham 1936*

| | WHITE | BLACK | | WHITE | BLACK |
|---|---|---|---|---|---|
| 1 | P–Q4 | P–Q4 | 14 | NxKP | NxN |
| 2 | P–QB4 | P–QB3 | 15 | QxN† | B–K2 |
| 3 | N–KB3 | N–B3 | 16 | B–Q5 | R–Q1 |
| 4 | P–K3 | P–K3 | 17 | B–N5 | RxB |
| 5 | B–Q3 | PxP | 18 | RxR | O–O |
| 6 | BxBP | P–B4 | 19 | R–Q7 | B–Q1 |
| 7 | O–O | P–QR3 | 20 | R–K1 | B–B2 |
| 8 | Q–K2 | P–QN4 | 21 | Q–K3 | N–N1 |
| 9 | B–N3 | N–B3 | 22 | R–K7 | BxN |
| 10 | R–Q1 | Q–N3 | 23 | QxB | P–R3 |
| 11 | N–B3 | B–N2 | 24 | B–B4 | B–Q3 |
| 12 | P–Q5! | PxP | 25 | R–N7 | Q–Q1 |
| 13 | P–K4 | PxP | 26 | R–Q1 | Resigns |

*Queen's Gambit Accepted Game 2*

*WHITE: Sherwin* *BLACK: Kramer*

*New York 1954-55*

| WHITE | BLACK | WHITE | BLACK | WHITE | BLACK |
|---|---|---|---|---|---|
| 1 P–Q4 | P–Q4 | 14 B–KB4 | R–B1 | 27 B–B4 | R–B7 |
| 2 P–QB4 | PxP | 15 P–QR4! | PxP | 28 R–R5 | Q–K3 |
| 3 N–KB3 | N–KB3 | 16 QRxP | B–K2 | 29 R–K5 | Q–B1 |
| 4 P–K3 | P–K3 | 17 N–N5 | O–O | 30 R/1–K1 | B–B3 |
| 5 BxP | P–B4 | 18 NxN† | BxN | 31 QxP | B–N4 |
| 6 O–O | P–QR3 | 19 NxRP | P–N3 | 32 Q–KR3 | P–Q6 |
| 7 Q–K2 | P–QN4 | 20 NxR | QxN | 33 R–Q5 | RxNP |
| 8 B–N3 | B–N2 | 21 Q–N4 | N–K2 | 34 P–N4 | B–B5 |
| 9 N–B3 | Q–B2 | 22 B–Q6 | R–B3 | 35 R/5–K5 | B–N4 |
| 10 R–Q1 | N–B3 | 23 P–K5 | Q–B1 | 36 PxN | P–Q7 |
| 11 P–Q5 | PxP | 24 Q–N3 | P–B5 | 37 BxP | RxB |
| 12 P–K4 | P–Q5 | 25 PxB | N–B4 | 38 Q–R6 | Q–B1 |
| 13 N–Q5 | Q–Q1 | 26 Q–R3 | PxB | 39 QxR | Resigns |

PRACTICAL VARIATIONS 1–5:

1 P–Q4, P–Q4 2 P–QB4, PxP 3 N–KB3, N–KB3 4 P–K3, P–K3 5 BxP, P–B4 6 Q–K2, P–QR3 7 O–O, N–B3 8 N–B3

| | *1* | *2* | *3* | *4* | *5* |
|---|---|---|---|---|---|
| *8* | — — | — — | — — | — — | — — |
| | P–QN4[1] | — — | — — | — — | — — |
| *9* | B–N3 | — — | — — | — — | — — |
| | B–N2[2] | — — | — — | B–K2[13] | Q–B2 |
| *10* | R–Q1[3] | — — | — — | PxP | R–Q1 |
| | Q–B2[4] | — — | — — | BxP | B–K2[15] |
| *11* | P–Q5 | — — | — — | P–K4 | PxP |
| | PxP | — — | — — | P–N5 | BxP |
| *12* | P–K4[5] | — — | — — | P–K5 | P–KR3[16] |
| | PxP[6] | — — | P–Q5 | PxN | O–O |
| *13* | NxKP | — — | N–Q5 | PxN | P–K4 |
| | NxN | — — | Q–Q1[10] | NPxP | B–N2 |
| *14* | QxN† | — — | B–KB4 | Q–B4 | P–K5 |
| | B–K2 | Q–K2[8] | R–B1 | Q–N3 | N–Q2 |
| *15* | B–KB4 | Q–KB4 | P–QR4 | QxBP[14] | B–KB4 |
| | Q–B1 | N–Q1 | PxP[11] | ± | B–K2 |
| *16* | B–Q5[7] | R–K1 | QRxP | | N–K4 |
| | ± | N–K3 | B–K2 | | N–B4 |
| *17* | | Q–KN4 | N–N5 | | NxN |
| | | P–B5 | O–O | | BxN |
| *18* | | B–N5[9] | NxN† | | QR–B1 |
| | | ± | BxN | | B–K2 |
| *19* | | | NxRP[12] | | P–QR4[17] |
| | | | ± | | ± |

*Notes to practical variations 1-5:*

[1] For 8 . . . PxP see Idea Var. 1.

[2] 9 . . . PxP 10 PxP, NxP 11 NxN, QxN 12 N–Q5!, NxN 13 R–Q1 favors White. A game Balbochan–Evans continued 13 . . . N–B6 14 PxN, Q–N3 15 Q–K5, B–N2 16 B–K3, Q–B3 17 B–Q5, Q–B1 18 BxB, QxB 19 P–QR4 with a better game for White. If 9 . . . P–N5, White moves effectively 10 P–Q5, N–QR4 11 B–R4†, B–Q2 12 PxP, PxP 13 R–Q1!, PxN 14 RxB, NxR 15 N–K5, R–R2 16 PxP, K–K2 17 P–K4, N–KB3 18 B–KN5, Q–B2 19 B–B4, Q–N3 20 R–Q1, P–N3 21 B–KN5, B–N2 22 N–Q7, RxN 23 RxR†, K–B1 24 BxN, BxB 25 P–K5 and Black resigns (Alekhine–Book, Margate 1938).

[3] Instead, 10 P–Q5 is also strong, as shown in Donner–van Scheltinga, Amsterdam 1954: 10 P–Q5, PxP 11 P–K4, P–Q5 12 P–K5, N–KN5!? 13 N–N5, P–B5 14 QxN, PxN, and now White should have played 15 B–B2 with a dangerous attack.

[4] For 10 . . . Q–N3 see Idea Var. 2; for 10 . . . P–B5 see Idea Var. 3.

[5] A typical tactical idea in this line.

[6] The best for Black seems to be . . . O–O–O (Stumpers–van Steenis, Leiden 1946), although 13 NxP, NxN 14 BxN still favors White.

[7] Najdorf–Christoffel, Groningen 1946.

[8] Nor does this move save the situation.

[9] Kotov–O'Kelly, Groningen 1946.

[10] Nor is Black well off in the wild position arising from 13 . . . NxN 14 PxN†, N–K2 15 P–QR4, P–B5 16 NxP, when 16 . . . BxP 17 PxP, PxB 18 N–B5, R–Q1 19 PxP, P–B3 20 RxB, RxR 21 P–R7 leads to a great advantage for White.

[11] If 15 . . . P–B5, White gets the advantage after 16 PxP, P–Q6 17 PxN, PxQ 18 PxB, PxR(Q)† 19 RxQ.

[12] See Game 2.

[13] Rendering P–Q5 harmless at the expense of a tempo.

[14] Euwe–Alekhine, Match Game, Amsterdam 1937.

[15] Now that White's King Rook no longer protects his King Bishop Pawn the text move is justified. White maintains some advantage.

[16] Necessary; the immediate P–K4 is premature because of N–KN5.

[17] White's development is superior and he commands greater space.

---

## part 2—ACCELERATED FIANCHETTO

### OBSERVATIONS ON KEY POSITION 2

Since the Modern Variation clearly favors White, Black must obviously choose some other line, and it is the Accelerated Fianchetto which deserves priority. Black achieves nothing by immediately exerting pressure on White's Queen Pawn, as was demonstrated in Part 1, and his seventh move 7 . . . N–QB3 is the culprit. Instead, the immediate fianchetto of the Queen Bishop controls his Q4 and K5 and restricts White's chances for a quick breakthrough in the center.

1 P–Q4, P–Q4
2 P–QB4, PxP
3 N–KB3, N–KB3
4 P–K3, P–K3
5 BxP, P–B4
6 O–O, P–QR3
7 Q–K2, P–QN4

KEY POSITION 2

IDEA VARIATIONS 4 AND 5:

(4) 8 B–Q3, PxP 9 PxP, B–K2 10 P–QR4, PxP! 11 RxP, B–N2 12 N–B3, O–O 13 B–KN5 with a satisfactory game for Black.

(5) 8 B–N3, B–N2 9 R–Q1, QN–Q2 (under these circumstances the Knight is better placed here than at QB3) 10 N–B3, Q–B2 11 P–Q5, P–B5 12 PxP, PxP 13 B–B2, B–Q3 14 P–KR3, O–O 15 P–K4, N–B4 16 B–N5, N–R4, and Black has counterplay.

PRACTICAL VARIATIONS 6–11:

1 P–Q4, P–Q4 2 P–QB4, PxP 3 N–KB3, N–KB3 4 P–K3, P–K3 5 BxP, P–B4 6 O–O, P–QR3 7 Q–K2, P–QN4

| | *6* | *7* | *8* | *9* | *10* | *11* |
|---|---|---|---|---|---|---|
| 8 | B–Q3 | – – | – – | B–N3 | – – | – – |
| | N–B3[1] | – – | PxP![7] | B–N2 | – – | – – |
| 9 | PxP | P–QR4[3] | PxP[8] | P–QR4 | – – | – – |
| | BxP | NPxP[4] | B–K2[9] | QN–Q2[13] | – – | – – |
| *10* | P–QR3 | N–B3[5] | P–QR4 | PxNP | – – | – – |
| | B–N2 | N–QN5 | PxP | PxNP | – – | – – |
| *11* | P–QN4 | B–B4 | RxP[10] | RxR | – – | – – |
| | B–K2 | B–N2 | B–N2 | QxR | – – | – – |
| *12* | B–N2 | KR–Q1 | QN–Q2[11] | N–B3 | – – | – – |
| | O–O | Q–B2 | O–O | P–N5 | – – | – – |
| *13* | QN–Q2 | PxP | N–N3 | N–QN5 | – – | – – |
| | Q–N3 | BxP | B–B3 | Q–R4 | Q–N1[17] | – – |
| *14* | KR–B1 | NxP | R–R1 | P–K4 | P–K4 | – – |
| | KR–B1 | B–K2 | Q–N3[12] | B–K2[14] | B–K2 | – – |
| *15* | N–N5 | B–Q2 | ∓ | P–K5[15] | P–Q5 | – – |
| | P–R3 | O–O | | N–Q4 | PxP[18] | O–O[20] |
| *16* | KN–K4 | QR–B1 | | B–N5 | BxP | PxP |
| | NxN | Q–N1[6] | | B–R3 | BxB | B–B3[21] |
| *17* | BxN[2] | = | | BxN | PxB | QN–Q4[22] |
| | ± | | | BxN | O–O | PxN |
| *18* | | | | B–QB4 | QxB | PxN |
| | | | | BxB | QxN[19] | BxKP[23] |
| *19* | | | | QxB | ± | NxP |
| | | | | N–N3 | | R–Q1 |
| *20* | | | | Q–B1 | | B–B2! |
| | | | | P–R3[16] | | ± |
| | | | | = | | |

PRACTICAL VARIATIONS 12–16:

1 P–Q4, P–Q4 2 P–QB4, PxP 3 N–KB3, N–KB3 4 P–K3, P–K3 5 BxP, P–B4 6 O–O, P–QR3 7 Q–K2, P–QN4 8 B–N3, B–N2

| | *12* | *13* | *14* | *15* | *16* |
|---|---|---|---|---|---|
| *9* | P–QR4 | – – | N–B3[34] | – – | – – |
| | QN–Q2 | – – | QN–Q2 | – – | – – |
| *10* | PxNP | P–K4[27] | R–Q1 | – – | – – |
| | PxNP | PxQP[28] | Q–B2[35] | B–K2 | B–Q3[40] |
| *11* | RxR | P–K5[29] | P–K4[36] | P–K4 | P–K4[41] |
| | QxR | N–N5[30] | PxP | PxP | PxP |
| *12* | N–B3 | PxNP | NxQP[37] | NxQP | NxQP |
| | P–N5 | B–B4[31] | B–Q3 | Q–B2 | Q–N1[42] |
| *13* | N–QN5 | PxP | P–N3 | B–N5 | N–B3 |
| | Q–N1 | O–O | B–K4 | P–N5 | P–N5 |
| *14* | P–K4 | PxB?[32] | P–B3 | N–R4 | N–Q5 |
| | PxP[24] | RxR | O–O | Q–K4 | PxN |
| *15* | KNxP | Q–K4 | B–K3 | BxN | P–K5 |
| | N–B4![25] | NxBP | N–B4 | NxB | NxP |
| *16* | P–K5 | KxN | B–B2 | N–N6 | NxN |
| | N/3–Q2 | P–Q6† | QR–B1 | R–Q1 | O–O[43] |
| *17* | B–KB4 | K–N3 | R–Q2[38] | B–R4† | ∓ |
| | NxB | RxN | ± | K–B1 | |
| *18* | NxN | QxP | | B–B6 | |
| | B–K2 | RxB | | Q–B2 | |
| *19* | R–Q1 | RxR | | BxB | |
| | B–R3 | Q–B2 | | QxB[39] | |
| *20* | N–B7† | Q–N5 | | ± | |
| | QxN | B–B7† | | | |
| *21* | QxB | KxB | | | |
| | O–O[26] | QxR | | | |
| *22* | ± | QxN | | | |
| | | QxP† | | | |
| *23* | | N–Q2 | | | |
| | | QxP[33] | | | |
| | | = | | | |

*Notes to practical variations 6-16:*

[1] If 8 . . . B–N2 9 PxP, after which 9 . . . BxP fails against 10 BxP†. However, Black should play 9 . . . N–B3 which, after 10 P–QR3, leads to the text variation.

[2] Muller–Racek, Vienna 1958.

continued ▶

[3] The sharpest.

[4] Weak is 9 . . . P–N5, since it allows White the maneuver N–Q2–QB4, thus: 10 PxP, BxP 11 P–K4, P–K4 12 B–K3, BxB 13 QxB, O–O 14 QN–Q2, N–KR4 15 N–B4, N–B5 16 KR–Q1±. Also inferior is 9 . . . P–B5, which gives White too much freedom in the center after 10 B–B2, B–N2 11 PxP, PxP 12 RxR, QxR 13 N–B3 followed by P–K4.

[5] Nor is 10 RxP stronger, because of 10 . . . N–QN5 11 B–N5†, B–Q2 12 BxB†, QxB 13 N–B3, PxP 14 PxP, R–B1 15 N–K5, Q–N2 16 Q–B3 = (Grunfeld–Pilnik, Belgrade 1952). Worthwhile, however, is the finesse 10 B–B2!, N–QN5 11 BxP†, B–Q2 12 N–B3, with a promising position for White. A plausible continuation is 12 . . . PxP 13 NxP, B–K2 14 R–Q1, BxB 15 NxB, Q–B2 16 P–K4, O–O 17 B–N5±. Or Black may vary at his twelfth move and play 12 . . . B–K2, when follows 13 R–Q1, Q–B2 14 BxB†, NxB 15 P–Q5, PxP 16 NxP, NxN 17 RxN±. In the above line of play after White's 10 B–B2!, Black may play 10 . . . PxP after which 11 BxP, B–Q2 12 NxP, NxN 13 PxN causes Black's Queen Rook Pawn to become quite vulnerable.

[6] Wade-Pilnik, Stockholm 1952.

[7] The correct way of treating this variation.

[8] Black also has a satisfactory game after 9 NxP, B–K2 10 P–QR4, PxP.

[9] The safest continuation.

[10] There is no point in deferring the Pawn capture.

[11] For 12 N–B3 see Idea Var. 4.

[12] Barcza–Keres, Budapest 1952.

[13] Black's best move. The point is that after 10 PxNP, PxNP 11 RxR, QxR 12 QxP, Black gains the edge with 12 . . . BxN.

[14] Black cannot safely capture on his K5 because of 14 . . . NxP 15 N–N5, NxN 16 BxN with the strong threat BxP. Or if Black captures the King Pawn with his Bishop he is subjected to a strong attack: 14 . . . BxP 15 N–N5, B–N3 16 P–Q5.

[15] More suited to make things difficult for Black is 15 P–Q5.

[16] If 21 BxB, Black's King is better poised for the ending.

[17] The usually preferred move.

[18] For 15 . . . O–O, see Game 3.

[19] Florian–Pilnik, Helsinki 1952.

[20] Here, too, White maintains some advantage.

[21] The point of Black's preceding move. If 17 PxN, BxN. If 17 PxP†, K–R1 18 B–QB4, N–N3 with a satisfactory game for Black.

[22] To provoke a weakening of Black's Pawn structure.

[23] In this complicated variation it seems impossible to find a better move for Black. If 18 . . . B–B4 19 P–K5, BxN 20 PxB, NxP 21 P–K6, N–K4 22 P–B4 and White wins. In the above line if Black varies at his 21st move with 21 . . . Q–K4, then White gets the better of it with 22 R–K1, B–Q3 23 P–B4! If 18 . . . Q–N3 19 P–K5, BxN 20 PxN!, BxQ 21 PxB, Q–N1 22 PxR (Q)†

KxQ 23 B–N5, P–B3 24 R–B1 and wins—a fantastic variation

[24] White has the edge. Black may vary: 14 . . . NxP 15 N–N5!, NxN 16 BxN with a few threats. Or 14 . . . BxP 15 N–N5!, B–KB4 16 P–Q5 with an imminent attack.

[25] Necessary, because if 15 . . . B–K2 or 15 . . . B–B4 White obtains a dangerous attack with the sacrifice 16 BxP.

[26] Kopilov–Flohr, Moscow 1953.

[27] A sharp move, apt to create great complications.

[28] Best. Risky is 10 . . . NxP because of 11 P–Q5, PxQP 12 N–B3, P–B5 13 B–B2, B–K2 14 NxN, PxN 15 BxP, BxB 16 QxB, O–O 17 PxP with advantage for White.

[29] Kotov–Flohr, Budapest 1950, led to difficult complications after 11 PxP, N–B4 12 B–QB4, P–Q6 13 Q–K3.

[30] Worthy of examination for Black is 11 . . . N–Q4 so as to meet 12 PxP with 12 . . . P–Q6 13 QxP, N–B4 14 Q–Q1, PxP and Black stands well. In the above line if 14 Q–B4 Black plays N–N3 and has a good game.

[31] Better is 12 . . . N–B4 to meet 13 B–QB4 with 13 . . . P–Q6.

[32] This leads to very exciting complications. Preferable is 14 B–KB4, B–B3 15 N–Q2 with a slight plus for White.

[33] Petrosian–Smyslov, Moscow 1952. This wild game ended in a draw.

[34] Aiming at quick action in the center.

[35] If 10 . . . Q–N3 11 P–QR4, which is unpleasant for Black in view of 11 . . . P–N5 12 P–R5! followed by 13 N–QR4. Plausible, however, is 10 . . . P–N5 11 N–QR4, Q–R4. This remarkable maneuver occurred in Spasski–Keres, Candidates' Tournament, Amsterdam 1956, which continued 12 P–K4, Q–N4 13 Q–K1, BxP 14 N–K5, P–B5! 15 NxQBP, and now Black should have played 15 . . . B–Q4, but instead replied 15 . . . B–K2 and the game went on: 16 B–B4, O–O 17 N–Q6 with advantage for White. In the above game if Black varies on his 13th move with 13 . . . NxP, White counters effectively with 13 P–Q5!

[36] If 11 P–Q5?, NxP 12 NxN, BxN 13 BxB, PxB 14 RxP, B–K2 15 P–K4, O–O and Black is well off. In this line another good move for Black after White plays 11 P–Q5? is 11 . . . P–B5.

[37] The sacrifice 12 N–Q5 is fairly promising. A plausible continuation would be 12 . . . PxN 13 PxP†, K–Q1 14 NxP with difficult complications.

[38] Reshevsky–Najdorf, Match Game 1952.

[39] Smyslov–Keres, Budapest 1950.

[40] A new move which Smyslov successfully introduced against Petrosian with some success in a Candidates' Tournament in Yugoslavia.

[41] This move is inadequate. Best for White is 11 P–Q5, although 11 . . . P–K4 leads to a good game for Black.

[42] This strong move wins a Pawn by force.

[43] Black has a good Pawn plus.

## SUPPLEMENTARY VARIATIONS 1–13:

1 P–Q4, P–Q4 2 P–QB4, PxP 3 N–KB3, N–KB3 4 P–K3, P–K3 5 BxP, P–B4

| | 1 | 2 | 3 | 4 | 5 | 6 | 7 |
|---|---|---|---|---|---|---|---|
| 6 | O–O | — — | — — | — — | — — | — — | Q–K2[21] |
| | P–QR3 | — — | — — | — — | — — | — — | P–QR3[22] |
| 7 | Q–K2 | — — | — — | — — | — — | — — | PxP |
| | N–B3 | — — | — — | — — | — — | — — | BxP |
| 8 | R–Q1[1] | — — | — — | — — | — — | — — | P–K4[23] |
| | P–QN4 | — — | — — | — — | — — | — — | P–QN4 |
| 9 | B–N3 | — — | — — | PxP | — — | — — | B–Q3 |
| | P–B5![2] | — — | — — | Q–B2 | — — | — — | QN–Q2[24] |
| 10 | B–B2 | — — | — — | B–Q3 | — — | — — | O–O |
| | N–QN5![3] | — — | — — | BxP | — — | N–QN5! | B–N2 |
| 11 | N–B3 | — — | — — | P–QR4 | — — | N–B3 | QN–Q2 |
| | NxB | — — | — — | P–N5? | PxP | NxB | O–O |
| 12 | QxN[4] | — — | — — | QN–Q2 | RxP | QxN | P–K5 |
| | N–Q4[5] | B–N2 | — — | O–O[17] | N–QN5 | BxP | N–N5 |
| 13 | P–K4[6] | P–Q5[10] | — — | N–N3 | B–N5† | P–K4[20] | N–K4[25] |
| | N–N5 | PxP | Q–B2[13] | B–K2 | B–Q2 | = | ± |
| 14 | Q–K2 | P–K4 | P–K4[14] | P–K4 | BxB† | | |
| | N–Q6 | B–K2 | P–K4[15] | N–Q2 | NxB | | |
| 15 | B–K3 | P–K5[11] | B–N5 | B–K3 | B–Q2 | | |
| | B–N2[7] | N–Q2 | N–Q2 | N/2–K4 | P–QR4 | | |
| 16 | P–Q5 | NxQP | QR–B1 | NxN | R–QB1 | | |
| | P–K4[8] | O–O | B–Q3 | NxN | Q–N2 | | |
| 17 | P–QN3 | Q–B5 | N–K2 | QR–B1 | N–R3[19] | | |
| | B–N5 | N–B4 | P–B3[16] | Q–N1 | ± | | |
| 18 | Q–B2 | N–B6† | = | B–B5[18] | | | |
| | Q–R4 | BxN | | ± | | | |
| 19 | N–K2 | RxQ | | | | | |
| | O–O | BxR | | | | | |
| 20 | PxP | N–N5 | | | | | |
| | PxP | BxN | | | | | |
| 21 | N–B1[9] | BxB[12] | | | | | |
| | ± | ± | | | | | |

*Notes to supplementary variations 1–13:*

[1] Weaker than 8 N–B3. See Part 1.

[2] If 9 . . . PxP 10 NxP, Q–B2 11 P–QR4, P–N5 12 NxN, QxN 13 P–R5, B–Q2 14 N–Q2, B–K2 15 N–B4 with an initiative for White. In the above line if Black plays 9 . . . Q–B2 or 9 . . . Q–N3, then 10 N–B3, B–N2 leads to the Modern Variation. See Part 1.

[3] Black carries out his threat of exchanging the enemy Bishop.

[4] The issue is center and development versus the two Bishops.

[5] Intending to counter White's center advance by maneuvering the Knight, . . . N–N5–Q6.

| 8 | 9 | 10 | 11 | 12 | 13 |
|---|---|---|---|---|---|
| O–O | — — | — — | — — | — — | — — |
| PxP | P–QR3 | — — | — — | — — | — — |
| PxP[26] | Q–K2 | — — | P–QR4[35] | P–K4[37] | — — |
| QN–Q2[27] | PxP | QN–Q2 | N–B3 | NxP[38] | P–QN4[43] |
| N–B3 | PxP | P–QR4[33] | Q–K2 | P–Q5[39] | B–Q3[44] |
| N–N3 | B–K2 | P–QN3 | B–K2 | N–Q3[40] | B–N2 |
| B–N3 | R–Q1 | N–B3 | R–Q1 | PxP | R–K1[45] |
| B–K2 | P–QN4[29] | B–N2 | Q–B2 | BxP[41] | B–K2 |
| B–N5 | B–N3[30] | R–Q1 | N–B3 | BxB | PxP |
| O–O | B–N2 | Q–B2 | O–O | PxB | BxBP |
| Q–Q3 | P–QR4 | P–QN3 | P–QN3 | R–K1[42] | B–N5[46] |
| B–Q2 | P–N5 | B–K2 | B–Q2 | = | ± |
| N–K5 | QN–Q2 | B–N2 | B–N2[36] | | |
| QN–Q4 | P–QR4[31] | O–O | = | | |
| QR–Q1 | N–B4 | QR–B1[34] | | | |
| R–B1 | O–O[32] | ± | | | |
| P–B4 | = | | | | |
| N–QN5 | | | | | |
| Q–R3[28] | | | | | |
| ± | | | | | |

6 Inferior is 13 P–QN3, PxP 14 QxP, B–N2.

7 Euwe recommends 15 . . . B–N5 to hamper 16 P–Q5 or 16 P–QN3.

8 Better is 16 . . . PxP 17 PxP, B–K2 18 N–K1, NxN 19 QxN, O–O 20 P–Q6, BxQP! 21 B–B4, BxB 22 RxQ QRxR 23 Q–K7 with a slight advantage for White.

9 White wins the Queen Bishop Pawn (Landau–Euwe, Soest 1940).

10 Faulty is 13 P–K4 because of 13 . . . P–N5. In Szabo–Euwe, Groningen 1946, follows 14 P–K5, PxN 15 PxN, PxBP 16 Q–R4†, Q–Q2 17 QxBP, R–B1 18 Q–K2, R–KN1 with a strong attack for Black.

11 In Eliskases–Flohr, White played 15 PxP, resulting in a quick draw. Black may well continue 15 . . . O–O 16 P–Q6, BxP 17 B–B4, BxB 18 RxQ, QRxR with seemingly sufficient compensation for the Queen; however, this line has not been tested through in actual play. The column continuation offers White opportunities for attack.

12 White has an irresistible attack (Euwe–Grunfeld, Zandvoort 1936).

13 This move with the ensuing column continuation is considered to be Black's best. Weaker is 13 . . . Q–N3, whence follows 14 P–K4, B–B4 15 B–N5, O–O 16 P–QR4 with a clear advantage for White.

14 Or 14 PxP, PxP 15 N–Q4, K–B2 with a good enough game for Black (Knip-Kmoch, Amsterdam 1941).

continued ▸

[15] This closing of the center is Black's best.

[16] For 17 . . . O–O, see Game 4.

[17] White also obtains the better game after 12 . . . N–QR4 13 P–QN3, N–Q4 14 B–N2, N–B6 15 BxN, PxB 16 N–K4, NxP 17 QR–N1, N–R4 18 KR–QB1, B–K2 19 RxP (Euwe–Flohr, 8th Match Game 1932).

[18] Alekhine–Flohr, Bled 1931.

[19] White enjoys superiority in space.

[20] White still has some attacking chances.

[21] An entirely new idea. White wants to play PxP, precluding the exchange of Queens.

[22] 6 . . . PxP 7 PxP, N–B3 leads to Sup. Var. 8, note 27.

[23] 8 O–O, N–B3 9 P–K4, P–QN4 10 P–K5, PxB 11 PxN, PxP 12 QxP leads to sharp but balanced positions.

[24] If 9 . . . N–B3 10 N–B3!

[25] Taimanov–Bazin, Buenos Aires 1960.

[26] To keep an opening advantage White must allow the isolation of his Queen Pawn.

[27] As has been pointed out before, the move 7 . . . N–B3 is effectively countered by 8 Q–K2, NxP 9 NxN, QxN 10 R–Q1, with the better game for White.

[28] Black will experience difficulty on the Kingside.

[29] The Neo-Steinitz variation.

[30] Here, too, this is the best square for retreat. Instead, 10 B–Q3, O–O 11 P–QR4, PxP leads to variations treated in Part 2. The line 10 B–Q3, N–B3 11 P–QR4, P–N5 requires 12 B–K3 as a preparation for the maneuver QN–Q2–B4. In the above line 11 N–B3, N–QN5 12 B–N1, QN–Q4 offers even chances.

[31] An important move. Black must always be aware of the weakness at his QN3 if he allows White to play P–QR5. For instance, 12 . . . O–O 13 P–QR5, N–Q2 14 N–B4 with advantage for White.

[32] Black has a satisfactory game. Euwe–Najdorf, New York 1951, continued 14 KN–K5, QN–Q2 15 R–Q3. This last move of White's is too risky because of the continuation 15 . . . N–N3 16 R–N3, NxN 17 BxN, N–K5, and Black stands better. In the above line White should play 15 B–K3 followed by 16 QR–B1, effecting an even game.

[33] Now this move is more plausible because Black's Queen Knight is placed on Q2 rather than on QB3, which lessens the significance of the weakness on White's QN4. However, Black has a satisfactory game.

[34] White has a tiny edge.

[35] White hampers the development of Black's Queenside, but he weakens his own QN4.

[36] Recommended for Black is 12 . . . PxP 13 PxP, N–QR4 14 N–K5 with even chances. Inferior is 12 . . . QR–B1, which is met by White with the center push 13 P–Q5! Botvinnik–Euwe, Groningen 1946, continued 13 . . . PxP 14 NxP, NxN 15 BxN, B–N5 16 Q–B4, B–R4 17 BxN, QxB 18 N–K5, Q–K1 19 R–Q5, R–Q1, and White should now have played 20 P–KN4, maintaining his initiative.

[37] This Pawn sacrifice was introduced by Petrosian in his game against Sherwin, Portoroz 1958.

[38] The acceptance of the Pawn sacrifice is almost forced. In case Black declines, White assuredly obtains the edge.

[39] 8 Q–K2 also merits consideration, whence follows 8 . . .

N–Q3 9 PxP, NxB 10 QxN, Q–B2 11 P–QN4, or 8 . . . N–KB3 9 R–Q1, Q–B2 10 P–Q5, in both cases with attacking chances for White.

[40] 8 . . . PxP is met by 9 BxP, N–Q3 10 R–K1†, B–K2 11 B–N5, P–B3 12 B–B4 with advantage for White. Or 8 . . . P–QN4 9 PxP!, QxQ 10 PxP†, K–K2 11 RxQ, PxB 12 R–K1 with advantage.

[41] If 9 . . . NxB, then 10 PxP†.

[42] This sharp position offers even chances.

[43] Petrosian–Sherwin, Portoroz 1958, continued 7 . . . PxP 8 P–K5, KN–Q2 9 QxP, N–QB3 10 Q–K4, Q–B2 11 B–B4, P–QN4 12 B–QN3, N–B4 13 Q–K2, NxB 14 PxN, B–N2 15 N–B3. White maintains an advantage in space.

[44] If 8 B–N3, then 8 . . . NxP 9 P–Q5?, P–B5!

[45] 9 P–K5 is somewhat premature, for Black obtains good counterplay with 9 . . . KN–Q2 10 B–N5, Q–N3 11 PxP, BxP 12 B–KB4, N–QB3 (Petrosian-van Scheltinga, Beverwijk 1960).

[46] White's development is superior and his position less vulnerable.

## *Queen's Gambit Accepted Game 3*

*WHITE: Uhlmann* *BLACK: Stahlberg*

*Wageningen 1957*

| | WHITE | BLACK | | WHITE | BLACK | | WHITE | BLACK |
|---|---|---|---|---|---|---|---|---|
| 1 | P–Q4 | P–Q4 | 28 | Q–R4† | K–N1 | 55 | R–B8† | K–K3 |
| 2 | P–QB4 | PxP | 29 | B–Q2 | R–KR2 | 56 | R–K8† | K–Q4 |
| 3 | N–KB3 | N–KB3 | 30 | Q–QB4 | R–QB2 | 57 | K–B3 | N–Q3 |
| 4 | P–K3 | P–K3 | 31 | BxP | RxQ | 58 | R–KN8 | N–B2 |
| 5 | BxP | P–QR3 | 32 | BxQ | K–B2 | 59 | K–N2 | K–K3 |
| 6 | O–O | P–B4 | 33 | R–K1 | R–B7 | 60 | R–QN8 | K–Q2 |
| 7 | Q–K2 | P–QN4 | 34 | P–QN4 | R–N7 | 61 | R–N7† | K–K3 |
| 8 | B–N3 | B–N2 | 35 | R–K4 | P–B4 | 62 | B–B5 | N–K4 |
| 9 | P–QR4 | QN–Q2 | 36 | R–Q4 | N–B6 | 63 | R–QB7 | N–Q2 |
| 10 | PxP | PxP | 37 | R–QB4 | N–K5 | 64 | B–K3 | R–N5 |
| 11 | RxR | QxR | 38 | R–B7† | K–K3 | 65 | R–B6† | K–B4 |
| 12 | N–B3 | P–N5 | 39 | B–B5 | R–N8† | 66 | K–N3 | N–K4 |
| 13 | N–QN5 | Q–N1 | 40 | K–R2 | P–N4 | 67 | R–B7 | N–B5 |
| 14 | P–K4 | B–K2 | 41 | P–N3 | K–B3 | 68 | R–B5† | K–K5 |
| 15 | P–Q5 | O–O | 42 | K–N2 | R–N6 | 69 | BxP | NxP |
| 16 | PxP | B–B3 | 43 | R–B8 | K–N2 | 70 | P–B3† | K–Q5 |
| 17 | N/5–Q4 | PxN | 44 | B–Q4† | K–B2 | 71 | R–B5 | R–N8 |
| 18 | PxN | BxKP | 45 | R–QN8 | N–Q7 | 72 | P–R4 | N–B5 |
| 19 | NxP | R–Q1 | 46 | B–K3 | N–K5 | 73 | B–B4 | N–K6 |
| 20 | B–B2 | RxP | 47 | P–N5 | K–K3 | 74 | BxN† | KxB |
| 21 | BxB | RxN | 48 | P–N6 | K–Q2 | 75 | R–K5† | K–Q5 |
| 22 | BxP† | KxB | 49 | R–KB8 | K–K3 | 76 | R–K4† | K–Q4 |
| 23 | QxB | R–Q2 | 50 | R–KN8 | R–N7 | 77 | P–R5 | R–N8† |
| 24 | Q–K2 | Q–Q3 | 51 | K–B3 | R–N6 | 78 | K–B4 | R–KR8 |
| 25 | B–N5 | P–N3 | 52 | P–N4 | N–Q7† | 79 | K–N5 | R–R6 |
| 26 | P–R3 | N–Q4 | 53 | K–K2 | N–K5 | 80 | P–R6 | Resigns |
| 27 | Q–K4 | P–B3 | 54 | PxP† | KxP | | | |

*Queen's Gambit Accepted Game 4*

*WHITE: Stahlberg* *BLACK: Alexander*

*London 1951*

| WHITE | BLACK | WHITE | BLACK | WHITE | BLACK |
|---|---|---|---|---|---|
| 1 P–Q4 | P–Q4 | 11 N–B3 | NxB | 21 P–R5 | N–B4 |
| 2 N–KB3 | N–KB3 | 12 QxN | B–N2 | 22 N–R4 | K–B2 |
| 3 P–B4 | PxP | 13 P–Q5 | Q–B2 | 23 Q–K2 | R–KN1 |
| 4 P–K3 | P–K3 | 14 P–K4 | P–K4 | 24 PxP† | PxP |
| 5 BxP | P–B4 | 15 B–N5 | N–Q2 | 25 N/3–B5 | B–B1 |
| 6 O–O | N–B3 | 16 QR–B1 | B–Q3 | 26 NxP | RxN |
| 7 Q–K2 | P–QR3 | 17 N–K2 | O–O? | 27 Q–R5 | Q–Q2 |
| 8 R–Q1 | P–QN4 | 18 N–N3 | P–B3 | 28 BxN | RxB |
| 9 B–N3 | P–B5 | 19 B–K3 | P–N3 | 29 R–B3 | Resigns |
| 10 B–B2 | N–QN5 | 20 P–KR4 | QR–B1 | | |

## part 3—ALEKHINE VARIATION

1 P–Q4, P–Q4
2 P–QB4, PxP
3 N–KB3, P–QR3[A]
4 P–K3[B], B–N5[C]
5 BxP[D], P–K3[E]
6 Q–N3[F], BxN
7 PxB, P–QN4[G]
8 B–K2

KEY POSITION 3

### OBSERVATIONS ON KEY POSITION 3

[A] Preferred by Alekhine.

[B] 4 P–K4 is dubious because of 4 . . . P–QN4 5 P–QR4, B–N2, and White has lost the initiative. Nor is 4 P–QR4 good, since it weakens White's QN4. Black proceeds 4 . . . N–KB3 5 P–K3, B–N5 6 BxP, P–K3 with equality.

[C] This Bishop move leads to the Alekhine Variation proper. Black may also play 4 . . . P–K3 or 4 . . . N–KB3 transposing into variations previously examined. This tactic is sometimes adopted to circumvent the Mannheim Variation.

[D] An interesting try is 5 P–KR3, and then if Black proceeds carelessly with 5 . . . B–R4, White follows 6 P–KN4, B–N3 7 N–K5 and Black has a bad position. The line continues 7 . . . P–K3 8 B–N2, P–QB3 9 N–Q2 and White has the initiative. In the above line Black may vary with 7 B–K5 8 BxP!, B–Q4 9 BxB, QxB and, according to Van Seters, White stands better with 10 O–O. In the above line White would not improve by 9 Q–B3 because of 9 . . . N–KB3. The safest reply to 5 P–KR3 is 5 . . . BxN 6 QxB, N–QB3 7 N–B3, N–B3 8 BxP, P–K3.

[E] Practically forced in view of the threat BxP†.

[F] The continuation 6 P–Q5, which is of Russian origin, is best met by 6 . . . N–KB3 7 N–B3, PxP 8 NxP, QN–Q2.

[G] Also playable is 7 . . . R–R2 8 N–B3, N–KB3 9 O–O, P–B4 10 R–Q1, PxP 11 RxP, Q–B2 with an almost even game.

Black's Queenside is weakened by the advance of his Pawns there and the absence of his Queen Bishop. White must try to profit from this situation by playing P–QR4 and subsequently applying pressure along the Queen Bishop file. Black, though, has counterchances because of the weakening effect of the doubled Pawns on White's Kingside and center. A possible . . . P–QB4 followed by . . . PxP may cause White some difficulties.

IDEA VARIATIONS 6 AND 7:

(6) 8 . . . N–Q2 9 P–QR4, P–N5 10 P–B4, P–QB4; (better is 10 . . . KN–B3) 11 P–Q5!, PxP 12 QxQP, KN–B3 13 Q–N2, B–K2 14 N–Q2, O–O 15 P–K4! with a great advantage for White.

(7) 8 . . . P–QB4 9 PxP, BxP 10 Q–B3, B–B1 11 N–Q2, N–Q2 12 N–N3, KN–B3 13 B–Q2, R–B1 14 Q–R5, QxQ 15 BxQ, N–Q4 with a satisfactory game for Black.

PRACTICAL VARIATIONS 17–22:

1 P–Q4, P–Q4 2 P–QB4, PxP 3 N–KB3, P–QR3 4 P–K3, B–N5 5 BxP, P–K3 6 Q–N3, BxN 7 PxB, P–QN4 8 B–K2

| | *17* | *18* | *19* | *20* | *21* | *22* |
|---|---|---|---|---|---|---|
| *8* | – – | – – | – – | – – | – – | – – |
| | P–QB4 | – – | – – | – – | – – | N–Q2[18] |
| *9* | P–QR4[1] | – – | PxP | – – | – – | P–QR4 |
| | P–N5 | – – | BxP[7] | – – | QN–Q2[15] | P–N5 |
| *10* | PxP | – – | Q–B3 | R–N1[10] | P–B6 | P–B4[19] |
| | BxP | – – | B–K2[8] | N–K2[11] | N–B4 | KN–B3[20] |
| *11* | N–Q2 | O–O | QxP | RxP? | Q–B2 | B–B3 |
| | N–KB3 | N–KB3 | B–B3 | N–N3 | R–B1 | R–R2[21] |
| *12* | Q–B4[2] | N–Q2 | Q–N4 | Q–B3[12] | P–QR4[16] | B–B6[22] |
| | QN–Q2 | QN–Q2 | N–R3 | Q–K2 | RxP | ± |
| *13* | N–N3 | N–B4 | Q–K4[9] | B–Q2[13] | B–Q2 | |
| | B–K2 | O–O | = | P–N5[14] | P–N5 | |
| *14* | P–K4[3] | P–R5[5] | | ∓ | BxNP | |
| | O–O | N–Q4 | | | N–Q6† | |
| *15* | B–K3 | P–K4 | | | QxN | |
| | Q–N1 | N–K2 | | | R–B8† | |
| *16* | R–QB1 | K–R1[6] | | | K–Q2 | |
| | B–Q3[4] | ± | | | QxQ† | |
| | = | | | | BxQ | |
| | | | | | RxR[17] | |
| | | | | | ± | |

*Notes to practical variations 17-22:*

[1] Gaining control of QB4 by force. The text move is most likely stronger than PxP.

[2] The plausible 12 Q–B2, QN–Q2 13 N–B4, O–O 14 P–N3, R–B1 results in equality.

[3] H. Muller recommends 14 P–R5.

[4] The position is balanced by an equal number of weaknesses on both sides.

continued ▸

[5] For 14 Q–B2 see Game 5.

[6] Black is more vulnerable on both wings.

[7] Simple and best.

[8] A promising Pawn sacrifice. For . . . 10 B–B1 see Idea Var. 7.

[9] A very sharp position.

[10] Introduced by Van Foltys.

[11] Best. Inferior is 10 . . . K–B1 because of 11 Q–B3. 10 . . . P–N3 loses to 11 Q–B3. But worthy of consideration is 10 . . . Q–R5.

[12] Or 12 RxN, RPxR 13 Q–B3, RxP 14 QxB, R–R8† 15 B–B1, Q–Q6.

[13] If 13 RxN, B–N5.

[14] White has a difficult development and an awkward Rook.

[15] Black effectively develops his Queen Knight, but loses time recovering the Pawn.

[16] An interesting moment. White can proceed with 12 N–B3, meeting 12 . . . RxP with 13 NxP, when he has the better game.

[17] Barendregt–van Scheltinga, Amsterdam 1950, continued 18 B–B3?, N–B3 19 BxP, N–Q4 20 B–N5†, K–Q1 21 B–R5†, K–B1 22 P–K4, N–B2 with a decisive advantage for Black. However, 18 B–R5 followed by the capture of the Queen Rook Pawn gives White good winning chances.

[18] Too slow.

[19] A strong move which accentuates the white-square weakness in the Black camp.

[20] For 10 . . . P–QB4 see Idea Var. 6.

[21] 11 . . . P–B4 offers the exchange after 12 BxR, QxB 13 R–N1. White suffers from a weakness on his white squares, as shown in Weltmander–Gretajkin, Moscow 1954, which continued 13 . . . B–Q3 14 N–Q2, PxP 15 N–B4, B–K2 16 PxP, O–O 17 Q–N3, P–N3 18 Q–N2, N–Q4, and Black has a fighting game. In the above line Black may vary: 13 . . . PxP 14 PxP, B–Q3 15 B–K3, O–O 16 N–Q2, R–B1 (Iliotsky–Gretajkin, Moscow 1954).

[22] White has a bind.

### *Queen's Gambit Accepted Game 5*

*WHITE: Denker* — *BLACK: Lundin*

*Groningen 1946*

| | WHITE | BLACK | | WHITE | BLACK |
|---|---|---|---|---|---|
| 1 | P–Q4 | P–Q4 | 9 | P–QR4 | P–N5 |
| 2 | P–QB4 | PxP | 10 | PxP | BxP |
| 3 | N–KB3 | P–QR3 | 11 | O–O | N–Q2 |
| 4 | P–K3 | B–N5 | 12 | N–Q2 | KN–B3 |
| 5 | BxP | P–K3 | 13 | N–B4 | O–O |
| 6 | Q–N3 | BxN | 14 | Q–B2 | R–B1 |
| 7 | PxB | P–QN4 | 15 | P–N3 | N–Q4 |
| 8 | B–K2 | P–QB4 | 16 | B–N2 | B–K2 |

| | WHITE | BLACK | | WHITE | BLACK |
|---|---|---|---|---|---|
| 17 | K–R1 | B–B3 | 30 | QxN | N–B6 |
| 18 | QR–Q1 | BxB | 31 | NxN | PxN |
| 19 | QxB | N–B6 | 32 | RxP | QxP |
| 20 | R–Q6 | Q–B2 | 33 | Q–B2 | Q–R3 |
| 21 | RxRP | N–B3 | 34 | K–N2 | P–B4 |
| 22 | N–Q6 | QR–Q1 | 35 | P–B5 | R–B3 |
| 23 | N–N5 | Q–B1 | 36 | Q–N3† | K–B1 |
| 24 | N–Q4 | N/3–Q4 | 37 | R–Q3 | P–K5? |
| 25 | R–B6 | Q–Q2 | 38 | Q–N8† | K–B2 |
| 26 | R–B4 | R–B1 | 39 | R–Q7† | K–N3 |
| 27 | R–B1 | P–K4 | 40 | Q–N3† | K–R4 |
| 28 | N–N5 | RxR | 41 | RxP | R–N3 |
| 29 | PxR | NxB | 42 | RxP† | Resigns |

*Queen's Gambit Accepted Game 6*

*WHITE: Stahlberg* — *BLACK: Foltys*

*Amsterdam 1950*

| | WHITE | BLACK | | WHITE | BLACK |
|---|---|---|---|---|---|
| 1 | P–Q4 | P–Q4 | 23 | RxR | KxR |
| 2 | P–QB4 | PxP | 24 | B–Q4 | R–B3 |
| 3 | N–KB3 | P–QR3 | 25 | BxN | PxB |
| 4 | P–K3 | B–N5 | 26 | N–Q4 | R–N3 |
| 5 | BxP | P–K3 | 27 | K–N2 | K–Q2 |
| 6 | Q–N3 | BxN | 28 | K–B3 | K–K2 |
| 7 | PxB | P–QN4 | 29 | R–KN1 | B–B4 |
| 8 | B–K2 | P–QB4 | 30 | N–K2 | R–Q3 |
| 9 | PxP | N–Q2 | 31 | R–N7 | R–Q7 |
| 10 | P–B6 | N–B4 | 32 | RxP | RxP |
| 11 | Q–B2 | R–B1 | 33 | R–R8 | P–B4 |
| 12 | N–Q2 | Q–Q4 | 34 | P–R4 | R–R8 |
| 13 | O–O | N–B3 | 35 | P–R5 | B–R6 |
| 14 | P–B4 | QxBP | 36 | K–N2 | B–N7 |
| 15 | N–N3 | N–R5 | 37 | R–R8 | B–N2 |
| 16 | QxQ† | RxQ | 38 | R–KN8 | B–B1 |
| 17 | N–Q4 | R–N3 | 39 | N–Q4 | R–QB8 |
| 18 | P–N3 | N–B6 | 40 | R–R8 | R–B1 |
| 19 | B–N2 | NxB† | 41 | P–R6 | R–K1 |
| 20 | NxN | B–Q3 | 42 | P–R7 | B–N2 |
| 21 | QR–B1 | K–Q2 | 43 | N–B6† | Resigns |
| 22 | KR–Q1 | R–QB1 | | | |

## SUPPLEMENTARY VARIATIONS 14-24:

1 P–Q4, P–Q4 2 P–QB4, PxP

| | 14 | 15 | 16 | 17 | 18 | 19 |
|---|---|---|---|---|---|---|
| 3 | N–KB3 | – – | – – | – – | – – | – – |
| | N–KB3 | – – | – – | – – | – – | – – |
| 4 | P–K3 | – – | – – | Q–R4†[19] | – – | – – |
| | P–KN3[1] | – – | B–K3[14] | QN–Q2[20] | P–B3 | Q–Q2 |
| 5 | BxP[2] | – – | N–R3[15] | N–B3 | QxBP | QxBP |
| | B–N2 | – – | P–B4[16] | P–K3 | B–B4 | Q–B3[28] |
| 6 | O–O | – – | NxP | P–K4 | N–B3 | N–R3 |
| | O–O | – – | N–B3 | P–B4[21] | QN–Q2 | QxQ |
| 7 | N–B3 | – – | Q–R4 | P–Q5[22] | P–KN3 | NxQ |
| | KN–Q2[3] | – – | PxP | PxP | P–K3 | P–K3 |
| 8 | P–K4[4] | Q–K2[9] | QN–K5 | P–K5 | B–N2 | P–QR3 |
| | N–N3 | N–N3 | B–Q2 | P–QN4[23] | B–B7[26] | P–B4[29] |
| 9 | B–K2 | B–N3 | NxB | QxNP[24] | P–K3 | B–B4 |
| | B–N5 | N–B3[10] | NxN | R–QN1 | B–K2 | N–B3 |
| 10 | B–K3 | R–Q1[11] | NxP | Q–R4 | O–O | PxP |
| | N–B3 | N–R4 | NxN | P–Q5 | O–O | BxP |
| 11 | P–Q5[5] | B–B2 | QxN | PxN | P–QR3 | P–QN4 |
| | BxN | B–K3 | P–K4 | PxN | P–QR4 | B–K2 |
| 12 | BxB | P–QN3[12] | Q–QR4 | BxP[25] | Q–K2 | P–N5 |
| | N–K4 | N–Q4 | Q–N3[17] | ± | B–N3 | N–QN1 |
| 13 | B–K2 | NxN | B–Q2 | | P–K4[27] | N–Q6† |
| | N/4–B5 | QxN | QxP | | ± | BxN |
| 14 | B–B1[6] | B–N2 | R–Q1 | | | BxB[30] |
| | P–QB3[7] | B–N5 | O–O–O | | | ± |
| 15 | Q–N3[8] | P–N4[13] | B–R5 | | | |
| | ∓ | = | B–K2[18] | | | |
| | | | = | | | |

*Notes to supplementary variations 14–24:*

[1] The singular move of the Smyslov Variation. The fianchetto of Black's Bishop gives the game the character of a Grunfeld Defense.

[2] 5 N–R3 is artificial. After 5 . . . B–N2 6 NxP, O–O 7 B–K2, P–B4 8 O–O, N–B3 9 PxP, Black has an excellent game.

[3] This Smyslov maneuver makes this variation playable, though there are few examples illuminating the point. White's center may easily become a substantial asset.

[4] Weakens the Queen Pawn which now becomes a target.

[5] A weakening of White's center, but forced.

[6] Necessary, for after 14 B–Q4, NxNP 15 Q–Q2, N/7–B5, White has lost a Pawn; or 14 B–B5, NxNP 15 Q–N3, BxN 16 QxB, N/7–R5!

[7] Firing at White's center.

[8] After 15 PxP, QxQ 16 RxQ, PxP, Black has a good game, exerting pressure. Evans–Smyslov, Helsinki 1952, continued from the column line 15 . . . PxP 16 NxP, N–R4 17 Q–N5, NxN 18 PxN, P–QR3 19 Q–Q3, R–B1.

| 20 | 21 | 22 | 23 | 24 |
|---|---|---|---|---|
| – – | – – | – – | P–K3[43] | P–K4[47] |
| – – | B–N5[35] | P–QN4[39] | P–K4[44] | P–QB4[48] |
| – – | N–K5 | P–K3 | BxP[45] | P–Q5[49] |
| B–Q2[31] | B–R4 | P–QR3[40] | PxP | N–KB3 |
| QxBP | N–QB3 | P–QR4 | PxP | N–QB3 |
| P–K3 | N–Q2[36] | B–N2 | B–N5† | P–K3 |
| N–B3 | NxQBP | PxP[41] | N–B3 | BxP |
| N–R3 | KN–B3 | PxP | N–KB3 | PxP |
| P–K4 | Q–N3 | RxR | N–B3 | PxP |
| P–B4 | N–N3 | BxR | O–O | B–Q3 |
| B–K2[32] | P–K4 | P–QN3 | O–O | N–B3 |
| PxP | QxP | P–K3 | B–N5 | O–O |
| NxP | B–K3 | PxP | B–KN5 | O–O |
| R–B1 | Q–Q1[37] | PxP | N–B3[46] | P–QR3 |
| Q–Q3 | P–B3 | BxP | = | P–QR4 |
| N–QN5[33] | P–K3 | N–KB3 | | B–N5[50] |
| Q–N1 | R–Q1 | O–O | | = |
| P–K4 | Q–B1 | QN–Q2 | | |
| N–B3 | N–N5 | N–B3 | | |
| B–QB4 | NxN | B–K2 | | |
| O–O[34] | QxN[38] | Q–K2 | | |
| = | ± | N–K5[42] | | |
| | | = | | |

[9] Best. White completes his development before starting action in the center.

[10] Inferior is 9 . . . P–QR4 because of 10 P–QR4, N–B3 11 R–Q1, B–N5 12 P–R3, BxN 13 QxB, P–K3 14 B–Q2, Q–K2 15 B–K1, N–B1? 16 P–Q5 with a great advance for White (Geller–Plater, Bad Salzbrunnen 1957). See Game 7.

[11] Relatively better is 10 P–QR3 so as to retain the White Bishop on the diagonal QR2–KN8 where it supports a possible P–Q5.

[12] Stronger is 12 P–Q5. White then maintains some superiority in space, the point being that if Black captures the Queen Pawn he loses a piece.

[13] Muhring–Lehmann, Utrecht 1954.

[14] Introduced by Flohr, and satisfactory for Black. The unusual 4 . . . B–N5 was played in Szabo–Larsen, Portoroz 1958, which continued 5 BxP, P–K3 6 Q–N3, BxN 7 PxB, QN–Q2. Now if 8 QxP, P–B4 9 PxP, BxP 10 N–B3, O-O, threatening N–K4 with good counterchances. Szabo therefore proceeded with 8 N–B3, N–N3 9 B–K2, B–K2 10 P–B4, O–O 11 B–B3, keeping some advantage.

[15] Also plausible is 5 N–B3 or 5 QN–Q2.

[16] Tolush–Klamen, Moscow 1958, continued 5 . . . B–Q4 6 NxP, P–K3 7 P–QR3, P–B4 8 PxP, BxP 9 P–QN4, B–K2 10 B–N2, N–B3 with equality.

continued ▶

[17] A sharp move, designed to keep White's Bishop at bay.

[18] Not 15 . . . N–N3 16 Q–N4†, and not 15 . . . B–B4 16 B–R6! After the text move, however, 16 B–R6 is also promising. In a game Van Scheltinga–Flohr, Beverwijk 1960, White played 16 B–K2, resulting in a speedy draw.

[19] The so-called Mannheim Variation which, for some time, was considered White's best. The alternative 4 N–B3, QN–Q2 5 P–K4, N–N3 6 P–QR4, P–QR4 7 N–K5 gives White a fine game. But in the above line, Black has better: 4 . . . P–QR3 5 P–QR4, N–B3 6 P–K4, B–N5, when the difficulties are White's.

[20] 4 . . . N–B3 is unusual but not bad: 5 QxBP, B–K3 6 Q–N5, B–Q4! Or 5 P–K3, P–K3 6 BxP, B–Q3 and Black effects a speedy P–K4.

[21] Leads the game into more quiet channels.

[22] Very sharp. After 7 BxP, PxP 8 NxP, Black has a good enough game.

[23] An important Pawn sacrifice. Weak is 8 . . . P–Q5 9 PxN, PxN 10 BxP, QxP 11 B–KN5, Q–B4 12 O–O, and White has the advantage (Dittman–Dr. Herman, Leipzig 1958).

[24] Not 9 NxNP, N–K5 10 B–B4, B–K2 11 P–K6, O–O 12 PxN, BxP 13 Q–R6, B–KB3 14 R–QN1, P–N4 15 N–B7, PxB 16 NxR, QxN, which favors Black.

[25] For a long time this complicated position has been attacked by analysts. One discovery is that 12 . . . PxNP 13 BxP†, KxB 14 N–N5† leads to a winning advantage for White no matter what Black plays: if 14 . . . K–N1 White mates next move; if 14 . . . K–K1 15 P–B7† mates in a few moves; if 14 . . . KxP 15 Q–B6†, K–K4 16 Q–K6† and mate in two; and if 14 . . . K–N3 15 Q–K4†, K–R4 16 P–N4† and wins. Therefore Black must try 12 . . . R–N5, but White still maintains a decisive advantage. True, 13 Q–B2, as recommended by Keres, is not convincing because of 13 . . . NxP. However, White plays 13 Q–Q1, NxP 14 BxP†, K–K2 15 QxQ†, KxQ 16 PxP, or 13 . . . PxNP 14 BxP†, KxB 15 Q–Q5†, K–K1 16 P–B7†, K–K2 17 BxP, RxB 18 O–O with a winning attack.

[26] Threatening to win the Queen with 9 . . . N–N3, but this gesture is too easily parried to have any effect.

[27] See Game 8.

[28] This simplifying maneuver leaves Black with a cramped game.

[29] After this Black is handicapped by the weakness of his Q3 square. Alekhine gave 8 . . . P–QR4 as the better move.

[30] Alekhine–Fine, Kemeri 1937.

[31] A move which in combination with the ensuing system has undergone little testing.

[32] If 8 P–Q5, PxP 9 PxP, N–QN5.

[33] Also plausible is 10 . . . B–B4.

[34] The position is balanced.

[35] 3 . . . P–QB3 offers the possibility of a transposition into the Slav accepted. The text move is considered unsatisfactory.

[36] 5 . . . P–K3 leads to an inferior game for Black after 6 P–KN4, B–N3 7 P–KR4, P–KB3 8 Q–R4†, P–B3 9 NxB, PxN 10 QxBP with a superior game for White (Alekhine–Grunfeld, Semmering 1926).

[37] Not 9 . . . Q–Q2 10 BxN, RPxB 11 NxP! (Bogoljubov–Grekov, Kiev 1914).

[38] White's development is superior.

[39] This attempt to hold the gambit Pawn as long as possible is not nearly as bad as its reputation.

[40] Or 4 . . . P–QB3 5 P–QR4, Q–N3 6 PxP, PxP 7 P–QN3, PxP 8 QxP, P–N5 9 Q–Q5, B–N2 10 B–N5†, B–B3 11 N–K5 with advantage for White.

[41] Only 6 P–QN3 may lead to advantage for White: 6 . . . BPxP 7 PxP, PxP 8 RxR, BxR 9 BxP†.

[42] Grunfeld–Haberditz, Vienna 1948.

[43] A steady alternative to the usual 3 N–KB3.

[44] 3 . . . N–KB3 leads to the more usual variations.

[45] Favorable to Black is 4 PxP, QxQ† 5 KxQ, B–K3.

[46] Marshall–Janowski, New York 1924.

[47] Somewhat optimistic.

[48] Also possible is 3 . . . P–K4 4 PxP, QxQ† 5 KxQ, N–QB3 6 P–B4, B–N5† 7 N–B3, O–O–O†, and Black has the better of it. In the above line White would do better on his 4th move to play 4 BxP, PxP 5 Q–N3! Also, in the above line if 7 K–B2, O–O–O 8 BxP, B–Q8† 9 K–B3, B–N5 mate.

[49] 4 N–KB3, PxP 5 QxP, QxQ 6 NxQ, B–Q2 7 BxP leads to equality (Capablanca–Rubinstein, Kissengen 1928).

[50] White's powerful center is debited with an isolated Pawn, and Black retains a Queenside Pawn majority.

## *Queen's Gambit Accepted Game 7*

*WHITE: Golombek* *BLACK: Smyslov*

*Budapest 1952*

| | WHITE | BLACK | | WHITE | BLACK | | WHITE | BLACK |
|---|---|---|---|---|---|---|---|---|
| 1 | P–Q4 | P–Q4 | 21 | BxB | NxB | 41 | K–R3 | Q–Q7 |
| 2 | P–QB4 | PxP | 22 | QR–B1 | NxRP | 42 | QxQ | BxQ |
| 3 | N–KB3 | N–KB3 | 23 | NxP | QxN | 43 | N–B4 | B–B8 |
| 4 | P–K3 | P–KN3 | 24 | PxN | RxR | 44 | K–N2 | P–N6 |
| 5 | BxP | B–N2 | 25 | RxR | QxRP | 45 | K–B3 | P–N7 |
| 6 | O–O | O–O | 26 | R–N1 | R–B1 | 46 | N–R3 | P–N4 |
| 7 | N–B3 | KN–Q2 | 27 | P–N3 | R–B8† | 47 | P–B5 | P–N5† |
| 8 | Q–K2 | N–N3 | 28 | RxR | QxR† | 48 | K–K4 | B–Q7 |
| 9 | B–N3 | P–QR4 | 29 | K–N2 | Q–B3 | 49 | N–N1 | B–R4 |
| 10 | R–Q1? | P–R5 | 30 | Q–Q3 | P–QN4 | 50 | K–Q5 | K–B1 |
| 11 | B–B2 | N–B3 | 31 | N–Q2 | B–B6 | 51 | P–B6 | B–N3 |
| 12 | P–QR3 | B–Q2 | 32 | P–B3 | P–N5 | 52 | P–K6 | B–N8 |
| 13 | P–Q5 | N–R4 | 33 | N–B4 | Q–N4 | 53 | P–K7† | K–K1 |
| 14 | P–K4 | Q–K1 | 34 | P–B4 | K–N2 | 54 | K–K4 | BxP |
| 15 | B–B4 | N/3–B5 | 35 | K–B3 | Q–R4† | 55 | K–B4 | P–R5 |
| 16 | B–Q3 | P–K4 | 36 | K–N2 | Q–QB4 | 56 | KxP | PxP |
| 17 | PxP e.p. | QBxP | 37 | P–K5 | Q–B3† | 57 | K–R3 | B–N8 |
| 18 | BxP | R–B1 | 38 | K–R3 | P–R4 | 58 | N–B3 | B–Q5 |
| 19 | BxN | NxB | 39 | N–K3 | Q–K3† | 59 | N–Q5 | B–K4 |
| 20 | B–N5 | B–B5 | 40 | K–N2 | Q–R7† | | Resigns | |

*Queen's Gambit Accepted Game 8*

*WHITE: Bogoljubov* *BLACK: Alekhine*

*Mannheim 1934*

| | WHITE | BLACK | | WHITE | BLACK |
|---|---|---|---|---|---|
| 1 | P–Q4 | P–Q4 | 30 | PxP | N–B5 |
| 2 | N–KB3 | N–KB3 | 31 | B–B4 | NxP |
| 3 | P–B4 | PxP | 32 | P–N5 | B–Q1 |
| 4 | Q–R4† | P–B3 | 33 | B–K5 | R–R2 |
| 5 | QxBP | B–B4 | 34 | Q–R5 | N–B5 |
| 6 | N–B3 | P–K3 | 35 | PxP | NxB |
| 7 | P–KN3 | QN–Q2 | 36 | PxN | B–N3† |
| 8 | B–N2 | B–B7 | 37 | K–R1 | P–Q5† |
| 9 | P–K3 | B–K2 | 38 | Q–B3 | QxQ† |
| 10 | O–O | O–O | 39 | RxQ | R–B6 |
| 11 | P–QR3 | P–QR4 | 40 | R/3–B1 | P–Q6 |
| 12 | Q–K2 | B–N3 | 41 | P–B6 | R–B3 |
| 13 | P–K4 | Q–N3 | 42 | NxP | RxN |
| 14 | P–R3 | Q–R3 | 43 | PxR | PxP |
| 15 | Q–K3 | P–B4 | 44 | R–B6 | B–Q5 |
| 16 | P–K5 | N–Q4 | 45 | R–R8† | KxP |
| 17 | NxN | PxN | 46 | RxR | P–Q7 |
| 18 | B–Q2 | B–K5 | 47 | R–B7† | K–N3 |
| 19 | B–B3 | P–B5 | 48 | R–N8† | K–B4 |
| 20 | N–K1 | BxB | 49 | R–B8† | K–K5 |
| 21 | NxB | P–QN4 | 50 | R–B1 | BxP |
| 22 | P–B4 | Q–R3 | 51 | R–B4† | K–Q6 |
| 23 | Q–B3 | P–N5 | 52 | RxP | B–N6 |
| 24 | B–Q2 | N–N3 | 53 | K–N2 | B–K8 |
| 25 | P–N4 | Q–QB3 | 54 | R–QN1 | B–R5 |
| 26 | P–B5 | P–B3 | 55 | R–N3† | K–K7 |
| 27 | N–B4 | KR–B1 | 56 | R–N5 | K–K6 |
| 28 | PxP | BxP | 57 | R–Q5 | K–K7 |
| 29 | N–K6 | P–B6 | 58 | R–B7 | Resigns |

# chapter 22—Cambridge Springs Defense

This line arises after 1 P–Q4, P–Q4 2 P–QB4, P–K3 3 N–QB3, N–KB3 4 B–N5, QN–Q2 5 P–K3, P–B3 6 N–B3, Q–R4. The great American master, Harry Nelson Pillsbury, introduced it at Nuremberg in 1896. Hence it is also known as the Pillsbury Defense. It was only after the Cambridge Springs Tournament of 1904, however, that the defense made an impression.

Pillsbury's idea is based on counterattack: Black pins White's Queen Knight and can increase the pressure with . . . N–K5 and . . . B–QN5. White must also take into consideration the attack on his Queen Bishop on KN5 after PxP. Although in most cases Black enjoys excellent counterplay, the defense is little used today for no discernible reason other than the dictates of fashion.

---

## part 1—BOGOLJUBOV VARIATION

### OBSERVATIONS ON KEY POSITION 1

[A] Setting a well-known trap: after 5 PxP, PxP 6 NxP?, NxN 7 BxQ, B–N5†, White loses a piece.

[B] Now White actually threatens to win the Pawn. 5 PxP, PxP 6 P–K3 transposes into the Exchange Variation.

[C] 5 . . . B–K2 leads to the Orthodox Defense.

[D] If White wishes to avoid 6 . . . Q–R4, he can do so in several ways, as suggested in some of the supplementary variations.

[E] Considered best; 7 PxP is also important and is treated in Part 2. For 7 BxN, see Sup. Var. 1. 7 B–Q3?, N–K5! 8 BxN, PxB 9 N–K5, B–N5! is definitely favorable for Black.

[F] For 7 . . . PxP, see Sup. Var. 2.

[G] Not 8 Q–N3?, PxP! Teichmann's recommendation, 8 Q–B1, is too passive.

1 P–Q4, P–Q4
2 P–QB4, P–K3
3 N–QB3, N–KB3
4 B–N5, QN–Q2[A]
5 P–K3[B], P–B3[C]
6 N–B3[D], Q–R4
7 N–Q2[E], B–N5[F]
8 Q–B2[G]

KEY POSITION 1

Black has launched an attack on White's Queen Knight and now faces an important decision. The immediate 8 . . . N–K5 is not convincing after 9 QNxN, PxN 10 B–R4. But Black has two other systems at his disposal, each offering good chances. He can immediately bring his King into safety and then play for . . . P–K4. In this case he normally must make a temporary Pawn sacrifice. Or he can secure the Bishop-pair with 8 . . . PxP and then try to free his game with . . . P–QB4.

IDEA VARIATIONS 1 AND 2:

(1) 8 . . . O–O 9 B–K2 (for 9 B–R4, the so-called Argentine Variation, see Prac. Var. 1), P–K4 (an excellent Pawn sacrifice which White may well decline) 10 QPxP (after 10 O–O, B–Q3! 11 N–N3, Q–B2, the chances are even, nor does White get anywhere with 10 BxN, NxB 11 QPxP, N–K5), N–K5! 11 N/2xN, PxN 12 O–O, BxN 13 PxB (the end game resulting after 13 QxB, QxQ 14 PxQ, NxP offers equal chances), NxP 14 QxP, N–N3! (this move, suggested by Pachman, is the strongest; for 14 . . . P–B3, see Prac. Var. 2).

(2) 8 . . . PxP 9 BxN, NxB 10 NxP (after 10 BxP, P–K4!, Black finds it easier going), Q–B2 11 P–QR3 (for 11 P–KN3, see Game 1), B–K2 12 B–K2, O–O 13 O–O, R–Q1 14 P–QN4, P–QN3 =.

*Queen's Gambit Declined Game 1*

*WHITE: Alekhine* — *BLACK: Bogoljubov*

*Bad Nauheim 1936*

| | WHITE | BLACK | | WHITE | BLACK |
|---|---|---|---|---|---|
| 1 | P–Q4 | P–Q4 | 19 | N–R5 | P–QR3 |
| 2 | P–QB4 | P–K3 | 20 | N–B4 | P–QN3 |
| 3 | N–QB3 | N–KB3 | 21 | R–N1 | B–B3? |
| 4 | B–N5 | QN–Q2 | 22 | KR–QB1 | Q–R2 |
| 5 | P–K3 | P–B3 | 23 | Q–B2 | R–B2 |
| 6 | N–B3 | Q–R4 | 24 | P–QR4 | B–K2 |
| 7 | N–Q2 | B–N5 | 25 | P–R5 | PxP |
| 8 | Q–B2 | PxP | 26 | PxP | P–QB4 |
| 9 | BxN | NxB | 27 | N–N6 | B–QN4 |
| 10 | NxP | Q–B2 | 28 | P–Q5 | PxP |
| 11 | P–KN3 | O–O | 29 | BxP | B–B1 |
| 12 | B–N2 | B–Q2 | 30 | R–Q1 | R–Q3 |
| 13 | P–QR3 | B–K2 | 31 | B–B4 | RxR† |
| 14 | P–QN4 | N–Q4 | 32 | RxR | Q–N1 |
| 15 | O–O | NxN | 33 | Q–Q3 | Q–K1 |
| 16 | QxN | KR–Q1 | 34 | Q–Q8 | R–K2 |
| 17 | QR–B1 | B–K1 | 35 | QxQ | BxQ |
| 18 | KR–Q1 | QR–B1 | 36 | R–Q8 | B–B3 |

| WHITE | BLACK | WHITE | BLACK |
|---|---|---|---|
| 37 BxP | P–N3 | 43 P–K4 | B–R6 |
| 38 B–B4 | R–N2 | 44 R–K8 | B–KB1 |
| 39 K–B1 | K–N2 | 45 P–R6 | R–B2 |
| 40 K–K2 | B–K2 | 46 P–K5 | B–Q2 |
| 41 R–QB8 | B–N7 | 47 NxB | RxN |
| 42 P–B3 | P–R4 | 48 R–N8 | Resigns |

## PRACTICAL VARIATIONS 1 AND 2:

1 P–Q4, P–Q4 2 P–QB4, P–K3 3 N–QB3, N–KB3 4 B–N5, QN–Q2 5 P–K3, P–B3 6 N–B3, Q–R4 7 N–Q2, B–N5 8 Q–B2

| | *1* | *2* |
|---|---|---|
| *8* | – – | – – |
| | O–O | – – |
| *9* | B–R4 | B–K2 |
| | P–B4![1] | P–K4 |
| *10* | N–N3 | QPxP |
| | Q–R5 | N–K5 |
| *11* | BxN | N/2xN |
| | NxB | PxN |
| *12* | QPxP | O–O |
| | BxN†[2] | BxN |
| *13* | QxB | PxB |
| | N–K5 | NxP |
| *14* | Q–R5 | QxP |
| | QxQ | P–B3 |
| *15* | NxQ | B–B4?[4] |
| | NxQBP | B–B4![5] |
| *16* | PxP | ∓ |
| | PxP[3] | |
| | = | |

*Notes to practical variations 1 and 2:*

[1] Best, according to Alekhine. The Pawn sacrifice 9 . . . P–K4 is dubious.

[2] Also 12 . . . Q–B3 13 PxP, PxP is considered to be satisfactory for Black.

[3] The simplified position facilitates Black's task despite the isolated Pawn.

[4] An interesting error. Correct is 15 B–R4!, B–K3! with equal chances.

[5] This is the game Grunfeld–Bogoljubov, Mahrisch-Ostrau 1929. White faces loss of material.

## part 2—EXCHANGE VARIATION

1 P–Q4, P–Q4
2 P–QB4, P–K3
3 N–QB3, N–KB3
4 B–N5, QN–Q2
5 P–K3, P–B3
6 N–B3, Q–R4
7 PxP

Key Position 2

OBSERVATIONS ON KEY POSITION 2

This position may lead to great complications. The pin of the Queen Knight again plays an important part in making White's job anything but simple. Actually two systems are available to White, namely, 8 Q–N3 and 8 Q–Q2. In the former case Black can get good chances with a fierce Pawn sacrifice. In the latter case White usually sacrifices a Pawn to justify his set-up. At the present time there is doubt as to which of these methods is preferable.

IDEA VARIATIONS 3 AND 4:

(3) 7 . . . NxP (this move is consistent in combination with 6 . . . Q–R4; other possibilities are discussed in Prac. Var. 3-5) 8 Q–N3, B–N5 9 R–B1 (threatening to get the advantage with 10 P–QR3), P–K4! (this Pawn sacrifice is of Yugoslav origin) 10 B–QB4 (bad is 10 PxP, N–B4! 11 Q–B2, N–R5 etc.; also 10 NxP, N/2xN 11 PxN, B–K3 offers better chances to Black), N/2–N3 (leading to great complications; also playable is 10 . . . PxP) 11 BxN, NxB 12 NxP, B–K3 (not 12 . . . P–B3 13 N–B4!) 13 N–B4 (better than 13 P–QR3, NxN, which is advantageous for Black), NxN! 14 NxQ!, NxP† 15 QxB/4, NxQ 16 K–Q2, P–B3 17 B–B4, O–O–O with a difficult game and chances for both sides.

(4) 7 . . . NxP 8 Q–Q2, N/2–N3 (the sharpest; after 8 . . . B–N5 9 R–B1, O–O 10 P–K4, NxN 11 PxN, B–R6 12 R–QN1, P–K4 13 B–Q3, R–K1 14 O–O, P–QN3 15 Q–K2!, White has slightly the better of it) 9 B–Q3 (the most important continuation; other moves are unproductive), NxN 10 PxN, N–Q4 11 R–QB1 (also 11 O–O deserves consideration, e.g., 11 . . . QxBP! 12 Q–K2, B–Q3 13 QR–B1, Q–R4 14 B–N1, N–B6 15 Q–Q2, B–N5 with a position difficult to assess), NxP 12 O–O, B–N5 13 P–QR3, QxP 14 R–R1, Q–N6 15 N–K5 (the most aggressive continuation, according to Alekhine; for 15 B–B2?, see Game 2), N–K5 16 Q–K2, NxB 17 Q–R5, B–K2 18 QR–N1, Q–B6 19 QR–B1, Q–N5 20 R–N1, Q–Q3 21 P–B4, P–KN3 22 Q–R6, B–B1 23 QxN, B–N2. White has fair attacking chances, but it is open to question whether this is sufficient compensation for his Pawns.

*Queen's Gambit Declined Game 2*

*WHITE: Alekhine* *BLACK: Euwe*

*25th Match Game 1935*

| WHITE | BLACK | WHITE | BLACK |
|---|---|---|---|
| 1 P–Q4 | P–Q4 | 14 R–R1 | Q–N6 |
| 2 P–QB4 | P–K3 | 15 B–B2? | Q–Q4 |
| 3 N–KB3 | N–KB3 | 16 P–K4 | NxP |
| 4 N–B3 | P–B3 | 17 QxB | NxB |
| 5 B–N5 | QN–Q2 | 18 N–K5 | P–QR4 |
| 6 P–K3 | Q–R4 | 19 Q–R3 | P–B3 |
| 7 PxP | NxP | 20 B–N6†? | PxB |
| 8 Q–Q2 | N/2–N3 | 21 NxNP | N–B6†! |
| 9 B–Q3 | NxN | 22 QxN | QxQ |
| 10 PxN | N–Q4 | 23 PxQ | R–R4 |
| 11 R–QB1 | NxBP | 24 N–B4 | R–KB4 |
| 12 O–O | B–N5 | 25 N–Q3 | RxP and |
| 13 P–QR3 | QxP | | Black won |

PRACTICAL VARIATIONS 3-5:

1 P–Q4, P–Q4 2 P–QB4, P–K3 3 N–QB3, N–KB3 4 B–N5, QN–Q2 5 P–K3, P–B3 6 N–B3, Q–R4 7 PxP

| | 3 | 4 | 5 |
|---|---|---|---|
| 7 | – – | – – | – – |
| | KPxP | BPxP | N–K5 |
| 8 | B–Q3 | BxN! | PxKP |
| | N–K5 | NxB | PxP |
| 9 | O–O! | B–Q3[3] | B–R4![4] |
| | NxB[1] | ± | NxN |
| 10 | NxN | | PxN |
| | B–K2 | | QxP† |
| 11 | P–B4! | | N–Q2[5] |
| | N–B3 | | ± |
| 12 | Q–K1 | | |
| | Q–N3 | | |
| 13 | R–N1 | | |
| | B–Q2 | | |
| 14 | N–B3[2] | | |
| | ± | | |

*Notes to practical variations 3–5:*

[1] Or 9 . . . NxN 10 PxN, QxBP 11 P–K4, PxP 12 R–K1 with a promising game for White.

[2] Janowski–Bogoljubov, New York 1924.

[3] White has good prospects.

[4] Better than 9 Q–R4!?, QxQ 10 NxQ, B–N5† 11 K–Q1, P–N4! etc.

[5] Black's development is inferior.

## SUPPLEMENTARY VARIATIONS 1-7:

1 P–Q4, P–Q4 2 P–QB4, P–K3 3 N–QB3, N–KB3 4 B–N5, QN–Q2

| | *1* | *2* | *3* | *4* | *5* | *6* | *7* |
|---|---|---|---|---|---|---|---|
| *5* | P–K3 | – – | – – | – – | – – | – – | N–B3 |
| | P–B3 | – – | – – | – – | – – | – – | P–B3 |
| *6* | N–B3 | – – | – – | B–Q3 | Q–B2 | P–QR3 | P–K4 |
| | Q–R4 | – – | B–K2 | Q–R4 | Q–R4 | B–K2 | PxP |
| *7* | BxN | N–Q2 | B–Q3 | B–R4 | PxP | N–B3 | NxP |
| | NxB | PxP[2] | O–O | PxP[7] | NxP | O–O[11] | B–K2[13] |
| *8* | B–Q3 | BxN | O–O | BxBP | P–K4 | Q–B2 | N–B3 |
| | B–N5 | NxB | P–KR3 | P–QN4 | NxN | PxP | O–O |
| *9* | Q–N3 | NxP[3] | B–R4 | B–QN3 | B–Q2! | BxP | Q–B2 |
| | PxP | Q–B2 | P–B4![6] | B–N2 | Q–R5[9] | N–Q4 | P–K4![14] |
| *10* | BxBP | R–B1[4] | = | N–B3 | QxN | BxB | O–O–O[15] |
| | O–O | N–Q4 | | P–B4 | P–QR4 | QxB | PxP |
| *11* | O–O | B–Q3 | | PxP | N–B3 | N–K4 | NxP |
| | BxN | NxN | | BxP | B–N5 | N/4–B3 | Q–R4 |
| *12* | PxB | PxN | | O–O | Q–B1 | N–N3 | B–K3 |
| | P–QN3 | B–K2 | | O–O[8] | O–O | P–QN3 | N–B4[16] |
| *13* | N–K5 | O–O | | | P–QR3 | O–O | = |
| | B–N2 | O–O | | | BxB† | P–B4[12] | |
| *14* | B–K2 | Q–R5 | | | QxB | = | |
| | P–B4[1] | P–KN3 | | | P–K4[10] | | |
| *15* | = | Q–R6 | | | = | | |
| | | B–B3![5] | | | | | |
| | | = | | | | | |

*Notes to supplementary variations 1-7:*

[1] With a fully satisfactory game for Black.

[2] Suggested by Rubinstein.

[3] 9 BxP is also good, since 9 . . . P–K4 fails against 10 Q–N3!

[4] A measure against . . . P–QB4.

[5] Black's Bishop-pair compensates for his inferior development.

[6] Black's game is promising (Tartakower–Spielmann, Semmering 1926).

[7] Better than 7 . . . N–K5 8 N–K2! ±.

[8] With chances for both sides.

[9] Most likely stronger than 9 . . . P–K4 10 PxN, PxP 11 PxP, B–N5 12 QR–N1, which is slightly better for White (Kotov–Eliskases, Stockholm 1952).

[10] Black has no serious problems.

[11] Also good is 7 . . . N–K5 or 7 . . . P–KR3 8 B–R4, N–K5! etc.

[12] Black has a satisfactory game.

[13] The most solid reply; 7 . . . P–KR3 is also playable.

[14] Suggested by Lundin; 9 . . . P–QN3 10 O–O–O is promising for White.

[15] Exchanging on K5 is favorable to Black. The text move leads to an even game.

[16] Alekhine–Lundin, Orebro 1935.

# chapter 23—Catalan Opening

This opening derives its name from Catalonia, Spain, where it seems to have had its debut. It was so designated by Dr. Tartakover.

The moves 1 P–Q4, N–KB3 2 P–QB4, P–K3 3 P–KN3 constitute the Catalan, and it is White's 3rd move, a prelude to the fianchetto of the King Bishop, which is the distinguishing trait. Its virtues are manifold. To begin with, on the negative side, it avoids the obstreperous Nimzo-Indian or Queen's Indian and, significantly, gives White the direction of the opening. On the positive side, many of its evolving patterns yield White an advantage.

Its basic feature is the pressure of White's King Bishop (at KN2) on Black's Q4. This can be met in different ways, each with varying plus and minus factors. Black will have the opportunity during the course of the game, for example, to capture White's Queen Bishop Pawn with his Queen Pawn. In this case, he will undoubtedly benefit from the absence of the Queen Bishop Pawn and, as will be shown, obtain good chances. In turn, however, he must perforce reckon with the extended scope of White's King Bishop on the long diagonal. Or Black may prefer to support his center with . . . P–QB3, and rest his case on a passive but reasonably secure position.

Capture and non-capture of White's Queen Bishop Pawn by Black's Queen Pawn are the principal subdivisions of the Catalan, the Catalan Accepted, and the Catalan Declined. Their sharp and interesting lines commend themselves to the attention of the combative chess player.

---

## part 1—CATALAN ACCEPTED

### OBSERVATIONS ON KEY POSITION 1

[A] Other moves here are 3 . . . P–B4 4 P–Q5!, the modern Benoni. But 3 . . . P–B4 4 N–KB3, PxP 5 NxP, P–Q4 reaches easy equality. For 3 . . . B–N5†, see Sup. Var. 1.

[B] Precise play, though 4 N–KB3 is also feasible.

Black abandons the center for a momentary Pawn plus. By utilizing White's loss of time in recovering the Pawn, Black can obtain active Queenside counterplay beginning with 5 . . . QN–Q2! or exert pressure on the center with the maneuver . . . B–Q2–B3. Each line yields him satisfactory chances.

1 P–Q4, N–KB3
2 P–QB4, P–K3
3 P–KN3, P–Q4[A]
4 B–N2[B], PxP
5 Q–R4†

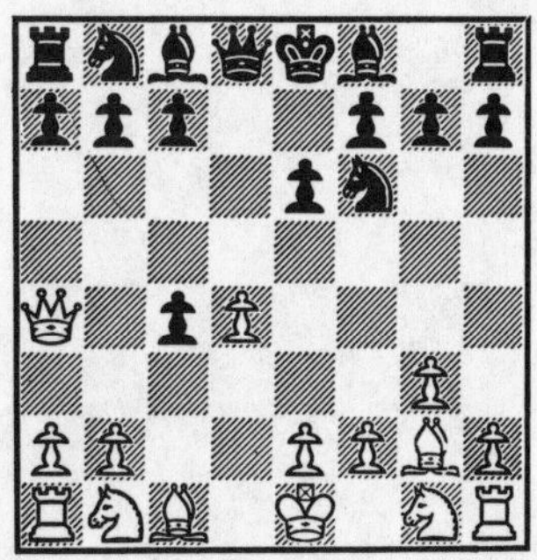

KEY POSITION 1

IDEA VARIATIONS 1–3:

(1) 5 . . . QN–Q2 6 QxBP, P–QR3 7 Q–B2!, P–B4 8 N–KB3, P–QN4 (O'Kelly recommends 8 . . . P–QN3 to avoid complications, and then if 9 N–K5, N–Q4; not so good, however, is 8 . . . PxP 9 NxP, Q–N3 10 N–N3, B–N5† 11 B–Q2, N–K4 12 O–O, when Black's position is uncomfortable, as in Smyslov–O'Kelly, Groningen 1946) 9 N–K5, N–Q4 10 BxN (if 10 NxN, QxN 11 PxP, B–N2 12 O–O, R–B1 with advantage to Black; see Game 1), PxB 11 NxN, QxN 12 PxP, B–N2 13 O–O, Q–B3 14 P–QN4, P–QR4 (14 . . . P–Q5 is a good alternative) 15 B–R3!, P–Q5 16 P–B3, P–R4. Black enjoys attacking chances. That they are equal to White's Pawn plus is debatable. Practical examples are lacking.

If 6 QN–Q2, P–B4! 7 NxP, PxP 8 B–B4, B–K2 9 N–Q6†, K–B1!, or if 6 N–KB3, P–QR3 7 N–B3, R–QN1!, and Black's position is excellent. After 6 QxBP, P–QR3 7 N–KB3, P–QN4 8 Q–B6, R–QN1 9 O–O, B–N2, Black's game is easy. See Prac. Var. 2.

(2) 5 . . . B–Q2 6 QxBP, B–B3 7 P–B3, QN–Q2 8 P–K4, N–N3 (if 8 . . . B–K2 9 N–K2, P–QR3 10 QN–B3, O–O 11 B–K3, N–N3 12 Q–Q3±) 9 Q–Q3, Q–Q2 10 N–B3, B–N5 11 B–K3 (if 11 B–Q2, R–Q1 12 KN–K2, BxN 13 BxB, B–N4 14 Q–K3±), B–N4 12 Q–B2, P–B4 13 O–O–O! (the line is Bouwmeester–Kottnauer, Beverwijk 1954, up to 13 O–O–O; it continued with 13 . . . N–B5 14 B–B2, B–R3 15 PxP, Q–B3 16 KN–K2, BxP 17 N–Q4!, Q–B1 18 Q–R4†±), BxN 14 QxB, N–R5 15 Q–R3 with chances for both sides.

(3) 5 . . . B–Q2 6 QxBP, B–B3 7 N–KB3, QN–Q2 8 N–B3, N–N3 9 Q–Q3, B–N5 10 O–O, O–O 11 R–Q1 (11 P–QR3 gets the "two Bishops," but 11 . . . BxN 12 PxB, B–K5 leaves Black with adequate compensation in the pressure on the white squares), P–KR3 12 B–Q2, Q–K2 13 P–QR3, BxN 14 QxB, KR–Q1 (if 14 . . . N–K5, then 15 Q–N4!) 15 B–K1, QR–B1 with equal chances (Smyslov–Keres, The Hague 1948).

*Catalan Opening Game 1*

*WHITE: Dunkelblum* — *BLACK: Euwe*

*Belgium–Netherlands, Antwerp 1950*

| WHITE | BLACK | WHITE | BLACK |
|---|---|---|---|
| 1 P–Q4 | N–KB3 | 7 Q–B2 | P–B4 |
| 2 P–QB4 | P–K3 | 8 N–KB3 | P–QN4 |
| 3 P–KN3 | P–Q4 | 9 N–K5 | N–Q4 |
| 4 B–N2 | PxP | 10 NxN | QxN |
| 5 Q–R4† | QN–Q2 | 11 PxP | B–N2 |
| 6 QxBP | P–QR3 | 12 O–O | R–B1 |

| | WHITE | BLACK | | WHITE | BLACK |
|---|---|---|---|---|---|
| 13 | Q–N3 | BxP | 24 | R/7–Q4 | P–K4 |
| 14 | B–Q2 | O–O | 25 | N–Q5 | R–Q2 |
| 15 | R–Q1 | Q–K2 | 26 | Q–K3 | PxR |
| 16 | N–B3 | N–B3 | 27 | RxP | KR–Q1 |
| 17 | BxB | QxB | 28 | N–K7† | K–B1 |
| 18 | B–K1 | R–B2 | 29 | N–B6 | Q–B4 |
| 19 | R–Q3 | N–N5 | 30 | RxR | QxQ† |
| 20 | QR–Q1 | Q–R1 | 31 | KxQ | RxR |
| 21 | R–Q7? | NxBP! | 32 | N–N4 | P–QR4 |
| 22 | BxN | BxB† | | | Black Won |
| 23 | KxB | Q–R2† | | | |

PRACTICAL VARIATIONS 1–7:

1 P–Q4, N–KB3 2 P–QB4, P–K3 3 P–KN3, P–Q4 4 B–N2, PxP 5 Q–R4†

| | *1* | *2* | *3* | *4* | *5* | *6* | *7* |
|---|---|---|---|---|---|---|---|
| *5* | – – | – – | – – | – – | – – | – – | – – |
| | QN–Q2 | – – | – – | – – | B–Q2 | – – | – – |
| *6* | QxBP | – – | – – | – – | QxBP | – – | – – |
| | P–QR3 | – – | – – | – – | B–B3[5] | – – | – – |
| *7* | N–KB3 | – – | Q–B2 | – – | P–B3 | N–KB3 | – – |
| | P–QN4 | – – | P–B4 | – – | Q–Q4[6] | B–Q4 | – – |
| *8* | Q–B6 | – – | N–KB3 | – – | Q–B3[7] | Q–R4† | Q–Q3! |
| | R–R2 | R–QN1 | P–QN4 | – – | P–K4[8] | B–B3[11] | P–B4[13] |
| *9* | O–O![1] | O–O | P–QR4[2] | PxP | PxP | Q–Q1 | N–B3 |
| | B–N2 | B–N2 | B–N2 | BxP[4] | N–N5![9] | P–K4![12] | B–B3 |
| *10* | Q–B2 | Q–B2 | O–O | N–K5 | P–K4 | O–O | O–O |
| | P–B4 | P–B4 | R–B1 | R–QN1 | Q–N4! | PxP | QN–Q2 |
| *11* | P–QR4 | P–QR4! | PxNP | N–B6 | P–QR3[10] | QxP | R–Q1 |
| | ± | Q–N3! | PxNP | Q–B2 | NxKP | QxQ | Q–N3![14] |
| *12* | | = | Q–N3 | NxR | B–B1 | = | P–K4! |
| | | | Q–N3 | BxP† | Q–B4 | | PxP |
| *13* | | | N–R3 | K–Q1 | B–K3 | | NxP |
| | | | B–B3![3] | QxN | QxQ† | | B–B4 |
| *14* | | | = | ∓ | NxQ | | NxB![15] |
| | | | | | QN–Q2 | | ± |
| | | | | | = | | |

*Notes to practical variations 1-7:*

[1] If 9 B–B4, then B–N2! is strong.

[2] Alekhine's original intention. For the stronger 9 N–K5 see Idea Var. 1.

[3] 13 . . . B–QR3? 14 N–B4!, PxN 15 QxQ, NxQ 16 RxB ± (Keres–Platz, Budapest 1952).

[4] Better than 9 . . . NxP 10 B–K3! ±.

[5] Kevitz suggests 6 . . . N–B3 7 N–KB3, N–QR4 8 Q–Q3, P–B4. Black may play for center pressure with . . . Q–N3 and . . . R–Q1, or for a Queenside majority by a timely . . . P–B5 and P–QN4.

continued ▸

[6] This interesting continuation derives from Czechoslovakian chess circles.

[7] If 8 Q–Q3, then P–K4!

[8] The point of the system.

[9] Aggressive reinforcement compared to 9 . . . KN–Q2, recommended by the Dutch theorist Van den Berg, after which 10 P–K4! gives White a good game.

[10] 11 B–B1?, Q–N3!

[11] 8 . . . Q–Q2 also suffices for equality.

[12] For 9 . . . QN–Q2, see Game 2.

[13] Nor can 8 . . . B–K5 9 Q–K3! P–B4 10 PxP, Q–R4† 11 N–B3, BxP 12 Q–B4! keep White from getting the better game.

[14] Unfavorable is 11 . . . PxP 12 NxP, BxB 13 KxB, B–K2 14 Q–B3! (Alekhine–Rabar, 1942).

[15] This promising Pawn sacrifice derives from Hans Muller. After 14 . . . BxP† 15 K–B1, PxN 16 N–R4, Q–R4 17 KxB, QxN 18 Q–Q6, White has fine chances.

## *Catalan Opening Game 2*

*WHITE: Smyslov* *BLACK: Taimanov*

*Tchigorin Memorial Tournament, Leningrad 1951*

| WHITE | BLACK | WHITE | BLACK | WHITE | BLACK |
|---|---|---|---|---|---|
| 1 P–Q4 | N–KB3 | 15 N–Q3 | B–Q3 | 29 B–Q6 | R–Q2 |
| 2 P–QB4 | P–K3 | 16 N–B5! | KBxN | 30 B–K5 | P–B3 |
| 3 P–KN3 | P–Q4 | 17 PxB | QxQ | 31 R–Q3! | N–R5 |
| 4 B–N2 | PxP | 18 KRxQ | N–R5 | 32 PxB | PxB |
| 5 Q–R4† | B–Q2 | 19 BxBP | KR–B1 | 33 PxP | RxR |
| 6 QxBP | B–B3 | 20 B–Q6 | NxBP | 34 BxR | K–B1 |
| 7 N–KB3 | B–Q4 | 21 R–Q4 | B–Q4 | 35 R–K1 | R–Q1 |
| 8 Q–R4† | B–B3 | 22 B–B1 | R–B3 | 36 B–B2 | N–B6 |
| 9 Q–Q1 | QN–Q2 | 23 B–K7 | BxN | 37 RxP | K–K2 |
| 10 O–O | P–KR3 | 24 BxN | B–K5 | 38 B–N3 | R–Q7 |
| 11 QN–Q2 | B–N5 | 25 B–K7 | B–Q4 | 39 R–QB5 | N–K7† |
| 12 N–B4 | O–O | 26 P–QN4! | N–K5 | 40 K–B1 | N–Q5 |
| 13 B–B4 | N–N3 | 27 P–B3 | N–B6 | 41 R–B7† | K–K1 |
| 14 QN–K5 | B–K5 | 28 P–K4 | R–B2 | 42 RxQNP | Resigns |

## *Catalan Opening Game 3*

*WHITE: Minev* *BLACK: O'Kelly*

*Lasker Memorial Tournament, Berlin 1962*

| WHITE | BLACK | WHITE | BLACK | WHITE | BLACK |
|---|---|---|---|---|---|
| 1 P–Q4 | N–KB3 | 10 N–Q6† | BxN | 19 QPxN | PxP |
| 2 P–QB4 | P–K3 | 11 BxB | B–N2 | 20 PxP | O–O |
| 3 P–KN3 | P–Q4 | 12 N–B3 | P–B5 | 21 R–N3 | Q–B3 |
| 4 B–N2 | PxP | 13 P–KN4 | N/2–B3 | 22 RxR | RxR |
| 5 Q–R4† | QN–Q2 | 14 B–B5 | N–B5 | 23 Q–Q4 | P–B6 |
| 6 N–Q2 | P–B4 | 15 KR–N1 | NxB† | 24 P–K4 | P–B7 |
| 7 NxP | P–QR3 | 16 RxN | N–K5 | Resigns. | |
| 8 B–B4 | P–QN4 | 17 P–N4 | P–QR4 | | |
| 9 Q–Q1 | N–Q4 | 18 P–QR3 | NxB | | |

*Catalan Opening Game 4*

*WHITE: Botvinnik* *BLACK: Vidmar*

*Groningen Tournament 1946*

| | WHITE | BLACK | | WHITE | BLACK | | WHITE | BLACK |
|---|---|---|---|---|---|---|---|---|
| 1 | P–Q4 | P–Q4 | 21 | B–B1 | N–B3! | 41 | R–N7† | K–R1 |
| 2 | N–KB3 | N–KB3 | 22 | NxN | BxN | 42 | P–N4 | P–K4 |
| 3 | P–B4 | P–K3 | 23 | P–QR4 | B–K1 | 43 | P–Q5 | R/B8–B4 |
| 4 | P–KN3 | PxP | 24 | P–R5 | N–R1 | 44 | R–R7† | K–N1 |
| 5 | Q–R4† | Q–Q2 | 25 | P–R6 | P–QN3 | 45 | R–N7† | K–R1 |
| 6 | QxBP | Q–B3 | 26 | P–QN4 | K–N1 | 46 | RxP | R–QN1 |
| 7 | QN–Q2 | QxQ | 27 | R–B3 | P–QB3 | 47 | RxR† | KxR |
| 8 | NxQ | B–N5† | 28 | QR–B1 | P–B3 | 48 | P–R7† | K–N2 |
| 9 | B–Q2 | BxB† | 29 | N–N1 | B–Q2 | 49 | N–Q6† | KxP |
| 10 | KNxB | N–B3 | 30 | N–R3 | N–B2 | 50 | N–K8 | K–N3 |
| 11 | P–K3 | N–QN5 | 31 | P–N5 | NxNP | 51 | NxP | R–B6† |
| 12 | K–K2 | B–Q2 | 32 | BxN | PxB | 52 | K–B2 | R–B2 |
| 13 | B–N2 | B–B3 | 33 | R–B7 | R–QB1? | 53 | P–R4 | R–B2 |
| 14 | P–B3 | N–Q2 | 34 | R–N7† | K–R1 | 54 | N–R5 | K–B2 |
| 15 | P–QR3 | N–Q4 | 35 | RxB! | RxR | 55 | P–N5 | PxP |
| 16 | P–K4 | N/4–N3 | 36 | NxP | KR–QB1 | 56 | PxP | R–R2 |
| 17 | N–R5 | B–N4† | 37 | RxNP | P–R3 | 57 | N–B6 | R–R7† |
| 18 | K–K3 | O–O–O | 38 | RxP† | K–N1 | 58 | K–N3 | R–R8 |
| 19 | KR–QB1 | N–N1 | 39 | R–N7† | K–R1 | 59 | K–N2 | R–R1 |
| 20 | P–N3 | B–Q2 | 40 | R–R7† | K–N1 | 60 | P–N6 | Resigns |

---

## part 2—CATALAN DECLINED

### OBSERVATIONS ON KEY POSITION 2

1 P–Q4, N–KB3
2 P–QB4, P–K3
3 P–KN3, P–Q4
4 B–N2, B–K2
5 N–KB3, O–O
6 O–O

KEY POSITION 2

Black's decision to maintain the center leads to a closed position. Black, of course, may capture the Bishop Pawn later on. But this plan is ineffective. His general procedure should be to consolidate the center via . . . P–QB3, develop his Queen Bishop on the wing, and "break" with . . . P–QB4 at the right time. Success in these goals will give him an easy game.

Although White enjoys some superiority in space, he will find it difficult to turn this to account. Even White's eventual P–K4 hardly enhances his prospects. White, too, often develops his Queen Bishop on the wing.

### IDEA VARIATIONS 4 AND 5:

(4) 6 . . . QN–Q2 7 N–B3, PxP! 8 P–K4, P–B3 (Alekhine suggests 8 . . . P–B4 9 P–Q5, PxP 10 P–K5, P–Q5! 11 PxN, BxP, whereupon Black has sufficient compensation for the piece) 9 P–QR4, P–QR4 (Botvinnik–Lasker, Moscow 1936; also good is 9 . . . P–QN3, e.g., 10 Q–K2,

B–R3 11 P–N3, B–N5! 12 B–N2, P–B4 with equality) 10 Q–K2, N–N3 11 R–Q1, B–N5 12 N–K5, Q–K2 13 B–K3, B–Q2 14 NxQBP, NxN 15 QxN, P–K4! (Botvinnik–Lasker continued 15 . . . P–QN4 16 Q–K2!, QR–N1? 17 PxP, PxP 18 P–K5! and Black was lost) 16 PxP, N–N5. Black has near-equality.

6 . . . QN–Q2 is the strongest continuation. For other moves see Prac. Var. 10–12. An interesting gambit is initiated by 7 N–B3. Weaker than 7 . . . PxP is 7 . . . P–B3 8 Q–Q3!, P–QN3 9 P–N3, B–N2 10 P–K4, PxKP? 11 NxP, P–B4 12 N–B3. Now White has a good game, as in Botvinnik–Tylor, Nottingham 1936.

(5) 6 . . . QN–Q2 7 QN–Q2 (less sharp with fewer chances), P–B3 8 P–N3 (also important is 8 Q–B2, P–QN3 9 P–K4, B–N2!, e.g., 10 P–N3, R–B1 11 R–Q1, Q–B2 12 B–N2, KR–Q1 13 QR–B1, Q–N1=; now if 14 Q–Q3, N–B4! or 14 . . . P–QR4 15 N–K5, Q–R1 with equal chances), P–QN3 9 B–N2, B–N2 (better than 9 . . . B–R3 10 R–B1, R–B1 11 R–B2, P–B4 12 Q–R1±) 10 R–B1 (10 P–K3, R–B1 11 Q–K2, R–B2 12 KR–Q1, Q–R1 13 N–K5, NxN! 14 PxN, N–Q2 is too shallow a line for White to obtain real prospects), R–B1 11 P–K3, Q–B2 (Black should not precipitate . . . P–B4; in Keres–Kotov, Zurich 1953, Black experienced difficulties after 11 . . . P–B4 12 Q–K2, BPxP 13 NxP!, N–B4 14 KR–Q1) 12 Q–K2, Q–N1 13 KR–Q1, KR–Q1 14 N–K5 (up to this point the line is Najdorf–Foltys, Amsterdam 1950), NxN! 15 PxN, N–Q2=.

PRACTICAL VARIATIONS 8–12:

1 P–Q4, N–KB3 2 P–QB4, P–K3 3 P–KN3, P–Q4 4 B–N2, B–K2 5 N–KB3, O–O 6 O–O

| | *8* | *9* | *10* | *11* | *12* |
|---|---|---|---|---|---|
| *6* | — — | — — | — — | — — | — — |
| | QN–Q2 | — — | PxP | P–B4 | P–B3 |
| 7 | Q–B2[1] | P–N3 | Q–B2! | PxQP | N–B3 |
| | P–B3 | P–B4! | P–QR3[5] | NxP[6] | QN–Q2[7] |
| *8* | R–Q1[2] | P–K3 | P–QR4! | N–B3! | Q–Q3![8] |
| | P–QN3 | P–QN3 | N–B3 | NxN | ± |
| *9* | P–N3 | B–N2 | R–Q1 | PxN | |
| | B–N2 | B–N2[4] | N–QR4 | PxP | |
| *10* | N–B3 | = | QN–Q2 | PxP | |
| | R–B1 | | P–QN4 | B–Q2 | |
| *11* | P–K4 | | PxP | N–K5 | |
| | NxP[3] | | PxP | ± | |

| | 8 | 9 | 10 | 11 | 12 |
|---|---|---|---|---|---|
| 12 | NxN | | P–N3! | | |
| | PxN | | ± | | |
| 13 | QxP | | | | |
| | ± | | | | |

*Notes to practical variations 8–12:*

[1] For 7 N–B3 and 7 QN–Q2 see Idea Var. 4 and 5 respectively.

[2] For 8 B–B4, see Game 5.

[3] Better is 11 . . . Q–B2.

[4] Black has equality (Pachman).

[5] 7 . . . P–QN4? 8 P–QR4, P–B3 9 PxP, PxP 10 N–N5! and wins. 7 . . . QN–Q2 8 QN–Q2 also favors White.

[6] 7 . . . KPxP transposes into the Tarrasch Defense.

[7] Now 7 . . . PxP is wrong because of 8 N–K5. For 7 . . . P–QN3 see Game 6.

[8] See Botvinnik–Tylor in Idea Var. 4.

*Catalan Opening Game 5*

*WHITE: Novotelnov* *BLACK: Averbach*

*USSR Championship 1951*

| WHITE | BLACK | WHITE | BLACK | WHITE | BLACK |
|---|---|---|---|---|---|
| 1 P–Q4 | N–KB3 | 12 BPxP | KPxP | 23 P–QR4 | P–KR4! |
| 2 P–QB4 | P–K3 | 13 NxP | NxN | 24 N–B4 | P–R5 |
| 3 N–KB3 | P–Q4 | 14 PxN | PxP | 25 Q–B2 | P–R6 |
| 4 P–KN3 | B–K2 | 15 Q–R4 | N–B4! | 26 Q–K2 | N–Q5 |
| 5 B–N2 | O–O | 16 QxQP | N–K3 | 27 Q–B1 | Q–B1? |
| 6 O–O | QN–Q2 | 17 Q–K4 | R–B4! | 28 BxN | BxB |
| 7 Q–B2 | P–B3 | 18 B–K3 | BxP | 29 R–Q2 | Q–N5 |
| 8 B–B4 | P–QN3 | 19 Q–N1 | BxB | 30 QR–Q1? | BxBP† |
| 9 KN–Q2 | B–N2 | 20 KxB | R–Q4 | 31 QxB | QxR† |
| 10 P–K4 | R–B1 | 21 R–Q1 | B–B3 | Resigns | |
| 11 QN–B3 | P–B4! | 22 K–N1 | R–K1 | | |

*Catalan Opening Game 6*

*WHITE: Szabo* *BLACK: Book*

*Saltsjobaden 1948*

| WHITE | BLACK | WHITE | BLACK | WHITE | BLACK |
|---|---|---|---|---|---|
| 1 N–KB3 | P–Q4 | 9 PxP | BPxP | 17 Q–N4 | P–KN3 |
| 2 P–KN3 | N–KB3 | 10 B–B4 | KN–Q2 | 18 BxP | B–Q6 |
| 3 B–N2 | P–K3 | 11 R–B1 | NxN | 19 BxR | B–KB4 |
| 4 O–O | B–K2 | 12 BxN | P–QN4 | 20 Q–K2 | B–N4 |
| 5 P–B4 | O–O | 13 P–K4! | P–N5 | 21 P–KR4 | BxN |
| 6 P–Q4 | P–B3 | 14 N–K2 | Q–R4 | 22 BxB | N–Q2 |
| 7 N–B3 | P–QN3 | 15 PxP | PxP | 23 B–B3 | B–K3 |
| 8 N–K5 | B–R3 | 16 N–B4! | BxR | 24 B–Q6! | Resigns |

## part 3—CATALAN GAMBIT

1 P–Q4, N–KB3
2 P–QB4, P–K3
3 P–KN3, P–Q4
4 B–N2, PxP
5 N–KB3

KEY POSITION 3

OBSERVATIONS ON KEY POSITION 3

With 5 N–KB3 White temporarily abandons the Bishop Pawn, accentuating development. Although Black can hardly hope to keep the Pawn, he can rally his forces for counterplay during the time it takes White to recover the lost material. In most variations, . . . P–QB4 plays a vital role. While the Catalan Gambit is currently in vogue, it is by no means certain that it is preferable to 5 Q–R4†.

IDEA VARIATIONS 6 AND 7:

(6) 5 . . . P–QR3 6 N–K5, P–B4 7 B–K3.

Until recently 5 . . . P–QR3 was considered best for Black. An alternative to 6 N–K5 is 6 O–O, e.g., 6 . . . P–QN4 7 P–QR4 (or 7 N–K5, N–Q4!=), B–N2 8 N–B3!, P–N5 (safer is 8 . . . P–B3=). If 9 N–N1 in reply to 8 . . . P–N5, then P–B4 10 QN–Q2, PxP 11 NxBP, B–B4 12 B–N5, P–R3 13 BxN, QxB 14 R–B1, N–Q2 15 P–K3! with good chances for the Pawn. See Game 7.

After 5 . . . P–QR3 6 N–K5, P–B4, Haberditz suggests 7 B–K3 rather than 7 P–K3, PxP or 7 N–R3, PxP 8 QNxP, B–B4!, after which Black stands well. 7 . . . N–Q4 in answer to 7 B–K3 could continue 8 PxP, NxB 9 QxQ†, KxQ 10 PxN, K–K1 11 P–B6, PxP 12 NxP/4 with advantage for White. Another line favorable to White is 8 . . . Q–R4† 9 Q–Q2, QxQ† 10 BxQ, BxP 11 NxBP, while if 8 . . . BxP, then 9 BxB, Q–R4† 10 N–B3, NxN 11 Q–Q2, QxB 12 QxN, recovering the Pawn with a good game. But 8 . . . Q–B2! and the position seems satisfactory for Black.

(7) 5 . . . P–B4 6 O–O (if 6 Q–R4†, B–Q2! 7 QxBP, B–B3 8 PxP, QN–Q2 9 P–QN4, P–QR4, Black has a good game), N–B3 7 Q–R4 (7 N–K5, N–Q4!), B–Q2 (7 . . . N–Q2 seems better; e.g., 8 PxP, BxP 9 QxBP, O–O 10 N–B3, P–QR3 11 N–K4, B–K2 with equal chances) 8 PxP (8 QxBP, P–QN4! is dangerous), N–QR4 9 Q–B2, BxP 10 N–K5 (to be considered is 10 B–Q2, e.g., 10 . . . R–QB1 11 B–B3, O–O? 12 N–N5!, P–KN3 13 Q–Q2 with good attacking chances), R–QB1 11 N–QB3, P–QN4 12 B–N5, Q–N3 13 QR–Q1 (Barcza-Richter). White has a fine initiative for the Pawn.

## *Catalan Opening Game 7*

*WHITE: Bolbochan* *BLACK: Duckstein*

*Match Game, Vienna 1956*

| WHITE | BLACK | WHITE | BLACK | WHITE | BLACK |
|---|---|---|---|---|---|
| 1 P–Q4 | N–KB3 | 8 N–B3! | P–N5 | 15 P–K3! | O–O |
| 2 P–QB4 | P–K3 | 9 N–N1 | P–B4 | 16 PxP | B–R2 |
| 3 P–KN3 | P–Q4 | 10 QN–Q2 | PxP | 17 N–R5 | B–Q4 |
| 4 B–N2 | PxP | 11 NxBP | B–B4 | 18 N–B6 | KR–B1 |
| 5 N–KB3 | P–QR3 | 12 B–N5! | P–R3 | 19 KN–K5! | N–B1 |
| 6 O–O | P–QN4 | 13 BxN | QxB | 20 N–N4 | Q–N4 |
| 7 P–QR4 | B–N2 | 14 R–B1 | N–Q2 | 21 BxB | Resigns |

PRACTICAL VARIATIONS 13–17:

1 P–Q4, N–KB3 2 P–QB4, P–K3 3 P–KN3, P–Q4 4 B–N2, PxP 5 N–KB3

| | *13* | *14* | *15* | *16* | *17* |
|---|---|---|---|---|---|
| *5* | – – | – – | – – | – – | – – |
| | P–B3 | B–N5†[2] | – – | QN–Q2 | – – |
| *6* | N–K5 | B–Q2[3] | – – | QN–Q2[7] | O–O |
| | B–N5† | B–K2! | – – | N–N3 | P–B3 |
| *7* | B–Q2! | Q–B2 | – – | O–O | P–QR4 |
| | QxP | B–Q2 | – – | P–B4 | P–QN4 |
| *8* | BxB | N–K5 | O–O | NxP | PxP |
| | QxN | N–B3! | B–B3 | NxN | PxP |
| *9* | N–R3[1] | QxBP[4] | QxBP | Q–R4† | N–B3 |
| | ± | NxN | B–Q4 | B–Q2 | Q–N3 |
| *10* | | PxN | Q–B2 | QxN | P–N3 |
| | | N–Q4![5] | N–B3 | Q–N3 | B–N5 |
| *11* | | BxN | B–B3 | P–N3[8] | N–R2 |
| | | PxB | B–K5[6] | ± | B–K2 |
| *12* | | QxQP | = | | PxP |
| | | Q–B1! | | | PxP |
| *13* | | O–O | | | N–Q2[9] |
| | | B–B3 | | | ± |
| | | ∓ | | | |

*Notes to practical variations 13–17:*

[1] A typical gambit with good attacking chances.

[2] One of the best systems for Black and recommended by Bronstein.

[3] Or 6 QN–Q2, P–B3! and 7 . . . P–QN4.

[4] Or 9 NxN, BxN 10 BxB†, PxB 11 QxBP, Q–Q4! with a satisfactory game for Black.

[5] Analysis by Najdorf.

[6] Petrosian–Bronstein, Zurich 1953.

[7] For 6 Q–R4, see Game 8.

[8] Najdorf–Kramer, Amsterdam 1950.

[9] Fine–Euwe, New York 1951.

### *Catalan Opening Game 8*

*WHITE: Eliskases* *BLACK: Prins*

*Interzonal Tournament, Stockholm 1952*

| | WHITE | BLACK | | WHITE | BLACK |
|---|---|---|---|---|---|
| 1 | P–Q4 | N–KB3 | 15 | P–K4! | N–B3 |
| 2 | P–QB4 | P–K3 | 16 | B–K3 | BxP |
| 3 | P–KN3 | P–Q4 | 17 | QR–B1 | P–QN3 |
| 4 | B–N2 | QN–Q2 | 18 | Q–B3 | Q–N2 |
| 5 | N–KB3 | PxP | 19 | KR–Q1 | BxB |
| 6 | Q–R4 | B–K2? | 20 | QxB | B–Q2 |
| 7 | QxBP | O–O | 21 | NxB | NxN |
| 8 | O–O | R–N1 | 22 | P–K5! | Q–R2 |
| 9 | N–B3 | P–QR3 | 23 | P–R5! | KR–Q1 |
| 10 | P–QR4 | N–N3 | 24 | R–Q6 | K–B1 |
| 11 | Q–N3 | N/N–Q4 | 25 | R/1–Q1 | R/N–B1 |
| 12 | N–K5! | P–B4! | 26 | PxP | Q–N1 |
| 13 | NxN | NxN | 27 | RxN! | Resigns |
| 14 | PxP | Q–B2 | | | |

SUPPLEMENTARY VARIATIONS 1–5:

1 P–Q4, N–KB3 2 P–QB4, P–K3 3 P–KN3

| | *1* | *2* | *3* | *4* | *5* |
|---|---|---|---|---|---|
| *3* | – – | – – | – – | – – | – – |
| | B–N5† | – – | P–Q4 | – – | P–K4!? |
| *4* | B–Q2 | N–Q2! | B–N2 | – – | N–KB3[4] |
| | Q–K2 | P–B4 | B–N5† | – – | PxP |
| *5* | B–N2 | P–QR3 | B–Q2 | QN–Q2! | NxP |
| | O–O | BxN† | B–K2![3] | O–O | P–Q4 |
| *6* | N–KB3 | QxB | Q–B2 | Q–B2 | B–N2 |
| | BxB† | PxP | O–O | N–B3 | PxP |
| *7* | QxB | N–B3 | = | N–KB3 | Q–R4† |
| | P–Q4 | N–B3 | | N–K5 | P–B3 |
| *8* | O–O | NxP | | O–O | QxBP |
| | N–B3 | N–QR4[1] | | P–B4 | B–K2 |
| *9* | N–K5 | Q–N4![2] | | P–N3 | O–O |
| | ± | P–Q4 | | ± | O–O |
| *10* | | N–N5 | | | ± |
| | | NxP | | | |
| *11* | | B–B4! | | | |
| | | ± | | | |

*Notes to supplementary variations 1–5:*

[1] The absence of Black's King Bishop is significant.

[2] 9 P–N3?, P–Q4! (Donner–Trifunovic, Buenos Aires 1955).

[3] The White Bishop is not well posted at Q2.

[4] The continuation 4 PxP, N–N5! transposes into a kind of Budapest gambit, in which White's P–KN3 is by no means a reinforcement.

# chapter 24—Irregular Queen's Gambit Declined

There are several ways to decline the Queen's Gambit (1 P–Q4, P–Q4 2 P–QB4) other than 2 . . . P–K3 and 2 . . . P–QB3. While none of these other defenses is considered fully satisfactory, it is anything but easy to demonstrate their inadequacy.

## SYMMETRICAL DEFENSE: 2 . . . P–QB4 (PRAC. VAR. 1–5)

There are a number of little tactical points which come to the surface if White reacts too energetically; in this case, Black always obtains a satisfactory game (see Prac. Var. 1). By adopting a more restrained line, however, White is able to obtain an advantage.

## TCHIGORIN DEFENSE: 2 . . . N–QB3 (PRAC. VAR. 6–8)

Tchigorin's own results with this defense were quite good, his opponents never finding the strongest antidote. Since his day, however, several systems have been developed which tend to favor White.

## MARSHALL DEFENSE: 2 . . . N–KB3 (PRAC. VAR. 9–10)

Although this line definitely is unsatisfactory for Black against best play, he does obtain counterchances if White advances P–K4 prematurely.

## ALBIN COUNTER GAMBIT: 2 . . . P–K4 (PRAC. VAR. 11–14)

This is a sharp defense, the strength of which White must not underestimate. Black obtains excellent practical chances for the Pawn. A remarkable feature of the positions produced by this gambit is the frequency with which White can turn the tables by sacrificing the exchange (see Prac. Var. 11 and 14). This is a possibility which occurs time and time again.

## PRACTICAL VARIATIONS 1–14:
### 1 P–Q4, P–Q4 2 P–QB4

| | 8 | 9 | 10 | 11 | 12 | 13 | 14 |
|---|---|---|---|---|---|---|---|
| 2 | — — | — — | — — | — — | — — | — — | — — |
| | — — | N–KB3[24] | — — | P–K4 | — — | — — | — — |
| 3 | N–KB3 | PxP | — — | PxKP | — — | — — | — — |
| | B–N5 | NxP[25] | — — | P–Q5 | — — | — — | — — |
| 4 | Q–R4[20] | P–K4[26] | N–KB3[30] | N–KB3[34] | — — | — — | — — |
| | BxN | N–KB3 | B–B4[31] | N–QB3[35] | — — | — — | — — |
| 5 | KPxB | B–Q3[27] | Q–N3 | QN–Q2[36] | — — | — — | — — |
| | P–K3 | P–K4 | N–QB3 | B–KN5 | B–K3 | B–QN5 | P–B3[41] |
| 6 | N–B3[21] | PxP | QN–Q2[32] | P–KN3 | P–KN3 | P–QR3 | PxP |
| | KN–K2[22] | N–N5 | N–N3 | Q–Q2 | Q–Q2 | BxN† | QxP |
| 7 | PxP | N–KB3 | P–K4 | B–N2 | B–N2[38] | BxB | P–KN3 |
| | PxP | N–QB3 | B–N3 | O–O–O | R–Q1 | B–N5 | B–KB4 |
| 8 | B–QN5 | B–KN5[28] | P–Q5 | P–KR3 | O–O | Q–N3 | B–N2 |
| | P–QR3 | B–K2 | N–N1 | B–KB4 | KN–K2 | KN–K2 | N–N5[42] |
| 9 | BxN† | BxB | P–QR4 | P–QR3 | Q–R4 | P–KN3 | O–O |
| | NxB | QxB | P–QR4 | P–B3 | N–N3 | O–O | N–B7[43] |
| 10 | O–O[23] | N–B3 | N–K5 | PxP | P–QR3 | B–N2 | R–N1 |
| | ± | N/3xP | N/1–Q2 | NxP | B–K2 | R–QN1 | N–N5 |
| 11 | | NxN | B–N5 | P–QN4 | P–QN4 | O–O | P–QR3! |
| | | NxN | Q–B1 | R–K1 | O–O | N–N3 | BxR |
| 12 | | B–K2 | N/2–B4[33] | B–N2 | B–N2[39] | P–R3[40] | NxB[44] |
| | | P–QB3[29] | ± | B–Q6[37] | ± | ± | ± |
| | | = | | ± | | | |

---

*Notes to practical variations 1–14:*

[1] 3 . . . QxP 4 N–KB3, PxP 5 N–B3, Q–QR4 6 NxP concedes White too great a lead in development.

[2] Black has at least equality: 13 K–Q2, NxR 14 N–B3, P–QN3 15 B–Q3, B–N2 16 NxP, N–N6† 17 PxN, PxN.

[3] This unusual move assures White a lasting advantage.

[4] If 6 . . . P–K3, White obtains a slight edge after both 7 N–QR3, BxP 8 R–B1, N–R3 9 N–N5, O–O 10 P–K4, N–B3 and 7 N–QB3, BxP 8 NxN, PxN 9 R–B1, N–Q2 10 P–K3, P–Q5 11 P–K4.

[5] 13 NxN, PxN 14 R–B5, O–O† 15 K–K3, R–K1 16 P–KN3 favors White.

[6] 7 . . . BxP 8 R–B1±.

[7] White has a slight edge (e.g., 12 . . . NxN† 13 PxN, RxP 14 B–B3! and 15 BxKP).

[8] In this line, symmetry does not work against the second player; but see column 5.

[9] Gaining equality by seizing the center.

[10] For 5 . . . P–QR3, see Game 1.

[11] The alternative continuations, 6 . . . N–N5 7 Q–R4†, N/5–B3 8 NxN, NxN 9 B–K3 and 6 . . . N–B2 7 N–QB3,

| 1 | 2 | 3 | 4 | 5 | 6 | 7 |
|---|---|---|---|---|---|---|
| — — | — — | — — | — — | — — | — — | — — |
| P–QB4 | — — | — — | — — | — — | N–QB3 | — — |
| PxQP | — — | — — | N–KB3 | — — | N–QB3 | — — |
| N–KB3[1] | — — | — — | N–KB3 | — — | PxP[14] | N–B3 |
| PxP | — — | — — | PxQP | — — | P–Q5[15] | N–B3 |
| QxP | — — | — — | PxQP[8] | — — | N–R4 | B–N5[18] |
| QxQ | — — | — — | QxP | NxP | Q–R4†?[16] | PxP |
| NxQ | — — | — — | QxP | NxP[10] | P–B3 | KNxP |
| P–K4 | B–Q2[3] | — — | N–B3 | P–K4 | P–QN4 | P–K4 |
| N–N5 | P–K4[4] | — — | QxQ | N–KB3[11] | P–QN4! | BxN |
| N–QR3 | N–QB3 | N–QR3 | NxQ | B–N5†[12] | QxN | PxB |
| P–K3! | NxN | QN–B3[6] | P–QR3 | B–Q2 | QxQ | NxN |
| B–K3 | BxN | N–N5 | P–KN3 | P–K5 | PxQ | PxN |
| N–Q2 | N–B3 | P–QR3 | B–Q2 | BxB | P–N5 | P–K4 |
| N–N5 | N–B3 | P–K4 | B–N2 | NxB | N–Q1 | P–Q5[19] |
| BxP | P–B3 | PxN | P–K4[9] | QxQ† | PxP[17] | ± |
| N–B7† | R–B1 | PxN | N–B2 | KxQ | ∓ | |
| K–Q1 | BxP | N–Q5 | B–B3 | N–Q4 | | |
| NxR | BxP | R–B1 | P–K4 | N/1–B3 | | |
| BxB | BxP† | RxP | QN–Q2 | NxN† | | |
| PxB | KxB | N–B3![7] | O–O | PxN | | |
| N–B7†[2] | NxB[5] | ± | R–QB1 | N–R3[13] | | |
| = | ± | | = | ± | | |

P–K4 8 N/4–N5, QxQ† 9 KxQ, NxN 10 NxN, N–R3 11 B–QB4 also favor White.

[12] Suggested by Pachman, this move is stronger than the routine 7 N–QB3.

[13] After 13 B–K3, P–QN3 14 K–B2, P–K3 15 KR–Q1, White's edge is clear.

[14] 3 . . . P–K4 is not commendable because of 4 PxQP, NxP 5 P–K3, N–B4 6 Q–B2 (threatening 7 B–N5†), N–Q3 7 N–B3±.

[15] 4 N–B3 is safer; after 4 . . . N–B3 5 P–K4, B–N5 6 B–K3, BxN 7 PxB, White has bright prospects.

[16] 5 B–B4 is preferable, e.g., 5 . . . P–K3 6 P–K4, PxP 7 NxP, B–Q3 8 BxB, PxB 9 BxP with an excellent game for White.

[17] Black has more then sufficient compensation for the piece (Vienna–St. Petersburg, Postal Game 1897–98).

[18] 4 . . . B–B4 5 PxP, KNxP 6 Q–N3, P–K3 7 P–K4!, NxN 8 PxB, N–Q4 9 P–QR3! strongly favors White.

[19] White's strong center and two Bishops are sure to cause Black trouble.

[20] After 4 P–K3, P–K3, Black is safe.

**continued ▸**

[21] This simple developing move assures White a lasting advantage.

[22] Bronstein's idea, but still not good enough to rehabilitate the defense. For the older 6 . . . B–N5, see Game 2.

[23] Black is skating on thin ice. After 10 . . . Q–Q3, so as to meet 11 Q–N3 with 11 . . . O–O–O, there may follow 11 R–K1†, B–K2 12 B–B4!, QxB 13 RxB†!

[24] With this move Black abandons the center, a policy rarely commendable.

[25] 3 . . . QxP 4 N–QB3, Q–QR4 5 N–B3, N–B3 and now 6 B–Q2! favors White. For 6 P–K3, see Game 3.

[26] Premature.

[27] 5 N–QB3 is met effectively by 5 . . . P–K4.

[28] Not 8 B–KB4 because of 8 . . . N–N5!

[29] Grunfeld–Becker, Breslau 1925.

[30] Eliminating any counterplay by means of . . . P–K4.

[31] 3 . . . P–KN3, leading to a kind of Grunfeld Defense, is much more prudent.

[32] Not 6 QxP because of 6 . . . N/4–N5.

[33] Takacs–Havasi, Budapest 1926.

[34] 4 P–K3?, B–N5† 5 B–Q2, PxP! 6 BxB?, PxP† 7 K–K2, PxN/N†! is Lasker's famous trap.

[35] For 4 . . . P–QB4, see Game 4.

[36] 5 P–KN3, also good, usually transposes into the column.

[37] Bondarevski–Mikenas, Moscow 1950, continued 13 O–O, BxKP 14 Q–R4, BxR 15 RxB, K–N1 16 P–N5, N–Q1 17 NxP after White has ample compensation for the exchange.

[38] Against White's deployment, Black strains at the leashes for equality.

[39] White remains a Pawn to the good.

[40] Black regains the Pawn after 12 . . . BxN 13 PxB, QNxP 14 P–B4, N–Q2 15 Q–Q1, but his position is none too enviable.

[41] Consistent, but too venturesome.

[42] 8 . . . O–O–O 9 N–R4 also favors White.

[43] Or 9 . . . B–B7 10 Q–K1, B–N3 11 N–N3, N–B7 12 Q–R5, NxR 13 QNxP! with White for choice (Bogoljubov).

[44] After 12 . . . N–B3 13 P–QN4, White's harmonious development and two Bishops assure a lasting initiative.

*Irregular Queen's Gambit Declined Game 1*

*WHITE: Alekhine* *BLACK: Wolf*

*Bad Pistyan 1922*

| | WHITE | BLACK | | WHITE | BLACK |
|---|---|---|---|---|---|
| 1 | P–Q4 | P–Q4 | 11 | Q–B3 | R–N1 |
| 2 | N–KB3 | P–QB4 | 12 | B–K3 | P–N3 |
| 3 | P–B4 | PxQP | 13 | QN–Q2 | B–N2 |
| 4 | PxP | N–KB3 | 14 | B–Q4 | BxB |
| 5 | NxP | P–QR3? | 15 | QxB | B–N4 |
| 6 | P–K4! | NxKP | 16 | BxB† | PxB |
| 7 | Q–R4† | B–Q2 | 17 | O–O | R–R5 |
| 8 | Q–N3 | N–B4 | 18 | P–QN4 | Q–Q1 |
| 9 | Q–K3 | P–KN3 | 19 | P–QR3 | N/1–Q2 |
| 10 | N–KB3 | Q–B2 | 20 | KR–K1 | K–B1 |

| | WHITE | BLACK | | WHITE | BLACK |
|---|---|---|---|---|---|
| 21 | P–Q6 | N–K3 | 31 | R–K1 | Q–Q3 |
| 22 | RxN! | PxN | 32 | P–K8/N† | NxN |
| 23 | N–N5 | Q–N1 | 33 | QxN | QxN |
| 24 | NxKP† | K–B2 | 34 | Q–K5† | K–B2 |
| 25 | N–N5† | K–B1 | 35 | P–KR4! | RxP |
| 26 | Q–Q5 | R–N2 | 36 | Q–K8† | K–N2 |
| 27 | N–K6† | K–N1 | 37 | R–K7† | K–R3 |
| 28 | NxR† | KxN | 38 | Q–B8† | K–R4 |
| 29 | PxP | N–B3 | 39 | R–K5† | K–N5 |
| 30 | QxP | R–R2 | 40 | R–N5† | Resigns |

*Irregular Queen's Gambit Declined Game 2*

*WHITE: Alekhine* *BLACK: Colle*

*Baden–Baden 1925*

| | WHITE | BLACK | | WHITE | BLACK |
|---|---|---|---|---|---|
| 1 | P–Q4 | P–Q4 | 32 | Q–N4† | K–R1 |
| 2 | P–QB4 | N–QB3 | 33 | P–B5 | NxP |
| 3 | N–KB3 | B–N5 | 34 | BxN | PxB |
| 4 | Q–R4 | BxN | 35 | QxP | Q–Q1 |
| 5 | KPxB | P–K3 | 36 | PxP | R–Q3 |
| 6 | N–B3 | B–N5 | 37 | Q–B4 | K–R2 |
| 7 | P–QR3 | BxN† | 38 | Q–K4† | K–R1 |
| 8 | PxB | N–K2 | 39 | Q–K3 | K–N2 |
| 9 | R–QN1 | R–QN1 | 40 | Q–Q3 | P–QR4 |
| 10 | B–Q3 | PxP | 41 | R–K3 | R–N1 |
| 11 | BxBP | O–O | 42 | R–R3 | Q–Q2 |
| 12 | O–O | N–Q4 | 43 | Q–K3 | P–B4 |
| 13 | Q–B2 | N/3–K2 | 44 | R–N3† | K–R2 |
| 14 | B–Q3 | P–KR3 | 45 | RxR | KxR |
| 15 | P–QB4 | N/4–N3 | 46 | Q–N3† | K–R2 |
| 16 | R–Q1 | N/N–B1 | 47 | Q–N3 | K–N2 |
| 17 | P–B4 | P–QN3 | 48 | P–R3 | Q–Q1 |
| 18 | B–N2 | P–QB3 | 49 | Q–N3† | K–R2 |
| 19 | Q–K2 | N–Q3 | 50 | Q–K5 | Q–Q2 |
| 20 | Q–K5 | N–K1 | 51 | R–Q3 | P–B3 |
| 21 | P–QR4 | R–N2 | 52 | Q–Q4 | Q–Q1 |
| 22 | R–K1 | N–B3 | 53 | Q–QB4 | Q–Q2 |
| 23 | QR–Q1 | R–Q2 | 54 | R–Q4 | K–N2 |
| 24 | B–B2 | P–R3 | 55 | Q–Q3 | K–B2 |
| 25 | Q–K2 | Q–N1 | 56 | P–N4 | K–B1 |
| 26 | P–Q5 | BPxP | 57 | PxP | Q–K1 |
| 27 | BxN | PxB | 58 | R–K4 | Q–R4 |
| 28 | Q–N4† | K–R1 | 59 | R–N4 | Q–B2 |
| 29 | Q–R | K–N2 | 60 | Q–K3 | Q–R2 |
| 30 | Q–N4† | K–R1 | 61 | R–N6 | Resigns |
| 31 | Q–R4 | K–N2 | | | |

*Irregular Queen's Gambit Declined Game 3*

*WHITE: Euwe* — *BLACK: Bogoljubov*

*4th Match Game 1928*

| | WHITE | BLACK | | WHITE | BLACK |
|---|---|---|---|---|---|
| 1 | P–Q4 | N–KB3 | 24 | NxB | N–K5! |
| 2 | P–QB4 | P–Q4 | 25 | NxN | PxN |
| 3 | PxP | QxP | 26 | R–B1 | QR–N1† |
| 4 | N–QB3 | Q–R4 | 27 | K–R1 | R–R6 |
| 5 | N–B3 | N–B3 | 28 | B–Q2 | R/1–KR1 |
| 6 | P–K3? | P–K4 | 29 | QR–Q1 | RxP† |
| 7 | P–Q5? | N–QN5 | 30 | K–N1 | R/7–R2 |
| 8 | B–N5† | P–B3 | 31 | R–B2 | R–R8† |
| 9 | Q–R4 | QxQ | 32 | K–N2 | R/8–R7† |
| 10 | BxQ | P–QN4 | 33 | K–N1 | RxR |
| 11 | B–N3 | N–Q6† | 34 | BxP† | NxB |
| 12 | K–K2 | P–K5 | 35 | R–Q7† | K–B3 |
| 13 | N–KN5 | P–N5 | 36 | KxR | N–Q6† |
| 14 | N/3xP | B–R3 | 37 | K–N1 | R–N1† |
| 15 | K–B3 | PxP | 38 | K–R2 | B–B1 |
| 16 | B–R4† | K–K2 | 39 | RxP | N–K4 |
| 17 | N–Q2 | P–R3 | 40 | B–Q1 | N–B6† |
| 18 | N–R3 | P–N4 | 41 | BxN | PxB |
| 19 | P–N4 | P–R4 | 42 | R–R4 | R–N7† |
| 20 | NxP | PxP† | 43 | K–R1 | RxP |
| 21 | K–N2 | B–R3 | 44 | R–B4† | K–K2 |
| 22 | P–B4 | PxP e.p.† | 45 | K–N1 | R–N7† |
| 23 | N/2xP | BxN | | Resigns | |

*Irregular Queen's Gambit Declined Game 4*

*WHITE: Tarrasch* — *BLACK: Tartakover*

*Berlin 1920*

| | WHITE | BLACK | | WHITE | BLACK |
|---|---|---|---|---|---|
| 1 | P–Q4 | P–Q4 | 14 | NxN | QxN |
| 2 | P–QB4 | P–K4 | 15 | N–B3 | Q–QB4 |
| 3 | PxKP | P–Q5 | 16 | B–B4! | B–Q3 |
| 4 | N–KB3 | P–QB4 | 17 | BxN! | PxB |
| 5 | P–K3 | N–QB3 | 18 | BxB | RxB |
| 6 | PxP | PxP | 19 | N–K5 | R/1–Q1 |
| 7 | B–Q3 | KN–K2 | 20 | Q–R4 | P–Q6! |
| 8 | QN–Q2! | B–N5 | 21 | P–QN4 | Q–Q5 |
| 9 | Q–N3 | Q–B2 | 22 | NxQBP! | RxN |
| 10 | O–O | O–O–O | 23 | QxR† | K–N1 |
| 11 | R–K1 | N–N3 | 24 | P–B5 | P–Q7 |
| 12 | P–KR3 | B–K3 | 25 | R/K–Q1 | B–B4 |
| 13 | B–K4 | N/NxP | 26 | Q–N5† | K–B2! |

| | WHITE | BLACK | | WHITE | BLACK |
|---|---|---|---|---|---|
| 27 | Q–R5† | K–N1 | 34 | Q–B7 | R–QN4 |
| 28 | P–N5 | B–B7 | 35 | QxB† | KxP |
| 29 | P–N6! | R–Q2 | 36 | P–QR4 | R–QB4 |
| 30 | PxP† | K–R1 | 37 | Q–N4 | QxR |
| 31 | P–B6 | R–Q4 | 38 | RxQ | R–B8† |
| 32 | P–B7! | B–B4 | 39 | Q–Q1 | Resigns |
| 33 | P–B8(Q) | BxQ | | | |

*Irregular Queen's Gambit Declined Game 5*

*WHITE: Euwe* *BLACK: Kostic*

*Beverwijk 1952*

| | WHITE | BLACK | | WHITE | BLACK |
|---|---|---|---|---|---|
| 1 | P–Q4 | P–Q4 | 18 | Q–K2 | P–QB4 |
| 2 | P–QB4 | P–K4 | 19 | PxP | N–Q6 |
| 3 | PxKP | P–Q5 | 20 | QR–Q1 | NxQBP |
| 4 | N–KB3 | N–QB3 | 21 | Q–B3 | P–B4 |
| 5 | P–KN3 | B–K3 | 22 | N–K2 | N–K5 |
| 6 | QN–Q2 | Q–Q2 | 23 | N–B4 | Q–QB3 |
| 7 | B–N2 | KN–K2 | 24 | N–Q5 | B–Q3 |
| 8 | O–O | N–N3 | 25 | Q–K2 | R–B1 |
| 9 | P–QR3 | B–K2 | 26 | P–B3 | N–N4 |
| 10 | P–QN4 | R–Q1 | 27 | R–B1 | P–N4 |
| 11 | B–N2 | O–O | 28 | P–B5 | QxN |
| 12 | R–B1 | B–R6 | 29 | KR–Q1 | QxP† |
| 13 | N–N3 | BxB | 30 | QxQ | NxQ |
| 14 | KxB | Q–N5 | 31 | PxB | N–N4 |
| 15 | N/NxP | N/BxKP | 32 | RxR | RxR |
| 16 | NxN | NxN | 33 | P–Q7 | R–Q1 |
| 17 | P–K3 | Q–N3 | 34 | B–B3 | Resigns |

# chapter 25—Manhattan Variation

1 P–Q4, P–Q4
2 P–QB4, P–K3
3 N–QB3, N–KB3
4 B–N5, QN–Q2
5 N–B3, B–N5
6 PxP[A], PxP
7 P–K3, P–B4[B]

KEY POSITION

This defense arises after 1 P–Q4, P–Q4 2 P–QB4, P–K3 3 N–QB3, N–KB3 4 B–N5, QN–Q2 5 N–B3, B–N5. It is played when White no longer can proceed with KN–K2. Thus, if 5 P–K3, B–N5 6 B–Q3 followed by 7 KN–K2, Black's attack on the Queen Knight is futile. In the main line Black tries to reinforce the Cambridge Springs Defense by saving the move . . . P–QB3 and later playing . . . P–QB4. White, however, can transpose into the Exchange Variation and then Black's Bishop on QN5 is not so well placed. Today the defense is outmoded.

## OBSERVATIONS ON KEY POSITION

[A] The simplest counter-measure. Both 6 P–QR3, BxN† 7 PxB, P–B4! and 6 Q–R4, Q–K2 7 BxN, BxN†! are satisfactory for Black.

[B] The point of Black's counterplay.

Since 8 PxP, Q–R4 is not commendable for White, Black is able to play . . . P–QB5 and establish a Queen-side Pawn majority. But White's majority in the center is of greater significance giving him excellent chances for attack. Hence there is little in the position in the diagram to entice the Black player.

## IDEA VARIATION:

(1) 8 B–Q3, P–B5 (8 . . . PxP 9 NxP/4 is inferior; for 8 . . . Q–R4, see Prac. Var. 1) 9 B–B2 (threatening 10 P–K4 and preparing for a strong Pawn sacrifice; 9 B–B5 is also good), Q–R4 10 O–O (the consistent continuation), BxN 11 PxB, QxBP (concerning the superior 11 . . . N–K5, see Prac. Var. 2) 12 Q–N1, O–O 13 P–K4!, PxP (after 13 . . . NxP 14 B–K7, R–K1? 15 B–N4!, Black's Queen is lost) 14 B–Q2, Q–R6 15 B–N4, Q–R3 16 BxR, PxN 17 B–N4 (if 17 B–K7?, Q–K3!), PxP 18 R–K1 with a winning advantage for White. The threat is 19 BxP†!

PRACTICAL VARIATIONS 1 AND 2:

1 P–Q4, P–Q4 2 P–QB4, P–K3 3 N–QB3, N–KB3 4 B–N5, QN–Q2 5 N–B3, B–N5 6 PxP, PxP 7 P–K3, P–B4

| | *1* | *2* |
|---|---|---|
| *8* | B–Q3 | – – |
| | Q–R4 | P–B5 |
| *9* | O–O[1] | B–B2 |
| | BxN[2] | Q–R4 |
| *10* | PxB | O–O |
| | QxBP | BxN |
| *11* | R–B1 | PxB |
| | Q–R4 | N–K5 |
| *12* | PxP[3] | Q–K1 |
| | ± | QxBP![4] |
| *13* | | BxN |
| | | QxQ |
| *14* | | KRxQ |
| | | PxB |
| *15* | | N–Q2 |
| | | P–KR3 |
| *16* | | B–B4 |
| | | P–B4[5] |
| | | ± |

*Notes to practical variations 1 and 2:*

[1] The sharpest line; 9 Q–B2 is also good.

[2] 9 . . . P–B5 leads to the Idea Var. If 9 . . . PxP 10 NxP/4, BxN 11 PxB, QxP 12 N–N5, and White has excellent compensation for his Pawn.

[3] White builds a strong attack.

[4] Not 12 . . . NxQBP? 13 P–K4!.

[5] Black has the slightly inferior game, but can probably hold his own.

# chapter 26—Meran Defense

The "Meran" derives its name from the international tournament staged at that resort in 1924. Here it was that the great Akiba Rubinstein unveiled his new conception to the world, startling his opponent and quickly wresting the upper hand from him.

Ever since that game, analysts have delighted in attempts at refutation. In spite of prolonged analytical investigation, however, definite conclusions as to the value of the defense have yet to be reached. Just when all possibilities appear exhausted, new variations are uncovered, driving the analysts back into their studies.

The Meran is a sharp defense; Black must be fully acquainted with all its intricacies before adopting it over the board.

---

## part 1—BLUMENFELD VARIATION

1 P–Q4, P–Q4
2 P–QB4, P–QB3
3 N–KB3, N–B3
4 N–B3, P–K3
5 P–K3, QN–Q2
6 B–Q3, PxP
7 BxBP, P–QN4
8 B–Q3[A], P–QR3[B]
9 P–K4, P–B4
10 P–K5[C], PxP
11 NxNP, NxP
12 NxN, PxN

KEY POSITION 1

### OBSERVATIONS ON KEY POSITION 1

[A] 8 B–N3 offers Black an easy time after 8 . . . P–N5! 9 N–K2, B–N2 10 O–O, B–K2 11 N–N3, O–O 12 P–K4, P–B4. 8 B–K2 is too modest to cause Black much trouble.

[B] Wade's 8 . . . B–N2 yields White good chances after 9 P–K4, P–N5 10 N–QR4, P–B4 11 P–K5, N–Q4 12 NxP!, NxN 13 PxN, Q–R4 14 Q–K2, P–QR3 15 O–O, BxP 16 N–N5! (Pachman–Vesely, Prague 1953).

[C] Reynold's Variation — 10 P–Q5 — offers Black a satisfactory game after 10 . . . P–K4; neither 11 O–O, P–B5 12 B–B2, B–Q3 nor 11 P–QN3, B–Q3 12 O–O, O–O 13 P–QR4, P–B5! 14 PxP, P–N5! is of much promise to White.

This is a configuration of almost bewildering complexity. To avoid disadvantage, both White and Black must act with energy and determination.

At first glance it appears that White easily obtains the advantage with 13 BxP†; this, however, proves not to be the case. Considerable experience has established that White's best course of action is to develop quickly and play for the attack. For this purpose two moves serve best: Rellstab's 13 O–O and Stahlberg's 13 Q–B3.

### IDEA VARIATIONS 1–3:

(1) 13 BxP†, B–Q2 14 BxB† (14 NxB, Q–R4† 15 B–Q2, QxB 16 NxN†, PxN 17 Q–K2=) NxB 15 NxN, B–N5† 16 B–Q2, Q–R4 17 P–QR3, BxB† 18 QxB, KxN 19 QxQ, RxQ, and Black's prospects are bright in view of his lead in development.

(2) 13 O–O, Q–Q4 14 Q–K2, R–N1 (14 . . . B–N2

15 BxP†, K–Q1 16 P–B4, B–B4 17 K–R1, K–K2 18 B–B4, Q–Q3 19 P–B5 also favors White; correct is 14 . . . B–R3, for which see Prac. Var. 1) 15 B–N5, B–Q3 (after 15 . . . B–K2 16 P–B4, O–O 17 R–B3, White's attack is very strong) 16 P–B4, BxN 17 PxB, N–Q2 18 RxP!!, KxR 19 Q–R5†, P–N3 20 R–B1† and wins.

(3) 13 Q–B3, B–N5† 14 K–K2, Q–Q4 (here 14 . . . R–QN1 deserves the nod; see Prac. Var. 2) 15 QxQ, NxQ 16 BxP†, K–B1 (or 16 . . . K–K2 17 R–Q1!, B–B4 18 N–B6†, K–Q3 19 NxP, BxN 20 RxB, K–B4 21 R–QR4! with a pull for White, as in Euwe–Wolthius, Amsterdam 1942) 17 B–Q2, P–B3 18 N–Q3, BxB 19 KxB, B–R3 20 B–B6, R–Q1 21 BxN, RxB± (Fontein–Lenton, Netherlands–England 1938).

PRACTICAL VARIATIONS 1–3:

1 P–Q4, P–Q4 2 P–QB4, P–QB3 3 N–KB3, N–B3 4 N–B3, P–K3 5 P–K3, QN–Q2 6 B–Q3, PxP 7 BxBP, P–QN4 8 B–Q3, P–QR3 9 P–K4, P–B4 10 P–K5, PxP 11 NxNP, NxP 12 NxN, PxN

| | *1* | *2* | *3* |
|---|---|---|---|
| *13* | O–O | Q–B3 | – – |
| | Q–Q4 | B–N5†[5] | – – |
| *14* | Q–K2 | K–K2 | – – |
| | B–R3[1] | R–QN1 | – – |
| *15* | B–N5[2] | Q–N3[6] | – – |
| | B–K2 | Q–Q4 | Q–Q3[9] |
| *16* | P–B4[3] | N–B3 | N–B3 |
| | O–O | P–K4 | QxQ |
| *17* | R–B3 | QxP†[7] | RPxQ |
| | B–N2 | QxQ† | B–Q3 |
| *18* | R–R3[4] | NxQ | B–KB4[10] |
| | P–KN3 | R–N3 | BxB |
| *19* | = | B–Q2 | PxB |
| | | BxB | B–Q2 |
| *20* | | KxB[8] | NxP |
| | | ± | K–K2 |
| *21* | | | QR–QB1 |
| | | | KR–QB1[11] |
| | | | = |

*Notes to practical variations 1–3:*

[1] Best. Inferior alternatives are discussed in Idea Var. 2.

[2] 15 P–QR4, B–Q3 16 PxP, B–N2 is satisfactory for Black (Spielmann–Bogoljubov, 3d Match Game 1932).

[3] Here, too, 16 P–QR4 is of no promise, e.g., 16 . . . O–O 17 PxP, B–N2 18 P–B4, P–R3 19 B–R4, RxR 20 RxR, R–R1= (Alekhine–Bogoljubov, Alysczech 1934).

[4] 18 R–N3 followed by the advance of the King Rook Pawn offers White better attacking chances.

[5] If 13 . . . Q–R4†, the continuation 14 B–Q2, B–N5! favors Black. Correct for White is 14 K–K2. See Game 1.

[6] Reshevsky's move, considered White's best.

[7] 17 QxP is strongly countered by 17 . . . P–K5!

[8] Landau–Schmidt, Stockholm 1937. See Game 2.

[9] Black's best.

[10] 18 NxP, B–Q2 19 B–Q2, N–N5 is satisfactory for Black.

[11] Szabo–Stahlberg, Saltsjobaden 1948.

*Meran Defense Game 1*

*WHITE: Reshevsky* *BLACK: Botvinnik*

*Moscow 1955*

| | WHITE | BLACK | | WHITE | BLACK | | WHITE | BLACK |
|---|---|---|---|---|---|---|---|---|
| 1 | P–Q4 | P–K3 | 15 | Q–B6† | K–K2 | 29 | P–R5 | R/1–B3 |
| 2 | P–QB4 | P–Q4 | 16 | B–Q2 | P–N5 | 30 | K–K2 | R–Q3 |
| 3 | N–QB3 | P–QB3 | 17 | QxB† | KxQ | 31 | K–K1 | N–B2 |
| 4 | P–K3 | N–B3 | 18 | N–B4† | K–Q2 | 32 | RxR† | KxR |
| 5 | N–B3 | QN–Q2 | 19 | NxQ | RxN | 33 | B–B3! | P–B3 |
| 6 | B–Q3 | PxP | 20 | KR–QB1 | B–R3 | 34 | R–R1 | N–R3 |
| 7 | BxBP | P–QN4 | 21 | BxB | RxB | 35 | R–R3 | K–B2 |
| 8 | B–Q3 | P–QR3 | 22 | R–B4 | N–Q4 | 36 | RxP | N–B4 |
| 9 | P–K4 | P–B4 | 23 | RxQP | R–QN1 | 37 | R–N5 | N–R5 |
| 10 | P–K5 | PxP | 24 | K–Q3 | P–R4 | 38 | B–Q4 | P–K4 |
| 11 | NxNP | NxP | 25 | K–B4? | P–N6 | 39 | K–Q1! | R–B5 |
| 12 | NxN | PxN | 26 | P–QR4 | R–B3† | 40 | B–K3 | K–B3 |
| 13 | Q–B3 | Q–R4† | 27 | K–Q3 | R–B7 | 41 | R–N8 | K–B2 |
| 14 | K–K2 | B–Q3 | 28 | R–QN1 | R/1–QB1 | | Resigns | |

*Meran Defense Game 2*

*WHITE: Landau* *BLACK: Schmidt*

*Stockholm 1937*

| | WHITE | BLACK | | WHITE | BLACK |
|---|---|---|---|---|---|
| 1 | P–Q4 | P–Q4 | 21 | KR–K1 | B–K3 |
| 2 | P–QB4 | P–QB3 | 22 | P–QR3 | R–R1 |
| 3 | N–KB3 | N–B3 | 23 | N–B3 | R–R5 |
| 4 | P–K3 | P–K3 | 24 | R–K5! | B–B5 |
| 5 | N–B3 | QN–Q2 | 25 | R–QB5 | P–N3 |
| 6 | B–Q3 | PxP | 26 | N–K5 | R–R1 |
| 7 | BxBP | P–QN4 | 27 | P–B3 | BxB |
| 8 | B–Q3 | P–QR3 | 28 | KxB | R–Q1 |
| 9 | P–K4 | P–B4 | 29 | R–B6 | N–Q2 |
| 10 | P–K5 | PxP | 30 | RxR | NxN† |
| 11 | NxNP | NxP | 31 | K–K2! | P–Q6† |
| 12 | NxN | PxN | 32 | K–B2! | R–Q4 |
| 13 | Q–B3 | B–N5† | 33 | R–N8† | K–N2 |
| 14 | K–K2 | R–QN1 | 34 | P–QN3 | R–B4 |
| 15 | Q–N3 | Q–Q4 | 35 | K–K3 | N–B3 |
| 16 | N–B3 | P–K4 | 36 | R–QB8 | R–B6 |
| 17 | QxP† | QxQ† | 37 | R–Q1 | R–B7 |
| 18 | NxQ | R–N3 | 38 | RxP | N–Q5 |
| 19 | B–Q2 | BxB | 39 | RxR | NxR† |
| 20 | KxB | O–O | 40 | K–Q2 | Resigns |

SUPPLEMENTARY VARIATIONS 1–6:

1 P–Q4, P–Q4 2 P–QB4, P–QB3 3 N–KB3, N–B3 4 N–B3, P–K3 5 P–K3, QN–Q2 6 B–Q3, PxP 7 BxBP, P–QN4 8 B–Q3

| | *1* | *2* | *3* | *4* | *5* | *6* |
|---|---|---|---|---|---|---|
| *8* | – – | – – | – – | – – | – – | – – |
| | P–N5 | P–QR3 | – – | – – | – – | – – |
| *9* | N–K4[1] | O–O | P–K4 | – – | – – | – – |
| | B–K2[2] | P–B4 | P–N5 | P–B4 | – – | – – |
| *10* | NxN† | P–QR4 | N–QR4 | P–K5 | – – | – – |
| | NxN | P–N5 | P–B4 | N–KN5[9] | PxP | – – |
| *11* | P–K4 | N–K4 | P–K5 | N–N5[10] | NxNP | – – |
| | P–B4 | B–N2 | N–Q4 | PxP | N–N5 | PxN[18] |
| *12* | PxP | NxP[5] | O–O | NxBP | Q–R4[14] | PxN |
| | BxP | NxN | B–N2[7] | Q–R5[11] | B–N2[15] | Q–N3[19] |
| *13* | O–O | PxN | B–N5 | P–KN3 | QNxP | PxP! |
| | B–K2[3] | BxP[6] | B–K2 | Q–R4[12] | Q–N3 | BxP |
| *14* | Q–K2 | = | BxB | NxR | O–O | O–O |
| | O–O | | QxB | PxN | B–B4 | N–B4 |
| *15* | R–Q1[4] | | R–B1 | B–K4 | P–KR3 | B–KB4[20] |
| | ± | | PxP | B–N5 | BxKN[16] | B–N2 |
| *16* | | | R–K1 | K–B1 | PxN | R–K1 |
| | | | O–O | R–R2 | B–Q4[17] | NxB |
| *17* | | | B–K4[8] | B–B4 | ± | QxN |
| | | | ± | P–N4 | | BxN |
| *18* | | | | P–KR3[13] | | QxB[21] |
| | | | | ± | | ± |

*Notes to supplementary variations 1–6:*

[1] Stronger than 9 N–QR4, P–B4 10 PxP, NxP, which is comfortable for Black.

[2] 9 . . . P–B4 10 Q–R4, PxP 11 NxN†, PxN 12 B–K4, R–QN1 13 NxP favors White. Recent analysis indicates, however, that Black can equalize with 9 . . . NxN 10 BxN, B–N2, e.g., 11 Q–R4, Q–N3 12 O–O, B–K2 13 N–Q2, QR–B1, when Black is out of danger.

[3] Not 13 . . . O–O because of 14 P–K5, N–Q2 15 BxP†!

[4] White leads in development.

[5] Of no promise whatsoever. 12 N/4–Q2! offers White more chances, as in 12 . . . B–K2 13 P–R5, O–O 14 N–B4, B–K5!, and Black just barely holds his own. In this line 13 . . . Q–B2 14 N–B4 favors White.

[6] Black has solved all his opening problems.

[7] This is an improvement on the older 12 . . . B–K2, after which 13 PxP, NxBP 14 NxN, BxN 15 N–N5 is to White's advantage.

continued ▸

[8] White has a slight edge.

[9] Tricky but dubious.

[10] The refutation.

[11] Far weaker for Black is 12 . . . KxN 13 QxN, NxP 14 Q–R5†, K–N1 15 QxN, PxN 16 B–K4, R–R2 17 O–O, when White has a winning advantage.

[12] Or 13 . . . Q–R6 14 N–K4!, Q–N7 15 QxN!

[13] Van den Berg–Been, Beverwijk 1946.

[14] Strongest. After the immediate 12 N/5xP, Black conveniently equalizes with 12 . . . B–N5† 13 B–Q2, BxB† 14 QxB, B–N2.

[15] Trifunovic's astonishing 12 . . . N/4xKP?! founders on 13 NxN, NxN 14 N–B7†, K–K2 15 Q–N4†, K–B3 16 N–K8†!!, QxN 17 QxP±.

[16] 15 . . . NxBP 16 RxN, B/2xN 17 RxB, BxN† 18 K–R1, R–R2 19 B–Q2 favors White.

[17] Trifunovic–Gligoric, Amsterdam 1950, ended in a draw after 17 N–N3, O–O 18 QxN, BxN 19 BxP†, KxB 20 Q–Q3†, K–N1 21 QxB, QxQ 22 PxQ, KR–N1. White's best try is probably 17 N–B3.

[18] This capture was undeservedly in vogue for a number of years. It is inferior to other lines.

[19] Best. Other moves are also in White's favor, e.g., 12 . . . B–N2 13 O–O, PxP 14 BxNP, R–KN1 15 B–KB4, R–R4 16 P–QR4, RxB 17 PxR (Botvinnik–Simagin, USSR Championship 1951).

[20] To maintain control of K5.

[21] Szabo–Foltys, Budapest 1948, continued with 18 . . . O–O 19 QR–B1, QR–B1 20 Q–KN3, K–R1 21 P–KR4!, and White has a distinct edge.

---

## part 2—SEMI—MERAN

1 P–Q4, P–Q4
2 P–QB4, P–QB3
3 N–KB3, N–B3
4 N–B3, P–K3
5 P–K3, QN–Q2
6 B–Q3

KEY POSITION 2

### OBSERVATIONS ON KEY POSITION 2

The Meran Defense with its wild variations requiring a plethora of "book" knowledge is not to everyone's taste. Hence, the possibilities of avoiding this defense — for both White and Black — gain in significance. Avoidance on the part of Black by omitting 6 . . . PxP leads to what is known as the Semi-Meran.

In the diagrammed position, Black has at his disposal three reasonable moves other than 6 . . . PxP; these are 6 . . . B–K2, 6 . . . B–Q3 and 6 . . . B–N5.

Each leads to a different course, depending on the resultant center formation.

(1) 6 . . . B–K2 gives White a free hand in the center for the moment. Experience shows, however, that White achieves little if he quickly proceeds with P–K4 aiming to profit from his more active position. In this case, Black usually obtains adequate counterplay by means of . . .

QPxKP soon followed by . . . P–QB4. For this reason, White does better to abstain from an early P–K4, choosing instead a more subtle line of play.

(2) 6 . . . B–Q3 looks most natural, but it has the drawback of allowing White's P–K4 with considerably more force than in the previous variation. The main point is that White often can take advantage of the somewhat exposed position of the Bishop.

(3) 6 . . . B–N5 (the Romih Variation) momentarily prevents 7 P–K4. If the Bishop is attacked by 7 P–QR3, the seemingly consistent 7 . . . BxN is not advisable, since it cedes to White a strong center as well as a pair of Bishops. Black's best course is to retreat his attacked Bishop via QR4 to QB2; on QB2 the Bishop is better placed than on Q3, and the value of Black's counterstroke, . . . P–K4, is greatly enhanced.

IDEA VARIATIONS 4–6:

(4) 6 . . . B–K2 7 O–O, O–O 8 P–K4, PxKP 9 NxP, P–QN3 10 Q–K2, B–N2 11 R–Q1, Q–B2 12 B–N5, P–B4 13 PxP, PxP, and Black's position is entirely satisfactory.

(5) 6 . . . B–Q3 7 P–K4, PxKP 8 NxP, NxN 9 BxN, O–O 10 O–O, P–QB4 11 B–B2!, P–QN3 12 Q–Q3, P–N3 13 B–R6, R–K1 14 QR–Q1 with a substantial superiority for White. See *Game 3.*

(6) 6 . . . B–N5 7 P–QR3, B–R4 8 Q–B2, O–O 9 B–Q2, B–B2 10 O–O, PxP 11 BxP, P–K4 12 B–R2, P–KR3 13 QR–K1, R–K1 with a steady position for Black.

*Meran Defense Game 3*

*WHITE: Euwe* — *BLACK: Winter*

*Nottingham 1936*

| | WHITE | BLACK | | WHITE | BLACK |
|---|---|---|---|---|---|
| 1 | P–Q4 | P–Q4 | 10 | O–O | P–QB4? |
| 2 | P–QB4 | P–QB3 | 11 | B–B2! | P–QN3 |
| 3 | N–KB3 | N–B3 | 12 | Q–Q3 | P–N3 |
| 4 | N–B3 | P–K3 | 13 | B–R6 | R–K1 |
| 5 | P–K3 | QN–Q2 | 14 | QR–Q1 | B–B1 |
| 6 | B–Q3 | B–Q3 | 15 | PxP! | BxB? |
| 7 | P–K4 | PxKP | 16 | P–B6 | Q–B3? |
| 8 | NxP | NxN | 17 | PxN | Resigns |
| 9 | BxN | O–O | | | |

## PRACTICAL VARIATIONS 4–11:

1 P–Q4, P–Q4 2 P–QB4, P–QB3 3 N–KB3, N–B3 4 N–B3, P–K3 P–K3 5 P–K3, QN–Q2 6 B–Q3

| | 4 | 5 | 6 | 7 | 8 | 9 | 10 | 11 |
|---|---|---|---|---|---|---|---|---|
| 6 | – – | – – | – – | – – | – – | – – | – – | – – |
| | B–K2[1] | B–Q3[6] | – – | – – | B–N5 | – – | – – | – – |
| 7 | O–O | O–O | P–K4![12] | – – | O–O | – – | P–QR3 | – – |
| | O–O | O–O | PxBP? | PxKP | O–O | – – | B–R4[21] | – – |
| 8 | P–QN3[2] | P–K4 | BxP | NxP | B–Q2 | Q–B2 | Q–B2[22] | – – |
| | P–QN3[3] | PxBP | P–K4 | NxN | B–Q3[18] | PxP! | Q–K2 | O–O |
| 9 | B–N2 | BxP | PxKP | BxN | P–QN3 | BxP | B–Q2 | O–O |
| | B–N2 | P–K4! | QNxP | O–O[14] | Q–K2 | B–Q3 | PxP | B–B2 |
| 10 | Q–K2 | B–KN5[7] | NxN | O–O | Q–B2 | B–Q3 | BxBP | P–QN3 |
| | Q–B2 | Q–K2 | BxN | Q–B2[15] | P–K4 | Q–K2 | P–K4 | Q–K2 |
| 11 | N–K5[4] | R–K1 | QxQ† | B–B2 | PxQP | N–K2 | O–O | B–N2[25] |
| | P–B4 | N–N3 | KxQ | P–KR3 | BPxP | P–B4 | O–O | ± |
| 12 | P–B4 | B–N3 | BxP | R–K1[16] | PxP | P–K4 | B–R2[23] | |
| | PxQP | P–KR3[8] | BxN† | R–K1 | NxP | PxP | B–B2 | |
| 13 | KPxP | B–KR4[9] | PxB | B–Q2 | N–Q4 | N/2xP | QN–N5 | |
| | PxP | B–KN5 | NxP | P–QB4 | NxB | N–K4 | B–N3 | |
| 14 | PxP | P–KR3 | O–O[13] | PxP | QxN | NxN | B–N4 | |
| | QR–B1 | BxN | ± | NxP | Q–K4 | BxN | P–B4 | |
| 15 | QR–Q1[5] | QxB | | Q–K2[17] | P–B4 | N–B3 | PxBP | |
| | ± | QN–Q2[10] | | ± | Q–K2[19] | Q–B2[20] | BxP | |
| 16 | | P–Q5[11] | | | = | = | BxB | |
| | | ± | | | | | NxB | |
| 17 | | | | | | | KR–QB1[24] | |
| | | | | | | | ± | |

*Notes to practical variations 4–11:*

[1] This move offers better chances for equality than 6 . . . B–Q3, according to Bogoljubov.

[2] Tchigorin's antidote.

[3] 8 . . . PxP favors White because of 9 PxP!

[4] See Game 4 for 11 QR–Q1. In that game the text position was reached by transposition.

[5] White's more active position is the plus factor.

[6] Favored by Tchigorin.

[7] Other moves are even less effective.

[8] After 12 . . . B–KN5 13 P–KR3, BxN 14 QxB, Black must proceed with 14 . . . QN–Q2 and not with 14 . . . PxP, which fails against 15 P–K5!, e.g., 15 . . . BxP 16 N–K4, Q–Q1 17 Q–B5, QN–Q2 18 P–B4! with a winning attack (Szabo–Honfi, Budapest 1950).

[9] After 13 PxP, BxP 14 NxB, QxN 15 B–R4, N–R4 Black is comfortable.

[10] 15 . . . P–N4 is too venturesome. After 16 B–N3, KN–Q2 17 Q–B5, K–N2 18 PxP, both 18 . . . NxP 19 QR–Q1! and 18 . . . BxP 19 P–B4! yield White the edge.

[11] Black is somewhat cramped.

[12] White's most energetic continuation.

[13] White has the superior game. If now 14 . . . NxQBP, Grunfeld gives 15 B–N2, R–B1 16 B–N3, N–K7† 17 K–R1, P–KN3 18 QR–Q1†, K–B2 19 B–K5†, K–N3 20 B–QB4, N–B5 21 B–Q6 with a winning attack.

[14] 9 . . . N–B3 10 B–B2, B–N5† 11 B–Q2, Q–R4 12 O–O, BxB 13 NxB clearly favors White. Worth notice is 9 . . . P–K4 10 O–O, PxP 11 QxP, Q–B3 12 Q–Q1, N–K4 13 R–K1, B–KN5 14 B–N5, Q–K3 15 Q–B2, P–B3 16 N–Q4, Q–B2 17 B–Q2, O–O–O, but this, too, leaves White with the better game.

[15] For 10 . . . P–QB4, see Game 3.

[16] Threatening 13 Q–Q3. An immediate 12 Q–Q3 is adequately answered by 12 . . . P–KB4.

[17] White's superiority is in space.

[18] By moving his Bishop to Q3 by way of QN5, Black has succeeded in circumventing Prac. Var. 6. If now 9 P–K4, Black can safely reply with . . . PxBP, but the advance of the King Pawn may nevertheless be White's best.

[19] Kotov–Botvinnik, Moscow 1955.

[20] The column is a Russian analysis which has received no over-the-board test.

[21] 7 . . . BxN† 8 PxB leads to a positional advantage for White after 8 . . . O–O 9 O–O, Q–B2 10 N–Q2, P–K4 11 B–N2, P–K5 12 B–K2, P–QN4 13 PxNP, PxP 14 P–QR4, PxP 15 P–QB4! (Euwe–Alekhine, 3d Match Game 1937).

[22] White's strongest weapon against the Romih Variation.

[23] Najdorf's innovation, which causes Black a deal of difficulty.

[24] Foltys–Donner, Amsterdam 1950.

[25] Black's position is cramped. 11 . . . P–K4 is effectively met by 12 PxQP.

*Meran Defense Game 4*

*WHITE: Euwe* — *BLACK: Winter*

*Nottingham 1936*

| | WHITE | BLACK | | WHITE | BLACK |
|---|---|---|---|---|---|
| 1 | P–Q4 | P–Q4 | 14 | PxP | PxP |
| 2 | P–QB4 | P–QB3 | 15 | B–R6 | B–QB3 |
| 3 | N–KB3 | N–B3 | 16 | B–N5 | B–N2 |
| 4 | N–B3 | P–K3 | 17 | P–K4! | B–KB3 |
| 5 | P–K3 | QN–Q2 | 18 | BxB | NxB |
| 6 | B–Q3 | B–K2 | 19 | PxP | NxP |
| 7 | O–O | O–O | 20 | Q–K5 | Q–R4 |
| 8 | P–QN3 | P–QN3 | 21 | B–B4 | N–B3 |
| 9 | B–N2 | B–N2 | 22 | N–N5 | QR–K1 |
| 10 | Q–K2 | P–B4 | 23 | Q–B4 | P–KR3? |
| 11 | QR–Q1 | N–K5 | 24 | NxP! | B–R3 |
| 12 | PxBP | NxN | 25 | N–Q6† | Resigns |
| 13 | BxN | NPxP | | | |

## part 3—ANTI—MERAN GAMBIT

1 P–Q4, P–Q4
2 P–QB4, P–QB3
3 N–KB3, N–B3
4 N–B3, P–K3
5 B–N5, PxP[A]
6 P–K4[B], P–N4
7 P–K5[C], P–KR3
8 B–R4, P–N4
9 KNxP, PxN[D]
10 BxNP, QN–Q2

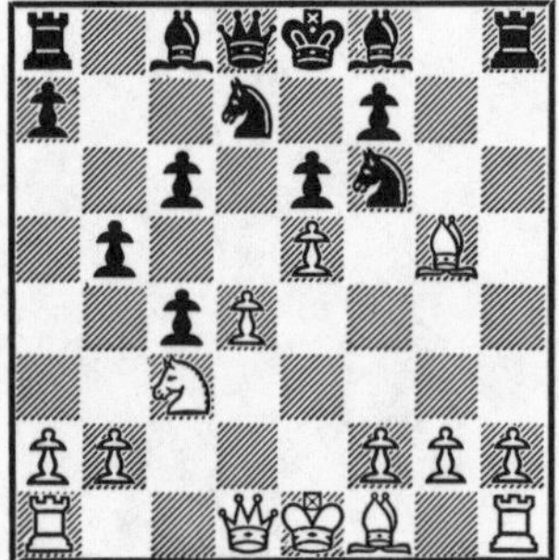

KEY POSITION 3

[A] 5 . . . QN–Q2 transposes into the Cambridge Springs Defense; 5 . . . B–K2 leads to a kind of Orthodox.

[B] Also worth consideration is 6 P–QR4, B–N5 7 P–K4 with these possibilities:

(1) 7 . . . P–N4 8 P–K5, P–KR3 9 B–R4, P–N4 10 PxN, PxB 11 N–K5, QxBP 12 B–K2, and White has a slight edge (compare Prac. Var. 17).

(2) 7 . . BxN† 8 PxB, Q–R4 9 P–K5, N–K5 10 R–B1, N–Q2 11 B–K3, N–N3, and it is questionable whether White has enough for the Pawn.

(3) 7 . . . P–B4 8 BxP, PxP 9 NxP, P–KR3 10 B–K3, NxP 11 O–O, N–KB3 (Bronstein–Botvinnik, 24th Match Game 1951). Keres now suggests 12 N/4–N5! as advantageous for White, e.g., 12 . . . QxQ? 13 N–B7†, K–Q1 14 KRxQ†, KxN 15 N–N5†, K–B3 16 QR–B1 with an overwhelming attack.

[C] Petrosian–Neikirch, Portoroz 1958, went on with 7 Q–B2, P–KR3 8 B–R4, P–N4 9 B–N3, P–KN5 10 N–K5, QxP 11 B–K2, B–N5. This is a difficult line offering approximately even chances.

[D] The consequences of 9 . . . N–Q4?! 10 NxBP, QxB 11 NxR, B–N5 12 Q–Q2, P–B4 13 O–O–O are obscure.

1 P–Q4, P–Q4
2 P–QB4, P–QB3
3 N–KB3, N–B3
4 N–B3, P–K3
5 B–N5, PxP
6 P–K4, P–N4
7 P–K5, P–KR3
8 B–R4, P–N4
9 PxN, PxB
10 N–K5, QxBP[A]

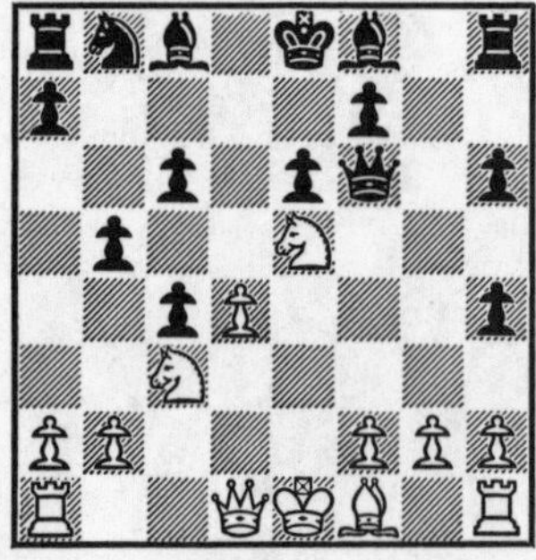

KEY POSITION 4

[A] Definitely not 10 . . . N–Q2 because of 11 NxKBP!, KxN 12 Q–R5†.

### OBSERVATIONS ON KEY POSITIONS 3 AND 4

Avoidance of the Meran can take place on White's 5th or Black's 6th move. Part 2 dealt with avoidance on Black's 6th turn; Part 3 discusses avoidance on White's 5th.

Both key positions feature wild play which reduces material considerations to a secondary factor.

Key position 3 is double-edged. White, in fact, must play with extreme alertness to avoid a disadvantage.

In key position 4 the attacking chances are all White's. Black, on the other hand, is two Pawns to the good. If he can consolidate his position before White makes too much progress, victory is his.

The value of the Anti-Meran Gambit is still in dispute, but while formerly the gambit generally was considered to be in Black's favor, today the opposite judgment prevails.

### IDEA VARIATIONS 6 AND 7 (KEY POSITION 3):

(6) 11 Q–B3, B–QN2 12 B–K2, Q–N3! 13 BxN, P–B4! 14 N–K4, R–KN1 15 Q–B4, PxP 16 B–R5, N–B4 17 BxP†, K–Q2!∓ (Zollner–Junge, Warsaw 1942).

(7) 11 P–KN3, B–QN2 12 B–N2, R–KN1 13 BxN, NxB 14 PxN, Q–N3 15 O–O, O–O–O 16 Q–R5, R–N3 17 P–QR4, P–R3 18 PxP, BPxP 19 P–Q5±.

IDEA VARIATION 8 (Key Position 4):

(8) 11 P–KN3, N–Q2 12 P–B4, PxP 13 PxP, NxN 14 QPxN, Q–N3? (correct is 14 . . . Q–Q1!) 15 Q–B3, B–Q2 16 O–O–O, R–Q1 17 B–N2 with a winning position for White (Pachman–van Scheltinga, Hilversum 1947).

PRACTICAL VARIATIONS 12–17:

1 P–Q4, P–Q4 2 P–QB4, P–QB3 3 N–KB3, N–B3 4 N–B3, P–K3 5 B–N5, PxP 6 P–K4, P–N4 7 P–K5, P–KR3 8 B–R4, P–N4

| | *12* | *13* | *14* | *15* | *16* | *17* |
|---|---|---|---|---|---|---|
| *9* | KNxP | – – | – – | – – | PxN | – – |
| | PxN | – – | – – | – – | PxB | – – |
| *10* | BxNP | – – | – – | – – | N–K5 | – – |
| | QN–Q2 | – – | – – | – – | QxBP | – – |
| *11* | P–KN3 | – – | PxN | – – | P–KN3 | B–K2 |
| | B–QN2 | Q–R4[4] | B–QN2 | – – | N–Q2 | N–Q2[17] |
| *12* | B–N2 | PxN | B–K2 | P–KN3[11] | P–B4[14] | O–O[18] |
| | R–KN1[1] | P–N5 | Q–N3 | Q–N3[12] | NxN | NxN |
| *13* | BxN | N–K4 | P–QR4[8] | B–N2 | BPxN[15] | PxN |
| | NxB | B–QR3 | P–N5[9] | O–O–O | Q–N4 | QxP |
| *14* | PxN | Q–B3[5] | P–R5 | O–O | Q–B3 | B–B3 |
| | QxBP[2] | O–O–O | Q–R3 | N–K4 | B–QN2 | B–QN2 |
| *15* | P–QR4 | B–K2[6] | N–K4 | Q–K2 | NxNP[16] | R–K1 |
| | P–N5 | B–QN2 | O–O–O | QxP | ± | Q–Q3[19] |
| *16* | N–K4 | O–O | Q–B2 | B–K3 | | = |
| | Q–B4 | Q–Q4 | P–B4 | Q–Q6 | | |
| *17* | Q–K2 | B–K3[7] | BxP | KR–Q1 | | |
| | O–O–O | = | Q–B3 | QxQ | | |
| *18* | QxP | | B–Q3 | RxR† | | |
| | B–N2 | | P–N6[10] | KxR | | |
| *19* | QxP | | = | NxQ[13] | | |
| | BxP | | | ± | | |
| *20* | O–O | | | | | |
| | Q–K4[3] | | | | | |
| | ± | | | | | |

*Notes to practical variations 12–17:*

[1] 12 . . . Q–R4 13 PxN, O–O–O 14 Q–B2, N–N3 15 O–O, RxQP 16 KR–Q1, RxR† 17 QxR, N–Q4 18 N–K4, P–N5 19 P–QR3! favors White (Lilienthal–Botvinnik, Moscow 1944).

[2] For the inferior 14 . . . Q–N3, see Idea Var. 7. Black does not fear 15 NxP because of 15 . . . O–O–O!

[3] White's attack is facile, although Black's desperate counterchances must not be discounted.

[4] 11 . . . Q–N3 is not good because of 12 PxN, B–QN2 13 B–N2, P–B4 14 P–Q5!±.

continued ▸

[5] There is much to say for 14 P–N3, e.g., 14 . . . O–O–O 15 Q–B2, N–N3 16 B–K3, P–B6 17 BxB†, QxB 18 Q–K2, when an exchange of Queens favors White. 14 B–N2 is definitely weak because of 14 . . . P–B6.

[6] Here, too, White must not fianchetto his Bishop, e.g., 15 B–N2?, P–B6 16 NxP, N–N1! 17 N–K4, RxQP 18 B–K3, P–N6† 19 N–B3, B–R6! and wins.

[7] White threatens 18 N–N5 with effect. One possible continuation is 17 . . . R–N1 18 KR–B1, P–B4 19 N–Q2, PxP 20 QxQ, PxQ 21 BxQP with about even chances.

[8] For 13 O–O, see Game 5.

[9] 13 . . . O–O–O merits consideration.

[10] White must not play 19 QxNP, which fails against 19 . . . P–B5!

[11] This counter-fianchetto is White's surest means of obtaining the advantage.

[12] Definitely not 12 . . . P–B4? because of 13 P–Q5, P–N5 14 BxP, PxN 15 PxKP±. Nor is 12 . . . P–N5 satisfactory because of 13 N–K4, P–B4 14 Q–N4!±.

[13] Smyslov–Botvinnik, 5th Match Game 1954.

[14] Bronstein recommends 12 Q–K2; see Game 6.

[15] This is stronger than 13 QPxN, Q–Q1! 14 QxQ†, KxQ 15 B–N2, B–QN2 16 NxP, PxN 17 BxB, R–QN1, when Black has the edge. For 13 . . . Q–N3 in this line, see Idea Var. 8.

[16] Black's position is more vulnerable.

[17] 11 . . . B–QN2 12 B–B3, P–R3 13 O–O is good for White.

[18] If 12 NxP/6, B–QN2 13 B–B3, P–R3 14 O–O, B–N2! 15 P–R4, P–N5 16 N–K4, Q–B5 17 P–KN3, PxP 18 RPxP, Q–B2∓.

[19] The end game resulting from 16 NxP, QxQ 17 QRxQ, PxN 18 BxB, R–Q1! offers equal chances. Black must play for an exchange of Queens to stem the tide of White's attack.

### *Meran Defense Game 5*

*WHITE: Denker* *BLACK: Botvinnik*

*Radio Match 1945*

| | WHITE | BLACK | | WHITE | BLACK |
|---|---|---|---|---|---|
| 1 | P–Q4 | P–Q4 | 14 | P–QR4 | P–N5 |
| 2 | P–QB4 | P–K3 | 15 | N–K4 | P–B4 |
| 3 | N–QB3 | P–QB3 | 16 | Q–N1 | Q–B2 |
| 4 | N–KB3 | N–B3 | 17 | N–N3 | PxP |
| 5 | B–N5 | PxP | 18 | BxP | Q–B3 |
| 6 | P–K4 | P–N4 | 19 | P–B3 | P–Q6 |
| 7 | P–K5 | P–KR3 | 20 | Q–B1 | B–B4† |
| 8 | B–R4 | P–N4 | 21 | K–R1 | Q–Q3 |
| 9 | NxKNP | PxN | 22 | Q–B4 | RxP†! |
| 10 | BxNP | QN–Q2 | 23 | KxR | R–R1† |
| 11 | PxN | B–QN2 | 24 | Q–R4 | RxQ† |
| 12 | B–K2 | Q–N3 | 25 | BxR | Q–B5! |
| 13 | O–O | O–O–O | | Resigns | |

*Meran Defense Game 6*

*WHITE: Bronstein* *BLACK: Botvinnik*

*USSR Championship 1951*

| | WHITE | BLACK | | WHITE | BLACK |
|---|---|---|---|---|---|
| 1 | P–Q4 | P–Q4 | 26 | P–N5 | PxP |
| 2 | P–QB4 | P–QB3 | 27 | PxP | Q–Q1 |
| 3 | N–QB3 | N–B3 | 28 | QxP† | K–R1 |
| 4 | N–B3 | P–K3 | 29 | Q–N4 | Q–K1 |
| 5 | B–N5 | PxP | 30 | P–N6 | B–R3 |
| 6 | P–K4 | P–N4 | 31 | QxRP | K–N2 |
| 7 | P–K5 | P–KR3 | 32 | P–Q7 | Q–Q1 |
| 8 | B–R4 | P–N4 | 33 | QxP | B–N4 |
| 9 | PxN | PxB | 34 | P–QR4 | Q–K2 |
| 10 | N–K5 | QxP | 35 | Q–N4 | Q–B3 |
| 11 | P–KN3 | N–Q2 | 36 | K–R2 | P–N5 |
| 12 | Q–K2 | NxN | 37 | R–KN1 | P–N6† |
| 13 | PxN | Q–K2 | 38 | K–R3 | B–K6 |
| 14 | B–N2 | B–QN2 | 39 | Q–R5 | B–R3 |
| 15 | O–O–O | B–N2 | 40 | QxP? | R–Q1? |
| 16 | P–B4 | O–O | 41 | R–Q1 | KxP |
| 17 | R–Q6 | QR–Q1 | 42 | Q–N1† | K–R2 |
| 18 | R/1–Q1 | RxR | 43 | K–N4 | R–N1† |
| 19 | PxR | Q–Q1 | 44 | K–B5 | B–K6† |
| 20 | N–K4 | Q–R4 | 45 | QxB | Q–N3† |
| 21 | K–N1 | Q–N3 | 46 | KxP | QxQ |
| 22 | Q–N4? | P–KB4 | 47 | P–Q8/Q | RxQ |
| 23 | Q–N6 | P–B4 | 48 | RxR | Q–K3† |
| 24 | P–KN4 | BxN† | 49 | R–Q5 | P–R4 |
| 25 | BxB | PxB | 50 | P–R4 | White resigns |

*Meran Defense Game 7*

*WHITE: Euwe* *BLACK: Van Steenis*

*Amsterdam 1941*

| | WHITE | BLACK | | WHITE | BLACK | | WHITE | BLACK |
|---|---|---|---|---|---|---|---|---|
| 1 | P–Q4 | P–Q4 | 12 | B–B4 | B–K2 | 23 | Q–B4 | B–N1 |
| 2 | P–QB4 | P–QB3 | 13 | O–O | N–Q4 | 24 | RxN | PxR |
| 3 | N–KB3 | N–B3 | 14 | P–K4 | NxP | 25 | BxP† | P–K4 |
| 4 | N–B3 | P–K3 | 15 | B–N2 | N–B7 | 26 | BxP† | BxB |
| 5 | P–K3 | P–QR3 | 16 | PxP | O–O | 27 | QxKP† | K–R3 |
| 6 | P–B5 | QN–Q2 | 17 | QR–Q1 | NxP | 28 | N–K4 | P–QN4 |
| 7 | P–QN4 | N–K5 | 18 | Q–N4 | BxP | 29 | P–N4 | BxP |
| 8 | NxN | PxN | 19 | N–K4 | B–R2 | 30 | N–B6 | B–B4 |
| 9 | N–Q2 | P–B4 | 20 | P–B6 | P–KN3 | 31 | N–N8† | RxN |
| 10 | P–B3 | PxP | 21 | N–N5 | P–B4 | 32 | PxR/Q | Q–N4† |
| 11 | QxP | N–B3 | 22 | P–B7† | K–N2 | 33 | Q–N3 | Resigns |

## SUPPLEMENTARY VARIATIONS 7–13:

1 P–Q4, P–Q4 2 P–QB4, P–QB3 3 N–KB3, N–B3 4 N–B3, P–K3 5 P–K3

| | 7 | 8 | 9 | 10 | 11 | 12 | 13 |
|---|---|---|---|---|---|---|---|
| 5 | – – | – – | – – | – – | – – | – – | – – |
| | QN–Q2 | – – | N–K5[11] | P–QR3[14] | – – | – – | – – |
| 6 | Q–B2[1] | N–K5[7] | B–Q3[12] | B–Q3[15] | Q–B2[19] | P–B5[23] | – – |
| | B–Q3[2] | NxN[8] | P–KB4 | PxP[16] | PxP[20] | P–QN3 | QN–Q2 |
| 7 | P–K4[3] | PxN | N–K5 | BxP | BxP | PxP | P–QN4[25] |
| | PxKP | N–Q2 | Q–R5 | P–QN4 | QN–Q2 | QN–Q2 | P–KN3[26] |
| 8 | NxP | P–B4 | P–KN3 | B–N3[17] | P–K4[21] | N–QR4 | B–N2 |
| | NxN | B–K2[9] | Q–R6 | P–B4 | P–QN4 | NxP | B–N2 |
| 9 | QxN | PxP | B–B1 | O–O | B–Q3 | B–Q2 | B–K2 |
| | P–K4![4] | BPxP | Q–R3 | B–N2 | P–B4 | KN–Q2 | O–O |
| 10 | P–B5[5] | B–Q3 | B–N2 | Q–K2 | P–K5 | QR–B1 | O–O |
| | B–K2 | N–B4 | N–Q2 | QN–Q2 | PxP | B–N2[24] | Q–K2 |
| 11 | NxP | B–B2 | NxQN | R–Q1[18] | NxNP | ± | N–QR4 |
| | NxN | P–QR4 | BxN | ± | PxN | | N–K5[27] |
| 12 | QxN | O–O | Q–N3 | | PxN | | B–Q3 |
| | O–O[6] | P–KN3 | P–QN3 | | Q–N3[22] | | P–B4 |
| 13 | ∓ | P–K4 | P–B3 | | ∓ | | N–K5[28] |
| | | P–Q5 | NxN | | | | ± |
| 14 | | N–R4 | PxN[13] | | | | |
| | | P–N3 | ± | | | | |
| 15 | | NxN | | | | | |
| | | PxN[10] | | | | | |
| | | = | | | | | |

*Notes to supplementary variations 7–13:*

[1] Stoltz' continuation, much favored by Taimanov.

[2] After 6 . . . B–K2 7 P–QN3, O–O 8 B–N2 White has considerable pressure.

[3] Nor does 7 P–QN3 offer any advantage, e.g., 7 . . . O–O 8 B–K2, P–K4 9 PxQP, NxP 10 NxN, PxN 11 PxP, NxP 12 O–O, B–KN5 followed by 13 . . . R–B1, and Black has a satisfactory game. 7 B–Q2 followed by O–O–O gives the game a sharp turn.

[4] 9 . . . N–B3 10 Q–B2, B–N5† 11 B–Q2 yields a slight edge to White.

[5] This line is too risky. White does better to content himself with equality, as in 10 PxP, NxP 11 NxN, Q–R4† 12 B–Q2, QxN 13 QxQ†, BxQ 14 O–O–O.

[6] White faces difficulties owing to the exposed position of his Queen.

[7] Rubinstein's anti-Meran.

[8] 6 . . . B–K2 leads to equality after 7 B–Q3, O–O 8 P–B4, P–B4!

[9] 8 . . . B–B4 is a promising alternative.

[10] Tartakover–Maroczy, Nice 1930.

[11] Known as the Meran Stonewall, this variation is not quite sufficient for equality.

[12] 6 PxP, KPxP 7 NxN, PxN 8 N–Q2 also favors White.

[13] Flohr–Tartakover, Bled 1931.

[14] The Accelerated Meran. Black postpones . . . QN–Q2 in order to hasten the characteristic Meran Pawn action.

[15] White accepts the challenge.

[16] 6 . . . P–QN4 is also playable, e.g., 7 P–QN3, QN–Q2 8 O–O, B–N2 9 P–B5, B–K2 (Bronstein–Botvinnik, 18th Match Game 1951.)

[17] After 8 B–Q3, P–B4 9 O–O, PxP 10 PxP, B–N2 Black stands very well (Lasker–Reshevsky, Nottingham 1935).

[18] The opening has transposed into the Queen's Gambit Accepted.

[19] 6 PxP, KPxP rather favors Black, while 6 N–K5 is adequately met by 6 . . . P–B4.

[20] 6 . . . QN–Q2 7 P–QN3 leads to a game similar in strategy to that of Prac. Var. 4.

[21] 8 P–QR4!

[22] Flohr–Yudovitch, Moscow 1945.

[23] The traditional "refutation."

[24] Black experiences difficulty freeing his Queenside.

[25] 7 N–QR4, P–KN3 leads to equality after 8 B–K2, B–N2 9 O–O, O–O 10 B–Q2, N–K5!

[26] For the inferior 7 . . . N–K5, see Game 7.

[27] 11 . . . P–K4 is premature because of 12 NxP!, NxN 13 PxN, N–Q2 14 P–B4, P–B3 15 P–K4!

[28] White has a tiny pull.

# chapter 27—Orthodox Defense

The Orthodox Defense arises after 1 P–Q4, P–Q4 2 P–QB4, P–K3 3 N–QB3, N–KB3 4 B–N5, B–K2. The name was suggested by Tarrasch, who poked fun at all systems except his own. In spite of Tarrasch, however, the Orthodox Defense has held its own to this day, although admittedly many modern tournament players prefer the Indian Defenses.

Black has good chances for equality, but cannot expect to find strong attacking opportunities. This probably explains the current popularity of sharper defenses, such as the King's Indian or Dutch.

With the move 2 . . . P–K3, Black temporarily locks in his Queen Bishop and consequently must strive to develop this piece later in some sound manner. This can be done in two ways, namely, via the diagonal QB1–KR6 by means of . . . P–K4 (usually preceded by . . . QPxP in order to avoid the isolation of the Queen Pawn), or via the flank by means of . . . P–QN3. In the latter case the advance . . . P–QB4 is vital in order to maintain equality in the center.

By and large the Orthodox Defense is considered satisfactory for Black, although in most cases White retains some initiative. Among the modern grandmasters who have successfully adopted this system are Stahlberg, Trifunovic and Eliskases. In former years, Capablanca was one of its chief exponents.

1 P–Q4, P–Q4
2 P–QB4, P–K3
3 N–QB3[A], N–KB3[B]
4 B–N5[C], B–K2[D]
5 P–K3[E], O–O[F]
6 N–B3, QN–Q2[G]
7 R–B1[H], P–B3[I]
8 B–Q3[J], PxP[K]
9 BxP, N–Q4[L]
10 BxB[M], QxB
11 O–O[N], NxN
12 RxN[O], P–K4

KEY POSITION 1

---

## part 1—CLASSICAL VARIATION

### OBSERVATIONS ON KEY POSITION 1

[A] For 3 N–KB3, see Sup. Var. 10.

[B] Two subvariations are the Janowski, 3 . . . P–QR3 4 PxP!, PxP 5 B–B4, N–KB3 6 P–K3, B–Q3 7 BxB, QxB 8 B–Q3±, and the Alapin, 3 . . . P–QN3 4 PxP!, PxP 5 N–KB3, B–N2 6 P–K4!±. 3 . . . PxP at this point is definitely inferior, e.g., 4 P–K4, P–QB4 5 N–B3, N–KB3 6 BxP, PxP 7 NxP, B–B4 8 B–K3±.

[C] 4 B–B4, P–B4! 5 P–K3, P–QR3 6 PxBP, BxP achieves nothing for White. For 4 PxP and 4 N–B3, see Parts 5 and 6 respectively.

[D] 4 . . . P–B4 is discussed in Sup. Var. 9.

[E] 5 N–B3 in most cases transposes into the main line. But if 5 . . . P–KR3 6 BxN, BxB 7 P–K4 is possible.

[F] Here or on the next move, Lasker's Defense . . . N–K5 is worth considering. It is usual, however, to interpolate . . . P–KR3. See Part 4.

G 6 . . . P–QN3 7 BxN, BxB 8 PxP, PxP 9 B–Q3, B–N2 10 P–KR4! is considered promising for White. Black must keep an eye on the possibility of White's sacrificing his Bishop on KR7.

H Most usual: 7 Q–B2 and 7 B–Q3 are treated under Sup. Var. 7 and 8 respectively.

I 7 . . . P–B4 is not exactly faulty, but after 8 PxBP!, Q–R4! 9 PxP, NxP 10 BxB, NxB the position is not easy for Black. See also Sup. Var. 5 and 6.

J See also Sup. Var. 4.

K The preparation for the liberating action. See also Sup. Var. 3.

L This move, which is characteristic of the Orthodox Defense, is known as "Capablanca's freeing maneuver." 9 . . . P–QN4 10 B–Q3, P–QR3 11 P–K4! is advantageous for White.

M Better than 10 N–K4, P–B3!, when Black has a good game. For other moves see Sup. Var. 1 and 2.

N Also important is 11 N–K4. See Part 2.

O 12 PxN, P–B4! leads to nothing.

Black gains some freedom. The exchange of two minor pieces makes the defense easier, and Black has opened the diagonal for his Queen Bishop. Hence his strategy has been successful. White nonetheless enjoys a slight lead in development which he must try to exploit. There are several systems serving this aim which will be examined more closely. Black's overall job is not yet easy.

IDEA VARIATIONS 1–3:

(1) 13 Q–B2 (this continuation, offering White typical chances, is most usual at present; alternatives are treated in Idea Var. 2 and 3 and Prac. Var. 1–3), P–K5 (best, as 13 . . . PxP 14 PxP, N–N3 15 R–K3!, Q–Q1 16 B–N3, N–Q4 17 R–K5 is promising for White; for 14 . . . N–B3 in this variation, see Game 1) 14 N–Q2, N–B3 15 R–B1 (another move which strongly merits consideration, according to Vukovic, is 15 B–N3 as a preparation for R–B5–K5), K–R1 (Stahlberg's recommendation, which prepares for 16 . . . B–K3, is most likely Black's best) 16 P–QN4, QxP 17 NxP, NxN 18 QxN, and White has a slight advantage.

(2) 13 Q–N1 (similar to 13 Q–B2 in that White maintains the tension in the center; after . . . P–K5 White's Queen is well placed on QN1 in view of the Queenside action beginning with P–QN4), PxP (13 . . . P–K5 is not now commendable because of 14 N–Q2, N–B3 15 P–QN4!±) 14 PxP, N–N3 15 B–N3, Q–B3 16 R–K1,

B–B4 (16 . . . B–K3 17 BxB, PxB also appears playable) 17 Q–B1, QR–K1. White still has some initiative.

(3) 13 PxP, NxP 14 NxN, QxN 15 P–B4! (in this line, which was inaugurated by Rubinstein, White has exchanged even more material, but the problem of Black's Queen Bishop, as will be seen, has become more acute), Q–B3 (the best retreat; 15 . . . Q–K5 16 Q–K2!, B–B4 17 B–Q3, Q–Q4 18 P–K4, Q–Q5† 19 K–R1, KR–K1 20 R–B4, Q–Q2 21 Q–QB2, B–K3 22 R–QB3 offers White good attacking chances, while actually weak is 15 . . . Q–K2 16 P–B5!; see Game 2) 16 P–B5 (the point; Black's Queen Bishop is again locked in and must be developed via the flank), P–QN4 17 B–N3, P–N5 (if 17 . . . B–N2 then 18 Q–B3 is strong) 18 R–B5, KR–K1! (Eliskases' move; bad is 18 . . . QxNP? 19 P–B6! etc.) 19 Q–B1, B–N2=.

*Orthodox Queen's Gambit Game 1*

*WHITE: Pirc* *BLACK: Tartakover*

*Noordwijk 1938*

| | WHITE | BLACK | | WHITE | BLACK |
|---|---|---|---|---|---|
| 1 | P–Q4 | P–Q4 | 12 | RxN | P–K4 |
| 2 | P–QB4 | P–K3 | 13 | Q–B2 | PxP |
| 3 | N–QB3 | N–KB3 | 14 | PxP | N–B3? |
| 4 | B–N5 | B–K2 | 15 | R–K1 | Q–Q3 |
| 5 | P–K3 | O–O | 16 | N–N5! | B–Q2 |
| 6 | N–B3 | QN–Q2 | 17 | Q–N3 | N–N5 |
| 7 | R–B1 | P–B3 | 18 | BxP† | K–R1 |
| 8 | B–Q3 | PxP | 19 | R–R3 | N–R3 |
| 9 | BxP | N–Q4 | 20 | Q–Q3 | B–B4 |
| 10 | BxB | QxB | 21 | QxB! | P–KN3 |
| 11 | O–O | NxN | 22 | RxN! | Resigns |

*Orthodox Queen's Gambit Game 2*

*WHITE: Euwe* *BLACK: Sir G. A. Thomas*

*Hastings 1934–35*

| | WHITE | BLACK | | WHITE | BLACK | | WHITE | BLACK |
|---|---|---|---|---|---|---|---|---|
| 1 | P–Q4 | P–Q4 | 10 | BxB | QxB | 19 | RxQBP | QxP† |
| 2 | P–QB4 | P–K3 | 11 | O–O | NxN | 20 | K–R1 | B–N2 |
| 3 | N–QB3 | N–KB3 | 12 | RxN | P–K4 | 21 | R/6xP | Q–K5 |
| 4 | B–N5 | B–K2 | 13 | NxP | NxN | 22 | Q–Q2! | K–R1 |
| 5 | P–K3 | O–O | 14 | PxN | QxP | 23 | BxP | QR–B1 |
| 6 | N–B3 | QN–Q2 | 15 | P–B4 | Q–K2? | 24 | R/6–B2 | KR–Q1 |
| 7 | R–B1 | P–B3 | 16 | P–B5! | P–QN4 | 25 | Q–N5 | R–Q3 |
| 8 | B–Q3 | PxP | 17 | B–N3 | P–N5 | 26 | B–Q5!! | Resigns |
| 9 | BxP | N–Q4 | 18 | P–B6! | PxP | | | |

PRACTICAL VARIATIONS 1–4:

1 P–Q4, P–Q4 2 P–QB4, P–K3 3 N–QB3, N–KB3 4 B–N5, B–K2 5 P–K3, O–O 6 N–B3, QN–Q2 7 R–B1, P–B3 8 B–Q3, PxP 9 BxP, N–Q4 10 BxB, QxB 11 O–O, NxN 12 RxN, P–K4

| | 1 | 2 | 3 | 4 |
|---|---|---|---|---|
| *13* | P–K4 | P–Q5 | R–K1 | B–N3 |
| | PxP | P–K5![4] | P–K5! | PxP[9] |
| *14* | NxP[1] | N–Q4 | N–Q2 | PxP |
| | N–K4[2] | P–QB4![5] | K–R1![7] | N–B3 |
| *15* | B–N3 | N–B5 | Q–N1 | R–K1 |
| | P–B4 | Q–K4 | P–KB4[8] | Q–Q3[10] |
| *16* | N–K2 | N–N3 | = | = |
| | N–B3[3] | N–B3[6] | | |
| | = | = | | |

*Notes to practical variations 1–4:*

[1] 14 QxP, P–QN4 and 15 . . . P–QB4 is good for Black.

[2] 14 . . . QxP 15 R–K1 offers White promising chances.

[3] Black has solved all his major problems.

[4] 13 . . . PxP? 14 QxP favors White.

[5] 14 . . . PxP 15 BxP gives White good chances.

[6] A complicated game.

[7] After 14 . . . N–B3 15 Q–N1, B–B4 16 P–QN4, White has the edge.

[8] With even chances (Pachman).

[9] Best. 13 . . . P–K5 14 N–Q2, N–B3 15 R–B5! gives White a plus.

[10] White's superior development can be contained (Pachman).

---

## part 2—ALEKHINE VARIATION

OBSERVATIONS ON KEY POSITION 2

This line was introduced by Alekhine in his match with Capablanca in Buenos Aires 1927, and has been repeatedly adopted since. Taimanov has scored remarkable successes with it.

With 11 N–K4 White postpones castling to avoid exchanging pieces. This is motivated by his superiority in space. The Knight maneuver, however, also loses time. With the knowledge of some particular finesses in the position, Black can successfully enforce . . . P–K4.

1 P–Q4, P–Q4
2 P–QB4, P–K3
3 N–QB3, N–KB3
4 B–N5, B–K2
5 P–K3, O–O
6 N–B3, QN–Q2
7 R–B1, P–B3
8 B–Q3, PxP
9 BxP, N–Q4
10 BxB, QxB
11 N–K4

KEY POSITION 2

IDEA VARIATIONS 4 AND 5:

(4) 11 . . . N/4–B3 12 N–N3, P–K4! (for 12 . . . Q–N5† see Idea Var. 5, and for 12 . . . P–B4? see Game 3) 13 O–O, PxP (13 . . . P–KN3 did not work out well in Smyslov–Rabar, Helsinki 1952, where 14 B–N3, PxP

15 QxP followed) 14 N–B5 (meriting a try, according to Alekhine, is 14 PxP, in which experience is lacking), Q–Q1 15 N/3xP (Taimanov prefers 15 N/5xQP), N–K4 16 B–N3, BxN 17 NxB, P–KN3! (better than 17 . . . Q–N3? 18 Q–Q6! etc.; see Game 4) 18 Q–Q4 (18 Q–Q6 is now ineffective because of 18 . . . R–K1), QxQ 19 NxQ, QR–Q1 with a completely even game.

11 . . . N/4–B3 is Lasker's move, which is Black's best. 11 . . . N/2–B3 weakens Black's control of his K4. In the game Alekhine–Treybal there followed 12 N–N3, Q–N5† 13 Q–Q2, QxQ† 14 KxQ, R–Q1 15 KR–Q1±. For other moves (11 . . . Q–N5†, 11 . . . P–QN3 and 11 . . . P–K4!?), see Prac. Var. 5, 6 and 7.

(5) 11 . . . N/4–B3 12 N–N3, Q–N5† (as was played six times by Capablanca in his match with Alekhine) 13 Q–Q2, QxQ† 14 KxQ, P–B4 (most likely better than 14 . . . R–Q1 15 KR–Q1, P–QN3 16 P–K4, B–N2 17 P–K5, N–K1 18 K–K3, P–QB4? 19 P–Q5! with advantage to White) 15 PxP, NxP 16 P–QN4, N/4–K5† (better than 16 . . . R–Q1† 17 K–K2, N/4–K5 18 NxN, NxN 19 N–K5, which offers White an end-game advantage [Taimanov–Sanchez, Stockholm 1952]) 17 NxN, NxN† 18 K–K2, B–Q2 19 N–K5, B–R5 with approximate equality, according to Stahlberg.

*Orthodox Queen's Gambit Game 3*

*WHITE: Szabo* *BLACK: Vaitonis*

*Stockholm 1952*

| | WHITE | BLACK | | WHITE | BLACK |
|---|---|---|---|---|---|
| 1 | P–Q4 | P–Q4 | 18 | N–Q6 | QR–N1 |
| 2 | P–QB4 | P–K3 | 19 | N–KN5 | N–N5 |
| 3 | N–QB3 | N–KB3 | 20 | Q–N3 | N–R3 |
| 4 | N–B3 | B–K2 | 21 | N/6xBP! | NxN |
| 5 | B–N5 | QN–Q2 | 22 | BxP | B–K1 |
| 6 | P–K3 | O–O | 23 | R–B7 | R–Q2 |
| 7 | R–B1 | P–B3 | 24 | RxR | NxR |
| 8 | B–Q3 | PxP | 25 | R–Q1 | Q–K2 |
| 9 | BxP | N–Q4 | 26 | RxN | R–Q1 |
| 10 | BxB | QxB | 27 | RxR | QxR |
| 11 | N–K4 | N/4–B3 | 28 | P–KR3 | P–KR3 |
| 12 | N–N3 | P–B4? | 29 | NxN | BxN |
| 13 | O–O | PxP | 30 | BxB† | KxB |
| 14 | QxP | N–N3 | 31 | Q–B3† | K–N1 |
| 15 | B–N3 | R–Q1 | 32 | QxP | Q–R4 |
| 16 | Q–K5 | B–Q2 | 33 | Q–N3† | K–R1 |
| 17 | N–B5 | Q–B1 | 34 | K–R2 | Resigns |

*Orthodox Queen's Gambit Game 4*

*WHITE: Alekhine* *BLACK: Lasker*

*Zurich 1934*

| | WHITE | BLACK | | WHITE | BLACK | | WHITE | BLACK |
|---|---|---|---|---|---|---|---|---|
| 1 | P–Q4 | P–Q4 | 10 | BxB | QxB | 19 | KR–Q1 | QR–Q1 |
| 2 | P–QB4 | P–K3 | 11 | N–K4 | N/4–B3 | 20 | Q–N3 | P–N3 |
| 3 | N–QB3 | N–KB3 | 12 | N–N3 | P–K4 | 21 | Q–N5! | K–R1 |
| 4 | N–B3 | B–K2 | 13 | O–O | PxP | 22 | N–Q6 | K–N2 |
| 5 | B–N5 | QN–Q2 | 14 | N–B5 | Q–Q1 | 23 | P–K4! | N–KN1 |
| 6 | P–K3 | O–O | 15 | N/3xP | N–K4 | 24 | R–Q3 | P–B3 |
| 7 | R–B1 | P–B3 | 16 | B–N3 | BxN | 25 | N–B5† | K–R1 |
| 8 | B–Q3 | PxP | 17 | NxB | Q–N3? | 26 | QxP! | Resigns |
| 9 | BxP | N–Q4 | 18 | Q–Q6! | N/4–Q2 | | | |

PRACTICAL VARIATIONS 5–7:

1 P–Q4, P–Q4 2 P–QB4, P–K3 3 N–QB3, N–KB3 4 B–N5, B–K2 5 P–K3, O–O 6 N–B3, QN–Q2 7 R–B1, P–B3 8 B–Q3, PxP 9 BxP, N–Q4 10 BxB, QxB 11 N–K4

| | 5 | 6 | 7 |
|---|---|---|---|
| *11* | – – | – – | – – |
| | Q–N5† | P–QN3[2] | P–K4!? |
| *12* | Q–Q2 | O–O | O–O[4] |
| | QxQ† | B–N2 | PxP |
| *13* | KxQ | Q–K2 | QxP |
| | R–Q1 | QR–Q1 | N/2–N3 |
| *14* | KR–Q1 | P–QR3 | B–N3 |
| | N/4–B3 | N/4–B3 | B–N5 |
| *15* | NxN†! | N–N3 | N–N3 |
| | NxN | P–B4[3] | BxN |
| *16* | B–N3[1] | = | PxB |
| | ± | | Q–B3 |
| *17* | | | QxQ |
| | | | NxQ |
| *18* | | | N–B5 |
| | | | QR–Q1 |
| *19* | | | KR–Q1[5] |
| | | | ± |

*Notes to practical variations 5–7:*

[1] Alekhine–Capablanca, 6th Match Game. White maintains a long-lasting initiative.

[2] Unusual but apparently not bad.

[3] Taimanov–Moisejev, Moscow 1953.

[4] 12 PxP, N/2xP 13 BxN, PxB 14 QxP, NxN† 15 PxN, B–K3 offers Black good chances for the Pawn.

[5] White has a slight edge, as in Najdorf–Stahlberg, Zurich 1953.

## part 3—NEO-ORTHODOX VARIATION

1 P–Q4, P–Q4
2 P–QB4, P–K3
3 N–QB3, N–KB3
4 B–N5, B–K2
5 P–K3, O–O
6 N–B3, P–KR3[A]
7 B–R4[B]

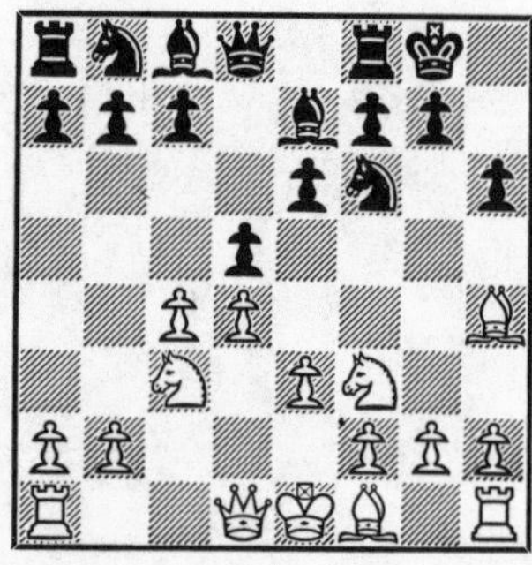

KEY POSITION 3

OBSERVATIONS ON KEY POSITION 3

[A] The first step to variations which are most usual today.

[B] 7 B–B4, P–B4! 8 PxBP, BxP 9 PxP, NxP 10 NxN, PxN 11 B–K2, N–B3 gives Black an excellent game. Nor does 7 BxN lead to anything, e.g., 7 . . . BxB 8 Q–B2, P–B4 9 PxBP, Q–R4 10 B–K2, PxP 11 O–O!, BxN 12 QxB, QxQ 13 PxQ, N–Q2.

With 6 . . . P–KR3 Black has denied his KN4 to the enemy and has also secured his King Rook Pawn against attacks on the diagonal (White's QN1–KR7). But Black's problem Queen Bishop must develop via the flank. There are two ways of proceeding.

(1) *The Lasker Method* (*7 . . . N–K5*): This practically forces the exchange of several minor pieces, thereby making the defense considerably easier. It is a good weapon if Black is striving for a draw.

(2) *The Tartakover Method* (*7 . . . P–QN3*): This method usually leads to complicated and interesting play with chances in the balance. The struggle gets its character from White's counter to Black's plan. According to present views, Black has sufficient counterplay.

IDEA VARIATIONS 6 AND 7:

(6) 7 . . . N–K5 8 BxB, QxB 9 Q–B2, P–QB3 10 B–K2 (or 10 NxN, PxN 11 QxP, Q–N5†, and Black recovers his Pawn with a fine game), N–Q2 11 O–O, NxN (better than 11 . . . P–KB4 12 N–K5! etc.) 12 QxN, PxP 13 BxP (if 13 QxP, P–K4), P–QN3 14 P–K4, B–N2 15 KR–K1, P–QB4 (best; after 15 . . . KR–B1 16 QR–Q1, P–R3 17 B–N3, White maintains a slight edge) 16 P–Q5, PxP 17 PxP, Q–B3! 18 QxQ, NxQ 19 QR–Q1, QR–Q1 20 R–K7, BxP with equal chances.

9 Q–B2 is considered to be White's best chance. 9 B–Q3, NxN! 10 PxN, PxP 11 BxP, N–Q2 12 O–O, P–QN3 and 9 NxN, PxN 10 N–Q2, P–KB4 11 R–B1, N–Q2 12 Q–B2, P–B3 13 P–B5, P–K4 are both easier for Black. For 9 PxP and 9 R–B1, see Prac. Var. 8 and 9 respectively.

(7) 7 . . . P–QN3 8 PxP (most usual, but 8 B–Q3 is not bad either, e.g., 8 . . . B–N2 9 O–O, PxP 10 BxP, QN–Q2 11 Q–K2, N–K5 12 B–KN3!, NxB 13 RPxN, P–QB4 14 KR–Q1 with a good game for White, as in Gligoric–Unzicker, Dubrovnik 1950), NxP (8 . . . PxP 9 B–Q3, B–K3! 10 N–K5, KN–Q2 is also playable) 9 BxB (if 9 B–N3, P–QB4), QxB (for 9 . . . NxB, see Prac. Var. 10) 10 NxN, PxN 11 R–B1 (also promising is 11 B–Q3; see Prac. Var. 11), B–K3! (an unusual but correct development of the Bishop; after 11 . . . B–N2 12 B–K2, P–QB4 13 PxP, PxP 14 O–O, N–Q2 15 P–QN4!, White has the edge) 12 Q–R4, P–QB4 13 Q–R3 (for 13 PxP, see Game 5), R–B1 14 B–K2, Q–B1 (Russian analysts have kept themselves busy with 14 . . . Q–N2; 14 . . . K–B1 also seems to be good) 15 PxP, PxP 16 O–O, N–Q2 17 N–Q2 (to prepare for P–K4). White has a slight edge.

*Orthodox Queen's Gambit Game 5*

*WHITE: Pomar* — *BLACK: Kottnauer*

*Hastings 1959–60*

| | WHITE | BLACK | | WHITE | BLACK |
|---|---|---|---|---|---|
| 1 | P–Q4 | P–Q4 | 20 | N–K5 | QR–N1 |
| 2 | P–QB4 | P–K3 | 21 | B–B6? | Q–B2 |
| 3 | N–QB3 | N–KB3 | 22 | P–B4 | R–N5 |
| 4 | B–N5 | B–K2 | 23 | Q–R3 | Q–N3 |
| 5 | P–K3 | P–KR3 | 24 | B–R4 | P–B5 |
| 6 | B–R4 | O–O | 25 | R–K1 | P–Q5! |
| 7 | N–B3 | P–QN3 | 26 | PxBP | PxP |
| 8 | PxP | NxP | 27 | P–B5 | RxQBP |
| 9 | BxB | QxB | 28 | RxR | QxR |
| 10 | NxN | PxN | 29 | N–Q3 | Q–Q5 |
| 11 | R–B1 | B–K3 | 30 | NxR | P–K7† |
| 12 | Q–R4 | P–B4 | 31 | K–R1 | Q–B7 |
| 13 | PxP | PxP | 32 | Q–B1 | PxN |
| 14 | B–N5 | R–B1 | 33 | B–B6 | B–B5! |
| 15 | O–O | Q–N2 | 34 | R–N1? | N–N5 |
| 16 | P–QN3 | P–QR3 | 35 | B–K4 | Q–R5 |
| 17 | B–K2 | N–Q2 | 36 | P–KR3 | Q–N6 |
| 18 | KR–Q1 | P–QR4 | | Resigns | |
| 19 | B–N5 | N–B3 | | | |

PRACTICAL VARIATIONS 8–11:

1 P–Q4, P–Q4 2 P–QB4, P–K3 3 N–QB3, N–KB3 4 B–N5, B–K2 5 P–K3, O–O 6 N–B3, P–KR3 7 B–R4

| | 8 | 9 | 10 | 11 |
|---|---|---|---|---|
| 7 | – – | – – | – – | – – |
| | N–K5 | – – | P–QN3 | – – |
| 8 | BxB | – – | PxP | – – |
| | QxB | – – | NxP | – – |
| 9 | PxP | R–B1 | BxB | – – |
| | NxN | P–QB3 | NxB | QxB |
| 10 | PxN | B–Q3 | B–K2 | NxN |
| | PxP | NxN | N–Q2![6] | PxN |
| 11 | Q–N3 | RxN | O–O | B–Q3 |
| | Q–Q3![1] | PxP | P–QB4! | B–K3 |
| 12 | P–B4 | RxP | PxP | O–O |
| | PxP | N–Q2 | NxP | P–QB4 |
| 13 | BxP | B–B2 | P–QN4 | PxP |
| | N–B3 | R–Q1 | N–Q2 | PxP |
| 14 | Q–B3[2] | Q–Q3 | Q–Q6 | P–K4 |
| | B–N5 | N–B1[5] | N–N3[7] | P–Q5[8] |
| 15 | N–Q2[3] | ± | = | ± |
| | QR–Q1 | | | |
| 16 | O–O | | | |
| | N–K2 | | | |
| 17 | KR–B1 | | | |
| | P–QB4![4] | | | |
| | = | | | |

*Notes to practical variations 8–11:*

[1] Bernstein's move, which is the best. Other methods have not met with success in practical play, e.g., 11 . . . R–Q1 12 P–B4, N–B3 13 PxP, Q–N5† 14 N–Q2±.

[2] 14 B–K2! possibly offers White better chances, e.g., 14 . . . B–K3 15 Q–B3!, Q–N5 16 K–Q2! etc.

[3] For 15 O–O, see Game 6.

[4] Black has solved his opening problems.

[5] White controls more space.

[6] Stronger than 10 . . . B–N2 11 O–O, N–Q2 12 Q–R4±.

[7] With equal chances (Alekhine).

[8] So far the game Filip–Podgorny, 1948. Pachman points out that White now obtains excellent chances with 15 N–Q2 followed by P–B4.

*Orthodox Queen's Gambit Game 6*

*WHITE: Euwe* *BLACK: Eliskases*

*Noordwijk 1938*

| WHITE | BLACK | WHITE | BLACK |
|---|---|---|---|
| 1 P–Q4 | P–Q4 | 4 B–N5 | B–K2 |
| 2 P–QB4 | P–K3 | 5 P–K3 | P–KR3 |
| 3 N–QB3 | N–KB3 | 6 B–R4 | O–O |

| WHITE | BLACK | WHITE | BLACK |
|---|---|---|---|
| 7 N–B3 | N–K5 | 30 BxN | RxB |
| 8 BxB | QxB | 31 Q–B5 | R–K1 |
| 9 PxP | NxN | 32 K–N2 | P–N3 |
| 10 PxN | PxP | 33 PxP | Q–K3! |
| 11 Q–N3 | Q–Q3 | 34 Q–K5† | QxQ |
| 12 P–B4 | PxP | 35 PxQ | RxP |
| 13 BxP | N–QB3 | 36 PxP | R–QR4 |
| 14 Q–B3 | B–N5 | 37 P–QR4 | P–N4 |
| 15 O–O | BxN | 38 PxP | PxP |
| 16 PxB | QR–Q1 | 39 R–N7? | P–N5 |
| 17 K–R1 | Q–B3 | 40 RxP | P–R3! |
| 18 B–K2 | KR–K1 | 41 R–B8† | K–R2 |
| 19 QR–K1 | R–Q2 | 42 R–B7† | K–N1 |
| 20 R–KN1 | N–K2 | 43 R–Q7 | P–N6 |
| 21 R–N2 | N–B4 | 44 R–Q1 | R–N4 |
| 22 R/1–KN1 | K–R1 | 45 K–B3 | P–N7 |
| 23 R–N4 | P–KN3 | 46 R–QN1 | P–QR4 |
| 24 R–B4 | P–KN4 | 47 K–K2 | P–R5 |
| 25 R–K4 | R/2–K2 | 48 K–Q3 | P–R6 |
| 26 R/1–N4 | P–B3 | 49 K–B2 | P–R7 |
| 27 RxR | RxR | 50 RxP | R–B4† |
| 28 P–B4 | N–Q3 | Resigns | |
| 29 B–B3 | N–K5 | | |

---

## part 4—ANTI-NEO-ORTHODOX VARIATION

1 P–Q4, P–Q4
2 P–QB4, P–K3
3 N–QB3, N–KB3
4 B–N5, B–K2
5 P–K3, O–O
6 R–B1[A], P–KR3
7 B–R4

KEY POSITION 4

### OBSERVATIONS ON KEY POSITION 4

[A] This has been tried as an improvement of White's set-up. If now 6 . . . QN–Q2 then 7 N–B3, P–B3, transposing into the Classical Variation (Part 1). The text move aims at a deployment which offers White the chance to act more effectively against the Lasker and Tartakover methods.

Once again we encounter 7 . . . N–K5 (Lasker) and 7 . . . P–QN3 (Tartakover). In both cases Black's job is more difficult because White can play his Queen or King Bishop to KB3 effectively while his King Knight develops via K2 and KB4. White's chances for initiative are better than in the variations treated in Part 3.

### IDEA VARIATIONS 8 AND 9:

(8) 7 . . . N–K5 8 BxB, QxB 9 PxP (the point of the Anti-Lasker Variation; the position now is similar in character to the Exchange Variation, discussed in Part 5),

NxN 10 RxN, PxP 11 B–Q3, P–QB3 12 N–K2 (the characteristic development of the Knight; after 12 N–B3, B–N5, Black's game is easier; for 12 B–N1, see Prac. Var. 12), N–Q2 13 O–O, N–B3 14 Q–N1! (preparing for the minority attack on the Queenside; 14 N–B4 leads to an even game after 14 . . . B–N5 15 Q–B2, N–R4 16 NxN, BxN, as in Reshevsky–Euwe, AVRO 1938), R–K1 (14 . . . P–QR4 is another possibility) 15 P–QN4, P–QR3 16 P–QR4, Q–Q3 17 KR–B1. White has the edge. Idea Var. 8 is exemplified by Taimanov–Goldenov, Moscow 1952.

(9) 7 . . . P–QN3 8 PxP (most usual; also promising is 8 BxN, BxB 9 PxP, PxP 10 Q–B3!, B–K3 11 B–B4!, followed, as in a game Bronstein–Geller, by 11 . . . P–B3 12 B–N3, Q–Q2 13 KN–K2, N–R3 14 N–B4 with strong pressure on Black's position), NxP (perhaps under the circumstances 8 . . . PxP serves well; after 9 B–Q3, B–N2 10 P–B3, P–B4 11 N–K2, White's advantage is minimal) 9 NxN, PxN 10 BxB, QxB 11 B–K2 (the King Bishop will have an excellent square in KB3; weaker is 11 Q–B2 because of 11 . . . P–QB4! 12 PxP, P–Q5! etc.; for 11 N–K2, see Prac. Var. 13), P–QB4 (after 11 . . . Q–N5†; 12 Q–Q2, QxQ† 13 KxQ, P–QB3 14 N–B3, B–N2 15 N–K5!, R–B1 16 P–QN4, the end game is practically untenable for Black, as was shown in the game Najdorf–Pilnik, Mar del Plata 1955) 12 B–B3, B–N2 (the Bishop is better placed here than on K3 in view of White's coming maneuver KN–K2–B4) 13 N–K2, R–Q1 (after 13 . . . N–Q2, White's best is 14 O–O; for 13 . . . P–B5, see Game 7) 14 O–O. White has a slight pull.

*Orthodox Queen's Gambit Game 7*

*WHITE: Euwe* *BLACK: Minev*

*Amsterdam 1954*

| | WHITE | BLACK | | WHITE | BLACK |
|---|---|---|---|---|---|
| 1 | P–Q4 | P–Q4 | 10 | BxB | QxB |
| 2 | P–QB4 | P–K3 | 11 | B–K2 | B–N2 |
| 3 | N–QB3 | N–KB3 | 12 | B–B3 | P–B4 |
| 4 | B–N5 | B–K2 | 13 | N–K2 | P–B5 |
| 5 | P–K3 | P–KR3 | 14 | P–QN3 | P–QN4 |
| 6 | B–R4 | O–O | 15 | N–B3 | Q–Q2 |
| 7 | R–B1 | P–QN3 | 16 | PxP | NPxP |
| 8 | PxP | NxP | 17 | O–O | R–K1 |
| 9 | NxN | PxN | 18 | R–N1 | B–B3 |

| | WHITE | BLACK | | WHITE | BLACK |
|---|---|---|---|---|---|
| 19 | Q–B1 | N–R3 | 30 | RxP | K–Q3 |
| 20 | Q–R3 | N–B2 | 31 | RxB† | KxR |
| 21 | Q–R5 | P–B4 | 32 | R–QB1 | QR–N1 |
| 22 | R–N4 | KR–Q1 | 33 | NxP† | K–Q3 |
| 23 | KR–N1 | N–K3 | 34 | R–B2 | KR–QB1 |
| 24 | P–N3 | Q–QB2 | 35 | N–B3 | N–B2 |
| 25 | QxQ | NxQ | 36 | P–N4! | P–N3 |
| 26 | K–B1 | K–B1 | 37 | P–R5! | R–B1 |
| 27 | K–K1 | K–K2 | 38 | PxNP | PxP |
| 28 | K–Q2 | K–K3 | 39 | N–K4† | K–K3 |
| 29 | P–KR4 | N–R3 | 40 | BxP† | Resigns |

## PRACTICAL VARIATIONS 12 AND 13:

1 P–Q4, P–Q4 2 P–QB4, P–K3 3 N–QB3, N–KB3 4 B–N5, B–K2 5 P–K3, O–O 6 R–B1, P–KR3 7 B–R4

| | *12* | *13* |
|---|---|---|
| *7* | – – | – – |
| | N–K5 | P–QN3 |
| *8* | BxB | PxP |
| | QxB | NxP |
| *9* | PxP | NxN |
| | NxN | PxN |
| *10* | RxN | BxB |
| | PxP | QxB |
| *11* | B–Q3 | N–K2 |
| | P–QB3 | B–N2[2] |
| *12* | B–N1 | N–B4 |
| | N–Q2 | P–QB4 |
| *13* | N–B3 | PxP |
| | R–Q1![1] | R–Q1! |
| *14* | = | B–N5! |
| | | PxP[3] |
| *15* | | O–O |
| | | N–R3 |
| *16* | | Q–R5 |
| | | Q–B3! |
| *17* | | KR–Q1[4] |
| | | QxP |
| *18* | | QR–N1 |
| | | Q–B3[5] |
| | | = |

*Notes to practical variations 12–13:*

[1] Weaker is 13 . . . N–B3? 14 N–K5!, B–K3 15 P–B4, QR–Q1 16 O–O, KR–K1 17 P–KN4! with a strong attack for White (Euwe–Spanjaard, Baarn 1939). After the text move Black has sufficient counterplay.

[2] 11 . . . B–R3 is simply answered by 12 N–B4, BxB 13 KxB.

[3] 14 . . . P–Q5 15 O–O, PxKP 16 Q–K2 favors White.

[4] Or 17 BxN, BxB 18 NxP, QxP 19 R–K1, QxP 20 N–B7, QR–B1 21 R–R1, B–K7! etc.

[5] Taimanov–Szabo, Moscow 1956. Black is able to maintain the balance.

## part 5—EXCHANGE VARIATION

1 P–Q4, P–Q4
2 P–QB4, P–K3
3 N–QB3, N–KB3
4 PxP[A], PxP[B]
5 B–N5[C], P–B3
6 Q–B2[D], B–K2
7 P–K3[E], QN–Q2[F]
8 B–Q3

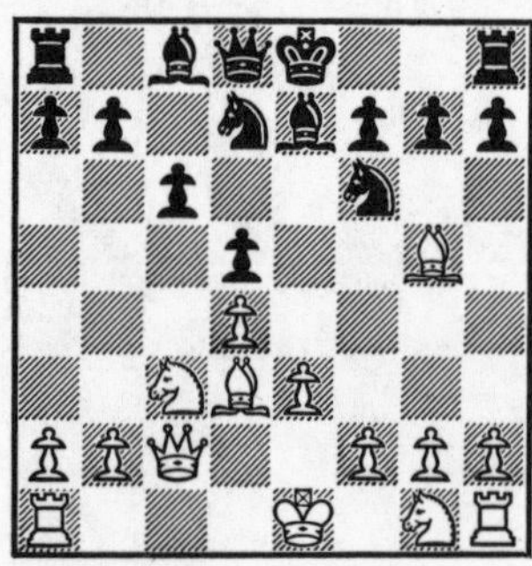

KEY POSITION 5

OBSERVATIONS ON KEY POSITION 5

[A] This exchange, may be deferred.

[B] 4 . . . NxP is questionable. In Teschner–Trifunovic, Bled 1956, there followed 5 P–K4, NxN 6 PxN, P–QB4 7 R–N1!, PxP 8 PxP, N–B3 9 B–QN5, B–K2 10 N–K2, with an excellent game for White.

[C] Another possibility is 5 N–B3, B–K2 6 B–B4, but after 6 . . . P–B3 7 Q–B2, P–KN3! 8 P–K3, B–KB4 9 B–Q3, BxB 10 QxB, QN–Q2 11 P–KR3, N–B1, Black has sufficient counterplay (Kotov–Stahlberg, Zurich 1953).

[D] Most accurate. White prevents 6 . . . B–KB4.

[E] If 7 N–B3, Black can again proceed with 7 . . . P–KN3, e.g., 8 P–K3, B–KB4 9 B–Q3, BxB 10 QxB, O–O 11 BxN!, BxB 12 P–QN4, and White has only a slight edge.

[F] 7 . . . N–K5? fails against 8 BxB, QxB 9 NxP! Nor is 7 . . . B–KN5 8 B–Q3, B–R4 9 KN–K2, B–N3 10 N–B4, BxB 11 NxB satisfactory for Black.

This position occurs most frequently in the Exchange Variation. White has good chances on the Queenside, where he can launch the minority attack with P–QN4–N5. Black on the other hand, must strive to free himself by means of . . . N–K5 or possibly . . . N–K1 or . . . N–KR4. Later he may start an attack on the Kingside by means of P–KB4–5. Normally White maintains a slight but lasting advantage.

IDEA VARIATIONS 10 AND 11:

(10) 8 . . . P–KR3 9 B–R4 (weaker is 9 B–KB4, e.g., 9 . . . N–R4! 10 B–K5, NxB 11 PxN, P–Q5! etc.), O–O (9 . . . N–R4 is also playable here) 10 N–B3 (for 10 KN–K2, see Prac. Var. 15), R–K1 11 O–O (sounder than 11 O–O–O, N–K5! 12 BxB, QxB 13 BxN, PxB 14 N–Q2, N–B3 with a good game for Black), N–K5! (11 . . . N–B1 is too passive; see Prac. Var. 16) 12 BxB (or 12 BxN, BxB 13 B–R7†, K–R1 14 B–Q3, B–K2 with an even game), QxB 13 BxN (if 13 QR–N1, N–Q3! 14 P–QN4, P–QN4!), PxB 14 N–Q2, N–B3=.

8 . . . O–O is not to be recommended because of 9 P–KN4! — a continuation which, by the way, is little known but would seem to offer White strong attacking chances. For 8 . . . N–R4, see Idea Var. 11, and for 8 . . . N–B1, see Prac. Var. 14.

(11) 8 . . . N–R4 (also a good continuation) 9 BxB (if 9 P–KR4, Black's best continuation is 9 . . . P–KN3), QxB 10 KN–K2 (forestalling 10 . . . N–B5 and safer than the venturesome 10 BxP, P–KN3 11 BxP, with which no experience can be cited; worth considering is 10 O–O–O, as in 10 . . . N–N3 11 N–B3, B–N5; 12 QR–N1!, BxN 13 PxB, O–O–O 14 N–R4, NxN 15 QxN, K–N1 16 K–N1, Q–R5 with balanced chances), P–KN3 11 O–O (for 11 O–O–O, see Prac. Var. 17), P–KB4 (11 . . . O–O is also good; see Game 8) 12 QR–N1 (12 KR–K1, O–O also leads to an even game), O–O; 13 P–QN4, P–QR3 14 P–QR4, P–B5. The line is taken from Bouwmeester–Euwe, Amsterdam, 1950. Black has a satisfactory game.

*Orthodox Queen's Gambit Game 8*

*WHITE: Kottnauer* — *BLACK: Euwe*

*Amsterdam 1950*

| | WHITE | BLACK | | WHITE | BLACK |
|---|---|---|---|---|---|
| 1 | P–QB4 | P–K3 | 18 | Q–B5 | Q–K3 |
| 2 | N–QB3 | P–Q4 | 19 | N–N6 | R–QN1 |
| 3 | P–Q4 | N–KB3 | 20 | P–B3 | R–Q1 |
| 4 | B–N5 | QN–Q2 | 21 | P–K4? | PxP |
| 5 | P–K3 | P–B3 | 22 | PxP | N–N5! |
| 6 | PxP | PxKP | 23 | B–B4 | Q–Q3 |
| 7 | B–Q3 | B–K2 | 24 | QxQ | RxQ |
| 8 | Q–B2 | N–R4 | 25 | QR–Q1 | B–K3 |
| 9 | BxB | QxB | 26 | R–Q3? | QR–Q1 |
| 10 | KN–K2 | P–KN3 | 27 | KR–Q1 | BxB |
| 11 | O–O | O–O | 28 | NxB | R–K3 |
| 12 | N–N3(?) | NxN | 29 | N–Q2 | N–K4! |
| 13 | RPxN | N–B3 | 30 | P–Q5 | NxR |
| 14 | KR–K1 | Q–Q3 | 31 | PxR | N–K4! |
| 15 | P–R3 | K–N2 | 32 | PxP | NxP |
| 16 | P–QN4 | P–QR3 | 33 | K–B2 | R–Q6 |
| 17 | N–R4 | P–KR4 | | Resigns | |

PRACTICAL VARIATIONS 14–17:

1 P–Q4, P–Q4 2 P–QB4, P–K3 3 N–QB3, N–KB3 4 PxP, PxP 5 B–N5, P–B3 6 Q–B2, B–K2 7 P–K3, QN–Q2 8 B–Q3

| | *14* | *15* | *16* | *17* |
|---|---|---|---|---|
| *8* | – – | – – | – – | – – |
| | N–B1 | P–KR3 | – – | N–R4 |
| *9* | N–B3[1] | B–R4 | – – | BxB |
| | N–K3 | O–O | – – | QxB |
| *10* | B–R4[2] | KN–K2 | N–B3 | KN–K2 |
| | P–KN3 | N–K1 | R–K1 | P–KN3 |
| *11* | O–O | B–N3 | O–O | O–O–O |
| | O–O[3] | N/2–B3 | N–B1 | P–KB4 |
| *12* | QR–N1 | O–O | QR–N1[6] | N–B4!?[8] |
| | P–QR4 | B–Q3[5] | N–K5 | NxN |
| *13* | P–QR3 | = | BxB | PxN |
| | N–N2 | | QxB | O–O[9] |
| *14* | P–QN4 | | P–QN4![7] | = |
| | PxP | | ± | |
| *15* | PxP | | | |
| | B–KB4 | | | |
| *16* | P–N5[4] | | | |
| | ± | | | |

*Notes to practical variations 14–17:*

[1] 9 KN–K2, N–K3 10 B–R4, P–KN3 11 P–B3 deserves consideration.

[2] 10 P–KR4, P–KR3 11 BxN, BxB is satisfactory for Black.

[3] 11 . . . N–N2 is effectively answered by 12 P–QN4!

[4] Szabo–Stahlberg, Zurich 1953.

[5] With practically even chances, although the onus of proving equality is on Black.

[6] Also good is 12 BxN, BxB 13 P–QN4 etc.

[7] The minority attack is shaping up.

[8] 12 P–KR3, O–O 13 P–KN4, N–N2 leads to a good game for Black.

[9] Black is sufficiently safe.

1 P–Q4, P–Q4
2 P–QB4, P–K3
3 N–QB3, N–KB3
4 N–B3, P–B4[A]

KEY POSITION 6

## part 6—HALF-CLASSICAL VARIATION

### OBSERVATIONS ON KEY POSITION 6

[A] Of course, there are several other possibilities. After 4 . . . QN–Q2 or 4 . . . B–K2, White can proceed with either 5 PxP or 5 B–N5, leading to well-known positions. Interesting for Black is 4 . . . B–N5, the so-called Ragosin system, which has been adopted of late by Fischer. It may go 5 PxP, PxP 6 B–N5, P–KR3 7 BxN (if 7 B–R4, P–KN4! leads to complications),

QxB 8 Q–R4†, N–B3 9 P–K3, O–O 10 B–K2, B–K3 11 O–O, P–QR3 12 KR–B1, B–Q3 13 Q–Q1, when White has a slight edge, as shown in Olafsson–Petrosian, Candidate's Tournament 1959.

The game may develop in several ways. White can either remove the tension in the center by means of 5 PxP or maintain the tension for the time being by means of 5 PxQP. These are the most important possibilities. 5 P–K3 leads to the so-called Closed Variation of the Tarrasch Defense, which offers little chance for initiative. The two first mentioned possibilities usually create a complicated struggle with chances for both sides. Most often White maintains a slight advantage in the center.

Black has to watch out for tactical turns as well as unfavorable transpositions into the Tarrasch Defense.

IDEA VARIATIONS 12 AND 13:

(12) 5 PxQP (most usual), NxP (5 . . . KPxP is a variation of the Tarrasch which is definitely unfavorable for Black, and apparently 5 . . . BPxP is equally untrustworthy; see Prac. Var. 18 and Game 9) 6 P–K3 (after 6 P–KN3, N–QB3! 7 B–N2, NxP 8 KNxN, NxN!, Black has no difficulties [Alekhine–Euwe, 30th Match Game 1937]; for 6 P–K4, see Prac. Var. 19), N–QB3 7 B–B4 (also possible is 7 B–Q3; see Prac. Var. 20), PxP (better than 7 . . . NxN 8 PxN, PxP 9 KPxP, B–K2 10 O–O, O–O 11 Q–K2±, as in Stahlberg–Szabo, Helsinki 1952) 8 PxP, B–K2 9 O–O, O–O 10 R–K1 (after 10 BxN, PxB 11 Q–N3, Black, according to Pachman, has sufficient counterplay in 11 . . . B–KN5), NxN (bad is 10 . . . P–QN3? 11 NxN, PxN 12 B–QN5!, as illustrated in Botvinnik–Alekhine, AVRO 1938) 11 PxN, P–QN3 12 B–Q3, B–N2 13 Q–B2, P–N3 (13 . . . P–KR3 is effectively met with 14 Q–K2!) 14 B–KR6, R–K1 15 Q–Q2, R–QB1 16 QR–B1, B–B3 (weaker is 16 . . . Q–B2 because of 17 P–KR4!, as in Najdorf–Sliwa, Moscow 1956) 17 Q–B4, B–N2 (for 17 . . . N–R4?, see Game 10) 18 B–KN5, Q–B2 19 Q–R4, N–K2, and Black holds his own.

(13) 5 B–N5 (this continuation is known for its two famous games between Pillsbury and Lasker in 1896 and 1904), PxQP (practically forced; 5 . . . PxBP 6 P–K4, PxP 7 NxP! favors White) 6 KNxP (after 6 QxP, Black's safest is 6 . . . B–K2; Donner–Euwe, Beverwijk 1950, continued with 7 PxP, PxP 8 P–K3, N–B3 9 B–N5, O–O

10 Q–QR4, N–K5! 11 NxN, PxN, and Black obtained good counterplay for the Pawn), P–K4; 7 N–B3 (too risky is 7 N/4–N5, P–QR3! 8 Q–R4, B–Q2 and it is Black for choice; in this variation 8 NxP? is refuted by 8 . . . PxN 9 NxN†, QxN and Black wins), P–Q5 8 N–Q5, B–K2! 9 BxN, BxB 10 P–K4, PxP e.p. 11 N/5xP (11 PxP, P–K5! favors Black), QxQ† 12 RxQ, P–K5 13 N–Q4, N–B3=.

*Orthodox Queen's Gambit Game 9*

*WHITE: Geller* *BLACK: Keres*

*Zurich 1953*

| | WHITE | BLACK | | WHITE | BLACK |
|---|---|---|---|---|---|
| 1 | P–Q4 | P–Q4 | 15 | B–KR4 | N–K5 |
| 2 | P–QB4 | P–K3 | 16 | B–N3 | NxN |
| 3 | N–QB3 | N–KB3 | 17 | PxN | B–B3! |
| 4 | N–B3 | P–B4 | 18 | QxR† | QxQ |
| 5 | PxQP | BPxP | 19 | RxQ† | RxR |
| 6 | QxP | PxP | 20 | RxP | R–QB1! |
| 7 | P–K4! | N–B3 | 21 | R–Q3? | N–N5! |
| 8 | B–QN5 | NxP | 22 | R–K3 | NxP |
| 9 | O–O | N–B3 | 23 | P–R3 | BxN |
| 10 | R–K1† | B–K2 | 24 | PxB | NxP |
| 11 | Q–K5? | O–O | 25 | B–Q7 | R–Q1 |
| 12 | Q–K2 | R–K1 | 26 | B–B5 | P–KN3 |
| 13 | B–N5 | B–KN5 | 27 | B–Q3 | N–Q8 |
| 14 | QR–Q1 | P–KR3 | | Resigns | |

*Orthodox Queen's Gambit Game 10*

*WHITE: Bolbochan* *BLACK: Pachman*

*Moscow 1956*

| | WHITE | BLACK | | WHITE | BLACK |
|---|---|---|---|---|---|
| 1 | P–Q4 | P–Q4 | 12 | B–Q3 | B–N2 |
| 2 | P–QB4 | P–K3 | 13 | Q–B2 | P–N3 |
| 3 | N–QB3 | N–KB3 | 14 | B–R6 | R–K1 |
| 4 | N–B3 | P–B4 | 15 | Q–Q2 | R–QB1 |
| 5 | PxQP | NxP | 16 | QR–B1 | B–B3 |
| 6 | P–K3 | N–QB3 | 17 | Q–B4 | N–R4? |
| 7 | B–B4 | PxP | 18 | N–K5 | N–B3 |
| 8 | PxP | B–K2 | 19 | N–N4 | B–R5 |
| 9 | O–O | O–O | 20 | P–N3 | B–K2 |
| 10 | R–K1 | NxN | 21 | B–QB4 | R–B2? |
| 11 | PxN | P–QN3 | 22 | QxP†! | Resigns |

PRACTICAL VARIATIONS 18–20:

1 P–Q4, P–Q4 2 P–QB4, P–K3 3 N–QB3, N–KB3 4 N–B3, P–B4

| | 18 | 19 | 20 |
|---|---|---|---|
| 5 | PxQP | – – | – – |
| | BPxP | NxP | – – |
| 6 | QxP | P–K4 | P–K3 |
| | PxP | NxN | N–QB3 |
| 7 | P–K4! | PxN | B–Q3 |
| | N–B3 | PxP | PxP[8] |
| 8 | B–QN5 | PxP | PxP |
| | P–QR3[1] | B–N5† | B–K2 |
| 9 | PxP[2] | B–Q2 | O–O |
| | PxB | BxB† | O–O |
| 10 | PxN | QxB | Q–K2! |
| | QxQ | O–O | N–B3[9] |
| 11 | NxQ | B–B4[4] | R–Q1 |
| | PxP | N–B3[5] | N–QN5 |
| 12 | NxBP | O–O | B–QB4 |
| | B–N2 | P–QN3 | P–QN3 |
| 13 | N–Q4 | KR–Q1 | N–K5 |
| | BxP | B–N2 | B–N2[10] |
| 14 | R–KN1[3] | Q–B4 | = |
| | ± | Q–B3[6] | |
| 15 | | Q–K3 | |
| | | KR–Q1 | |
| 16 | | P–K5 | |
| | | Q–R3![7] | |
| | | = | |

*Notes to practical variations 18–20:*

[1] 8 . . . NxP 9 O–O, N–B3 10 B–N5!, B–K2 11 BxN, BxB 12 Q–B5! leads to very promising possibilities for White. See also Game 9. 8 . . . B–Q2 (Vukovic) can be well answered by 9 BxN, BxB 10 PxP, BxP 11 O–O!

[2] Better than 9 BxN†, PxB 10 N–K5, B–N2 11 PxP, NxP 12 O–O, B–K2 13 NxQBP!?, BxN 14 QxP, B–B3! 15 R–K1†, K–Q2 and White's attack peters out.

[3] Tactically and materially White has the edge (Vukovic).

[4] 11 B–K2 also deserves consideration.

[5] Better than 11 . . . N–Q2 12 O–O, P–QN3 13 QR–Q1± (Keres–Fine, Ostend 1937).

[6] Simplest. The exchange of Queens is not bad for Black.

[7] Reshevsky–Fine, Hastings 1937–38.

[8] 7 . . . NxN 8 PxN, B–K2 9 Q–B2, P–KN3 10 P–KR4! is very good for White.

[9] The acceptance of the Pawn sacrifice after 10 . . . N/4–N5 11 B–K4! is very dangerous for Black.

[10] Najdorf–Fine, 1949.

## SUPPLEMENTARY VARIATIONS 1–10:
### 1 P–Q4, P–Q4 2 P–QB4, P–K3

| | 1 | 2 | 3 | 4 | 5 |
|---|---|---|---|---|---|
| 3 | N–QB3 | – – | – – | – – | – – |
| | N–KB3 | – – | – – | – – | – – |
| 4 | B–N5 | – – | – – | – – | – – |
| | B–K2 | – – | – – | – – | – – |
| 5 | P–K3 | – – | – – | – – | – – |
| | O–O | – – | – – | – – | – – |
| 6 | N–B3 | – – | – – | – – | – – |
| | QN–Q2 | – – | – – | – – | – – |
| 7 | R–B1 | – – | – – | – – | – – |
| | P–B3 | – – | – – | – – | P–QR3[19] |
| 8 | B–Q3 | – – | – – | Q–B2[15] | PxP[20] |
| | PxP | – – | P–KR3 | N–K5[16] | PxP |
| 9 | BxP | – – | B–R4[9] | BxB | B–Q3 |
| | N–Q4 | – – | PxP | QxB | P–B3 |
| 10 | B–B4 | P–KR4 | BxP | B–Q3 | Q–B2[21] |
| | NxB[1] | NxN | P–QN4[10] | NxN | = |
| 11 | PxN | RxN[6] | B–Q3 | QxN[17] | |
| | N–N3 | P–QN3[7] | P–R3 | PxP | |
| 12 | B–N3 | B–N3 | P–R4![11] | BxP | |
| | N–Q4 | B–N2[8] | PxP[12] | P–QN3[18] | |
| 13 | Q–Q2 | = | NxP | = | |
| | Q–Q3[2] | | Q–R4† | | |
| 14 | N–K5[3] | | N–Q2[13] | | |
| | NxN | | B–N5 | | |
| 15 | PxN[4] | | N–B3 | | |
| | P–QB4 | | P–B4 | | |
| 16 | O–O | | N–N3[14] | | |
| | P–QN4[5] | | ± | | |
| 17 | ∓ | | | | |

*Notes to supplementary variations 1–10:*

[1] 10 . . . NxN also deserves consideration, e.g., 11 PxN, P–QN3 12 O–O, B–N2 13 P–K4, N–B3 14 Q–K2, P–B4 with even chances.

[2] Better than 13 . . . NxN 14 QxN, Q–Q3 15 Q–K3!±.

[3] Or 14 P–N3, NxN! 15 QxN, P–QN3! and Black has a good game.

[4] Not 15 QxN? because of 15 . . . R–Q1!

| 6 | 7 | 8 | 9 | 10 |
|---|---|---|---|---|
| – – | – – | – – | – – | N–KB3 |
| – – | – – | – – | – – | N–KB3 |
| – – | – – | – – | – – | B–N5 |
| – – | – – | – – | P–B4!?[33] | B–N5†[39] |
| – – | – – | – – | PxQP | N–B3 |
| – – | – – | – – | BPxP[34] | PxP |
| – – | – – | – – | QxP[35] | P–K4 |
| – – | – – | – – | B–K2 | P–B4 |
| – – | Q–B2 | B–Q3 | P–K4 | P–K5[40] |
| P–QN3 | P–B4[26] | PxP[31] | N–B3 | PxP |
| PxP | PxQP[27] | BxP | Q–Q2[36] | Q–R4† |
| PxP[22] | NxP[28] | P–B4 | NxKP | N–B3 |
| B–N5[23] | BxB | O–O | NxN | O–O–O |
| B–N2 | QxB[29] | P–QR3 | PxP | B–Q2! |
| O–O[24] | NxN | P–QR4 | BxB | N–K4 |
| P–QR3 | PxN | P–QN3 | QxB | B–K2 |
| B–QR4 | PxP | Q–K2 | QxP[37] | PxN |
| P–B4 | NxP | B–N2 | P–B4[37] | PxP |
| PxP[25] | B–K2[30] | KR–Q1 | B–N5! | B–R4 |
| ± | ± | Q–B2[32] | QxN† | R–QB1![41] |
| | | = | QxQ | K–N1 |
| | | | PxQ | N–R4[42] |
| | | | R–B1 | Q–B2 |
| | | | B–Q2 | P–K4 |
| | | | N–K2![38] | NxQP |
| | | | ± | PxN |
| | | | | RxP |
| | | | | Q–N3 |
| | | | | RxB[43] |
| | | | | = |

[5] Black has the Bishop-pair and better Pawn structure.

[6] After 11 PxN, P–QN3 Black has no difficulties.

[7] Risky is 11 . . . P–B3 12 BxP†, K–R1 13 B–KB4, B–N5. White has compensation for the exchange.

[8] Black has a satisfactory game.

[9] 9 B–B4 is not bad, e.g., 9 . . . N–R4 10 B–K5!, NxB 11 PxN, P–KN3 12 O–O, and White has a slight edge.

[10] If now 10 . . . N–Q4 then 11 B–KN3!

continued ▸

[11] Other moves offer little chance for any advantage.

[12] 12 . . . P–N5 is best answered by 13 BxN, BxB 14 N–K4, P–K4 15 N–B5!±.

[13] Stronger than 14 N–B3, P–B4 15 O–O, PxP 16 NxP, B–N2 with an even game.

[14] White's deployment of his forces is superior.

[15] This is called a tempo-stroll variation (marking time). White wishes to avoid B–Q3 and then BxP.

[16] The Lasker method is simplest here.

[17] Bad is 11 BxP†?, K–R1 12 PxN, P–KB4!

[18] White cannot stave off the eventual liberating . . . P–QB4.

[19] Analyzed by the Swiss master Henneberger.

[20] The exchange method is best. Other moves offer practically no chance for advantage.

[21] Theoretically even, but Black's defense is difficult. See also Part 5.

[22] 8 . . . NxP? costs a Pawn after 9 NxN!

[23] 9 B–Q3 followed by 10 O–O, 11 N–K5 and 12 P–B4 is the Pillsbury Attack.

[24] 10 Q–R4, P–QR3 produces little.

[25] Since 12 . . . PxP? is not good because of 13 BxQN! QxB 14 N–QR4!, White has a slight pull.

[26] Best; 7 . . . P–B3 8 R–Q1 is promising for White.

[27] 8 R–Q1, Q–R4 9 B–Q3, P–KR3 10 B–R4, PxBP! 11 BxBP, N–N3 is satisfactory for Black. According to Pachman, 8 O–O–O, Q–R4 9 K–N1 is worth some consideration.

[28] Weaker is 8 . . . KPxP 9 R–Q1, P–B5 10 B–K2±.

[29] 9 . . . NxB can be strongly met by 10 O–O–O!

[30] White maintains a slight initiative.

[31] 7 . . . P–B4 is equally good.

[32] With an even game, although Black must play with care to maintain equality.

[33] This sharp line is accredited to the Dutch analysts Been and Koomen.

[34] Canal's Variation, 5 . . . Q–N3, is also interesting, e.g., 6 PxKP, PxQP 7 PxP†, KxP 8 N–R4, Q–R4† 9 B–Q2, B–QN5 10 Q–N3†, N–Q4 11 BxB, QxB† 12 QxQ, NxQ 13 R–Q1!, and it is questionable whether Black has enough compensation for the Pawn.

[35] 6 Q–R4†, QN–Q2! 7 BxN, QxB 8 N–N5, N–N3! favors Black.

[36] Best, according to present-day views.

[37] 11 . . . O–O is sufficient after 12 P–B3, N–N5 13 Q–B4 (Korchnoi).

[38] Black's isolated Pawn is a handicap.

[39] Again, of course, many transpositions are possible. The text move leads to the famous Vienna Variation. Another important alternative is 4 . . . P–KR3, e.g., 5 BxN, QxB 6 Q–N3, P–B3 7 N–B3, QN–Q2 8 P–K4, PxP 9 NxP, Q–B4! 10 B–Q3, Q–R4† 11 N–B3, and White has a slight edge.

[40] Most likely 7 BxP is even stronger. See Games 11 and 12.

[41] 12 . . . N–N5? 13 QxN! is a surprising possibility.

[42] Or 13 . . . P–N4 14 QxNP, P–B6 15 NxQP!

[43] Whites best chance. 17 Q–B3?, B–KB4! 18 P–KN4, B–N3 favors Black. White obtains good chances for the exchange.

*Orthodox Queen's Gambit Game 11*

*WHITE: Alekhine* *BLACK: Bogoljubov*

*Warsaw 1941*

| | WHITE | BLACK | | WHITE | BLACK |
|---|---|---|---|---|---|
| 1 | P–Q4 | P–Q4 | 11 | K–B1 | QxB† |
| 2 | P–QB4 | P–K3 | 12 | K–N1 | B–Q2 |
| 3 | N–KB3 | N–KB3 | 13 | R–B1 | Q–R3 |
| 4 | B–N5 | B–N5† | 14 | NxP! | PxN |
| 5 | N–B3 | PxP | 15 | R–B8† | K–B2 |
| 6 | P–K4 | P–B4 | 16 | RxR | PxB |
| 7 | BxP | PxP | 17 | Q–R5† | K–K2 |
| 8 | NxP | Q–R4 | 18 | Q–B5† | K–B2 |
| 9 | BxN | BxN† | 19 | RxP† | K–N1 |
| 10 | PxB | QxP† | 20 | Q–K7 | Resigns |

*Orthodox Queen's Gambit Game 12*

*WHITE: Stahlberg* *BLACK: Sefc*

*Trencianske Teplice 1949*

| | WHITE | BLACK | | WHITE | BLACK |
|---|---|---|---|---|---|
| 1 | P–Q4 | P–Q4 | 14 | R–B1 | Q–R3 |
| 2 | P–QB4 | P–K3 | 15 | B–R6 | N–B3 |
| 3 | N–KB3 | N–KB3 | 16 | P–K5! | N–Q4 |
| 4 | B–N5 | B–N5† | 17 | P–KR4! | B–Q2 |
| 5 | N–B3 | PxP | 18 | Q–B2! | R–N3 |
| 6 | P–K4 | P–B4 | 19 | P–R5! | R–N5 |
| 7 | BxP | PxP | 20 | QxP | K–K2 |
| 8 | NxP | Q–R4 | 21 | R–R4! | R/5–N1 |
| 9 | BxN | BxN† | 22 | B–N7 | Q–R6 |
| 10 | PxB | QxP† | 23 | B–B6† | K–B1 |
| 11 | K–B1 | QxB† | 24 | R–B7!! | NxB |
| 12 | K–N1 | N–Q2 | 25 | PxN | Q–Q3 |
| 13 | BxP | R–KN1 | 26 | P–R6! | Resigns |

# chapter 28—Queen Pawn Games
## Without Early P-QB4

The openings collectively known as Queen Pawn Games are distinguished from the Queen's Gambit by White's omission of P–QB4, at least in the very early stage of play. In these openings, White usually makes no attempt quickly to seize the initiative. This is not to say White does not seek an opening advantage. As in many of the slow-moving debuts, Black must beware of overestimating his chances. His impetuous tactics may boomerang.

The Colle System (Prac. Var. 1–2) is characterized by an early P–K3, soon to be followed by P–K4. Hence, White readily achieves the general mobilization of his minor pieces. White's plan is excellent, but its effective execution is a different matter. With proper caution, Black faces fewer problems than in the regular Queen's Gambit.

In playing the Classical Variation (Prac. Var. 3), White virtually transposes into the Black side of the Queen's Gambit, except that he enjoys more freedom than Black in the analogous position. For he has a move in hand. As for achieving an opening advantage, White's chance comes only against reckless play.

The Bishop's Defense (Prac. Var. 4–5) is marked by Black's early development of his Queen Bishop. Attempts by White quickly to profit from this sortie come to nought. By developing normally, possibly by transposing into a favorable variation of the Slav Defense, White may obtain a tiny edge.

The Queen's Bishop Game (Prac. Var. 6), identified by White's B–KB4, is one of the most promising of these openings. Black's best policy is to lead into the Exchange Variation of the Caro–Kann Defense, an option at his disposal.

Prac. Var. 7 is a Black effort to head off the Colle System by saving a move, getting in . . . P–K4 in one turn rather than two with . . . P–K3 and . . . P–K4. The column favors White, though Black's play conceivably may be improved.

The Blackmar–Diemer Gambit (Prac. Var. 8) arises after 2 P–K4 or 3 P–K4. The gambit is hoary, though recently stanchly advocated by the German, Diemer. He has had considerable success with it for the past ten years.

Profound theoretical knowledge by Black is required to avoid its pitfalls.

Prac. Var. 9, apart from dealing with some transpositional possibilities in the Blackmar–Diemer Gambit, illustrates a line in which White achieves P–K4 without sacrificing a Pawn. White, however, gains no advantage.

PRACTICAL VARIATIONS 1–9:

1 P–Q4, P–Q4

| | *1* | *2* | *3* | *4* | *5* | *6* | *7* | *8* | *9* |
|---|---|---|---|---|---|---|---|---|---|
| *2* | N–KB3 | – – | – – | – – | – – | – – | – – | P–K4 | N–QB3 |
| | N–KB3 | – – | – – | – – | – – | – – | P–QB4[27] | PxP[32] | N–KB3 |
| *3* | P–K3 | – – | – – | – – | – – | B–B4 | P–K3[28] | N–QB3[33] | P–B3[41] |
| | P–K3 | – – | – – | B–B4 | – – | P–B4[23] | N–KB3 | N–KB3 | B–B4 |
| *4* | QN–Q2 | – – | B–Q3 | P–B4 | B–Q3 | P–K3 | P–B3[29] | P–B3[34] | B–N5 |
| | P–B4 | – – | P–B4 | P–K3! | P–K3 | P–K3[24] | QN–Q2 | PxP[35] | P–B3 |
| *5* | P–B3[1] | – – | P–QN3 | Q–N3[17] | BxB[20] | P–B3 | QN–Q2 | NxP[36] | Q–Q2 |
| | N–B3 | QN–Q2[8] | N–B3 | Q–B1[18] | PxB | Q–N3 | Q–B2[30] | P–KN3[37] | QN–Q2 |
| *6* | B–Q3 | B–Q3[9] | B–N2 | N–B3 | Q–Q3 | Q–B1 | B–Q3 | B–QB4 | P–K4 |
| | B–Q3 | B–K2[10] | B–Q3 | P–B3 | Q–B1 | N–B3 | P–K4 | B–N2 | PxP |
| *7* | O–O | O–O | O–O | B–Q2 | P–QN3 | P–KR3[25] | P–K4! | N–K5 | Q–B4 |
| | O–O | O–O | O–O[13] | QN–Q2 | N–R3! | B–Q2 | PxKP | O–O | Q–R4 |
| *8* | PxP[2] | P–K4 | P–QR3[14] | R–B1 | O–O | B–K2 | QNxP | B–KN5 | O–O–O |
| | BxP | PxKP[11] | Q–K2 | B–Q3 | B–K2 | R–B1 | NxN | QN–Q2[38] | P–K3 |
| *9* | P–K4[3] | NxP | N–K5[15] | B–K2 | P–B4 | O–O | BxN | O–O | BxN |
| | Q–B2[4] | NxN[12] | R–Q1 | O–O | O–O | B–K2 | N–B3 | P–B4[39] | NxB |
| *10* | Q–K2[5] | BxN | N–Q2 | O–O | N–B3[21] | QN–Q2 | B–B2 | NxN | PxP |
| | N–KN5![6] | N–B3 | N–Q2 | P–KR3[19] | P–B3 | O–O | BPxP | BxN! | B–N3 |
| *11* | P–KR3 | B–B2 | P–KB4 | ∓ | B–N2 | Q–N1[26] | O–O! | PxP | B–Q3 |
| | KN–K4 | P–QN3 | N–B1[16] | | N–K5 | ± | PxP | Q–B2[40] | B–N5 |
| *12* | NxN | = | = | | KR–B1 | | NxP[31] | = | KN–K2 |
| | NxN | | | | R–Q1 | | ± | | P–K4![42] |
| *13* | N–B3 | | | | Q–K2 | | | | ∓ |
| | N–N3[7] | | | | Q–K3[22] | | | | |
| | = | | | | = | | | | |

*Notes to practical variations 1–9:*

[1] Starting point of the Colle System.

[2] The exchange must precede the advance of the King Pawn to avoid an isolated Queen Pawn (8 P–K4, PxQP 9 BPxP, PxP).

[3] White has achieved his initial objective.

[4] To prevent P–K5. 9 . . . PxP merely assists White. After 10 NxP, NxN 11 BxN, QxQ 12 RxQ, White's advantage is clear, thanks to his Queenside Pawn majority (Colle–Rubinstein, Berlin 1926). As for 9 . . . P–K4, this move also offers White the initiative with 10 Q–K2.

continued ▸

[5] 10 PxP, PxP 11 N–N3, B–N3 yields White little. The text move renews the threat of P–K5.

[6] After 10 . . . B–Q3 11 R–K1, N–KN5 12 P–KR3, N/5–K4 13 NxN, NxN 14 PxP, PxP 15 N–B3, White's edge is minimal.

[7] After 14 PxP, PxP, White must defend against 15 . . . BxRP, followed by 16 . . . Q–N6†.

[8] So as to meet PxP by . . . NxP.

[9] The thematic move to enforce P–K4.

[10] Another satisfactory continuation is 6 . . . B–Q3 7 O–O, O–O 8 P–K4, PxQP 9 BPxP, PxP 10 NxP, NxN 11 BxN, Q–N3! For 8 R–K1 in this line, see Game 1.

[11] Not 8 . . . PxQP because of 9 P–K5.

[12] 9 . . . PxP 10 NxP favors White.

[13] Castling is advisable before undertaking complications here.

[14] Preventing 8 . . . N–QN5. After 8 QN–Q2, Black proceeds comfortably with 8 . . . Q–K2, threatening not only 9 . . . PxP, followed by 10 . . . B–R6, but also 9 . . . P–K4. As for 8 N–K5, this sortie is met by 8 . . . Q–B2 9 P–KB4, PxP 10 PxP, N–QN5.

[15] Otherwise 9 . . . P–K4.

[16] Now that Black's critical King Rook Pawn has been properly protected, his game is satisfactory; he can play 12 . . . P–B3, followed possibly by . . . B–Q2 and . . . B–K1.

[17] White's Queenside attack is innocuous.

[18] The best defense. Even after 5 . . . N–B3 6 P–B5!, Q–B1! 7 B–N5, N–Q2 8 O–O, B–K2 9 Q–R4, N/3–N1 10 P–QN4, P–QB3, Black holds his own. 6 QxP? in this line is met by . . . N–QN5!

[19] Black's plus is in space.

[20] Not best. Correct is the transposition into the Slav Defense by means of 5 P–B4, P–B3 6 O–O, after which White has a minimal edge.

[21] 10 PxP is met by . . . N–QN5, followed by 11 . . . N/5xQP.

[22] See Game 2.

[23] 3 . . . P–K3 4 P–K3 gives White a chance for an initiative. The same is true after 3 . . . B–B4 4 P–B4, P–K3 5 Q–N3, Q–B1 6 P–K3.

[24] Safest is 4 . . . PxP 5 PxP, with transposition into the Exchange Variation of the Caro–Kann.

[25] So as to answer . . . N–KR4 with B–R2.

[26] This is approximately Prac. Var. 5 with colors reversed.

[27] The Queen's Gambit in reverse—not too promising for Black.

[28] 3 P–B4 leads to the Symmetrical Variation of the Queen's Gambit Declined.

[29] Transposition into the ordinary Queen's Gambit is also possible here.

[30] 5 . . . P–K3 leads to the Colle System. 5 . . . P–KN3 deserves serious consideration: 6 B–Q3, B–N2 7 O–O, O–O 8 Q–K2 (8 P–QN4!), R–K1 9 P–K4, P–K4! 10 PxKP, NxP/5

11 NxN, PxN 12 BxP, NxP∓ (Colle–Fairhurst, Scarborough 1927).

[31] Black's over-enterprising play has boomeranged.

[32] 2 . . . P–K3 is the French Defense; 2 . . . P–QB3 the Caro–Kann.

[33] Blackmar consistently continued with 3 P–KB3. It is weaker than the text because of 3 . . . P–K4! 4 P–Q5, B–KB4.

[34] For 4 B–N5 (by transposition) see Game 3.

[35] Hans Mueller's 4 . . . B–B4 permits the dangerous 5 P–KN4, B–N3 6 P–KR4. It remains to be seen whether this attack is sound.

[36] 5 QxP, QxP 6 B–K3, Q–KN5 favors Black.

[37] The steadiest continuation. Other possibilities are:

1) 5 . . . P–K3 6 B–N5, B–K2, when both 7 B–Q3, QN–Q2 8 O–O, O–O 9 Q–K1, P–KR3 10 Q–R4 and 7 Q–Q2, O–O 8 B–Q3, QN–Q2 9 Q–B4, P–QN3 10 Q–R4, R–K1 11 N–K5 (Diemer–Fuller, Hastings 1957) offer White good attacking chances.

2) 5 . . . P–B4 6 P–Q5, P–KN3 7 B–KB4, P–QR3 8 P–QR4, B–N2 9 B–B4, O–O 10 O–O with ample compensation for the Pawn.

3) 5 . . . B–N5 6 P–KR3, B–R4 7 P–KN4, B–N3 8 N–K5 with excellent prospects for White.

[38] 8 . . . N–B3 merits further consideration.

[39] Black must react vigorously. After 9 . . . P–B3 10 B–N3, White has excellent prospects: e.g., 10 . . . NxN? 11 PxN, Q–N3† 12 K–R1, N–N5 13 P–K6!, N–B7† 14 RxN, QxR 15 PxP†, RxP 16 Q–Q8†, B–B1 17 N–K4! (17 B–R6?, B–R6!). For 9 . . . N–N3 see Game 4.

[40] 12 P–QN4 is best met by 12 . . . B–B3.

[41] On 3 P–K4, Black's safest is . . . PxP, transposing into Prac. Var. 8.

[42] If 13 PxP, N–Q2.

## *Colle System Game 1*

*WHITE: Colle* — *BLACK: O'Hanlon*

*Nice 1930*

| | WHITE | BLACK | | WHITE | BLACK |
|---|---|---|---|---|---|
| 1 | P–Q4 | P–Q4 | 11 | BxN | PxP |
| 2 | N–KB3 | N–KB3 | 12 | BxP†!? | KxB |
| 3 | P–K3 | P–K3 | 13 | N–N5† | K–N3? |
| 4 | B–Q3 | P–B4 | 14 | P–KR4 | R–R1? |
| 5 | P–B3 | B–Q3 | 15 | RxP†! | N–B3 |
| 6 | QN–Q2 | QN–Q2 | 16 | P–R5† | K–R3 |
| 7 | O–O | O–O | 17 | RxB | Q–R4 |
| 8 | R–K1 | R–K1 | 18 | NxP† | K–R2 |
| 9 | P–K4 | PxKP | 19 | N–N5† | K–N1 |
| 10 | NxP | NxN | 20 | Q–N3† | Resigns |

*Bishop's Defense Game 2*

*WHITE: Alekhine* *BLACK: Euwe*

*17th Match Game 1935*

| | WHITE | BLACK | | WHITE | BLACK |
|---|---|---|---|---|---|
| 1 | P–Q4 | P–Q4 | 15 | P–B5 | R–K1 |
| 2 | N–KB3 | N–KB3 | 16 | P–QN4 | P–B5 |
| 3 | P–K3 | B–B4 | 17 | PxP | NxN |
| 4 | B–Q3 | P–K3 | 18 | QxQ | NxQ |
| 5 | BxB | PxB | 19 | RxN | NxBP |
| 6 | Q–Q3 | Q–B1 | 20 | R–N3 | P–QR3 |
| 7 | P–QN3 | N–R3 | 21 | P–N3 | N–K3 |
| 8 | O–O | B–K2 | 22 | P–QR4 | B–B3 |
| 9 | P–B4 | O–O | 23 | R–Q1 | N–B2 |
| 10 | N–B3 | P–B3 | 24 | K–B1 | R–K5 |
| 11 | B–N2 | N–K5 | 25 | B–B1 | QR–K1 |
| 12 | KR–B1 | R–Q1 | 26 | B–B4 | N–K3 |
| 13 | Q–K2 | Q–K3 | 27 | B–K3 | N–B2 |
| 14 | P–QR3 | N–B2 | | Draw | |

*Blackmar-Diemer Gambit Game 3*

*WHITE: Spasski* *BLACK: Filip*

*Amsterdam 1956*

| | WHITE | BLACK | | WHITE | BLACK |
|---|---|---|---|---|---|
| 1 | P–Q4 | N–KB3 | 26 | N–B3 | N–K4 |
| 2 | N–QB3 | P–Q4 | 27 | K–B4 | P–B3 |
| 3 | B–N5 | B–B4 | 28 | N–R4 | P–N3 |
| 4 | P–B3 | B–N3 | 29 | N–B3 | B–K1 |
| 5 | P–K4 | PxP | 30 | P–QN4 | P–KR4 |
| 6 | Q–Q2 | P–K3 | 31 | P–N3 | N–N3† |
| 7 | PxP | B–N5 | 32 | K–K3 | P–R5 |
| 8 | Q–K3 | N–N5 | 33 | PxP | RxP |
| 9 | Q–Q2 | N–KB3 | 34 | R–KB1 | R–R6† |
| 10 | Q–K3 | N–N5 | 35 | K–Q2 | N–K4 |
| 11 | Q–B4 | QxP | 36 | R–B2 | B–N3 |
| 12 | N–K2 | BxN† | 37 | R–N2 | B–B2 |
| 13 | NxB | P–KR3 | 38 | N–Q1 | N–B6† |
| 14 | QxN | PxB | 39 | BxN | RxB |
| 15 | QxP | N–Q2 | 40 | P–K5 | R–B5 |
| 16 | B–K2 | RxP | 41 | PxP† | KxP |
| 17 | RxR | Q–N8† | 42 | P–R3 | R–Q5† |
| 18 | B–B1 | QxR | 43 | K–B1 | P–K4 |
| 19 | O–O–O | Q–R3 | 44 | N–K3 | B–R4 |
| 20 | QxQ | PxQ | 45 | R–N8 | P–K5 |
| 21 | B–K2 | O–O–O | 46 | R–QB8 | K–K4 |
| 22 | R–R1 | R–R1 | 47 | R–B8 | B–B6 |
| 23 | K–Q2 | K–Q1 | 48 | K–N2 | R–Q2 |
| 24 | K–K3 | K–K2 | 49 | K–B3 | Draw |
| 25 | N–N5 | P–QB3 | | | |

*Blackmar-Diemer Gambit Game 4*

*WHITE: Diemer* *BLACK: Sutterer*

*Rastatt 1952*

| | WHITE | BLACK | | WHITE | BLACK |
|---|---|---|---|---|---|
| 1 | P–Q4 | P–Q4 | 11 | Q–Q2 | N/N–Q4 |
| 2 | P–K4 | PxP | 12 | QR–K1 | N–B2 |
| 3 | N–QB3 | N–KB3 | 13 | N–K4! | N–K3 |
| 4 | P–B3 | PxP | 14 | P–B3 | NxN |
| 5 | NxP | P–KN3 | 15 | RxN | NxB |
| 6 | B–QB4 | B–N2 | 16 | QxN | B–B3 |
| 7 | N–K5 | O–O | 17 | Q–R6 | Q–Q3 |
| 8 | B–KN5 | QN–Q2 | 18 | R–R4! | BxR |
| 9 | O–O | N–N3 | 19 | NxBP | Resigns |
| 10 | B–N3 | P–B3 | | | |

*Semi-Tarrasch Game 5*

*WHITE: Keres* *BLACK: Geller*

*Match Game, Moscow 1962*

| | WHITE | BLACK | | WHITE | BLACK |
|---|---|---|---|---|---|
| 1 | P–Q4 | N–KB3 | 16 | P–Q5 | PxP |
| 2 | P–QB4 | P–K3 | 17 | PxP | Q–K2 |
| 3 | N–KB3 | P–Q4 | 18 | N–K5 | P–B3 |
| 4 | N–B3 | P–B4 | 19 | Q–R5 | P–N3 |
| 5 | BPxP | NxP | 20 | NxP | PxN |
| 6 | P–K3 | N–QB3 | 21 | KBxP | Q–N2 |
| 7 | B–B4 | NxN | 22 | R–Q3 | B–Q3 |
| 8 | PxN | B–K2 | 23 | P–B4 | Q–R1 |
| 9 | O–O | O–O | 24 | Q–N4 | B–B4† |
| 10 | P–K4 | P–QN3 | 25 | K–R1 | R–QB2 |
| 11 | B–N2 | B–N2 | 26 | B–R7† | K–B2 |
| 12 | Q–K2 | N–R4 | 27 | Q–K6† | K–N2 |
| 13 | B–Q3 | R–B1 | 28 | R–N3† | KxB |
| 14 | QR–Q1 | PxP | 29 | Q–R3 mate | |
| 15 | PxP | B–N5 | | | |

*Semi-Tarrasch Game 6*

*WHITE: Najdorf* *BLACK: Portisch*

*Varna Olympics 1962*

| | WHITE | BLACK | | WHITE | BLACK | | WHITE | BLACK |
|---|---|---|---|---|---|---|---|---|
| 1 | P–Q4 | P–Q4 | 9 | B–Q3 | NxN | 17 | Q–R5 | P–B3 |
| 2 | P–QB4 | P–K3 | 10 | PxN | NxP | 18 | QxP | K–B2 |
| 3 | N–QB3 | N–KB3 | 11 | NxN | QxN | 19 | B–K2 | Q–KN4 |
| 4 | N–B3 | P–B4 | 12 | B–N5† | K–K2 | 20 | B–QB1 | BxP† |
| 5 | BPxP | NxP | 13 | O–O | QxP | 21 | KxB | Q–K4† |
| 6 | P–K3 | PxP | 14 | Q–K2 | B–Q3 | 22 | P–B4 | Resigns |
| 7 | PxP | B–N5 | 15 | B–N2 | Q–R4 | | | |
| 8 | Q–B2 | N–QB3 | 16 | KR–Q1 | R–Q1 | | | |

# chapter 29—Slav Defense

The characteristic theme of this defense is the protection of Black's attacked Queen Pawn by 2 . . . P–QB3. An analysis of this continuation was published as early as 1590, but it was not until 1920 that a detailed investigation of its possibilities began. It is known as the "Slav" in deference to the great labor lavished upon the defense by masters of Slavic descent, notably, Alapin, Alekhine, Bogoljubov, Treybal and Vidmar.

Black's general idea is to protect his Queen Pawn without locking in his Queen Bishop. This plan, however, cannot easily be carried out in full; before developing his Queen Bishop, Black must first relinquish the center by . . . PxBP. This line of play leads to the main line of the Slav, the so-called Slav Accepted: 1 P–Q4, P–Q4 2 P–QB4, P–QB3 3 N–KB3, N–B3 4 N–B3, PxP. If White wishes to avoid this complicated line, he can play 4 P–K3 instead of 4 N–B3, thus adopting the Slav Declined.

In addition, White has the further option of 3 N–QB3 which leads to the Marshall Variation. Black, too, has much room for deviation. He may play 3 . . . P–K3, the Semi-Slav, or he may decide to restrict his Bishop one move later (3 . . . N–B3 4 N–B3, P–K3) thereby inviting the complexities of the Meran Defense.

It is interesting to note that the Slav Defense has been a favorite weapon of three World Champions: Botvinnik, Euwe and Smyslov.

---

## part 1—SLAV ACCEPTED

1 P–Q4, P–Q4
2 P–QB4, P–QB3
3 N–KB3, N–B3
4 N–B3, PxP[A]
5 P–QR4, B–B4
6 N–K5

KEY POSITION 1

### OBSERVATIONS ON KEY POSITION 1

[A] A necessary evil. An immediate 4 . . . B–B4 is countered by 5 Q–N3, or perhaps 5 PxP followed by 6 Q–N3, in both cases to White's advantage.

White's last move, which at first glance may seem to be a somewhat clumsy way to recover the Pawn, is actually the starting point of a deviously calculated plan: to proceed with P–B3 and P–K4 taking advantage of Black's exposed Bishop which literally becomes cornered.

Black, for his part, will seek to punish White for his general neglect of development. A tense clash almost always ensues.

IDEA VARIATIONS 1–3:

(1) 6 . . . P–K3 7 B–N5, B–K2? (6 . . . B–QN5! is necessary) 8 P–B3, P–KR3 9 P–K4, B–R2 10 B–K3, QN–Q2 11 NxP/4, O–O 12 B–K2, P–B4 13 PxP, BxBP 14 BxB, NxB 15 P–QN4 with a distinct advantage to White, thanks to Black's blocked-in Bishop (Alekhine–Bogoljubov, Wiesbaden 1929).

(2) 6 . . . P–K3 7 P–B3, B–QN5! 8 P–K4, BxP 9 PxB, NxP 10 Q–B3, QxP 11 QxP†, K–Q1 12 QxKNP?? (12 B–N5† is correct), BxN† 13 PxB, Q–B7† 14 K–Q1, NxP mate.

(3) 6 . . . QN–Q2 7 NxP/4, Q–B2 8 P–B3? (in these circumstances, 8 P–KN3 is called for), P–K4 9 P–K4, PxP 10 QxP, B–K3 with Black for choice.

PRACTICAL VARIATIONS 1–4:

1 P–Q4, P–Q4 2 P–QB4, P–QB3 3 N–KB3, N–B3 4 N–B3, PxP 5 P–QR4, B–B4 6 N–K5

| | 1 | 2 | 3 | 4 |
|---|---|---|---|---|
| 6 | — — | — — | — — | — — |
| | QN–Q2 | — — | P–K3[8] | — — |
| 7 | NxP/4 | — — | P–B3[9] | — — |
| | Q–B2 | — — | B–QN5[10] | — — |
| 8 | P–KN3[1] | — — | P–K4[11] | B–N5[16] |
| | P–K4[2] | — — | BxP | P–B4[17] |
| 9 | PxP | — — | PxB | PxP |
| | NxP | — — | NxP | Q–Q4![18] |
| 10 | B–B4 | — — | B–Q2[12] | QxQ |
| | N/3–Q2 | — — | QxP | PxQ |
| 11 | B–N2 | — — | NxN | P–K4 |
| | R–Q1[3] | — — | QxN†[13] | PxP |
| 12 | Q–B1[4] | — — | Q–K2 | NxQBP |
| | P–B3 | — — | BxB† | O–O |
| 13 | O–O | — — | KxB | BxN |
| | B–K3 | — — | Q–Q4† | PxB |
| 14 | NxN | N–K4! | K–B2 | O–O–O |
| | NxN | B–QN5 | N–R3 | PxP |
| 15 | P–R5 | P–R5 | NxP/4![14] | N–Q5 |
| | P–QR3 | O–O | O–O–O | N–B3 |
| 16 | N–K4 | R–R4[7] | Q–K3 | PxP |
| | B–QN5 | ± | N–B4 | BxP |
| 17 | N–B5[5] | | B–K2 | NxP† |
| | B–B1 | | Q–B4† | K–R1 |
| 18 | R–R4 | | K–B1 | R–Q5 |
| | BxP[6] | | N–Q6†[15] | N–Q5![19] |
| | ∓ | | = | = |

*Notes to practical variations 1–4:*

[1] 8 Q–N3 has been tried and found wanting. After 8 . . . P–K4 9 PxP, N–B4 10 Q–R2, N–R3! 11 P–K4, NxP 12 NxN, BxN 13 N–Q6†, BxN 14 PxB, QxP 15 BxN, BxP, Black has a decisive advantage (Petrov–Capablanca, Semmering–Baden 1937). For 8 P–B3?, see Idea Var. 3.

[2] This advance, known as the Carlsbad Variation, gives White the opportunity for a dangerous pin, but is Black's only hope for counterplay.

[3] 11 . . . P–B3 is inferior, e.g., 12 O–O, B–K3 13 NxN, PxN 14 B–K3, B–QB4 15 Q–B1, BxB 16 QxB, Q–N3 17 P–R5!, QxQ 18 PxQ, P–QR3 19 N–K4, K–K2 20 R–R4! with advantage to White (Klein–Capablanca, Margate 1935). No better in this line is 13 . . . NxN 14 Q–Q4, B–K2 15 QR–B1, Q–N1 16 N–K4, O–O 17 N–N5!±.

continued ▸

[4] 12 Q–Q4, P–B3 13 QxP, B–B4 is far too risky.

[5] Fine–Capablanca, Semmering–Baden 1937, was called a draw after 17 B–Q2, BxB 18 NxB, O–O 19 Q–B3, Q–Q3 20 N–K4, Q–Q5 21 N–B5, B–B1 22 Q–N3†, Q–B5.

[6] See Game 1.

[7] For 16 P–R6, see Game 2.

[8] The Wiesbaden Variation—more logical and stronger than 6 . . . QN–Q2.

[9] For 7 B–N5, see Idea Var. 1.

[10] 7 . . . P–B4 is insufficient because of 8 PxP, QxQ† 9 KxQ, BxP 10 P–K4, B–KN3 11 BxP, N–B3 12 NxN, PxN 13 B–B4 with White for choice (Alekhine–Bogoljubov, Wiesbaden 1929).

[11] Risky because of the ensuing sacrifice.

[12] For 10 Q–B3, see Idea Var. 2.

[13] 11 . . . BxB† 12 QxB, QxN/4 favors White because of 13 O–O–O.

[14] Best. The continuation 15 R–Q1, Q–R4 16 NxP/4, QxP† 17 P–N3 (Reshevsky–Smyslov, The Hague 1948) gives Black the edge after 17 . . . N–N5†! 18 K–B3, N–Q4†.

[15] 19 BxN, RxB 20 Q–K5, Q–B7! is satisfactory for Black, according to Keres. Inferior is 20 . . . QxQ 21 NxQ, R–K6 22 NxKBP, R–B1 23 K–Q2, R–QN6 24 KR–KB1, when White has the superior game (Tolush–Furman, Moscow 1952).

[16] The most important continuation.

[17] 8 . . . P–KR3 is also playable. After 9 BxN, both 9 . . . QxB 10 P–K4, B–R2 11 BxP, O–O 12 Q–N3, P–B4 13 N–N4!, Q–R5†! 14 P–N3, Q–K2 and 9 . . . PxB 10 NxP/4, P–QB4 11 PxP, QxQ† 12 RxQ, B–B7 13 R–B1, B–N6 (Euwe–Alekhine, 11th Match Game 1937) give Black a satisfactory game.

[18] Only this strong move allows Black to maintain the balance.

[19] After this surprising stroke, White can do no better than to play for a draw with 19 N–K4, BxN 20 PxB, QR–Q1 21 N–K5, RxR 22 PxR. In the column, however, 15 N–Q6 seems to favor White.

## *Slav Defense Game 1*

*WHITE: Vidmar* — *BLACK: Euwe*

*Nottingham 1936*

| | WHITE | BLACK | | WHITE | BLACK | | WHITE | BLACK |
|---|---|---|---|---|---|---|---|---|
| 1 | P–Q4 | P–Q4 | 11 | B–N2 | R–Q1 | 21 | Q–B2 | P–N4 |
| 2 | P–QB4 | P–QB3 | 12 | Q–B1 | P–B3 | 22 | BxP† | QxB |
| 3 | N–KB3 | N–B3 | 13 | O–O | B–K3 | 23 | BxN | B–R2 |
| 4 | N–B3 | PxP | 14 | NxN | NxN | 24 | B–B3 | P–N4 |
| 5 | P–QR4 | B–B4 | 15 | P–R5 | P–QR3 | 25 | R/4–R1 | P–QB4 |
| 6 | N–K5 | QN–Q2 | 16 | N–K4 | B–QN5 | 26 | Q–B1 | P–B5 |
| 7 | NxP/4 | Q–B2 | 17 | N–B5 | B–B1 | 27 | N–K1 | B–N2 |
| 8 | P–KN3 | P–K4 | 18 | R–R4 | BxP | 28 | N–B3 | P–KN5 |
| 9 | PxP | NxP | 19 | N–Q3 | O–O | 29 | N–N5 | Q–B4 |
| 10 | B–B4 | N/3–Q2 | 20 | B–K4 | B–N3 | | Resigns | |

*Slav Defense Game 2*

*WHITE: Euwe* *BLACK: Alekhine*

*1st Match Game 1937*

| | WHITE | BLACK | | WHITE | BLACK |
|---|---|---|---|---|---|
| 1 | P–Q4 | P–Q4 | 26 | RxR | N–B5 |
| 2 | P–QB4 | P–QB3 | 27 | B–B5 | R–K3 |
| 3 | N–KB3 | N–B3 | 28 | B–Q4 | RxP |
| 4 | N–B3 | PxP | 29 | BxP | P–N5! |
| 5 | P–QR4 | B–B4 | 30 | K–B1! | R–B7 |
| 6 | N–K5 | QN–Q2 | 31 | R–N7† | K–B1 |
| 7 | NxP/4 | Q–B2 | 32 | RxNP | NxP |
| 8 | P–KN3 | P–K4 | 33 | BxN | RxB |
| 9 | PxP | NxP | 34 | R–B4 | R–N3 |
| 10 | B–B4 | N/3–Q2 | 35 | K–K2 | K–B2 |
| 11 | B–N2 | P–B3 | 36 | R–KR4 | K–N3 |
| 12 | O–O | R–Q1 | 37 | R–KB4 | R–N6 |
| 13 | Q–B1 | B–K3 | 38 | R–B4 | R–N3 |
| 14 | N–K4 | B–QN5 | 39 | K–K3 | K–B4 |
| 15 | P–R5 | O–O | 40 | P–N4† | K–K3 |
| 16 | P–R6 | PxP? | 41 | P–B4 | K–Q4 |
| 17 | NxN | NxN | 42 | R–Q4† | K–K3 |
| 18 | N–B5 | BxN | 43 | P–B5† | K–K2 |
| 19 | QxB | P–N4 | 44 | R–K4† | K–B2 |
| 20 | B–K3 | B–Q4 | 45 | P–R4 | R–N8 |
| 21 | RxP | BxB | 46 | K–B4 | R–B8 |
| 22 | KxB | R–B2 | 47 | R–R4 | P–R3 |
| 23 | R/1–QR1 | Q–Q3 | 48 | R–R7† | K–N1 |
| 24 | QxQ | RxQ | 49 | P–N5 | Resigns |
| 25 | RxRP | RxR | | | |

## part 2—SLAV ACCEPTED (DUTCH VARIATION)

1 P–Q4, P–Q4
2 P–QB4, P–QB3
3 N–KB3, N–B3
4 N–B3, PxP
5 P–QR4, B–B4
6 P–K3[A], P–K3[B]
7 BxP, B–QN5
8 O–O, O–O

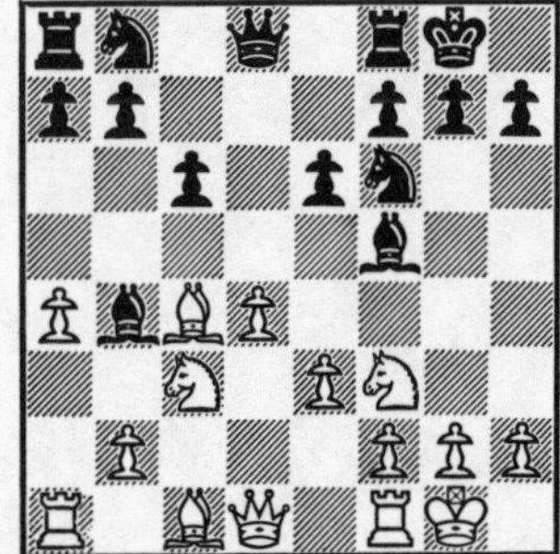

KEY POSITION 2

### OBSERVATIONS ON KEY POSITION 2

[A] The Dutch Variation, less artificial than 6 N–K5. In recapturing the Pawn, White furthers his development.

[B] 6 . . . B–Q6 7 BxB, PxB 8 QxP cedes White the advantage, while the continuation 6 . . . N–R3 7 BxP, N–QN5 8 O–O, P–K3 9 Q–K2 also favors White.

White must attempt to emphasize his center Pawn majority by means of P–K4. The realization of this advance, however, is time-consuming, and Black can make good use of this time to extend his own influence in the center. He may play for . . . P–K4 himself, or failing this, induce White to play P–K5. In either case, the situation in the center becomes stabilized, greatly easing the pressure on Black's game.

IDEA VARIATIONS 4–6:

(4) 9 Q–K2, B–N5 10 R–Q1, QN–Q2 11 P–K4, Q–K2 12 P–KR3, B–KR4 13 P–N4, B–N3 14 N–KR4, P–K4 15 N–B5, BxKN 16 KPxB, PxP 17 QxQ, BxQ 18 RxP with an end game that clearly favors White (Flohr–Yanofsky, Saltsjobaden 1948).

(5) 9 Q–K2, B–N5 10 P–KR3, BxKN 11 QxB, QN–Q2 12 R–Q1, P–K4! 13 P–Q5, BxN 14 PxP, P–K5 15 Q–B5 (15 Q–K2 is slightly better), B–K4 16 PxN, Q–B2 17 B–N3, P–KN3= (Reshevsky–Smyslov, Moscow 1948).

(6) 9 Q–K2, QN–Q2 10 P–K4, B–N3 11 B–Q3, B–KR4 12 B–KB4, R–K1 13 P–K5 (otherwise Black proceeds with P–K4), N–Q4 14 NxN, BPxN 15 Q–K3, B–N3 16 B–KN5, B–K2 17 KBxB, BPxB!, and Black is safe (Panno–Filip, Amsterdam 1956).

PRACTICAL VARIATIONS 5–9:

1 P–Q4, P–Q4 2 P–QB4, P–QB3 3 N–KB3, N–B3 4 N–B3, PxP 5 P–QR4, B–B4 6 P–K3, P–K3 7 BxP, B–QN5 8 O–O, O–O

| | *5* | *6* | *7* | *8* | *9* |
|---|---|---|---|---|---|
| *9* | N–K5[1] | Q–K2[4] | – – | – – | – – |
| | P–B4! | N–K5[5] | B–N5[8] | QN–Q2[13] | – – |
| *10* | P–N4[2] | P–N4[6] | R–Q1[9] | P–K4 | – – |
| | B–N3 | B–N3 | QN–Q2 | B–N3 | – – |
| *11* | N–R2 | N–K5 | P–K4 | B–Q3[14] | – – |
| | B–QR4 | NxN | Q–K2 | P–B4 | B–KR4 |
| *12* | NxB | PxN | P–R3 | P–K5 | P–K5[16] |
| | RPxN | BxP | BxKN[10] | PxP | N–Q4 |
| *13* | PxP | NxB | QxB | PxN | N–K4[17] |
| | N–B3 | RPxN | P–K4 | PxN | R–K1 |
| *14* | R–N1 | R–N1 | P–Q5 | BPxP | N–N3 |
| | N–N5! | Q–K2 | N–K1[11] | KxP | B–N3 |
| *15* | NxN | P–B4 | PxP | R–Q1 | BxB |
| | BxN | P–QB4[7] | PxP[12] | Q–B2[15] | BPxB[18] |
| *16* | Q–B3 | = | ± | = | = |
| | Q–K2[3] | | | | |
| | = | | | | |

*Notes to practical variations 5–9:*

[1] Enabling Black to achieve equality without much difficulty. Two rarely played alternatives, 9 N–R4 and 9 N–K2, also give Black little trouble, e.g., 9 N–R4, B–N5 10 P–B3, N–Q4! or 9 N–K2, QN–Q2 10 N–N3, B–N3 11 N–R4, P–B4!

[2] 10 N–R2 is still less promising. After 10 . . . B–R4 11 PxP, QxQ 12 RxQ, B–B2! Black stands well (Capablanca–Euwe, Nottingham 1936).

[3] Saemisch–Euwe, Nauheim 1937.

[4] Most usual. After 9 Q–N3, Q–K2 10 B–Q2, P–B4!, Black is out of danger.

[5] 9 . . . P–B4 is now a mistake because of 10 N–R2!, B–R4 11 PxP, N–B3 12 R–Q1, Q–K2 13 N–Q4!, when White keeps his extra Pawn.

[6] Credit for this surprising thrust belongs to Saemisch. 10 B–Q3, as played in a few games of the 1937 Euwe–Alekhine match, is also worthwhile. Some possible continuations are: 10 . . . BxN 11 PxB, NxQBP 12 Q–B2, BxB 13 QxB, N–Q4 14 B–R3, R–K1 15 QR–N1, when White's strong pressure compensates for his sacrificed Pawn (Euwe–Alekhine, 17th Match Game 1937), and 10 . . . NxN? 11 PxN, BxP 12 BxB, PxB 13 R–N1, Q–B1 14 B–R3, R–Q1 15 N–N5! with a crushing attack (Najdorf–Kashdan, Radio Match, Buenos Aires–New York 1947). In this latter line 12 . . . BxR fails to 13 B–N1!, and Black's Bishop will bite the dust.

[7] Alekhine–Euwe, 26th Match Game 1937, continued 16 PxP, N–B3 17 B–R3, P–R4 18 QR–B1, B–N5 19 BxB, PxB 20 B–N5, KR–Q1 21 KR–Q1, RxR† 22 QxR, P–K4 23 Q–Q6, Q–R5 with about even chances.

[8] Preventing 10 P–K4.

[9] For 10 P–KR3, see Idea Var. 5.

[10] For the inferior 12 . . . B–KR4, see Idea Var. 4 as well as Game 3.

[11] This is stronger than 14 . . . N–N3 15 B–N3, PxP, when White retains the edge with 16 P–R5!, e.g., 16 . . . N–B5 17 B–N5!, BxN 18 QxB, QR–B1 19 BxKN, QxB 20 RxP (Pachman–Paoli, Trencianske–Teplice 1949).

[12] White has but a slight advantage. Black's play along the Queen Knight file will balance the weakness of his Queen Bishop Pawn.

[13] Introduced by Smyslov. Black speculates on White's Pawn center becoming increasingly vulnerable.

[14] 11 P–K5, N–Q4 12 NxN, BPxN 13 B–Q3, P–QR3 14 BxB, BPxB is satisfactory for Black (Boleslavski–Smyslov, Zurich 1953).

[15] 16 PxP, BxP 17 B–N2, BxB/7 18 QxB†, K–N1 19 QR–B1 offers White sufficient compensation for the Pawn (Smyslov–Penrose, Amsterdam 1954).

[16] For 12 B–KB4, see Idea Var. 6.

[17] After 13 NxN, BPxN 14 Q–K3, Black must play 14 . . . R–K1 in order to be able to protect his King Rook Pawn by . . . N–B1. For the consequences of 14 . . . Q–K2, see Game 4.

[18] Najdorf–Euwe, Leipzig 1960. After 16 P–R4, P–KR3 17 B–Q2, B–K2 18 Q–K4, N–B1 19 Q–N4, Q–N3, the game hangs in the balance.

*Slav Defense Game 3*

*WHITE: Euwe* *BLACK: Enevoldsen*

*Copenhagen 1949*

| | WHITE | BLACK | | WHITE | BLACK |
|---|---|---|---|---|---|
| 1 | P–Q4 | P–Q4 | 20 | R–Q1 | N/3–Q2 |
| 2 | P–QB4 | P–QB3 | 21 | N–Q3 | N–QB3 |
| 3 | N–KB3 | N–B3 | 22 | NxB | NxN |
| 4 | N–B3 | PxP | 23 | B–QN5 | KR–B1 |
| 5 | P–QR4 | B–B4 | 24 | R–R3 | Q–N2? |
| 6 | P–K3 | P–K3 | 25 | B–K3! | N–K4? |
| 7 | BxP | B–QN5 | 26 | P–B4! | N/K–Q2 |
| 8 | O–O | O–O | 27 | P–N4 | P–R3 |
| 9 | Q–K2 | B–N5 | 28 | PxN | PxB |
| 10 | P–R3 | B–KR4 | 29 | RxR | RxR |
| 11 | R–Q1 | Q–K2 | 30 | QxP | QxQ |
| 12 | P–K4 | QN–Q2 | 31 | NxQ | NxP |
| 13 | P–R5 | P–KR3 | 32 | BxN | BxP |
| 14 | P–R6 | PxP | 33 | N–B3 | B–B3 |
| 15 | BxQRP | N–N1 | 34 | R–Q6 | R–R8† |
| 16 | P–N4 | B–N3 | 35 | K–B2 | B–N2 |
| 17 | N–K5 | P–B4! | 36 | R–Q8† | K–R2 |
| 18 | B–QB4 | PxP | 37 | R–Q7 | Resigns |
| 19 | RxQP | B–QB4 | | | |

*Slav Defense Game 4*

*WHITE: Gligoric* *BLACK: Smyslov*

*Kiev 1959*

| | WHITE | BLACK | | WHITE | BLACK |
|---|---|---|---|---|---|
| 1 | P–Q4 | P–Q4 | 17 | P–N4! | PxN |
| 2 | P–QB4 | P–QB3 | 18 | PxB | P–B3 |
| 3 | N–KB3 | N–B3 | 19 | KPxP | NxP |
| 4 | N–B3 | PxP | 20 | PxP | N–K5 |
| 5 | P–QR4 | B–B4 | 21 | P–B3 | N–Q7 |
| 6 | P–K3 | P–K3 | 22 | R–B2 | N–N6 |
| 7 | BxP | B–QN5 | 23 | BxP!! | QxB† |
| 8 | O–O | QN–Q2 | 24 | R–N2 | Q–K6† |
| 9 | Q–K2 | O–O | 25 | K–R1 | K–N2 |
| 10 | P–K4 | B–N3 | 26 | Q–R7† | K–B3 |
| 11 | B–Q3 | B–KR4 | 27 | Q–R4† | K–N2 |
| 12 | P–K5 | N–Q4 | 28 | Q–R7† | K–B3 |
| 13 | NxN | BPxN | 29 | P–N7! | QxBP |
| 14 | Q–K3 | Q–K2? | 30 | PxR/Q† | BxQ |
| 15 | N–N5 | P–KR3 | 31 | R–K1 | Resigns |
| 16 | Q–R3! | P–KN3 | | | |

## SUPPLEMENTARY VARIATIONS 1–9:

1 P–Q4, P–Q4 2 P–QB4, P–QB3 3 N–KB3, N–B3 4 N–B3, PxP

| | 1 | 2 | 3 | 4 | 5 | 6 | 7 | 8 | 9 |
|---|---|---|---|---|---|---|---|---|---|
| 5 | P–QR4 | – – | – – | – – | – – | – – | P–K4[18] | P–K3 | – – |
| | B–B4 | – – | – – | P–K3 | N–R3[12] | B–N5 | P–QN4 | P–QN4 | – – |
| 6 | N–R4 | P–K3 | – – | P–K4 | P–K3 | N–K5 | P–K5 | P–QR4 | – – |
| | B–B1[1] | P–K3 | – – | B–N5 | B–KN5 | B–R4 | N–Q4 | P–N5[21] | – – |
| 7 | P–K4!?[2] | BxP | – – | P–K5[8] | BxP | P–KN3[15] | P–QR4 | N–QN1 | N–R2[23] |
| | P–K4 | B–QN5 | – – | N–K5[9] | P–K3 | P–K3 | P–K3 | B–R3 | P–K3 |
| 8 | BxP | O–O | – – | Q–B2 | P–R3 | B–N2[16] | PxP[19] | Q–B2 | BxP |
| | PxP | QN–Q2 | – – | Q–Q4 | B–R4 | B–QN5 | NxN | P–K3 | B–N2 |
| 9 | P–K5 | Q–N3 | N–R4 | B–K2 | O–O[13] | O–O | PxN | BxP | O–O |
| | PxN! | P–QR4! | O–O[6] | P–QB4 | N–QN5 | O–O | PxP | BxB | B–K2 |
| 10 | BxP† | N–R2 | P–B3 | O–O | B–K2 | NxP/4 | N–N5 | QxB | Q–K2 |
| | KxB | B–K2![5] | B–N3 | NxN | B–K2 | P–R4 | B–N2 | Q–Q4 | O–O |
| 11 | QxQ | = | P–K4 | PxN | P–K4 | P–R3 | Q–R5 | QN–Q2 | R–Q1 |
| | PxP | | P–K4 | PxP | B–N3[14] | QN–Q2 | P–N3 | QN–Q2 | P–QR4[24] |
| 12 | Q–B7† | | NxB | PxP[10] | ± | P–N4 | Q–N4 | Q–K2 | B–Q2 |
| | K–K3![3] | | RPxN | P–B6 | | B–N3 | B–K2[20] | N–K5[22] | QN–Q2 |
| 13 | QxB† | | B–K3 | B–Q2[11] | | B–N5 | ∓ | = | N–B1[25] |
| | QN–Q2 | | Q–K2 | ± | | P–R3 | | | Q–N3 |
| 14 | QxNP | | Q–K2 | | | B–R4 | | | = |
| | PxR(Q) | | PxP | | | B–R2![17] | | | |
| 15 | QxP† | | BxP[7] | | | = | | | |
| | K–B2 | | ± | | | | | | |
| 16 | P–K6† | | | | | | | | |
| | K–N1 | | | | | | | | |
| 17 | O–O | | | | | | | | |
| | Q–K4 | | | | | | | | |
| 18 | QxR | | | | | | | | |
| | QxP[4] | | | | | | | | |
| | ∓ | | | | | | | | |

*Notes to supplementary variations 1–9:*

[1] Both simplest and best.

[2] White actually has nothing better than 7 N–B3. The text is a sharp attempt to seize the initiative. 7 P–K3 is weak. After 7 . . . P–K4 8 PxP, QxQ† 9 NxQ, B–N5† 10 B–Q2, BxB† 11 KxB, N–K5†, Black has the edge.

[3] The hidden resource! 13 BxP fails against 13 . . . N–R3 followed by 14 . . . B–N5†.

[4] Larsen–Teschner, Wageningen 1957.

[5] After 11 QxP, White can do no better than draw, e.g., 11 . . . R–QN1 12 Q–R6 (not 12 QxP, R–N3), R–R1 13 QxBP, R–QB1 (Smyslov–Flohr, Moscow 1947).

continued ▸

[6] The continuation 9 . . . B–N5 10 P–B3, N–Q4 11 PxB, QxN 12 Q–B3, O–O 13 B–Q2= comes into serious consideration (Ragozin–Kaliwoda, 2d World's Championship Postal Tournament). Black can meet 11 Q–K1 with 11 . . . B–K2.

[7] Botvinnik–Smyslov, 12th Match Game 1954.

[8] 7 B–N5 is best met by 7 . . . P–B4!

[9] After 7 . . . N–Q4 8 B–Q2, White's advantage is even more pronounced, e.g., 8 . . . BxN 9 PxB, P–QN4 10 N–N5!, P–B3 11 KPxP, NxP/3 12 B–K2, P–QR3 13 B–B3, and White has a powerful attack (Alekhine–Bogoljubov, 1st Match Game 1929).

[10] Also promising for White is 12 NxP, B–B4 13 N–B3, N–Q2 14 R–Q1, Q–B3 15 BxP, O–O 16 N–N5 (Alekhine–Bogoljubov, Nottingham 1936).

[11] Alekhine–Euwe, 19th Match Game 1935.

[12] Smyslov's innovation.

[13] 9 BxN, PxB offers Black counterplay along the Queen Knight file; his weak Queen Bishop Pawn can be exchanged by . . . P–QB4.

[14] See Game 5.

[15] 7 P–B3 followed by either 8 P–K4 or 8 P–KN4 is worth trying.

[16] After 8 P–R5, best is 8 . . . B–QN5 9 Q–R4, N–Q4!

[17] 15 P–K4 now fails against 15 . . . P–KN4 followed by 16 . . . BxN.

[18] In spite of Geller's continued approval, this gambit is questionable.

[19] 8 B–K2 is an interesting alternative which, in a game Geller–Smyslov, Budapest 1952, gave White a decisive edge after 8 . . . B–N2 9 O–O, P–QR3 10 N–K4, N–Q2 11 N/3–N5, B–K2 12 B–R5, O–O 13 Q–N4, N–B2 14 NxRP! Black, however, can improve on this line with 10 . . . P–KR3.

[20] White's compensation for the Pawn is nebulous, e.g., 13 B–K2, N–Q2 14 B–B3, Q–B1! 15 B–R3, QBxB 16 NxB, Q–R3!∓ (Szabo–Petrosian, Budapest 1955). In this line Black must avoid 14 . . . Q–B2 15 N–K4, N–N3 16 B–R6, R–KN1 17 B–N5, BxN 18 KBxB, N–Q4 19 BxN!, which is promising for White. Geller against Flohr (Moscow 1951) sought to strengthen White's attack with 14 P–KR4, but after 14 . . . P–KR4! 15 Q–N3, N–N3, it is still Black for choice.

[21] Alekhine's antidote, and Black's best procedure against 5 P–K3.

[22] Stahlberg–Euwe, Stockholm 1937. After 13 NxN, QxN 14 O–O, B–K2 15 B–Q2, O–O 16 KR–B1, P–QB4, Black stands well.

[23] More forceful than 7 N–N1.

[24] 11 . . . QN–Q2 12 P–K4 favors White (Alekhine–Tarrasch, Hastings 1922).

[25] Reshevsky–Smyslov, USA–USSR Radio Match 1945.

*Slav Defense Game 5*

*WHITE: Gligoric* *BLACK: Smyslov*

*Bled 1959*

| | WHITE | BLACK | | WHITE | BLACK |
|---|---|---|---|---|---|
| 1 | P–Q4 | P–Q4 | 20 | R–R3 | P–N3 |
| 2 | P–QB4 | P–QB3 | 21 | R–B1 | R–B1 |
| 3 | N–KB3 | N–B3 | 22 | N/3–N5 | P–QB4 |
| 4 | N–B3 | PxP | 23 | Q–N3 | BxN |
| 5 | P–QR4 | N–R3 | 24 | NxB | Q–K7 |
| 6 | P–K3 | B–N5 | 25 | BxN | RPxB |
| 7 | BxP | P–K3 | 26 | R–KB3 | QxNP |
| 8 | P–KR3 | B–R4 | 27 | R–Q1 | P–B3 |
| 9 | O–O | N–QN5 | 28 | NxP | Q–B7 |
| 10 | B–K2 | B–K2 | 29 | R–K1 | P–B5 |
| 11 | P–K4 | B–N3 | 30 | Q–N4 | Q–Q7 |
| 12 | P–K5 | N/3–Q4 | 31 | R–KB1 | P–B4 |
| 13 | N–K1 | P–QR4 | 32 | QxNP | Q–R3 |
| 14 | B–R5 | Q–N3 | 33 | QxP | P–N3 |
| 15 | BxB | RPxB | 34 | R–KN3 | N–K2 |
| 16 | N–B3 | R–Q1 | 35 | Q–B6 | R–B3 |
| 17 | B–Q2 | O–O | 36 | P–Q5 | R–B1 |
| 18 | N–K4 | R–Q2 | 37 | P–Q6 | R–B1 |
| 19 | Q–N3 | Q–R3 | 38 | PxN | Resigns |

## part 3—SLAV DECLINED

### OBSERVATIONS ON KEY POSITION 3

Since no variation of the Slav Accepted guarantees White anything more than a minimal advantage, some masters prefer to avoid its well analyzed lines and seek complications in less charted territory.

In this position, White obviously must try to profit from the early sortie of Black's Queen Bishop. He may do so either by striking at Black's Queen Knight Pawn or by launching an aggressive action along the QR4–K8 diagonal. Neither system, however, poses a real threat to Black's security, and equality is usually his without much difficulty. A word of caution, though: if Black is not wary, he may fall prey to any one of a number of White traps.

1 P–Q4, P–Q4
2 P–QB4, P–QB3
3 N–KB3, N–B3
4 P–K3, B–B4
5 PxP, PxP

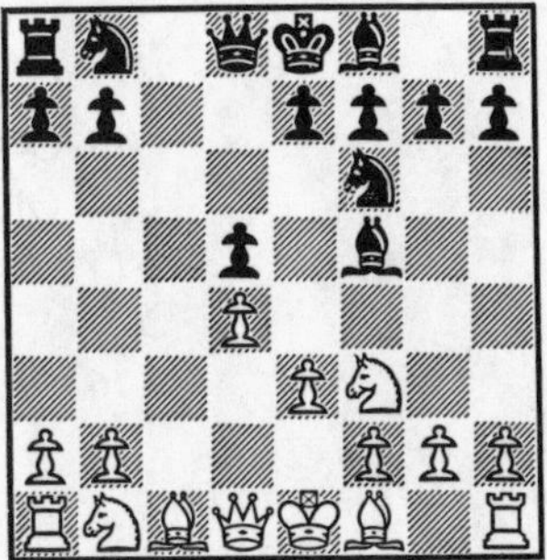

KEY POSITION 3

IDEA VARIATIONS 7 AND 8:

(7) 6 N–B3, P–K3 7 N–K5, QN–Q2? (7 . . . KN–Q2! is necessary; see Prac. Var. 10) 8 P–KN4!, NxN (8 . . . B–N3 9 P–KR4, P–KR3 10 NxB, PxN 11 B–Q3 also leads to great advantage for White) 9 PxN, NxP 10 Q–R4†, K–K2 11 Q–N4†, and White must win.

(8) 6 Q–N3, Q–B1 7 N–R3, P–K3 8 B–Q2, N–B3 9 R–B1, N–Q2! 10 B–N5, B–K2 11 Q–R4, O–O 12 BxN, PxB 13 RxP, Q–N2=. Black has ample compensation for his Pawn.

PRACTICAL VARIATIONS 10–15:

1 P–Q4, P–Q4 2 P–QB4, P–QB3 3 N–KB3, N–B3 4 P–K3, B–B4 5 PxP, PxP

| | *10* | *11* | *12* | *13* | *14* | *15* |
|---|---|---|---|---|---|---|
| 6 | N–B3 | Q–N3 | – – | – – | – – | – – |
| | P–K3 | Q–B1 | – – | Q–B2 | – – | – – |
| 7 | N–K5[1] | N–R3[5] | – – | B–N5† | N–B3 | N–R3 |
| | KN–Q2[2] | P–K3 | – – | B–Q2 | P–K3 | N–B3 |
| 8 | Q–N3 | B–Q2 | – – | N–B3 | B–Q2 | B–Q2 |
| | Q–B1 | N–B3 | – – | P–K3 | N–B3 | P–K3 |
| 9 | B–Q2 | R–B1 | – – | BxB† | R–B1 | R–B1 |
| | N–QB3 | N–K5[6] | N–Q2! | QNxB | P–QR3 | N–K5 |
| *10* | R–B1 | B–N5 | B–N5 | B–Q2 | Q–R4 | B–N5 |
| | N/2xN[3] | NxB | B–K2 | P–QR3 | R–B1![11] | NxB |
| *11* | PxN | KxN | Q–R4 | O–O | N–K5 | NxN[12] |
| | B–K2 | B–Q3 | O–O | B–Q3 | N–Q2 | B–K2[13] |
| *12* | B–K2 | BxN† | BxN | KR–B1 | = | Q–R4 |
| | O–O | PxB | PxB | Q–N3 | | O–O |
| *13* | N–N5 | N–QN5 | QxBP[8] | Q–B2 | | BxN |
| | Q–Q2 | B–N1[7] | QxQ | QR–B1 | | PxB |
| *14* | O–O | ± | RxQ | P–QR4 | | O–O[14] |
| | QR–B1[4] | | QR–N1 | O–O | | Q–N3 |
| *15* | = | | B–B1[9] | P–R5 | | N–N3 |
| | | | = | Q–B2 | | KR–B1[15] |
| *16* | | | | Q–N1 | | ∓ |
| | | | | Q–N1[10] | | |
| | | | | = | | |

*Notes to practical variations 10–15:*

[1] For 7 Q–N3, see Game 6.

[2] 7 . . . QN–Q2 is a blunder; see Idea Var. 7.

[3] 10 . . . B–K2 11 NxN, QxN 12 N–R4 slightly favors White.

[4] Alekhine–Euwe, 11th Match Game 1935.

[5] 7 N–B3, P–K3 8 N–K5 leads to Prac. Var. 10.

[6] After 9 . . . B–K2? 10 N–K5, O–O 11 B–N5, Black loses a Pawn without compensation.

[7] Landau–Euwe, Rotterdam 1936. White can now win a Pawn with 14 R–B3! (14 . . . P–QR3 15 KR–QB1).

[8] 13 RxP, Q–N2=.

[9] 15 . . . BxN 16 PxB offers Black at least equality.

[10] Alekhine–Euwe, 28th Match Game 1937.

[11] The text move equalizes. Inferior is 10 . . . N–Q2 11 B–N5, R–B1 12 BxN, QxB 13 O–O with White for choice (Stahlberg–Van Scheltinga, Buenos Aires 1939).

[12] 11 KxN, R–B1 12 Q–R4, Q–N3 13 N–K5, B–Q3! 14 NxN, PxN 15 RxP, RxR 16 BxR†, K–K2 17 Q–N5, R–QN1 is satisfactory for Black.

[13] Or 11 . . . R–B1 12 O–O, P–QR3 13 BxN†, PxB 14 R–B3, B–Q3 15 KR–B1, O–O 16 Q–R4, BxP† 17 K–R1, B–Q3 18 RxP, Q–K2 19 N–B3, RxR 20 RxR, with drawn result (Reshevsky–Capablanca, Semmering 1937).

[14] Both 14 RxP, Q–N2 15 Q–N5, QR–N1 and 14 QxP, QxQ 15 RxP, KR–N1 16 N–N3, P–QR4 favor Black.

[15] Vidmar–Gligoric, Laibach 1946.

*Slav Defense Game 6*

*WHITE: Euwe* — *BLACK: Alekhine*

*16th Match Game 1935*

| | WHITE | BLACK | | WHITE | BLACK | | WHITE | BLACK |
|---|---|---|---|---|---|---|---|---|
| 1 | P–Q4 | P–Q4 | 23 | K–R1 | P–N3 | 45 | R–KN2 | K–Q5 |
| 2 | P–QB4 | P–QB3 | 24 | B–N3 | R–B4 | 46 | KxP | P–B5 |
| 3 | N–KB3 | N–B3 | 25 | P–B3 | P–QR4 | 47 | PxP | RxP |
| 4 | P–K3 | B–B4 | 26 | P–K4 | P–R5 | 48 | K–N5 | R–K5 |
| 5 | PxP | PxP | 27 | B–Q5 | R/7–N4 | 49 | K–B5 | R–K4† |
| 6 | N–B3 | P–K3 | 28 | P–KR3 | K–N2 | 50 | K–B4 | R–K1 |
| 7 | Q–N3 | Q–B1 | 29 | R–B2 | NxB | 51 | K–B3 | K–Q6 |
| 8 | B–Q2 | N–B3 | 30 | RxR | RxR | 52 | R–N2 | R–B1† |
| 9 | R–B1 | B–K2 | 31 | PxN | RxP | 53 | K–N3 | K–B6 |
| 10 | B–N5 | O–O | 32 | R–B2 | K–B3 | 54 | R–N7 | R–B8 |
| 11 | O–O | Q–Q1 | 33 | R–K2 | R–K4 | 55 | R–N8 | R–QR8 |
| 12 | N–QR4 | N–QR4 | 34 | R–QB2 | R–K6 | 56 | K–B3 | RxP |
| 13 | BxN | QxB | 35 | K–R2 | R–R6 | 57 | K–K3 | R–R7 |
| 14 | N–B5 | BxN | 36 | K–N3 | K–K4 | 58 | R–B8†? | K–N7 |
| 15 | PxB | N–K5 | 37 | R–Q2 | P–R3 | 59 | R–N8† | K–B8 |
| 16 | Q–R4 | QxQ | 38 | P–R4 | P–R4 | 60 | R–B8† | K–N8 |
| 17 | BxQ | KR–B1 | 39 | R–K2† | K–Q3 | 61 | R–N8† | R–N7 |
| 18 | P–B6 | PxP | 40 | K–B4 | P–B3 | 62 | R–QR8 | R–N6† |
| 19 | BxP | QR–N1 | 41 | R–QB2 | K–Q4 | 63 | K–Q4 | P–R6 |
| 20 | N–Q4 | RxP | 42 | P–N3 | P–N4†? | 64 | K–B4 | K–N7 |
| 21 | NxB | PxN | 43 | PxP | PxP† | 65 | R–R8 | R–B6† |
| 22 | BxP? | N–B6 | 44 | KxNP | RxBP | | Resigns | |

## SUPPLEMENTARY VARIATIONS 10–13:

1 P–Q4, P–Q4 2 P–QB4, P–QB3

| | *10* | *11* | *12* | *13* |
|---|---|---|---|---|
| *3* | PxP[1] | – – | N–KB3 | – – |
| | PxP | – – | N–B3 | – – |
| *4* | N–QB3 | – – | P–K3 | – – |
| | N–KB3 | – – | P–KN3 | B–B4 |
| *5* | N–B3[2] | – – | N–B3 | B–Q3[12] |
| | N–B3 | – – | B–N2 | P–K3[13] |
| *6* | B–B4 | – – | B–K2[9] | O–O[14] |
| | P–K3 | B–B4[6] | O–O | QN–Q2 |
| *7* | P–K3 | P–K3 | O–O | N–B3 |
| | B–K2 | P–K3 | P–K3 | BxB |
| *8* | B–Q3 | Q–N3 | P–QN3 | QxB |
| | O–O | B–QN5 | QN–Q2[10] | B–N5 |
| *9* | O–O[3] | B–QN5[7] | B–R3 | B–Q2 |
| | N–KR4 | O–O | R–K1 | BxN[15] |
| *10* | B–K5 | O–O | Q–B2 | BxB |
| | P–B4![14] | BxN | PxP | O–O |
| *11* | R–B1 | BxN | BxP[11] | N–Q2 |
| | N–B3[5] | BxNP[8] | ± | P–B4[16] |
| | = | = | | ± |

*Notes to supplementary variations 10–13:*

[1] The Exchange Variation.

[2] On 5 Q–N3 Black has the satisfactory answer 5 . . . N–B3 6 N–B3, N–QR4!

[3] Or 9 P–KR3, B–Q2 10 O–O, Q–N3! 11 Q–K2, KR–QB1 12 QR–B1, B–K1 13 KR–Q1, Q–Q1 with equality. In this line 10 . . . P–QR3 11 R–B1, B–K1 12 B–N1, N–KR4 13 B–R2, P–B4 14 N–QR4, B–Q3 15 N–B5 gives White the edge (Botvinnik–Smyslov, Moscow 1946).

[4] The correct rejoinder. 10 . . . P–B3 is faulty because of 11 N–KN5! with a winning advantage.

[5] Capablanca–Lasker, New York 1924.

[6] This symmetrical continuation often leads to lifeless positions of a drawish nature.

[7] Or 9 P–QR3, BxN† 10 PxB, O–O 11 QxNP, Q–R4! etc.

[8] Botvinnik–Trifunovic, Moscow 1947, the game in which this variation was introduced, led to a quick draw after 12 BxNP, BxR 13 RxB, Q–N3 14 BxR, RxB. For 8 B–N5 (omitting 8 Q–N3) see Botvinnik–Tal, Chess Review, 1961, page 172.

[9] After 6 Q–N3. O–O 7 B–Q2, both 7 . . . Q–N3 and 7 . . . P–K3 8 B–Q3, QN–Q2 9 O–O, P–N3 are satisfactory for Black. For 9 . . . N–N3 in this latter line, see Game 7.

[10] If 8 . . . Q–R4, then 9 Q–Q2!, threatening 10 NxP.

[11] Van Scheltinga–Cortlever, Amsterdam 1958.

[12] This is stronger than 5 PxP. See Part 3.

[13] Hoping for 6 BxB, PxB, which increases Black's control of the center.

[14] After 6 N–B3, BxB 7 QxB, B–N5 8 O–O, O–O 9 B–Q2, Black easily equalizes, as in 9 . . . N–R3 10 P–QR3, BxN 11 BxB, PxP 12 QxP, Q–Q4 13 Q–K2, N–K5 (Pirc–Trifunovic, Belgrade 1950).

[15] 9 . . . O–O? fails against 10 NxP!, while after 9 . . . B–R4 10 P–QN4!, B–B2 11 P–K4, PxBP 12 QxP, P–K4 13 B–K3!, White has a slight edge (Pirc–Euwe, 3d Match Game 1949).

[16] After 12 PxBP, NxP 13 Q–Q4, R–B1 14 QR–Q1, PxP 15 NxP, QxQ 16 BxQ, White enjoys the slightly better end game (Bondarevski–Gligoric, Saltsjobaden 1948).

*Slav Defense Game 7*

*WHITE: Fine* *BLACK: Lilienthal*

*Moscow 1937*

| WHITE | BLACK | WHITE | BLACK | WHITE | BLACK |
|---|---|---|---|---|---|
| 1 P–Q4 | P–Q4 | 14 P–K5 | N–N3 | 27 P–R5 | R–B5 |
| 2 P–QB4 | P–QB3 | 15 Q–K2 | P–KB4 | 28 R–K2 | PxP |
| 3 N–KB3 | N–B3 | 16 PxP e.p. | RxP | 29 Q–N3† | Q–N2 |
| 4 P–K3 | P–KN3 | 17 N–K4 | R–B4 | 30 R–Q3 | P–R5 |
| 5 N–B3 | B–N2 | 18 B–N4 | R–Q4 | 31 QxQ† | KxQ |
| 6 Q–N3 | O–O | 19 N–K5 | R–Q1 | 32 P–KN3 | PxP |
| 7 B–Q2 | P–K3 | 20 QR–B1 | N–Q4 | 33 RxP† | K–B1 |
| 8 B–Q3 | QN–Q2 | 21 B–R3 | N–K2 | 34 P–B3 | N–B3 |
| 9 O–O | N–N3 | 22 Q–B3 | N–Q4 | 35 R–R2 | RxN |
| 10 KR–Q1 | PxP | 23 Q–KN3 | B–R3 | 36 PxR | NxP |
| 11 BxBP | NxB | 24 R–B2 | B–B1 | 37 R–N4 | N–B3 |
| 12 QxN | N–Q2 | 25 P–KR4 | BxB | 38 R–KB2 | Resigns |
| 13 P–K4 | Q–B2 | 26 QxB | R–B1 | | |

---

## part 4—SEMI-SLAV (NOTEBOOM VARIATION)

1 P–Q4, P–Q4
2 P–QB4, P–QB3
3 N–KB3, P–K3
4 N–B3, PxP
5 P–QR4[A], B–N5
6 P–K3[B], P–QN4
7 B–Q2, P–QR4[C]
8 PxP, BxN
9 BxB, PxP
10 P–QN3[D], B–N2[E]

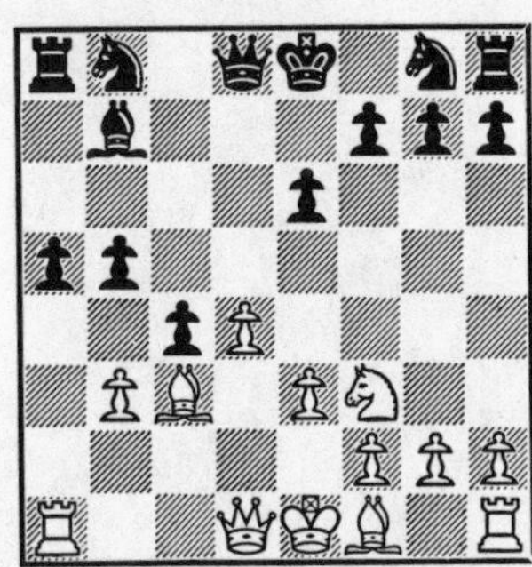

KEY POSITION 4

### OBSERVATIONS ON KEY POSITION 4

[A] After 5 P–K3, P–QN4 6 P–QR4, P–N5 7 N–K4, B–R3 8 Q–B2, Q–Q4 Black has an excellent game.

[B] The disadvantage of 6 P–K4 is seen in the variation 6 . . . P–QN4 7 B–Q2, P–QR4 8 PxP, BxN 9 BxB, PxP 10 P–QN3, when 10 . . . B–N2, hitting White's King Pawn, gains Black a vital tempo.

[C] The most enterprising continuation. Also worth consideration is 7 . . . Q–K2 8 PxP, BxN 9 BxB, PxP. In this position, of course, White cannot play the thematic 10 P–QN3 because of 10 . . . P–N5 followed by 11 . . . P–B6. However, he has better; see Game 8. White's best on 7 . . . Q–K2 may well be 8 Q–B2, e.g., 8 . . . N–KB3 9 PxP, BxN 10 QxB, PxP 11 P–QN3, N–K5 12 Q–R5, NxB 13 NxN, O–O 14 QxNP± (Denker–Christoffel, Groningen 1946).

D The characteristic countermeasure against Black's pawn set-up.

E The point of the Noteboom Variation: Black now obtains two connected passed Pawns.

Black pins his hopes on his two dangerous passed and connected Queenside Pawns. It is incumbent upon White to counter quickly in the center, else Black gains too free a hand. White's slight lead in development, not surprisingly, often proves the deciding factor.

*Slav Defense Game 8*

*WHITE: Van Scheltinga* *BLACK: Alexander*

*Hilversum 1947*

| | WHITE | BLACK | | WHITE | BLACK |
|---|---|---|---|---|---|
| 1 | P–Q4 | P–Q4 | 22 | QxR | N–N3 |
| 2 | P–QB4 | P–K3 | 23 | Q–B6 | B–Q2 |
| 3 | N–QB3 | P–QB3 | 24 | Q–Q6 | QxQ |
| 4 | N–B3 | PxP | 25 | NxQ | N–R5 |
| 5 | P–QR4 | B–N5 | 26 | P–B4 | P–QR3 |
| 6 | P–K3 | P–QN4 | 27 | R–N1 | K–B1 |
| 7 | B–Q2 | Q–K2 | 28 | R–N7 | N–B4 |
| 8 | PxP | BxN | 29 | R–B7 | K–K2 |
| 9 | BxB | PxP | 30 | N–B8† | K–Q1 |
| 10 | P–Q5 | N–KB3 | 31 | RxN | BxN |
| 11 | PxP | PxP | 32 | P–K4 | K–Q2 |
| 12 | N–Q4 | O–O | 33 | P–K5 | B–N2 |
| 13 | NxNP | N–K5 | 34 | P–N3 | B–B6 |
| 14 | BxBP | NxP | 35 | R–R5 | B–N2 |
| 15 | Q–R5 | N–K5 | 36 | K–B2 | K–B3 |
| 16 | R–KB1 | RxR† | 37 | K–K3 | K–N3 |
| 17 | KxR | NxB | 38 | R–R1 | K–B4 |
| 18 | PxN | N–B3 | 39 | K–Q3 | B–N7 |
| 19 | K–N1 | P–N3 | 40 | K–B3 | B–N2 |
| 20 | Q–N4 | N–K4? | 41 | R–Q1 | Resigns |
| 21 | Q–K4 | NxB | | | |

IDEA VARIATIONS 9 AND 10:

(9) 11 PxP, P–N5 12 B–N2, N–KB3 13 B–Q3, B–K5 14 Q–B2 (better is 14 BxB, NxB 15 Q–B2, P–B4), BxB 15 QxB, P–R5 with Black for choice.

(10) 11 P–Q5!, N–KB3 12 PxBP, P–N5 13 BxN, QxB 14 Q–R4†, N–Q2 15 N–Q4, PxP 16 P–B5, R–QB1 17 B–N5 and White wins.

## PRACTICAL VARIATIONS 16–20:

1 P–Q4, P–Q4 2 P–QB4, P–QB3 3 N–KB3, P–K3 4 N–B3, PxP 5 P–QR4, B–N5 6 P–K3, P–QN4 7 B–Q2, P–QR4 8 PxP, BxN 9 BxB, PxP 10 P–QN3, B–N2

| | *16* | *17* | *18* | *19* | *20* |
|---|---|---|---|---|---|
| *11* | PxP | – – | – – | P–Q5! | – – |
| | P–N5 | – – | – – | N–KB3[5] | – – |
| *12* | B–N2 | – – | – – | PxBP | – – |
| | N–KB3 | – – | – – | P–N5 | – – |
| *13* | B–Q3 | – – | – – | BxN | – – |
| | QN–Q2 | – – | B–K5! | QxB[6] | – – |
| *14* | Q–B2 | – – | N–K5[3] | Q–R4†[7] | – – |
| | O–O | – – | O–O | N–Q2[8] | K–B1! |
| *15* | P–K4 | – – | P–B3 | N–Q4 | N–Q4 |
| | P–K4 | – – | BxB | K–K2[9] | PxP |
| *16* | PxP[1] | O–O! | NxB | P–Q6† | Q–N5 |
| | N–B4 | PxP[2] | QN–Q2 | KxP | B–B3 |
| *17* | R–Q1 | P–K5 | O–O[4] | R–Q1 | Q–B5† |
| | KNxP | N–N5 | = | KR–Q1 | Q–K2 |
| *18* | ∓ | BxP† | | P–B5† | RxP |
| | | K–R1 | | NxP | QxQ |
| *19* | | B–K4 | | Q–N5[10] | RxQ |
| | | ± | | ± | K–K2[11] |
| | | | | | ± |

*Notes to practical variations 16–20:*

[1] 16 P–Q5, R–K1 17 P–B5, BxP! also favors Black (18 P–B6, P–N6).

[2] Also satisfactory for White is 16 . . . N–R4 17 P–B5.

[3] See Idea Var. 9 for alternate lines.

[4] A difficult struggle.

[5] After 11 . . . P–B3, White proceeds with 12 PxBP, P–N5 13 BxNP!, PxB 14 RxR, BxR 15 Q–R4†, N–Q2 16 PxP±.

[6] 13 . . . PxB 14 N–Q4, PxP 15 P–B5 also favors White.

[7] White's best try for an opening advantage.

[8] 14 . . . K–K2 15 N–Q4, PxP 16 Q–N5 gives White a decisive advantage.

[9] For 15 . . . PxP, see Idea Var. 10.

[10] White has a winning position (Spanjaard–Cortlever, Amsterdam 1950).

[11] White has the edge, but his task is far from simple. He faces problems after both 20 RxB, NxR 21 NxN†, K–Q3 22 NxP, PxP and 20 PxP, R–R8† 21 K–Q2, B–Q2.

## part 5—MARSHALL VARIATION

1 P–Q4, P–Q4
2 P–QB4, P–QB3
3 N–QB3, P–K3
4 P–K4[A], PxKP
5 NxP, B–N5†
6 B–Q2![B], QxP[C]
7 BxB, QxN†
8 B–K2[D]

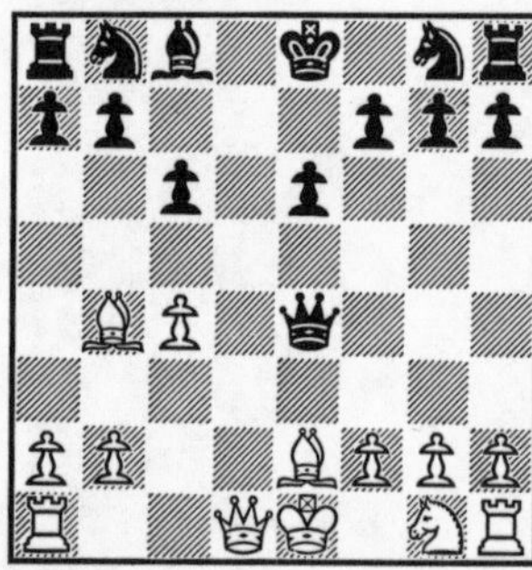

KEY POSITION 5

### OBSERVATIONS ON KEY POSITION 5

[A] For 4 P–K3, see Sup. Var. 14–16. The text move culminates in a Pawn sacrifice which offers White good attacking chances.

[B] The point of the variation. The meek 6 N–B3 offers White practically no chance for an advantage after 6 . . . P–QB4! 7 B–K3, N–KB3.

[C] Black accepts the challenge. 6 . . . BxB† 7 QxB, N–B3 8 NxN†, QxN is simpler, but offers White a positional advantage.

[D] Some years ago Canal suggested 8 N–K2, but this line is adequately countered by 8 . . . N–Q2 9 Q–Q6, P–QB4! 10 BxP, NxB 11 QxN, B–Q2 12 P–B3, P–QN3, when Black's position is satisfactory.

White is a Pawn down while another (the King Knight Pawn) is about to fall. In return he has a substantial lead in development and his Queen Bishop is menacingly posted, Black does best, therefore, to abstain from further material gain in an attempt to consolidate his position.

### IDEA VARIATIONS 11–13:

(11) 8 . . . QxNP 9 B–KB3, Q–N4 10 N–K2, N–QR3 11 R–KN1, Q–KB4 12 B–B8!, N–B3 13 BxNP, R–KN1 14 Q–Q4!±.

(12) 8 . . . N–QR3 9 B–B3, N–K2 10 BxP, R–KN1! (not 10 . . . QxNP? 11 B–B6, QxR 12 Q–Q6, O–O 13 Q–N3†, N–N3 14 B–KB3 and White wins) 11 B–B3, QxNP? (better is 11 . . . N–Q4!) 12 Q–Q2, QxR 13 O–O–O, and White has the edge; see Game 9.

(13) 8 . . . P–QB4 9 BxP, QxNP 10 B–B3, Q–N4 11 B–K3, Q–R4† 12 B–Q2, Q–B2 13 N–K2, N–QB3 14 B–B3, N–K4 15 N–Q4, B–Q2!∓ (Kovacs–Van Scheltinga, Amsterdam 1954).

*Slav Defense Game 9*

*WHITE: Bronstein* *BLACK: Kotov*

*Budapest 1950*

| | WHITE | BLACK | | WHITE | BLACK |
|---|---|---|---|---|---|
| 1 | P–Q4 | P–Q4 | 7 | BxB | QxN† |
| 2 | P–QB4 | P–K3 | 8 | B–K2 | N–QR3 |
| 3 | N–QB3 | P–QB3 | 9 | B–B3 | N–K2 |
| 4 | P–K4 | PxKP | 10 | BxP | R–KN1 |
| 5 | NxP | B–N5† | 11 | B–B3 | QxNP |
| 6 | B–Q2 | QxP | 12 | Q–Q2 | QxR |

| | WHITE | BLACK | | WHITE | BLACK |
|---|---|---|---|---|---|
| 13 | O–O–O | N–Q4 | 23 | B–R5 | B–B3 |
| 14 | N–B3 | QxR† | 24 | Q–Q6† | K–B3 |
| 15 | BxQ | NxB | 25 | N–R6 | R–N8† |
| 16 | QxN | K–K2 | 26 | K–Q2 | K–N2 |
| 17 | N–K5 | B–Q2 | 27 | N–N4 | RxN |
| 18 | Q–R3† | P–B4 | 28 | Q–K7† | K–R3 |
| 19 | Q–KB3 | QR–Q1 | 29 | BxR | RxP† |
| 20 | QxP† | K–Q3 | 30 | K–K3 | R–B8 |
| 21 | Q–B4 | QR–KB1 | 31 | P–KR4 | K–N3 |
| 22 | N–B7† | K–K2 | 32 | B–R5† | Resigns |

## PRACTICAL VARIATIONS 21–24:

1 P–Q4, P–Q4 2 P–QB4, P–QB3 3 N–QB3, P–K3 4 P–K4, PxKP 5 NxP, B–N5† 6 B–Q2!, QxP 7 BxB, QxN† 8 B–K2

| | *21* | *22* | *23* | *24* |
|---|---|---|---|---|
| *8* | — — | — — | — — | — — |
| | N–QR3[1] | — — | P–QB4[9] | — — |
| *9* | B–B3 | B–Q6[6] | BxP | — — |
| | N–K2 | P–QN3[7] | QxNP | — — |
| *10* | BxP | N–B3 | B–B3[10] | — — |
| | R–KN1 | B–N2 | Q–N4[11] | — — |
| *11* | B–QB3 | N–K5 | Q–Q6[12] | B–Q6[14] |
| | N–Q4![2] | P–B3 | N–Q2 | N–QB3[15] |
| *12* | PxN | O–O | B–K3 | BxN† |
| | QxNP | PxN | Q–QR4† | PxB |
| *13* | PxKP | B–R5† | P–N4 | N–B3[16] |
| | BxP | P–N3 | Q–K4[13] | = |
| *14* | B–B6[3] | R–K1[8] | = | |
| | QxR[4] | ± | | |
| *15* | Q–Q6 | | | |
| | RxN† | | | |
| *16* | K–Q2 | | | |
| | Q–Q4†[5] | | | |
| | = | | | |

*Notes to practical variations 21–24:*

[1] For 8 . . . QxNP, see Idea Var. 11.

[2] At this point 11 . . . QxNP favors White; see Idea Var. 12.

[3] 14 B–KB3 offers Black the choice between 14 . . . QxR and 14 . . . QxN†.

[4] Worth consideration is 14 . . . R–N3 15 B–R4, QxR 16 Q–Q6, QxN† with chances for Black.

[5] Black has a satisfactory game, according to Yudovitch: 17 QxQ, BxQ 18 RxR, K–Q2 19 BxN, PxB.

[6] White's most promising continuation.

continued ▸

[7] 9 . . . QxNP 10 Q–Q2!, QxR? 11 Q–N5 is too risky.

[8] With a slight advantage for White (Ragosin–Schaposchnikov, Correspondence Game 1952). After 14 . . . Q–R5 15 B–KN4, R–Q1 16 RxP, N–B2? 17 BxP, N–K2 18 BxN/B! White's advantage is decisive. Black fares better in this line with 16 . . . N–B4.

[9] Suggested by Euwe and certainly Black's best.

[10] Or 10 Q–Q6, N–Q2 11 O–O–O, Q–B3!, when Queens are exchanged.

11 The point of 8 . . . P–QB4 becomes clear. In retreating his Queen, Black gains a tempo on the attacked enemy Bishop.

[12] For 11 B–K3, see Idea Var. 13.

[13] Black has a satisfactory game. White's Bishops are a measure of compensation for his Pawn minus.

[14] Considered White's best.

[15] Not 11 . . . N–K2 which favors White after 12 BxQN, RxB 13 Q–Q6!

[16] White has good attacking chances for the Pawn, but Black's position is sound. See Game 10.

*Slav Defense Game 10*

*WHITE: Golz* — *BLACK: Van Scheltinga*

*Budapest 1960*

| | WHITE | BLACK | | WHITE | BLACK |
|---|---|---|---|---|---|
| 1 | P–Q4 | P–Q4 | 24 | Q–K5? | QxQ |
| 2 | P–QB4 | P–K3 | 25 | BxQ | R–QB1! |
| 3 | N–QB3 | P–QB3 | 26 | R–N1 | R–B5 |
| 4 | P–K4 | PxP | 27 | N–B3 | K–Q2 |
| 5 | NxP | B–N5† | 28 | B–Q4 | P–B3 |
| 6 | B–Q2 | QxP | 29 | R–N2 | P–QR3 |
| 7 | BxB | QxN† | 30 | B–K3 | R/1–QB1 |
| 8 | B–K2 | P–QB4 | 31 | N–K1 | P–Q5 |
| 9 | BxP | QxNP | 32 | B–Q2 | P–K4 |
| 10 | B–B3 | Q–N4 | 33 | R–N3 | K–Q3 |
| 11 | B–Q6 | N–QB3! | 34 | P–N5 | PxP |
| 12 | BxN† | PxB | 35 | RxP | R–QR1 |
| 13 | N–B3 | Q–KB4 | 36 | R–N2 | K–B2 |
| 14 | Q–K2 | N–B3 | 37 | B–N4 | P–K5 |
| 15 | R–KN1 | B–R3 | 38 | P–QR3 | P–B4 |
| 16 | P–N3 | R–Q1 | 39 | P–B3 | R–R3 |
| 17 | R–Q1 | N–K5 | 40 | PxP | PxP |
| 18 | N–R4 | Q–R4† | 41 | K–B2 | R–B3† |
| 19 | P–N4 | Q–R6 | 42 | K–K2 | P–Q6† |
| 20 | QxN | Q–B6† | 43 | K–Q1 | R–KB8 |
| 21 | K–B1 | BxP† | 44 | B–Q2 | R–R5 |
| 22 | K–N2 | B–Q4 | 45 | R–R2 | K–B3 |
| 23 | RxB | BPxR | 46 | B–K3 | K–Q4 |

| | WHITE | BLACK | | WHITE | BLACK |
|---|---|---|---|---|---|
| 47 | R–R1 | P–R3 | 56 | RxR | KxB |
| 48 | K–Q2 | R–R8 | 57 | R–KN1 | R–N7 |
| 49 | B–B4 | P–N4 | 58 | RxP† | K–B3 |
| 50 | B–N3 | P–R4 | 59 | R–Q5 | R–K7† |
| 51 | B–N8 | P–R5 | 60 | K–B4 | P–Q7 |
| 52 | K–K3 | R–R1 | 61 | P–R4 | P–K6 |
| 53 | B–B7 | R–R2 | 62 | P–R5 | R–K8 |
| 54 | B–N8 | R–QN2 | | Resigns | |
| 55 | B–K5 | RxN† | | | |

## SUPPLEMENTARY VARIATIONS 14-21:

1 P–Q4, P–Q4 2 P–QB4, P–QB3

| | *14* | *15* | *16* | *17* | *18* | *19* | *20* | *21* |
|---|---|---|---|---|---|---|---|---|
| 3 | N–KB3 | – – | – – | N–QB3 | – – | – – | – – | – – |
| | P–K3 | – – | – – | P–K3 | PxP | – – | P–K4[19] | N–B3 |
| 4 | P–K3 | – – | – – | P–K3 | P–K4[14] | – – | PxQP[20] | P–K3 |
| | N–B3 | P–KB4[5] | – – | P–KB4 | P–K4[15] | – – | BPxP | P–KN3[23] |
| 5 | QN–Q2[1] | N–B3 | – – | P–B4[12] | BxP | N–B3 | N–B3[21] | P–B4[24] |
| | P–B4[2] | N–Q2[6] | B–Q3 | N–B3 | PxP | PxP | P–K5 | B–N2 |
| 6 | B–K2[3] | B–Q3 | B–Q3 | N–B3 | N–B3 | QxP | N–Q2[22] | N–B3 |
| | N–B3 | Q–B3 | N–KR3 | B–K2 | PxN[16] | NxQ | = | O–O |
| 7 | O–O | Q–B2 | N–K5 | B–K2[13] | BxP† | B–QN5 | | B–K2 |
| | B–Q3 | N–R3[7] | BxN | ± | K–K2 | B–K3 | | B–B4 |
| 8 | P–QR3 | O–O | PxB | | Q–N3 | N–B3 | | O–O |
| | PxQP | B–Q3?[8] | O–O | | PxP | P–B3 | | QN–Q2 |
| 9 | KPxP | PxP | O–O[10] | | BxP | P–QN4 | | N–K5 |
| | P–QR4 | KPxP | N–N5 | | Q–N3[17] | P–QR4[18] | | ± |
| *10* | B–Q3 | P–K4![9] | P–B4 | | ∓ | ± | | |
| | O–O[4] | ± | PxP | | | | | |
| *11* | = | | B–K2[11] | | | | | |
| | | | ± | | | | | |

*Notes to supplementary variations 14–21:*

[1] 5 B–Q3, QN–Q2 6 O–O leads to a kind of Meran Defense (q.v.), distinguished therefrom by the postponement of development of White's Queen Knights. After 6 . . . PxP 7 BxBP, B–Q3 8 QN–Q2, O–O 9 B–Q3, P–B4 10 N–B4, B–K2 Black obtains approximately even chances. In this variation if 9 B–N3, correct for Black is 9 . . . B–B2.

[2] Appearances to the contrary, this move is no loss of time. Black quickly brings pressure to bear on White's center; White, meanwhile, is hampered by the placement of his Queen Knight.

[3] After 6 B–Q3, N–B3, Black threatens to win the enemy Queen Pawn.

continued ▸

[4] Alekhine–Vidmar, Semmering 1926. Black's game is certainly not inferior.

[5] The Slav–Stonewall, preferably adopted only when White has locked in his Queen Bishop by P–K3.

[6] 5 . . . N–KB3 6 B–Q3, N–K5 leads to the Meran–Stonewall (q.v.).

[7] Black must be ready to answer PxP with . . . KPxP. Recapture with the Queen Bishop Pawn yields White the open Queen Bishop file.

[8] Correct is 8 . . . B–K2 with even chances.

[9] A stock sacrifice against this type of Stonewall. After 10 . . . BPxP 11 BxP, PxB 12 NxP, Q–B1 13 R–K1, White has a winning attack.

[10] 9 PxP is also good.

[11] But not 11 BxQBP because of 11 . . . Q–R5 12 P–KR3, NxP/4.

[12] The Counter–Stonewall, which always leads to a slight edge for White.

[13] White has some initiative. He can soon launch a Queenside assault with P–B5 followed by P–QN4–5.

[14] The strongest continuation. After 4 P–K3, P–QN4, as well as after 4 P–QR4, P–K4!, Black stands well.

[15] Black must react with vigor. The alternate line of 4 . . . P–QN4 5 P–QR4, P–N5 6 N–R2 is very promising for White.

[16] 6 . . . B–B4 comes into consideration, but 6 . . . P–QN4 is faulty. See Game 11.

[17] It appears that White lacks an effective continuation for the attack (10 BxN, RxB!).

[18] See Game 12.

[19] The Winawer Counter-Gambit, which has thus far defied refutation.

[20] 4 PxKP, P–Q5 5 N–K4, Q–R4† 6 N–Q2, N–Q2! is satisfactory for Black.

[21] After 5 PxP, P–Q5 6 N–K4, Q–R4† 7 N–Q2, N–QB3, Black again emerges with a good game, but worth serious consideration is 5 P–K4, PxKP 6 B–N5†.

[22] After 6 N–K5, P–B3?, White wins with 7 Q–R4†, K–K2 8 Q–N3! With 6 . . . N–QB3!, however, Black yields White only a minute edge: 7 NxN, PxN 8 B–B4.

[23] 4 . . . P–K3 5 N–B3 leads to the Meran. 4 . . . B–B4 is effectively met by 5 PxP, PxP 6 Q–N3, which is another argument in favor of the Marshall Variation.

[24] 5 N–B3 leads to the Schlechter Variation (Sup. Var. 12).

[25] White maintains some initiative.

*Slav Defense Game 11*

*WHITE: Alekhine* *BLACK: Euwe*

*6th Match Game 1937*

| | WHITE | BLACK | | WHITE | BLACK |
|---|---|---|---|---|---|
| 1 | P–Q4 | P–Q4 | 13 | Q–B2 | Q–B4 |
| 2 | P–QB4 | P–QB3 | 14 | N–B5 | N–K4 |
| 3 | N–QB3 | PxP | 15 | B–B4 | N–R4 |
| 4 | P–K4 | P–K4 | 16 | BxP† | KxB |
| 5 | BxP | PxP | 17 | QxQ | BxQ |
| 6 | N–B3 | P–QN4? | 18 | BxN | R–N4 |
| 7 | NxNP | B–R3 | 19 | B–Q6 | B–N3 |
| 8 | Q–N3 | Q–K2 | 20 | P–QN4 | R–Q1 |
| 9 | O–O | BxN | 21 | QR–Q1 | P–QB4 |
| 10 | BxB | N–B3 | 22 | PxP | BxP |
| 11 | B–QB4 | QN–Q2 | 23 | R–Q5 | Resigns |
| 12 | NxP | R–QN1 | | | |

*Slav Defense Game 12*

*WHITE: Keres* *BLACK: Euwe*

*8th Match Game 1939*

| | WHITE | BLACK | | WHITE | BLACK |
|---|---|---|---|---|---|
| 1 | P–Q4 | P–Q4 | 19 | RxBP | NxP |
| 2 | P–QB4 | P–QB3 | 20 | R–B2 | N–Q2 |
| 3 | N–QB3 | PxP | 21 | K–K2 | P–QR4 |
| 4 | P–K4 | P–K4 | 22 | R–Q1 | N/5–N3 |
| 5 | N–B3 | PxP | 23 | P–QN3 | P–R5 |
| 6 | QxP | QxQ | 24 | PxP | RxRP |
| 7 | NxQ | B–QB4 | 25 | R–B6 | R–R7† |
| 8 | B–K3 | N–B3 | 26 | K–K1 | P–B4 |
| 9 | P–B3 | P–QN4 | 27 | P–K5 | NxP |
| 10 | P–QR4 | P–N5 | 28 | PxN | RxP |
| 11 | N–Q1 | B–R3 | 29 | R–Q8† | K–B2 |
| 12 | R–B1 | N/3–Q2 | 30 | R–B7† | K–N3 |
| 13 | P–B4 | O–O | 31 | R–Q6† | K–R4 |
| 14 | BxP | R–K1 | 32 | P–N4† | K–R5 |
| 15 | N–KB2 | BxN | 33 | RxP | RxB† |
| 16 | BxB/4 | BxB | 34 | K–B1 | P–R4 |
| 17 | RxB | P–QB4 | 35 | R–R6! | Resigns |
| 18 | B–K3 | N–N3 | | | |

# chapter 30—Tarrasch Defense

This debut, which Tarrasch himself called the normal defense, arises after 1 P–Q4, P–Q4 2 P–QB4, P–K3 3 N–QB3, P–QB4, and offers Black freedom for his pieces. Its drawback is that Black in most cases must acquiesce in the isolation of his Queen Pawn, which is why the defense has been unpopular. Lately, however, interest has been reviving, insofar as fresh examination has shown that White's task is anything but simple. Thus even grandmasters like Tal and Keres have been experimenting anew with this old system.

---

## part 1—PRAGUE VARIATION

1 P–Q4, P–Q4
2 P–QB4, P–K3
3 N–QB3, P–QB4
4 PxQP[A], KPxP[B]
5 N–B3[C], N–QB3[D]
6 P–KN3[E], N–B3[F]
7 B–N2

KEY POSITION 1

OBSERVATIONS ON KEY POSITION 1

[A] The most important continuation. For 4 P–K3 and 4 N–B3 see respectively Sup. Var. 1 and 2.

[B] An interesting possibility is 4 . . . BPxP, the so-called Hennig–Schara Gambit. See Sup. Var. 3.

[C] For 5 P–K4 and 5 PxP, see Sup. Var. 4 and 5.

[D] If 5 . . . N–KB3 the answer 6 B–N5! is definitely unfavorable for Black.

[E] Schlechter's innovation, also played with great success by Rubinstein, was considered for a long time the refutation of the defense. Other moves lead to little. For instance: 6 B–N5, B–K2 7 BxB, KNxB 8 P–K3, PxP 9 NxP/4, O–O 10 B–K2, Q–N3∓ or 6 B–K3, P–B5! 7 P–KN3, B–QN5 8 B–N2, KN–K2∓.

[F] Better than 6 . . . B–K3; see Game 1. 6 . . . P–B5 is treated in Part 2.

Both sides can easily complete their development. White can isolate Black's Queen Pawn by means of PxP, but must carefully consider the consequences of Black's . . . P–Q5. Black, for his part, generally can prevent the isolation of his Queen Pawn by means of . . . P–B5. But experience shows that White's center majority then carries more weight. Usually the fluidity of the center is maintained for some time. In most cases Black must eventually acquiesce in the isolation of the Queen Pawn, but it is problematical just how disadvantageous this will turn out to be.

*Tarrasch Defense Game 1*

*WHITE: Rubinstein* *BLACK: Capablanca*

*San Sebastian 1911*

| | WHITE | BLACK | | WHITE | BLACK |
|---|---|---|---|---|---|
| 1 | P–Q4 | P–Q4 | 22 | B–N4 | R–Q3! |
| 2 | N–KB3 | P–QB4 | 23 | KR–K1 | RxR |
| 3 | P–QB4 | P–K3 | 24 | RxR | R–QN3! |
| 4 | PxQP | KPxP | 25 | R–K5 | RxP |
| 5 | N–B3 | N–QB3 | 26 | RxP | N–B3 |
| 6 | P–KN3 | B–K3 | 27 | B–K6† | K–B1 |
| 7 | B–N2 | B–K2 | 28 | R–B5† | K–K1 |
| 8 | O–O | R–B1 | 29 | B–B7† | K–Q2 |
| 9 | PxP | BxP | 30 | B–B4 | P–QR3 |
| 10 | N–KN5! | N–B3 | 31 | R–B7† | K–Q3 |
| 11 | NxB | PxN | 32 | RxKNP | P–N4 |
| 12 | B–R3 | Q–K2 | 33 | B–N8 | P–QR4 |
| 13 | B–N5 | O–O | 34 | RxP | P–R5 |
| 14 | BxN | QxB | 35 | P–R4 | P–N5 |
| 15 | NxP!! | Q–R3 | 36 | R–R6† | K–B4 |
| 16 | K–N2 | QR–Q1 | 37 | R–R5† | K–N3 |
| 17 | Q–B1!! | PxN | 38 | B–Q5? | P–N6? |
| 18 | QxB | Q–Q7 | 39 | PxP! | P–R6 |
| 19 | Q–N5! | N–Q5 | 40 | BxN! | RxP |
| 20 | Q–Q3! | QxQ | 41 | B–Q5 | P–R7 |
| 21 | PxQ | KR–K1 | 42 | R–R6† | Resigns |

IDEA VARIATIONS 1 AND 2:

(1) 7 . . . B–K2 (probably the strongest; for other continuations, see Prac. Var. 1–3) 8 O–O, O–O 9 B–B4 (rather little known, but apparently offering White a good chance for a lasting initiative), PxP (as played in the game Petrosian–Geller, Amsterdam 1956; favorable for White, according to Petrosian, is 9 . . . B–K3 10 PxP, P–Q5 11 N–QN5, BxBP 12 R–QB1, Q–N3 13 P–QR4, while 9 . . . P–B5 is met strongly by 10 N–K5 followed by P–N3) 10 NxP/4, Q–N3 11 NxN, PxN (Black's isolani no longer exists, but the hanging Pawns at QB3 and Q4 are anything but an asset) 12 Q–B2, B–K3 (trying for . . . P–QB4) 13 R–QB1± (stronger than 13 B–K3, as played by Petrosian).

(2) 7 . . . B–K2 8 O–O, O–O 9 B–N5 (probably weaker than 9 B–B4, as in Idea Var. 1, but more usual; for good alternatives, see Prac. Var. 4–6), B–K3 (9 . . . P–B5 10 N–K5! favors White) 10 PxP (for a long time 10 R–B1 was considered strongest; it seems, however, that in this case Black obtains sufficient counterplay by means of 10 . . . N–K5 11 BxB, QxB 12 PxP, KR–Q1!), BxP (10 . . . P–Q5 is dubious because of 11 N–QR4±) 11 N–QR4 (11 R–B1! is preferable to the text, e.g., 11 . . . B–N3 12 R–B2, P–KR3 13 B–R4!, R–K1 14 R–Q2, P–N4 15 NxNP, PxN 16 BxNP, Q–K2 17 BxP, B–R6 18 Q–R4! and White's attack is overwhelming, as in Dely–Bilek, Budapest 1959), B–N3! 12 NxB, PxN 13 N–Q4, P–R3 14 B–B4, Q–Q2 15 P–QR3, B–R6! Idea Var. 2 is taken from Tal–Keres, Belgrade 1959, in which Black obtained good counterplay.

PRACTICAL VARIATIONS 1–6:

1 P–Q4, P–Q4 2 P–QB4, P–K3 3 N–QB3, P–QB4 4 PxQP, KPxP 5 N–B3, N–QB3 6 P–KN3, N–B3 7 B–N2

| | *1* | *2* | *3* | *4* | *5* | *6* |
|---|---|---|---|---|---|---|
| *7* | – – | – – | – – | – – | – – | – – |
| | PxP | B–N5 | B–K3 | B–K2 | – – | – – |
| *8* | NxP/4 | B–N5![5] | O–O | O–O | – – | – – |
| | B–QB4[1] | B–K2[6] | B–K2 | O–O | – – | – – |
| *9* | N–N3![2] | PxP | PxP | B–K3 | P–QR3 | PxP |
| | B–N3 | P–Q5 | BxP[9] | N–KN5![13] | B–K3 | P–Q5[17] |
| *10* | O–O![3] | BxN[7] | N–QR4 | B–B4 | PxP | N–QR4[18] |
| | B–K3 | BxB | B–K2 | B–K3 | BxP | B–B4 |
| *11* | B–N5 | N–K4 | B–K3 | PxP | P–QN4 | B–B4[19] |
| | O–O | B–K2 | N–K5![10] | BxP | B–K2 | B–K5![20] |
| *12* | N–R4! | O–O | R–B1![11] | N–K1 | B–N2 | R–B1 |
| | P–KR3 | O–O | O–O | B–Q5![14] | R–B1[15] | Q–Q4 |
| *13* | NxB | Q–N3[8] | N–Q4 | = | N–Q4 | P–N3 |
| | PxN | ± | NxN | | NxN | QR–Q1 |
| *14* | B–K3 | | QBxN[12] | | QxN | Q–Q2 |
| | N–K4 | | ± | | P–QR4[16] | Q–R4[21] |
| *15* | B–Q4! | | | | = | = |
| | N–B5 | | | | | |
| *16* | N–Q2[4] | | | | | |
| | ± | | | | | |

*Notes to practical variations 1–6*:

[1] 8 . . . Q–N3 9 NxN!, PxN 10 O–O also offers White the better chances.

[2] The text is stronger than 9 NxN, PxN 10 O–O, which is also good for White. 9 B–K3, Q–N3! favors Black.

[3] White does better to decline the sacrifice. After 10 NxP, NxN 11 QxN, Q–B3, Black has good chances.

[4] Black's Pawn structure is a serious handicap.

[5] Better than 8 N–K5, B–B4! etc.

[6] Not 8 . . . PxP 9 BxN!±.

[7] 10 N–QR4 is a good try.

[8] Grunfeld–Wagner, 1923.

[9] 9 . . . P–Q5 10 N–QN5!, BxBP 11 P–QN4! is risky for Black.

[10] Black's best chance.

[11] 12 N–Q4, NxN 13 BxN, O–O 14 N–B3, NxN 15 BxN, B–B3 is easier for Black.

[12] Black has the inferior position and the isolani.

[13] 9 . . . B–K3 is dubious, as shown in Petrosian–Keres, Amsterdam 1956, where 10 PxP, N–KN5 11 B–Q4, NxB 12 NxN± followed.

[14] Black's easy game compensates for the isolani.

[15] 12 . . . N–K5 is also playable.

[16] The weaknesses balance out.

[17] If 9 . . . BxP 10 N–QR4: (a) 10 . . . B–K2 11 N–Q4 with a slightly better game for White, or (b) 10 . . . B–N3! 11 NxB, QxN 12 B–N5, QxP 13 R–N1, QxRP 14 BxN, PxB, and White lacks sufficient counterplay for his two-Pawn deficit. His best in this line is probably 11 B–N5.

[18] After 10 N–QN5, BxP 11 B–B4, N–Q4!, Black has a good game.

[19] Introduced by Fine. Other moves have not turned out well in practical play.

[20] 11 . . . Q–Q2 followed by 12 . . . QR–Q1 maintains the Queen Pawn and offers Black good chances.

[21] Black's counterplay is worth the Pawn.

---

## part 2—SWEDISH VARIATION

### OBSERVATIONS ON KEY POSITION 2

1 P–Q4, P–Q4
2 P–QB4, P–K3
3 N–QB3, P–QB4
4 PxQP, KPxP
5 N–B3, N–QB3
6 P–KN3, P–B5[A]
7 B–N2[B], B–QN5!
8 O–O, KN–K2![C]

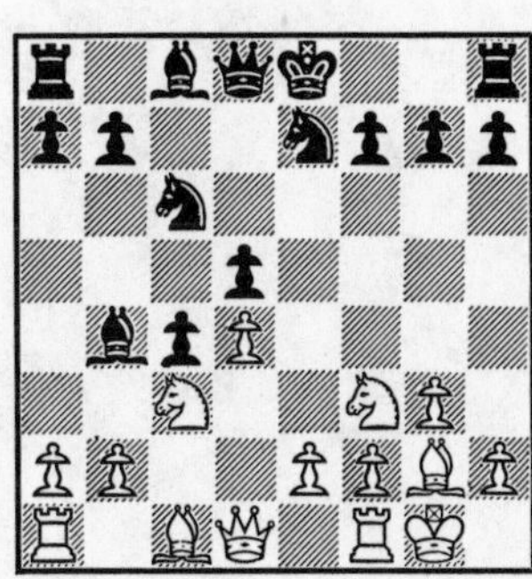

KEY POSITION 2

[A] The Swedish Variation. Both Stoltz and Stahlberg have examined this line extensively and introduced it in practical play.

[B] Too ambitious is 7 P–K4, PxP 8 N–KN5, QxP 9 B–B4, B–QN5 10 QxQ, NxQ 11 BxP, B–K3∓, according to Stahlberg.

[C] Weak is 8 . . . N–B3 because of 9 N–K5! The text move completes the Swedish set-up.

By means of the advance . . . P–QB5, Black establishes a Queenside Pawn majority. In doing this, he also avoids a weakening of his Pawn structure. The diagrammed position nevertheless offers White the better chances. With the thrust P–K4 White starts a vigorous action in the center, and his Kingside pieces join the fray quickly. All in all, the Swedish Variation is no improvement over the Prague.

IDEA VARIATIONS 3 AND 4:

(3) 9 N–K5 (this little known recommendation by Van Scheltinga offers White fine chances; for 9 P–K4, see Idea Var. 4, and for 9 P–QR3, see Prac. Var. 7), O–O 10 NxN, PxN 11 P–K4 (11 B–Q2 also merits consideration), B–K3 12 P–K5, R–N1 13 N–K2! (Van Scheltinga-Stahlberg, Amsterdam 1950; White clearly has the edge after 13 . . . B–R4 14 P–N3, R–K1 15 B–Q2).

(4) 9 P–K4, PxP (for 9 . . . O–O, see Game 2) 10 NxP, B–KB4 (for 10 . . . O–O 11 Q–B2!, see Prac. Var. 8) 11 N–K5, NxN (best; after either 11 . . . NxP 12 P–QR3, B–R4 13 NxQBP or 11 . . . QxP 12 QxQ, NxQ 13 P–QR3, White gets the better game) 12 PxN, N–B3 13 B–KN5, QxQ 14 KRxQ, P–KR3 (14 . . . NxP fails against 15 R–Q5!) 15 B–B4±.

*Tarrasch Defense Game 2*

*WHITE: Olafsson* *BLACK: Szabo*

*Portoroz 1958*

| | WHITE | BLACK | | WHITE | BLACK |
|---|---|---|---|---|---|
| 1 | P–QB4 | P–QB4 | 14 | NxN | B–KB4 |
| 2 | N–QB3 | P–K3 | 15 | B–N5 | P–B3 |
| 3 | N–B3 | P–Q4 | 16 | B–Q2 | BxB |
| 4 | PxP | PxP | 17 | QxB | Q–N3 |
| 5 | P–Q4 | N–QB3 | 18 | KR–K1 | KR–K1 |
| 6 | P–KN3 | P–B5 | 19 | P–Q6 | K–R1 |
| 7 | B–N2 | B–QN5 | 20 | N–B3 | KR–Q1 |
| 8 | O–O | KN–K2 | 21 | N–Q5 | Q–B4 |
| 9 | P–K4 | O–O | 22 | Q–B4 | B–N3 |
| 10 | PxP | KNxP | 23 | N–B7 | QR–B1 |
| 11 | N–KN5! | N–B3 | 24 | QR–Q1 | Q–N3 |
| 12 | P–Q5! | N–QR4 | 25 | B–R3 | R–QN1 |
| 13 | N/5–K4 | NxN | 26 | P–Q7 | N–B3 |

| WHITE | BLACK | WHITE | BLACK |
|---|---|---|---|
| 27 N–K6 | QxP | 36 R–QB5 | K–B2 |
| 28 NxR | RxN | 37 RxP | K–K2 |
| 29 Q–B7 | Q–N3 | 38 P–B4 | R–QR1 |
| 30 QxQ? | PxQ | 39 R–Q4 | K–Q1 |
| 31 R–N1 | N–K4? | 40 B–K6 | R–R6 |
| 32 RxN | PxR | 41 P–B5 | R–K6 |
| 33 RxP | B–K5 | 42 R–KN4 | P–N3 |
| 34 R–K6 | B–B3 | and Black resigns | |
| 35 RxP | K–N1 | | |

PRACTICAL VARIATIONS 7 AND 8:

1 P–Q4, P–Q4 2 P–QB4, P–K3 3 N–QB3, P–QB4 4 PxQP, KPxP 5 N–B3, N–QB3 6 P–KN3, P–B5 7 B–N2, B–QN5 8 O–O, KN–K2

| | 7 | 8 |
|---|---|---|
| *9* | P–QR3 | P–K4 |
| | B–R4 | PxP |
| *10* | P–K4 | NxP |
| | O–O | O–O |
| *11* | PxP | Q–B2! |
| | KNxP | Q–Q4[3] |
| *12* | NxN | B–K3 |
| | QxN | N–N3 |
| *13* | N–N5 | N–R4! |
| | QxP | Q–QN4[4] |
| *14* | Q–B2[1] | NxN |
| | Q–Q6 | RPxN |
| *15* | Q–R4 | P–QR3 |
| | B–N3 | B–K2 |
| *16* | B–K4 | P–Q5 |
| | Q–N6 | N–R4 |
| *17* | BxP† | P–Q6 |
| | K–R1 | B–Q1 |
| *18* | QxQ | N–B3[5] |
| | PxQ | ± |
| *19* | B–K4[2] | |
| | ± | |

*Notes to practical variations 7 and 8:*

[1] Better than 14 Q–R5, as in Szabo–Bronstein, Amsterdam 1956.

[2] White has a slight end game advantage.

[3] Not 11 . . . NxP 12 NxN, QxN 13 B–K3! etc.

[4] If 13 . . . NxP? then 14 Q–Q1! wins a piece.

[5] White has the superior development.

*Tarrasch Defense Game 3*

*WHITE: Pirc* — *BLACK: Alekhine*

*Bled 1931*

| | WHITE | BLACK | | WHITE | BLACK |
|---|---|---|---|---|---|
| 1 | P–Q4 | P–Q4 | 14 | QxR | B–QR6! |
| 2 | P–QB4 | P–K3 | 15 | Q–N3 | BxR |
| 3 | N–QB3 | P–QB4 | 16 | QxB/3 | QxP |
| 4 | PxQP | BPxP | 17 | Q–Q3 | B–N5! |
| 5 | Q–R4† | B–Q2 | 18 | N–B3 | BxN |
| 6 | QxQP | PxP | 19 | Q–B5† | K–N1 |
| 7 | QxQP | N–QB3 | 20 | QxB | Q–K8† |
| 8 | B–N5 | N–B3 | 21 | K–B2 | R–QB1 |
| 9 | Q–Q2 | P–KR3 | 22 | Q–N3† | N–K4† |
| 10 | BxN? | QxB | 23 | K–N3 | Q–Q8† |
| 11 | P–K3 | O–O–O | 24 | K–R3 | R–B4! |
| 12 | O–O–O? | B–KN5 | | Resigns | |
| 13 | N–Q5 | RxN! | | | |

SUPPLEMENTARY VARIATIONS 1–5:

1 P–Q4, P–Q4 2 P–QB4, P–K3 3 N–QB3, P–QB4

| | *1* | *2* | *3* | *4* | *5* |
|---|---|---|---|---|---|
| *4* | P–K3[1] | N–B3 | BPxP | – – | – – |
| | N–KB3 | PxQP[4] | BPxP[6] | KPxP | – – |
| *5* | N–B3 | KNxP | Q–R4†[7] | P–K4[12] | PxP[15] |
| | N–B3 | P–K4 | B–Q2[8] | PxKP | P–Q5[16] |
| *6* | PxBP[2] | N/4–N5 | QxQP | P–Q5 | N–R4 |
| | BxP | P–Q5 | PxP | P–B4 | P–QN4! |
| *7* | P–QR3 | N–Q5 | QxQP | B–KB4 | PxP e.p. |
| | P–QR3 | N–QR3 | N–KB3[9] | B–Q3 | PxP |
| *8* | B–K2 | P–K4 | Q–Q1![10] | B–QN5†![13] | P–QN3 |
| | O–O | N–B3 | N–B3 | K–B2 | N–KB3 |
| *9* | O–O | Q–R4 | N–B3 | N–R3 | P–K3 |
| | PxP | B–Q2 | B–QB4[11] | N–KB3 | B–Q2 |
| *10* | Q–B2 | B–N5[5] | = | B–B4 | QxP |
| | P–K4 | ± | | P–QR3 | N–B3 |
| *11* | BxP | | | P–R4[14] | Q–N2![17] |
| | B–KN5 | | | = | N–K5[18] |
| *12* | N–KN5 | | | | P–QR3! |
| | P–R3[3] | | | | P–QN4 |
| *13* | ± | | | | B–Q3 |
| | | | | | Q–R4† |
| *14* | | | | | K–K2 |
| | | | | | B–KB4 |
| *15* | | | | | Q–N1![19] |
| | | | | | ± |

*Notes to supplementary variations 1–5:*

[1] This is called the "Closed Variation." It is not a bad line, but is rather passive.

[2] After 6 P–QR3, Black's best continuation is 6 . . . PxQP 7 KPxP, B–K2.

[3] White has a slight initiative.

[4] Stronger is 4 . . . N–KB3, which transposes into the Semi-Tarrasch Defense.

[5] In this line 10 QxN? fails against 10 . . . B–N5†!

[6] The Hennig–Schara Gambit.

[7] 5 QxP, N–QB3 6 Q–Q1, PxP 7 QxP, B–K3 8 QxQ†, RxQ is difficult for White.

[8] Bad is 5 . . . Q–Q2 because of 6 N–N5!

[9] For 7 . . . N–QB3, see Game 3.

[10] Not 8 QxNP?, N–B3 9 Q–N3, N–Q5 10 Q–Q1, B–KB4 11 P–K4, NxP 12 Q–R4†, K–K2 13 Q–R3†, K–B3!∓ (analysis by Tartakower).

[11] Black has some compensation for the Pawn.

[12] The dangerous Marshall Gambit.

[13] An improvement by Tolush. After 8 N–R3, P–QR3 9 P–B3 N–KB3 10 PxP, PxP (Burn–Tarrasch, 1905), Black stands well.

[14] White has good chances for the Pawn.

[15] The old Tarrasch Gambit.

[16] The simple 5 . . . N–KB3 is possibly better.

[17] Only this move justifies White's set-up. After 11 QxP?, B–N5† 12 B–Q2, BxB† 13 KxB, Q–K2, Black has a winning advantage.

[18] Or 11 B–N5†, 12 B–Q2, BxB† 13 QxB, N–K5 14 Q–N2, Q–K2 15 P–QR3 (analysis by Henneberger).

[19] Analysis by Haberditz.

# chapter 31—Benoni Defense

The Benoni Defense made its academic debut in an obscure work published in Frankfort by A. Reinganun in 1825. It failed to make its over-the-board appearance, however, until 1843, when St. Amant tested the defense in his match with Staunton. Thereafter the line was again relegated to obscurity and seen only infrequently until it was revived by Spielmann in the Bad Pistyan Tournament of 1912.

A favorite with two World Champions, Alekhine and Tal, the Benoni is a forceful defense giving rise to extremely active positions rich in rapid-fire tactics. Often both sides skate on thin ice where sure footing is nowhere in sight.

---

## part 1—BLOCKADE SYSTEM

1 P–Q4, P–QB4
2 P–Q5[A], P–K4
3 P–K4, P–Q3

KEY POSITION 1

OBSERVATIONS ON KEY POSITION 1

[A] Less commendable is any of the following:

(1) 2 PxP, P–K3 3 P–QB4, BxP N–QB3, N–KB3= (Meyer–Schmid, Nuremburg 1952).

(2) 2 P–K3, N–KB3 3 N–KB3, PxP 4 PxP, P–KN3 5 B–Q3, B–N2 6 P–B3, P–Q3 7 P–KR3, O–O 8 O–O, N–B3= (Lee–Blackburne, London 1899).

(3) 2 N–KB3, PxP 3 NxP, P–Q4 4 P–QB4, P–K4 5 N–B2, P–Q5! 6 P–K3, N–QB3 7 PxP, PxP 8 B–Q3, N–B3 9 O–O, B–K2 10 R–K1, B–KN5! 11 P–B3, B–K3 12 P–QN3, O–O 13 B–N2, Q–B2∓ (Menchik–Alekhine, Hastings 1937).

(4) 2 P–K4, PxP with transposition into the Sicilian Defense.

This variation, a favorite with Alekhine, is characterized by the double advance of Black's King Pawn and the consequent closing of the center. For both sides, the major problem is the advance of the King Bishop Pawn and its lasting effect on the Pawn formation.

Although presently not in vogue, the Blockade Variation is more difficult to meet than the modern treatment of the Benoni, 2 . . . P–Q3.

IDEA VARIATIONS 1 AND 2:

(1) 4 P–QB4, P–B4 (for 4 . . . N–KB3, see Part 3) 5 PxP (5 N–QB3, N–KB3 6 B–Q3, P–KN3 7 B–N5, P–KR3 8 BxN, QxB 9 PxP, PxP 10 Q–R5†, Q–B2 [Vajda-Tschepurnov, Paris 1924], or, in this line, 6 . . . PxP 7 NxP, P–KN3 8 KN–K2 (Gilg–Kipke, Oeynhausen 1922], in each case with a minimal plus for White), BxP 6 N–QB3, N–KB3 7 KN–K2, B–K2 8 N–N3, QB–B1 9 B–Q3, O–O 10 O–O, P–QR3 11 Q–K2, P–QN3 12 KN–K4, NxN 13 BxN, N–Q2 14 P–B4!± (Mueller-Gygli, 1934).

(2) 4 P–KN3, P–B4 5 N–QB3, N–KB3 6 B–N2, B–K2 7 P–QR4 (7 KN–K2, P–QN4! [Gygli–Alekhine, Zurich 1934]), O–O 8 KN–K2, PxP 9 NxP, B–B4 10 Q–Q3, Q–B1=.

PRACTICAL VARIATIONS 1–4:

1 P–Q4, P–QB4 2 P–Q5, P–K4 3 P–K4, P–Q3

| | *1* | *2* | *3* | *4* |
|---|---|---|---|---|
| *4* | P–KB4 | N–QB3 | B–Q3! | – – |
| | PxP[1] | P–QR3[5] | N–K2[9] | P–KN3 |
| *5* | BxP | P–QR4 | N–K2[10] | P–QB4[14] |
| | Q–R5†[2] | P–B4[6] | N–N3 | B–N2 |
| *6* | P–N3 | P–B4! | O–O | N–K2 |
| | Q–K2 | N–KB3 | P–QR3 | N–K2 |
| *7* | B–N5†[3] | PxKP | P–QR4 | O–O[15] |
| | N–Q2 | QPxP | B–K2 | O–O |
| *8* | N–KB3 | PxP | N–R3 | QN–B3 |
| | QxP† | BxP | O–O | P–B4 |
| *9* | K–B2 | B–KN5 | N–B4 | P–B4! |
| | Q–N5 | B–Q3 | N–Q2 | N–Q2 |
| *10* | R–K1† | KN–K2 | B–Q2[11] | PxBP |
| | K–Q1 | QN–Q2[7] | P–N3 | NPxP |
| *11* | N–B3 | N–N3 | P–QB3 | PxP |
| | P–KR3 | B–N3 | R–N1 | NxKP |
| *12* | Q–Q3 | B–Q3 | P–QN4 | B–N5 |
| | KN–B3 | BxB | N–B3 | P–KR3 |
| *13* | P–QR3 | QxB | PxP | B–R4 |
| | Q–R4 | Q–B2 | NPxP[12] | N/4–N3 |
| *14* | K–N2 | N–B5 | R–N1 | B–N3 |
| | P–R3 | O–O | B–Q2 | P–R3 |
| *15* | P–QN4 | NxB | Q–B2 | Q–B2 |
| | Q–B2 | QxN | Q–B2 | Q–B2 |
| *16* | BxN | O–O | Q–R2 | QR–K1 |
| | BxB?[4] | P–B5![8] | N–R4 | B–Q2 |
| *17* | ± | = | P–N3[13] | P–KR3 |
| | | | ± | P–N4[16] |
| | | | | ± |

*Notes to practical variations 1–4:*

[1] 4 . . . P–B4 5 N–QB3, N–KB3 6 N–B3, P–QR3 7 PxKP, QPxP 8 B–N5, B–Q3 9 PxP, BxP 10 B–Q3, BxB 11 QxB, O–O 12 O–O, QN–Q2 favors White (Ahues–Richter, Salzbrunn 1933). The analyst Dr. E. Schmidt gives also 4 . . . P–B4 5 B–Q3, BPxP 6 BxP, N–KB3 7 N–QB3, B–K2 8 N–B3, O–O 9 PxP, PxP 10 O–O±.

[2] 5 . . . N–K2, with the following possibilities, deserves consideration:

1) 6 N–Q2!, N–N3 7 B–N3, B–K2 8 KN–B3, O–O 9 B–Q3, N–Q2 10 N–B4, N–B3 11 P–QR4, N–R4 12 KN–Q2, N/4–B5! 13 O–O, NxB 14 PxN, P–B3 15 N–B3, N–K4=. In this line 9 N–B4 is answered by 9 . . . N–Q2!

*continued* ▸

2) 6 N–QB3, N–N3 7 B–N3, P–QR3 8 P–QR4, B–K2 9 N–B3, B–N5 10 B–K2, N–Q2=.

[3] If instead 7 N–QB3, then P–KN4! 8 B–K3, N–Q2 9 N–B3, P–KR3 10 Q–Q2, KN–B3 11 O–O–O, N–N5 12 B–K2, B–N2∓ (Bogoljubov–Alekhine, 9th Match Game 1934). Alekhine himself recommended 7 N–KB3, and if 7 . . . QxP† then 8 K–B2, N–KB3 9 B–R3!, K–Q1 10 N–QB3±; or if 7 . . . B–KN5, simply 8 QN–Q2. Note that 7 B–Q3 is strongly met by 7 . . . P–KN4!

[4] 17 PxP!, QxP 18 B–K3, Q–B2 19 P–QR4, B–K2 20 P–R5 and White has a winning position (Toth–Grob, Belgrade 1950). Necessary was 16 . . . NxB!

[5] Or, if 4 . . . P–KN3, then either:

1) 5 P–KN3, B–N2 6 B–N2, N–K2 7 KN–K2, O–O 8 O–O, P–QR3 9 P–QR4, N–Q2 10 B–K3, P–B4 11 Q–Q2 followed by QR–K1 and P–KB4 etc.± or
2) 5 P–B4, B–N2 6 N–B3, B–N5 7 PxP, BxN 8 QxB, BxP 9 B–N5†, N–Q2 10 O–O, Q–K2 11 BxN†, QxB 12 B–B4± (Stahlberg–Seitz, Lodz 1938). For 4 . . . B–K2, see Game 1.

[6] Black can also try 5 . . . B–K2, e.g., 6 B–Q3, B–N4 7 N–B3, BxB 8 QxB, N–K2 9 N–K2, N–Q2 10 N–N3, N–KB3 11 Q–N5, O–O= (Galia–Hein, Vienna 1955). For 5 . . N–KB3, see Game 2.

[7] 10 . . . Q–N3! puts White in difficulties.

[8] Euwe–Alekhine, Hilversum 1935.

[9] Inferior is 4 . . . B–K2 5 N–K2, P–KN3 6 O–O, P–B4 7 P–KB4!, PxKP 8 BxP, N–KB3 9 QN–B3, NxB 10 NxN, PxP 11 BxP, O–O 12 Q–Q2, and White has excellent chances (Saunders–Tartakover, Scarborough 1929).

[10] Another equally commendable system is 5 P–QB4, N–N3 6 P–KN3, B–K2 7 P–KR4!, P–KR3 8 N–QB3, N–Q2 9 N–B3, N–B3 10 N–R2, B–Q2 11 N–B1, N–B1 12 N–K3, P–KN3 13 B–K2, P–KR4 14 B–Q2 (Rubinstein–Spielmann, Stockholm 1919).

[11] 10 P–R5 is a good alternative.

[12] 13 . . . QPxP 14 P–B4!±.

[13] Kmoch–Alekhine, Amsterdam 1936.

[14] Worth consideration is Nimzowitsch's recommendation of 5 P–QR4 followed by N–QR3–B4. If Black counters with . . . P–B4, White plays P–KB3. 5 N–K2 is also good, e.g., 5 . . . P–B4 6 P–KB4! or 5 . . . N–KR3 6 N–N3 (Alatortsev–Ryumin, Moscow 1935).

[15] If 7 N–N3, P–KR4.

[16] 18 P–N3!, P–N5 19 N–Q1, R–B2 20 B–R2± (Reshevsky–Seitz, Great Yarmouth 1934).

### *Benoni Defense Game 1*

*WHITE: Alekhine* *BLACK: Tartakover*

*Dresden 1929*

| WHITE | BLACK | WHITE | BLACK |
|---|---|---|---|
| 1 P–Q4 | P–QB4 | 5 B–Q3 | B–N4 |
| 2 P–Q5 | P–Q3 | 6 N–B3 | BxB |
| 3 P–K4 | P–K4 | 7 QxB | N–KR3 |
| 4 N–QB3 | B–K2 | 8 P–KR3 | P–B4 |

| WHITE | BLACK | WHITE | BLACK |
|---|---|---|---|
| 9 Q–N5! | O–O | 33 N–K5 | K–N2 |
| 10 QxQ | RxQ | 34 R–R7† | K–R3 |
| 11 N–KN5 | P–KN3 | 35 R–QB7 | N–Q6 |
| 12 P–B4 | PxBP | 36 NxN | BxN |
| 13 O–O | N–R3 | 37 N–B7† | K–R4 |
| 14 RxP | N–QN5 | 38 P–Q6 | B–N3 |
| 15 R–R4 | NxB | 39 P–Q7 | BxN |
| 16 RxN | NxP | 40 R–B8 | B–K3 |
| 17 RxP | N–B5 | 41 RxR | BxQP |
| 18 PxP | BxP | 42 R–B7 | B–R5 |
| 19 RxP | R–K1 | 43 K–B2 | K–N3 |
| 20 N–R7 | R–K6 | 44 R–QR7 | B–B7 |
| 21 N–B6† | K–B1 | 45 R–R6† | K–N2 |
| 22 N–R7† | K–N1 | 46 K–K3 | K–B2 |
| 23 N–QN5 | P–N4 | 47 K–Q4 | K–N2 |
| 24 N–B6† | K–R1 | 48 K–K5 | B–Q6 |
| 25 R–KB1! | BxBP | 49 R–R3 | B–B7 |
| 26 R–B1 | N–R4 | 50 R–KN3 | K–N3 |
| 27 R–QB7! | B–N3 | 51 P–R4 | K–R4 |
| 28 NxQP | R–KB1 | 52 RxP† | KxP |
| 29 N–N4 | R–K7 | 53 K–B4 | B–Q8 |
| 30 RxRP | RxP | 54 P–N3† | K–R6 |
| 31 RxP | N–N6 | 55 P–N4 | Resigns |
| 32 RxR | NxR | | |

*Benoni Defense Game 2*

*WHITE: Grunfeld* *BLACK: Palda*

*Klosterneuburg 1934*

| WHITE | BLACK | WHITE | BLACK |
|---|---|---|---|
| 1 P–Q4 | P–QB4 | 15 NxN | N–Q2 |
| 2 P–Q5 | P–K4 | 16 B–K3 | K–R1 |
| 3 P–K4 | P–Q3 | 17 Q–B7 | R–N1 |
| 4 N–QB3 | P–QR3 | 18 P–Q6 | B–B3 |
| 5 P–QR4 | N–KB3 | 19 R–KB1 | Q–N1 |
| 6 P–KN3! | B–K2 | 20 QxQ† | KxQ |
| 7 B–N2 | O–O | 21 BxP | P–QN3 |
| 8 KN–K2 | N–K1 | 22 B–K3 | B–N2 |
| 9 O–O | P–B4 | 23 P–QN4! | K–B2 |
| 10 P–B4! | PxKP | 24 P–B4 | P–QR4 |
| 11 PxP | RxR† | 25 P–B5 | PxNP |
| 12 QxR | PxP | 26 NxB | NxP |
| 13 NxP | N–KB3 | 27 N–Q7† | Resigns |
| 14 N/2–B3 | NxN | | |

*Benoni Defense Game 3*

*WHITE: Donner* *BLACK: Balcerovski*

*Varna Olympics 1962*

| WHITE | BLACK | WHITE | BLACK |
|---|---|---|---|
| 1 P–Q4 | P–QB4 | 9 P–KN3 | B–K2 |
| 2 P–Q5 | P–K4 | 10 P–R4 | O–O |
| 3 P–K4 | P–Q3 | 11 B–Q2 | P–N3 |
| 4 N–QB3 | N–K2 | 12 N–Q1 | N–Q2 |
| 5 N–KB3 | B–N5 | 13 N–K3 | N–B3 |
| 6 P–KR3 | BxN | 14 P–KR5 | N–R1 |
| 7 QxB | P–QR3 | 15 N–B5 | R–R2 |
| 8 P–QR4 | N–N3 | 16 P–R6 | Resigns |

---

## part 2—2 . . . P-Q3 SYSTEM

1 P–Q4, P–QB4
2 P–Q5, P–Q3[A]

KEY POSITION 2

OBSERVATIONS ON KEY POSITION 2

[A] The alternatives 2 . . . P–KN3 and 2 . . . P–K3 are treated separately in Sup. Var. 1–5.

This system differs essentially from the Blockade Variation in that the position is not locked with . . . P–K4. Black thus maintains the option of striking at the hostile center with a timely . . . P–K3. This treatment, currently in fashion, has among its devotees the German grandmaster and correspondence player of renown, Lothar Schmid, who has employed it with considerable success in numerous tournament and postal games.

IDEA VARIATION 3:

(3) 3 N–QB3, N–KB3 (for 3 . . . P–KN3, see Prac. Var. 6–8) 4 P–K4, P–QR3 5 P–QR4, P–KN3 6 N–B3, B–N2 7 N–Q2, O–O 8 B–K2, P–K3 9 O–O, PxP 10 PxP, QN–Q2 11 N–B4, N–N3 12 N–R3, R–K1 13 B–B3, B–Q2 14 B–B4, NxRP 15 NxN, BxN 16 N–B4, B–N4 17 NxP, BxR 18 NxR, NxN 19 KxB, BxP 20 R–N1, Q–B3 21 B–N3, R–Q1 22 Q–K2, N–Q3 23 P–B4, B–R6! (23 . . . B–B6 24 R–N6! etc.) (Haag–Kluger, Balatonfured, 1959). White must play for the draw.

PRACTICAL VARIATIONS 5–8:

1 P–Q4, P–QB4 2 P–Q5, P–Q3

| | *5* | *6* | 7 | 8 |
|---|---|---|---|---|
| *3* | P–QB4 | P–K4[8] | – – | – – |
| | P–KN3 | P–KN3 | – – | – – |
| *4* | N–QB3[1] | P–KB4 | N–KB3 | – – |
| | B–N2 | B–N2 | B–N2 | – – |

| | 5 | 6 | 7 | 8 |
|---|---|---|---|---|
| 5 | P–K4 | N–KB3 | P–B4 | N–B3 |
| | N–KB3 | P–K3[9] | N–Q2 | N–KB3 |
| 6 | B–K2[2] | N–B3[10] | N–B3 | B–K2[17] |
| | P–K3[3] | N–K2[11] | KN–B3 | N–R3[18] |
| 7 | B–N5 | B–N5† | B–K2 | O–O[19] |
| | O–O | B–Q2 | O–O | N–B2 |
| 8 | N–B3 | BxB† | O–O | P–QR4 |
| | PxP | QxB | P–QR3[14] | P–QR3 |
| 9 | BPxP[4] | O–O | P–QR4[15] | N–Q2 |
| | P–KR3 | N–R3[12] | R–N1 | B–Q2 |
| 10 | B–R4[5] | B–K3 | P–R3 | N–B4[20] |
| | P–KN4 | BxN | N–K1 | P–QN4 |
| 11 | B–N3 | PxP | B–B4 | P–K5![21] |
| | P–N4 | QxP | N–K4 | ± |
| 12 | Q–B2[6] | PxB | Q–Q2 | |
| | P–QN5 | QxKP | NxN† | |
| 13 | N–Q1 | R–K1 | BxN | |
| | NxKP | Q–B3 | Q–R4 | |
| 14 | QxN | B–B2 | B–N5 | |
| | P–B4 | P–B3 | B–B3 | |
| 15 | Q–B2 | R–K6 | B–K3 | |
| | P–KB5 | R–Q1 | B–Q2 | |
| 16 | O–O | Q–K2 | B–K2 | |
| | N–Q2[7] | Q–B2[13] | P–K4[16] | |
| | ± | ± | ± | |

*Notes to practical variations 5–8:*

[1] The game Rubinstein–Spielmann, Pistyan 1912, took the following interesting course: 4 P–K4, B–N2 5 B–Q3, P–K3 6 N–QB3, N–K2 7 KN–K2, PxP 8 KPxP, N–Q2 9 P–B4, N–KB3 10 N–N3, P–KR4! 11 O–O, P–R5 12 KN–K4, NxN 13 BxN, B–Q5† 14 K–R1, N–B4 15 BxN, BxB 16 R–K1†, K–B1 and White should now have played 17 P–KR3. Even so, Black's Bishop-sweep gives him an edge.

[2] On 6 P–B4, not 6 . . . QN–Q2 7 N–B3, O–O 8 B–K2, Q–B2 9 O–O, P–QR3 10 P–KR3, P–N3 11 Q–Q3, B–N2 12 B–K3± (Euwe–Saemisch, Budapest 1921), but 6 . . . O–O! 7 N–B3, B–N5 8 P–KR3, BxN 9 QxB, QN–Q2 10 P–KN4, P–K3 11 PxP, PxP 12 B–Q2, N–K1 13 O–O–O, Q–B3 14 P–KR4, Q–B2 (Burn–Tchigorin, Vienna 1898), and White cannot be satisfied with this position.

[3] For 6 . . . O–O 7 B–N5!, see Part 2, Prac. Var. 5, of the King's Indian Defense.

[4] Or 9 KPxP, B–N5 10 O–O, BxN 11 BxB, QN–Q2 12 Q–Q2, R–K1 13 Q–B4, R–K4 14 Q–R4, Q–N3 15 QR–N1, P–QR3 16 B–Q1± (Szabo–Pilnik, Amsterdam 1956).

[5] 10 B–KB4, P–QN4 11 N–Q2, P–QR3 12 O–O, R–K1 13 B–Q3, Q–K2 14 R–K1, QN–Q2 15 N–B3, N–N5∓ (Gligoric–Malich, Munich 1958).

continued ▸

[6] 12 N–Q2, P–QR3 13 O–O, R–K1 14 Q–B2 (Reshevsky–Szabo, Israel 1959) is also good.

[7] For the continuation, see Game 4.

[8] For 3 N–QB3, see Idea Var. 3.

[9] 5 . . . N–KB3 is inferior because after 6 B–N5†!, B–Q2 7 BxB†, QNxB 8 Q–K2 White will be able to force a favorable breakthrough with P–K5. 5 . . . N–Q2 is answered by 6 N–QB3, Q–N3 7 N–Q2, P–QR3 8 Q–B3, N–R3 9 N–B4, Q–B2 10 P–QR4, P–B4 11 B–Q3, PxP 12 N/3xP, O–O 13 O–O etc.±.

[10] The game Van Scheltinga–Schmid, Dublin 1957, continued 6 PxP, PxP 7 P–K5!, P–Q4 8 P–B4, N–K2 9 N–B3, P–QR3, and in this position White can keep the advantage with either 10 P–KR4! or 10 B–K2. Black does better, however, to answer 6 PxP with 6 . . . BxP; if 7 P–B4, simply 7 . . . N–QB3, or if 7 N–N5, then 7 . . . N–K2.

[11] 6 . . . P–QR3 is superior.

[12] Or 9 . . . PxP 10 NxP, O–O 11 P–B3, QN–B3 12 B–K3, and now not 12 . . . KR–K1? 13 BxP! (Mueller–Eysser, Aachen 1938), but 12 . . . QR–Q1.

[13] 17 B–R4!, P–KN4 18 R–K1, R–Q2 19 PxP, K–B2 20 PxP, N–B4 21 N–N5†, K–N3 22 Q–N4, Resigns (Cohn–Mieses, Breslau 1912).

[14] 8 . . . N–K1 9 B–N5!, B–B3 10 B–B4, N–N3 11 P–KR3, P–K4 12 PxP e.p., BxP 13 Q–N3, Q–B2 14 KR–K1± (Saemisch–Wagner, Swinemunde 1930).

[15] The modern remedy 9 B–N5 can also be applied, e.g., 9 . . . P–KR3 10 B–B4, K–R2 11 P–KR3, N–K1 12 Q–Q2 (Szabo–Paoli, Team Match 1960).

[16] After 17 PxP e.p., PxP 18 KR–Q1, R–Q1 19 P–B3, B–B3 20 N–Q5, QxQ 21 NxB†, NxN 22 RxQ, White has the superior position (Rubinstein–L. Steiner, Dresden 1926).

[17] Inferior is 6 B–N5†, QN–Q2 7 P–QR4, O–O 8 O–O, P–QR3 9 B–K2, R–N1 10 R–K1, N–K1 11 B–B4, N–B2 12 B–B1, R–K1 13 Q–Q2, P–QN4 14 P–R3, N–B3 15 QR–Q1 (Tal–Benko, Bled 1959), and now 15 . . . P–N5! gives Black a satisfactory game. Pirc's suggestion 6 . . . B–Q2 followed by . . . N–QR3 is worth investigating.

[18] After 6 . . . O–O 7 O–O, N–R3 8 N–Q2, N–B2 9 P–QR4, P–N3 10 N–B4, B–QR3, there can follow:

1) 11 B–B4, R–N1 12 P–QN3, N–Q2 13 Q–Q2, P–B4 14 QR–Q1, PxP 15 NxKP (Smyslov–Schmid, Helsinki 1952), and Black can now obtain a reasonable position with 15 . . . N–B3 or 15 . . . B–N2. In this variation, 12 . . . N–R4 is inferior, e.g., 13 B–Q2, N–B5 14 B–B3, P–K4 15 P–N3± (Rabar–Lehmann, Munich 1954).
2) 11 B–N5, BxN 12 BxB, P–QR3 13 R–K1, N–Q2 14 Q–Q2, R–K1 15 B–B1, R–N1 16 R–R2, P–QN4? 17 PxP, PxP 18 R/1–R1, N–K4 19 N–Q1, and White has a positional advantage (Johansson–Fuderer, Amsterdam 1954).

[19] Not as sharp is 7 B–N5, P–KR3 8 B–KB4, N–B2 (Tal–Schmid, Hamburg 1960).

[20] Much inferior is 10 P–R5, N–N4! 11 N/3–N1, O–O 12 B–B3, N–Q5, and Black has bright prospects (Keres–Schmid, Wien–Baden 1957).

[21] An important improvement for White! Prior to Botvinnik–Schmid, Leipzig 1960 (see Game 5), the only known continuation was 11 N–N6, P–N5! 12 NxR, QxN 13 N–N1, NxKP 14 B–B3, P–B4 15 N–Q2, N–KN4 (Hayes–Schmid, Dyckhoff Memorial Correspondence Tournament), and Black had a powerful initiative. Instead of the Botvinnik–Schmid continuation 11 . . . PxKP 12 PxP, PxP?, Schmid suggests 12 . . . NxNP as an improvement, e.g., 13 NxN, BxN 14 NxP, BxB 15 QxB, QxP 16 RxP, RxR 17 QxR, O–O 18 N–B6, R–K1 or 13 NxP, NxN 14 PxN, N–K5, and in both cases Black has drawing chances.

*Benoni Defense Game 4*

*WHITE: Bobozoff* — *BLACK: L. Szabo*

*Balatonfured 1958*

| | WHITE | BLACK | | WHITE | BLACK | | WHITE | BLACK |
|---|---|---|---|---|---|---|---|---|
| 1 | P–QB4 | P–KN3 | 14 | QxN | P–B4 | 27 | N–K5 | BxN |
| 2 | N–QB3 | B–N2 | 15 | Q–B2 | P–KB5 | 28 | BxN | BxB |
| 3 | P–Q4 | P–QB4 | 16 | O–O | N–Q2 | 29 | BxQ | B–B7† |
| 4 | P–Q5 | P–Q3 | 17 | N–K3! | N–N3 | 30 | K–R1 | QRxB |
| 5 | P–K4 | N–KB3 | 18 | QR–Q1 | Q–K2 | 31 | P–Q7 | R–Q1 |
| 6 | B–K2 | P–K3 | 19 | KR–K1 | PxN | 32 | R–B1 | P–K6 |
| 7 | B–N5 | O–O | 20 | PxP | B–B4 | 33 | QxBP | B–B4 |
| 8 | N–B3 | PxP | 21 | P–K4! | B–R2 | 34 | RxB | PxR |
| 9 | BPxP | P–KR3 | 22 | Q–B1 | N–Q2 | 35 | QxBP | K–N1 |
| 10 | B–R4 | P–KN4 | 23 | P–K5! | PxP | 36 | QxP | B–N5 |
| 11 | B–N3 | P–N4 | 24 | P–Q6 | Q–K1 | 37 | R–K1 | RxP |
| 12 | Q–B2 | P–QN5 | 25 | B–B4† | K–R1 | 38 | Q–N6 | K–R2 |
| 13 | N–Q1 | NxKP | 26 | B–N5 | P–K5 | 39 | P–KR3 | Resigns |

*Benoni Defense Game 5*

*WHITE: Botvinnik* — *BLACK: Schmid*

*Leipzig 1960*

| | WHITE | BLACK | | WHITE | BLACK |
|---|---|---|---|---|---|
| 1 | P–Q4 | P–QB4 | 16 | PxN | Q–B1 |
| 2 | P–Q5 | P–Q3 | 17 | B–KB4! | PxP |
| 3 | P–K4 | P–KN3 | 18 | NxB | NxN |
| 4 | N–KB3 | B–N2 | 19 | B–QN5 | B–Q5 |
| 5 | B–K2 | N–KB3 | 20 | P–B3! | P–K4 |
| 6 | N–B3 | N–R3 | 21 | PxB | PxB |
| 7 | O–O | N–B2 | 22 | BxN† | QxB |
| 8 | P–QR4 | P–QR3 | 23 | Q–K2† | K–B1 |
| 9 | N–Q2 | B–Q2 | 24 | Q–K5 | K–N1 |
| 10 | N–B4 | P–QN4 | 25 | R–N1 | P–B3 |
| 11 | P–K5! | PxKP | 26 | QxQBP | K–N2 |
| 12 | PxP | PxP? | 27 | RxP | R–K1 |
| 13 | RxR | QxR | 28 | R–N1 | P–B6 |
| 14 | NxKP | P–N5 | 29 | PxP | Q–R6 |
| 15 | P–Q6! | PxN | 30 | Q–B6 | Resigns |

## part 3—HROMADKA SYSTEM

1 P–Q4, N–KB3
2 P–QB4, P–B4
3 P–Q5A

KEY POSITION 3

OBSERVATIONS ON KEY POSITION 3

A 3 P–K3, PxP 4 PxP, P–Q4 transposes into the well-known Panov Attack.

The interpolation of White's P–QB4 distinguishes this treatment of the defense from those previously examined. The difference is more than one of mere appearance; note that White is unable to post a Knight on his QB4.

IDEA VARIATION 4:

(4) 3 . . . P–QN4 (a somewhat daring gambit) 4 PxP (4 N–KB3 is also good), B–N2 (4 . . . P–QR3 5 P–K3, P–K3 6 N–QB3, PxNP 7 BxP favors White) 5 N–QB3, Q–R4 6 B–Q2, P–K3 7 P–K4, PxP 8 PxP, Q–B2 9 B–QB4, P–Q3 10 KN–K2!, QN–Q2 11 O–O, N–K4 12 P–QN3, B–K2 13 N–N3, Q–Q2 14 P–B4, NxB 15 PxN, O–O 16 Q–B2± (Stahlberg–Stoltz, 1933).

PRACTICAL VARIATIONS 9–12:

1 P–Q4, N–KB3 2 P–QB4, P–B4 3 P–Q5

| | *9* | *10* | *11* | *12* |
|---|---|---|---|---|
| *3* | – – | – – | – – | – – |
| | P–K4 | – – | P–Q3 | – – |
| *4* | N–QB3 | – – | N–QB3 | – – |
| | P–Q3 | – – | P–KN3 | – – |
| *5* | P–K4[1] | – – | P–K4 | – – |
| | B–K2 | P–KN3 | P–QN4[16] | B–N2 |
| *6* | B–Q3[2] | B–K2[7] | PxP | P–B4[22] |
| | P–QR3[3] | B–N2[8] | B–KN2 | O–O[23] |
| *7* | KN–K2 | B–N5[9] | B–K2 | N–B3 |
| | QN–Q2 | N–R3[10] | P–QR3[17] | P–K3 |
| *8* | N–N3[4] | N–B3 | N–B3 | B–K2 |
| | P–KN3 | N–B2[11] | O–O | PxP |
| *9* | O–O | N–Q2! | PxP | BPxP |
| | P–KR4 | B–Q2[12] | BxP[18] | R–K1 |
| *10* | KN–K2 | P–QR4 | BxB[19] | N–Q2 |
| | P–R5 | P–N3[13] | NxB | N–R3[24] |
| *11* | B–Q2 | N–N5 | O–O | O–O |
| | N–R4 | BxN[14] | N–Q2[20] | R–N1 |
| *12* | Q–B1 | BPxB | B–N5 | B–B3 |
| | P–KN4 | O–O | R–N1 | P–QN4 |

| | *9* | *10* | *11* | *12* |
|---|---|---|---|---|
| *13* | P–KN4 | P–QN4! | Q–Q2 | P–QR4 |
| | PxP e.p. | P–KR3 | R–K1 | PxP |
| *14* | BPxP | BxN! | QR–N1 | N–B4 |
| | N/2–B3 | QxB | Q–R4 | R–N5 |
| *15* | N–Q1[5] | O–O | KR–B1 | RxP |
| | B–R6 | KR–Q1 | N–B2 | R–K2 |
| *16* | R–B3 | N–B4 | B–R6! | P–K5 |
| | N–N5[6] | B–B1[15] | B–B3[21] | N–K1[25] |
| | ∓ | ± | ± | ± |

*Notes to practical variations 9–12:*

[1] The alternatives 5 P–KN3 and 5 N–B3 merit attention:

1) 5 P–KN3, B–K2 6 B–N2, O–O 7 P–K4, N–K1 8 KN–K2, P–B4 9 O–O, PxP 10 NxP, B–B4 11 P–B4± or 8 . . . N–Q2 9 O–O, P–QR3 10 B–K3± (Becker–Grunfeld, Vienna 1922, and Geller–Ljublinszkij, Moscow 1951).

2) 5 N–B3, B–B4 6 P–KN3, P–KR3 7 B–N2, P–KN4 8 N–Q2!± (Bogoljubov–Hromadka, Pistyan 1922).

[2] After 6 P–B3, O–O 7 B–K3, N–K1 8 Q–Q2, P–B4 (Moisejew–Panov, Moscow 1935) Black has a good game.

[3] Or 6 . . . O–O 7 KN–K2, N–K1 8 N–N3, P–KN3 9 O–O, N–N2 10 P–QR3, P–B4 11 P–B4, PxBP 12 BxP, P–KN4 13 B–Q2, P–B5 14 N–R5.

[4] Better is 8 P–QR3.

[5] After 15 BxP, Black can recover the Pawn with 15 . . . NxQP. Stronger, however, is 15 . . . B–R6 16 R–B3 (or 16 R–K1), N–N5 with a rapidly developing attack. 15 K–N2 is impractical because of 15 . . . B–R6†!

[6] See Game 6.

[7] Equally commendable is 6 B–Q3, B–N2 7 KN–K2, O–O 8 P–KR3, N–R3 9 B–N5± (Reshevsky–Horowitz, New York 1956).

[8] Also playable is 6 . . . N–R3 7 B–N5, P–KR3 8 B–R4, B–N2 9 N–B3, N–B2 10 O–O, O–O 11 R–N1, P–KN4.

[9] Or 7 N–B3, O–O 8 B–N5, P–KR3 9 B–R4, P–KN4 10 B–N3, N–R4 11 N–Q2, N–B5 12 O–O, Q–K2 13 B–N4!, BxB 14 QxB, P–B4 15 PxP, P–KR4 16 Q–Q1, RxP 17 BxN, NPxB 18 Q–B2± (Portisch–Bobozoff, Balatonfured 1958) For 9 B–Q2, see the King's Indian Defense, Part 2, Prac. Var. 5, in which the identical position is reached by transposition.

[10] Another possibility is 7 . . . P–KR3 8 B–K3, O–O 9 P–KN4!, N–K1 10 Q–Q2, K–R2 11 P–KR4, N–R3 12 O–O–O, N/3–B2 13 N–KB3, P–R3 14 QR–N1, P–B3 15 P–N5± (Alster–Hofmann, Bratislava 1959).

[11] Correct is 8 . . . P–KR3 9 B–Q2, B–N5 10 P–QR3, BxN 11 BxB, N–Q2 12 N–QN5, Q–K2 13 Q–B2, P–R4 14 P–KR4, B–R3= (Szabo–Panno, Amsterdam 1956).

[12] The book of the Amsterdam 1956 tournament suggests 9 . . . P–QR3 as an improvement.

continued ▸

[13] 10 . . . P–QR3 11 P–R5, and White has a firm grip on the Queenside.

[14] The tournament book recommends 11 . . . NxN. If 11 . . . B–QB1, then 12 P–R5±.

[15] See Game 7.

[16] Interesting, but incorrect.

[17] Omitting . . . P–QR3 is inferior, e.g., 7 . . . O–O 8 N–B3, B–N2 9 O–O, QN–Q2 10 N–Q2!± (Ragosin–Menchik, Moscow 1935).

[18] 9 . . . NxRP 10 O–O, N–Q2 was tried in the game Kellner–Opocenski, Vienna 1947. It is no better than 9 . . . BxP.

[19] Although 10 O–O, Q–B2 11 R–K1, QN–Q2 12 BxB, RxB (Taimanov–Bronstein, Bad Neuhausen 1953) gives Black some chances, White can safely proceed with 13 B–B4 followed by 14 Q–Q2 or 14 Q–B2.

[20] 11 . . . R–N1 is sharper.

[21] After 17 P–QR3, R–N6 18 Q–B2, R/1–N1 19 N–Q2, R/6–N2 20 N–B4, Q–R3 21 Q–R4!, QxQ 22 NxQ, N–N4 23 P–QN4!, White maintains his advantage (Bronstein–Lundin, Saltjobaden 1948).

[22] See the King's Indian Defense, Part 2, for related lines. The text is easily subject to transpositions.

[23] After 6 . . . QN–Q2 7 N–B3, O–O 8 B–Q3, White controls more space.

[24] Exciting play results from 10 . . . P–KR4, e.g., 11 O–O, N–N5 12 BxN, PxB 13 P–KN3, P–B4 14 R–K1, B–Q5† 15 K–N2, P–R3 16 P–QR4, Q–B3 17 R–R3, B–Q2 18 Q–N3, P–QN4 19 PxP, Q–R1 20 P–R4, PxP e.p.† 21 K–R2, Q–R4 22 Q–Q1. The result is still unclear.

[25] 17 N–K4, RxR 18 QxR, PxP 19 P–Q6, R–K3 20 N–N5, RxP 21 NxR, NxN 22 PxP, BxP 23 B–Q5± (Pantaleew–Prachow, 14th Bulgarian Championship 1960).

*Benoni Defense Game 6*

*WHITE: Bisguier* *BLACK: Panno*

*Buenos Aires 1955*

| | WHITE | BLACK | | WHITE | BLACK | | WHITE | BLACK |
|---|---|---|---|---|---|---|---|---|
| 1 | P–Q4 | N–KB3 | 13 | P–KN4 | PxP e.p. | 25 | RxN | P–B4 |
| 2 | P–QB4 | P–B4 | 14 | BPxP | QN–B3 | 26 | R/3–Q2 | B–Q1 |
| 3 | P–Q5 | P–K4 | 15 | N–Q1 | B–R6 | 27 | N–K3 | P–B5 |
| 4 | N–QB3 | P–Q3 | 16 | R–B3 | N–N5 | 28 | NxB | QxN |
| 5 | P–K4 | B–K2 | 17 | N/2–B3 | Q–Q2 | 29 | R–R6 | B–B2 |
| 6 | B–Q3 | P–QR3 | 18 | B–K1 | O–O–O | 30 | R/2–R2 | PxP |
| 7 | KN–K2 | QN–Q2 | 19 | Q–Q2 | QR–N1 | 31 | R–N2 | R–B1 |
| 8 | N–N3 | P–KN3 | 20 | QR–B1 | N–B5! | 32 | BxP | Q–B6 |
| 9 | O–O | P–KR4 | 21 | R–QB2 | NxRP! | 33 | K–R2 | Q–K6 |
| 10 | KN–K2 | P–R5 | 22 | QxN2 | B–N5 | 34 | R–K2 | Q–Q6 |
| 11 | B–Q2 | N–R4 | 23 | R–K3 | RxQ | 35 | R–N6 | B–R4 |
| 12 | Q–B1 | P–KN4 | 24 | RxR | NxB | | Resigns | |

*Benoni Defense Game 7*

*WHITE: Petrosian* *BLACK: Pilnik*

*Amsterdam 1956*

| | WHITE | BLACK | | WHITE | BLACK |
|---|---|---|---|---|---|
| 1 | P–Q4 | N–KB3 | 26 | R–K1 | PxP |
| 2 | P–QB4 | P–B4 | 27 | PxP | N–R2 |
| 3 | P–Q5 | P–K4 | 28 | N–B4 | R–R7 |
| 4 | N–QB3 | P–Q3 | 29 | B–N2 | Q–B3 |
| 5 | P–K4 | P–KN3 | 30 | R–KB1 | N–N4 |
| 6 | N–B3 | B–N2 | 31 | Q–N3 | R/1–R1 |
| 7 | B–N5 | N–R3 | 32 | P–R4 | N–R2 |
| 8 | B–K2 | N–B2 | 33 | RxNP | R–R8 |
| 9 | N–Q2! | B–Q2 | 34 | R–B6 | R/1–R7 |
| 10 | P–QR4 | P–N3 | 35 | Q–K3 | Q–Q1 |
| 11 | N–N5 | BxN | 36 | RxR | RxR† |
| 12 | BPxB | O–O | 37 | K–R2 | N–B3 |
| 13 | P–QN4! | P–KR3 | 38 | P–B3 | Q–N1 |
| 14 | BxN! | QxB | 39 | Q–N3 | N–Q2 |
| 15 | O–O | KR–Q1 | 40 | P–N6 | N–B4 |
| 16 | N–B4 | B–B1 | 41 | Q–N2 | R–R5 |
| 17 | P–N3! | PxP | 42 | Q–N5 | R–R7 |
| 18 | Q–N3 | K–N2 | 43 | R–B7 | P–N4 |
| 19 | KR–B1 | P–KR4 | 44 | N–K3! | PxP |
| 20 | N–K3 | N–K1 | 45 | N–B5† | K–N1 |
| 21 | QxP | KR–B1 | 46 | PxP | R–R3 |
| 22 | R–B6! | Q–Q1 | 47 | P–N7 | R–R2 |
| 23 | QR–QB1 | N–B3 | 48 | R–B8 | QxP |
| 24 | B–B1! | KR–N1 | 49 | Q–K8 | N–Q2 |
| 25 | B–R3 | P–R3 | 50 | NxP | Resigns |

---

## part 4—TAL VARIATION

1 P–Q4, N–KB3
2 P–QB4, P–B4
3 P–Q5, P–K3
4 N–QB3, PxP[A]
5 PxP

KEY POSITION 4

### OBSERVATIONS ON KEY POSITION 4

[A] 4 . . . N–R3 is original but most unconvincing, e.g., 5 P–K4, PxP 6 BPxP, N–B2? 7 P–Q6, N–K3 8 P–K5, N–N1 9 B–QB4, P–B3 10 P–B4, PxP ¶11 BxN, PxB 12 PxP, B–Q2 13 N–B3, P–KN3 14 O–O, B–N2 15 N–K4, Q–B1 16 Q–B2, P–QN3 17 N/4–N5, N–R3 18 NxRP± (Moeller-Nielsen, Copenhagen 1910). 6 . . . P–Q3 is necessary.

This line of play is distinctly divided from other systems of the Benoni by Black's early . . . P–K3. Black aims for play on the half-open King file combined with sharp action on the Queenside. The net result of this debut is complicated, enterprising play, and it is therefore not difficult to understand why the recent World Champion, Mikhail Tal, is its most ardent advocate.

PRACTICAL VARIATIONS 13–16:

1 P–Q4, N–KB3 2 P–QB4, P–B4 3 P–Q5, P–K3 4 N–QB3, PxP 5 PxP

| | *13* | *14* | *15* | *16* |
|---|---|---|---|---|
| *5* | – – | – – | – – | – – |
| | P–Q3[1] | – – | – – | – – |
| *6* | N–KB3[2] | P–K4 | – – | – – |
| | P–KN3[3] | P–KN3[9] | – – | – – |
| *7* | B–N5[4] | P–B4 | B–K2 | B–Q3[20] |
| | B–N2 | B–N2 | B–N2 | B–N2 |
| *8* | N–Q2 | B–N5†[10] | N–B3 | KN–K2 |
| | P–KR3[5] | KN–Q2[11] | O–O | O–O |
| *9* | B–R4 | B–Q3 | O–O[14] | O–O |
| | P–KN4 | O–O | R–K1[15] | R–K1[21] |
| *10* | B–N3 | N–B3 | N–Q2[16] | P–KR3 |
| | N–R4 | N–R3 | N–R3[17] | QN–Q2 |
| *11* | N–B4[6] | O–O | R–N1[18] | N–N3 |
| | NxB | N–B2 | B–Q2 | P–QR3 |
| *12* | RPxN | Q–B2[12] | R–K1 | P–QR4 |
| | O–O | R–N1 | R–N1 | Q–B2 |
| *13* | P–K3 | P–QN3 | P–QN3 | P–B4 |
| | Q–K2 | P–QN4 | P–QN4 | P–B5 |
| *14* | B–K2 | B–N2 | B–N2 | B–B2 |
| | R–Q1 | P–B5 | N–B2 | N–B4 |
| *15* | O–O | PxP | Q–B2 | K–R1 |
| | N–Q2 | PxP | Q–K2 | B–Q2 |
| *16* | P–QR4[7] | BxP | N–Q1 | Q–B3[22] |
| | N–K4[8] | NxP[13] | B–R3![19] | K–R1[23] |
| | = | ± | ∓ | ± |

*Notes to practical variations 13–16:*

[1] An immediate fianchetto is also playable: 5 . . . P–KN3 6 N–KB3, B–N2 7 B–N5, O–O 8 P–K3, P–Q3 9 N–Q2, P–KR3 10 B–R4, R–K1 11 B–K2, N–R3 12 N–B4, N–B2 13 P–R4, P–N3 14 O–O, B–R3 15 P–QN3, Q–K2 16 R–R2, QR–Q1 17 R–K1, B–N2 18 R–Q2, P–KN4 19 B–N3, P–KR4 20 P–R3, P–R5 21 B–R2, N–N5∓ (Simagin–Tolush, USSR 1960). See also Prac. Var. 20 and Game 11.

[2] 6 P–KN3, P–KN3 7 B–N2, B–N2 8 N–B3, O–O 9 O–O, with the following possibilities, also merits attention:

1) 9 . . . R–K1 10 N–Q2, P–N3 11 P–QR4!, B–QR3 12 N–N5, BxN 13 PxB, QN–Q2 14 P–R3!, R–K2 15 R–R4, N–K1 16 N–K4, N/2–B3 17 N–B3, N–B2 18 Q–Q3, N–Q2 19 P–B4, P–QR3 20 PxP, P–QN4 21 R–K4± (Heemsoth–Gligoric, Hastings 1960).

2) 9 . . . N–K1 10 B–N5, P–B3 11 B–B4, N–Q2 12 Q–B1, P–QR3 13 P–KR4, P–QN4 14 B–R6, Q–K2 15 R–K1, P–N5 16 BxB, KxB 17 N–R4, N–B2 18 N–Q2, R–QN1 19 P–N3, B–N2 20 P–K4, N–K4 21 N–N2± (Romani–Bialas, Biel 1960).

[3] Inferior is 6 . . . B–B4 7 P–K4!, B–N3 8 B–K2, QN–Q2 9 N–Q2!, P–KR4 10 P–B4, N–N5 11 N–B3, P–B4 12 P–KR3, PxP 13 PxN, PxN 14 BxP, Q–K2† 15 K–B2, O–O–O 16 PxP± (Tartakover–Norman, Hastings 1927). But 6 . . . B–K2 is worth a try, e.g., 7 N–Q2, O–O 8 N–B4, N–K1 9 B–B4, B–B3 10 P–K3, N–Q2! (Kotov–Tolush 1957), or 7 P–KN3, O–O 8 B–N2, N–K1 9 O–O, B–B3 10 N–Q2, N–Q2 11 R–N1, Q–R4 12 Q–B2, P–QN4 13 P–QR3, B–N2= (Boleslavski–Tolush, Moscow 1956).

[4] After 7 P–KN3, B–N2 8 B–N2, O–O 9 O–O, R–K1 10 N–Q2, P–QR3 11 P–QR4, QN–Q2 12 P–KR3, R–N1 13 N–B4, N–N3 14 N–R3, B–Q2 15 P–R5, N–B1 16 N–B4, Q–B2 17 R–K1, B–N4 18 Q–N3, BxN! 19 QxB, N–Q2 20 Q–KR4, P–N3 21 PxP, RxP 22 R–R4, N–K2 23 Q–QB4, Q–N2 24 N–K4, N–KB3 25 P–K3, N–B4 (Averbach–Korchnoi, Moscow 1956), Black has equalized. But White fares better with 10 B–B4, P–QR3 11 P–QR4, Q–B2 12 Q–Q2, QN–Q2 13 KR–B1, P–B5 14 B–R6, B–R1 15 Q–B4, QR–N1 16 P–KR3, P–QN4 17 PxP, PxP 18 N–Q4, N–R4 19 Q–R4, P–N5 20 N–Q1, N–K4 21 N–B6!± (Smyslov–Tolush, Leningrad 1951).

Another interesting move at White's disposal is the Nimzowitsch-like 7 N–Q2, e.g., 7 . . . B–N2 8 N–B4, O–O 9 B–B4, N–K1 10 Q–Q2, and now:

1) 10 . . . BxN 11 PxB, P–QN4 12 N–N2, P–QR4 13 P–K4!, Q–K2 14 B–Q3, P–N5 15 O–O, N–Q2 16 N–B4± (Borisenko–Tal, Moscow 1956).
2) 10 . . . P–N3 11 P–K3, B–QR3 12 P–QR4, BxN 13 BxB, P–QR3 14 O–O, N–Q2 15 QR–N1, P–B4 16 B–KN3, Q–K2 17 KR–K1, N–K4 18 B–B1, N–KB3 19 P–K4, NxKP 20 NxN, PxN 21 RxP, Q–Q2 22 Q–K2, Q–B4 23 R–K1 (Taimanov–Suetin, Leningrad 1960), P–KN4! If 14 . . . Q–K2 in this line, then 15 QR–N1, N–Q2 16 KR–B1, P–B4 17 P–QN4, N–K4 18 B–B1, P–KN4 19 B–N3, N–N3 20 P–B4 (Borisenko–Folugajevsky, Moscow 1956). In each case, White's initiative is cancelled.

[5] 8 . . . P–QR3 9 P–K4, P–KR3 10 B–R4, P–QN4 11 Q–B2 (Portisch–Honfi, Budapest 1960) is less solid.

[6] 11 Q–R4†, forcing 11 . . . K–B1, deserves serious consideration. 11 . . . B–Q2?, 12 Q–K4† wins the Queen Pawn.

[7] 16 P–K4, answering 16 . . . N–K4 with 17 N–K3 followed by P–B4, is Tolush's worthwhile suggestion.

[8] 17 NxN, QxN 18 P–R5, R–N1 19 R–R2, B–Q2 20 N–N5, BxN 21 BxB, P–N3 22 P–R6, QR–B1= (Botvinnik–Tal, 2nd Match Game 1960).

[9] 6 . . . B–K2 is a seldom seen sideline. One example is 7 N–B3, O–O 8 B–K2, N–R3 9 O–O, N–B2 10 R–K1, R–N1 11 P–QR4, P–QR3 12 P–R5, N–Q2 13 B–B4, P–B3 14 N–Q2, P–QN4 15 PxP e.p., NxNP 16 N–N3, R–K1 17 N–R5, B–Q2 18 N–B6! (Lokvenc–Leinweber, Vienna 1960). If 8 . . . QN–Q2 (in lieu of 8 . . . N–R3), then best is 9 O–O, N–K1 10 N–Q2, B–B3 11 P–B4!±.

[10] An extremely complicated alternative is 8 N–B3, O–O 9 B–K2, R–K1 10 P–K5, PxP 11 PxP, N–N5 12 P–K6, PxP 13 O–O, PxP 14 NxP, B–K3 15 B–QB4, N–K4 16 B–KN5!, NxN†

continued ▸

17 QxN, QxB 18 QR–K1, R–KB1 (Niemela–Tal, Riga 1959), and White can continue 19 QxR†. After 19 . . . BxQ 20 RxB, N–B3 21 N–B7, Black's Rook cannot be saved, owing to the disastrous threat of the discovered check. There are innumerable variants to this line, some of which are noted below:

1) 10 N–Q2.
2) 10 . . . KN–Q2 (Lehmann–Toran, Munich, 1954).
3) Keres' suggestion, 14 B–KN5, e.g., 14 . . . Q–Q3 15 P–KR3, N–K6 16 BxN, RxB 17 NxP±.
4) 15 . . . N–QB3 16 B–KN5, N–KB3 17 N–K5 (Kotov-Burchall, Stockholm 1960), and Black must now play 17 . . . QNxN.
5) 19 Q–K4.

[11] 8 . . . B–Q2 is strongly met by 9 P–K5!

[12] 12 N–Q2 has also been tried:

1) 12 . . . P–QN4 13 NxP, NxN 14 BxN, R–N1 15 P–QR4, N–B3 (O'Kelly–Van Seters, 1959), and now White's strongest course of action is 16 B–K2 followed by 17 B–B3. Black has a reasonable game.
2) 12 . . . N–KB3 13 P–KR3, R–K1 14 Q–B3, R–N1 15 P–QR4, N–R3 16 N–B4± (Taimanov–Trifunovic, Leningrad 1957).

[13] In the game Alster–Clarke, Wageningen 1957, there followed 17 BxN, Q–N3† 18 R–B2, QxB 19 QxQ, RxQ 20 RxR, BxN 21 QR–N1, BxR 22 RxB, N–B4 23 R–Q2, B–K3 24 BxB, PxB 25 RxP, RxP 26 N–N5, R–KN5 27 NxKP, NxN 28 RxN±.

[14] 9 B–KB4 is also good, e.g., 9 . . . N–R3 10 N–Q2, N–B2 11 P–QR4, P–N3 12 O–O, N/3–K1 13 N–B4, B–QR3 14 R–K1 (Karaklaic–Schumacher, Brussels 1960). If 9 . . . N–R4, then 10 B–KN5.

[15] For the inferior 9 . . . B–N5, see Game 8.

[16] 10 Q–B2, N–R3 11 B–KB4, N–QN5 12 Q–N1, NxKP! 13 NxN, B–B4 14 N/3–Q2, NxP∓ (Averbach–Tal, Riga, 1958).

[17] 10 . . . P–QR3 is a playable alternative, e.g., 11 P–QR4, P–N3 12 P–B4, R–R2 13 B–B3, R/2–K2, but 10 . . . P–N3 11 P–B3, N–R3 12 N–B4, N–B2 13 B–KB4, B–B1 14 P–QR4 favors White (Lemaire–Wade, Australia 1954).

[18] Other possibilities:

1) 11 P–B3, N–B2 12 P–QR4, P–N3 13 N–N5, P–QR3 14 NxN, QxN 15 N–B4, B–N2 16 B–B4, QR–Q1 17 Q–B2, and Black has a satisfactory game (Niephaus–Bialas, Nuremberg 1959).
2) 11 R–K1, N–B2 12 P–QR4, P–N3 13 Q–B2?, N–N5! (Gurgenidze–Tal, 24th USSR Championship). Better is 13 P–B3!

[19] 17 P–B3, N–R4 18 N–B1, NxP! 19 PxN, B–B4 20 Q–B3, B–N2 21 Q–B1, BxR 22 BxB, KxB 23 QxB, N–B5 24 N/Q–K3, Q–K4! with complications in Black's favor (Gligoric-Tal, Belgrade 1959).

[20] Weaker is 7 N–B3, P–QR3 8 P–QR4, B–N5 9 B–K2, BxN 10 BxB, QN–Q2 11 O–O, B–N2 12 B–B4, Q–N1 13 B–K2, O–O 14 B–N3, R–K1 15 Q–B2, Q–B2 16 P–B4, P–B5! 17 K–R1, QR–B1 18 P–R5, Q–Q1 19 KR–K1, R–B4∓ (Wexler–Bronstein, Mar del Plata 1960).

[21] For 9 . . . P–QR3, see Game 9.

[22] 16 P–K5 is a forceful alternative: 16 . . . PxP 17 PxP, QxP 18 B–B4, Q–K2 19 Q–Q2!

[23] In the game Ojanen–Keres, Team Match 1960, there followed 17 B–K3, N–N1 18 QR–Q1, P–QN4 19 PxP, PxP 20 P–K5!, PxP 21 P–B5, P–R4 22 P–Q6, Q–R4 23 N/B–K4±.

*Benoni Defense Game 8*

*WHITE: Smyslov* *BLACK: Filip*

*Vienna 1957*

| | WHITE | BLACK | | WHITE | BLACK |
|---|---|---|---|---|---|
| 1 | P–Q4 | N–KB3 | 21 | B–B3 | BxN |
| 2 | P–QB4 | P–B4 | 22 | QxB | PxP |
| 3 | P–Q5 | P–K3 | 23 | B–N4 | N/R–B3 |
| 4 | N–QB3 | PxP | 24 | B–K6† | K–R2 |
| 5 | PxP | P–Q3 | 25 | P–R4 | R–N1 |
| 6 | P–K4 | P–KN3 | 26 | P–KN4 | P–KR4 |
| 7 | N–B3 | B–N2 | 27 | P–N5 | N–N5 |
| 8 | B–K2 | O–O | 28 | P–B5 | KR–KB1 |
| 9 | O–O | B–N5 | 29 | PxP† | KxP |
| 10 | P–KR3! | BxN | 30 | BxN/4 | PxB |
| 11 | BxB | P–QR3 | 31 | P–R5†! | KxRP |
| 12 | B–B4 | N–K1 | 32 | Q–N7 | P–N6 |
| 13 | P–QR4 | N–Q2 | 33 | BxP | K–N5 |
| 14 | B–K2 | Q–B2 | 34 | R–KN1 | R–R1† |
| 15 | R–B1 | R–N1 | 35 | B–R2† | K–R5 |
| 16 | P–QN3! | N/1–B3 | 36 | QR–KB1 | QR–N1 |
| 17 | Q–B2 | KR–K1 | 37 | R–B4† | K–R5 |
| 18 | B–R2 | P–R3 | 38 | Q–B7† | R–N3 |
| 19 | K–R1 | N–R2 | 39 | Q–B5 | Resigns |
| 20 | P–B4! | P–B4 | | | |

*Benoni Defense Game 9*

*WHITE: Penrose* *BLACK: Tal*

*Leipzig 1960*

| | WHITE | BLACK | | WHITE | BLACK | | WHITE | BLACK |
|---|---|---|---|---|---|---|---|---|
| 1 | P–Q4 | N–KB3 | 14 | B–B2 | N–B4 | 27 | QxN | QxQ |
| 2 | P–QB4 | P–K3 | 15 | Q–B3 | KN–Q2 | 28 | NxQ | RxP |
| 3 | N–QB3 | P–B4 | 16 | B–K3 | P–QN4 | 29 | N–N6 | R–N6 |
| 4 | P–Q5 | PxP | 17 | PxP | R–N1 | 30 | NxBP | R–Q1 |
| 5 | PxP | P–Q3 | 18 | Q–B2 | PxP | 31 | P–Q6 | R–B6 |
| 6 | P–K4 | P–KN3 | 19 | P–K5! | PxP | 32 | R–B1 | RxR |
| 7 | B–Q3 | B–N2 | 20 | P–B5! | B–N2 | 33 | RxR | B–Q4 |
| 8 | KN–K2 | O–O | 21 | QR–Q1 | B–QR1 | 34 | N–N6 | B–N6 |
| 9 | O–O | P–QR3 | 22 | QN–K4 | N–R5 | 35 | N–K4 | P–R3 |
| 10 | P–QR4 | Q–B2 | 23 | BxN | PxB | 36 | P–Q7 | B–B1 |
| 11 | P–R3 | QN–Q2 | 24 | PxP | BPxP | 37 | R–B8 | B–K2 |
| 12 | P–B4 | R–K1 | 25 | Q–B7† | K–R1 | 38 | B–B5 | B–R5 |
| 13 | N–N3 | P–B5 | 26 | N–QB5 | Q–R2 | 39 | P–N3 | Resigns |

## part 5—BLUMENFELD VARIATION

1 P–Q4, N–KB3
2 P–QB4, P–K3
3 N–KB3, P–B4

KEY POSITION 5

OBSERVATIONS ON KEY POSITION 5

If Black wishes, he may decline White's invitation to the Queen's Gambit (3 . . . P–Q4), the Queen's Indian (3 . . . P–QN3) or the Bogo-Indian (3 . . . B–N5†), and instead choose to play the Blumenfeld Variation. The Blumenfeld was introduced into tournament play in 1922, but still shows no sign of age, being every bit as sprightly today as it was four decades ago. Black's immediate engagement of the center on the bias introduces intriguing patterns and problems.

IDEA VARIATIONS 5 AND 6:

(5) 4 P–KN3, PxP 5 NxP, P–Q4 6 B–N2, P–K4 7 N–KB3, and now: (a) 7 . . . P–K5 8 KN–Q2, PxP 9 Q–R4†, B–Q2 10 QxBP, P–K6!∓ (Ed. Lasker–Capablanca, Lake Hopatcong 1926); (b) 7 . . . P–Q5 8 O–O, N–B3 9 P–K3, B–K2 10 PxP, PxP 11 QN–Q2, B–K3 12 R–K1, O–O 13 P–N3, Q–Q2 14 B–N2, QR–Q1 15 P–QR3, P–QR4∓ (Saigon–Tal, Moscow 1954); (c) 7 . . . N–B3 8 PxP, NxP 9 NxP!±; (d) 7 . . . B–N5† 8 B–Q2, BxB† 9 QxB, P–K5 10 N–K5, Q–K2 11 Q–Q4±.

(6) 4 P–K3, P–Q4 5 P–QR3, BPxP 6 KPxP, B–K2 7 N–B3, O–O 8 B–B4, N–B3 9 R–B1, N–K5 10 B–Q3, NxN 11 RxN, PxP 12 RxP, Q–R4†!, and Black's position is satisfactory (Keres–Tal, 24th USSR Championship); or 5 N–B3, N–B3 6 B–Q3, B–K2 7 O–O, O–O 8 P–QN3, PxQP 9 KPxP, P–QN3 10 B–N2, B–R3 11 R–K1!, PxP 12 PxP, R–B1 13 Q–R4!± (Grunfeld–Alekhine, Pistyan 1922).

PRACTICAL VARIATIONS 17–20:

1 P–Q4, N–KB3 2 P–QB4, P–K3 3 N–KB3, P–B4

| | *17* | *18* | *19* | *20* |
|---|---|---|---|---|
| 4 | N–B3 | P–Q5 | – – | – – |
| | PxP | P–QN4[8] | – – | PxP |
| 5 | NxP | PxKP | B–N5![12] | PxP |
| | B–N5[1] | BPxP | PxQP[13] | P–KN3[18] |
| 6 | Q–N3[2] | PxP | PxQP | N–B3 |
| | B–B4[3] | P–Q4 | P–KR3![14] | B–N2 |
| 7 | N–B3[4] | B–N5[9] | BxN | B–N5 |
| | P–QN3[5] | B–K2 | QxB | O–O |
| 8 | B–N5 | P–K3 | Q–B2 | P–K3 |
| | B–N2 | O–O | P–Q3 | R–K1 |

| | *17* | *18* | *19* | *20* |
|---|---|---|---|---|
| *9* | P–K3 | B–K2 | P–K4 | N–Q2 |
| | N–B3 | QN–Q2 | P–R3 | P–Q3 |
| *10* | B–K2 | N–B3 | P–QR4 | B–K2 |
| | P–KR3 | B–N2 | P–N5 | P–QR3 |
| *11* | B–R4 | O–O | KN–Q2[15] | P–QR4 |
| | Q–K2[6] | Q–K1 | B–K2 | QN–Q2 |
| *12* | P–QR3 | Q–B2 | N–B4 | O–O |
| | P–KN4 | B–Q3 | QN–Q2 | Q–B2 |
| *13* | B–N3 | KR–K1 | QN–Q2 | Q–B2 |
| | N–KR4 | R–B1 | O–O | N–N3 |
| *14* | O–O–O | QR–Q1 | B–Q3 | B–B3! |
| | NxB | B–N1 | P–QR4 | P–B5?[19] |
| *15* | RPxN | B–R4[10] | O–O | BxN |
| | O–O–O | K–R1 | N–K4 | BxB |
| *16* | Q–R4 | B–B1 | NxN[16] | P–R5 |
| | K–N1[7] | P–K4[11] | PxN[17] | N–Q2 |
| | ± | = | ± | ± |

*Notes to practical variations 17-20:*

[1] Or 5 . . . N–B3 6 P–K3, B–N5! 7 Q–B2, P–Q4 8 NxN, PxN 9 B–Q2, O–O 10 B–K2, P–K4 11 PxP, PxP 12 O–O, B–N2 13 KR–Q1, Q–K2∓ (Pavey–Keres, New York 1954). If 7 Q–N3 in this variation, then 7 . . . B–B4 8 N–B3, O–O 9 B–K2, P–QN3! 10 O–O, B–N2 11 P–QR3, R–B1 12 R–Q1, Q–K2∓ (Porreca–Barcza, Belgrade 1954). In answer to 5 . . . N–B3, however, White does better to play 5 N/4–N5, e.g., 6 . . . B–N5 7 B–B4, or 6 . . . B–B4 7 B–B4, O–O 8 B–B7!

[2] 6 B–Q2 is too passive. After 6 . . . O–O 7 P–K3, P–Q4 8 Q–N3, B–B4 9 N–B3, N–B3 (Machate–Spielmann, Magdeburg 1927), Black has good play. For 6 . . . N–B3, see Game 10.

[3] Or 6 . . . N–R3 7 B–Q2, P–QN3 8 P–K3, B–N2 9 B–K2, O–O 10 O–O, B–K2 11 QR–Q1, N–B4 12 Q–B2, P–Q4 13 PxP, NxP 14 B–B3, N–N5 15 Q–N1, BxB 16 PxB, B–B3 17 N–K4, N–Q4 18 N–K2, N–Q2 19 K–R1= (Bogoljubov–Przepiorka, Pistyan 1922). In this position, Black's best move is 19 . . . P–KN3, and if White abstains from 20 NxB, then 20 . . . B–N2. A simpler plan for Black in this line is 10 . . . BxN followed by 11 . . . P–Q4. 7 P–K3 is strongly met by 7 . . . N–K5 (Boleslavski–Szabo, Zurich 1953).

[4] More aggressive than 7 B–K3 or 7 P–K3.

[5] In answer to either 7 . . . O–O (Rubinstein–Teichmann, Teplitz–Schonau 1922) or 7 . . . N–B3 (Menchik–Spielmann, Carlsbad 1929), White should continue with 8 B–N5, and not 8 P–K3 as was played in each of the cited games. 7 . . . P–Q4 is inferior, since after 8 PxP, PxP 9 B–N5, B–K3 10 BxN, PxB 11 O–O–O Black's Pawn formation is wrecked.

[6] 11 . . . B–K2 gives Black even fewer prospects.

[7] Gruenfeld–Spielmann, Wiener Trebitsch 1929, continued 17 N–Q4, BxN 18 PxB, R–QB1 19 K–N1, N–R4 20 P–B5!, BxP 21 PxP!, PxP 22 Q–N5!, and White's attack insured a win.

continued ▸

[8] Blumenfeld's spirited innovation! In exchange for a Pawn, Black obtains a powerful center.

[9] 7 P–K3 is a tenuous alternative, e.g., 7 . . . B–Q3 8 N–B3, O–O 9 B–K2, B–N2 and now:

1) 10 P–QN3, QN–Q2 11 B–N2, Q–K2 12 O–O, QR–Q1, 13 Q–B2, P–K4∓ (Tarrasch–Alekhine, Pistyan 1922).
2) 10 O–O, Q–K2 11 Q–B2, QN–Q2 12 P–QR4, P–K4 13 N–R4! (Cherubim–A. Thomas, Hastings 1959).
   Both 9 P–K4 and 10 P–K4 are best met with . . . QN–Q2.

[10] A clever move whose aim is to meet 15 . . . N–K5 with 16 NxN, PxN 17 N–Q2, N–K4 18 B–N3!

[11] There followed 17 P–K4, P–Q5 18 N–N1, P–B5 19 QN–Q2 (Cholmov–Portisch, Balatonfured 1959) and the tournament book now suggests 19 . . . Q–N3, answering 20 BxP with 20 . . . N–B4!

[12] Black's best on 5 N–B3 is 5 . . . P–N5.

[13] Alternatives prove to be inferior:

1) 5 . . . P–KR3 6 BxN, QxB 7 N–QB3, P–N5 8 N–QN5, N–R3 9 P–K4!, QxP 10 B–Q3, Q–B3 11 P–K5, Q–Q1 12 PxP!, QPxP 13 B–K4 and White soon won (Grunfeld–Bogoljubov, Vienna 1922).
2) 5 . . . Q–R4† 6 Q–Q2, QxQ† 7 QNxQ, PxBP 8 BxN, PxB 9 P–K4, P–B4 10 BxP, B–N2 11 O–O, B–KR3 12 KR–K1, O–O 13 QR–Q1, K–R1 14 N–N3± (Grunfeld–Rabinowitsch, Moscow 1925). If 7 . . . PxQP, then 8 BxN, PxB 9 PxQP, B–N2 10 P–K4, P–B4 11 BxP, and White still holds an edge (Auer–Florian, Vienna 1949).

[14] According to Spielmann, the only move to justify the variation. Also satisfactory, however, is 6 . . . P–Q3 7 P–K4, P–QR3 8 P–QR4, B–K2 9 PxP, NxKP 10 BxB, QxB 11 B–K2, O–O 12 O–O, B–N2 13 N–B3, N–KB3 14 R–K1, Q–B2 (Litmanowicz–Pytlakowski, Salzbrunn 1952).

[15] The natural 11 QN–Q2 may even be superior. The game Kmoch–Spielmann, Semmering 1926, continued 11 . . . B–N5 12 B–K2, QN–Q2, and White's prospects are excellent after 13 N–KN1!, N–K4 14 BxB, NxB 15 KN–B3 followed by N–B4.

[16] Or 16 P–B4, NxN 17 NxN, Q–Q5† 18 K–R1, B–R3 and 19 . . . BxN. Also worth consideration in this line is 16 . . . NxB 17 QxN, Q–N3. In each case, White has a slight pull.

[17] 17 N–B4, R–Q1 18 QR–B1, Q–N4 19 KR–Q1, P–N3 20 B–B1, B–B1 (Ljubliky–Tolush, Moscow 1952). Black barely holds. 16 . . . QxN (instead of 16 . . . PxN) is inferior, e.g., 17 P–B4, Q–Q5† 18 K–R1 and now:

1) 18 . . . B–N5 19 P–R3, B–R4 20 P–N4, B–N3 21 P–B5.
2) 18 . . . B–B3 19 QR–N1, B–N5 20 N–N3, Q–K6 21 QR–K1±.

[18] For 5 . . . P–Q3, see Prac. Var. 13-16.

[19] Suspect. Kmoch suggests 14 . . . B–B4, and if 15 P–K4, then 15 . . . B–QB1. See Game 11.

## SUPPLEMENTARY VARIATIONS 1-5:

1 P–Q4, P–QB4 2 P–Q5

| | 1 | 2 | 3 | 4 | 5 |
|---|---|---|---|---|---|
| 2 | — — | — — | — — | — — | — — |
| | P–KN3 | P–K3 | — — | — — | — — |
| 3 | P–K4 | P–K4 | — — | — — | N–QB3! |
| | B–N2 | N–KB3 | — — | — — | N–B3 |
| 4 | P–KB4[1] | N–QB3 | — — | — — | P–KN3 |
| | N–QR3 | P–Q3[4] | — — | — — | P–Q3 |
| 5 | N–KB3 | N–B3 | — — | — — | B–N2 |
| | N–B2 | B–K2 | PxP! | — — | B–K2 |
| 6 | P–B4 | B–N5† | PxP | — — | PxP |
| | P–Q3 | QN–Q2 | B–K2 | B–N5 | PxP |
| 7 | B–Q3 | PxP | B–K2 | B–K2 | P–K4 |
| | P–K3 | PxP | O–O | BxN | N–B3 |
| 8 | O–O | N–N5[5] | O–O | BxB | KN–K2 |
| | PxP | ± | P–QR3 | B–K2 | O–O |
| 9 | BPxP | | P–QR4 | O–O | O–O |
| | N–B3 | | P–QN3 | O–O | N–K1 |
| 10 | N–B3 | | N–Q2 | B–B4 | P–QR4! |
| | O–O | | QN–Q2 | QN–Q2 | N–B2 |
| 11 | Q–B2 | | N–B4 | R–K1 | N–N5 |
| | R–K1 | | N–K4 | N–K1! | P–QR3 |
| 12 | B–Q2 | | N–K3 | B–K2 | NxN |
| | B–Q2 | | R–K1 | P–QR3[7] | QxN |
| 13 | QR–K1[2] | | P–B4 | = | N–B4 |
| | P–QN4 | | N–N3 | | B–Q2 |
| 14 | Q–N1 | | B–Q3 | | B–K3±[8] |
| | P–N5 | | B–B1[6] | | ± |
| 15 | N–Q1 | | ± | | |
| | P–QR4 | | | | |
| 16 | N–B2 | | | | |
| | N–N4 | | | | |
| 17 | B–B1 | | | | |
| | R–QB1 | | | | |
| 18 | N–Q2[3] | | | | |
| | ± | | | | |

*Notes to supplementary variations 1-5:*

[1] 4 P–Q6!, PxP 5 N–QB3 (Swiderski–Blackburne, Ostend 1907) is an aggressive alternative.

[2] Better is 13 P–QR4.

[3] 18 . . . N–Q5 19 N–B4, B–N4 20 B–Q2 (Burn–Pollock, Hastings 1895).

[4] 4 . . . PxP? 5 P–K5!, N–N1 6 QxP± (Alster–Letelier, 1956).

[5] Pillsbury–Mumelter, blindfold simultaneous exhibition, 1902.

[6] Orbaan–Uhlmann, Wageningen 1957.

[7] Filip–Barcza, Sofia 1957.

[8] Panno–Barcza, Munich 1958.

*Benoni Defense Game 10*

*WHITE: Blau* *BLACK: Tal*

*Zurich 1959*

| | WHITE | BLACK | | WHITE | BLACK |
|---|---|---|---|---|---|
| 1 | N–KB3 | N–KB3 | 19 | P–B3 | KR–Q1 |
| 2 | P–Q4 | P–K3 | 20 | P–K3 | B–Q4 |
| 3 | P–B4 | P–B4 | 21 | B–R3? | N–N5 |
| 4 | N–B3 | PxP | 22 | O–O | P–QR4 |
| 5 | NxP | B–N5 | 23 | B–N2 | P–R5 |
| 6 | B–Q2 | N–B3 | 24 | KR–B1 | N–Q6 |
| 7 | N–B2 | B–B4 | 25 | R/1–B2 | P–KN3 |
| 8 | B–K3 | BxB | 26 | K–B1 | P–QN4! |
| 9 | NxB | O–O | 27 | NxP | QR–N1 |
| 10 | P–KN3 | P–Q4! | 28 | N–B3 | B–K3 |
| 11 | PxP | PxP | 29 | R–R7 | NxP |
| 12 | N/KxP | NxN | 30 | NxP | N–Q8! |
| 13 | QxN | Q–N3 | 31 | R–B1 | R–Q7 |
| 14 | Q–N5 | QxQ | 32 | K–N1 | NxP |
| 15 | NxQ | N–N5 | 33 | B–KB1 | R–R7 |
| 16 | R–B1 | B–B4! | 34 | R–R6 | NxB |
| 17 | N–Q4 | NxP | 35 | KxN | B–B5† |
| 18 | R–B7 | B–K5 | | Resigns | |

*Benoni Defense Game 11*

*WHITE: Botvinnik* *BLACK: Tal*

*Eighth Match Game, Moscow 1960*

| | WHITE | BLACK | | WHITE | BLACK | | WHITE | BLACK |
|---|---|---|---|---|---|---|---|---|
| 1 | P–Q4 | N–KB3 | 15 | BxN | BxB | 29 | PxB | N–B4 |
| 2 | P–QB4 | P–K3 | 16 | P–R5 | N–Q2 | 30 | PxP | B–Q2 |
| 3 | N–KB3 | P–B4 | 17 | N/3–K4 | B–K4 | 31 | Q–B3 | QxQ |
| 4 | P–Q5 | PxP | 18 | QxP | Q–Q1 | 32 | PxQ | B–N4! |
| 5 | PxP | P–KN3 | 19 | Q–R2 | P–B4 | 33 | KR–K1 | N–K5 |
| 6 | N–B3 | B–N2 | 20 | N–B3 | P–KN4 | 34 | QR–B1 | R/N–B1 |
| 7 | B–N5 | O–O | 21 | N–B4 | P–N5 | 35 | N–R5! | BxB |
| 8 | P–K3 | R–K1 | 22 | B–K2 | Q–B3 | 36 | RxB | NxP |
| 9 | N–Q2 | P–Q3 | 23 | N–R4 | K–R1 | 37 | RxN! | RxR |
| 10 | B–K2 | P–QR3 | 24 | P–KN3 | P–R4 | 38 | NxP | R/1xP |
| 11 | P–QR4 | QN–Q2 | 25 | P–B4 | B–Q5! | 39 | RxR | RxR |
| 12 | O–O | Q–B2 | 26 | Q–R3 | R–QN1 | 40 | NxP | R–Q6 |
| 13 | Q–B2 | N–N3 | 27 | N/R–N6 | P–R5 | 41 | N–B7† | Resigns |
| 14 | B–B3 | P–B5? | 28 | QR–Q1 | BxN | | | |

# chapter 32—Budapest Defense

The Budapest Defense was conceived in the year 1917 by the Budapest masters Abonyi, Breyer, and Barasz and was introduced into serious competition in the Four Master Tournament at Berlin in 1918. Its popularity soon waned, however, and since the Carlsbad Tournament of 1923 its appearance in tournaments has been sporadic. For a time the Fajarowicz Variation (3 . . . N–K5), dating from 1928, seemed to offer Black some chances, but in this line, too, the latest analysis favors White.

1 P–Q4, N–KB3
2 P–QB4, P–K4
3 PxP[A]

KEY POSITION

## OBSERVATIONS ON KEY POSITION

[A] If 3 N–KB3?, P–K5! 4 KN–Q2, P–Q4 5 PxP, QxP 6 P–K3, B–QN5 7 N–B3, BxN 8 PxB, O–O 9 Q–N3, Q–KN4 10 B–R3, R–K1 11 P–N3, P–QN3 12 B–KN2, B–R3! 13 P–QB4, N–B3 14 Q–B3, QR–Q1 15 O–O, P–R4 16 P–B4, PxP e.p. 17 RxP, N–KN5 18 N–B1, N–R4! 19 P–R3, N–KB3 20 N–Q2, B–N2! (Menchik–Tartakover, Paris 1929), and Black won in a few more moves. In this line, however, White does much better with 11 B–B4!, e.g., 11 . . . Q–N3 12 O–O, N–B3 13 P–B4.

White may decline the gambit with 3 P–K3, an improvement on the variation treated above, e.g., 3 . . . PxP 4 PxP, P–Q4! 5 PxP. This same position was reached by transposition (1 P–K4, P–K4 2 P–Q4, PxP 3 P–QB3, P–Q4 4 KPxP, N–KB3 5 PxP) in Reti–Schlechter, Baden 1914. The continuation was 5 . . . B–N5† 6 B–Q2, BxB† 7 QxB, O–O 8 N–KB3, N–K5 9 Q–B4, QxP 10 B–Q3, Q–R4† 11 QN–Q2, NxN 12 QxN, R–K1†, and a draw was recorded on the 31st move. Another try in this variation is 5 N–KB3, e.g., 5 . . . B–Q3 6 P–B5 (N–B3!), B–K2 7 B–Q3, P–QN3 8 PxP, RPxP 9 N–B3, O–O 10 O–O, B–KN5 11 P–KR3, B–R4 12 P–KN4, B–N3 13 N–K5, BxB 14 QxB, P–B3 15 B–N5?, NxP! ∓ (Tartakover–Botvinnik, Groningen 1946).

With the forceful advance 2 . . . P–K4, Black sacrifices a Pawn which, after 3 PxP, N–N5, White does best to return. In doing this, material equality is restored but White achieves a lasting positional edge.

As for the Fajarowicz Variation (3 . . . N–K5), White has various methods by which to maintain the initiative. See Prac. Var. 3–5.

PRACTICAL VARIATIONS 1–5:
1 P–Q4, N–KB3 2 P–QB4, P–K4 3 PxP

| | 1 | 2 | 3 | 4 | 5 |
|---|---|---|---|---|---|
| 3 | – – | – – | – – | – – | – – |
| | N–N5 | – – | N–K5 | – – | – – |
| 4 | B–B4[1] | N–KB3 | N–Q2[15] | N–KB3[22] | P–QR3! |
| | N–QB3[2] | N–QB3 | N–B4[16] | N–QB3 | N–QB3 |
| 5 | N–KB3 | P–K3[10] | KN–B3 | QN–Q2 | N–KB3 |
| | B–N5†[3] | B–B4[11] | N–B3 | B–N5 | P–Q3 |
| 6 | QN–Q2![4] | B–K2 | P–KN3[17] | P–QR3![23] | Q–B2! |
| | Q–K2[5] | O–O[12] | Q–K2[18] | BxN† | B–B4 |
| 7 | P–QR3 | O–O | B–N2 | NxB![24] | N–B3 |
| | N/5xKP | R–K1[13] | P–KN3[19] | NxN | NxBP |
| 8 | NxN[6] | N–B3 | N–QN1 | BxN | QxB |
| | NxN | KNxP/4 | NxP[20] | NxP | NxR |
| 9 | P–K3 | P–QN3 | O–O | B–B3 | P–K6 |
| | BxN† | P–QR4 | NxN† | P–B3[25] | PxP |
| 10 | QxB | N–QR4 | PxN! | P–K4 | QxP† |
| | P–Q3 | B–K2 | B–N2 | Q–K2 | Q–K2 |
| 11 | B–K2 | B–N2 | R–K1 | P–B4 | Q–Q5 |
| | O–O | B–B3 | N–K3 | N–N3 | P–KR3 |
| 12 | O–O | P–B5! | N–B3 | Q–B3 | P–KN3 |
| | B–B4[7] | P–Q4 | O–O | O–O | P–KN4 |
| 13 | KR–Q1[8] | PxP e.p. | N–Q5 | B–Q3 | B–N2 |
| | B–K5 | PxP | Q–Q1 | P–N3 | NxP |
| 14 | QR–B1 | Q–Q2 | P–B4 | P–KR4 | PxN |
| | N–N3 | P–QN4 | P–QB3 | B–N2 | B–N2 |
| 15 | B–N3 | NxN | N–B3 | P–R5 | B–R3 |
| | QR–Q1 | NxN | P–Q3 | N–R1 | N–K4 |
| 16 | P–N4 | BxP | B–K3 | P–R6 | B–Q2![27] |
| | P–N3 | N–B6† | Q–B2[21] | P–N3[26] | ± |
| 17 | Q–B3 | PxN | ± | ± | |
| | P–KB4 | B–R6 | | | |
| 18 | P–B5![9] | K–R1[14] | | | |
| | ± | ± | | | |

[1] The attempt to maintain the Pawn with 4 P–B4? is inferior because of 4 . . . B–B4, e.g., 5 N–KR3, P–Q3 6 PxP, O–O! 4 P–K4 is currently out of fashion, but was once quite popular:

1) 4 . . . P–Q3 5 B–K2! See Game 1.
2) 4 . . . NxKP 5 P–B4, and now (a) 5 . . . N–N3 6 N–KB3, B–B4? 7 P–B5; (b) 5 . . . N/4–B3! 6 B–K3, B–N5† 7 N–B3, Q–K2 (if 7 . . . P–Q3, then 8 B–Q3) 8 B–Q3, P–B4 9 Q–R5†!, P–N3 10 Q–B3, PxP 11 BxKP, BxN† 12 PxB, O–O 13 B–Q5†, K–R1 14 N–R3, P–Q3 15 O–O± (Alekhine–Seitz, Hastings 1926); (c) 5 . . . N/4–B3! 6 B–K3, N–R3! 7 N–QB3, B–B4 8 BxB, NxB 9 N–B3, O–O 10 B–Q3, P–Q3 11 O–O, NxB 12 QxN, P–B4! 13 QR–K1, PxP=.

[2] Somewhat compromising is Abonyi's recommended 4 . . . P–KN4. White's best answer is 5 B–Q2. If 5 B–N3, there follows 5 . . . B–N2 6 N–KB3, N–QB3 7 N–B3, N/5xKP 8 NxN, NxN 9 P–K4, P–Q3 10 B–K2, B–K3 11 O–O, Q–Q2 12 N–Q5, O–O–O 13 Q–Q2, P–KR3 (Gligoric–Bakonyi, Budapest 1948).

[3] Quite daring is 5 . . . P–B3, e.g., 6 PxP, QxP 7 Q–Q2, B–N5 8 N–B3, BxN 9 PxB, P–Q3 10 P–K3, P–QN3 11 B–K2, B–N2 12 O–O, N–K2 13 N–Q4!, N–K4 (Eliskases–Bogoljubov, 11th Match Game 1939). 14 N–N5 now forces the reply 14 . . . K–Q1, after which White has the edge.

[4] After 6 N–B3, Black fares well, e.g., 6 . . . Q–K2 7 Q–Q5, BxN† 8 PxB, Q–R6 9 Q–Q2, Q–R4! 10 P–K4, N/5xKP 11 N–Q4, P–Q3 12 N–N3, Q–R5 13 BxN, NxB 14 Q–Q4, P–KB3 15 P–B5, QxQ 16 PxQ, N–B2 17 PxP, NxP 18 B–Q3, O–O 19 O–O, R–K1= (Schobloch–Zimmermann, Correspondence Game 1919). Inferior for Black in this line is 9 . . . Q–B4? 10 P–K3, Q–R4 11 R–QN1, P–QR3 12 P–B5!± (Bogoljubov–Tartakover, Kissingen 1928). The point is that 10 . . . N/5xKP fails against 11 NxN, NxN 12 Q–Q4!±. Worth a trial by White is 9 R–B1 (instead of 9 Q–Q2).

[5] 6 . . . P–B3 7 PxP, QxP is too risky. After both 8 P–K3, QxP 9 R–QN1, QxP 10 B–Q3, O–O 11 P–B5! (Winter–Goldstein, London 1927) and 8 P–KN3!, QxP 9 B–N2, P–Q3 10 O–O, O–O 11 N–N3, Q–B3 12 N–N5 (Rubinstein–Tartakover, Kissingen 1928), White stands well.

[6] Catastrophic is 8 PxB??, N–Q6 mate!

[7] Other moves of the Bishop also saddle Black with an uphill struggle, e.g., 13 . . . B–K3 13 P–B5, P–KB3 14 PxP, PxP 15 Q–N4, R–B2 16 P–K4, P–Q4 (Ritzen–Grunfeld, Correspondence Game 1918) or 13 . . . B–Q2 13 P–B5, B–B3 14 PxP, QxP 15 Q–B3 (Nikolac–Vukcevic, Sarajevo 1954). In this latter line Black may vary with 14 . . . PxP 15 Q–N4, KR–K1.

[8] Another option at White's disposal is 13 B–N3. After 13 . . . B–K5 14 P–N4, K–R1 15 P–B3, B–B3 16 P–N5, B–K1 17 P–B5, R–Q1 18 PxP, RxP 19 Q–B3, N–Q6 (Vidmar-Opocensky, Sliac 1932), White plays 20 P–K4 with the better game.

[9] Flohr–Richter, Hamburg 1930.

[10] Though rarely essayed, this variation by Nimzowitsch guarantees White a lasting advantage.

[11] Nor does 5 . . . B–N5† 6 B–Q2, BxB† 7 QxB, N/5xKP 8 NxN, NxN 9 N–B3, O–O 10 B–K2, P–Q3 11 O–O, B–K3 12 P–QN3, P–KB4 13 P–B4, N–N3 14 B–B3! improve Black's chances.

[12] After 6 . . . N/5xKP both 7 NxN, NxN 8 O–O, O–O 9 N–B3, P–Q3 10 N–R4, B–N3 11 P–QN3, P–KB4 12 Q–Q5†, N–B2 13 B–N2, Q–K2 14 K–R1, P–B3 15 Q–Q2, B–B2 16 P–B4! (Alekhine and Sterk vs. Abonyi, Erdey, A. Steiner, and Vajda, Consultation Game, Budapest 1927) and 7 N–B3, P–Q3 8 O–O, O–O 9 P–QN3, R–K1 10 N–QR4, B–N3 11 NxB, RPxN 12 N–Q4, B–Q2 13 Q–Q2, Q–R5 14 P–R4 (Foltys–Bakonyi, Budapest 1948) give White the edge.

[13] With 7 . . . N/5xKP Black can transpose into the variations of the previous note.

continued ▸

[14] After 18 . . . BxB 19 QxB, R–K4 20 R–KN1, P–N3 21 R–N3, Black resigned (Nimzowitsch–Helling, Berlin 1928).

[15] If 4 Q–Q5, then 4 . . . P–KB4!

[16] 4 . . . B–N5 5 N–B3 leads to Prac. Var. 4.

[17] After 6 P–QR3, P–QR4? 7 N–N3, P–R3 8 B–B4, N–K3 9 B–N3, B–B4 10 P–K3, P–Q3 11 PxP, Q–B3 12 NxB, NxN 13 PxP, QxP? 14 B–K5!, Black is lost (Bogoljubov–Richter, Swinemuende 1931). Black's correct reply to 6 P–QR3 is 6 . . . Q–K2!, and if 7 P–QN4, then 7 . . . NxKP!

[18] 6 . . . P–Q4 is of no avail. After 7 PxP, QxP 8 B–N2, NxP 9 O–O, P–QR4 10 NxN, QxN 11 N–B4, White still has a pull (Keres–Mikula, Correspondence Game 1938). But 6 . . . P–KN3 is worth a try, e.g., 7 N–N3, N–K3 8 B–Q2, B–N2 9 B–B3, P–QR4 10 B–N2, P–R5 11 QN–Q2, P–Q3 12 PxP, BxB 13 PxB, QxP 14 N–K4, Q–K2 15 Q–Q2, P–B4 16 N/4–N5, N–R4 17 NxN, BxN 18 N–K5, O–O.

[19] The rash 7 . . . P–KN4 founders on 8 O–O, P–N5 9 N–R4, NxP 10 P–N4!, N–R3 11 P–QR3, P–Q3 12 Q–B2, N–N3 13 B–N2, KR–N1 14 N–B5, Q–N4 15 P–K4, when White has a clear edge (Eliskases–Pitschak, Mahrisch–Ostrau, 1933).

[20] 8 . . . B–N2 is effectively countered by 9 B–N5.

[21] See Game 2.

[22] Still another good line is 4 Q–B2, e.g., 4 . . . B–N5† 5 QN–Q2, P–Q4 6 PxP e.p., B–KB4 7 P–QR3, BxN† 8 BxB, NxQP 9 Q–N3, B–K3 10 P–K3± (Stoltz–Meyer, Correspondence Game 1954), or 4 . . . P–Q4 5 PxP e.p., B–B4 and now 6 N–QB3!, NxQP 7 P–K4!, NxKP 8 B–Q3!, NxP 9 BxB, NxR 10 N–B3, B–B4 11 N–K4, Q–K2 12 B–N5!, P–KB3 13 O–O–O± (Kottnauer–Martin, Czechoslovakia–France Match 1946). White's point is that 6 . . . N–N6 fails against 7 Q–R4†, and if 7 . . . B–Q2, then 8 N–N5! Black's best chance in this line is 12 . . . B–N5† 13 K–K2, P–KB3 14 B–K3, but even in this case White has a margin.

[23] 6 P–KN3 also merits consideration. After 6 . . . P–Q3 follows 7 PxP, QxP 8 B–N2, (8 P–QR3, Q–B4!), B–K3 9 P–QR3, BxN† 10 NxB, NxN 11 QxN!, N–Q5 12 Q–B3, O–O–O 13 B–K3, B–N5 14 P–R3!± (Watzl–Kunerth, Correspondence Game 1942).

[24] The text is an improvement on 7 BxB, Q–K2 8 B–B4, P–KN4! 9 Q–Q5, PxB 10 QxN/4, P–Q3 11 QxBP, PxP 12 Q–R6, B–Q2 13 Q–N5, Q–K3 14 P–K3, P–KR3 15 Q–R4, R–KN1 16 P–KR3, N–K2, which gives Black too much play (Riedmiller–Fitzinger, Vienna 1942).

[25] 9 . . . Q–K2 10 P–K3, O–O 11 B–K2, P–Q3 12 O–O, B–B4 13 P–B5!, PxP 14 Q–Q5!, KR–K1 15 QxNP, B–Q6 16 BxB, NxB 17 QR–Q1, P–B5 18 Q–B6 also favors White (Spielmann–Weil, Vienna 1937).

[26] Pomar–Steiner, Madrid 1951, continued 17 O–O–O, N–B2 18 Q–N4, N–Q3 19 QR–K1, Q–B2 20 P–KB5, K–R1 21 P–K5, and Black resigned on the 30th move.

[27] Reshevsky–Bisguier, New York 1955. White should win without much difficulty.

*Budapest Defense Game 1*

*WHITE: Reshevsky* *BLACK: Denker*

*Syracuse 1934*

| | WHITE | BLACK | | WHITE | BLACK |
|---|---|---|---|---|---|
| 1 | P–Q4 | N–KB3 | 11 | P–K5! | PxP |
| 2 | P–QB4 | P–K4 | 12 | PxP | N–KN1 |
| 3 | PxP | N–N5 | 13 | B–K3 | P–B3 |
| 4 | P–K4 | P–Q3 | 14 | B–Q3 | PxP |
| 5 | B–K2! | NxKP | 15 | N–KN5! | N–B3 |
| 6 | P–B4 | N–N5 | 16 | RxN! | BxR |
| 7 | N–KB3 | N–QB3 | 17 | Q–R5† | P–N3 |
| 8 | O–O | B–Q2 | 18 | BxP† | PxB |
| 9 | N–B3 | B–K2 | 19 | QxP† | K–K2 |
| 10 | P–KR3 | N–B3 | | . . . . | Resigns |

*Budapest Defense Game 2*

*WHITE: Alekhine* *BLACK: Tartakover*

*London 1932*

| | WHITE | BLACK | | WHITE | BLACK |
|---|---|---|---|---|---|
| 1 | P–Q4 | N–KB3 | 17 | QR–B1 | B–Q2 |
| 2 | P–QB4 | P–K4 | 18 | Q–Q2 | QR–Q1 |
| 3 | PxP | N–K5 | 19 | KR–Q1 | B–B1 |
| 4 | N–Q2 | N–B4 | 20 | N–K4 | N–B4 |
| 5 | KN–B3 | N–B3 | 21 | NxP | N–R5 |
| 6 | P–KN3 | Q–K2 | 22 | P–QB5 | NxNP |
| 7 | B–N2 | P–KN3 | 23 | R–K1 | P–QN4? |
| 8 | N–QN1 | NxP | 24 | PxP e.p.! | QxN |
| 9 | O–O | NxN† | 25 | QxQ | RxQ |
| 10 | PxN! | B–N2 | 26 | PxP | B–N2 |
| 11 | R–K1 | N–K3 | 27 | B–B5 | R(3)–Q1 |
| 12 | N–B3 | O–O | 28 | BxR | KxB |
| 13 | N–Q5 | Q–Q1 | 29 | BxP | BxB |
| 14 | P–B4 | P–QB3 | 30 | RxB | R–R1 |
| 15 | N–B3 | P–Q3 | 31 | R–N6! | RxP |
| 16 | B–K3 | Q–B2 | 32 | R–N8 mate | |

# chapter 33—Dutch Defense

Although the precise origin of the Dutch Defense is lost in obscurity, an extensive treatment of the opening is found in a 1779 treatise, *Nouvel essai sur les echecs,* by Elias Stein, a resident of Holland.

Of the half-closed defenses, the Dutch is certainly one of the most important. Black aims to initiate an attack against White's Kingside, avoiding an early exchange of pieces by building up his forces behind a wall of Pawns.

The main idea for Black is to gain control of his K5 and to avoid simplification of the center. White, on the other hand, seeks to control his Q5, to break open the center, and to carry the battle to the Queen's wing. These opposing aims create an asymmetrical position leading to extremely lively play.

In the hands of an aggressive player the Dutch is always a dangerous weapon, so that it behooves White to acquaint himself with the many ramifications of the opening.

Except for Botvinnik, who employed it most successfully, the Dutch found little favor with chessmasters prior to World War II. During the past decade, however, the Russian analysts have explored the defense more closely and have demonstrated the efficacy of several lines of play for Black aside from the popular Stonewall Variation.

1 P–Q4, P–KB4
2 P–QB4, P–K3[A]
3 N–KB3, N–KB3
4 P–KN3, B–K2
5 B–N2, O–O
6 O–O, P–Q4[B]

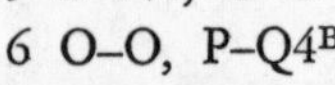

KEY POSITION 1

---

## part 1—OLD STONEWALL VARIATION

### OBSERVATIONS ON KEY POSITION 1

[A] This position frequently arises after 1 P–Q4, P–K3 2 P–QB4. Now if 2 . . . P–KB4, Black has avoided the annoying Staunton Gambit (see Part 7). Furthermore, with 1 . . . P–K3 Black retains the option of playing 2 . . . N–KB3 in reply to 2 P–QB4, 2 N–KB3 or 2 P–KN3. Of course if 1 P–Q4, P–K3 2 P–K4, the opening becomes a French Defense.

B Also possible is 6 . . . P–B3 7 N–B3, P–Q4, and Black has avoided the variation 6 . . . P–Q4 7 P–N3, P–B3 8 B–QR3.

If 6 . . . P–B3 7 P–N3, Black can try to transpose into the Old Dutch Defense with 7 . . . P–Q3. See Part 2.

By fianchettoing his King Bishop, White reveals his intention of defending his Kingside and directing his attention to the hostile Queen's wing and to the center. White can storm the Queen's wing with P–QN4–5, usually preceded by P–QB5 or by QBPxQP. In the latter case, Black as a rule will recapture with his King Pawn, thereby activating his Queen Bishop; however, if Black's Queen Knight is still on QN1, Black may well recapture with his Queen Bishop Pawn, and then develop his Knight to QB3.

In the center White aims for P–K4. This breakthrough is often prepared by transferring the King Knight to Q3 and then playing P–B3. In most cases White need not fear . . . QPxQBP as this merely accelerates his chances for P–K4.

It should be noted that Black's Queen Bishop is very much a "bad" Bishop. White, by exchanging his own Queen Bishop against Black's King Bishop or against Black's Knight on KB3, may sometimes reach a favorable end game.

Another weakness in Black's position is his K4. White therefore frequently plays B–KB4, keeping the square under observation and preventing . . . P–K4. White, of course, could achieve the same end by fianchettoing his Queen Bishop at N2. But then there is the danger that the Bishop might become comparatively inactive, as it could take little part in the defense of the Kingside.

Black's chances are to be found in a Kingside assault, usually by means of . . . P–KN4, . . . KN–K5, . . . Q–K1 and . . . Q–R4. If White plays P–QB5, however, Black is well advised to give preference to the counter-thrust . . . P–K4. A third plan for Black is the development of his "bad" Bishop via QR3.

IDEA VARIATIONS 1–5:

(1) 7 N–B3, P–B3 8 R–N1, Q–K1 (8 . . . K–R1! is to be considered) 9 P–B5, Q–R4 10 P–QN4, N–K5 11 Q–B2, N–Q2 12 P–N5, B–B3 13 B–B4, Q–K1 (preparing the counter-thrust in the center) 14 B–B7, R–B2 15 B–R5, P–K4!=

(2) 7 N–B3, P–B3 8 Q–B2, Q–K1 9 B–B4, Q–R4 10 QR–K1, QN–Q2 11 N–Q2, P–KN4 12 B–B7, N–K1 13 B–K5, NxB 14 PxN, P–B5. Black's action on the Kingside has upset White's plans. White's Pawn at K5 is weak and he is unable to play P–K4.

(3) 7 P–N3, P–B3 8 B–QR3, P–QN3 9 BxB, QxB 10 N–K5, B–N2 11 N–Q2, QN–Q2 12 NxN (White cannot very well keep his K5 under control: 12 P–B4, NxN 13

---

PRACTICAL VARIATIONS 1–23:

1 P–Q4, P–KB4 2 P–QB4, P–K3 3 N–KB3, N–KB3 4 P–KN3, B–K2 5 B–N2, O–O 6 O–O, P–Q4

| | 1 | 2 | 3 | 4 | 5 |
|---|---|---|---|---|---|
| 7 | N–B3 | — — | — — | — — | — — |
| | P–B3 | — — | — — | — — | — — |
| 8 | B–B4 | — — | — — | — — | — — |
| | Q–K1 | — — | — — | — — | QN–Q2 |
| 9 | Q–B2 | — — | — — | — — | P–B5 |
| | Q–R4 | — — | — — | — — | N–R4 |
| 10 | QR–Q1 | — — | P–B5 | QR–N1[4] | Q–Q2 |
| | QN–Q2 | — — | QN–Q2 | QN–Q2 | NxB |
| 11 | P–N3 | — — | P–QN4 | P–B5 | PxN |
| | N–K5 | K–R1 | N–K5 | N–K5 | ± |
| 12 | N–K5 | K–R1[2] | NxN | P–QN4 | |
| | B–B3[1] | R–KN1 | BPxN | P–KN4 | |
| 13 | = | P–K3 | N–K5 | B–B7 | |
| | | P–KN4 | B–B3 | R–B3 | |
| 14 | | B–B7[3] | NxN | P–KR3 | |
| | | ± | BxN | R–R3 | |
| 15 | | | Q–Q2 | ∓ | |
| | | | P–K4 | | |
| | | | = | | |

PxN, N–N5∓), NxN 13 P–K3, QR–B1 14 R–B1, P–B4. The problem of Black's Queen Bishop is solved, and Black's position is completely satisfactory.

(4) 7 QN–Q2, P–B3 8 P–N3, Q–K1 9 N–K5, QN–Q2 10 N–Q3 (the position of White's Knights is very effective: the Knight on Q3 controls KB4 and prepares for the thrust P–QN4, while the Knight on Q2 can often be transferred advantageously to KB3, where it will exert even more pressure on K5), P–QN3 11 P–QN4, N–K5 12 Q–N3, B–B3 13 N–B3, B–R3 14 PxP, BPxP 15 P–N5±.

(5) 7 N–B3, P–B3 8 R–N1, N–K5 9 Q–B2, Q–K1 10 P–QN4, N–Q2 11 P–B5, P–QN4 12 PxP e.p., QNxP 13 N–K5, B–N2 14 B–B4, N–Q3 15 N–Q3, N/N–B5 with a difficult game and chances for both sides.

---

| *6* | *7* | *8* | *9* | *10* | *11* |
|---|---|---|---|---|---|
| N–B3 | – – | – – | – – | – – | – – |
| P–B3 | – – | – – | – – | – – | – – |
| Q–N3 | Q–Q3 | – – | – – | N–K5 | – – |
| K–R1 | Q–K1 | – – | N–K5[7] | QN–Q2 | Q–K1 |
| N–K5 | N–K5 | – – | N–K5 | N–Q3 | P–N3 |
| QN–Q2 | Q–R4 | QN–Q2 | N–Q2 | PxP | N–K5 |
| NxN | P–B3 | PxP | NxN | N–B4 | B–N2 |
| NxN | QN–Q2 | KPxP | BxN | N–N3 | N–Q2 |
| R–Q1 | B–B4 | QxP | P–B3 | P–K4 | N–Q3[9] |
| N–N3 | ± | NxN | NxN | = | ± |
| PxP[5] | | QxN/5 | PxN | | |
| KPxP | | N–N5 | PxP | | |
| N–R4 | | Q–B7 | QxQBP | | |
| N–B5[6] | | B–Q1 | Q–N3[8] | | |
| = | | Q–Q6 | ± | | |
| | | B–K2 | | | |
| | | = | | | |

continued ▸

PRACTICAL VARIATIONS 1–23:

1 P–Q4, P–KB4 2 P–QB4, P–K3 3 N–KB3, N–KB3 4 P–KN3, B–K2 5 B–N2, O–O 6 O–O, P–Q4

| 12 | 13 | 14 | 15 | 16 | 17 |
|---|---|---|---|---|---|
| N–B3 | – – | – – | – – | – – | – – |
| P–B3 | – – | – – | – – | – – | – – |
| P–N3 | – – | R–N1[10] | – – | B–N5 | – – |
| N–K5 | Q–K1 | K–R1! | – – | QN–Q2 | – – |
| B–N2 | B–N2 | PxP | P–B5[12] | P–K3 | – – |
| N–Q2 | QN–Q2 | BPxP | N–K5 | Q–K1 | – – |
| Q–B2 | P–K3 | B–B4 | Q–B2 | Q–B2 | – – |
| B–B3 | N–K5 | N–B3! | N–Q2 | K–R1 | – – |
| $=$ | N–K2 | N–K5 | P–QN4 | N–K2 | PxP |
| | P–QR4 | B–Q2 | B–B3[13] | P–KR3 | KPxP |
| | N–B4 | R–B1 | $\mp$ | BxN | QxP?? |
| | QN–B3 | R–B1[11] | | BxB | N–K5 |
| | N–K5 | $=$ | | PxP | Q–N4 |
| | $\pm$ | | | KPxP | N–K4 |
| | | | | N–B4 | $\mp$ |
| | | | | P–KN4 | |
| | | | | N–Q3 | |
| | | | | R–KN1[14] | |
| | | | | $=$ | |

*Notes to practical variations 1–23:*

[1] 12 . . . N–N4 13 P–B3, N–R6† 14 BxN, QxB 15 P–K4 is to White's advantage.

[2] Or 12 P–K3, N–K5 13 B–B7$\pm$.

[3] 14 . . . N–K1 15 B–K5†, NxB 16 NxN, N–B3 17 P–B3, B–Q3 18 P–K4, N–Q2 19 P–KN4 (Yudovitch–Botvinnik, Leningrad 1934).

[4] 10 P–QR3 leads only to equality after 10 . . . QN–Q2 11 P–QN4, PxP.

[5] 12 P–B5, N–Q2$\mp$.

[6] Capablanca–Botvinnik, Moscow 1936.

[7] 8 . . . QN–Q2? 9 PxP!$\pm$.

[8] Grunfeld prefers White's game, although Pachman claims the position is level. After 14 B–B4, White may have a slight pull.

| *18* | *19* | *20* | *21* | *22* | *23* |
|---|---|---|---|---|---|
| – – | P–N3 | – – | – – | – – | QN–Q2 |
| – – | P–B3 | – – | – – | – – | P–B3 |
| – – | B–QR3 | – – | – – | – – | N–K5 |
| – – | P–QN3 | QN–Q2 | BxB | – – | QN–Q2 |
| PxP | BxB | Q–B1 | NxB | – – | N–Q3 |
| KPxP | QxB | N–K5 | Q–K1 | Q–K2 | Q–K1 |
| P–K3 | N–K5 | QN–Q2 | N–B2 | Q–B1 | Q–B2 |
| P–KR3 | B–N2 | BxB | QN–Q2 | QN–Q2 | P–KN4 |
| BxN | N–Q2 | QxB | PxP | Q–N2 | N–B3 |
| NxB | QN–Q2 | P–QN3 | KPxP | N–K5 | N–K5 |
| R–N1 | NxN | QR–B1 | N–N4 | P–K3 | R–N1 |
| N–K5 | NxN | B–N2 | N–K5 | N–Q3 | B–B3 |
| N–K5 | P–K3 | KR–Q1 | P–K3 | N–K5 | P–QN4 |
| B–Q3 | QR–B1 | Q–B3 | P–QR4 | ± | P–N4? |
| P–B4 | R–B1 | PxP | N–Q3[16] | | P–B5 |
| ± | = | KPxP | ± | | P–QR4 |
| | | N–K1[15] | | | P–QR3[17] |
| | | = | | | ± |

---

[9] Steinitz–Zukertort, London 1872. White has a minimal advantage.

[10] If 8 Q–B2, not 8 . . . QN–Q2 9 PxP, BPxP 10 B–B4±, but 8 . . . Q–K1 which transposes into Prac. Var. 1 after 9 B–B4.

[11] Keres–Botvinnik, Moscow 1948.

[12] 9 Q–B2 immediately is preferable.

[13] Had Black continued in routine fashion with 8 . . . Q–K1, White could have completed his development with 12 B–B4. Now, however, this move would be strongly met by 12 . . . P–KN4!

[14] See Game 1.

[15] 15 . . . P–QR4 16 N/2–B3, P–B5 17 N–Q3, PxP 18 RPxP, QR–K1= (Szabo–Botvinnik, Budapest 1952).

[16] Botvinnik–Ragosin, Moscow 1939.

[17] Geller–Szabo, Budapest 1952. See Game 2.

*Dutch Defense Game 1*

*WHITE: Botvinnik* *BLACK: Smyslov*

*22nd Match Game 1958*

| | WHITE | BLACK | | WHITE | BLACK |
|---|---|---|---|---|---|
| 1 | P–Q4 | P–KB4 | 21 | NxN | QxN |
| 2 | P–KN3 | N–KB3 | 22 | QR–K1 | R–N2 |
| 3 | B–N2 | P–K3 | 23 | R–B2 | P–N3 |
| 4 | N–KB3 | B–K2 | 24 | Q–B3 | Q–Q3 |
| 5 | O–O | O–O | 25 | R–B2 | B–Q2 |
| 6 | P–B4 | P–B3 | 26 | P–QN4 | P–KR4 |
| 7 | N–B3 | P–Q4 | 27 | K–R1? | P–R5 |
| 8 | B–N5 | QN–Q2 | 28 | PxP | PxP |
| 9 | P–K3 | Q–K1 | 29 | P–B4 | QR–KN1 |
| 10 | Q–B2 | K–R1 | 30 | B–B3 | B–K1 |
| 11 | N–K2 | P–KR3 | 31 | Q–Q2 | Q–R3 |
| 12 | BxN | BxB | 32 | Q–K2 | P–R6 |
| 13 | PxP | KPxP | 33 | R/2–B1 | R–N7! |
| 14 | N–B4 | P–KN4 | 34 | BxR | RxB |
| 15 | N–Q3 | R–KN1 | 35 | Q–B3 | Q–R5 |
| 16 | Q–B3 | B–K2 | 36 | P–N5 | B–R4 |
| 17 | KN–K5 | N–B3 | 37 | QxR | PxQ† |
| 18 | P–B3 | B–K3 | 38 | K–N1 | P–B4 |
| 19 | N–B5 | BxN | | Resigns | |
| 20 | QxB | N–Q2 | | | |

*Dutch Defense Game 2*

*WHITE: Geller* *BLACK: Szabo*

*Budapest 1952*

| | WHITE | BLACK | | WHITE | BLACK |
|---|---|---|---|---|---|
| 1 | P–Q4 | P–K3 | 16 | PxP | P–N5 |
| 2 | N–KB3 | P–KB4 | 17 | N/B–K5 | NxN |
| 3 | P–KN3 | N–KB3 | 18 | PxN | B–Q1 |
| 4 | B–N2 | B–K2 | 19 | B–R6 | R–B2 |
| 5 | O–O | O–O | 20 | P–B3 | B–N4 |
| 6 | P–B4 | P–Q4 | 21 | BxB | NxB |
| 7 | QN–Q2 | P–B3 | 22 | PxP | KR–R2 |
| 8 | N–K5 | QN–Q2 | 23 | PxP | PxP |
| 9 | N–Q3 | Q–K1 | 24 | Q–Q2 | N–B2 |
| 10 | Q–B2 | P–KN4 | 25 | Q–B4 | R–R7 |
| 11 | N–B3 | N–K5 | 26 | Q–K3 | Q–K2 |
| 12 | R–N1 | B–B3 | 27 | B–R3 | N–N4 |
| 13 | P–QN4 | P–N4 | 28 | BxP | P–Q5 |
| 14 | P–B5 | P–QR4 | 29 | QxP | RxP |
| 15 | P–QR3 | PxP | 30 | BxB | R/1–R7 |

| WHITE | BLACK | WHITE | BLACK |
|---|---|---|---|
| 31 N–N2 | RxKP | 34 QxR | N–K5 |
| 32 QR–Q1 | R–K7 | 35 Q–B4 | RxN |
| 33 R–Q2 | RxR | 36 B–K6†! | Resigns |

---

## part 2—OLD DUTCH DEFENSE

1 P–Q4, P–KB4
2 P–QB4, P–K3
3 N–KB3, N–KB3
4 P–KN3, B–K2
5 B–N2, O–O
6 O–O, P–Q3

KEY POSITION 2

OBSERVATIONS ON KEY POSITION 2

In this line Black aims for an early advance of his King Pawn, making no effort to prevent P–K4 on White's part. As in the Stonewall Variation, Black's key move is often . . . Q–K1 with the intent of keeping the hostile King's wing under pressure.

White has three systems from which he may choose. He can proceed with P–K4 after N–QB3 and R–K1; he can proceed with P–K4 after N–QB3 and Q–B2; or, finally, he may fianchetto his Queen Bishop hoping to hamper Black's coming . . . P–K4.

The ensuing positions are rife with tactical possibilities, the slightest slip on either side often proving fatal.

IDEA VARIATIONS 6 AND 7:

(6) 7 N–B3, Q–K1 8 P–N3 (formerly considered White's strongest move; the system introduced by Black's next move is a recommendation of the Russian theorist, Simagin), P–QR4 9 B–QR3, N–R3 (the point; Black intends to transfer his Knight to QN5) 10 R–K1, N–QN5 (attempts to prevent P–K4 rebound to White's favor: 10 . . . Q–N3 11 N–K5! or 10 . . . N–K5 11 NxN, PxN 12 N–Q2, P–Q4 13 BxB, QxB 14 P–B3±) 11 P–K4, PxP 12 NxP, NxN 13 RxN, Q–N3 14 Q–K2±. In this variation White has cleverly combined two attacking systems.

(7) 7 N–B3, P–QR4 8 R–K1, N–K5 9 Q–B2, N–QB3?! (an enterprising Pawn sacrifice difficult to refute) 10 NxN (10 P–QR3, NxN 11 PxN, P–K4 and Black has a good game), N–N5 11 Q–N1, PxN 12 QxP, P–K4 (for a long time this position was considered favorable for Black; Illivitsky's 13 P–KN4!, however, turns the tables, though White's task is still far from easy).

## PRACTICAL VARIATIONS 24–33:

1 P–Q4, P–KB4 2 P–QB4, P–K3 3 N–KB3, N–KB3 4 P–KN3, B–K2 5 B–N2, O–O 6 O–O, P–Q3.

| | 24 | 25 | 26 | 27 | 28 |
|---|---|---|---|---|---|
| 7 | N–B3 | – – | – – | – – | – – |
| | Q–K1 | – – | – – | – – | – – |
| 8 | R–K1 | – – | – – | – – | – – |
| | Q–N3[1] | – – | N–K5 | – – | – – |
| 9 | P–K4 | – – | Q–B2 | – – | – – |
| | PxP | – – | Q–N3 | – – | – – |
| 10 | NxP | – – | B–K3 | – – | – – |
| | NxN | – – | NxN | – – | – – |
| 11 | RxN | – – | QxN | – – | – – |
| | N–B3[2] | – – | N–Q2? | B–B3 | – – |
| 12 | Q–K2 | R–K1 | P–B5! | QR–Q1 | P–QN4 |
| | B–B3 | N–N5 | N–B3 | N–B3 | R–K1 |
| 13 | B–Q2 | P–QR3 | PxP | Q–N3 | P–B5 |
| | P–K4 | N–B7 | PxP | P–QR4[6] | P–K4 |
| 14 | PxP | N–R4 | Q–N3 | P–B5! | PxQP |
| | NxP[3] | BxN[4] | N–Q4[5] | P–R5[7] | BPxP[8] |
| 15 | B–B3 | = | ± | = | ± |
| | = | | | | |

*Notes to practical variations 24–33:*

[1] 8 . . . P–Q4 transposes into Part 1.

[2] Both 11 . . . QxR? 12 N–R4! and 11 . . . P–K4 12 R–K1 favor White.

[3] For 14 . . . PxP, see Game 3.

[4] See Game 4.

[5] 15 B–Q2, P–N3? 16 B–N5!, BxB 17 NxB, B–N2 18 P–K4±. Better is 15 . . . R–N1 16 KR–QB1, B–Q2 17 N–K1,

| *29* | *30* | *31* | *32* | *33* |
|---|---|---|---|---|
| N–B3 | – – | – – | – – | – – |
| Q–K1 | – – | – – | – – | – – |
| Q–B2 | – – | – – | P–N3 | – – |
| Q–R4 | – – | – – | P–QR4! | Q–R4 |
| P–K4 | B–N5 | P–N3! | B–N2[9] | B–QR3 |
| P–K4! | P–KR3! | N–B3 | N–R3 | N–B3 |
| PxKP | BxN | B–QR3 | P–QR3 | Q–B2 |
| QPxP | BxB | P–QR4 | P–B3 | B–Q2 |
| N–Q5 | P–K4 | QR–Q1 | Q–B2 | P–Q5! |
| NxN | N–B3 | N–QN5 | P–QN4 | ± |
| KPxN | QR–Q1 | Q–N1 | ∓ | |
| N–Q2 | P–K4 | P–KN4 | | |
| ∓ | = | B–N2 | | |
| | | N–K1 | | |
| | | N–Q2 | | |
| | | ± | | |

B–QB3 18 N–Q3, when White enjoys only a slight edge.

[6] Or 13 . . . P–K4 14 P–B5†, K–R1=.

[7] 15 Q–R3, R–R3 16 PxP, PxP 17 P–Q5, N–R4 18 Q–N4, P–K4 19 QR–B1, P–B5 20 B–N6, P–K5 21 BxN, PxN 22 PxP/3, BxP=.

[8] 15 PxP, PxP 16 QR–B1, N–B3 17 P–N5, N–Q1 18 KR–Q1, N–B2 19 Q–N4, B–K3 20 N–R4, BxN 21 QxB, P–K5 22 R–B7±.

[9] For 9 B–QR3, see Idea Var. 6.

### *Dutch Defense Game 3*

*WHITE: Aronson* *BLACK: Tal*

*USSR Championship 1957*

| | WHITE | BLACK | | WHITE | BLACK |
|---|---|---|---|---|---|
| 1 | P–Q4 | P–K3 | 20 | P–N5 | N–Q1 |
| 2 | P–QB4 | P–KB4 | 21 | B–Q5† | K–R1 |
| 3 | N–KB3 | N–KB3 | 22 | P–B4 | PxP |
| 4 | N–B3 | B–K2 | 23 | Q–Q2 | Q–QN3† |
| 5 | P–KN3 | O–O | 24 | B–Q4 | Q–N3 |
| 6 | B–N2 | P–Q3 | 25 | QxP | K–R2 |
| 7 | O–O | Q–K1 | 26 | QxP | B–N8 |
| 8 | R–K1 | Q–N3 | 27 | B–K5 | N–K3 |
| 9 | P–K4 | PxP | 28 | Q–Q6 | Q–B4 |
| 10 | NxP | NxN | 29 | B–B4 | N–N4 |
| 11 | RxN | N–B3 | 30 | Q–N4 | B–K5 |
| 12 | Q–K2 | B–B3 | 31 | BxB | RxB |
| 13 | B–Q2 | P–K4 | 32 | R–KB1 | R–K7 |
| 14 | PxP | PxP | 33 | Q–Q6 | RxQRP |
| 15 | B–B3 | B–B4 | 34 | Q–Q5 | Q–B7 |
| 16 | N–R4 | BxN | 35 | P–B5 | R–Q1 |
| 17 | RxB | QR–K1 | 36 | B–Q6 | R–K1 |
| 18 | Q–K3 | P–KR3 | | White overstepped the | |
| 19 | P–QN4 | Q–B3 | | time limit | |

### *Dutch Defense Game 4*

*WHITE: Neikirch* *BLACK: Larsen*

*Interzonal Tournament, Portoroz 1958*

| | WHITE | BLACK | | WHITE | BLACK |
|---|---|---|---|---|---|
| 1 | P–Q4 | P–KB4 | 19 | K–N3 | N–B4† |
| 2 | P–KN3 | N–KB3 | 20 | K–N2 | P–N3 |
| 3 | B–N2 | P–K3 | 21 | B–N5 | B–N2† |
| 4 | P–QB4 | P–Q3 | 22 | K–B1 | P–B4 |
| 5 | N–KB3 | B–K2 | 23 | PxP | NPxP |
| 6 | O–O | O–O | 24 | Q–R4 | P–R4 |
| 7 | N–B3 | Q–K1 | 25 | R–B1 | R–B2 |
| 8 | R–K1 | Q–N3 | 26 | R–B3 | N–Q5 |
| 9 | P–K4 | NxP | 27 | B–K3 | B–B3 |
| 10 | NxN | PxN | 28 | Q–Q1 | P–K4 |
| 11 | RxP | N–B3 | 29 | Q–N1 | N–B4 |
| 12 | R–K1 | N–N5 | 30 | P–N3 | R–N1 |
| 13 | P–QR3 | N–B7 | 31 | Q–Q1 | R/2–N2 |
| 14 | N–R4 | BxN | 32 | P–QR4 | K–B2 |
| 15 | B–K4 | NxKR | 33 | R–Q3 | R–N3 |
| 16 | BxQ | N–B6† | 34 | K–K2 | B–K5 |
| 17 | K–N2 | PxB | 35 | R–B3 | R–KR1 |
| 18 | PxB | NxP† | 36 | Q–KN1 | N–Q5 |

| WHITE | BLACK | WHITE | BLACK |
|---|---|---|---|
| 37 BxN | BPxB | 56 K–K3 | K–B4 |
| 38 R–N3 | P–Q6† | 57 Q–B5† | K–N5 |
| 39 K–K3 | B–B4 | 58 Q–N5† | K–B6 |
| 40 Q–K1 | R–N5 | 59 Q–Q5 | R/5–QN5 |
| 41 Q–KR1 | R–QB1 | 60 Q–N2 | P–Q4 |
| 42 Q–Q5† | K–K2 | 61 Q–Q2† | K–B5 |
| 43 P–B4 | R–B4 | 62 P–R4 | R–B6 |
| 44 Q–N8 | RxNP | 63 P–R5 | R/5–N6 |
| 45 QxP† | K–Q1 | 64 K–B3 | P–Q5 |
| 46 RxP | BxR | 65 Q–R6 | P–Q7† |
| 47 QxB | PxP† | 66 K–K2 | R–Q6 |
| 48 KxP | K–B2 | 67 Q–B6† | K–N5 |
| 49 Q–N7† | K–N3 | 68 Q–Q6† | KxP |
| 50 Q–Q4 | K–B3 | 69 Q–B6 | K–R6 |
| 51 Q–K4† | K–Q2 | 70 Q–B5 | K–N7 |
| 52 Q–R7† | K–B1 | 71 K–Q1 | P–R5 |
| 53 Q–N8† | K–N2 | 72 P–R6 | K–R8 |
| 54 Q–B7† | K–N3 | Resigns | |
| 55 Q–Q7 | RxP† | | |

## part 3—LENINGRAD SYSTEM

1 P–Q4, P–KB4
2 P–QB4[A], N–KB3
3 P–KN3, P–KN3
4 B–N2, B–N2
5 N–KB3[B], O–O
6 O–O, P–Q3

KEY POSITION 3

### OBSERVATIONS ON KEY POSITION 3

[A] For the time being White can omit this move, thus, 2 P–KN3, P–KN3 3 B–N2, B–N2 4 N–QB3 (Taimanov's recommendation), N–KB3 5 B–N5, N–B3! with a difficult game and chances for both players. Another system worth a try is 2 N–KB3 followed by 3 P–KN3 and 4 P–QN3.

[B] The development of the Knight to KR3 deserves further investigation. 1 P–Q4, P–KB4 2 P–KN3, P–KN3 3 B–N2, B–N2 4 N–KR3, N–QB3 5 P–Q5, N–K4 6 N–B3, N–KB3 7 P–K4, P–Q3 8 N–B4, P–B3 9 O–O, O–O 10 KPxP, BxP 11 QN–K2!† (Pachman–Alexander, 1955).

In sharp contrast with other variations of the Dutch Defense, the Leningrad system offers active play for Black's Bishops. The King Bishop is powerfully posted on KN2 commanding the long KR1–QR8 diagonal, while the Queen Bishop awaits only the removal of Black's King Bishop Pawn (usually by a later . . . PxKP) to play an important role in the game. In these circumstances it is obvious that Black is not obliged, as in the Old Dutch, to strive for . . . P–K4, or, as in the Stonewall, to seek other diagonals for his Queen Bishop.

It must be noted that examples of the Leningrad System in tournament play are comparatively rare. The Leningrad masters, Vinogradov, Kopylov and Korchnoi, have employed it with considerable success, and outside of the Soviet Union, the frequent winner of the British championship, Alexander is its most consistent adherent.

IDEA VARIATIONS 8 AND 9:

(8) 7 N–B3, N–B3 8 P–Q5 (this advance is compulsory for White if he wants to achieve an advantage: 8 P–K3, P–K4!═), N–QR4 (for the more customary 8 . . . N–K4, see Prac. Var. 34 and 35) 9 Q–Q3 (9 Q–R4! is stronger; see Prac. Var. 36), P–B4 (to prevent 10 P–QR4) 10 N–KN5 (too optimistic; better is 10 P–N3) P–QR3 11 R–N1, R–N1 12 B–Q2, Q–K1 13 P–N3, P–N4 14 P–QR3, N–N5 with forceful counterplay for Black (Benko–Tal, Candidates' Tournament 1959; see Game 5).

(9) 7 N–B3, P–B3 8 P–N3, N–R3 9 B–N2, B–Q2 10 R–K1, Q–R4 11 P–K4, PxP 12 NxP, QR–K1. White has the sounder position, but Black's is quite resilient. The chances are about equal.

*Dutch Defense Game 5*

*WHITE: Benko* — *BLACK: Tal*

*Candidates' Tournament, Bled 1959*

| | WHITE | BLACK | | WHITE | BLACK |
|---|---|---|---|---|---|
| 1 | N–KB3 | P–KB4 | 16 | PxP | R–N6 |
| 2 | P–KN3 | N–KB3 | 17 | RxR | NxR |
| 3 | B–N2 | P–KN3 | 18 | R–N1 | N–Q5 |
| 4 | P–QB4 | B–N2 | 19 | P–K3 | NxN† |
| 5 | N–B3 | O–O | 20 | BxN | N–K4 |
| 6 | O–O | P–Q3 | 21 | Q–K2 | NxB† |
| 7 | P–Q4 | N–B3 | 22 | QxN | P–K4 |
| 8 | P–Q5 | N–QR4 | 23 | Q–Q1 | P–K5 |
| 9 | Q–Q3 | P–B4 | 24 | Q–R4 | Q–K2 |
| 10 | N–KN5 | P–QR3 | 25 | Q–B6 | P–B5! |
| 11 | R–N1 | R–N1 | 26 | R–N8 | B–R6! |
| 12 | B–Q2 | Q–K1 | 27 | RxR† | QxR |
| 13 | P–N3 | P–N4 | 28 | KPxP | Q–N1 |
| 14 | P–QR3 | N–N5 | 29 | N–K2 | Q–N8† |
| 15 | N–B3 | PxP | | and in this lost position White forfeited. | |

PRACTICAL VARIATIONS 34–38:

1 P–Q4, P–KB4 2 P–QB4, N–KB3 3 P–KN3, P–KN3 4 B–N2, B–N2 5 N–KB3, O–O 6 O–O, P–Q3

| | *34* | *35* | *36* | *37* | *38* |
|---|---|---|---|---|---|
| *7* | N–B3 | – – | – – | – – | – – |
| | N–B3 | – – | – – | P–B3 | – – |
| *8* | P–Q5 | – – | – – | Q–B2 | P–N3 |
| | N–K4 | – – | N–QR4 | Q–B2 | N–R3 |
| *9* | NxN | Q–N3 | Q–R4! | R–K1[3] | B–N2 |
| | PxN | KN–Q2 | P–B4 | N–R3 | B–Q2 |
| *10* | P–K4 | B–K3 | PxP e.p. | P–K4? | R–K1 |
| | P–K3 | R–K1 | NxP/3 | PxP | Q–R4 |
| *11* | PxKP | QR–Q1 | R–Q1 | NxP | P–K4 |
| | P–B3[1] | N–B1 | N–QR4 | B–B4 | PxP |
| *12* | PxP | N–Q4 | P–B5 | ∓ | NxP |
| | PxP | K–R1 | B–Q2 | | QR–K1 |
| *13* | R–K1[2] | B–N5 | Q–R3 | | = |
| | ± | ± | N–K1 | | |
| *14* | | | B–N5 | | |
| | | | ± | | |

*Notes to practical variations 34–38:*

[1] Or 11 . . . BxP 12 PxP, BxQBP 13 R–K1, QxQ 14 NxQ±.

[2] In Pachman's opinion White has the better game. After 13 . . . P–K5, however, the situation is far from clear.

[3] 9 P–Q5! is sharper, e.g., 9 . . . PxP 10 PxP, N–R3 11 N–Q4±. In this line, if 10 . . . NxP?, then 11 Q–N3, again with advantage to White.

## part 4—ANTI-STONEWALL VARIATION

1 P–Q4, P–KB4
2 P–QB4, P–K3
3 P–KN3, N–KB3
4 B–N2, B–K2
5 N–QB3, O–O
6 Q–N3[A]

KEY POSITION 4

### OBSERVATIONS ON KEY POSITION 4

[A] 6 P–Q5, P–K4! 7 P–K4, P–Q3 offers Black no difficulties.

White's 6 Q–N3 serves a double purpose. It prevents 6 . . . P–Q4 and exerts direct pressure on Black's Queen Knight Pawn. Black, however, can easily avoid this variation by substituting for his 5th move (. . . O–O) 5 . . . P–Q3 or 5 . . . P–Q4.

IDEA VARIATION 10:

(10) 6 . . . P–B4 (best is probably 6 . . . K–R1; see Prac. Var. 39 and 40) 7 P–Q5, P–K4 8 P–K4, P–Q3? (somewhat better is 8 . . . PxP; see Prac. Var. 41) 9 PxP, BxP 10 QxP, QN–Q2 11 Q–N3 and White maintains the extra Pawn without much risk.

*Dutch Defense Game 6*

*WHITE: Porath* *BLACK: Larsen*

*Chess Olympics, Moscow 1956*

| | WHITE | BLACK | | WHITE | BLACK |
|---|---|---|---|---|---|
| 1 | N–KB3 | P–KB4 | 18 | PxP | R–Q2 |
| 2 | P–QB4 | N–KB3 | 19 | P–Q5 | NxP |
| 3 | N–B3 | P–KN3 | 20 | B–B4 | K–R2 |
| 4 | P–QN3 | B–N2 | 21 | BxN | BxN† |
| 5 | B–N2 | P–Q3 | 22 | BxB | PxB |
| 6 | P–Q4 | P–B3 | 23 | P–N4 | RxP |
| 7 | P–K3 | Q–R4 | 24 | PxP | PxP |
| 8 | P–QR3 | O–O | 25 | R–Q1 | N–B3 |
| 9 | B–K2 | P–K4 | 26 | P–N5 | N–Q1 |
| 10 | P–QN4 | Q–B2 | 27 | P–B3 | N–K3 |
| 11 | P–Q5 | P–KR3 | 28 | PxP | BPxP |
| 12 | P–B5? | P–K5! | 29 | R–KB1 | N–N4 |
| 13 | N–Q4? | PxBP | 30 | R–B5 | P–Q5 |
| 14 | Q–N3 | PxN | 31 | P–KR4 | N–B6† |
| 15 | P–Q6† | B–K3 | 32 | K–K2 | R–QB1 |
| 16 | QxB† | Q–B2 | 33 | B–N4 | R–KN3 |
| 17 | QxQ† | RxQ | | Resigns | |

*Dutch Defense Game 7*

*WHITE: Vidmar* *BLACK: Guimard*

*Groningen 1946*

| | WHITE | BLACK | | WHITE | BLACK | | WHITE | BLACK |
|---|---|---|---|---|---|---|---|---|
| 1 | P–Q4 | P–K3 | 12 | N–B4 | R–QN1 | 23 | PxB | RxBP |
| 2 | P–QB4 | P–KB4 | 13 | P–QR3 | B–Q3 | 24 | Q–B6 | RxBP! |
| 3 | N–QB3 | N–KB3 | 14 | P–QN4 | N–Q4! | 25 | KxR | R–B1† |
| 4 | P–KN3 | B–K2 | 15 | N/3xN | PxN | 26 | K–K1 | Q–B6 |
| 5 | B–N2 | O–O | 16 | Q–B2 | P–N4 | 27 | K–Q2 | Q–N7† |
| 6 | Q–N3 | K–R1 | 17 | N–Q3 | P–B5 | 28 | K–B1 | QxR† |
| 7 | N–R3 | P–Q4 | 18 | N–K5 | Q–R4 | 29 | K–B2 | QxP† |
| 8 | PxP | PxP | 19 | PxP | PxP | 30 | K–N1 | Q–R6 |
| 9 | BxP | N–B3 | 20 | B–N2 | B–K3 | 31 | Q–B5 | R–B8† |
| 10 | BxN | PxB | 21 | Q–B3 | P–B6! | 32 | K–B2 | B–B4† |
| 11 | Q–B4 | Q–K1 | 22 | PxP | BxN | | Resigns | |

PRACTICAL VARIATIONS 39–42:

1 P–Q4, P–KB4 2 P–QB4, P–K3 3 P–KN3, N–KB3 4 B–N2, B–K2 5 N–QB3, O–O 6 Q–N3

| | *39* | *40* | *41* | *42* |
|---|---|---|---|---|
| *6* | – – | – – | – – | – – |
| | K–R1 | – – | P–B4 | N–B3 |
| *7* | N–R3 | – – | P–Q5 | P–Q5 |
| | P–Q4[1] | – – | P–K4 | N–K4 |
| *8* | PxP | – – | P–K4 | PxP[2] |
| | PxP | – – | PxP | PxP |
| *9* | NxP | BxP | NxP | B–B4 |
| | NxN | N–B3 | NxN | N/3–Q2 |
| *10* | QxN | BxN | BxN | R–Q1 |
| | QxQ | PxB | P–Q3 | Q–K1 |
| *11* | BxQ | Q–B4 | Q–Q3 | N–N5 |
| | R–Q1 | Q–K1 | P–KR3 | B–Q1 |
| *12* | B–N3 | N–B4 | N–K2 | = |
| | RxP | QR–N1 | N–Q2 | |
| *13* | B–KB4 | P–QR3 | O–O | |
| | ± | B–Q3 | ± | |
| | | ∓ | | |

*Notes to practical variations 39–42:*

[1] An attractive attempt to neutralize the tension, but not quite satisfactory.

[2] 8 N–R3, N–B2 9 PxP, PxP=.

---

## part 5—CLOSED VARIATION

1 P–Q4, P–KB4
2 P–QB4, P–K3
3 P–KN3, B–K2
4 B–N2, N–KB3
5 N–QB3, O–O
6 P–K3[A]

KEY POSITION 5

### OBSERVATIONS ON KEY POSITION 5

[A] 6 N–R3, P–Q3! (if 6 . . . P–Q4, White's Knight becomes powerfully posted at KB4) 7 O–O, Q–K1 8 P–K4, PxP 9 NxP, NxN 10 BxN, P–K4! and Black has a good game.

This position occurred in the 1st, 16th, and 22nd games of the match between Botvinnik and Bronstein in 1951. White's intention is to develop his King Knight to K2, thus facilitating the moves P–KB3 and P–K4. Black's characteristic maneuver . . . Q–K1–R4 is now without meaning, as White can neutralize its force with N–KB4. Another advantage in the development of the King Knight to K2 is seen when Black chooses to play the Old Dutch; White's Knight is far less exposed than on KR3.

IDEA VARIATIONS 11 AND 12:

(11) 6 . . . P–Q4 (the Stonewall and the Old Dutch are about equal here) 7 KN–K2, P–B3 (threatening . . . PxP under certain circumstances) 8 Q–Q3 (for 8 P–N3, see Prac. Var. 44–46), N–QR3 (8 . . . QN–Q2 9 PxP, BPxP favors White, as Black can no longer develop his Queen Knight to QB3 without waste of time) 9 P–QR3, N–B2 10 O–O, P–QN3 11 P–B3 with good chances for White.

(12) 6 . . . P–Q3 7 KN–K2, P–K4 8 P–Q5, P–B4 9 O–O (9 PxP e.p., PxP=) N–R3 (if 9 . . . P–K5, White's best is 10 P–N3) 10 P–K4, and White has a small advantage.

PRACTICAL VARIATIONS 43–46:

1 P–Q4, P–KB4 2 P–QB4, P–K3 3 P–KN3, B–K2 4 B–N2, N–KB3 5 N–QB3, O–O 6 P–K3

| | *43* | *44* | *45* | *46* |
|---|---|---|---|---|
| *6* | — — | — — | — — | — — |
| | P–Q3 | P–Q4 | — — | — — |
| 7 | KN–K2 | KN–K2 | — — | — — |
| | P–B3 | P–B3 | — — | — — |
| *8* | O–O | P–N3 | — — | — — |
| | P–K4 | N–K5 | — — | B–Q3 |
| *9* | P–Q5 | O–O | — — | O–O |
| | Q–K1 | N–Q2 | — — | Q–K2 |
| *10* | P–K4 | B–N2 | — — | Q–B2 |
| | N–R3[1] | QN–B3 | — — | N–K5 |

| | *43* | *44* | *45* | *46* |
|---|---|---|---|---|
| *11* | = | Q–Q3 | — — | B–N2[4] |
| | | B–Q2 | P–KN4 | ± |
| *12* | | P–B3 | P–B3[2] | |
| | | NxN | NxN | |
| *13* | | NxN | NxN | |
| | | B–K1 | P–N5 | |
| *14* | | = | PxNP | |
| | | | NxP[3] | |
| | | | ± | |

*Notes to practical variations 43–46:*

[1] Inferior is 10 . . . Q–R4 11 KPxP, BxP 12 P–B5!, BPxP 13 Q–N3±.

[2] For 12 PxP, see Game 8.

[3] 15 P–K4!, BPxP 16 NxKP, PxN 17 BxP, and Boleslavski gives the following impressive variations:

1) 17 . . . N–B3 18 BxRP†, NxB 19 Q–N6†, K–R1 20 P–Q5†, R–B3 21 P–Q6, QxP 22 RxR, NxR 23 BxN†, BxB 24 QxB†, K–N1 25 R–KB1 and wins. Subvariations are: 20 . . . N–B3 21 R–B4 and mate follows; and 20 . . . B–B3 21 RxB, NxR 22 R–KB1 and wins.

2) 17 . . . B–B3 18 P–KR3, N–R3 19 BxP†, K–R1 20 Q–N6 and then 20 . . . BxP† 21 K–R1, N–B4 22 RxN, RxR 23 BxB†, P–K4 24 R–K1! Black is lost, e.g., 24 . . . QxB?? 25 Q–N8 mate. If 24 . . . PxB 25 B–N8!!, Q–Q2! 26 B–K6, QxB 27 RxQ, BxR 28 Q–R6†. Or 24 . . . Q–N4 25 BxP†, RxB 26 RxR etc.

[4] For 11 N–Q1, see Game 9.

*Dutch Defense Game 8*

*WHITE: Bronstein* *BLACK: Botvinnik*

*22d Match Game 1951*

| | WHITE | BLACK | | WHITE | BLACK | | WHITE | BLACK |
|---|---|---|---|---|---|---|---|---|
| 1 | P–Q4 | P–K3 | 14 | BxN | P–N5 | 27 | R/2–R2 | Q–B1 |
| 2 | P–QB4 | P–KB4 | 15 | PxP | NxP | 28 | N–Q3 | QR–N1 |
| 3 | P–KN3 | N–KB3 | 16 | B–R3 | N–R3 | 29 | PxP | RPxP |
| 4 | B–N2 | B–K2 | 17 | N–B4 | B–Q3 | 30 | R–R7 | R–K2 |
| 5 | N–QB3 | O–O | 18 | P–QN4 | P–R3 | 31 | N–K5 | B–K1 |
| 6 | P–K3 | P–Q4 | 19 | P–R4 | Q–K2 | 32 | P–N4! | PxP |
| 7 | KN–K2 | P–B3 | 20 | QR–N1 | P–N4 | 33 | BxN | PxB |
| 8 | P–N3 | N–K5 | 21 | B–KN2 | N–N5 | 34 | B–R4 | RxN |
| 9 | O–O | N–Q2 | 22 | B–Q2 | N–B3 | 35 | PxR | BxKP |
| 10 | B–N2 | QN–B3 | 23 | R–N2 | B–Q2 | 36 | R–KB1 | Q–N1 |
| 11 | Q–Q3 | P–KN4 | 24 | R–R1 | N–K5 | 37 | B–N3! | B–N2 |
| 12 | PxP | KPxP | 25 | B–K1 | KR–K1 | 38 | QxQ† | Resigns |
| 13 | P–B3 | NxN | 26 | Q–N3 | K–R1 | | | |

*Dutch Defense Game 9*

*WHITE: Bronstein* *BLACK: Botvinnik*

*16th Match Game 1951*

| | WHITE | BLACK | | WHITE | BLACK | | WHITE | BLACK |
|---|---|---|---|---|---|---|---|---|
| 1 | P–Q4 | P–K3 | 26 | B–N2 | R–KN1 | 51 | K–N2 | Q–Q1 |
| 2 | P–QB4 | P–KB4 | 27 | B–QB3 | N/4–K5 | 52 | K–B1 | Q–B3 |
| 3 | P–KN3 | N–KB3 | 28 | B–K1 | PxP | 53 | R–Q3 | P–R4 |
| 4 | B–N2 | B–K2 | 29 | PxP | N–R4 | 54 | P–R4 | R–N1 |
| 5 | N–QB3 | O–O | 30 | N/4–Q3 | N/4–B3 | 55 | R–Q1 | Q–N2 |
| 6 | P–K3 | P–Q4 | 31 | Q–N1 | B–KR4 | 56 | Q–KB3 | K–R3 |
| 7 | KN–K2 | P–B3 | 32 | R–N2 | B–K1 | 57 | K–N2 | R–QR1 |
| 8 | P–N3 | B–Q3 | 33 | R–R2 | RxR | 58 | R–Q3 | R–R7† |
| 9 | O–O | Q–K2 | 34 | QxR | B–N1 | 59 | K–B1 | R–R8 |
| 10 | Q–B2 | N–K5 | 35 | Q–N2 | P–R3 | 60 | Q–N2 | Q–N5 |
| 11 | N–Q1 | N–R3 | 36 | N–B4 | K–R2 | 61 | Q–KR2 | Q–N1 |
| 12 | N–N2 | B–Q2 | 37 | K–R1 | N–N5 | 62 | P–N5 | Q–QR1 |
| 13 | P–B5 | B–B2 | 38 | NxN | RxN | 63 | Q–QN2 | Q–R4 |
| 14 | N–Q3 | B–K1 | 39 | B–R3 | R–N4 | 64 | R–K3 | PxP |
| 15 | P–QN4 | N–N1 | 40 | Q–R1 | B–KB2 | 65 | R–K2 | Q–R5 |
| 16 | B–N2 | P–QR4 | 41 | B–N2 | R–N1 | 66 | K–N2 | R–Q8 |
| 17 | P–QR3 | N–Q2 | 42 | B–KB3 | N–B3 | 67 | B–B2 | Q–B5 |
| 18 | N–K5 | KN–B3 | 43 | Q–N2 | N–N5 | 68 | P–B6 | QxBP |
| 19 | N–B1 | P–KN4 | 44 | Q–K2 | N–B3 | 69 | Q–N4 | Q–K1 |
| 20 | P–B3 | P–N5 | 45 | R–N1 | N–K5 | 70 | R–B2 | R–Q6 |
| 21 | N/1–Q3 | PxBP | 46 | R–B1 | Q–K1 | 71 | B–K1 | Q–KN1 |
| 22 | BxP | N–K5 | 47 | Q–Q3 | BxN | 72 | Q–K7 | RxP† |
| 23 | QR–K1 | QN–B3 | 48 | KPxB | B–R4 | 73 | BxR | QxB† |
| 24 | N–B4 | K–R1 | 49 | Q–R3 | BxB | 74 | K–R1 | Q–K8† |
| 25 | R–K2 | N–N4 | 50 | RxB | R–N2 | 75 | K–R2 | . . . |
| | | | | | | | Draw | |

# part 6—NON-FIANCHETTO VARIATION

1 P–Q4, P–KB4
2 P–QB4, P–K3
3 N–QB3, B–N5
4 Q–B2[A], N–KB3
5 P–K3, O–O
6 B–Q3, P–Q3[B]

KEY POSITION 6

OBSERVATIONS ON KEY POSITION 6

[A] Most common, but 4 Q–N3 and 4 P–K3 can both be played.

[B] 6 . . . P–QN3 is worth a try, e.g., 7 P–B3, B–N2 8 B–Q2, P–B4! 9 KN–K2, N–B3=.

In this variation White foregoes the fianchetto of his King Bishop in favor of its development to Q3. By exerting pressure on Black's King Bishop Pawn, White hopes to prevent the normal freeing move . . . P–K4. Black must be careful not to give White free rein as, in that event, White's control of the center forms the basis for a dangerous Kingside assault.

IDEA VARIATIONS 13 AND 14:

(13) 7 B–Q2, P–B4 8 N–B3, N–B3 (stronger is 8 . . . BxN 9 BxB, P–QN3 followed by . . . B–N2) 9 O–O–O, B–Q2 10 P–KR3, PxP 11 PxP, R–K1 12 P–KN4±. White has the ideal position — control of the center and good Kingside attacking chances.

(14) 7 KN–K2, P–B4 8 P–QR3 (8 P–Q5, BxN† favors Black), BxN† 9 NxB, N–B3 10 PxP, PxP 11 P–QN3, B–Q2 12 B–N2, N–K4 13 B–K2 (better is 13 O–O–O!; see Prac. Var. 47), B–B3 14 P–B3, N–R4 15 N–Q1 (if 15 O–O, then 15 . . . Q–N4∓), N–N3 16 Q–B3, Q–N4 17 P–KN3, P–K4 with excellent counterchances for Black.

PRACTICAL VARIATIONS 47-50:

1 P–Q4, P–KB4 2 P–QB4, P–K3 3 N–QB3, B–N5 4 Q–B2, N–KB3 5 P–K3, O–O 6 B–Q3, P–Q3

| | *47* | *48* | *49* | *50* |
|---|---|---|---|---|
| 7 | KN–K2 | – – | – – | N–B3 |
| | P–B4 | – – | – – | P–B4 |
| 8 | P–QR3 | – – | P–Q5 | B–Q2 |
| | BxN† | B–R4 | BxN† | N–B3 |
| 9 | NxB | P–Q5 | NxB | O–O–O |
| | N–B3 | PxP | PxP | B–Q2 |

| | 47 | 48 | 49 | 50 |
|---|---|---|---|---|
| 10 | PxP | PxP | PxP | P–KR3 |
| | PxP | N–N5 | N–N5 | PxP[2] |
| 11 | P–QN3 | N–B4 | O–O | PxP |
| | B–Q2 | N–K4 | N–R3 | R–B1 |
| 12 | B–N2 | B–K2 | ∓ | P–N4 |
| | N–K4 | Q–K2 | | N–K2 |
| 13 | O–O–O! | O–O | | PxP |
| | NxB† | N–R3 | | NxP |
| 14 | RxN | P–QN3 | | P–Q5 |
| | Q–K2 | B–Q2 | | ± |
| 15 | KR–Q1 | B–N2 | | |
| | B–B3 | N–B2[1] | | |
| | ± | ± | | |

*Notes to practical variations 47–50:*

[1] 16 QR–Q1, P–QN4 17 N–N1 (Taimanov–Botvinnik, 3rd Match Game 1953).

[2] Better is 10 . . . BxN 11 BxB, P–QR3 12 P–KN4, N–K2=.

---

## part 7—STAUNTON GAMBIT

### OBSERVATIONS ON KEY POSITION 7

1 P–Q4, P–KB4
2 P–K4, PxP[A]
3 N–QB3, N–KB3

KEY POSITION 7

[A] Declining the gambit is not advisable: 2 . . . P–Q3 3 PxP, BxP 4 Q–B3, Q–B1 5 B–Q3 and White has the superior position.

Latest analysis indicates that the Staunton Gambit, although yielding no clear advantage, is certainly a playable alternative to the more routine lines. White, in addition to obtaining sharp attacking chances for his Pawn, places his opponent at a psychological disadvantage. Black, in choosing to play the Dutch Defense, is in effect announcing his aggressive intentions. When forced to play against the Staunton, he must instead resign himself to an accurate and stubborn defense, in all probability not suited to his nature.

One of White's trumps in this opening is the control of the QR2–KN8 diagonal by his King Bishop Generally, . . . P–K3 is not a sufficient countermeasure; White can frequently re-open the diagonal with a timely P–Q5. For this reason, Black normally prefers to close the diagonal by playing . . . P–Q4, thus accepting a permanent weakness at his K4.

IDEA VARIATIONS 15 AND 16:

(15) 4 P–B3, P–Q4 (for alternatives, see Prac. Var. 64–66) 5 PxP, PxP 6 B–N5, B–B4 7 B–QB4 (seizing the key diagonal!), N–B3 8 KN–K2, Q–Q2 9 O–O, P–K3 (weaker is 9 . . . P–K4? because of 10 BxN, PxB 11 N–Q5, B–N2 12 RxB, QxR 13 NxQBP† and White wins) 10 Q–K1, O–O–O 11 R–Q1 with good chances for White.

(16) 4 B–KN5, P–KN3 5 P–B3, PxP 6 NxP, P–Q4 (this strengthening of the center is absolutely necessary) 7 N–K5 (taking immediate advantage of Black's weak square), B–N2 8 Q–Q2, O–O 9 O–O–O. White has more than adequate compensation for his Pawn. It should be noted that 9 . . . N–N5 fails because of 10 NxQP!

*Dutch Defense Game 10*

*WHITE: Reti* *BLACK: Euwe*

*Match 1920*

| WHITE | BLACK | WHITE | BLACK |
|---|---|---|---|
| 1 P–Q4 | P–KB4 | 10 R–QN1 | NxP |
| 2 P–K4 | PxP | 11 NxN! | QxR† |
| 3 N–QB3 | N–KB3 | 12 K–B2 | QxR |
| 4 B–KN5 | P–KN3 | 13 BxP | P–Q3 |
| 5 P–B3 | PxP | 14 BxP | N–B3 |
| 6 NxP | B–N2 | 15 B–N5 | B–Q2 |
| 7 B–Q3 | P–B4? | 16 BxN | PxB |
| 8 P–Q5 | Q–N3 | 17 Q–K2† | Resigns |
| 9 Q–Q2 | QxP? | | |

*Dutch Defense Game 11*

*WHITE: Reshevsky* *BLACK: Botvinnik*

*World Championship 1948*

| WHITE | BLACK | WHITE | BLACK |
|---|---|---|---|
| 1 P–Q4 | P–K3 | 8 P–K4 | PxP |
| 2 P–QB4 | P–KB4 | 9 N–B4 | P–B3 |
| 3 P–KN3 | N–KB3 | 10 QNxP | NxN |
| 4 B–N2 | B–K2 | 11 BxN | P–K4 |
| 5 N–KR3 | O–O | 12 N–N2 | N–Q2 |
| 6 O–O | P–Q3 | 13 N–K3 | PxP |
| 7 N–B3 | Q–K1 | 14 QxP | N–K4 |

| WHITE | BLACK | WHITE | BLACK |
|---|---|---|---|
| 15 P–B4 | N–N5 | 25 Q–B7 | Q–QB4 |
| 16 NxN | BxN | 26 R–K1 | R–QB1 |
| 17 R–K1 | B–B3 | 27 QxNP | B–Q5 |
| 18 Q–Q3 | Q–R4 | 28 K–B2? | BxR† |
| 19 B–Q2 | KR–K1 | 29 RxB | Q–Q5 |
| 20 QR–N1? | R–K2? | 30 Q–N3 | Q–Q7† |
| 21 B–N4 | QR–K1 | 31 K–N1 | Q–B8† |
| 22 BxQP | R–K3 | 32 K–B2 | Q–Q7† |
| 23 R–K3 | RxQB? | Draw | |
| 24 QxR | R–Q1 | | |

*Dutch Defense Game 12*

*WHITE: Bogoljubov* *BLACK: Alekhine*

*Hastings 1922*

| WHITE | BLACK | WHITE | BLACK |
|---|---|---|---|
| 1 P–Q4 | P–KB4 | 27 N–Q2 | P–QN4 |
| 2 P–QB4 | N–KB3 | 28 N–Q1 | N–Q6 |
| 3 P–KN3 | P–K3 | 29 RxP | P–N5! |
| 4 B–N2 | B–N5† | 30 RxR | PxQ! |
| 5 B–Q2! | BxB | 31 RxQ | P–B7! |
| 6 NxB | N–B3 | 32 RxR† | K–R2 |
| 7 KN–B3 | O–O | 33 N–B2 | P–B8(Q)† |
| 8 O–O | P–Q3 | 34 N–B1 | N–K8 |
| 9 Q–N3 | K–R1 | 35 R–R2 | QxBP |
| 10 Q–B3 | P–K4 | 36 R–QN8 | B–N4 |
| 11 P–K3 | P–QR4 | 37 RxB | QxR |
| 12 P–N3 | Q–K1 | 38 P–N4 | N–B6† |
| 13 P–QR3 | Q–R4 | 39 BxN | PxB |
| 14 P–KR4 | N–KN5 | 40 PxP | Q–K7 |
| 15 N–N5 | B–Q2 | 41 P–Q5 | K–N1 |
| 16 P–B3 | N–B3 | 42 P–R5 | K–R2 |
| 17 P–B4 | P–K5 | 43 P–K4 | NxKP |
| 18 KR–Q1 | P–R3 | 44 NxN | QxN |
| 19 N–R3 | P–Q4 | 45 P–Q6 | PxP |
| 20 N–B1 | N–K2 | 46 P–B6 | PxP |
| 21 P–R4 | N–B3 | 47 R–Q2 | Q–K7 |
| 22 R–Q2 | N–QN5 | 48 RxQ | PxR |
| 23 B–R1 | Q–K1 | 49 K–B2 | PxN(Q)† |
| 24 R–KN2 | PxP | 50 KxQ | K–N2 |
| 25 PxP | BxP | and Black won | |
| 26 N–B2 | B–Q2 | | |

## PRACTICAL VARIATIONS 51–69:
### 1 P–Q4, P–KB4 2 P–K4, PxP 3 N–QB3, N–KB3

| | 51 | 52 | 53 | 54 | 55 | 56 | 57 | 58 | 59 |
|---|---|---|---|---|---|---|---|---|---|
| 4 | B–KN5 | – – | – – | – – | – – | B–KN5 | – – | – – | – – |
| | P–K3 | P–KN3 | – – | – – | – – | P–B3 | – – | – – | N–B3[7] |
| 5 | NxP | P–B3 | – – | P–KR4 | – – | P–B3 | – – | – – | P–Q5 |
| | B–K2 | PxP | P–Q4 | B–N2 | P–Q4 | Q–R4 | PxP | – – | N–K4 |
| 6 | BxN[1] | NxP | PxP | P–R5 | P–R5 | B–Q2![4] | NxP | – – | Q–Q4 |
| | BxB | P–Q4![2] | PxP | NxP[3] | B–B4 | P–K6 | P–KN3 | P–Q4[6] | N–B2 |
| 7 | N–KB3 | N–K5! | B–QB4 | RxN | BxN | BxP | Q–Q2 | B–Q3 | BxN |
| | P–Q4 | B–N2 | N–B3 | PxR | PxB | P–K4 | B–N2 | B–N5 | KPxB |
| 8 | NxB† | Q–Q2 | B–N5 | QxP† | P–KN4 | Q–Q2[5] | O–O–O | P–KR3 | NxP |
| | PxN | O–O | B–Q2 | K–B1 | B–K3 | B–N5 | ± | BxN | P–KB4![8] |
| 9 | Q–Q2 | O–O–O | KN–K2 | N–Q5 | PxP | KN–K2 | | QxB | N–N3 |
| | N–B3 | ± | P–QR3 | N–B3 | Q–Q2 | O–O | | QN–Q2 | P–KN3 |
| 10 | O–O–O | | BxN | B–QB4 | ∓ | O–O–O | | O–O–O | O–O–O |
| | B–Q2 | | BxB | ± | | ± | | ± | B–R3† |
| 11 | B–N5 | | O–O | | | | | | K–N1 |
| | Q–K2 | | B–N2 | | | | | | O–O |
| 12 | KR–K1 | | N–B4 | | | | | | N–B3 |
| | O–O–O | | ± | | | | | | = |
| | = | | | | | | | | |

*Notes to practical variations 51–69:*

[1] Yet to be tested is 6 NxN†, BxN 7 P–KR4 with sharp play.

[2] 6 . . . B–N2 7 B–QB4, P–B3 8 P–Q5±. For 6 . . . B–N2 7 B–Q3, see Game 10.

[3] Better is 6 . . . P–Q4 7 P–R6, B–B1 8 Q–Q2=.

[4] 6 Q–Q2, P–K4! with equality.

[5] 8 PxP, QxKP 9 Q–Q2, B–N5 leads to a level game.

[6] Or 6 . . . P–K3 7 B–Q3, B–K2 8 N–K5!±.

| 60 | 61 | 62 | 63 | 64 | 65 | 66 | 67 | 68 | 69 |
|---|---|---|---|---|---|---|---|---|---|
| — — | — — | P–B3 | — — | — — | — — | — — | P–KN4 | — — | — — |
| — — | — — | P–Q4 | — — | N–B3 | PxP | — — | P–KR3! | P–Q4[12] | — — |
| — — | — — | B–N5 | — — | PxP | NxP | — — | P–N5 | P–N5 | — — |
| — — | — — | B–B4 | N–B3 | P–K4 | P–Q4 | P–K3 | PxP | N–N1 | B–N5 |
| — — | — — | PxP | PxP | PxP | N–K5! | B–Q3 | BxP | P–B3 | B–K2 |
| — — | — — | PxP | KNxP | NxP/4 | P–KN3[11] | B–K2 | P–Q4! | PxP | BxB |
| — — | B–R4 | Q–K2[9] | NxN | N–B3 | B–KB4 | Q–K2 | P–B3 | QxP | QxB |
| — — | P–KN4 | N–B3 | PxN | P–Q3 | B–N2 | P–B4 | B–B4 | N–QB3 | KN–Q2 |
| O–O–O | B–N3 | BxN | P–Q5 | B–KB4 | Q–Q2 | PxP | ∓ | B–K3 | NxQP |
| B–Q3 | B–N2 | KPxB | N–K4 | N–N3[10] | O–O | BxP | | P–K4 | N–QB3 |
| NxP | O–O–O | O–O–O | Q–Q4 | B–N3 | O–O–O | B–KN5 | | = | QxP |
| B–K4 | O–O | B–Q3 | N–B2 | N–R4 | ± | O–O | | | P–K4 |
| Q–K3 | NxP | NxP | B–K3 | B–B2 | | KR–B1 | | | PxP |
| P–KB4 | P–B3 | O–O | P–K3 | N/4–B5 | | ± | | | N–B4 |
| P–KB4 | NxN† | NxB | B–QB4 | B–Q4 | | | | | Q–N2 |
| PxN | PxN | PxN | ± | P–B3 | | | | | N–Q5 |
| QxKP | = | = | | Q–Q2 | | | | | N–K3 |
| ± | | | | ± | | | | | Q–Q2 |
| | | | | | | | | | ∓ |

---

[7] 4 . . . P–QN3 5 B–QB4, P–K3 6 P–Q5!±.

[8] Stronger than 8 . . . B–Q3 9 NxB†, NxN 10 B–Q3, Q–K2† 11 K–Q2!±.

[9] For 7 B–QB4, see Idea Var. 15.

[10] Or 9 . . . NxN 10 QxN, B–N5 11 Q–B2, B–K2 12 B–B4±.

[11] 6 . . . B–B4 is met by 7 P–KN4!, e.g., 7 . . . B–K3 8 P–N5, N–K5 9 B–R3!±.

[12] Inferior is 4 . . . P–K3 5 P–N5, N–Q4 6 NxP±.

## SUPPLEMENTARY VARIATIONS 1–7:
## 1 P–Q4, P–KB4

| | *1* | *2* | *3* | *4* | *5* | *6* | *7* |
|---|---|---|---|---|---|---|---|
| *2* | B–N5 | N–QB3 | P–KN3 | P–QB4 | – – | – – | Q–Q3[10] |
| | P–KN3! | P–Q4 | P–K3 | P–K3 | – – | – – | P–K3 |
| *3* | N–QB3[1] | P–B3 | B–N2 | P–KN3 | – – | – – | P–KN4 |
| | B–N2 | N–KB3 | N–KB3 | N–KB3 | – – | – – | PxP |
| *4* | P–K4 | P–K4 | N–KR3 | B–N2 | – – | – – | P–KR3 |
| | PxP | QPxP | B–K2 | B–N5† | – – | – – | PxP |
| *5* | NxP | PxP | O–O | B–Q2! | – – | – – | NxP |
| | P–Q4! | PxP[2] | O–O | BxB† | Q–K2 | B–K2 | ± |
| *6* | N–QB3 | ∓ | P–QB4 | QxB[6] | B–B3[8] | Q–N3! | |
| | N–KB3 | | P–Q3[3] | O–O | O–O | P–Q4[9] | |
| *7* | B–Q3 | | N–B3 | N–QB3 | P–QR3 | B–N4! | |
| | N–B3 | | Q–K1 | P–Q3 | BxB† | BxB† | |
| *8* | KN–K2 | | P–K4[4] | N–B3 | NxB | QxB | |
| | O–O | | PxP[5] | N–B3[7] | P–Q3 | N–B3 | |
| *9* | O–O | | ∓ | R–Q1 | = | Q–R4! | |
| | P–K4! | | | ± | | O–O | |
| *10* | | | | | | N–KB3 | |
| | | | | | | ± | |

*Notes to supplementary variations 1–7:*

[1] 3 P–KR4, B–N2 4 N–KR3, P–B4! favors Black.

[2] Transposing into the Staunton Gambit; see Part 7.

[3] 6 . . . P–Q4 is strongly met by 7 N–B3, P–B3 8 N–B4! etc.

[4] More precise is 8 N–B4.

[5] See Game 11.

[6] For 6 NxB, see Game 12.

[7] After 8 . . . N–K5, there follows 9 NxN, PxN 10 N–N5, P–Q4 11 R–QB1±.

[8] Recommended by Vidmar. Other moves offer no more.

[9] 6 . . . P–B3 7 N–QB3, P–Q3 8 P–K4 also gives White the edge.

[10] Ulvestad's idea.

# chapter 34—Grunfeld-Indian Defense

The characteristic moves of this opening are 1 P–Q4, N–KB3 2 P–QB4, P–KN3 3 N–QB3[1], P–Q4.

The singular idea of the defense, Black's 3 . . . P–Q4, was conceived about 1922 when the Viennese grandmaster, Ernst Grünfeld, was attempting to bolster Black's counterplay in the regular King's Indian. By this early thrust together with a later exchange of the Queen Pawn, Black exposes the enemy Queen Pawn to direct pressure on the Queen file as well as on the long diagonal (Black's KR1–QR8). The action is particularly effective in conjunction with the challenging . . . P–QB4.

On the minus side of the position, from Black's point of view, the exchange of Black's Queen Pawn for White's Queen Bishop Pawn leaves White temporarily in control of the center.

The ensuing play is sharp and precise. Black tries to eliminate White's tenuous hold on the center, while White hopes to be able to fortify it. Along these lines the issue is drawn. Success or failure in the early action is reflected in the entire course of the game.

Up to now experience credits the defense for an interesting and even scintillating middle game.

[1] For 3 P–KN3, B–N2 4 B–N2, P–Q4 5 PxP, NxP see Part 7, "Counter-Thrust Variation," of the King's Indian Defense.

---

## part 1—GRUNFELD GAMBIT

1 P–Q4, N–KB3
2 P–QB4, P–KN3
3 N–QB3, P–Q4
4 B–B4[A], B–N2[B]
5 P–K3, O–O[C]
6 PxP, NxP
7 NxN, QxN
8 BxP

KEY POSITION 1

### OBSERVATIONS ON KEY POSITION 1

[A] One of the sharpest lines.

[B] Other possibilities are (1) 4 . . . P–B3 (Slav fianchetto), (2) 4 . . . N–R4? 5 B–K5, P–KB3 6 B–N3, NxB 7 RPxN± and (3) 4 . . . PxP? 5 P–K4±.

[C] The following Pawn sacrifice is consistent with his plans.

Acceptance of the Pawn leaves White lagging in development. Black must exploit this factor by rapid mobilization of his forces. The two methods he can use begin with (1) 8 . . . N–R3 and (2) 8 . . . N–B3.

The first method enables Black to recover the Pawn rather easily, though hardly with a plus in position. The second is more enterprising. Here Black plays with abandon, finally sacrificing a piece. The appraisal of this plan, however, is not definitive.

IDEA VARIATIONS 1–3:

(1) 8 . . . N–R3 9 BxN (other moves are weak, e.g., 9 B–N3, B–B4 10 N–K2, Q–R4† 11 N–B3, N–N5 12 R–B1, NxP 13 R–R1, NxN∓, as in Fairhurst–Pachman, Dublin 1957), QxNP (also important is 9 . . . PxB; see Idea Var. 2) 10 Q–B3, QxQ 11 NxQ, PxB 12 R–QB1, P–QR4 (heading for a draw after 13 BxP, B–N2 14 K–K2, B–R3† 15 K–Q2, B–N2; for 12 . . . B–N5, see Game 1) 13 R–KN1, P–R5 14 R–N5±.

(2) 8 . . . N–R3 9 BxN, PxB 10 N–B3 (inferior is 10 Q–B3?, e.g., 10 . . . Q–QN4! 11 QxR, QxP 12 R–Q1, Q–B6† 13 R–Q2, B–N5! and Black wins), B–N2! (after 10 . . . Q–N2 11 B–N3, QxP 12 O–O, B–K3 13 Q–Q2!, White has the initiative; for 10 . . . B–N5, see Game 2. 11 O–O, QR–B1 12 B–N3, R–B3, and, according to Yugoslav analyst Vukovic, Black has sufficient compensation for the Pawn.

(3) 8 . . . N–B3 9 N–K2 (the powerful Keres move; 9 N–B3, B–N5 or 9 B–K2, B–B4! 10 B–B3, Q–N4! is easier for Black), B–N5 10 P–B3, BxBP (unfavorable for Black is 10 . . . QR–B1 11 N–B3!) 11 PxB, QxBP 12 R–KN1, QxP 13 B–B4, Q–K5 14 B–N2, Q–B4 15 BxN (it is dangerous to postpone the exchange, e.g., 15 Q–Q2, P–K4! 16 BxN, KPxB 17 B–B3, KR–K1 with a strong attack), PxB 16 Q–Q2 (more or less the most important position of the Gambit Variation; the analysis is by Trifunovic), P–B4! (for 16 . . . KR–Q1, see Prac. Var. 4) 17 P–Q5 (if 17 R–N5, Black obtains fine counterplay with 17 . . . Q–K5 18 PxP, P–K4 19 B–K3, QR–Q1), KR–Q1 18 O–O–O, P–K3 19 Q–B2 (better than 19 P–Q6, QR–N1 20 P–N3, P–B5! etc.), QxQ† 20 KxQ, PxP with a difficult game and chances for both sides.

*Grunfeld-Indian Defense Game 1*
*WHITE: Najdorf* — *BLACK: Lilienthal*
*Candidates' Tournament, Budapest 1950*

| WHITE | BLACK | WHITE | BLACK |
|---|---|---|---|
| 1 P–Q4 | N–KB3 | 6 PxP | NxP |
| 2 P–QB4 | P–KN3 | 7 NxN | QxN |
| 3 N–QB3 | P–Q4 | 8 BxP | N–R3 |
| 4 B–B4 | B–N2 | 9 BxN | QxNP |
| 5 P–K3 | O–O | 10 Q–B3 | QxQ |

| | WHITE | BLACK | | WHITE | BLACK |
|---|---|---|---|---|---|
| 11 | NxQ | PxB | 27 | R–Q1 | P–N5 |
| 12 | R–QB1 | B–N5 | 28 | P–N4 | B–R5 |
| 13 | N–Q2 | KR–B1 | 29 | R–Q4 | P–K4 |
| 14 | O–O | B–Q2 | 30 | R–Q2 | P–B5 |
| 15 | R–B3 | P–B4? | 31 | N–B4 | P–N6 |
| 16 | KR–B1 | P–K3 | 32 | RPxP | PxNP |
| 17 | P–QR3 | K–B2 | 33 | PxP | RxP |
| 18 | K–B1 | K–K2 | 34 | R–KR2 | B–N4 |
| 19 | K–K1 | P–N4 | 35 | RxP† | K–K3 |
| 20 | R–B5 | K–K1 | 36 | RxP | K–Q4 |
| 21 | N–B4 | B–B1 | 37 | P–R4 | BxN |
| 22 | B–Q6 | RxR | 38 | R–Q7† | K–K5 |
| 23 | PxR | BxB | 39 | KxB | RxP |
| 24 | NxB† | K–K2 | 40 | P–N5 | PxP† |
| 25 | K–Q2 | B–B3 | 41 | PxP | Resigns |
| 26 | K–B3 | R–KN1 | | | |

*Grunfeld-Indian Defense Game 2*

*WHITE: Najdorf* *BLACK: Unzicker*

*Interzonal Tournament, Göteborg 1955*

| | WHITE | BLACK | | WHITE | BLACK | | WHITE | BLACK |
|---|---|---|---|---|---|---|---|---|
| 1 | P–QB4 | N–KB3 | 27 | PxB | R–N2 | 53 | K–N2 | K–R2 |
| 2 | N–QB3 | P–Q4 | 28 | P–Q5 | P–B3 | 54 | R–K6 | K–N2 |
| 3 | P–Q4 | P–KN3 | 29 | P–K4 | K–B2 | 55 | R–QR6 | R–B4 |
| 4 | B–B4 | B–N2 | 30 | K–N2 | P–QR4 | 56 | N–N2 | R–B6 |
| 5 | P–K3 | O–O | 31 | R–B8 | B–Q3 | 57 | R–R5 | K–N3 |
| 6 | PxP | NxP | 32 | N–B4 | B–B5 | 58 | R–Q5 | B–B2 |
| 7 | NxN | QxN | 33 | R–QR8 | RxP | 59 | N–Q3 | K–B3 |
| 8 | BxP | N–R3 | 34 | RxP† | K–K1 | 60 | N–B5 | K–N3 |
| 9 | BxN | PxB | 35 | RxP | R–Q6 | 61 | N–K4 | R–R6 |
| 10 | N–B3! | B–N5 | 36 | R–R8† | K–K2 | 62 | R–N5† | K–R3 |
| 11 | O–O | Q–N2 | 37 | R–R7† | K–K1 | 63 | R–QB5 | B–B5 |
| 12 | B–N3 | QxP | 38 | R–R6 | K–K2 | 64 | R–B6† | K–N2 |
| 13 | Q–N3 | QxQ | 39 | N–R5 | P–B4 | 65 | R–B6 | B–B2 |
| 14 | PxQ | B–Q2 | 40 | RxP | PxP | 66 | R–B5 | K–N3 |
| 15 | KR–B1 | QR–B1 | 41 | R–K6† | K–B2 | 67 | R–N5† | K–R3 |
| 16 | P–R3 | B–N4 | 42 | RxKP | B–Q7 | 68 | R–N8 | B–K4 |
| 17 | N–Q2 | KR–Q1 | 43 | N–B4 | RxP | 69 | R–K8 | B–B5 |
| 18 | N–K4 | B–B1 | 44 | K–N3 | B–B6 | 70 | R–KB8 | B–K4 |
| 19 | B–B7 | R–K1 | 45 | N–K3 | R–QR4 | 71 | R–K8 | B–B5 |
| 20 | B–R5 | P–R3 | 46 | R–QB4 | B–B3 | 72 | R–KB8 | B–K4 |
| 21 | B–N4 | RxR† | 47 | R–B7† | K–N3 | 73 | P–B4 | R–R7† |
| 22 | RxR | R–N1 | 48 | R–B6 | K–N2 | 74 | K–B3 | R–R6† |
| 23 | N–Q2 | R–N2 | 49 | K–N4 | P–R4† | 75 | K–K2 | BxP |
| 24 | R–B8 | B–Q2 | 50 | K–B3 | B–N4 | 76 | R–B6† | K–N2 |
| 25 | R–Q8 | BxP | 51 | N–B4 | R–B4† | 77 | RxB | RxP |
| 26 | BxP | RxB | 52 | K–N3 | B–B5† | | Draw | |

PRACTICAL VARIATIONS 1-4:

1 P–Q4, N–KB3 2 P–QB4, P–KN3 3 N–QB3, P–Q4 4 B–B4, B–N2 5 P–K3, O–O 6 PxP, NxP 7 NxN, QxN 8 BxP

| | *1* | *2* | *3* | *4* |
|---|---|---|---|---|
| *8* | – – | – – | – – | – – |
| | N–R3 | – – | N–B3 | – – |
| *9* | BxN | – – | N–K2 | – – |
| | QxNP | PxB | B–N5 | – – |
| *10* | Q–B3 | Q–B3? | P–B3 | BxBP |
| | QxQ | Q–QN4! | QR–B1? | PxB |
| *11* | NxQ | N–K2[3] | N–B3! | QxBP |
| | PxB | Q–N5† | Q–Q2! | R–KN1 |
| *12* | R–KN1[1] | N–B3 | B–KB4! | QxP |
| | B–N2 | B–N2 | P–K4 | B–B4 |
| *13* | K–K2 | Q–K2 | BxP | Q–K5 |
| | P–B3 | BxNP | NxB | B–N2 |
| *14* | KR–Q1 | R–KN1 | PxN | Q–B4 |
| | QR–B1 | B–B6! | QxQ† | BxN |
| *15* | QR–B1 | Q–Q3 | RxQ | PxB |
| | B–Q4[2] | QR–B1[4] | B–K3 | Q–Q2 |
| *16* | = | ∓ | P–B4 | KR–Q1 |
| | | | ± | O–O–O |
| *17* | | | | P–K4 |
| | | | | BxP![5] |
| *18* | | | | ± |

1 P–Q4, N–KB3
2 P–QB4, P–KN3
3 N–QB3, P–Q4
4 B–B4, B–N2
5 P–K3, O–O

KEY POSITION 2

*Notes to practical variations 1–4:*

[1] For 12 R–QB1 see Idea Var. 1.

[2] Stahlberg–Donner, 1954.

[3] 11 Q–K2 is met by . . . Q–N2. For 11 QxR see Idea Var. 2.

[4] Correspondence Game, DeCarbonnel–Koch, 1955. Black won quickly.

[5] Bolbochan–Marini, 1950. The game continued 18 . . . BxB 19 R–N5, Q–B7 20 RxB, QxRP 21 Q–K3, R–Q4 22 N–B4!

## part 2—GRUNFELD GAMBIT DECLINED

OBSERVATIONS ON KEY POSITION 2

White need not play to accept the gambit Pawn, for he enjoys several alternatives, each leading to a lively game. In any case, however, Black is obliged to enforce the characteristic counter-thrust, . . . P–QB4, to restore the balance in the center. If successful in this respect, Black will do well. Black can also rely on . . . P–QB3 for a safe but passive defense.

IDEA VARIATIONS 4–6:

(4) 6 N–B3 (this is convenient for Black, as it permits the immediate . . . P–B4), P–B4! 7 QPxP (for Abraham's move, 7 B–K5, see Prac. Var. 5) Q–R4 (if 7 . . . N–K5, the correct reply is 8 NxP) 8 Q–N3, N–K5 9 B–K5, NxN 10 BxN, BxB† 11 QxB, QxQ† 12 PxQ, PxP 13 BxP, N–Q2, with an even game (Gligoric–Boleslavski, Warsaw 1947).

(5) 6 R–B1, P–B4 (here, too, this is a key move, although Black must be familiar with the ensuing finesses; 6 . . . P–B3 also will do) 7 QPxP, B–K3! (7 . . . Q–R4 leads to great complications; see Prac. Var. 6 and 7 and Game 3) 8 N–B3 (the end game after 8 Q–N3, N–R3 9 QxP, NxP favors Black, as does 8 PxP, NxP 9 NxN, BxN 10 P–QN3, Q–R4† 11 Q–Q2, QxQ† 12 KxQ, R–Q1), N–B3 (better than 8 . . . Q–R4 9 Q–R4, QxP 10 Q–N5 etc.) 9 B–K2 (9 Q–R4 is well met by 9 . . . N–K5!, as in Ragosin–Botvinnik, 1940), Q–R4 10 O–O, PxP 11 N–KN5, QR–Q1 12 Q–R4, QxQ 13 NxQ, B–Q2 14 BxP, P–K4 15 B–KN3, N–QR4 16 B–N3, NxB 17 PxN, N–Q4 and Black has a good game. White's extra Pawn is of little significance.

(6) 6 Q–N3 (the best way to decline the gambit), P–B4 (after 6 . . . PxP 7 BxP, Black probably can play 7 . . . N–B3 with impunity, but 7 . . . P–B4 8 PxP, Q–R4 9 N–B3!, QxBP 10 N–K5 seems to favor White; for 6 . . . P–B3 7 N–B3, Q–R4!, see Prac. Var. 8) 7 BPxP (QPxP also offers a chance for a slight advantage, e.g., 7 . . . N–K5! 8 PxP, Q–R4 9 N–K2, NxQBP [9 . . . N–R3! is better] 10 Q–Q1!, Q–N5 11 Q–Q2!, QxP 12 QxQ, N–Q6† 13 K–Q2, NxQ 14 N–Q4 etc.; for 10 . . . P–K4 in this line see Game 4), PxP 8 PxP, QN–Q2 (the Pawn sacrifice, 8 . . . P–K3, is too risky, as shown in Reshevsky–Szabo, Zurich 1953) 9 B–K2, N–N3 10 B–B3, B–B4 (or 10 . . . B–N5 11 BxB, NxB 12 N–B3, N–B3 13 P–Q6) 11 R–Q1, Q–Q2 12 P–KR3, P–KR4 13 KN–K2, QR–Q1 with an even game.

*Grunfeld-Indian Defense Game 3*

*WHITE: Tolush* *BLACK: Botvinnik*

*Moscow Tournament 1939*

| | WHITE | BLACK | | WHITE | BLACK | | WHITE | BLACK |
|---|---|---|---|---|---|---|---|---|
| 1 | P–Q4 | N–KB3 | 14 | R–Q1 | R–Q1 | 27 | BxR | N–K4 |
| 2 | P–QB4 | P–KN3 | 15 | Q–B1 | Q–R4† | 28 | K–K2 | Q–N4† |
| 3 | N–QB3 | P–Q4 | 16 | R–Q2 | R–Q4! | 29 | B–Q3 | NxB |
| 4 | B–B4 | B–N2 | 17 | N–K2 | RxP | 30 | RxN | P–QR4 |
| 5 | P–K3 | O–O | 18 | N–B3 | BxN | 31 | KR–Q1 | Q–B5 |
| 6 | R–B1 | P–B4 | 19 | PxB | RxP | 32 | K–B3 | P–QN4 |
| 7 | QPxP | Q–R4 | 20 | Q–N2 | R–R6 | 33 | R–Q7 | P–R5 |
| 8 | PxP | R–Q1 | 21 | Q–N5 | Q–B6 | 34 | R–R7 | P–N5! |
| 9 | Q–Q2 | NxP | 22 | Q–N2 | Q–B4 | 35 | R–Q8† | K–N2 |
| 10 | B–B7!? | QxB | 23 | Q–N1 | BxP | 36 | R/8–QR8 | P–R6 |
| 11 | NxN | RxN! | 24 | RxB | Q–R4† | 37 | P–N3 | Q–N4 |
| 12 | QxR | B–K3 | 25 | R–Q2 | R–R8 | | Resigns | |
| 13 | Q–Q2 | N–B3 | 26 | B–Q3 | RxQ† | | | |

*Grunfeld-Indian Defense Game 4*

*WHITE: Reshevsky* *BLACK: Kashdan*

*1st Match Game 1942*

| | WHITE | BLACK | | WHITE | BLACK |
|---|---|---|---|---|---|
| 1 | P–Q4 | N–KB3 | 20 | NPxP | PxP |
| 2 | P–QB4 | P–KN3 | 21 | BxP | N–Q2 |
| 3 | N–QB3 | P–Q4 | 22 | O–O | QR–K1 |
| 4 | B–B4 | B–N2 | 23 | B–Q4 | N–K4 |
| 5 | P–K3 | O–O | 24 | K–R1 | P–QR3 |
| 6 | Q–N3 | P–B4!? | 25 | P–Q6! | K–R1 |
| 7 | QPxP | N–K5 | 26 | P–N4! | Q–Q1 |
| 8 | PxP | Q–R4 | 27 | N–Q5 | P–N5?! |
| 9 | N–K2 | NxQBP | 28 | N–B7 | PxP |
| 10 | Q–Q1 | P–K4 | 29 | BxBP! | NxB |
| 11 | B–N5 | P–B3 | 30 | BxB† | KxB |
| 12 | P–QR3 | N–K5 | 31 | NxR† | QxN |
| 13 | B–R4 | P–KN4 | 32 | R–B7† | K–N1 |
| 14 | B–N3 | P–B4 | 33 | R–K7! | Q–N3 |
| 15 | P–B3 | NxN | 34 | Q–Q5† | K–R1 |
| 16 | NxN | P–B5 | 35 | RxN | |
| 17 | B–B2 | P–K5 | | In a losing position, | |
| 18 | R–B1 | B–B4 | | Black overstepped the | |
| 19 | B–K2 | KPxP | | time limit. | |

PRACTICAL VARIATIONS 5–8:

1 P–Q4, N–KB3 2 P–QB4, P–KN3 3 N–QB3, P–Q4 4 B–B4, B–N2 5 P–K3, O–O

| | 5 | 6 | 7 | 8 |
|---|---|---|---|---|
| 6 | N–B3 | R–B1 | – – | Q–N3 |
| | P–B4! | P–B4 | – – | P–B3[9] |
| 7 | B–K5 | QPxP | – – | N–B3 |
| | QPxP | Q–R4[2] | – – | Q–R4[10] |
| 8 | BxP | PxP | – – | N–Q2[11] |
| | N–B3 | R–Q1 | – – | QN–Q2 |
| 9 | O–O | Q–R4[3] | B–B4[5] | B–K2 |
| | PxP | QxQ | B–K3 | N–R4![12] |
| 10 | PxP | NxQ | P–QN4 | BxN |
| | P–N3! | NxP | QxNP | PxP |
| 11 | Q–K2 | B–QN5 | Q–N3 | Q–Q1! |
| | B–N2[1] | NxB | QxQ | QxB |
| 12 | = | PxN | BxQ | QxQ |
| | | B–K3[4] | NxP[6] | PxQ |
| 13 | | = | NxN | NxP |
| | | | RxN![7] | P–N3 |
| 14 | | | BxR | N–K4 |
| | | | BxB | B–QR3![13] |
| 15 | | | N–B3 | = |
| | | | N–B3! | |
| 16 | | | O–O | |
| | | | BxP[8] | |
| | | | = | |

*Notes to practical variations 5–8:*

[1] Abrahams–Flohr, 1939.

[2] For 7 . . . B–K3, see Idea Var. 5.

[3] Weak is 9 Q–Q2?, NxP 10 B–B7, QxB! 11 NxN, RxN 12 QxR, B–K3 13 Q–Q2, N–B3. Black has a strong attack.

[4] Capablanca–Reshevsky, 1938.

[5] Suggested by the late Dutch master, Landau.

[6] 12 . . . B–Q2 is met by 13 KN–K2.

[7] 13 . . . BxN 14 R–Q1 favors White.

[8] Black has compensation for the exchange.

[9] Other possibilities are treated under Idea Var. 6.

[10] 7 . . . PxP 8 BxP, QN–Q2 9 O–O favors White. Kotov–Kashdan, 1945.

[11] Thought to be White's best chance.

[12] A move that curiously offers Black a satisfactory game.

[13] Black has sufficient counterplay.

## part 3—EXCHANGE VARIATION

1 P–Q4, N–KB3
2 P–QB4, P–KN3
3 N–QB3, P–Q4
4 PxP, NxP
5 P–K4, NxN[A]
6 PxN

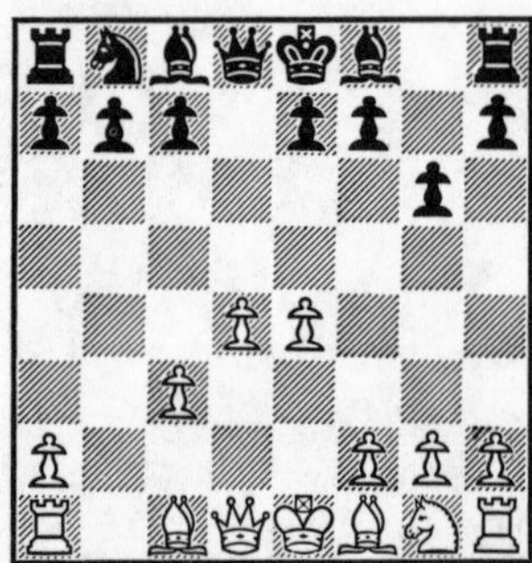

KEY POSITION 3

OBSERVATIONS ON KEY POSITION 3

[A] Other moves deserve little consideration: e.g., 5 . . . N–N3 6 P–KR3!, B–N2 7 N–B3, O–O 8 B–K3, N–B3 9 B–K2, P–K4 10 P–Q5 with a clear advantage for White.

The Exchange Variation is the oldest line of the Grunfeld-Indian insofar as it was adopted in the inaugural game. It fell into disuse, however, until 1948, when it was revived because of new insight into its potentialities for both sides. By now, it is safe to say that the original problems have worn rather thin. White can obtain a strong center, the defender has adequate counterplay and will keep White's Q4 under constant observation.

This variation illustrates the basic ideas of the Grunfeld–Indian exceptionally well, particularly in its emphasis on such significant factors as Black's open Queen Bishop file and Pawn majority on the Queenside.

IDEA VARIATIONS 7–9:

(7) 6 . . . B–N2 (at first 6 . . . P–QB4 was considered best, for after the text move it was feared that 7 B–R3 gave White the edge; Trifunovic, however, exposed this fallacy as follows: 7 . . . QN–Q2! 8 B–B4, P–B4 9 Q–N3, O–O 10 N–B3, P–QR3 with a playable game for the defender) 7 B–QB4 (no other move yields an advantage; e.g., 7 N–B3, P–QB4 8 B–K2, O–O 9 B–K3, Q–R4! 10 Q–Q2, R–Q1 11 QR–B1, PxP 12 PxP, QxQ† 13 NxQ, N–B3 14 P–Q5, N–Q5 with an even game), P–QB4 8 N–K2, N–B3 9 B–K3, O–O 10 O–O, Q–B2 (also usual is 10 . . . PxP 11 PxP, B–N5; see Prac. Var. 9) 11 R–B1, R–Q1 12 P–B4 (for 12 P–KR3, see Game 5), B–N5 (also tenable is the consistent 12 . . . P–K3) 13 P–B5, N–R4! (not 13 . . . NPxP? 14 BxP†!). Black has a satisfactory game.

(8) 6 . . . B–N2 7 B–QB4, O–O 8 N–K2, N–B3 (a fine rejoinder, suggested by Simagin; Black intends to complete the development of his Queenside first and later play . . . P–QB4 with increasing effect) 9 B–KN5 (probably too bold is 9 P–KR4, as in N–R4 10 B–Q3, P–QB4! with a good game for Black, although 10 B–N3

may be stronger; for 9 O–O, see Game 6), N–R4 10 B–N3 (correctly assuming that the exchange on White's QN3 favors White), P–N3 11 O–O, B–R3 and the chances are about even.

(9) 6 . . . B–N2 7 B–QB4, O–O 8 N–K2, P–N3 (this system lost favor since Fuderer–Filip, Goteborg 1955) 9 P–KR4! (9 O–O, B–N2 10 P–B3, P–B3 offers White little promise), B–QR3 (the point of the preceding move, but 9 . . . P–K4 also merits attention; e.g., 10 P–R5, KPxP 11 PxNP, RPxP 12 PxP, Q–K2 with a counterattack against White's center) 10 BxB, NxB 11 P–R5, P–QB4 12 RPxP, RPxP (not 12 . . . BPxP 13 Q–N3†, K–R1 14 N–B4! etc.) 13 Q–Q3, Q–B1 14 Q–N3, PxP 15 PxP (premature is 15 Q–R4?, P–B4!).

Fuderer–Filip now followed with 15 . . . N–N5 (Black should have tried 15 . . . Q–K3) 16 Q–R4, P–B3 (nor is 16 . . . P–B4 17 Q–R7†, K–B2 18 B–R6, R–KN1 19 O–O! satisfactory) 17 Q–R7†, K–B2 18 B–R6, R–KN1 19 N–B4! and White's attack decided.

*Grunfeld–Indian Defense Game 5*

*WHITE: Gligoric* *BLACK: Smyslov*

*USSR vs. Yugoslavia, Kiev* 1959

| | WHITE | BLACK | | WHITE | BLACK |
|---|---|---|---|---|---|
| 1 | P–Q4 | N–KB3 | 21 | N–N3 | P–QN4 |
| 2 | P–QB4 | P–KN3 | 22 | P–QR4 | P–QR3 |
| 3 | N–QB3 | P–Q4 | 23 | R–QN1 | QR–N1 |
| 4 | PxP | NxP | 24 | B–Q2 | NPxP |
| 5 | P–K4 | NxN | 25 | R–QR1 | B–R1 |
| 6 | PxN | B–N2 | 26 | BxRP | Q–B2 |
| 7 | B–QB4 | P–QB4 | 27 | R–R2 | R–N3 |
| 8 | N–K2 | O–O | 28 | PxP | KPxP |
| 9 | O–O | N–B3 | 29 | B–B1 | N–Q4 |
| 10 | B–K3 | Q–B2 | 30 | N–K2 | P–QR4 |
| 11 | R–B1 | R–Q1 | 31 | B–B2 | R–N6! |
| 12 | P–KR3 | P–N3 | 32 | BxR | PxB |
| 13 | P–B4 | P–K3 | 33 | R–R4 | B–B1 |
| 14 | Q–K1 | B–N2 | 34 | B–N2 | N–K6! |
| 15 | Q–B2 | N–R4 | 35 | KR–QR1 | N–B5 |
| 16 | B–Q3 | P–B4! | 36 | N–N3 | B–K2 |
| 17 | P–K5 | P–B5 | 37 | N–B1 | Q–B3 |
| 18 | B–B2 | N–B3 | 38 | RxN | Q–R8† |
| 19 | P–N4 | N–K2 | 39 | K–N3 | P–R4 |
| 20 | K–R2 | Q–B3 | | Resigns | |

### *Grunfeld–Indian Defense Game 6*

*WHITE: Toran* *BLACK: Larsen*

*Hoogoven Tournament, Beverwijk 1959*

| | WHITE | BLACK | | WHITE | BLACK | | WHITE | BLACK |
|---|---|---|---|---|---|---|---|---|
| 1 | P–Q4 | N–KB3 | 16 | RPxP | RPxP | 30 | Q–R7 | PxP |
| 2 | P–QB4 | P–KN3 | 17 | P–Q5 | N–R4 | 31 | B–B2 | R–QB1 |
| 3 | N–QB3 | P–Q4 | 18 | B–Q3 | P–QB3 | 32 | B–N3 | Q–K2 |
| 4 | PxP | NxP | 19 | R–R1 | R–R1 | 33 | R–Q1 | B–B3 |
| 5 | P–K4 | NxN | 20 | B–B5! | KR–N1 | 34 | Q–R6 | Q–N2 |
| 6 | PxN | B–N2 | 21 | P–Q6! | B–QB1! | 35 | BxP† | KxB |
| 7 | B–QB4 | O–O | 22 | Q–N1 | Q–K3 | 36 | Q–R2† | K–K2 |
| 8 | N–K2 | N–B3 | 23 | Q–N4 | N–N6 | 37 | Q–Q2 | B–R6 |
| 9 | O–O | P–N3 | 24 | RxR | RxR | 38 | N–N3 | K–B1 |
| 10 | B–K3 | Q–Q2 | 25 | N–B1 | NxB | 39 | N–R5 | Q–K2 |
| 11 | R–B1 | B–N2 | 26 | QxN | B–Q2 | 40 | Q–R6† | K–N1 |
| 12 | B–QN5 | P--QR3 | 27 | P–QB4 | B–KB1 | 41 | Q–R3 | B–Q2 |
| 13 | B–R4 | P–QN4 | 28 | PxP | BxP | 42 | Q–N3† | K–R1 |
| 14 | B–B2 | QR–Q1 | 29 | Q–N6 | R–N1 | 43 | P–N3 | . . . . |
| 15 | P–QR4 | P–K4 | | | | | Resigns | |

PRACTICAL VARIATIONS 9–12:

1 P–Q4, N–KB3 2 P–QB4, P–KN3 3 N–QB3, P–Q4 4 PxP, NxP 5 P–K4, NxN 6 PxN

| | *9* | *10* | *11* | *12* |
|---|---|---|---|---|
| *6* | – – | – – | – – | – – |
| | B–N2 | – – | – – | P–QB4 |
| *7* | B–QB4 | – – | N–B3 | B–N5† |
| | P–QB4 | – – | P–QB4 | B–Q2 |
| *8* | N–K2 | – – | B–K2 | B–QB4 |
| | PxP | O–O | O–O | B–N2 |
| *9* | PxP | O–O | O–O | N–K2 |
| | N–B3 | N–Q2 | P–N3 | O–O |
| *10* | B–K3 | B–KN5[4] | B–K3 | O–O |
| | O–O[1] | P–KR3 | B–N2 | PxP |
| *11* | O–O | B–K3 | P–K5 | PxP[8] |
| | B–N5 | Q–B2 | PxP | = |
| *12* | P–B3 | R–B1 | PxP | |
| | N–R4 | P–R3 | N–R3 | |
| *13* | B–Q5! | Q–Q2[5] | Q–R4 | |
| | B–B1 | K–R2 | N–B2[7] | |
| *14* | B–N5! | B–Q3 | ∓ | |
| | P–KR3 | P–QN4 | | |
| *15* | B–R4 | N–B4 | | |
| | P–KN4 | P–K4 | | |
| *16* | B–B2 | N–Q5[6] | | |
| | P–K3 | ± | | |
| *17* | B–QN3 | | | |
| | NxB | | | |
| *18* | PxN | | | |
| | B–Q2[2] | | | |
| *19* | N–N3 | | | |
| | P–B4![3] | | | |
| | = | | | |

*Notes to practical variations 9–12:*

[1] Interesting is 10 . . . Q–R4† 11 B–Q2, Q–R6! 12 R–QN1, O–O, and now not 13 P–Q5, N–K4 14 B–N4, Q–B6! but 13 O–O with a satisfactory game for White.

[2] More accurate is 18 . . . P–N3 and 19 . . . B–N2.

[3] Fuderer–Unzicker in 1955 continued with the inferior 19 . . . B–QB3 20 N–R5, P–B4? (better 20 . . . B–R1) 21 P–Q5! and White won quickly. With the text move, Black holds his own.

[4] Introduced by Bronstein in the second game of his match with Botvinnik in 1951.

[5] Also strong is Loewenfisch's 13 N–B4!

[6] Bronstein–Botvinnik, 1951.

[7] Rubinstein–Alekhine, 1924.

[8] With a game similar to Prac. Var. 9.

---

## part 4—TWO PAWNS GAME

1 P–Q4, N–KB3
2 P–QB4, P–KN3
3 N–QB3, P–Q4
4 N–B3, B–N2
5 Q–N3, PxP[A]
6 QxBP, O–O[B]
7 P–K4[C]

KEY POSITION 4

### OBSERVATIONS ON KEY POSITION 4

[A] 5 . . . P–B4 fails against 6 BPxP, PxP 7 Q–R4†! etc. 5 . . . P–B3, the Slav Defense, leads to equality.

[B] Not 6 . . . B–K3? 7 Q–N5†, P–B3 8 QxNP! etc.

[C] 7 B–B4, N–R3 or 7 . . . P–B3 8 P–K4, P–QN4 9 Q–N3, Q–R4 is good for Black.

This method is most frequently encountered against the Grunfeld–Indian Defense. White has a strong center but must guard against a breach. Black, on the other hand, has a plus in development and must bring pressure against the enemy Queen Pawn. In this connection the thrust . . . P–QB4 is of great significance and constitutes the key to the most important lines of the defense. Many systems have been devised against White's set-up.

(1) *The Smyslov System (Idea Var. 10)*:

Black plays 7 . . . B–N5, followed by the maneuver KN–Q2–QN3. This converts Black's King Knight from a defensive piece to an aggressive one and keeps open the Queen file and the long diagonal (Black's KR1–QR8) for concentrated action. Black's Queen Knight may go to B3 with additional direct pressure on the enemy Queen Pawn, or it may go to QR3 as a preparation for . . . P–QB4 and increased tension. The Smyslov system is currently considered to offer Black excellent chances for equality. See Game 7.

(2) *The Prins System (Idea Var. 11):*

Here Black plays 7 . . . N–R3 and White cannot prevent the freeing . . . P–QB4. But the line is double-edged in that it requires impeccable technique on the part of the defender.

(3) *The Boleslavski System (Idea Var. 12):*

The objectives here are different from the foregoing. Black's prime target is to enforce . . . P–K4 in conjunction with the dispossession of White's Queen Knight from its central post. The latter is accomplished by means of 7 . . . P–B3, 8 . . . P–QN4, 9 . . . Q–R4 and 10 . . . P–N5. The usual thrust . . . P–QB4 may still play an important role later.

Insufficient experience with this line thus far prevents a definitive verdict as to its validity. It seems, however, that with accurate play, White's chances are superior.

*Grunfeld–Indian Defense Game 7*

*WHITE: Botvinnik* *BLACK: Fischer*

*Varna Olympics 1962*

| | WHITE | BLACK | | WHITE | BLACK |
|---|---|---|---|---|---|
| 1 | P–Q4 | N–KB3 | 35 | R–K3 | R–K2 |
| 2 | P–QB4 | P–KN3 | 36 | R–B3† | K–N2 |
| 3 | N–QB3 | P–Q4 | 37 | R–B3 | R–K5 |
| 4 | N–B3 | B–N2 | 38 | B–Q1 | R–Q5 |
| 5 | Q–N3 | PxP | 39 | B–B2 | K–B3 |
| 6 | QxBP | O–O | 40 | K–B3 | K–N4 |
| 7 | P–K4 | B–N5 | 41 | K–N3 | N–K5† |
| 8 | B–K3 | KN–Q2 | 42 | BxN | RxB |
| 9 | B–K2 | N/1–B3 | 43 | P–R3 | R–K2 |
| 10 | R–Q1 | N–N3 | 44 | R–KB3 | R–QB2 |
| 11 | Q–B5 | Q–Q3 | 45 | P–QR4 | R–B4 |
| 12 | P–KR3 | BxN | 46 | R–B7 | R–R4 |
| 13 | PxB | KR–Q1 | 47 | RxKRP | RxP |
| 14 | P–Q5 | N–K4 | 48 | P–R4† | K–B4 |
| 15 | N–N5 | Q–KB3 | 49 | R–B7† | K–K4 |
| 16 | P–B4 | N/5–Q2 | 50 | R–KN7 | R–R8 |
| 17 | P–K5 | QxBP | 51 | K–B3 | P–QN4 |
| 18 | BxQ | NxQ | 52 | P–R5 | R–R6† |
| 19 | NxBP | QR–B1 | 53 | K–N2 | PxP |
| 20 | P–Q6 | PxP | 54 | R–N5† | K–Q3 |
| 21 | PxP | BxP | 55 | RxNP | P–R5 |
| 22 | O–O | N/3–Q2 | 56 | P–B4 | K–B3 |
| 23 | R–Q5 | P–N3 | 57 | R–N8 | P–R6† |
| 24 | B–B3 | N–K3 | 58 | K–R2 | P–R4 |
| 25 | NxN | PxN | 59 | P–B5 | K–B2 |
| 26 | R–Q3 | N–B4 | 60 | R–N5 | K–Q3 |
| 27 | R–K3 | P–K4 | 61 | P–B6 | K–K3 |
| 28 | BxP | BxB | 62 | R–N6† | K–B2 |
| 29 | RxB | RxP | 63 | R–R6 | K–N3 |
| 30 | R–K7 | R–Q2 | 64 | R–B6 | P–R5 |
| 31 | RxR | NxR | 65 | R–R6 | K–B2 |
| 32 | B–N4 | R–B2 | 66 | R–B6 | R–QN6 |
| 33 | R–K1 | K–B2 | 67 | R–R6 | P–R6 |
| 34 | K–N2 | N–B4 | 68 | K–N1 | Draw |

IDEA VARIATIONS 10–12:

(10) 7 . . . B–N5 8 B–K3 (generally adjudged as the strongest continuation), KN–Q2 (the characteristic maneuver of this system; inferior is 8 . . . N–B3 9 P–Q5!, BxN 10 PxB, N–K4 11 Q–K2, P–B3 12 P–B4, QN–Q2 13 B–N2! with great advantage to White) 9 R–Q1 (the alternative 9 Q–N3, BxN 10 PxB, QN–B3 11 R–Q1, P–K4 is satisfactory for Black, and so would seem to be the so-called Yugoslav Variation, 9 . . . P–B4: 10 P–Q5!, N–R3! 11 N–Q2, P–K3! 12 P–KR3 [see Game 8 for 12 P–Q6], PxP 13 PxP, B–B4 14 P–N4, P–B5 15 BxBP, QN–B4 16 Q–R3, B–Q6), N–N3 (Pachman suggests 9 . . . P–K4 10 PxP, N–QB3, but overlooks the correct 10 P–Q5; playable, however, is 9 . . . N–QB3, as in 10 B–K2, BxN 11 PxB, N–N3 12 Q–B5, P–B4 13 P–Q5, N–K4 with balanced chances) 10 Q–N3, N–B3 11 P–Q5, N–K4 12 B–K2, NxN† 13 PxN, B–R4 (the best retreat) 14 P–KR4 (Smyslov–Botvinnik, 11th Match Game 1958; 14 P–B4 is also worth a try), Q–Q2 (another possibility is 14 . . . Q–N1 followed by . . . P–QB3), 15 P–R4 (Botvinnik now played 15 . . . P–R4 but ran into difficulties after 16 N–N5, N–B1 17 B–Q4; hence, according to Loewenfisch, he should have accepted the Pawn offer [15 . . . BxN† and 16 . . . NxRP]).

(11) 7 . . . N–R3 8 B–K2 (premature is 8 P–QN4, P–B3! 9 P–QR3, B–K3 10 Q–Q3, N–Q2 11 B–K3, N–N3; Black has a slight edge), P–B4! 9 P–Q5 (better than 9 PxP?, B–K3! 10 Q–N5, R–B1! etc.; see Game 9 for 9 O–O?), P–K3 10 O–O (10 P–Q6 is met by 10 . . . P–K4 11 O–O, QxP 12 R–Q1, Q–B2∓), PxP 11 PxP, Q–N3! (one of the points of this position; Black must always bear in mind the maneuver . . . Q–N3–N5) 12 P–QR3 (if 12 B–B4, R–K1!), B–B4 13 N–KR4, B–Q2! (for 13 . . . B–B7?, see Game 10).

(12) 7 . . . P–B3 8 B–K2 (best; after 8 Q–N3, Black may even play . . . P–K4, e.g., 9 PxP, N–N5 10 B–K2, Q–N3 11 QxQ, PxQ 12 B–KB4, N–Q2 13 P–K6, PxP 14 B–Q6, R–K1=), P–QN4 9 Q–N3, Q–R4 10 B–Q2!, P–N5 11 N–QR4, NxP 12 BxP, Q–KB4 (the Pawn sacrifice is Black's best chance; 12 . . . Q–Q1 13 O–O, P–QR4 14 B–R3, N–R3 15 QR–B1 gives White a clear advantage, as in Flohr–Lilienthal, 1947) 13 O–O!, B–K3 14 Q–R3, B–Q4 15 BxP, R–K1. Black has compensation for the Pawn.

### *Grunfeld–Indian Defense Game 8*

*WHITE: Stahlberg* *BLACK: Szabo*

*Zurich 1953*

| | WHITE | BLACK | | WHITE | BLACK |
|---|---|---|---|---|---|
| 1 | P–Q4 | N–KB3 | 22 | NxN | RxN! |
| 2 | P–QB4 | P–KN3 | 23 | QR–B1 | RxQP |
| 3 | N–QB3 | P–Q4 | 24 | QxP | RxP |
| 4 | N–KB3 | B–N2 | 25 | QxRP | P–Q6 |
| 5 | Q–N3 | PxP | 26 | Q–K3 | P–Q7 |
| 6 | QxBP | O–O | 27 | QR–Q1 | KR–Q1 |
| 7 | P–K4 | B–N5 | 28 | P–KN4 | Q–R5 |
| 8 | B–K3 | KN–Q2 | 29 | R–B2 | R–Q6 |
| 9 | Q–N3 | P–B4!? | 30 | Q–B4 | Q–K2 |
| 10 | P–Q5 | N–R3 | 31 | Q–R4 | Q–B3 |
| 11 | N–Q2 | P–K3 | 32 | Q–N4 | Q–N4 |
| 12 | P–Q6 | B–Q5! | 33 | K–N2 | R/6–Q5 |
| 13 | BxN | PxB | 34 | Q–N3 | P–KR4! |
| 14 | N–B4 | R–N1 | 35 | P–KR3 | P–R5 |
| 15 | Q–B2 | P–K4 | 36 | P–B4 | Q–K2 |
| 16 | N–Q5 | Q–R5 | 37 | R–B3 | R–Q6 |
| 17 | O–O | B–K3 | 38 | RxR | Q–K7† |
| 18 | P–KN3 | Q–R4 | 39 | K–N1 | RxR |
| 19 | P–B3 | BxN | 40 | Q–N8† | K–R2 |
| 20 | PxB | N–N3 | | Resigns | |
| 21 | BxB | KPxB | | | |

### *Grunfeld–Indian Defense Game 9*

*WHITE: G. Kramer* *BLACK: Najdorf*

*New York 1948-49*

| | WHITE | BLACK | | WHITE | BLACK |
|---|---|---|---|---|---|
| 1 | P–Q4 | N–KB3 | 19 | B–B3 | B–QB3 |
| 2 | P–QB4 | P–KN3 | 20 | N–N4 | N–B7! |
| 3 | N–QB3 | P–Q4 | 21 | NxB | NxR! |
| 4 | Q–N3 | PxP | 22 | B–Q2 | PxN |
| 5 | QxBP | B–N2 | 23 | RxN | P–Q6 |
| 6 | N–B3 | O–O | 24 | Q–R6 | Q–Q5† |
| 7 | P–K4 | N–R3 | 25 | K–R1 | QxP |
| 8 | B–K2 | P–B4 | 26 | Q–B4† | K–R1 |
| 9 | O–O? | PxP | 27 | P–KR3 | P–B4 |
| 10 | R–Q1 | P–K4! | 28 | P–QR4 | Q–Q5 |
| 11 | NxKP | N–Q2 | 29 | QxQ | BxQ |
| 12 | NxN | BxN | 30 | B–KN4 | R–B2 |
| 13 | N–Q5 | R–B1 | 31 | B–QR5 | R–B2 |
| 14 | Q–N3 | N–B4 | 32 | B–N6 | R–B7 |
| 15 | Q–R3 | R–K1 | 33 | P–R5 | P–Q7 |
| 16 | P–B3 | P–B4 | 34 | K–R2 | R–K8 |
| 17 | QxP | PxP | 35 | K–N3 | RxR |
| 18 | PxP | NxP | | Resigns | |

*Grunfeld–Indian Defense Game 10*

*WHITE: Kotov* *BLACK: Lilienthal*

*Candidates' Tournament, Budapest 1950*

| | WHITE | BLACK | | WHITE | BLACK |
|---|---|---|---|---|---|
| 1 | P–Q4 | N–KB3 | 20 | P–Q6 | P–QN4 |
| 2 | P–QB4 | P–KN3 | 21 | Q–Q5 | QR–B1 |
| 3 | N–QB3 | P–Q4 | 22 | B–K3 | R–B3 |
| 4 | N–B3 | B–N2 | 23 | B–N5 | R/3–B1 |
| 5 | Q–N3 | PxP | 24 | B–K7 | P–R3 |
| 6 | QxBP | O–O | 25 | N–R4 | P–B5 |
| 7 | P–K4 | N–R3 | 26 | P–QN4 | P–B6 |
| 8 | B–K2 | P–B4 | 27 | QR–B1 | P–B7 |
| 9 | P–Q5 | P–K3 | 28 | R–Q2 | RxB |
| 10 | O–O | PxP | 29 | PxR | QxP |
| 11 | PxP | Q–N3 | 30 | NxP | Q–B3 |
| 12 | P–QR3 | B–B4 | 31 | Q–KB5 | R–B5? |
| 13 | N–KR4 | B–B7? | 32 | QxP | Q–N7? |
| 14 | B–Q1 | BxB | 33 | N–K7† | K–B1 |
| 15 | RxB | N–K1 | 34 | R–K1! | R–K5 |
| 16 | N–K4 | N–Q3 | 35 | R–Q8† | KxN |
| 17 | NxN | QxN | 36 | RxR† | KxR |
| 18 | N–B3 | KR–K1 | 37 | R–K8† | Resigns |
| 19 | R–N1 | Q–Q2 | | | |

PRACTICAL VARIATIONS 13–17:

1 P–Q4, N–KB3 2 P–QB4, P–KN3 3 N–QB3, P–Q4 4 N–B3, B–N2 5 Q–N3, PxP 6 QxBP, O–O 7 P–K4

| | 13 | 14 | 15 | 16 | 17 |
|---|---|---|---|---|---|
| 7 | – – | – – | – – | – – | – – |
| | B–N5 | – – | – – | N–R3 | P–N3? |
| 8 | B–K3 | – – | – – | B–N5 | P–K5! |
| | KN–Q2 | – – | – – | P–R3 | B–QR3 |
| 9 | O–O–O | B–K2 | N–Q2 | B–R4 | PxN![8] |
| | QN–B3 | N–N3 | N–N3 | P–B4 | BxQ |
| 10 | P–KR3 | Q–B5 | Q–Q3 | P–Q5 | PxB |
| | BxN | P–B3 | P–QB3[5] | P–K3 | KxP |
| 11 | PxB | R–Q1 | P–B3 | P–Q6!? | BxB |
| | N–N3 | N/1–Q2 | B–K3 | P–K4! | ± |
| 12 | Q–B5 | Q–QR5 | R–Q1 | R–Q1 | |
| | P–B4 | P–K4[3] | N–R3! | B–K3 | |

| | 13 | 14 | 15 | 16 |
|---|---|---|---|---|
| 13 | N–K2 | P–Q5 | P–QR3 | Q–R4 |
| | Q–Q3 | PxP | Q–Q2 | N–QN5 |
| 14 | P–K5 | QNxP | Q–B2[6] | NxP |
| | Q–Q4![1] | NxN | ± | P–R3 |
| 15 | QxQ†[2] | QxN | | R–Q2 |
| | NxQ | B–K3[4] | | P–KN4 |
| 16 | N–B3 | = | | B–N3 |
| | NxB | | | N–R4[7] |
| 17 | PxN | | | ∓ |
| | P–B5 | | | |
| | ∓ | | | |

*Notes to practical variations 13–17:*

[1] Smyslov–Botvinnik, 6th Match Game 1957. White obtained a great advantage after 14 . . . QxQ? 15 PxQ, N–B5 16 P–B4, KR–Q1 17 B–N2.

[2] After 15 P–N3, KR–Q1 16 N–B4, QxQ 17 PxQ, RxR† 18 KxR, N–Q2 19 N–K6, P–B5!, Black has a good game.

continued ▸

[3] Played by Smyslov in the 4th Match Game vs. Botvinnik, 1958. The idea is 13 NxP, BxB 14 NxB, NxN 15 PxN, Q–R5 etc.

[4] In the aforesaid game, Black had no inferiority.

[5] 10 . . . N–B3 is now less effective because of 11 P–B3, B–Q2 12 N–N3.

[6] So far Botvinnik–Smyslov, The Hague 1948. It continued 14 . . . N–B2? 15 N–N3, B–B5 16 B–K2±. Best for Black is probably 14 . . . BxP.

[7] Szabo–Pachman, 1949.

[8] This combination is standard in positions of this type. White "sacrifices" the Queen for three minor pieces, which usually is a bargain.

---

## part 5—THREE KNIGHTS' VARIATION

1 P–Q4, N–KB3
2 P–QB4, P–KN3
3 N–QB3, P–Q4
4 N–B3, B–N2

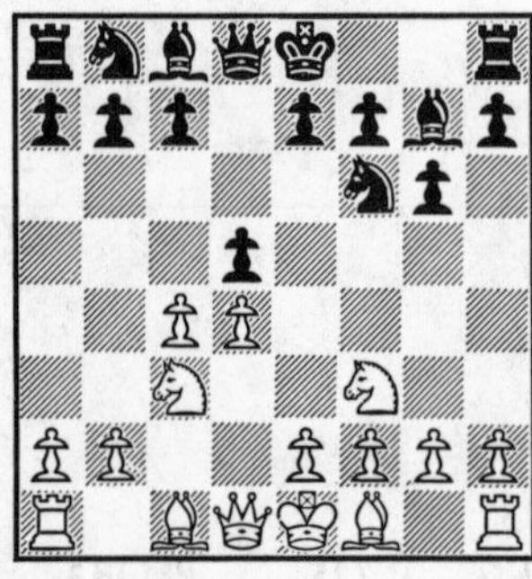

KEY POSITION 5

OBSERVATIONS ON KEY POSITION 5

Besides 5 Q–N3, there are several other continuations which lately have commanded White's attention. They are ways of attempting to gain and maintain the center. Their drawback usually lies in Black's willingness to abandon the center in return for superior mobility. As of the present, no particular line offers the first player much promise.

IDEA VARIATIONS 13–15:

(13) 5 B–N5 (pioneered by Lasker and lately favored by Petrosian), N–K5! (the indicated reaction) 6 PxP, NxB 7 NxN, P–K3 8 N–B3 (or 8 Q–R4†, P–B3! 9 PxBP, NxP 10 N–B3, B–Q2, and Black recovers the Pawn with a good game; for 8 Q–Q2, PxP 9 Q–K3†, K–B1, see *Chess Review* for July and October of 1961), PxP 9 P–K3, O–O 10 B–K2 (to anticipate the pinning by . . . B–N5, but 10 B–Q3 is also good; see Game 11), P–QB3 11 O–O, Q–K2 12 P–QR3, P–KB4= (Kluger–Uhlmann, 1959).

(14) 5 Q–R4†, B–Q2 (better than 5 . . . P–B3 6 PxP, NxP 7 P–K4 etc.) 6 Q–N3, B–B3 (6 . . . PxP 7 QxBP is another possibility) 7 P–K3, P–K3! (else 8 N–K5 and White gets the edge) 8 N–K5, PxP 9 BxP, BxP 10 R–KN1 (the sacrifice on KB7 is too risky), B–B3 11 BxP, PxB 12 QxP†, Q–K2 13 Q–B8† with a draw (Pachman).

(15) 5 B–B4, O–O 6 R–B1, PxP (for 6 . . . P–B4, see Prac. Var. 19 and Game 12) 7 P–K3 (after 7 P–K4, P–B4 8 PxP, Q–R4, Black has no problems), B–K3! (better than 7 . . . P–B4 8 BxP, PxP 9 NxP, QN–Q2 10 B–KN3 etc.) 8 N–KN5, B–Q4 9 NxB, NxN 10 B–N3, P–QB4∓.

*Grunfeld–Indian Defense Game 11*

*WHITE: Petrosian* *BLACK: Krogius*

*USSR Championship, Tiflis 1959*

| | WHITE | BLACK | | WHITE | BLACK |
|---|---|---|---|---|---|
| 1 | P–Q4 | N–KB3 | 21 | N–B5 | KR–Q1 |
| 2 | N–KB3 | P–KN3 | 22 | PxP | PxP |
| 3 | P–B4 | B–N2 | 23 | Q–R4 | Q–B3 |
| 4 | N–B3 | P–Q4 | 24 | K–N2 | R–QR1 |
| 5 | B–N5 | N–K5 | 25 | N–N7 | R–K1 |
| 6 | PxP | NxB | 26 | N–R5 | P–N4 |
| 7 | NxN | P–K3 | 27 | P–KR3 | Q–B4 |
| 8 | N–B3 | PxP | 28 | NxP | Q–K5 |
| 9 | P–K3 | O–O | 29 | R–B5 | P–B4 |
| 10 | B–Q3 | N–B3 | 30 | Q–B2 | NxN |
| 11 | O–O | N–K2 | 31 | RxN | P–B5 |
| 12 | P–QN4 | B–B4 | 32 | KPxP | PxP |
| 13 | BxB | NxB | 33 | P–N4 | BxP |
| 14 | P–N5 | Q–Q3 | 34 | Q–Q2 | B–N2 |
| 15 | Q–N3 | N–K2 | 35 | R–K1 | Q–R5 |
| 16 | QR–B1 | K–R1? | 36 | QxQP | RxR |
| 17 | R–B2 | P–KR3 | 37 | NxR | R–KB1 |
| 18 | KR–B1 | P–QB3 | 38 | N–B3 | K–R1 |
| 19 | N–QR4 | QR–N1 | 39 | R–B7 | P–R3 |
| 20 | P–N3 | K–R2 | 40 | N–R4 | Resigns |

*Grunfeld–Indian Defense Game 12*

*WHITE: Petrosian* *BLACK: Benko*

*Curacao Candidates' Tournament 1962*

| | WHITE | BLACK | | WHITE | BLACK |
|---|---|---|---|---|---|
| 1 | P–Q4 | N–KB3 | 13 | BxP† | KxB |
| 2 | P–B4 | P–KN3 | 14 | RxB | RxR |
| 3 | N–QB3 | P–Q4 | 15 | N/3–N5† | K–N1 |
| 4 | N–B3 | B–N2 | 16 | QxN | Q–QB3 |
| 5 | B–B4 | O–O | 17 | N–Q6 | Q–Q2 |
| 6 | R–B1 | P–B4 | 18 | QxQ | NxQ |
| 7 | QPxP | PxP | 19 | NxR | RxN |
| 8 | P–K4 | Q–R4 | 20 | P–B4 | R–B7 |
| 9 | P–K5 | R–Q1 | 21 | K–K2 | B–R3 |
| 10 | B–Q2 | N–N5 | 22 | N–B3 | RxP |
| 11 | BxP | QxBP | 23 | P–N3 | P–KN4 |
| 12 | N–K4 | Q–N3 | | Draw | |

PRACTICAL VARIATIONS 18–20:

1 P–Q4, N–KB3 2 P–QB4, P–KN3 3 N–QB3, P–Q4 4 N–B3, B–N2

| | *18* | *19* | *20* |
|---|---|---|---|
| *5* | B–N5 | B–B4 | PxP |
| | N–K5 | O–O | NxP |
| *6* | PxP | R–B1 | Q–R4† |
| | NxN | P–B4 | N–B3[4] |
| *7* | PxN | QPxP | N–K5 |
| | QxP | B–K3![2] | NxN[5] |
| *8* | P–K3 | N–Q4 | PxN |
| | P–QB4 | N–B3 | B–Q2 |
| *9* | B–N5† | NxB | = |
| | B–Q2 | PxN | |
| *10* | P–B4 | P–K3 | |
| | Q–K5 | Q–R4 | |
| *11* | Q–N1[1] | Q–R4 | |
| | ± | QxP[3] | |
| | | = | |

*Notes to practical variations 18–20:*

[1] Petrosian's idea, offering strong pressure on the Queenside. Little is achieved by 11 O–O?, BxB 12 PxB, N–Q2 (Alekhine–Grunfeld, 1922).

[2] Inferior is 7 . . . Q–R4? 8 PxP, R–Q1 9 B–Q2!, QxBP 10 P–K4±.

[3] Ragosin–Mikenas, 1940.

[4] 6 . . . B–Q2 is also good.

[5] Better than 7 . . . Q–Q3 8 NxN, QxN 9 QxQ†, PxQ 10 P–K3±.

---

## part 6—4 P-K3 VARIATION

1 P–Q4, N–KB3
2 P–QB4, P–KN3
3 N–QB3, P–Q4
4 P–K3, B–N2
5 N–B3[A], O–O

KEY POSITION 6

OBSERVATIONS ON KEY POSITION 6

[A] Unusual but not bad is 5 P–B4, e.g., . . . O–O 6 N–B3, P–B4 7 QPxP, Q–R4 8 PxP, NxP 9 QxN, BxN† 10 B–Q2= (Pirc–Alatortzev, 1935).

In this system, White fortifies his center and obtains a safe and sound position. Black, on the other, faces no perils if he follows the principles of sound development.

IDEA VARIATIONS 16 AND 17:

(16) 6 Q–N3 (most usual; for 6 B–K2, see Game 13), PxP (see also Prac. Var. 21 and 22) 7 BxP, KN–Q2

distinctly weak is 7 . . . QN–Q2 because of 8 N–KN5!, P–K3 9 BxP, PxB 10 NxKP, Q–K2 11 NxP†, K–R1 12 NxR, N–N5 13 B–Q2!; it is noteworthy that both Keres and Eliskases overlooked this possibility in their game at Semmering in 1937) 8 O–O (overambitious is 8 P–KR4!?, N–QB3! 9 P–R5, N–R4 10 Q–R4, NxB 11 QxN/4, N–N3∓), N–N3 9 B–K2, B–K3 10 Q–B2, N–B3!∓ (Pachman).

(17) 6 P–QN4 (Makagonov's move), P–B3 7 B–Q2! (Troianescu–Botvinnik, 1952, continued 7 Q–N3?, PxP 8 BxP, P–QN4 9 B–K2, P–QR4 10 O–O, B–K3 11 Q–N2, PxP 12 QxP, N–R3∓), B–N5 8 P–KR3, BxN 9 QxB, PxP 10 BxP, QN–Q2=.

*Grunfeld–Indian Defense Game 13*

*WHITE: Sokolski* *BLACK: Botvinnik*

*USSR Championship, Leningrad 1938*

| | WHITE | BLACK | | WHITE | BLACK |
|---|---|---|---|---|---|
| 1 | P–QB4 | N–KB3 | 22 | N–R1 | P–Q5 |
| 2 | N–QB3 | P–Q4 | 23 | Q–K2 | N–K4 |
| 3 | P–Q4 | P–KN3 | 24 | PxP | PxP |
| 4 | N–B3 | B–N2 | 25 | RxR | BxR |
| 5 | P–K3 | O–O | 26 | R–K1 | P–Q6 |
| 6 | B–K2 | P–K3 | 27 | Q–Q1 | B–N5 |
| 7 | O–O | P–N3 | 28 | Q–R1 | P–Q7 |
| 8 | PxP | PxP | 29 | RxN | P–Q8(Q) |
| 9 | P–QN3 | B–N2 | 30 | R–K8† | RxR |
| 10 | B–N2 | QN–Q2 | 31 | QxQ/6 | B–K7 |
| 11 | Q–B2 | P–QR3 | 32 | N–N3 | B–N2 |
| 12 | QR–B1 | R–B1 | 33 | Q–B6 | B–N4 |
| 13 | KR–Q1 | Q–K2 | 34 | Q–B1 | QxQ |
| 14 | Q–N1 | KR–Q1 | 35 | BxQ | R–K8 |
| 15 | B–B1 | P–B4 | 36 | B–K3 | R–R8 |
| 16 | PxP | PxP | 37 | P–QR4 | B–Q6 |
| 17 | N–K2 | B–R3 | 38 | P–B4 | R–N8 |
| 18 | B–R3 | N–N5 | 39 | K–B2 | BxB |
| 19 | Q–Q3 | KN–K4 | 40 | NxB | RxP |
| 20 | NxN | QxN | | Resigns | |
| 21 | N–N3 | Q–B3 | | | |

*Grunfeld–Indian Defense Game 14*

*WHITE: Alatortzev* *BLACK: Flohr*

*Leningrad–Moscow Tournament 1939*

| | WHITE | BLACK | | WHITE | BLACK |
|---|---|---|---|---|---|
| 1 | P–Q4 | N–KB3 | 11 | P–K3 | N–Q2 |
| 2 | P–QB4 | P–KN3 | 12 | P–B3 | NxP |
| 3 | N–QB3 | P–Q4 | 13 | B–N4 | R–QB1 |
| 4 | B–N5 | N–K5 | 14 | K–N1 | N–R3 |
| 5 | NxN | PxN | 15 | B–R5 | O–O |
| 6 | Q–Q2 | B–N2 | 16 | P–QN3 | N–B4 |
| 7 | O–O–O | P–KR3 | 17 | B–K2 | P–QN4 |
| 8 | B–B4 | P–QB4 | 18 | PxNP | PxP |
| 9 | PxP | QxQ† | | Resigns | |
| 10 | BxQ | B–K3 | | | |

PRACTICAL VARIATIONS 21–23:

1 P–Q4, N–KB3 2 P–QB4, P–KN3 3 N–QB3, P–Q4 4 P–K3, B–N2 5 N–B3, O–O

| | *21* | *22* | *23* |
|---|---|---|---|
| *6* | Q–N3 | – – | PxP |
| | P–K3 | P–B3 | NxP |
| *7* | B–Q2 | B–Q2 | B–B4 |
| | P–N3 | PxP[2] | N–N3[3] |
| *8* | PxP | BxP | B–N3 |
| | PxP | QN–Q2 | N–R3! |
| *9* | B–K2 | O–O | N–K4 |
| | P–B4[1] | N–N3 | P–B4! |
| *10* | PxP | B–K2 | NxP |
| | PxP | B–K3 | NxN |
| *11* | O–O | Q–B2 | PxN |
| | N–B3 | B–B5 | N–Q2 |
| *12* | KR–Q1 | ± | P–B6 |
| | R–N1 | | PxP[4] |
| | = | | ∓ |

*Notes to practical variations 21–23:*

[1] 9 . . . B–N2 is also good.

[2] 7 . . . P–K3 8 B–Q3, QN–Q2 leads to a difficult position with some initiative for White.

[3] Relatively best. 7 . . . NxN 8 PxN, P–B4 9 O–O, Q–B2 10 B–N3 gives White a slight edge.

[4] Despite his weak Bishop Pawn, Black's position is better.

## SUPPLEMENTARY VARIATIONS 1–6:

1 P–Q4, N–KB3 2 P–QB4, P–KN3 3 N–QB3, P–Q4

| | *1* | *2* | *3* | *4* | *5* | *6* |
|---|---|---|---|---|---|---|
| *4* | B–B4 | PxP | Q–N3 | B–N5 | P–KN3 | Q–R4† |
| | B–N2 | NxP | PxP | N–K5 | PxP! | B–Q2 |
| *5* | Q–R4† | P–KN3 | QxBP | PxP[11] | Q–R4† | Q–N3 |
| | B–Q2[1] | B–N2 | B–K3[9] | NxB | KN–Q2 | N–B3! |
| *6* | Q–N3 | B–N2 | Q–Q3![10] | P–KR4 | B–N2[13] | N–B3 |
| | N–B3![2] | NxN | B–N2 | N–K5! | B–N2 | N–QR4 |
| *7* | QxP[3] | PxN | P–K4 | NxN | N–B3 | Q–N4 |
| | R–QN1[4] | P–QB4 | P–B3 | QxP | N–B3! | N–B3 |
| *8* | QxBP | P–K3 | N–B3 | QN–B3 | ∓ | Q–N3 |
| | QxQ | N–B3 | O–O | Q–QR4 | | N–QR4[14] |
| *9* | BxQ | N–K2 | B–K2 | P–K3 | | = |
| | RxP | B–Q2[6] | N–K1 | B–N2[12] | | |
| *10* | O–O–O! | O–O | O–O | ∓ | | |
| | R–N5[5] | QR–B1 | N–Q3 | | | |
| *11* | = | B–R3 | Q–B2 | | | |
| | | Q–R4![7] | B–B5 | | | |
| *12* | | Q–N3 | ± | | | |
| | | Q–R3! | | | | |
| *13* | | N–B4 | | | | |
| | | P–N3 | | | | |
| *14* | | KR–K1 | | | | |
| | | N–R4[8] | | | | |
| | | ∓ | | | | |

*Notes to supplementary variations 1–6:*

[1] Or 5 . . . P–B3 6 BxN, RxB 7 QxP, B–K3, and Black has sufficient compensation for the Pawn.

[2] Bad is 6 . . . B–B3? because of the surprising 7 P–K4!

[3] 7 PxP, QNxP 8 Q–Q1, N–N4 favors Black.

[4] Dubious is 7 . . . NxQP, 8 O–O–O, N–K3 9 B–K5, R–N1 10 Q–R6±.

[5] Black enjoys counterplay for the Pawn.

[6] The ensuing plan is Bronstein's. Black postpones castling to speed up his Queenside action.

[7] Maneuvering for a favorable regrouping.

[8] Geller–Bronstein, Amsterdam 1956.

[9] Stronger is 5 . . . B–N2!, leading to the lines discussed in Part 4.

[10] 6 Q–N5†, N–B3 7 N–B3, N–Q4!∓.

[11] Weaker is 5 NxN, PxN 6 P–K3 (for 6 Q–Q2, see Game 14), P–QB4! 7 Q–Q2, B–Q2 8 P–Q5, Q–N3 9 O–O–O, N–R3 10 P–B3, N–N5∓.

[12] Simkin–Spasski, 1950. Black obtained the advantage.

[13] Or 6 QxBP, N–N3 7 Q–Q3, B–N2 8 N–B3, O–O 9 B–N2, N–B3∓.

[14] With a draw by repetition of moves (Pachman).

# chapter 35—King's Indian Defense

This defense (1 P–Q4, N–KB3 2 P–QB4, P–KN3), which is marked by the fianchetto of Black's King Bishop originated in the latter half of the nineteenth century. Introduced in the Leipzig Tournament of 1879, the defense subsequently proved popular in numerous international events. Hastings 1895, Baden–Baden 1925, Moscow 1925 and New York 1927 are but a few of the great tournaments in which the King's Indian made its appearance with some regularity. After 1927, however, the defense surprisingly vanished from tournament play only to reappear vigorously in the late 1940's.

In the eyes of the enterprising player, the major advantage of this difficult opening is that its closed nature involves the minimum exchange of pieces and the maximum amount of complications. As a result, the positions arrived at give rise to a wide variety of combinational possibilities. This fact alone assures the continued popularity of the defense among self-reliant and imaginative players who are willing to take their chances amid the vicissitudes of mid-game fortune:

---

## part 1—SAEMISCH VARIATION

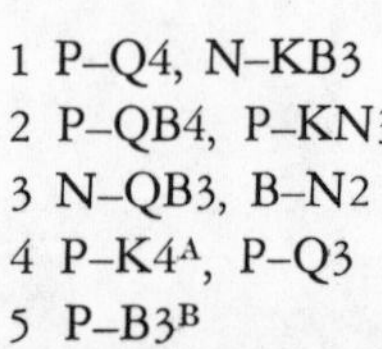
1 P–Q4, N–KB3
2 P–QB4, P–KN3
3 N–QB3, B–N2
4 P–K4[A], P–Q3
5 P–B3[B]

KEY POSITION 1

### OBSERVATIONS ON KEY POSITION 1

[A] An old idea recently revived is 4 B–N5. Some examples:

(1) 4 . . . O–O 5 P–K3, P–B3 6 N–B3, P–Q4 7 Q–N3, Q–R4 8 PxP, NxP 9 B–QB4, NxN 10 PxN, Q–B2 11 O–O, P–N3 12 B–B4, Q–Q1 13 P–QR4± (Gereben–Uhlmann, Hastings 1959).

(2) 4 . . . P–Q3 5 P–K3, P–B4 6 N–B3, Q–R4 7 Q–Q2, O–O 8 B–K2, P–KR3 9 B–R4!, N–B3 10 P–KR3, P–QR3 11 O–O, R–N1 12 P–QR3, PxP 13 PxP, Q–Q1 14 QR–Q1, B–Q2 15 KR–K1, R–B1 16 P–QN4± (Benko–Gligoric, Bled 1959).

(3) 4 . . . P–Q3 5 P–K3, P–B4 6 N–B3, P–KR3 7 B–R4, P–KN4 8 B–N3, N–R4 9 PxP, NxB 10 RPxN, PxP 11 QxQ†, KxQ 12 O–O–O†= (Benko–Fischer, Bled 1959, and Smyslov–Petrosian, Belgrade 1959).

(4) 4 . . . P–Q3 5 N–KB3, N–B3 6 P–Q5, N–QN1 7 P–K4, QN–Q2 8 N–Q4, N–B4 9 P–B3, P–QR4 10 Q–Q2, O–O 11 B–K2, P–K4 12 N–B2, K–R1 13 P–KN4!, B–Q2 14 P–KR4± (Saemisch–Yates, Moscow 1925).

(5) 4 . . . P–B4 5 PxP (5 P–Q5!, P–Q3 6 P–K4 is preferable), N–R3 6 P–KN3, NxP 7 B–N2, P–Q3 8 R–B1, O–O 9 P–QN4? (9 N–B3 is best answered by 9 . . . N/4–K5), N–K3 10 B–Q2, P–QR4 11 P–QR3, PxP 12 PxP, N–Q5∓ (Smyslov–Gligoric, Belgrade 1959).

B The continuation 5 P–B4, known as the Four Pawn Attack, was introduced in the game Schwarz–Paulsen, Leipzig 1879, the earliest known example of the King's Indian Defense. Later it was adopted in the game Englisch–Tarrasch, Hamburg 1885. Some recent examples are treated below:

(1) 5 P–B4, P–B4 6 P–Q5, O–O 7 N–B3, P–K3! 8 B–K2, PxP 9 KPxP, R–K1 10 O–O, N–N5 11 R–K1, B–Q5†? 12 NxB (12 K–B1, Q–R5!), PxN 13 QxP, Q–R5 14 B–Q2!± (Filip–Szabo, Amsterdam 1956). In this variation 11 . . . B–B4 is slightly better but not quite sufficient, e.g., 12 P–KR3, N–K6 13 BxN, RxB 14 Q–Q2, R–K1 15 B–Q3, and White enjoys an advantage in development. An immediate 11 . . . N–K6 is best met by 12 Q–Q2 followed by 13 B–Q3. 11 . . . N–KR3 followed by 12 . . . N–B4 deserves consideration, according to Euwe.

(2) 5 P–B4, P–B4 6 P–Q5, O–O 7 N–B3, P–K3! 8 B–K2, PxP 9 KPxP, R–K1 10 O–O, B–B4 11 N–KR4, N–K5 12 NxB, PxN 13 NxN, PxN 14 B–K3, BxP 15 R–N1, Q–B3 16 Q–N3, B–Q5 17 BxB, QxB†= Antoschin–Boleslavski, Moscow 1956).

(3) 5 P–B4, P–B4 6 P–Q5, O–O 7 N–B3, P–K3! 8 B–K2, PxP 9 BPxP, R–K1 10 N–Q2, P–QR3 11 P–QR4, N–KN5!∓ (analysis by Euwe).

The formation chosen by White had already been adopted in the 1890's, but it was Saemisch who in 1925 first molded it into a logical system. White will use his strong center as the basis for a Kingside assault. (Game 1 is a rather lurid example of this.) At the proper moment Black must counter with . . . P–KB4. It should be noted that if White plays carelessly, Black may even work up a promising Queenside attack.

IDEA VARIATIONS 1 AND 2:

(1) 5 . . . P–B4? 6 PxP, PxP 7 QxQ†, KxQ 8 B–K3, KN–Q2 9 KN–K2, N–QB3 10 O–O–O, P–N3 11 P–B4, P–K4 12 N–Q5, B–N2 13 PxP, N/3xP 14 B–N5†, K–B1 15 N/2–B3, P–B3 16 B–B4, BxN 17 RxB, P–QR3 18 B–K2, K–B2 19 KR–Q1± (Szabo–Euwe, Amsterdam 1954).

(2) 5 . . . QN–Q2 6 B–K3, P–B4? 7 KN–K2, P–QR3 8 Q–Q2, Q–R4 9 N–B1!, PxP 10 BxP, N–B4 11 P–QR3, N–K3 12 B–K3, B–Q2 13 B–K2, Q–B2 14 O–O, O–O 15 N–N3, N–B4 16 NxN, PxN 17 P–B4, B–B3 18 B–B3, QR–Q1 19 Q–B2± (Jezek–Gilg, Wien-Baden 1957).

6 . . . P–K4 7 KN–K2!, O–O 8 Q–Q2, PxP 9 NxP, R–K1 10 O–O–O, N–B1 11 P–KN4, N–K3 12 N–B2, P–N3 13 B–R6, B–R1 14 P–KR4, B–QN2 15 P–R5, Q–K2 16 N–K3 gives White a clear positional edge (Benko–Dorn, Badgastein 1948). In this line, in Saemisch–te Kolste, Baden-Baden 1925, Black tried 9 . . . N–B4, but after 10 B–K2, N–K3 11 N–B2, White had a great advantage.

PRACTICAL VARIATIONS 1-4:

1 P–Q4, N–KB3 2 P–QB4, P–KN3 3 N–QB3, B–N2 4 P–K4, P–Q3 5 P–B3

| | *1* | *2* | *3* | *4* |
|---|---|---|---|---|
| *5* | – – | – – | – – | – – |
| | P–K4[1] | – – | O–O | – – |
| *6* | P–Q5[2] | KN–K2[7] | B–K3[11] | – – |
| | O–O[3] | QN–Q2[8] | P–K4[12] | – – |
| *7* | B–N5[4] | B–N5 | P–Q5 | KN–K2! |
| | P–KR3 | P–B3[9] | P–B3[13] | P–B3 |
| *8* | B–K3 | Q–Q2 | Q–Q2[14] | Q–Q2 |
| | N–R4[5] | O–O | PxP | QN–Q2[19] |
| *9* | Q–Q2 | P–Q5! | BPxP | O–O–O[20] |
| | P–KB4 | P–B4 | P–QR3 | Q–R4[21] |
| *10* | PxP! | P–KN4 | P–KN4! | K–N1 |
| | PxP | P–QR3 | QN–Q2[15] | N–N3[22] |
| *11* | O–O–O | N–N3 | KN–K2 | N–B1 |
| | Q–B3 | R–K1 | P–KR4 | B–K3 |
| *12* | B–Q3 | P–KR4 | B–N5[16] | P–Q5 |
| | N–R3 | Q–R4 | PxP | PxP[23] |
| *13* | KN–K2 | B–R6 | PxP | N–N3! |
| | N–B4 | N–B1 | N–B4 | Q–N5 |
| *14* | B–QB2 | P–R5 | N–N3 | BPxP |
| | P–B5? | Q–B2 | BxP | B–Q2 |
| *15* | BxN | B–Q3 | P–N4[17] | N–N5! |
| | PxB | P–N4 | N/4–Q2 | QxQ |
| *16* | N–K4 | O–O–O | P–KR3 | RxQ |
| | Q–R3[6] | PxP[10] | B–B6[18] | BxN[24] |
| | ± | ± | ± | ± |

*Notes to practical variations 1–4:*

[1] Other possibilities:

1) 5 . . . QN–Q2 6 B–K3 (6 B–N5, as played in Tolush–Rellstab, Vienna 1957, is best answered by 6 . . . P–B3 followed by 7 . . . P–K4), O–O 7 Q–Q2, P–B3 8 KN–K2, P–K4, reaching Prac. Var. 4 by transposition.

2) 5 . . . QN–Q2 6 B–K3, P–B3 7 Q–Q2, P–K4 8 P–Q5, P–B4 9 KN–K2, P–QR3 10 P–KN4, R–QN1 11 N–N3 (Letelier–Najdorf, Montevideo 1954), Q–R4!

3) 5 . . . P–B3 (the latest try) 6 B–K3, P–K4 7 Q–Q2, O–O 8 P–Q5 (Marthaler–Walter, Biel 1960). See Prac. Var. 3.

4) 5 . . . P–B3 6 B–K3, P–QR3 7 B–Q3, P–QN4 8 Q–Q2, PxP 9 BxP, P–Q4 10 B–N3, PxP 11 NxP, O–O 12 N–K2, P–QR4 13 O–O, P–R5 14 B–QB4, QN–Q2 15 QR–B1± (Botvinnik–Smyslov, 6th Match Game 1958).

[2] The exchange 6 PxP, PxP 7 QxQ†, KxQ gains nothing for White, e.g., 8 B–K3, B–K3 9 N–R3?, BxN 10 PxB, P–B3 (Filip–Panno, Amsterdam 1956) or 8 B–N5, P–B3 9 P–B4 (Lutikov–Gufeld, 1959). 9 . . . K–K1! should now be played.

[3] 6 . . . N–R4 is a popular alternative, e.g., 7 B–K3, P–KB4 8 KN–K2 (or 8 PxP, PxP 9 P–B4, N–KB3), O–O 9 Q–Q2, P–QR3 10 O–O–O, P–QN4 11 KPxP, PxKBP 12 N–N3, N–KB3 13 B–N5, Q–K1 14 P–KR4, P–N5 15 N–N1, N–R4 16 NxN, QxN 17 B–K2, P–B5 18 P–N4, Q–B2 19 B–Q3!± (Ivkov–Fischer, Mar del Plata 1959). For 8 Q–Q2 in this variation, see Game 2.

[4] 7 B–K3 is also possible. See Prac. Var. 3.

[5] After 8 . . . K–R2 9 Q–Q2, P–QR4 10 P–KN4, N–N1 11 P–KR4, N–R3 (Maricic–Desler, correspondence game), White has the edge.

[6] Taimanov–Kashdan, USSR vs USA 1955, continued 17 P–Q6!, QxBP 18 N/2–B3, Q–Q5 19 Q–K2, Q–K6† 20 QxQ, PxQ 21 P–Q7 and Black resigned.

[7] By maintaining the tension in the center, not only are White's chances for advantage increased, but his choice of continuations is greater.

[8] 6 . . . O–O 7 B–N5, P–B3 8 Q–Q2, P–QR3 9 P–Q5, PxP 10 NxP, N–B3 11 N/2–B3, N–Q5 12 B–Q3, P–N4 13 PxP, PxP 14 O–O± (Botvinnik–Roessel, Wageningen 1958). If 8 . . . QN–Q2 in this line, White does best with 9 P–Q5! (not 9 R–Q1, Q–R4, as in Kieninger–Uhlmann, Belgrade 1956), transposing into Prac. Var. 2.

[9] Or 7 . . . P–KR3 8 B–K3, PxP 9 NxP, N–K4 10 Q–Q2, B–Q2 11 B–K2, O–O 12 O–O, K–R2 13 K–R1, N–N1 14 P–B4, N–QB3 15 QR–Q1, R–K1± (Palme–Galia, Badgastein 1948).

[10] After 17 B–N1, B–R1 18 QR–N1, R–N1 19 N–B5!, White has the advantage. See Game 3.

[11] 6 B–N5 is often played here, e.g., 6 . . . P–KR3 7 B–K3, P–K4 8 KN–K2, PxP 9 NxP, QN–Q2 (if 9 . . . P–B3 then 10 N–B2) 10 Q–Q2, K–R2 11 B–K2, N–B4 12 O–O–O, N–K3 with chances for both sides. However, if this line is played, White does better to transpose into Prac. Var. 1 with 8 P–Q5! But Black has a stronger defense against 6 B–N5 in 6 . . . P–B4!, e.g., 7 P–Q5, QN–Q2 8 Q–Q2, R–K1 9 P–KN4, Q–R4! 10 B–R6, B–R1 11 P–KR4, N–K4 12 P–R5, P–K3 13 O–O–O, PxP 14 KPxP, P–QN4! 15 PxP, P–R3 with an overwhelming position for Black (Watzl–Heemsoth, Dyckhoff Memorial Correspondence Tournament, 1954-56).

[12] 6 . . . P–B3 7 B–Q3 (for 7 Q–Q2, P–K4 8 P–Q5, see Prac. Var. 3), P–K4 8 P–Q5, PxP 9 BPxP, N–K1 10 KN–K2, P–B4 11 QR–B1 (Q–Q2!), N–Q2 12 P–QR3, B–R3!= (Pfeiffer–Geller, Hamburg 1960). Another possibility is 6 . . . QN–Q2, e.g., 7 Q–Q2 (7 N–R3 is also playable) 7 . . . P–K4 8 P–Q5, N–R4 9 O–O–O, P–KB4 10 PxP (or 10 B–Q3, N–B4 11 B–QB2± (Kotov–Szabo, Zurich 1953), PxP 11 N–R3, QN–B3? 12 B–KN5, Q–K1 13 B–Q3, Q–B2 14 KR–N1, P–B3 15 QR–B1± (Rejfir–Lokvenc, Prague 1955).

[13] 7 . . . P–B4 is inferior. After 8 Q–B2, N–K1 9 O–O–O, P–B4 10 PxP, PxP (Spasski–Boleslavski, Leningrad 1956) as well as after 8 B–Q3, N–R4 9 Q–Q2, P–B4 10 PxP, PxP 11 KN–K2 P–QR3 12 O–O–O (Szabo–Esposito, Buenos Aires 1955), White has excellent attacking prospects. However, 7 . . . N–R4 is a resource, as in 8 Q–Q2, P–KB4 9 PxP, PxP 10 O–O–O, P–QR3! 11 B–N5, Q–K1 12 N–R3, N–Q2 (Szabo–Bronstein, 1955), and Black has nothing further to fear.

continued ▸

[14] 8 KN–K2, PxP 9 BPxP, P–QR3 10 Q–Q2, QN–Q2 11 P–KN4, as played in the game Pachman–Gligoric, Buenos Aires 1960, leads to the column by transposition.

[15] Or 10 . . . N–K1 11 O–O–O, P–B4 12 NPxP, PxP 13 K–N1, P–B5 14 B–B2, B–B3 15 P–KR4, N–N2 16 B–R3± (Pachman–Gligoric, Dublin 1957).

[16] Neither 12 P–N5 nor 12 PxP offers much promise for White. A new continuation appeared in the game Tal–Gligoric, Bled 1959: 12 P–KR3, N–R2 13 P–KR4!, PxP 14 PxP, N/R–B3 15 B–R3, N–N3 16 B–N5, N–B5 17 Q–Q3!±

[17] This is White's best chance. If 15 P–KR3 then 15 . . . B–Q2! 16 P–KR4, Q–R4 17 R–QN1, Q–N5 18 P–R5, Q–Q5 19 Q–N2, N–N5! 20 R–Q1 (Pachman–Gligoric, Buenos Aires 1960), and now Black should play 20 . . . N–K6, e.g., 21 Q–R2, NxR.

[18] This 10th Match Game, Botvinnik–Tal, continued 17 R–R2, P–QR4, at which point White could have obtained a positional advantage with 18 Q–K3! thus: 18 . . . PxP 19 N–N5, B–R4 20 NxB, PxN 21 NxP. Black perhaps does better in this variation to answer 17 R–R2 with 17 . . . Q–N3, e.g., 18 R–B2, B–R4.

[19] If 8 . . . PxP then 8 BxP! (9 NxP can be answered by 9 . . . P–Q4!), or if 8 . . . Q–R4 then 9 O–O–O, P–QN4 10 PxNP, BPxP 11 PxP, PxP 12 N–Q5, QxQ† 13 RxQ, NxN 14 PxN± Bronstein–Panno, Amsterdam 1956.

[20] Another possibility is 9 P–Q5:

1) 9 . . . PxP 10 BPxP, N–N3 11 P–QN3, N–R4 12 P–N3, P–B4 13 B–N2, N–Q2 14 B–N5, B–B3= (Olafsson–Uhlmann, Wageningen 1957). In this line if 11 N–B1 then 11 . . . N–KR4 12 N–N3, P–B4=.

2) 9 . . . PxP 10 NxP, NxN 11 BPxN, P–B4 12 N–B3, N–B3 13 B–Q3, B–Q2 14 P–QR4, P–B5 15 B–KB2, P–KN4 16 B–N5, P–QR3 17 BxB, QxB 18 P–KR3, QR–B1 19 Q–Q3, P–KR4 (Van Scheltinga–Reshevsky, Helsinki 1952). Black's prospective break on . . . KN5 and command of the open Queen Bishop file give him a relatively easy game.

3) 9 . . . PxP 10 NxP, NxN 11 QxN!, N–N3 12 Q–Q3, B–K3 13 P–QN3 followed by 14 N–B3±.

[21] Both 9 . . . Q–B2 and 9 . . . P–QR3 are inferior to the text. For example: 9 . . . Q–B2 10 K–N1, R–K1 11 P–KN4, N–B1 12 P–Q5, P–B4 13 N–N3, P–QR3 14 P–KR4, R–K2 15 P–R5± (Muller–Dorn, Vienna 1938) and 9 . . . P–QR3 10 P–Q5, P–B4 11 P–KN4, P–QN4 12 N–N3, N–N3 13 P–KR4!, KN–Q2 14 P–R5, R–K1 15 BPxP, N–B1 16 B–R6, PxNP 17 BxP, B–Q2 18 N–B5!± (Sliwa–Uhlmann, Dresden 1956).

[22] The continuation 10 . . . P–QN4 11 PxP, PxP 12 N–B1 also favors White.

[23] Black must sacrifice a Pawn with 12 . . . B–Q2.

[24] In the game Sliwa–Najdorf, Goteborg 1955, there followed 17 BxB, N–K1 18 N–R5, R–N1 19 R–B2, P–B4 20 BxN/8 and Black resigned.

*King's Indian Defense Game 1*

*WHITE: Hort* *BLACK: R. Byrne*

*Varna Olympics 1962*

| | WHITE | BLACK | | WHITE | BLACK |
|---|---|---|---|---|---|
| 1 | P–QB4 | P–KN3 | 10 | P–KR4 | P–K4 |
| 2 | N–QB3 | B–N2 | 11 | P–R5 | NxRP |
| 3 | P–Q4 | N–KB3 | 12 | P–KN4 | N/4–B3 |
| 4 | P–K4 | P–Q3 | 13 | B–R6 | KPxP |
| 5 | P–B3 | P–QR3 | 14 | BxB | KxB |
| 6 | B–K3 | P–B3 | 15 | Q–R6† | K–R1 |
| 7 | Q–Q2 | P–QN4 | 16 | NxQP | N–K4 |
| 8 | B–Q3 | QN–Q2 | 17 | NxBP | NxB† |
| 9 | KN–K2 | O–O | 18 | K–Q2 | Resigns |

*King's Indian Defense Game 2*

*WHITE: Spasski* *BLACK: Tal*

*Moscow 1956*

| | WHITE | BLACK | | WHITE | BLACK |
|---|---|---|---|---|---|
| 1 | P–Q4 | N–KB3 | 20 | B–QB2 | P–N4 |
| 2 | P–QB4 | P–KN3 | 21 | PxNP | R–QN1 |
| 3 | N–QB3 | B–N2 | 22 | PxP | BxP |
| 4 | P–K4 | P–Q3 | 23 | BxKP | BxB |
| 5 | P–B3 | P–K4 | 24 | NxB | QxQP |
| 6 | P–Q5 | N–R4 | 25 | QxQ | NxQ |
| 7 | B–K3 | P–KB4 | 26 | NxQP | QR–Q1 |
| 8 | Q–Q2 | N–R3 | 27 | BxP | NxP |
| 9 | O–O–O | N–KB3 | 28 | B–Q4! | N–N3 |
| 10 | PxP | PxP | 29 | R–K7! | NxR |
| 11 | B–Q3 | O–O | 30 | BxN† | K–N1 |
| 12 | KN–K2 | Q–K2 | 31 | BxR† | KxB |
| 13 | QR–K1 | P–B4 | 32 | R–B1† | K–N1 |
| 14 | N–N3 | N–K1 | 33 | R–Q1 | R–KB1 |
| 15 | N–R5 | N/3–B2 | 34 | P–QR4 | R–B7 |
| 16 | P–KN4 | K–R1 | 35 | N–B4! | RxRP |
| 17 | KR–N1 | Q–B2 | 36 | R–Q7 | N–B4 |
| 18 | NxB | NxN | 37 | RxQRP | N–Q5 |
| 19 | P–B4 | P–K5 | 38 | R–QB7 | Resigns |

*King's Indian Defense Game 3*

*WHITE: Tal* *BLACK: Tolush*

*USSR Championship 1957*

| WHITE | BLACK | WHITE | BLACK |
|---|---|---|---|
| 1 P–QB4 | N–KB3 | 22 B–R6† | K–N1 |
| 2 N–QB3 | P–KN3 | 23 P–B4 | PxBP |
| 3 P–K4 | P–Q3 | 24 QxP | Q–Q1 |
| 4 P–Q4 | B–N2 | 25 PxP | NxP |
| 5 P–B3 | P–K4 | 26 Q–R2 | N/2–K4 |
| 6 KN–K2 | QN–Q2 | 27 B–B4 | N–B1? |
| 7 B–N5 | P–B3 | 28 Q–R6 | N/4–N3 |
| 8 Q–Q2 | O–O | 29 B–N5 | P–B3 |
| 9 P–Q5 | P–B4 | 30 P–K5! | RxP |
| 10 P–KN4 | P–QR3 | 31 BxN | R–N2 |
| 11 N–N3 | R–K1 | 32 N–K4! | BPxB |
| 12 P–KR4 | Q–R4 | 33 R–B1 | RxN |
| 13 B–R6 | N–B1 | 34 BxR | R–N2 |
| 14 P–R5 | Q–B2 | 35 R–B6 | BxP |
| 15 B–Q3 | P–QN4 | 36 R/1–B1 | N–Q2 |
| 16 O–O–O | PxBP | 37 RxP | Q–K2 |
| 17 B–N1 | B–R1 | 38 RxP | K–R1 |
| 18 QR–N1 | R–N1 | 39 BxP | N–N1 |
| 19 N–B5! | N/3–Q2 | 40 B–B5† | K–N1 |
| 20 B–N5! | B–N2 | 41 B–K6† | BxB |
| 21 NxB | KxN | 42 RxB | Resigns |

---

## part 2—CLASSICAL VARIATION

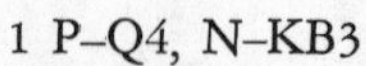

1 P–Q4, N–KB3
2 P–QB4, P–KN3
3 N–QB3, B–N2
4 P–K4, P–Q3
5 B–K2A

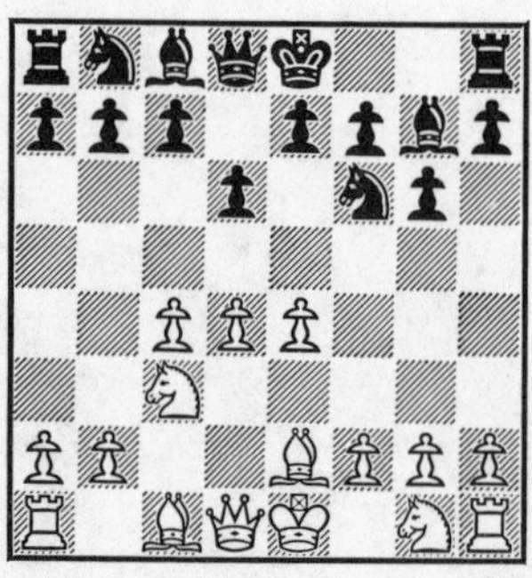

KEY POSITION 2

### OBSERVATIONS ON KEY POSITION 2

A The seldom played move 5 B–Q3 places no difficulties in Black's way. For examples: 5 . . . P–K4 6 KN–K2, O–O 7 P–B3, PxP followed by 8 . . . P–B3 and 9 . . . P–Q4= or 5 . . . O–O 6 KN–K2, N–B3 7 O–O, P–K4 8 P–Q5, N–Q5, 9 NxN, PxN 10 N–K2, R–K1 11 NxP, NxKP 12 BxN, RxB 13 B–K3, B–N5! 14 Q–Q3, Q–K2 with the threat of 15 . . . BxN∓.

In developing his Bishop at K2, White adopts a variation which proved quite successful in the 1953 Candidates' Tournament at Zurich and later, in somewhat altered form, in the 1959 Candidates' Tournament in Yugoslavia. In its latest form the variation leads to a double-edged game in which Black makes use of . . . P–KB4 in preparing a Kingside attack, while White pins his hopes on the Queenside. Present opinion holds that Black is faced with a difficult uphill struggle for equality.

IDEA VARIATIONS 3 AND 4:

(3) 5 . . . P–K4 6 P–Q5, P–QR4 7 B–N5, N–R3 8 P–KR3, Q–Q2 9 N–B3, O–O 10 P–KN4, N–K1 11 Q–Q2, P–R5 12 O–O–O, P–R6 13 P–QN3, N–B4 14 QR–N1, P–QB3 15 P–R4, N–B2 16 B–R6, PxP 17 BxB, KxB 18 KPxP, P–B3 19 P–N5± (Taimanov–Bronstein, Moscow 1956).

An alternative to 6 . . . P–QR4 is 6 . . . P–B4 7 B–N5, N–R3 (if 7 . . . P–KR3 then 8 B–K3, O–O 9 P–KN4!) 8 N–B3, P–R3 9 B–Q2, B–N5 10 P–QR3, BxN 11 BxB, N–Q2 12 N–N5, Q–K2 13 Q–B2, P–R4 14 P–KR4, B–R3 15 BxB RxB 16 O–O–O, N–B3 17 Q–Q2, R–R1= (Szabo–Panno, Amsterdam 1956). In this variation, 8 . . . N–B2 is inferior, e.g., 9 N–Q2, B–Q2 10 P–QR4, P–N3 11 N–N5, BxN 12 BPxB, O–O 13 P–QN4± (Petrosian–Pilnik, Amsterdam 1956).

(4) 5 . . . QN–Q2 6 P–B4, P–K4 7 BPxP, PxP 8 P–Q5, O–O 9 N–B3, N–B4 10 Q–B2, P–QR4 11 O–O, N–K1 12 B–K3, Q–K2. White's advantage is minimal.

Another possibility is 6 B–K3 (N–B3!), P–K4 7 Q–Q2 (7 N–B3, O–O 8 P–KR3 is also playable) O–O 8 P–Q5, N–B4 9 P–B3, P–QR4 10 P–KN4, R–K1 11 P–KR4, KN–Q2 12 P–R5 (Dr. Voellmy and others vs. Eliskases, handicap game 1935). White has a dangerous attack.

PRACTICAL VARIATIONS 5–8:

1 P–Q4, N–KB3 2 P–QB4, P–KN3 3 N–QB3, B–N2 4 P–K4, P–Q3 5 B–K2

| | 5 | 6 | 7 | 8 |
|---|---|---|---|---|
| 5 | — — | — — | — — | — — |
| | O–O | — — | — — | — — |
| 6 | B–N5[1] | N–B3 | — — | — — |
| | P–B4[2] | P–K4[9] | — — | — — |
| 7 | P–Q5[3] | O–O | P–Q5! | — — |
| | P–QR3[4] | N–B3![10] | QN–Q2[16] | — — |
| 8 | P–QR4[5] | P–Q5[11] | B–N5[17] | — — |
| | Q–R4[6] | N–K2 | P–KR3 | — — |
| 9 | B–Q2 | P–QN4[12] | B–R4 | — — |
| | P–K4[7] | N–R4[13] | P–R3 | P–KN4 |
| 10 | P–KN4! | P–N3 | N–Q2 | B–N3 |
| | N–K1 | P–KB4 | Q–K1 | N–R4 |
| 11 | P–R4 | N–KN5 | O–O | O–O |
| | P–B4 | N–KB3 | N–R2 | N–B5 |
| 12 | P–R5! | P–B5![14] | P–QN4 | N–Q2[21] |
| | P–B5 | PxKP | N–N4[18] | P–KB4[22] |
| 13 | P–N5 | QNxP | P–B3[19] | PxP |
| | R–B2 | NxN | P–KB4 | NxB† |
| 14 | B–N4 | NxN | B–B2 | QxN |
| | Q–Q1 | N–B4 | Q–K2 | N–B3 |
| 15 | BxB | B–KN5 | R–B1 | P–B5![23] |
| | QxB | Q–K1 | N–B3 | ± |
| 16 | N–B3[8] | Q–Q2[15] | P–B5[20] | |
| | ± | = | ± | |

*Notes to practical variations 5–8:*

[1] The Four Pawn Attack leads to great complications: 6 P–B4, P–B4 7 N–B3, PxP 8 NxP, N–B3 and now:

1) 9 B–K3, N–Q2 10 O–O, NxN 11 BxN, P–K4 12 PxP, NxP 13 Q–Q2, B–K3 14 P–QN3, P–QR3 15 QR–Q1,

continued ▸

Q–K2 16 B–K3, N–B3 17 R–B2± (Fuderer–Gligoric, Agram 1953).

2) 9 B–K3, N–N5 10 BxN, BxN (not 10 . . . BxB? because of 11 NxN etc.) 11 B/3xB, BxB 12 Q–Q2, NxB 13 QxN, P–K4 14 PxP, PxP 15 QxKP, R–K1 16 Q–N3, B–B4 17 O–O, BxP 18 Q–B2± (Uhlmann–Donner, Wageningen 1957). In this line, however, 14 . . . Q–R5†! equalizes.

3) 9 B–K3, B–Q2 10 O–O, N–N5 (after 10 . . . P–QR3 11 Q–Q2, White, in Teschner–Troianescu, Wageningen 1957, converted his positional advantage into a win; preferable was 10 . . . R–B1, as played in Dittmann–Beni, Vienna 1956) 11 BxN, BxB 12 NxN (sharper than 12 Q–Q2), Q–Q2 13 NxKP†± (Capablanca–Marotti, London 1922).

4) 9 B–K3, B–N5! (this appears to be Black's best line) 10 N–B3!, P–K4! with chances for both sides (Uhlmann–Geller, Dresden 1959).

5) In view of the last variation, 9 N–B2 comes into consideration, e.g., 9 . . . Q–N3? 10 B–K3! or 9 . . . B–K3 10 R–QN1, R–B1 11 B–K3 (Haberditz–Heinicke, Graz 1941). In this continuation Pachman gives 9 . . . B–K3 10 O–O, N–QR4=.

[2] In Averbach–Fischer, Portoroz 1958, 6 . . . P–KR3 was played, with the continuation 7 B–K3, P–B4 8 P–Q5, P–K3 9 P–KR3, PxP 10 KPxP, R–K1 11 N–B3, B–B4=. In a later game against Juchtmann, Averbach improved this line with 9 Q–Q2, PxP 10 KPxP, K–R2 11 P–KR3, R–K1 12 B–Q3! 6 . . . P–KR3 7 B–K3, P–B4 also appeared in Szabo–Olaffson, Prague–Marienbad 1954, where White's attack proved decisive.

Black has still another possibility in 6 . . . QN–Q2. For example:

1) 7 P–B4 etc.

2) 7 N–B3, P–B3 8 O–O, P–K4 9 Q–Q2, R–K1 10 QR–Q1, Q–K2 11 P–Q5, P–B4 12 P–KR3, P–QR3 13 N–R2, Q–B1 14 P–QR3, K–R1 15 P–QN4± (Stahlberg–Pilnik, Beverwijk 1956).

3) 7 Q–Q2, P–B3 8 P–KR4, P–KR4 9 N–R3, P–K4 10 P–Q5, N–N3 11 P–B3± (Grois–Kaliwoda, Prein 1960).

Finally, it should be mentioned that 6 . . . P–K4? fails here against 7 PxP, PxP 8 QxQ, RxQ 9 N–Q5.

[3] If 7 PxP then 7 . . . Q–R4!, while 7 N–B3? is simply answered by 7 . . . PxP 8 NxP, N–B3∓.

[4] Black has other moves at his disposal, as the following examples show:

1) 7 . . . P–K3 8 Q–Q2, PxP 9 KPxP, R–K1 10 N–B3, B–N5 11 O–O, QN–Q2 12 P–KR3, BxN 13 BxB, Q–N3 14 QR–Q1, P–QR3 15 Q–B2, R–K4= (Unzicker–Najdorf, Moscow 1956).

2) 7 . . . P–K3 8 N–B3, PxP 9 KPxP (or 9 BPxP, R–K1 10 N–Q2, P–QR3 Malich–Gromek, Marienbad 1959) B–N5 10 O–O, BxN 11 BxB, QN–Q2 12 Q–Q2, R–K1 13 Q–B4± (Szabo–Pilnik, Amsterdam 1956).

3) 7 . . . P–KR3 8 B–B4!, QN–Q2 9 Q–Q2, K–R2 10 N–B3, N–N5 11 O–O, N/2–K4 12 NxN, NxN 13 B–N3, P–B4 14 PxP, BxP 15 QR–K1 with good chances for White (Stahlberg–Matanovic, Beverwijk 1955).

4) 7 . . . P–KR3 8 B–B4!, QN–Q2 9 Q–Q2, K–R2 10 N–B3, P–QR3 11 O–O, Q–R4 12 Q–B2, R–QN1 13 P–QR4, N–N5 14 N–K1, N/4–K4 15 B–Q2, P–KN4 16 R–R3, and White, in Johannsson–Reshevsky, Munich 1958, accepted a premature draw on the 18th move!

5) 7 . . . P–K4? 8 P–KN4!

6) 7 . . . P–K4? 8 N–B3, P–KR3 9 B–Q2, N–K1 10 P–KR4±.

7) 7 . . . Q–R4 8 B–Q2, P–K3 9 N–B3, PxP 10 KPxP, B–N5! 11 O–O, BxN 12 BxB, QN–Q2 13 Q–B2, KR–K1 14 B–K2, R–K2 15 P–B4, QR–K1 16 B–Q3= (Pachman–Ujtelky, Prague 1957).

[5] Or 8 N–B3, P–QN4! 9 Q–B2, PxP 10 N–Q2, QN–Q2 11 O–O, N–N3 12 NxP, NxN 13 B/2xN, N–K1± (Rabar–Ivkov, Zagreb 1955).

[6] If 8 . . . QN–Q2 then 9 N–B3, N–K1 10 O–O, N–K4 11 N–Q2, P–B3 12 B–K3, R–N1 13 P–B4, N–B2 14 Q–B2, P–N3 15 KR–N1!± (Bronstein–Pilnik, Belgrade 1954). Or 8 . . . P–K3 9 Q–Q2, Q–R4 10 R–R3, PxP 11 KPxP, QN–Q2 12 N–B3 (Averbach–Fuchs, Dresden 1956), Black should now play 12 . . . R–K1 and reply to 13 O–O with 13 . . . N–B1. In Szabo–Spasski, 1959, Black played 8 . . . P–KR3, with the continuation 9 B–B4, P–K4 10 PxP e.p., BxP 11 BxQP, R–K1. Now, instead of 12 P–K5, N–N5, as in the actual game, White should have played 12 N–B3 to obtain a good game.

[7] 9 . . . P–K3 deserves consideration, e.g., 10 P–KN4 (10 N–B3 is safer) PxP 11 KPxP, Q–Q1 12 P–R4, R–K1 13 K–B1, QN–Q2 14 P–R5, N–K5 15 NxN, RxN 16 PxP, BPxP 17 R–QR3, N–B3 18 P–B3, R–K1 19 Q–K1, P–N3! 20 Q–R4, R–R2! (Ciocaltea–Gligoric, Moscow 1956). Black has a satisfactory game.

[8] See Game 4.

[9] 6 . . . B–N5 can lead to the following variations: 7 B–K3, P–K4 (if 7 . . . N–B3 then 8 O–O, P–K4 9 P–Q5) 8 P–Q5 (Grunfeld–Takacs, Meran 1924, and Portisch–Gurgenidse, Budapest 1959) or 7 O–O, QN–Q2 8 P–KR3, or 7 O–O, KN–Q2 8 B–K3, P–K4 9 P–Q5. In each case White retains a minimal initiative.

[10] Also good is the oft-played 7 . . . P–B3. For example:

1) 8 R–K1, PxP 9 NxP, R–K1 10 B–B1, N–N5 11 P–KR3, Q–B3!= (Smyslov–Geller, Zurich 1953).

2) 8 R–K1, QN–Q2 9 P–Q5, P–B4! 10 P–QR3, N–K1 11 B–N5, P–B3 12 B–Q2, P–B4 etc.= (Bronstein–Petrosian, Amsterdam 1956).

3) 8 R–K1, QN–Q2 9 B–B1!, R–K1 10 P–Q5, P–B4 11 P–KN3, R–B1 12 R–N1, N–K1 13 P–QR3, P–B4? 14 N–N5, N/2–B3 15 PxP, PxP 16 N–K6!± (Pachman–Uhlmann, Prague 1958).

4) 8 R–K1, Q–N3 9 P–Q5, P–B4 10 P–QR3 (Trifunovic–Orbaan, Wageningen 1957), N–K1!

continued ▸

5) 8 R–K1, Q–N3 9 PxP, PxP 10 B–K3, Q–B2 11 N–Q2, R–Q1 12 R–QB1, QN–Q2 13 Q–B2, N–B1, and Black has a satisfactory game (Teschner–Keres, Hamburg 1960).

6) 8 R–K1, Q–N3 9 B–B1, B–N5 10 P–Q5, P–B4 11 P–QR3, P–QR4 12 R–N1, N–R3 13 B–N5, P–R3 14 B–Q2, N–K1 15 P–R3, B–Q2= (Panno–Donner, Buenos Aires 1955).

The old continuation, 7 . . . QN–Q2, has disappeared from the tournament player's opening repertoire, since Black faces great difficulties after 8 R–K1, R–K1 9 B–B1!, P–B3 10 P–Q5, P–B4 11 P–QR3, R–B1 12 P–KN3, N–K1 13 P–QN4± (Reshevsky–Gligoric, 1952). 9 . . . PxP is also unsatisfactory in this line, e.g., 10 NxP, P–B3 11 B–B4. It should be noted, however, that if White plays 9 P–Q5 (instead of 9 B–B1!) Black equalizes with 9 . . . N–B4.

[11] Reshevsky's recommendation, 8 B–K3, is best answered with 8 . . . R–K1, e.g., 9 PxP, PxP 10 QxQ, NxQ (if 10 . . . RxQ, then 11 B–N5) 11 N–QN5, N–K3 12 N–N5, R–K2 13 NxQRP, N–B5 14 BxN, PxB 15 NxB, RxB 16 P–B3, N–Q2 17 QR–N1, R–R1 18 P–QR3, B–Q5† 19 K–R1, P–R3 20 N–R3, P–KN4 21 N–B2, R–K3 and, according to Najdorf, Black's active position is full compensation for his sacrificed Pawn. Or 9 P–Q5, N–Q5 10 NxN, PxN 11 BxP, NxKP 12 BxB, KxB= (Reshevsky–Najdorf, 1953). The *Tournament Book* of Wageningen 1957 cites a third possibility: 9 PxP, PxP 10 QxQ, NxQ 11 N–QN5, N–K3 12 N–N5, R–K2 13 KR–Q1! But this is not enough for an advantage.

[12] The older treatment, 9 N–K1, N–Q2, gives Black too many chances. For example:

1) 10 N–Q3, P–KB4 11 B–Q2, N–KB3 12 P–B3, P–B5 13 P–B5, P–KN4 14 R–B1, N–N3 15 N–N5, P–QR3! 16 N–R3, P–N5! 17 B–K1, P–N6! (Pachman–Padevsky, Dresden 1956).

2) 10 N–Q3, P–KB4 11 P–B3, P–B5 12 B–Q2, P–KN4 13 R–B1, N–KN3! 14 N–N5, P–QR3 15 N–R3, N–B3 16 P–B5, P–N5 17 PxQP, PxQP 18 N–B4, P–N6 (Reshevsky–Lombardy, US Championship 1957–58).

3) 10 B–K3, P–KB4 11 P–B3, P–B5 12 B–B2, P–KN4 13 N–Q3, N–KB3! 14 P–B5, N–N3! 15 R–B1, R–B2 16 PxP, PxP 17 N–N5, P–N5.

4) 10 B–K3, P–KB4 11 P–B3, P–B5 12 B–B2, P–KN4 13 N–Q3, N–KB3! 14 P–B5, N–N3! 15 R–B1, R–B2 16 PxP, PxP 17 R–B2, B–B1 18 Q–Q2, P–N5 19 KR–B1, P–N6! with a powerful attack (Taimanov–Najdorf, Zurich 1953).

5) 10 B–K3, P–KB4 11 P–B3, P–B5 12 B–B2, P–KN4 13 N–Q3, N–KB3! 14 P–B5, N–N3! 15 R–B1, R–B2 16 Q–N3, P–N5! 17 PxNP, NxNP 18 BxN, BxB 19 QxP, P–B6 (Eliskases–Gligoric, Mar del Plata 1953), and White found himself in difficult straits.

[13] On 9 . . . N–K1 there follows 10 P–B5, P–B4 11 N–KN5, K–R1 12 R–N1!, PxKP 13 B–N4!, N–B4 14 N/5xKP, P–KR3 15 Q–Q3± (Pachman–Flores, Santiago de Chile 1959). In this line if 10 . . . P–QR4 then 11 B–R3, RPxP 12 BxP, PxP 13 BxP,

N–Q3 14 Q–N3±. Playable for Black is 9 . . . P–QR4, e.g., 10 B–R3, N–Q2! 11 PxP, RxP 12 B–N4, R–R1 13 P–QR4, B–R3 14 P–R5, P–KB4 15 N–Q2, N–KB3 16 B–Q3, P–B4 17 PxP e.p., NxBP= (Bronstein–Robatsch, Gotha 1957).

[14] Weaker is 12 P–B3, P–B5 13 P–B5, P–QR4 (13 . . . N–R4? 14 P–KN4, B–B3 15 N–K6) 14 N–N5, RPxP 15 Q–N3, P–R3 16 N–K6, BxN 17 PxB, PxNP 18 PxNP, PxP 19 B–K3, P–N3 20 QR–Q1, Q–N1 21 P–B4, P–B3 22 PxP, PxN 23 B–KB4, N–R4, and Black won (Larsen–Dittmann, Reykjavik 1957).

[15] In Trifunovic–Larsen, Wageningen 1957, there followed 16 . . . N–Q5! 17 PxP, B–R6 18 PxP!, Q–B2 19 P–B3, BxR 20 RxB, QxQP 21 K–N2, QR–B1=.

[16] The text is considered Black's best reply; other continuations, treated below, definitely give White the edge:

1) 7 . . . N–R3 8 N–Q2 (8 B–N5 also merits some attention), P–B4 9 P–QR3, N–K1 10 P–KR4, P–B4 11 P–R5, N–B3 12 PxNP, PxNP 13 N–B3, N–B2 14 N–KN5, Q–K2 15 Q–Q3, P–B5 16 B–Q2± (Larsen–Gligoric, Portoroz 1958).

2) 7 . . . N–R4 8 P–KN3!, N–Q2 9 B–K3 (better than 9 B–N5, after which Black equalizes with 9 . . . N/2–B3 10 P–KR3, P–B4 11 Q–Q2, P–QR3 etc.), N/4–B3 10 N–Q2, P–B3 11 P–KR4, N–K1 12 P–KN4, P–KB4 13 NPxP, NPxP 14 KPxP, N/2–B3 15 P–R5, P–KR3 16 Q–B2, PxP 17 PxP, P–N4 18 BxNP, N–N5 19 N/2–K4, BxP 20 B–Q3± (Petrosian–Olafsson, Portoroz 1958). In this line 8 N–KN1 is inferior, e.g., 8 . . . N–Q2! 9 BxN, PxB 10 QxP, N–B4 11 N–B3, P–B4, and Black has excellent counterplay for his sacrificed Pawn (Szabo–Boleslavski, Budapest 1950).

3) 7 . . . P–QR4 8 O–O, N–R3 (or 8 . . . QN–Q2 9 Q–B2, N–R4! 10 P–KN3, N–B4) and now Pachman–Reshevsky, Munich 1958, continued 9 N–K1, N–B4 10 Q–B2, N–K1 11 B–K3, P–B4. Stronger for White than 8 O–O, however, is 8 B–N5, as in 8 . . . P–R3 9 B–R4, N–R3 10 N–Q2, P–KN4 11 B–N3, N–B4 12 O–O, P–B3 13 K–R1, B–Q2 14 P–B3, P–R5 15 P–QN4, PxP e.p. 16 PxP, Q–N3 17 Q–B2, N–R3 18 B–B2, and White enjoys a great advantage in space (Szabo–Ciocaltea, Bucharest 1960).

4) 7 . . . P–B4 8 B–N5 (again this move is stronger than 8 O–O, e.g., 8 . . . N–R3 9 N–K1, N–K1=, as in Lundin–Rabar, Helsinki 1952), P–KR3 9 B–Q2, N–K1 10 P–KR4, P–B4 11 P–R5!, P–KN4 12 PxP± (Petrosian–Nikolaijewsky, 1957).

[17] Neither 8 Q–B2, P–QR4 9 P–KR3, P–B3 (Szabo–Najdorf, 1950) nor 8 O–O, N–B4 9 N–Q2, P–QR4 10 Q–B2, B–R3! (Sakellaropoulos–Boleslavski, Helsinki 1952) causes Black any difficulties.

[18] The aggressive 12 . . . P–KB4 is met by 13 PxP, RxP (13 . . . PxP? 14 B–R5) 14 B–N4±. After 12 . . . B–B3, Tal–Fischer, Zagreb 1959, continued 13 BxB, N/RxB 14 N–N3, Q–K2 15 Q–Q2, K–R2 16 Q–K3, N–KN1 17 P–B5, P–B4 18 PxBP, NPxP 19 P–B4!±.

[19] Even stronger is 13 R–B1. See Game 5.

continued ▸

[20] Tal–Fischer, Bled 1959, continued 16 . . . B–Q2 17 Q–B2, N–R4 18 P–N5, PxKP 19 N/2xP, NxN 20 PxN, N–B5 21 P–B6, Q–N4! 22 B–B3, PxBP 23 QPxP!±.

[21] If 12 N–K1, P–KB4 13 PxP, NxB† 14 QxN, N–B3 15 P–KR4, BxP 16 PxP, PxP 17 N–B2, B–N3 18 N–K3, Q–Q2 19 P–B5, N–R4∓ (Matulovic–Gligoric, Yugoslav Championship 1959).

[22] Here 12 . . . N–B4! is more promising. For example:

1) 13 P–N4?, N/4–Q6 14 P–QR3, NxB† 15 QxN, N–B5 16 Q–Q1, P–KR4! 17 P–B3, P–N5 18 PxP, BxP 19 Q–B2, B–R3! (O'Kelly–Gligoric, Madrid 1960).
2) 13 B–N4, NxKP 14 N/2xN, P–KB4 15 BxBP, BxB 16 P–B3, Q–K1 17 P–N4, Q–N3 18 K–R1, P–QR4 19 P–QR3, P–N5! 20 P–B5, NxNP!∓.
3) 13 N–N3, P–N3 14 NxN, NxB† 15 QxN, NPxN 16 P–QR3, P–B4 17 PxP, BxP 18 P–N4± (Szabo–Gligoric, Budapest 1960). The game was drawn after 18 . . . P–K5! 19 QR–B1, PxP 20 PxP, P–QR4 21 PxP, RxP 22 NxP, Q–R1 23 KR–K1, R–R7 24 R–B2, R–R8 25 QR–B1, R–R7.

[23] Smyslov–Benko, Zagreb 1959, continued 15 . . . BxP 16 QR–B1, PxP 17 Q–B4, N–Q2 18 P–N4!, P–N3 19 N–N3, Q–K2 20 N–N5, Q–B2 21 PxP, PxP 22 N/5xBP±.

### *King's Indian Defense Game 4*

*WHITE: Averbach* *BLACK: Panno*

*USSR vs. Argentina 1954*

| | WHITE | BLACK | | WHITE | BLACK | | WHITE | BLACK |
|---|---|---|---|---|---|---|---|---|
| 1 | P–Q4 | N–KB3 | 12 | P–R5! | P–B5 | 23 | R–R1 | R–QN1 |
| 2 | P–QB4 | P–KN3 | 13 | P–N5 | R–B2 | 24 | BxP! | Q–B2 |
| 3 | N–QB3 | B–N2 | 14 | B–N4 | Q–Q1 | 25 | Q–R2 | N–Q2 |
| 4 | P–K4 | P–Q3 | 15 | BxB | QxB | 26 | Q–R3 | N–B1 |
| 5 | B–K2 | O–O | 16 | N–B3 | B–B1 | 27 | RxN† | KxR |
| 6 | B–N5 | P–B4 | 17 | K–K2 | R–N2 | 28 | Q–K6 | R–N1 |
| 7 | P–Q5 | P–QR3 | 18 | R–R4 | N–Q2 | 29 | N–R4 | B–Q1 |
| 8 | P–QR4 | Q–R4 | 19 | PxP | PxP | 30 | NxP† | K–N2 |
| 9 | B–Q2 | P–K4 | 20 | Q–R1 | B–K2 | 31 | NxP! | Resigns |
| 10 | P–KN4! | N–K1 | 21 | R–R8† | K–B2 | | | |
| 11 | P–R4 | P–B4 | 22 | Q–R6 | N–B1 | | | |

### *King's Indian Defense Game 5*

*WHITE: Petrosian* *BLACK: Gligoric*

*Belgrade 1959*

| | WHITE | BLACK | | WHITE | BLACK |
|---|---|---|---|---|---|
| 1 | P–Q4 | N–KB3 | 3 | N–QB3 | B–N2 |
| 2 | P–QB4 | P–KN3 | 4 | P–K4 | P–Q3 |

| WHITE | BLACK | WHITE | BLACK |
|---|---|---|---|
| 5 N–B3 | O–O | 26 P–QR3 | PxP |
| 6 B–K2 | P–K4 | 27 PxP | R–N3 |
| 7 P–Q5 | QN–Q2 | 28 N/2xN | PxN |
| 8 B–N5 | P–KR3 | 29 BxP | B–B4 |
| 9 B–R4 | P–R3 | 30 BxB | NxB |
| 10 N–Q2 | Q–K1 | 31 Q–R5 | R–B3 |
| 11 O–O | N–R2 | 32 R–N1† | K–R1 |
| 12 P–QN4 | N–N4 | 33 QR–K1 | Q–B2 |
| 13 R–B1 | P–KB4 | 34 QxQ | RxQ |
| 14 P–B3 | Q–K2 | 35 R–K4 | K–R2 |
| 15 K–R1 | N–B3 | 36 NxP | R–R7 |
| 16 P–B5 | N–R4 | 37 N–Q4? | NxN |
| 17 P–B6! | P–N3 | 38 RxN | R–K2 |
| 18 PxP | PxP | 39 P–B5! | R/2–K7 |
| 19 P–N3! | B–B3 | 40 R–R4 | R–KB7 |
| 20 P–B4 | N–N2 | 41 P–N5 | R/R–N7 |
| 21 N–B4 | PxP | 42 P–N6!! | RxNP |
| 22 PxP | P–N4 | 43 R/4–KN4 | R–N1 |
| 23 N–Q2 | N–K5 | 44 R–N7† | K–R1 |
| 24 BxB | RxB | 45 R/7–N6 | Resigns |
| 25 B–B3 | P–QR4 | | |

## part 3—MODERN TREATMENT

OBSERVATIONS ON KEY POSITION 3

This sprightly deployment of White's Queen Bishop has been the subject of much theoretical analysis since its initial appearance in the 1953 Candidates' Tournament at Zurich. At present it is in great vogue, although it is doubtful whether the variation is as effective as 5 B–K2, O–O 6 B–N5 (Prac. Var. 5).

1 P–Q4, N–KB3
2 P–QB4, P–KN3
3 N–QB3, B–N2
4 P–K4, P–Q3
5 B–N5

KEY POSITION 3

IDEA VARIATIONS 5 AND 6:

(5) 5 . . . QN–Q2 6 P–B4, O–O 7 N–B3, P–B4 8 P–Q5, P–KR3 9 B–R4, Q–R4 10 Q–Q2, R–K1 11 B–Q3, N–B1 12 O–O, P–R3 13 P–K5, N/3–R2 14 QR–K1, B–Q2 15 P–K6!± (Haggqvist–Edback, Stockholm 1957).

(6) 5 . . . P–B3 6 B–K2, O–O 7 P–KR4, P–K4 8 P–Q5, Q–K2 9 Q–B1!, N–R3 10 P–R5, N–B2 11 B–R6, N/2–K1 12 N–R3 (Walter–Dintheer, Zurich 1958). At this point Black should continue with 12 . . . B–N5 and reply to 13 P–B3 with 13 . . . BxN.

PRACTICAL VARIATIONS 9–12:

1 P–Q4, N–KB3 2 P–QB4, P–KN3 3 N–QB3, B–N2 4 P–K4, P–Q3 5 B–N5

| | 9 | 10 | 11 | 12 |
|---|---|---|---|---|
| 5 | – – | – – | – – | – – |
| | P–KR3 | P–B4 | – – | O–O |
| 6 | B–R4[1] | P–Q5! | – – | Q–Q2[17] |
| | P–B4[2] | O–O[7] | – – | QN–Q2[18] |
| 7 | P–Q5 | B–Q3[8] | N–B3 | B–Q3 |
| | O–O[3] | P–QR3[9] | P–K3[14] | P–B4 |
| 8 | B–Q3[4] | P–B4[10] | N–Q2 | P–Q5 |
| | P–K3 | P–N4 | P–KR3 | P–QR3 |
| 9 | PxP[5] | N–B3 | B–R4 | N–B3 |
| | BxP | PxP[11] | P–R3[15] | P–N4[19] |
| 10 | P–B4 | BxP | P–R4 | PxP |
| | N–B3 | B–N5 | QN–Q2 | N–N3 |
| 11 | KN–K2 | O–O | B–K2 | O–O |
| | P–KN4 | QN–Q2 | R–K1 | B–N5 |
| 12 | PxP | Q–K1[12] | P–B4 | PxP! |
| | N–KN5 | P–R3 | Q–N3 | BxN |
| 13 | Q–Q2 | B–R4 | R–R3 | PxB |
| | N/3–K4 | N–N3 | P–K4 | P–B5 |
| 14 | O–O | N–Q2 | P–B5 | B–K2 |
| | N–N3 | B–B1 | PxP | RxP |
| 15 | P–KN3! | QR–Q1 | PxP | P–N4! |
| | N/5–K4 | Q–B2 | P–K5 | N–R4 |
| 16 | N–Q5[6] | P–KR3 | P–R5 | P–QR4[20] |
| | ± | P–K3[13] | Q–B2[16] | ± |
| | | ± | = | |

*Notes to practical variations 9–12:*

[1] Inferior is 6 B–K3, e.g., 6 . . . N–N5 7 B–B1, P–QB4 8 P–Q5, B–Q5 9 N–R3, N–K4 10 N–B4, Q–R4 11 B–Q2, P–KN4 (Bisguier–Rabar, Goteborg 1955).

[2] Weaker is 6 . . . QN–Q2 7 P–B4, P–K4 (P–B4!) 8 QPxP, PxP 9 N–B3, Q–K2 10 N–Q5, Q–B4 11 P–QN4! (Golz–Uhlmann, Dresden 1956) or 6 . . . O–O 7 B–Q3, N–B3 8 KN–K2, P–K4 9 P–Q5, N–Q5 10 P–B3, P–B4 11 Q–Q2, P–QR3 12 NxN, KPxN 13 N–K2, R–K1 14 B–N3, N–R4 15 B–B2, P–B4 (Zinn–Karastojcev, Warna 1960).

[3] To be considered is 7 . . . Q–R4, e.g., 8 P–B3, P–R3 9 P–R4, QN–Q2 10 R–R3 (better is 10 B–Q3! followed by KN–K2), P–KN4 11 B–B2, N–K4 (Tschukajew–Keres, Moscow 1959), and Black stands very well. Or 8 B–Q3, QN–Q2 9 P–B4, P–QN4! 10 PxP, P–B5 11 B–QB2, P–QR3 (Tolush–Wasjukow, Leningrad–Moscow 1960). White should now play 12 KN–K2 or 12 PxP.

[4] If 8 N–B3 then 8 . . . P–K3 9 N–Q2 transposes into Prac. Var. 11.

[5] Or 9 KN–K2, PxP 10 KPxP, QN–Q2 11 P–B4, P–R3 12 O–O, P–QN4 13 PxP, Q–N3 14 K–R1, R–K1 15 P–KR3, B–N2 16 Q–N3, P–B5! 17 BxBP, N–B4 18 Q–B2, PxP 19 BxN, PxB 20 BxB, KxB 21 P–B5, N–Q6 (Cholmov–Neikirch, Balatonfured 1959). White stands well.

[6] White has the edge. See Game 6.

[7] After 6 . . . N–R3 7 B–Q3, N–B2 8 KN–K2, P–QR3 9 P–QR4, R–QN1 10 O–O, O–O 11 Q–B2, B–Q2 12 P–KR3, P–N4 13 P–B4!, N–K1 14 RPxP, PxP 15 R–R7 (Bronstein–Najdorf, Zurich 1953), White has a favorable game.

[8] Pachman–Alster, Prague 1953, continued 7 P–B4, Q–R4 8 B–Q3, P–N4 9 PxP, P–QR3 10 PxP, BxP 11 KN–K2, QN–Q2 12 BxB, RxB 13 O–O, Q–N3 14 Q–Q2, KR–N1 15 QR–N1, P–B5† 16 K–R1, N–B4 17 N–N3. An alternative is 7 Q–Q2, e.g., 7 . . . P–K4 8 O–O–O, N–R3 9 P–B3, N–B2 (Sanz–Gumprich, Dyckhoff Memorial Correspondence Tournament 1954-56) or 7 . . . R–K1? 8 O–O–O, P–QR3 9 P–B4, P–N4 10 PxP, PxP 11 BxP, B–Q2 12 B–Q3, N–R3 13 P–K5! (Lehman–Lambert, 1953) or 7 . . . P–QR3 8 B–Q3, P–K4 9 KN–K2, QN–Q2 10 O–O, Q–K1 (Hottes–Geller, Hamburg 1960).

[9] 7 . . . P–KR3 8 B–R4 transposes into Prac. Var. 9.

[10] White achieves less with 8 P–QR4, e.g., 8 . . . Q–R4 9 KN–K2, P–K3 10 PxP (Golz–Zirngible, Leipzig 1959), PxP 11 O–O, N–B3.

[11] 9 . . . QN–Q2 10 O–O, R–N1 11 P–K5, N–K1 12 Q–K2, P–B3 13 P–K6, N–N3 14 P–B5! (Bisguier–Baker, New York 1958).

[12] Simultaneously breaking the pin and threatening 13 Q–R4. More natural, however, is 12 P–KR3.

[13] In the game Bisguier–Matanovic, Munich 1958, there followed 17 PxP, BxP, and White now could have maintained his advantage with 18 B–Q3.

[14] Eibensteiner–Kunert, Linz 1924, continued 7 . . . QN–Q2 8 B–Q3, N–N5! 9 O–O, N/5–K4 10 NxN, NxN 11 P–B4. Best now for Black is 11 . . . N–N5, e.g., 12 Q–B3, B–Q5† 13 K–R1, P–B3 14 B–R4, P–KN4! 7 . . . Q–R4 was played in Sanguinetti–Fuchs, Munich 1958, and there followed 8 N–Q2, P–QR3 9 P–QR4, P–R3 10 B–R4, P–K3 11 B–K2, PxP 12 BPxP, Q–B2 13 O–O, QN–Q2 14 Q–B2, R–K1 15 P–B4±.

[15] Or 9 . . . N–R3 10 B–K2, N–B2 (Kluger–Szabo).

[16] Najdorf–Panno, Mar del Plata 1957, followed a very interesting course: 17 Q–B2, P–K6 18 N/2–K4, NxN 19 NxN, BxP 20 RxP, QxP† 21 K–B1, B–Q5 22 R–N3†, K–B1 23 NxP, Q–R8† 24 B–Q1, R–K6 25 RxR, BxR 26 P–KN4, Q–K4 and only owing to a blunder on Black's 31st move did White obtain an advantage.

[17] Other moves lead to variations which have been previously discussed, such as 6 P–B3, P–B4! (Prac. Var. 3, footnote 11), 6 B–K2 (Prac. Var. 5 and 6), and 6 N–B3, P–B4 7 P–Q5 (Prac. Var. 11).

[18] For 6 . . . P–B4 7 P–Q5, see Prac. Var. 10, footnote 8.

[19] An audacious Pawn sacrifice which is not quite sound.

[20] Black can offer no resistance to the coming advance of White's two connected passed Pawns. See Game 7.

*King's Indian Defense Game 6*

*WHITE: Uhlmann* *BLACK: Gligoric*

*Buenos Aires 1960*

| | WHITE | BLACK | | WHITE | BLACK |
|---|---|---|---|---|---|
| 1 | P–Q4 | N–KB3 | 19 | KPxB | P–N4 |
| 2 | P–QB4 | P–KN3 | 20 | PxP | R–K1 |
| 3 | N–QB3 | B–N2 | 21 | B–K4 | R–N1 |
| 4 | P–K4 | P–Q3 | 22 | P–QR4 | R–N2 |
| 5 | B–N5 | P–KR3 | 23 | N–N3 | N–N3 |
| 6 | B–R4 | P–B4 | 24 | QR–K1 | R/2–K2 |
| 7 | P–Q5 | O–O | 25 | Q–N2 | N–R5 |
| 8 | B–Q3 | P–K3 | 26 | Q–R3 | N–N3 |
| 9 | PxP | BxP | 27 | Q–R5 | Q–R4 |
| 10 | P–B4 | N–B3 | 28 | BxN! | BPxB |
| 11 | KN–K2 | P–KN4 | 29 | RxR! | PxQ |
| 12 | PxP | N–KN5 | 30 | RxR† | K–R2 |
| 13 | Q–Q2 | N/3–K4 | 31 | R–K6 | Q–Q7 |
| 14 | O–O | N–N3 | 32 | P–N6† | K–R3 |
| 15 | P–KN3! | N/5–K4 | 33 | N–B5† | K–N4 |
| 16 | N–Q5 | N/3xB | 34 | P–R4† | K–N5 |
| 17 | PxN | PxP | 35 | R–K4† | Resigns |
| 18 | PxP | BxN | | | |

*King's Indian Defense Game 7*

*WHITE: Pietzch* *BLACK: Gligoric*

*Madrid 1960*

| | WHITE | BLACK | | WHITE | BLACK |
|---|---|---|---|---|---|
| 1 | P–Q4 | N–KB3 | 16 | P–QR4 | P–B4 |
| 2 | P–QB4 | P–KN3 | 17 | B–R6 | BxB |
| 3 | N–QB3 | B–N2 | 18 | QxB | P–B5 |
| 4 | P–K4 | P–Q3 | 19 | P–K5! | N–N2 |
| 5 | B–N5 | O–O | 20 | KR–Q1 | PxP |
| 6 | Q–Q2 | QN–Q2 | 21 | P–R5 | N–Q2 |
| 7 | B–Q3 | P–B4 | 22 | P–Q6! | RxQP |
| 8 | P–Q5 | P–QR3 | 23 | BxP† | K–R1 |
| 9 | N–B3 | P–N4 | 24 | N–K4 | N–KB4 |
| 10 | PxP | N–N3 | 25 | Q–R3 | R–Q5 |
| 11 | O–O | B–N5 | 26 | RxR | NxR |
| 12 | PxP! | BxN | 27 | N–N5 | N–KB3 |
| 13 | PxB | P–B5 | 28 | P–R6! | N–B7 |
| 14 | B–K2 | RxP | 29 | R–QB1 | Q–Q7 |
| 15 | P–N4! | N–R4 | 30 | RxN | QxR |

| WHITE | BLACK | WHITE | BLACK |
|---|---|---|---|
| 31 N–B7† | RxN | 37 Q–R1 | K–R3 |
| 32 BxR | K–N2 | 38 P–R7 | Q–Q7 |
| 33 B–K6 | P–K5 | 39 P–R8(Q) | Q–N4† |
| 34 PxP | NxP | 40 K–B1 | Q–N7† |
| 35 Q–B1 | N–B6 | 41 K–K1 | Resigns |
| 36 B–B4 | P–B6 | | |

---

## part 4—OLD FIANCHETTO

OBSERVATIONS ON KEY POSITION 4

This system, much in vogue at one time, is marked by the fianchetto of White's King Bishop in conjunction with the development of his King Knight to K2. A distinct disadvantage of the formation is White's lack of pressure on K5, allowing Black to play . . . P–K4 without a preparatory . . . QN–Q2. The first known example of this set-up is found in Von Bardeleben–Riemann, Nuremberg 1883.

1 P–Q4, N–KB3
2 P–QB4, P–KN3
3 N–QB3, B–N2
4 P–K4, P–Q3
5 P–KN3

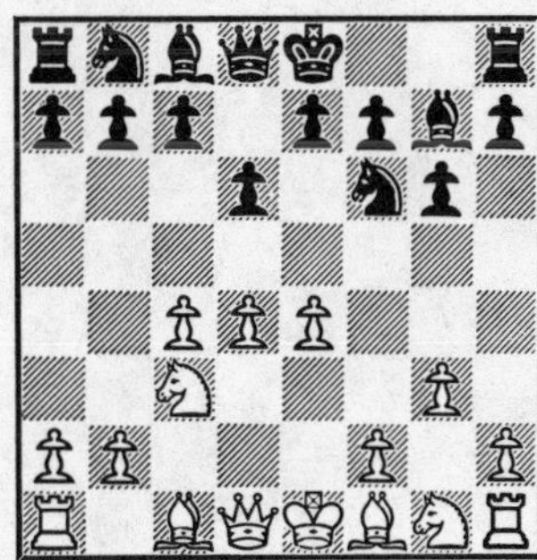

KEY POSITION 4

IDEA VARIATIONS 7 AND 8:

(7) 5 . . . N–B3 (or 5 . . . QN–Q2 6 B–N2, P–K4 7 KN–K2, O–O 8 O–O, P–B3 9 P–KR3, PxP 10 NxP, reaching a type of position discussed in Part 5; the transposition can be avoided by 8 P–Q5) 6 P–Q5!, N–K4 (if 6 . . . N–QN1 7 B–N2, P–K4 8 KN–K2, QN–Q2 9 P–KR3, P–KR3 10 B–K3± (Winter-Bogoljubov, Nottingham 1936) 7 P–B4, N/4–Q2 8 B–N2, O–O 9 KN–K2, P–K4 (if 9 . . . P–B3 10 B–K3, as in Mendes-Paoli, Vienna 1952–53) 10 O–O, P–N3 11 P–B5!, P–QR4 12 P–KR3, N–K1 13 B–K3, N–B4 14 P–R3, B–Q2 15 P–QN4± (Grunfeld–Weiss, Vienna 1941).

(8) 5 . . . O–O 6 B–N2, P–B4 7 P–Q5, QN–Q2 (more in the modern manner is 7 . . . P–K3 8 KN–K2, PxP 9 BPxP, P–QR3 10 P–QR4, QN–Q2 11 O–O [Becker–Carls, Dresden 1926, and Nowetelnow–Plater, Moscow 1947]) 8 P–B4! (positionally necessary but capable of being deferred, e.g., 8 KN–K2, N–K4 9 P–N3, B–N5 10 P–B4!), N–N3 9 Q–Q3, P–K3 10 KN–K2, PxP 11 BPxP, N–K1 12 P–QR4, P–B4 13 P–R5, PxP 14 NxP, N–Q2 15 N–N5!, N/2–B3 16 N–K6± (Grunfeld–deGroot, Amsterdam 1936).

PRACTICAL VARIATIONS 13–16:

1 P–Q4, N–KB3 2 P–QB4, P–KN3 3 N–QB3, B–N2 4 P–K4, P–Q3 5 P–KN3

| | *13* | *14* | *15* | *16* |
|---|---|---|---|---|
| *5* | — — | — — | — — | — — |
| | O–O[1] | — — | — — | — — |
| *6* | B–N2 | — — | — — | — — |
| | P–B4 | P–K4! | — — | — — |
| *7* | P–Q5 | KN–K2[7] | — — | — — |
| | P–K4[2] | PxP | N–B3 | QN–Q2 |
| *8* | KN–K2 | NxP | P–Q5 | P–Q5![16] |
| | N–R4[3] | N–B3 | N–Q5![12] | P–QR4[17] |
| *9* | O–O | N–B2[8] | O–O![13] | O–O |
| | B–Q2[4] | B–K3[9] | R–K1[14] | N–B4 |
| *10* | B–K3 | P–N3 | B–K3 | P–B3[18] |
| | N–R3 | Q–Q2 | NxN† | N–K1[19] |
| *11* | Q–Q2 | O–O | QxN | B–K3 |
| | N–B2 | B–R6 | N–N5 | P–B4 |
| *12* | P–B4 | P–B3 | B–B1 | Q–Q2[20] |
| | PxP | BxB | P–KB4 | N–B3 |
| *13* | NxP | KxB | P–B3 | K–R1 |
| | N–B3 | P–QR3[10] | N–B3 | B–Q2 |
| *14* | P–KR3 | B–N2 | B–K3 | QR–Q1 |
| | P–QN4[5] | N–R2 | N–R4 | PxP |
| *15* | P–K5 | Q–Q2 | P–B5[15] | NxP |
| | QPxP | P–QN4 | ± | QNxN |
| *16* | N–Q3![6] | N–K3 | | PxN |
| | ± | P–B3[11] | | N–N5[21] |
| | | ± | | = |

*Notes to practical variations 13-16:*

[1] After 5 . . . P–B4 6 P–Q5, P–K4 7 B–N2, P–QR3 (7 . . . O–O leads to Prac. Var. 13) 8 KN–K2, QN–Q2 9 P–KR3, R–N1 10 P–QR4, N–N1 11 B–K3, N–K2 12 Q–Q2± (Grunfeld–Danek, Vienna 1932). But Black does better with 6 . . . O–O 7 B–N2, P–K3 8 KN–K2, PxP 9 BPxP, R–K1 10 P–QR4, N–R3 11 P–B3, N–QN5 12 B–K3, P–N3 13 Q–Q2, B–QR3 14 O–O, N–Q2 15 P–B4, P–B4 16 N–N5, BxN 17 PxB, N–KB3 18 P–K5, N–N5 19 QR–Q1, PxP 20 PxP, NxB 21 QxN, RxP 22 Q–B2, Q–Q3 23 N–B4, B–R3 24 KR–K1, QR–K1∓ (Donner–Czerniak, Venice 1950). Black also has the edge in this variation after 10 . . . P–N3, e.g., 11 O–O, P–QR3 12 P–KR3, QN–Q2 13 B–K3, R–N1 (Krogius–Kopylov, 17th USSR Championship). Better for White is 12 P–B3.

[2] For 7 . . . QN–Q2 or 7 . . . P–K3, see Idea Var. 8.

[3] Other continuations:

1) 8 . . . N–K1 9 O–O, P–B4 10 B–K3, N–Q2 11 PxP, PxP 12 P–B4, P–K5 13 P–KN4, N/2–B3 14 PxP, N–N5 15 B–Q2, BxP 16 P–KR3, N–R3 17 N–N3, B–Q5† 18

K–R2, P–K6 19 B–K1, R–B1 20 Q–R5± (Beni–Wenzel, Vienna 1951).

2) 8 . . . N–K1 9 O–O, P–B4 10 PxP, PxP 11 P–B4, N–Q2 12 Q–B2, N/2–B3 13 N–Q1, P–K5 14 N–K3, P–KR4 15 B–Q2, N–N5± (L. Schmid–Kovacs, 1953).

3) 8 . . . QN–Q2 9 O–O, N–K1 10 B–K3, P–QR3 11 Q–Q2, P–N3 12 QR–K1, R–R2 13 P–B4!, PxP 14 PxP, P–B4 15 PxP, PxP 16 N–N3, N/2–B3 17 B–R3± (Fine–Stahlberg, Match 1937).

4) 8 . . . P–QR3 9 P–QR4, QN–Q2 10 O–O, N–R4 11 B–K3, P–B4 12 PxP (Q–Q2!), PxP 13 P–B4, PxP 14 NxP, NxN 15 PxN, N–B3 16 P–KR3, B–Q2 17 Q–Q3, Q–K1 18 QR–N1, Q–N3 19 P–N4, N–K5∓ (Reshevsky–Najdorf, 12th Match Game 1952).

[4] Horowitz–Petrosian, 1955, continued 9 . . . N–Q2 10 B–K3, P–B4 11 P–B4 (Q–Q2!), PxBP 12 NxP, NxN 13 BxN, N–K4 with good play for Black.

[5] 14 . . . Q–K2 is met by 15 N–Q3 with the threat of 16 P–K5 (15 . . . N–R4 16 P–KN4).

[6] In Konig-Prins, Hastings 1937, there followed 16 . . . PxP 17 NxKP, N/3xP 18 B–N5!, Q–K1 19 NxN, QxN 20 B–B6, Q–R4 21. P–KN4, BxP 22 PxB, QxP 23 Q–R6!, and Black resigned.

[7] 7 P–Q5 deserves serious consideration, e.g., 7 . . . P–QR4 8 KN–K2, N–R3 9 O–O, Q–K2 (for 9 . . . N–B4, see Prac. Var. 16) 10 P–B3 followed by 11 B–K3.

[8] Or 9 NxN, PxN 10 O–O, N–Q2! 11 Q–B2, Q–B3 12 N–K2, R–K1 13 R–N1, Q–K2 14 B–Q2, N–B4 15 QR–K1, P–QR4= (Najdorf–Bronstein, Budapest 1950). In this line White achieves more with 11 P–B4, as in 11 . . . B–QR3 12 R–K1, N–B4 13 N–QR4± (Lundin–Platz, Helsinki 1952).

[9] Or 9 . . . N–K4 10 P–N3, N/3–Q2 11 N–Q4, N–B4 12 O–O, P–B3 13 P–KR3, P–QR4 14 B–K3, R–K1 15 Q–B2, P–R5 16 KR–Q1, PxP 17 PxP, RxR 18 RxR, N/K–Q6= H. Steiner–Geller, Saltsjobaden 1952).

[10] Better is 13 . . . N–KR4!, e.g., 14 B–N2, P–B4= (Botvinnik–Yudowitsch, 11th USSR Championship).

[11] 17 QR–Q1, QR–Q1 18 N–K2±. See Game 8.

[12] Inferior is 8 . . . N–K2, e.g., 9 O–O, N–R4 10 B–K3, P–KB4 11 P–B3, P–N3 12 P–QN4, P–R4 13 P–QR3, B–QR3 14 Q–N3, Q–Q2 15 RPxP, NPxP 16 N–N5, KR–N1 17 P–QR4, N–KB3 18 B–Q2, B–N2 19 P–B5± (Beni–Prameshuber, Vienna 1951) or 9 O–O, N–Q2 10 B–K3, P–KB4 11 P–B3±.

[13] Better than 9 NxN, PxN 10 N–K2 (not 10 QxP?, NxKP!), R–K1 11 P–B3, P–B4 12 PxP e.p., PxP 13 NxP, Q–N3 14 N–B2, P–Q4! 15 B–K3, Q–R3 16 BPxP, PxP 17 PxP, B–B4 18 K–B2, BxN 19 QxB, RxB! 20 KxR, R–K1† 21 K–B2, N–N5†! 22 PxN, B–Q5† (Birzoi–Gavrila, 1958), and White resigned. In this variation, 14 B–K3 is met with 14 . . . P–Q4!, e.g., 15 O–O, QxP 16 NxP, PxKP 17 PxP, N–N5 (Evans–Lambert, Ragusa 1950).

[14] 9 . . . P–B4 is incorrect because of 10 PxP e.p., PxP 11 NxN, PxN 12 N–K2!, R–K1 13 NxP, NxP 14 NxP, Q–B2 15 Q–Q5, B–N2 16 BxN, QR–B1 17 Q–Q3! After 9 . . . NxN† 10 QxN, Q–K2 11 P–KR3!, P–QR4 12 B–K3, P–N3 13 P–N3, N–Q2, White has but a slight edge.

continued ▸

[15] If 15 Q–Q2 then 15 . . . P–B5! 16 PxP, NxP 17 BxN, PxB 18 QxP, R–K4!∓ (Beni–Poschauko, Vienna 1951).

[16] 8 O–O, R–K1 9 P–Q5, P–QR4 10 P–KR3, N–B4 11 B–K3± (Christoffel–Yanofsky, Groningen 1946). Or 8 O–O, P–B3 9 P–Q5, P–B4 10 P–KR3, P–QR3 11 B–K3± (Game 9). In this line if 9 . . . Q–K2 10 P–KR3, N–K1 11 B–K3, P–QB4 12 Q–Q2±.

[17] 8 . . . N–K1 can be answered by 9 O–O, P–KB4 10 P–KB4.

[18] Heemsoth–Henning, German Correspondence Championship 1951-54, continued 10 P–KR3, K–R1 11 B–K3, N–N1 12 Q–Q2, P–B4 13 PxP, PxP 14 P–B4, P–K5 15 K–R2, N–B3 16 N–Q1, B–Q2 17 N–Q4, Q–K1=.

[19] Or 10 . . . KN–Q2 11 B–K3, P–B4 12 Q–B2, P–N3 13 P–KR3, PxP 14 PxP, N–B3 15 P–QR3, N/4–Q2 16 P–QN4± (Castaldi–Nestler, Florenz 1953).

[20] Also to be considered is 12 P–QR3, P–N3 13 P–QN4, N–Q2 14 Q–Q3±.

[21] Petrosian–Geller, Saltsjobaden 1952.

### *King's Indian Defense Game 8*

*WHITE: Kotov* — *BLACK: Barcza*

*Saltsjobaden 1952*

| | WHITE | BLACK | | WHITE | BLACK |
|---|---|---|---|---|---|
| 1 | P–Q4 | N–KB3 | 17 | QR–Q1 | QR–Q1 |
| 2 | P–QB4 | P–KN3 | 18 | N–K2! | Q–B2 |
| 3 | N–QB3 | B–N2 | 19 | B–B3 | Q–K2 |
| 4 | P–K4 | P–Q3 | 20 | N–Q4 | N–K1 |
| 5 | P–KN3 | O–O | 21 | N/4–B5! | PxN |
| 6 | B–N2 | P–K4 | 22 | NxP | Q–B2 |
| 7 | KN–K2 | PxP | 23 | NxB | NxN |
| 8 | NxP | N–B3 | 24 | B–B6! | K–R1 |
| 9 | N–B2 | B–K3 | 25 | Q–N5 | R–KN1 |
| 10 | P–N3 | Q–Q2 | 26 | P–KR4 | QR–K1 |
| 11 | O–O | B–R6 | 27 | P–R5 | R–K4! |
| 12 | P–B3 | BxB | 28 | BxR | PxB |
| 13 | KxB | P–QR3 | 29 | Q–B6! | N–B1 |
| 14 | B–N2 | N–R2 | 30 | P–R6 | N–K2 |
| 15 | Q–Q2 | P–QN4 | 31 | R–Q2! | Resigns |
| 16 | N–K3 | P–B3 | | | |

### *King's Indian Defense Game 9*

*WHITE: Grunfeld* — *BLACK: Kaliwoda*

*Hartberg 1948*

| | WHITE | BLACK | | WHITE | BLACK |
|---|---|---|---|---|---|
| 1 | P–Q4 | N–KB3 | 5 | KN–K2! | P–KN3 |
| 2 | P–QB4 | P–Q3 | 6 | P–KN3 | B–N2 |
| 3 | N–QB3 | QN–Q2 | 7 | B–N2 | O–O |
| 4 | P–K4 | P–K4 | 8 | O–O | P–B3 |

| | WHITE | BLACK | | WHITE | BLACK |
|---|---|---|---|---|---|
| 9 | P–Q5 | P–B4 | 19 | N/BxP | N–B4 |
| 10 | P–KR3 | P–QR3 | 20 | NxN | BxN |
| 11 | B–K3 | P–R3 | 21 | N–N3! | R–K1 |
| 12 | Q–Q2 | K–R2 | 22 | NxB | PxN |
| 13 | K–R2 | N–KN1 | 23 | B–B2 | RxR |
| 14 | P–B4 | PxP | 24 | RxR | N–Q2 |
| 15 | PxP | N–N3 | 25 | Q–Q3! | Q–B1 |
| 16 | P–N3 | P–B4 | 26 | B–R4 | K–N1 |
| 17 | QR–K1 | N–K2 | 27 | B–K7 | N–K4 |
| 18 | N–N3 | PxP | 28 | RxN | Resigns |

---

## part 5—MODERN FIANCHETTO

### OBSERVATIONS ON KEY POSITION 5

1 P–Q4, N–KB3
2 P–QB4, P–KN3
3 P–KN3, B–N2
4 B–N2, O–O
5 N–QB3, P–Q3[A]

KEY POSITION 5

[A] It is interesting to note that this exact position arose by transposition in the games Schwarz–L. Paulsen, 1881, and W. Paulsen–Riemann, 1882.

Although adopted by former world champion Alekhine in the tournaments of Karlsbad 1923 and New York 1924, this system until recently had not found as much favor as the variation treated in Part 4. There White's Knight is developed at K2, allowing Black much counterplay; here it is usually brought to KB3 to exert pressure on Black's K4. Latest theoretical investigation of this line reveals excellent chances for White.

### IDEA VARIATION 9:

(9) 6 P–K3, QN–Q2 (6 . . . P–K4 7 KN–K2, Q–K2 8 O–O, P–K5 9 P–KR3, P–KR4 10 N–B4, P–B3 11 P–QN4, QN–Q2 12 Q–K2, KR–K1 13 B–R3, P–QR3, and White's position is somewhat uncomfortable) 7 KN–K2, P–K4 8 P–N3 (8 O–O, R–K1 9 Q–B2, PxP 10 NxP, P–QR4= or 8 O–O, P–B3 9 P–N3, R–K1 10 B–R3, PxP 11 NxP, N–B4, as in Golombek–Pirc, Belgrade 1952), R–K1 9 B–R3, P–KR4 10 P–KR3, P–QR3 11 PxP, PxP, and Black has a satisfactory position (Botvinnik–Smyslov, 20th Match Game 1954).

PRACTICAL VARIATIONS 17-20:

1 P–Q4, N–KB3 2 P–QB4, P–KN3 3 P–KN3, B–N2 4 B–N2, O–O 5 N–QB3, P–Q3

| | 17 | 18 | 19 | 20 |
|---|---|---|---|---|
| 6 | N–B3![1] | – – | – – | – – |
| | QN–Q2 | – – | – – | – – |
| 7 | O–O | – – | – – | – – |
| | P–K4[2] | – – | – – | – – |
| 8 | P–K4[3] | – – | – – | – – |
| | P–B3[4] | – – | – – | PxP |
| 9 | P–KR3 | R–K1 | B–K3 | NxP |
| | Q–N3[5] | Q–B2[10] | N–N5 | N–B4[16] |
| 10 | P–Q5[6] | P–KR3 | B–N5 | P–B3[17] |
| | PxP[7] | R–K1[11] | Q–N3 | P–QR4[18] |
| 11 | BPxP | B–K3 | P–KR3 | B–K3 |
| | N–B4 | P–N3 | PxP | P–R5 |
| 12 | N–K1 | R–QB1 | N–R4 | R–B2 |
| | B–Q2 | B–N2 | Q–R3 | P–B3 |
| 13 | N–Q3 | K–R2 | PxN | N–B2 |
| | NxN | QR–Q1 | P–N4 | Q–K2 |
| 14 | QxN | Q–B2 | NxP | R–Q2 |
| | KR–B1 | Q–N1 | PxN | KN–Q2! |
| 15 | R–N1[8] | Q–N1 | B–K7![13] | R–B1[19] |
| | N–R4 | N–B1 | R–K1[14] | B–K4 |
| 16 | B–K3 | P–Q5 | BxP[15] | B–B2[20] |
| | Q–N5[9] | P–B4[12] | ± | R–K1[21] |
| | = | = | | = |

*Notes to practical variations 17–20:*

[1] 6 P–K4 is discussed in Prac. Var. 13-16.

[2] The seldom played 7 . . . P–B4 deserves some consideration: 8 P–Q5, N–N5 9 N–Q2, N–N3 10 P–KR3, N–K4 11 Q–N3, P–B4 12 P–B4, N–B2 13 P–QR4, P–QR4 14 P–K4, PxP 15 N/2xP± (Glass–Wolf, Vienna 1931) or 8 P–Q5, P–QR3 9 P–QR4, R–N1 10 P–R3, Q–B2 11 P–K4, P–K3 (Beni–Auer, Wolfsberg 1953). In this latter line, another try is 9 N–Q2, R–N1 10 P–QR4, Q–B2 11 P–K4, P–K3 (Kovacs–Beni, Wolfsberg 1953).

[3] Other possibilities are:

1) 8 P–N3, R–K1 9 Q–B2, P–B3 10 B–R3, PxP 11 NxP, P–Q4 12 PxP, NxP 13 NxN, BxN 14 QR–Q1, B–N2 15 N–K3, Q–R4 16 N–B4, Q–R3 and now 17 B–N2, N–B3 18 B–QB3, B–K3 19 N–Q6± (Pirc–Pilnik, Belgrade 1952) or 17 P–K4, N–B3 18 B–B1± (Blau–Lokvenc, Vevey 1953).

2) 8 P–N3, PxP 9 NxP, N–B4 10 B–N2, R–K1 11 Q–B2, N–K3 12 QR–Q1± (Alekhine–Saemisch, 1921).

3) 8 P–KR3, P–B3 9 PxP, PxP 10 B–K3, Q–K2 and White now has a choice among 11 Q–Q2 (Pachman–Gligoric,

Moscow 1947), 11 Q–N3 (Kovacs–Lokvenc, Wolfsberg 1953), or 11 Q–B1 (Guimard–Donner, Goteborg 1955).

[4] 8 . . . R–K1 has no independent value. Unusual is 8 . . . P–QR4, e.g., 9 B–K3, R–K1 10 P–KR3, PxP 11 NxP, N–B4 12 Q–B2, P–B3 13 N–N3 (Botvinnik–Sale, Amsterdam 1954) or 9 P–Q5, N–B4 10 Q–K2.

[5] Clarke–Szabo, Wageningen 1957, continued 9 . . . Q–R4 10 P–Q5, PxP 11 BPxP, P–QN4 and White could have obtained good chances with 12 P–QR3 (12 . . . P–N5 13 N–QR2). In this line, however, White does better with either 10 B–K3 or 10 Q–B2!, as in 10 B–K3, PxP 11 BxP! (Guimard–Boleslavski, Buenos Aires 1955) or 10 Q–B2!, PxP 11 NxP, N–N3 12 N/3–K2, R–K1 13 P–QR4!± (Gligoric–Szabo, Budapest 1957). The very popular 9 . . . R–K1 can be well answered with 10 B–K3, P–QR4 11 Q–B2, P–R5 12 KR–Q1, Q–R4 13 QR–N1!, PxP 14 NxP, N–B4 15 P–QN4 (Korchnoi–Ivkov, Hastings 1956).

[6] The inferior 10 R–K1 is met by 10 . . . PxP 11 NxP, N–N5. But 10 R–N1! merits attention, e.g., 10 . . . PxP 11 NxP, NxP 12 NxN, BxN 13 P–QN4, N–K4 14 P–B5!, PxP 15 PxP, Q–Q1 16 B–R6± (Reshevsky–Lombardy, 1959).

[7] Better is 10 . . . N–B4 11 Q–B2, PxP 12 BPxP, B–Q2 13 B–K3, P–QR4 with a satisfactory game for Black.

[8] Simpler is 15 Q–K2 (15 . . . N–R4 16 B–K3).

[9] The sixth game of the Botvinnik–Tal match, Moscow 1960, continued 17 Q–K2, R–B5 18 KR–B1, R/1–QB1, and White should now have played 19 P–QR3, e.g., 19 . . . Q–N6 20 Q–Q1!, QxQ 21 RxQ with 22 B–KB1 to follow. Thus if 21 . . . P–QR3? 22 B–KB1, R/5–B2 23 B–N6 or 21 . . . P–N3 22 B–KB1, R/5–B2 23 N–N5!, BxN 24 BxB, and White will soon be able to assume control of the Queen Bishop file after 25 B–R6.

[10] 9 . . . N–K1 10 B–N5, P–B3 11 B–K3, Q–K2 12 Q–Q2, P–KB4 13 P–B5, Q–B2 14 PxBP, NPxP 15 BPxP, P–K5 16 N–N5, Q–B3 (Larsen–Olafsson, Portoroz 1958) 17 P–B3!, PxP 18 NxBP and White has an excellent position. In this variation 17 . . . P–KR3 fails against 18 PxP!, PxN 19 P–K5.

[11] The surrender of the center with 10 . . . PxP gives White good chances. Smyslov–Plater, Moscow 1947, continued 11 NxP, N–N3 12 P–N3, R–K1 13 B–N5.

[12] White has a slight edge; Black's position is solid, but under pressure. In Grunfeld–Paoli, Vienna 1952-53, there followed 17 N–N1, K–R1 18 Q–B2, B–B1 19 KN–K2, B–Q2 20 P–KN4, P–KR4 21 P–N5, N–N1 22 N–KN1, N–R2 23 N–B3, B–KB1 24 R–KN1, P–R3 25 P–QR4.

[13] This position arose in the 14th game of the Botvinnik–Smyslov match, Moscow 1954 (see Game 11). The text move, recommended by Unzicker in *Schach-Echo,* is an improvement on Botvinnik's 15 NxP.

[14] Or 16 . . . N–K4! 17 P–B5!, BxP 18 Q–B2, N–Q6 (or . . . N–B5) 19 NxP! with advantage to White, although Black has some chances.

[15] 16 . . . QxP now fails against 17 NxP!, when White wins the exchange in favorable circumstances.

[16] Or 9 . . . R–K1 10 P–KR3, N–B4 11 R–K1, P–QR4 12 Q–B2, P–B3 13 B–K3, P–R5 14 QR–Q1, KN–Q2 (14 . . . Q–R4 is answered by 15 B–B4!) 15 R–K2! (stronger than 15 P–B4, as

continued ▸

played in the game Panno-Sherwin, Copenhagen 1953), Q–R4 16 R/2–Q2, Q–N5 17 N–N1± (Averbach–Dittmann, Dresden 1956). In this variation 12 . . . KNxP? is a mistake because of 13 NxN, BxN 14 B–N5, Q–Q2 15 N–B6†, BxN 16 BxB, and White's position is overwhelming (Grois–Galia, Vienna 1959).

[17] 10 P–KR3 is equally playable and leads to variations discussed in the previous note.

[18] If 10 . . . KN–Q2 then 11 B–K3, P–B3 12 Q–Q2, P–QR4 13 QR–Q1, N–K4 14 P–N3, P–R5? (Kotov–Geller, Moscow 1949), and now 15 P–B4!, N–N5 16 NxP, Q–K1 17 N–Q4 gives White the edge.

[19] If 15 RxP then 15 . . . P–R6! and Black has the advantage.

[20] White must be careful. 16 P–B4, BxN 17 PxB, NxP favors Black.

[21] After 17 N–K3, N–B1 18 N–K2, Q–B2 19 R–N1 (19 Q–B2 is also playable), P–R6 20 P–N3, P–R4 21 Q–B2, B–K3 22 N–B3, N–R2 23 P–QN4, White's game is solid though passive. In Averbach–Gligoric, Zurich 1953, White's position gradually deteriorated, but only because of some inferior Pawn maneuvers on his part.

### *King's Indian Defense Game 10*

*WHITE: Botvinnik* — *BLACK: Tal*

*6th Match Game, Moscow 1960*

| WHITE | BLACK | WHITE | BLACK |
|---|---|---|---|
| 1 P–QB4 | N–KB3 | 25 RxQ | PxQ |
| 2 N–KB3 | P–KN3 | 26 R–N3 | R–Q5! |
| 3 P–KN3 | B–N2 | 27 B–K1 | B–K4† |
| 4 B–N2 | O–O | 28 K–N1 | B–B5 |
| 5 P–Q4 | P–Q3 | 29 NxP | RxR |
| 6 N–B3 | QN–Q2 | 30 NxR/4 | RxB† |
| 7 O–O | P–K4 | 31 B–B1 | B–K5 |
| 8 P–K4 | P–B3 | 32 N–K2 | B–K4 |
| 9 P–KR3 | Q–N3 | 33 P–B4 | B–B3 |
| 10 P–Q5 | PxP | 34 RxP | BxP |
| 11 BPxP | N–B4 | 35 R–QB7 | BxP |
| 12 N–K1 | B–Q2 | 36 RxQRP | B–B5 |
| 13 N–Q3 | NxN | 37 R–R8† | K–B2 |
| 14 QxN | KR–B1 | 38 R–R7† | K–K3 |
| 15 R–N1 | N–R4 | 39 R–R3 | P–Q4 |
| 16 B–K3 | Q–N5 | 40 K–B2 | B–R5† |
| 17 Q–K2 | R–B5 | 41 K–N2 | K–Q3 |
| 18 KR–B1 | QR–QB1 | 42 N–N3 | BxN |
| 19 K–R2? | P–B4! | 43 BxB | PxB! |
| 20 PxP | BxP | 44 KxB | K–Q4 |
| 21 R–QR1 | N–B5! | 45 R–R7 | P–B6 |
| 22 PxN | PxP | 46 R–QB7 | K–Q5 |
| 23 B–Q2 | QxP | Resigns | |
| 24 QR–N1 | P–B6! | | |

*King's Indian Defense Game 11*
*WHITE: Botvinnik* *BLACK: Smyslov*
*14th Match Game, Moscow 1954*

| | WHITE | BLACK | | WHITE | BLACK |
|---|---|---|---|---|---|
| 1 | P–Q4 | N–KB3 | 18 | R–B1 | Q–N5! |
| 2 | P–QB4 | P–KN3 | 19 | P–R3 | QxQNP |
| 3 | P–KN3 | B–N2 | 20 | QxRP | B–N2 |
| 4 | B–N2 | O–O | 21 | R–N1? | N–B6† |
| 5 | N–QB3 | P–Q3 | 22 | K–R1 | BxB |
| 6 | N–B3 | QN–Q2 | 23 | RxQ | NxB† |
| 7 | O–O | P–K4 | 24 | K–R2 | N–B6† |
| 8 | P–K4 | P–B3 | 25 | K–R3 | BxR |
| 9 | B–K3 | N–N5 | 26 | QxP | B–K5 |
| 10 | B–N5 | Q–N3 | 27 | P–R4 | K–N2 |
| 11 | P–KR3 | PxP | 28 | R–Q1 | B–K4 |
| 12 | N–QR4 | Q–R3 | 29 | Q–K7 | R–B1 |
| 13 | PxN | P–N4 | 30 | P–R5 | R–B7 |
| 14 | NxP | PxN | 31 | K–N2 | N–Q5† |
| 15 | NxP | QxN | 32 | K–B1 | B–B6 |
| 16 | P–K5 | QxP | 33 | R–N1 | N–B3 |
| 17 | BxR | NxP | | Resigns | |

## part 6—YUGOSLAV VARIATION

OBSERVATIONS ON KEY POSITION 6

1 P–Q4, N–KB3
2 P–QB4, P–KN3
3 P–KN3, B–N2
4 B–N2, O–O
5 N–QB3, P–Q3
6 N–B3

KEY POSITION 6

Credit for introducing this modern treatment goes to the Yugoslav chess masters. Actually, two systems fall under its broad heading, 6 . . . P–B4 and 6 . . . N–B3. In practice, however, transposition from one into the other is a common occurrence.

IDEA VARIATIONS 10 AND 11:

These examples begin with move 5 . . . of the foregoing and reach the main line by transposition.

(9) 5 . . . P–B4 6 N–B3, N–B3 (6 . . . P–Q4 transposes into the Grunfeld) 7 O–O, P–Q3 8 P–K3, B–B4 9 P–N3, Q–B1 (9 . . . P–Q4, recommended by Mueller, fails against 10 PxQP, N–QN5 if 10 . . . PxP 11 PxN, PxN 12 PxNP±) 11 B–N2, N/3xP 12 NxN, NxN 13 Q–K2±) 10 B–N2, N–K5 11 R–B1, NxN (or 11 . . . PxP 12 PxP) 12 BxN, B–K5 13 P–Q5!, BxB 14 RxB, N–Q1 15 N–Q2, BxB 16 KxB± (Botvinnik–Najdorf, Amsterdam 1954).

(10) 5 . . . P–B4 6 P–Q5, P–K4 7 N–R3, P–Q3 8 O–O, QN–Q2 9 P–K4, P–KR3 10 P–B4, PxP 11 PxP, R–K1 12 Q–Q3, P–R3 13 P–R4, N–N5 14 N–K2, Q–R5

15 R–R3, R–N1 16 R–N3, P–QN4! 17 RPxP, N–N3 18 R–R3, PxP 19 PxP, B–Q2 20 P–N4, PxP 21 R–N3, N–R5 22 RxP, N–B4∓ Guimard–Najdorf, Havana 1952.

An alternative to 7 N–R3 is 7 B–N5, P–KR3 (7 . . . P–Q3 8 Q–Q2) 8 BxN, QxB 9 P–Q6, N–B3 10 P–K3, K–R1 11 KN–K2, P–N3 12 O–O, B–N2 13 Q–R4, QxP 14 QR–Q1, Q–K3 15 N–N5, QR–Q1 16 N/2–B3, K–R2 17 N–Q6, R–QN1 18 N/3–N5, Q–K2 19 NxB, RxN 20 N–Q6, R–QN1= (DeJong–Euwe, 1954) But in this line, 10 . . . P–N3 11 B–Q5, K–R1 12 N–K4, Q–Q1 13 P–KR4± (Euwe–Najdorf, Zurich 1953). Or 7 P–K4, P–Q3 8 KN–K2, as in the Fine–Stahlberg match. Cf. Prac. Var. 13, footnote 3.

PRACTICAL VARIATIONS 21–24:

1 P–Q4, N–KB3 2 P–QB4, P–KN3 3 P–KN3, B–N2 4 B–N2, O–O 5 N–QB3, P–Q3 6 N–B3!

| | *21* | *22* | *23* | *24* |
|---|---|---|---|---|
| *6* | – – | – – | – – | – – |
| | P–B4 | – – | N–B3 | – – |
| *7* | O–O[1] | – – | O–O | – – |
| | N–B3 | – – | P–QR3[12] | – – |
| *8* | P–Q5[2] | – – | P–Q5[13] | P–KR3 |
| | N–QR4![3] | – – | N–QR4! | R–N1[18] |
| *9* | Q–Q3 | N–Q2! | N–Q2 | P–N3[19] |
| | P–QR3[4] | P–QR3[8] | P–B4 | P–QN4 |
| *10* | P–K4[5] | Q–B2[9] | Q–B2 | P–K3 |
| | P–K3[6] | B–Q2[10] | R–N1[14] | N–QR4 |
| *11* | P–KR3 | P–N3 | P–N3 | PxP! |
| | PxP | P–QN4 | P–QN4 | PxP |
| *12* | BPxP | B–N2 | B–N2[15] | B–N2 |
| | P–QN4 | R–N1 | PxP | P–N5 |
| *13* | B–B4 | QR–N1 | PxP | N–K2 |
| | P–N5 | Q–B2 | B–R3! | B–QR3 |
| *14* | N–Q1 | KR–B1 | P–B4[16] | R–K1 |
| | R–K1 | PxP | P–K4 | Q–Q2 |
| *15* | R–K1 | PxP | QR–K1 | R–QB1 |
| | P–B5 | B–B4 | PxP | KR–B1 |
| *16* | Q–B2 | P–K4 | PxP | N–B4 |
| | R–R2[7] | B–Q2[11] | R–K1[17] | P–B3[20] |
| | ∓ | ± | ∓ | ± |

*Notes to practical variations 21–24:*

[1] The older 7 P–Q5 is also playable, e.g., B–Q2 8 O–O (Johner–Reti, Teplitz–Schonau 1922) or 7 . . . P–K4 8 O–O, N–R3 9 P–K4 (Lokvenc–Wagner, Dresden 1926) or 7 . . .

N–R3 8 O–O, N–B2 9 N–Q2, R–N1 10 Q–B2, P–K4 11 PxP e.p., BxP 12 P–N3, P–Q4 13 PxP, N/2xP 14 B–N2, P–N3= (Botvinnik–Padewski, Moscow 1956).

[2] Simplification with 8 PxP, PxP 9 B–B4 (or 9 B–K3) is no longer popular. 8 P–KR3, however, deserves consideration, e.g., 8 . . . B–Q2 9 P–K3, Q–B1 10 K–R2, R–Q1 11 Q–K2± (Olafsson–Clarke, Wageningen 1957) or 8 . . . PxP 9 NxP, NxN 10 QxN, N–Q2 11 Q–Q2! followed by 12 P–N3±.

[3] The once popular reply 8 . . . N–N1 is answered with 9 B–B4, P–KR3 10 Q–Q2, K–R2 11 P–K4, N–R4 12 B–K3, N–Q2 13 QR–K1 (Alekhine).

[4] Another line is 9 . . . P–K4 10 PxP e.p., BxP 11 N–Q2 with the following possibilities: 11 . . . P–QR3 12 R–N1, N–B3 13 P–K4, N–KN5 14 Q–K2, N–Q5 15 Q–Q1, N–K4 16 P–N3, P–B4 17 N–K2, N–Q6 18 NxN, BxN (Castagna–Filipovic, St. Radegand 1960) or 11 . . . N–B3 12 N/2–K4, N–K1 13 B–N5, Q–Q2 14 QR–Q1, N–K4 15 Q–B2, R–B1 16 N–Q5, BxN 17 RxB, P–B4 18 N–B3, P–KR3 19 B–B4, N–QB3 (Euwe–Bouwmeester, Beverwijk 1958).

[5] Antoschin–Chasin, Moscow 1956, continued 10 N–Q2, N–Q2 11 P–B4, P–QN4 12 PxP, PxP 13 QxQNP, B–QR3 14 Q–R4, BxN 15 PxB, BxP 16 R–K1, B–Q6 17 P–B4.

[6] If 10 . . . N–K1 then 11 KR–K1 (Euwe–Yanofsky, Munich 1958). Other possibilities are 10 . . . P–QN4 11 P–K5, PxBP 12 Q–K2, N–K1 and 10 . . . P–QN4 11 PxP, PxP 12 NxP, P–B5 13 Q–B2, B–QR3 14 N–B3, Q–B2 15 B–N5, KR–N1.

[7] Rossetto–Tal, Portoroz 1958. See Game 12.

[8] Also good is 9 . . . P–K4 10 P–QR3, P–N3 11 P–QN4, N–N2 12 R–N1, N–K1 13 N/2–K4, P–B4 14 N–KN5, P–K5 15 Q–N3, Q–B3 16 N–Q1, P–KR3= (Olafsson–Fischer, Belgrade 1959) or 9 . . . B–N5 10 Q–B2, P–QR3 11 P–KR3, B–Q2 12 P–N3, P–QN4 13 B–N2, PxP 14 PxP, R–N1 15 QR–N1, P–K4 16 N–Q1, B–R3 17 B–QB3, Q–B2= (Uhlmann–Bilek, Balatonfured 1959).

[9] 10 P–K4? is inferior: 10 . . . R–K1 11 P–QR3, N–Q2! 12 Q–B2, N–K4! 13 P–N3, P–QN4 (Rinder–Bhend, Zagreb 1955) or 10 . . . P–K3 11 R–N1?, PxP 12 BPxP, P–QN4 13 P–QN4, PxP 14 RxP, B–Q2 15 N–K2, R–B1 16 B–QR3, R–K1 17 N–Q4, N–N5! (Bergraser–Smyslov, Munich 1958). 10 P–QR3 (with the threat of P–QN4) is playable, e.g., 10 . . . Q–B2 11 Q–B2, B–Q2 12 R–N1, P–QN4 13 P–N3, QR–N1 14 B–N2, PxP 15 PxP (Simagin–Golowke, Moscow 1959).

[10] 10 . . . B–N5 11 P–KR3 transposes into the game Uhlmann–Bilek (see note 8).

[11] Smyslov–Malich, Munich 1958, continued 17 N–Q1, P–K4 18 B–QB3, N–N5 19 P–KR3, N–R3 20 R–N2, RxR 21 QxR, B–KB3 22 P–B4±.

[12] The Panno Variation. Unfavorable for Black is 7 . . . B–B4: 8 P–N3, N–K5 9 B–N2, NxN 10 BxN, B–K5 11 R–B1, P–Q4 12 P–K3! or, in this line, 9 . . . Q–Q2 10 R–B1, N–N5 11 NxN, BxN 12 Q–Q2 (Najdorf–Spasski and Donner–Spasski, Goteborg 1955). Interesting are both 7 . . . R–N1 8 Q–Q3, N–Q2 9 B–K3, P–QR3 10 QR–B1 (Stahlberg–Donner, Wageningen 1957) and 7 . . . B–N5 8 P–KR3 (8 P–Q5, N–QR4!) BxN 9 BxB, N–Q2 10 P–K3, P–K4 11 P–Q5, N–K2 12 P–K4= (Stahlberg–Olafsson, Wageningen 1957).

continued ▸

[13] Or 8 P–N3, B–N5 9 B–N2, R–N1 10 P–KR3, B–Q2 11 R–QB1, P–QN4 12 PxP, PxP 13 P–Q5, N–R2 14 N–Q4, P–N5 15 N–R4, P–K4= (Ilivetski–Pilnik, Goteborg 1955). 8 Q–Q3 merits consideration, e.g., 8 . . . N–Q2 9 R–Q1, R–N1 10 B–K3, P–R3 11 QR–B1, K–R2 12 Q–N1±.

[14] For 10 . . . B–Q2, see Prac. Var. 22. Another possibility is 10 . . . P–K3 11 P–N3, R–N1 12 B–N2, P–QN4 13 PxKP, PxKP 14 PxP, PxP 15 N/3–K4, B–N2 16 NxN†, BxN 17 B–KR3, Q–K2 (Simagin–Scherbakow). Black has no difficulties.

[15] 12 PxP, PxP 13 B–N2 appears playable, e.g., 13 . . . P–N5 14 N–Q1, B–QR3 (B–KR3!) 15 R–K1 (Donner–Larsen, Wageningen 1957) or 13 . . . B–B4 14 P–K4, B–Q2 15 P–QR4, P–N5 16 N–N5! Black's sharpest, however, is 13 . . . B–QR3!

[16] 14 P–K3 is strongly answered by 14 . . . B–B4!

[17] After 17 N–Q1, best is 17 . . . N–R4! 18 P–K3, R–N2 with R/2–K2 to follow. For 17 . . . R–N2? see Game 13.

[18] If 8 . . . B–Q2 then 9 B–K3, R–N1 10 P–QR4!, R–K1 11 P–R5, Q–B1 12 P–Q5± (Grunfeld–Lokvenc, Vienna 1957).

[19] Inferior to the text are both 9 P–K4, P–QN4 10 P–K5, N–K1 11 Q–K2, N–QR4 12 P–B5, P–N5 13 N–K4, P–Q4 14 N/4–Q2, P–B4 15 R–Q1, P–K3 16 N–B1, P–R3 (Larsen–Olafsson match, 1956) and 9 B–K3, P–QN4 10 PxP (if 10 N–Q2 then 10 . . . B–Q2), PxP 11 P–Q5, N–QR4 12 P–QN4, N–B5 13 B–R7, R–N2 14 B–Q4, P–K4∓ (Smyslov–Petrosian, Amsterdam 1956). In this line, 11 R–B1, N–QR4 12 P–N3, P–N5 was played in the game Stahlberg–Panno, Goteborg 1955.

[20] Idigoras–Panno, Mar del Plata 1955, continued 17 P–KR4!, Q–R2 18 R–B2, N–N2 19 P–R5, P–B4 20 PxNP, RPxP 21 B–KR3, R–B1 22 N–N5, B–R3? (N–Q1!) 23 NxNP!±.

*King's Indian Defense Game 12*

*WHITE: Rossetto* — *BLACK: Tal*

*Portoroz 1958*

| WHITE | BLACK | WHITE | BLACK | WHITE | BLACK |
|---|---|---|---|---|---|
| 1 P–QB4 | N–KB3 | 15 R–K1 | P–B5 | 29 Q–R3 | BxB |
| 2 N–KB3 | P–KN3 | 16 Q–B2 | R–R2 | 30 KxB | Q–B5 |
| 3 P–KN3 | B–N2 | 17 B–K3 | R/2–K2 | 31 QxP | B–B1 |
| 4 B–N2 | O–O | 18 N–Q2 | P–N6 | 32 Q–QB6 | Q–K5† |
| 5 O–O | P–Q3 | 19 PxP | NxNP | 33 K–N1 | N–K4! |
| 6 P–Q4 | N–B3 | 20 R–R4 | NxQP! | 34 N–B3 | N–B6† |
| 7 N–B3 | P–QR3 | 21 PxN | B–B4 | 35 K–R1 | Q–K4 |
| 8 P–Q5 | N–QR4 | 22 QxP | NxN | 36 K–N2 | N–R5† |
| 9 Q–Q3 | P–B4 | 23 QxP | N–K5 | 37 K–N1 | B–Q3 |
| 10 P–K4 | P–K3 | 24 Q–N6 | Q–B1 | 38 R–Q1 | Q–R7† |
| 11 P–KR3 | PxP | 25 P–KN4 | N–B4 | 39 K–B1 | RxB |
| 12 BPxP | P–QN4 | 26 R–R7 | RxR | Resigns | |
| 13 B–B4 | P–N5 | 27 QxR | N–Q6 | | |
| 14 N–Q1 | R–K1 | 28 R–B1 | B–K5 | | |

*King's Indian Defense Game 13*

*WHITE: Botvinnik* *BLACK: Donner*

*Wageningen 1958*

| | WHITE | BLACK | | WHITE | BLACK |
|---|---|---|---|---|---|
| 1 | P–QB4 | N–KB3 | 22 | Q–B3 | P–B4 |
| 2 | N–KB3 | P–KN3 | 23 | B–B3 | B–B1 |
| 3 | P–KN3 | B–N2 | 24 | N–Q3 | R–KB2 |
| 4 | B–N2 | O–O | 25 | R–B2 | N–N2 |
| 5 | O–O | P–Q3 | 26 | R/2–K2 | R/1–B1 |
| 6 | N–QB3 | P–QR3 | 27 | N–KB1 | Q–R4 |
| 7 | P–Q4 | N–B3 | 28 | QxQ | NxQ |
| 8 | P–Q5 | N–QR4 | 29 | R–QB2 | R–N2 |
| 9 | N–Q2 | P–B4 | 30 | N–Q2 | N–K1 |
| 10 | Q–B2 | R–N1 | 31 | R–B3! | R–N3 |
| 11 | P–N3 | P–QN4 | 32 | R–R3 | N–QN2 |
| 12 | B–N2 | PxP | 33 | R–N1! | RxR |
| 13 | PxP | B–R3! | 34 | NxR | N–B2 |
| 14 | P–B4 | P–K4 | 35 | N–Q2 | K–B2 |
| 15 | QR–K1 | PxP | 36 | K–B2 | K–K2 |
| 16 | PxP | R–K1! | 37 | P–R4! | P–R3 |
| 17 | N–Q1 | R–N2? | 38 | B–Q1 | B–Q2 |
| 18 | B–QB3! | B–Q2 | 39 | R–N3 | N–R4 |
| 19 | P–K3 | N–R4 | 40 | R–N6 | R–QR1 |
| 20 | N–B2 | B–N2 | 41 | NxP! | PxN |
| 21 | BxB | NxB | 42 | P–Q6† | Resigns |

---

## part 7—COUNTER-THRUST VARIATION

1 P–Q4, N–KB3
2 P–QB4, P–KN3
3 P–KN3, B–N2
4 B–N2, P–Q4
5 PxP, NxP

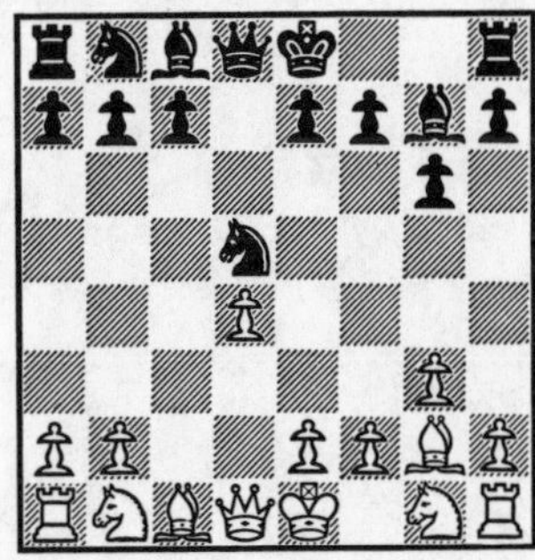

KEY POSITION 7

### OBSERVATIONS ON KEY POSITION 7

The popular reply of . . . P–Q4 as a counter to White's Kingside fianchetto was first adopted in the Carlsbad Tournament of 1923. This system, akin to Grunfeld's Defense, must not be underrated; it offers Black good counterplay.

### IDEA VARIATION 12:

The move . . . P–Q4 often occurs before Black's fourth turn, as given above. In the example which follows, it is played on Black's third. The key position is reached by transposition.

(12) 3 . . . P–Q4 4 PxP, QxP? (correct is . . . NxP) 5 N–KB3, B–N2 6 B–N2, O–O (also insufficient is 6

. . . P–B3 7 O–O, O–O 8 N–B3, Q–QR4 9 B–Q2, Q–R4 10 Q–N3, QN–Q2 11 P–K4, N–N3 12 P–K5, B–K3 13 PxN!, BxQ 14 BPxB, KxP 15 PxB± [Stahlberg–Storm-Herseth, Stockholm 1937]) 7 N–B3! (if 7 O–O, Q–KR4 8 Q–N3, N–B3 9 N–B3, N–K1 10 R–Q1, R–N1 11 B–K3, N–Q3 12 P–Q5, N–R4 13 Q–N4, P–N3= [Nimzowitsch–Tartakover, Berlin 1928]), Q–KR4 8 P–KR3, N–B3 9 N–KN5!, R–Q1 10 B–B3, RxP 11 Q–N3, and Black resigned (Grunfeld–Nagy, Debreczin 1924).

PRACTICAL VARIATIONS 25–28:

1 P–Q4, N–KB3 2 P–QB4, P–KN3 3 P–KN3, B–N2 4 B–N2, P–Q4 5 PxP, NxP

| | *25* | *26* | *27* | *28* |
|---|---|---|---|---|
| *6* | P–K4 | – – | N–KB3![13] | – – |
| | N–N3 | N–N5! | O–O | – – |
| *7* | N–K2 | P–Q5 | O–O | – – |
| | O–O[1] | P–QB3 | N–N3 | P–QB4 |
| *8* | O–O | N–K2 | N–B3[14] | P–K4[17] |
| | P–QB3[2] | PxP![7] | N–B3[15] | N–N3[18] |
| *9* | QN–B3 | PxP | P–Q5 | P–Q5 |
| | N–R3[3] | B–B4[8] | N–N5 | P–K3 |
| *10* | P–N3[4] | Q–R4†[9] | P–K4 | N–K1[19] |
| | N–B2 | N/1–B3 | P–QB3 | PxP |
| *11* | B–QR3 | O–O | Q–N3 | PxP |
| | B–N5 | B–B7 | N–Q6 | N–B3! |
| *12* | P–B3[5] | Q–R3 | B–K3 | N–QB3 |
| | B–B1 | NxQP | P–QB4 | N–N5?[20] |
| *13* | Q–Q2 | Q–B5 | N–K1 | P–QR3 |
| | P–QR4[6] | BxN | P–B5 | BxN |
| *14* | = | BxN[10] | Q–B2 | PxN |
| | | B–B4 | NxN | BxP/5 |
| *15* | | B–N5[11] | KRxN | N–B2 |
| | | R–QB1 | P–K3 | Q–B3[21] |
| *16* | | KR–K1 | PxP | NxB |
| | | O–O[12] | BxP[16] | PxN[22] |
| | | ∓ | ± | ± |

*Notes to practical variations 25–28:*

[1] If 7 . . . P–QB4 then 8 P–Q5, P–K3 9 O–O, O–O 10 N/2–B3, PxP 11 PxP, N/1–Q2 12 N–K4!, N–B3 13 N/1–B3, N/N3–Q2 14 P–Q6 (Euwe–Keres, Zurich 1953). Or 7 . . . N–B3 8 P–Q5, N–K4? (N–N1!) 9 P–B4, N–N5 10 P–KR3, N–KB3 11 N/1–B3, P–K3 12 B–K3± (Beni–Nestler, Vienna 1957).

[2] Euwe–Robatsch, 1956, continued 8 . . . P–K3? 9 QN–B3, N–B3 10 P–K5!, N–N5 11 N–K4, P–KR3 12 N–B6†, K–R1 13 P–KR4!, P–B4 14 N–N4±.

[3] 9 . . . P–K4 merits some attention, e.g., 10 P–Q5, PxP 11 PxP, B–B4 12 N–K4, N–R3 13 N/2–B3, Q–Q2 14 Q–N3, QR–B1 or 10 PxP, BxP 11 B–R6, B–N2 12 BxB, KxB 13 QxQ, RxQ 14 KR–Q1, R–K1= (Grunfeld–Kopetzky, Vienna 1950).

[4] 10 P–QR4 is sharper.

[5] Another possibility is 12 P–R3, BxN 13 QxB, QxP 14 QR–B1!

[6] The best is now 14 KR–Q1, P–R5 15 P–B4, PxP 16 PxP, B–K3 17 Q–B2. For 14 QR–B1, see Game 14.

[7] This offers more than 8 . . . O–O e.g., 9 O–O, P–K3 10 P–QR3!, N/5–R3 11 QN–B3, BPxP 12 PxP, PxP 13 NxP, N–B3 14 N/2–B3± Pachman–Filip, 2d Match Game 1954.

[8] After 9 . . . O–O there follows 10 P–QR3, N/5–R3 11 O–O, N–Q2 12 QN–B3± (Euwe–Barcza, Venice 1948).

[9] 10 O–O is more solid, e.g., O–O 11 QN–B3, QN–R3! 12 B–B4, N–Q6 13 P–Q6!, NxB 14 NxN, N–B4 15 PxP, QxP= (Stahlberg–Pachman, Prague 1954). If 10 . . . N–B7? then 11 P–KN4!, NxR 12 PxB, Q–B1 13 QN–B3, QxP 14 B–B4, N–B7 15 BxN, RxB 16 N–N3, Q–B5 17 QxN, O–O 18 R–K1± (Beinweber–Beni, Vienna 1959).

[10] Porath–Barcza, Moscow 1956, continued 14 RxB, P–K3 15 N–B3, Q–N3! 16 QxQ, NxQ 17 N–N5, O–O 18 N–Q6, N–Q4 19 NxNP, QR–N1 20 N–B5, KR–B1∓.

[11] After 15 BxN†, PxB 16 QxBP†, B–Q2 Black has two Bishops and stands well.

[12] Black wins after 17 N–B3, P–KR3 18 B–K3 (18 BxKP, NxB 19 QxN, RxN!) N–R4 19 QxRP, RxN 20 KR–Q1, R–Q6 (Szabo–Olafsson, Dallas 1957).

[13] 6 N–QB3 leads to a variation of the Grunfeld Defense favoring Black: 6 . . . NxN 7 PxN, P–QB4 8 P–K3, N–B3 9 N–K2, B–Q2 10 O–O, R–QB1 11 B–QR3, Q–R4! 12 Q–N3, Q–R3 13 N–B4, P–N3 (Geller–Bronstein, Amsterdam 1956) or, in this line, 8 . . . O–O 9 N–K2, N–B3 10 O–O, Q–R4 11 P–QR4, PxP 12 BPxP, B–K3 13 R–N1 (Filip–Fuchs, Prague 1958).

[14] Or 8 P–K4, N–B3 9 P–Q5, N–N1 10 N–B3, P–QB3 11 P–QR4, PxP 12 P–R5!, N–B5 13 PxP, N–R3 14 Q–R4, N–Q3! 15 B–K3, B–Q2 (Zimmermann–Leepin, Zurich 1949).

[15] Spanjaard–Wolk, Amersfoort 1959, continued 8 . . . P–QR4 9 P–K4, P–QB3 10 B–N5 (10 B–B4 is better), P–KR3 11 B–K3, N–B5 with a satisfactory game for Black.

[16] See Game 15.

[17] If 8 PxP, N–R3 9 N–N5, N/4–N5 10 N–QB3, P–R3! 11 N–B3, QxQ 12 RxQ, B–K3∓ (Panno–Szabo, Amsterdam 1956). If 8 N–B3, PxP 9 NxP, NxN 10 PxN, Q–B2 (N–B3!) 11 Q–N3, N–B3, and White can now obtain good chances with either 12 NxN (Keres–Mikenas, Hastings 1937) or 12 KR–Q1 (Szabo–Flohr, Budapest 1950).

[18] This is stronger than 8 . . . N–B3, e.g., 9 P–K5, N–Q4 10 PxP, N–B3 (10 . . . N–R3 11 Q–K2!) 11 P–QR3!, N–B2 12 Q–N3, N–R3 (12 . . . B–K3 13 Q–K3) 13 B–K3, Q–B2 14 N–B3, B–K3 15 Q–R4± (Stahlberg–Szabo, Amsterdam 1954).

[19] After 10 PxP, BxKP Black stands very well, nor can White achieve anything with the dubious Pawn sacrifice, 10 N–B3, BxN 11 PxB, PxP.

[20] Necessary is 12 . . . N–Q5!=.

continued ▸

[21] 15 . . . P–QR4 is better: 16 NxB, RPxN.

[22] Donner–Lehmann, Ostende 1956, continued 17 B–K3, B–B4 18 B–Q4, Q–Q3 19 P–N4, B–Q2 20 R–K1, KR–K1 21 Q–B3, P–QR4 22 QR–Q1, P–R5? (N–B5!) 23 R–K6!±.

### *King's Indian Defense Game 14*

*WHITE: Reshevsky* — *BLACK: Gligoric*

*Dubrovnik 1950*

| | WHITE | BLACK | | WHITE | BLACK |
|---|---|---|---|---|---|
| 1 | P–Q4 | N–KB3 | 26 | N–B4 | N–B2? |
| 2 | P–QB4 | P–KN3 | 27 | B–R5 | KR–B1 |
| 3 | P–KN3 | B–N2 | 28 | BxN | RxB |
| 4 | B–N2 | P–Q4 | 29 | NxB | QxN |
| 5 | PxP | NxP | 30 | P–B4 | Q–B1 |
| 6 | P–K4 | N–N3 | 31 | Q–B3 | P–K3 |
| 7 | N–K2 | O–O | 32 | P–QN4 | Q–Q1 |
| 8 | O–O | P–QB3 | 33 | B–B3 | R–Q2 |
| 9 | QN–B3 | N–R3 | 34 | P–N4 | R–R5 |
| 10 | P–N3 | N–B2 | 35 | P–B5 | R–R1 |
| 11 | B–QR3 | B–N5 | 36 | PxKP | PxP |
| 12 | P–B3 | B–B1 | 37 | Q–B4 | Q–K2 |
| 13 | Q–Q2 | P–QR4 | 38 | P–QN5 | PxP |
| 14 | QR–B1 | P–R5! | 39 | RxP | R–B2 |
| 15 | B–N4 | PxP | 40 | Q–K2 | R/1–B1 |
| 16 | PxP | B–K3 | 41 | Q–K4 | Q–R5 |
| 17 | R–N1 | N–B1 | 42 | R–KB1 | B–R3 |
| 18 | KR–Q1 | N–R3 | 43 | RxP | RxR |
| 19 | B–QR3 | N–B2 | 44 | QxR | B–K6† |
| 20 | Q–B1 | N–Q3 | 45 | K–R1 | R–B1 |
| 21 | P–K5 | N/3–N4 | 46 | Q–Q7 | Q–R6 |
| 22 | NxN | NxN | 47 | QxKP† | K–R1 |
| 23 | B–N4 | Q–Q2 | 48 | Q–B4 | BxP |
| 24 | R–N2 | KR–Q1 | 49 | B–N2 | Resigns |
| 25 | Q–B5 | B–B1 | | | |

### *King's Indian Defense Game 15*

*WHITE: Benko* — *BLACK: Reshevsky*

*First Match Game 1960*

| | WHITE | BLACK | | WHITE | BLACK |
|---|---|---|---|---|---|
| 1 | P–Q4 | N–KB3 | 9 | P–Q5 | N–N5 |
| 2 | P–QB4 | P–KN3 | 10 | P–K4 | P–QB3 |
| 3 | P–KN3 | B–N2 | 11 | Q–N3 | N–Q6 |
| 4 | B–N2 | P–Q4 | 12 | B–K3 | P–QB4 |
| 5 | PxP | NxP | 13 | N–K1 | P–B5 |
| 6 | N–KB3! | O–O | 14 | Q–B2 | NxN |
| 7 | O–O | N–N3 | 15 | KRxN | P–K3 |
| 8 | N–B3 | N–B3 | 16 | PxP | BxP |

| WHITE | BLACK | WHITE | BLACK |
|---|---|---|---|
| 17 QR–Q1 | Q–K2 | 28 P–B4 | PxP |
| 18 N–Q5 | NxN | 29 QxNP | PxP |
| 19 PxN | B–N5 | 30 PxP | RxP |
| 20 P–B3 | B–B4 | 31 Q–R8† | B–B1 |
| 21 QxP | QR–B1 | 32 B–B6 | Q–K3 |
| 22 Q–N5 | P–QR3 | 33 P–Q7 | Q–K7 |
| 23 Q–N6 | KR–K1 | 34 QxB† | KxQ |
| 24 B–B2 | Q–Q2 | 35 P–Q8(Q)† | K–N2 |
| 25 RxR† | RxR | 36 B–Q4† | K–R3 |
| 26 P–Q6 | R–K7 | 37 Q–B6† | Resigns |
| 27 P–N3 | P–N4 | | |

---

## part 8—OLD INDIAN DEFENSE

### OBSERVATIONS ON KEY POSITION 8

1 P–Q4, N–KB3
2 P–QB4, P–Q3
3 N–KB3ᴬ

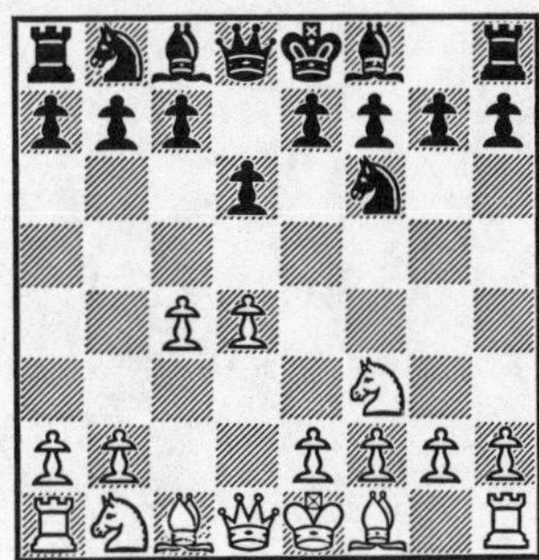

KEY POSITION 8

A 3 N–QB3 is also very popular, after which some possible continuations are as follows:

(1) 3 . . . P–K4 4 PxP (for 4 N–B3, QN–Q2, see Prac. Var. 30), PxP 5 QxQ†, KxQ and now:

*a.* 6 B–N5, P–B3 7 N–B3, QN–Q2 8 P–KN3!, K–B2 9 B–R3, B–N5 10 B–Q2, R–K1 11 R–QB1, P–QR4 12 O–O, N–N3 13 BxB, NxB 14 P–QR3, BxN 15 BxB, N–Q2 16 P–B5!± (Keller–Auer, Vienna 1953).

*b.* 6 N–B3, KN–Q2 7 P–KN3, P–KB3 8 B–N2, P–B3 9 O–O, K–B2=.

*c.* 6 N–B3, KN–Q2 7 B–K3, P–QB3 8 O–O–O, P–B3 9 P–KN4!, K–K1 10 P–N5, N–B4 11 P–KR4, B–K3 12 P–N3, P–QR4 12 P–R5, QN–Q2 14 PxP, PxP 15 B–R3 (Bertok–Udovcic, Laibach 1960).

(2) 3 . . . QN–Q2 4 P–K4, P–K4 and now:

*a.* 5 P–Q5, N–B4 6 P–B3, B–K2 (Capablanca–Ryumin, Moscow 1936).

*b.* 5 KN–K2, B–K2 6 P–KN3.

*c.* 5 N–B3, B–K2 6 B–Q3, O–O 7 O–O, P–B3 8 P–KR3!, Q–B2 9 B–K3, R–K1 10 N–KR4! with good chances for White (Schlechter–Tarrasch, Monte Carlo 1903). In this line 6 P–KN3 followed by B–N2 also merits some attention.

Strictly speaking, the Old Indian, rooted in this position, is not part of the King's Indian insofar as Black intends to develop his King Bishop at K2 instead of fianchettoing it. In other respects, however, the characteristic . . . P–Q3, preparing to strike at the center with . . . P–K4, initiaties a familiar motif. The Russian grandmaster Tchigorin, who was particularly fond of this opening system, played it for the first time in his career when he opposed the German master E. Cohn in the Karlsbad Tournament of 1907. Previously the Old Indian made its debut at the 1903 Monte Carlo Tournament. In modern master play it is still seen with fair frequency, and although Black is not believed to have prospects fully the equal of those in the King's Indian, he achieves a flexible set-up with many good plans at his disposal for reducing White's advantage to a minimum.

## IDEA VARIATIONS 13 AND 14:

(13) 3 . . . B–B4 4 P–KN3, P–KR3 5 B–N2, P–B3 6 N–B3, Q–B1 7 O–O, QN–Q2 8 R–K1, P–K4 (not 8 . . . N–K5? because of 9 Q–B2, NxNP 10 P–K4! and White wins a piece) 9 P–K4, B–R2 10 P–N3, B–K2 11 B–N2, O–O 12 R–B1, R–K1 13 Q–Q2, Q–B2 14 QR–Q1, QR–Q1 15 N–KR4, B–B1 16 P–Q5± (Grunfeld–Bruckner, Vienna 1933).

(14) 3 . . . B–B4 4 N–B3, P–KR3 5 P–K3, QN–Q2 6 B–Q3, BxB 7 QxB and now:

*a.* 7 . . . P–KN3 8 O–O, B–N2 9 P–K4, P–K4 10 B–K3, O–O 11 QR–Q1, R–K1 12 PxP, PxP 13 Q–K2, P–B3 14 B–B5!± (Godai–Leinweber, Vienna 1946).

*b.* 7 . . . P–K4 8 O–O, P–KN3? (B–K2) 9 P–B5!, P–B3 10 P–N3, Q–B2 11 PxQP, BxP 12 B–N2, QR–Q1 13 N–K4!± (Kotov–Kottnauer, vs. Prague 1946).

## PRACTICAL VARIATIONS 29–32:

1 P–Q4, N–KB3 2 P–QB4, P–Q3 3 N–KB3

| | 29 | 30 | 31 | 32 |
|---|---|---|---|---|
| 3 | – – | – – | – – | – – |
| | B–N5 | QN–Q2 | – – | – – |
| 4 | N–B3 | N–B3 | – – | – – |
| | QN–Q2[1] | P–K4 | – – | – – |
| 5 | P–K4[2] | P–KN3 | P–K4! | B–N5 |
| | P–K4 | B–K2 | B–K2[16] | B–K2[22] |
| 6 | B–K2 | B–N2 | P–KN3[17] | P–K3 |
| | B–K2[3] | O–O | O–O | O–O |
| 7 | B–K3 | O–O | B–N2 | Q–B2 |
| | O–O | P–B3[8] | R–K1 | P–B3![23] |
| 8 | O–O[4] | P–K4[9] | O–O | B–Q3 |
| | B–R4[5] | Q–B2 | P–B3 | PxP[24] |
| 9 | N–Q2 | P–KR3[10] | P–N3[18] | PxP |
| | PxP[6] | R–K1[11] | Q–B2 | R–K1 |
| 10 | BxP | B–K3 | B–N2[19] | O–O |
| | BxB | N–B1[12] | N–B1 | P–KR3 |
| 11 | QxB | R–B1 | P–KR3 | B–Q2 |
| | R–K1 | P–KR3[13] | N–N3[20] | N–B1 |
| 12 | P–B4 | P–Q5! | Q–B2 | P–KR3 |
| | B–B1 | B–Q2[14] | B–Q2 | N–K3 |
| 13 | QR–Q1 | N–Q2 | N–Q1! | QR–K1 |
| | P–QR3 | P–KN4 | P–B4 | P–Q4 |
| 14 | Q–B3 | P–B4! | PxKP | PxP |
| | P–B3 | NPxP | PxP | PxP |
| 15 | P–KN4 | NPxP | N–K3 | Q–N3 |
| | N–B4 | K–R2 | QR–Q1 | B–B1 |
| 16 | BxN/5 | PxKP | QR–K1 | R–K2 |
| | PxB[7] | PxKP[15] | B–Q3[21] | Q–Q3[25] |
| | ± | ± | ± | ± |

*Notes to practical variations 29–32:*

[1] Also possible is 4 . . . N–B3 5 P–K4, P–K4 6 P–Q5, N–N1 7 P–KR3, B–R4 8 B–Q3, KN–Q2 9 B–K3, B–K2 10 N–K2 (Tartakover–Poulsen, Ragusa 1950) or 4 . . . P–KN3 5 P–K4, B–N2 6 P–KR3, BxN 7 QxB, O–O 8 B–K2, KN–Q2 9 Q–Q3, N–QB3 10 B–K3, P–K4 11 P–Q5, N–Q5! 12 O–O, P–KB4 (Rubinstein–Reti, Stockholm 1919). In this line, if 5 . . . BxN 6 QxB, KN–Q2, White does best with 7 B–K3. 7 P–K5? is inferior, e.g., 7 . . . N–QB3 8 PxP, NxP 9 Q–K4, P–K4 10 PxP, QxP 11 N–Q5, Q–Q3 12 B–B4, N–QB3, and Black stands well (Pachman–Petrosian, Portoroz 1958).

[2] Colle–Janowski, 1926, continued 5 P–KN3, P–K4 6 B–N2, B–K2 7 O–O, O–O 8 PxP, PxP 9 Q–B2, B–Q3.

[3] If 6 . . . P–KN3 then 7 B–K3, B–N2 8 P–Q5, N–KR4 9 P–KR3!, BxN 10 BxB, N–B5 11 P–KN3, N–R4 12 BxN, PxB 13 QxP± (Grunfeld–Bogoljubov, Budapest 1921).

[4] Or 8 P–KR3, BxN 9 BxB, R–K1 10 P–KN3!, PxP 11 QxP. In this line 10 P–Q5 allows Black equality after 10 . . . N–B1 11 P–KN3, N/3–Q2 12 Q–Q2, N–QN3 13 P–N3, N/1–Q2 (Grunfeld–Lasker, Moscow 1925).

[5] After 8 . . . P–B3 9 N–Q2, BxB 10 QxB White has the edge (Mikenas–Flohr, Hastings 1937–38).

[6] Rather than surrender the center, Black should play 9 . . . BxB.

[7] Petrosian–Larsen, Copenhagen 1960, continued 17 P–K5, N–Q2 18 N/2–K4, Q–B2 19 R–Q3, QR–Q1 20 KR–Q1, N–N3 21 P–N3, N–B1 22 P–N5, B–K2 23 Q–R5, RxR 24 RxR, R–Q1 25 N–B6† with a winning game for White.

[8] Or 7 . . . R–K1 8 P–N3, N–B1 (if 8 . . . P–B3 then 9 Q–B2!) 9 B–N2, N–N3 10 P–KR3, B–Q2 11 Q–B2, Q–B1 12 K–R2, P–KR4 13 QR–Q1, P–R5 14 B–B1!, N–R2 15 P–K4± (Maroczy–Spencer, Weston-super-Mare 1922).

[9] Or 8 P–N3, R–K1 9 Q–B2!, B–B1 10 P–K4!± .

[10] Equally playable is 9 P–N3, R–Q1 (for 9 . . . R–K1, see Prac. Var. 31) 10 B–N2, N–B1 11 P–KR3, N–K3 12 Q–Q2 and White has a great advantage in space.

[11] Or 9 . . . P–QN3 10 B–K3, R–K1 11 R–B1, B–R3 12 P–N3, QR–Q1 13 R–K1, N–B1 14 Q–Q2, Q–N1 15 K–R2, N–N3 16 P–Q5± (Muller–Grob, Vienna 1947). In this line 15 N–KR4! gives White an even greater advantage.

[12] If 10 . . . B–B1 11 K–R2, P–QN3 12 R–B1, B–N2 13 Q–B2± (Rubinstein–Przepiorka, Marienbad 1925) or if 10 . . . B–B1 11 R–B1, P–KN3 12 P–Q5!± (Grunfeld–Mattison, Debreczin 1925).

[13] If 11 . . . B–Q2 12 P–B5, PxQP 13 PxP, QxP 14 NxP, Q–N1 15 K–R2!±.

[14] Better, according to Tartakover, is 12 . . . P–KN4!, e.g., 13 N–Q2, N–N3.

[15] Botvinnik–Tartakover, Nottingham 1936, continued 17 P–B5, PxP 18 NxP, Q–B3 19 N–QB4, N–N3 20 N–Q6±.

[16] Two other possibilities are:

1) 5 . . . PxP 6 NxP followed by (a) 6 . . . P–B3 7 B–B4!, N–N3 8 B–K2± or (b) 6 . . . P–KN3 7 B–K3, B–N2 8 P–B3!, O–O 9 Q–Q2, N–B4 10 B–K2=.
2) 5 . . . P–B3 6 B–K2, B–K2 7 O–O, Q–B2 8 R–N1,

continued ▸

N–B1 9 R–K1, N–N3 10 P–KR3, O–O 11 P–QN4, P–QR3 12 P–QR4±.

[17] Also good for White is 6 B–K2, O–O 7 P–KR3, e.g., 7 . . . R–K1 8 B–K3, B–B1 9 P–Q5, N–B4 10 N–Q2, P–QR4 11 P–QR3, P–QN3 12 P–QN4± (Bogoljubov–Kieninger, Pyrmont 1933) or 7 . . . P–B3 8 Q–B2, Q–B2 9 B–K3, R–K1 10 P–Q5, N–B1 11 B–Q3, B–Q2 12 QR–B1, P–B4 13 P–KN4± (Gygli–Lokvenc, Schaffhausen 1948).

[18] 9 P–KR3, Q–B2 leads to Prac. Var. 30.

[19] Or 10 P–KR3, P–QR3 11 P–QR4, B–B1 12 B–K3, P–B4 13 P–Q5, P–QN3 14 N–K1, P–N3 15 N–Q3, B–KN2 16 Q–Q2 (Eliskases–Kieninger, Harzburg 1938).

[20] 11 . . . P–KR3 followed by . . . P–KN4 and . . . N–N3 deserves serious consideration.

[21] See Game 16.

[22] Keres–Boleslavski, Neuhausen 1953, continued 5 . . . P–KR3 6 B–R4, P–KN4 (6 . . . B–K2! is more solid) 7 PxP!

[23] If 7 . . . P–KR3 8 P–KR4, PxP 9 NxP, N–K4 10 O–O–O, P–B3 11 P–B3, N–R4 12 BxB, QxB 13 B–Q3± (Spielmann–Tartakover, Vienna 1913). For 7 . . . PxP, see Game 17.

[24] Or 8 . . . P–KR3 9 B–R4, R–K1 10 O–O–O, PxP 11 NxP, N–K4 12 B–K2, N–N3 13 B–N3, Q–N3 14 R–Q2, P–Q4 15 PxP, PxP 16 N–R4 (Canal–Szabados, Venice 1947).

[25] After 17 B–B1, P–R3 18 KR–K1, P–QN4 19 B–B5, B–Q2 20 P–R3, QR–B1 21 Q–Q1, N–B2 22 BxB, NxB 23 N–K5 (Euwe–Petrosian, Zurich 1953), White had a clear advantage, but agreed to a premature draw in this position.

### *King's Indian Defense Game 16*

*WHITE: Najdorf* *BLACK: Tartakover*

*Dubrovnik 1950*

| | WHITE | BLACK | | WHITE | BLACK |
|---|---|---|---|---|---|
| 1 | P–Q4 | N–KB3 | 19 | N–N1 | N–K2 |
| 2 | P–QB4 | P–Q3 | 20 | NxN† | BxN |
| 3 | N–QB3 | P–K4 | 21 | N–B3 | P–QR3 |
| 4 | N–B3 | QN–Q2 | 22 | P–B4! | PxP |
| 5 | P–K4 | B–K2 | 23 | PxP | N–R4 |
| 6 | P–KN3 | O–O | 24 | N–Q5 | Q–Q2 |
| 7 | B–N2 | R–K1 | 25 | P–B5 | B–R5 |
| 8 | O–O | P–B3 | 26 | B–KB3 | Q–Q3 |
| 9 | P–N3 | Q–B2 | 27 | P–K5 | Q–R3 |
| 10 | B–N2 | N–B1 | 28 | B–B1 | B–N4 |
| 11 | P–KR3 | N–N3 | 29 | BxB | QxB† |
| 12 | Q–B2 | B–Q2 | 30 | Q–N2 | N–B5! |
| 13 | N–Q1! | P–B4 | 31 | NxN | QxN |
| 14 | PxKP | PxP | 32 | B–Q5! | Q–Q5† |
| 15 | N–K3 | QR–Q1 | 33 | Q–B2 | QxQ† |
| 16 | QR–K1 | B–Q3 | 34 | RxQ | R–K2 |
| 17 | N–B5 | B–KB1 | 35 | P–K6 | PxP |
| 18 | N–Q2! | B–B1 | 36 | PxP | P–KN3 |

| | WHITE | BLACK | | WHITE | BLACK |
|---|---|---|---|---|---|
| 37 | K–N2 | P–QN4 | 55 | R–N7 | B–B4 |
| 38 | K–N3 | K–N2 | 56 | RxP | K–Q5 |
| 39 | R–B7† | RxR | 57 | K–Q2 | R–R6! |
| 40 | PxR | B–Q2 | 58 | R–R8 | RxNP |
| 41 | K–B4 | K–B3 | 59 | R–Q8† | K–K4 |
| 42 | P–KR4 | P–N5 | 60 | B–Q3 | R–N7† |
| 43 | R–K5 | P–QR4 | 61 | K–B3 | R–KR7 |
| 44 | B–K4 | KxP | 62 | BxB | PxB |
| 45 | RxP | P–R5 | 63 | R–KR8 | P–B5 |
| 46 | R–B7 | PxP | 64 | P–R5! | P–B6 |
| 47 | PxP | K–K3! | 65 | K–Q3 | K–B5 |
| 48 | R–N7 | R–KB1† | 66 | P–R6 | R–R8! |
| 49 | K–K3 | R–B8 | 67 | P–R7 | P–B7 |
| 50 | RxP | K–K4 | 68 | K–Q4 | K–B6 |
| 51 | B–B3 | R–K8† | 69 | R–KB8† | K–K7! |
| 52 | K–Q2 | R–KB8 | 70 | R–K8† | K–Q7! |
| 53 | B–K2 | R–B7 | 71 | R–KB8 | K–K7 |
| 54 | K–K1 | R–R7 | | Draw | |

*King's Indian Defense Game 17*

*WHITE: Flohr* *BLACK: Petrosian*

*USSR Championship, Moscow* 1949

| | WHITE | BLACK | | WHITE | BLACK |
|---|---|---|---|---|---|
| 1 | P–Q4 | N–KB3 | 23 | Q–Q4 | P–QN4 |
| 2 | P–QB4 | P–Q3 | 24 | R–B3 | N/1–Q2 |
| 3 | N–QB3 | P–K4 | 25 | B–N5 | R–B2 |
| 4 | N–B3 | QN–Q2 | 26 | PxQP | NxP |
| 5 | B–N5 | B–K2 | 27 | RxR | QxR |
| 6 | P–K3 | O–O | 28 | B–B3 | N/4–N3 |
| 7 | Q–B2 | PxP | 29 | B–R6 | R–K1 |
| 8 | NxP | N–K4 | 30 | K–N1 | N–K4 |
| 9 | B–K2 | N–N3 | 31 | B–K2 | P–N4 |
| 10 | P–KR4! | P–B3 | 32 | K–R1 | Q–N3 |
| 11 | N–B5 | BxN | 33 | R–R1 | Q–B3 |
| 12 | QxB | Q–B2 | 34 | R–R5 | QxP |
| 13 | O–O–O | KR–K1 | 35 | RxP† | K–B2 |
| 14 | P–R5 | N–B1 | 36 | R–N7†? | K–K3 |
| 15 | R–R3! | P–Q4 | 37 | B–N4† | NxB |
| 16 | R–N3 | P–KN3 | 38 | QxN† | K–Q4 |
| 17 | PxNP | BPxP | 39 | Q–Q4† | K–K3 |
| 18 | B–B4 | Q–B1 | 40 | Q–K4† | K–B3 |
| 19 | Q–B2 | B–N5 | 41 | Q–Q4† | K–K3 |
| 20 | B–R6! | Q–K3 | 42 | Q–K4† | K–B3 |
| 21 | Q–N3 | BxN | 43 | QxBP† | Resigns |
| 22 | QxB | R–K2 | | | |

# chapter 36—Nimzo-Indian Defense

This opening arises after 1 P–Q4, N–KB3 2 P–QB4, P–K3 3 N–QB3, B–N5. With his pin, Black avoids the Queen's Gambit without permitting P–K4.

The inaugural game of the Nimzo-Indian, as far as is known, is Rubinstein–Alekhine, Leningrad 1914. It was primarily Nimzowitsch, however, who extensively analyzed and championed this defense.

In modern tournament play, the Nimzo–Indian is of major importance, and there is hardly a master who has not been confronted with it on one occasion or another. As for the systems of meeting 3 . . . B–N5, most usual today is 4 P–K3. In any case, the theory of this continuation has undergone tremendous expansion in recent years and investigation still continues. No doubt the Nimzo-Indian will keep players and analysts busy for many years to come.

---

## part 1—ZURICH VARIATION

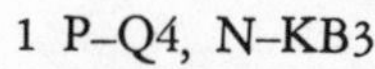
1 P–Q4, N–KB3
2 P–QB4, P–K3
3 N–QB3, B–N5
4 Q–B2[A], N–B3[B]
5 N–B3[C], P–Q3[D]

KEY POSITION 1

### OBSERVATIONS ON KEY POSITION 1

[A] Once again threatening P–K4.

[B] Deeply analyzed by Swiss masters, this system received its first practical test in the Zurich Tournament of 1934. For 4 . . . P–Q4 and 4 . . . P–B4, see Parts 2 and 3. See also Sup. Var. 1–7.

[C] The safest reply to 5 P–K3 is 5 . . . P–Q3, which leads to positions similar to the text.

[D] 5 . . . O–O 6 B–N5, P–KR3 7 B–R4! favors White. A move meriting more attention is 5 . . . P–Q4; best then seems to be 6 B–N5, PxP 7 P–K3, Q–Q4 8 BxN, PxB 9 N–Q2, and White maintains the initiative.

With his last two moves, Black has been preparing for . . . P–K4, which White cannot long prevent. White usually plays for the exchange of the enemy King Bishop, so that he emerges from the opening with the two Bishops. This advantage has little significance as long as the position remains closed. White has little chance for initiative, even with accurate play.

### IDEA VARIATIONS 1 AND 2:

(1) 6 B–Q2 (considered best; for 6 P–QR3, see Idea Var. 2), Q–K2 7 P–QR3, BxN 8 BxB, P–QR4 (preventing White from gaining the upper hand on the Queenside with 9 P–QN4) 9 R–Q1 (most likely White's best; after 9 P–K3, P–K4 10 PxP, PxP 11 P–KR3, O–O 12 B–K2, P–KN3, Black has a satisfactory game, as in Van Scheltinga–

Reshevsky, Amsterdam 1950), P–K4 (the consistent continuation; instead, 9 . . . P–R5 10 P–K3, P–K4 11 PxP, PxP 12 B–K2, O–O 13 R–Q5! offers White fine chances) 10 P–QN4, PxNP 11 PxNP, P–K5 12 P–Q5, PxN 13 PxN with a good game for White. The acceptance of the Pawn sacrifice, 13 . . PxKP 14 BxP, PxP 15 O–O, is very dangerous for Black.

(2) 6 P–QR3, BxN† 7 QxB, P–QR4 8 P–QN3, O–O 9 B–N2 (better than 9 P–N3, e.g., 9 . . . R–K1! 10 B–N2, P–K4 11 P–Q5, N–K2 12 N–Q2, P–B3! 13 PxP, NxP!∓, as in O'Kelly–Reshevsky, New York 1951), R–K1 (this is the correct reply; 9 . . . N–K5 10 Q–B2, P–B4 11 P–N3, Q–K2 12 B–N2, P–K4 13 PxP, PxP 14 R–Q1! favors White) 10 R–Q1 (after 10 P–N3, P–K4, Black experiences no further difficulties), Q–K2 11 P–Q5, N–N1 12 PxP, PxP 13 P–N3, P–QN3 14 B–N2, B–N2 15 O–O, and White's edge is slight indeed.

In the foregoing line, 7 . . . P–QR4 in reply to 7 QxB is most usual. Also playable is 7 . . . Q–K2, e.g., 8 P–QN4, P–K4! 9 PxP, NxKP 10 NxN, PxN 11 B–N2, P–K5, and Black has nothing to fear.

8 P–QN3 following 7 . . . P–QR4 is Fine's suggestion. Worth further investigation is 8 B–N5 (see Game 2). After 8 P–Q5, N–QN1 9 PxP, Black's best is 9 . . . PxP.

*Nimzo-Indian Defense Game 1*

*WHITE: Euwe* *BLACK: Kramer*

*Netherlands Championship 1952*

| | WHITE | BLACK | | WHITE | BLACK |
|---|---|---|---|---|---|
| 1 | P–Q4 | N–KB3 | 19 | B–K1 | N–B1 |
| 2 | P–QB4 | P–K3 | 20 | RxR | RxR |
| 3 | N–QB3 | B–N5 | 21 | Q–N3† | K–R1 |
| 4 | Q–B2 | N–B3 | 22 | P–B6 | PxP |
| 5 | N–B3 | P–Q3 | 23 | Q–R4 | B–Q6 |
| 6 | B–Q2 | O–O | 24 | BxB | RxB |
| 7 | P–QR3 | BxN | 25 | QxRP | Q–Q2 |
| 8 | BxB | R–K1 | 26 | K–B2 | P–R3 |
| 9 | P–QN4 | P–K4 | 27 | P–QR4 | N–K3 |
| 10 | PxP | NxP | 28 | P–R5 | K–R2 |
| 11 | P–K3 | B–N5 | 29 | P–R6 | P–QB4 |
| 12 | NxN | PxN | 30 | Q–N7 | RxP |
| 13 | P–B3 | B–R4 | 31 | P–R7 | Q–Q5 |
| 14 | B–K2 | B–N3 | 32 | P–R8(Q) | N–B5 |
| 15 | Q–N2 | N–Q2 | 33 | K–B1 | RxB† |
| 16 | O–O | P–KB3 | 34 | RxR | Q–Q6† |
| 17 | P–B5 | Q–K2 | 35 | K–N1 | Resigns |
| 18 | KR–Q1 | KR–Q1 | | | |

*Nimzo-Indian Defense Game 2*

*WHITE: Wolthuis* *BLACK: Van Scheltinga*

*Maastricht 1946*

| | WHITE | BLACK | | WHITE | BLACK |
|---|---|---|---|---|---|
| 1 | P–Q4 | N–KB3 | 43 | R–K6† | K–B2 |
| 2 | P–QB4 | P–K3 | 44 | R–K7† | K–B3 |
| 3 | N–QB3 | B–N5 | 45 | R/KxN | RxP |
| 4 | Q–B2 | N–B3 | 46 | R–KR7 | R–Q7† |
| 5 | N–B3 | P–Q3 | 47 | K–K3 | RxQP |
| 6 | P–QR3 | BxN† | 48 | R–R6† | R–N3 |
| 7 | QxB | P–QR4 | 49 | RxR† | NxR |
| 8 | B–N5 | P–R3 | 50 | B–B4 | K–K4 |
| 9 | B–R4 | P–KN4 | 51 | B–Q5 | R–KB3 |
| 10 | P–Q5 | N–QN1 | 52 | K–Q3 | R–B7 |
| 11 | B–N3 | P–K4 | 53 | K–B3 | N–B5 |
| 12 | N–Q2 | N–R4 | 54 | B–B4 | KxP |
| 13 | BxP | PxB | 55 | R–K7† | K–B4 |
| 14 | QxP† | K–Q2 | 56 | R–QN7 | K–K4 |
| 15 | Q–B5† | K–K1 | 57 | RxP | R–B6† |
| 16 | Q–K5† | K–Q2 | 58 | K–B2 | K–Q5 |
| 17 | P–KR4 | R–K1 | 59 | B–R6 | R–B7† |
| 18 | Q–B5† | K–K2 | 60 | K–N3 | N–Q4 |
| 19 | Q–K5† | K–Q2 | 61 | R–N5 | R–B3 |
| 20 | Q–Q4 | N–KB3 | 62 | RxP | R–N3† |
| 21 | PxP | PxP | 63 | K–R2 | R–R3 |
| 22 | R–R6 | N–N1 | 64 | B–N7 | N–K6 |
| 23 | Q–N4† | K–K2 | 65 | R–QN5 | K–B5 |
| 24 | QxP† | K–B1 | 66 | P–R4 | R–R2 |
| 25 | QxQ | RxQ | 67 | B–R6 | N–Q4 |
| 26 | R–R4 | P–KB4 | 68 | K–R3 | K–Q4 |
| 27 | P–B3 | P–B3 | 69 | B–N7 | R–R6† |
| 28 | P–K4 | PxKP | 70 | R–N3 | N–K6 |
| 29 | BPxP | PxP | 71 | R–B3 | R–R3 |
| 30 | BPxP | N–Q2 | 72 | P–R5? | N–B5† |
| 31 | N–B4 | P–N3 | 73 | K–N4 | NxNP |
| 32 | B–Q3 | B–R3 | 74 | R–B8 | N–Q6† |
| 33 | K–Q2 | BxN | 75 | K–N5 | R–R4† |
| 34 | BxB | N–K4 | 76 | K–N6 | N–N5 |
| 35 | B–K2 | N–KB3 | 77 | B–B6 | R–KN4 |
| 36 | R–QB1 | K–K2 | 78 | B–N5 | R–N3† |
| 37 | K–K3 | R–KN1 | 79 | K–N7 | K–Q4 |
| 38 | K–Q4 | R–N4 | 80 | B–B4† | K–Q3 |
| 39 | R–B7† | N/3–Q2 | 81 | R–B7 | R–N4 |
| 40 | R–R6 | R/1–KN1 | 82 | P–R6 | NxP |
| 41 | P–Q6† | K–Q1 | 83 | BxN | R–QB4 |
| 42 | B–R6 | K–K1 | | Draw | |

PRACTICAL VARIATIONS 1–3:

1 P–Q4, N–KB3 2 P–QB4, P–K3 3 N–QB3, B–N5 4 Q–B2, N–B3 5 N–B3, P–Q3

| | 1 | 2 | 3 | | 1 | 2 | 3 |
|---|---|---|---|---|---|---|---|
| 6 | B–Q2 | – – | P–QR3 | 10 | P–QN4! | PxP | NxN |
| | P–K4 | O–O | BxN† | | P–K5 | PxP | PxN |
| 7 | P–QR3! | P–QR3 | QxB | 11 | P–N5![2] | P–QN4 | QxP |
| | BxN | BxN | O–O | | PxN | B–N5 | R–K1 |
| 8 | BxB | BxB | P–QN4 | 12 | PxN[3] | P–N5![5] | Q–N2 |
| | Q–K2[1] | Q–K2[4] | P–K4[6] | | ± | ± | Q–Q6[8] |
| 9 | PxP | P–K3 | PxP | | | | ± |
| | PxP | P–K4 | NxP[7] | | | | |

*Notes to practical variations 1–3:*

[1] 8 . . . P–K5 9 P–Q5! gives White too great a pull.

[2] 11 N–Q4 is met by 11 . . . P–K6!

[3] The freedom of White's Bishops on an open board is the plus factor.

[4] For 8 . . . R–K1, see Game 1. 8 . . . P-QR4 9 P-K4!, P–K4! 10 PxP, PxP 11 NxP, Q–K1! 12 P–B4! favors White.

[5] E.g., 12 . . . BxN 13 PxB, N–Q5 14 Q–Q1, P–B4 15 B–QN2, N–B4 16 Q–B2, N–R5 17 O–O–O±.

[6] This gambit is Black's most thematic continuation. After 8 . . . R–K1 9 B–N2!, P–K4 10 PxP, NxKP 11 NxN, PxN 12 P–K3, White has the better game.

[7] 9 . . . N–K5 is no stronger, e.g., 10 Q–K3!, P–B4 11 B–N2, NxP 12 NxN, PxN 13 P–N3, and White has the better game. In this line, 11 . . . B–K3 deserves consideration.

[8] 13 B–N5, N–N5 14 P–B3 leaves Black with insufficient compensation for his Pawn. Two possibilities are mentioned by Lilienthal: 14 . . . Q–B4 15 Q–B1, N–K4 16 K–B2, N–N5† 17 K–N1± and 14 . . . N–K4 15 PxQ, NxQP† 16 K–Q2, NxQ 17 P–QR4±.

---

## part 2—4...P-Q4 VARIATION

### OBSERVATIONS ON KEY POSITION 2

Black's last move leads to a Queen's Gambit, differing only by the interpolation of the unusual moves Q–B2 and . . . B–N5. Surprisingly, however, the game may now become extremely complicated, both sides firing blazing tactical salvos. White's safest continuation is 5 PxP, but this line offers him less than the intricate 5 P–QR3. Adoption of this latter continuation, it should be stressed, requires a thorough knowledge of the many dangerous possibilities at Black's disposal.

1 P–Q4, N–KB3
2 P–QB4, P–K3
3 N–QB3, B–N5
4 Q–B2, P–Q4

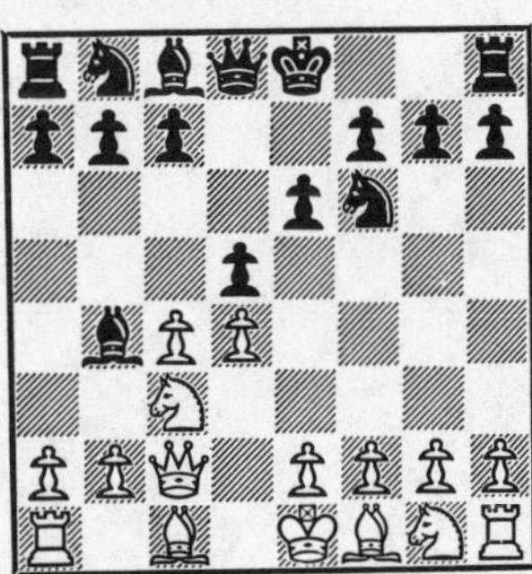

KEY POSITION 2

IDEA VARIATIONS 3 AND 4:

(3) 5 P–QR3 (both 5 N–B3 and 5 B–N5 are answered by 5 . . . PxP, when Black has excellent prospects; for the steadier 5 PxP, see Idea Var. 4), BxN†! (with 5 . . . . B–K2 Black can return to Queen's Gambit lines, although White remains with the extra tempo P–QR3) 6 QxB, N–K5 (another possibility is 6 . . . PxP 7 QxP, O–O 8 B–N5, P–B3 9 N–B3, QN–Q2 [Euwe–Capablanca, Carlsbad 1929], after which White has the edge; for the Botvinnik Variation, 6 . . . N–B3, see Sup. Var. 1) 7 Q–B2, N–QB3 (an extremely sharp line; see Prac. Var. 4 and Game 3 for 7 . . . P–QB4 and Prac. Var. 5 for 7 . . . O–O) 8 P–K3 (strangely enough, this move is stronger than 8 N–B3, after which 8 . . . P–K4 is more effective than in the text, as seen in the two following continuations: 9 PxKP, B–B4 10 Q–R4, O–O 11 P–K3, P–Q5! with fine chances for Black, and 9 P–K3, B–B4 10 Q–R4, O–O 11 PxQP, QxP 12 Q–N5, QxQ 13 BxQ, N–R4 [Grunfeld–Fine, Zandvoort 1936], leaving Black with a slight edge), P–K4 (the only consistent continuation) 9 PxQP! (best; other moves make Black's life simple), QxP 10 B–B4, Q–R4†, 11 P–N4, NxNP 12 QxN!, N–B7† 13 K–K2, Q–K8† (not 13 . . . NxR because of 14 N–B3!, and after 14 . . . B–Q2 15 NxP, O–O–O 16 NxB, RxN 17 B–N2, White's advantage is decisive) 14 K–B3, NxR 15 B–N2, O–O (ingenious but insufficient is 15 . . . B–K3?, e.g., 16 P–Q5, O–O–O 17 PxB, PxP 18 K–N3!, KR–B1 19 BxP! [Pachman], RxP 20 BxP†, K–N1 21 K–R3, R–B8 22 B–N4! and Black is helpless) 16 K–N3, B–Q2 (16 . . . P–KR3 17 P–R3, B–Q2 18 K–R2, P–QN4 19 N–B3, QxBP 20 R–KB1, QxB 21 BxP† and White wins) 17 P–R3 (flashy but inferior is 17 N–B3; after 17 . . . QxR 18 N–N5, P–KN3 19 QxKP, QR–K1 20 Q–B6, RxP†!, Black stands well), and White has a won game.

(4) 5 PxP, PxP (5 . . . NxP 6 P–K4, NxN 7 PxN, B–K2 8 N–B3, P–QB4 9 B–QB4±; for 5 . . . QxP, see Prac. Var. 6) 6 B–N5 (6 P–QR3, BxN† 7 PxB, P–B4 8 N–B3, Q–R4 9 N–Q2, B–Q2 10 N–N3, Q–R5 11 Q–N2, N–R3 12 P–K3, PxP followed by . . . P–QN3 yields Black approximate equality; inferior for White in this line is 8 P–B3, Q–B2 9 R–R2!, P–KR3! 10 P–K3, O–O 11 B–Q3, P–QN3∓ [Pachman]), P–KR3 7 B–R4, P–B4! 8 PxP, P–KN4! 9 B–N3, N–K5 10 B–K5, O–O and Black has good chances.

*Nimzo-Indian Defense Game 3*

*WHITE: Euwe* *BLACK: Najdorf*

*Mar del Plata 1947*

| WHITE | BLACK | WHITE | BLACK | WHITE | BLACK |
|---|---|---|---|---|---|
| 1 P–Q4 | N–KB3 | 14 NxP | NxN | 27 KPxB | N–Q5 |
| 2 P–QB4 | P–K3 | 15 BPxN | N–B7† | 28 Q–Q5 | N–B4 |
| 3 N–QB3 | B–N5 | 16 K–B2 | Q–N4 | 29 QxP | N–K6 |
| 4 Q–B2 | P–Q4 | 17 P–KR4 | Q–R3 | 30 R–K1 | Q–B6 |
| 5 P–QR3 | BxN† | 18 P–N4 | B–K5 | 31 R–K2 | Q–Q5 |
| 6 QxB | N–K5 | 19 P–N5 | Q–N3 | 32 P–N3! | R–K1 |
| 7 Q–B2 | P–QB4 | 20 R–Q1 | P–B3 | 33 Q–R6 | R–Q1 |
| 8 QPxP | N–B3 | 21 Q–N3† | K–R1 | 34 Q–K6 | NxB† |
| 9 PxP | PxP | 22 PxP | RxP† | 35 KxB | Q–R8† |
| 10 N–B3 | B–B4 | 23 BxR | QxB† | 36 K–B2 | QxP |
| 11 P–QN4 | O–O | 24 K–N1 | R–KB1 | 37 Q–B7 | QxNP |
| 12 B–N2 | N–N6? | 25 R–R3 | P–KR3 | 38 R–K8† | Resigns |
| 13 Q–B3 | P–Q5 | 26 R–KB3? | BxR | | |

PRACTICAL VARIATIONS 4–6:

1 P–Q4, N–KB3 2 P–QB4, P–K3 3 N–QB3, B–N5 4 Q–B2, P–Q4

| | *4* | *5* | *6* |
|---|---|---|---|
| *5* | P–QR3 | – – | PxP |
| | BxN† | – – | QxP |
| *6* | QxB | – – | N–B3[11] |
| | N–K5 | – – | P–B4[12] |
| *7* | Q–B2 | – – | B–Q2 |
| | P–QB4 | O–O | BxN |
| *8* | PxBP | N–B3[8] | BxB |
| | N–QB3 | P–QN3 | PxP[13] |
| *9* | PxP![1] | B–B4 | NxP |
| | PxP | B–R3 | O–O |
| *10* | N–B3 | PxP | P–K3 |
| | B–B4[2] | PxP | P–K4 |
| *11* | P–QN4! | BxP[9] | N–B3 |
| | O–O[3] | Q–K2[10] | N–B3 |
| *12* | B–N2 | = | B–K2 |
| | P–QN3[4] | | B–N5 |
| *13* | P–N5 | | P–KR3 |
| | PxP | | B–R4 |
| *14* | PxN | | O–O |
| | Q–R4† | | KR–Q1[14] |
| *15* | N–Q2 | | = |
| | QR–N1![5] | | |
| *16* | R–Q1 | | |
| | P–B5![6] | | |
| *17* | P–B3 | | |
| | N–B7 | | |
| *18* | Q–B3[7] | | |
| | ± | | |

*Notes to practical variations 4–6:*

[1] Additional possibilities are: (a) 9 P–K3, Q–R4† 10 B–Q2, NxB 11 QxN, PxP 12 BxP, QxBP 13 R–B1, Q–KN4 14 P–B4±: (b) 9 N–B3, Q–R4† 10 N–Q2, N–Q5 11 Q–Q3!, P–K4! 12 P–QN4, Q–R5 13 R–R2!, NxN! 14 QxN!= (Bronstein–Boleslavski, Saltsjobaden 1948).

continued ▸

[2] Simpler, but insufficient for equality, is 10 . . . Q–R4† 11 B–Q2.

[3] 11 . . . P–Q5 12 P–KN4!±.

[4] For 12 . . . N–N6?, see Game 3. 12 . . . P–Q5 is again best answered by 13 P–KN4.

[5] A suggestion of the Czech analyst Katetov.

[6] If 16 . . . P–Q5, then 17 P–B7!

[7] With complications.

[8] 8 P–K3 may be an improvement. After 8 . . . P–QN3 9 B–Q3, B–R3 10 P–QN3!, White has the upper hand.

[9] 11 QxP, QxQ 12 BxQ, N–B3∓.

[10] Black has sufficient compensation for his Pawn.

[11] 6 P–K3 makes matters still easier for Black, e.g., 6 . . . P–B4 7 P–QR3, BxN† 8 PxB, O–O 9 N–B3, PxP 10 BPxP, P–QN3 11 B–B4, Q–B3 12 B–Q3, QxQ=.

[12] 6 . . . O–O is also playable. After 7 B–Q2, BxN Black has approximate equality.

[13] 8 . . . N–B3 is inferior. The position resulting from 9 R–Q1, O–O 10 P–QR3! may prove troublesome for Black.

[14] Flohr–Reshevsky, AVRO 1938.

---

## part 3—PIRC VARIATION

1 P–Q4, N–KB3
2 P–QB4, P–K3
3 N–QB3, B–N5
4 Q–B2, P–B4
5 PxP[A], O–O[B]

KEY POSITION 3

### OBSERVATIONS ON KEY POSITION 3

[A] After 5 P–K3 or 5 N–B3, Black equalizes with 5 . . . P–Q4.

[B] For 5 . . . BxP and 5 . . . BxN†, see Sup. Var. 2 and 3 respectively.

This system, worked out by the Yugoslavian grandmaster Vasja Pirc, is the reason why the once popular 4 Q–B2 is no longer played. Black quickly completes his development so that he may profit from White's castling difficulty. No resource has been found so far to provide White with good chances. Donner's suggestion of 6 B–B4 most likely constitutes White's best try for some initiative.

### IDEA VARIATIONS 5 AND 6:

5) 6 B–N5, N–R3 (still more enterprising is 6 . . . P–KR3, e.g., 7 B–R4, N–R3 8 P–K3, NxP 9 N–K2, P–Q4 10 O–O–O, B–Q2 11 PxP, R–B1 12 K–N1, P–K4!, and Black has good chances for his Pawn) 7 P–QR3 (7 P–B3, NxP 8 P–K4, Q–R4∓), BxN† 8 QxB, NxP 9 BxN (9 P–B3 is surprisingly met by 9 . . . KN–K5!, while after 9 Q–B2, P–QR4 10 P–B3, P–R5, Black also enjoys the advantage), QxB 10 QxQ, PxQ 11 P–QN4,

N–R5 12 O–O–O, P–QR4 13 K–B2, P–Q4!∓ (Euwe-Pirc, 2nd Match Game, Bled 1949).

The pin, 6 B–N5, appears most natural, but involves some tactical drawbacks. 6 N–B3 and 6 P–QR3 are discussed in Prac. Var. 7 and 8 respectively. 6 P–K3 is too passive. After 6 . . . N–R3 7 N–K2, NxP 8 P–QR3, BxN† 9 NxB, P–QR4 10 B–K2, the game is lifeless. For 6 B–B4, see Idea Var. 6.

(6) 6 B–B4, BxP 7 P–K3, N–B3 8 N–B3, P–Q4 (8 . . . P–QN3, of which no tournament examples are known, is probably a better try) 9 R–Q1 (for 9 P–QR3, see Game 4), Q–R4 10 P–QR3, N–K5 (10 . . . R–Q1 11 N–Q2, PxP 12 NxP, RxR† 13 QxR, Q–Q1 14 QxQ†, NxQ 15 N–R4! offers White a slight but distinct advantage [Euwe–Kupper, Zurich 1954]) 11 B–Q3!, NxN 12 BxP†, K–R1 13 PxN, P–KN3 14 BxP, PxB 15 N–K5! and White has a dangerous attack.

Besides 6 . . . BxP other possibilities are 6 . . . N–R3 7 B–Q6, R–K1 8 P–QR3, BxBP 9 BxB, NxB 10 P–QN4 and 6 . . . Q–R4 7 P–K3, BxN† 8 QxB, QxQ† 9 PxQ. In both cases White has the better game.

*Nimzo-Indian Defense Game 4*

*WHITE: Euwe* — *BLACK: Taimanov*

*Zurich 1953*

| | WHITE | BLACK | | WHITE | BLACK |
|---|---|---|---|---|---|
| 1 | P–Q4 | N–KB3 | 20 | Q–R7† | K–B1 |
| 2 | P–QB4 | P–K3 | 21 | RxB | PxN |
| 3 | N–QB3 | B–N5 | 22 | RxB | QxR |
| 4 | Q–B2 | P–B4 | 23 | Q–R8† | K–K2 |
| 5 | PxP | O–O | 24 | QxR | Q–Q8† |
| 6 | B–B4 | BxP | 25 | B–B1 | Q–N6 |
| 7 | P–K3 | N–B3 | 26 | P–R3 | QxNP |
| 8 | N–B3 | P–Q4 | 27 | P–QR4 | Q–N3 |
| 9 | P–QR3 | Q–K2 | 28 | Q–R8 | K–B3 |
| 10 | B–N5 | R–Q1 | 29 | P–R4 | Q–B4? |
| 11 | R–Q1 | PxP | 30 | P–KR5 | P–N5 |
| 12 | RxR† | QxR | 31 | P–R6 | Q–KN4 |
| 13 | BxP | B–K2 | 32 | P–R7 | P–N6 |
| 14 | O–O | B–Q2 | 33 | Q–KN8 | PxP† |
| 15 | R–Q1 | Q–K1 | 34 | KxP | N–K2 |
| 16 | BxN | BxB | 35 | P–R8 (Q) | NxQ |
| 17 | N–K4 | B–K2 | 36 | QxN | Q–R5† |
| 18 | N/3–N5 | P–KR3! | | Draw | |
| 19 | N–Q6 | BxN/3 | | | |

PRACTICAL VARIATIONS 7–8:

1 P–Q4, N–KB3 2 P–QB4, P–K3 3 N–QB3, B–N5 4 Q–B2, P–B4 5 PxP, O–O

| | 7 | 8 |
|---|---|---|
| *6* | N–B3 | P–QR3 |
| | N–R3 | BxBP |
| *7* | P–QR3[1] | N–B3 |
| | BxN† | N–B3[5] |
| *8* | QxB | P–QN4[6] |
| | NxP | B–K2 |
| *9* | P–KN3[2] | P–K3[7] |
| | P–QN3[3] | P–QN3 |
| *10* | B–N2 | B–N2 |
| | B–R3![4] | B–N2 |
| *11* | = | B–Q3[8] |
| | | R–B1 |
| *12* | | O–O |
| | | P–KR3 |
| *13* | | KR–Q1 |
| | | P–QR4[9] |
| *14* | | P–N5 |
| | | N–N1[10] |
| | | ∓ |

*Notes to practical variations 7–8:*

[1] If 7 B–Q2, then 7 . . . NxP and after 8 P–K3, P–QN3 9 B–K2, B–R3! 10 P–QR3, BxN 11 BxB, R–B1 (Pirc–Bonderevski, Saltsjobaden 1948) or 8 P–QR3, BxN 9 BxB, N/4–K5 and Black has no worries. In this latter line 9 . . . P–QN3 demands precise play after 10 N–N5!. Reshevsky–Euwe, Amsterdam 1950, continued 10 . . . R–K1 11 P–QN4, P–KR3!

[2] 9 P–K3, P–QN3 10 B–K2, B–R3 11 P–QN4, N/4–K5 12 Q–N3, P–Q4∓.

[3] Also promising is 9 . . . N/4–K5 and if 10 Q–B2, then 10 . . . Q–R4†.

[4] Najdorf–Pachman, Prague 1946.

[5] After 7 . . . P–Q4 8 PxP, PxP 9 B–N5, Q–N3 10 P–K3, N–K5! 11 R–B1!, White's chances are slightly better.

[6] If 8 B–N5, Black replies 8 . . . N–Q5!, e.g., 9 NxN, BxN 10 P–K3, Q–R4!∓.

[7] An unsatisfactory alternative for White is 9 P–N3, P–Q4 10 PxP, PxP, when Black's isolated Pawn is more than compensated by his active position.

[8] 11 B–K2, R–B1 12 O–O, Q–B2 13 N–KN5! is preferable.

[9] 13 . . . P–QR3 14 Q–K2, Q–B2 15 QR–B1, P–Q3 16 N–QN5! favors White.

[10] Najdorf–Reshevsky, 5th Match Game, New York 1952.

1 P–Q4, N–KB3
2 P–QB4, P–K3
3 N–QB3, B–N5
4 P–QR3, BxN†
5 PxB

KEY POSITION 4

## part 4—SAEMISCH VARIATION

### OBSERVATIONS ON KEY POSITION 4

For decades now, the Saemisch Variation has been known as White's most venturesome continuation against the Nimzo-Indian. Black has the choice of several lines of play, but which is best remains debatable. 5 . . . P–B4, postponing the advance of the Queen Pawn, is considered the most important variation. Since 1960, however, much attention has been focussed on 5 . . . N–K5, a move that Tal repeatedly adopted with success against Botvinnik in their first match for the world title.

IDEA VARIATIONS 7 AND 8:

(7) 5 . . . N–K5 6 Q–B2 (Botvinnik–Tal, 14th Match Game 1960, continued 6 N–R3, P–QB4! 7 P–K3, Q–R4 8 B–Q2, PxP 9 BPxP, NxB 10 QxN, QxQ† 11 KxQ, P–QN3 12 B–Q3, B–R3 and Black has a satisfactory game; for 6 P–K3, P–KB4!? 7 Q–R5†, see Game 5), P–KB4 7 N–R3 (7 P–K3, P–QN3 8 B–Q3, B–N2 9 N–R3, Q–R5 10 O–O, P–KN4 also offers Black good chances), O–O (after 7 . . . P–Q3 8 P–B3, N–KB3 9 P–K4, White has the initiative: Botvinnik–Tal, 16th Match Game 1960) 8 P–B3, N–KB3 9 P–K4, PxP 10 PxP, P–K4! and Black has excellent counterplay (Botvinnik–Tal, 18th Match Game, 1960.)

5 . . . N–K5 6 Q–B2, P–KB4 7 P–B3, Q–R5† 8 P–N3, NxNP 9 PxN, QxR 10 N–R3! is a new experiment. See *Chess Review,* page 78, March 1963.

(8) 5 . . . P–B4 6 P–K3 (6 P–B3 is an enterprising and popular alternative; see Prac. Var. 10), P–QN3 7 N–K2 (according to Vukovic, 7 B–Q3, B–N2 8 P–B3, O–O 9 N–K2, N–B3 10 P–K4, N–K1 [avoiding the pin by B–KN5] 11 O–O, N–R4 12 N–N3, PxP 13 PxP, R–B1 14 P–B4, NxP 15 P–B5, P–B3 offers White excellent attacking prospects if he continues with 16 P–QR4 and not, as in Game 6, with 16 R–B4), N–B3 (after 7 . . . B–R3 8 N–N3, Q–B2 9 P–K4!, PxP 10 PxP, BxP 11 P–K5, N–Q4 12 Q–N4, White's attacking chances compensate for his Pawn minus) 8 N–N3, B–R3 (8 . . . O–O 9 P–K4, N–K1 is safer) 9 P–K4, O–O 10 B–N5, P–R3 11 P–KR4!, PxP (11 . . . P–Q3 is also playable) 12 PxP, PxB 13 PxP, P–N3 14 P–K5 (better than 14 PxN, QxP 15 P–K5, when 15 . . . NxKP gives Black three Pawns for his piece as well as a good position), N–R2 15 N–K4, K–N2 16 Q–N4, R–R1 17 N–B6, NxNP (in this way Black eliminates all danger; determined defensive players may prefer 17 . . . P–Q3) 18 RxR, QxR 19 QxN, Q–R3=.

5 . . . P–B4 is most usual. 5 . . . P–Q4 6 B–N5, P–B4 7 PxQP, KPxP 8 N–B3 slightly favors White. Hardly to be recommended for Black is 5 . . . P–QN3 6 P–B3, P–Q4 7 B–N5, B–R3 8 P–K4!, P–KR3 9 B–R4! For 5 . . . P–Q3 and 6 . . . O–O, see Prac. Var. 11.

6 . . . P–QN3 in reply to 6 P–K3 is O'Kelly's innovation. Black quickly seizes the QR1–KR8 diagonal in order to provoke P–KB3. This last move would cost White a tempo in that his aggressive configuration normally demands P–K4 followed by P–KB4. Two further possibilities for Black are 6 . . . Q–R4 and 6 . . . N–B3. The Queen sortie appears playable, although tournament examples are few. The early development of the Knight is not bad. After 7 B–Q3, P–K4! 8 N–K2, P–K5 9 B–N1, P–QN3 10 N–N3, B–R3, Black achieves equality (Spasski–Tal, Riga 1958). For 6 . . . O–O, possibly Black's best, see Prac. Var. 9.

*Nimzo-Indian Defense Game 5*

*WHITE: Botvinnik* — *BLACK: Tal*

*20th Match Game, Moscow 1960*

| | WHITE | BLACK | | WHITE | BLACK |
|---|---|---|---|---|---|
| 1 | P–QB4 | N–KB3 | 15 | BPxP | N–N5 |
| 2 | P–Q4 | P–K3 | 16 | P–KR3 | Q–B7† |
| 3 | N–QB3 | B–N5 | 17 | K–Q2 | QxQ |
| 4 | P–QR3 | BxN† | 18 | BxQ | N–B7 |
| 5 | PxB | N–K5 | 19 | KR–KB1 | NxB |
| 6 | P–K3 | P–KB4 | 20 | RxR† | KxR |
| 7 | Q–R5† | P–N3 | 21 | KxN | B–K3 |
| 8 | Q–R6 | P–Q3 | 22 | N–N3 | N–Q2 |
| 9 | P–B3 | N–KB3 | 23 | N–B1 | P–QR3 |
| 10 | P–K4 | P–K4 | 24 | B–B2 | K–N2 |
| 11 | B–N5 | Q–K2 | 25 | N–Q2 | R–KB1 |
| 12 | B–Q3 | R–B1 | 26 | B–K3 | P–N3 |
| 13 | N–K2 | Q–B2 | 27 | R–QN1 | N–B3 |
| 14 | Q–R4 | PxKP | | Draw | |

*Nimzo-Indian Defense Game 6*

*WHITE: Geller* — *BLACK: Euwe*

*Zurich 1953*

| | WHITE | BLACK | | WHITE | BLACK | | WHITE | BLACK |
|---|---|---|---|---|---|---|---|---|
| 1 | P–Q4 | N–KB3 | 10 | O–O | N–QR4 | 19 | PxP | NxB |
| 2 | P–QB4 | P–K3 | 11 | P–K4 | N–K1 | 20 | QxN | QxP |
| 3 | N–QB3 | B–N5 | 12 | N–N3 | PxP | 21 | QxP† | K–B2 |
| 4 | P–K3 | P–B4 | 13 | PxP | R–B1 | 22 | B–R6 | R–KR1?! |
| 5 | P–QR3 | BxN† | 14 | P–B4 | NxP | 23 | QxR | R–B7 |
| 6 | PxN | P–QN3 | 15 | P–B5 | P–B3 | 24 | R–QB1? | RxP† |
| 7 | B–Q3 | B–N2 | 16 | R–B4 | P–QN4 | 25 | K–B1 | Q–N6 |
| 8 | P–B3 | N–B3 | 17 | R–R4 | Q–N3 | 26 | K–K1 | Q–B6 |
| 9 | N–K2 | O–O | 18 | P–K5 | NxKP | | Resigns | |

## PRACTICAL VARIATIONS 9–11:

1 P–Q4, N–KB3 2 P–QB4, P–K3 3 N–QB3, B–N5 4 P–QR3, BxN† 5 PxB

| | 9 | 10 | 11 |
|---|---|---|---|
| 5 | – – | – – | – – |
| | P–B4 | – – | P–Q3[15] |
| 6 | P–K3 | P–B3 | P–B3[16] |
| | O–O | P–Q4[7] | O–O |
| 7 | B–Q3 | PxQP[8] | P–K4 |
| | N–B3[1] | NxP[9] | P–K4 |
| 8 | N–K2[2] | PxP[10] | B–Q3[17] |
| | P–QN3 | P–B4[11] | N–B3 |
| 9 | P–K4 | P–QB4[12] | N–K2 |
| | N–K1 | Q–B3![13] | N–Q2 |
| 10 | B–K3[3] | B–N5 | O–O |
| | B–R3![4] | QxB | P–QN3 |
| 11 | N–N3[5] | PxN | B–K3 |
| | N–R4 | PxP | B–R3 |
| 12 | Q–K2 | QxP | N–N3 |
| | R–B1[6] | N–B3[14] | N–R4 |
| | = | ∓ | Q–K2 |
| 13 | | | Q–K1 |
| | | | P–B4 |
| 14 | | | P–KB3 |
| | | | R–B3 |
| 15 | | | K–R1[18] |
| | | | BPxP[19] |
| | | | ± |

*Notes to practical variations 9–11:*

[1] 7 . . . P–QN3 8 P–K4! is distinctly inferior.

[2] 8 P–K4?! is daring but doubtful. Szabo–Smyslov, Moscow 1956, continued 8 . . . PxP 9 PxP, NxQP 10 P–K5, Q–R4† 11 K–B1, N–K1∓.

[3] 10 O–O, B–R3 11 Q–R4, Q–B1 12 B–K3, P–Q3 13 QR–Q1, N–R4 14 PxP, QPxP 15 P–K5, Q–B3 16 Q–B2, P–B4 favors Black.

[4] Weaker is 10 . . . P–Q3 11 N–N3!, Q–Q2 12 O–O, B–R3 13 P–B4, P–B4 14 Q–R4, when White has the initiative.

[5] 11 PxP is strongly answered by 11 . . . N–K4! At a later stage PxP is equally ineffective, e.g., 11 Q–R4, Q–B1 12 O–O, N–R4 13 PxP, P–Q3! (Szabo–Portisch, 1960).

[6] White's inferior Pawn structure affords Black good counterplay.

[7] 5 . . . P–Q3 gives rise to positions similar to Prac. Var. 11.

[8] 7 P–K3 has not vanished from the tournament arena without good cause. After 7 . . . O–O 8 PxQP, NxP 9 B–Q2, N–QB3 10 B–Q3, PxP 11 BPxP, P–K4!, Black has the edge (Lilienthal–Botvinnik, Moscow 1935).

[9] 7 . . . PxP has recently gained in popularity, but results are not encouraging for Black, e.g., 8 P–K3, B–B4 9 N–K2, O–O 10 P–N4, and now neither 10 . . . B–Q2 11 N–N3 nor 10 . . . NxP 11 PxN, Q–R5† 12 K–Q2, B–K5 13 R–KN1, PxP 14 KPxP, Q–N4† 15 K–K1, Q–R5† 16 R–N3 offers Black bright prospects.

[10] Additional possibilities are: (a) 8 Q–Q2, Q–R4! 9 B–N2, N–N3! 10 P–K3, N–R5∓ and (b) 8 Q–Q3, PxP 9 BPxP, P–QN3 10 P–K4, B–R3 11 Q–Q1, BxB 12 KxB, N–K2 13 N–K2, O–O 14 B–N2, QN–B3 15 K–B2, R–B1 16 Q–Q3, N–R4 17 QR–QB1, Q–Q2=.

[11] 8 . . . Q–R4 can also be ventured. After 9 P–K4, both 9 continued ▸

. . . NxP 10 Q–Q2, N–B3 11 B–N2, N–R5 12 BxP, R–KN1 13 B–B6, QxQ† 14 KxQ, NxP 15 K–K3 and 9 . . . N–K2 10 B–K3, O–O 11 Q–N3, N–R3 12 B–QN5 favor White, but 9 . . . N–KB3 (DiCamillo) deserves serious consideration.

[12] 9 P–K4!?, PxP 10 Q–B2 is best met by 10 . . . P–K6!

[13] Preferable to 9 . . . Q–R5† 10 P–N3, QxBP 11 P–K4, Q–B6† 12 B–Q2, Q–K4 13 B–N2, PxP 14 P–B4, when White has vigorous attacking chances.

[14] Black's lead in development amply compensates for his Pawn.

[15] 5 . . . O–O is unusual, yet by no means bad, e.g., 6 P–B3, N–K1 7 P–K4, P–QN3 8 B–Q3, N–QB3 9 P–QR4, B–R3 10 B–R3, P–Q3 11 P–B4, N–R4= or 6 P–K3, P–Q3 7 B–Q3, P–K4 8 N–K2, P–K5 9 B–N1, B–K3 10 N–N3, BxP 11 NxP, NxN 12 BxN, P–QB3=.

[16] Black's sharpest riposte to 6 Q–B2 is 6 . . . P–K4! 7 P–K4, N–B3!

[17] 8 B–N5!, N–B3 9 N–K2, P–QN3 10 P–N4! offers White more hope, in Pachman's judgment.

[18] An improvement upon 15 . . . PxBP 16 BxP!, Q–B2 17 N–B5!

[19] Thanks to his advantage in space, White has the better game.

*Nimzo-Indian Defense Game 7*

*WHITE: Donner* *BLACK: Matanovic*

*Beverwijk 1963*

| | WHITE | BLACK | | WHITE | BLACK |
|---|---|---|---|---|---|
| 1 | P–Q4 | N–KB3 | 24 | Q–B7 | Q–B3 |
| 2 | P–QB4 | P–K3 | 25 | QxBP | N–K3 |
| 3 | N–QB3 | B–N5 | 26 | Q–K3 | P–QR3 |
| 4 | P–QR3 | BxN† | 27 | N–Q6 | R–K2 |
| 5 | PxB | O–O | 28 | K–N1 | Q–N4 |
| 6 | P–B3 | P–Q3 | 29 | QxQ | NxQ |
| 7 | P–K4 | P–K4 | 30 | P–B5 | N–K3 |
| 8 | N–K2 | QN–Q2 | 31 | P–B6 | PxP |
| 9 | N–N3 | R–K1 | 32 | NxB | RxN |
| 10 | B–K3 | N–B1 | 33 | BxP | R–R1 |
| 11 | Q–Q2 | Q–K2 | 34 | B–B4 | N–B4 |
| 12 | K–B2 | P–B4 | 35 | P–R6 | R–B2 |
| 13 | B–K2 | N–N3 | 36 | K–B2 | K–B1 |
| 14 | P–QR4 | Q–B2 | 37 | K–K3 | K–K2 |
| 15 | P–R5 | N–K2 | 38 | P–N3 | P–B3 |
| 16 | B–N5 | N–Q2 | 39 | P–B4 | R/1–R2 |
| 17 | BxN | RxB | 40 | R–R5 | N–Q2 |
| 18 | N–B5 | R–K1 | 41 | B–K2 | P–R3 |
| 19 | PxKP | PxP | 42 | R–QN1 | P–N4 |
| 20 | KR–Q1 | N–B1 | 43 | PxNP | RPxP |
| 21 | N–Q6 | R–K2 | 44 | P–R4 | PxP |
| 22 | N–N5 | Q–B3 | 45 | PxP | Resigns |
| 23 | Q–Q8 | R–K1 | | | |

# part 5—NORMAL VARIATION

1 P–Q4, N–KB3
2 P–QB4, P–K3
3 N–QB3, B–N5
4 P–K3[A], O–O[B]
5 N–B3[C], P–Q4[D]
6 B–Q3[E], P–B4[F]
7 O–O, N–B3
8 P–QR3, BxN
9 PxB, PxBP[G]
10 BxP, Q–B2

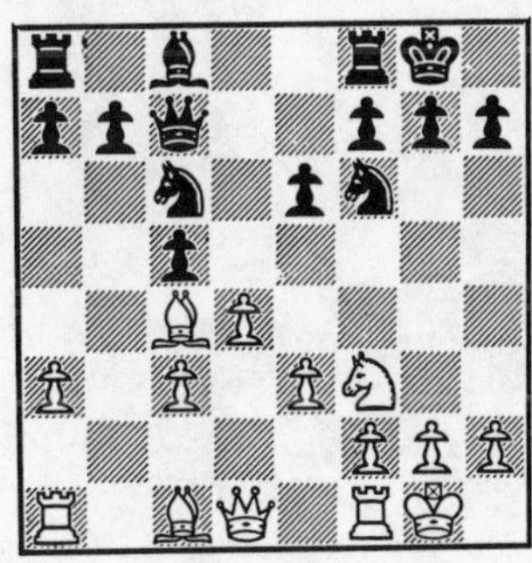

KEY POSITION 5

## OBSERVATIONS ON KEY POSITION 5

[A] At present this modest looking move is considered White's most potent weapon against the Nimzo-Indian Defense.

[B] 4 . . . P–Q4 is sharply met by 5 P–QR3! After 5 . . . BxN† 6 PxB, P–B4 7 PxQP, KPxP (7 . . . NxP 8 B–Q2±) 8 B–Q3, O–O 9 N–K2, P–QN3 10 O–O, B–R3 11 P–B3, BxB 12 QxB, White's position is particularly promising. 5 . . . B–K2 is not much better, e.g., 6 N–B3, O–O 7 B–Q3, P–QN3 8 O–O, P–B4 9 Q–K2, N–B3 10 R–Q1, BPxP 11 KPxP±.

[C] 5 B–Q3 normally transposes into the text.

[D] After 5 . . . P–B4 6 B–Q3, Black's best is to return to the text with 6 . . . P–Q4. Bad for Black is 5 . . . P–QN3 because of 6 P–Q5!

[E] 6 B–K2 is an important alternative. After 6 . . . P–B4 7 O–O, N–B3 8 PxQP, both 8 . . . KPxP 9 PxP, BxP 10 P–QR3, P–QR3 11 P–QN4, B–Q3 12 B–N2, B–N5 13 R–B1 (Gligoric–Euwe, Zurich 1953) and 8 . . . BPxP 9 PxN, PxN 10 Q–N3!, Q–K2 11 N–K5! (Bronstein–Szabo, Zurich 1953) slightly favor White.

[F] 6 . . . N–B3 7 O–O, PxP 8 BxP, B–Q3 9 N–QN5! (Gligoric–Fischer, Leipzig 1960) gives White the edge.

[G] Alternatives are: (1) 9 . . . Q–B2 10 BPxP!, KPxP 11 B–N2, P–B5 12 B–B2, R–K1 13 N–R4, N–KN5 14 P–N3, N–K2± (Bronstein–Szabo, Amsterdam 1956). In this line 10 Q–B2? is met by 10 . . . N–QR4! (2) 9 . . . P–QN3 10 BPxP, KPxP 11 N–K5!, Q–B2 12 NxN, QxN 13 P–B3, P–QR4! 14 Q–K2, P–B5 15 B–B2, P–QN4 16 Q–K1!± (Taimanov).

This position has been a center of controversy for some years now. White has the two Bishops and must aim for an open game; he does so by playing for P–K4. On the other hand, Black has no trouble completing his development and has many chances for counterplay in the center. Theory has probed deeply, but whether White can force an advantage remains an open question. Practice alone will provide the answer.

## IDEA VARIATIONS 9 AND 10:

(9) 11 B–Q3, P–K4 12 Q–B2, R–K1! (best; both 12 . . . R–Q1 13 P–R3, P–QN3 14 P–K4! and 12 . . . B–N5 13 NxP, NxN 14 PxN, QxP 15 P–B3!, B–Q2 16 R–K1! favor White, with 16 P–K4 in this latter line failing to 16 . . . B–R5!; for 12 . . . Q–K2, see Prac. Var. 12) 13 P–K4 (for 13 NxP, see Game 8) P–B5 (13 . . . KPxP 14 PxP, B–N5! introduces enormous complications) 14 BxP, PxP 15 PxP, N–QR4 (15 . . . RxP is far too dangerous, e.g., 16 B–Q3, R–K2 17 P–Q5!, NxP 18 BxP†, K–R1 19 B–N5! and White has a great advantage) 16 B–Q3, QxQ

17 BxQ, NxP 18 R–K1, B–B4 19 B–B4, N–Q3 20 B–R4, P–QN4!= (Donner–Larsen, The Hague 1958)

(10) 11 B–N2, P–K4 12 P–R3 (12 B–R2 also merits consideration; see Prac. Var. 14), B–B4 13 B–N5, P–K5 14 N–R4, B–Q2! (better than 14 . . . B–K3 15 P–QB4, PxP 16 PxP, QR–Q1? 17 P–Q5, N–K4 18 Q–N3, B–Q2 19 Q–N3, which greatly favors White) 15 P–QB4, PxP 16 PxP, Q–B5 17 P–N3, Q–Q3 18 P–Q5 (18 K–R2, Q–K3 19 P–N4, Q–Q3†∓), N–K4 19 BxB, N/3xB 20 Q–Q4, P–B4!, and Black has good counterplay (Uhlmann–Szabo, Wageningen 1957).

*Nimzo-Indian Defense Game 8*

*WHITE: Gligoric* *BLACK: Euwe*

*Leipzig 1960*

| | WHITE | BLACK | | WHITE | BLACK |
|---|---|---|---|---|---|
| 1 | P–Q4 | N–KB3 | 15 | P–B3 | B–K3 |
| 2 | P–QB4 | P–K3 | 16 | R–K1 | QR–Q1 |
| 3 | N–QB3 | B–N5 | 17 | R–N1 | P–B5 |
| 4 | P–K3 | P–B4 | 18 | B–B1 | N–Q2 |
| 5 | B–Q3 | P–Q4 | 19 | P–K4 | N–B4 |
| 6 | N–B3 | O–O | 20 | B–K3 | N–N6? |
| 7 | O–O | N–B3 | 21 | P–B4 | Q–B2 |
| 8 | P–QR3 | BxN | 22 | P–B5 | B–B1 |
| 9 | PxB | PxBP | 23 | Q–B2 | RxP? |
| 10 | BxP | Q–B2 | 24 | B–N6 | QxB |
| 11 | B–Q3 | P–K4 | 25 | QxQ | PxQ |
| 12 | Q–B2 | R–K1 | 26 | RxR | BxP |
| 13 | NxP | NxN | 27 | R–Q1! | R–R1 |
| 14 | PxN | QxP | 28 | RxP and White won | |

PRACTICAL VARIATIONS 12–15:

1 P–Q4, N–KB3 2 P–QB4, P–K3 3 N–QB3, B–N5 4 P–K3, O–O 5 N–B3, P–Q4 6 B–Q3, P–B4 7 O–O, N–B3 8 P–QR3, BxN 9 PxB, PxBP 10 BxP, Q–B2

| | *12* | *13* | *14* | *15* |
|---|---|---|---|---|
| *11* | B–Q3 | Q–K2[4] | B–R2 | B–N5[11] |
| | P–K4 | P–K4 | P–K4 | P–QR3[12] |
| *12* | Q–B2 | P–Q5[5] | P–R3[8] | B–Q3[13] |
| | Q–K2 | P–K5! | P–K5 | P–K4 |
| *13* | PxKP | PxN[6] | N–R2 | Q–B2 |
| | NxP | N–N5! | B–B4 | R–K1[14] |
| *14* | NxN | P–N3 | B–N2 | P–K4 |
| | QxN | PxN | QR–Q1 | P–B5 |

| | 12 | 13 | 14 | 15 |
|---|---|---|---|---|
| 15 | P–B3[1] | QxP | Q–K2 | BxP |
| | B–K3 | N–K4[7] | R–Q2[9] | PxP |
| 16 | R–K1[2] | ∓ | P–KB4 | PxP |
| | KR–Q1 | | PxP e.p. | N–QR4 |
| 17 | R–N1 | | RxP | N–K5![15] |
| | P–B5 | | B–N3[10] | B–K3 |
| 18 | B–B1 | | ∓ | B–Q3 |
| | N–Q4! | | | QxQ |
| 19 | B–Q2 | | | BxQ |
| | Q–B2 | | | QR–B1 |
| 20 | P–K4 | | | B–Q3 |
| | N–K2 | | | N–N6 |
| 21 | B–K3 | | | R–N1 |
| | N–B3 | | | NxQP |
| 22 | P–B4 | | | RxP[16] |
| | P–B3[3] | | | ± |
| | = | | | |

*Notes to practical variations 12–15:*

[1] 15 P–K4? fails against 15 . . . P–B5! 16 BxP, N–N5 17 P–N3, Q–KR4∓. On 15 R–K1 Black's simplest, according to Pachman, is 15 . . . P–B5! 16 BxP, B–B4 17 Q–K2, QxBP 18 B–N2, Q–B7. Donner's 15 P–KB4! may be best, e.g., 15 . . . Q–K2 16 P–B4, R–K1 17 R–K1, N–K5 18 B–N2, P–B3 19 B–K5!±.

[2] After 16 P–K4, P–B5 17 B–K2, Q–B4† 18 K–R1, N–Q2 (Botvinnik–Euwe, Amsterdam 1954), Black's position is satisfactory.

[3] Pachman–Rabar, Goteborg 1955.

[4] An inferior continuation.

[5] 12 PxKP is relatively better.

[6] 13 N–Q2, N–K4 also favors Black.

[7] There are many holes in White's position.

[8] For 12 Q–B2, see Game 9.

[9] 15 . . . R–Q3 is a plausible alternative, e.g., 16 P–QR4, P–QN3 17 KR–Q1, KR–Q1 18 N–B1, N–QR4.

[10] Black has a fair game. The sacrificial line 18 RxN?!, PxR 19 Q–B2, P–B4 20 P–K4, N–K2! 21 KPxP, NxP 22 N–N4, K–N2 seems dubious for White.

[11] Additional alternatives are: (a) 11 P–QR4, P–QN3! 12 B–R3, B–N2 13 B–K2, KR–Q1 14 Q–B2, N–QR4∓; (b) 11 R–K1, P–K4 12 P–Q5, N–QR4! 13 P–Q6, Q–N3 14 NxP, NxB 15 NxN, Q–R3 and Black recovers the Pawn with a good game; (c) 11 B–K2, R–Q1 12 B–N2, P–K4 13 Q–B2, B–N5=.

[12] Both 11 . . . B–Q2 and 11 . . . P–QN3 are reasonable sidelines.

[13] White hopes to cash in on the slight weakness he has provoked in the enemy camp.

continued ▸

[14] In this position 13 . . . Q–K2 probably serves better, e.g., 14 PxKP, NxP 15 NxN, QxN 16 P–KB4, Q–K2 17 P–B4, P–QN4=.

[15] After 17 . . . NxB 18 QxN, QxQ 19 NxQ, NxP 20 N–N6!±, White's policy pays off.

[16] The tricky 22 . . . NxKP is adequately countered by 23 R–N4.

*Nimzo-Indian Defense Game 9*

*WHITE: Taimanov* *BLACK: Euwe*

*Zurich 1953*

| | WHITE | BLACK | | WHITE | BLACK |
|---|---|---|---|---|---|
| 1 | P–Q4 | N–KB3 | 22 | P–B4 | PxP e.p. |
| 2 | P–QB4 | P–K3 | 23 | P–K4 | QR–K1 |
| 3 | N–QB3 | B–N5 | 24 | B–N5 | RxKP |
| 4 | P–K3 | P–B4 | 25 | BxN | RxB |
| 5 | B–Q3 | P–Q4 | 26 | RxP | RxQBP |
| 6 | N–B3 | O–O | 27 | R–K1 | R–N5† |
| 7 | O–O | N–B3 | 28 | K–B2 | R–Q5 |
| 8 | P–QR3 | BxN | 29 | R–K7 | RxQP |
| 9 | PxB | PxBP | 30 | P–B6 | RxP |
| 10 | BxP | Q–B2 | 31 | RxR | PxR |
| 11 | B–R2 | P–K4 | 32 | RxNP | P–QR4 |
| 12 | Q–B2 | B–N5 | 33 | R–N5 | P–R5 |
| 13 | P–Q5? | N–K2 | 34 | R–R5 | R–Q5 |
| 14 | P–B4 | BxN | 35 | RxBP | R–Q6 |
| 15 | PxB | Q–Q2 | 36 | R–QR5 | RxP |
| 16 | B–N1 | N–N3 | 37 | R–R7 | R–R8 |
| 17 | Q–B5 | QxQ | 38 | K–N3 | P–R6 |
| 18 | BxQ | N–R5 | 39 | K–N4 | P–R7 |
| 19 | B–K4 | NxB | 40 | K–R5 | P–B4 |
| 20 | PxN | P–B4 | 41 | K–R6 | P–B5 |
| 21 | PxP | P–K5 | | Resigns | |

1 P–Q4, N–KB3
2 P–QB4, P–K3
3 N–QB3, B–N5
4 P–K3, O–O
5 N–B3, P–Q4
6 B–Q3, P–B4
7 O–O

KEY POSITION 6

## part 6—SEMI-NORMAL VARIATION

### OBSERVATIONS ON KEY POSITION 6

In addition to 7 . . . N–B3 (treated in Part 5), Black has a number of other satisfactory continuations at his disposal, many of which have the practical advantage of being little analyzed. Analyzed or not, however, the most promising of these from the objective standpoint is 7 . . . PxBP followed by 8 . . . P–QN3.

IDEA VARIATIONS 11 AND 12:

(11) 7 . . . QN–Q2 (recent experience indicates that this move is inadequate) 8 P–QR3! (both 8 Q–K2, P–QR3 9 P–QR3, B–R4! and 8 PxQP, KPxP 9 P–QR3, B–R4 are more convenient for Black), PxQP (after 8 . . . BxN 9 PxB, PxBP 10 BxP, Q–B2 11 Q–K2, P–K4, White, with 12 P–K4!, can profit from Black's failure to exert sufficient pressure on White's Q4; 8 . . . QPxP 9 PxB, PxQP fails against 10 BxP†±, while 8 . . . B–R4 is adequately countered by 9 Q–B2!, P–QR3 10 P–QN3) 9 NxP/5!± (Tal–Tolush, Riga 1958); see Game 10.

(12) 7 . . . PxBP 8 BxP, QN–Q2 9 Q–Q3!, P–QR3 10 P–QR4, R–K1 11 R–Q1, PxP 12 PxP, N–N3 13 B–N3, B–Q2 14 N–K5, B–B3 15 Q–R3, and White has excellent attacking chances.

9 Q–Q3! is unusual, but quite promising. Other possibilities are: (a) 9 Q–K2, P–QN3 10 P–Q5, BxN 11 PxP, N–K4 12 PxB!, NxN† 13 QxN, BxP 14 BxB, PxB 15 P–K4, Q–B2!= and (b) 9 Q–N3, PxP! 10 QxB, PxN 11 QxBP, Q–B2=.

9 . . . Q–K2 in reply to 9 Q–Q3! followed by 10 R–Q1, P–QR3 11 P–QR4, B–R4 12 P–QN3, BxN 13 QxB, P–QN3 14 PxP, NxP 15 B–R3 gives White a slight edge (Furman–Stoljar, Moscow 1957).

*Nimzo-Indian Defense Game 10*

*WHITE: Tal* — *BLACK: Tolush*

*Riga 1958*

| | WHITE | BLACK | | WHITE | BLACK |
|---|---|---|---|---|---|
| 1 | P–Q4 | N–KB3 | 15 | R–K1 | RxR† |
| 2 | P–QB4 | P–K3 | 16 | QxR | P–QN3 |
| 3 | N–QB3 | B–N5 | 17 | B–Q4 | B–N2 |
| 4 | P–K3 | P–QB4 | 18 | R–Q1 | Q–K1 |
| 5 | B–Q3 | P–Q4 | 19 | B–K5 | Q–N4 |
| 6 | N–B3 | O–O | 20 | BxN | PxB |
| 7 | O–O | QN–Q2 | 21 | Q–K4! | QxP |
| 8 | P–QR3 | PxQP | 22 | N–Q4 | P–B4 |
| 9 | NxP/5! | PxN | 23 | Q–K5! | N–K2 |
| 10 | PxB | PxBP | 24 | Q–B6 | B–Q4 |
| 11 | BxP | N–N3 | 25 | N–B6! | QxB |
| 12 | B–N3 | PxP | 26 | NxN† | K–B1 |
| 13 | BxP | N/N–Q4 | 27 | R–K1! | B–K3 |
| 14 | B–B5 | R–K1 | 28 | NxP | Resigns |

PRACTICAL VARIATIONS 16 AND 17:

1 P–Q4, N–KB3 2 P–QB4, P–K3 3 N–QB3, B–N5 4 P–K3, O–O 5 N–B3, P–Q4 6 B–Q3, P–B4 7 O–O

| | *16* | *17* |
|---|---|---|
| 7 | – – | – – |
| | PxBP | P–QN3 |
| *8* | BxP | PxQP |
| | P–QN3[1] | KPxP |
| *9* | Q–K2[2] | N–K5![9] |
| | B–N2 | B–N2 |
| *10* | R–Q1[3] | B–Q2[10] |
| | PxP[4] | N–B3 |
| *11* | PxP[5] | P–QR3 |
| | KBxN[6] | BxN |
| *12* | PxB | BxB |
| | N–Q4 | NxN |
| *13* | Q–Q3! | PxN |
| | N–Q2[7] | N–K5 |
| *14* | N–N5 | BxN |
| | N/2–B3[8] | PxB |
| *15* | = | Q–N4! |
| | | Q–K2 |
| *16* | | KR–Q1[11] |
| | | ± |

*Notes to practical variations 16 and 17:*

[1] Another line of interest is Bronstein's remarkable 8 . . . B–Q2, e.g., 9 PxP, B–B3! 10 N–QN5, P–QR3 11 N/5–Q4, BxP 12 B–Q2, B–Q4 13 R–B1, B–K2 14 Q–N3, QN–Q2 15 B–N4, B/2xB 16 QxB, Q–N3= (Petrosian–Bronstein, Moscow 1957). 9 P–QR3, BxN 10 PxB, B–B3 11 R–K1!, QN–Q2 12 B–Q3, B–K5 13 B–B1 followed by 14 N–Q2 and 15 P–K4 gives White only a slight edge.

[2] 9 P–QR3 is sharper. After 9 . . . PxP 10 PxP, BxN 11 PxB, B–N2 12 Q–K2, QN–Q2 13 N–K5, Q–B2 14 P–B4, QR–B1 15 B–Q3, QxP 16 B–N2, White's aggressive position more than compensates for his Pawn.

[3] 10 PxP also offers White some advantage, e.g., 10 . . . BxN 11 PxB, PxP 12 B–Q3!, QN–Q2 13 P–K4!

[4] If 10 . . . QN–Q2, then 11 P–Q5!

[5] 11 N–QN5 is not a bad alternative.

[6] Donner–Matanovic, Leipzig 1960, continued 11 . . . QN–Q2 12 P–Q5, PxP 13 NxP, R–K1 14 Q–B2, NxN 15 BxN, BxB 16 RxB, Q–K2 17 B–N5!, when White has good chances. Black, however, can improve on this line and obtain sufficient counterplay, e.g., 12 . . . BxN 13 PxP, BxN! 14 PxQB, PxP 15 PxB, Q–B2 16 BxP†, K–R1 (Donner–Portisch, Leipzig 1960).

[7] Stronger than 13 . . . Q–B2 14 N–N5! (Szabo–Portisch, 1958).

[8] Black has a tenable game, although White's Bishops are a tiny edge.

[9] 9 B–Q2, B–N5 10 P–QR3, KBxN 11 BxB, P–B5 gives Black fine chances. For 9 PxP, see Game 11.

[10] More accurate than 10 P–QR3, PxP 11 PxP, B–K2.

[11] Bishops of opposite colors notwithstanding, White's occupation of the Queen file is a plus factor.

## *Nimzo-Indian Defense Game 11*

*WHITE: Gligoric* *BLACK: Keres*

*Zurich 1953*

| | WHITE | BLACK | | WHITE | BLACK |
|---|---|---|---|---|---|
| 1 | P–Q4 | N–KB3 | 37 | B–Q5 | N–B4 |
| 2 | P–QB4 | P–K3 | 38 | RxP | N–Q6 |
| 3 | N–QB3 | B–N5 | 39 | R–KB7 | K–N4 |
| 4 | P–K3 | O–O | 40 | P–R4† | KxP |
| 5 | B–Q3 | P–B4 | 41 | B–K4 | R–B6! |
| 6 | N–KB3 | P–Q4 | 42 | K–R2 | N–B4 |
| 7 | O–O | P–QN3 | 43 | RxP† | K–N4 |
| 8 | PxQP | KPxP | 44 | B–N1 | R–B8 |
| 9 | PxP | PxP | 45 | R–QB7 | RxB |
| 10 | N–K2 | N–B3 | 46 | RxN† | K–B5 |
| 11 | P–QN3 | B–N5 | 47 | K–N2 | R–N5 |
| 12 | B–N2 | P–Q5 | 48 | R–QR5 | P–N4 |
| 13 | PxP | BxN | 49 | R–R8 | K–B4 |
| 14 | PxB | NxP | 50 | P–R4 | K–N3 |
| 15 | NxN | PxN | 51 | P–R5 | R–QR5 |
| 16 | BxP | N–R4 | 52 | K–B3 | K–N2 |
| 17 | K–R1 | Q–R5 | 53 | P–R6 | R–B5† |
| 18 | R–KN1 | B–Q3 | 54 | K–K3 | R–QR5 |
| 19 | P–B4 | N–B3 | 55 | P–B3 | K–R2 |
| 20 | Q–B3 | BxP | 56 | K–Q3 | R–KB5 |
| 21 | R–N2 | QR–Q1 | 57 | R–QB8 | RxP† |
| 22 | B–N2 | KR–K1 | 58 | K–B4 | R–QR6 |
| 23 | R/1–KN1 | P–N3 | 59 | K–N5 | K–N3 |
| 24 | B–B4 | N–K5 | 60 | R–B4 | K–B4 |
| 25 | B–QB1 | N–Q7 | 61 | R–QR4 | R–N6† |
| 26 | Q–B6 | K–N2? | 62 | K–B6 | R–N1 |
| 27 | B–Q5 | Q–B3 | 63 | P–R7 | R–QR1 |
| 28 | R–N4 | Q–K4 | 64 | K–N7 | RxP† |
| 29 | B–QN2 | QxB | 65 | RxR | P–N5 |
| 30 | RxB | R–K2 | 66 | K–B6 | K–K5 |
| 31 | RxP† | RxR | 67 | R–R3 | K–B5 |
| 32 | BxR | Q–B3 | 68 | R–R4† | K–B6 |
| 33 | B–Q5 | QxQ | 69 | R–R3† | K–B7 |
| 34 | BxQ | R–QB1 | 70 | R–R2† | K–B6 |
| 35 | R–Q1 | NxP! | 71 | R–R3† | Draw |
| 36 | R–Q7† | K–R3 | | | |

## part 7—BRONSTEIN VARIATION

1 P–Q4, N–KB3
2 P–QB4, P–K3
3 N–QB3, B–N5
4 P–K3, P–QN3
5 N–K2, B–R3[A]

KEY POSITION 7

OBSERVATIONS ON KEY POSITION 7

[A] 5 . . . B–N2 is no longer played because of 6 P–QR3! Two possible continuations follow: 6 . . . B–K2 7 P–Q5!, O–O 8 P–K4!, P–Q3 9 P–KN3, P–B3 10 PxKP, PxP 11 N–Q4± (Euwe–O'Kelly, Groningin 1946) and 6 . . . BxN† 7 NxB, P–Q4 8 B–K2, PxP 9 O–O!, B–R3 10 P–K4!, again with advantage to White. In the latter line 7 . . . O–O is met by 8 B–Q3!

Introduced by Bronstein in his 1951 match against Botvinnik, and repeatedly adopted by Smyslov in his matches with Botvinnik, this variation has been the subject of close scrutiny. Black's basic idea is to exert pressure on White's Queen Bishop Pawn. He may increase this pressure by a later . . . P–Q4.

As an exchange of "white-bound" Bishops constitutes a slight strategic victory for Black, White's proper procedure is to refrain from BPxQP, protecting his QB Pawn by means of P–QN3. In this case, Black must play for . . . P–QB4 and a consequent liquidation in the center.

IDEA VARIATIONS 13 AND 14:

(13) 6 P–QR3 (adopted to the exclusion of almost every other continuation; for the infrequently played 6 N–N3, see Prac. Var. 19), BxN† (introduced by Donner and consistently essayed by Smyslov) 7 NxB, P–Q4 8 P–QN3 (after 8 PxP, BxB 9 KxB, White's advantage is negligible), O–O 9 B–K2 (or 9 P–QR4, P–B4 10 B–R3, PxBP 11 NPxP, N–B3 12 N–N5 with approximately even chances, as in Botvinnik–Smyslov, 13th Match Game 1957), PxP 10 PxP, N–B3 11 P–QR4, Q–Q2 12 N–N5, KR–Q1 13 B–N2, N–QR4 14 Q–B2, P–B3 15 N–R3, Q–K2= (Botvinnik–Smyslov, 15th Match Game 1957).

(14) 6 P–QR3, B–K2 7 N–B4 (better than 7 N–N3, P–Q4 8 PxP, BxB 9 NxB, PxP 10 N–N3, Q–Q2, which is quite satisfactory for Black [Botvinnik–Bronstein, 19th Match Game 1961]), P–Q4 8 PxP (after 8 P–QN3, O–O 9 Q–B3, P–B3 10 P–KN4?!, P–B4! 11 PxQP, B–N2!, Black has good play), BxB 9 KxB (for 9 PxP?!, see Prac. Var. 18), PxP 10 P–KN4, P–KN4! (10 . . . P–B3 is weak; see Game 12) 11 N–Q3, P–KR4 12 PxP, RxP 13 N–K5 (13 Q–B3 deserves the nod), P–B3 14 Q–B3, Q–B1 with equality.

*Nimzo-Indian Defense Game 12*

*WHITE: Botvinnik* — *BLACK: Smyslov*

*Second Match Game, Moscow 1954*

| | WHITE | BLACK | | WHITE | BLACK |
|---|---|---|---|---|---|
| 1 | P–Q4 | N–KB3 | 16 | P–R5 | R–K1 |
| 2 | P–QB4 | P–K3 | 17 | N–Q6 | R–K3 |
| 3 | N–QB3 | B–N5 | 18 | P–Q5 | RxN |
| 4 | P–K3 | P–QN3 | 19 | BxR | QxP |
| 5 | N–K2 | B–R3 | 20 | Q–B3 | QxQP |
| 6 | P–QR3 | B–K2 | 21 | QxQ | PxQ |
| 7 | N–B4 | P–Q4 | 22 | R–B1 | N–R3 |
| 8 | PxP | BxB | 23 | P–N4 | P–R3 |
| 9 | KxB | PxP | 24 | R–R3 | K–R2 |
| 10 | P–KN4! | P–B3? | 25 | R–Q3 | N–B3 |
| 11 | P–N5 | KN–Q2 | 26 | P–N5 | N–B4 |
| 12 | P–KR4 | B–Q3 | 27 | BxN | PxB |
| 13 | P–K4 | PxP | 28 | RxBP | R–QN1 |
| 14 | NxP | BxN | 29 | P–R4 | R–N2 |
| 15 | BxB | O–O | 30 | R/3–QB3 | Resigns |

PRACTICAL VARIATIONS 18 AND 19:

1 P–Q4, N–KB3 2 P–QB4, P–K3 3 N–QB3, B–N5 4 P–K3, P–QN3 5 N–K2, B–R3

| | *18* | *19* |
|---|---|---|
| *6* | P–QR3 | N–N3 |
| | B–K2 | O–O |
| *7* | N–B4 | P–K4 |
| | P–Q4 | P–Q4![4] |
| *8* | PxP | P–K5 |
| | BxB | N–K5![5] |
| *9* | PxP?! | NxN[6] |
| | B–R3 | PxN |
| *10* | PxP† | B–K2 |
| | KxP | N–B3 |
| *11* | P–K4[1] | B–K3 |
| | P–B4 | N–R4[7] |
| *12* | B–K3 | = |
| | N–B3 | |
| *13* | Q–N3† | |
| | P–B5 | |
| *14* | Q–Q1 | |
| | B–Q3![2] | |
| *15* | P–K5 | |
| | NxKP | |
| *16* | PxN | |
| | BxKP[3] | |
| | ∓ | |

*Notes to practical variations 18 and 19:*

[1] Insufficient for White is 11 Q–N3†, K–K1 12 N–K6, Q–Q2!

[2] Otherwise White's attack is overwhelming.

[3] Lombardy-Keres, Mar del Plata 1957.

[4] Alternatives favor White. Two examples are: 7 . . . P–Q3 8 B–Q2, P–B4 9 P–QR3, B–R4 10 P–Q5, PxP 11 BPxP (Resh-

continued ▸

evsky–Keres, Zurich 1953) and 7 . . . P–B4 8 P–Q5, PxP 9 BPxP, BxB 10 KxB, P–Q3 11 B–N5 (Reshevsky–Evans, New York 1955).

[5] Suggested by Filip and Pachman.

[6] 9 Q–B2 fails against 9 . . . P–QB4!

[7] Black has powerful counterplay.

---

## part 8—5 B-Q3 VARIATION

1 P–Q4, N–KB3
2 P–QB4, P–K3
3 N–QB3, B–N5
4 P–K3, P–QN3
5 B–Q3, B–N2

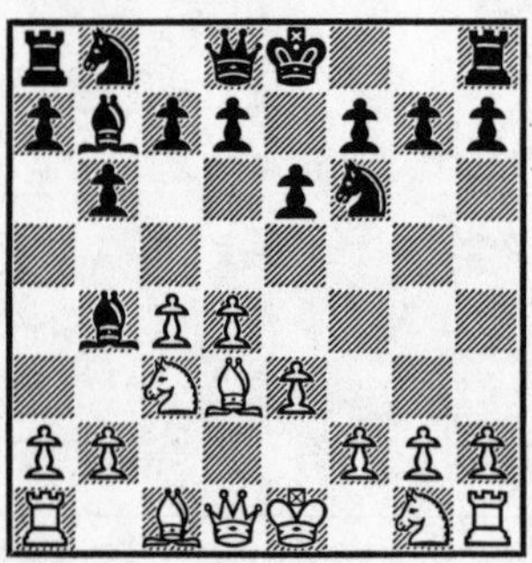

KEY POSITION 8

### OBSERVATIONS ON KEY POSITION 8

Owing to the early development of his King Bishop, White faces some minor difficulty along the KR1–QR8 diagonal. These difficulties are usually resolved by 6 N–B3, leading to several lines of play. There are two significant continuations, one based on . . . P–Q4 and the other on . . . P–QB4. Both systems offer Black fair chances for equality, although complications may arise.

### IDEA VARIATIONS 15 AND 16:

(15) 6 N–B3 (too bold an alternative is 6 N–K2, BxP 7 R–KN1, B–K5!, when 8 BxB, NxB 9 RxP fails against 9 . . . NxP!, while 8 RxP, B–N3 is hardly commendable; for 6 P–B3, see Prac. Var. 21), O–O (6 . . . N–K5! is a little known option; after 7 O–O, BxN! 8 PxB, NxQBP 9 Q–B2, BxN 10 PxB, Q–N4† 11 K–R1, Q–KR4 12 R–KN1, QxBP† 13 R–N2, P–KB4! 14 QxN, Black has a perpetual check starting with 14 . . . Q–Q8†, while if 7 Q–B2, P–KB4 8 O–O, BxN 9 PxB, O–O, Black has equalized) 7 O–O, P–Q4 8 PxP (other moves offer little; here is a single example: 8 B–Q2, PxP 9 BxP, QN–Q2! 10 Q–K2, P–B4 11 P–QR3, BxN 12 BxB, N–K5= [Taimanov–Averbach, Moscow 1951]), PxP (not 8 . . . NxP because of 9 Q–B2) 9 P–QR3 (after 9 N–K5, sufficient for Black, according to Taimanov, is 9 . . . P–B4 10 P–QR3, PxP 11 PxP, B–K2), BxN (both 9 . . . B–Q3 and 9 . . . B–K2 are effectively answered by 10 P–QN4) 10 PxB, R–K1 11 B–N2, N–B3 12 P–B4, N–QR4= (Petrosian–Filip, Goteborg 1955).

(16) 6 N–B3, O–O 7 O–O, P–B4 8 N–QR4 (a sharp attempt to take advantage of the position of Black's King Bishop; both 8 B–Q2, PxP 9 PxP, P–Q4 10 PxP, NxP and 8 P–QR3, BxQN 9 PxB, B–K5 10 B–K2, N–B3 offer little to White), PxP 9 P–QR3 (the simple 9 PxP may be even better; if then 9 . . . P–Q4, White plays 10 P–B5 with advantage), B–K2 10 PxP, Q–B2 (10 . . . N–K5 is worth consideration) 11 P–QN4!, N–N5 (11 . . .

P–QR4 12 P–N5, P–Q4 13 P–B5!, PxP 14 PxP, BxP 15 B–N2 assures White ample return for his Pawn) 12 P–N3, P–B4 13 N–B3, P–QR3 14 R–K1, N–QB3 15 B–B1, QR–K1! (for 15 . . . N–Q1, see Game 13) with approximate equality.

*Nimzo-Indian Defense Game 13*

*WHITE: Botvinnik* *BLACK: Bronstein*

*5th Match Game, Moscow 1951*

| | WHITE | BLACK | | WHITE | BLACK | | WHITE | BLACK |
|---|---|---|---|---|---|---|---|---|
| 1 | P–Q4 | N–KB3 | 15 | B–B1 | N–Q1 | 29 | N–B5 | N–B5 |
| 2 | P–QB4 | P–K3 | 16 | B–B4 | B–Q3 | 30 | R–Q1? | K–R1 |
| 3 | N–QB3 | B–N5 | 17 | BxB | QxB | 31 | R–K1? | NxP |
| 4 | P–K3 | O–O | 18 | B–N2 | N–B2 | 32 | N–Q6 | B–B3 |
| 5 | B–Q3 | P–B4 | 19 | P–B5 | Q–B2 | 33 | R–R1 | N–B7 |
| 6 | N–B3 | P–QN3 | 20 | QR–B1 | QR–K1 | 34 | RxP | P–Q5! |
| 7 | O–O | B–N2 | 21 | N–QR4 | P–QN4 | 35 | N/3xP | BxB |
| 8 | N–QR4 | PxP | 22 | N–B3 | P–B5! | 36 | KxB | N–N5! |
| 9 | P–QR3 | B–K2 | 23 | P–Q5 | PxNP | 37 | N–B5 | P–Q6 |
| 10 | PxP | Q–B2 | 24 | BPxP | PxP | 38 | R–Q6 | RxN |
| 11 | P–QN4 | N–N5 | 25 | Q–Q4 | N–B3 | 39 | RxP | N/7–K6† |
| 12 | P–N3 | P–B4 | 26 | N–KR4 | R–K4! | | Resigns | |
| 13 | N–B3 | P–QR3 | 27 | RxR | QxR | | | |
| 14 | R–K1 | N–QB3 | 28 | QxQ | NxQ | | | |

PRACTICAL VARIATIONS 20 AND 21:

1 P–Q4, N–KB3 2 P–QB4, P–K3 3 N–QB3, B–N5 4 P–K3, P–QN3 5 B–Q3, B–N2

| | 20 | 21 | | 20 | 21 |
|---|---|---|---|---|---|
| *6* | N–B3 | P–B3 | *12* | P–B3 | QBxN |
| | O–O | P–K4[3] | | N–KB3 | PxB |
| *7* | O–O | KN–K2[4] | *13* | B–R3 | O–O |
| | KBxN | PxP | | P–Q3 | BxN |
| *8* | PxB | PxP | *14* | N–Q3 | PxB |
| | B–K5 | P–Q4 | | P–B4 | P–B4 |
| *9* | BxB[1] | Q–R4† | *15* | N–B4 | B–B2 |
| | NxB | N–B3 | | N–B3 | N–K2 |
| *10* | Q–B2 | B–N5 | *16* | P–K4![2] | QxBP |
| | P–KB4 | PxP | | ± | O–O–O[5] |
| *11* | N–K5 | B–K4 | | | = |
| | Q–K1 | Q–Q2 | | | |

*Notes to practical variations 20 and 21:*

[1] Also playable is 9 B–K2. After 9 . . . P–B4 10 N–Q2, B–N2 11 N–N3, P–Q3 12 P–B3, QN–Q2 13 P–K4, P–K4 14 P–QR4, P–QR4 15 P–Q5 White's chances are excellent (Bori-

continued ▶

senko–Smyslov, 1950). In this line, however, Konstantinopolsky suggests as an improvement for Black the more active 11 . . . Q–B2 12 P–B3, P–Q4. And, at an even earlier stage, Black may well do better to play 10 . . . B–N3.

[2] Reshevsky–Alekhine, AVRO 1938.

[3] 6 . . . P–B4 is an attractive alternative.

[4] Better than 7 PxP, N–N5!

[5] Bondarevski–Ragosin, Match Game 1946. Black has active counterplay.

---

## part 9—RUBINSTEIN VARIATION

1 P–Q4, N–KB3
2 P–QB4, P–K3
3 N–QB3, B–N5
4 P–K3

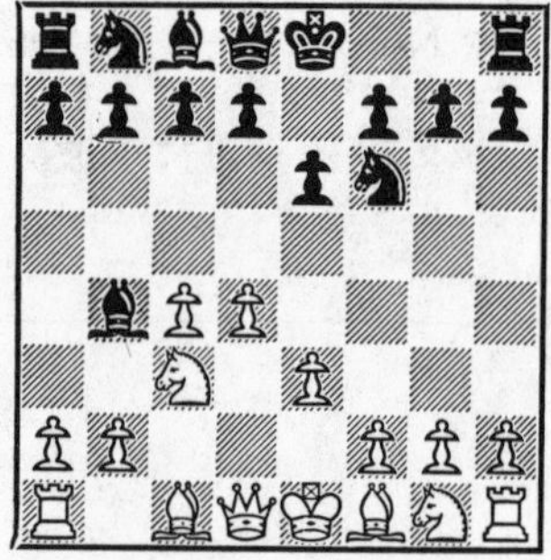

KEY POSITION 9

OBSERVATIONS ON KEY POSITION 9

The idea of this variation is to prepare a timely P–QR3 by first proceeding with KN–K2. Naturally enough this plan can be adopted in several forms. This section treats a number of divergent lines which exhibit the characteristic maneuver of KN–K2.

IDEA VARIATIONS 17–19:

(17) 4 . . . O–O 5 N–K2 (although strongly favored by Reshevsky, this line, if properly countered, offers White little chance for the initiative), P–Q4 (after 5 . . . P–Q3 6 P–QR3, BxN† 7 NxB, P–K4 8 B–K2, White has a promising game) 6 P–QR3, B–K2 (6 . . . BxN† 7 NxB, P–QN3 8 P–QN4! favors White, as in Reshevsky–Van den Berg, Amsterdam 1950) 7 PxP (nor is 7 N–N3, PxP 8 BxP, P–B4 of greater promise; for 7 N–B4, see Game 14), PxP (7 . . . NxP is also good, e.g., 8 Q–B2, N–Q2! 9 B–Q2, N/4–B3 10 N–N3, P–B4!= or 8 P–KN3, N–Q2 9 B–N2, N/4–B3 10 N–N3, P–B4!= or 8 P–KN3, N–Q2 9 B–N2, N/2–N3 10 O–O, R–K1 11 P–N3, P–QR4, when Black has nothing to fear) 8 P–QN4, R–K1 (if 8 . . . P–QR4, then 9 P–N5) 9 N–N3, QN–Q2 (9 . . . P–B3 10 B–Q3, P–QN4 is equally satisfactory for Black [Reshevsky–Gligoric, New York 1952]) 10 B–Q3, P–B3 11 P–N5, PxP (most probably stronger than 11 . . . P–B4 12 O–O, P–QN3 13 B–Q2, B–B1 14 P–QR4! [Reshevsky–Lombardy, New York 1956]) 12 NxNP, P–QR3 13 N–B3, P–QN4 14 O–O, N–N3, and Black has a good game.

(18) 4 . . . P–B4 5 N–K2, PxP (recent experience indicates this as best; after 5 . . . P–Q4 6 P–QR3, PxQP 7 PxB!, PxN 8 NxP, White has a slight edge) 6 PxP, P–Q4 (6 . . . N–K5 merits attention) 7 P–B5 (7 P–QR3,

B–K2 8 P–B5, O–O 9 P–QN4, P–QN3 10 P–KN3, PxP 11 QPxP, P–QR4! 12 R–QN1, PxP 13 PxP, N–B3 favors Black [Gligoric–Szabo, Helsinki 1952]), N–K5 (Spasski has experimented with 7 . . . N–B3, but 8 P–QR3, B–R4 9 P–QN4, B–B2 10 P–N3! gives White a slight edge) 8 B–Q2, NxB (safer than 8 . . . N–QB3 9 NxN, PxN 10 BxB, NxB 11 N–B3!, QxP 12 QxQ, after which White has the brighter end-game prospects) 9 QxN, P–QN3 10 P–QR3, BxN 11 NxB, PxP 12 B–N5†, B–Q2 13 PxP, P–QR4 14 O–O, P–R5 15 Q–Q4, BxB 16 QxNP, BxR 17 QxR†, K–K2 18 QxQ†, KxQ=.

(19) 4 . . . N–B3 (Taimanov's pet line) 5 N–K2, P–Q4 (after 5 . . . P–K4 6 P–QR3, BxN† 7 NxB, PxP 8 PxP, P–Q4, White has the effective 9 P–B5!) 6 P–QR3, B–K2 7 PxP, PxP 8 N–B4, O–O 9 B–K2, B–B4 (the immediate 9 . . . B–K3 is stronger) 10 P–KN4!, B–K3 11 NxB, PxN 12 O–O, Q–Q2 13 P–B4, and Black must face an uphill struggle (Botvinnik–Taimanov, 5th Match Game 1953).

*Nimzo-Indian Defense Game 14*

*WHITE: Olafsson* *BLACK: Reshevsky*

*Dallas 1957*

| | WHITE | BLACK | | WHITE | BLACK |
|---|---|---|---|---|---|
| 1 | P–Q4 | N–KB3 | 23 | NPxB | B–Q4 |
| 2 | P–QB4 | P–K3 | 24 | Q–R5 | Q–Q2 |
| 3 | N–QB3 | B–N5 | 25 | R–B1 | P–KR3 |
| 4 | P–K3 | O–O | 26 | K–N2 | Q–K2 |
| 5 | N–K2 | P–Q4 | 27 | Q–Q1 | Q–B2 |
| 6 | P–QR3 | B–K2 | 28 | P–R3 | B–N2 |
| 7 | N–B4 | P–B3 | 29 | K–R2 | K–R2 |
| 8 | PxP | BPxP | 30 | Q–N4! | P–N4? |
| 9 | B–K2 | P–QN3 | 31 | BxP! | QxR |
| 10 | O–O | B–N2 | 32 | Q–B5† | K–N2 |
| 11 | P–QN3 | N–B3 | 33 | QxBP† | K–R1 |
| 12 | B–N2 | R–B1 | 34 | Q–B6† | K–R2 |
| 13 | N–Q3 | N–K5 | 35 | B–B5† | K–N1 |
| 14 | NxN | PxN | 36 | Q–N6† | K–B1 |
| 15 | N–B4 | N–R4 | 37 | QxP† | K–K1 |
| 16 | R–B1 | RxR | 38 | Q–K6† | K–B1 |
| 17 | BxR | Q–B2 | 39 | Q–B6† | K–K1 |
| 18 | B–Q2?! | R–B1 | 40 | Q–R8† | K–K2 |
| 19 | BxN | PxB | 41 | Q–N7† | K–K1 |
| 20 | B–B4 | K–R1 | 42 | QxB | R–B2 |
| 21 | P–QR4 | B–Q3 | 43 | QxP† | Resigns |
| 22 | P–N3 | BxN | | | |

PRACTICAL VARIATIONS 22 AND 23:

1 P–Q4, N–KB3 2 P–QB4, P–K3 3 N–QB3, B–N5 4 P–K3

| | 22 | 23 | | 22 | 23 |
|---|---|---|---|---|---|
| 4 | – | – | 9 | B–N5[3] | PxP[9] |
| | N–B3 | P–B4 | | P–K4[4] | BxP |
| 5 | N–B3 | B–Q3 | 10 | BxN | P–QR3 |
| | O–O | O–O | | PxP[5] | B–K3 |
| 6 | B–Q3 | KN–K2[7] | 11 | PxP | P–QN4 |
| | P–Q4 | P–Q4 | | PxB | B–Q3 |
| 7 | O–O | O–O | 12 | B–N5 | N–N5 |
| | PxP[1] | N–B3 | | P–KR3 | B–N1 |
| 8 | BxP | PxQP[8] | 13 | B–R4[6] | B–N2 |
| | B–Q3[2] | KPxP | | ± | N–K4![10] |
| | | | | | = |

*Notes to practical variations* 22 *and* 23:

[1] The Ragosin system, particularly favored by Fischer.

[2] 8 . . . Q–K1 is effectively countered by 9 N–K5! (Taimanov).

[3] Gligoric–Fischer, Leipzig 1960, continued 9 N–QN5. After 9 . . . B–K2 10 P–KR3, P–QR3 11 N–B3, P–QN4 12 B–Q3, B–N2 13 Q–K2 with a lasting initiative. But 9 . . . P–K4 is to be considered.

[4] Otherwise White proceeds with 10 P–K4.

[5] Best. Now White must not play to win a Pawn with either 11 BxP, BxB 12 NxP, Q–Q2 13 P–B3!, B–K4 or 11 NxP, PxB 12 NxP, Q–K1 13 N–Q4, B–N2, when Black would have a strong initiative.

[6] White has a superior Pawn skeleton and the better development.

[7] Too modest. 6 N–B3 is preferable.

[8] 8 P–QR3, BPxP 9 PxB, PxN 10 PxBP, PxP 11 BxP, Q–B2 yields Black an excellent game.

[9] P–QR3, PxP 10 PxP, B–Q3! =

[10] Despite his isolated Pawn, Black enjoys full mobility.

1 P–Q4, N–KB3
2 P–QB4, P–K3
3 N–QB3, B–N5
4 N–B3

KEY POSITION 10

## part 10—THREE KNIGHTS' VARIATION

### OBSERVATIONS ON KEY POSITION 10

White's last move is an attempt to meet the Nimzo-Indian with straightforward development. The idea is certainly not bad, but offers few real chances against proper counterplay. In practice, 4 N–B3 often serves merely to transpose into more usual lines of play.

IDEA VARIATIONS 20 AND 21:

(20) 4 . . . P–B4 (not 4 . . . O–O 5 Q–N3!, N–B3 6 P–QR3 with White for choice) 5 P–Q5 (most usual today; after 5 Q–N3, N–K5! or 5 PxP, BxN† 6 PxB, Q–R4, Black has a satisfactory game), P–Q3 (for 5 . . . PxP, see Game 15; interesting is 5 . . . N–K5 6 Q–B2, Q–B3 7 B–Q2, BxN 8 PxB, NxB, when White's active position amply compensates for his weakened Pawn structure) 6 B–Q2, O–O 7 P–K3, BxN 8 BxB, N–K5 with even chances (Szabo–Reshevsky, Dallas 1957).

(21) 4 . . . P–Q4 5 Q–R4† (for 5 P–K3, P–B4, see Parts 5 and 6; 5 B–N5 and PxP lead to the Queen's Gambit), N–B3 6 N–K5, B–Q2 7 NxB, QxN 8 P–K3, P–K4 9 PxKP, P–Q5 10 P–QR3!, BxN† 11 PxB, PxKP! 12 BxP (12 PxN?, PxP† 13 KxP, Q–B4† favors Black), N–KN5 13 B–Q4, KNxKP! 14 P–B4, NxB 15 QxQ†, KxQ with equality (Spielmann–Fine, Zandvoort 1936).

*Nimzo-Indian Defense Game 15*

*WHITE: Szabo* *BLACK: Donner*

*Wageningen 1957*

| | WHITE | BLACK | | WHITE | BLACK |
|---|---|---|---|---|---|
| 1 | P–QB4 | N–KB3 | 21 | QxN | N–B3 |
| 2 | P–Q4 | P–K3 | 22 | Q–B6 | Q–Q2 |
| 3 | N–QB3 | B–N5 | 23 | Q–B3 | N–K5 |
| 4 | N–B3 | P–B4 | 24 | Q–K2 | R–N1 |
| 5 | P–Q5 | PxP | 25 | P–B3 | Q–N4 |
| 6 | PxP | P–Q3 | 26 | Q–Q1 | Q–N6 |
| 7 | P–K3 | QN–Q2 | 27 | B–B1 | QxQ |
| 8 | P–QR3 | BxN† | 28 | RxQ | N–B6 |
| 9 | PxB | O–O | 29 | RxP | N–K7† |
| 10 | P–B4 | P–QN4 | 30 | K–B2 | NxB |
| 11 | PxP | N–N3 | 31 | RxN | R–N7† |
| 12 | B–N2 | QNxP | 32 | K–N3 | RxP |
| 13 | B–B4 | N–N3 | 33 | P–K4 | R/6–R7 |
| 14 | B–Q3 | P–QR3 | 34 | RxP | RxP† |
| 15 | O–O | PxP | 35 | K–B4 | P–N4† |
| 16 | BxP | B–R3 | 36 | RxP† | RxR |
| 17 | BxB | RxB | 37 | KxR | RxP |
| 18 | Q–Q3 | R–R5 | 38 | K–B6 | R–R3† |
| 19 | N–N5 | N/N–Q4 | 39 | K–K7 | R–R4 |
| 20 | NxRP | NxN | 40 | R–Q5! | Resigns |

PRACTICAL VARIATIONS 24 AND 25:

1 P–Q4, N–KB3 2 P–QB4, P–K3 3 N–QB3, B–N5 4 N–B3

| | 24 | 25 | | 24 | 25 |
|---|---|---|---|---|---|
| 4 | – – | – – | 10 | B–N2 | |
| | P–QN3[1] | BxN† | | R–QN1[4] | |
| 5 | Q–B2[2] | PxB | 11 | P–QN4 | |
| | B–N2 | P–Q3[6] | | O–O | |
| 6 | P–QR3 | N–Q2[7] | 12 | O–O | |
| | BxN† | P–K4 | | P–KB4 | |
| 7 | QxB | P–K4 | 13 | B–N2 | |
| | N–K5[3] | N–B3 | | Q–K2 | |
| 8 | Q–B2 | B–N2 | 14 | QR–Q1 | |
| | P–Q3 | O–O[8] | | N/2–B3[5] | |
| 9 | P–KN3 | = | | ∓ | |
| | N–Q2 | | | | |

*Notes to practical variations 24–25:*

[1] This is actually a position of the Queen's Indian Defense. For a more detailed study of its complexities, refer to that opening.

[2] For 5 B–N5! and other possibilities, see the Queen's Indian. 5 Q–N3, Q–K2 6 P–N3, B–N2 7 B–N2 favors Black after 7 . . . N–B3!

[3] Nimzowitsch preferred 7 . . . P–Q3. After 8 B–N5, QN–Q2 9 P–K3, N–K5! 10 BxQ, NxQ 11 B–R4, N–K5 Black has achieved equality.

[4] Taking the sting out of a possible 11 N–N5 or 11 N–Q2.

[5] Mueller–Alekhine, Kecskemet 1927.

[6] 5 . . . P–QN3 is also good. See Game 16.

[7] Alternatives are 6 Q–B2, Q–K2 7 P–K4, P–K4 8 N–Q2, N–B3 9 B–N2= and 6 P–N3, O–O 7 B–N2, Q–K2 8 B–QR3, P–B4!∓.

[8] White's center Pawns abreast compensate for his awkward doubled Pawns.

*Nimzo-Indian Defense Game 16*

*WHITE: Bogoljubov* *BLACK: Nimzowitsch*

*Carlsbad 1929*

| | WHITE | BLACK | | WHITE | BLACK |
|---|---|---|---|---|---|
| 1 | P–Q4 | N–KB3 | 9 | R–K1 | P–Q3 |
| 2 | P–QB4 | P–K3 | 10 | Q–B2 | B–K5 |
| 3 | N–QB3 | B–N5 | 11 | Q–N3 | N–B3 |
| 4 | N–B3 | BxN† | 12 | B–B1 | P–K4 |
| 5 | PxB | P–QN3 | 13 | PxP | NxP |
| 6 | P–N3 | B–N2 | 14 | NxN | RxN |
| 7 | B–N2 | O–O | 15 | B–B4 | R–K1 |
| 8 | O–O | R–K1 | 16 | P–B3 | B–N2 |

| WHITE | BLACK | WHITE | BLACK |
|---|---|---|---|
| 17 QR–Q1 | N–Q2 | 35 R/B–K2 | RxR |
| 18 P–K4 | Q–B3 | 36 BxR | R–K1 |
| 19 B–N2 | N–K4 | 37 K–B2 | R–K4 |
| 20 R–Q2 | R–K2 | 38 R–Q5 | P–KN4 |
| 21 R/1–Q1 | B–B3 | 39 RxR | PxR |
| 22 R–KB2 | R/1–K1 | 40 P–B5 | PxP |
| 23 B–KB1? | P–KR3? | 41 B–R6 | P–K5 |
| 24 B–K2 | K–R1 | 42 P–QR4 | K–N2 |
| 25 Q–R3 | Q–K3 | 43 P–R5 | PxP |
| 26 Q–B1 | P–B4 | 44 KxP | K–B3 |
| 27 PxP | QxP/4 | 45 K–K3 | K–K4 |
| 28 Q–Q2 | Q–B2 | 46 B–B4 | B–N5 |
| 29 Q–Q4 | N–N3 | 47 B–R6 | P–R4 |
| 30 B–Q3 | NxB | 48 B–B4 | P–R5 |
| 31 QxN | QxQ | 49 B–R6 | B–Q8 |
| 32 PxQ | R–KB1 | 50 B–N7 | P–N5 |
| 33 P–KB5 | B–Q2 | Resigns | |
| 34 R/1–Q2 | BxP | | |

## part 11—SPIELMANN VARIATION

1 P–Q4, N–KB3
2 P–QB4, P–K3
3 N–QB3, B–N5
4 Q–N3

KEY POSITION 11

### OBSERVATIONS ON KEY POSITION 11

This line enjoyed a brief popularity in the years following the First World War, but is entirely out of fashion today. The one obvious advantage of 4 Q–N3 over 4 Q–B2 is that by attacking the advanced Bishop, White somewhat restricts Black's freedom of choice; on N3, however, White's Queen is more vulnerable.

### IDEA VARIATIONS 22 AND 23:

(22) 4 . . . P–B4 5 PxP, N–B3 (the main continuation, but 5 . . . N–R3! also serves very well; Eliskases–Botvinnik, Moscow 1936, continued 6 P–QR3, BxBP! 7 N–B3, P–QN3 8 B–N5, B–N2 9 P–K3, B–K2 with a good game for Black) 6 N–B3, N–K5 (aiming for complications) 7 B–Q2, NxB 8 NxN, BxP (best; after 8 . . . P–B4 9 P–N3! White has a distinct advantage, according to Trifunovic) 9 P–K3 (9 P–N3 merits consideration), P–QN3 10 O–O–O, B–N2 11 B–K2, and White has a slight initiative.

(23) 4 . . . P–B4 5 PxP, N–B3 6 N–B3, N–K5 7 B–Q2, NxQBP 8 Q–B2, P–B4! (Black must keep control of K5) 9 P–QR3 (in Bogoljubov–Nimzowitsch, San Remo

1930, there followed 9 P–K3, O–O 10 B–K2, P–QN3 11 O–O–O, P–QR4! 12 P–QR3?, P–R5! with advantage to Black; the text is an important improvement), BxN 10 BxB, O–O 11 P–QN4, N–K5 12 B–N2 (for 12 P–K3, see Game 17), P–QN3 13 P–N3, B–N2 14 B–N2 and White has a slight edge.

*Nimzo-Indian Defense Game 17*

*WHITE: Stahlberg* *BLACK: Alekhine*

*Hamburg 1930*

| | WHITE | BLACK | | WHITE | BLACK |
|---|---|---|---|---|---|
| 1 | P–Q4 | N–KB3 | 17 | KR–Q1 | R–Q1 |
| 2 | P–QB4 | P–K3 | 18 | P–QR4? | P–B5 |
| 3 | N–QB3 | B–N5 | 19 | P–R5 | PxKP |
| 4 | Q–N3 | P–B4 | 20 | QxP | N–B4 |
| 5 | PxP | N–B3 | 21 | Q–B3 | P–Q3! |
| 6 | N–B3 | N–K5 | 22 | PxP | PxP |
| 7 | B–Q2 | NxQBP | 23 | N–K1 | P–K4 |
| 8 | Q–B2 | P–B4 | 24 | R–R7 | N–Q5 |
| 9 | P–QR3 | BxN | 25 | Q–K3 | R–Q2 |
| 10 | BxB | O–O | 26 | R–R2 | R/2–KB2 |
| 11 | P–QN4 | N–K5 | 27 | P–B3 | R–B5 |
| 12 | P–K3 | P–QN3 | 28 | B–Q3 | Q–R4! |
| 13 | B–Q3? | NxB | 29 | B–B1 | Q–N4! |
| 14 | QxN | B–N2 | 30 | R–KB2 | P–R3! |
| 15 | O–O | N–K2 | 31 | K–R1 | RxP!! |
| 16 | B–K2 | Q–K1 | | Resigns | |

PRACTICAL VARIATIONS 26 AND 27:

1 P–Q4, N–KB3 2 P–QB4, P–K3 3 N–QB3, B–N5 4 Q–N3

| | 26 | 27 |
|---|---|---|
| *4* | — — | — — |
| | N–B3 | Q–K2[7] |
| *5* | N–B3[1] | P–QR3[8] |
| | P–Q3[2] | BxN† |
| *6* | P–Q5[3] | QxB |
| | BxN† | P–QN3[9] |
| *7* | QxB | P–B3 |
| | PxP | P–Q4 |
| *8* | PxP | PxP |
| | NxP[4] | NxP |
| *9* | QxP | Q–B2! |
| | Q–B3 | Q–R5† |
| *10* | QxQ | P–N3 |
| | NxQ | QxQP |
| *11* | P–QN3 | P–K4 |
| | N–K5 | N–K2[10] |
| *12* | B–N2 | B–KB4[11] |
| | KR–N1[5] | ± |
| *13* | N–Q2 | |
| | N–B4![6] | |
| | = | |

*Notes to practical variations 26 and 27:*

[1] 5 P–Q5 merits investigation.

[2] Worth testing is 5 . . . P–QR4. After 6 P–QR3, P–R5 7 Q–B2, BxN† 8 PxB!, P–Q3 9 P–K4, P–K4 10 P–KR3, O–O

11 B–K3, the game is approximately even. On 5 . . . P–Q4 White's best is 6 B–N5!

[3] For 6 P–QR3, BxN† 7 QxB, see Part I.

[4] If 8 . . . N–K2, then 9 P–K4.

[5] For 12 . . . O–O, see Game 18.

[6] Black's free-wheeling Knights are as good as White's Bishops.

[7] Unusual, but not bad.

[8] On 5 N–B3, Pachman recommends 5 . . . N–K5!

[9] 6 . . . P–Q3 7 N–B3, QN–Q2 is more promising.

[10] 11 . . . N–K6? 12 Q–Q3 wins.

[11] White has more than sufficient compensation for his Pawn.

*Nimzo-Indian Defense Game 18*

*WHITE: Euwe* *BLACK: Kramer*

*Hoogoven 1950*

| WHITE | BLACK | WHITE | BLACK |
|---|---|---|---|
| 1 P–Q4 | N–KB3 | 22 B–N2 | B–Q4 |
| 2 P–QB4 | P–K3 | 23 R–QB5 | K–K3 |
| 3 N–QB3 | B–N5 | 24 P–KR4 | R–K4 |
| 4 Q–N3 | N–B3 | 25 B–R3 | P–N3 |
| 5 N–B3 | P–Q3 | 26 R–B1 | R–Q3 |
| 6 P–Q5 | BxN† | 27 P–N5† | P–B4 |
| 7 QxB | PxP | 28 P–R5 | R–Q2 |
| 8 PxP | NxP | 29 P–R6 | N–K2 |
| 9 QxP | Q–B3 | 30 RxQP | P–B4 |
| 10 QxQ | NxQ | 31 R–Q3 | R–K5 |
| 11 P–QN3 | N–K5 | 32 P–B3 | R–KR5 |
| 12 B–N2 | O–O | 33 R–KR1 | P–QB5 |
| 13 N–Q2 | NxN | 34 PxP | BxP/5 |
| 14 KxN | P–B3 | 35 RxR | KxR |
| 15 R–B1 | B–K3 | 36 P–K4 | B–K3 |
| 16 P–KN4 | P–Q4 | 37 B–B6 | R–B5 |
| 17 R–KN1 | K–B2 | 38 BxN | KxB |
| 18 R–N3 | R–KN1 | 39 P–N6 | PxP |
| 19 R–KB3 | P–Q5 | 40 P–R7 | R–KR5 |
| 20 P–KR3 | QR–Q1 | 41 B–N2 | Resigns |
| 21 R–KB4 | R–N4 | | |

---

## part 12—SPASSKI VARIATION

### OBSERVATIONS ON KEY POSITION 12

Some years ago Spasski scored a series of notable victories with this variation. Since that time, however, many of its menacing problems have been solved. Recent investigation reveals that Black definitely need not fear this line if he is familiar with its intricacies.

1 P–Q4, N–KB3
2 P–QB4, P–K3
3 N–QB3, B–N5
4 B–N5

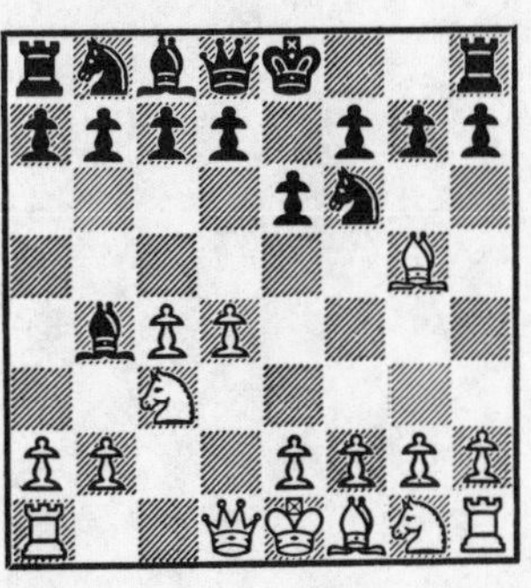

KEY POSITION 12

IDEA VARIATIONS 24 AND 25:

(24) 4 . . . P–B4 (the interpolation of 4 . . . P–KR3 is even stronger) 5 P–Q5, P–N4 (under these circumstances, a promising gambit) 6 P–K4, P–KR3 7 BxN, QxB 8 R–B1, O–O 9 BPxP, PxP 10 QxP, Q–QN3 11 B–B4, B–N2 12 Q–B5, P–QR3 13 P–QR4? (correct is 13 PxP, BxP 14 BxB, RxB 15 N–K2 which leads to equality), PxP 14 PxP, BxN† 15 PxB, R–R5! with advantage to Black (Steiner–Unzicker, Stockholm 1952).

(25) 4 . . . P–KR3 5 B–R4, P–B4 6 P–Q5 (6 P–K3, Q–R4 7 Q–N3, N–K5 is certainly not to White's advantage), P–Q3 (for 6 . . . P–QN4, see Game 19; a remarkable alternative is 6 . . . P–KN4! 7 B–N3, N–K5 8 B–K5, O–O, which led to a quick win for Black in the game Clarke–Niephaus, Wageningen 1957) 7 P–K3, PxP 8 PxP, QN–Q2 9 B–Q3! (better than 9 B–QN5, P–QR3 10 BxN†, BxB 11 N–K2, P–KN4!, when Black dominates the board), Q–R4 10 N–K2, NxP (declining the Pawn gives White a distinct advantage; see Game 20) 11 O–O, NxN 12 PxN, BxP 13 NxB, QxN 14 B–K2!, O–O 15 B–K7, R–K1 16 QxP!, Q–K4 17 QxQ, NxQ 18 BxP and White has a slight edge (Korchnoi–Gipslis, Riga 1955).

*Nimzo-Indian Defense Game 19*

*WHITE: Korchnoi* — *BLACK: Durasevic*

*Belgrade 1956*

| | WHITE | BLACK | | WHITE | BLACK |
|---|---|---|---|---|---|
| 1 | P–Q4 | N–KB3 | 14 | P–QN4 | P–N4! |
| 2 | P–QB4 | P–K3 | 15 | B–N3 | R–B1 |
| 3 | N–QB3 | B–N5 | 16 | PxB | RxN |
| 4 | B–N5 | P–B4 | 17 | Q–Q2 | NxP |
| 5 | P–Q5 | P–KR3 | 18 | QxP | QxP |
| 6 | B–R4 | P–QN4! | 19 | Q–N4 | QxQ |
| 7 | P–K4 | P–Q3 | 20 | PxQ | R–K1 |
| 8 | Q–B2 | O–O | 21 | P–B3 | R–K6† |
| 9 | PxKP | N–B3! | 22 | K–Q1 | B–N6† |
| 10 | N–B3 | BxP | 23 | K–B1 | R–B1† |
| 11 | PxP | N–Q5 | 24 | K–N2 | R–B7† |
| 12 | NxN | PxN | 25 | K–R3 | R–Q7 |
| 13 | P–QR3 | B–R4 | | Resigns | |

*Nimzo-Indian Defense Game 20*

*WHITE: Spasski* *BLACK: Filip*

*Göteborg 1955*

| | WHITE | BLACK | | WHITE | BLACK |
|---|---|---|---|---|---|
| 1 | P–Q4 | N–KB3 | 21 | P–QR4 | P–B3 |
| 2 | P–QB4 | P–K3 | 22 | R/1–KB1 | R–B2 |
| 3 | N–QB3 | B–N5 | 23 | B–R5 | R–N2 |
| 4 | B–N5 | P–KR3 | 24 | P–R5 | R–KB1 |
| 5 | B–R4 | P–B4 | 25 | N–Q1 | R–N4 |
| 6 | P–Q5 | PxP | 26 | B–K2 | N–N3 |
| 7 | PxP | P–Q3 | 27 | R/4–B2 | N–K4 |
| 8 | P–K3 | QN–Q2 | 28 | N–K3 | R–N2 |
| 9 | B–Q3 | O–O | 29 | BxN | QPxB |
| 10 | N–K2 | N–K4 | 30 | P–Q6 | Q–Q1 |
| 11 | O–O | BxN | 31 | B–B4 | B–B3 |
| 12 | NxB | N–N3 | 32 | N–B5 | R–N4 |
| 13 | B–N3 | Q–K2 | 33 | P–KR4 | R–N3 |
| 14 | P–K4 | B–Q2 | 34 | BxN† | R/1xB |
| 15 | R–K1 | N–K4 | 35 | N–K7 | BxP |
| 16 | B–K2 | P–KN4 | 36 | NxR/6 | RxN |
| 17 | R–KB1 | K–R2? | 37 | P–R5 | R–N2 |
| 18 | Q–Q2 | N–N1 | 38 | RxP | RxP† |
| 19 | P–B4 | PxP | 39 | QxR | BxQ |
| 20 | RxP | P–R3 | 40 | R–B8 | Resigns |

PRACTICAL VARIATION 28:

1 P–Q4, N–KB3 2 P–QB4, P–K3 3 N–QB3, B–N5 4 B–N5

| *28* | *28* |
|---|---|
| *4* – – | *8* P–K3[1] |
| P–KR3 | P–Q3 |
| *5* B–R4 | *9* Q–B2 |
| P–B4 | QN–Q2 |
| *6* P–Q5 | *10* B–Q3 |
| BxN† | Q–K2 |
| *7* PxB | *11* P–B3 |
| P–K4 | P–KN4[2] |
| | = |

*Notes to practical variation 28:*

[1] The Russian theoretician, Zak, suggests 8 P–Q6!?

[2] Keres–O'Kelly, Budapest 1952.

continued ▶

## SUPPLEMENTARY VARIATIONS 1–12:
### 1 P–Q4, N–KB3 2 P–QB4, P–K3 3 N–QB3, B–N5

| | 1 | 2 | 3 | 4 | 5 | 6 |
|---|---|---|---|---|---|---|
| 4 | Q–B2 | — — | — — | — — | — — | — — |
| | P–Q4 | P–B4 | — — | P–QN3? | P–Q3 | BxN† |
| 5 | P–QR3 | PxP | — — | P–K4 | B–N5 | QxB |
| | BxN† | BxP | BxN† | BxN† | QN–Q2[11] | N–K5 |
| 6 | QxB | N–B3 | QxB | PxB | P–K3 | Q–B2 |
| | N–B3[1] | N–B3 | N–K5 | P–Q3 | P–QN3 | P–Q4 |
| 7 | N–B3[2] | B–N5 | Q–Q4![8] | P–B4 | B–Q3 | N–B3! |
| | N–K5 | P–QN3[5] | Q–R4† | P–K4 | B–N2 | P–QB4 |
| 8 | Q–N3![3] | P–K3 | K–Q1! | B–Q3 | P–B3 | PxBP |
| | N–R4 | B–N2 | P–B4 | Q–K2 | BxN† | QN–B3 |
| 9 | Q–R4† | B–K2 | P–B3 | N–B3 | QxB | P–K3 |
| | P–B3 | QR–B1 | N–KB3 | N–B3 | P–B4 | O–O |
| 10 | P–B5[4] | O–O | B–Q2[9] | O–O | N–R3 | B–Q2![13] |
| | ± | B–K2 | ± | B–N2 | P–KR3 | ± |
| 11 | | QR–Q1 | | R–N1 | B–B4 | |
| | | P–Q3 | | O–O–O | Q–K2 | |
| 12 | | R–Q2 | | P–QB5![10] | B–N3 | |
| | | P–QR3 | | ± | P–K4 | |
| 13 | | KR–Q1 | | | PxKP | |
| | | O–O[6] | | | PxP | |
| 14 | | B–B4 | | | O–O–O[12] | |
| | | N–K1[7] | | | ± | |
| | | ± | | | | |

*Notes to supplementary variations 1–12:*

[1] Successfully adopted by Botvinnik on several occasions.

[2] After 7 P–K3, P–K4! 8 PxKP, N–K5 9 Q–Q3, N–B4 10 Q–B2, PxP, Black has no particular difficulties (Kotov–Szabo, Budapest 1950).

[3] 8 Q–B2?, P–K4! favors Black. See Part 2.

[4] The column is suggested by Hans Mueller.

[5] Two alternatives also in White's favor are 7 . . . P–KR3 8 B–R4, B–K2 9 R–Q1, O–O 10 P–K3, P–Q4 11 B–K2, Q–R4 12 N–Q2!, R–Q1 13 O–O (Rubinstein–Ahues, Berlin 1926) and 7 . . . N–Q5 8 NxN, BxN 9 N–N5!, B–B4 10 O–O–O! In this latter line if 9 P–K3, Black equalizes with 9 . . . Q–R4!

[6] Not 13 . . . Q–B2 14 B–B4!±.

[7] White has a slight superiority in space, but its utilization remains a problem.

[8] A suggestion of Haberditz. 7 Q–QR3 is a worthwhile alternative.

[9] Black's early incursion is repulsed.

[10] Noteboom–Flohr, Hastings 1929.

[11] 5 . . . N–B3 is met by 6 O–O–O.

[12] Alekhine–Nimzowitsch, New York 1927.

| 7 | 8 | 9 | 10 | 11 | 12 |
|---|---|---|---|---|---|
| — — | P–K3 | — — | B–Q2 | P–B3 | P–KN3 |
| O–O | O–O | — — | O–O | P–Q4[22] | P–B4 |
| P–QR3[14] | N–B3 | — — | N–KB3 | P–QR3 | P–Q5 |
| BxN† | P–Q4 | — — | P–QN3[20] | B–K2[23] | N–K5 |
| QxB | B–Q3 | — — | P–K3 | P–K4 | B–Q2[25] |
| P–QN3! | P–B4 | — — | B–N2 | PxKP | BxN |
| N–B3[15] | O–O | — — | B–Q3 | PxP | BxB |
| B–N2 | N–B3 | — — | P–Q4 | P–K4! | NxB |
| B–N5 | P–QR3 | — — | PxP | P–Q5 | PxN |
| P–Q3 | B–R4 | PxQP | PxP | B–QB4 | P–Q3[26] |
| P–K3 | N–K2[17] | KPxP | QR–B1 | B–N5 | ∓ |
| QN–Q2 | PxBP | PxP | P–QR3 | P–KR3 | |
| Q–B2 | BxP | BxP | N–K2 | B–R4 | |
| Q–K1 | B–N3 | BxN | B–Q3 | P–QR4 | |
| N–Q2 | PxP | PxB | N–N3 | B–Q3 | |
| P–B4![16] | BxP | Q–R4 | R–K1[21] | Q–Q3![24] | |
| = | P–QN4 | Q–B2 | ∓ | = | |
| | QxQ | P–K4 | | | |
| | RxQ | B–K3[19] | | | |
| | B–K2 | ± | | | |
| | B–N2[18] | | | | |
| | ± | | | | |

[13] Rubinstein–Nimzowitsch, Kissingen 1928.

[14] Too sharp is 5 P–K4, P–Q3 6 P–K5, PxP 7 PxP, N–N5!, when Black stands well.

[15] Nor does 7 B–N5, B–N2 8 P–B3, N–B3! offers White an advantage.

[16] Reshevsky–Keres, Moscow 1948.

[17] After 9 BPxP, KPxP 10 PxP, BxN 11 PxB, B–N5! 12 P–B4, P–Q5!, Black has sufficient counterplay.

[18] Spasski–Krogius, Riga 1958.

[19] White's last few moves were suggested by Donner. If now 13 . . . N–KN5, White replies 14 N–N5!

[20] The simple 5 . . . P–Q4 is also good.

[21] Black has a minimal initiative.

[22] After 4 . . . P–Q3 5 P–K4, O–O 6 N–K2, P–K4 7 P–QR3, White has an excellent game. O'Kelly recommends 4 . . . P–B4 5 P–Q5, P–QN4!

[23] For 5 . . . BxN†, see Prac. Var. 10. Simagin suggests 5 . . . B–Q3?! and if 6 P–K4, then 6 . . . P–B4.

[24] Portisch–Szabo, Budapest 1960.

[25] Not 6 Q–B2?, Q–B3!∓.

[26] White's Pawn structure is permanently damaged.

# chapter 37—Queen's Indian Defense

## (including Bogo-Indian and Queen's Indian Knight's Game)

The moves 1 P–Q4, N–KB3 2 P–QB4, P–K3 3 N–KB3, P–QN3 constitute the Queen's Indian Defense. Its rationale is White's neglect of his K4 by 3 N–KB3, instead of covering it with 3 N–QB3. Black immediately focuses attention on that square by the coming fianchetto of the Queen Bishop, which he will augment with moves like . . . P–Q4 and/or . . . P–KB4. To boot, Black has . . . P–QB4 in reserve in many positions to maintain the center tension. On the other side, White need not surrender the square. He may in due time challenge its control and/or attempt to enforce P–Q5 and lock the opposing Bishop out of the game. Should White succeed in doing so, he will retain a lasting initiative.

Today the Queen's Indian is in reasonably good repute. Black has several lines which offer chances for equality. From White's point of view, it is a question which line grants him the most latitude. The classic deployment with P–KN3 has had remarkably few supporters in recent years.

1 P–Q4, N–KB3
2 P–QB4, P–K3[A]
3 N–KB3, P–QN3
4 P–KN3, B–N2[B]
5 B–N2, B–K2[C]
6 O–O[D], O–O
7 N–B3[E], N–K5
8 Q–B2[F], NxN[G]
9 QxN[H]

KEY POSITION 1

## part 1—CLASSICAL VARIATION

### OBSERVATIONS ON KEY POSITION 1

[A] 2 . . . P–QN3 immediately is inferior. For instance, 3 N–QB3, B–N2 4 Q–B2!, P–Q4 5 PxP, NxP 6 N–B3, P–K3 7 P–K4, NxN 8 PxN with a clear advantage for White in space, the center and mobility.

[B] At present 4 . . . B–R3 is also usual. See Sup. Var. 2.

[C] Other moves sometimes tried in this position are:

(1) 5 . . . P–Q4 6 O–O, B–K2 7 N–B3. See Part 2.

(2) 5 . . . P–B4 6 P–Q5!, PxP 7 N–R4!±.

(3) 5 . . . B–N5†. See Part 3.

[D] If 6 N–B3, N–K5!

E This is considered strongest. Other possibilities are:

(1) 7 Q–B2, N–B3 8 N–B3, P–Q4 9 PxP, N–QN5! leading to an even game.

(2) 7 P–N3, P–B4! 8 B–N2, PxP 9 NxP, BxB 10 KxB, P–Q4 with equal chances.

(3) 7 P–Q5!?. See Sup. Var. 1.

F If 8 NxN, BxN 9 B–B4, P–QB3!

G 8 . . . P–Q5 also seems playable — but experience is lacking.

H Not 9 N–N5?, NxP†! Good for Black is 9 PxN, P–KB4! 10 P–Q5, Q–B1.

This is the most frequently occurring position in the Queen's Indian Defense. Black still controls K5, but White is ready to challenge this with 10 Q–B2 or 10 Q–Q3. Black can simply play 9 . . . P–Q4, but this has the drawback that it locks in the fianchettoed Bishop. Hence, more usual are the continuations 9 . . . P–KB4 and 9 . . . B–K5. In the former case, the counter-advance P–Q5 plays an important role leading to sharp positions offering chances for White. Against . . . B–K5 White must operate more conservatively, with precise play yielding some prospects for an initiative.

IDEA VARIATIONS 1 AND 2:

(1) 9 . . . P–KB4 10 P–Q5 (the sharpest, although also worth considering is the quiet 10 P–N3; see Prac. Var. 1), B–KB3 (10 . . . PxP 11 N–K1 is good for White) 11 Q–Q2 (11 Q–B2 also merits attention, as in 11 . . . P–B3 [a Yugoslav suggestion] 12 PxKP, PxP 13 P–K4! with good chances for White), Q–K1 12 N–Q4!, BxN (12 . . . N–R3 13 R–Q1, BxN 14 QxB, P–K4 15 Q–B3, P–Q3 16 P–QN4 favors White; see Game 1) 13 QxB, P–K4 14 Q–B3, P–Q3 15 P–QN4±.

(2) 9 . . . B–K5 10 N–K1 (or 10 B–B4, e.g., 10 . . . P–Q3 11 Q–K3, B–N2 12 KR–Q1, N–Q2 13 P–QN4, N–B3 14 P–QR4, N–R4 with chances for both sides), BxB 11 NxB, P–QB3 (the immediate 11 . . . P–Q4 is dubious because of 12 PxP, PxP 13 B–B4, P–QB4 14 PxP, PxP 15 KR–Q1 with strong pressure against Black's center) 12 P–Q5 (otherwise Black can conveniently play 12 . . . P–Q4), BPxP 13 PxP, N–R3 14 N–B4, Q–B1 15 Q–B3, Q–B2 (15 . . . P–K4 is strongly answered by 16 P–Q6, BxP 17 N–Q5!±) 16 P–K4, N–B4 with approximately even chances.

*Queen's Indian Defense Game 1*

*WHITE: Fuderer* *BLACK: Geller*

*Chess Olympics, Amsterdam 1954*

| WHITE | BLACK | WHITE | BLACK |
|---|---|---|---|
| 1 P–Q4 | N–KB3 | 19 P–K3 | B–B1 |
| 2 P–QB4 | P–K3 | 20 B–N2 | Q–R4? |
| 3 N–KB3 | P–QN3 | 21 P–B4! | N–N1 |
| 4 P–KN3 | B–N2 | 22 P–B5! | N–Q2 |
| 5 B–N2 | B–K2 | 23 PxQP | PxQP |
| 6 O–O | O–O | 24 R–Q2 | N–B3 |
| 7 N–B3 | N–K5 | 25 P–N5! | PxP |
| 8 Q–B2 | NxN | 26 KPxP | N–K5 |
| 9 QxN | P–KB4 | 27 BxN | PxB |
| 10 P–Q5 | B–KB3 | 28 BxP | P–K6 |
| 11 Q–Q2 | Q–K1 | 29 BxR | KxB |
| 12 N–Q4! | N–R3 | 30 P–N4! | BxP |
| 13 R–Q1 | BxN | 31 R–KN2 | P–K7 |
| 14 QxB | P–K4 | 32 R–K1 | R–K2 |
| 15 Q–B3 | P–Q3 | 33 P–Q6 | R–Q2 |
| 16 P–QN4 | Q–R4 | 34 Q–B8† | K–B2 |
| 17 B–B3 | Q–N3 | 35 R/1xP | B–K3 |
| 18 B–R3 | QR–K1 | 36 P–B5 | Resigns |

PRACTICAL VARIATIONS 1–3:

1 P–Q4, N–KB3 2 P–QB4, P–K3 3 N–KB3, P–QN3 4 P–KN3, B–N2 5 B–N2, B–K2 6 O–O, O–O 7 N–B3, N–K5 8 Q–B2, NxN 9 QxN

| | *1* | *2* | *3* |
|---|---|---|---|
| *9* | – – | – – | – – |
| | P–KB4 | P–Q3 | Q–B1[8] |
| *10* | P–N3[1] | Q–Q3[5] | B–B4[9] |
| | B–KB3 | N–B3 | P–Q3 |
| *11* | B–N2 | R–Q1 | KR–K1 |
| | Q–B1[2] | P–QR4 | B–K5 |
| *12* | Q–Q2 | P–K4 | B–R3![10] |
| | P–Q3 | P–K4 | P–QB3 |
| *13* | N–K1 | B–K3 | N–Q2 |
| | N–Q2 | Q–B1 | B–N3 |
| *14* | R–Q1 | P–QR3 | P–K4 |
| | P–QR4 | PxP[6] | N–Q2 |
| *15* | P–Q5 | NxP | B–K3 |
| | BxB[3] | NxN | Q–B2 |
| *16* | PxP | BxN | P–B4[11] |
| | N–B4 | P–KB4 | ± |
| *17* | QxB[4] | P–B4![7] | |
| | = | ± | |

*Notes to practical variations 1–3:*

[1] 10 P–Q5 leads to Idea Var. 1.

[2] Smyslov's move, which is most solid. Not bad either is 11 . . . N–B3, e.g., 12 QR–Q1, N–K2 13 N–K1, BxB 14 NxB, P–KN4 or 12 N–K5, NxP 13 QxN, BxB 14 KxB, P–Q3 15 Q–K3, in both cases with an even game.

[3] Better than 15 . . . P–K4 16 P–K4!, PxP 17 B–KR3!±.

[4] Filip–Smyslov, Amsterdam 1956.

[5] Also 10 Q–B2, P–KB4 11 P–Q5!, P–K4 12 P–K4 offers White a slight edge.

[6] 14 . . . P–R5 is preferable, according to Pachman.

[7] Lundin–Yanofsky, Groningen 1946.

[8] Although adopted by Smyslov on several occasions, this move seems insufficient for equality.

[9] Also good is 10 Q–B2; see Game 2.

[10] The well-known method in positions of this type: White avoids the exchange of Bishops.

[11] Larsen–O'Kelly, Hastings 1956–57.

## *Queen's Indian Defense Game 2*

*WHITE: Bouwmeester* *BLACK: Van Seters*

*Amsterdam vs. Brussels 1952*

| WHITE | BLACK | WHITE | BLACK |
|---|---|---|---|
| 1 P–Q4 | N–KB3 | 20 NxP | QxN |
| 2 P–QB4 | P–K3 | 21 QxB | N–B4 |
| 3 N–KB3 | P–QN3 | 22 QxQ† | KxQ |
| 4 P–KN3 | B–N2 | 23 B–B7 | R–Q2 |
| 5 B–N2 | B–K2 | 24 KR–Q1 | R–QB1 |
| 6 O–O | O–O | 25 P–Q6 | R/1xB |
| 7 N–B3 | N–K5 | 26 B–Q5† | K–B3 |
| 8 Q–B2 | NxN | 27 PxR | RxP |
| 9 QxN | Q–B1? | 28 R–B4 | P–QR4 |
| 10 Q–B2 | P–Q4 | 29 P–B4 | R–K2 |
| 11 PxP | PxP | 30 K–B2 | K–B4 |
| 12 B–B4 | P–QB3 | 31 K–B3 | P–R4 |
| 13 N–K5 | R–Q1 | 32 P–KR3 | K–B3 |
| 14 QR–B1 | Q–K3 | 33 R–QB2 | R–QB2 |
| 15 P–K4 | P–QB4 | 34 R–K2 | P–KN3 |
| 16 PxBP | BxP? | 35 P–N4 | PxP |
| 17 P–QN4! | BxP | 36 PxP | P–QR5 |
| 18 Q–B7 | N–Q2 | 37 P–N5† | K–N2 |
| 19 PxP | Q–B4 | 38 R–K8 | Resigns |

## part 2—CLOSED DEFENSIVE SYSTEM

1 P–Q4, N–KB3
2 P–QB4, P–K3
3 N–KB3, P–QN3
4 P–KN3, B–N2
5 B–N2, B–K2
6 O–O, O–O
7 N–B3

KEY POSITION 2

### OBSERVATIONS ON KEY POSITION 2

In addition to 7 . . . N–K5 there are some other continuations which offer satisfactory chances. Since Black is obliged to prevent White's P–K4, he must generally resort to . . . P–Q4, which gives the position a more or less closed character.

After the exchange of Pawns on Q5, White usually obtains some pressure on the half-open QB file and some prospects on the Queenside. Thus, if he intends to treat the defense actively, Black must try to get in . . . P–QB4; then he must acquiesce in hanging Pawns in the center. This gives him good chances in the central zone, though the hanging Pawns remain vulnerable.

### IDEA VARIATIONS 3 AND 4:

(3) 7 . . . P–Q4 (with the exception of 7 . . . N–K5, this is the most popular continuation) 8 N–K5! (nothing is to be gained by other moves, such as 8 PxP, NxP 9 R–K1, P–QB4!, with an even game), P–B3 (also important is 8 . . . Q–B1; see Prac. Var. 4 and Game 3) 9 P–K4! (without this Pawn offer, White has little opportunity for an advantage; for 9 PxP, BPxP, see Game 4), PxBP 10 NxP/4, B–R3 11 P–N3, P–QN4 (Black must proceed consistently, for otherwise White maintains a clear positional advantage) 12 N–K3! (12 N–K5, P–N5 13 N–K2, P–B4! is satisfactory for Black), P–N5 13 N–K2, BxN (now 13 . . . P–B4 is bad because of 14 P–K5!) 14 QxB, QxP 15 B–N2, Q–N3 16 N–B4, Q–N4 17 BxN, PxB (better than 17 . . . BxB 18 P–K5, B–K2 19 QR–Q1 etc.) 18 QR–Q1, and White has a strong attack for the Pawn (Smyslov–Guimard, Groningen 1946).

(4) 7 . . . Q–B1 (unusual but not bad) 8 P–N3 (8 Q–B2 may well be answered by 8 . . . P–B4; see Prac. Var. 6), P–Q4 (the characteristic set-up: weak is 8 . . . P–B4 because of 9 P–Q5!) 9 PxP, PxP (if 9 . . . NxP, then 10 B–N2, P–QB4 11 R–B1!) 10 Q–B2, QN–Q2 11 B–B4, P–QR3 12 N–K5, Q–Q1 13 R–B1. White maintains some initiative.

### *Queen's Indian Defense Game 3*

*WHITE: Lundin* *BLACK: Botvinnik*

*Groningen 1946*

| | WHITE | BLACK | | WHITE | BLACK |
|---|---|---|---|---|---|
| 1 | P–Q4 | N–KB3 | 28 | B–N3? | P–B5! |
| 2 | P–QB4 | P–K3 | 29 | B–B2 | QxQ |
| 3 | N–KB3 | P–QN3 | 30 | PxQ | P–N5! |
| 4 | P–KN3 | B–N2 | 31 | R–K1 | R–QB2 |
| 5 | B–N2 | B–K2 | 32 | R–K5 | N–N4 |
| 6 | O–O | O–O | 33 | K–R2 | B–QB1 |
| 7 | N–B3 | P–Q4 | 34 | P–KR4 | P–KR3 |
| 8 | N–K5 | Q–B1 | 35 | PxP | PxP |
| 9 | PxP | NxP | 36 | K–N1 | B–Q2 |
| 10 | NxN | PxN | 37 | R/2–K2 | K–B1 |
| 11 | Q–N3 | Q–K3 | 38 | R–B2 | R–QR2 |
| 12 | N–Q3! | R–Q1 | 39 | B–B1 | P–R5! |
| 13 | B–K3 | P–QB3 | 40 | PxP | RxP |
| 14 | KR–Q1 | N–Q2 | 41 | R–N2 | N–B6 |
| 15 | QR–B1 | N–B3 | 42 | R–K1 | R–KR2 |
| 16 | R–B2 | N–K5 | 43 | R–R1 | K–B2 |
| 17 | R/1–QB1 | QR–B1 | 44 | B–K1 | N–N4 |
| 18 | N–B4 | Q–Q2 | 45 | B–K2 | NxP |
| 19 | Q–R4 | P–QR4 | 46 | B–Q1 | P–B4! |
| 20 | Q–N3 | P–QN4 | 47 | BxR | NxP†! |
| 21 | Q–Q3? | P–KN4 | 48 | K–B2 | BxP! |
| 22 | N–R5 | P–KB4 | 49 | B–Q1 | N–K4! |
| 23 | P–B3 | N–Q3 | 50 | BxB | NxB† |
| 24 | B–B2 | R–B1 | 51 | K–N1 | RxN |
| 25 | P–N3 | R–KB2 | 52 | R–N2 | B–B3 |
| 26 | P–KR3 | Q–K3 | | Resigns | |
| 27 | P–KN4 | Q–N3 | | | |

### *Queen's Indian Defense Game 4*

*WHITE: Saemisch* *BLACK: Nimzowitsch*

*Copenhagen 1923*

| | WHITE | BLACK | | WHITE | BLACK | | WHITE | BLACK |
|---|---|---|---|---|---|---|---|---|
| 1 | P–Q4 | N–KB3 | 10 | B–B4 | P–QR3! | 19 | R–N1 | B–Q3 |
| 2 | P–QB4 | P–K3 | 11 | R–B1 | P–QN4 | 20 | P–K4 | BPxP |
| 3 | N–KB3 | P–QN3 | 12 | Q–N3 | N–B3! | 21 | QxN | RxP |
| 4 | P–KN3 | B–N2 | 13 | NxN | BxN | 22 | Q–N5 | QR–KB1 |
| 5 | B–N2 | B–K2 | 14 | P–KR3 | Q–Q2 | 23 | K–R1 | R/1–B4 |
| 6 | N–B3 | O–O | 15 | K–R2 | N–R4 | 24 | Q–K3 | B–Q6 |
| 7 | O–O | P–Q4 | 16 | B–Q2 | P–B4! | 25 | QR–K1 | P–R3!! |
| 8 | N–K5 | P–B3 | 17 | Q–Q1 | P–N5! | | Resigns | |
| 9 | PxP | BPxP | 18 | N–N1 | B–QN4 | | | |

PRACTICAL VARIATIONS 4–6:

1 P–Q4, N–KB3 2 P–QB4, P–K3 3 N–KB3, P–QN3 4 P–KN3, B–N2 5 B–N2, B–K2 6 O–O, O–O 7 N–B3

| | 4 | 5 | 6 |
|---|---|---|---|
| 7 | – – | – – | – – |
| | P–Q4 | – – | Q–B1 |
| 8 | N–K5 | – – | Q–B2 |
| | Q–B1[1] | N–K5[5] | P–B4 |
| 9 | PxP | PxP | P–N3[8] |
| | NxP[2] | PxP[6] | PxP |
| 10 | NxN[3] | NxN | NxP |
| | PxN | PxN | BxB |
| 11 | Q–N3 | Q–B2! | KxB |
| | Q–K3 | P–KB4 | N–B3 |
| 12 | N–Q3! | B–K3 | R–Q1 |
| | R–Q1 | N–R3 | P–Q4[9] |
| 13 | B–K3 | QR–B1[7] | = |
| | P–QB3 | ± | |
| 14 | QR–B1[4] | | |
| | ± | | |

*Notes to practical variations 4–6:*

[1] Threatening to obtain a good position with 9 . . . PxP 10 NxP/4, P–B4. Inferior is 8 . . . QN–Q2 9 PxP, PxP 10 Q–R4!, and White has the edge.

[2] More comfortable than 9 . . . PxP.

[3] After 10 P–K4, NxN 11 PxN, N–Q2, Black has a satisfactory position.

[4] For 14 KR–Q1, see Game 3.

[5] Introduced by Capablanca. For 8 . . . P–B3, see Idea Var. 3.

[6] Or 9 . . . NxN 10 PxN, PxP 11 P–QB4±.

[7] Euwe–Capablanca, AVRO 1938.

[8] 9 PxP, PxP rather favors Black.

[9] If 13 PxP, N–QN5!

1 P–Q4, N–KB3
2 P–QB4, P–K3
3 N–KB3, P–QN3
4 P–KN3, B–N2
5 B–N2, B–N5†

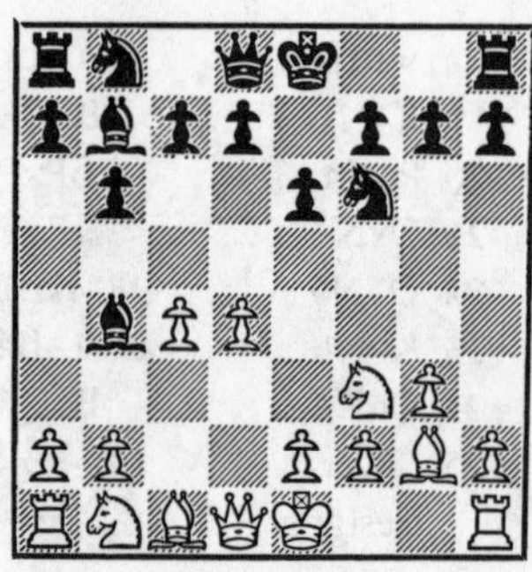

KEY POSITION 3

## part 3—THE SYSTEM WITH 5...B-N5+

OBSERVATIONS ON KEY POSITION 3

This system has been favored by Bogoljubov and Nimzowitsch, and even more by Capablanca. The check in itself is not quite logical, for after the exchange of the Bishop one of Black's active defenders is eliminated. Even so, Black still gets satisfactory chances in some variations.

IDEA VARIATIONS 5–7:

(5) 6 B–Q2 (6 QN–Q2 [Prac. Var. 7] has disap-

peared from practical play; 6 N–B3 leads to the Nimzo–Indian), BxB† 7 QxB (after QNxB, P–B4!, Black has little difficulty), O–O (after 7 . . . P–Q3 8 N–B3, Black must not reply 8 . . . N–K5?, e.g., 9 Q–B4!, NxN? 10 N–N5! and White wins; Black must keep an eye on this sort of thrust in this variation) 8 N–B3, P–Q3 (a common mistake is 8 . . . N–K5? because of 9 Q–B2, NxN 10 N–N5!, winning the exchange) 9 Q–B2, Q–K2 10 O–O, P–B4 (for 10 . . . QN–Q2, see Prac. Var. 8) 11 QR–Q1 (11 P–K4, N–B3! leads to an equal game), N–B3 12 P–N3!, QR–B1 13 Q–N2±.

(6) 6 B–Q2, Q–K2 (this has little independent significance) 7 O–O, BxB (otherwise 8 B–N5 is somewhat unpleasant for Black) 8 QxB, O–O 9 N–B3, P–Q3 (herewith the essence of Idea Var. 5 is reached; weaker would be 9 . . . N–K5 10 NxN, BxN 11 Q–B4!, P–Q4 12 PxP, PxP 13 QR–B1 with advantage for White).

(7) 6 B–Q2, B–K2 (a more or less surprising move based on the idea that White's Bishop does not serve best on Q2) 7 O–O, O–O 8 N–B3, P–Q4 (if 8 . . . N–K5, then 9 P–Q5!) 9 PxP (after 9 N–K5, P–B3, White's advance, 10 P–K4, is not playable because of 10 . . . PxBP, and White's Queen Pawn is loose; cf. Idea Var. 3), NxP (for 9 . . . PxP, see Prac. Var. 9) 10 R–K1, P–QB4 11 P–K4, NxN 12 BxN, PxP 13 NxP, QN–Q2=.

PRACTICAL VARIATIONS 7–9:

1 P–Q4, N–KB3 2 P–QB4, P–K3 3 N–KB3, P–QN3 4 P–KN3, B–N2 5 B–N2, B–N5†

| | 7 | 8 | 9 |
|---|---|---|---|
| *6* | QN–Q2 | B–Q2 | – – |
| | O–O[1] | BxB† | B–K2 |
| 7 | O–O | QxB | O–O |
| | P–Q4[2] | O–O | O–O |
| 8 | Q–B2 | N–B3 | N–B3 |
| | QN–Q2 | P–Q3[4] | P–Q4 |
| *9* | P–QR3 | Q–B2 | PxP |
| | B–K2 | Q–K2 | PxP[7] |
| *10* | P–QN4 | O–O | Q–B2 |
| | P–B4 | QN–Q2[5] | QN–Q2[8] |
| *11* | PxQP | P–K4 | R–B1 |
| | KPxP | QR–B1 | R–K1[9] |
| *12* | QPxP | KR–K1 | B–B4 |
| | PxP | P–K4 | P–B3[10] |
| *13* | PxP | P–Q5 | = |
| | NxP[3] | P–B3 | |
| *14* | = | PxP | |
| | | BxP | |
| *15* | | Q–K2[6] | |
| | | ± | |

*Notes to practical variations 7–9:*

[1] Other good continuations are 6 . . . N–K5 and 6 . . . P–B4.

[2] Weak is 7 . . . BxQN. See Game 5.

continued ▸

[3] Flohr–Alekhine, AVRO 1938.
[4] For 8 . . . N–K5, see Game 6.
[5] Stronger is 10 . . . P–B4. See Idea Var. 5.
[6] Black's backward Queen Pawn is a handicap.
[7] For 9 . . . NxP, see Idea Var. 7.
[8] Better than 10 . . . N–K5? 11 NxN, PxN 12 N–K5±.
[9] Premature is 11 . . . P–B4, e.g., 12 PxP, PxP 13 B–N5!, R–K1 14 N–K1! followed by 15 N–Q3 with strong pressure against Black's hanging Pawns.
[10] If is difficult to expose a weakness.

*Queen's Indian Defense Game 5*

*WHITE: Alekhine* — *BLACK: Alexander*

*Nottingham 1936*

| | WHITE | BLACK | | WHITE | BLACK |
|---|---|---|---|---|---|
| 1 | P–Q4 | N–KB3 | 15 | N–R4 | Q–Q2 |
| 2 | P–QB4 | P–K3 | 16 | B–KR3 | P–N3 |
| 3 | N–KB3 | B–N5† | 17 | P–B3 | N–B4 |
| 4 | QN–Q2 | P–QN3 | 18 | Q–N5 | Q–N2 |
| 5 | P–KN3 | B–N2 | 19 | P–QN4 | N/4–Q2 |
| 6 | B–N2 | O–O | 20 | P–K4! | NxKP |
| 7 | O–O | BxQN? | 21 | Q–B1! | N/5–B3 |
| 8 | QxB | P–Q3 | 22 | BxP! | K–R1 |
| 9 | P–N3 | QN–Q2 | 23 | B–K6 | B–R3 |
| 10 | B–N2 | R–N1 | 24 | KR–K1 | N–K4 |
| 11 | QR–Q1! | N–K5 | 25 | P–B4! | N–Q6 |
| 12 | Q–K3 | P–KB4 | 26 | RxN | BxR |
| 13 | P–Q5! | PxP | 27 | P–N4 | Resigns |
| 14 | PxP | N/2–B3 | | | |

*Queen's Indian Defense Game 6*

*WHITE: Euwe* — *BLACK: Flohr*

*Second Match Game 1932*

| | WHITE | BLACK | | WHITE | BLACK |
|---|---|---|---|---|---|
| 1 | P–Q4 | N–KB3 | 13 | P–B4 | N/2–B3 |
| 2 | P–QB4 | P–K3 | 14 | QR–B1 | NxN |
| 3 | N–KB3 | P–QN3 | 15 | QxN | R–B1 |
| 4 | P–KN3 | B–N2 | 16 | P–QN4 | P–B3 |
| 5 | B–N2 | B–N5† | 17 | R–QB2 | N–Q2 |
| 6 | B–Q2 | BxB† | 18 | Q–R3 | NxN |
| 7 | QxB | O–O | 19 | BPxN | P–QR3 |
| 8 | N–B3 | N–K5 | 20 | Q–K3 | Q–K2 |
| 9 | Q–B2 | P–KB4 | 21 | P–QR3 | R–R1 |
| 10 | N–K5! | P–Q4 | 22 | Q–N3 | K–R1 |
| 11 | PxP | PxP | 23 | P–QR4 | P–QN4 |
| 12 | O–O | N–Q2 | 24 | P–R5 | Q–K3 |

| WHITE | BLACK | WHITE | BLACK |
|---|---|---|---|
| 25 B–R3 | Q–R3! | 36 Q–N5 | B–B1 |
| 26 BxP | P–N3 | 37 P–K4 | PxP |
| 27 B–N4 | RxR† | 38 BxP | B–Q2 |
| 28 KxR | R–B1† | 39 R–B2 | Q–B2 |
| 29 K–N1 | Q–N4 | 40 B–Q3 | B–K1 |
| 30 B–B3 | P–R4 | 41 R–KR2 | R–R1 |
| 31 Q–B3 | K–N2 | 42 Q–B6† | QxQ |
| 32 Q–Q2 | Q–K2 | 43 PxQ† | K–N1 |
| 33 R–B1 | P–R5 | 44 RxR† | KxR |
| 34 B–N2 | PxP | 45 B–K4 | K–N1 |
| 35 PxP | Q–K3 | 46 P–Q5! | Resigns |

## part 4—NON-FIANCHETTO SYSTEMS

1 P–Q4, N–KB3
2 P–QB4, P–K3
3 N–KB3, P–QN3

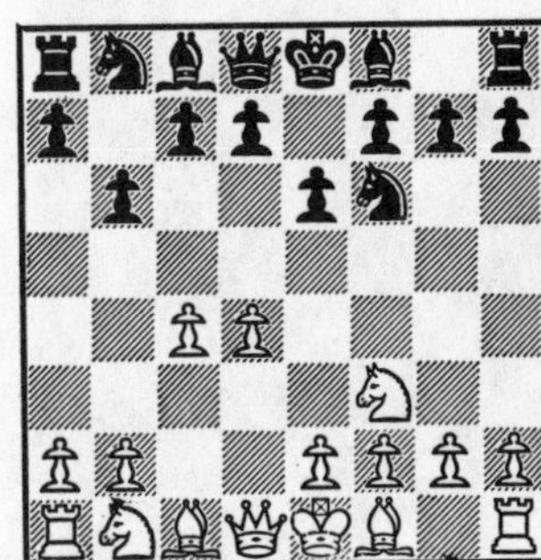

KEY POSITION 4

### OBSERVATIONS ON KEY POSITION 4

Since experience has shown that White's 4 P–KN3 is not unfavorable for Black, other systems of countering the Queen's Indian Defense have been tried in recent years. The moves most often seen are 4 P–K3 and 4 B–N5. The examination of these continuations is in the early stage. So far nothing has been found other than that the variations give rise to complicated positions with chances for both sides. Black has nothing to fear, provided he is well aware of some important finesses.

### IDEA VARIATIONS 8 AND 9:

(8) 4 B–N5 (the sharpest continuation), B–N2 5 N–B3, B–N5 (most frequently played; also possible is 5 . . . P–KR3 6 B–R4, B–K2 7 Q–B2, P–Q4) 6 P–K3, P–KR3 7 B–R4, P–KN4 (recent tournament experience does not encourage this line of play; probably stronger is 7 . . . BxN† 8 PxB, P–Q3, as in Prac. Var. 10) 8 B–N3, N–K5 9 Q–B2, BxN† 10 PxB, P–Q3 11 B–Q3, P–B4 (Tal–Gligoric, Candidates' Tournament 1959, continued 11 . . . NxB 12 RPxB, N–Q2 13 P–R4, P–QR4 14 R–QN1, P–KN5 15 N–R4, N–B3 16 P–Q5!, and White has fine attacking chances) 12 P–Q5! (a characteristic Pawn sacrifice in this line), PxP 13 PxP, BxP 14 N–Q4! (the point of White's 12th move), Q–B3 15 P–B3!, NxB 16 PxN, N–Q2 17 BxP, N–B4 (White also has a strong initiative after 17 . . . O–O–O 18 Q–R4!) 18 N–N5 with good chances for White. See Game 7.

(9) 4 P–K3 (the idea behind this move is to prepare for P–K4 with B–Q3 and N–B3), B–N2 5 B–Q3, B–K2 (in these circumstances 5 . . . B–N5† can be met by 6 QN–Q2) 6 N–B3, P–B4 (O–O is also playable; see Prac. Var. 11) 7 O–O, PxP 8 PxP, P–Q4 9 PxP (White tries to profit from Black's uncastled position, but most likely 9 P–QN3 is stronger; see Prac. Var. 12), NxP 10 B–QN5†, B–B3 11 Q–R4, Q–Q2 12 NxN (12 N–K5 is met by 12 . . . NxN!), QxN (not 12 . . . BxB 13 QxB!) 13 BxB, NxB 14 B–K3 (or 14 N–K5, P–QN4!), O–O. Black has a slight edge.

*Queen's Indian Defense Game 7*

*WHITE: Tal* — *BLACK: Duckstein*

*Zurich 1959*

| | WHITE | BLACK | | WHITE | BLACK |
|---|---|---|---|---|---|
| 1 | P–Q4 | P–K3 | 30 | NxR | R–R2 |
| 2 | N–KB3 | N–KB3 | 31 | N–N4 | K–K3 |
| 3 | P–B4 | B–N5† | 32 | K–Q2 | P–N4 |
| 4 | N–B3 | P–QN3 | 33 | R–K1 | P–R4 |
| 5 | B–N5 | B–N2 | 34 | K–K3 | R–R1 |
| 6 | P–K3 | P–KR3 | 35 | P–KB4 | P–N5 |
| 7 | B–R4 | P–KN4 | 36 | P–B5† | K–B2 |
| 8 | B–N3 | N–K5 | 37 | PxP | PxP |
| 9 | Q–B2 | P–Q3 | 38 | K–Q4 | P–N6 |
| 10 | B–Q3 | BxN† | 39 | PxP | R–QN1 |
| 11 | PxB | P–KB4 | 40 | K–Q5 | R–N5 |
| 12 | P–Q5! | PxP | 41 | N–K5†! | K–B3 |
| 13 | PxP | BxP | 42 | N–B6! | RxNP |
| 14 | N–Q4 | Q–B3 | 43 | P–K5† | PxP |
| 15 | P–B3 | NxB | 44 | KxN | KxP |
| 16 | PxN | N–Q2 | 45 | NxP | RxP |
| 17 | BxP | N–B4 | 46 | R–K2 | R–QR6 |
| 18 | N–N5 | Q–N2 | 47 | K–Q4 | R–R5† |
| 19 | B–N6† | K–Q2 | 48 | N–B4 | K–B5 |
| 20 | B–B5† | B–K3 | 49 | K–Q3 | P–N5 |
| 21 | BxB† | NxB | 50 | R–K3 | R–R8 |
| 22 | N–Q4 | N–B4 | 51 | P–N3† | K–B4 |
| 23 | Q–B5† | K–K2 | 52 | R–K5† | K–B3 |
| 24 | Q–Q5 | Q–B3 | 53 | R–K4 | K–N4 |
| 25 | O–O–O | QR–KB1 | 54 | N–K3 | R–R6† |
| 26 | P–K4 | Q–B2 | 55 | K–Q4 | K–R4 |
| 27 | N–B5† | K–Q2 | 56 | K–K5 | R–R8 |
| 28 | QxQ† | RxQ | 57 | K–B6 | Resigns |
| 29 | RxP | RxR | | | |

## PRACTICAL VARIATIONS 10–13:

1 P–Q4, N–KB3 2 P–QB4, P–K3 3 N–KB3, P–QN3

| | *10* | *11* | *12* | *13* |
|---|---|---|---|---|
| *4* | B–N5 | P–K3 | – – | B–B4 |
| | B–N2 | B–N2 | – – | B–N2 |
| *5* | N–B3 | B–Q3 | – – | P–K3 |
| | B–N5 | B–K2 | – – | N–K5! |
| *6* | P–K3 | N–B3 | – – | B–Q3 |
| | P–KR3 | O–O[5] | P–B4 | B–N5† |
| *7* | B–R4 | O–O | O–O | QN–Q2 |
| | BxN†[1] | P–Q4[6] | PxP | P–KB4 |
| *8* | PxB | Q–K2 | PxP | O–O |
| | P–Q3 | QN–Q2 | P–Q4 | O–O[11] |
| *9* | B–Q3 | P–QN3 | P–QN3 | = |
| | QN–Q2 | P–QR3 | O–O | |
| *10* | O–O | B–N2 | B–N2 | |
| | Q–K2[2] | B–Q3 | N–B3 | |
| *11* | N–Q2 | P–K4[7] | R–B1[9] | |
| | P–KN4[3] | NxP | R–B1 | |
| *12* | B–N3 | NxN | R–K1 | |
| | P–KR4 | PxN | N–QN5 | |
| *13* | P–KR3 | BxP | B–B1 | |
| | O–O–O[4] | BxB | N–K5[10] | |
| *14* | = | QxB | = | |
| | | Q–K2 | | |
| *15* | | QR–K1[8] | | |
| | | ± | | |

*Notes to practical variations 10–13:*

[1] Inferior is 7 . . . O–O, e.g., 8 B–Q3, P–Q3 9 Q–N3, BxN† 10 QxB, QN–Q2 11 O–O–O, Q–K2 12 N–Q2!, when White has a strong attack (Alekhine–Wheatcroft, 1938). For 7 . . . P–KN4, see Idea Var. 8.

[2] 10 . . . P–KN4 11 B–N3, N–K5 12 N–Q2, NxN 13 QxN, P–KB4 14 P–B4, Q–K2 15 QR–K1, N–B3 16 P–B5, O–O–O 17 P–K4 leads to a good game for White, as shown in Larsen–Donner, Munich 1958.

[3] 11 . . . P–K4 is well met by 12 B–K4!

[4] A difficult game with chances for both sides.

[5] 6 . . . P–B4 leads to Idea Var. 9.

[6] If 7 . . . P–B4, then 8 P–Q5!

[7] White's best chance. After 11 QR–Q1, N–K5!, Black stands well.

[8] Kotov–Reshevsky, Zurich 1953. White exercises some pressure.

[9] 11 Q–K2 may cost a Pawn after 11 . . . N–QN5 12 B–N1, PxP 13 PxP, BxN followed by 14 . . . QxP. It is questionable whether White gets enough compensation.

[10] See Game 8. Black has counterplay.

[11] White's initiative is gone (analysis by Pachman).

*Queen's Indian Defense Game 8*

*WHITE: Keres* *BLACK: Smyslov*

*Zurich 1953*

| | WHITE | BLACK | | WHITE | BLACK |
|---|---|---|---|---|---|
| 1 | P–QB4 | N–KB3 | 16 | N–K5? | NxN |
| 2 | N–QB3 | P–K3 | 17 | RxN | B–B3 |
| 3 | N–B3 | P–B4 | 18 | R–R5 | P–N3 |
| 4 | P–K3 | B–K2 | 19 | R/3–KR3 | PxP! |
| 5 | P–QN3 | O–O | 20 | RxP | P–B6 |
| 6 | B–N2 | P–QN3 | 21 | Q–QB1! | QxP |
| 7 | P–Q4 | PxP | 22 | Q–R6 | KR–Q1 |
| 8 | PxP | P–Q4 | 23 | B–B1 | B–N2 |
| 9 | B–Q3 | N–B3 | 24 | Q–N5 | Q–B3 |
| 10 | O–O | B–N2 | 25 | Q–N4 | P–B7 |
| 11 | R–B1 | R–B1 | 26 | B–K2 | R–Q5 |
| 12 | R–K1 | N–QN5 | 27 | P–B4 | R–Q8† |
| 13 | B–B1 | N–K5 | 28 | BxR | Q–Q5† |
| 14 | P–QR3 | NxN | | Resigns | |
| 15 | RxN | N–B3 | | | |

---

## part 5—**BOGO-INDIAN SYSTEM**

1 P–Q4, N–KB3
2 P–QB4, P–K3
3 N–KB3, B–N5†

Key Position 5

OBSERVATIONS ON KEY POSITION 5

The Bogo–Indian, also called the Bogo system, is an unusual opening, but by no means bad for Black. Black's leading idea is that the exchange of pieces in general cases the burden of defense. Concerning his center formation, Black reserves the choice of . . . P–Q4 or . . . P–Q3. In most cases . . . P–Q3 gets the preference, because . . . P–Q4 may cause a weakness on the Black squares in consequence of the disappearance of Black's King Bishop.

In many instances Black can still proceed with the fianchetto of his Queen Bishop. In these cases we arrive at the variations treated in Part 3.

IDEA VARIATIONS 10 AND 11:

(10) 4 B–Q2, BxB† (4 . . . Q–K2 is also good; see Prac. Var. 14) 5 QxB (stronger than 5 NxB, P–Q3! 6 P–K4, O–O 7 B–Q3, P–K4!, when 8 PxP, PxP 9 NxP, N–B3! leads to a good game for Black, e.g., 10 QN–B3, NxN 11 NxN, Q–Q5!), N–K5! (this continuation, attributed to Gligoric, appears best, but 5 . . . P–Q3 is also playable) 6 Q–B2, P–KB4 7 P–KN3, O–O 8 B–N2, P–Q3 9 O–O, Q–K2 with a satisfactory game for Black (Foltys–Gligoric, Prague 1946).

(11) 4 QN–Q2, O–O (other possibilities are 4 . . . P–QN3, transposing into Prac. Var. 7, and 4 . . . P–Q4, e.g., 5 P–K3, O–O 6 P–QR3, B–K2 with even chances) 5 P–QR3, BxN† 6 QxB, P–QN3 (transposition into the Queen's Indian is simplest for Black) 7 Q–B2, B–N2 8 B–N5, P–Q3 9 P–K3, P–KR3 10 B–R4, QN–Q2 with about equal chances.

PRACTICAL VARIATIONS 14–16:

1 P–Q4, N–KB3 2 P–QB4, P–K3 3 N–KB3, B–N5†

| | *14* | *15* | *16* |
|---|---|---|---|
| *4* | B–Q2 | – – | – – |
| | Q–K2 | BxB† | – – |
| *5* | P–KN3 | QxB | NxB |
| | N–B3[1] | P–Q4[6] | P–Q3! |
| *6* | B–N2 | N–B3 | P–KN3[8] |
| | BxB†[2] | O–O | P–QN3 |
| *7* | QNxB | P–K3 | B–N2 |
| | P–Q3 | QN–Q2 | B–N2 |
| *8* | O–O | R–B1 | O–O |
| | O–O | P–B3 | O–O |
| *9* | P–K4 | B–Q3[7] | Q–B2 |
| | P–QR4![3] | ± | Q–K2 |
| *10* | P–N3[4] | | P–K4 |
| | P–K4 | | P–B4[9] |
| *11* | P–Q5 | | = |
| | N–N1 | | |
| *12* | N–K1 | | |
| | N–R3[5] | | |
| | = | | |

*Notes to practical variations 14–16:*

[1] This has frequently occurred in practical play, but 5 . . . BxB† 6 QxB, N–K5, transposing into Idea Var. 10, is actually better.

[2] Forcing White to recapture with the Knight because after 7 QxB, N–K5 8 Q–B2, Black has the bothersome counter 8 . . . Q–N5†.

[3] This is stronger than 9 . . . P–K4. See Game 9.

[4] Or 10 P–K5, PxP 11 PxP, N–Q2 12 Q–K2, N–B4 with an even game.

[5] Black can hold his own.

[6] See also Idea Var. 10.

[7] White has the superior development.

[8] For 6 P–K4, see Idea Var. 10.

[9] The chances are even, according to Pachman.

*Queen's Indian Defense Game 9*

*WHITE: Euwe* *BLACK: Flohr*

*AVRO 1938*

| | WHITE | BLACK | | WHITE | BLACK |
|---|---|---|---|---|---|
| 1 | P–Q4 | N–KB3 | 17 | KR–K1 | B–R6 |
| 2 | P–QB4 | P–K3 | 18 | B–R1 | PxP |
| 3 | N–KB3 | B–N5† | 19 | PxP | N–B2 |
| 4 | B–Q2 | Q–K2 | 20 | N–N2 | BxN |
| 5 | P–KN3 | N–QB3 | 21 | BxB | P–R3 |
| 6 | B–N2 | BxB† | 22 | N–B1 | KR–B1 |
| 7 | QNxB | P–Q3 | 23 | N–K3 | N–R3 |
| 8 | O–O | O–O | 24 | P–B5! | PxP |
| 9 | P–K4 | P–K4 | 25 | N–B4 | Q–Q1 |
| 10 | P–Q5 | N–N1 | 26 | NxP | QNxP |
| 11 | P–QN4 | B–N5 | 27 | P–Q6 | RxR |
| 12 | Q–B2 | P–B3 | 28 | QxP† | K–R2 |
| 13 | N–R4 | PxP | 29 | RxR | QxP |
| 14 | KPxP | P–QR4 | 30 | B–K4† | K–R1 |
| 15 | P–QR3 | N–R3 | 31 | N–N6† | K–R2 |
| 16 | Q–N3 | Q–Q2 | 32 | N–K7† | Resigns |

---

## part 6—**QUEEN'S INDIAN KNIGHT'S GAME**

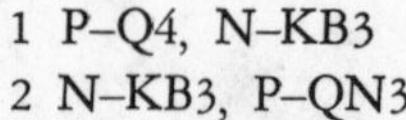

1 P–Q4, N–KB3
2 N–KB3, P–QN3

KEY POSITION 6

OBSERVATIONS ON KEY POSITION 6

Here are those variations where White omits an immediate P–QB4. This usually precludes P–Q5 in answer to . . . P–QB4. Consequently, Black's job is easier in general than in the regular Queen's Indian.

In practical play this line is rarely used. In most cases White proceeds with 3 P–QB4 and Black with 3 . . . P–K3, reverting to the usual variations. The remaining general characteristics of this position are the same as discussed previously.

IDEA VARIATIONS 12 AND 13:

(12) 3 N–B3 (rarely played, but by no means bad), B–N2 (3 . . . P–Q4 is probably better, after which Black can reply to 4 B–N5 with 4 . . . N–K5!) 4 B–N5, P–Q4 (Black does well to prevent 5 P–K4) 5 N–K5, P–K3 6 P–K3 (the Pawn sacrifice 6 P–K4, PxP 7 B–N5†, P–B3 8 B–QB4 also deserves consideration), B–K2 7 Q–B3, O–O 8 B–Q3 with good chances for White.

(13) 3 P–KN3, B–N2 4 B–N2, P–B4! 5 O–O (5 PxP, PxP 6 P–B4?, P–N3 is not commendable; see Game 10), PxP 6 NxP (6 QxP, N–B3 7 Q–KB4, P–Q4 leads to a good game for Black), BxB 7 KxB, P–N3 (7 . . . P–Q4 8 P–QB4, PxP 9 Q–R4†, Q–Q2 10 N–N5, Q–B3† is also satisfactory for Black) 8 P–QB4 (without this move White can hope for no advantage), Q–B1! (after 8 . . . B–N2 9 N–QB3, Q–B1, the reply 10 Q–Q3! is promising for White) 9 P–N3 (9 Q–Q3 now is simply answered by 9 . . . N–B3 10 P–N3, Q–N2 11 P–B3, P–Q4!), B–N2 10 N–QB3, Q–N2† 11 P–B3, P–Q4!= (Capablanca–Botvinnik, Nottingham 1936).

*Queen's Indian Defense Game 10*

*WHITE: Rubinstein* *BLACK: Nimzowitsch*

*Marienbad 1925*

| WHITE | BLACK | WHITE | BLACK |
|---|---|---|---|
| 1 P–Q4 | N–KB3 | 19 BxN | PxB |
| 2 N–KB3 | P–QN3 | 20 K–B2 | P–B4 |
| 3 P–KN3 | P–B4 | 21 QxP | B–N2 |
| 4 B–N2 | B–N2 | 22 R–QN1 | B–Q5 |
| 5 PxP | PxP | 23 K–N2 | BxN |
| 6 P–B4 | P–N3 | 24 NxB | RxN |
| 7 P–N3 | B–N2 | 25 QxP | RxP† |
| 8 B–N2 | O–O | 26 R–B2 | RxR† |
| 9 O–O | N–B3 | 27 QxR | RxP |
| 10 N–B3 | P–QR4 | 28 P–QR3 | RxP |
| 11 Q–Q2 | P–Q3 | 29 Q–K2 | R–R1 |
| 12 N–K1 | Q–Q2 | 30 P–B5 | Q–R3 |
| 13 N–B2 | N–QN5! | 31 QxQ | NxQ |
| 14 N–K3 | BxB | 32 R–R1 | N–B2 |
| 15 KxB | Q–N2† | 33 RxR† | NxR† |
| 16 P–B3 | B–R3 | White soon | |
| 17 N/B–Q1 | P–R5 | resigned | |
| 18 PxP | KR–K1 | | |

## PRACTICAL VARIATIONS 17–19:

1 P–Q4, N–KB3 2 N–KB3, P–QN3

| | *17* | *18* | *19* |
|---|---|---|---|
| 3 | P–K3 | B–B4 | B–N5 |
| | B–N2 | P–K3 | B–N2[5] |
| 4 | QN–Q2 | P–K3 | QN–Q2 |
| | P–K3 | B–N2 | P–B4! |
| 5 | B–Q3 | QN–Q2 | P–K3 |
| | P–B4 | N–R4 | P–K3[6] |
| 6 | O–O | B–N3 | = |
| | N–B3 | P–Q3 | |
| 7 | P–B3[1] | B–Q3 | |
| | B–K2 | QN–Q2 | |
| 8 | P–K4 | Q–K2 | |
| | PxP | B–K2 | |
| 9 | NxP[2] | P–B3 | |
| | O–O[3] | P–QB4[4] | |
| | = | = | |

*Notes to practical variations 17–19:*

[1] A sort of Colle system.

[2] 9 PxP is answered by 9 . . . N–QN5 10 B–N1, B–R3 11 R–K1, N–Q6∓.

[3] With sharp play.

[4] Romi–Capablanca, Paris 1938. Black has no problems.

[5] Better than 3 . . . N–K5 4 B–R4, B–N2 5 QN–Q2, NxN 6 QxN with some initiative for White (Alekhine).

[6] Black's game is relatively easy.

## SUPPLEMENTARY VARIATIONS 1-5:

1 P–Q4, N–KB3 2 P–QB4, P–K3 3 N–KB3, P–QN3

| | *1* | *2* | *3* | *4* | *5* |
|---|---|---|---|---|---|
| 4 | P–KN3 | – – | – – | P–QR3 | B–B4 |
| | B–N2 | B–R3[6] | – – | B–N2 | B–N2 |
| 5 | B–N2 | Q–R4[7] | – – | N–B3 | QN–Q2 |
| | B–K2 | B–K2[8] | – – | B–K2 | N–K5 |
| 6 | O–O | N–B3 | – – | B–B4 | P–QR3 |
| | O–O | O–O[9] | – – | P–Q4 | P–KB4 |
| 7 | P–Q5!?[1] | P–K4 | B–N2 | = | P–K3 |
| | PxP[2] | P–Q4 | P–B3 | | P–B4[15] |
| 8 | N–Q4 | BPxP | B–B4[11] | | ∓ |
| | P–B3![3] | BxB | Q–B1[12] | | |
| 9 | PxP | KxB | O–O | | |
| | NxP | PxP | P–Q4 | | |

| | 1 | 2 | 3 |
|---|---|---|---|
| 10 | BxN | P–K5 | N–K5 |
| | PxB | N–K5 | Q–N2 |
| 11 | N–QB3 | K–N2[10] | PxP[13] |
| | B–KB3 | ± | BPxP |
| 12 | N/4–N5 | | KR–B1 |
| | P–Q5![4] | | P–QN4 |
| 13 | NxQP | | Q–Q1 |
| | P–Q4[5] | | R–B1[14] |
| | = | | = |

*Notes to supplementary variations 1–5:*

[1] With this interesting move, White scored a surprising success in the game O'Kelly–Euwe, Beverwijk 1958.

[2] Other moves are hardly better.

[3] This is considered the best reply. An alternative is 8 . . . B–B3 with the following possibilities:

1) 9 NxB, PxN 10 N–B3, PxP 11 Q–R4, P–QN4 12 Q–R5 with a promising game for White. Stronger, however, is 10 . . . P–Q5! (Vukovic).
2) PxP, BxP 10 BxB, NxB 11 P–K4, N–KB3 12 P–K5, N–K1 13 Q–B3, P–QB3 14 R–Q1 with more than sufficient compensation for the Pawn. In this line if 13 . . . N–QB3, then 14 N–B5, R–N1 15 N–B3 is very strong for White.

[4] With this counter-sacrifice Black completely frees his game.

[5] Black's position certainly is not inferior.

[6] Interest in this old line of play was revived after some special Soviet researches. It offers sufficient chances.

[7] Little is achieved with other moves, e.g., 5 QN–Q2, P–B4 6 B–N2, N–B3 7 PxP, PxP 8 O–O, B–K2 9 P–N3, O–O with an even game (Nedelkovic–Bronstein, Belgrade 1954).

[8] Also interesting is 5 . . . P–B3 6 N–B3, P–QN4!? 7 PxP, PxP 8 NxP, Q–N3. Black has some compensation for the Pawn.

[9] After 6 . . . B–N2 (to prevent 7 P–K4) 7 B–N2, O–O 8 B–N5! is promising for White (Bronstein–Petrosian, Portoroz 1958).

[10] White's development is superior.

[11] For 8 N–K5?, Q–K1!, see Game 11. The text move threatens 9 BxN, winning a piece.

[12] The Pawn sacrifice 8 . . . P–QN4 9 PxP, PxP 10 NxP, N–Q4 is insufficient after 11 O–O! In this variation 10 . . . Q–N3 is answered by 11 N–B7, QxNP 12 O–O.

[13] The sharp 11 P–QN4 offers good chances.

[14] Black has sufficient counterplay.

[15] Black has the better prospects (Marchand–Euwe, Goteborg 1920).

*Queen's Indian Defense Game 11*

*WHITE: Stahlberg* *BLACK: Taimanov*

*Zurich 1953*

| | WHITE | BLACK | | WHITE | BLACK |
|---|---|---|---|---|---|
| 1 | P–Q4 | N–KB3 | 22 | NxN | PxN |
| 2 | P–QB4 | P–K3 | 23 | P–QR3 | P–R4! |
| 3 | N–KB3 | P–QN3 | 24 | P–Q5 | R/1–B5 |
| 4 | P–KN3 | B–R3 | 25 | R–Q1 | PxP |
| 5 | Q–R4 | B–K2 | 26 | B–Q2 | Q–KB3 |
| 6 | B–N2 | O–O | 27 | QR–N1 | P–R5 |
| 7 | N–QB3 | P–B3 | 28 | Q–R4 | Q–B4 |
| 8 | N–K5? | Q–K1! | 29 | QxRP | B–B1 |
| 9 | O–O | P–Q4 | 30 | Q–N8 | P–N4 |
| 10 | R–K1 | P–QN4! | 31 | PxP | PxP |
| 11 | PxNP | PxP | 32 | Q–B4 | QxQ |
| 12 | Q–Q1 | P–N5 | 33 | PxQ | P–Q5 |
| 13 | N–N1? | N–B3 | 34 | P–N3 | R–B3 |
| 14 | NxN | QxN | 35 | PxP | P–B4 |
| 15 | N–Q2 | Q–N3 | 36 | P–R3 | R–QR3 |
| 16 | P–K3 | QR–B1 | 37 | QR–B1 | RxR |
| 17 | B–B1 | R–B3 | 38 | RxR | R–R7 |
| 18 | BxB | QxB | 39 | B–K1 | R–N7 |
| 19 | N–B3 | KR–B1 | 40 | K–N2 | RxP |
| 20 | Q–N3 | N–K5 | 41 | R–B8 | R–N8 |
| 21 | N–Q2? | R–B7? | 42 | B–Q2 | P–K6 |
| | | | | Resigns | |

*Queen's Indian Defense Game 12*

*WHITE: Pomar* *BLACK: Kupper*

*Munich 1958*

| | WHITE | BLACK | | WHITE | BLACK |
|---|---|---|---|---|---|
| 1 | P–Q4 | N–KB3 | 15 | B–B4 | B–B4 |
| 2 | P–QB4 | P–K3 | 16 | N–B5 | K–R1 |
| 3 | N–KB3 | P–QN3 | 17 | P–K6 | Q–Q1 |
| 4 | P–KN3 | B–N2 | 18 | PxQP | NxP |
| 5 | B–N2 | B–K2 | 19 | QxP | N/1–B3 |
| 6 | O–O | O–O | 20 | N–B3 | Q–B1 |
| 7 | P–Q5!? | PxP | 21 | Q–B3 | Q–R3 |
| 8 | N–Q4 | B–B3 | 22 | N–Q5 | Q–N2 |
| 9 | PxP | BxP | 23 | P–QN4 | BxP |
| 10 | BxB | NxB | 24 | NxKNP | KxN |
| 11 | P–K4 | N–KB3 | 25 | B–K5 | Q–B3 |
| 12 | P–K5 | N–K1 | 26 | B–N2 | QR–K1 |
| 13 | Q–B3 | P–QB3 | 27 | Q–N4† | K–R1 |
| 14 | R–Q1 | Q–B2 | 28 | NxB | Resigns |

# Section Three: OTHER OPENINGS

# chapter 38—Bird's Opening

The opening move 1 P–KB4 is in reality an old debut with a modern character. White starts by taking control of an important center square without actually occupying the center. Tartakover had a certain predilection for this opening, which now constitutes an important part of the Danish Grandmaster Larsen's opening repertoire.

In general, however, for no obvious reason, 1 P–KB4 has never become popular. Since the Dutch Defense is resorted to fairly often, Bird's Opening, which is really the Dutch with a move in hand, can hardly be bad. Perhaps the fact that Black can adopt the From Gambit has had some deterrent influence.

---

## part 1—DUTCH DEFENSE IN REVERSE

1 P–KB4, P–Q4[A]
2 N–KB3[B], N–KB3[C]
3 P–K3[D]

KEY POSITION 1

OBSERVATIONS ON KEY POSITION 1

[A] An important alternative is the From Gambit 1 . . . P–K4. See Part 2. For other moves, see supplementary variations.

[B] White has plenty of choice. Playable is 2 P–QN3 or 2 P–KN3 or 2 P–K3. There is little theory on these systems.

[C] The most usual. As for a single alternative, there is the Dutch Stonewall in reverse: 2 . . . P–KN3 3 P–K3, B–N2 4 P–Q4, N–KB3 5 B–K2.

[D] Interesting is 3 P–KN3, aiming at a type of Leningrad system. There are few examples to the point.

The character of the struggle is quickly determined. White aims at control of the central squares of Black color. He usually augments his strategy by means of a Queenside fianchetto. He may also proceed with P–Q4, building a Stonewall formation, or P–Q3, transposing into an Old Dutch in reverse. For the two latter systems, reference must be made to the Dutch Defense.

The main line, White's anticipated fianchetto, can be met by Black in several ways; the most usual are 3 . . . B–KN5, tending to eliminate White's Knight, or 3 . . . P–KN3, preparing the neutralization of White's fianchetto.

IDEA VARIATIONS 1 AND 2:

(1) 3 . . . B–N5 4 P–KR3 (the most enterprising reaction, but 4 B–K2 is certainly just as good; see Game 2), BxN 5 QxB, QN–Q2 (threatening to obtain an excellent game by 6 . . . P–K4) 6 N–B3 (but 6 P–Q4, N–K5 7 B–Q3, P–KB4 8 O–O, P–K3 9 P–B4, P–QB3 is satisfactory for Black [Brinckmann–Kmoch, Kecskemet 1927]), P–B3 (the simplest; also playable is 6 . . . P–K3, followed

by 7 . . . B–N5) and Black has a good game, notwithstanding White's pair of Bishops.

For 3 . . . B–B4, 3 . . . P–K3, or 3 . . . P–B4 see Prac. Var. 1, 2, and 3. Game 1 illustrates 3 . . . P–B4.

(2) 3 . . . P–KN3 4 P–QN3 (as mentioned before, 4 P–Q4 and 4 P–Q3 lead to known positions of the Dutch Defense, but in reverse), B–N2 5 B–N2, O–O 6 B–K2, P–B4 7 O–O, N–B3 8 N–K5, B–Q2 (8 . . . Q–B2 leads again in reverse into known positions of the Queen's Indian Defense) 9 P–Q3, P–Q5! 10 NxN, BxN and Black has a satisfactory game (Tartakover–Pirc, Cheltenham 1951).

*Bird's Opening Game 1*

*WHITE: Tartakover* *BLACK: Spielmann*

*Vienna 1910*

| | WHITE | BLACK | | WHITE | BLACK | | WHITE | BLACK |
|---|---|---|---|---|---|---|---|---|
| 1 | P–KB4 | P–Q4 | 13 | P–B4 | P–B3 | 25 | N–K5 | Q–N4 |
| 2 | P–K3 | N–KB3 | 14 | PxP | PxP | 26 | NxB | PxN |
| 3 | N–KB3 | P–B4 | 15 | P–K4 | P–Q5 | 27 | RxP† | K–Q2 |
| 4 | P–QN3 | P–K3 | 16 | P–QN4 | P–KN4 | 28 | RxN | KxR |
| 5 | B–N2 | N–B3 | 17 | PxBP | BxP/4 | 29 | Q–N4† | K–B3 |
| 6 | B–N5 | B–Q2 | 18 | PxP | R–N1 | 30 | R–B1† | K–N2 |
| 7 | O–O | B–Q3 | 19 | QR–B1 | B–R2 | 31 | Q–K6 | KR–B1 |
| 8 | P–Q3 | Q–B2 | 20 | N–N3 | N–N2 | 32 | BxP† | RxB |
| 9 | Q–K2 | O–O–O | 21 | N–B5 | BxN | 33 | Q–K7† | K–N3 |
| 10 | QN–Q2 | P–QR3 | 22 | RxB | N–K3 | 34 | QxR | Resigns |
| 11 | BxN | BxB | 23 | R–B4 | PxP | | | |
| 12 | P–N3 | N–K1 | 24 | R/1–B1 | Q–N3 | | | |

*Bird's Opening Game 2*

*WHITE: Larsen* *BLACK: Petrosian*

*Portoroz 1958*

| | WHITE | BLACK | | WHITE | BLACK | | WHITE | BLACK |
|---|---|---|---|---|---|---|---|---|
| 1 | P–KB4 | N–KB3 | 15 | N–Q3 | B–K2 | 29 | R–R6 | R–Q6 |
| 2 | N–KB3 | P–Q4 | 16 | P–B5 | Q–Q2 | 30 | RxRP | R–K1 |
| 3 | P–K3 | B–N5 | 17 | N–R4 | N–B2 | 31 | N–N2 | P–N4 |
| 4 | B–K2 | QN–Q2 | 18 | B–N3 | B–Q3 | 32 | R–B1 | R–Q3 |
| 5 | N–K5 | BxB | 19 | BxB | QxB | 33 | P–KR4 | R/3xKP |
| 6 | QxB | P–K3 | 20 | QR–Q1 | QR–K1 | 34 | R/1–B7 | N–Q3 |
| 7 | O–O | B–Q3 | 21 | QPxP | NxP/4 | 35 | RxP | R–QB1 |
| 8 | P–Q4 | O–O | 22 | N–B4 | P–QN4 | 36 | R/KR–N7† | K–R1 |
| 9 | N–Q2 | P–B4 | 23 | Q–N2 | R–Q1 | 37 | P–R5 | N–K1 |
| 10 | P–B3 | R–B1 | 24 | P–N4 | N–K5 | 38 | R/N–KB7 | N–Q3 |
| 11 | P–KN4 | N–K1 | 25 | PxP | P–N3 | 39 | R–R7† | K–N1 |
| 12 | N/2–B3 | N/2–B3 | 26 | NxQP | NxN | 40 | P–R6 | N–K1 |
| 13 | B–Q2 | N–K5 | 27 | QxN | NxBP | 41 | R/KR–KB7 | Resigns |
| 14 | B–K1 | P–B3 | 28 | RxQ | NxQ | | | |

## PRACTICAL VARIATIONS 1–3:
1 P–KB4, P–Q4 2 N–KB3, N–KB3 3 P–K3

| | 1 | 2 | 3 |
|---|---|---|---|
| 3 | — — | — — | — — |
| | B–B4 | P–K3 | P–B4 |
| 4 | P–QN3 | P–QN3 | P–QN3[5] |
| | P–K3 | B–K2 | N–B3[6] |
| 5 | B–N2 | B–N2 | B–N5 |
| | QN–Q2 | QN–Q2 | B–Q2[7] |
| 6 | P–N3 | B–Q3 | B–N2 |
| | B–Q3 | O–O[2] | P–K3 |
| 7 | B–N2 | O–O | O–O |
| | Q–K2 | P–QN3 | B–K2[8] |
| 8 | O–O | N–B3 | P–Q3 |
| | P–K4! | B–N2 | O–O |
| 9 | PxP | N–K2 | BxN[9] |
| | NxP | N–B4![3] | BxB |
| 10 | NxN | N–N3 | N–K5[10] |
| | BxN | NxB | ± |
| 11 | P–Q4 | PxN | |
| | B–N5![1] | P–B4[4] | |
| | = | = | |

*Notes to practical variations 1–3:*

[1] Nimzowitsch–Petersen, 1928.

[2] Other good moves are 6 . . . N–K5 and 6 . . . N–B4.

[3] The famous game, Lasker–Bauer, Amsterdam 1889, continued 9 . . . P–B4 10 N–N3, Q–B2 11 N–K5, NxN 12 BxN, Q–B3 13 Q–K2, P–QR3? 14 N–R5, NxN 15 BxP†, KxB 16 QxN† K–N1 17 BxP!!, with a winning attack.

[4] Black's Bishops and less awkward Pawn structure counterbalance White's attacking chances.

[5] After 4 B–N5†, Black's best is 4 . . . B–Q2. Black is generally better off if he avoids the exchange of his Queen Knight for White's King Bishop.

[6] After this move White can carry out his plan. Best for Black is most likely 4 . . . P–KN3. See Idea Var. 2.

[7] Also plausible is 5 . . . Q–N3.

[8] For 7 . . . B–Q3, see Game 2.

[9] Otherwise Black can maintain his Knight.

[10] White has good attacking chances, as the games of Nimzowitsch often demonstrate.

---

1 P–KB4, P–K4
2 PxP[A], P–Q3[B]
3 PxP[C], BxP
4 N–KB3[D]

KEY POSITION 2

# part 2—FROM GAMBIT

## OBSERVATIONS ON KEY POSITION 2

[A] Convenient for Black is 2 P–Q3, PxP 3 BxP, P–Q4. White may transpose into the King's Gambit with 2 P–K4.

[B] Better than 2 . . . P–KB3? 3 P–K4!

[C] Here, too, White can transpose into the King's Gambit by 3 N–KB3, PxP 4 P–K4. But not 3 P–Q4?, PxP 4 PxP, QxQ† 5 KxQ, N–QB3 and Black has the better of it.

[D] The only good defense to the threat of 4 . . . Q–R5†. But 4 P–KN3 is weak because Black then initiates a strong attack by 4 . . . P–KR4!

Black has some advance in development and good attacking chances for the Pawn. He can proceed in two basically different ways, . . . N–KR3–N5 or . . . P–KN4–N5. Both lines of attack take advantage of the weakening of White's Kingside caused by the disappearance of his King Bishop Pawn. The attack leads to rather difficult positions with tactical chances for both sides.

Alertness and exactitude in calculation are required by both sides.

IDEA VARIATIONS 3 AND 4:

(3) 4 . . . N–KR3 5 P–Q4, N–N5 6 Q–Q3! P–QB4! 7 Q–K4†, B–K3 8 N–N5 (8 P–Q5 leads to nothing after 8 . . . N–KB3!; also good for Black is 8 B–N5, Q–N3!), BxP! (a new point, which actually follows From's original idea) 9 NxB, Q–R5† 10 K–Q2, PxN 11 RxB (creating great complications; for 11 QxP†, see Game 3), Q–N4† 12 K–B3, and the chances are hard to assess.

The move 4 . . . N–KR3 aims at . . . N–N5, possibly followed by . . . NxRP. From himself considered this continuation of the attack as Black's best. Yet this line has long been considered inferior because of Lipke's method of counterplay. Recently, however, improvements for Black have been found, and the assessment of the variation for the time being is an open question. From's line can also start with 4 . . . N–KB3, in which case Black has the additional option of proceeding positively by anchoring his King Knight on K5. See Prac. Var. 4.

Lipke's move, 6 Q–Q3!, has long been considered the refutation of Black's system, but the strong rejoinder 6 . . . P–QB4! was turned up in a recent investigation by Czech analysts. Faulty is 6 . . . NxRP? because of 7 Q–K4†—Lipke's point—and White wins. The alternative, 6 . . . N–QB3 7 N–B3, O–O 8 P–K4, R–K1 9 B–K2, also favors White.

(4) 4 . . . P–KN4 (Emanuel Lasker's continuation, which is most usual) 5 P–Q4, P–N5 6 N–N5!? P–KB4 7 P–K4, P–KR3 8 P–K5, B–K2 (consistent; in any event, White gets an edge upon 8 . . . PxN 9 PxB) 9 N–KR3, PxN 10 Q–R5†, K–B1 11 B–QB4, Q–K1 12 QxP/3 (Pirc–Aitken, Munich 1954). This is the game in which White's chances for attack proved excellent.

6 N–N5!? is aimed at an interesting sacrifice of a piece. This move was repeatedly and successfully adopted by Tartakover. But 6 N–K5 is weak because of 6 . . .

BxN 7 PxB, QxQ† and Black has excellent counterplay. After 6 N–N5!?, White gets the better of it, according to Alekhine, if Black plays 6 . . . Q–K2 (7 Q–Q3, P–KB4 8 P–KR3!).

*Bird's Opening Game 3*

*WHITE: Filip* *BLACK: Fichtl*

*Czechoslovakia 1958*

| WHITE | BLACK | WHITE | BLACK | WHITE | BLACK |
|---|---|---|---|---|---|
| 1 P–KB4 | P–K4 | 16 K–Q3 | NxB | 31 B–B3 | RxP |
| 2 PxP | P–Q3 | 17 NxN | QxR | 32 N–N7 | R–Q7† |
| 3 PxP | BxP | 18 R–R5 | QxRP | 33 K–B5 | R–K4 |
| 4 N–KB3 | N–KB3 | 19 PxP | Q–B2 | 34 P–N3 | P–KR4 |
| 5 P–Q4 | N–N5 | 20 P–KN4 | P–KN3 | 35 PxP | PxP |
| 6 Q–Q3 | P–QB4! | 21 R–Q5 | R–K1 | 36 N–Q6 | R–B7† |
| 7 Q–K4† | B–K3 | 22 N–K4 | Q–K2 | 37 N–B4 | R–B6 |
| 8 N–N5 | BxP | 23 B–N2 | QxQ | 38 B–R1 | R–B8 |
| 9 NxB | Q–R5† | 24 NxQ | R–K2 | 39 B–B3 | R–B6 |
| 10 K–Q2 | PxN | 25 NxP† | K–B2 | 40 K–N4 | RxB |
| 11 QxP† | K–Q1 | 26 N–R5 | R/1–K1 | 41 P–Q6† | K–B1! |
| 12 K–B3 | N–KB3 | 27 P–B6 | N–N3 | 42 NxR | R–B3 |
| 13 Q–Q6† | QN–Q2 | 28 P–K4 | NxR | 43 K–B5 | P–R5 |
| 14 RxB | Q–K8† | 29 PxN | R–K6† | 44 P–B7 | K–N2! |
| 15 B–Q2 | N–K5† | 30 K–Q4 | R–K7 | Resigns | |

PRACTICAL VARIATION 4:

1 P–KB4, P–K4 2 PxP, P–Q3 3 PxP, BxP 4 N–KB3

| 4 | 4 |
|---|---|
| 4 – – | 7 NxN |
| N–KB3 | BxN |
| 5 P–Q4[1] | 8 P–K3 |
| N–K5[2] | O–O[5] |
| 6 N–B3[3] | ± |
| B–KB4[4] | |

*Notes to practical variation 4:*

[1] After 5 P–KN3, Black's best is 5 . . . N–N5. For 5 . . . P–KR4, see Game 4.

[2] For 5 . . . N–N5, see Idea Var. 3. Worth trying is 5 . . . N–B3 6 B–N5, P–KR3 7 BxN, QxB 8 P–K4, B–N5, and Black has counterplay.

[3] 6 Q–Q3, P–KB4 gives Black a good game. 6 P–KN3 is playable for White.

[4] Now 6 . . . P–KB4 is unsatisfactory because of 7 NxN, PxN 8 B–N5!

[5] Black has some compensation for the Pawn.

### *Bird's Opening Game 4*

*WHITE: Tartakover* *BLACK: Prins*

*Zandvoort 1936*

| | WHITE | BLACK | | WHITE | BLACK |
|---|---|---|---|---|---|
| 1 | P–KB4 | P–K4 | 11 | RxB | PxR |
| 2 | PxP | P–Q3 | 12 | N–B3 | NxN |
| 3 | PxP | BxP | 13 | PxN | O–O |
| 4 | N–KB3 | N–KB3 | 14 | QxP | R–K1 |
| 5 | P–KN3 | P–KR4 | 15 | Q–Q3 | N–Q2 |
| 6 | P–Q4 | P–R5 | 16 | N–N5 | N–B3 |
| 7 | PxP | N–K5 | 17 | B–K6† | K–R1 |
| 8 | Q–Q3 | B–KB4 | 18 | N–B7† | K–N1 |
| 9 | B–R3 | B–N3 | 19 | B–N3! | K–B1 |
| 10 | R–N1! | Q–K2 | 20 | N–R8! | Resigns |

SUPPLEMENTARY VARIATIONS 1–4:

| | *1* | *2* | *3* | *4* |
|---|---|---|---|---|
| *1* | – – | – – | – – | – – |
| | P–KB4[1] | P–K3[4] | P–QB4 | N–KB3 |
| *2* | P–K4 | N–KB3 | N–KB3 | P–K3 |
| | PxP | P–KB4 | P–KN3 | P–KN3 |
| *3* | P–Q3 | P–K4 | P–K3 | P–QN3 |
| | PxP[2] | P–Q4 | B–N2 | B–N2 |
| *4* | BxP | PxBP | P–Q4 | B–N2 |
| | N–KB3 | PxP | PxP | P–Q3 |
| *5* | N–KB3 | P–Q4 | PxP | Q–B1 |
| | P–K3 | N–KB3[5] | P–Q3 | O–O |
| *6* | N–B3[3] | = | B–Q3 | N–KB3 |
| | ± | | Q–N3 | B–N5 |
| *7* | | | P–B3 | B–K2 |
| | | | N–KR3 | N–B3 |
| *8* | | | O–O | O–O |
| | | | O–O | P–K4 |
| *9* | | | K–R1[6] | PxP |
| | | | B–B4[7] | NxP[8] |
| | | | = | = |

*Notes to supplementary variations 1–4:*

[1] Neither usual nor commendable.

[2] Worthy of consideration is 3 . . . P–Q4.

[3] White has good attacking chances.

[4] This move has little independent significance as have Sup. Var. 3 and 4.

[5] Pure symmetry, with the first move of little importance.

[6] Also deserving consideration is 9 N–R3.

[7] Black has no structural weakness and fair prospects.

[8] Nimzowitsch–Euwe, Karlsbad 1929.

# chapter 39—English Opening

The English Opening comprises those lines which arise from 1 P–QB4, N–KB3. Transposition into the King's Indian or Nimzo–Indian is possible at many points. Also, Black may play P–K4, transposing into the Sicilian in reverse, or Sicilian Attack. The latter is discussed in a separate chapter.

The subsidiary variations of the English occur but rarely and consequently have not been profoundly investigated.

---

## part 1—SICILIAN VARIATION

1 P–QB4, N–KB3
2 N–QB3[A], P–K3[B]
3 P–K4[C], P–B4[D]

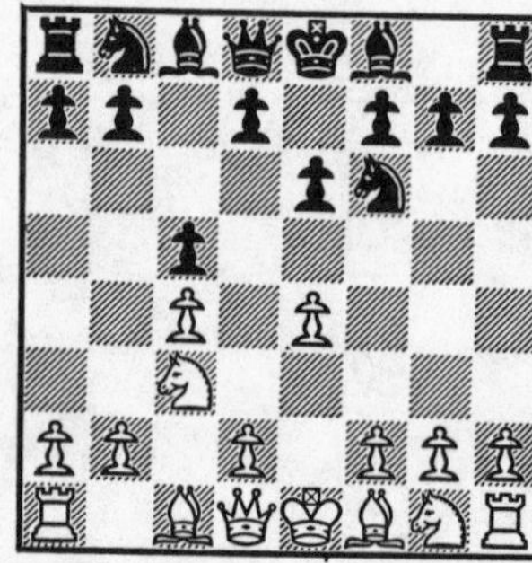

KEY POSITION 1

### OBSERVATIONS ON KEY POSITION 1

[A] Most usual. 2 P–KN3 and 2 N–KB3 also deserve consideration.

[B] For the important alternative 2 . . . P–Q4 see Part 2. Other possibilities for Black's second move are treated in Sup. Var. 2–4.

[C] The characteristic move 3 P–Q4 establishes the Nimzo–Indian Defense.

[D] Supposedly Black's best. For 3 . . . P–Q4 see Sup. Var. 1.

The struggle for the center is in full swing. Both White and Black generally aim at P–Q4. However, the immediate 4 P–Q4 is poor because of 4 . . . PxP 5 QxP, N–B3 and Black has the initiative. White therefore must proceed in a more subtle manner. Black may easily get the worst of it if he plays too passively; but by proceeding carefully and actively, he gets excellent chances for equality.

### IDEA VARIATIONS 1 AND 2:

(1) 4 P–K5 (the sharpest; White dislodges the Knight, but his advanced Pawn becomes vulnerable), N–N1 5 P–Q4 (for 5 P–B4, see Prac. Var. 2), PxP 6 QxP, N–QB3 7 Q–K4, P–Q3 (speculative is 7 . . . P–B4 8 Q–K2, KN–K2 9 P–B4; see Game 1) 8 N–B3, Q–R4! (this move, suggested by Kan, leads comfortably to equality) 9 PxP, N–B3 10 Q–B4, Q–N5 and Black recovers the Pawn safely.

(2) 4 P–KN3 (this move calls for an accurate defense; for 4 N–B3 see Prac. Var. 1), N–B3 (better than 4 . . . P–Q4 5 BPxP, PxP 6 P–K5 and White has the edge) 5 B–N2, P–Q4! (this move involves the sacrifice of a Pawn; with other moves, however, Black has difficulty with his development) 6 KPxP, PxP 7 PxP (if 7 NxP, NxN 8 PxN, N–N5, with consequences similar to the main line), N–QN5 and Black has sufficient compensation for the Pawn, more so in view of the vulnerability of White's Pawn on Q5.

*English Opening Game 1*

*WHITE: Aronin* *BLACK: Smyslov*

*USSR Championship 1950*

| WHITE | BLACK | WHITE | BLACK |
|---|---|---|---|
| 1 P–QB4 | P–K3 | 30 B–N5 | R–B4 |
| 2 N–QB3 | N–KB3 | 31 BxP | K–K2 |
| 3 P–K4 | P–B4 | 32 B–K3 | QxB |
| 4 P–K5 | N–N1 | 33 QxQ† | KxQ |
| 5 P–Q4 | PxP | 34 P–R3 | BxP |
| 6 QxP | N–QB3 | 35 PxB | R–B6 |
| 7 Q–K4 | P–B4 | 36 B–B1 | R–N6 |
| 8 Q–K2 | KN–K2 | 37 P–R6 | PxP |
| 9 N–B3 | N–N3 | 38 R–R1 | R–N3 |
| 10 B–Q2 | P–QR3 | 39 R–R2 | BxP |
| 11 O–O–O | Q–B2 | 40 B–Q2 | P–R5 |
| 12 R–K1 | B–B4 | 41 B–N4 | B–B6 |
| 13 P–KR4 | N–Q5 | 42 K–B2 | P–R4 |
| 14 NxN | BxN | 43 R–R3 | R–N7† |
| 15 P–B4 | P–N4 | 44 K–B3 | R–B7 |
| 16 P–R5 | N–K2 | 45 K–Q4 | B–N5 |
| 17 Q–Q3 | B–B7 | 46 R–Q3 | K–B3 |
| 18 R–Q1 | B–N2 | 47 K–B3 | K–N4 |
| 19 Q–Q6 | Q–B1 | 48 R–Q6 | R–B6† |
| 20 R–R3 | B–B4 | 49 K–Q2 | RxBP |
| 21 Q–Q3 | PxP | 50 RxP | R–K5 |
| 22 QxQBP | N–Q4 | 51 K–Q3 | P–R5 |
| 23 NxN | BxN | 52 R–K7 | P–R3 |
| 24 Q–B2 | Q–N2 | 53 B–Q6 | P–R6 |
| 25 K–N1 | QR–B1 | 54 P–K6 | B–K7† |
| 26 R–QB3 | K–B2 | 55 K–Q2 | B–B5 |
| 27 B–B1 | B–N5 | 56 R–KR7 | R–Q5† |
| 28 RxR | RxR | Resigns | |
| 29 Q–R4 | P–R4 | | |

PRACTICAL VARIATIONS 1 AND 2:

1 P–QB4, N–KB3 2 N–QB3, P–K3 3 P–K4, P–B4

| | 1 | 2 |
|---|---|---|
| 4 | N–B3[1] | P–K5 |
| | N–B3 | N–N1 |
| 5 | P–Q4 | P–B4 |
| | PxP | N–QB3[5] |
| 6 | NxP | N–B3 |
| | B–N5 | P–Q3 |
| 7 | NxN[2] | PxP |
| | QPxN! | BxP |
| 8 | QxQ† | P–Q4 |
| | KxQ | N–B3![6] |
| 9 | P–B3[3] | PxP |
| | P–K4 | BxQBP |
| 10 | B–Q2 | QxQ† |
| | P–QR4 | KxQ[7] |
| 11 | O–O–O | = |
| | K–B2[4] | |
| | = | |

*Notes to practical variations 1 and 2:*

[1] A solid continuation which has, however, little promise for White.

[2] 7 P–B3?, P–Q4 favors Black. Or 7 Q–Q3, P–Q4 8 KPxP, PxP 9 B–N5, Q–K2† is satisfactory for Black.

[3] Or 9 P–K5, N–Q2! 10 B–B4, BxN† 11 PxB, P–QB4 and Black stands better. Or 9 B–N5, BxN† 10 PxB, P–KR3 11 BxN†, PxB 12 O–O–O†, K–K2 and Black has the edge.

[4] Black enjoys reasonably easy development.

[5] Also sufficient is 5 . . . P–Q3 6 PxP, BxP 7 P–Q4!, PxP 8 N–N5, B–N5†.

[6] Stronger than 8 . . . PxP 9 NxP, N–B3 10 N/4–N5, B–N1 11 QxQ†, KxQ 12 B–K3 with advantage for White.

[7] Black has the easier game.

---

## part 2—EXCHANGE VARIATION

1 P–QB4, N–KB3
2 N–QB3, P–Q4[A]
3 PxP, NxP
4 P–KN3[B]

Key Position 2

OBSERVATIONS ON KEY POSITION 2

[A] This method gained popularity after the Botvinnik–Smyslov match in 1958.

[B] Here 4 P–K4 has a surprising drawback: 4 . . . N–N5 5 B–B4, B–K3 6 BxB, PxB 7 KN–K2, N–Q6†. For 4 N–B3 see Sup. Var. 3.

Black must now decide whether or not to exchange his Knight. Recent experience has shown that he is better off after the exchange, the game then assuming a character similar to the Exchange Variation in the Grunfeld Defense. This method, adopted in the Botvinnik–Smyslov match, 1958, in most cases led to satisfactory games for Black.

IDEA VARIATIONS 3 AND 4:

(3) 4 . . . P–QB4 5 B–N2, N–B2 (here 5 . . . NxN is

possible, but after 6 NPxN, P–KN3 is dubious because of 7 Q–R4† and Black has some difficulties; however, in the above line Black may try 6 . . . P–K3) 6 P–Q3 (more to the point than 6 N–B3, N–B3 7 P–N3, P–K4 8 B–N2, B–K2 9 R–QB1, P–B3! and Black stands well), P–K4 (less commendable is 6 . .. N–B3? 7 BxN†!, PxB 8 Q–R4 and White has the better game) 7 P–B4 (White has good chances [Filip–Ragosin, Prague 1956]).

(4) 4 . . . NxN 5 NPxN, P–KN3 6 B–KN2, B–N2 (this move had long been considered inferior, but the old assessment has been revised in view of some of the games of the 1958 Botvinnik–Smyslov match) 7 B–QR3 (played by Botvinnik in the 10th game of his match with Smyslov; in later games he showed preference for 7 R–QN1 and 7 Q–N3. See Prac. Var. 3 and 4. N–Q2 8 N–B3, P–QB4 9 Q–R4 (to ward off 9 . . . Q–R4), O–O 10 R–QN1, P–QR3 11 P–B4 with chances for both sides.

PRACTICAL VARIATIONS 3 AND 4:

1 P–QB4, N–KB3 2 N–QB3, P–Q4 3 PxP, NxP 4 P–KN3

| | 3 | 4 |
|---|---|---|
| 4 | – – | – – |
| | NxN | – – |
| 5 | NPxN | – – |
| | P–KN3 | – – |
| 6 | B–KN2 | – – |
| | B–N2 | – – |
| 7 | R–QN1 | Q–N3 |
| | N–Q2[1] | N–B3![4] |
| 8 | P–QB4[2] | N–B3 |
| | O–O | O–O |
| 9 | N–B3 | O–O |
| | R–N1[3] | N–R4[5] |
| | = | = |

*Notes to practical variations 3 and 4:*

[1] In order to meet 8 BxP with 8 . . . BxB 9 RxB, N–N3!

[2] In a later game Botvinnik played 8 N–B3 and after 8 . . . O–O 9 O–O, P–K4 10 P–Q4! obtained an edge.

[3] With approximately equal chances, although White's position is easier to manage.

[4] A substantial improvement. The continuation 8 BxN†, PxB is not unfavorable for Black.

[5] Again equal. But Black's Knight does not obstruct the development of his other men.

## SUPPLEMENTARY VARIATIONS 1–4:
### 1 P–QB4, N–KB3 2 N–QB3

| | *1* | *2* | *3* | *4* |
|---|---|---|---|---|
| *2* | – – | – – | – – | – – |
| | P–K3 | P–B3 | P–B4 | – – |
| *3* | P–K4 | P–K4 | N–B3 | – – |
| | P–Q4 | P–Q4[5] | P–Q4 | P–K3 |
| *4* | P–K5 | P–K5 | PxP | P–KN3 |
| | P–Q5[1] | P–Q5! | NxP | P–QN3 |
| *5* | PxN | PxN | P–K4[7] | B–N2 |
| | PxN | PxN | N–N5[8] | B–N2 |
| *6* | NPxP | NPxP | B–B4 | O–O |
| | QxP | KPxP | N–Q6†[9] | B–K2 |
| *7* | P–Q4 | P–Q4 | K–K2 | P–Q4 |
| | P–QN3[2] | B–Q3 | N–B5†[10] | PxP |
| *8* | N–B3 | B–Q3 | K–B1 | QxP |
| | B–N2 | O–O[6] | N–K3[11] | N–B3[12] |
| *9* | B–K2 | = | ± | Q–B4 |
| | QN–Q2[3] | | | O–O |
| *10* | O–O | | | R–Q1 |
| | P–KR3[4] | | | Q–N1 |
| *11* | = | | | QxQ |
| | | | | QRxQ |
| *12* | | | | B–B4 |
| | | | | QR–B1 |
| *13* | | | | N–K5[13] |
| | | | | ± |

*Notes to supplementary variations 1–4:*

[1] Also sufficient is 4 . . . KN–Q2.

[2] Worth consideration is 7 . . . P–B4 8 N–B3, P–KR3 9 B–K2, PxP 10 PxP, B–N5† with only a tiny edge for White.

[3] Or 9 . . . P–KR3 10 N–K5, B–Q3 11 Q–R4†, K–K2! with equality.

[4] White enjoys a minimal initiative.

[5] Also playable is 3 . . . P–K4 4 N–B3, B–N5.

[6] Chances are equal. But the unbalanced Pawn structure leads to a struggle.

[7] Introduced by Nimzowitsch. Alternatives are 5 P–KN3 and 5 P–K3, in both cases favoring White.

[8] A dubious line for Black is 5 . . . NxN 6 NPxN, P–KN3 7 Q–R4†.

[9] Not good for Black is 6 . . . B–K3 7 BxB, PxB 8 O–O, QN–B3 9 N–N5. In the above line Black may vary with 7 . . . N–Q6† 8 K–B1, PxB 9 N–N5 and White has a slight margin.

[10] The safest. 7 . . . NxB† leads to complications.

[11] White's advantage is in development which requires sharp play to exploit.

[12] This win of a tempo could better be postponed in this manner: 8 . . . O–O 9 R–Q1, Q–B1 10 B–B4, R–Q1 11 QR–B1, N–B3 12 Q–Q3, P–Q4 and Black has achieved equality.

[13] White has a tiny edge.

*English Opening Game 2*

*WHITE: Van der Hoek* *BLACK: Euwe*

*The Hague 1942*

| | WHITE | BLACK | | WHITE | BLACK | | WHITE | BLACK |
|---|---|---|---|---|---|---|---|---|
| 1 | P–QB4 | N–KB3 | 10 | P–Q3 | Q–K3 | 19 | PxB | R–Q7 |
| 2 | P–KN3 | P–B3 | 11 | P–Q4 | O–O | 20 | Q–KB4 | QR–Q1 |
| 3 | B–N2 | P–Q4 | 12 | P–K4 | Q–K2 | 21 | P–N4 | B–Q3 |
| 4 | P–N3? | PxP | 13 | R–N1 | PxP | 22 | Q–N5 | RxB |
| 5 | PxP | Q–Q5 | 14 | NxP | N–N3 | 23 | RxR | Q–K4 |
| 6 | N–QB3 | QxP | 15 | Q–N3 | B–QB4 | 24 | KR–N1 | QxP† |
| 7 | N–B3 | QN–Q2 | 16 | N–R4 | NxN | 25 | K–B1 | B–B5 |
| 8 | O–O | P–K4 | 17 | QxN | R–Q1 | | Resigns | |
| 9 | B–N2 | B–Q3 | 18 | N–B5 | BxN | | | |

*English Opening Game 3*

*WHITE: Petrosian* *BLACK: Szabo*

*Zurich 1953*

| | WHITE | BLACK | | WHITE | BLACK | | WHITE | BLACK |
|---|---|---|---|---|---|---|---|---|
| 1 | P–QB4 | N–KB3 | 15 | N–Q2 | P–B4 | 29 | Q–KN2 | NxBP |
| 2 | N–QB3 | P–B4 | 16 | N–N3 | QR–B1 | 30 | PxN | RxP |
| 3 | N–B3 | P–Q4 | 17 | BxNP | R–QB2 | 31 | QxR | QxKP† |
| 4 | PxP | NxP | 18 | B–N2 | P–B5 | 32 | Q–K2 | QxR† |
| 5 | P–KN3 | NxN | 19 | B–QB1 | B–QB3 | 33 | Q–B1 | Q–R7 |
| 6 | NPxN | P–KN3 | 20 | BxB | RxB | 34 | B–K3 | QxP† |
| 7 | Q–R4† | N–Q2 | 21 | N–Q2 | PxP | 35 | Q–B2 | Q–R6 |
| 8 | P–R4 | P–KR3 | 22 | PxP | N–B1 | 36 | K–Q2 | P–K5 |
| 9 | QR–N1 | B–N2 | 23 | R–N8 | N–Q3 | 37 | N–B6† | K–R1 |
| 10 | B–KN2 | O–O | 24 | RxR† | QxR | 38 | NxKP | Q–K3 |
| 11 | P–B4 | P–K4 | 25 | P–K4 | Q–B1 | 39 | K–Q3 | Q–Q2† |
| 12 | P–Q3 | N–N3 | 26 | N–B1 | P–KR4 | 40 | K–K2 | Q–K3 |
| 13 | Q–B2 | B–Q2 | 27 | N–K3 | R–R3 | 41 | N–Q2 | Resigns |
| 14 | B–K3 | Q–K2 | 28 | N–Q5 | Q–N5 | | | |

*English Opening Game 4*

*WHITE: Keres* *BLACK: Fine*

*USA–USSR, Moscow 1944*

| | WHITE | BLACK | | WHITE | BLACK | | WHITE | BLACK |
|---|---|---|---|---|---|---|---|---|
| 1 | P–QB4 | P–QB4 | 12 | P–B4 | P–K4 | 23 | Q–KR3 | N–B3 |
| 2 | N–KB3 | N–KB3 | 13 | QR–Q1 | KPxP | 24 | B–B4 | QR–B1 |
| 3 | N–B3 | P–Q4 | 14 | PxP | P–N3 | 25 | NxBP! | Q–Q2 |
| 4 | PxP | NxP | 15 | P–Q5 | B–N2 | 26 | QxQ | NxQ |
| 5 | P–K3 | NxN | 16 | Q–N3 | QR–N1 | 27 | N–Q6 | QR–Q1 |
| 6 | NPxN | P–KN3 | 17 | B–B1 | P–QN4 | 28 | B–K3 | N–N3 |
| 7 | Q–R4† | N–Q2 | 18 | PxP | PxP | 29 | BxP | N–R5 |
| 8 | B–R3 | Q–B2 | 19 | BxP | B–QR3 | 30 | B–R3 | N–B6 |
| 9 | B–K2 | B–N2 | 20 | P–QR4 | BxB | 31 | N–N7 | NxR |
| 10 | O–O | O–O | 21 | PxB | Q–N2 | 32 | NxR | Resigns |
| 11 | P–Q4 | P–QR3 | 22 | N–N5 | QxNP | | | |

# chapter 40—Indian In Reverse

The Indian in Reverse finds itself today at the peak of its popularity. This opening, offering White numerous chances for favorable transposition into other lines, has been adopted on important occasions by nearly every leading modern master.

In this section only the independent variations arising from 1 N–KB3, P–Q4 are treated. Much of the further course of the game depends upon Black. Several good continuations are at his disposal; his choice is a matter of personal preference.

Reti and Nimzowitsch both championed the Indian in Reverse. By adopting with White a set-up originally designed for Black, they hoped to make their extra tempo tell. Certainly not bad strategy, but, in spite of this, White's chances in this kind of opening must not be overestimated. If Black proceeds with caution, he faces few problems.

---

## part 1—WING GAMBIT ACCEPTED

1 N–KB3, P–Q4
2 P–B4[A], PxP

KEY POSITION 1

### OBSERVATIONS ON KEY POSITION 1

[A] For the important alternative, 2 P–KN3, see Part 5.

With his last move Black abandons the center. It is his idea to make his opponent lose some time in the recovery of the Pawn, while he, in the meantime, proceeds with his development. For Black to obtain equality in the center, he usually must play for . . . P–QB4. The relationship of this system to the Queen's Gambit Accepted is very clear. With proper play, Black obtains a level game.

IDEA VARIATIONS 1 AND 2:

(1) 3 P–K3, P–QB4 4 BxP, N–KB3 5 O–O, P–QR3 6 P–QN3 (6 P–Q4, P–K3 leads to the Queen's Gambit Accepted), P–K3 (for 6 . . . P–QN4, see Game 1) 7 B–N2, N–B3 8 P–QR4, B–K2 9 N–K5, N–QR4! with approximately even chances (Keres–Fine, Zandvoort 1936).

3 P–K3 is most usual. (The continuation 3 Q–R4† leads to the Mannheim Variation of the Queen's Gambit Accepted or to variations of the Catalan Accepted.) Worthy of consideration is 3 . . . N–QB3. After BxP, P–K4 5 Q–N3, N–R3 6 P–Q4, P–K5, Black can hold his own. The continuation 3 . . . P–QN4 4 P–QR4, P–QB3 5 PxP, PxP 6 P–QN3, P–QR4 leads to a game similar in spirit to the Noteboom Variation of the Semi-Slav.

(2) 3 N–R3, P–QB4 4 NxP, N–QB3 5 P–QN3, P–K4! (the Pawn is immune: 6 N/4xP, NxN 7 NxN, Q–Q5, and Black wins) 6 B–N2, P–B3 7 P–N3, KN–K2 8 B–N2, N–Q4 (Alekhine recommended 8 . . . N–B4) 9 O–O, B–K2 10 N–R4, O–O, and Black has a satisfactory game. See Game 2.

3 N–R3 is White's best chance, according to Alekhine; his opinion notwithstanding, the line is seldom seen today: 3 . . . P–QB4 is the correct reply. For alternatives, see Prac. Var. 1 and 2.

*Indian in Reverse Game 1*

*WHITE: Keres* *BLACK: Euwe*

*Twelfth Match Game 1940*

| WHITE | BLACK | WHITE | BLACK |
|---|---|---|---|
| 1 N–KB3 | P–Q4 | 13 P–Q4! | P–K3 |
| 2 P–B4 | PxP | 14 PxP! | BxP |
| 3 P–K3 | P–QB4 | 15 N–Q4! | BxN |
| 4 BxP | N–KB3 | 16 QxB! | Q–N2? |
| 5 O–O | P–QR3 | 17 Q–N4! | N–Q4 |
| 6 P–QN3 | P–QN4?! | 18 Q–Q6 | N–K2 |
| 7 B–K2 | B–N2 | 19 R–B1 | P–N5 |
| 8 B–N2 | QN–Q2 | 20 N–B4 | N–KB4 |
| 9 P–QR4 | Q–N3? | 21 Q–B4 | BxP |
| 10 PxP | PxP | 22 N–Q6† | NxN |
| 11 RxR† | BxR | 23 QxN | Resigns |
| 12 N–R3 | B–B3 | | |

## PRACTICAL VARIATIONS 1 AND 2:

1 N–KB3, P–Q4 2 P–B4, PxP

| | *1* | *2* |
|---|---|---|
| *3* | N–R3 | N–R3 |
| | N–KB3 | P–K4[2] |
| *4* | NxP | NxKP |
| | P–K3 | BxN |
| *5* | P–KN3 | Q–R4†[3] |
| | QN–Q2 | P–QN4[4] |
| *6* | B–N2 | QxB[5] |
| | N–N3 | B–N2 |
| *7* | P–N3![1] | P–K3[6] |
| | ± | Q–Q3 |
| *8* | | QxQ |
| | | PxQ |
| *9* | | N–B3 |
| | | N–QB3 |
| *10* | | P–QN3! |
| | | P–Q4 |
| *11* | | PxP |
| | | NPxP[7] |
| *12* | | P–Q3![8] |
| | | ± |

*Notes to practical variations 1 and 2:*

[1] Alekhine's move, which leads to an advantage for White. Less clear is 7 O–O, NxN 8 Q–R4†, B–Q2! 9 QxN, B–B3.

[2] After 3 . . . P–QR3 4 NxP, P–QN4 5 N–K3, B–N2 6 P–KN3, P–K3 7 B–N2, N–KB3 8 O–O, QN–Q2 9 P–Q3, B–Q3 10 B–Q2, O–O 11 P–QR4!, White has a slight edge.

[3] But not 5 PxB, as 5 . . . Q–Q5 wins for Black.

[4] The point of Black's strategy.

[5] 6 QxP†?, P–B3 costs White a piece.

[6] 7 P–Q3 deserves consideration.

[7] If 11 . . . QPxP, then 12 P–QR4! is promising for White.

[8] White has the edge. 12 . . . N–N5? fails against 13 R–QN1!

### *Indian in Reverse Game 2*

*WHITE: Botvinnik* — *BLACK: Fine*

*Nottingham 1936*

| WHITE | BLACK | WHITE | BLACK |
|---|---|---|---|
| 1 N–KB3 | P–Q4 | 8 B–N2 | N–Q4 |
| 2 P–B4 | PxP | 9 O–O | B–K2 |
| 3 N–R3 | P–QB4 | 10 N–R4 | O–O |
| 4 NxP | N–QB3 | 11 Q–N1! | R–B2 |
| 5 P–QN3 | P–B3 | 12 N–B5 | B–K3! |
| 6 B–N2 | P–K4 | 13 P–B4 | PxP |
| 7 P–N3 | KN–K2 | 14 PxP | N–N3 |

| WHITE | BLACK | WHITE | BLACK |
|---|---|---|---|
| 15 B–K4 | BxN | 26 P–QR3 | R/2–Q2 |
| 16 PxB | NxP | 27 K–N2 | P–QN3 |
| 17 B–QB3! | N–Q5! | 28 K–B3 | N–B2 |
| 18 NxN | PxN | 29 K–K3 | N–R3 |
| 19 BxP† | K–B1! | 30 R–QB3 | N–B4 |
| 20 B–N4 | P–Q6!! | 31 R–KB2 | R–Q5 |
| 21 BxB† | RxB | 32 P–B5 | R–R5 |
| 22 QxQP | QxQ | 33 R–N2 | R/5–Q5 |
| 23 PxQ | N–N3 | 34 R–KB2 | R–R5 |
| 24 B–K4 | R–Q1 | 35 R–N2 | R/5–Q5 |
| 25 QR–B1 | N–Q4 | Draw | |

## part 2—WING-ORTHODOX DEFENSE

1 N–KB3, P–Q4
2 P–QB4, P–K3
3 P–KN3A, N–KB3B
4 B–N2

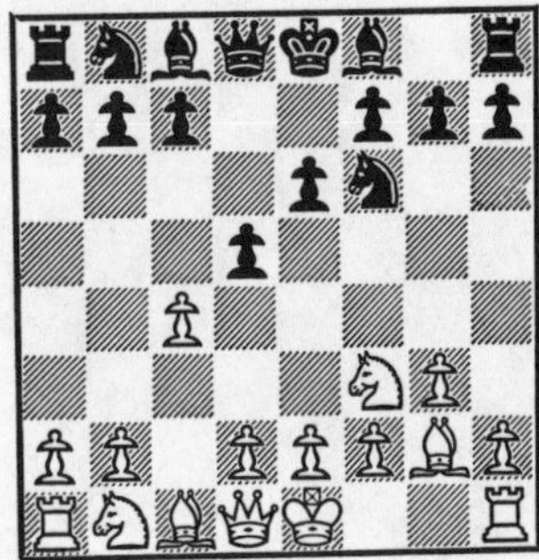

KEY POSITION 2

### OBSERVATIONS ON KEY POSITION 2

A For 3 P–Q4, see the Queen's Gambit.

B The immediate 3 . . . PxP is best met by 4 B–N2. Of less promise is 4 Q–R4† because of 4 . . . B–Q2 5 QxBP, P–B4 6 N–K5, N–QB3. 3 . . . P–Q5 is not commendable, for after 4 P–Q3, N–KB3 5 B–N2, P–B4 6 P–K4!, White has a fine game.

Black is confronted in this position with the same problem he faces in the Orthodox Defense to the Queen's Gambit: how to develop his Queen Bishop. As in the Queen's Gambit, several solutions present themselves.

White does well to bear in mind the possibility of favorably transposing into the Catalan system if the opportunity presents itself.

### IDEA VARIATIONS 3 AND 4:

(3) 4 . . . PxP (except for 4 . . . B–K2, Black's most important line; for alternatives, see Prac. Var. 3 and 4) 5 Q–R4† (no stronger, if as strong, is 5 O–O, which leads only to equality after 5 . . . QN–Q2 6 N–R3, N–N3! 7 NxP, NxN 8 Q–R4†, B–Q2 9 QxN, B–B3), QN–Q2 (after 5 . . . B–Q2 6 QxBP, B–B3 7 O–O, White has a slight advantage, but Black may try Kevitz's line, 5 . . . B–Q2 6 QxBP, N–B3, and now, if 7 P–Q4, then 7 . . . N–QR4, intending 8 . . . R–B1 or 8 . . . P–B4 and a subsequent Queen-side Pawn storm. For 5 . . . Q–Q2, see Game 3) 6 O–O, P–QR3 (also good is 6 . . . P–B4 7 QxBP, P–QR3, after which White obtains but a minimal edge) 7 QxBP, P–QN4 8 Q–B2, B–N2 9 P–QR4, and White has a slight advantage in space (Smyslov–Szily, Budapest 1952).

(4) 4 . . . B–K2 5 O–O, O–O 6 P–N3 (the plausible 6 Q–B2 rather favors Black after 6 . . . P–B4! 7 P–Q3, N–QB3), P–B4 (most natural; for 6 . . . P–Q5, see Game 4) 7 PxP (at this point it is wise to anticipate 7 . . . P–Q5), NxP (7 . . . PxP 8 P–Q4 transposes into the Tarrasch Defense) 8 B–N2, N–QB3 9 P–Q4 (the artificial 9 N–R3 leads to a good game for Black after 9 . . . B–B3 10 BxB, NxB, while 9 N–B3 offers about even chances), P–QN3 10 N–B3, NxN 11 BxN, B–N2 12 PxP, BxP. The chances are equal.

PRACTICAL VARIATIONS 3 AND 4:

1 N–KB3, P–Q4 2 P–B4, P–K3 3 P–KN3, N–KB3 4 B–N2

| | *3* | *4* |
|---|---|---|
| *4* | – – | – – |
| | P–QB4 | P–Q5 |
| *5* | PxP | P–QN4! |
| | NxP[1] | P–B4[6] |
| *6* | O–O | B–N2 |
| | QN–B3 | Q–N3[7] |
| *7* | P–Q4 | Q–N3 |
| | N–B3[2] | N–B3 |
| *8* | N–K5![3] | P–N5 |
| | B–Q2[4] | N–QR4[8] |
| *9* | NxN | Q–B2 |
| | BxN | B–Q3 |
| *10* | BxB† | P–K3[9] |
| | PxB | ± |
| *11* | Q–R4[5] | |
| | ± | |

*Notes to practical variations 3 and 4:*

[1] 5 . . . PxP, leading to the Tarrasch Defense, is preferable.

[2] 7 . . . B–K2 8 PxP, BxP 9 Q–B2 also favors White.

[3] 8 B–K3 is met with 8 . . . N–KN5.

[4] 8 . . . NxN 9 PxN gives White the advantage.

[5] White has a substantial superiority insofar as Black's Pawn formation constitutes a permanent weakness.

[6] 5 . . . BxP? 6 Q–R4†, N–B3 7 N–K5 gives White a winning advantage.

[7] 6 . . . N–B3 is worth trying, but after 7 P–N5, N–K2, White still maintains a strong initiative.

[8] After 8 . . . N–K2 9 P–K3, N–B4 10 B–KR3!, White also has the edge.

[9] Kotov–Taimanov, Zurich 1953.

*Indian in Reverse Game 3*

*WHITE: Botvinnik* *BLACK: Gereben*

*Budapest 1952*

| | WHITE | BLACK | | WHITE | BLACK | | WHITE | BLACK |
|---|---|---|---|---|---|---|---|---|
| 1 | P–QB4 | P–K3 | 15 | O–O | P–R5 | 29 | N–N4 | R–R4 |
| 2 | N–KB3 | N–KB3 | 16 | N–B1 | B–Q1 | 30 | R–N3 | B–Q2 |
| 3 | P–KN3 | P–Q4 | 17 | N–Q3 | B–K2 | 31 | N–Q3 | R–Q1 |
| 4 | B–N2 | PxP | 18 | BxB | KxB | 32 | N–K5 | B–K1 |
| 5 | Q–R4† | Q–Q2 | 19 | P–B5! | N–Q4 | 33 | P–KR3 | P–R4 |
| 6 | QxBP | Q–B3 | 20 | N/B–K5 | N–B6 | 34 | K–B2 | R–R3 |
| 7 | P–QN3 | QxQ | 21 | B–B3 | P–B3 | 35 | B–B3 | R–R4 |
| 8 | PxQ | QN–Q2 | 22 | N–QB4 | N–N4 | 36 | R–KN1 | P–N3 |
| 9 | N–B3 | B–N5 | 23 | P–K3 | K–Q1 | 37 | P–N4! | RPxP |
| 10 | N–QN5 | B–R4 | 24 | KR–B1 | P–R6 | 38 | PxP | PxP |
| 11 | B–QR3 | P–QR3 | 25 | B–N2 | K–B2 | 39 | NxP/4 | NxN† |
| 12 | N/5–Q4 | B–N3 | 26 | P–B4 | P–B4 | 40 | RxN/4 | B–B2 |
| 13 | N–N3 | P–B3 | 27 | QR–N1 | N–B3 | 41 | N–B4 | R–R5 |
| 14 | P–Q4 | P–QR4 | 28 | N–N6 | R–R3 | 42 | N–K5 | Resigns |

*Indian in Reverse Game 4*

*WHITE: Botvinnik* *BLACK: Stahlberg*

*Amsterdam 1954*

| | WHITE | BLACK | | WHITE | BLACK | | WHITE | BLACK |
|---|---|---|---|---|---|---|---|---|
| 1 | P–QB4 | P–K3 | 18 | P–Q4! | Q–B1 | 35 | P–QN4! | N–Q6 |
| 2 | P–KN3 | P–Q4 | 19 | N–Q2 | P–B4 | 36 | P–B5! | NxNP |
| 3 | B–N2 | N–KB3 | 20 | N–K4 | BxP | 37 | P–B6 | R–Q4 |
| 4 | N–KB3 | B–K2 | 21 | BxB | PxB | 38 | P–B7 | RxN |
| 5 | O–O | O–O | 22 | RxP | N–B4 | 39 | R–B8† | KxR |
| 6 | P–QN3 | P–Q5 | 23 | N–Q6! | Q–B3† | 40 | P–B8/Q† | K–K2 |
| 7 | P–K3! | N–B3 | 24 | Q–B3 | QxQ† | 41 | Q–B7† | K–K3 |
| 8 | PxP | NxP | 25 | KxQ | R–Q2 | 42 | QxNP | N–Q4† |
| 9 | B–N2 | NxN† | 26 | R/1–Q1 | P–B3 | 43 | K–B3 | R–R4 |
| 10 | QxN | QR–N1 | 27 | K–K3 | P–K4 | 44 | QxRP | RxP |
| 11 | Q–K2 | P–QN3 | 28 | R–Q5 | N–K3 | 45 | P–R4 | N–K2 |
| 12 | N–B3 | B–N2 | 29 | N–N5! | R–K2 | 46 | P–R5 | R–Q7 |
| 13 | QR–Q1! | BxB | 30 | R–Q7 | R/1–B2 | 47 | P–R6 | P–B4 |
| 14 | KxB | P–B3 | 31 | RxR | RxR | 48 | Q–N7 | P–K5† |
| 15 | N–K4! | R–N2 | 32 | R–Q6 | K–B2 | 49 | K–N2 | P–K6 |
| 16 | N–N5 | N–Q2 | 33 | R–B6 | R–Q2 | 50 | P–R7 | Resigns |
| 17 | N–B3 | B–B3 | 34 | R–B8 | N–B4 | | | |

# part 3—SLAV-WING SYSTEM

1 N–KB3, P–Q4
2 P–B4, P–QB3
3 P–QN3[A], N–B3[B]
4 P–N3

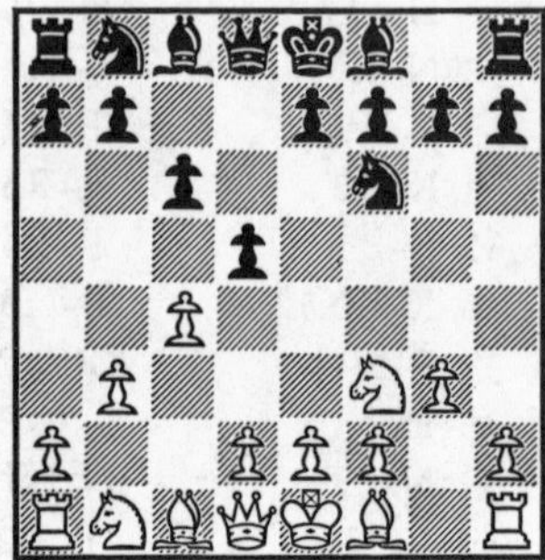

KEY POSITION 3

## OBSERVATIONS ON KEY POSITION 3

[A] A necessary preparation for the fianchetto of the King Bishop, as the Queen Bishop Pawn needs protection. For 3 P–Q4, see the Slav Defense.

[B] Preferable to 3 . . . P–Q5, which gives White the edge after 4 P–K3, P–QB4 5 P–QN4!

Because his Queen Bishop has an open diagonal, Black's task here is easier than in the Wing-Orthodox Defense. He can obtain a satisfactory game in several ways, the most usual being 4 . . . B–B4, the New York Variation. Excellent alternatives are 4 . . . P–KN3 and 4 . . . P–K3.

## IDEA VARIATIONS 5 AND 6:

(5) 4 . . . B–B4 5 B–KN2, P–K3 (more accurate than 5 . . . QN–Q2, which is strongly met by 6 PxP!) 6 B–N2 (after 6 N–R4, B–K5 7 P–B3?, BxN 8 RxB, P–KN4!, Black wins a piece), QN–Q2 7 O–O, P–KR3 (not bad, according to recent findings, is 7 . . . B–Q3, e.g., 8 P–Q3, O–O 9 N–B3 [for 9 QN–Q2, see Game 5], Q–K2 10 R–K1, KR–Q1! 11 P–KR3, B–R6, and Black has almost even chances) 8 P–Q3 (8 P–Q4 is met most simply by 8 . . . B–Q3), B–K2 (if 8 . . . B–B4, then 9 N–B3! is best) 9 QN–Q2 (9 N–B3, serving as a preparation for a later P–K4, is not commendable in this position: e.g., 9 . . . O–O 10 Q–B2, B–R2 11 P–K4, PxKP 12 PxP, N–B4 13 QR–Q1, Q–N3! 14 N–Q4, P–QR4), O–O 10 R–B1, P–QR4 11 P–QR3 (to meet 11 . . . P–R5 with 12 P–QN4), R–K1 12 R–B2, B–R2 13 Q–R1 (Capablanca-Lilienthal, Moscow 1936). The chances are equal.

(6) 4 . . . B–B4 (for other moves, see Prac. Var. 5 and 6) 5 B–KN2, P–K3 6 B–N2, QN–Q2 7 O–O, B–K2 8 N–B3, O–O 9 N–KR4 (a risky maneuver; steadier is 9 P–Q3, which leads into the channels of Idea Var. 5), B–KN5 10 P–KR3, B–R4 11 P–KN4, P–Q5! 12 N–N1, BxP! Black gets two Pawns and fine attacking chances for the piece. See Game 6.

*Indian in Reverse Game 5*

*WHITE: Reti* — *BLACK: Lasker*

*New York 1924*

| WHITE | BLACK | WHITE | BLACK |
|---|---|---|---|
| 1 N–KB3 | P–Q4 | 4 P–N3 | N–B3 |
| 2 P–B4 | P–QB3 | 5 B–KN2 | QN–Q2 |
| 3 P–QN3 | B–B4 | 6 B–N2 | P–K3 |

| | WHITE | BLACK | | WHITE | BLACK |
|---|---|---|---|---|---|
| 7 | O–O | B–Q3 | 27 | PxP | NxN |
| 8 | P–Q3 | O–O | 28 | BxN | B–B3 |
| 9 | QN–Q2 | P–K4 | 29 | BxP | R–B4 |
| 10 | PxP | PxP | 30 | B–R6 | B–N3 |
| 11 | R–B1 | Q–K2 | 31 | Q–N7 | Q–Q1 |
| 12 | R–B2 | P–QR4 | 32 | P–QN4 | R–B2 |
| 13 | P–QR4 | P–R3 | 33 | Q–N6 | R–Q2 |
| 14 | Q–R1 | KR–K1 | 34 | QxQ† | RxQ |
| 15 | KR–B1 | B–R2 | 35 | P–K3 | PxP |
| 16 | N–B1 | N–B4 | 36 | K–N2 | BxN |
| 17 | RxN! | BxR | 37 | PxB | B–B4 |
| 18 | NxP | QR–B1 | 38 | B–N7 | B–K3 |
| 19 | N–K3 | Q–K3 | 39 | K–B3 | B–N6 |
| 20 | P–R3 | B–Q3? | 40 | B–B6 | R–Q3 |
| 21 | RxR | RxR | 41 | B–N5 | R–B3† |
| 22 | N–B3? | B–K2 | 42 | K–K3 | R–K3† |
| 23 | N–Q4 | Q–Q2 | 43 | K–B4 | R–K7 |
| 24 | K–R2 | P–R4 | 44 | B–B1 | R–B7 |
| 25 | Q–R1 | P–R5 | 45 | B–K3 | B–Q4 |
| 26 | NxP | PxP† | | Resigns | |

*Indian in Reverse Game 6*

*WHITE: Smyslov* *BLACK: Bronstein*

*Zurich 1953*

| | WHITE | BLACK | | WHITE | BLACK |
|---|---|---|---|---|---|
| 1 | P–QB4 | N–KB3 | 22 | K–R1 | P–B4 |
| 2 | P–KN3 | P–B3 | 23 | PxP | PxP |
| 3 | N–KB3 | P–Q4 | 24 | B–B3 | N–N6† |
| 4 | P–N3 | B–B4 | 25 | K–N1 | B–B3! |
| 5 | B–KN2 | P–K3 | 26 | BxB | QxB |
| 6 | O–O | QN–Q2 | 27 | Q–K1 | P–B5? |
| 7 | B–N2 | B–K2 | 28 | N–N4 | Q–Q5† |
| 8 | N–B3 | O–O | 29 | K–N2 | QR–K1 |
| 9 | N–KR4 | B–KN5 | 30 | Q–KN1 | Q–N7 |
| 10 | P–KR3 | B–R4 | 31 | Q–QB1 | Q–Q5 |
| 11 | P–KN4 | P–Q5 | 32 | Q–B3 | Q–Q3 |
| 12 | N–N1 | BxP! | 33 | P–B5 | Q–N3 |
| 13 | PxB | NxP | 34 | Q–B4† | K–R1 |
| 14 | P–K4 | NxP | 35 | R–R3 | P–KR4 |
| 15 | RxN | BxN | 36 | K–R2 | Q–R2 |
| 16 | R–B3 | N–K4 | 37 | N–B2 | P–KN4 |
| 17 | R–R3 | B–N4 | 38 | Q–Q4† | K–N1 |
| 18 | N–R3 | N–N3 | 39 | Q–B4† | K–R1 |
| 19 | N–B2 | N–B5 | 40 | Q–Q4† | K–N1 |
| 20 | R–R2 | P–Q6 | 41 | R–KN1 | Draw |
| 21 | N–K3 | N–K7† | | | |

PRACTICAL VARIATIONS 5 AND 6:

1 N–KB3, P–Q4 2 P–B4, P–QB3 3 P–QN3, N–KB3 4 P–N3

| | 5 | 6 | | 5 | 6 |
|---|---|---|---|---|---|
| 4 | – – | – – | 7 | B–N2 | O–O |
| | P–K3 | P–KN3 | | O–O | QN–Q2 |
| 5 | B–KN2 | B–KN2 | 8 | P–Q4![2] | P–Q3[5] |
| | QN–Q2[1] | B–N2 | | N–K5 | R–K1 |
| 6 | O–O | B–N2 | 9 | QN–Q2 | QN–Q2 |
| | B–Q3 | O–O[4] | | P–KB4[3] | P–K4[6] |
| | | | | = | ∓ |

*Notes to practical variations 5 and 6:*

[1] Bronstein's 5 . . . P–QR4 merits closer investigation.

[2] If 8 P–Q3, then 8 . . . P–K4!

[3] Black has a satisfactory game. White's best now is 10 N–K5.

[4] Equally sufficient is 6 . . . Q–N3, as played in Smyslov–Szabo, Zurich 1953.

[5] Nor do alternatives offer any advantage.

[6] Kostich–Spielmann, Bled 1931.

## part 4—WING-BLUMENFELD

1 N–KB3, P–Q4
2 P–B4, P–Q5[A]

KEY POSITION 4

OBSERVATIONS ON KEY POSITION 4

[A] This system, never popular, may also be called the Benoni in Reverse.

Experience has shown that, although Black cannot easily maintain his Pawn on Q5, the line is not necessarily disadvantageous for him if he plays accurately. He must strive particularly for . . . P–K4, keeping White's potentially dangerous center Pawn majority at bay.

IDEA VARIATIONS 7 AND 8:

(7) 3 P–K3 (much weaker is 3 P–QN4, which is met by 3 . . . P–KB3!; see Prac. Var. 7), N–QB3! (the alternative lines, 3 . . . PxP 4 BPxP and 3 . . . P–QB4 4 P–QN4! [Blumenfeld], both yield White a substantial advantage) 4 PxP (now 4 P–QN4 is weak, e.g., 4 . . . PxP 5 BPxP, NxP 6 P–Q4, P–K4! 7 P–QR3, N–QB3! 8 P–Q5, P–K5!), NxP 5 NxN, QxN 6 N–B3, P–K4 (another possibility is 6 . . . N–B3 7 P–Q3, P–K4! 8 B–K3, Q–Q1 9 B–K2, and White stands but slightly better; for 6 . . . B–N5, see Game 7) 7 P–Q3, B–QB4 8 B–K3, Q–Q3 9 N–N5 (if 9 N–K4, then 9 . . . B–N5†), Q–K2 10 BxB, QxB 11 P–Q4, PxP 12 QxP, QxQ 13 NxQ, B–N5 14 P–B3 (after 14 N–N5, O–O–O 15 NxP†, K–N1 16 N–N5, N–B3, Black has the edge), O–O–O 15 O–O–O,

B–Q2 (Katetov–Alekhine, Prague 1943) with equality.

(8) 3 P–K3, N–QB3 4 PxP, NxP 5 NxN, QxN 6 N–B3, P–K4 7 P–Q3, P–QB3 (most likely the simplest way to obtain equality) 8 B–K3, Q–Q3 (Flohr's move; Black aims for . . . N–KR3 followed by . . . N–KB4) 9 P–Q4 (after 9 B–K2, N–R3! Black stands well), PxP 10 QxP (if 10 BxP, then 10 . . . B–B4 followed by . . . O–O–O), QxQ 11 BxQ, B–K3 with equality.

*Indian in Reverse Game 7*

*WHITE: Keres* *BLACK: Euwe*

*Norway 1938*

| WHITE | BLACK | WHITE | BLACK | WHITE | BLACK |
|---|---|---|---|---|---|
| 1 N–KB3 | P–Q4 | 15 P–N5 | N–R2 | 29 K–N2 | PxP |
| 2 P–B4 | P–Q5 | 16 P–B5 | B–K2 | 30 PxP | B–B2 |
| 3 P–K3 | N–QB3 | 17 P–Q5! | O–O | 31 R–Q1 | R–KR5 |
| 4 PxP | NxP | 18 PxBP | QxP | 32 R–Q2 | R–R8 |
| 5 NxN | QxN | 19 QxQ | PxQ | 33 P–B4! | B–N5 |
| 6 N–B3 | B–N5 | 20 R–Q7 | KR–K1 | 34 PxP | B–N3 |
| 7 Q–R4† | P–B3 | 21 B–R6 | P–K4 | 35 P–R3 | BxN† |
| 8 P–Q3 | N–B3 | 22 R–B7 | N–B1 | 36 KxB | P–KR5 |
| 9 B–K3 | Q–Q2 | 23 B–N7 | QR–N1 | 37 P–K6 | R–K8 |
| 10 P–Q4 | P–K3 | 24 BxP | N–K3 | 38 K–Q4 | K–B1 |
| 11 P–B3 | B–KB4 | 25 BxR | NxR | 39 B–B2 | NxP† |
| 12 O–O–O | B–Q3 | 26 B–Q7 | P–R4 | 40 K–Q5 | N–B2† |
| 13 P–KN4! | B–N3 | 27 P–B6 | R–N5 | 41 K–B5 | Resigns |
| 14 P–KR4! | P–KR4 | 28 P–N3 | P–B3 | | |

PRACTICAL VARIATION 7:

1 N–KB3, P–Q4 2 P–B4, P–Q5

| 7 | 7 |
|---|---|
| 3 P–QN4 | 6 Q–K2 |
| P–KB3![1] | Q–K2 |
| 4 P–K3[2] | 7 N–N1 |
| P–K4 | N–B3 |
| 5 PxP | 8 Q–K3 |
| P–K5![3] | NxNP[4] |
| | ∓ |

*Notes to practical variation 7:*

[1] The only good reply. For 3 . . . P–KN3, see Game 8.

[2] Black also has the better chances after 4 B–N2, P–K4 5 P–QR3, P–QB4 6 PxP, BxP.

[3] The point of the defense.

[4] Lokvenc–Addicks, Prague 1931.

*Indian in Reverse Game 8*

*WHITE: Euwe* — *BLACK: Alekhine*

*8th Match Game 1936*

| | WHITE | BLACK | | WHITE | BLACK |
|---|---|---|---|---|---|
| 1 | N–KB3 | P–Q4 | 22 | P–B6! | PxP |
| 2 | P–B4 | P–Q5 | 23 | QxP | N–K4 |
| 3 | P–QN4 | P–KN3 | 24 | Q–Q2 | Q–R3 |
| 4 | P–K3! | P–QR4 | 25 | P–R5 | NxP |
| 5 | P–N5 | P–QB4 | 26 | N–B5! | NxN |
| 6 | PxP | B–N2 | 27 | BxN | Q–N4 |
| 7 | P–Q3 | PxP | 28 | BxKP | R–QB1 |
| 8 | P–N3 | N–Q2 | 29 | B–B1! | Q–N6 |
| 9 | QN–Q2 | N–B4 | 30 | R–R3 | Q–Q4 |
| 10 | N–N3 | Q–N3? | 31 | P–N7 | R–N1 |
| 11 | NxN | QxN | 32 | P–R6 | B–QB1 |
| 12 | B–KN2 | N–R3 | 33 | PxB (Q) | QRxQ |
| 13 | O–O | O–O | 34 | B–N2 | Q–Q2 |
| 14 | P–QR4 | R–K1 | 35 | B–B5 | RxR† |
| 15 | R–K1 | B–B4 | 36 | QxR | P–R4 |
| 16 | B–QR3 | Q–B2 | 37 | P–R7 | R–R1 |
| 17 | P–B5 | QR–Q1 | 38 | Q–K4 | P–Q6 |
| 18 | N–N5 | B–B3 | 39 | RxP | Q–N2 |
| 19 | N–K4 | B–N2 | 40 | QxBP | Q–N8† |
| 20 | Q–Q2 | N–N5 | 41 | B–B1 | RxP |
| 21 | P–N6 | Q–B1 | 42 | BxR | Resigns |

## part 5—**KING'S INDIAN IN REVERSE**

1 N–KB3, P–Q4
2 P–KN3[A], N–KB3[B]
3 B–N2

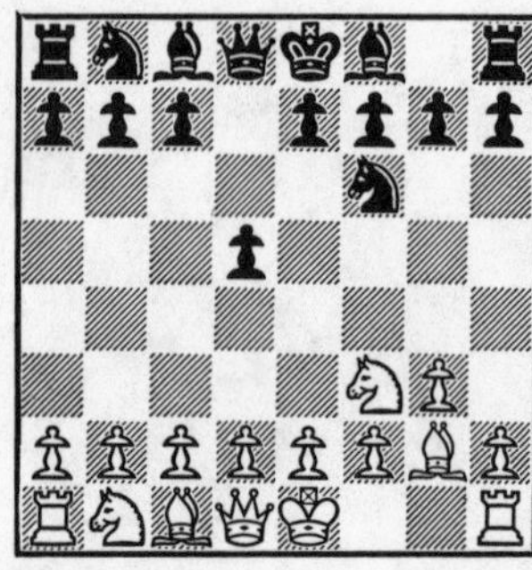

KEY POSITION 5

### OBSERVATIONS ON KEY POSITION 5

[A] Sometimes called the Barcza System.

[B] Needless to say, in this position as in reply to White's second move, Black has numerous satisfactory choices at his disposal. One interesting possibility is 2 . . . P–B4 which can become a Grunfeld in reverse: 3 B–N2, N–QB3 4 P–Q4, N–KB3 5 O–O, P–K3 6 P–B4, QPxP 7 Q–R4, N–Q2! with equality.

This position frequently occurs in today's tournament play. Black's most important lines of defense are those with 3 . . . P–KN3 and 3 . . . B–B4. Acting with appropriate care, Black certainly has sufficient counterplay in both these variations.

### IDEA VARIATIONS 9 AND 10:

(9) 3 . . . B–B4 (for the more passive 3 . . . P–K3,

see Prac. Var. 8) 4 O–O, P–K3 (too ambitious is 4 . . . QN–Q2; Smyslov–Euwe, Zurich 1953, continued 5 P–Q3, P–B3 6 QN–Q2, P–KR3 7 P–K4, PxP 8 PxP, NxP 9 N–Q4 with fine prospects for White) 5 P–Q3, P–B3 (after 5 . . . P–KR3 6 QN–Q2, B–B4 7 Q–K1, O–O 8 P–K4, White has a clear edge) 6 QN–Q2, N–R3 (an idea of Smyslov's: Black intends to answer 7 Q–K1 with 7 . . . N–QN5) 7 P–QR3, B–K2 with equality. See Game 9.

(10) 3 . . . P–KN3 4 O–O, B–N2 5 P–Q3, O–O 6 QN–Q2, P–B4 (for 6 . . . N–B3, see Prac. Var. 9) 7 P–K4, P–K3 8 R–K1, N–B3 9 PxP (more enterprising is 9 P–B3, perhaps later followed by P–K5), NxP (9 . . . PxP is effectively met by 10 P–Q4 and, if 10 . . . PxP, then 11 N–N3) 10 N–B4, Q–B2 11 P–QR4, R–Q1 12 Q–K2, N–Q5, and Black has good chances for equality. For the inferior 12 . . . P–N3, see Game 10.

*Indian in Reverse Game 9*

*WHITE: Zvetkov* — *BLACK: Smyslov*

*Amsterdam 1954*

| | WHITE | BLACK | | WHITE | BLACK |
|---|---|---|---|---|---|
| 1 | N–KB3 | N–KB3 | 25 | B–K2 | P–QB4 |
| 2 | P–KN3 | P–Q4 | 26 | Q–K1 | Q–B3 |
| 3 | B–N2 | P–B3 | 27 | P–KB3 | R–Q3 |
| 4 | O–O | B–B4 | 28 | Q–B2 | R/1–Q1 |
| 5 | P–Q3 | P–K3 | 29 | P–N3 | P–B4 |
| 6 | QN–Q2 | N–R3 | 30 | PxBP | BxP |
| 7 | P–QR3 | B–K2 | 31 | B–B1 | R–B3 |
| 8 | Q–K1 | N–B4 | 32 | Q–N2 | R/1–KB1 |
| 9 | N–Q4 | B–N3 | 33 | R–K1 | Q–Q3 |
| 10 | N/4–N3 | N/3–Q2 | 34 | Q–K2 | R–K1 |
| 11 | P–K4 | O–O | 35 | B–N2 | B–N3 |
| 12 | NxN | BxN | 36 | Q–K3 | P–KR3 |
| 13 | N–N3 | B–N3 | 37 | QR–Q1 | K–R2 |
| 14 | B–K3 | R–K1 | 38 | R–Q2 | R/3–K3 |
| 15 | Q–K2 | P–B3 | 39 | R/2–K2 | B–B4 |
| 16 | KR–K1 | Q–B2 | 40 | Q–Q2 | R/3–K2 |
| 17 | P–QR4 | BxB | 41 | Q–K3 | P–Q5 |
| 18 | QxB | B–B2 | 42 | Q–Q2 | P–KN4 |
| 19 | N–B5 | P–K4 | 43 | Q–B1 | K–N2 |
| 20 | NxN | QxN | 44 | Q–Q2 | B–N3 |
| 21 | Q–B5 | P–QN3 | 45 | B–R3 | Q–B3 |
| 22 | Q–N4 | QR–B1 | 46 | R–KB1 | B–B2 |
| 23 | KR–Q1 | QR–Q1 | 47 | R/2–B2 | B–Q4 |
| 24 | B–B3 | B–K3 | 48 | B–N2 | Draw |

*Indian in Reverse Game 10*

*WHITE: Reshevsky* *BLACK: Sherwin*

*New York 1955*

| WHITE | BLACK | WHITE | BLACK |
|---|---|---|---|
| 1 N–KB3 | N–KB3 | 16 P–R5! | N–K2? |
| 2 P–KN3 | P–KN3 | 17 NxBP! | KxN |
| 3 B–N2 | B–N2 | 18 QxP† | K–B1 |
| 4 O–O | O–O | 19 B–B4! | Q–Q2 |
| 5 P–Q3 | P–Q4 | 20 BxB | QxB |
| 6 QN–Q2 | P–B4 | 21 B–Q6 | RxB |
| 7 P–K4 | P–K3 | 22 QxR | R–K1 |
| 8 R–K1 | N–B3 | 23 R–R4! | P–KN4 |
| 9 PxP | NxP | 24 R/4–K4 | PxP |
| 10 N–B4 | Q–B2 | 25 R/1–K3! | Q–N3 |
| 11 P–QR4 | R–Q1 | 26 R–B3† | K–N1 |
| 12 Q–K2 | P–N3 | 27 Q–Q7 | R–KB1 |
| 13 P–B3 | P–KR3 | 28 RxN | RxR |
| 14 N/3–K5 | NxN | 29 RxB† | Resigns |
| 15 NxN | B–N2 | | |

PRACTICAL VARIATIONS 8 AND 9:
1 N–KB3, P–Q4 2 P–KN3, N–KB3 3 B–N2

| | 8 | 9 |
|---|---|---|
| *3* | — — | — — |
| | P–K3 | P–KN3 |
| *4* | O–O | O–O |
| | B–K2 | B–N2 |
| *5* | P–Q3 | P–Q3 |
| | O–O | O–O |
| *6* | QN–Q2 | QN–Q2 |
| | P–QN3![1] | N–B3 |
| *7* | P–K4 | P–K4[3] |
| | PxP | PxP |
| *8* | N–N5 | PxP |
| | B–N2 | P–K4 |
| *9* | N/2xP | R–K1 |
| | NxN | Q–K2[4] |
| *10* | NxN | ± |
| | Q–B1[2] | |
| | ∓ | |

*Notes to practical variations 8 and 9:*

[1] Stronger than 6 . . . P–B4, as played in Petrosian–Barcza, Budapest 1952: 7 P–K4, N–B3 8 R–K1, P–QN3 9 P–K5, N–Q2 10 N–B1, B–R3 11 P–KR4, Q–K1 12 B–R3!

[2] Taimanov–Eliskases, Saltsjobaden 1952.

[3] If 7 P–B3, then 7 . . . P–K4! and Black has the initiative (Phillips–Unzicker, Hastings 1954).

[4] Botvinnik–O'Kelly, Budapest 1952.

SUPPLEMENTARY VARIATIONS 1–4:

1 N–KB3, P–Q4

| | 1 | 2 | 3 | 4 |
|---|---|---|---|---|
| 2 | P–B4 | P–QN3[4] | – – | P–QN4[11] |
| | N–KB3[1] | N–KB3[5] | – – | N–KB3[12] |
| 3 | PxP | B–N2 | – – | B–N2 |
| | QxP[2] | P–B4[6] | P–K3 | P–K3[13] |
| 4 | N–B3 | P–K3 | P–K3 | P–QR3 |
| | Q–QR4 | P–KN3[7] | QN–Q2 | P–QR4 |
| 5 | P–Q4 | P–B4[8] | P–B4 | P–N5 |
| | P–B3 | PxP | P–B3 | P–B4 |
| 6 | B–Q2 | PxP[9] | B–K2 | PxP e.p. |
| | Q–B2 | B–N2 | B–Q3[10] | PxP |
| 7 | R–B1 | B–K2 | = | = |
| | P–K3[3] | O–O | | |
| 8 | P–KN3! | O–O | | |
| | B–K2 | N–B3 | | |
| 9 | B–N2 | = | | |
| | O–O | | | |
| 10 | O–O | | | |
| | QN–Q2 | | | |
| 11 | P–K4 | | | |
| | ± | | | |

*Notes to supplementary variations 1–4:*

[1] Both gratuitous and unsatisfactory.

[2] 3 . . . NxP leads to the Knight's Defense of the Queen's Gambit.

[3] Or 7 . . . B–B4.

[4] This is the Queen's Indian in reverse, a favorite of Nimzowitsch's.

[5] 2 . . . P–KB3 is weak because of 3 P–Q4!

[6] Bogoljubov's 3 . . . B–N5 is also good.

[7] If 4 . . . N–B3, then 5 B–N5!

[8] 5 B–N5† is best met by 5 . . . B–Q2!

[9] To set up a center Pawn majority.

[10] 7 P–Q4 leads to a kind of Semi-Meran.

[11] Known as "Santasiere's Folly."

[12] Reasonable is 2 . . . B–B4, or 2 . . . P–K3 3 P–QR3, B–Q3 followed by . . . N–Q2 and . . . P–K4. The same program may serve also after 2 . . . B–B4. White's P–QN4 and P–QR3 do little to further White's game.

[13] 3 . . . P–KN3 is a worthwhile alternative.

# chapter 41—Reti System

In this section are treated all independent openings arising from 1 N–KB3, N–KB3 2 P–B4. A very close kinship, however, exists between these variations and those arising from 1 N–KB3, P–Q4 and, owing to the numerous possibilities for transposition from one to the other, it is quite difficult to separate the two.

---

## part 1—SYMMETRICAL VARIATION

1 N–KB3, N–KB3
2 P–B4, P–B4
3 P–Q4[A], PxP[B]
4 NxP

KEY POSITION 1

OBSERVATIONS ON KEY POSITION 1

[A] The best chance for maintaining the initiative. After 3 P–KN3, P–KN3 4 B–N2, B–N2 5 O–O, O–O 6 N–B3, Black can almost equalize with 6 . . . P–Q4!

[B] Also playable is 3 . . . P–K3 which leads to the Benoni Defense after 4 P–Q5.

Black must now aim to restore the balance in the center by means of . . . P–Q4. He may either prepare this advance with 4 . . . P–K3 or play it directly at the crucial moment. Both methods offer Black chances for equality.

IDEA VARIATIONS 1 AND 2:

(1) 4 . . . P–K3 (an immediate 4 . . . P–Q4 is premature, e.g., 5 PxP, NxP 6 P–K4±) 5 N–QB3 (after 5 P–KN3, P–Q4 6 B–N2, P–K4 Black has nothing to fear), B–N5 6 N–N5! (this move, Najdorf's innovation, is White's best chance) P–Q4 (consistent, but probably inferior to 6 . . . O–O) 7 B–B4, N–R3 8 P–K3, O–O 9 P–QR3±.

For 6 B–Q2 instead of Najdorf's 6 N–N5!, see Prac. Var. 1. 6 Q–N3, N–R3 7 P–K3, N–K5! 8 B–K2, Q–R4 favors Black. See Game 1.

(2) 4 . . . P–KN3 (for 4 . . . N–B3, see Prac. Var. 2) 5 N–QB3 (4 P–B3, P–Q4 offers White little promise), P–Q4! (this advance is always plausible when White has played N–QB3; compare the Grunfeld Defense) 6 PxP, NxP 7 N/4–N5, NxN 8 QxQ†, KxQ 9 NxN, B–N2 10 B–Q2, B–K3 and Black has almost achieved equality.

*Reti System Game 1*

*WHITE: Boleslavski* *BLACK: Szabo*

*Zurich 1953*

| | WHITE | BLACK | | WHITE | BLACK |
|---|---|---|---|---|---|
| 1 | P–Q4 | N–KB3 | 23 | P–B3 | R–N3 |
| 2 | P–QB4 | P–K3 | 24 | BxN | PxB |
| 3 | N–KB3 | P–B4 | 25 | B–Q5 | R–N7 |
| 4 | N–B3 | PxP | 26 | R–B3 | RxP |
| 5 | NxP | B–N5 | 27 | R–N3 | B–Q2 |
| 6 | Q–N3 | N–R3 | 28 | R–N7 | K–Q3 |
| 7 | P–K3 | N–K5 | 29 | BxP | B–B3 |
| 8 | B–K2 | Q–R4 | 30 | R–N1 | P–QR4 |
| 9 | O–O | N/3–B4 | 31 | B–Q5 | BxB |
| 10 | Q–B2 | BxN | 32 | R–Q1 | P–R5 |
| 11 | PxB | QxBP | 33 | RxB† | K–B3 |
| 12 | QxQ | NxQ | 34 | P–R4 | R–QB7 |
| 13 | B–B3 | K–K2 | 35 | RxP | P–R6 |
| 14 | N–N3 | N/6–R5 | 36 | R–K6† | K–N2 |
| 15 | B–R3 | P–Q3 | 37 | R–K7† | K–N3 |
| 16 | N–R5 | P–K4 | 38 | R–K6† | K–R4 |
| 17 | KR–B1 | QR–N1 | 39 | R–K8 | P–R7 |
| 18 | QR–N1 | B–B4! | 40 | R–R8† | K–N5 |
| 19 | RxP† | NxR | 41 | K–R2 | K–N6 |
| 20 | NxN | RxN! | 42 | R–N8† | KxP |
| 21 | BxR | R–QN1 | | Resigns | |
| 22 | B–B6 | N–B4 | | | |

PRACTICAL VARIATIONS 1 AND 2:

1 N–KB3, N–KB3; 2 P–B4, P–B4 3 P–Q4, PxP 4 NxP

| | *1* | *2* | | *1* | *2* |
|---|---|---|---|---|---|
| *4* | – – | – – | 7 | P–K3 | N–N3 |
| | P–K3 | N–B3 | | N–B3 | B–K2 |
| *5* | N–QB3 | N–QB3 | 8 | B–K2[1] | B–N2 |
| | B–N5 | P–K3[3] | | P–Q4 | O–O |
| *6* | B–Q2 | P–KN3 | 9 | PxP | O–O |
| | O–O | B–N5 | | PxP[2] | P–Q3[4] |
| | | | | ∓ | = |

*Notes to practical variations 1 and 2:*

[1] 8 N–B2 is probably a little stronger (Taimanov–Pachman, Stockholm 1952).

[2] Black has the initiative.

[3] 5 . . . P–KN3 6 P–K4 transposes into the Sicilian Defense. 5 . . . P–Q4 6 PxP, NxP 7 N/4xN slightly favors White.

[4] White's best now is 10 N–Q2.

# part 2— QUEEN'S INDIAN DEFENSIVE METHOD

1 N–KB3, N–KB3
2 P–B4, P–QN3
3 P–KN3[A], B–N2
4 B–N2

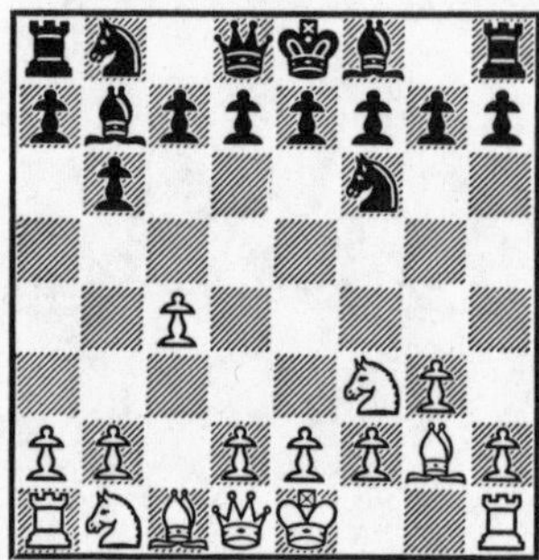

KEY POSITION 2

## OBSERVATIONS ON KEY POSITION 2

[A] For 3 P–Q3, see Game 2.

As early as here Black faces an important decision. He can play 4 . . . P–K4 because of the pin on White's King Knight, or the more routine 4 . . . P–K3 which often leads to the Queen's Indian Defense. Both methods seem quite adequate, although extensive analysis has not yet been lavished on many of the resulting positions.

## IDEA VARIATIONS 3 AND 4:

(3) 4 . . . P–K3 5 O–O, B–K2 6 N–B3, O–O (6 . . . P–B4 is dubious; see Prac. Var. 4) 7 P–Q3, P–Q4 (best; if instead 7 . . . P–B4 then 8 P–K4!± [Reti–Grunfeld, Semmering 1926]) 8 N–K5, QN–Q2 with a satisfactory game for Black.

In the foregoing 7 P–Q3 is passive as against the more dynamic 7 P–Q4; see the Queen's Indian Knight Game. The text move gives the opening its independent significance.

(4) 4 . . . P–K4 (also worthwhile is 4 . . . P–B4; see Prac. Var. 3) 5 N–B3, B–N5 6 Q–N3 (to prevent a weakening of the Pawn formation; after 6 O–O, KBxN! 7 NPxB, P–Q3 8 P–Q4, P–K5 Black, according to Alekhine, has the edge), P–QR4 7 P–QR3 and White's advantage is minimal.

## PRACTICAL VARIATIONS 3 AND 4:

1 N–KB3, N–KB3 2 P–B4, P–QN3 3 P–KN3, B–N2 4 B–N2

| | *3* | *4* |
|---|---|---|
| *4* | — — | — — |
| | P–B4 | P–K3 |
| *5* | O–O | O–O |
| | P–N3 | B–K2 |
| *6* | N–B3 | N–B3 |
| | B–N2 | P–B4 |
| *7* | P–Q3[1] | P–Q4![3] |
| | O–O[2] | PxP[4] |
| *8* | = | NxP |
| | | BxB |
| *9* | | KxB |
| | | P–Q4 |
| *10* | | Q–R4†![5] |
| | | ± |

[1] Better is 7 P–Q4 transposing into the Queen's Indian.

[2] Pirc–Klein, Hastings 1938.

[3] The best chance. The continuations 7 P–Q3, P–Q4! and 7 P–N3, P–Q4! are comfortable for Black.

[4] White threatened 8 P–Q5.

[5] White's prospects are good.

*Reti System Game 2*

*WHITE: Reshevsky* *BLACK: Keres*

*The Hague 1948*

| WHITE | BLACK | WHITE | BLACK |
|---|---|---|---|
| 1 N–KB3 | N–KB3 | 22 B–Q2 | P–B4 |
| 2 P–B4 | P–QN3 | 23 B–N5 | R–K1 |
| 3 P–Q3 | P–N3 | 24 P–R3 | PxP? |
| 4 P–K4 | P–Q3 | 25 NxP/4 | BxN |
| 5 N–B3 | B–KN2 | 26 QxB | N–B3 |
| 6 P–Q4 | O–O | 27 Q–K3 | N/1–Q2 |
| 7 B–K2 | B–N2 | 28 Q–N3 | R–N1 |
| 8 Q–B2 | P–K4 | 29 B–K3 | N–B4 |
| 9 PxP | PxP | 30 Q–B2 | R–R1 |
| 10 B–K3 | R–K1 | 31 N–N5 | R–K1 |
| 11 O–O | QN–Q2 | 32 P–R4 | P–K5 |
| 12 KR–Q1 | P–B3 | 33 N–R3 | R–Q1 |
| 13 P–QN4 | Q–K2 | 34 N–B4 | R–Q3 |
| 14 QR–N1 | N–B1 | 35 P–R5! | P–KN4 |
| 15 P–QR4 | Q–B2 | 36 N–Q5 | NxN |
| 16 P–N5 | KR–Q1 | 37 PxN | P–R3 |
| 17 RxR | RxR | 38 BxN | PxB |
| 18 P–R5 | N–N5 | 39 QxKP | B–Q5? |
| 19 RPxP | RPxP | 40 Q–K8† | K–N2 |
| 20 B–N5 | P–B3 | 41 R–N8 | Resigns |
| 21 PxP | BxP | | |

## part 3—KING'S INDIAN DEFENSIVE METHOD

### OBSERVATIONS ON KEY POSITION 3

1 N–KB3, N–KB3
2 P–B4, P–KN3

KEY POSITION 3

With his last move, Black adopts the King's Indian set-up, and unless White proceeds with P–Q4, the first player abandons all hope for an opening advantage. As is demonstrated in this section, Black has no difficulties whatsoever against other lines of play.

### IDEA VARIATIONS 5 AND 6:

(5) 3 P–QN3, B–N2 4 B–N2, O–O 5 P–N3, P–Q3 (or 5 . . . P–B3 6 B–N2, P–Q4=; worth trying is 5 . . . P–B4) 6 B–N2, N–B3 7 O–O, P–K4 8 P–Q3 (now 8 P–Q4 is questionable, e.g., 8 . . . P–K5! 9 KN–Q2, P–K6 10 PxP, N–KN5∓), B–Q2! (better than 8 . . . N–KR4 which leads only to equality after 9 N–B3, P–B4 10

P–K3) 9 N–B3 (9 P–KR3; is powerfully met by 9 . . . Q–B1, and if 10 K–R2 then 10 . . . P–K5!∓; or if 10 P–KN4 then 10 . . . P–KR4!±), Q–B1 10 R–K1, B–R6 11 B–R1, P–KR3 and Black has a good game.

(6) 3 P–QN4 (Reti's innovation) B–N2 (Pachman recommends 3 . . . P–QR4, but his analysis is not convincing; White must proceed 4 P–N5, B–N2 5 B–N2, P–Q3 6 P–KN3!) 4 B–N2, O–O 5 P–N3, P–N3 (after 5 . . . P–Q4 6 PxP White has a slight advantage in space) 6 B–N2, B–N2 7 O–O, P–Q3 8 P–Q3, QN–Q2 9 QN–Q2, P–K4 10 Q–B2, KR–K1=. See Game 3.

*Reti System Game 3*

*WHITE: Reti* *BLACK: Capablanca*

*New York 1924*

| | WHITE | BLACK | | WHITE | BLACK |
|---|---|---|---|---|---|
| 1 | N–KB3 | N–KB3 | 17 | Q–B3? | KPxP |
| 2 | P–B4 | P–KN3 | 18 | KPxP | N/3–Q2? |
| 3 | P–QN4 | B–N2 | 19 | Q–Q2! | PxP |
| 4 | B–N2 | O–O | 20 | BxP | QxP |
| 5 | P–N3 | P–N3 | 21 | BxB | KxB |
| 6 | B–N2 | B–N2 | 22 | Q–N2†! | K–N1 |
| 7 | O–O | P–Q3 | 23 | RxP | Q–B4 |
| 8 | P–Q3 | QN–Q2 | 24 | R/1–Q1 | R–R2 |
| 9 | QN–Q2 | P–K4 | 25 | N–K3 | Q–R4 |
| 10 | Q–B2 | R–K1 | 26 | N–Q4! | BxB |
| 11 | KR–Q1 | P–QR4 | 27 | KxB | Q–K4? |
| 12 | P–QR3 | P–R3 | 28 | N–B4 | Q–QB4 |
| 13 | N–B1 | P–B4! | 29 | N–B6 | R–B2 |
| 14 | P–N5 | N–B1 | 30 | N–K3 | N–K4 |
| 15 | P–K3 | Q–B2 | 31 | R/1–Q5! | Resigns |
| 16 | P–Q4 | B–K5 | | | |

PRACTICAL VARIATION 5:

1 N–KB3, N–KB3 2 P–B4, P–KN3

| | 5 |
|---|---|
| 3 | P–KN3 |
| | B–N2 |
| 4 | B–N2 |
| | P–B3[1] |
| 5 | P–N3[2] |
| | N–K5 |
| 6 | P–Q4 |
| | Q–R4†[3] |
| | ∓ |

*Notes to practical variation 5:*

[1] Most simple, but 4 . . . P–Q3 is also good, e.g., 5 O–O, O–O 6 N–B3, QN–Q2 7 P–Q3, P–B4=.

[2] Questionable. Better is 5 P–Q4.

[3] Black already holds the initiative.

## SUPPLEMENTARY VARIATIONS 1–3:

1 N–KB3

| | *1* | *2* | *3* |
|---|---|---|---|
| *1* | – – | – – | – – |
| | N–KB3 | – – | P–KB4 |
| *2* | P–B4 | – – | P–K4[5] |
| | P–Q3 | – – | PxP |
| *3* | P–KN3 | – – | N–N5 |
| | P–K4 | B–N5[3] | N–KB3[6] |
| *4* | B–N2[1] | B–N2 | P–Q3 |
| | P–B3 | P–B3 | P–Q4! |
| *5* | P–Q3 | P–Q3 | PxP |
| | B–K2 | P–K4 | P–KR3 |
| *6* | QN–Q2 | QN–Q2 | N–KB3 |
| | O–O | QN–Q2 | PxP[7] |
| *7* | O–O | P–N3 | QxQ† |
| | QN–Q2 | B–K2 | KxQ |
| *8* | P–N3 | B–N2 | N–K5 |
| | Q–B2 | O–O | B–K3[8] |
| *9* | B–N2 | O–O[4] | = |
| | R–K1 | ± | |
| *10* | Q–B2[2] | | |
| | ± | | |

*Notes to supplementary variations 1–3:*

[1] 4 P–N3 is inferior. After 4 . . . P–K5 5 N–R4, P–Q4 6 PxP, NxP Black has the edge.

[2] Reti–Hromadka, Mahrisch–Ostrau 1923.

[3] For 3 . . . B–B4, see Game 4.

[4] White has a minimal advantage.

[5] Other moves lead to the Dutch Defense, or unusual forms of the Indian in reverse.

[6] For 3 . . . P–K4, see Game 5.

[7] If 6 . . . NxP?, then 7 N–K5!±.

[8] White's compensation is in Black's broken Pawn structure and Black's inability to castle.

*Reti System Game 4*

*WHITE: Reti* — *BLACK: Gruber*

*Vienna 1923*

| | WHITE | BLACK | | WHITE | BLACK |
|---|---|---|---|---|---|
| 1 | N–KB3 | N–KB3 | 15 | P–B4 | PxP |
| 2 | P–B4 | P–Q3 | 16 | PxP | P–KB4 |
| 3 | P–KN3 | B–B4 | 17 | K–R1 | N–B3 |
| 4 | B–N2 | P–B3 | 18 | R–KN1! | N–R4 |
| 5 | P–N3 | Q–B1 | 19 | B–KB3 | N/4xP |
| 6 | P–KR3 | P–K4 | 20 | N–Q5! | NxN |
| 7 | B–N2 | N–R3 | 21 | PxN | B–N4 |
| 8 | N–B3 | P–R3 | 22 | PxN! | QxP |
| 9 | P–Q3 | B–K2 | 23 | Q–B3 | B–B3 |
| 10 | Q–Q2 | N–B2 | 24 | Q–Q2 | K–R1 |
| 11 | N–Q1 | O–O | 25 | R–N2 | R–B2 |
| 12 | N–K3 | B–R2 | 26 | R/1–KN1 | B–K4 |
| 13 | O–O | N–Q2 | 27 | P–Q4 | B–B3 |
| 14 | N–R2 | N–K3 | 28 | P–Q5 | Resigns |

*Reti System Game 5*

*WHITE: Robatsch* — *BLACK: Larsen*

*Moscow 1956*

| | WHITE | BLACK | | WHITE | BLACK |
|---|---|---|---|---|---|
| 1 | N–KB3 | P–KB4 | 11 | N–QN5 | N–B4 |
| 2 | P–K4 | PxP | 12 | Q–B3 | P–Q4 |
| 3 | N–N5 | P–K4 | 13 | N–B6† | QxN |
| 4 | P–Q3 | P–K6! | 14 | NxP† | K–Q1 |
| 5 | BxP | N–QB3 | 15 | NxR | P–K5 |
| 6 | Q–R5† | P–N3 | 16 | PxP | QxP |
| 7 | Q–B3 | Q–B3 | 17 | Q–Q1 | NxB |
| 8 | Q–N3 | KN–K2 | 18 | PxN | Q–B6† |
| 9 | N–QB3 | P–KR3 | 19 | K–B2 | B–QB4 |
| 10 | N/5–K4 | Q–B2 | | Resigns | |

# chapter 42—Sicilian Attack

The Sicilian Attack or Sicilian in reverse, as it is sometimes called, arises when Black answers 1 P–QB4 with 1 . . . P–K4. This opening occurs rather frequently in modern tournament play, and in many variations offers White good chances for maintaining the initiative.

The late German master, Carl Carls of Bremen, was a great expert in handling this debut. Hence the opening is also known as the Bremen System.

Nimzowitsch and Reti, who were fond of 1 P–QB4, also contributed greatly to the development of this opening. And Botvinnik, its latter-day exponent, handles the Sicilian Attack with particular skill and refinement.

The most recent systems of the Sicilian Defense — the Najdorf and the Boleslavski — have yet to be investigated in so far as their adaptability to an attacking system is concerned. In this area there is much room for experiment.

---

## part 1—FOUR KNIGHTS' GAME

1 P–QB4, P–K4
2 N–QB3, N–KB3
3 N–B3, N–B3[A]

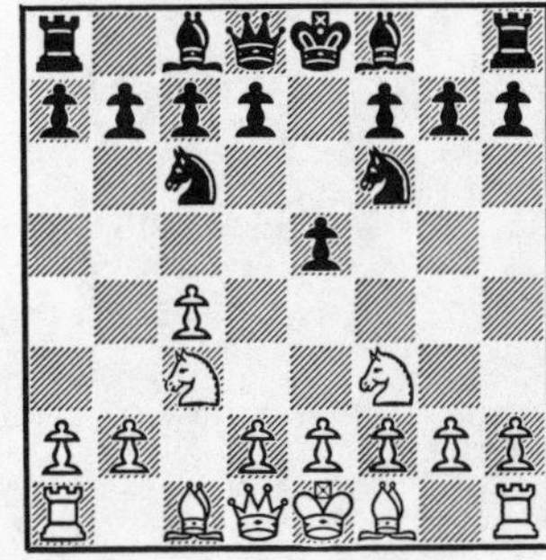

KEY POSITION 1

### OBSERVATIONS ON KEY POSITION 1

[A] Some interesting transpositions are possible. 3 . . . P–Q3 4 P–Q4, QN–Q2 5 P–K4, P–KN3, for example, is a King's Indian.

White now has two main lines at his disposal. He can assume a temporizing attitude and proceed after . . . P–Q4 in the steps of the ordinary Sicilian, or he can aim to seize the initiative by means of P–Q4 himself. The latter method is the most usual, although it cannot be said with certainty that it deserves the preference — most likely it is a matter of taste.

### IDEA VARIATIONS 1 AND 2:

(1) 4 P–QR3 (as in many variations of the Sicilian Defense, a very useful temporizing move), P–Q4 (naturally, neither 4 . . . P–Q3 nor 4 . . . B–K2 is bad, but these continuations have little independent value) 5 PxP, (5 P–Q4 is a curious alternative best met by 5 . . . PxQP) NxP 6 P–Q3 (the Dragon set-up 6 P–KN3 is inconsistent

with 4 P–QR3, while 6 P–K3, NxN 7 NPxN, P–K5 8 N–Q4, N–K4 leads to an approximately even game; worth trying, though, is 6 P–K4 leading to completely unexplored territory), B–K2 7 P–K3 (White has achieved the Scheveningen Variation of the Sicilian Defense a tempo to the good; his chances for obtaining an advantage, however, are slim).

(2) 4 P–Q4, PxP 5 NxP, B–N5 (5 . . . B–B4 is probably not as bad as its reputation; in fact after 6 NxN, NPxN 7 P–KN3, P–KR4! Black has good counterchances) 6 B–N5 (after 6 P–KN3, N–K5! or 6 N–B2, BxN† 7 PxB, P–Q4 Black has no further difficulties), P–KR3 (6 . . . BxN† is also good, followed by 7 . . . P–KR3, and if then 7 . . . N–K4 8 P–B4!; see Game 2) 7 B–R4, BxN† (also playable is 7 . . . P–Q3 8 P–K3, Q–K2 9 B–K2, P–KN4) 8 PxB, P–Q3 (8 . . . N–K4 is dangerous because of 9 P–B4!) 9 P–B3, O–O 10 P–K4, N–K4 11 B–K2, N–N3 12 B–B2, N–Q2 13 Q–Q2, N–N3 14 N–N3, B–K3= (Botvinnik–Pirc, Moscow 1935).

4 . . . P–K5, the so-called Bradley Beach Variation, never became popular. One possible continuation is 5 N–Q2, NxP 6 N/2xP, N–K3 7 P–KN3, NxN 8 NxN, B–N5†! 9 B–Q2, BxB† 10 QxB, O–O 11 N–B3 with a slightly more comfortable game for White. For 5 . . . B–N5 in this line, see Game 1.

*Sicilian Attack Game 1*

*WHITE: Botvinnik* *BLACK: Ragosin*

*Match 1940*

| | WHITE | BLACK | | WHITE | BLACK |
|---|---|---|---|---|---|
| 1 | P–QB4 | P–K4 | 17 | P–KR4! | P–Q4 |
| 2 | N–QB3 | N–KB3 | 18 | PxP | PxP |
| 3 | N–B3 | N–B3 | 19 | B–Q1! | B–K5 |
| 4 | P–Q4 | P–K5 | 20 | RxP | N–N3 |
| 5 | N–Q2 | B–N5 | 21 | Q–KB2 | R–K3 |
| 6 | P–K3 | O–O | 22 | RxR! | PxR |
| 7 | B–K2 | R–K1 | 23 | P–R5! | N–B1 |
| 8 | O–O | BxN | 24 | Q–N3† | K–B2 |
| 9 | PxB | P–Q3 | 25 | R–B1† | B–B4 |
| 10 | P–B3! | PxP | 26 | Q–B4 | N–Q2 |
| 11 | BxP! | RxP | 27 | B–B2 | Q–QN1 |
| 12 | N–N3! | R–K1 | 28 | Q–R6 | Q–KN1 |
| 13 | B–N5 | N–K2 | 29 | BxB | PxB |
| 14 | Q–Q2! | P–B3 | 30 | RxP† | K–K2 |
| 15 | QR–K1 | B–B4 | 31 | R–N5 | Q–K3 |
| 16 | BxN | PxB | 32 | R–N7† | Resigns |

*Sicilian Attack Game 2*

*WHITE: Kottnauer* *BLACK: Euwe*

*Groningen 1946*

| | WHITE | BLACK | | WHITE | BLACK | | WHITE | BLACK |
|---|---|---|---|---|---|---|---|---|
| 1 | P–QB4 | P–K4 | 12 | O–O | P–Q3 | 23 | Q–K3 | Q–Q3 |
| 2 | N–QB3 | N–KB3 | 13 | QR–N1 | P–B3 | 24 | B–R3 | BxB |
| 3 | N–B3 | N–B3 | 14 | Q–Q2 | R–K1 | 25 | RxR | QxP |
| 4 | P–Q4 | PxP | 15 | P–K4 | N–B1 | 26 | K–B2 | QxP† |
| 5 | NxP | B–N5 | 16 | KR–K1 | N–Q2? | 27 | K–K1 | Q–N8† |
| 6 | B–N5 | BxN† | 17 | N–B5 | P–Q4 | 28 | K–Q2 | B–N5 |
| 7 | PxB | N–K4 | 18 | BPxP | PxP | 29 | QxP | Q–Q8† |
| 8 | P–B4! | N–N3 | 19 | PxP? | RxR† | 30 | K–K3 | Q–K7† |
| 9 | P–N3 | P–KR3 | 20 | RxR | QxN | 31 | K–Q4 | K–R2 |
| 10 | BxN | QxB | 21 | R–K8† | N–B1 | | Resigns | |
| 11 | B–N2 | O–O | 22 | Q–K1 | Q–B3 | | | |

PRACTICAL VARIATIONS 1–3:

1 P–QB4, P–K4 2 N–QB3, N–KB3 3 N–B3, N–B3

| | *1* | *2* | *3* |
|---|---|---|---|
| *4* | P–K3 | P–K4 | P–KN3 |
| | P–Q4[1] | B–N5![4] | P–KN3[8] |
| *5* | PxP | P–Q3 | B–N2 |
| | NxP | P–Q3 | B–N2 |
| *6* | B–N5 | P–KN3[5] | P–Q4 |
| | NxN | B–QB4 | PxP |
| 7 | NPxN | P–KR3[6] | NxP |
| | B–Q3![2] | B–K3 | O–O |
| *8* | P–Q4 | B–N2 | O–O |
| | B–Q2 | P–KR3 | R–K1 |
| *9* | P–K4 | P–R3 | P–K3 |
| | PxP | P–QR4[7] | N–K4 |
| *10* | PxP | = | P–N3[9] |
| | B–N5† | | ± |
| *11* | B–Q2 | | |
| | BxB† | | |
| *12* | QxB | | |
| | O–O | | |
| *13* | O–O[3] | | |
| | ± | | |

*Notes to practical variations 1–3:*

[1] Well worth consideration is 4 . . . B–N5, e.g., 5 N–Q5, P–K5! 6 NxB, NxN! and Black stands well.

[2] 7 . . . P–K5 is an alternative.

[3] White has a slight superiority in the center.

[4] 4 . . . B–B4 5 NxP! is promising for White.

continued ▸

[5] 6 B–K2 is simple, but White cannot then hope for more than equality.

[6] 7 B–N2, N–KN5 8 O–O, P–B4 rather favors Black (Nimzowitsch–Mieses, Hanover 1926).

[7] The game is even, but certainly not drawish.

[8] 4 . . . P–Q4 leads to variations treated in Part 2. 4 . . . B–K2 5 P–Q4! is good for White.

[9] White's domination of his Q5 plus the sweep of his King Bishop are in his favor.

---

## part 2—DRAGON SYSTEM

1 P–QB4, P–K4
2 N–QB3, N–KB3
3 P–KN3, P–Q4[A]
4 PxP, NxP
5 B–N2, N–N3[B]

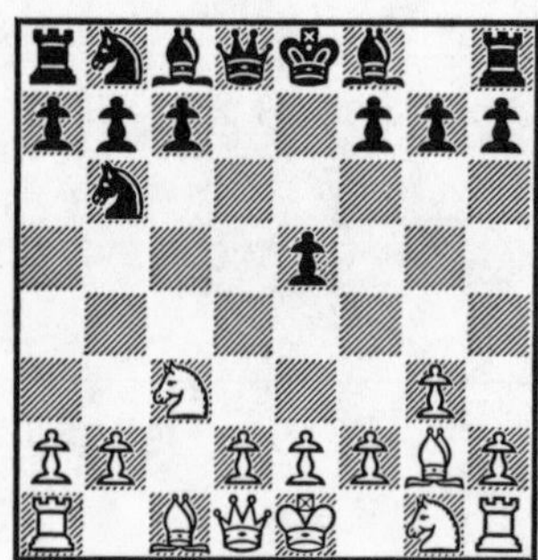

KEY POSITION 1

### OBSERVATIONS ON KEY POSITION 2

[A] Keres strongly favors 3 . . . P–B3. Then 4 N–B3!, P–K5 5 N–Q4, P–Q4 6 PxP, PxP 7 P–Q3 leads to a difficult game with about equal chances.

[B] Best. After both 5 . . . NxN 6 NPxN, P–B3 7 N–B3 and 5 . . . B–K3 6 N–B3, N–QB3 7 O–O White has the edge. For 5 . . . N–K2, see Game 3.

White enjoys a slight lead in development while Black holds some superiority in the center. There are two important lines emerging from this key position. The classical method continues with 6 N–B3, leading to a normal Dragon Variation with colors reversed. In recent years White has also experimented with the Simagin system in reverse, consisting of 6 P–Q3 followed by 7 N–R3 and 8 P–B4. Neither system offers White any definite advantage by force, but there is much room for Black to go wrong.

### IDEA VARIATIONS 3 AND 4:

(3) 6 P–Q3, B–K2 7 N–R3, B–KB4 (best; for 7 . . . N–B3, see Game 4) 8 P–B4 (the point of White's maneuvering), Q–Q2 9 N–B2, N–B3 10 O–O. There is very little over-the-board experience with this position, but the chances appear about balanced.

(4) 6 N–B3, N–B3 7 O–O, B–K2 8 P–Q3, O–O 9 B–K3, P–B4 10 Q–B1 (as in analogous positions of the ordinary Dragon, White can also play 10 N–QR4 or 10 P–QN4 to advantage), B–B3 11 B–B5 and White has a slight edge.

In the Chess Olympics at Moscow 1956, Botvinnik unveiled 8 P–QR3 against Benkner. Black's best reply then is 8 . . . P–QR4. Another possibility for White is 8 P–QR4. See Prac. Var. 5.

PRACTICAL VARIATIONS 4–6:

1 P–QB4, P–K4 2 N–QB3, N–KB3 3 P–KN3, P–Q4 4 PxP, NxP 5 B–N2, N–N3

| | 4 | 5 | 6 |
|---|---|---|---|
| 6 | N–R3 | N–B3 | – – |
| | B–KB4! | N–B3 | – – |
| 7 | O–O[1] | O–O | – – |
| | Q–Q2 | B–K2 | – – |
| 8 | N–KN5 | P–QR4 | P–Q3 |
| | B–K2 | P–QR4! | B–K3 |
| 9 | P–Q3 | P–Q3 | B–K3[4] |
| | N–B3[2] | O–O! | O–O![5] |
| 10 | = | B–K3 | N–K4 |
| | | P–B4[3] | P–B4 |
| | | = | = |

*Notes to practical variations 4–6:*

[1] 7 P–B4 is unsatisfactory now because of 7 . . . BxN 8 BxB, PxP∓.

[2] Owing to his lead in development, Black stands well.

[3] Black's position is slightly more comfortable than in Idea Var. 4.

[4] Not 9 N–K4, P–B4! 10 N/4–N5, B–N1! ∓.

[5] 9 . . . Q–Q2? 10 P–Q4! favors White.

*Sicilian Attack Game 3*

*WHITE: Olafsson* *BLACK: Duckstein*

*Wageningen 1957*

| | WHITE | BLACK | | WHITE | BLACK |
|---|---|---|---|---|---|
| 1 | P–QB4 | P–K4 | 13 | KR–B1 | N/4–Q5 |
| 2 | N–QB3 | N–KB3 | 14 | BxN | PxB |
| 3 | P–KN3 | P–Q4 | 15 | Q–N2 | P–Q6 |
| 4 | PxP | NxP | 16 | P–K3 | K–N1 |
| 5 | B–N2 | N–K2 | 17 | QR–N1 | N–R2 |
| 6 | N–B3 | QN–B3 | 18 | N–B5 | BxN |
| 7 | O–O | N–B4 | 19 | PxB | P–B3 |
| 8 | P–QN4! | P–QR3 | 20 | N–Q4 | B–B2 |
| 9 | B–N2 | B–K3 | 21 | Q–N6 | K–R1 |
| 10 | N–K4 | P–B3 | 22 | B–R3 | N–B1 |
| 11 | P–QR3 | Q–Q2 | 23 | BxQ | NxQ |
| 12 | Q–B2 | O–O–O? | 24 | BxP | Resigns |

*Sicilian Attack Game 4*

*WHITE: Uhlmann* *BLACK: Hanninen*

*Wageningen 1957*

| WHITE | BLACK | WHITE | BLACK | WHITE | BLACK |
|---|---|---|---|---|---|
| 1 P–QB4 | P–K4 | 10 N–B2 | PxP | 19 N–K4 | QxP |
| 2 N–QB3 | N–KB3 | 11 BxP | P–B4 | 20 RxP | Q–K4 |
| 3 P–KN3 | P–Q4 | 12 QR–B1 | P–N4!? | 21 RxB† | QxR |
| 4 PxP | NxP | 13 B–Q2 | P–KR4 | 22 BxP | Q–K4 |
| 5 B–N2 | N–N3 | 14 P–K4! | P–R5 | 23 Q–B3 | K–Q2 |
| 6 P–Q3 | B–K2 | 15 PxBP | PxP? | 24 Q–B7† | K–B3 |
| 7 N–R3 | N–B3 | 16 PxB | PxN† | 25 R–B2† | K–N4 |
| 8 O–O | B–K3 | 17 RxP | Q–Q3 | 26 Q–N3† | K–R3 |
| 9 P–B4 | Q–Q2 | 18 BxN† | QxB | 27 N–B5† | Resigns |

## part 3—VIENNA DEFENSE

1 P–QB4, P–K4
2 N–QB3, N–QB3
3 P–KN3[A]

Key Position 3

### OBSERVATIONS ON KEY POSITION 3

[A] 3 N–B3 is also possible of course. Black's safest reply is then 3 . . . N–B3, transposing into Part 1.

White's last move is motivated by his desire to dominate Q5, Black's control of which has been considerably decreased by 2 . . . N–QB3. The fact gives the ensuing struggle its salient character. White usually proceeds with KN–K2, keeping the diagonal of his King Bishop open. If White then succeeds in achieving P–Q4 with impunity, the scales become heavily tipped in his favor.

### IDEA VARIATIONS 5 AND 6:

(5) 3 . . . P–KN3 (most usual) 4 B–N2, B–N2 5 P–K3 (for other ideas in treating this type of position, refer to the Closed Variation of the Sicilian Defense), P–Q3 6 KN–K2, KN–K2 7 P–Q4! (without this advance, White achieves little; after 7 P–Q3, O–O 8 O–O, B–B4 9 N–Q5, R–N1 the chances are approximately even), PxP 8 PxP, O–O 9 O–O, B–N5 (for 9 . . . N–B4, see Game 5), 10 P–KR3, BxN 11 NxB and White has the edge.

(6) 3 . . . P–B4 (interesting, but not quite satisfactory) 4 B–N2, N–B3 5 P–K3, B–K2 (5 . . . P–KN3 is a worthwhile alternative) 6 KN–K2!± (6 P–Q4 is premature; after 6 . . . P–K5 7 P–B3, O–O 8 PxP, PxP 9 NxP, NxN 10 BxN, B–N5† 11 B–Q2, White's game is endangered by 11 . . . Q–K2!).

### *Sicilian Attack Game 5*

*WHITE: Botvinnik* *BLACK: Reshevsky*

*AVRO 1938*

| | WHITE | BLACK | | WHITE | BLACK | | WHITE | BLACK |
|---|---|---|---|---|---|---|---|---|
| 1 | P–QB4 | P–K4 | 14 | P–QN4 | N–Q2 | 27 | N–B5 | Q–K1 |
| 2 | N–QB3 | N–QB3 | 15 | Q–N3 | N–Q5 | 28 | NxB | KxN |
| 3 | P–KN3 | P–KN3 | 16 | NxN | BxN | 29 | R–Q7† | R–B2 |
| 4 | B–N2 | B–N2 | 17 | QR–Q1 | B–N2 | 30 | B–K5! | K–N1 |
| 5 | P–K3 | P–Q3 | 18 | KR–K1 | PxP | 31 | RxP | RxR |
| 6 | KN–K2 | KN–K2 | 19 | PxP | N–B3 | 32 | BxR | R–R8† |
| 7 | P–Q4 | PxP | 20 | P–KR3 | P–R4 | 33 | K–R2 | R–R2 |
| 8 | PxP | O–O | 21 | P–B5! | B–B4 | 34 | B–K5 | R–KB2 |
| 9 | O–O | N–B4 | 22 | N–N5! | B–Q2 | 35 | P–B7 | N–Q2 |
| 10 | P–Q5 | N–K4 | 23 | P–B6 | PxP | 36 | Q–B2! | R–B1 |
| 11 | P–N3 | P–QR4 | 24 | PxP | B–B1 | 37 | P–B8(Q) | Resigns |
| 12 | B–N2 | N–Q2 | 25 | NxQP! | B–K3 | | | |
| 13 | P–QR3 | N–B4! | 26 | RxB! | PxR | | | |

## PRACTICAL VARIATIONS 7 AND 8:

1 P–QB4, P–K4 2 N–QB3, N–QB3 3 P–KN3

| | 7 | 8 |
|---|---|---|
| *3* | – – | – – |
| | B–B4[1] | P–Q3 |
| *4* | B–N2 | B–N2 |
| | P–Q3 | N–B3[4] |
| *5* | P–K3 | P–K3 |
| | KN–K2[2] | B–K2 |
| *6* | P–QR3 | KN–K2 |
| | P–QR4 | O–O |
| *7* | KN–K2 | O–O[5] |
| | O–O | ± |
| *8* | O–O | |
| | B–Q2 | |
| *9* | P–R3[3] | |
| | ± | |

*Notes to practical variations 7 and 8:*

[1] Not advisable. The Bishop has too little scope on QB4.

[2] Or 5 . . . N–B3 6 KN–K2, O–O 7 O–O, R–K1 8 P–Q4, B–N3 9 P–KR3, B–KB4 10 P–Q5, N–K2 11 P–KN4!, when White has good attacking chances (Korchnoi–S. Szabo, Bucharest 1953).

[3] After the eventual P–Q4, Black's position will be cramped.

[4] For 4 . . . B–Q2, see Game 6.

[5] White's is somewhat freer.

*Sicilian Attack Game 6*

*WHITE: Darga* *BLACK: Keller*

*Chaumont 1958*

| WHITE | BLACK | WHITE | BLACK |
|---|---|---|---|
| 1 P–QB4 | P–K4 | 10 P–B5! | P–Q4 |
| 2 N–QB3 | N–QB3 | 11 P–K4 | B–N5 |
| 3 P–KN3 | P–Q3 | 12 Q–R4 | P–Q5 |
| 4 B–N2 | B–Q2 | 13 P–K5 | N–K2 |
| 5 N–B3 | Q–B1 | 14 N–Q5! | NxN |
| 6 O–O | P–KN3 | 15 QxP† | B–Q2 |
| 7 P–Q4! | PxP | 16 QxN | O–O |
| 8 NxP | B–N2 | 17 QxP | Resigns |
| 9 NxN | PxN | | |

## part 4—DUTCH DEFENSIVE SYSTEM

1 P–QB4, P–K4
2 N–QB3, P–Q3
3 P–KN3[A], P–KB4[B]
4 B–N2, N–KB3

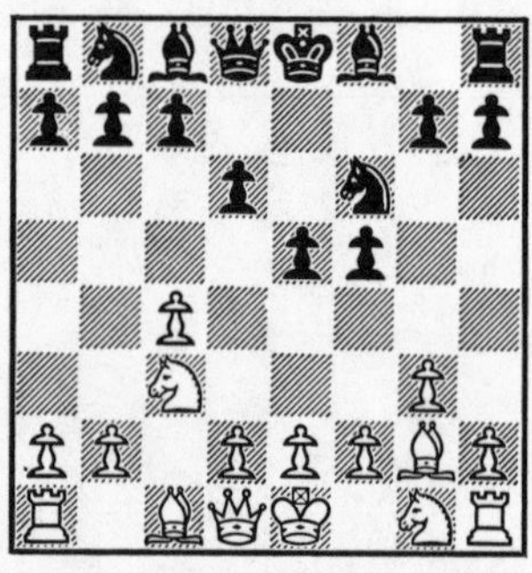

KEY POSITION 4

### OBSERVATIONS ON KEY POSITION 4

[A] White need not necessarily fianchetto his King Bishop; the continuation 3 N–B3 is just as good, e.g., 3 . . . P–KB4 4 P–Q4, P–K5 5 N–KN5, B–K2 6 N–R3, N–KB3 7 P–K3, N–R3 8 B–K2, P–B3 9 O–O, N–B2 10 P–B3, O–O 11 B–Q2 and White maintains the initiative. For 5 N–Q2 in this line, see Game 7.

[B] The characteristic Pawn advance of this system.

This position has occurred but rarely in tournament play. Both sides must act vigorously. White, if given a free hand, may castle long and initiate a powerful King-side assault. Black, for his part, must not hesitate at critical moments to part with a Pawn to keep his counter-attack alive.

### IDEA VARIATION 7:

(7) 5 P–Q4! (practically the only move worth serious consideration; for the passive 5 P–Q3, see Prac. Var. 9), B–K2 (the continuation 5 . . . PxP 6 QxP, N–B3 7 Q–Q2 is greatly to White's advantage; he best proceeds by placing his King Knight on KB4 and following up with the fianchetto of his Queen Bishop) 6 P–K3, O–O 7 KN–K2, K–R1 8 Q–B2, Q–K1 9 P–N3, N–B3 10 B–R3, PxP 11 PxP, P–B5! (in order to answer 12 P–Q5 with 12 . . . P–B6 13 KBxP, N–K4) 12 O–O–O (better than 12 PxP, N–KR4 13 B–K4, NxBP 14 BxRP, N–N7† 15 K–Q1, RxP which clearly favors Black), P–B6! (consistent; inferior is 12 . . . N–KR4; see Game 8) 13 BxP, N–KN5 14 BxN, BxB 15 P–B4, B–B3 and Black has good chances for the Pawn.

*Sicilian Attack Game 7*

*WHITE: Boleslavski* *BLACK: Bronstein*

*Zurich 1953*

| | WHITE | BLACK | | WHITE | BLACK | | WHITE | BLACK |
|---|---|---|---|---|---|---|---|---|
| 1 | P–QB4 | P–K4 | 18 | PxN | N–B3 | 35 | P–R5 | Q–B3 |
| 2 | N–QB3 | P–Q3 | 19 | B–QB3 | B–QN2 | 36 | R–R2 | P–N4 |
| 3 | N–B3 | P–KB4 | 20 | Q–N2 | N–N5 | 37 | R–KB1 | Q–N3 |
| 4 | P–Q4 | P–K5 | 21 | Q–B1 | B–N2 | 38 | RPxP | RPxP |
| 5 | N–Q2 | P–B3 | 22 | P–KR3 | BxB | 39 | R–R7 | R/1–Q2 |
| 6 | P–K3 | N–B3 | 23 | QxB | N–B3 | 40 | R–R8 | N–B3 |
| 7 | B–K2 | P–KN3 | 24 | B–B4 | QR–Q1 | 41 | Q–N2 | P–N5 |
| 8 | O–O | B–R3 | 25 | R–Q2 | P–KR3 | 42 | PxP | QxP |
| 9 | P–QN4 | O–O | 26 | N–B1 | K–R2 | 43 | R–Q1 | Q–R4 |
| 10 | P–N5 | R–K1 | 27 | N–K2 | Q–B1 | 44 | Q–KB2 | Q–N3 |
| 11 | N–N3 | QN–Q2 | 28 | R/1–Q1 | R–Q3 | 45 | R–QB8 | N–N5 |
| 12 | Q–B2 | Q–B2 | 29 | Q–N3 | R/1–Q1 | 46 | Q–K1 | R–R2 |
| 13 | B–Q2 | P–B4 | 30 | N–B3 | Q–K2 | 47 | R–B6 | R–R6 |
| 14 | PxP | PxP | 31 | R/2–KB2 | B–B1 | 48 | R–B1 | Q–B3 |
| 15 | N–Q5 | Q–Q3 | 32 | N–K2 | B–K3 | 49 | B–K2 | Draw |
| 16 | QR–Q1 | P–N3 | 33 | N–B3 | B–B2 | | | |
| 17 | P–B4 | NxN | 34 | P–QR4 | N–K1 | | | |

*Sicilian Attack Game 8*

*WHITE: Stolz* *BLACK: H. Steiner*

*Saltsjobaden 1952*

| | WHITE | BLACK | | WHITE | BLACK |
|---|---|---|---|---|---|
| 1 | P–QB4 | P–K4 | 20 | PxB | B–B4 |
| 2 | N–QB3 | P–Q3 | 21 | Q–R6† | B–R2 |
| 3 | P–KN3 | P–KB4 | 22 | N–K3! | R–B3 |
| 4 | B–N2 | N–KB3 | 23 | Q–N5 | R–N3 |
| 5 | P–Q4 | B–K2 | 24 | P–Q5! | RxQ |
| 6 | P–K3 | O–O | 25 | RPxR | N–K2 |
| 7 | KN–K2 | K–R1 | 26 | N–N4! | Q–QB1 |
| 8 | Q–B2 | Q–K1 | 27 | P–N6 | QxN |
| 9 | P–N3 | N–B3 | 28 | RxB† | K–N1 |
| 10 | B–R3 | PxP | 29 | RxN† | K–B1 |
| 11 | PxP | P–B5 | 30 | R–B7† | K–K1 |
| 12 | O–O–O | N–KR4? | 31 | R–K1 | QxNP |
| 13 | B–K4 | P–KN3 | 32 | R/1xN† | K–Q1 |
| 14 | N–Q5 | Q–Q1 | 33 | B–B6? | QxB |
| 15 | B–QN2 | P–B6 | 34 | RxQ | Forfeit |
| 16 | N/2–B4 | B–N4 | | Black overstepped the time limit. | |
| 17 | BxNP! | PxB | | | |
| 18 | QxP | N–N2 | | | |
| 19 | P–KR4 | BxN† | | | |

## PRACTICAL VARIATION 9:

1 P–QB4, P–K4 2 N–QB3, P–Q3 3 P–KN3, P–KB4 4 B–N2, N–KB3

| | 9 | | 9 |
|---|---|---|---|
| 5 | P–Q3 | 8 | B–Q2[1] |
| | P–KN3 | | P–B3 |
| 6 | N–R3 | 9 | K–R1 |
| | B–N2 | | K–R1 |
| 7 | O–O | 10 | P–B4[2] |
| | O–O | | P–K5![3] |
| | | | ∓ |

*Notes to practical variation 9:*

[1] White promotes his own downfall with this passive move. Far better is 8 P–B4 immediately, e.g., 8 . . . P–K5 9 PxP, PxP 10 N–KN5.

[2] Better now is 10 P–B3 followed by 11 N–B2.

[3] Golombek–Botvinnik, Budapest 1952.

## SUPPLEMENTARY VARIATIONS 1–3:

1 P–QB4, P–K4

| | 1 | 2 | 3 |
|---|---|---|---|
| 2 | N–KB3[1] | – – | – – |
| | P–K5[2] | – – | – – |
| 3 | N–Q4 | – – | – – |
| | N–QB3[3] | – – | – – |
| 4 | NxN | N–B2 | P–K3 |
| | QPxN | N–B3 | NxN |
| 5 | P–Q4[4] | N–B3 | PxN |
| | PxP e.p. | B–B4 | P–Q4 |

| | 1 | 2 | 3 |
|---|---|---|---|
| 6 | QxP | P–K3[6] | P–Q3[9] |
| | QxQ | P–Q3[7] | N–B3 |
| 7 | PxQ[5] | P–Q3 | N–B3 |
| | = | PxP | PxQP |
| 8 | | BxP | BxP |
| | | B–K3 | B–K2 |
| 9 | | O–O[8] | = |
| | | P–Q4 | |
| | | = | |

*Notes to supplementary variations 1–3:*

[1] This offers White little hope for the initiative.

[2] Other moves are of no independent significance.

[3] 3 . . . P–QB4 is best met by 4 N–N5!

[4] 5 N–B3, N–B3 6 P–K3, B–KB4! is satisfactory for Black.

[5] With Queens exchanged and Pawn structures sound, there is little to explore.

[6] After 6 P–QN3, O–O 7 P–N3 Black frees his game with 7 . . . P–Q4!, and if 8 PxP, then 8 . . . N–KN5!

[7] 6 . . . P–Q4? PxP as well as 6 . . . N–K4 7 P–Q4 favors White.

[8] 9 P–K4? fails against 9 . . . N–KN5!

[9] 6 N–B3 is most safely answered by 6 . . . P–QB3.

# chapter 43—Irregular and Unusual Openings

Once called a "joke opening" by Capablanca, 1 . . . P–KN3 (the "Fianchetto del Rey" in an earlier terminology and currently renamed the Robatsch Defense after the Austrian player who has done most to popularize it) is a sort of factotum which can be used against practically any White opening move including 1 P–K4, 1 P–Q4, 1 P–QB4, 1 N–KB3, etc.

The old masters shrank in horror from a fianchetto on the first move, and even some hypermoderns might blanch a bit at the idea; but so far no specific refutation of the Robatsch has been found, and all that can be said is that White, faced by no particular problems and free to choose almost any methodical development, should maintain a minimal initiative at worst. If he attempts, however, to overrun the Black position without further ado, he may run into disagreeable resistance.

The advantage of the Robatsch over the Pirc, its close kin, is supposedly a degree of flexibility. For one point, the Black King Knight may go to K2 instead of KB3, especially if a previous . . . P–K4 has been bypassed with White's P–Q5. Then, with the Knight at K2, Black may enjoy the ready-made break, . . . P–KB4.

To be sure, any value that Black may get out of this possibility is offset by the extreme latitude granted to White from the opening gun. An attack on White's King Pawn by . . . N–KB3, for example, would compel an immediate decision as to a defense. Black's failure to introduce this kind of tension gives White ample time to set up whatever positional pattern he prefers. As a contemporary instance of the continuing hypermodern challenge to classicism, the Robatsch is primarily a weapon for those who have a flair for Nimzowitschian strategies requiring patience, tenacity, and resourceful defense.

Somewhat similar considerations apply to 1 P–KN3, the Robatsch in reverse — a favorite of Benko's and therefore often called the Benko Opening. The difference is that White has the move in hand and may be able to transpose into some favorable line unless Black is exceedingly cautious and alert. That the opening tends to demand position play of a high order from both players is illustrated in Game 2.

### *Game 1*

*WHITE: Botvinnik* *BLACK: Lombardy*

*Munich 1958*

| | WHITE | BLACK | | WHITE | BLACK |
|---|---|---|---|---|---|
| 1 | P–QB4 | P–KN3 | 22 | B–K2 | N–N6 |
| 2 | P–K4 | B–N2 | 23 | B–Q3 | N–Q1 |
| 3 | P–Q4 | P–Q3 | 24 | K–B2 | B–B2 |
| 4 | N–QB3 | P–K4 | 25 | R–KN1 | N–R4 |
| 5 | PxP | PxP | 26 | B–Q2 | B–B1 |
| 6 | QxQ† | KxQ | 27 | B–K3 | B–R3 |
| 7 | B–N5† | P–B3 | 28 | R–B3 | B–B1 |
| 8 | O–O–O† | N–Q2 | 29 | N/3–K2 | P–QN4 |
| 9 | B–K3 | P–B3 | 30 | PxP | P–B4 |
| 10 | P–KN3 | K–B2 | 31 | P–N6† | PxP |
| 11 | P–B4 | N–R3 | 32 | N–N5† | K–N2 |
| 12 | P–KR3 | N–B2 | 33 | N/2–B3 | N–QB3 |
| 13 | N–B3 | B–R3 | 34 | P–R3 | KR–Q1 |
| 14 | R–K1 | R–K1 | 35 | B–QB1 | QR–B1 |
| 15 | R–R2 | N–B1 | 36 | K–N1 | N–N2 |
| 16 | R–KB2 | PxP | 37 | B–B1 | N–K3 |
| 17 | PxP | N–K3 | 38 | R–B2 | N/K–Q5 |
| 18 | N–R2 | P–KB4 | 39 | P–KR4 | N–R4 |
| 19 | P–K5 | N–N2 | 40 | R–N3 | N/4–N6 |
| 20 | N–B3 | N–R4 | | Draw | |
| 21 | N–Q4 | B–K3 | | | |

### *Game 2*

*WHITE: Benko* *BLACK: Fischer*

*Curacao 1962*

| | WHITE | BLACK | | WHITE | BLACK |
|---|---|---|---|---|---|
| 1 | P–KN3 | N–KB3 | 14 | P–B4 | R–N1 |
| 2 | B–N2 | P–KN3 | 15 | Q–Q2 | P–QN4 |
| 3 | P–K4 | P–Q3 | 16 | PxP e.p. | PxP |
| 4 | P–Q4 | B–N2 | 17 | P–QN4 | N–K3 |
| 5 | N–K2 | O–O | 18 | P–N5 | NxN |
| 6 | O–O | P–K4 | 19 | BxN | BxB† |
| 7 | QN–B3 | P–B3 | 20 | QxB | P–QB4 |
| 8 | P–QR4 | QN–Q2 | 21 | Q–Q2 | B–N2 |
| 9 | P–R5 | PxP | 22 | QR–Q1 | R–K3 |
| 10 | NxP | N–B4 | 23 | P–K5 | BxB |
| 11 | P–R3 | R–K1 | 24 | KxB | Q–N2† |
| 12 | R–K1 | KN–Q2 | 25 | K–B2 | R–Q1 |
| 13 | B–K3 | Q–B2 | 26 | PxP | N–B3 |

| | WHITE | BLACK | | WHITE | BLACK |
|---|---|---|---|---|---|
| 27 | RxR | PxR | 34 | P–N4 | P–K4 |
| 28 | Q–K2 | K–B2 | 35 | PxP | R–B2† |
| 29 | Q–B3 | Q–N1 | 36 | K–N2 | Q–R5 |
| 30 | N–K4 | NxN | 37 | R–KB1 | RxR |
| 31 | QxN | R–Q2 | 38 | RxR | QxP† |
| 32 | Q–B6 | Q–Q1 | 39 | Q–N2 | Q–K6 |
| 33 | K–B3 | K–N2 | 40 | Q–K2 | Resigns |

*Game 3*

*WHITE: Bronstein* *BLACK: O'Kelly*

*Beverwyk 1963*

| | WHITE | BLACK | | WHITE | BLACK |
|---|---|---|---|---|---|
| 1 | P–KN3 | N–KB3 | 17 | N–N4 | P–R5 |
| 2 | B–N2 | P–Q4 | 18 | Q–Q2 | P–B5 |
| 3 | N–KB3 | P–K3 | 19 | PxP | BxP |
| 4 | O–O | B–K2 | 20 | B–N5 | P–R6 |
| 5 | P–Q3 | P–B4 | 21 | P–N3 | B–R3 |
| 6 | QN–Q2 | N–B3 | 22 | QR–B1 | N–R2 |
| 7 | P–K4 | O–O | 23 | BxB | QxB |
| 8 | R–K1 | Q–B2 | 24 | N–N5 | N–N4 |
| 9 | P–K5 | N–Q2 | 25 | BxP | R–Q1 |
| 10 | Q–K2 | P–QN4 | 26 | BxR | NxP |
| 11 | P–KR4 | P–QR4 | 27 | QxR† | QxQ |
| 12 | N–B1 | B–R3 | 28 | RxN | N–B6 |
| 13 | N/1–R2 | P–N5 | 29 | B–B3 | P–B4 |
| 14 | P–R5 | KR–B1 | 30 | NxKP | Q–Q7 |
| 15 | P–R6 | P–N3 | | .... | Resigns |
| 16 | B–B4 | Q–Q1 | | | |

---

## "OFFBEAT" OPENINGS

What was said earlier about the Fianchetto del Rey (Robatsch in Reverse) and the Robatsch Defense (special examples of which are presented in Prac. Var. 2 and 3 of this chapter) applies in some measure to all irregular and unusual openings: they are primarily a weapon for those with the patience, stubbornness and defensive resourcefulness required by Nimzowitschian strategies.

But there may be additional reasons for the occasional use of "off-beat" openings. Precisely because they are seldom ventured, they may enable a tournament player who has familiarized himself with their intricacies to gain some time on the clock while his more conventional opponent consumes precious minutes trying to figure out how best to take advantage of what, by definition, are not standard, well-established lines. Apart from this consideration, the "natural" player may feel that he is able to improvise more effectively than a pure theoretician; perhaps a student of human nature, such as Dr. Emanuel Lasker, has particular psychological reasons for springing a surprise; or quite simply, a jaded player may nibble at an odd opening pretty much as he might sample an exotic food. Surely the mavericks of chess like Nimzowitsch, Tartakover and Reti must have grinned inwardly as they confounded the pillars of orthodoxy with rank heresies.

One thing is certain: "book knowledge," while indispensable to the mastery of chess, will not automatically defeat any and all departures from the norm. Even so absured a pattern as the "Hippopotamus," which consists largely in moving as many Pawns as possible to the third rank, cannot be guaranteed to fall of its own weight. The proper reaction to such outright violations of principle is not impetuosity or exorcism but the application of calm, watchful technique. An unsound opening, far from beating itself, must be beaten by unremitting thought and effort. And then, of course, one must be positive that it is really unsound and not just "off-beat" or novel.

The remainder of this chapter consists in brief discussions of infrequently played openings, followed by practical variations and notes. Alapin's Opening (1 P–K4, P–K4 2 N–K2), Anderssen's Opening (1 P–QR3) and the Queen's Fianchetto Defense (1 . . . P–QN3) merit no allocation of space because, for the best of reasons, they are seen about as rarely as Halley's Comet.

## DUNST OPENING

Extensively analyzed and often adopted by the New York master, T. A. Dunst, the move 1 N–QB3, formerly called the Queen's Knight's Opening, can give rise to unique variations as well as transpositions into familiar territory (the Vienna, the Sicilian, the Caro-Kann, etc.). The following brief comments will be confined to the idiosyncratic possibilities of the opening.

When Black replies with 1 . . . P–Q4 and then essays the characteristic center-locking advance 2 . . . P–Q5 in answer to 2 P–K4, the result is a positional kind of game in which White will usually aim for an auspicious P–KB4.

An entirely different set-up stems from 1 N–QB3, P–Q4 2 P–K4, PxP 3 NxP, while still another line is what the Italians have called the "Ruy Lopez of the Queenside": 1 N–QB3, N–KB3 2 P–Q4, P–Q4 3 B–N5. If 1 . . . P–K4, White is under no necessity of transposing into the Vienna with 2 P–K4 but instead may choose the distinctive 2 N–B3. If, then, 2 . . . N–QB3, the policy of avoiding a King's Pawn transposition can be pursued with 3 P–Q4. See Prac. Var. 1. Interestingly, Black can hardly attempt a Dutch formation with 1 . . . P–KB4 because of the strong immediate response 2 P–K4!

The opening is sound and playable, but affords Black a wide array of defenses and makes no attempt to confront him with thorny problems requiring immediate solution.

## PARIS OPENING

The Paris Opening, 1 N–KR3, begins with a violation of principle. On the very first move, White's King Knight is brought to the rim of the board instead of the center. On R3 he not only has less mobility but after 1 . . . P–Q4 offers himself as a target for the Black Queen Bishop. While Black's forthright threat of 2 . . . BxN, which would disrupt White's Kingside Pawn formation, can be met for the moment by 2 P–KN3, Black may proceed methodically to line up on the Knight with 3 . . . B–B4 and 4 . . . Q–Q2. Then White will be forced to move the Knight with consequent loss of time.

In case Black fails to exploit the awkward Knight development, White may capitalize the more favorable aspect of the move. Since the Knight on R3 does not block White's King Bishop Pawn, that Pawn may effectively advance to KB4, attack the adverse center and open White's King Bishop file. See Prac. Var. 4.

It may be noted in passing that 1 N–QR3 (the Durkin Attack) can satisfy the penchant for oddity as well as 1 N–KR3. R. T. Durkin has done surprisingly well with this in various postal and New Jersey tournaments and T. A. Dunst has brought off a few successful experiments. After 1 . . . P–Q4 White may play 2 P–QB4 or 2 P–QB3 (intending, in the latter case, 3 N–B2 followed by P–Q4), while against 1 . . . P–K4, the bizarre 2 N–B4 is in the spirit of the opening. Apart from its possible shock value, however, the Durkin Attack is hardly to be recommended as a reliable weapon.

## POLISH OPENING

Called the Polish Opening or the Orang-Utan, the esoteric 1 P–QN4 was added to opening repertoire by the Viennese master Englisch about half a century ago. It was a favorite of Tartakover's and more recently has been investigated by Sokolsky and Pachman. The latter advocates the reply 1 . . . P–QR4, giving the opening an altogether weird appearance. A. E. Santasiere plays 1 N–KB3 as a prefatory move and refers to a later P–QN4 (against 1 . . . P–Q4, for example) as "Santasiere's Folly." Among contemporary masters who will occasionally resort to 1 P–QN4 is Sidney Bernstein of New York.

The obvious defects of the Polish are that it initiates a wing demonstration when emphasis should be placed on center control and provides a ready-made target which may easily become a source of permanent concern. On the other hand, the move readies a promising fianchetto, while the advanced Pawn will inhibit enemy expansion on the Queenside. Thus the Polish Opening appeals to those who like to fish in troubled waters, but serves no purpose where there is a preference for sounder and more conservative methods.

Entirely valueless is the Polish Defense (1 . . . P–QN4 in answer to 1 P–Q4, 1 P–K4, 1 N–KB3 etc.), introduced by A. Wagner at Stanislau in 1913. Unless Black is intent on committing suicide, he has no business indulging in such weakening, time-wasting antics in the opening. See Prac. Var. 7 for an illustration of how quickly Black can find himself saddled with grave, self-created difficulties.

## SARAGOSSA OPENING

The Saragossa Opening, 1 P–QB3, attributed to Juncosa of Saragossa, lends itself to numerous transpositions in addition to its inherent character as a Caro-Kann in reverse.

1 P–QB3, P–Q4 2 P–Q4 is a Queen Pawn which becomes a Colle after 2 . . . N–KB3 3 N–B3, P–K3.

1 P–QB3, P–K4 2 P–Q4, PxP 3 PxP, P–Q4 is the Exchange Variation of the Queen's Gambit, while 1 P–QB3, P–QB4 2 P–Q4, PxP 3 PxP, P–Q4 reverts to the Exchange Variation of the Slav Defense.

Other transpositions are the Exchange Variation of the Caro-Kann Defense (1 P–QB3, P–QB3 2 P–K4, P–Q4 3 PxP, PxP 4 P–Q4) and the Ponziani (1 P–QB3, P–K4 2 P–K4, N–QB3 3 N–B3).

It is evident that Black enjoys great latitude and can face the opening phase of the game without qualms.

## THE "SPIKE"

1 P–KN4, the "Spike" or Kolibri Opening, is a defiant, almost contemptuous beginning, as though to show that White can get away with anything on his first move, including this self-inflicted wound on his strategic King-side. White appears to be saying to his opponent, "See in what low esteem I hold you. I can toy with you, I can play the most preposterous opening, and you are impotent to exact a penalty." If this is indeed the message intended by 1 P–KN4, the move belongs to the realm of psychology rather than logic. It is rarely encountered in master chess for the good and sufficient reason that there is a limit to the risks that can be taken even by the most daring performer on a flying trapeze.

## VAN'T KRUYS OPENING

Named after a Dutch player who lived about 1860, the Van't Kruys Opening, 1 P–K3, has little independent significance. Once in a while it may evoke an original and downright wild position, but for the most part it is marked by the absence of clash and tension, and is often a prelude to transposition into some lackadaisical line of one of the regular openings.

A simple transposition into a Queen's Pawn Game is effected with 1 P–K3, P–Q4 2 P–Q4, and a tame variation of the French Defense is reached after 1 P–K3, P–K4 2 P–Q4, PxP 3 PxP, P–Q4. In this line 2 P–QB4 metamorphizes into an English, in which Black should not unwarily permit White to obtain a Sicilian Four Knights in reverse: 2 . . . N–KB3 3 N–QB3, P–Q4 4 PxP, NxP 5 N–B3! Other possibilities are Bird's Opening (1 P–K3, P–Q4 2 P–KB4) and a line in the Reti (1 P–K3, P–Q4 2 P–QB4, P–QB3 3 N–KB3). Black's choice of first moves is practically unlimited, since almost anything will do. 1 . . . P–QB4, 1 . . . P–Q3, 1 . . . P–K3, 1 . . . P–KB4; 1 . . . N–KB3 and 1 . . . P–KN3 are all playable replies.

| | Dunst Opening | Robatsch in Reverse | Fianchetto del Rey (Robatsch Defense) | Paris Opening | Polish Opening I |
|---|---|---|---|---|---|
| | 1 | 2 | 3 | 4 | 5 |
| 1 | N–QB3 | P–KN3 | P–K4 | N–KR3 | P–QN4 |
| | P–K4[1] | P–KN3[4] | P–KN3 | P–Q4 | P–K4 |
| 2 | N–B3 | B–N2 | P–Q4 | P–KN3 | B–N2 |
| | N–QB3 | B–N2 | B–N2 | P–K4 | P–KB3[15] |
| 3 | P–Q4 | P–Q4 | N–QB3 | P–KB4[9] | P–K4[16] |
| | PxP | P–Q3 | P–Q3 | BxN[10] | BxP |
| 4 | NxP | P–K4 | P–B4 | BxB | B–B4 |
| | N–B3[2] | N–KB3 | N–KB3 | PxP | N–K2 |
| 5 | B–N5 | N–K2 | N–B3 | O–O | P–B4 |
| | P–Q4 | O–O | O–O | PxP | P–Q4 |
| 6 | P–K4 | O–O | B–Q3 | PxP[11] | PxQP |
| | B–K2 | QN–Q2 | B–N5 | B–Q3[12] | B–Q3[17] |
| 7 | B–N5 | QN–B3 | P–KR3 | P–K4! | PxP |
| | B–Q2 | P–B3 | BxN | Q–N4[13] | PxP |
| 8 | PxP | P–QR4 | QxB | Q–B3 | Q–R5† |
| | NxP | P–QR4 | N–B3 | QxP† | N–N3 |
| 9 | NxN/5 | P–N3 | Q–B2[6] | QxQ | N–KB3[18] |
| | BxB | R–K1 | N–Q2[7] | BxQ | ± |
| 10 | Q–K2† | B–QR3 | B–K3[8] | B–B8[14] | |
| | N–K2[3] | Q–B2[5] | ± | ± | |
| | ± | ± | | | |

*Notes to practical variations 1–10:*

[1] The alternative, 1 . . . P–Q4, is an attempt to transpose into a Queen's Pawn Game in which White's Queen Knight is supposedly misplaced because he blocks the Queen Bishop Pawn. Actually, White need not permit this transposition insofar as the immediate presence of the White Knight on QB3 supports the thrust P–K4 and has the effect of turning the opening into a King's Pawn formation. An example of this is seen in a Vienna line that was in vogue during the reign of Steinitz: 1 N–QB3, P–Q4 2 P–K4, P–Q5 3 QN–K2, P–K4 4 N–N3, B–K3 5 P–Q3, P–QB4 6 P–KB4, PxP 7 BxP, N–QB3 8 N–B3, N–B3 9 B–K2, N–KN5 10 Q–Q2, B–Q3=.

[2] Plausible, but inferior to the development of the King Bishop to B4 or N5.

[3] 10 . . . B–K2 also fails after 11 O–O–O, when White has a plethora of threats. One possibility, for example, is 11 . . . NxN 12 BxB†, QxB 13 RxN, and White's superiority in development is crushing. The moves in the column are taken from Dunst–Gresser, Marshall Chess Club Championship, 1950-51. The game continued: 11 Q–K5!, BxB 12 NxP†, K–B1 13 N/7–K6†, Resigns.

[4] Emulating White is no attempt at refutation.

[5] Benko–Tal, Curacao 1962. The game continued with 11

| *Polish Opening* II | *Polish Defense* | *Saragossa Opening* | *"Spike"* | *Van't Kruys Opening* |
|---|---|---|---|---|
| 6 | 7 | 8 | 9 | 10 |
| – – | P–Q4 | P–QB3 | P–KN4 | P–K3 |
| P–Q4 | P–QN4 | P–Q4 | P–Q4[27] | P–QB4 |
| B–N2 | P–K4[22] | P–Q4 | B–N2 | P–QB4 |
| N–KB3[19] | B–N2 | P–QB4 | BxP | N–QB3 |
| P–K3 | P–KB3[23] | P–K3 | P–QB4 | N–QB3 |
| P–K3 | P–QR3[24] | N–Q2 | P–QB3[28] | P–KN3 |
| P–N5 | P–QB4 | P–KB4 | PxP | P–B4[32] |
| B–K2 | PxP | KN–B3 | N–KB3[29] | B–N2 |
| P–KB4 | BxP | N–Q2 | N–QB3 | N–B3 |
| O–O | P–K3 | P–KN3 | P–K4[30] | P–K4[33] |
| B–Q3 | N–B3[25] | KN–B3 | PxP e.p. | PxP |
| P–QR3[20] | ± | B–N2 | BxP | NxP |
| P–QR4 | | B–Q3 | P–Q4 | B–K2![34] |
| PxP | | O–O | QN–Q2 | NxN† |
| PxP | | O–O | P–K4 | BxN[35] |
| RxR | | Q–B2 | B–K2 | Q–R5† |
| BxR | | N–K5 | KN–K2[31] | P–N3 |
| P–B4[21] | | N–K1[26] | ± | QxBP[36] |
| = | | = | | = |

Q–Q2, P–K4 12 QR–Q1, PxP 13 NxP, N–B4 14 P–B3, P–N3 15 N/4–K2, B–B1 16 B–N2, Q–K2 17 N–Q4, B–QN2 18 KR–K1, B–N2 19 P–B4, QR–Q1 20 B–B3, Q–Q2 21 Q–N2!±.

[6] If 9 B–K3, P–K4 10 QPxP, PxP 11 P–B5, N–Q5 12 Q–B2, PxP with adequate play for Black.

[7] If 9 . . . N–QN5 10 B–B1 (10 B–B4, NxKP!).

[8] Penrose–Robatsch, Hastings 1961-62.

[9] The Paris Gambit. 3 B–N2, B–KB4, followed by 4 . . . Q–Q2, favors Black.

[10] After 3 . . . P–K5 4 B–N2, B–KB4 5 P–Q3, White has fair prospects.

[11] The Compromised Paris Gambit is 6 P–K4, PxP† 7 K–R1, etc.

[12] 6 . . . Q–N4 7 R–B3, B–Q3 8 P–Q3±.

[13] If 7 . . . BxP? 8 Q–B3! If 7 . . . PxKP 8 Q–N4.

[14] Analysis by Tartakover.

[15] To fortify the King Pawn. But the move has an artificial appearance, and, in fact, exposes Black's KN1–QR7 diagonal.

2 . . . BxP 3 BxP, N–KB3, followed by . . . N–QB3, gives Black a free and easy development, even though this is in line with White's plan to exchange a center Pawn for an outside one.

Of course, 2 . . . N–QB3 fails against 3 P–N5.

[16] The gambit. But 3 P–QR3, P–Q4 is good for Black.

**continued ▸**

[17] 6 . . . PxP is risky: 7 Q–B3, B–Q3 8 N–K2, N–N3 9 P–Q4, Q–K2 10 B–B1, B–KB4 11 B–Q3± (Tartakover–Colle, Mardiov 1926).

[18] Tartakover–Reti, Vienna 1919.

[19] 2 . . . B–B4 3 P–K3, P–K3 4 P–KB4, N–KB3 5 N–KB3, BxNP 6 N–B3, QN–Q2 7 N–K2, N–N5 8 P–B3, B–K2 9 P–KR3, N–B4 10 N–N3, B–R5 11 NxB, QxN 12 Q–B3, NxP 13 Q–B2, NxB, Resigns (Capablanca–Kevitz, Brooklyn 1924).

[20] Or 6 . . . P–B4.

[21] Tartakover–Maroczy, New York 1924.

[22] To neutralize the effect of the coming fianchetto. 2 N–KB3 is also good.

[23] So that Black's Queen Bishop will bite on granite. With a move in hand, this move is safer than the same move played by Black against the Polish Opening. White now can continue also with 3 BxP, BxP 4 N–KB3, followed by N–QB3.

[24] Somewhat better is 3 . . . P–N5.

[25] 6 . . . P–Q4? 7 Q–N3, N–QB3 8 PxP, NxP 9 QxB, R–N1? 10 QxRP, R–R1 11 B–N5†, K–K2 12 P–Q6†, Resigns (Euwe–Abrahams, Bournemouth 1939).

[26] The line employed by Black is the most efficient against the Colle System or Stonewall Attack. Black will swing his King Knight to Q3 and his Queen Knight to KB3 with a view to occupying his K5 at the proper moment.

[27] 1 . . . P–K4 is equally good.

[28] If 3 P–K3, White recovers the Pawn: 4 Q–R4†, followed by PxP±.

[29] If 4 . . . PxP 5 Q–N3.

[30] Better is 5 . . . PxP 6 Q–N3, P–K3 7 QxNP, QN–Q2∓. If then 8 N–N5, R–B1!

[31] Correspondence game, Keres–Nieman, 1934.

[32] Risky. Steadier is 4 P–Q4.

[33] More conservative is 5 . . . N–B3, e.g., 6 P–Q4, PxP 7 PxP, P–Q4.

[34] Another sacrifice in truer gambit style is 7 P–Q4, e.g., . . . NxN† 8 QxN, PxP 9 PxP, BxP 10 N–N5. Simple and good is 7 NxN, BxN 8 Q–B3.

[35] Obviously not 8 PxN, Q–R5† 9 K–B1, P–Q3, threatening mate in a few moves.

[36] Levine–Borochow, California 1958. White has fine chances for the Pawn. In the game, 10 B–Q5 was played.

# INDEX

## F



## G



## H



## I



## K

## R